MICROECONOMICS

Third Edition

Hugh Gravelle and Ray Rees

An imprint of **Pearson Education**

Harlow, England • London • New York • Boston • San Francisco • Toronto • Sydney • Singapore • Hong Kong
Tokyo • Seoul • Taipei • New Delhi • Cape Town • Madrid • Mexico City • Amsterdam • Munich • Paris • Milan

Pearson Education Limited
Edinburgh Gate
Harlow
Essex CM20 2JE
England

and Associated Companies throughout the world

Visit us on the World Wide Web at:
www.pearsoned.co.uk

First published 1981
Second edition published 1992
Third edition published 2004

© Pearson Education Limited 2004

ISBN: 978-0-582-40487-8

British Library Cataloguing-in-Publication Data
A catalogue record for this book is available from the British Library

Library of Congress Cataloging-in-Publication Data

Gravelle, Hugh.
   Microeconomics / Hugh Gravelle and Ray Rees. — 3rd ed.
       p.   cm.
   Includes bibliographical references and index.
   ISBN 0-582-40487-8
     1. Microeconomics.   I. Rees, Ray, 1943-   II. Title.

   HB171.5.G786 2004
   338.5—dc22   2004049279

12
12

Typeset in 9.5/12pt stone serif by 35
Printed and bound by Ashford Colour Press, Gosport, Hants, UK

The publisher's policy is to use paper manufactured from sustainable forests.

Contents

Preface to the third edition

We seem to be able to produce a new edition of this book every eleven years or so. This is undoubtedly not an optimal interval from the point of view of maximizing sales revenue, but it is an interesting one over which to observe the changes in microeconomic theory and in the way it is taught. In the time that elapsed between the first and second editions, the increasing emphasis on game theory and the economics of uncertainty and asymmetric information, at the expense of the more traditional topics in consumption, production and general equilibrium theory, was quite marked. That tendency has strengthened over the period since the second edition appeared, and this is reflected in the content and organization of this third edition. We have added a new chapter on game theory, and have considerably extended and restructured the chapters on uncertainty and asymmetric information. In order to keep the length of the book within reasonable bounds, we have deleted some material that we thought was unlikely these days to be covered in an advanced microeconomics course, and replaced the chapter on the mathematics of optimization by a number of shorter appendices. In addition, the discussions of the literature and suggestions for further reading previously at the end of each chapter have been gathered into a set of notes at the end of the book, which has not only saved space but, we hope, has allowed us to improve them.

The aims and approach of the book have remained the same. We have tried to provide a comprehensive exposition of modern microeconomic theory, beginning at the intermediate level and ending at an appropriate level for graduate students. We aim to cover the ground between the standard intermediate micro course, taught largely in two dimensions with little explicit use of mathematics, and the advanced doctoral course. This book is meant to fit between, say, Hal Varian's excellent *Intermediate Microeconomics*, and Mas-Colell, Whinston and Green's magisterial *Microeconomic Theory*. We have again placed major emphasis on trying to give the student an intuitive understanding of the economic content of the models, and of their purpose and nature, as well as a clear account of their mathematics.

We are very grateful to the many users of this book, students as well as teachers, who have over the years sent us corrections and suggestions for improvement. We would like particularly to thank Patricia Apps and Klaus Schmidt, who have commented in depth on some of the new material we have prepared for this edition. We are also grateful to Paula Harris of Pearson Education for her good-natured stoicism in the face of missed deadlines, and for her encouragement finally to finish this book.

H.S.E.G.
R.R.

Preface to the third edition

1 The nature and scope of microeconomics

A. Concepts and methods

Microeconomics is a set of models constructed with the aim of helping us understand the process by which scarce resources are allocated among alternative uses, and of the role of prices and markets in this process. In its purest form, it is a philosophical inquiry into the processes of resource allocation. However, with understanding usually comes the ability to predict and to control, and this has certainly been the case in microeconomics. The concepts and models economists have developed, in conjunction with the necessary empirical data, provide the basis for the analysis of policies by governments wishing to influence the allocation of resources. Through the development of 'operations research', 'management science' and 'business economics', concepts from microeconomics have also been applied to assist decision-taking in business.

A good way of providing an introductory overview of microeconomics is to set out its basic elements.

1. Goods and services or commodities

These are the central objects of economic activity, since 'economic activity' consists of the production and exchange of commodities. We distinguish commodities from each other by one or more of three characteristics: their *attributes*, which determine the way they meet the needs of consumers and producers; the *location* at which they are made available; and the *date* at which they are made available. For example, coal and crude oil have different attributes, as do the services of a hairdresser and those of an accountant (though in each case the broad category of resource from which the commodities derive – 'land' in one case and 'labour' in the other – is the same). Equally important is the fact that crude oil in Dubai available tomorrow is a different commodity from crude oil available tomorrow at a refinery in western Europe; while coal in London today is a different commodity from coal in London this time next year. The basis of the distinction between commodities is that they cannot be regarded as perfect substitutes in production or consumption – a businessman who goes along to his accountant for advice on a tax problem would not be just as happy to be offered a haircut instead.

Commodities are not necessarily physical objects or labour services. For example, Chapters 19 and 21 are concerned with markets for insurance and for financial capital. The purchase of a share in a company quoted on the stock exchange entitles the purchaser to a future stream of dividend payments. The purchaser of car insurance buys a promise from the insurer to reimburse her for any costs incurred if she has an accident. As the insurance example suggests, and as we will see in Chapter 19, the definition of such commodities requires an extension of the set of relevant characteristics defining commodities to include the 'state of the world' in which the commodity will be delivered. For the first half of the book we deal with markets where there is no uncertainty and the characterization of commodities by their attributes, location and date is sufficient.

In most of microeconomics we usually assume a *finite* set of possible bundles of attributes, a finite set of possible locations – we do not regard geographical space as continuous, but rather divided up into small areas – and a finite set of dates. We do not regard calendar time as continuous, but rather divided up into equal discrete time intervals, and moreover not as extending indefinitely far into the future, but instead we assume some definite, though possibly very distant, time horizon. These assumptions ensure that there is a finite number of commodities. Alternatively, we could assume a *continuum* of commodities: given any one commodity, we could always define another which is as close as we like to the first in attributes, location or time. Moreover, this commodity continuum need not be bounded – we could picture commodities as points in a space which stretches to infinity, since we could always define commodities available later in time. Since the assumptions required to establish a finite set of commodities do not seem to do serious injustice to reality, while considerably simplifying the analysis, we usually adopt them.

2. Prices

Associated with each commodity is a price, which may be expressed in one of two ways. First, we may choose one commodity in the economy as a *numeraire*, i.e. as the commodity in terms of which all prices are to be expressed. For example, suppose we choose gold. Then the price of each commodity is the number of units of gold which exchange for one unit of that commodity. The price of gold is 1. In general, we are free to choose *any* commodity as numeraire, so that prices could just as well be expressed in terms of the number of units of some kind of labour service, or the number of bottles of beer, or Armani suits, which exchange for one unit of each other commodity. It might be argued that in reality different commodities may have different degrees of suitability for use in market transactions. Commodities which are not easily divisible, and which are bulky and subject to physical decay, will tend not to be used as a means of payment. However, it is important to note that a numeraire is not intended to represent a *means of exchange*, or 'money', in this sense. We are simply using it as a *unit of account*, or a *unit of measurement* for prices in the economy, and *nothing need be implied about the mechanism by which transactions actually take place*. Given the choice of numeraire, prices are effectively *commodity rates of exchange* – they express the rate at which the numeraire exchanges for each other commodity. They have the dimension (units of the numeraire/units of the commodity). They are therefore not independent of the units in which we measure commodities. For example, if we double the unit in which we measure each commodity *except* for the numeraire we would have to double prices.

The second way in which prices might be expressed does not involve a numeraire. Instead, we suppose there to be some unit of account which is not a quantity of some commodity, but an abstract unit used in making bookkeeping entries. If one unit of a commodity is sold, the account is credited with a certain number of units of account, whereas, if the commodity is bought, the same number of units is debited from the account. The price of the commodity is then the number of units debited or credited per unit of the commodity. We find it useful to give this unit of account a name, and so we could call it the pound sterling, or the US dollar, for example. If different accounts are kept in different units, then rates of exchange between units of account must be established before transfers from one account to another can be made. Clearly, there is no actual commodity corresponding to the unit of account, say the pound sterling. A cheque made out for £x is an instruction to credit one account and debit another, i.e. to transfer x units of account between accounts. Notes and coin have no intrinsic worth (until perhaps they cease to be used in exchange and acquire intrinsic worth – become commodities themselves – to numismatists), but are simply tokens representing numbers of units of account which are passed around directly and form part (usually a relatively small part) of the credit side of one's accounts.

The seemingly abstract definition of prices in terms of units of account is the way prices are usually expressed, and has come about because of the development of the modern banking system. There is a straightforward correspondence between prices expressed in terms of units of account and prices expressed as commodity rates of exchange. Suppose prices are expressed in £ sterling: $p_1, p_2, \ldots p_n$. By taking any one such price, say the nth, and forming the n ratios

$$r_1 = p_1/p_n; \qquad r_2 = p_2/p_n; \qquad \ldots \qquad r_n = p_n/p_n = 1 \qquad \text{[A.1]}$$

we can interpret each r_j, $j = 1, 2, \ldots n$, as the number of units of commodity n which will exchange for one unit of commodity j, i.e. as commodity rates of exchange with n as the numeraire. Each r_j will be in dimensions (units of good n/units of good j):

$$p_j/p_n = (£/\text{units of good } j \div £/\text{units of good } n)$$
$$= (\text{units of good } n/\text{units of good } j), \qquad j = 1, 2, \ldots, n \qquad \text{[A.2]}$$

Thus, each r_j is the number of units of good n we could buy if we sold a unit of good j and spent the proceeds (p_j units of account) on good n.

3. Markets

The everyday notion of a market is as a specific place where certain types of commodities are bought and sold, for example a cattle market, or a fruit and vegetable market. The concept of a market in economics is much more general than this: a market exists whenever two or more individuals are prepared to enter into an exchange transaction, regardless of time or place. Thus, if two poachers meet in the middle of a forest in the dead of night, one with a catch of salmon and the other with a bag of pheasants, and they decide to negotiate an exchange of fish for fowl, we would say that a market exists. The word 'market' denotes exchange. The central problem in microeconomics is the analysis of how markets operate, since we view the process of resource allocation as a market process – a resource allocation is brought about by the workings of markets.

It is important to distinguish between *forward* and *spot* markets. On a spot market, an agreement is made under which delivery of a commodity is completed within the current period; on a forward market, delivery will be made at some future period. (Some markets may do both, e.g. the market in leasehold accommodation, where what may be sold is a flow of housing services over possibly a very large number of years.) We could envisage an economy in which at a given point in time there exists a market for every commodity, which means there is a complete system of spot and forward markets. In such an economy, contracts would be entered into for all future exchanges of commodities as well as for all current exchanges, and so market activity could cease entirely after the first period: the rest of the time would be spent simply fulfilling the contracts already concluded. Real economies do not possess such complete market systems. In any one period, markets exist for delivery of commodities within the period, and some forward markets exist for future delivery, but only relatively few. Hence, at any one time only a relatively small subset of all commodities can be exchanged. There is a sequence of market systems, one in each period, and exchange activity takes place continually.

This picture of the economy raises a number of interesting questions. How will the outcomes on markets at one period be influenced by expectations about the outcomes in later periods? What will be the relationship, if any, between spot prices of commodities with the same physical attributes but different dates of delivery (e.g. the price of crude oil now and its price this time next year)? Can income (which we can take here to be the proceeds of sales of commodities, including of course labour services) be transferred between time periods and, if so, how? What are the consequences of the fact that the future cannot be known with certainty?

The analysis of the full implications of the view of the economy as a time sequence of market systems is complex and still incomplete. We take it in three stages. We first analyse an 'atemporal economy', which could be thought of as an economy existing for just a single time period. We then extend the analysis to an 'intertemporal economy' by considering an economy which will exist over more than one period, but make the assumption of *certainty* – all relevant facts about the future are known at each point in time. We then take the final step of relaxing this certainty assumption and allowing incomplete information about data relating to the future. It is the analysis of this last kind of economy which is not yet complete. As long as we assume certainty, analysis of an intertemporal economy can be made formally identical to that of the atemporal economy, or, alternatively, identical to that of the kind of economy in which there is a complete system of spot and forward markets existing at any one time (see Chapter 11). At a more advanced level of analysis, it is usual to merge stages one and two, and analyse an economy which could be interpreted either atemporally or intertemporally. Indeed, on certain quite strong assumptions it is possible to do the same for the economy with uncertainty (see Chapter 21). However, in this book we shall take one stage at a time.

4. Economic agents

The basic units of analysis in microeconomics are the individual economic agents or decision-takers (hence the term *micro*economics), who are usually classified either as *consumers* or *firms*. A consumer is regarded as an individual who may initially own certain stocks of commodities, his 'initial endowment' (counted as part of his wealth), and who has to choose an amount of each commodity (which may of course be zero) to consume. This amount, in conjunction with his initial endowment, will determine the quantity of each commodity he will want to buy or sell on the relevant market. An alternative and less general formulation is to ignore the selling side of the consumer's activities, and assume his initial endowment takes the form of 'income', expressed in units of account or in terms of some numeraire. We then analyse simply his consumption (equals purchasing) decision, assuming also that he holds zero stocks of all the goods he might want to consume. This somewhat restrictive view of the consumer's activities is useful as a way of developing certain tools of analysis, but clearly can only be provisional, if we also want to say anything about the supply of commodities such as labour services.

A firm is also usually regarded as an individual decision-taker, undertaking the production of commodities by combining inputs in technological processes. These inputs will usually themselves be commodities, some of which the firm may own as part of its initial endowment, and some of which it may buy on the relevant markets. In certain cases, however, important inputs may not be commodities, e.g. sunshine in the production of wine. The crux of the distinction between consumers and firms is the nature of their economic activity: consumers buy and sell commodities in order to consume; firms buy inputs and produce commodities in order to sell.

In reality the counterparts of these theoretical abstractions are more complex. 'Consumer units' are usually groups of two or more people comprising a 'household' and decisions on purchases and sales may well be group decisions. Provided that the household acts in its decision-taking in a way which corresponds reasonably closely to certain principles of rationality and consistency, it may be *enough for the purposes of our theory* to regard it as a single abstract decision-taker, 'the consumer'. However, for some purposes the treatment of the household as a single decision-taker is inadequate. We show, in Chapter 4, that it is possible to extend the theory of 'the' consumer to cover multi-person households with two or more decision-takers.

In the case of the firm, the empirical counterpart of the theoretical entity may be thought even less like a single individual. Although many owner-controlled or *entrepreneurial* firms exist, economic activity is dominated by large corporations, with complex structures of organization and decision-taking. We can apply the same argument as before: it is a simplifying theoretical abstraction to ignore the organizational characteristics of firms for the purpose of our analysis of the general resource allocation process. This is defensible as long as the explanations and predictions we make about the decisions of firms in this process are not shown to be false by the evidence of firms' behaviour. However, there is a great deal of argument and some evidence to suggest that certain aspects of the organizational structure of firms *do* lead them to behave differently from the predictions of the theory of the firm as a single decision-taker. Accordingly in Chapters 7 and 20 we examine theories which take some account of the organizational characteristics of modern corporations.

The classification of the set of economic agents into consumers and firms reflects the basic conceptual distinction between the activities of production and consumption. We can have a less rigid separation between types of economic agents. For example, if the decision-taker controlling the firm is a person, the *entrepreneur*, then she is necessarily a consumer as well as a producer. We could then construct a theory which has the producer taking consumption decisions as well as production decisions. This leads to a view of an economy of consumers, some of whom have access to production possibilities – they possess the knowledge, skills and initial endowment of commodities which enable them to produce as well as exchange. Such an economy is amenable to analysis by the methods developed for the economy in which we preserve the distinction between consumers and producers. Indeed, if we make the assumption that inputs of 'managerial services' can be bought and sold on a market, there is no essential difference between the two economies.

An alternative way of blurring the distinction between consumers and producers is to regard the consumer as a kind of producer. A model of the consumer as a producer could regard her as buying market goods and services, and combining them with her own time and effort, to 'produce' certain consumption services, which are the real objects of consumption. For example, a rail journey from A to B involves the purchase of a transportation service on the market, together with an input of the traveller's time, to produce the consumption service of a trip from A to B. The method of analysis developed for production by firms could be used to analyse the consumer's choices of market commodities when they are regarded as inputs into the production of consumption services. Such models have wide application and help us understand why, as real incomes increase, consumers appear to substitute time- and labour-saving commodities for others. They are useful whenever we want to bring to the forefront of the analysis the fact that time is a scarce resource.

5. Rationality

Whatever the distinction made between consumers and producers in microeconomic models, two central elements remain. First is the adoption of the individual decision-taker as the basic unit of analysis. Second is the hypothesis that this decision-taker is *rational*. The concept of rationality is so pervasive that its meaning must be clearly expressed. In rational decision-taking:

(a) The decision-taker sets out *all* the *feasible* alternatives, rejecting any which are not feasible;

(b) He takes into account whatever information is readily available, or worth collecting, to assess the consequences of choosing each of the alternatives;

(c) In the light of their consequences he ranks the alternatives in order of preference, where this ordering satisfies certain assumptions of completeness and consistency (discussed in Chapter 2);

(d) He chooses the alternative highest in this ordering, i.e. he chooses the alternative with the consequences he prefers over all others available to him.

These 'requirements of rationality' seem to be quite consistent with the everyday sense in which rationality is used. People *can* behave irrationally in this sense: in taking a decision, they may ignore *known* feasible alternatives, they may allow themselves to be influenced by infeasible alternatives, they may ignore or not bother to collect information on the consequences of their decisions, they may contradict themselves in the ranking of the alternatives, and they may even choose an alternative whose consequences *they have already told us* they regard as less attractive than those of another alternative. That is to say, the assumption of rationality is an *hypothesis*, rather than a *tautology* – it may be false for a particular decision-taker.

However, it is not always easy to conclude that a decision-taker is behaving irrationally. The important principle here is (b) above, relating to the use and acquisition of information. The collection of information, and the process of decision-taking itself, absorbs resources and therefore imposes costs. Given that all the information which could possibly be relevant to a decision is not readily and costlessly available, we may often observe behaviour which is rational on the basis of principles (a) – (d), but may be labelled irrational by a careless observer. For example, a consumer may habitually use the same supermarket rather than shopping around other supermarkets to find better bargains. This might appear to violate principle (a), but could be explained by the arguments that habit is essentially a way of economizing on time and effort, and that the consumer's expectation of the gain he would make by shopping around does not seem to him to justify the cost and bother involved.

The danger in this kind of explanation is apparent in the example: with a little ingenuity, just about any kind of behaviour could be made to appear rational. This is a danger we have to avert, if the concept of rationality is not to become an empty tautology – we have to accept that people may at times be irrational. It is difficult to test the rationality assumption directly by observing, or asking individuals about, the process of decision-taking. A better approach is to test the predictions it generates about decisions and especially how they change in response to changes in observable features of the decision-taker's environment.

To summarize the discussion of this chapter so far, the basic elements of microeconomics are: *rational* individual decision-takers; commodities; markets; prices.

6. Method of analysis

The core of microeconomic theory follows through a systematic line of development. We begin with models of the individual decision-takers, a 'typical' or representative consumer and a 'typical' or representative firm. The assumption of rationality implies that these models take the form of *optimization problems*: the decision-taker is assumed to seek the *best* alternative out of the feasible set of alternatives open to her. By specifying these optimization problems and then solving them, we are able to attribute certain characteristics and properties to the decision-taker's choices. Moreover, by examining the way in which the optimal choices vary with changes in underlying parameters of the decision problem (especially prices), we can trace out *behaviour relationships* such as demand and supply curves.

A major purpose of the models of individual decisions is to allow us to place restrictions on these behaviour relationships, or at least to clarify the assumptions under which particular restrictions (e.g. that demand curves have negative slopes) can be made.

The next step in the development of the theory is to aggregate the individual behaviour relationships over groups of economic agents – usually the set of buyers in a market on the one hand and the set of sellers in a market on the other. These aggregated relationships then form the basis for an analysis of the operation of a single market taken in isolation, and also of systems of several interrelated markets. At the most general, we consider the system of markets for the economy as a whole, and analyse the way in which a resource allocation is determined by the simultaneous interaction of this market system.

The method of analysis is the *equilibrium methodology*. The equilibrium of a system is defined as a situation in which the forces determining the state of that system are in balance, so that there is no tendency for the variables of the system to change. (Strictly speaking, this is the method of *static* equilibrium analysis. We could allow variables and parameters to vary with time, and look for *equilibrium time-paths*, in a dynamic analysis.) An equilibrium of a system of economic agents, which may be a single market or a whole economy, exists when two conditions are satisfied:

(a) individual decision-takers have no wish to change their planned decisions;

(b) the plans of decision-takers are consistent or compatible and hence can be realized.

The significance of the equilibrium concept is that it provides a *solution principle*. Once we have defined the forces operating within a given economic system, for example a model of a single market, we ask the question: what will the outcome of the interaction of those forces be? The answer is provided by the concept of equilibrium: we find the characteristics of the equilibrium state of the system, and take this as the outcome we seek. But if we want to use the equilibrium state as a prediction of the outcome of the workings of the system, we first have to answer a number of fundamental questions:

(a) *Existence*. Does the system in fact *possess* an equilibrium state, i.e. given the forces operating within the system, is there a state in which they would be in balance, or is no such state of balance is possible?

(b) *Stability*. Suppose that an equilibrium state does exist. Then, given that the system may not initially be in this state, would it tend to converge to it? If it does, then we call the system stable. The equilibrium state loses much of its interest if the system is not stable, since it is unlikely ever actually to be attained.

(c) *Uniqueness*. A system may possess more than one equilibrium state, and the different possible equilibria may have different properties and implications. It is therefore important to know for a given system whether there is only one possible equilibrium state.

Questions of the existence, stability and uniqueness of an equilibrium state are necessarily raised by an equilibrium methodology, and will be considered in a variety of contexts throughout this book.

Having described the basic concepts of microeconomics, the overall structure of the theory and its method of analysis, we conclude this introductory chapter with some comments on the view of the economic and social system which is implicit in modern microeconomic analysis.

B. The economic and social framework

We do not say very much in the rest of this book about the institutional, political and legal framework within which our economic analysis is set. Much of microeconomic theory implicitly assumes a certain kind of framework and is concerned with examining the economic forces which operate within it. Despite this the theory can offer deep insights into a variety of institutional frameworks. Some fundamental economic issues exist whatever the institutional form and one means of comparing alternative systems is in terms of the way in which these problems manifest themselves and are dealt with.

Three facts of economic life appear in all types of society. The first is *relative scarcity* of resources: however abundant in absolute terms are the resources possessed by a society, the individuals in the society want to consume more goods and services than can be produced from those resources. Second, there are gains from *specialization*: the output of goods and services will be greater if individuals specialize in different aspects of the production process and each does not attempt to produce all the commodities they consume. Third, *information is decentralized*: no single individual initially knows all the economically relevant information. This information includes both the characteristics of individuals, such as their preferences and their endowments of resources (widely defined to include their skills, productivity, the quality of goods they have to sell) and the actions they take (for example how hard or carefully they work). Given these facts, every society is faced with the problems of organizing exchange and coordinating the separate decisions of the large numbers of consumers and producers.

The decisions taken by individuals in an economy are constrained both by *technology* and by the set of *property rights*. Technological constraints arise from the fundamental physical laws which determine what outputs of goods and services can be produced from given sets of resources. Property rights are the rules (whether formal and legal or informal custom) which specify which individuals are allowed to do what with resources and the outputs of those resources. Property rights define which of the technologically feasible economic decisions individuals are *permitted* to make.

The institutional frameworks of economies can be classified by the sets of property rights with which they are associated. The microeconomic theory in this book was originally developed to examine how the basic economic problems are solved in a *decentralized private ownership economy*. In such an economy the set of property rights vests ownership of resources and commodities in individuals. All resources are owned by specified individuals who have the right to use them for a wide variety of purposes and can sell that right to other individuals. Decisions are decentralized in the sense that there is no agency or individual in the economy with the right to tell any individual what she must do with the resources she owns. The state's role in such economic models is minimal: it is tacitly assumed to enforce and define the set of private ownership rights and to provide the institutions this requires: a police force and civil and criminal courts.

Microeconomic analysis has relevance beyond its application to such an economy. The concepts and models developed in this book can be used to examine the behaviour of individuals in economies with a wider role for the state and with other institutional frameworks. Economies with different institutional frameworks impose different constraints on decisions because of the differences in the sets of property rights, but the basic microeconomic methodology is unchanged. Individuals in such economies can still be modelled as rational agents optimizing subject to constraints, and so we can make predictions about how their behaviour responds to changes in their environment. We can still define an equilibrium in such economies as a situation in which individuals make optimal decisions which are mutually consistent and thus can be implemented. The equilibrium we investigate may not look like the equilibrium of the simple decentralized private ownership economy, but we can still investigate the circumstances under which it will exist, be stable and be unique, compare the equilibria which arise as conditions change and make welfare judgements about the resulting allocations. Thus, for example, in an economy with prices fixed by a central authority, equilibrium may be compatible with consumers spending considerable lengths of time waiting in line in order to acquire commodities. This situation could not be an equilibrium in an unregulated market economy, but this does not mean that we cannot use microeconomic theory to examine it.

Microeconomic theory has been used to examine the allocation of resources in anarchic societies without public enforcement of property rights, in feudal economies, slave economies, centrally planned economies, cooperative economies and in mixed economies where private ownership is combined with a large state sector and extensive regulation of individual decision-making. In short, the micro-economic methodology we set out can be used to analyse economic decisions in a wide range of institutional frameworks and to examine the consequences of changes in those frameworks.

CHAPTER

2

The theory of the consumer

The central assumption in the theory of the consumer is optimization: given the feasible set of consumption bundles, the bundle chosen is the one the consumer prefers. The purpose of the theory is first to characterize the bundle of goods which will be chosen, and second to predict how the optimal choice will change in response to changes in the feasible set.

In analysing the consumer's optimal choice, we proceed in three steps. We first construct a model of the consumer's preferences, which allows us to specify certain properties of the consumer's ranking of consumption bundles. We then examine how the prices of commodities, in conjunction with the consumer's income (or initial endowment of commodities in a more general model), determine the feasible set of consumption bundles. Finally, by applying the model of the consumer's preference ordering to the feasible set, we are able to determine the characteristics of the optimal choice.

A. The preference ordering

A consumption bundle is denoted by a vector:

$$x = (x_1, x_2, \ldots, x_n)$$

where x_i, $i = 1, 2, \ldots, n$, is the amount of the ith good in the bundle. Each x_i is assumed to be non-negative – the consumer can consume only zero or a positive quantity of each good – and also is taken to be perfectly divisible – goods do not come in lumpy discrete amounts.

The meaning of the terms 'preference' and 'indifference' is taken as understood; we take it for granted that everyone knows what is meant by the statement, 'I prefer this to that', or, 'I am indifferent between this and that'. We assume that the consumer can make statements such as, 'I prefer consumption bundle x' to x''', or, 'I am indifferent between x' and x'''. More formally, we introduce the symbol $\gtrsim$ which is read 'is preferred or indifferent to', or 'is at least as good as', or 'is no worse than', so that $x' \gtrsim x''$ means that the consumer regards x' as at least as good as x''. This symbol is called the *preference–indifference relation.*

The consumer ranks the consumption bundles in the feasible set in order of preference, and chooses the one which is highest in the ranking. This preference ranking can be thought of as being arrived at by repeated application of the preference–indifference relation to successive pairs of consumption bundles. For the purpose of our theory, we want the preference ranking to have certain properties, which give it a particular, useful structure. We build these properties up by making a number of assumptions, first about the preference–indifference relation itself, and then about some aspects of the preference ranking to which it gives rise.

As a preliminary, suppose the consumer told us that

$$x' \gtrsim x'' \quad \text{and} \quad x'' \gtrsim x'$$

in words, 'x' is preferred or indifferent to x''', and 'x'' is preferred or indifferent to x'''. Since we would regard him as talking nonsense – violating the meaning of the word 'preferred' – if he told us that x' is preferred to x'' *and* x'' is preferred to x', this must mean that x' is indifferent to x''. We write 'x' is indifferent to x''', as $x' \sim x''$. Suppose, alternatively, the consumer told us that:

$$x' \gtrsim x'' \quad \text{and } not \quad x'' \gtrsim x'$$

This must mean that x' is preferred to x'' and this is written $x' > x''$. Thus we have as implications of the meaning of the preference–indifference relation:

(a) $x' \gtrsim x''$ *and* $x'' \gtrsim x'$ implies $x' \sim x''$

(b) $x' \gtrsim x''$ and *not* $x'' \gtrsim x'$ implies $x' > x''$.

We can now proceed to the assumptions which give the desired properties to the consumer's preference ordering.

Assumption 1. Completeness.   For *any pair* of bundles x' and x'', either $x' \gtrsim x''$ or $x'' \gtrsim x'$ (or both).

This assumption says in effect that the consumer is able to express a preference or indifference between any pair of consumption bundles however alike or unalike they may be. This ensures that there are no 'holes' in the preference ordering. It also implies that, given some bundle x', every other bundle can be put into one of three sets:

1. the set of bundles preferred or indifferent to x': the 'better set' for x';
2. the set of bundles indifferent to x': the 'indifference set' of x';
3. the set of bundles to which x' is preferred or indifferent: the 'worse set' for x'.

These sets, and especially set 2, play an important part in what follows.

Assumption 2. Transitivity.   For any three bundles x', x'', x''', if $x' \gtrsim x''$ and $x'' \gtrsim x'''$ then $x' \gtrsim x'''$.

This is a consistency requirement on the consumer. Given the first two statements, if the third did not hold, so that $x''' > x'$, we would feel there was an inconsistency in preferences. The assumption has an important implication for the 'indifference sets' just defined, in that it implies that no bundle can belong to more than one such set. For suppose that $x' \sim x''$, so that x'' belongs to the indifference set of x'; and also that $x'' \sim x'''$, so x'' belongs to the indifference set of x'''. If $x' \sim x'''$, then there is no problem, since all three bundles are in the same indifference set. But suppose $x''' > x'$. Then x'' must be in two indifference sets, that of x' and that of x'''. But then we have

$$x' \sim x'' \quad \text{and} \quad x'' \sim x''' \quad \text{but} \quad x''' > x'$$

which violates the assumption of transitivity. Thus given this assumption, no bundle can belong to more than one indifference set: *the transitivity assumption implies that indifference sets have no intersection.*

Assumption 3. Reflexivity. $x' \gtrsim x'$.

In words, any bundle is preferred or indifferent to itself. Since we can interchange the two sides of the relation, the assumption has the implication that a bundle is indifferent to itself, which seems trivially true. However, its implication is less trivial: it ensures that every bundle belongs to at least one indifference set, namely that containing itself, if nothing else.

These three properties of the preference–indifference relation imply that every bundle (completeness) can be put into one indifference set (reflexivity) and no more than one indifference set (transitivity). Thus we can *partition* any given set of consumption bundles, by use of the relation, into non-intersecting indifference sets, which provide us with a useful way of representing a particular preference ordering. The indifference sets can be ranked in order of preference on the basis of the ranking of the bundles they contain. The following assumptions we make about the consumer's preferences are chiefly designed to give these sets a particular structure.

Assumption 4. Non-satiation. A consumption bundle x' will be preferred to x'' if x' contains more of at least one good and no less of any other, i.e. if $x' > x''$.

This assumption establishes a relationship between the quantities of goods in a bundle and its place in the preference ordering – the more of each good it contains the better. Moreover, this is held to be true however large the amounts of the goods in the bundle, hence the term 'non-satiation' – the consumer is assumed never to be satiated with goods. This assumption is much stronger than we need to make in two respects. It first implies that none of the goods is in fact a 'bad', a commodity such as garbage or aircraft noise which one would prefer to have less of. Second, it assumes that the consumer is never satiated in *any* good. We could generalize by allowing some goods to be bads, and by assuming non-satiation only in at least one good, without changing anything of significance in the results of the theory. For simplicity, however, we adopt the stronger assumption here.

The non-satiation assumption has two important consequences for the nature of indifference sets, which are best expressed geometrically. In Fig. 2.1, x_1 and x_2 are goods, and $x' = (x_1', x_2')$ is a consumption bundle. Because of assumption 4, all

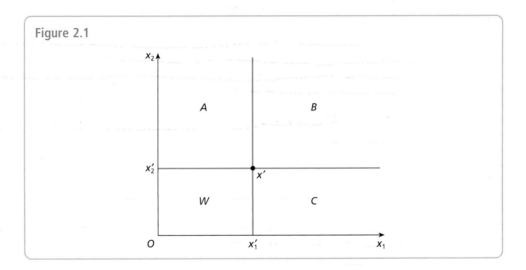

Figure 2.1

bundles in the area B (including the boundaries, except for x' itself) must be preferred to x', and all points in the area W (again including the boundaries except for x') must be inferior to x'. The first consequence of the assumption is that points in the indifference set for x' (if there *are* any besides x') must lie in areas A and C. In other words, if we imagine moving between bundles in the indifference set, we can only do so by *substituting* or *trading off* the goods – giving more of one good must require taking away some of the other good in order to stay within the indifference set. The second consequence is that an indifference set is never 'wider' than a single point – its geometric representation can never be an area or band, though it may be a single point, an unconnected set of points or a curve. For suppose x' was contained in an indifference set which was a band. Then some bundles indifferent to it must lie in areas B and W, which violates assumption 4. Thus the assumption implies that an indifference set cannot be thick at point x', or, by extending the argument, at any point contained in it.

None of the assumptions we have made so far, however, implies that there must be more than one point in an indifference set, or, if there is more than one point, that these make up a continuous line or curve. For example, as is shown in Appendix 1 to this chapter, the so-called *lexicographic ordering* satisfies assumptions 1 to 4, but its indifference sets each consist of only one point. We know that from the point of view of solving optimization problems, continuity is a very important property, and since we shall in effect be using indifference sets (or their geometric representation in the two-good case: indifference curves) to model the consumer's problem, it is a property we should like them to possess. Hence we make the assumption of continuity.

Assumption 5. Continuity. The graph of an indifference set is a continuous surface.

This implies that the surface, or curve in two dimensions, has no gaps or breaks at any point. In terms of the consumer's choice behaviour, given two goods in his consumption bundle, we can reduce the amount he has of one good, and however small this reduction is, we can always find an increase in the other good which will exactly compensate him, i.e. leave him with a consumption bundle indifferent to the first. The reader should confirm diagrammatically that this is possible only if the indifference surface is everywhere continuous. (See Appendix 2 for a more formal treatment of this assumption.)

We now want to place some restrictions on the shape of the indifference surfaces or curves. From assumption 4 we already know that they must be negatively sloped, and now we say something about their curvature. Recall the earlier definition of the better set of a point x', as the set of bundles which are preferred or indifferent to x'. Then we make the assumption:

Assumption 6. Strict convexity. Given any consumption bundle x', its better set is strictly convex.

Figure 2.2 illustrates for the two-good case. The better set for the point x' is the set of points on the indifference curve I' and in the shaded area, and this is drawn as strictly convex. There is an important technical reason for making this assumption: we know (from Appendix E at the end of the book) that, given also that the feasible set is convex, the consumer's optimal point will as a result be a unique local – and therefore a global – optimum, and this is useful when we analyse the consumer's responses to changes in the feasible set.

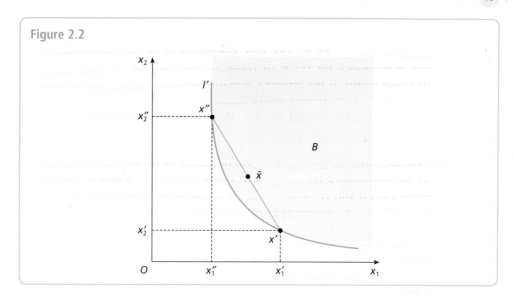

Figure 2.2

There is also a basis for the assumption in terms of economic behaviour. It can be expressed in two ways. From Fig. 2.2 it is clear that, if we move the consumer along the indifference curve leftward from point x', reducing the quantity of x_1 by small, equal amounts, we have to compensate, to keep him on the indifference curve, by giving him larger and larger increments of x_2. In other words, the curvature implies that the smaller the amount of x_1 and larger the amount of x_2 held by the consumer, the more valuable are marginal changes in x_1 relative to marginal changes in x_2. This is a plausible feature of consumer preferences.

A second way of rationalizing the curvature is as follows. In Fig. 2.2, $x' \sim x''$. Consider the straight line joining these two points. Any point on this line, for example $\bar{x}$, is a convex combination of x' and x'', in that it can be expressed as

$$\bar{x} = kx' + (1 - k)x'' \qquad 1 \geqslant k \geqslant 0 \qquad [A.1]$$

i.e. the bundle $\bar{x}$ contains an amount of x_1 given by $kx_1' + (1 - k)x_1''$, and an amount of x_2 given by $kx_2' + (1 - k)x_2''$. So, for example, if $k = \frac{1}{2}$, $\bar{x}$ lies halfway along the line, and contains half of x_1' plus half of x_1'', and half of x_2' plus half of x_2''. We call such a convex combination a mixture of x' and x''.

It follows from the strict convexity assumption that any mixture along the line will be preferred to x' and x'' (in fact this is the formal *definition* of strict convexity of the better set – see Appendix B). Thus, the consumer always prefers a mixture of two consumption bundles which are indifferent to each other, to either one of those bundles. Again it is argued that this preference for mixtures is a commonly observed aspect of consumer behaviour.

A weaker convexity assumption than assumption 6 can be made: we could assume that the better set is convex but not strictly convex. This means that we allow the possibility of linear segments in the indifference curves, as Fig. 2.3 illustrates. The better sets for points x', x'' and x''' respectively are each convex but none is strictly convex. Linearity in the indifference curve over some range implies that, within this range, the valuation of marginal decreases in one good relative to marginal increments in the other remains constant – successive equal reductions in the amount of

Figure 2.3

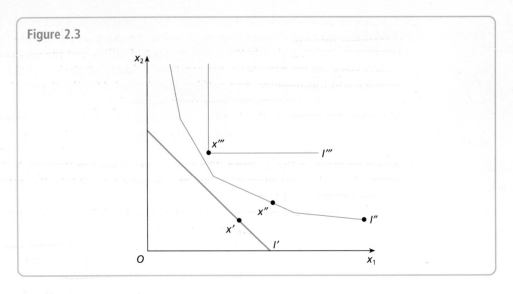

one good are compensated by successive equal increases in the amount of the other. Alternatively, a mixture of two indifferent bundles, in the sense just defined, is indifferent to the two, rather than preferred to them. The reason for excluding such linearity by the strict convexity assumption is, as we shall see, to ensure that the solution to the consumer's problem is a unique point and not a set of infinitely many points.

As a result of these six assumptions, we can represent the preference ordering of the consumer by a set of continuous convex-to-the-origin indifference curves or surfaces, such that each consumption bundle lies on one and only one of them. Moreover, as a result of assumption 4 we can say that bundles on a higher indifference surface are preferred to those on a lower. Thus, the best consumption bundle open to a consumer is the one lying on the highest possible indifference surface. We therefore have part of the analytical apparatus we need to solve the consumer's choice problem.

The utility function

Historically the word 'utility' was used in economics to denote the subjective sensations – satisfaction, pleasure, wish-fulfilment, cessation of need, etc. – which are derived from consumption, and the experience of which is the object of consumption. The economists in the late nineteenth century who were concerned with constructing a theory of consumer choice went further than this definition and regarded utility as something which could be measured in the same way as weight can be measured. They thought it possible to speak of the total quantity of utility derived from consuming a given bundle of goods, of subtracting such quantities from each other, and discussing how these differences changed as consumption varied. Thus was developed the 'law of diminishing marginal utility'. However, even then some of these economists were unhappy about this measurability and it came increasingly under attack as the theory developed. The position which is generally accepted now is that the subjective sensations grouped under the name 'utility' are not capable of being treated as quantities in this sense. An important reason for the adoption of that position was the demonstration that, for the purpose of constructing a theory of consumer choice, not only the measurement of utility, but the very concept itself, is unnecessary. As we have seen, we can base a theory of choice on the concepts of preference and indifference, and *nothing more is needed* for the theory than the set of indifference curves (or surfaces) with their assumed properties.

However, for some methods of analysis it is useful to have a function which provides a numerical representation of the preference ordering. That is, it is useful to have a rule for associating with each consumption bundle a real number which indicates its place in the ranking. The reason is that we can then apply the standard method of constrained maximization of a function to obtain the solution to the consumer's choice problem.

A suitable rule of association or function can be defined in the following way. On the assumptions made about the consumer's preferences we can partition the consumption bundles into indifference sets and can rank these sets. A rule or function $u(x)$ which assigns a real number u to each bundle x is said to *represent* the consumer's preferences if all bundles in the same indifference set have the same number and bundles in preferred indifference sets have higher numbers, i.e.

(a) $u(x') = u(x'')$ if and only if $x' \sim x''$

(b) $u(x') > u(x'')$ if and only if $x' > x''$

Any function satisfying these simple requirements is a *utility function* for the consumer.

A utility function is merely a way of attaching numbers to the consumer's indifference sets such that the numbers increase as higher or more preferred sets are reached. It reflects only the *ordering* of the bundles by the consumer and so is an *ordinal* function. Since we only require that the consumer can rank bundles and the utility function is a numerical representation of this ordering, no significance attaches to the size of the difference between numbers attached to different bundles. We are concerned only with the *sign* of the difference, i.e. whether $u(x') \gtreqless u(x'')$ or whether x' is preferred or indifferent to x'' or x'' preferred to x'.

There are an infinite number of ways of attaching numbers to bundles which are consistent with the requirements (a) and (b) above: the utility function is not unique. For example, given four consumption bundles x', x'', x''', x'''', any one of the columns in the following table is an acceptable numerical representation of the preference ordering $x' \sim x'' > x''' > x''''$.

	$u(x)$	$v(x)$	$w(x)$
x'	3	10 000	500
x''	3	10 000	500
x'''	2	2	499
x''''	1	1.5	1.9

where $v(x)$ and $w(x)$ denote functions which obey the rule in (a)–(b) above, but which differ from $u(x)$. To put this more formally, we could regard the function $v(x)$ as being derived from $u(x)$ by applying, at each x, some *rule of transformation*, such as, for example, 'When $x = x'$ multiply $u(x')$ by $333\frac{1}{3}$ to obtain $v(x)$'. That is in general we write:

$$v(x) = T[u(x)] \qquad \text{[A.2]}$$

where $T[\cdot]$ denotes the rule of transformation we devise. The only restriction we place on this transformation rule is that when u increases, v must increase, because then v will correctly represent the preference ordering. Such a transformation is called '*positive monotonic*', because v must always increase with u. Hence, we say that the function $u(x)$ is unique up to a positive monotonic transformation, meaning that we can always derive another permissible representation of the preference ordering by applying some positive monotonic transformation T to $u(x)$. Examples of such transformations are:

$$v(x) = e^{u(x)}$$
$$v(x) = 3 + 2u(x) \qquad\qquad [A.3]$$
$$v(x) = 5 + \log u(x)$$

where the transformation T is defined by a simple function. As the table above showed, we do not *have* to define T in such a simple way.

So far we have taken it for granted that a function $u(x)$ which gives a numerical representation of a preference ordering actually does exist. What do we have to assume in order to ensure that the function exists? Consider first assumptions 1–3 above, on completeness, transitivity and reflexivity. Recall that they resulted in a family of indifference sets such that every consumption bundle belonged to one and only one set. We might then reason intuitively that, since that $u(x)$ function effectively assigns numbers to indifference sets, there can be no problem. We would, however, be wrong. It can be shown that we may have a preference ordering satisfying assumptions 1–3 (and 4), but for which no numerical representation exists – we cannot apply to it the rule for assigning numbers to consumption bundles that we set out earlier. An ordering for which this is true is the lexicographic ordering discussed in Appendix 1. The existence of this counter-example tells us that assumptions 1–4 are not sufficient to guarantee existence of a numerical representation of a preference ordering. The further assumption which solves the problem is that of continuity. It can be shown (see Appendix 2) that if assumption 5 holds, so that the indifference surfaces are continuous, a continuous numerical representation $u(x)$ can always be constructed for the preference ordering.

We can now consider the relation between the function $u(x)$ and the indifference sets, which are the fundamental expressions of the consumer's preference ordering. Consider the set of consumption bundles which satisfy

$$u(x) = u^0 \qquad\qquad [A.4]$$

where u^0 is some given number. Since these consumption bundles yield the same value of the function they must constitute an indifference set. A set of values of the independent variables in a function which yield a constant value of the function is said to define a *contour* of that function. Hence the indifference sets are contours of the function $u(x)$, and the assumptions 4 and 6 which define the shape of the indifference sets can just as well be interpreted as defining the properties of the contours of $u(x)$. This implies that $u(x)$ is what we called in Appendix B a *strictly quasi-concave* function. In addition, we know that a consumption bundle which yields a higher value of the function than another will always be preferred, and so we can interpret the desire to choose the preferred alternative in some given set of alternatives as equivalent to maximizing the function $u(x)$ over that set. Thus we can represent the consumer's choice problem as one of constrained maximization of a strictly quasi-concave function.

Figure 2.4

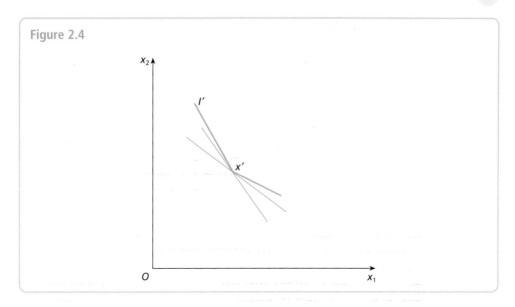

In formulating the consumer's choice problem in this way, it is useful if we can use methods of differentiation to find solutions. The assumptions made so far do not imply differentiability: for example, Fig. 2.4 shows a contour which satisfies all the assumptions but is not differentiable at x' – the slope of the contour is not uniquely defined at that point, which is a corner. To rule out such cases, we make the assumption of differentiability (since differentiability implies continuity, we could regard assumption 7 as replacing assumption 5).

Assumption 7. Differentiability. Utility functions are differentiable to any required order.

This assumption rules out cases in which the slope of an indifference surface or curve makes a sudden jump, as in Fig. 2.4. We now examine more closely the interpretation of the slope of an indifference curve.

Recall that in discussing assumption 6 we used the idea of successive small reductions in x_1 being compensated by small increments in x_2 just enough to stay on the indifference curve. This can be thought of as defining a 'required rate of compensation', whose (absolute) value increases as we move leftward along the indifference curve. As usual with ratios of *finite* changes, there is an ambiguity arising out of the arbitrariness of the size of the change, and so we find it useful to go to the limit and define the derivative

$$\left.\frac{dx_2}{dx_1}\right|_{u\ constant} = \lim_{\Delta x_1 \to 0}\left(\frac{\Delta x_2}{\Delta x_1}\right) \qquad [A.5]$$

where the notation on the left-hand side is intended to emphasize that we are constraining the changes in x_1 and x_2 to keep the value of the function u constant. In effect, we view the indifference curve as defining x_2 as a function of x_1, which could be called an 'indifference function' or 'contour function'. Then the derivative we have defined above is the slope of this function at a point. Figure 2.5 illustrates this.

Figure 2.5

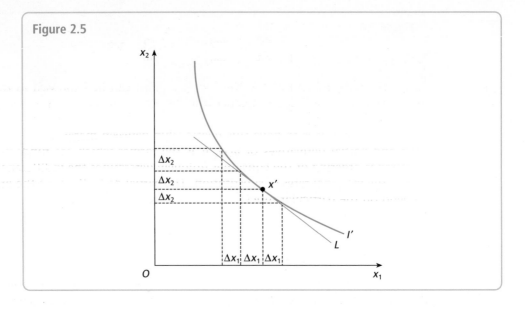

The slope of the tangent L to the indifference curve at x' gives the value of the above derivative at x'. As we take points leftward along the indifference curve, the absolute value of the derivative increases. The figure also shows a sequence of finite changes; the ratio $\Delta x_2 / \Delta x_1$ gives the *average* rate of change of x_2 with respect to x_1 over an arc of the curve, and its value will depend on the size of the change Δx_1.

Important derivatives in economics are always called the marginal something or other, and this is no exception. We define the *marginal rate of substitution* of good 2 for good 1, written MRS_{21}, as

$$MRS_{21} = -\frac{dx_2}{dx_1}\bigg|_{u \text{ constant}} \quad\quad\quad\quad\quad\quad [A.6]$$

The negative sign occurs because we wish MRS_{21} to be positive. Assumption 6 implies that MRS_{21} varies inversely with x_1. We also define the marginal rate of substitution of good 1 for good 2, written MRS_{12}, as:

$$MRS_{12} = -\frac{dx_1}{dx_2}\bigg|_{u \text{ constant}} \quad\quad\quad\quad\quad\quad [A.7]$$

which refers to the slope of an indifference curve relative to the x_2 axis. Since the two are reciprocals of each other, it is enough to work always with just one of them, and MRS_{21} will usually be taken.

Along an indifference surface we have:

$$u(x) = u^0$$

where u^0 is a given constant. Let u_i, $i = 1, 2, \ldots, n$ be the partial derivative $\partial u/\partial x_i$ or the *marginal utility* of good i: the rate at which the utility changes as good i is increased with other goods held constant. If $u_i \neq 0$, the Implicit Function Theorem implies that there is a function $\phi^i(\cdot)$ such that

$$x_i = \phi^i(x_1, \ldots, x_{i-1}, x_{i+1}, \ldots, x_n) \quad\quad\quad\quad [A.8]$$

where

$$\frac{\partial \phi^i}{\partial x_j} = -\frac{dx_i}{dx_j}\bigg|_{u \text{ constant}} = \frac{u_j}{u_i} = MRS_{ij} \qquad [A.9]$$

Thus the marginal rate of substitution at a point can be expressed as the ratio of marginal utilities at that point. Since u_i and u_j are in general functions of all n goods, so is MRS_{ij}.

Useful though it is to have this relationship between marginal rates of substitution and partial derivatives of $u(x)$, it is the former which are fundamental. The preference ordering of the consumer uniquely determines the indifference sets and hence the marginal rates of substitution. The partial derivatives, on the other hand, depend on the particular function used to represent the consumer's preferences, or to label the indifference sets.

Properties of marginal utility

If x_i increases with the amounts of all other goods held constant the consumer achieves a better bundle and hence the utility number must increase, so that marginal utility of the ith good is positive: $u_i(x) > 0$. The *sign* of the marginal utility of a good is the same for all numerical representations of the consumer's preferences (i.e. for all utility functions) but the size of the marginal utility is not. If u is a utility function and $v = T[u(x)]$ is a transformation of u with the property that $T' = dT/du > 0$ then $v(x)$ is also a utility function. The partial derivative of v with respect to x_i is

$$\frac{\partial v}{\partial x_i} = v_i = T' \cdot \frac{\partial u}{\partial x_i} = T'u_i \qquad [A.10]$$

and, since by assumption $T' > 0$, the sign of v_i is the sign of u_i but $v_i \neq u_i$ unless $T' = 1$.

The rate of change of marginal utility of x_i with respect to x_i is the second partial derivative of u with respect to x_i: $u_{ii} = \partial^2 u/\partial x_i^2$. Neither the sign nor the magnitude of the rate of change of u_i are the same for all representations of preferences. For example, with the function v considered in the previous paragraph,

$$v_{ii} = \frac{\partial^2 v}{\partial x_i^2} = \frac{\partial}{\partial x_i}(T'u_i) = T'u_{ii} + T''u_i u_i$$

The sign of v_{ii} is the same as the sign of u_{ii} only if $T'' = d^2T/du^2 = 0$, but the only restriction on T is that $T' > 0$. Statements about increasing or diminishing marginal utility are therefore meaningless, because we can always find a function to represent the consumer's preferences which contradicts the statement.

Equation [A.9] makes the important point that ratios of marginal utilities are invariant to permissible transformations of the utility function since they must all equal the marginal rate of substitution, which is determined by the consumer's preferences. Using the utility functions u and v above and [A.10], we see that

$$MRS_{ij} = \frac{v_j}{v_i} = \frac{T'u_j}{T'u_i} = \frac{u_j}{u_i} \qquad [A.11]$$

Our warnings about the meaninglessness of statements about the size of changes in utility are valid for the preferences which satisfy the assumptions of this chapter but, as we will see in Chapter 17, if certain additional restricting assumptions about an individual's preferences are made, it becomes sensible to talk of the rate of change of marginal utility. These extra assumptions are unnecessary for our present purposes and so we do not adopt them until they are needed when we study decision-making under uncertainty.

EXERCISE 2A

1. Show that if indifference curves intersect the consumer is inconsistent.

2. Construct a set of indifference curves which satisfy all the assumptions of this section, *except*:

   (a) one of the 'goods' is in fact a bad; or

   (b) the consumer may reach a point at which he is satiated with one good but not the other; or

   (c) the consumer may reach a point at which he is satiated with both goods (a 'bliss point'); or

   (d) there is a quantity for each good up to which it is a good, and beyond which it is a bad.

   Give concrete examples of goods which may fit each case.

3. Discuss the relationship between the non-satiation assumption and the idea of scarcity which underlies microeconomics.

4. Draw indifference curves relating to:

   (a) red and blue matches with identical incendiary properties;

   (b) left and right shoes of the same size, quality, design, etc.;

   and state whether the corresponding utility function is strictly quasi-concave. Comment on the way in which the MRS_{21} varies along these indifference curves. Explain why goods in case (a) are called 'perfect substitutes', and those in (b) 'perfect complements'.

5. Ms A's indifference curves for water and diamonds satisfy the assumption of strict convexity, and she is endowed with a great deal of water and very few diamonds. Which of the following does this imply?

   (a) Diamonds are more valuable to her than water.

   (b) She would give up a lot of water to get one more diamond.

   (c) She would give up more water for an extra diamond than would be the case if she had a combination, indifferent to the first, of less water and more diamonds.

B. The feasible set

We initially assume that the consumer has a given money income M, faces constant prices for all of the goods in the utility function and cannot consume negative quantities of any good. Then (see Appendix A) the consumer's feasible set defined by these assumptions is the set of bundles satisfying

$$p_1 x_1 + p_2 x_2 + \ldots + p_n x_n = \sum p_i x_i \leq M \qquad [\text{B.1}]$$
$$x_1 \geq 0, \, x_2 \geq 0, \ldots, x_n \geq 0$$

where p_i is the price of good i.

Figure 2.6

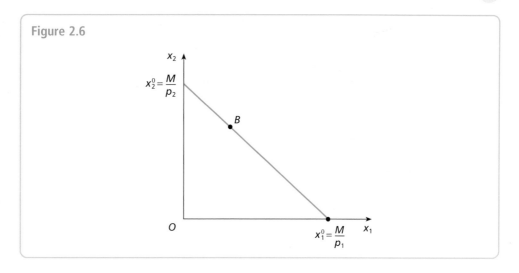

The feasible set in the two-good case is shown in Fig. 2.6 as the triangular area $Ox_1^0 x_2^0$. $x_1^0 = M/p_1$ is the maximum amount of x_1 that can be bought with income M at a price of p_1. x_2^0 is analogously defined. The budget constraint is $p_1 x_1 + p_2 x_2 \leqslant M$ in this two-good case, or:

$$x_2 \leqslant (M - p_1 x_1)/p_2 \qquad \text{[B.2]}$$

which is satisfied by all points on or below the line B from x_1^0 to x_2^0. B, the upper boundary of the feasible set, is known as the consumer's *budget line* and is defined by

$$x_2 = (M - p_1 x_1)/p_2 \qquad \text{[B.3]}$$

The slope of the budget line is

$$\left.\frac{dx_2}{dx_1}\right|_{M \text{ constant}} = -\frac{p_1}{p_2} \qquad \text{[B.4]}$$

where the notation on the left-hand side is to remind us that this is the rate at which a consumer with fixed income can exchange x_1 for x_2 on the market. A one-unit reduction in purchases of x_1 reduces expenditure by p_1, and so, since 1 unit of x_2 costs p_2, the consumer can buy p_1/p_2 extra units of x_2. Therefore 1 unit of x_1 exchanges for p_1/p_2 units of x_2.

The consumer's feasible set has a number of properties relevant for the analysis of the optimal consumption decision (see Appendix B). It is:

(a) *bounded*, from below by the non-negativity constraints on the x_i and from above by the budget constraint, provided that M is finite and no price is zero. If, for example, $p_1 = 0$ then the budget line would be a line parallel to the x_1 axis through the point $x_2^0 = M/p_2$, and the feasible set would be unbounded to the right: since x_1 would be a free good the consumer could consume as much of it as he wished;

(b) *closed*, since any bundle on the budget line B or the quantity axes is available;

(c) *convex*, since for any two bundles x' and x'' in the feasible set, any bundle $\bar{x}$ lying on a straight line between them will also be in the feasible set. Since $\bar{x}$ lies between x' and x'', and they both satisfy the non-negativity constraints, $\bar{x}$ will also satisfy these constraints. $\bar{x}$ will cost no more than the consumer's income: lying between x' and x'' it must cost no more than the more expensive of them, say x'. But since x' lies within the feasible set, so must $\bar{x}$. Hence $\bar{x}$ is in the feasible set;

(d) *non-empty*: provided that $M > 0$ and at least one price is finite the consumer can buy a positive amount of at least one good.

Consider the effects of changes in M and p_i on the feasible set, in preparation for section D where we examine their effects on the consumer's optimal choice. If money income increases from M_0 to M_1, the consumer's feasible set expands as the budget line moves outward parallel with its initial position, as in Fig. 2.7(a). With $M = M_0$ the intercepts of the budget line B_0 on the x_1 and x_2 axes respectively are M_0/p_1 and M_0/p_2 and with $M = M_1$ they are M_1/p_1 and M_1/p_2. A doubling of M, for example, will double the value of the intercepts, since $M_1/p_2 = 2M_0/p_2$ when $M_1 = 2M_0$. The slope of the budget line is $-p_1/p_2$ and is unaffected by changes in M.

Consider next an increase in p_1, as shown in Fig. 2.7(b). Since M and p_2 are unchanged the budget line will still have the same M/p_2 intercept on the x_2 axis. An increase in p_1 will cause the budget line to pivot about M_0/p_2 and become more steeply sloped as p_1/p_2 becomes larger. In Fig. 2.7(b) a rise in p_1 to p_1' shifts the x_1 intercept from M_0/p_1 to M_0/p_1' where $M_0/p_1 > M_0/p_1'$ since $p_1 < p_1'$.

Equal proportionate increases in all prices cause the budget line to shift inwards towards the origin as in Fig. 2.7(c). Suppose p_1 and p_2 increase from p_1 and p_2 to kp_1 and kp_2 where $k > 1$. Then the slope of the new budget line is unchanged: $-kp_1/kp_2 = -p_1/p_2$, and the new intercepts are $M/kp_1 < M/p_1$ and $M/kp_2 < M/p_2$.

Finally, if all prices and M change in the same proportion the budget line is unchanged. The intercept on the ith axis after all prices and M change by the factor k is $kM/kp_i = M/p_i$ so the intercept is unaffected, as is the slope, which is $-kp_1/kp_2 = -p_1/p_2$.

Figure 2.7

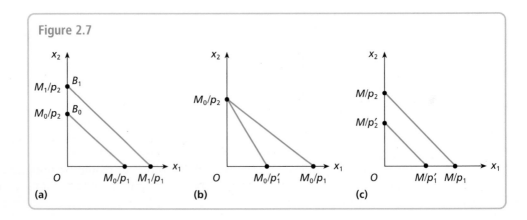

EXERCISE 2B

1. Suppose that the price of one of the commodities bought by the consumer rises as he buys larger quantities. What effect will this have on his feasible set? What interpretation can be given to the slope of his budget line? Can you show in the diagram the relationship between the average price (expenditure divided by quantity bought) and the marginal price?

2. Many public utilities sell their products on multi-part tariffs. The consumer must pay a connection charge for the right to consume (say) electricity, irrespective of the amount consumed. The price paid for the first n units will exceed the price paid for any units consumed in excess of n. Draw the feasible set for the consumer, with electricity on one axis and a consumption good on the other. Distinguish between the average and marginal prices of electricity and investigate the effects of changes in the connection charge and the price of electricity.

3. Draw the feasible set of the consumer in Question 2a, Exercise 2A, assuming that the 'bad' is garbage and that there is a given price per bag of garbage removed, and a given amount of garbage produced per period by the consumer.

C. The consumption decision

Given the assumptions of the previous two sections, the consumer's problem of choosing the most preferred bundle from those available can be formally stated as

$$\max_{x_1,\ldots,x_n} u(x_1, x_2, \ldots, x_n) \quad \text{s.t.} \sum_i p_i x_i \leqslant M, \qquad x_i \geqslant 0, \qquad i = 1, \ldots, n \qquad \text{[C.1]}$$

We can derive the conditions which the solution to this problem must satisfy by a diagrammatic analysis of the two-good case. We leave to the latter part of this section a brief confirmation of our results using more rigorous methods.

From the assumptions of section A we can represent the consumer's preferences by a utility function which has indifference curves or contours like those of Fig. 2.8.

Figure 2.8

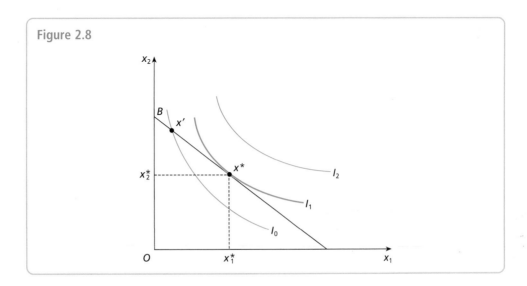

All commodities are assumed to have positive marginal utility so that bundles on higher indifference curves are preferred to those on lower indifference curves. This assumption (a consequence of assumption 4 in section A) also means that the consumer will spend all his income since he cannot be maximizing u if he can buy more of some good with positive marginal utility. The consumer will therefore choose a bundle on his budget line B.

In Fig. 2.8 there is a *tangency solution* where the optimal bundle x^* is such that the highest attainable indifference curve I_1 is tangent to the budget line and the consumer consumes some of both goods. The slope of the indifference curve is equal to the slope of the budget line at the optimum:

$$\left.\frac{dx_2}{dx_1}\right|_{u \text{ constant}} = \left.\frac{dx_2}{dx_1}\right|_{M \text{ constant}}$$

The negative of the slope of the indifference curve is the marginal rate of substitution MRS_{21}; and the negative of the slope of the budget line is the ratio of the prices of x_1 and x_2. Hence the consumer's equilibrium condition can be written as

$$MRS_{21} = \frac{u_1}{u_2} = \frac{p_1}{p_2} \qquad \text{[C.2]}$$

The consumer is in equilibrium (choosing an optimal bundle) when the rate at which he *can* substitute one good for another on the market is equal to the rate at which he is just content to substitute one good for another.

We can interpret this property of the optimal choice in a somewhat different way. If the consumer spent an extra unit of money on x_1 he would be able to buy $1/p_1$ units of x_1. $u_1\Delta x_1$ is the gain in utility from an additional Δx_1 units of x_1. Hence u_1/p_1 is the gain in utility from spending an additional unit of money on x_1. u_2/p_2 has an analogous interpretation. The consumer will therefore be maximizing utility when he allocates his income between x_1 and x_2 so that the marginal utility of expenditure on x_1 is equal to the marginal utility of expenditure on x_2:

$$\frac{u_1}{p_1} = \frac{u_2}{p_2} \qquad \text{[C.3]}$$

This is exactly the condition obtained by multiplying both sides of [C.2] by u_2/p_1.

If the consumer's income were increased by a small amount he would be indifferent between spending it on x_1 or x_2: in either case utility would rise by $u_1/p_1 = u_2/p_2$. Hence, if we call the rate at which the consumer's utility increases as income increases the marginal utility of income, denoted by u_M, we have

$$\frac{u_1}{p_1} = \frac{u_2}{p_2} = u_M \qquad \text{[C.4]}$$

A more plausible optimum when there are many goods would be a *corner point solution*, where the optimal bundle x^* does not contain positive amounts of all goods, as in Fig. 2.9 where no x_2 is purchased. In this case the indifference curve at x^* is steeper than the budget line, i.e. has a smaller slope (remembering that the indifference curve and the budget line are negatively sloped). Hence

$$\left.\frac{dx_2}{dx_1}\right|_{u \text{ constant}} < \left.\frac{dx_2}{dx_1}\right|_{M \text{ constant}} \qquad \text{[C.5]}$$

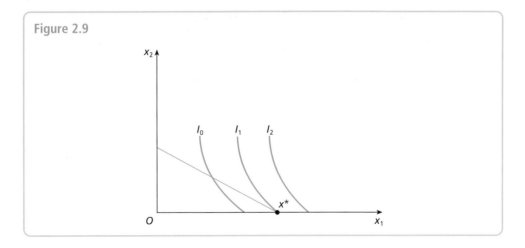

Figure 2.9

and therefore

$$\left.\frac{-dx_2}{dx_1}\right|_{u\ \text{constant}} = MRS_{12} = \frac{u_1}{u_2} > \frac{p_1}{p_2} = \left.\frac{-dx_2}{dx_1}\right|_{M\ \text{constant}} \quad \text{✗}$$ [C.6]

Rearranging, this condition can be written

$$u_M = \frac{u_1}{p_1} > \frac{u_2}{p_2}$$ [C.7]

The marginal utility of expenditure on the good purchased, x_1, is greater than the marginal utility of expenditure on x_2, the good not purchased. Because of the higher marginal utility of expenditure on x_1 than on x_2 the consumer would like to move further down the budget line substituting x_1 for x_2 but is restrained by the fact that consumption of negative amounts of x_2 is not possible.

A more formal analysis

Since the consumer's preferences satisfy the assumptions of section A, the objective function in problem [C.1] above is continuous and strictly quasi-concave. From section B the feasible set for the problem, defined by the budget and non-negativity constraints, is non-empty, closed, bounded and convex. From the Existence, Local–Global and Uniqueness Theorems (see Appendices C, D, E), the consumer's optimization problem has a unique solution and there are no non-global local solutions.

Since there is at least one good with positive marginal utility the consumer spends all income and hence the budget constraint can be written as an equality constraint: $M - \Sigma\, p_i x_i = 0$. If we assume that the solution will be such that some of all goods will be consumed ($x_i^* > 0$ ($i = 1, \ldots, n$) where x_i^* is the optimal level of x_i), then the non-negativity constraints are non-binding and we have a problem to which can be applied the method of Lagrange outlined in Appendix G. The Lagrange function derived from [C.1] is

$$L = u(x_1, \ldots, x_n) + \lambda[M - \Sigma\, p_i x_i]$$ [C.8]

and the first-order conditions for a solution to [C.1] are

$$\frac{\partial L}{\partial x_i} = u_i - \lambda p_i = 0 \qquad i = 1, \ldots, n \qquad \text{[C.9]}$$

$$\frac{\partial L}{\partial \lambda} = M - \Sigma p_i x_i^* = 0 \qquad \text{[C.10]}$$

If [C.9] is rewritten as $u_i = \lambda p_i$ and the condition on good i is divided by that on good j, we have

$$\frac{u_i}{u_j} = \frac{p_i}{p_j} \qquad \text{[C.11]}$$

or: the marginal rate of substitution between two goods is equal to the ratio of their prices as in condition [C.3] above. Alternatively, [C.9] can be rearranged to give

$$\frac{u_1}{p_1} = \frac{u_2}{p_2} = \ldots = \frac{u_n}{p_n} = \lambda \qquad \text{[C.12]}$$

which is the n-good extension of the condition [C.4] derived earlier.

The value of the Lagrange multiplier λ is the rate at which the objective function increases as the constraint parameter increases. In this case the objective function is the utility function and the constraint parameter is the individual's money income so that λ is the rate at which utility increases as money income increases:

$$\lambda = \frac{du^*}{dM} = u_M \qquad \text{[C.13]}$$

The Lagrange multiplier can be interpreted as the marginal utility of money income. This interpretation is supported by [C.12] since, as we argued above, u_i/p_i is the rate at which utility increases as more money is spent on good i.

Corner solutions

If the assumption that $x_i^* > 0$ for all i is dropped, the first order conditions for [C.1] are derived by maximization of the Lagrangean [C.8] subject to the direct non-negativity constraints on the choice variables. The conditions which must be satisfied by a solution to C.1 are

$$\frac{\partial L}{\partial x_i} = u_i - \lambda^* p_i \leq 0, \qquad x_i^* \geq 0, \qquad x_i^*(u_i - \lambda^* p_i) = 0$$
$$i = 1, 2, \ldots, n \qquad \text{[C.14]}$$

plus condition [C.10].

If [C.14] is rearranged to give

$$\lambda^* \geq \frac{u_i}{p_i}, \qquad x_i^* \geq 0, \qquad x_i^*\left(\frac{u_i}{p_i} - \lambda^*\right) = 0 \qquad \text{[C.15]}$$

it can be given a straightforward economic interpretation: if the marginal utility of expenditure on good i, (u_i/p_i), is less than the marginal utility of money at the optimal point, λ^*, then good i will not be bought since the consumer will get greater utility by expenditure on other goods. The same result can be derived from [C.7], where $x_2 = 0$, since $u_1/p_1 = u_M > u_2/p_2$, or $u_2 - u_M p_2 < 0$.

EXERCISE 2C

1. If a consumer buys electricity on a multi-part tariff, as in Question 2, Exercise 2B, are the conditions of the Existence, Local–Global and Uniqueness Theorems satisfied?

2. Derive and interpret the equilibrium conditions for the types of preferences postulated in Questions 2 and 4, Exercise 2A.
   (*Note*: what must be assumed about the price of a 'bad'?)

3. Explain why a consumer would:
   (a) not choose a point inside his budget line;
   (b) not choose the bundle x′ in Fig. 2.8.

4. Suppose that, as well as paying a price per unit of a good, the consumer has to pay a 'transactions cost' for using a market. Analyse the implications for the consumer's optimal choice of assuming:
   (a) the transactions cost is paid as a lump sum;
   (b) the transactions cost is proportional to price but independent of the quantity bought;
   (c) the transactions cost is charged per unit of the good bought, but decreases the greater the amount bought.

5. Is the marginal utility of money income, λ^* or u_M, uniquely defined?

D. The comparative statics of consumer behaviour

The solution to the consumer's optimization problem depends on the consumer's preferences, prices and money income. We can write the solution, which we call the *demand for goods*, as a function of prices and money income:

$$x_i^* = D_i(p_1, p_2, \ldots, p_n, M) = D_i(p, M) \qquad i = 1, \ldots, n \qquad \text{[D.1]}$$

where $p = (p_1, p_2, \ldots, p_n)$ is the vector of prices, and the form of the *Marshallian demand function* D_i depends on the consumer's preferences.

The properties of feasible sets and the objective function enable us to place restrictions on the form of the demand functions. First, provided that p, M are finite and positive, the optimization problem must have a solution, since the requirements of the Existence Theorem are satisfied. Second, the differentiability of the indifference curves and the linearity of the budget constraint imply that the optimal bundle will vary continuously in response to changes in prices and income, and that the demand functions are *differentiable*. Third, the conditions of the Uniqueness Theorem are satisfied and so the demand relationships are functions rather than correspondences: a *unique* bundle is chosen at each (p, M) combination.

We now consider the *comparative statics* properties of the model. We investigate the effects of changes in the exogenous variables (prices, money income) on the equilibrium values of the endogenous variables (the consumer's demand for goods). We want to predict what happens to the optimal bundle $x^* = (x_1^*, x_2^*, \ldots, x_n^*) = (D_1, D_2, \ldots, D_n)$ as the feasible set varies.

We consider first changes in the consumer's money income. In Fig. 2.10, B_1 is the initial budget line, x^* the initial bundle chosen. An increase in M, with p_1, p_2 constant, will shift the budget line outward parallel with itself, say to B_2 where $x′$ is chosen. A further increase in M will shift the budget line to B_3 where $x″$ is chosen.

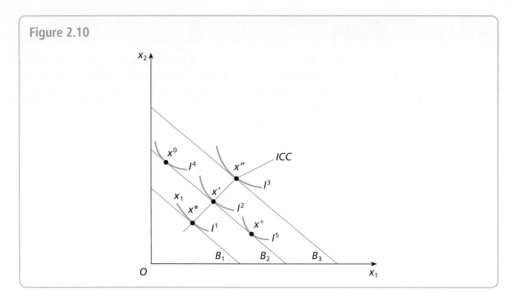

Figure 2.10

The *income consumption curve* is the set of optimal points traced out as income varies in this way, with prices constant. In the case illustrated both x_1 and x_2 are *normal goods*, for which demand increases as money income rises. However, with different preferences the consumer might have chosen x^0 or x^+ on B_2. If x^0 had been chosen (if I^4 and not I^2 had been the consumer's indifference curve) then the demand for x_1 would have fallen as money income rose. x_1 would then be known as an *inferior good*. A rise in M may lead to a rise, a fall, or no change in the demand for a good. Without knowledge of preferences we cannot predict whether a particular good will be inferior or normal. The theory of consumer behaviour cannot be tested by considering the effect of changes in M on the demand for a single good, since any effect is compatible with the theory.

The theory does predict, however, that *all* goods cannot be inferior. If the consumer reduces demand for all goods when income rises he will be behaving inconsistently. To show this, let x^* be the bundle chosen with an initial money income of M_1 and x' the bundle chosen when money income rises to M_2. If $x' \ll x^*$ i.e. if the demand for all goods is reduced, then x' must cost less than x^* since prices are held constant. x' was therefore available when x^* was chosen. But when x' was chosen x^* was still attainable (since money income had increased). The consumer therefore preferred x^* over x' with a money income of M_1 and x' over x^* with money income $M_2 > M_1$. He is therefore inconsistent: his behaviour violates the *transitivity assumption* of section A, and our model would have to be rejected.

We now turn to the effects of changes in prices on the consumer's demands. Figure 2.11 shows the implications of a fall in the price of x_1 with money income held constant. B_1 is the initial budget line, x^* the initial optimal bundle. A fall in p_1, say from p_1 to p_1', causes the budget line to shift to B_2. x' is the optimal bundle on B_2, x'' the optimal bundle on B_3, which results from a further fall in p_1 from p_1' to p_1''. The *price consumption curve* (PCC) is traced out as the set of optimal bundles as p_1 varies. In this case the demand for both goods increases as p_1 falls. However, with different preferences the optimal bundle might have been x^0 or x^+ on B_2. If x^0 was the optimal bundle with $p_1 = p_1'$ then x_1 would be a *Giffen good*, the demand for which falls as its

Figure 2.11

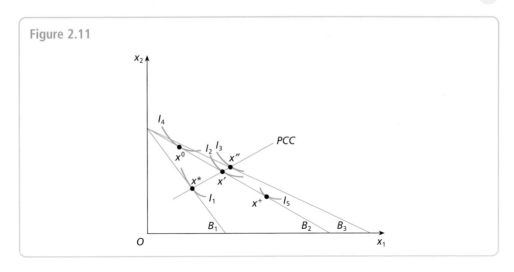

price falls. We conclude that the demand for a good may fall, rise or remain unchanged as a result of a change in a price facing the consumer. Once again the model yields no definite (refutable) prediction about the effect on a *single* endogenous variable (the demand for a good) of a change in *one* of the exogenous variables (in this case a price). It is again possible, however, to predict (by reasoning similar to that employed in the case of a change in M) that a fall in price will not lead to a reduction in demand for *all* goods, and the reader should supply the argument.

Income and substitution effects

The analysis of the effect of price changes on the consumer's demands (optimal choices) has suggested that demand for a good may increase, decrease or remain unchanged, when its price rises; in other words anything may happen. We now examine the effect of a change in the price of good 1 in more detail in order to see if it is possible to make more definite (refutable) predictions. We proceed by making a conceptual experiment. All we can actually observe is the change in quantity demanded following a price change. However, we can carry out a hypothetical analysis which decomposes the overall demand change into two components. We then use this decomposition to say something more definite about consumer behaviour.

In Fig. 2.12, it can be seen that the fall in price of good 1 does two things:

(a) it reduces the expenditure required to achieve the initial utility level I_1, allowing the higher utility level I_2 to be achieved with the same expenditure. There has been an increase in the consumer's *real income*;

(b) it changes the relative prices facing the consumer.

In Fig. 2.12 we accordingly break down the change in demand for x_1 into:

(a) *the income effect*, which is the change resulting solely from the change in real income, with relative prices held constant; and

(b) *the own substitution effect*, which results solely from the change in p_1 with real income held constant.

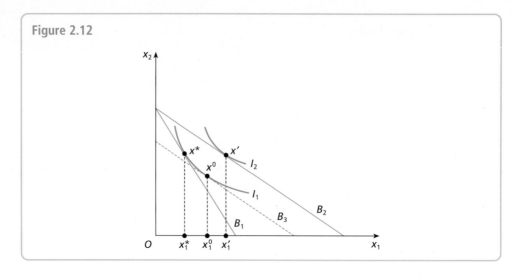

Figure 2.12

x^* and x' are the optimal bundles before and after the fall in p_1, B_1 and B_2 the corresponding budget lines. The *compensating variation* in money income is that change in M which will make the consumer just as well off after the price fall as he was before. In other words, there will be some reduction in M after the price fall which will 'cancel out' the real income gain and return the consumer to the initial indifference curve I_1. The budget line is shifted inwards (reducing M) parallel with the post-price fall budget line B_2 until at B_3 it is just tangent to the original indifference curve I_1. The consumer confronted with this budget line would choose bundle x^0. The difference between x^* and x^0 is due to a change in relative prices with real income (utility) held constant. The difference between x^0 and x' is due to the change in money income with relative prices held constant. x_1^*, x_1' and x_1^0 are the amounts of x_1 contained in the bundles x^*, x', x^0 and

(a) $x_1^0 - x_1^*$ is the own substitution effect;

(b) $x_1' - x_1^0$ is the income effect;

(c) $(x_1^0 - x_1^*) + (x_1' - x_1^0) = x_1' - x_1^*$ is the total *price effect*.

The purpose of carrying out this experiment in hypothetical compensation is to demonstrate that the own substitution effect will always be positive in the case of a price fall and negative for a price rise. The absolute value of the slope of the indifference curve declines from left to right, i.e. as more x_1 and less x_2 is consumed the curve flattens. The fall in p_1 flattens the slope of the budget line, and hence the budget line B_3 *must* be tangent with I_1 to the right of x^*, i.e. at a bundle containing more x_1.

The income effect is positive in the particular case illustrated in Fig. 2.12. The income effect reinforces the own substitution effect since x' contains more x_1 than x^0. If x_1 had been inferior the income effect of the price fall would have been negative and in the opposite direction to the own substitution effect, so that the price effect would be smaller than the own substitution effect. In Fig. 2.13(a) the income effect partially offsets the substitution effect but the price effect is still positive: a fall in p_1 leads to a rise in the demand for x_1. In Fig. 2.13(b) the negative income effect more than offsets the positive substitution effect and x_1 is a Giffen good. Hence inferiority is a necessary, but not sufficient, condition for a good to be a Giffen good.

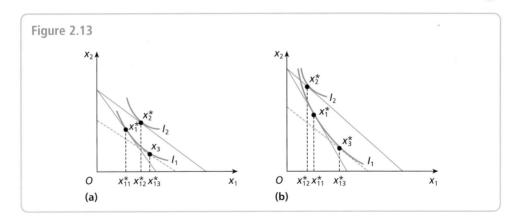

Figure 2.13

This decomposition of the price effect has generated two further predictions:

1. *A normal good cannot be a Giffen good.* Hence, if we observe that a consumer increases demand for a good when money income rises (other things including prices being held constant), we would predict that, if its price should fall, he will want to buy more of it. If we then observe that he reduces his demand for the good when its price falls (and all other prices are constant and his money income is reasonably close to its original level), then the optimizing model of consumer behaviour has yielded a false prediction.

2. *The own substitution effect is always of opposite sign to the price change.*

The above decomposition of the price effect into an income and substitution effect is based on the definition, made by Hicks, of unchanged *real income* as an unchanged *utility level*. Slutsky suggested an alternative definition of a constant real income as the ability to purchase the bundle of goods bought before the price change. This *constant purchasing power* definition has the advantage that it does not require detailed knowledge of the consumer's indifference map.

Figure 2.14 reproduces Fig. 2.11 with some additions to show the relationship between the Hicks and Slutsky definitions of a constant real income. The budget line B_4 just enables the consumer to buy x^*, the initially optimal bundle, at the lower price of p_1. Confronted with this budget line, the consumer actually chooses x^+. The price effect has been decomposed into an income effect $(x_1' - x_1^+)$ and an own substitution effect $(x_1^+ - x_1^*)$. The income effect will again be positive, negative or zero depending on the form of the indifference map. The substitution effect will, as in the Hicksian case, always lead to a rise in demand for a good whose price has fallen. x^+ cannot lie to the left of x^* on B_4 because this would mean that the consumer is now choosing x^+ when x^* is still available, having previously rejected x^+ in favour of x^*. The transitivity assumption would be violated by such behaviour. The Slutsky definition yields a prediction (the sign of the substitution effect) which can be tested without specific knowledge of the consumer's indifference curves to 'cancel out' the income effect.

Our consideration of the comparative static properties of the model has shown that it does not yield refutable predictions about the overall change in demand for individual goods induced by *ceteris paribus* changes in a price or money income. In other words,

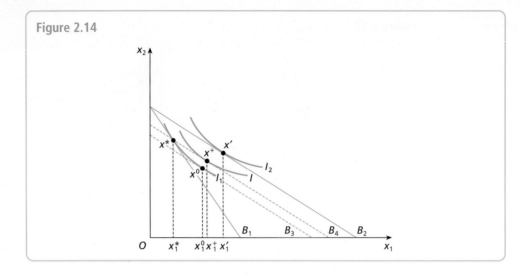

Figure 2.14

$$\frac{\partial x_i^*}{\partial p_j} = \frac{\partial D_i}{\partial p_j} \gtreqless 0 \qquad i, j = 1, 2, \ldots, n$$

and

$$\frac{\partial x_i^*}{\partial M} = \frac{\partial D_i}{\partial M} \gtreqless 0 \qquad i = 1, 2, \ldots, n$$

for every good and price. Only by considering the effect of changes in p_j or M on *all* goods, or by considering the effect of changes in p_j and M on a single good or by making more specific assumptions about the consumer's preferences can definite predictions be generated.

Consider, however, the consequences of equal proportionate changes in all prices and M. Suppose M increases to kM ($k > 1$) and prices to kp_1 and kp_2. The slope of the budget line will be unaffected. The intercept on the x_1 axis is M/p_1 before the changes in M and prices and $kM/kp_1 = M/p_1$ after the change. Similarly for the intercept on the x_2 axis. Hence the equal proportionate changes in M and all prices alter neither the slope nor the intercepts on the budget line and so the feasible set is unaltered. If the feasible set is unchanged then so is the optimal bundle.

The model therefore predicts that the consumer will not suffer from *money illusion*; he will not alter his behaviour if his purchasing power and relative prices are constant, irrespective of the absolute level of prices and money income. More formally, the demand function D_i for every commodity is *homogeneous of degree zero* in prices and money income, since we have

$$x_i^* = D_i(kp, kM) = k^0 D_i(p, M) = D_i(p, M) \qquad [\text{D.2}]$$

Demand curves

We complete this section on comparative statics by deriving the demand curve from the utility maximization model. The individual's *demand curve* for a good shows how desired or planned purchases of it vary as its price varies, other prices and income being held constant. As we have seen, a distinction can be drawn between constant

Figure 2.15

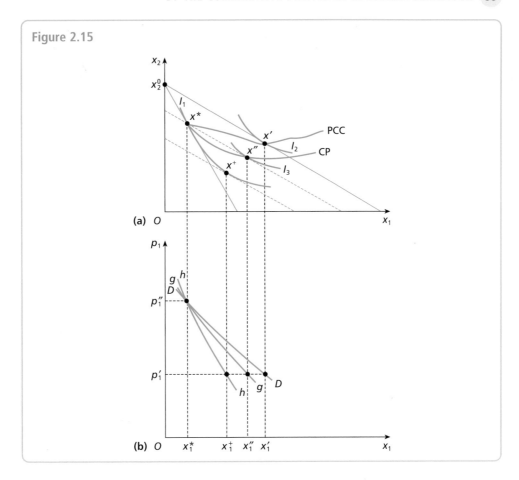

real and constant *money* income and there are also two possible definitions of constant real income. Figure 2.15 shows the derivation of three demand curves, corresponding to the different assumptions about what is held constant, from the consumer's indifference map. The upper part of Fig. 2.15 is Fig. 2.14 with two additions. The PCC (price consumption curve) shows the bundles chosen as p_1 varies with M constant (i.e. as the budget line pivots through x_2^0). The constant purchasing power consumption curve (CP) shows the bundles chosen as p_1 varies, with the consumer's money income varying so as just to enable the consumer to purchase the original bundle x^* (i.e. the Slutsky definition of constant real income is adopted and so the budget line pivots through x^*). The indifference curve I_1 shows how consumption varies as p_1 varies, with M varying to keep the consumer's utility level constant (i.e. the Hicks definition of constant real income is adopted and so the budget line slides round I_1). These three curves therefore show the change in the demand for x_1 (and x_2) as p_1 changes, with income (variously defined) and p_2 held constant. The lower half of the figure uses the information contained in the three curves to plot demand curves for x_1.

The *Marshallian constant money income demand curve DD* shows the effect of changes in p_1 with M (and p_2) held constant. It plots the information contained in the price consumption curve. For example, a fall in p_1 from p_1'' to p_1' with M constant causes the consumer to shift from bundle x^* to x' and his demand for x_1 to rise from x_1^* to x_1'.

The *constant purchasing power demand curve gg* corresponds to the CP curve. The fall in p_1 from p_1'' to p_1' with purchasing power constant causes the consumer to shift from x^* to x'' and his demand to increase from x_1^* to x_1''.

The *Hicksian constant utility demand curve hh* is derived from the indifference curve I_1. The fall in p_1 with utility constant at its initial level $u(x^*)$ causes the consumer to shift from x^* to x^+, and his demand to increase from x_1^* to x_1^+.

The constant money income demand curve plots the whole price effect and the other two curves plot only the two versions of the substitution effect. Hence the constant utility and purchasing power demand curves will be steeper than the constant money income demand curve when x_1 is a normal good, because they do not plot the income effect of the price change. When x_1 is inferior the relative steepness of the various demand curves is reversed. This analysis is taken further in Chapter 3, with the help of duality theory.

EXERCISE 2D

1. Derive the demand curve of the consumer of Question 3, Exercise 2B, for garbage disposal. Decompose the effects of a price change into income and substitution effects.

2. Examine the responses of an electricity consumer to changes in the connection charge and prices of electricity.

3. Examine the income and substitution effects in the cases given in Question 4, Exercise 2A.

4. Explain the difference between the Hicks and Slutsky definitions of real income, and apply this to explain why, in Fig. 2.15, the demand curve *hh* is steeper than the demand curve *gg*.

5. *Why* do we decompose the price effect into income and substitution effects?

6. Examine the properties of the demand functions of a consumer with the following utility functions:

   (a) $u(x) = x_1^{\alpha_1} x_2^{\alpha_2} \dots x_n^{\alpha_n}$ ($\alpha_i > 0$, all i; $\Sigma \alpha_i = 1$) (Cobb–Douglas)

   (b) $u(x) = (x_1 - k_1)^{\alpha_1}(x_2 - k_2)^{\alpha_2} \dots (x_n - k_n)^{\alpha_n}$ ($\alpha_i > 0$, all i; $\Sigma \alpha_i = 1$; $k_i > 0$, all i) (Stone–Geary)

   (c) $u(x) = \Sigma_i f_i(x_i)$ ($f_i' > 0$) (additive separable)

   (d) $u(x) = f(x_1) + x_2$ ($f' > 0$; $f'' < 0$) (quasi-linear)

   What interpretation can be given to the k_i in case (b)?

E. Offer curves and net demand curves

We now consider the case of a consumer who has preferences satisfying the assumptions of section A, and is endowed, not with a given money income, but with fixed amounts of commodities which she can consume or sell on the market in order to finance purchases of other commodities. The feasible set is defined by the non-negativity requirements on consumption and by the constraint that the market value of the bundle consumed cannot exceed the market value of the consumer's initial endowments. Her budget constraint is therefore:

$$\Sigma p_i x_i \leq \Sigma p_i \bar{x}_i = W \qquad i = 1, 2, \dots, n \qquad \text{[E.1]}$$

Figure 2.16

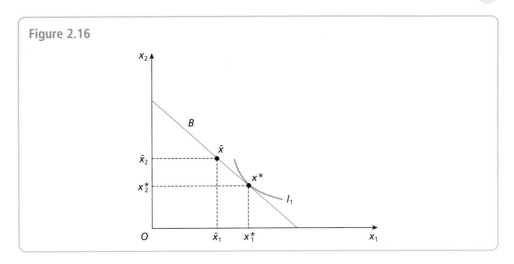

where $\bar{x}_i$ is her *initial endowment of good i*. $\sum p_i \bar{x}_i = W$ is the market value of the initial endowment, or the proceeds which could be obtained if the consumer sold all her initial endowments at the ruling market prices.

If x_i (the amount of commodity i *consumed*) differs from her endowment $\bar{x}_i$, then

(a) if $\hat{x}_i = x_i - \bar{x}_i > 0$, the consumer buys $\hat{x}_i$ of commodity i;

(b) if $\hat{x}_i = x_i - \bar{x}_i < 0$, she sells $\hat{x}_i$ of the commodity.

$\hat{x}_i$ is the *net demand* for commodity i. We can rewrite the budget constraint as:

$$\sum p_i \hat{x}_i = \sum p_i (x_i - \bar{x}_i) \leqslant 0 \qquad \text{[E.2]}$$

The sum of her expenditures on the quantities of goods she buys (which will be a positive component of the overall sum) cannot exceed the sum of the proceeds from the quantities of goods she sells (a negative component of the overall sum).

In the two-good case shown in Fig. 2.16 the budget line B is defined by

$$p_1 x_1 + p_2 x_2 = p_1 \bar{x}_1 + p_2 \bar{x}_2 = W \quad \text{or} \quad p_1(x_1 - \bar{x}_1) + p_2(x_2 - \bar{x}_2) = 0 \qquad \text{[E.3]}$$

and has a slope of $-(p_1/p_2)$. B must pass through $\bar{x} = (\bar{x}_1, \bar{x}_2)$, the endowed bundle, since whatever prices she faces the consumer will always have the possibility of consuming her endowment, i.e. neither buying nor selling on the market. The feasible set is similar in shape to the case of the consumer endowed with a fixed money income M, but there are significant differences as regards the effect of changes in prices:

(a) The market value of the endowment $W = \sum p_i \bar{x}_i$ will increase or decrease as the price of a commodity increases or decreases.

(b) Since the consumer is always able to consume her initial endowment vector $\bar{x}$, a change in a single price will cause the budget line to rotate through $\bar{x}$, rather than through an intercept on one of the axes.

(c) An equal proportionate change in all prices leaves the budget line unaffected, though the nominal value of the endowments varies in the same proportion. The budget line must still pass through $\bar{x}$, and its slope will be unaffected by such price changes and hence its position is unchanged. Only change in *relative* prices or in the initial endowments will alter the consumer's feasible set and therefore the consumer's demand or supply of a commodity. In the terminology of section D, her demand functions will again be *homogeneous of degree zero in prices*.

It is clear from the way in which the budget constraint [E.1] was written that the consumer's optimization problem in this case is formally identical to that considered previously, so we will not dwell on the equilibrium conditions and the possibility of corner solutions. We restrict ourselves to examining the comparative static properties of tangency solutions and the derivation of supply and demand curves.

In Fig. 2.16, $x^* = (x_1^*, x_2^*)$ is the optimal consumption bundle on B, where the indifference curve I_1 is tangent to the budget line. Since $x_1^* > \bar{x}_1$ and $\bar{x}_2 > x_2^*$ the consumer is maximizing utility by selling commodity 2, which gives her receipts of $p_2(\bar{x}_2 - x_2^*)$, and buying commodity 1 at a cost of $p_1(x_1^* - \bar{x}_1)$.

Increases in p_1 relative to p_2 will make the budget line rotate clockwise about $\bar{x}$ and the optimal bundle will vary as p_1/p_2 changes, as the upper half of Fig. 2.17 illustrates. With the budget line at B_2 the optimal bundle is the endowed bundle $\bar{x}$, and the consumer does not trade at all on the market. A further increase in p_1/p_2 will shift the budget line to B_3 where the optimal bundle is x' and the consumer is now selling commodity 1 and buying commodity 2.

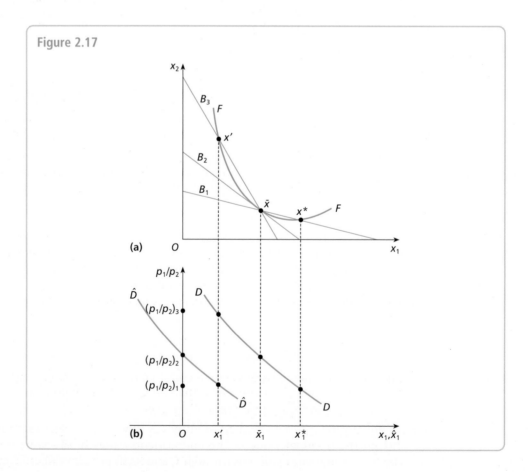

Figure 2.17

The line *FF* in Fig. 2.17 is the locus of optimal bundles traced out as p_1/p_2 varies with $\bar{x}$ fixed and is called the *offer curve*, since it shows the amounts (positive or negative) of the two goods which the consumer offers on the market at different relative prices. The consumer's *consumption demand curve DD* in the lower half of Fig. 2.17, which plots the consumption of x_1 as a function of p_1/p_2, is derived from the offer curve. As p_1 increases relative to p_2 the consumer reduces consumption of commodity 1, from x_1^* to $\bar{x}_1$ and then to x_1' as she moves along *FF* from x^* to $\bar{x}$ and x'. $(p_1/p_2)_1$, $(p_1/p_2)_2$ and $(p_1/p_2)_3$ are the price ratios at which x^*, $\bar{x}$ and x' are chosen.

The $\hat{D}\hat{D}$ curve in part (b) of Fig. 2.17 is the consumer's *net demand curve* and plots the net demand $\hat{x}_1 = x_1 - \bar{x}_1$, the amount of commodity 1 that she buys or sells on the market, against (p_1/p_2). It is derived by taking the horizontal distance between the *DD* curve and a vertical line through $x_1 = \bar{x}_1$ at each price ratio. Notice that when $(p_1/p_2) > (p_1/p_2)_2$ the consumer's net demand is negative: she supplies commodity 1 to the market.

In the illustrations above the effect of a fall in the relative price of a commodity was to increase the consumer's demand for it. However, with a different indifference map the *DD* and $\hat{D}\hat{D}$ curves could have been positively sloped, indicating that rises in the relative price of commodity 1 reduce the amount of the commodity supplied to the market. Hence a *ceteris paribus* change in a single price may increase, decrease or leave unchanged the individual's consumption of any single commodity. Similarly, a *ceteris paribus* change in the initial endowment may increase, decrease or leave unchanged the consumption of commodity *i*.

The consumption decision in terms of net demands

The consumer's optimization problem studied earlier had the levels of consumption $(x_1, \ldots, x_n)$ as choice variables, but it is possible to formulate the problem with the consumer's net demands $(\hat{x}_1, \ldots, \hat{x}_n)$ as the choice variables. Since this particular approach will be used in Chapter 12 on general equilibrium, it is useful to show here that it is equivalent to the model of section C.

The consumer's utility function $u(x)$ can be rewritten as a function of the net demands $\hat{x}_i$ since from the definitions $\hat{x}_i \equiv x_i - \bar{x}_i$ we have $x_i \equiv \hat{x}_i + \bar{x}_i$ and so

$$u(x_1, \ldots, x_n) = u(\hat{x}_1 + \bar{x}_1, \ldots, \hat{x}_n + \bar{x}_n) \qquad [E.4]$$

Since the initial endowments $\bar{x}_i$ are constants, u varies only as the $\hat{x}_i$ vary:

$$u(\hat{x}_1 + \bar{x}_1, \ldots, \hat{x}_n + \bar{x}_n) = \hat{u}(\hat{x}_1, \ldots, \hat{x}_n) \qquad [E.5]$$

and

$$\frac{\partial \hat{u}}{\partial \hat{x}_i} = \frac{\partial u}{\partial \hat{x}_i} = \frac{\partial u}{\partial \hat{x}_i}\frac{\partial \hat{x}_i}{\partial x_i} = \frac{\partial u}{\partial x_i} \qquad [E.6]$$

$\hat{u}$ will have all the properties possessed by u such as continuity, quasi-concavity, etc.

The feasible set can also be rewritten in terms of the $\hat{x}_i$, as was shown in [E.2].

The non-negativity constraints on the x_i are replaced by

$$x_i = \hat{x}_i + \bar{x}_i \geqslant 0 \qquad [E.7]$$

or

$$\hat{x}_i \geqslant -\bar{x}_i \qquad i = 1, \ldots, n$$

i.e. the supply of a good cannot exceed the endowment of that good. The consumer's optimization problem can now be written in terms of the net demands as (compare [C.1]):

$$\max \hat{u}(\hat{x}_1, \ldots, \hat{x}_n)$$
$$\text{s.t. } \Sigma p_i \hat{x}_i \leqslant 0 \qquad \qquad \qquad \qquad \text{[E.8]}$$
$$\hat{x}_i \geqslant -\hat{x}_i \qquad i = 1, \ldots, n$$

Proceeding, as in section C, to assume that the direct constraints [E.7] do not bind at the solution, the Lagrange function of the problem may be written

$$L = \hat{u}(\hat{x}_1, \ldots, \hat{x}_n) - \lambda \Sigma p_i \hat{x}_i$$

First-order conditions are

$$\frac{\partial L}{\partial \hat{x}_i} = \hat{u}_i - \lambda p_i = 0 \qquad i = 1, \ldots, n \qquad \text{[E.9]}$$

$$\frac{\partial L}{\partial \lambda} = -\Sigma p_i \hat{x}_i = 0 \qquad \qquad \qquad \text{[E.10]}$$

and from [E.6] we see that [E.9] is identical to [C.7], so that we would be able to derive exactly the same equilibrium conditions and comparative static properties as in section C.

This reformulation of the problem in terms of net demands rather than consumption bundles is, in terms of the diagrammatic analysis of Fig. 2.17, equivalent to shifting the origin to $\bar{x}$ so that $\hat{x}_1 = x_1 - \bar{x}_1$ and $\hat{x}_2 = x_2 - \bar{x}_2$ are measured along the axes. The budget line now passes through the new origin and the consumer's indifference map is unaffected. The reader should redraw Fig. 2.15 and the upper part of 2.16 in this way to confirm that nothing of substance is affected by the relabelling.

EXERCISE 2E

1. Show that, when the consumer is a net seller of good x_1, a fall in price of this good can result in a fall in demand for it, even given that it is a normal good. Explain intuitively why this is the case. Show that it does not happen if the consumer is a net buyer of the good.

2. How would you interpret the slope of the consumer's offer curve?

3. Explain why, at every point on the offer curve, there is tangency between an indifference curve and the budget line generating that point.

4. Discuss the relevance of the model examined in this section to:

   (a) a market in stocks and shares;

   (b) a market in new and secondhand cars;

   (c) the case where x_1 is bread and x_2 is leisure time, with $\bar{x}_1 = 0$ and $\bar{x}_2 = 24$ hours per day.

Appendix 1: The lexicographic ordering

The lexicographic ordering shows the need for the continuity assumption if we wish to work with a numerical representation of the consumer's preference ordering, i.e. with a utility function. The lexicographic ordering can be shown to satisfy the first four assumptions set out in section A but to be incapable of being represented by a utility function. On the other hand, it can be shown to give rise to well-defined demand functions, which implies that the continuity assumption is not necessary for their existence.

When consumption bundles consist of two goods, the ordering takes the following form. The consumer's preferences are such that, given two bundles $x' = (x_1', x_2')$ and $x'' = (x_1'', x_2'')$:

(a) $x_1' > x_1''$ implies $x' > x''$

(b) $x_1' = x_1''$ and $x_2' > x_2''$ implies $x' > x''$

The consumer always prefers a bundle with more of the first good in it, regardless of the quantity of the second good; only if the bundles contain the same amount of the first good does the quantity of the second matter. An illustration would be the case of a drunkard who would always prefer a combination of beer and bread with more beer in it to one with less, regardless of the amount of bread, but if the amounts of beer are the same, prefers the one with more bread. It is called a 'lexicographic ordering' because it is analogous to the way words are ordered in a dictionary: words beginning with A always come before those beginning with B, but if two words begin with A then the second letter determines their order.

The indifference sets corresponding to this ordering are found with the help of Fig. 2.18. Take the bundle $x' = (x_1', x_2')$, and ask: what points are preferred to it, and to what points is it preferred? The area B, *including* the points on the solid line above

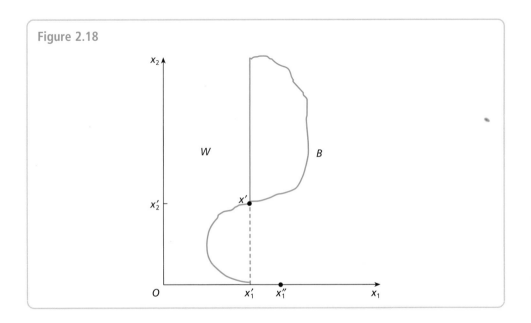

Figure 2.18

x', must all be preferred to x', since points to the right of x' contain more x_1, while points along the solid line contain as much x_1 and more x_2. The area W, *including* the points on the broken line below x', must all be such that x' is preferred to them, since points to the left of x' contain less x_1, while points on the broken line contain as much x_1 but less x_2. But if all the points in B are preferred to x', and x' is preferred to all the points in W, there can be no other points indifferent to x', and so the indifference set for x' consists only of this single point. Since x' was chosen arbitrarily, this is true for every point in the space: each lies in an indifference set consisting only of itself.

The lexicographic ordering does not satisfy the assumption of continuity, since the indifference set is a point and not a continuous curve. If we reduce the amount of x_1 in the bundle, by however small an amount, we can find no amount of x_2 to compensate for the change (the drunkard cannot be bribed by any amount of bread to give up even a sip of beer). We now show that it is not possible to represent the lexicographic ordering by a utility function.

First, if we divide the real line into non-empty, disjoint bounded intervals, the set of these intervals is *countable*. That is, we can put them into a one-to-one correspondence with the set of positive integers $\{1, 2, 3, \dots\}$. On the other hand, the points on the real line itself or some interval of it, e.g. its positive half, are *not* countable. It follows that any argument which leads to the conclusion that the positive half of the real line is countable must be false. We can show that the assumption that a utility function exists for the lexicographic ordering does just that.

Suppose that a utility function $u(x_1, x_2)$ exists, which gives a numerical representation of the lexicographic ordering. Refer to Fig. 2.18. Setting $x_1 = x_1'$, the function will take on the values $u(x_1', x_2)$ for all $x_2 \geqslant 0$ along the vertical line in the figure. This set of values has a lower bound at $u(x_1', 0)$, and it must have an upper bound because the u-values for any $x_1 = x_1'' > x_1'$ must be greater. Hence this set of values represents a non-empty bounded interval on the real line. Now choosing a value $x_1'' > x_1'$ we can in the same way associate with it a non-empty bounded interval of real numbers. Moreover, however close to x_1' we choose x_1'', it must always be the case that the intervals are disjoint, since $u(x_1'', x_2) > u(x_1', x_2)$ for every x_2, since $x_1'' > x_1'$. We can repeat this argument for every value of x_1 on the horizontal axis: to each corresponds a unique non-empty bounded interval on the real line. But this means we have put the positive half of the real line into one-to-one correspondence with a set of non-empty disjoint intervals of the real line, implying that the former is countable. This is false, and therefore so is the initial assumption that the utility function exists.

As we suggested earlier, the fact that the lexicographic ordering does not possess a numerical representation does not mean the consumer's choice problem cannot be solved nor even that a continuous demand function does not exist. Remember that continuity assumptions are usually sufficient rather than necessary. Thus consider our beer drinker with lexicographic preferences, an income of M and facing price p_1 for beer and price p_2 for bread. He will *always* spend his entire income on beer and nothing on bread. Hence his demand functions are

$$x_1 = M/p_1, \qquad x_2 = 0$$

which are well-defined and continuous. His demand curve for beer is just a rectangular hyperbola in (x_1, p_1) space and his demand function for bread in (x_2, p_2) space is the vertical axis.

EXERCISE A1

1. Suppose that the consumer has lexicographic preferences, but must consume a minimum level of x_2 for subsistence. Show how this affects his demand functions.

2. Likewise, show how the analysis is affected by the assumption that the consumer reaches a satiation level for x_1, but not for x_2.

3. Generalize the statement of the lexicographic ordering to n goods. What would be the demand functions with and without subsistence and satiation levels of each good?

4. How plausible do you find the assumption that a consumer has a lexicographic preference ordering with respect to:

   (a) each good taken separately;

   (b) groups of goods, e.g. food, clothing, shelter, entertainment?

Appendix 2: Existence of a utility function

The lexicographic ordering satisfies completeness, reflexivity, transitivity and non-satiation, but no utility function can be constructed to represent it. We now show that adding the assumption of continuity guarantees that a continuous, increasing utility function can be found to represent the preference ordering. We do this by actually constructing such a function.

In Fig. 2.19, since the indifference curves are continuous, they intersect the 45° line as shown in the figure. For any point such as x^0, associate with it the real number $u(x^0)$, a coordinate of the point at which the indifference curve through x^0 cuts the 45° line (either coordinate will do). The u-values are a numerical representation of this utility function: indifferent bundles have the same u-value, preferred bundles have higher u-values. We now put this more formally.

First, we need to state the continuity axiom in a more precise form. The better set of any point x^0 is $B(x^0) = \{x \mid x \succsim x^0\}$, and the worse set is $W(x^0) = \{x \mid x^0 \succsim x\}$. Then the continuity assumption is

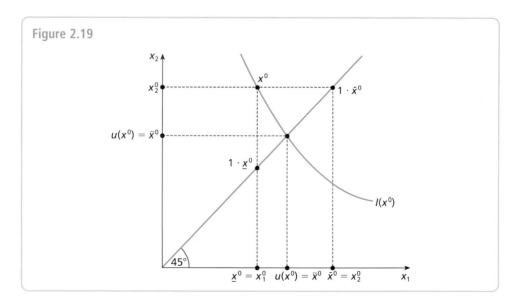

Figure 2.19

For all bundles x^0 the sets $B(x^0)$ and $W(x^0)$ are closed.

The lexicographic ordering violates this assumption. Recall that a closed set is one which contains its boundary points, i.e. points having the property that every neighbourhood of them contains points which are, and points which are not, in the set. In Fig. 2.18, the boundary of $B(x')$ and $W(x')$ is the vertical line through x'. Points on the dotted line below x' are not in $B(x')$, points on the solid line above x' are not in $W(x')$, and so neither of these sets is closed. Loosely, this means that one can move from a point strictly preferred to x', to a point strictly inferior to x', without passing through a point indifferent to x', however close to x' these points may be. In this loose sense there is a 'jump' in the preference ordering. The continuity assumption removes this possibility.

We now construct the utility function. First, we show that associated with any x^0 is a unique number $u(x^0)$, then that this has the properties of a utility function, and finally that this function is continuous.

Existence of $u(x^0)$: Given any bundle $x^0 = (x_1^0, \ldots, x_n^0)$, choose the smallest and largest components, and denote them by $\underline{x}^0$ and $\bar{x}^0$ respectively. If $\mathbf{1}$ is the n-vector $(1, \ldots, 1)$, then we have $\mathbf{1} \cdot \bar{x}^0 \succsim x^0 \succsim \mathbf{1} \cdot \underline{x}^0$ (Fig. 2.19 illustrates).

If $\bar{x}^0 = \underline{x}^0$ then the proposition holds trivially so we ignore this case. Consider the non-empty interval of real numbers $[\underline{x}^0, \bar{x}^0]$. We claim that there exists a number $\tilde{x}^0 \in [\underline{x}^0, \bar{x}^0]$ such that $\mathbf{1} \cdot \tilde{x}^0 \sim x^0$. Suppose not. Then for every $x \in [\underline{x}^0, \bar{x}^0]$ we have either $\mathbf{1} \cdot x > x^0$ or $x^0 > \mathbf{1} \cdot x$. Moreover, the transitivity and non-satiation assumptions imply that those x-values for which $\mathbf{1} \cdot x > x^0$ form a sub-interval of numbers strictly greater than the complementary sub-interval for which $x^0 > \mathbf{1} \cdot x$. This implies that the former sub-interval has a lower bound, and so a greatest lower bound; likewise the latter sub-interval has a least upper bound. Moreover, these bounds must be the same. Denote this common bound by b. Thus we can partition $[\underline{x}^0, \bar{x}^0]$ into $[\underline{x}^0, b]$ and $(b, \bar{x}^0]$, or $[\underline{x}^0, b)$ and $[b, \bar{x}^0]$. In each case, $\mathbf{1} \cdot b$ is a boundary point of $W(x^0)$ and $B(x^0)$, and is either not contained in $W(x^0)$ or not contained in $B(x^0)$. But this contradicts the assumption that these sets are closed. So there does exist $\tilde{x}^0$ such that $\mathbf{1} \cdot \tilde{x}^0 \sim x^0$, and we take $u(x^0) = \tilde{x}^0$. The non-satiation assumption implies that $u(x^0)$ is unique.

We now have to show that the $u(x)$ numbers constructed in this way satisfy the definition of a utility function, which is, for any two bundles x^0, x',

$$u(x^0) \geqslant u(x') \Leftrightarrow x^0 \succsim x'$$

Proof

(a) $u(x^0) \geqslant u(x') \Rightarrow x^0 \succsim x'$. Suppose not, i.e. $u(x^0) \geqslant u(x')$ but $x' > x^0$. Then $\mathbf{1} \cdot u(x^0) \geqslant \mathbf{1} \cdot u(x')$, where $\mathbf{1}$ is again an n-vector of ones. We then have by transitivity

$$\mathbf{1} \cdot u(x') \sim x' > x^0 \sim \mathbf{1} \cdot u(x^0)$$

which by non-satiation gives the contradiction

$$u(x') > u(x^0)$$

(b) $x^0 \succsim x' \Rightarrow u(x^0) \geqslant u(x')$. Suppose not, i.e. $x^0 \succsim x'$ but $u(x') > u(x^0)$. Then $\mathbf{1} \cdot u(x') > \mathbf{1} \cdot u(x^0)$ and the chain $x' \sim \mathbf{1} \cdot u(x') > \mathbf{1} \cdot u(x^0) \sim x^0$ gives the contradiction.

Finally, to prove that $u(x)$ is a continuous function it is convenient to take the following property of continuous functions.

A function $u(x)$, $x \in \mathbb{R}^n_+$, is continuous on $\mathbb{R}^n_+$ if and only if for each pair of subsets of function values, U_1 and U_2, if U_1 and U_2 are separated then $u^{-1}(U_1)$ and $u^{-1}(U_2)$ are separated.

Two sets are separated if no point in one set is a boundary point of the other. Thus, for example, the pairs of sets $[0, 3/4]$ and $[1, 2]$, and $[0, 1)$ and $(1, 2]$ are separated, while the pair $[0, 1]$ and $(1, 2]$ are not.

Then, take any bundle x^0 and its corresponding utility value $u(x^0)$, and form the intervals $U_1 = [\underline{u}, u(x^0))$, $U_2 = (u(x^0), \bar{u}]$ where $\underline{u} < u(x^0)$ and $\bar{u} > u(x^0)$ are arbitrary. Then clearly U_1 and U_2 are separated. The set $u^{-1}(U_1) = \{x | u(x) \in U_1\}$ is a subset of the interior of $W(x^0)$, and the set $u^{-1}(U_2) = \{x | u(x) \in U_2\}$ is a subset of the interior of $B(x^0)$. Since these subsets lie on either side of $I(x^0)$, which belongs to neither of them, they are also separated. Since x^0, $\underline{u}$ and $\bar{u}$ were arbitrary, the function $u(x)$ is continuous.

The above discussion of the existence of a continuous, increasing utility function used a specific construction and also made use of the non-satiation assumption. It is possible to drop the assumption and still prove existence of a continuous utility function, but it requires more advanced mathematical methods.

Consumer theory: duality

In the previous chapter we defined the consumer problem as that of choosing a vector x to solve the problem max $u(x)$ s.t. $px = M$, where p is a price vector and M money income. From the solution we derived *Marshallian* demand functions $x_i = D_i(p, M)$ $(i = 1, \ldots, n)$, which express demands as functions of prices and money income. We observed that we cannot place restrictions on the signs of the partial derivatives of these functions: $\partial D_i/\partial M \gtreqless 0$, $\partial D_i/\partial p_j \gtreqless 0$ $(i, j = 1, \ldots, n)$. In particular the demand for a good does not necessarily vary inversely with its own price. However, as a result of a diagrammatic analysis, we *were* able to say that this will be true of normal goods, or of inferior goods whose income effects are weaker than their substitution effects. We now put this analysis on a more rigorous and general basis. We also consider the problem, central to many applications of consumer theory, of deriving a money measure of the costs and benefits incurred by a consumer as a result of price changes. In doing so, we develop the methods and concepts of *duality theory*, an approach to the analysis of optimization problems which permits an elegant and concise derivation of comparative static results.

A. The expenditure function

The expenditure function is derived from the problem of minimizing the total expenditure necessary for the consumer to achieve a specified level of utility u:

$$\min_{x_1, \ldots, x_n} \Sigma \, p_i x_i \quad \text{s.t.} \quad \text{(i) } u(x_1, \ldots, x_n) \geqslant u$$

$$\text{(ii) } x_i \geqslant 0, \qquad i = 1, \ldots, n \qquad \text{[A.1]}$$

If all prices are positive the first constraint in [A.1] will be satisfied as an equality in the solution, since if $u(x) > u$ expenditure can be reduced without violating the constraint. If it is further assumed that all x_i are strictly positive in the solution, we can write the Lagrange function for the problem (with μ as the Lagrange multiplier) as

$$L = \Sigma \, p_i x_i + \mu[u - u(x_1, \ldots, x_n)] \qquad \text{[A.2]}$$

and the necessary conditions for a minimum of L, also the necessary conditions for a solution of [A.1], are

$$\frac{\partial L}{\partial x_i} = p_i - \mu u_i = 0 \qquad i = 1, \ldots, n \qquad \text{[A.3]}$$

$$\frac{\partial L}{\partial \mu} = u - u(x_1, \ldots, x_n) = 0 \qquad \text{[A.4]}$$

Figure 3.1

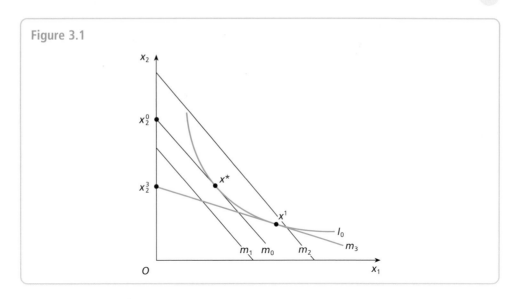

The conditions on the x_i bear a striking resemblance to [C.9] in Chapter 2. Writing them as $p_i = \mu u_i$ and dividing the condition on x_i by the condition on x_j gives

$$\frac{p_i}{p_j} = \frac{u_i}{u_j} \qquad \text{[A.5]}$$

which is identical with Chapter 2 [C.2]: the ratio of prices is equated to the marginal rate of substitution. This is not surprising as examination of the two-good case in Fig. 3.1 indicates. The indifference curve I_0 shows the combinations of x_1 and x_2 which give a utility level of u and the feasible set for the problem is all points on or above I_0. The lines m_0, m_1, m_2, are isoexpenditure lines similar to the budget lines of earlier diagrams. m_0, for example, plots all bundles costing m_0, i.e. satisfying the equation $p_1 x_1 + p_2 x_2 = m_0$. The problem is to find the point in the feasible set which is on the lowest isoexpenditure line. This will, in the tangency solution shown here, be where the indifference curve I_0 is tangent to the isoexpenditure line m_0. The problem confronting the *utility-maximizing* consumer is to move along the budget line until the highest indifference curve is reached. The *expenditure-minimizing* problem is to move along the indifference curve until the lowest isoexpenditure line is reached.

The optimal x_i^* in problem [A.1] depend on the prices and the utility level u:

$$x_i^* = H_i(p_1, \ldots, p_n, u) = H_i(p, u) \qquad i = 1, \ldots, n \qquad \text{[A.6]}$$

and $H_i(p, u)$ is the *Hicksian* demand function for x_i. Substituting the optimal values of the x_i in $\Sigma\, p_i x_i$ gives

$$\Sigma\, p_i x_i^* = \Sigma\, p_i H_i(p, u) = m(p, u) \qquad \text{[A.7]}$$

$m(p, u)$ is the *expenditure function*, showing the minimum level of expenditure necessary to achieve a given utility level as a function of prices and the required utility level.

The Hicksian demand function is also called the *compensated demand function*. In considering the effect of a change in price on demand with utility held constant (the partial derivative $\partial H_i / \partial p_j$ ($i, j = 1, \ldots, n$)) we automatically make whatever changes in expenditure are required to compensate for the effects of the price change on real income or utility. This is illustrated in Fig. 3.1. Assume p_2 remains constant while p_1 falls to give a new family of isoexpenditure lines, with slopes corresponding to that of m_3 in the figure. x^1 is the new expenditure minimizing consumption bundle, and the change from x^* to x^1 is the effect of making the relative price change with m varying to keep u constant. The optimal expenditure line slides round the indifference curve from m_0 to m_3 as the optimal bundle changes from x^* to x^1. The minimized total expenditure can be read off from the intercepts of m_0 and m_3 on the x_2 axis. The fall in p_1 lowers m from $p_2 x_2^0$ to $p_2 x_2^3$.

Provided the indifference curves are strictly convex to the origin the optimal x_i (and hence the expenditure function) vary smoothly and continuously with the prices of the goods. Hence the $H_i(p, u)$ functions have continuous derivatives with respect to the prices. The demand *curve* we derive from the Hicksian demand *function* was represented by curve hh in Fig. 2.15. The slope of the Hicksian or compensated demand curve, $\partial H_i / \partial p_i$ $(i = 1, \ldots, n)$, is the *substitution effect of the price change*, since by definition $\partial H_i / \partial p_i$ is taken with u held constant.

The expenditure function gives the smallest expenditure, at a given price vector, that is required to achieve a particular 'standard of living' or utility level, and describes how that expenditure will change as prices or the required utility level change. The assumptions made in Chapter 2 concerning the nature of the consumer's preference ordering and indifference sets imply certain properties of the expenditure function:

(a) The expenditure function is concave in prices

Choose two price vectors p' and p'', and k such that $0 \le k \le 1$. Define $\bar{p} = kp' + (1 - k)p''$. We have to prove that (see the definition of concavity in Appendix B):

$$m(\bar{p}, u) \ge km(p', u) + (1 - k)m(p'', u)$$

for *given u*.

Proof

Let x' and x'' solve the expenditure minimization problem when the price vector is respectively p' and p''. By definition of the expenditure function, $p'x' = m(p', u)$ and $p''x'' = m(p'', u)$. Likewise, let $\bar{x}$ solve the problem when the price vector is $\bar{p}$, so that $\bar{p}\bar{x} = m(\bar{p}, u)$. Since x' and x'' are solutions to their respective expenditure minimization problems we must have

$$p'\bar{x} \ge p'x' \quad \text{and} \quad p''\bar{x} \ge p''x'' \quad \text{[A.8]}$$

Multiplying through the first inequality by k and the second by $1 - k$ and summing, gives

$$kp'\bar{x} + (1 - k)p''\bar{x} \ge kp'x' + (1 - k)p''x'' \quad \text{[A.9]}$$

But by definition of $\bar{p}$ this implies

$$(kp' + (1 - k)p'')\bar{x} = \bar{p}\bar{x} \ge kp'x' + (1 - k)p''x'' \quad \text{[A.10]}$$

which is the result we want.

Figure 3.2 illustrates the proof of this important result. It is obvious that, when the isoexpenditure lines at which x' and x'' are optimal solutions are shifted so as to pass through point $\bar{x}$, they must yield higher expenditure, thus giving the key inequalities in [A.8]. The rest of the proof then follows by simple algebra.

Figure 3.2

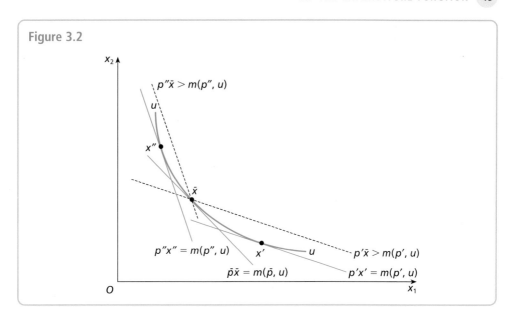

The figure could in one sense be misleading. The inequalities (which in this case are *strict*) appear to follow from the convexity of the indifference curves. Note, however, that the inequalities in [A.8] follow simply from the fact that x' (respectively x'') minimizes px at price vector p' (respectively p'') while $\bar{x}$ may not – [A.8] then follows from the definition of a minimum. Thus the proof of concavity of the expenditure function does *not depend* on convexity of preferences. However, the property of *uniqueness* of solutions like x' and x'', and the differentiability of Hicksian demands and of the expenditure function, do. Note that strict convexity of preferences implies strict concavity of the expenditure function at an interior solution to problem [A.1], since it implies uniqueness of the solution and hence strict inequalities in [A.8].

Figure 3.3 illustrates the strict concavity of the expenditure function when the price vectors p' and p'' differ only in respect of one price, p_i. The slope of the expenditure function at a point is equal to the compensated demand for good i at the price p_i:

(b) Shephard's lemma: $\partial m(p, u)/\partial p_i = x_i^* = H_i(p, u)$

The proof is just a version of the Envelope Theorem (Appendix J). Differentiating [A.7] with respect to the *i*th price gives

$$\frac{\partial m}{\partial p_i} = x_i^* + \sum_{j=1}^{n} p_j \frac{\partial x_j^*}{\partial p_i} = x_i^* + \mu \sum_{j=1}^{n} u_j \frac{\partial x_j^*}{\partial p_i} = x_i^* \qquad [\text{A.11}]$$

The second equality uses the fact that $p_i = \mu u_i$ from the first-order condition [A.3]. Since utility is held constant when p_i varies, differentiating the constraint [A.4] with respect to p_i shows that $\sum_{j=1}^{n} u_j \partial x_j^*/\partial p_i^* = 0$ which gives the third equality in [A.11].

Thus the partial derivative of the expenditure function with respect to the *i*th price is the compensated demand for the *i*th good. In Fig. 3.3, the slope of the curve at price p_i' is $x_i' = H_i(p_1', \ldots, p_i', \ldots, p_n', u)$. This can be put intuitively as follows. Suppose a consumer buys 12.5 units of gas a week at a cost of £1 per unit. The price

Figure 3.3

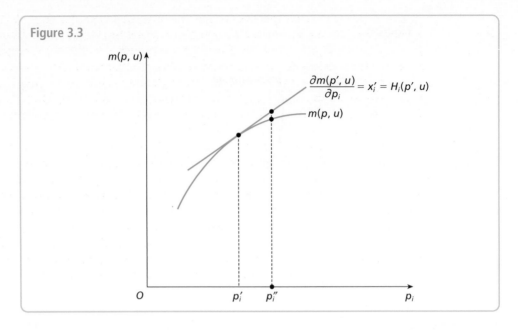

of gas then rises by 1p per unit. Shephard's lemma says that, *to a first approximation*, to maintain the same utility level or standard of living her expenditure must increase by $H_i\Delta p_i = 12.5p$: just enough to maintain consumption at the initial price level. The qualification 'to a first approximation' is important. For *finite* price changes Fig. 3.3 shows that $H_i\Delta p_i$ overstates the required increase in expenditure, since the expenditure function is strictly concave. As a good's price goes up, the consumer substitutes *away* from the good in question, and this reduces the amount of expenditure otherwise required to keep utility constant. Recall from Chapter 2 the distinction between Hicks and Slutsky compensated demands. Shephard's lemma tells us that for small enough price changes this distinction can be ignored.

(c) $\partial m/\partial p_i \geqslant 0$ with strict inequality if $x_i^* > 0$

This follows immediately from Shephard's lemma. Since at least one good must be bought, the expenditure function is non-decreasing in the price vector p and strictly increasing in at least one price. Higher prices mean higher expenditure to reach a given utility.

(d) The expenditure function is homogeneous of degree 1 in prices

Take a given u value and price vector p^0, and let $m^0 = m(p^0, u) = p^0x^0$ where x^0 is the expenditure-minimizing bundle at p^0, that is $p^0x^0 \leqslant p^0x$ for all bundles x yielding utility of u or more. But this imples that $kp^0x^0 \leqslant kp^0x$ for all bundles yielding at least u and so x^0 is optimal at prices p^0 and kp^0. Then $m(kp^0, u) = kp^0x^0 = km(p^0, u)$. Since *relative* prices do not change, the optimal bundle is not changed: it has merely become more or less expensive depending on whether $k > 1$ or $k < 1$.

(e) The expenditure function is increasing in u

Higher utility at given prices requires higher expenditure. Rather than use the envelope theorem again, recall that the Lagrange multiplier $\mu > 0$ in [A.2] is equal to the derivative $\partial m/\partial u$ (see Appendix G). μ is the 'marginal cost of utility', since it represents the rate of change of *minimized* expenditure with respect to the required utility level. μ is the reciprocal of the Lagrange multiplier λ in the corresponding utility maximization problem, i.e. μ is the inverse of the 'marginal utility of income' (see Question 3, Exercise 3A). Note that, although the assumptions underlying ordinal utility theory allow the sign of μ to be established, we cannot say that μ is necessarily increasing, or decreasing, with u, because both are possible for different, permissible utility functions (see Question 3, Exercise 3A).

It is important to be clear about the relation between expenditure and utility. The essential facts about the consumer's preference ordering are contained in the structure of her indifference sets or curves. The minimum expenditure required to reach a given indifference set at given prices is unaffected by any number we attach to that indifference set to indicate its place in the ordering. On the other hand, once we have chosen a numerical representation of the preference ordering – a utility function – this will imply a particular relationship between expenditure m and utility u. But the properties we set out above hold for all permissible utility functions, and the only general restriction we can place on the relation between m and u (for a given price vector) is that it is monotonically increasing.

EXERCISE 3A

1. *Cobb–Douglas utility function.* A consumer has the utility function $u = x_1^a x_2^b$, $a + b = 1$. Derive her Hicksian demand functions and expenditure function. Confirm that the expenditure function possesses the properties set out in this section. Then derive the expenditure function for the utility function $v = u^2$ and compare it with the one you obtained previously. In particular, compare the values $\partial m/\partial u$ in each case.

2. If goods are perfect complements the consumer's utility function can be written: $u = \min(x_1, x_2)$. If the goods are perfect substitutes the utility function can be written $u = ax_1 + bx_2$. Discuss the nature of the expenditure function in each of these cases.

3. Consider the problems:

$$\max u(x) \quad \text{s.t. } px = m; \qquad \min px \quad \text{s.t. } u = u(x)$$

where u is a strictly quasi-concave utility function and p is the same price vector in each case. With m given, let u^* be the optimized utility in the first problem, with every $x_i^* > 0$. Then let u^* be the value of the utility constraint in the second problem. Then show:

   (a) the solution vector in the second problem is identical to that in the first;

   (b) $\lambda^* = 1/\mu^*$, where λ^* and μ^* are the optimal values of the Lagrange multipliers in the first and second problems respectively;

   (c) these results hold for any positive monotonic transformation of the utility function.

4. *Stone–Geary utility function.* A consumer has the utility function

$$u = (x_1 - c_1)^a (x_2 - c_2)^b, \quad a + b = 1$$

where the c_i are interpreted as minimum subsistence levels of x_i, $i = 1, 2$. Derive the consumer's Hicksian demand functions and expenditure function, and compare them with the results obtained in Question 1.

5. *Quasi-linear utility function.* A consumer has the utility function

$$u = f(x_1) + x_2$$

where $f(\cdot)$ is increasing and strictly concave. Derive the Hicksian demand functions and expenditure function and discuss their properties. Illustrate on an indifference curve diagram.

B. The indirect utility function, Roy's identity and the Slutsky equation

The indirect utility function is derived from the consumer problem of maximizing $u(x_1, \ldots, x_n)$ subject to the budget constraint $\sum p_i x_i \leq M$ and non-negativity constraints. We saw in section 2D that the x_i which are optimal for this problem will be functions of the p_i and M: $x_i^* = D_i(p_1, \ldots, p_n, M) = D_i(p, M)$. The *maximized* value of $u(x_1, \ldots, x_n) = u(x_1^*, \ldots, x_n^*)$ will therefore also be a function of the p_i and M:

$$u(x_1^*, \ldots, x_n^*) = u(D_1(p, M), \ldots, D_n(p, M))$$
$$= u^*(p, M) \qquad \text{[B.1]}$$

u^* is known as the *indirect utility function* since utility depends indirectly on prices and money income via the maximization process, in contrast to the utility function $u(x_1, \ldots, x_n)$ where u depends directly on the x_i. We can use u^* to investigate the effects of changes in prices and money income on the consumer's utility.

From the interpretation of the Lagrange multiplier (section 2B), the effect of an increase in money income on the maximized utility is

$$\frac{\partial u^*}{\partial M} = \lambda \qquad \text{[B.2]}$$

The effect of a change in p_i on u^* can also be found as a version of the Envelope Theorem. Differentiating u^* with respect to p_i:

$$\frac{\partial u^*}{\partial p_i} = \sum u_k \frac{\partial x_k^*}{\partial p_i} = \lambda \sum p_k \frac{\partial x_k^*}{\partial p_i} \qquad \text{[B.3]}$$

The budget constraint must still be satisfied so that

$$\frac{d}{dp_i} \left(\sum p_k x_k^* \right) = \frac{dM}{dp_i} = 0$$

and so

$$\sum p_k \frac{\partial x_k^*}{\partial p_i} + x_i^* = 0$$

or

$$-x_i^* = \sum p_k \frac{\partial x_k^*}{\partial p_i}$$

Substitution of this in [B.3] gives Roy's identity:

$$\frac{\partial u^*}{\partial p_i} = -\lambda x_i^* = -\frac{\partial u^*}{\partial M} x_i^* \qquad \text{[B.4]}$$

The expression on the right-hand side of [B.4] has the following intuitive explanation. An increase in p_i is a reduction in the purchasing power of the consumer's money income M, and by Shephard's lemma, to the first order, her purchasing power falls at the rate $-x_i^*$ as p_i varies. λ is the marginal utility of money income. The product of λ and $-x_i^*$ is the rate at which utility varies with money income, times the rate at which (the purchasing power of) money income varies with p_i, and so this product yields the rate of change of utility with respect to p_i.

Since $\lambda > 0$, Roy's identity shows that an increase in the price of a good a consumer buys reduces her (maximized) utility or standard of living to a greater extent, the larger the quantity of it she buys.

The indirect utility function tells us that utility depends, via the maximization process, on the price–income situation the consumer faces. Note that [B.2] implies that the indirect utility function is monotonically increasing in income, M. Thus we can invert the indirect utility function $u = u^*(p, M)$ to obtain the expenditure function $M = m(p, u)$. A given solution point for a given price vector can be viewed equivalently as resulting from minimizing expenditure subject to the given utility level or maximizing utility subject to the given expenditure level. We can choose either to solve the utility maximization problem, obtain the indirect utility function and invert it to obtain the expenditure function, *or* to obtain the expenditure function and then invert it to obtain the indirect utility function (see Question 3, Exercise 3B). The two functions are *dual to each other*, and contain essentially the same information: the forms of the functions and their parameters are completely determined by the form of the original (direct) utility function. But then, since each of these three functions contains the same information, we can choose any one of them as the representation of the consumer's preferences that we wish to work with.

Duality can be used to give a neater derivation of Roy's identity. Setting $M = m(p, u)$, rewrite the indirect utility function as

$$u = u^*(p, m(p, u)) \qquad [B.5]$$

Then differentiating through with respect to p_i, *allowing m to vary in such a way as to hold u constant*, gives

$$0 = \frac{\partial u^*}{\partial p_i} + \frac{\partial u^*}{\partial M} \frac{\partial m}{\partial p_i} \qquad [B.6]$$

which, using Shephard's lemma and [B.2], gives Roy's identity [B.4] directly.

Since the indirect utility function is ordinal and not cardinal, we cannot restrict it to be convex or concave (unlike the expenditure function), but we can show that it is *quasi-convex* in prices and income, a property that is useful in many applications.

Figure 3.4 illustrates quasi-convexity in prices and income. A function is quasi-convex if, given any point in its (convex) domain, the *worse set* of that point, i.e. the

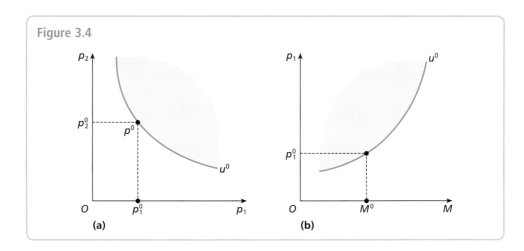

Figure 3.4

set of points giving the same or lower values of the function, is convex. Take the case of two goods, where the indirect utility function is $u*(p_1, p_2, M)$. In part (a) of the figure, $p^0 = (p_1^0, p_2^0)$ is some arbitrary point, and the indifference curve u^0, or contour of the indirect utility function, through that point is convex to the origin if the function is quasi-convex. The worse set $W(p^0) = \{(p_1, p_2); u*(p_1, p_2, M^0) \leq u*(p_1^0, p_2^0, M^0)\}$ lies to the north-east of p^0 (higher prices imply lower utility) and is convex. In (b) of the figure, the contour u^0 through the point (p_1^0, M^0) is convex from below, because the worse set $W(p_1^0, M^0) = \{(p_1, M); u*(p_1, p_2^0, M) \leq u*(p_1^0, p_2^0, M^0)\}$ lies to the north-west of the point (higher price and lower income implies lower utility) and is convex. (Be sure you can explain the negative and positive slopes of these contours, respectively.) Similarly for any point (p_2^0, M^0).

To prove that the indirect utility function is quasi-convex in prices and income, choose two points in the domain of the function, (p^0, M^0) and (p', M'), such that

$$u*(p^0, M^0) = u^0 \geq u' = u*(p', M') \qquad [\text{B.7}]$$

so that (p', M') is in the worse set of (p^0, M^0). We have to show that any convex combination of these two price–income vectors is also in this worse set of (p^0, M^0):

$$u*(\bar{p}, \bar{M}) \leq u^0 \qquad [\text{B.8}]$$

where

$$\bar{p} = kp^0 + (1-k)p', \quad \bar{M} = kM^0 + (1-k)M' \qquad k \in [0, 1] \qquad [\text{B.9}]$$

Now take any goods vector x that satisfies the budget constraint $\bar{p}x \leq \bar{M}$ or, given the definitions of $\bar{p}$ and $\bar{M}$

$$kp^0x + (1-k)p'x \leq kM^0 + (1-k)M' \qquad [\text{B.10}]$$

For this to hold either

$$p^0x \leq M^0 \qquad [\text{B.11}]$$

or

$$p'x \leq M' \qquad [\text{B.12}]$$

or both. Now x satisfying these inequalities cannot yield a higher utility value than the maximized utility at the corresponding budget constraint. Hence [B.11] implies $u*(\bar{p}, \bar{M}) \leq u^0$, and [B.12] implies $u*(\bar{p}, \bar{M}) \leq u'$ and since one or both of [B.11] and [B.12] must hold and $u' \leq u^0$ by assumption, we have established $u*(\bar{p}, \bar{M}) \leq u^0$ as required.

Figure 3.5 illustrates. Fix the price of good 2 as 1, so that the intercept on the x_2 axis shows total expenditure and the slope of the budget constraint is $-p_1$. B^0 in the figure corresponds to the budget constraint $p_1^0x_1 + x_2 = M^0$. B' corresponds to $p_1'x_1 + x_2 = M'$, and yields a lower utility value than B^0. $\bar{B}$ corresponds to $\bar{p}_1x_1 + x_2 = \bar{M}$ where $\bar{p}_1 = kp_1^0 + (1-k)p_1'$, $\bar{M} = kM^0 + (1-k)M'$. $\bar{B}$ also yields a lower value of utility than B^0. We have

$$M' < \bar{M} < M^0 \qquad [\text{B.13}]$$

$$p_1' < \bar{p}_1 < p_1^0 \qquad [\text{B.14}]$$

That $\bar{B}$ passes through the intersection point (x_1^0, x_2^0) of B^0 and B' follows by noting that if we sum

$$k(p_1^0x_1^0 + x_2^0) = kM^0 \qquad [\text{B.15}]$$

Figure 3.5

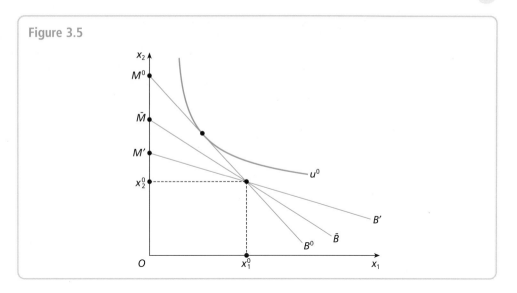

and

$$(1 - k)(p_1' x_1^0 + x_2^0) = M' \qquad [B.16]$$

we obtain

$$\bar{p}_1 x_1^0 + x_2^0 = \bar{M} \qquad [B.17]$$

Thus (p', M') and $(\bar{p}, \bar{M})$ are both in the worse set of (p^0, M^0) and $(\bar{p}, \bar{M})$ is a convex combination of (p^0, M^0) and (p', M').

The Slutsky equation

The Slutsky equation plays a central role in analysing the properties of demand functions. It is derived as follows. If we take as the constraint in the utility maximization problem the level of expenditure resulting from solution of the expenditure minimization problem (or equivalently take as the constraint in the latter problem the level of utility resulting from the solution to the former) then the solutions x_i^* to the two problems, the values of the Marshallian and Hicksian demand functions, will be identical. Setting $M = M(p, u)$, we can write for the ith good

$$H_i(p, u) = D_i(p, m(p, u)) \qquad [B.18]$$

Since [B.18] is an identity we can differentiate through with respect to the jth price, allowing expenditure to change in whatever way is required to keep utility constant, to obtain

$$\frac{\partial H_i}{\partial p_j} = \frac{\partial D_i}{\partial p_j} + \frac{\partial D_i}{\partial M} \frac{\partial m}{\partial p_j} \qquad [B.19]$$

Using Shephard's lemma and rearranging gives the *Slutsky equation*

$$\frac{\partial D_i}{\partial p_j} = \frac{\partial H_i}{\partial p_j} - x_j \frac{\partial D_i}{\partial M} \qquad [B.20]$$

Taking $i = j$, so that we consider the effect of a price change on its own demand, we see from [B.20] that the slope of the Marshallian demand function is the sum of two effects: the *substitution effect*, $\partial H_i/\partial p_i$, which is the slope of the Hicksian or compensated demand curve; and the *income effect*, $-x_i\partial D_i/\partial M$. Thus the Slutsky equation gives a precise statement of the conclusions of the diagrammatic analysis of Chapter 2. We show in a moment that $\partial H_i/\partial p_i \leq 0$. Then [B.20], again with $i = j$, establishes that if the good is normal, so that $\partial D_i/\partial M > 0$, the slope of its Marshallian demand curve is negative. If the good is inferior, so that $\partial D_i/\partial M \leq 0$, the slope is negative, positive or zero depending on the relative sizes of the absolute values $|\partial H_i/\partial p_i|$ and $|x_i\partial D_i/\partial M|$.

It is useful to express the Slutsky equation in elasticity form. Again taking $i = j$, multiplying through [B.20] by p_i/x_i, and the income term by M/M, gives

$$\varepsilon_{ii} = \sigma_{ii} - s_i\eta_i \qquad [B.21]$$

where ε_{ii} is the Marshallian demand elasticity, σ_{ii} is the Hicksian or compensated demand elasticity, η_i is the income elasticity of demand, and $s_i = p_ix_i/M$ is the share of good i in total expenditure. Thus the difference between Hicksian and Marshallian elasticities for a good will be smaller, the smaller its income elasticity and the less significant it is in the consumer's budget. With $i \neq j$, [B.20] becomes

$$\varepsilon_{ij} = \sigma_{ij} - s_j\eta_i \qquad [B.22]$$

which emphasizes that cross-price Marshallian demand elasticities depend both on compensated elasticities and on income elasticities weighted by expenditure shares. Equality of the Marshallian cross-price elasticities therefore requires strong restrictions on preferences (see Question 5, Exercise 3B).

We define the *Slutsky matrix* as the $n \times n$ matrix $[\partial H_i/\partial p_j]$ of Hicksian demand derivatives. It is a straightforward extension of Shephard's lemma and the properties of the expenditure function to show that this matrix is a *symmetric, negative semidefinite* matrix (Appendix I). From Shephard's lemma

$$\frac{\partial m(p, u)}{\partial p_i} = H_i(p, u) \qquad i = 1, \ldots, n$$

we have

$$\frac{\partial^2 m(p, u)}{\partial p_j\partial p_i} = \frac{\partial H_i}{\partial p_j} \qquad i, j = 1, \ldots, n \qquad [B.23]$$

Then, from *Young's Theorem*[1] we have immediately that $\partial H_i/\partial p_j = \partial H_j/\partial p_i$, and so the Slutsky matrix is symmetric. The Slutsky matrix $[\partial H_i/\partial p_j]$ is the matrix of second-order partials of the expenditure function and the concavity of the expenditure function implies that matrix is negative semi-definite. Since $\partial^2 m/\partial p_i^2 = \partial H_i/\partial p_i \leq 0$, by the definition of negative semi-definiteness (see Appendix I), the Hicksian demand curve cannot have a positive slope. We have seen earlier that strict convexity of preference and $x_i > 0$ at the optimum establish the stronger result that $\partial^2 m/\partial p_i^2 = \partial H_i/\partial p_i < 0$.

The Hicksian demand derivative $\partial H_i/\partial p_j$ is often used to define complements and substitutes. Two goods i and j are called *Hicksian complements* if $\partial H_i/\partial p_j < 0$ and *Hicksian substitutes* if $\partial H_i/\partial p_j > 0$. The advantage of this definition is that symmetry implies that the nature of the complementarity or substitutability between the goods cannot change if we take $\partial H_j/\partial p_i$ rather than $\partial H_i/\partial p_j$. This would *not* be true if we defined complements and substitutes in terms of the Marshallian demand derivatives (see Question 5, Exercise 3B).

Properties of demand functions

We have seen that it is possible to draw definite conclusions about the effects of price changes on the Hicksian demands. The Hicksian demand functions are not, however, directly observable since they depend on the consumer's utility level as well as prices. On the other hand, the Marshallian demand functions can be estimated from information on purchases, prices and money income. The Slutsky equation enables us to reformulate the predictions about the properties of Hicksian demand functions in terms of the observable Marshallian demand functions and thus to widen the set of testable predictions from consumer theory.

We can summarize the testable implications derived in this and the previous chapter:

(a) Marshallian demand functions are homogeneous of degree zero in prices and money income;

(b) the Marshallian demand functions satisfy the 'adding up' property: $\sum p_i x_i^* = M$;

(c) the Hicksian demand derivatives (cross-substitution effects) are symmetric: $\partial H_i/\partial p_j = \partial H_j/\partial p_i$ or, using the Slutsky equation, $\partial D_i/\partial p_j + x_j\partial D_i/\partial M = \partial D_j/\partial p_i + x_i\partial D_j/\partial M$;

(d) the Slutsky matrix $[\partial H_i/\partial p_j] = [\partial D_i/\partial p_j + x_j\partial D_i/\partial M]$ is negative semi-definite.

These are all the predictions about the Marshallian demand functions which can be made on the basis of the consumer preference axioms. (As we will see in sections D and E, more detailed predictions require stronger and less general specifications of preferences.) The converse question of whether a system of demand functions with these properties implies the existence of a utility function from which the demand functions could have been derived is known as the *integrability problem*. In the next section we will show that this is in fact so by considering the equivalent problem of retrieving an expenditure function (which also can be used to represent preferences) from a set of Marshallian demand functions which satisfy the above properties.

EXERCISE 3B

1. Show that the Hicksian demand function is homogeneous of degree zero in prices. Then, use the fact (Euler's Theorem) that if a function $f(x_1, \ldots, x_n)$ is homogeneous of degree zero, we have $\sum_{i=1}^n f_i x_i = 0$, to prove that $\sum_{j=1}^n (\partial H_i/\partial p_j)p_j = 0$. Interpret this in terms of the Slutsky matrix.

2. The consumer has the utility function $u = x_1^a x_2^{1-a}$. Find her indirect utility function. Confirm Roy's identity by:

   (a) differentiating the indirect utility function with respect to the price of good 1;

   (b) using the first-order conditions to obtain solutions for x_1 and λ, and therefore an expression for $-\lambda x_1$;

   (c) showing that (a) and (b) give the same result.

3. Invert the indirect utility function you obtain in Question 2 to express expenditure as a function of prices and utility. Then show that this is the expenditure function for this form of direct utility function.

4. (a) Show that the Marshallian demand functions satisfy the following restrictions:

   Cournot aggregation:　$\sum_{i=1}^{n} p_i \dfrac{\partial D_i}{\partial p_j} + x_j = 0$　　$j = 1, \ldots, n$

   Engel aggregation:　$\sum_{i=1}^{n} p_i \dfrac{\partial D_i}{\partial M} = 1$

   (*Hint*: use the adding up property and differentiate.)

   (b) Express these restrictions in elasticity form

   $$\Sigma_i s_i e_{ij} + s_j = 0 \qquad j = 1, \ldots, n$$
   $$\Sigma_i s_i \eta_i = 1$$

   where e_{ij} is the *cross-price elasticity* $(\partial D_i/\partial p_j)(p_j/x_i)$, η_i is the *income elasticity* $(\partial D_i/\partial M)(M/x_i)$ and $s_i = p_i x_i/M$ is the budget or expenditure share of the *i*th good.

   (c) Show that the homogeneity property implies

   $$\sum_{j=1}^{n} p_j \dfrac{\partial D_i}{\partial p_j} + M \dfrac{\partial D_i}{\partial M} = 0 \qquad i = 1, \ldots, n$$

   and express this in elasticity form

   $$\Sigma_j e_{ij} + \eta_i = 0 \qquad i = 1, \ldots, n$$

   (d) Show that if a set of Marshallian demand functions satisfies homogeneity, symmetry, and Engel aggregation they will also satisfy Cournot aggregation.

5. Show that if complements and substitutes are defined in terms of Marshallian demand derivatives, goods could be, say, complements on the basis of the sign of $\partial D_i/\partial p_j$, and substitutes on the basis of the sign of $\partial D_j/\partial p_i$. Give precise conditions under which this occurs.

6. Show that if the utility function $u(x)$ is an ordinal representation of preferences no restrictions can be placed on the signs of $\partial^2 u^*(p, M)/\partial M^2 = \partial \lambda/\partial M$ and $\partial^2 u^*(p, M)/\partial M\, \partial p_i = \partial \lambda/\partial p_i$. (*Hint*: consider positive monotonic transformations of the utility function $G(x) = g(u(x)), g' > 0$). Interpret the result. Is it possible to find a numerical representation of preferences $u(x)$ such that the marginal utility of income $\partial u^*/\partial M$ is constant with respect to all prices and income?

C. Measuring the benefits of price changes

We often wish to measure the benefit to consumers of a change in the price of a commodity. The price change may result, for example, from changes in tariffs on imported goods, or in the rate of purchase tax, and we may want to estimate the effect on consumers' welfare for public policy purposes. We know that a change in a price will alter the feasible set confronting a consumer, that a new optimal bundle of goods will result, and that the consumer will be on a new indifference curve. In the case of a price fall the consumer will be better off in the sense that he prefers the new bundle to the initial one. How can we measure this benefit? One suggestion might be by the change in the utility level of the consumer. But the utility functions we have used in the theory of the consumer are ordinal. Hence no significance attaches to the size of utility differences, only to their sign. This means that an ordinal utility measure would be essentially arbitrary. Furthermore, such utility measures would not be comparable among different individuals and we could not add utility differences for a measure of total benefit to all consumers.

Figure 3.6

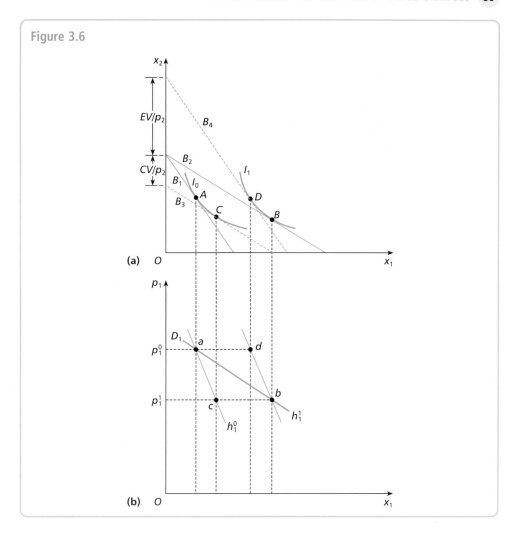

A measure which avoids this last problem is the consumer's own monetary valuation of the price change. Since the measure is expressed in terms of money, individual measures are at least commensurable and could *in principle* be added to form a measure of the aggregate benefit to all consumers of the good.

We stress 'in principle' because if the aggregate monetary measure is to be used for policy purposes, an important value judgement must be made before the individual monetary measures can be summed. This is that an extra £1 of benefit to an individual has the same social significance whichever individual it accrues to. This is particularly important in cost–benefit analysis if some individuals gain and others lose as a result of decisions. Then we have to make the value judgement that £1 of benefit to one individual can offset £1 of loss to another.

Figure 3.6 illustrates the effect of a fall in the price of good 1 from p_1^0 to p_1^1 with money income and the price of good 2 held constant. The consumer's initial bundle is A on I_0 and the bundle chosen after the fall in p_1 is B on I_1. The consumer is better off, but what is his monetary valuation of the change in utility? One answer is the maximum amount he would be prepared to pay for the opportunity of buying good 1 at the new price rather than at the old price. This is the *compensating variation* (*CV*) measure and is defined as the amount of money which must be taken from the consumer in the new situation in order to make him as well off as he was in the initial situation. It is identical to the compensating variation in money income used in section 2D to decompose the price effect into income and substitution effects. Notice that the definition used here applies equally well to price rises, in which case the compensating variation has the opposite sign: the consumer becomes worse off and must be given money to make him as well off with the new prices as he was with the old.

The *CV* measure is not the only plausible monetary measure of the gain to the consumer of a change in the price of a good. The *equivalent variation* (*EV*) is the amount of money which would have to be given to the consumer when he faces the initial price, to make him as well off as he would be facing the new price with his initial income. Again the definition allows for a rise as well as a fall in price. Both the *CV* and *EV* definitions allow for more than one price to change at the same time, but we will restrict ourselves to a single price change (See Question 4 for multiple price changes).

The *EV* and *CV* are shown in Fig. 3.6(a). *CV* is the change in *M* required to shift the budget line from B_2 to B_3 so that the consumer's utility level after the price fall is the same as it was before. *CV* is equal to p_2 times the difference in the x_2 intercept of B_2 and B_3. *EV* is the change in *M* required to shift the budget line from B_1 to B_4 so that facing the initial prices he can just achieve the utility level he would have had with the new prices. *EV* is equal to p_2 times the difference in the x_2 intercept of B_1 and B_4. Notice that *CV* is not in general equal to *EV*.

The distinction between *EV* and *CV* can be expressed in terms of the indirect utility function introduced in section B. In the initial situation the consumer faces prices $p^0 = (p_1^0, \ldots, p_n^0)$ with income M^0 and maximized utility is $u^*(p^0, M^0) = u^0$. With the new prices $p^1 = (p_1^1, \ldots, p_n^1)$ and the same income, maximized utility becomes $u^*(p^1, M^0) = u^1$. *CV* is the change in money income necessary to make utility when the consumer faces p^1 equal to the initial utility level when he faced p^0 with an income of M^0. Hence *CV* is defined by

$$u^*(p^0, M^0) = u^*(p^1, M^0 - CV) = u^0 \qquad [\text{C.1}]$$

EV is the change in *M* necessary to make utility when facing p^0 equal to utility when facing p^1 with income of M^0. *EV* is therefore defined by

$$u^*(p^0, M^0 + EV) = u^*(p^1, M^0) = u^1 \qquad [\text{C.2}]$$

We can also define *CV* and *EV* by using the expenditure function introduced in section A. The minimum level of expenditure necessary to achieve the consumer's initial utility level u_0 with the initial price vector p^0 is $m(p^0, u^0) = M^0$. The minimum level necessary to achieve this initial utility level when prices alter to p^1 is $m(p^1, u^0)$, so that the difference between $m(p^0, u^0)$ and $m(p^1, u^0)$ is the change in income necessary to ensure that the consumer is indifferent between facing prices p^0 with income M^0 and prices p^1 with a different income. This change in income is just the compensating variation, so that:

$$CV = M^0 - m(p^1, u^0) = m(p^0, u^0) - m(p^1, u^0) \qquad [\text{C.3}]$$

If only one price, say p_1, falls from p_1^0 to p_1^1 we must have

$$m(p^0, u^0) - m(p^1, u^0) = \int_{p_1^1}^{p_1^0} \frac{\partial m}{\partial p_1} dp_1$$

But we saw in section A that $\partial m/\partial p_1 = x_1^* = H_1(p, u^0)$ and so

$$CV = m(p^0, u^0) - m(p^1, u^0) = \int_{p_1^1}^{p_1^0} H_1(p, u^0) dp_1 \qquad [C.4]$$

$H_1(p, u^0)$ is the Hicksian constant utility demand function for x_1, and if all other prices are held constant we can draw, as in Fig. 3.6(b), the constant utility demand curve h_1^0, showing the relationship between p_1 and x_1 when utility is constant at $u = u^0$. For a price *fall* CV is the area $p_1^0 a c p_1^1$.

The consumer's market demand curve for x_1 is not, however, the constant utility demand curve but rather the constant money income demand curve, D_1. But from the Slutsky equation we saw that, since the constant utility demand curve plots the substitution effect of a price change and the constant money income demand curve plots the whole price effect (i.e. the substitution *and* income effects), the two curves will coincide if and only if the income effect is zero. Equivalently, the consumer's indifference curves in Fig. 3.6(a) must be vertically parallel.

When D_1 and h_1^0 coincide CV is the area between the price lines p_1^0 and p_1^1 under the consumer's market demand curve. If the income effect is non-zero then the area under the consumer's market demand curve between the price lines will not be equal to CV. In particular if x_1 is a normal good ($\partial D_1/\partial M > 0$) then D_1 will *exceed* h_1^0 for all $p_1 < p_1^0$ and the area under the D_1 curve between the price lines will exceed CV, as Fig. 3.6(b) illustrates.

Points A, B, C in Fig. 3.6(a) correspond to points a, b, c in Fig. 3.6(b) and D_1 cuts h_1^0 at a. If x_1 had been an inferior good then D_1 would have been below h_1^0 for $p_1 < p_1^0$ and CV would have been underestimated by the area under the D_1 curve between the price lines.

A similar approach can be used for EV. The value of the expenditure function $M^0 = m(p^1, u^1)$ is the minimum expenditure necessary to achieve the *new* post-price change utility level and $m(p^0, u^1)$ is that necessary to achieve the new level of utility with the initial prices. Hence in the case of a price fall from p_1^0 to p_1^1:

$$EV = m(p^0, u^1) - m(p^1, u^1) = \int_{p_1^1}^{p_1^0} H_1(p, u^1) dp_1 \qquad [C.5]$$

In Fig. 3.6(b) h_1^1 is the constant utility demand curve for $u = u^1$ and EV is the area under h_1^1 and between the price lines p_1^0, p_1^1. Since the income effect is non-zero, h_1^1 and D_1 intersect at b and the area under D_1 between the price lines is an *underestimate* of EV.

We can relate this discussion to the idea of *consumer surplus*. In early attempts to associate measures of consumer welfare with areas under demand curves, it was argued by Dupuit and by Marshall that the area under an individual's constant money income (Marshallian) demand curve up to the quantity being consumed gave a money measure of the benefit of that consumption. Subtracting the expenditure on the good from this area then gave the net benefit, or consumer surplus, derived from the good. We can examine this idea using the duality approach.

Consider the consumer's indirect utility function $u^*(p_1, \ldots, p_n, M)$, and let p_1^0 now denote the lowest price at which, given the remaining prices $p_2, \ldots, p_n$, the consumer's demand for good 1 is just zero. The actual price of good 1 is denoted $p_1^1 \leq p_1^0$. Roy's identity gives

$$\frac{\partial u^*}{\partial p_1} = -\lambda x_1 = -\lambda D_1(p_1, \ldots, p_n, M)$$

where λ is the marginal utility of income. Integrating over the interval $[p_1^1, p_1^0]$ gives

$$\int_{p_1^1}^{p_1^0} \frac{\partial u^*}{\partial p_1} \, dp_1 = -\lambda \int_{p_1^1}^{p_1^0} D_1(p_1, \ldots, p_n, M) \, dp_1 \qquad [C.6]$$

if and only if λ can be treated as a constant when p_1 changes. Thus we have

$$\frac{1}{\lambda}[u^*(p_1^1, \ldots, p_n, M) - u^*(p_1^0, \ldots, p_n, M)] = \int_{p_1^1}^{p_1^0} D_1(p_1, \ldots, p_n, M) \, dp_1 \qquad [C.7]$$

The left-hand side can be regarded as a *money measure* of the change in utility caused by a change in price from p_1^0 to p_1^1 (since λ is in units of utility/£ while u^* is in units of utility), while the right-hand side is the area under the Marshallian demand curve for good 1 between the prices p_1^0 and p_1^1.

Unfortunately it is in general not the case that a consumer's preferences can be represented by a utility function $u(x)$ such that the marginal utility of money income $\partial u^*/\partial M = \lambda$ is constant when a price changes. Using Roy's identity, we see that

$$\frac{\partial \lambda}{\partial p_i} = \frac{\partial^2 u^*}{\partial M \partial p_i} = \frac{\partial(-\lambda x_i)}{\partial M} = -x_i \frac{\partial \lambda}{\partial M} - \lambda \frac{\partial x_i}{\partial M} = 0 \qquad [C.8]$$

is necessary and sufficient for λ to be constant with respect to p_i. Multiplying through [C.8] by $M/\lambda x_i$ we can express the condition as

$$\eta_i = -\rho \qquad [C.9]$$

where η_i is the income elasticity of demand for good i and ρ is the elasticity of marginal utility of income. It is possible to specify preferences which can be represented by utility functions which satisfy [C.8] or [C.9]. In the example in Question 2 we have $\partial x_i/\partial M = 0 = \partial \lambda/\partial M$. However, [C.8] or [C.9] greatly restrict the preference orderings for which it is valid to use the area under the Marshallian demand curve $D_i(p, M)$ from p_1^0 to p_1^1 as a money measure of the change in utility arising from a change in p^1 from p_1^0 to p_1^1. The difficulties with using the areas under the Marshallian demand curves as welfare measures are compounded if more than one price changes. (See Question 4.)

We do, however, have money measures of benefits which do *not* require such restrictive assumptions, namely the *CV* and *EV*. In Fig. 3.7(b), h_1^0 and h_1^1 are the Hicksian demand curves corresponding to the pre- and post-price change utilities in Fig. 3.7(a), and D_1 the corresponding Marshallian demand. In exactly the same way as before, we can show that *CV* is given by the area $p_1^0 c p_1^1$ and *EV* by the area $p_1^0 d b p_1^1$. All that differs is that in the initial equilibrium $x_1 = 0$.

There would seem to be two problems with the Hicksian measures of the benefit or loss from price changes. One is that they are not unique – *CV* and *EV* in general differ, so which is 'right'? The other is that the Hicksian demand functions are not directly observable from market data, so how are *CV* and *EV* to be made operational?

The difference between *CV* and *EV* is inescapable without severe restrictions on preferences. If the income effect is not zero then the answer to the question 'how

Figure 3.7

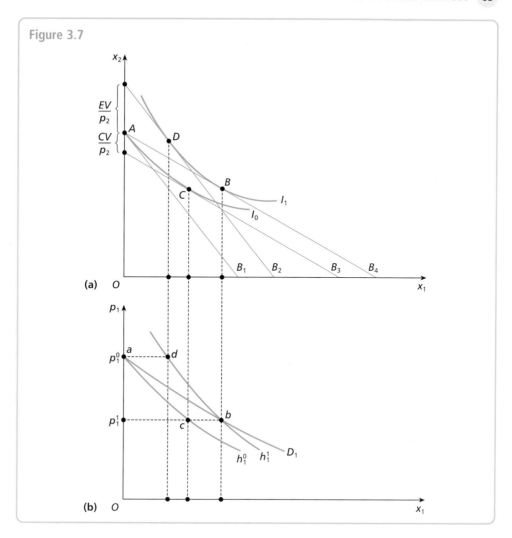

much income can we take from the consumer to cancel out the welfare gain result-ing from the fall in price from p_1^0 to p_1^1?' is bound to differ from the answer to the question 'how much income must we give the consumer to make him just as well off with price p_1^0 as he would be with price p_1^1?'

Which measure, CV or EV, is appropriate depends on which is the relevant ques-tion when a money measure of benefit is required. If, for example, a public project which reduces the price of good x_1 from p_1^0 to p_1^1 is financed by a lump-sum tax on each consumer, and each consumer's CV exceeds the tax she has to pay, then she must be better off. Another example is a subsidy to producers to reduce the price of good 1 from p_1^0 to p_1^1. If the cost of the subsidy per consumer (including administrative costs) exceeds each consumer's EV then consumers would prefer lump-sum payments to each consumer equal to her EV, since the same utility gain is achieved at a lower total cost.

The definitions of CV and EV in terms of the differences in values of the expendi-ture function also apply when many, or all, prices change. In [C.3] and [C.5] we can let the price vectors p^0 and p^1 differ with respect to as many prices as we wish. In each case we are finding an income change which makes the consumer indifferent between the two price vectors, with the *CV* corresponding to the pre-change utility level and the *EV* to the post-change utility level.

The choice of measure depends on the purpose of the measurement, but how are we actually to measure *CV*s or *EV*s in any given context? One approach might be to argue that, since the Hicksian demands are not directly observable, we should take the relevant area under the consumer's Marshallian demand function as *an approximation* to the appropriate measure. If income effects for the good are very small, one can claim that the approximation will be close. However, we can show that, if we have estimates of an individual's Marshallian demand functions, then such an approximation is unnecessary. Provided these functions satisfy the restrictions implied by consumer theory, the expenditure function can be 'retrieved' from the Marshallian demand functions, and once we have the expenditure function the *CV* and *EV* measures follow directly.

This can be proved by considering a version of a problem with a long history of study in economics, the *Integrability Problem*, the general form of which is as follows. Suppose that we have a given system of n partial differential equations

$$\frac{\partial y}{\partial x_i} = g_i(y, x) \qquad i = 1, \ldots, n \qquad \text{[C.10]}$$

where the g_i are given functions, y is a real variable and x is a vector of n real variables. A solution to the system is a function $y = f(x)$ which satisfies the n equations as an identity, i.e. they hold for all values of x. Such a function exists if the *Hurwicz–Uzawa integrability condition*

$$g_j(y, x)\frac{\partial g_i}{\partial y} + \frac{\partial g_i}{\partial x_j} = g_i(y, x)\frac{\partial g_j}{\partial y} + \frac{\partial g_j}{\partial x_i} \qquad \text{[C.11]}$$

is satisfied for every pair of variables x_i, x_j.

We can apply [C.11] to our problem as follows. Suppose that we have estimated a system of Marshallian demand functions for the consumer

$$x_i = D_i(p, M) \qquad i = 1, \ldots, n \qquad \text{[C.12]}$$

Taking the value of u *as a fixed parameter*, we can write

$$D_i(p, m(p, u)) = H_i(p, u) = \frac{\partial m}{\partial p_i} \qquad i = 1, \ldots, n \qquad \text{[C.13]}$$

where we use Shephard's lemma. The expenditure function $m(p, u)$ is unknown, but the problem of finding it is precisely that of solving a system of the type [C.10], with the price vector p identified as the vector x, M as the variable y and m as the function f. Applying the integrability condition [C.11] we can solve [C.13] for the expenditure function if

$$x_j\frac{\partial D_i}{\partial M} + \frac{\partial D_i}{\partial p_j} = x_i\frac{\partial D_j}{\partial M} + \frac{\partial D_j}{\partial p_i} \qquad i, j = 1, \ldots, n \qquad \text{[C.14]}$$

for all pairs of prices p_i, p_j (where we have used the fact that $x_i = D_i(p, M)$). But from the Slutsky equations, we see that [C.14] is precisely the condition that $\partial H_i/\partial p_j = \partial H_j/\partial p_i$, that is, that the Slutsky matrix be symmetric. Since this symmetry is implied by the theory, we conclude that we can obtain the consumer's expenditure function from the estimated Marshallian demand functions provided these also satisfy the restrictions implied by consumer theory: they must be homogeneous of degree zero in prices and income, satisfy the Slutsky equation, and satisfy the adding up condition that $\Sigma_i p_i D_i(p, M) = M$, so that expenditure just exhausts income at any price vector.

It may be no easy matter in practice actually to solve the given system of Marshallian demands for the expenditure function. In empirical demand analysis a simpler route is chosen. A particular functional form for the expenditure function (or equivalently the indirect utility function) is assumed, and the Marshallian demand functions corresponding to that form are estimated. It is then straight-forward to retrieve the expenditure function parameters from the estimated equations. The main drawback is that the estimated functions may not be those that best fit the data in the standard statistical sense.

There is one important caveat to the conclusion that exact measures of the benefit of price changes, *CV* and *EV*, can be derived from knowledge of a consumer's Marshallian demand functions, so that approximations by areas under the Marshallian demand function are unnecessary. In many cases where we wish to evaluate the benefits of policies, we are only able to estimate the *aggregate market* Marshallian demand function, rather than individual consumer demand functions. It is not in general possible to use this to infer anything about the parameters of individual Hicksian demand functions.

EXERCISE 3C

1. Restate the analysis of Fig. 3.6 and the interpretation of *CV* and *EV* for the case in which the price of good 1 increases from p_1^1 to p_1^0.

2. *Quasi-linear utility.* Suppose that the consumer's preferences can be represented by the quasi-linear utility function $u = f(x_1) + x_2$, $f' > 0$, $f'' < 0$.

    (a) Show that the consumer's indifference curves are vertically parallel, i.e. their slope depends only on x_1 and not on x_2.

    (b) Confirm that the income elasticity of demand for good 1 is zero and thus that the *CV* and *EV* for changes in p_1 are equal.

    (c) Show that the marginal utility of income is independent of p_1 so that the change in Marshallian consumer surplus is a measure of the change in utility caused by changes in p_1.

    (d) What is the relationship between the change in the Marshallian consumer surplus and the *EV* and *CV* measures in this case?

3. Calculate the *CV*, *EV* and the change in the Marshallian consumer surplus for a consumer with preferences represented by the utility function $u = x_1 x_2$ with income $M = 100$, $p_2 = 1$ and p_1 falling from 1 to $\frac{1}{4}$. Do this consumer's preferences satisfy the condition for the change in the Marshallian consumer surplus to be a valid measure of the change in utility?

4. *Multiple price changes.*

    (a) When more than one price changes the Marshallian measure is not well defined in general because it depends on the order in which the prices are assumed to change: it is a path dependent line integral. It is path independent only if the cross-price demand effects are equal: $\partial D_i(p, M)/\partial p_j = \partial D_j(p, M)/\partial p_i$. Show that if the Marshallian measure is to be well defined for all possible price changes the consumer's preferences must be such that all income elasticities are unity. (Note that this implies that preferences are homothetic – see section D.) (*Hint*: use the Slutsky equation.)

    (b) Show that the *CV* and *EV* measures are well defined for all possible price changes without any restriction on consumer preferences.

D. Composite commodities, separability and homotheticity

The analysis so far has developed the implications of the general set of assumptions on preferences and the budget constraint given in Chapter 2. We were able to place a number of restrictions on the forms of the demand and expenditure functions. However, for some purposes, especially applications of demand theory and empirical estimation of demand functions, further restrictions are useful. In this section we consider first an assumption about prices, and then some assumptions about the form of the utility or expenditure functions, which are useful in many circumstances.

Composite commodities

Suppose, for example, that we wish to analyse an individual's choice of labour supply and consumption goods. Although we could model her choice of the entire vector of consumption goods we are primarily interested in the trade-off between labour supply and 'consumption' in general. The only price in whose variations we are interested is the wage rate. It is then useful to treat the entire bundle of consumption goods as a single 'composite commodity'. The composite commodity theorem, due to Hicks, tells us that we can do this as long as we assume that the *relative prices* of the consumption goods remain constant throughout the analysis.

The composite commodity theorem

If the relative prices of a group of commodities $x_1, x_2, \ldots, x_g, g \leq n$, are fixed, then they can be treated for purposes of demand analysis as a single composite commodity with a price given by an appropriate index of the prices of the goods $p_1, \ldots, p_g$.

If the prices of the group of goods always move in proportion to each other then

$$p_2 = k_2 p_1, p_3 = k_3 p_1, \ldots, p_g = k_g p_1 \qquad k_i > 0, i = 2, \ldots, g \qquad [D.1]$$

for some constants k_i. Here the choice of good 1 as the 'group numeraire' is quite arbitrary. We can define the composite commodity as $x_c \equiv x_1 + \sum_{i=2}^{g} k_i x_i$ and we take as its price 'index' $p_c = p_1$ (see also Question 1, Exercise 3D). The idea of the theorem is that if we were to construct the consumer's preference ordering over consumption bundles consisting of the composite commodity and all other commodities, represent it by the utility function $\hat{u}(x_c, x_{g+1}, \ldots, x_n)$, and maximize this subject to the budget constraint $p_c x_c + \sum_{j=g+1}^{n} p_j x_j = M$, then we would obtain demand functions $D_c(p_c, p_{g+1}, \ldots, p_n, M), D_j(p_c, p_{g+1}, \ldots, p_n, M); j = g + 1, \ldots, n$, such that the D_j functions would be exactly those obtained from the corresponding problem with the original consumption bundle $(x_1, x_2, \ldots, x_g, \ldots, x_n)$, and the demand function for the composite commodity would be

$$D_c = D_1(p_1, \ldots, p_g, \ldots, p_n, M) + \sum_{i=2}^{g} k_i D_i(p_1, \ldots, p_g, \ldots, p_n, M)$$

Recall that, working with the direct utility function, the indirect utility function or the expenditure function are equivalent ways of analysing consumer demands because they contain the same information about preferences. We can prove the composite commodity theorem by using the indirect utility function (for an approach based on the expenditure function see Question 1). Taking the n commodities individually, the indirect utility function is $u = u^*(p_1, p_2, \ldots, p_n, M)$. Using [D.1] we can write this as

$$u = u^*(p_1, p_2, \ldots, p_n, M) = u^*(p_1, k_2 p_1, \ldots, k_g p_1, p_{g+1}, \ldots, p_n, M)$$
$$= v(p_1, p_{g+1}, \ldots, p_n, M) = v(p_c, p_{g+1}, \ldots, p_n, M) \qquad \text{[D.2]}$$

Hence applying Roy's identity we have

$$\frac{\partial v}{\partial p_c} = \frac{\partial u^*}{\partial p_1} + \sum_{i=2}^{g} k_i \frac{\partial u^*}{\partial p_i} = -\lambda \left[x_1 + \sum_{i=2}^{g} k_i x_i \right] = -\lambda x_c$$

$$= -\lambda D_c(p_c, p_{g+1}, \ldots, p_n, M)$$

$$\frac{\partial v}{\partial p_{g+j}} = \frac{\partial u^*}{\partial p_{g+j}} = -\lambda x_{g+j}$$

$$= -\lambda D_{g+j}(p_c, p_{g+1}, \ldots, p_n, M) \qquad j = 1, \ldots, n-g \qquad \text{[D.3]}$$

Thus the indirect utility function $v(\cdot)$ can be used in place of the indirect utility function $u^*(\cdot)$, and the demand functions depend on the price index, rather than the individual prices $p_1, \ldots, p_g$.

Separability

The composite commodity theorem tells us that we can group commodities together on the basis of a property of their relative prices. Knowing conditions under which it is possible to group commodities is important for empirical demand analysis, because data typically only exist for aggregates of commodities – food, clothing, transport, etc. – rather than for individual commodities such as meat, shirts etc. Unfortunately, it is often unreasonable to assume that the relative prices of the components of these aggregates have remained constant and so the composite commodity theorem cannot be applied. In such cases restrictions are placed on the form of the utility function, usually some kind of *separability* assumption. We consider two such assumptions: *weak separability* and *additive separability*.

Under weak separability the n commodities can be sorted into sub-groups, denoted by vectors x^k, $k = 1, \ldots, K$, in such a way that the preference ordering over the goods in one sub-group is independent of the quantities of goods in another sub-group. Another way of putting this is to say that the marginal rate of substitution between two goods in one sub-group is independent of the quantities of other goods in other subgroups. The utility function

$$u = u[v^1(x^1), v^2(x^2), \ldots, v^K(x^K)] \qquad \text{[D.4]}$$

expresses the idea of weak separability exactly. We have

$$MRS_{ij} = \frac{(\partial u/\partial v^k)(v_i^k)}{(\partial u/\partial v^k)(v_j^k)} = \frac{v_i^k(x^k)}{v_j^k(x^k)} \qquad k = 1, \ldots, K \qquad \text{[D.5]}$$

if goods i and j are in the same sub-group.

If we were to solve the problem of maximizing u subject to the budget constraint, we would find that we had K subsets of conditions of the form $v_i^k/v_j^k = p_i/p_j$, $k = 1, \ldots, K$, where the left-hand sides of these equations depend only on the quantities of goods in the kth sub-group and p_i is the price of the ith good in that sub-group.

If we knew the consumer's optimal amount of expenditure on each sub-group, say M_k, where $\sum_{k=1}^{K} M_k = M$, then we could solve separately for the demand functions of each sub-group and they could be written

$$x_i = D_i^k(p^k, M_k) \qquad k = 1, \ldots, K \qquad \text{[D.6]}$$

that is as functions *only* of the vector of prices of the goods in the sub-group, p^k, and expenditure on that sub-group.

We could only find the M_k from the full solution to the consumer's problem, but it is useful to know that the consumer's demand functions take the form [D.6]. We can then think of the consumer as first allocating optimally the expenditures M_k to each sub-group of goods, and then obtaining demands for the individual commodities by solving the problem

$$\max v^k(x^k) \quad \text{s.t.} \quad p^k x^k = M_k \qquad k = 1, \ldots, K \qquad \text{[D.7]}$$

From [D.7] we will have the K indirect utility functions $\phi^k(p^k, M^k)$, giving the overall indirect utility function

$$u = u^*(\phi^1(p^1, M_1), \ldots, \phi^K(p^K, M_K))$$

With the prices held constant, we can solve the problem for the optimal M_k

$$\max u \quad \text{s.t.} \quad \sum_{k=1}^{K} M_k = M$$

which tells us that at the optimal expenditure allocation

$$\frac{\partial u^*}{\partial \phi^k} \frac{\partial \phi^k}{\partial M_k} = \lambda \qquad k = 1, \ldots, K \qquad \text{[D.8]}$$

where λ is the Lagrange multiplier attached to the constraint in [D.8] and so is also the consumer's marginal utility of income. Thus expenditure is optimally allocated when the marginal utilities of expenditure allocated to each sub-group are equal. Inserting the optimal expenditures into the indirect utility functions ϕ^k and applying Roy's identity gives us the individual commodity demands.

When preferences satisfy additive separability the form of the utility function is

$$u = F[u_1(x_1) + u_2(x_2) + \ldots + u_n(x_n)] \qquad F'[\cdot] > 0 \qquad \text{[D.9]}$$

i.e. any positive monotonic transformation of a sum of individual utility functions. This functional form has a long history in economics, but has some strong and implausible implications. In particular, it can be shown that it rules out Hicksian complements and goods which are inferior (and so it also rules out Giffen goods). (See Question 4, Exercise 3D.) Nevertheless, two of the most widely used forms of utility function, $u = x_1^{a_1} x_2^{a_2} \ldots x_n^{a_n}$ and $u = (x_1 - c_1)^{a_1}(x_2 - c_2)^{a_2} \ldots (x_n - c_n)^{a_n}$ are of this form since we have the transformations

$$\log u = \sum_i a_i \log x_i, \qquad \log u = \sum_i a_i \log(x_i - c_i)$$

Homotheticity

A homothetic utility function takes the form

$$u = T[f(x_1, \ldots, x_n)] \qquad T' > 0 \qquad \text{[D.10]}$$

where f is a *linear homogeneous* function. A homothetic function is a positive monotonic transformation of a linear homogeneous function. In Chapter 5 we study the properties of linear homogeneous production functions in some depth and will not duplicate the discussion here. In the case of a utility function it is clearly not permissible to restrict attention to the linear homogeneous case because utility is not cardinally measurable. It makes sense to say that doubling inputs always doubles outputs, while it does not make sense to say doubling consumption quantities always doubles utility, since the utility function can always be transformed in such a way as to make this statement false.

However, we can exploit one parallel. In Chapter 5 it is shown that if the production function $y = f(x_1, \ldots, x_n)$ is linear homogeneous then the cost function $C = C(w_1, \ldots, w_n, y)$, where the w_i are the input prices, takes the form $C = c(w_1, \ldots, w_n)y$. That is, it can be factored into a unit cost function of input prices alone, and output. Now the cost minimization problem for the firm which gives that result is identical in structure to the expenditure minimization problem.

$$\min \sum p_i x_i \quad \text{s.t.} \ f(x_1, \ldots, x_n) = u \qquad \text{[D.11]}$$

where we choose f to be linear homogeneous. Thus, we can write the expenditure function as

$$m(p_1, \ldots, p_n, u) = a(p_1, \ldots, p_n)u \qquad \text{[D.12]}$$

Now, transforming the utility function f in [D.11] by some positive monotonic transformation $T[\cdot]$ cannot change the solution vector x^* for the problem, and hence the expenditure value $\sum p_i x_i^*$. It simply changes the value of u in the constraint and cannot alter the *form* of the function in [D.12]. That is, simply relabelling the consumer's indifference curves with a different set of numbers does not change the expenditure required to reach any specified indifference curve.

The expenditure function [D.12] has some very strong implications for the demand functions. Inverting $m(p, u)$ to get the indirect utility function $u^*(p, M)$ yields

$$u^*(p, M) = M/a(p) \qquad \text{[D.13]}$$

Applying Roy's identity to get the Marshallian demand functions we have

$$D_i(p, M) = \frac{-\partial u^*/\partial p_i}{\partial u^*/\partial M} = \frac{M}{a}\frac{\partial a}{\partial p_i} = M\frac{a_i(p)}{a(p)} \qquad \text{[D.14]}$$

so that demand for good i is proportional to income and the Engel curve plotting consumption against income, is a straight line through the origin. Since [D.14] implies that $\log x_i = \log M + \log(a_i/a)$ we see that the income elasticity of demand for good i is

$$\eta_i = \frac{\partial x_i/x_i}{\partial M/M} = \frac{\partial \log x_i}{\partial \log M} = 1 \quad i = 1, \ldots, n \qquad \text{[D.15]}$$

The expenditure or budget share $s_i = p_i x_i/M$ is also independent of income so that the consumer always spends a constant proportion of income on a commodity as income varies.

Quasi-homothetic preferences, due to Gorman, give an expenditure function of the form

$$m(p, u) = a(p_1, \ldots, p_n) + b(p_1, \ldots, p_n)u \qquad \text{[D.16]}$$

where a could be interpreted as a level of expenditure required for 'subsistence' ($u = 0$). Setting $M = m(p, u)$, invert the expenditure function to get the indirect utility function

$$u^\star = (M - a)/b \qquad\qquad\qquad \text{[D.17]}$$

Using Shephard's lemma in [D.16] and substituting from [D.17] gives

$$x_i = \frac{\partial a}{\partial p_i} + \frac{(M - a)}{b}\frac{\partial b}{\partial p_i} \qquad\qquad \text{[D.18]}$$

(Alternatively use Roy's identity on [D.1].) Thus, for given prices, the Engel curve relating x_i and M is again a straight line, but no longer a ray through the origin. The expenditure share $p_i x_i/M$ is no longer constant and expenditure elasticities of demand are no longer identical and equal to unity.

EXERCISE 3D

1. In the treatment of the composite commodity theorem, express the requirement that relative prices for a group of commodities remain unchanged by setting $p_i = kp_i^0$, $i = 1, \ldots, g$, where $k > 0$ is the same for all i but can itself vary, and p_i^0 is some constant base price. Show that the composite commodity theorem continues to hold, with k taken as the price of the composite commodity. Derive the expenditure function and show that it has the properties set out in section A, with k as the price of the composite commodity.

2. Consider the utility function $u = (\alpha_1 x_1^{-\beta} + \alpha_2 x_2^{-\beta})^{-1/\beta}$. What properties discussed in this section are true of this function?

3. Show that the Stone–Geary utility function $u = (x_1 - c_1)^\alpha (x_2 - c_2)^{1-\alpha}$, where c_1 and c_2 are subsistence consumption levels, has an expenditure function of the form [D.16].

4. Show that additive separability of the utility function rules out the possibilities that goods are (a) inferior and (b) Hicksian complements.

Note

1. Young's Theorem states that, if a function of n variables $f(x)$ has continuous second-order partial derivatives, then the cross-partial derivatives are equal: $f_{ij}(x) = f_{ji}(x)$.

CHAPTER 4

Further models of consumer behaviour

A. Revealed preference

We emphasized in Chapter 2 that utility functions are convenient numerical representations of preferences and that neither they nor the consumer's preferences are directly observable. This subjectivity of the foundations of consumer theory stimulated interest in the development of a theory of demand based solely on observable and measurable phenomena, namely the bundles actually bought by a consumer and the prices and money incomes at which they were bought. The emphasis in this approach is on assumptions about the consumer's *behaviour*, which can be *observed*, rather than on preferences, which cannot.

As in the utility theory of Chapter 2, we assume that the consumer faces a given price vector, p, and has a fixed money income, M. Our first behavioural assumption is that the consumer spends all income, which has similar implications to assumption 4 of section 2A.

The second assumption is that only one commodity bundle x is chosen by the consumer for each price and income situation. Confronted by a particular p vector and having a particular M, the consumer will always choose the same bundle.

The third assumption is that there exists one and only one price and income combination at which each bundle is chosen. For a given x there is some p, M situation in which x will be chosen by the consumer and that situation is unique.

The fourth and crucial assumption is that the consumer's choices are consistent. By this we mean that, if a bundle x^0 is chosen and a different bundle x^1 could have been chosen, then when x^1 is chosen x^0 must no longer be a feasible alternative.

To amplify this, let p^0 be the price vector at which x^0 is chosen. Then if x^1 could have been chosen when x^0 was actually chosen, the cost of x^1, p^0x^1, must be no greater than the cost of x^0, which is p^0x^0. This latter is also the consumer's money income $M_0 = p^0x^0$ when x^0 is chosen.

Similarly, let p^1 be the price vector at which x^1 is chosen. Then x^0 could not have been available at prices p^1, otherwise it would have been chosen. That is, its cost p^1x^0 must exceed the cost of x^1, p^1x^1, which equals the consumer's money income M_1 when x^1 is chosen. Hence this fourth assumption can be stated succinctly as

$$p^0x^0 \geqslant p^0x^1 \qquad \text{implies} \qquad p^1x^1 < p^1x^0 \qquad\qquad [\text{A.1}]$$

when x^0 is chosen at p^0, M_0 and x^1 at p^1, M_1. If x^0 is chosen when x^1 is purchasable x^0 is said to be *revealed preferred to* x^1. The statement [A.1] is usually referred to as the *weak axiom of revealed preference*.

This set of mild behavioural assumptions generates all the utility based predictions of section 2D concerning the consumer's demand functions. Consider first the sign of the substitution effect. Figure 4.1 shows the consumer's initial budget line B_0, defined by price vector p^0 and money income M_0. The bundle chosen initially on B_0

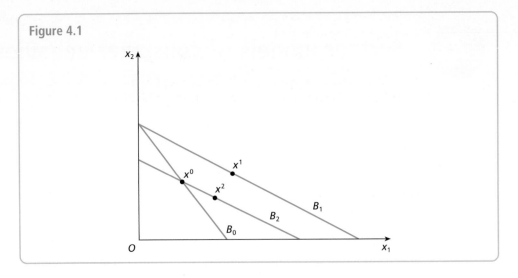

Figure 4.1

is x^0. B_1 is the budget line after a fall in p_1 with M unchanged, and x^1 the new bundle chosen on B_1. Our behavioural assumptions do not place any restrictions on the location of x^1 on B_1 (explain). (Neither do the preference assumptions of section 2A, as section 2D shows.) As in section 2D, it is useful to partition the price effect (x^0 to x^1) into a change in x due solely to relative price changes (the substitution effect) and a change due solely to a change in real income. Since we have forsworn the use of utility functions in this section we cannot use the indifference curve through x^0 to define a constant real income. Instead we adopt the constant purchasing power or Slutsky definition of constant real income (see section 2D). Accordingly, the consumer's money income is lowered until, facing the new prices, the initial bundle x^0 can just be bought. In Fig. 4.1 the budget line is shifted inward parallel with B_1, until at B_2 it passes through x^0. The consumer confronted with B_2 will buy the bundle x^2 to the right of x^0. Therefore x^0 to x^2 is the substitution effect and x^2 to x^1 the income effect of the fall in p_1.

We can now prove that if the consumer satisfies assumption [A.1] the substitution effect must always lead to an increase in consumption of the good whose price has fallen. This is easily done in the two-good example of Fig 4.1. x^2 must lie on B_2 (by the assumption that all income is spent) and hence there are three possibilities: x^2 can be to the left or the right of, or equal to, x^0. x^2 cannot be to the left of x^0 on B_2 because these bundles are inside the consumer's initial feasible set and were rejected in favour of x^0. x^2 cannot equal x^0 because the prices at which x^2 and x^0 are chosen differ and, by our second assumption, different bundles are chosen in different price-income situations. Therefore x^2 must contain more x_1 than (i.e. be to the right of) x^0.

This result can be extended to the n-good case, and the proof is instructive because similar arguments will be used in section 7D to derive comparative statics predictions in the theory of the firm. We can generalize the steps in the analysis of Fig. 4.1 as follows. p^0, x^0 are the initial price vector and consumption bundle, p^1 and x^1 are the new price vector and consumption bundle. The consumer's income is adjusted until at M_2 x^0 can just be purchased at the new prices, p^1, so that $p^1 x^0 = M_2$. Faced with price vector p^1 and the compensated money income, M_2, the consumer chooses

x^2, and because all income is spent we have that $p^1 x^2 = M_2$. Hence the compensating change in M ensures that

$$p^1 x^0 = M_2 = p^1 x^2 \qquad [A.2]$$

Now x^2 is chosen when x^0 is still available (i.e. they are both on the same budget plane) so that by our consistency assumption [A.1] we have

$$p^0 x^0 < p^0 x^2 \qquad [A.3]$$

or: x^2 was not purchasable when x^0 was bought. Rearranging [A.2] gives

$$p^1 x^0 - p^1 x^2 = p^1(x^0 - x^2) = 0 \qquad [A.4]$$

and similarly [A.3] gives

$$p^0 x^0 - p^0 x^2 = p^0(x^0 - x^2) < 0 \qquad [A.5]$$

Subtracting [A.5] from [A.4] gives

$$p^1(x^0 - x^2) - p^0(x^0 - x^2) = (p^1 - p^0)(x^0 - x^2) > 0$$

and multiplying by (-1) we have

$$(p^1 - p^0)(x^2 - x^0) < 0 \qquad [A.6]$$

This prediction applies irrespective of the number and direction of price changes, but in the case of a change in the jth price *only*, p^1 and p^0 differ only in p_j and so [A.6] becomes

$$\sum_i (p_i^1 - p_i^0)(x_i^2 - x_i^0) = (p_j^1 - p_j^0)(x_j^2 - x_j^0) < 0 \qquad [A.7]$$

Hence when p_j changes the substitution effect $(x_j^2 - x_j^0)$ is of opposite sign to the price change. The constant purchasing power demand curve will therefore slope downwards.

We can also derive the Slutsky equation of section 3B from the behavioural assumptions. Since $M_2 = p^1 x^0$ and $M_0 = p^0 x^0$ the compensating reduction in M is

$$\Delta M = M_0 - M_2 = p^0 x^0 - p^1 x^0 = (p^0 - p^1)x^0 = -(p^1 - p^0)x^0$$

and in the case of a change (Δp_i) in p_i only we have

$$\Delta M = -\Delta p_i x_i^0 \qquad [A.8]$$

The price effect of p_i on x_j is $(x_j^1 - x_j^0)$ and this can be partitioned into the substitution $(x_j^2 - x_j^0)$ and income $(x_j^1 - x_j^2)$ effects:

$$x_j^1 - x_j^0 = (x_j^2 - x_j^0) + (x_j^1 - x_j^2)$$

Dividing by Δp_i gives

$$\frac{x_j^1 - x_j^0}{\Delta p_i} = \frac{x_j^2 - x_j^0}{\Delta p_i} + \frac{x_j^1 - x_j^2}{\Delta p_i} \qquad [A.9]$$

But from [A.8] $\Delta p_i = -\Delta M / x_i^0$ and substituting this in the second term on the right-hand side of [A.9] yields

$$\frac{x_j^1 - x_j^0}{\Delta p_i} = \frac{x_j^2 - x_j^0}{\Delta p_i} - x_i^0 \cdot \frac{(x_j^1 - x_j^2)}{\Delta M}$$

or

$$\left.\frac{\Delta x_j}{\Delta p_i}\right|_M = \left.\frac{\Delta x_j}{\Delta p_i}\right|_{px} - x_i^0 \cdot \left.\frac{\Delta x_j}{\Delta M}\right|_p \qquad \text{[A.10]}$$

The $|_M$ notation indicates that money income is held constant in evaluating the rate of change of x_j with respect to p_i, and the similar notation on the right-hand side that purchasing power px and price vector p are being held constant in evaluating the rate of change of x_j with respect to p_i and M. [A.10] is the discrete purchasing power version of the Slutsky equation of section 3B.

It is possible to show that the utility maximizing theory of the consumer and the revealed preference theory are equivalent: all the predictions derived from the assumption about preferences in section 2A can also be derived from the assumption about behaviour made in this section. A consumer who satisfies the preference assumptions will also satisfy these behavioural assumptions. Similarly, if the consumer satisfies the behavioural assumptions, we can construct curves from observed choices which have all the properties of the indifference curves of section 2A. The consumer acts as if possessing preferences satisfying the preference assumptions. (Strictly the weak axiom needs to be strengthened slightly.) Since the two theories are equivalent we will not consider more of the predictions of the theory of revealed preference but will instead use the theory to investigate some properties of price indices.

Price indices

As we noted in section 3C, it is often useful to be able to measure the benefits to consumers of changes in prices of goods. For example, a government may wish to pay pensions which ensure at least a constant level of utility to its pensioners in a period when prices of goods bought by pensioners fluctuate. The pensions, i.e. money incomes, must therefore be adjusted as prices vary, but by how much?

Let x^0, x^1 be the bundles of goods bought by a consumer with incomes M_0, M_1 at price vectors p^0, p^1 respectively. (So that $p^0 x^0 = M_0$ and $p^1 x^1 = M_1$ and 0 denotes the initial or base period and 1 the current period.) Suppose the consumer satisfies our behavioural assumptions (or equivalently the preference assumptions of section 2A). Under what circumstances can we say that the consumer is better off in one price–income situation than another?

Suppose first that

$$p^1 x^1 \geqslant p^1 x^0 \qquad \text{[A.11]}$$

so that x^1 is revealed preferred to x^0, in that x^1 was chosen when x^0 was available. Dividing both sides of [A.11] by $p^0 x^0$ gives

$$MI = \frac{p^1 x^1}{p^0 x^0} \geqslant \frac{p^1 x^0}{p^0 x^0} = LP \qquad \text{[A.12]}$$

The left-hand side of [A.12] is an index of the consumer's money income and the right-hand side is an index of prices with base period quantities as weights, known as the *Laspeyres* price index. Hence, if the money income index is at least as large as the Laspeyres price index the consumer will be better off. Note that if the inequality in [A.12] was $<$ rather than $\geqslant$ nothing could be inferred from the relationship of the two indices.

Now assume that

$$p^0 x^0 \geqslant p^0 x^1 \qquad\qquad [A.13]$$

so that x^0 is revealed preferred to x^1. [A.13] is equivalent to

$$\frac{1}{p^0 x^0} \leqslant \frac{1}{p^0 x^1}$$

and hence to

$$MI = \frac{p^1 x^1}{p^0 x^0} \leqslant \frac{p^1 x^1}{p^0 x^1} = PP \qquad\qquad [A.14]$$

where PP is the *Paasche* current weighted price index. If the money income index is less than the Paasche price index the consumer is definitely worse off in the current period than in the base period. Again if $<$ replaces $\geqslant$ in [A.13] (so that $>$ replaces $\leqslant$ in [A.14]) nothing can be said about whether the individual is better or worse off.

In some circumstances therefore comparisons of price and money income indices do tell us whether a consumer is better or worse off as a result of changes in prices and his income, without requiring detailed information on his preferences.

Price indices are not, however, calculated for each individual using their own consumption levels as weights. The weights used are either total or average consumption bundles for particular groups (e.g. all pensioners, or the inhabitants of particular regions). Suppose that the Laspeyres price index and the money income index are calculated using the sum of consumption bundles and money incomes:

$$MI = \frac{\sum_s M_1^s}{\sum_s M_0^s} = \frac{\sum_s p^1 x^{s1}}{\sum_s p^0 x^{s0}} = \frac{p^1 \sum_s x^{s1}}{p^0 \sum_s x^{s0}} \qquad\qquad [A.15]$$

$$LP = \frac{p^1 \sum_s x^{s0}}{p^0 \sum_s x^{s0}} \qquad\qquad [A.16]$$

where M_0^s, x^{s0}, M_1^s, x^{s1} are the bundle and income of individuals in the base and current periods. What can be inferred from the relationship between [A.15] and [A.16]? Assume that MI exceeds LP and multiply both indices by $p^0 \sum x^{s0}$ to give

$$p^1 \sum_s x^{s1} > p^1 \sum_s x^{s0} \qquad\qquad [A.17]$$

which, taking a case involving two consumers, a and b, for simplicity, can be written

$$p^1 x^{a1} + p^1 x^{b1} > p^1 x^{a0} + p^1 x^{b0} \qquad\qquad [A.18]$$

Now [A.18] does *not* imply that $p^1 x^{a1} > p^1 x^{a0}$ and $p^1 x_1^{b1} > p^1 x^{b0}$, but merely that *at least one* of these inequalities holds, so that at least one of the consumers is better off in the current period. It is possible, however, that one of the consumers may be worse off. Hence $MI > LP$ does not imply that *all* members of the group for whom the indices are calculated are better off, merely that *some* of them are.

In some circumstances [A.18] will imply that *a and b* are better off in the current period. Suppose that the bundles bought by the consumers at given prices are proportional, i.e. that $x^{a1} = kx^{b1}$ and $x^{a0} = kx^{b0}$. Hence [A.18] is equivalent to

$$(1 + k)p^1 x^{b1} > (1 + k)p^1 x^{b0} \qquad\qquad [A.19]$$

and so

$$p^1 x^{b1} > p^1 x^{b0} \tag{A.20}$$

so that consumer b is better off. But multiplying both sides of [A.20] by k gives

$$p^1 k x^{b1} = p^1 x^{a1} > p^1 x^{a0} = p^1 k x^{b0}$$

and consumer a is better off as well. If the consumers in a group have preferences which ensure that each spends that same proportion of their income on the same good then price and money income indices can tell us, for some price and income changes, whether *all* consumers in the group are better or worse off. In order for the consumers to have equal proportionate expenditure patterns for all price vectors one of two conditions must be satisfied:

(a) consumers have identical preferences and identical incomes so that they buy identical bundles ($k = 1$ in the above example);

(b) consumers have identical *homothetic* preferences so that income consumption curves (see section 3D) are straight lines from the origin. Each good will have the same proportion of the consumer's income spent on it irrespective of income and income elasticities of demand for all goods will be unity.

The group of consumers for whom the indices are calculated must satisfy one of the above conditions if the indices are to be of use. This suggests that there may need to be many such indices and that the indices should be frequently updated. This latter suggestion implies that the periods being compared should be not too far apart, in order to minimize the errors from non-unitary income elasticities which can arise if incomes differ even though groups have identical tastes.

EXERCISE 4A

1. Show that a consumer who satisfies the preference assumptions of section 2A will also satisfy the behavioural assumptions. Can you relate the assumptions in the two sections? Which behavioural assumption, for example, plays a similar role to the transitivity assumption of section 2A?

2. Draw diagrams to show that $MI < LP$ and $MI > PP$ tell us nothing about which situation is preferred.

3. Suppose that the actual weights used in a price index are average consumption bundles for the group of consumers. Under what conditions does $MI > LP$ imply that *all* consumers are now better off?

4. Do the remarks in the last part of the section and the results obtained in Question 3 hold for Paasche price indices?

5. Laspeyres and Paasche quantity indices have the form

$$LQ = \frac{p^0 x^1}{p^0 x^0}, \quad PQ = \frac{p^1 x^1}{p^1 x^0}$$

If $LQ \geqslant 1$ or $PQ \leqslant 1$ can anything be said about whether the individual consuming x^0 and x^1 is better or worse off? Suppose the quantities were the total consumption of all members of an economy. Could anything be said about changes in standards of living using the indices?

6. Suppose that the government increases the income of its pensioners in proportion to the rise in the Laspeyres price index. Will they be better or worse off? What if the government used a Paasche price index? What if prices fell?

B. The consumer as a labour supplier

Our analysis in this and the two previous chapters has been concerned with the consumer's allocation of income among goods and has ignored the question of how the consumer allocates the time available in a given period. The problem is important. First, one of the main sources of the income spent on the goods consumed is the sale of the consumer's time in return for a wage. Second, time is a scarce resource and the consumption of goods requires an input of time as well as of money. In this section we will examine a simple model in which the consumer chooses the amount of time spent at work. In the following section we will enquire more closely into how the time not spent at work ('leisure' time) is allocated to the consumption of different goods and how this affects the consumer's labour supply decision.

The consumer's utility function depends on the bundle of goods consumed (x) and the amount of non-work time or leisure (L).

$$u = u(x, L) \qquad \text{[B.1]}$$

Since more leisure is assumed to be preferred to less, the marginal utility of leisure u_L is positive. The consumer is constrained in two ways. First she cannot spend more than her income M

$$\sum p_i x_i \leqslant M = wz + \bar{M} \qquad \text{[B.2]}$$

where z is the length of time spent at work, w is the wage rate (assumed constant) and $\bar{M}$ is non-work income from shares in firms, bond interest, government subsidies, etc. Since the marginal utility of at least one good is always positive (non-satiation assumption), [B.2] will be treated as an equality.

Second, the consumer in any given period of length T is constrained by her 'time budget'

$$T = z + L \qquad \text{[B.3]}$$

which says that the time she has available is divided between work and leisure. The consumer's problem is to maximize $u(x, L)$ subject to [B.2] and [B.3] by choice of x, L and z.

One way to proceed would be to use [B.3] to substitute $T - L$ for z in the constraint on expenditure [B.2] and to rearrange [B.2] as

$$\sum p_i x_i + wL \leqslant \bar{M} + wT \equiv F \qquad \text{[B.4]}$$

F is the individual's *full income*: the amount she would be able to spend if she used all her time endowment T to earn income. The problem of maximizing $u(x, L)$ subject to [B.4] is formally identical to the consumer problem studied in earlier chapters. We will therefore relegate this approach to the exercises and merely note that when the problem is set up in this way the wage rate w is clearly seen to be a price attached to the consumer's consumption of leisure.

An alternative approach is to assume for the remainder of this section that the goods prices p_i remain constant. Then we can use the Composite Commodity Theorem of section 3D to define the composite consumption commodity y with price p. Using the time constraint [B.3] to write L as $T - z$, we can equivalently and more simply represent preferences by the utility function $v(y, z)$ defined on the composite commodity and labour supply, rather than by [B.1]. The consumer prefers to have more of the composite consumption commodity to less and to supply less labour to more: $v_y > 0$, $v_z < 0$. In the upper part of Fig. 4.2 indifference curves are therefore positively sloped, as an increase in labour supplied must be compensated by an increase in the composite consumption commodity to keep utility constant. The indifference curves also reflect the assumption that preferences are quasi-concave.

We can formulate the consumer's problem of optimal choice of labour supply as

$$\max_{y, z} v(y, z) \quad \text{s.t.} \quad py = wz + \bar{M} \tag{B.5}$$

The Lagrangean is $v(y, z) + \lambda(\bar{M} + wz - py)$ and the first-order conditions on y, z

$$v_y - \lambda p = 0$$
$$v_z + \lambda w = 0$$

can be rearranged to give

$$-\frac{v_z}{v_y} = \frac{w}{p} \tag{B.6}$$

From [B.6] the marginal rate of substitution between consumption and labour supply must be equal to the *real wage* w/p. This condition and the budget constraint yield the Marshallian consumption demand and labour supply functions $y(w, p, \bar{M})$, $z(w, p, \bar{M})$ respectively.

In terms of Fig. 4.2, the consumer can initially purchase $\bar{M}/p$ of the composite consumption good without supplying any labour and $(\bar{M} + w_1 T)/p = F_1/p$ if she has no leisure and the wage rate is w_1. The budget constraint or wage line in (z, y) space has slope w_1/p and at the initial optimum the indifference curve I_1 is tangent to the budget constraint.

As the wage increases in Fig. 4.2 the wage line pivots about $\bar{M}/p$ and becomes steeper and the optimal position changes from A to B and then to C as the wage increases from w_1 to w_2 and then to w_3. In part (b) of Fig. 4.2 the labour supply curve shows the amount of labour supplied at the different wage rates, with points a, b and c on the supply curve S corresponding to the optimal positions A, B and C in part (a). The locus of optimal points in part (a) generates the supply curve in part (b). (Compare the relationship between the price consumption curve and the demand curve in Fig. 2.15 in Chapter 2.)

In Fig. 4.2 there is a *backward bending supply curve* with increases in w increasing the supply of labour at low wage rates but decreasing it at high wage rates. Since decreases in labour supplied imply increases in leisure demanded and w is the price of leisure, this apparently perverse response at high wage rates is analogous to a Giffen consumption good where an increase in price leads to an increase in demand. As with the Giffen good it is helpful to examine the effect of the change in wage rate in more detail.

The effect of changes in w on z supplied can be decomposed into income and substitution effects, as in the earlier analysis of the effects of changes in p_i on x_i demanded in section 2D. The 'wage effect' is the movement from A to B in Fig. 4.3. The wage line is then shifted downward parallel with itself until it is tangent to the initial indifference curve I_1 at D. The substitution effect AD shows the change due solely to the variation in w with utility held constant. DB is the income effect, showing the change due to the rise in utility with w held constant. $\Delta\bar{M}/p$ is the compensating variation in unearned income which will leave the consumer just as well off

Figure 4.2

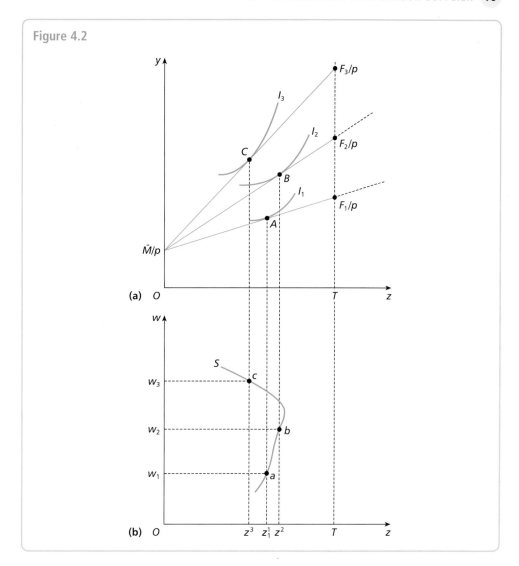

after the wage rise as she was before with her initial unearned income $\bar{M}$. The substitution effect of a wage rise is always to *increase* the supply of labour.

The wage line becomes steeper, and since the slope of I_1 rises as z rises, the point of tangency D between the wage line with slope w_2 and I_1 must be to the right of A.

No such restriction can be placed on the income effect. B may be to the right or (as in the figure) to the left of D. If B is to the left of D then z falls as income rises with constant w, or equivalently L rises as income rises, so that *leisure is a normal good*. Notice that if the supply of labour declines as w rises B in Fig. 4.3 would have to be to the left of A. Since A is always to the left of D the supply of labour would then *have* to fall (L rise) as income rises with constant w. Hence leisure being a normal good is a necessary, but not sufficient, condition for a backward bending, negatively sloped supply curve of labour.

That leisure is a normal good is plausible. Further, changes in the wage rate have a larger effect on the consumer's real income or utility than changes in the price of

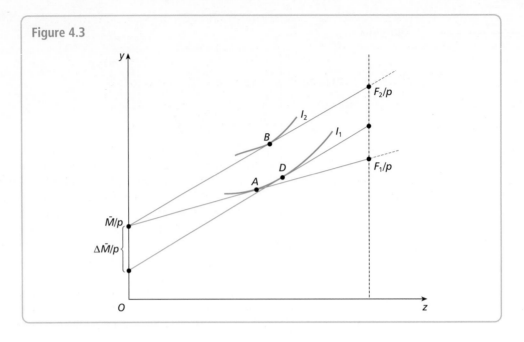

Figure 4.3

a consumption good, since expenditure on a consumption good is typically a small proportion of the consumer's income, whereas her earned income is likely to be a large proportion of her total income. Hence a backward bending supply curve for labour seems to be more likely than an upward sloping demand curve for a consumption good.

More formally, we can derive the Slutsky equation for labour supply using the same duality methods as for the Slutsky equation for consumption in section 3B.

The first step is to solve the minimization problem

$$\min_{y,z} \hat{M} = py - wz \quad \text{s.t.} \quad v(y, z) = v \tag{B.7}$$

That is, we find, at the given wage and price, the minimum non-wage income required to achieve a given utility level v. The Lagrangean is $py - wz + \mu[v(y, z) - v]$ and we can rearrange the first-order conditions on y, z to get [B.6]. Solving [B.6] and the utility constraint to obtain the Hicksian demand functions $\hat{y}(w, p, v)$, $\hat{z}(w, p, v)$, we get the minimized value of non-wage income (analogous to the expenditure function of Chapter 3):

$$\hat{M} = \hat{m}(w, p, v) = p\hat{y}(w, p, v) - w\hat{z}(w, p, v) \tag{B.8}$$

Applying the Envelope Theorem to [B.8] gives

$$\frac{\partial \hat{m}}{\partial w} = -\hat{z}(w, p, v) \tag{B.9}$$

Intuitively, for a given labour supply, the higher the wage, the less non-wage income is required to achieve a given level of utility.

We obtain the required Slutsky equation by setting the required utility level in the minimization problem [B.7] equal to the maximized utility achieved by solving problem [B.5]. The optimal labour supply is the same in both problems and we have the identity

$$z(w, p, m(w, p, v)) = \hat{z}(w, p, v) \qquad \text{[B.10]}$$

Differentiate through it to obtain, after rearrangement,

$$\frac{\partial z}{\partial w} = \frac{\partial \hat{z}}{\partial w} - \frac{\partial z}{\partial m} \cdot \frac{\partial m}{\partial w} = \frac{\partial \hat{z}}{\partial w} + z \frac{\partial z}{\partial m} \qquad \text{[B.11]}$$

using also [B.9]. It is easy to show that the substitution effect $\partial \hat{z}/\partial w > 0$, while, *if leisure is a normal good*, $\partial z/\partial m < 0$, since an increase in leisure implies a reduction in labour supply. Thus the slope of the labour supply curve could be positive or negative when leisure is a normal good, and is more likely to be negative, the weaker the substitution effect between labour supply (or equivalently leisure) and consumption, the larger is labour supply, and the stronger the effect of a change in income on labour supply (or leisure). This is illustrated in Fig. 4.2. The consumer has the non-wage income $\bar{M}$ as indicated, and the lines radiating from $\bar{M}/p$ show the budget constraint for increasing values of the wage rate.

The intuitive reason for the backward bending labour supply (positively sloped leisure demand) curve is easy to see. When the wage rate rises, the consumer would tend to substitute the relatively cheap good consumption for the now relatively dear good leisure. But, because she sells labour and the return to this has increased, she now has a higher income, and so she would want to increase her demand for leisure if it is a normal good. Thus the income and substitution effects work in opposite directions even though leisure is a normal good.

EXERCISE 4B

1. What is the effect on
   (a) the feasible set, and
   (b) the labour supply curve
   of (i) a proportional income tax; (ii) overtime payments; (iii) unemployment benefit; (iv) fixed hours of work?

2. What is the effect on labour supply of replacing a proportional income tax with a progressive (increasing marginal rate) income tax which yields the same tax revenue?

3. *Target income.* Suppose that a worker has a target income: she supplies just enough labour to produce a particular total income. Sketch her indifference curves and her labour supply curve. What is the effect of an increase in unearned income?

4. *Inflation and labour supply.*
   (a) What is the effect on labour supply of an equal proportionate change in all consumer prices, with the wage rate and unearned income held constant? [*Hint*: examine the effects of changes in p in Fig. 4.2.]
   (b) How will labour supply be affected by an equal proportionate change in all consumer prices and the wage rate? Compare with the effects of an equal proportionate change in all prices and money income on consumer demands.

5. *Consumer prices and labour supply.* Assume that the consumer's preferences are weakly separable in goods and in leisure. What effect will a change in the price of the *i*th consumer good have on the supply of labour?

C. Consumption and the allocation of time

In our discussions of the consumption decision so far we have assumed that the only requirement for the consumption and enjoyment of goods was money to purchase the goods. We now examine the implications of recognizing that the consumption of goods requires an input of the consumer's time, and that time is a scarce resource. Watching a film in a cinema, eating a meal or merely resting all require, in addition to the expenditure of money on cinema tickets, food or an armchair, an expenditure of time. Consumption decisions are therefore constrained by the time needed in the various consumption activities as well as by the consumer's money income. Increasing the time spent working will increase money income but will reduce the amount of time available for use in consuming the goods. The consumer's problem is therefore to allocate time *and* money income. We will consider a model which simultaneously examines the consumer's labour supply and consumption decisions.

The consumer's utility depends in the usual way on x, the bundle of goods consumed: $u = u(x)$. The consumption decision is constrained in two ways. First, the bundle of goods consumed cannot cost more than the consumer's income: $\sum p_i x_i \leqslant M = \bar{M} + wz$. Second, there is a time constraint: $T = \sum T_i + z$, where T_i is time spent consuming good i and z is work time. For simplicity we assume that there is a proportional relationship between the amount of good i and the length of time used in its consumption

$$T_i = t_i x_i \qquad \text{[C.1]}$$

t_i is the 'time price' of good i: the number of minutes required for consumption of one unit of good i.

The consumer's problem is (ignoring the non-negativity constraints)

$$\max_{x,z} u(x) \quad \text{s.t.} \quad \text{(i)} \ \sum p_i x_i \leqslant \bar{M} + wz$$

$$\text{(ii)} \ \sum t_i x_i + z = T \qquad \text{[C.2]}$$

Notice that T_i is not a choice variable. The proportionality assumption [C.1] implies that choice of a bundle of goods determines the length of time spent consuming each good. It would be possible to relax the proportionality assumption for many goods and allow for time spent in consuming goods to enter the utility function directly. This would, however, make the model rather complex and so we will limit ourselves to examining the implications of our very simple assumptions.

Using the time constraint in [C.2] we have $z = T - \sum t_i x_i$ and substituting in the expenditure constraint gives

$$\sum p_i x_i \leqslant \bar{M} + w(T - \sum t_i x_i)$$

or

$$\sum p_i x_i + w \sum t_i x_i = \sum (p_i + wt_i)x_i = \sum \rho_i x_i \leqslant \bar{M} + wT = F \qquad \text{[C.3]}$$

t_i is the time necessary for the consumption of one unit of good i and w is the money value of a unit of time so that wt_i is the *time cost*: the opportunity cost of the time used in consuming a unit of good i. p_i is the money price of the good. $\rho_i = p_i + wt_i$ is the *full price* of good i, reflecting the fact that additional consumption of good i reduces the labour supply and hence earned income. As in the previous section, F is the *full income* of the consumer: the maximum potential income if all time is used for earning. [C.3] is the *full budget* constraint of the consumer: the full cost of the goods consumed cannot exceed the consumer's *full* income. We assume that the consumer is not satiated so that at least one good has positive marginal utility and the budget constraint will always bind at the solution. Hence we will treat [C.3] as an equality constraint. Since choice of x also determines $z = T - \sum t_i x_i$ the consumer's choice of x to maximise $u(x)$ subject to [C.3] also gives her labour supply.

In the two-good case the constraint is, from [C.3]:

$$(p_1 + wt_1)x_1 + (p_2 + wt_2)x_2 = \bar{M} + wT$$

or

$$x_2 = [\bar{M} + wT - (p_1 + wt_1)x_1]/(p_2 + wt_2)$$

and so the slope of the full budget line F is

$$\frac{dx_2}{dx_1} = \frac{-(p_1 + wt_1)}{(p_2 + wt_2)} \tag{C.4}$$

The full budget line is drawn as F in Fig. 4.4. We can also draw the money and time budget constraints in the figure. For example, B' shows all bundles costing $\bar{M} + wz'$ and B'' all bundles costing $\bar{M} + wz''$, where $z'' > z'$. Similarly, all bundles along L' require a total time input in consumption of $T - z'$ and those along L'' a total consumption time input of $T - z''$. The B and L lines can be thought of as isoexpenditure and isoleisure contours. F is the locus of bundles satisfying both time and expenditure constraints simultaneously. For example, x' is on both B' and L' and x'' on both B'' and L''.

As in Chapter 2, the slope of the isoexpenditure lines is $-p_1/p_2$. Since, for given z along the L lines, variations in x_1 and x_2 must satisfy $t_1 dx_1 + t_2 dx_2 = 0$, the slope of the isoleisure lines is $-t_1/t_2$. Fig. 4.4 has been drawn so that

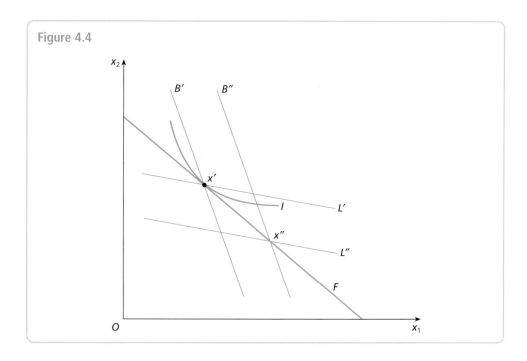

Figure 4.4

$$\frac{t_1}{t_2} < \frac{p_1}{p_2} \tag{C.5}$$

Good 1 is in this case relatively less expensive in terms of time than good 2 but relatively more expensive in terms of money. Alternatively, we can define the *time intensity* of the *i*th good as the proportion of the full price accounted for by the time cost; $wt_i/(p_i + wt_i)$. Writing [C.5] as $t_1 p_2 < t_2 p_1$, adding $t_1 wt_2$ to both sides and multiplying through by w yields

$$\frac{wt_1}{p_1 + wt_1} < \frac{wt_2}{p_2 + wt_2} \tag{C.6}$$

so that in Fig. 4.4 good 1 is less time-intensive than good 2. As the consumer moves down F he substitutes the less time-intensive x_1 for the more time-intensive x_2. He thereby consumes bundles with a greater money cost but with a smaller leisure time input, leaving him more time to earn the extra income required to pay for the more costly bundles.

Equilibrium of the consumer

The consumer is assumed to have preferences which satisfy the assumptions of section 2A and so we can analyse the choice by superimposing the indifference map on the feasible set as in Fig. 4.4. In the tangency solution at x' shown here, the slope of the indifference curve I is equal to the slope of the full budget line, or

$$\frac{u_1}{u_2} = \frac{p_1 + wt_1}{p_2 + wt_2} \tag{C.7}$$

The consumer's marginal rate of substitution is set equal to the ratio of full prices, rather than the ratio of money prices as in the model of Chapter 2. Choice of $x' = (x_1', x_2')$ determines total time spent on consumption $(t_1 x_1' + t_2 x_2')$ and at work $(T - t_1 x_1' - t_2 x_2' = z')$ and the amount of income earned (wz'), which together with unearned income is just sufficient to buy the bundle chosen $(\bar{M} + wz' = p_1 x_1' + p_2 x_2')$.

Comparative statics

The problem of maximizing the strictly quasi-concave $u(x)$ subject to $\sum p_i x_i = F$ is mathematically equivalent to the problem of maximizing $u(x)$ subject to $\sum p_i x_i = M$ which we examined in Chapter 2. We leave the reader to set up the Lagrangean and derive the first-order conditions. The Marshallian demands are a function of the vector of full prices ρ and the full income

$$x_i = x_i(\rho, F) \tag{C.8}$$

and so is the consumer's indirect utility:

$$v(\rho, F) = u(x(\rho, F)) \tag{C.9}$$

The reader should also check that the problem of minimizing the full cost $\sum p_i x_i$ of achieving a given utility level u will yield the Hicksian demands $h_i(\rho, u)$ and the full cost or expenditure function $c(\rho, u) = \sum p_i h_i(\rho, u)$.

We also leave it to the reader to apply the techniques of Chapter 2 to investigate the effects of changes in ρ and F (just replace p and M with ρ and F in the steps in

Figure 4.5

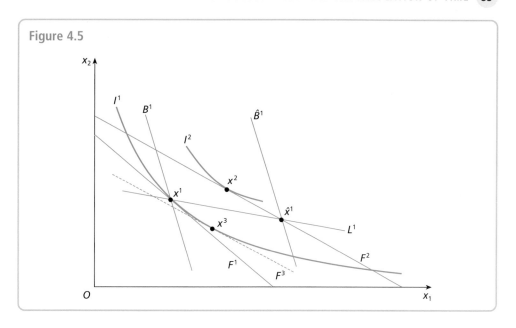

the arguments). Instead we examine the implications of a change in the wage rate. Since w influences all the full prices ($\rho_i = p_i + wt_i$) and the full income ($F = \bar{M} + wT$) its effects are more complicated than a change in income or a single price.

Initially, the consumer is at x^1 on F^1 in Fig. 4.5. Suppose that, following an increase in the wage, the consumer's new optimum bundle on F^2 is x^2, where more of both goods is consumed. The consumer's money income is larger at x^2 than at x^1 but x^2 lies on an isoleisure line above L^1 indicating that more time is devoted to consumption and the consumer's supply of labour has been reduced by the rise in w. Only if the optimum was to the right of $\hat{x}^1$ on F^2 would the rise in w lead to an increased supply of labour as the consumer chose a less time-consuming consumption bundle.

As in Chapter 2, the comparative static responses to changes in the exogenous variables such as the wage rate will depend on the consumer's preferences. However, we can use Fig. 4.5 to decompose the effect of the change in w into an income effect and a substitution effect. As in previous analysis we move the new (full) budget line inward until the consumer can just achieve his initial level of utility on I^1. Since the new budget line is flatter than the initial one, the compensated demand for goods will be to the right of the initial equilibrium at x^3, where F^3 is tangent to the initial indifference curve. Hence we can establish that the substitution effect of a rise in the wage rate will be to increase the demand for the less time-intensive good x_1. This compensated change in w will lead to a rise in the amount of labour supplied (since x^3 is on a lower isoleisure line than L^1). Thus the own substitution effect of the wage on the supply of labour leads to an increase in the supply of labour. Since the overall effect of the increase in w is to reduce the labour supply as the consumer moves from x^1 to x^2, the income effect is negative and sufficiently large to offset the substitution effect. Note that in the figure both goods are normal which explains the negative income effect of w on labour supply. (Is it necessary that both goods are normal for an increase in F to reduce labour supply?)

This analysis of the effect of a rise in the wage rate suggests some tentative explanations for two phenomena associated with rising real wages, i.e. with w rising faster than the money prices of goods. First, the substitution effect will lead to the substitution of goods which are less time-intensive for goods which are more time-intensive. Consumers will spend money in order to save time by buying higher-priced goods which have a smaller time cost. Examples include 'convenience' foods which require less time for preparation and the greater use of domestic appliances to economize on time. Second, the secular decline in the average number of hours worked per worker may be ascribed to the strength of the income effect of rising real wages. This more than offsets the substitution effect and leads to an increase in leisure time used for consumption of the larger basket of goods bought with the rising full income.

EXERCISE 4C

1. Prove, as asserted in the text, that a rise in w will indeed flatten the full budget line if and only if good 1 is less time-intensive than good 2. Investigate the effect on the demand for goods 1 and 2 and the supply of labour of an increase in the wage rate when good 1 is more time-intensive than good 2. Show that the wage own substitution effect on labour supply is positive.

2. Sketch the effect on the feasible set of changes in unearned income, money prices and the length of time required for consumption. Examine the resulting changes in the optimal bundle chosen by the consumer.

3. Use the indirect utility function and the cost function to examine the implications for the consumer's utility and the consumer's behaviour of an increase in (a) p_i; (b) t_i.

4. It is often suggested that individuals with larger incomes have smaller own money price elasticities of demand for goods. Give a rationale for this by examining the relationship between the money price elasticity of demand for a good and the consumer's wage rate.

5. How could the results of this section be used to evaluate the benefit to a consumer of, say, a new bridge which reduced the length of time taken to get to work?

D. Households

In the models of the consumer considered so far, the household consists of a single individual who supplies labour time to generate income to purchase a bundle of consumer goods. In the previous section we started to investigate the implications of a richer specification of the allocation of the consumer's time by assuming that the consumption of goods requires an input of time. We continue the investigation by assuming that individuals derive utility from both bought-in goods and from domestic outputs produced by bought-in goods and their leisure time. An example of a domestic output would be child care.

We also relax the assumption that the household is a single individual and recognize that many households are made up of two adults, with or without children. For some purposes the obvious unrealism of the standard single person household model does not matter, but there are many interesting issues, for example in labour supply, population, taxation and social policy, where it is relevant. For example, in the UK some years ago, a change was made in the way households were compensated for having children. Instead of a tax allowance which raised the income of the main earner (usually the father), a direct money payment, usually collected by the mother, was introduced. Supporters of the policy change argued that it was more likely to result in the money being spent on the child. Now we may or may not think that plausible, but the point is that we cannot even begin to analyse the issue at the usual level of rigour of economics unless we have a model of a two-adult household. Likewise, an important issue in the design of taxation is the treatment of two-income households, which are in the majority in the major developed economies. One system, joint taxation or 'income splitting', as for example in the USA and Germany, aggregates the income of the two earners and applies a progressive tax rate schedule to this aggregate. Thus the two earners face the same marginal rate of taxation, even if one income is much lower than the other. An alternative system, independent taxation, is used in the UK, Canada and Australia. Under independent taxation, the two incomes are taxed separately on a progressive rate schedule, so the lower income is likely to be taxed at a lower marginal rate. To compare analytically the effects of the two systems on labour supplies and individual welfare we need a model of a two-person household.

One way to model two-person households is to assume that the consumption and labour supply decisions of individuals in the household are determined by a cooperative bargaining game. (See Chapter 15 for an account of such games.) However, we take a more general approach. Regardless of how the household actually arrives at its decisions over labour supplies, consumption and household production, we assume that these decisions are *Pareto efficient*. This means that the household has exhausted all possibilities of making one person better off with the other no worse off, and has reached an allocation at which one could be made better off only at the expense of the other. Pareto efficiency seems to be a minimal requirement of joint rationality and provides the solution principle for the two-person household model. Chapter 13 discusses the concept in more detail.

We set up the simplest possible model. The two individuals have strictly quasi-concave utility functions:

$$u_i = u^i(x_i, y_i) \qquad i = 1, 2 \qquad [\text{D.1}]$$

where x_i is consumption of a composite market good and y_i consumption of a domestically produced good. Each individual has T units of time available, and spends $t_i \geq 0$ of it in producing the household good and supplies $T - t_i \geq 0$ units of labour. There is no pure leisure.

By combining their non-work time the household members produce a total amount y of the domestic good which is shared between them:

$$\sum_{i=1}^{2} y_i = y = h(t_1, t_2) \qquad [\text{D.2}]$$

The domestic production function is concave, so that increasing returns to scale (section 5B) are ruled out. Note that if one person has more of the domestic good the other will have less, for example a meal. It is also possible to model the production of a domestic 'public' good, such as a beautiful garden, where one person's consumption does not reduce the amount available for the other. (See Question 6, Exercise 4D.)

The price of the market consumption good is normalized at 1, and so the (net of tax) wage rates, w_i, are in units of the consumption good. The household's budget constraint is

$$\sum_{i=1}^{2} x_i = \sum_{i=1}^{2} w_i(T - t_i) \qquad [\text{D.3}]$$

We find the Pareto efficient allocations by maximizing the utility of one individual (say individual 1) subject to the other getting some specified utility level $\bar{u}^2$ and to the constraints [D.2] and [D.3]. Both members of the household have a reservation level of utility such that if their utility falls below it they leave the household. Hence $\bar{u}^2$ in the Pareto efficiency problem is at least as great as individual 2's reservation utility. We assume that there is a range of required utility levels $\bar{u}^2$ such that the corresponding maximized utility of individual 1 is at least as great as his reservation utility. Higher levels of $\bar{u}^2$ will lead to lower maximized levels of u_1. Factors such as bargaining strength, or love and caring determine the particular efficient allocation but we do not need to model this process more closely, we simply take it as given.

The Lagrangean for the household efficient allocation problem is

$$u^1(x_1, y_1) + \sigma[u^2(x_2, y_2) - \bar{u}^2] + \mu\left[h(t_1, t_2) - \sum_{i=1}^{2} y_i\right] + \lambda\left[\sum_{i=1}^{2} w_i(T - t_i) - \sum_{i=1}^{2} x_i\right] \quad \text{[D.4]}$$

Assume that both individuals consume some of both the market good and the domestically produced good and that both provide time to produce the domestic good. Assume further that individual 1 (the primary earner) always supplies some time to the market, whereas individual 2 (the secondary earner) may or may not do so. Then the optimal allocation satisfies the equality conditions on consumption of the two goods by the two individuals and the time allocation of the primary earner,

$$u_x^1(x_1, y_1) = \lambda = \sigma u_x^2(x_2, y_2)$$
$$u_y^1(x_1, y_1) = \mu = \sigma u_y^2(x_2, y_2)$$
$$\mu h_1(t_1, t_2) = \lambda w_1$$

the complementary slackness condition on the time allocation of the secondary earner,

$$\mu h_2(t_1, t_2) - \lambda w_2 \geq 0 \quad T - t_2 \geq 0 \quad [\mu h_2(t_1, t_2) - \lambda w_2](T - t_2) = 0$$

and the constraints. We can rearrange these conditions to get a set with intuitive economic interpretations:

$$\frac{u_y^1(x_1, y_1)}{u_x^1(x_1, y_1)} = \frac{\mu}{\lambda} = \frac{u_y^2(x_2, y_2)}{u_x^2(x_2, y_2)} \quad \text{[D.5]}$$

$$w_1 = \frac{\mu}{\lambda} h_1(t_1, t_2) \quad \text{[D.6]}$$

$$w_2 \leq \frac{\mu}{\lambda} h_2(t_1, t_2)$$

$$T - t_2 \geq 0$$

$$\left[w_2 - \frac{\mu}{\lambda} h_2(t_1, t_2)\right](T - t_2) = 0 \quad \text{[D.7]}$$

Since μ is the Lagrange multiplier attached to the production constraint it is in units of (1's utils)/(good y). λ is the multiplier attached to the budget constraint and is in units of (1's utils)/(good x). Thus μ/λ is in units of (good x/good y), and since x is the numeraire, this is in the units of the price of good y. We can interpret μ/λ as the implicit price of the household good at the optimal allocation and denote it by p.

The conditions then have a straightforward interpretation. Condition [D.5] says that the marginal rate of substitution between the two goods for each individual must equal the implicit price ρ of the domestically produced good in terms of the bought-in good. Hence the individuals' marginal rates of subsititution are equal to each other. This is the standard condition for Pareto efficiency in consumption.

The second condition [D.6] is that the primary earner allocates his time between market and household production so as to equate his marginal value product ($MVP_1 \equiv \rho h_1(t_1, t_2)$) in household production with his market wage. Alternatively we can write [D.6] as

$$\rho = \frac{w_1}{h_1(t_1, t_2)} \qquad \text{[D.8]}$$

Since one unit of time produces h_1 units of the household good, to produce an additional unit of y requires $1/h_1$ of time devoted to household production rather than to earning income. Hence the right-hand side of [D.8] is the marginal cost of the household good in terms of forgone household income. Thus the implicit price of the household good equals its marginal cost.

The Kuhn–Tucker complementary slackness condition [D.7] on t_2 covers two possibilities. First, the secondary earner allocates some time to working in the market ($0 < t_2 < T$), in which case the first weak inequality is satisfied as an equation and the condition has the same interpretation as for the primary earner. Second, or alternatively, she may specialize entirely in household production, in which case

$$w_2 \leqslant \rho h_2(t_1, t_2) \qquad \text{[D.9]}$$

If the opportunity cost (wage rate) of the time of the secondary earner is sufficiently small relative to the implicit value of the additional amount of the household good she can produce, the household does better by having her devote all her time to producing the household good.

Figure 4.6 illustrates the time allocation conditions, with MVP_2^0 showing the case in which the secondary earner supplies some time to the market, and MVP_2^1 the case in which she specializes in household production. The time allocations depend on the market wage rates, the implicit price of the domestic good, and marginal productivity of the individuals in household production.

From now on we assume for simplicity that both household members supply time to the labour market. From the conditions we can solve for the endogenous variables, consumptions and labour supplies, as functions of the exogenous variables, the two wage rates and the required utility level, $x_i(w_1, w_2, \bar{u}^2)$, $y_i(w_1, w_2, \bar{u}^2)$ and $t_i(w_1, w_2, \bar{u}^2)$. We can also solve for the implicit price $\rho(w_1, w_2, \bar{u}^2)$. We can then carry out the comparative statics analysis of the model in the usual way.

An alternative approach to the analysis is suggested by the Second Theorem of Welfare Economics (for a fuller discussion of the theorem, see Chapter 13). The theorem says that in certain types of economy, including the one we are modelling here, any Pareto efficient allocation can be achieved as a decentralized market equilibrium, given an appropriate initial distribution of income. We can use this proposition to formulate a simple approach to the comparative statics of the model. Suppose we know the price ρ corresponding to the above optimal allocation. Then we can say that the household chooses its time allocations as if it solves the problem

$$\max_{t_1, t_2} \pi(t_1, t_2) = \rho h(t_1, t_2) - w_1 t_1 - w_2 t_2 \qquad \text{[D.10]}$$

Figure 4.6

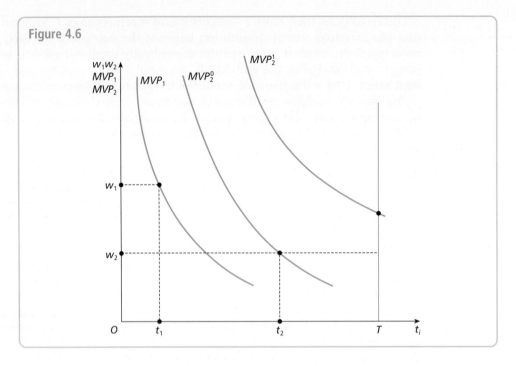

where π can be interpreted as the household's imputed net profit from production of the non-traded good. The reader should verify that the first-order conditions for [D.10] are equivalent to [D.6] and [D.7] and hence, for correct choice of ρ, give exactly the same time allocation. Now define the household's *full income* as

$$S = T\Sigma w_i + \pi \qquad [D.11]$$

Note that by adding π to both sides of the household's budget constraint in [D.3] we can write it as

$$\sum_{i=1}^{2} x_i + \sum_{i=1}^{2} \rho y_i = T\sum_{i=1}^{2} w_i + \pi = S \qquad [D.12]$$

Then, maximizing u_1 with respect to the consumption quantities x_i, y_i, subject only to the utility constraint $u_2 = \bar{u}^2$ and budget constaint [D.12], yields the initial optimal allocation. More interestingly, define each individual's share in full income s_i such that $\Sigma s_i = S$. Then if we solve the individual optimization problems

$$\max_{x_i, y_i} u_i = u^i(x_i, y_i) \quad \text{s.t. } x_i + \rho y_i = s_i \qquad [D.13]$$

then, provided the s_i are chosen so that exactly the required utility values are achieved, we again obtain the optimal consumptions in the earlier problem as the solution.

The advantage of this approach is that we obtain the demands $x_i(\rho, s_i)$ and $y_i(\rho, s_i)$ as functions simply of the price and income share, yielding also indirect utility functions $v^i(\rho, s_i)$ that are simply functions of the price and income share, and this greatly facilitates analysis of policy issues such as income taxation. Many interesting questions require models in which the household consists of more than one individual and in which individuals use their time to produce household, non-market goods. We have shown that it is possible to formulate simple and tractable models of such households.

EXERCISE 4D

1. Extend the model of this section to include:

    (a) a market good which is used as an input in household production;

    (b) pure leisure, the direct consumption of own time;

    (c) more than one market good, and more than one household good and interpret the resulting first-order conditions for an optimal allocation.

2. Show that, if there are constant returns to scale in household production, the implicit price of the household good is independent of the amount of it produced and consumed.

3. Derive and interpret the conditions for an optimal allocation when the market and household goods are perfect substitutes in consumption. Distinguish between this case and the case in which the household can buy in labour, at a lower wage than its own, which is a perfect substitute for its own labour in household production. What if this labour is a less than perfect substitute?

4. National income accounts do not include household production, and therefore underestimate the real output of the economy. Use the model of this section to discuss the issues involved in valuing household production.

5. Two households face identical wage rates and have identical utility functions of all household members. The primary earners in the households work the same number of hours on the market. In one household the secondary earner works full time in the market, but the secondary earner in the other supplies no market labour. How can you use the model of this section to account for this difference? Which household has higher welfare? What is the best income measure of their welfare?

6. Suppose that the domestic good is public in the sense that one person can increase their consumption of it without reducing the amount available for the other. For example, gardening produces an attractive garden which both can enjoy. How would this change the constraint [D.2] and what are the implications for the allocation of time? [*Hint*: see the discussion of public goods in section 13B.]

A. Introduction

In the last three chapters we examined the theory of the consumer at some length. Our aim was partly to explain and predict consumer behaviour and partly to derive some general results, which will be used in Chapters 8 and 12 as building blocks in constructing a theory of markets and of resource allocation in the economy as a whole.

A *pure exchange economy* is one in which economic agents have given endowments of goods and exchange goods among themselves to achieve preferred consumption patterns. In analysing the determination of prices and quantities exchanged in such an economy, it would be sufficient to use the consumer theory so far constructed – the model of section 2F would be directly applicable. However, the pure exchange economy lacks an important aspect of real economies, namely *production*. Production is the activity of combining goods and services called *inputs*, in technological processes which result in other goods and services called *outputs*. In the pure exchange economy, although each consumer can transform their endowed bundle of goods into some other bundle through exchange, this is not true for the group as a whole: the sum of consumptions of each good cannot exceed the sum of initial endowments of it. The existence of production possibilities adds another dimension to economic activity: it permits transformations of endowed bundles of goods into different bundles for the economy as a whole. Any attempt to explain resource allocation is incomplete unless it takes production into account. The firm is the institutional means by which production is organized in a market economy and theories of the firm arise out of the need to incorporate production into the theory of resource allocation.

Production can be wholly individualistic, being carried on by one person working with tools and raw materials. Some goods and services are produced in this way, for example, writing (though not publishing) a book, giving someone a haircut, painting a picture, but the overwhelming majority of goods and services (including some books, haircuts and paintings) are produced by *cooperating groups* of individuals. The reasons are not hard to find: *specialization* of individuals in parts of the production process can be carried further within a group than if one individual undertakes the whole process and, in many processes, there are gains from *teamwork* – the total output of a group when working as a team is greater than the sum of outputs of individuals working separately. However, the 'firm' as it has been traditionally conceived of in economics is more than simply a cooperating group of producers; it is a group with a particular *organizational structure*, and a particular set of *property rights*. For example, it is possible to conceive of a 'producers' cooperative' in which assets are owned in common – no individual has the right to exclusive use or disposal of any of the equipment, output, cash reserves, etc. of the cooperative and decisions are taken by majority vote. This would clearly not be a 'firm' as traditionally conceived. The essence of the latter is the existence of a central figure, the owner, employer or *entrepreneur*, who:

(a) enters into a contract with each of the individuals who supply productive services, which specifies the nature and duration of those services and the remuneration for them;

(b) either takes decisions, or has the right to insist that decisions are taken, in *her* interests, subject to her contractual obligations;

(c) has the right to the *residual income* from production, i.e. the excess of revenue over payments to suppliers of productive services made under the terms of their contracts;

(d) can transfer her right in the residual income, and her rights and obligations under the contracts with suppliers of productive services, to another individual;

(e) has the power to direct the activities of the suppliers of productive services, subject to the terms and conditions of their contracts;

(f) can change the membership of the producing group not only by terminating contracts but also by entering into new contracts and adding to the group.

The essential feature of the 'classical firm' is therefore a central figure, with whom all contracts are concluded, and who controls and directs in her own interests, subject to constraints arising out of the terms of the contract she has made.

Since we can conceive of different ways of organizing cooperating productive groups, it is of interest to ask why this particular form, the entrepreneurial firm, developed into the dominant form of organization of production. It is possible to give an historical account of this: in the transition from the feudal, largely agrarian economy of the late Middle Ages to the capitalist industrial economy of the nineteenth and twentieth centuries, an important role was played by wealthy men who had accumulated their wealth through trade, inheritance of land, or by being successful skilled craftsmen. These were able to respond to important developments in transport and production technology, especially mechanization and the use of steam power, by investing in plant and machinery, grouping workers together into factories, entering into contracts of employment with them, and financing production in advance of sales. Thus their ownership of wealth was translated into their ownership of the assets of the producing group and they became the buyers of labour power. The advent of the 'capitalist entrepreneur' thus shaped the organization of the producing group into that of the classical firm just described.

However, though this historical account may give a description of what happened, it does not constitute a complete explanation because it does not fully explain why it was this and not other forms of organization which came to dominate. Other organizational forms were certainly known and attempted, for example the early socialist experiments of Robert Owen. In addition, as Coase (1937) has emphasized, an alternative to organization within the firm which is always available is that of *organization through the market*. By this is meant the coordination of the myriad separate, individual decisions by the 'impersonal workings' of the price system. In this process there is no 'central planning' but only the self-interested planning of *individual* economic decision-takers, which interacts through the system of prices and markets to determine a resource allocation. In a phrase borrowed from

D.H. Robertson, Coase describes the firm as 'an island of conscious power' in this 'ocean of unconscious cooperation'. Within the firm there is centralized economic planning and administrative coordination replaces the price mechanism, although, of course, the firm is embedded in an external system of market forces which condition its operations. The question then is: why does the firm, viewed as a centrally planned system, replace coordination through the market, and become the dominant form of organization of the producer group?

An *explanation* of the dominant position of the classical firm in the organization of production must rest on a demonstration of the advantages which it has over other forms of organization, including that of the market. Coase argued that the firm superseded market organization because there are costs associated with use of the price mechanism and that administrative organization within the firm is, up to a point, less costly. The major types of costs involved in market transactions are those of acquiring information about prices and terms under which trade takes place; the costs of negotiating, writing and enforcing contracts; and the uncertainty which may exist about the conditions on markets in the future. In some kinds of activities and markets these costs might be minor, but in others they could greatly exceed the costs of organizing production within a firm, in which case we would expect the latter to dominate.

A second important reason for the dominance of the classical firm, not only over organization through the market but also over other forms of organization, such as that of the 'producer cooperative', has been advanced by Alchian and Demsetz (1972). When the producing group works as a team, there is the problem of measuring and rewarding each member's effort in such a way as to reward high productivity and penalize shirking. In the absence of such measurement and reward, the presumption is that it pays any one individual to minimize their effort, since the costs of doing so, in terms of reduced output, are spread over all the members of the team. Then, it is argued, the system under which a central individual monitors performance and apportions rewards stimulates productivity, as the retention by that individual of the residual income of the group provides an incentive to perform the monitoring function efficiently. To this we might add that, in terms of the speed with which decisions are arrived at, the costs absorbed in the decision-taking process, and the flexibility of response to changed circumstances, a system based on central direction rather than multilateral consultation and voting procedures is likely to have an advantage. (See the discussion in Chapter 13 on the problems of common access resources and voting procedures, and relate it to the question of the likely efficiency of a 'producers' cooperative'.) It can therefore be argued that the classical 'entrepreneurial firm' emerged as the dominant form of organization of production because it had advantages of efficiency and productivity over other forms of organization, whether the market or formal organizations with different systems of decision structure and property rights.

The characteristics of the 'classical firm' described above have determined the form of the 'theory of the firm' in economics, and hence the representation of how production is carried on in a private ownership economy. The firm is viewed as being faced with an optimization problem. Its choice variables are input and output levels and possibly other variables such as advertising and expenditure on research and development. Its objective is to maximize profit, defined as the excess of revenue over all opportunity costs, including those associated with the supply of capital and the managerial functions of planning, organizing and decision-taking. This formulation of the objective function appears quite natural, since the individual controlling the firm receives the profit as her income (over and above payment for her supply of productive services), and, viewing her as a consumer, her utility from consumption is greater the greater her income.

The constraints in the problem are of two types. First, the conditions on the markets which the firm enters as a seller of outputs or buyer of inputs will determine, through prices, the profitability of any production plan (i.e. a particular set of quantities of inputs and outputs), and hence also the way in which profits vary with the production plan. Market conditions determine the terms of the contracts into which the firm enters with buyers and suppliers of goods and productive services, and hence determine the amount of the residual income, or profit, which can be made. Second, the state of technology will determine which production plans are feasible, i.e. what amounts of inputs are required to produce given output levels, or conversely what outputs can be produced with given input levels.

The classical theory of the firm operates at a high level of abstraction, at least equivalent to that of the theory of the consumer in Chapters 2 and 3. In its basic formulation, the firm is assumed to know with certainty the market conditions and state of technology. The theoretical problem is then to formalize the firm's optimization problem; examine the nature of its solution and the way in which this solution varies with changes in the parameters of the problem; and then translate the results into explanations and predictions of the firm's behaviour. This will be the subject of this and the next two chapters. In Chapter 18 we consider the firm's decisions under uncertainty, and in Chapter 20 we will return to consider in more depth alternative theories about the nature of the firm itself.

EXERCISE 5A

1. Employment in the UK ports industry used to be subject to the 'casual system'. Twice each day, dock-workers and employers would assemble at a particular place at each port, and employers would hire the men they wanted for a specific job, the men being paid off once the job was completed, possibly the same day or a little later. Explain why this system of allocating labour resources in the ports industry could be called 'coordination by the market'. Why do you think it existed in the ports industry when in most other industries workers are employed on a regular weekly basis? Why do you think it came to an end?

2. Consider a group of n individuals each of whose production activities must be coordinated with the other $n - 1$ individuals. How many contracts are required under market coordination in which each individual contracts with every other individual? How many contracts are required if there is coordination via a central coordinator?

3. Set out as fully as possible the probable advantages and disadvantages of the producers' cooperative as compared with the conventional firm in the cases of:

   (a) a group of 6 potters producing handmade pottery;

   (b) a group of 200 workers producing motorcycles;

   (c) a group of 4000 workers producing a range of electrical and non-electrical components for motor cars.

B. The production function

The starting point for an analysis of the firm's production decision is the problem of minimizing the cost of producing a given level of output subject to technological constraints. This problem is an incomplete model of the firm because the level of output is taken as given, but it is important for two reasons. First, minimization of production cost is a necessary condition for the maximization of the objective functions of several important models of the firm. Second, as we shall see in Chapter 13, least-cost production is a necessary condition for the efficient allocation of resources, and hence our results provide criteria for making judgements about the efficiency of resource allocations. We now examine in some detail the technological constraints in the firm's cost minimization problem, and leave the analysis of the problem itself to the next chapter.

The firm typically transforms a large number of different types of inputs into a number of outputs, but to simplify the analysis we initially consider the case of a firm using two inputs (z_1, z_2) to produce a single output y. In most of this chapter we use a *production function* to summarize the technical constraints on the firm's production decisions but in the final section we briefly introduce the *production possibility set* as an alternative description of the feasible output and input combinations.

We initially restrict y and the input vector $z = (z_1, z_2)$ to be non-negative. (In section E we show how suitable redefinition of variables makes this restriction unnecessary.) The firm's *production function* $f(z_1, z_2)$ shows the maximum output which can be produced from the input combination (z_1, z_2). The technological constraint on the firm's behaviour is

$$0 \leqslant y \leqslant f(z_1, z_2) = f(z) \qquad \text{[B.1]}$$

If the firm's actual output from z is equal to the maximum feasible output it is *output efficient*. The possibility that the firm is output inefficient with $y < f(z)$ is allowed for primarily to investigate the circumstances in which the firm will *choose* to be output efficient. In what follows we will often make the implicit assumption that the firm is output efficient and write the technological constraint on the firm as $y = f(z)$.

One obvious restriction that is imposed on the technology is that it is impossible to produce output without using any inputs:

$$f(0, 0) = 0 \qquad \text{[B.2]}$$

There is *essentiality* if the production function satisfies [B.2]. More interestingly, if it is impossible to produce output without using a particular input, no matter how much of other inputs are used there is *strict essentiality*. For example, if input 1 is labour and labour is essential then

$$f(0, z_2) = 0 \qquad \text{[B.3]}$$

For much of what follows we assume that $f(z)$ is twice continuously differentiable. Unlike [B.2] or [B.3] this is a strong assumption which may not be satisfied in many interesting cases. We make the assumption because it simplifies many definitions and derivations of results. The *marginal product* MP_i of input i in the production of y is the rate at which the maximum feasible output of y changes in response to an

Figure 5.1

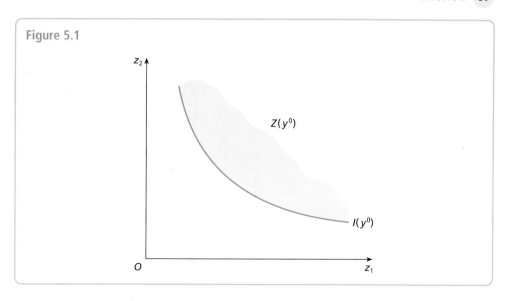

increase in z_i with the other input held constant. It is therefore the partial derivative of $f(z)$ with respect to z_i:

$$MP_i = \partial f_i(z_1, z_2)/\partial z_i = f_i(z)$$

We do not restrict the marginal product to be positive. For example, more fertilizer applied to a given amount of land will eventually reduce the crop. We do, however, make the plausible *productivity assumption* that there is always one input with a positive marginal product. Thus in the previous example if the marginal product of fertilizer is negative output can be increased by using the same amount of fertilizer on a bigger area of land.

The *input requirement set* $Z(y^0)$ for the output level y^0 is the set of input combinations which can produce at least y^0:

$$Z(y^0) = \{z \mid f(z) \geq y^0\} \qquad [\text{B.4}]$$

$Z(y^0)$ is the feasible set for the firm facing the problem of choosing z to minimize the cost of producing y^0. It is clearly closed because of the weak inequality in [B.4]. If $Z(y^0)$ is convex then the firm's production function is quasi-concave. In Fig. 5.1 the input requirement set for output level y^0 is the shaded area.

The *isoquant* $I(y^0)$ for the output level y^0 is the set of input combinations which can produce y^0 when used output-efficiently:

$$I(y^0) = \{z \mid f(z) = y^0\} \qquad [\text{B.5}]$$

The assumption that at least one marginal product is positive ensures that isoquants, like the indifference sets of section 2A, must be curves rather than areas. In Fig. 5.1 the isoquant for y^0 is the curve $I(y^0)$ which is the *boundary* of $Z(y^0)$. Those input combinations in the *interior* of $Z(y^0)$ can produce a larger output than y^0 and are therefore output-inefficient for y^0. The combinations on the boundary of the input requirement set are output-efficient for y^0.

An isoquant is a *contour* of the production function since it satisfies the relation:

$$f(z) = y^0 \qquad [\text{B.6}]$$

Figure 5.2

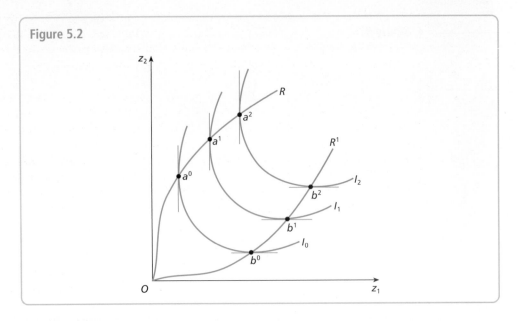

for some given y^0. This defines z_2 as an implicit function of z_1, and the Implicit Function Theorem (see Appendix G) gives

$$-\frac{dz_2}{dz_1}\bigg|_{dy=0} = \frac{f_1(z)}{f_2(z)} = \frac{MP_1}{MP_2}$$ [B.7]

The left-hand side of [B.7] is the negative of the slope of the isoquant and is the rate at which z_2 must be substituted for z_1 so as to keep output constant. It is the *marginal rate of technical substitution* of input 2 for input 1 and is denoted $MRTS_{21}$. It is directly analogous to the MRS_{21} of consumer theory. The utility function of consumer theory is an *ordinal* function whereas the production function involves a measure of output which is *cardinal* – the only degree of freedom in representing technology by a production function is in the choice of units of measurement of inputs or outputs. This gives the magnitude of marginal products f_i and their rates of change $f_{ij} = \partial f_i(z)/\partial z_j$ a significance which the magnitude of marginal utilities did not possess. Note that the $MRTS_{21}$ is independent of the units in which output is measured.

In Fig. 5.2 I_0, I_1 and I_2 are isoquants for successively greater output levels y^0, y^1 and y^2. (Note that a point on I_1 is in the interior of the input requirement set for y^0 and is therefore output-inefficient for output y^0 and output-efficient for output y^1.) The negatively sloped segments of the isoquants arise when both inputs have positive marginal products (see [B.7]).

Positively sloped portions of the isoquants occur when one of the inputs has a negative marginal product and the other a positive marginal product. For example, above a^0 on I_0 the marginal product of z_2 (say fertilizer) is negative and the reduction in output caused by further increases in z_2 must be offset by increases in the z_1 (say land) which has a positive marginal product.

At points like a^0, a^1 and a^2 the marginal product of z_2 is zero and at points like b^0, b^1 and b^2 the marginal product of z_1 is zero. The lines OR and OR^1, connecting the points at which MP_2 and MP_1 respectively are zero, are *ridge lines*. The area inside the ridge lines is known as the *economic region* because a cost-minimizing firm would always choose a point within it. This can be seen easily in Fig. 5.2. For example, for every point on the isoquant I_2 (corresponding to output y^2) outside the economic region, there is a point on I_2 inside the region where less of both inputs is used to produce y^2. Hence, as long as all inputs have non-negative prices and at least one has a positive price, a firm will incur a lower cost of producing y^2 inside the economic region than outside it.

The reason we bother to show the non-economic region outside the ridge lines is that it may be relevant in theories where the firm is not cost minimizing: it may, for example, have preferences which depend directly on the amount of an input used. Consideration of the non-economic region also leads to a distinction between output efficiency and *technical efficiency*. Production is technically inefficient if it is possible to produce a given output with less of at least one input and no more of another. Points on an isoquant for a given output level are output-efficient but unless they are in the economic region they are not technically efficient.

Elasticity of substitution

As we will see in the next chapter the shape of the isoquants has important implications for the effect of a change in input prices on the input mix used to produce a given output.

In particular, we will be interested in the *elasticity of substitution*

$$\sigma = \frac{\% \text{ change in } z_2/z_1}{\% \text{ change in } MRTS_{21}} = \frac{d(z_2/z_1)}{d(f_1/f_2)} \cdot \frac{(f_1/f_2)}{(z_2/z_1)} \qquad [B.8]$$

which captures the relationship between the input ratio and the curvature of the isoquants. Figure 5.3 illustrates. Consider the points a and b on the isoquant I_0. The change in the output ratio between a and b is shown by the difference between the slopes of the rays Ob and Oa. The corresponding change in the $MRTS_{21}$ is shown by the difference in the slopes of the lines tangent to I_0 at b and a. Now consider the isoquant I_1 and the points c and d. The slope of I_1 at c and d is equal to slope of I_0 at a and b respectively. The input mix is the same at c and a but the ratio z_2/z_1 is smaller at d than at b. Thus I_1 has a smaller elasticity of substitution than I_0: a smaller proportionate change in the input mix is associated with the same proportionate

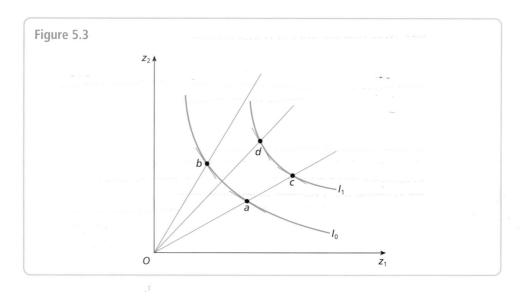

Figure 5.3

change in the slope of the isoquant. Intuitively: the smaller is the elasticity of substitution the more 'bowed in' will be the isoquants and the smaller the proportionate change in the input mix associated with any given proportionate change in the slope of the isoquant.

EXERCISE 5B

1. Explain what is meant by (a) technically efficient input combination and (b) an output-efficient input combination and show that for an input combination to be technically efficient it is necessary but not sufficient that it be output-efficient.

2. Why can isoquants have positively sloped regions while indifference curves do not?

3. Why can we adopt an assumption of diminishing marginal products when we could not adopt an assumption of diminishing marginal utility?

4. *Fixed Proportions Technology* (Leontief)

   (a) Process 1 uses at least β_{11} units of z_1 and β_{12} units of z_2 to produce one unit of output. Draw the isoquant for $y = 1$, and distinguish between the technical and output-efficient (z_1, z_2) points. Suppose that at least $y\beta_{11}$ units of z_1 and $y\beta_{12}$ units of z_2 are required to produce y units of output, so that the production function for process 1 is

   $$y = \min\left(\frac{z_1}{\beta_{11}}, \frac{z_2}{\beta_{12}}\right)$$

   Draw the isoquant map for the process. What does the economic region look like? (*Note*: min (...) is read: 'the smaller of' the terms in brackets.)

   (b) Suppose that y can also be produced from process 2, which requires at least $y\beta_{21}$ of z_1 and $y\beta_{22}$ of z_2 and that processes 1 and 2 are *additive* in that the output from one process is independent of the level at which the other process is used. Under what circumstances would it never be technically efficient to use process 2? A given level of y could be produced by different mixtures of the two processes using different total amounts of the inputs. Derive the isoquant for mixtures of the two processes (where a mixture uses $k\beta_{11} + (1 - k)\beta_{21}$ of z_1 and $k\beta_{12} + (1 - k)\beta_{22}$ of z_2 to produce 1 unit of output, with $0 \leqslant k \leqslant 1$). A mixture is a convex combination of processes.

   (c) Let there be three, four, . . . , n processes satisfying the above assumptions. Investigate the circumstances in which particular processes are never used. Show that as the number n of technically efficient processes becomes large the isoquant tends to the smooth shape assumed in this section.

5. The Cobb–Douglas production function is

   $$y = z_1^\alpha z_2^\beta \qquad \alpha > 0, \beta > 0$$

   Show that $MP_1 = \alpha y/z_1$, $MP_2 = \beta y/z_2$.
   What is the $MRTS_{21}$? How does it vary with: (a) y; (b) z_2/z_1?
   Draw the isoquant map.

6. The *CES* production function is

   $$y = A(\delta_1 z_1^\alpha + \delta_2 z_2^\alpha)^{1/\alpha}, \qquad \delta_1 + \delta_2 = 1, A > 0$$

   Show that

   $$MP_i = A^\alpha \delta_i \left[\frac{y}{z_i}\right]^{1-\alpha}$$

   What is the $MRTS_{21}$? How does it vary with (a) y; (b) z_2/z_1?

7. *Elasticity of substitution*

(a) Show that the elasticity of substitution can be written as

$$\sigma = \frac{f_1 f_2(z_1 f_1 + z_2 f_2)}{z_1 z_2[2f_{12} f_1 f_2 - f_{11}(f_2)^2 - f_{22}(f_1)^2]}$$

(*Hint*: define the input ratio as $r = z_2/z_1$, use the definition of the isoquant as $y^0 - f(z_1, rz_1) = 0$ to get z_1 as function of r : $z_1 = g(r)$ and write $MRTS_{21} = f_1(g(r), rg(r))/f_2(g(r), rg(r))$. Differentiate $MRTS_{21}$ with respect to r (using the implicit function theorem to get dg/dr.)

(b) Show that the elasticities of substitution of the Leontief, Cobb–Douglas and CES production functions are respectively zero, 1 and $1/(1 - \alpha)$. (*Hint*: in the latter two cases, rather than using the above expression for σ, use your earlier results concerning the MP_i and thus the $MRTS_{21}$ and remember the relationship between elasticities and logs.)

(c) Explain why the elasticity of substitution of the *linear production function*

$$y = a_1 z_1 + a_2 z_2, \quad a_1 > 0, \quad a_2 > 0$$

is infinite. Sketch the isoquants.

8. Show that the CES production function includes the following as special cases:

(a) the linear production function ($\alpha = 1$);

(b) the Cobb–Douglas production function (as $\alpha \to 0$);

(c) the Leontief production function (as $\alpha \to -\infty$).

C. Variations in scale

In this and the next section we examine the responses of output to changes in inputs. The sections are a preparation for the investigation in Chapter 6 of the relationship between output and cost minimizing input choices. Since cost minimization implies technical efficiency we restrict attention in these sections to firms which are output-efficient and operating in the economic region of the production function.

Changes in output can arise from

(a) changes in the scale of production by varying all inputs in the same proportion; or

(b) changes in relative input proportions.

The first corresponds to movements along a ray through the origin, such as OA or OB in Fig. 5.4, the second to a movement from one ray to another. For example, output can be increased by moving from z^0 on I_0 to the higher I_2 isoquant, either by doubling both inputs (moving to z^2), or varying the input proportion and moving to z^3 where z_2/z_1 has fallen. In this section we consider variations in scale and in the next an important case of variations in input proportions resulting from varying one input with the other held constant.

Starting from say z^0 on I_0 in Fig. 5.4 and multiplying each input by the *scale parameter* $s > 0$ is equivalent to a movement along the ray OA through z^0. If $s < 1$ the scale of production is reduced and there is a movement toward the origin. Conversely if $s > 1$ the scale of production is increased and there is a movement away from the origin. For example, when $s = \frac{1}{2}$ the point z^1 is reached and when $s = 2$ the point z^2 is reached.

Figure 5.4

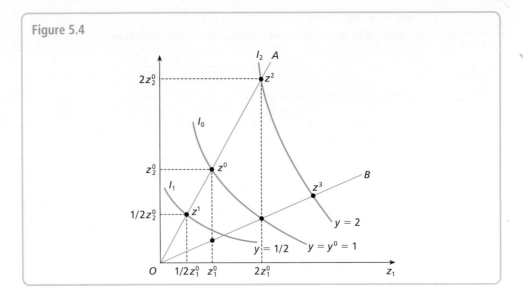

When we investigate the effects of scale variations from some initial input combination z we can write the production function as

$$y = f(sz) = y(s; z)$$

and consider how y varies with the scale parameter s with input proportions held constant at the values implied by the initial z.

The *elasticity of scale E* is the proportionate change in output y divided by the proportionate change in the scale of production s:

$$E = \frac{d \ln y}{d \ln s} = \frac{dy}{y} \cdot \frac{s}{ds} = \frac{dy}{ds} \cdot \frac{s}{y} \qquad \text{[C.1]}$$

It is a measure of the responsiveness of output to equal proportionate changes in all inputs. Output increases more or less proportionately with scale as E is greater or less than 1. There are said to be *increasing, constant* or *decreasing returns to scale* as $E > 1$, $E = 1$, or $E < 1$. Since dy/ds depends on the input mix as well as the scale parameter the returns to scale for a production function may depend on the input mix and the scale. Thus in Fig. 5.4 examination of the I_0 and I_2 isoquants shows that there are constant returns along OA and increasing returns along OB. In Fig. 5.5 output is plotted against the scale parameter (so that input proportions are held constant) and a number of possibilities are illustrated. There are increasing returns in part (a), constant returns in part (b), decreasing returns in part (c) and in part (d) there are initially increasing and then decreasing returns to scale.

Homogeneous and homothetic production functions

A production function is *homogeneous of degree t* if multiplying all inputs by the scale parameter s causes output to increase by the factor s^t. Formally if

$$f(sz) = s^t f(z) \qquad \text{[C.2]}$$

Figure 5.5

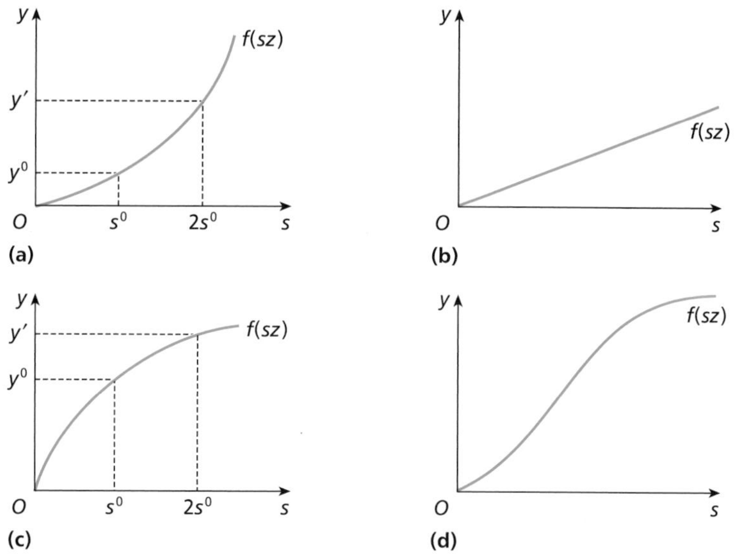

then the production function $y = f(z)$ is homogeneous of degree t. When $t = 1$ the production function is *linear homogeneous*. Many models assume that $f(z)$ is linear homogeneous because such functions have a number of properties which greatly aid analysis.

(a) Using [C.2] the elasticity of scale of a homogeneous function of degree t is

$$E = \frac{dy}{ds} \cdot \frac{s}{y} = \frac{df(sz)}{ds} \cdot \frac{s}{f(sz)} = \frac{ds^t f(z)}{ds} \cdot \frac{s}{s^t f(z)} = \left[ts^{t-1} f(z) \frac{s}{s^t f(z)} = t \right] \text{? Now!}$$

Since a linear homogeneous function has $t = 1$ we see that *the linear homogeneous production function has constant returns to scale at all input combinations.*

(b) [C.2] must hold for all z and so the partial derivatives with respect to z_i of both sides of [C.2] must be equal. Since the partial derivative of the left-hand side is

$$\frac{\partial f(sz_1, sz_2)}{\partial z_i} = \frac{\partial f(sz_1, sz_2)}{\partial (sz_i)} \cdot \frac{d(sz_i)}{dz_i} = f_i(sz)s \quad \text{? how}$$

and of the right-hand side is $s^t f_i(z)$ we have $f_i(sz)s = s^t f_i(z)$ or

$$f_i(sz) = s^{t-1} f_i(z) \tag{C.3}$$

Hence a function which is homogeneous of degree t has partial derivatives which are homogeneous of degree $t - 1$. Since $t = 1$ for a linear homogeneous function we have established that $f_i(sz) = f_i(z)$: *linear homogeneous production functions have marginal products which are independent of scale.* The marginal products will depend only on the input proportions and will be constant along rays from the origin.

(c) The slope of the isoquant at sz is $-f_1(sz)/f_2(sz)$ and at z is $-f_1(z)/f_2(z)$. Since [C.3] holds for all inputs i when the production function is homogeneous of degree t we see that *the slopes of the isoquants of a homogeneous production function depend only on the input proportions and are independent of the scale of production.* The slopes will be constant along rays from the origin and each isoquant is a radial expansion or contraction of every other isoquant. As we show in the next chapter this implies that input proportions for cost minimizing firms depend only on input prices and not on the level of output.

(d) Since [C.2] holds for all s if f is homogeneous the derivatives of both sides of [C.2] with respect to s must be equal. The derivative of the left-hand side of [C.2] is

$$\frac{df(sz_1, sz_2)}{ds} = \sum_i \frac{\partial f(sz_1, sz_2)}{\partial(sz_i)} \cdot \frac{d(sz_i)}{ds} = \sum_i f_i(sz)z_i = s^{t-1}\sum_i f_i(z)z_i$$

where the last step follows from [C.3]. The derivative of the right-hand side of [C.2] is $ts^{t-1}f(z)$ and so when f is homogeneous of degree t,

$$\sum_i f_i(z)z_i = tf(z) \tag{C.4}$$

This result is known as *Euler's Theorem*. When the production function is linear homogeneous [C.4] gives the *adding up property*: output is equal to the sum of the marginal products of the inputs times their level of use. Its significance is that if the price of each input is equal to the value of its marginal product (the price of output times the marginal product) then a profit maximizing firm will break even: its revenue will be equal to its costs.

A production function $g(z)$ is *homothetic* if it can be written as an increasing transformation of a linear homogeneous function of the inputs: $g(z) = F(f(z))$ where $f(z)$ is linear homogeneous, $F' > 0$ and $F(0) = 0$. Think of $f(z)$ as a 'composite' input and of $F(f)$ as a single input production function. An example of a homothetic production function is

$$y = \ln z_1^\alpha z_2^{1-\alpha} = \alpha \ln z_1 + (1 - \alpha)z_2, \qquad 0 < \alpha < 1 \tag{C.5}$$

where $F = \ln f$ and f is just a constant returns Cobb–Douglas production function.

Homothetic production functions are important because, unlike homogeneous functions, they can have variable returns to scale but they also have the useful property (c) of homogeneous functions. As the reader should check, in the example [C.5] of a homothetic production function, increasing all inputs by the factor s will increase output by the factor $\ln s$.

The elasticity of scale of the homothetic production function is

$$E = \frac{dg(sz)}{ds} \cdot \frac{s}{g(sz)} = \frac{dF(f(sz))}{df} \cdot \frac{df(sz)}{ds} \cdot \frac{s}{F(f(sz))} = \frac{dF}{df} \cdot \frac{df}{ds} \cdot \frac{s}{f} \cdot \frac{f}{F} = \frac{dF}{df} \cdot \frac{f}{F}$$

(remember that from the definition of homotheticity f is linear homogeneous so that $df/ds \cdot s/f = 1$). Thus the scale elasticity of a homothetic production function $F(f(z))$ is not constrained by the requirement that f is linear homogeneous. The scale elasticity of [C.5] for example is $1/F$ which decreases with the scale of production. The marginal product of input i if g is homothetic is

$$g_i(z) = F'(f(z))f_i(z)$$

and so the slope of the isoquant is

$$-g_1(z)/g_2(z) = -F'(f)f_1(z)/F'(f)f_2(z) = -f_1(z)/f_2(z)$$

Since f is linear homogeneous $-f_1/f_2$ depends only on the relative input proportions (property (c)) and so *the slopes of the isoquants of a homothetic production function are independent of scale.*

EXERCISE 5C

1. Do all homogeneous production functions of whatever degree have

    (a) marginal products, and

    (b) marginal technical rates of substitution

    which are independent of the level of output?

2. What are the degrees of returns to scale for the

    (a) linear production function;

    (b) Leontief production function;

    (c) Cobb–Douglas production function;

    (d) CES production function?

3. Show that all homogeneous functions are also homothetic. Give an example (not [C.5]) of a production function which is homothetic but not homogeneous of any degree.

4. *Elasticity of substitution and linear homogeneity.* Show that if $f(z_1, z_2)$ is linear homogeneous the expression for the elasticity of substitution in Question 7 of exercise 5B simplifies to $\sigma = f_1 f_2 / y f_{12}$. (*Hint*: use the fact that [C.4] implies $f_{11} z_1 + f_{21} z_2 = 0$ to substitute for f_{11} and f_{22}.)

D. Variations in input proportions

Figure 5.6 illustrates the effects of changes in input proportions when one input (z_2 in this case) is held fixed and the other is free to vary. In part (a) the isoquant map is shown and z_2 is assumed fixed at z_2^0. Variations in z_1 will lead to a movement along the line through z_2^0 parallel to the z_1 axis, and the output of y produced with $z_2 = z_2^0$ for different levels of z_1 can be read off from the isoquants. Part (b) plots the total curve $y = f(z_1, z_2^0)$ which results. If part (a) can be thought of as the contour map of the total product hill then part (b) shows a vertical slice through the hill at $z_2 = z_2^0$. Holding z_2 at different levels will give rise to different total product curves. Part (c) shows the average and marginal product of z_1 as a function of z_1 and is in turn derived from the total product curve of part (b).

The *average product* of z_1, $AP_1(z_1, z_2^0)$ is total product divided by z_1 : y/z_1. Consider in part (b) a ray from the origin to a point on the total product curve, for example the line OB. The slope of this line is the vertical distance BC divided by the horizontal distance OC. But $BC = y^0$ and $OC = z_1$ and hence: slope $OB = BC/OC = y^0/z_1 = AP_1(z_1, z_2^0)$. The AP_1 curve is, therefore, derived by plotting the slope of a ray from the origin to each point on the total product curve.

The marginal product curve MP_1 is derived by plotting the slope of the total product curve. Notice the relationship between the AP_1 and MP_1, with the MP_1 cutting the AP_1 from above at the point z_1' where AP_1 is at a maximum. It can be demonstrated that this relationship is no accident of draughtsmanship. The definition of the average product is:

$$AP_1 = \frac{y}{z_1} = \frac{f(z_1, z_2^0)}{z_1} \qquad \text{[D.1]}$$

Differentiating and setting equal to zero as a necessary condition for maximization yields

Figure 5.6

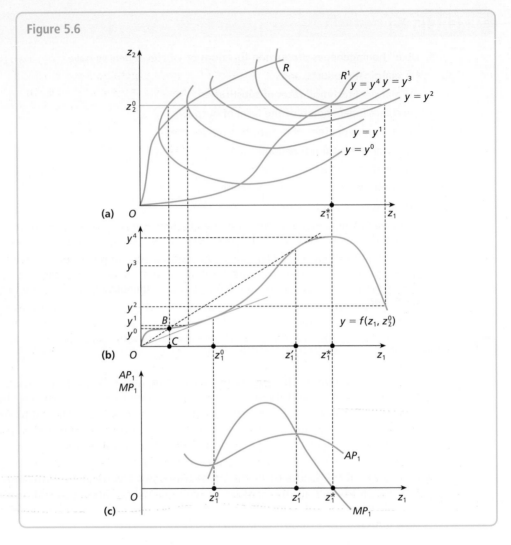

$$\frac{d}{dz_1}[AP_1] = \frac{1}{(z_1)^2}\left[\frac{\partial f}{\partial z_1} \cdot z_1 - f\right] = 0 \tag{D.2}$$

$$= \frac{1}{z_1}\left[f_1 - \frac{f}{z_1}\right] = \frac{1}{z_1}[MP_1 - AP_1] = 0 \tag{D.3}$$

Hence $MP_1 = AP_1$ is a necessary condition for AP_1 to be maximized.

EXERCISE 5D

1. What is the significance of the fact that in Fig. 5.6 the input level z_1^* is at the same time (a) a coordinate of a point on the ridge line, (b) the value of z_1 at which y is a maximum given $z_2 = z_2^0$, (c) the value of z_1 at which MP_1 is zero?

2. Explain why, in Fig. 5.6, AP_1 is at a minimum and $MP_1 = AP_1$ at z_1^0.

3. Redraw Fig. 5.6 taking a fixed level of z_1 rather than z_2.

E. The multi-product case

In the previous sections we have written the firm's production function in the *explicit* form $y = f(z_1, z_2)$, or, allowing for output inefficiency, $y \leqslant f(z_1, z_2)$. When the firm produces more than one output it is often more convenient to write the production function in its *implicit* form. Corresponding to the two explicit cases above we could have

$$y - f(z_1, z_2) = g(z_1, z_2, y) = 0$$

or

$$y - f(z_1, z_2) = g(z_1, z_2, y) \leqslant 0$$

The implicit and explicit forms are equivalent ways of describing the technical constraints on production provided that we restrict attention to the economic region of the explicit production function. (When isoquants are positively sloped the implicit production function is not well defined because given y and say z_2 there are two values of z_1 which satisfy $y - f(z) = 0$.)

The marginal products of the inputs and the marginal rate of technical substitution between them are derived from the implicit form by the implicit function rule of differentiation. Applying the rule we have, for example,

$$\frac{dy}{dz_1} = \frac{-g_{z_1}}{g_y} = -\left(\frac{-f_1}{1}\right) = f_1 = MP_1$$

It is convenient in many cases to adopt a slightly different notational convention. We have so far talked of y as an output and z_1 as an input and restricted both outputs and inputs to being non-negative. But what is an input for one firm may be an output for another, or a firm may change from producing a good to using it as an input, or it may use part of an output as an input (a power station uses electricity for lighting in producing electricity). To save relabelling the good when this happens it is easier to use the concept of the firm's *net output* of a good. (*Note*: this is quite different from the meaning of the term 'net output' as it occurs in, say, national income accounting, namely as the difference between a firm's revenue and the cost of bought-in inputs.) If the net output is positive the firm is producing the good, if it is negative the firm is 'consuming' it or using it as an input. The firm's net output of good i will be written as the variable y_i which is not constrained to be non-negative. If $y_i > 0$ good i is produced or supplied by the firm; if $y_i < 0$ good i is 'consumed' by the firm and if $y_i = 0$ the good is neither produced nor consumed. Using this labelling we can rewrite the implicit production constraint in the general case as

$$g(y_1, y_2, \ldots, y_n) = g(y) \leqslant 0 \tag{E.1}$$

with $y = (y_1, y_2, \ldots, y_n)$ now defined as the net output vector. The y_i are sometimes referred to as *netputs*.

When $g(y) < 0$ there is output inefficiency and when $g(y) = 0$ there is output efficiency. A technically infeasible net output vector is indicated by $g(y) > 0$. Notice that an *increase* in y_i means that if i is an input ($y_i < 0$) the use of the input has been *reduced*: y_i is measured along the negative part of the relevant axis if it is an input.

When $g(y) = 0$ it is technically infeasible to increase an output or reduce an input without reducing the level of some other net output, i.e. reducing some other output or increasing some other input. This implies that the partial derivatives g_i are always positive at $g(y) = 0$ to reflect the fact that *ceteris paribus* increases in y_i (reducing an input or increasing an input) are not technically feasible because they would lead to $g > 0$.

Again using the implicit function rule on $g(y) = 0$ and allowing only y_i and y_j to change, we have:

$$\frac{dy_i}{dy_j} = \frac{-g_j}{g_i} \qquad i, j = 1, 2, \dots, n \qquad \text{[E.2]}$$

This can be given a number of interpretations depending on whether y_i and y_j are positive or negative, as follows.

(a) $y_i < 0$ and $y_j < 0$.

Both goods are inputs so that dy_i/dy_j is the rate at which one input can be substituted for another when all other goods (inputs and outputs) are held constant. It is therefore the (negative of) the marginal rate of technical substitution, i.e. it is the slope of the isoquant, which in the multi-product case is the boundary of the set of y_i, y_j combinations which will just produce a given level of the firm's outputs with all other inputs held constant. For example, in the single-output, two-input case considered in previous sections we have (remembering that an *increase* in y_i means a *decrease* in z_1):

$$\frac{dy_2}{dy_1} = \frac{g_1}{g_2} = \frac{-f_1}{f_2} = -MRTS_{21} \qquad \text{[E.3]}$$

Figure 5.7(a) shows the isoquant for given levels of $y_3, \dots, y_n$ for a particular production function which has the convexity and smoothness properties of the explicit function of previous sections. Again all points in the shaded area are technically possible ($g(y) \leq 0$) but only points on the boundary of it are output efficient ($g(y) = 0$).

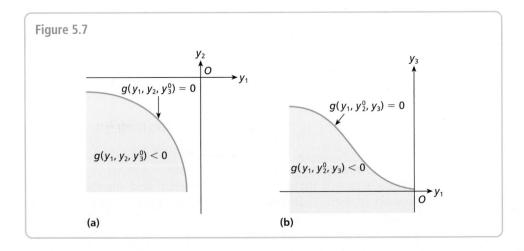

Figure 5.7

(a)

(b)

(b) $y_i > 0$, $y_j < 0$.

Good i is an output, j an input, so that dy_i/dy_j is the rate at which the output of i changes when input j is reduced with all other outputs and inputs held constant. It is therefore the negative of the marginal product of input j in the production of output i. Using our single output, two input example and remembering that $y_1 = -z_1$

$$\frac{dy_3}{dy_1} = \frac{-g_1}{g_3} = -f_1 = -MP_1 \qquad \text{[E.4]}$$

Figure 5.7(b) shows the relationship between an input (good 1) and an output (good 3) and corresponds to the total product curve of Fig. 5.6(b). All points in the shaded area are technically possible but only points on the upper boundary (the total product curve) are output efficient.

(c) $y_i > 0$, $y_j > 0$.

Both goods are outputs and so dy_i/dy_j is the rate at which the output of i varies as the output of j is increased when all inputs and all other outputs are held constant. This is the negative of the *marginal rate of transformation* of i into j or MRT_{ij}. In Fig. 5.8 both goods 1 and 2 are outputs, and the shaded area is the set of all technically possible combinations. The upper boundary of this shaded area is the set of output efficient points and is known as the *transformation curve*. Its slope is the marginal rate of transformation.

Increases in y_j require reductions in y_i. Different transformation curves are generated by fixing the other net outputs at different levels. A reduction in any other net output shifts the transformation curve out from the origin. In other words, decreases in other outputs or increases in inputs allow more of both good 1 and good 2 to be produced. We have assumed that the technology allows substitutability of outputs so that the transformation curve is negatively sloped. If the outputs must be produced in fixed proportions (as, for example, in some chemical processes) the transformation curves would be rectangular, indicating that an increase in the output of one good requires an increase in the level of inputs and cannot be made by reducing the output of the other good.

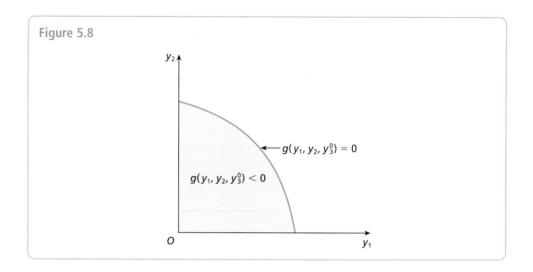

Figure 5.8

Joint products

In some cases where a firm produces more than one output it may be possible to relate the output of each product to a specific part of the bundle of inputs used by the firm, so that the firm has a production function for each output. For example if y_1 and y_2 are the levels of the firm's outputs and z_i^j is the amount of input i used in production of good j the firm's production possibilities could be written explicitly as

$$y_1 \leqslant f^1(z_1^1, z_2^1)$$
$$y_2 \leqslant f^2(z_1^2, z_2^2) \hspace{3cm} \text{[E.5]}$$

or implicitly as

$$y_1 - f^1(z_1^1, z_2^1) \leqslant 0$$
$$y_2 - f^2(z_1^2, z_2^2) \leqslant 0 \hspace{3cm} \text{[E.6]}$$

When it is possible to describe the technical constraints on the firm in this way the production function is *separable*. If the firm is producing several products and inputs *cannot* be assigned in this way the firm is said to be producing *joint products*. Notice that it is the way in which the inputs relate to outputs, *not* the number of products, which is the defining characteristic of joint production. When the production function is separable the firm could be regarded as the sum of several single-product plants, and if each of the constituent plants acts to minimize the cost of its own production, total costs are minimized. Production can be *decentralized* without increasing cost. When there is joint production, decentralization (instructing each product division to minimize cost) will not lead to minimum total cost because of the interdependence between the costs of each product. This point will be elaborated in the exercises in Chapter 6.

The production possibility set

An alternative and more general way of describing the technological constraints on the firm is by its *production set*, *PS*, which is the set of all possible input–output combinations. The *PS* is the set of all feasible net output bundles, or of all feasible *activities*. An *activity* of the firm is the firm's net output bundle: $y = (y_1, \ldots, y_n)$. The production function $g(y) \leqslant 0$ and the *PS* are equivalent descriptions of the technological constraints in the sense that the statement that y^0 is in the *PS* is equivalent to the statement $g(y^0) \leqslant 0$. If the activity y^0 is not technically possible then it is not in the *PS* and $g(y^0) > 0$. In terms of the figures in this section, the shaded areas (including their boundaries) can be thought of as slices through the *PS* and all points in the shaded areas are in the *PS*. The upper boundary of the *PS* is the set of points with the property that it is not possible to increase the net output of any good without reducing the net output of some other good (i.e. reducing an output or increasing an input). This upper boundary is therefore output-efficient and satisfies the equation $g(y) = 0$.

Cost

A. Introduction

Time dimension of production

In the previous chapter we did not consider in any detail exactly what is meant by 'inputs' and 'outputs' and in particular we did not discuss the time dimension of the firm's production function, preferring instead to talk loosely of 'levels' of outputs and inputs, in order to concentrate on the technical relationships involved. Output, however, is a *flow* and so must always have a time dimension: it is meaningless to say that a firm produces so many tons of a particular good unless we also specify the period of time (hour, day, month or year) over which the output was produced. y therefore has the dimension of a rate of flow of units of the good *per unit of time* or *per period*.

Input levels must be similarly interpreted. This is straightforward with inputs such as raw materials which are transformed or consumed by the firm. z_i would then have the dimension of the flow of the quantity of raw material of type i per period. Durable assets, however, such as machines, are, as the term implies, not consumed by the firm. In these cases we can think of the asset itself as embodying a *stock of productive services* and z_i is the *flow of productive services* of the asset used per period of time. For example with a machine of type i, z_i would be machine hours (the number of hours the machine is used) per day. The *capacity* of an asset is the maximum possible flow of productive services which can be used per period. In the example above, the capacity of the machine is 24 machine-hours per day (assuming no time has to be taken for cooling down, maintenance, etc.). As we will see in section C it is often necessary to distinguish carefully between capacity and actual usage.

In this chapter, an 'input' will always be measured as a rate of flow, either of some physical good (coal, crude oil, cotton) or of the *services* of some factor of production which is not itself used up in the production process (labour, machinery).

Long- and short-run decision-making

We concentrate on a two-input model and we assume that z_1 is a *variable input*: it can be varied at will by the firm. The firm can decide at the start of period 0, the 'present' time period, to use any level of z_1 in production in period 0 and can implement that decision. The other input z_2 takes time to vary: it takes one period to make available an increment of z_2, for example the flow of services from a machine or type of skilled labour. A decision taken 'now' at the start of period 0 to increase the amount of z_2 by Δz_2 will result in that increment becoming available for use in producing y at the start of period 1. As far as production in period 0 is concerned z_2 is a *constrained input*. The amount of z_2 used in period 0 certainly cannot be increased beyond the amount available at the start of period 0. On the other hand, the firm may or may not be able to *reduce* the amount of z_2 it uses in period 0. If the input is divisible the firm will be able to use less than the maximum amount unless there is some contractual limitation. Since contracts usually stipulate the amount of an input which will be *paid for* rather than the amount which must be used, divisibility will usually imply the possibility of using an input below capacity. For example, a firm may hire labour on a monthly contract, and be unable to increase or reduce the number of workers to whom it must pay a guaranteed wage within that period, but it may *if it chooses* use less than the maximum possible number of hours.

The distinction between fixed and variable inputs has a crucial implication for the firm's decision-making. The firm is always located in time at the start of period 0 (the present) and at that moment of time it must make two types of decision. First, given the desired output level for period 0, it must choose an actual level of z_1 for period 0, remembering that maximum z_2 is fixed in period 0. (When z_2 can be less than its maximum level the firm must also choose an *actual* level of z_2 to be used in period 0.) Second, given the planned or desired output level for period 1, it must *formulate a plan* specifying desired levels of z_1 and z_2 to be used in period 1. If the desired amount of z_2 in period 1 in the plan differs from the level of z_2 held by the firm at the start of period 0 it must begin to organize the required change at the start of period 0, so that it is available at the start of period 1. Thus the choices *implemented* by the firm in period 0 are the input levels actually used in period 0, and the change in the constrained input available for the next period.

To predict how the firm's behaviour will vary in response to changes in the desired output levels in periods 0 and 1 or changes in the costs of inputs, we must construct a model of the two kinds of decision taken by the firm at the start of period 0. In section B we consider the problem of finding desired levels of z_1 and z_2 to minimize the cost of producing the planned period 1 output. Both inputs are variable in this problem since the firm will be able to bring about any planned change in z_2 by the start of period 1. This is referred to as the *long-run* cost minimization problem. In section C we model the problem of setting z_1, with a fixed maximum z_2, so as to minimize the cost of producing the required period 0 output. This is the *short-run* cost minimization problem.

Adjustment costs

We assumed above that it was impossible to increase z_2 within period 0 but that z_1 was freely variable. This distinction is a crude recognition of the fact that in general there are differing *adjustment costs* for different types of inputs. Adjustment costs are those costs which arise solely from a change in the level of use of an input. Moreover, changes in input quantities have to be planned and organized over and above the management of ongoing activities. All this absorbs resources and hence imposes costs of adjustment.

For example, if a firm wishes to hire more labour it may have to advertise for new workers, but once the new workers are employed the advertisements are no longer necessary. The advertising cost is an adjustment cost: it is incurred solely because the firm wishes to hire more workers, since no advertisement is needed to retain workers already employed. Firms must shop around, search, and collect information just as consumers do.

If actual input levels differ from cost-minimizing levels, the firm will gain from changes in input levels. These changes will impose adjustment costs and so the firm must choose the *optimal rate of adjustment* by balancing the benefits (reduced production costs) against the adjustment costs of the changes.

Such problems are complicated (though not impossibly so) and we adopt here the crude simplification of regarding fixed and variable inputs as *polar cases* of adjustment costs. Variable inputs can be thought of as having zero adjustment costs and fixed inputs as having infinite adjustment costs for changes within period 0. The reader should remember that the terms 'long-run' and 'short-run' are based on these polar cases and that the rate of adjustment of inputs by the firm is not solely technologically determined: it depends on an economic decision balancing the benefits and costs of adjustment.

Opportunity costs

Before we can analyse the firm's cost minimization problems we must define the 'cost' of an input to the firm. The *marginal opportunity cost* of an input is the value of the alternative forgone by the use of an additional unit of that input by the firm. If the additional unit is not already owned or hired by the firm then it must be bought or rented, and the marginal opportunity cost is the market price or rental of the input. If the additional unit used is already owned or rented there is no additional cash outlay by the firm, but, since the unit could have been sold on the market, the market price is the value of the alternative (selling the unit rather than using it) which is forgone.

In the analysis of this chapter we interpret the 'cost' of an input as its marginal opportunity cost and assume that this is measured for variable inputs by the market price of the input. This assumption may not be valid for a number of reasons:

(a) If the market price of the input rises (falls) as the firm buys larger quantities of the input then the marginal opportunity cost of the input is greater (less) than its market price to the firm. The cost to the firm of an extra unit is the market price for that unit *plus* the effect of the change in price on the total cost of the units which the firm has already decided to buy. We leave the analysis of this case to Chapter 10 and assume throughout this chapter that input prices are fixed as far as the firm is concerned.

(b) The firm may face different market prices for the input depending on whether it wishes to buy or sell it. Purchase taxes may cause the buying price to exceed the selling price. Markets may be costly to use because of the costs of acquiring information, negotiation, etc., so that a seller may receive a net price below that paid by a buyer. These *transactions costs* may also include fees and commissions paid to agents and brokers. The contract under which an input was hired or bought may create a gap between buying and selling prices. For example, a firm may rent warehouse space under a contract which forbids the firm to re-let. The selling price is therefore zero but the purchase price of additional space is the market price. Again, consider a firm which hires labour under a contract which gives workers the right to a month's notice of dismissal, so that their wages are an inescapable cost over this period. The marginal opportunity cost of the input in the short-run decision problem in such cases is the selling price (zero in the two examples above) for quantities less than the amount already owned or rented and the buying price for larger quantities. In the long run (a month in the labour contract example), the marginal opportunity cost is the market price irrespective of the quantity the firm wishes to use.

The marginal opportunity cost of an input depends in general on the quantity which the firm wishes to use, the quantity which is already owned or contracted for, the costs of using the input market, and the terms of the contract under which inputs are traded. As the last two examples above indicate, *it will also depend on the time horizon of the decision for which the cost calculations are required,* i.e. on whether the decision is short- or long-run, or whether the input is fixed or variable.

EXERCISE 6A

1. If the firm can borrow and lend at the interest rate r per annum what is the opportunity cost of using an infinitely durable asset for one year, with and without a secondhand market in the durable asset? How would significant transaction costs (due to the need to dismantle and transport the asset each time it is sold) affect your answer? Suppose the asset had a finite life?

B. Long-run cost minimization

The firm's long-run cost minimization problem is to formulate a *plan* (an input combination) which will minimize the cost of producing *a specified output* during some period sufficiently far into the future for inputs to be considered fully variable. The firm is assumed to be able to buy inputs or sell inputs that it already owns, at a constant positive price, so that the total cost to be minimized is $\sum p_i z_i$. The production function constraining the minimization is assumed to be strictly quasi-concave and twice continuously differentiable. The long-run cost minimization problem is

$$\min_{z_1,\dots,z_n} \sum p_i z_i \quad \text{s.t. (i) } f(z_1, \dots, z_n) \geq y$$
$$\text{(ii) } z_i \geq 0 \qquad i = 1, \dots, n \qquad \text{[B.1]}$$

where y is the required output level.

Figure 6.1 illustrates a two-input version of the problem. The lines C^1, C^2, C^3 are *isocost* lines which show the combinations of the two inputs which have the same total cost. The C^1 line, for example, graphs the equation

Figure 6.1

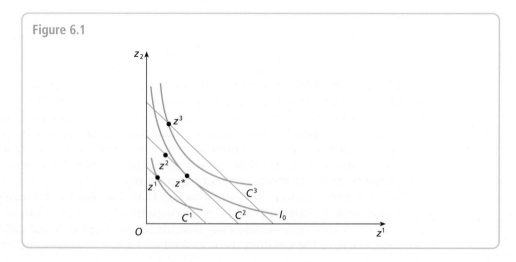

$$p_1 z_1 + p_2 z_2 = C^1$$

or

$$z_2 = \frac{C^1}{p_2} - \frac{p_1}{p_2} \cdot z_1$$

In this case, where the prices of the inputs are independent of the amounts of the inputs bought by the firm, the isocost lines are parallel straight lines with slope

$$\left. \frac{dz_2}{dz_1} \right|_{dC=0} = \frac{-p_1}{p_2} \qquad \text{[B.2]}$$

The further from the origin the higher are the total costs represented by the lines: z^2 on C^2 is an input bundle containing more of both inputs than z^1 on C^1. It must therefore cost more, and since all points on the same isocost line have the same total cost, all points on C^2 cost more than all points on C^1. I_0 is the isoquant for the required output and, as we argued in section 5B, the solution must be on this isoquant when input prices are positive. The problem is to choose the point on I_0 which has the lowest cost, i.e. is on the lowest isocost line. In this case the least cost input combination is z^* where I_0 is tangent to C^2. Combinations along lower isocost lines such as C^1 cost less than z^* but do not produce enough output: they are on lower isoquants. Combinations on higher isocost lines such as z^3 on C^3 satisfy the output constraint but have higher costs.

The slope of the isoquant is the negative of the marginal rate of technical substitution between z_1 and z_2 and, in the interior solution illustrated here, cost is minimized where

$$\frac{-p_1}{p_2} = \left. \frac{dz_2}{dz_1} \right|_{y=y^0} = -MRTS_{21} = \frac{-f_1}{f_2}$$

or

$$\frac{p_1}{p_2} = \frac{f_1}{f_2} \qquad \text{[B.3]}$$

The ratio of input prices is equal to the ratio of the marginal products. Rearranging this expression yields

$$\frac{p_1}{f_1} = \frac{p_2}{f_2} \qquad \text{[B.4]}$$

as a necessary condition for cost minimization. Now f_1 is the marginal product of z_1: the rate at which y increases as z_1 increases, and $1/f_1$ is the rate at which z_1 must increase to increase y; it is approximately the number of units of z_1 required to increase y by one unit. p_1 is the cost of an additional unit of z_1. p_1 times $1/f_1$ is therefore the cost of increasing the output of y by one unit by increasing the input of z_1. p_2/f_2 has a similar interpretation. When costs are minimized the firm would be indifferent between increasing y by increasing z_1 or z_2.

The effect on total cost is the same whichever input is varied so as to increase output by one unit, when inputs are chosen optimally. $p_1/f_1 = p_2/f_2 = LMC$ is therefore the *long-run marginal cost* of extra output to the firm: the rate at which cost increases as y increases when cost is minimized for every level of y and all inputs are variable.

In section 5B we introduced two distinct but related definitions of efficiency (output efficiency and technical efficiency) and we now introduce a third: *economic efficiency*. An input combination is economically efficient when it minimizes the cost of producing a given output. It is important to be clear about the relationships of these three types of efficiency: economic efficiency implies technical efficiency, which implies output efficiency, but none of the converse implications hold.

Method of Lagrange in the cost minimization problem

Since the solution to [B.1] will satisfy $y = f(z_1, \ldots, z_n)$ on our assumptions about input prices and technology, we can, if we also assume that all inputs are used in positive quantities in the solution, analyse the solution to [B.1] by forming the Lagrange function

$$L = \Sigma \, p_i z_i + \lambda [y - f(z_1, \ldots, z_n)] \qquad \text{[B.5]}$$

First-order conditions for a minimum of L are

$$\frac{\partial L}{\partial z_i} = p_i - \lambda f_i = 0 \qquad i = 1, \ldots, n$$

$$\frac{\partial L}{\partial \lambda} = y - f(z_1, \ldots, z_n) = 0 \qquad \text{[B.6]}$$

and by writing the conditions on z_i as $p_i = \lambda f_i$ and dividing the ith condition by the jth we have the n-input extension of [B.3]:

$$\frac{p_i}{p_j} = \frac{f_i}{f_j} \qquad j = 1, \ldots, n, \quad j \neq i \qquad \text{[B.7]}$$

We can, as in all economic problems using Lagrange techniques, give an economic interpretation to λ. The optimal value of λ is the rate at which the optimized value of the objective function increases as the constraint parameter is increased. (See Appendix F.) In [B.1] the objective function is total cost and the constraint parameter is output, so that the optimal value of λ is the rate at which cost increases as output increases, i.e. long-run marginal cost (*LMC*) so that

$$\lambda = \frac{\partial C}{\partial y} = LMC$$

where C is the minimized value of $\Sigma \, p_i z_i$. This interpretation is supported by writing the conditions [B.6] as

$$\frac{p_1}{f_1} = \ldots = \frac{p_n}{f_n} = \lambda = LMC \qquad \text{[B.8]}$$

and using the previous discussion of the two-input case in [B.4].

Cost function

The cost-minimizing input levels which solve [B.1] are the *conditional input demands* and are functions of the prices of the inputs and the output level required:

$$z_i^* = z_i(p_1, \ldots, p_n, y) = z_i(p, y) \qquad \text{[B.9]}$$

The input demands are conditional on the output of the firm so a full explanation of the firm's input demands must include a theory of its choice of output level. The results we derive from cost minimization can be used in any complete model of the firm which requires that the cost of producing the firm's optimal output be minimized.

The *cost function* relates the minimized cost of the firm to input prices and output:

$$C = \sum_i p_i z_i^* = pz(p, y) = C(p, y) \qquad [\text{B.10}]$$

We are interested in the effects of changes in input prices and output on the firm's conditional input demands and on its minimized cost. From [B.10] properties of $z(p, y)$ and $C(p, y)$ are clearly related.

The reader will have noticed that the firm's problem of minimizing the cost of producing a specified output y is remarkably similar in form to the consumer's problem in section 3A of minimizing the expenditure necessary to achieve a particular utility level. Indeed, if z denoted a consumption bundle, y utility, $f(z)$ the utility function and p the price vector of consumption goods, [B.1] would be identical to the consumer's expenditure minimization problem. This means that the results we derived concerning the expenditure minimization problem carry over directly to the firm's cost minimization problem. All that is required is a suitable relabelling so that instead of the Hicksian, constant utility demands $h_i(p, u)$ for goods by the consumer we refer to conditional input demands $z_i(p, y)$, and instead of the expenditure function $m(p, u)$ we refer to the firm's cost function $C(p, y)$.

In section 3A we examined the properties of the expenditure function. We restate some of them here in terms of the firm's cost function:

(a) $C(p, y)$ is increasing in y and non-decreasing in p;

(b) $C(p, y)$ is linear homogeneous in p: $C(kp, y) = kC(p, y)$;

(c) $C(p, y)$ is continuous and concave in p;

(d) Shephard's lemma: $\partial C(p, y)/\partial p_i = z_i(p, y)$.

We make extensive use of these properties in our analysis of the effects of p and y on the cost function and the conditional input demands.

Since we have already derived the properties in section 3A we leave it to the reader to apply the arguments in that section (with suitable relabelling) to the firm's cost function. We will, however, present an alternative proof of Shephard's lemma which is neater, though perhaps less intuitive, than the one given in section 3A. Consider the function

$$G(p, p^0, y) = C(p, y) - pz(p^0, y) \leqslant 0 \qquad [\text{B.11}]$$

This expression cannot be positive because $z(p^0, y)$ is the cost-minimizing input bundle at input prices p^0 and it cannot yield a smaller cost of producing y at some other price vector p than the bundle $z(p, y)$ which is cost-minimizing at p. However, at $p = p^0$, $z(p^0, y)$ is optimal, the cost function is $C(p^0, y) = p^0 z(p^0, y)$ and $G(p^0, p^0, y) = 0$. Thus $G(p, p^0, y)$ is maximized with respect to p at $p = p^0$. Hence at $p = p^0$ the partial derivatives of G with respect to p_i must be equal to zero:

$$\left. \frac{\partial G(p, p^0, y)}{\partial p_i} \right|_{p=p^0} = \left. \frac{\partial C(p, y)}{\partial p_i} \right|_{p=p^0} - z_i(p^0, y) = 0$$

Since $C_i(p^0, y) = z_i(p^0, y)$ must be true for all p^0 we have established Shephard's lemma.

Figure 6.2

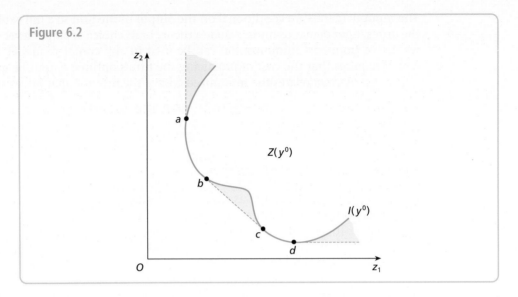

The cost function is useful because it contains all the economically relevant information about a cost-minimizing firm's technology. If we know the cost function we can discover the cost-minimizing input bundle $z(p, y)$ for any output y at any prices p by using Shephard's lemma. Thus we can find a set of input combinations which can be used to produce y and since we know that cost minimization implies that the firm is output-efficient this set must be a subset of the isoquant for y. There may be other input combinations which are also on the isoquant for y but because they are not cost minimizing at *any* p they are not economically relevant: no cost-minimizing firm would ever choose them. Figure 6.2 shows a rather bizarre technology in which the input requirement set $Z(y^0)$ is non-convex and the non-economic region is not empty (notice the positive sloped segments of the isoquant $I(y^0)$). The isoquant $I(y^0)$ is the whole of the lower boundary of $Z(y^0)$. As the reader should check by drawing negatively sloped isocost lines, no cost-minimizing firm facing positive input prices will ever choose to produce y^0 from an input combination in the segments of $I(y^0)$ north-east of a or d or between b and c. Such points on the isoquant are feasible but will never be chosen by a cost-minimizing firm which wished to produce y^0. The only input choices which can ever be observed are those between a and b and between c and d. These are identical with the input choices made by a cost-minimizing firm which faces a technology giving rise to an input requirement set $Z^*(y^0)$ consisting of the $Z(y^0)$ plus the shaded areas. Thus, although knowledge of the cost function does not tell us everything about the technology, it does convey all the information which is relevant for modelling cost-minimizing firms. Note that $Z^*(y^0)$ is convex even though $Z(y^0)$ is not, so that there is no loss in generality in assuming that cost-minimizing firms face quasi-concave production functions.

We assumed that $f(z)$ was strictly quasi-concave and twice continuously differentiable because these assumptions enable us to use calculus methods in studying optimization problems. We can summarize the economically relevant features of the technology in the cost function and the cost function has the properties listed above under much weaker conditions on the technology than are required to use Lagrangean methods to analyse cost-minimizing input choices directly.

Input choice and output level

Figure 6.3 illustrates the effects of changes in y on the optimal cost-minimizing input choices. z^0, z^1, z^2 are the input choices for producing output levels y^0, y^1, y^2 at minimum cost of C^0, C^1, C^2 respectively. The *expansion path EP* is the locus of optimal input combinations traced out as the required output varies with input prices held constant. Here *EP* is positively sloped indicating that increases in y cause increases in both inputs. However, with a different technology the expansion path can be negatively sloped over part of its range, as in Fig. 6.4. Here as y increases from y^0 to y^1 the amount of z_1 used declines from z_1^0 to z_1^1. Over this range z_1 is an *inferior* or *regressive* input and z_2 is *normal*. (Why must at least one input be normal?)

In section 5C we showed that if the production function is homothetic then the slopes of isoquants are constant along rays from the origin. Since [B.7] is necessary for cost minimization, we see that *if the production function is homothetic input proportions are the same at all output levels*, and the expansion path will be a ray from the origin. Only changes in relative input prices cause changes in input proportions.

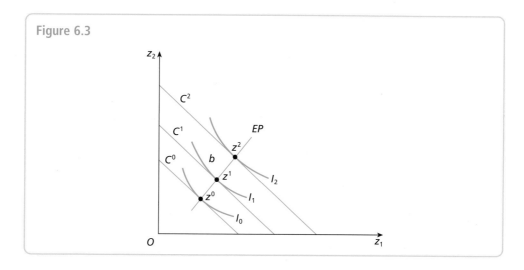

Figure 6.3

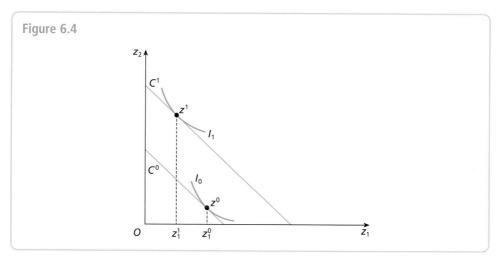

Figure 6.4

Long-run cost curves

The relationship between long-run cost and the level of output can be read off from the expansion path in Fig. 6.3 and graphed in Fig. 6.5(a). The isocost lines give total cost and the isoquants the output level for each point on EP. For example, the (minimized) cost of y^0 is C^0, of y^1 is C^1 and of y^2 is C^2. In Fig. 6.5(a) these outputs are plotted along the horizontal axis and the corresponding total costs along the vertical axis. LTC is the long-run total cost curve derived from minimizing cost for each level of output when all inputs are variable. As drawn, it embodies some particular assumptions about technology which will shortly be clarified.

The long-run average and marginal cost curves (LAC and LMC) which are plotted in part (b) of Fig. 6.5 are derived in turn from the LTC curve. The long-run average cost of producing y^0 is C^0/y^0 and this is the slope of the line OA in (a), which goes from the origin to the point on the LTC curve where $y = y^0$ and $C = C^0$. The LAC curve plots the *slopes of the rays* from the origin to the LTC curve. The fact that the rays get steadily flatter up to point B, and then steeper, accounts for the U-shaped LAC curve.

Figure 6.5

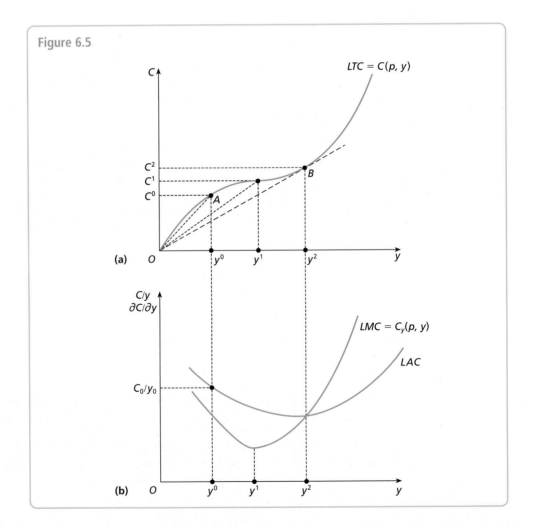

Since long-run marginal cost is the rate at which long-run cost increases as output increases ($LMC = \partial C/\partial y$) the LMC curve is derived by plotting the slope of the LTC curve from below at the point where LAC is at a minimum, since at output y^2 the ray from the origin OB is also tangent to the curve. It can be shown that this relationship must always hold by the same reasoning as was applied to the relationship between average and marginal product curves in section 5D. (See Question 1, Exercise 6B.) Note also that the output y^1 at which LMC is a minimum is the point of inflexion of the LTC curve, and that LAC is decreasing through this point (the rays in (a) are still getting flatter). Again the curvature of the LTC curve in (a), with its slope, though always positive, at first falling and then rising, implies the U-shaped LMC curve in (b).

Economies of scale and returns to scale

The *elasticity of cost with respect to output* is a measure of the responsiveness of cost to output changes. It is defined as the proportionate change in cost divided by the proportionate change in output:

$$E_y^c = \frac{\partial \ln C(p, y)}{\partial \ln y} = C_y(p, y)\frac{y}{C(p, y)} = \frac{LMC}{LAC} \qquad [\text{B.12}]$$

(remember that $C_y = LMC$ and $C/y = LAC$). The cost function has *economies of scale* if $LMC/LAC < 1$ and *diseconomies of scale* if $LMC/LAC > 1$. Since $LMC < LAC$ implies that LAC is decreasing with y, there are economies of scale when the LAC curve is falling. Conversely, there are diseconomies when the LAC curve is rising. In Fig. 6.5 there are economies of scale up to y^2 and diseconomies thereafter.

The relationship between output and costs depends on the underlying technology. Suppose that there are increasing returns to scale and $z(p, y^0)$ is cost minimizing for output y^0 at prices p. It will be possible to produce an output twice as large as y^0 from $sz(p, y^0)$ (defined by $f(s(z(p, y^0)) = 2y^0))$ where $s < 2$. Hence cost will less than double when output doubles and so there are economies of scale. (Note that if $sz(p, y^0)$ is not cost minimizing for $y = 2y^0$ the argument holds *a fortiori*.) Now suppose that there are *decreasing* returns to scale and $z(p, y^0)$ is cost minimizing for output y^0 at prices p. It will be possible to produce an output half as large as y^0 from $sz(p, y^0)$ (defined by $f(s(z(p, y^0)) = \frac{1}{2}y^0))$ where $s < \frac{1}{2}$. Hence cost will be more than halved when output is halved and so there are diseconomies of scale. Thus we have established

$$E_y^c = \frac{LMC}{LAC} \lesseqqgtr 1 \Leftrightarrow E \gtreqqless 1 \qquad [\text{B.13}]$$

where E is the elasticity of output with respect to scale.

Homotheticity and the cost function

Recall that a homothetic production function can be written in the form $g(z) = F(f(z))$ where $F' > 0$ and $f(z)$ is linear homogeneous. With a homothetic production function the cost-minimizing input proportions are independent of the output required so that, if $z(p, y^0)$ produces y^0 at minimum cost, $s(y)z(p, y^0)$ will produce y at minimum cost. $s(y)$ is the proportionate change in inputs required to produce y and so $C(p, y) = s(y)C(p, y^0)$. But $F(s(y)f(z(p, y^0))) = y$ implies that

$$s(y)f(z(p, y^0)) = F^{-1}(y) = a(y)$$

where $a(y) = F^{-1}(y)$ is the inverse of $F(\cdot)$. Hence the cost of producing y is

$$C(p, y) = s(y)C(p, y^0) = a(y)C(p, y^0)/f(z(p, y^0)) = a(y)b(p) \qquad \text{[B.14]}$$

where $b(p) = C(p, y^0)/f(z(p, y^0))$. (Compare the consumer's expenditure function in the case of homothetic preferences.) Thus *if the production function is homothetic then the cost function can be written in the form $C(p, y) = a(y)b(p)$*.

Homogeneous functions are homothetic so the reader can check that, when the production function is homogeneous of degree n, $a(y)$ has the form $y^{1/n}$. In particular, if the production function is linear homogeneous, cost is directly proportional to output since a proportional increase in output requires the same proportional increase in inputs. The reader is asked to show (see Question 5)

$$E_y^c = 1/E \qquad \text{[B.15]}$$

i.e. *the elasticity of cost with respect to output is the reciprocal of the scale elasticity if the production function is homothetic*. Since the cost-minimizing input proportions do not vary with output if the production function is homothetic, changes in output require only changes in scale. Hence the relationship between cost and output depends only on the relationship between output and scale. Cost varies proportionately with scale but output may vary proportionately more or less than scale. For example, with increasing returns ($E > 1$) costs will vary less than proportionately with output and there will be economies of scale ($E_y^c < 1$).

Input prices and conditional input demands

We can use the properties of the cost function to examine the relationship between the prices of inputs and the conditional input demands. The partial derivative of $C(p, y)$ with respect to p_i is $z_i(p, y)$ (property (d) – Shephard's lemma). Since the cost function is homogeneous of degree one in p (property (b)) the partial derivative of $C(b, y)$ with respect to p_i is homogeneous of degree zero (recall the discussion of homogeneous functions in section 5C). Hence $z_i(p, y)$ *is homogeneous of degree zero* and equal proportionate changes in all input prices have no effect on the cost-minimizing input choices: $z(sp, y) = z(p, y)$. If all input prices change in the same proportion the slopes of the isocost lines in Fig. 6.1 are unchanged and thus the z^* where the isocost line is tangent to the isoquant is also unchanged. Less informally (and not requiring any smoothness restrictions on technology): if $pz^* \leq pz$ for all z in $Z(y)$, so that z^* is cost-minimizing at p, then $spz^* \leq spz$ for all z in $Z(y)$ and z^* is also cost-minimizing at prices sp.

Next, suppose that p changes from p^0 to p^1 where p^1 is not necessarily proportional to p^0. The cost-minimizing input choice at p satisfies $pz(p, y) \leq pz$ for all z in $Z(y)$ and thus $z(p^1, y)$ cannot cost less at p^0 than $z(p^0, y)$:

$$p^0 z(p^0, y) - p^0 z(p^1, y) = p^0[z(p^0, y) - z(p^1, y)] \leq 0 \qquad \text{[B.16]}$$

Similarly, $z(p^0, y)$ cannot cost less at p^1 than $z(p^1, y)$:

$$p^1 z(p^0, y) - p^1 z(p^1, y) = p^1[z(p^0, y) - z(p^1, y)] \geq 0 \qquad \text{[B.17]}$$

Subtracting [B.17] from [B.16] gives

$$(p^0 - p^1)[z(p^0, y) - z(p^1, y)] \leq 0 \qquad \text{[B.18]}$$

so that *the sum of the price changes times the input demand changes cannot be positive*.

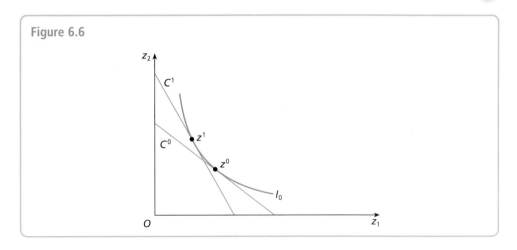

Figure 6.6

If only p_i changes the resulting change in $z_i(p, y)$ is the *own price input substitution effect*. [B.18] reduces to $(p_i^0 - p_i^1)[z_i(p^0, y) - z_i(p^1, y)] \leq 0$ and we can see that *the own price input substitution effect is non-positive*. Figure 6.6 illustrates for the case in which the isoquants are smooth. With input prices initially giving rise to isocost lines like C^0 the cost-minimizing input choice is z^0, where the isoquant I_0 is tangent to C^0. Let the price of z_1 increase. The isocost lines will pivot about their intercepts on the z_2 axis and will become steeper. The new optimal choice is z^1 where the isocost line C^1 is tangent to I_0. The increase in the relative price of input 1 must reduce the conditional demand, for it steepens the isocost lines and the isoquants become steeper as z_1 is reduced (z_2 is substituted for z_1).

We can reach the same conclusion by using Shephard's lemma and the concavity of the cost function (property (c)). Concavity places restrictions on the second-order partial derivatives of the cost function. In particular, the second-order own partials $C_{ii}(p, y)$ must be non-positive, which, using the fact that $C_i(p, y) = z_i(p, y)$ (Shephard's lemma), implies that

$$\frac{\partial z_i(p, y)}{\partial p_i} = \frac{\partial^2 C_i(p, y)}{\partial p_i^2} \leq 0 \qquad \text{[B.19]}$$

In section 5C we introduced the elasticity of substitution as a measure of the relationship between the slope of the isoquant and the input ratio z_1/z_2 and indicated that the concept is useful in analysing the demand for inputs. We must defer a full discussion to Chapter 10 since we do not yet have any model of the firm's choice of output but note from Fig. 6.6 that the effect of changes in relative input prices p_1/p_2 on the input proportions used to produce a given output depends on the curvature of the isoquant. Cost minimization requires that the slope of the isoquant be equal to the slope of the isocost line $-p_1/p_2$ and so the greater is the elasticity of substitution the greater will be the input substitution effects of changes in input prices.

Effects of input price changes on costs

The effect of a proportionate increase in p on the firm's total and average cost is straightforward since we know that $C(p, y)$ will change in the same proportion (property (b) – linear homogeneity) and thus so will $C(p, y)/y$. Thus the firm's total and average cost curves will shift upwards by the same proportion. Since long-run marginal cost is p_i/f_i (see [B.8]), its *LMC* curve will also be shifted up proportionately.

The effects on *LTC* and *LAC* of a change in the price of one input only are also fairly straightforward. Using Shephard's lemma, the *elasticity of cost with respect to p_i* is

$$E^c_{p_i} = \frac{\partial C(p, y)}{\partial p_i} \cdot \frac{p_i}{C(p, y)} = \frac{z_i(p, y)p_i}{C(p, y)} \qquad \text{[B.20]}$$

The responsiveness of cost to a change in the price of a single input is equal to the proportion of total cost accounted for by expenditure on that input. Since average cost is $C(p, y)/y$ and y is held constant in determining the effect of p_i on average cost, we leave it to the reader to establish that the *elasticity of average cost with respect to p_i is also equal to the expenditure share of input i*.

The effect of a given rise in p_i on the *LTC* and *LAC* curves will be to shift the *LTC* and *LAC* curves upward vertically by an amount dependent on the proportion of total cost which is spent on z_i. This does not mean that the curves shift by the same proportion for all output levels since the proportion of C spent on z_i may well vary with the output level. The effect of the change in p_i may be to increase or lower the output level at which *LAC* is a minimum and to increase or decrease the slope of the *LAC* curve at any output level. The precise effects will depend on the production function. For example, if it has linear expansion paths (MRTS constant along rays from the origin) then the proportion of total cost spent on the *i*th input will be constant since input proportions are constant along all expansion paths. Hence the *LTC* and *LAC* curves will shift vertically upward in the same proportion for all output levels and the output at which *LAC* is at a minimum will be unchanged.

The effect on the firm's *LMC* curve is less easy to predict without knowledge of the production function. The reason for this can be shown in Fig. 6.7. The initial input prices give rise to isocost lines C_0, C_2 and optimal input bundles z^0, z^2 for outputs of y^0 and y^1. The new higher price of p_1 gives isocost lines C_1, C_3 and optimal bundles z^1, z^3 for outputs of y^0 and y^1. The change in total cost for the change in output $\Delta y = y^1 - y^0$ with the initial lower price of z_1 is $\Delta C = C_2 - C_0$ and this can be measured in the diagram by p_2 times the distance AB. Similarly, with the higher price of z_1 the change in cost caused by a change in output from y^0 to y^1 is $\Delta C' = C_3 - C_1$

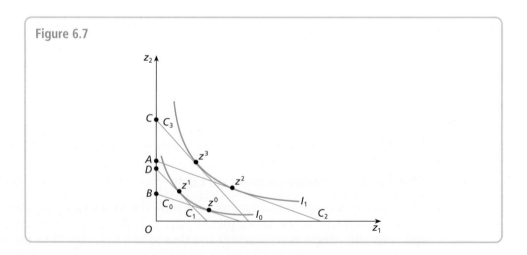

Figure 6.7

and is measured by p_2 times the distance DC. In Fig. 6.7, $\Delta C' > \Delta C$ and thus the effect of the rise in p_1 is to increase the marginal cost of Δy. However, with a differently shaped isoquant it is possible that $\Delta C' < \Delta C$. (Draw the diagram.) Hence it is impossible to predict the effect of a rise in p_i on marginal cost without knowledge of the production function.

Use of Shephard's lemma shows us exactly what is required for marginal cost $C_y(p, y)$ to increase or decrease with p_i. Since cross-partial derivatives do not depend on the order of differentiation

$$\frac{\partial^2 C(p, y)}{\partial y\, \partial p_i} = \frac{\partial^2 C(p, y)}{\partial p_i\, \partial y} = \frac{\partial z_i(p, y)}{\partial y} \qquad [\text{B.21}]$$

Now $\partial z_i(p, y)/\partial y$ is the effect on the demand for input i of an increase in output with input prices held constant and is positive or negative as z_i is a normal or regressive input. Hence *an increase in p_i increases marginal cost if and only if z_i is a normal input.*

If the expansion path is a ray from the origin, so that all inputs are normal, marginal cost must increase with p_i. Thus [B.21] implies that *if the production function is homothetic marginal cost increases with p_i.*

EXERCISE 6B

1. *Fixed proportions technology.* Illustrate the solution to the cost-minimization problem if the firm has the fixed proportions Leontief technology $y = \min(z_1/\beta_1, z_2/\beta_2)$. Show that the cost function is $C(p, y) = y(\beta_1 p_1 + \beta_2 p_2)$. Sketch the cost curves. Derive the conditional input demand functions.

2. *Linear technology.* Suppose the production function is $y = \alpha_1 z_1 + \alpha_2 z_2$. Sketch the firm's isoquants and the solution to its cost minimization problem. Show that the cost function is $C(p, y) = y \min(p_1/\alpha_1, p_2/\alpha_2)$. Sketch the cost curves. Derive the conditional input demand functions. Compare the results with those in Question 1.

3. *Cobb–Douglas technology.* Show that the cost function for a firm with the constant returns Cobb–Douglas production function $y = A z_1^{\alpha} z_2^{1-\alpha}$ of Question 5, Exercise 5B is $C(p, y) = y p_1^{\alpha} p_2^{1-\alpha} B$ where B is a function of A and α only. Sketch the cost curves. Derive the conditional input demands.

4. Assume that the firm owns z_1^0 units of z_1 and that the constant buying and selling prices of z_1 differ because of transaction costs. Draw the firm's isocost lines and sketch the solution to its cost-minimization problem. Show the expansion path and draw the long-run cost curves.

5. *Homotheticity and the cost function.* (a) Show that if the production function is homogeneous of degree n then the cost function can be written as $C(p, y) = y^{1/n} b(p)$. (b) Show that $E_y^c = 1/E$ if the production function is homothetic.

6. *Elasticity of substitution.* What is the relationship between the elasticity of substitution and the effect of a change in relative input prices on the firm's relative expenditure $(p_1 z_1/p_2 z_2)$ on its inputs in the case of a two-input production function?

7. *Indivisibility and the cost function.* Suppose that the firm uses a single indivisible input to produce y and that one unit of the input can produce $\bar{y}$ units of output. Thus to produce $0 < y \leqslant \bar{y}$ the firm must use one unit, to produce $\bar{y} < y \leqslant 2\bar{y}$ would require two units and so on. Assume that the input costs p per unit. Sketch the firm's total and average cost curves. What is marginal cost?

C. Short-run cost minimization

The short-run cost minimization problem is to choose a (z_1, z_2) pair to minimize the cost of a given output, when there are constraints on the adjustment of the fixed input z_2. The short-run cost function and associated curves show the relationship between y and minimized cost and are derived from the minimization problem. The constraints on z_2, and hence the short-run cost function, may take a variety of forms (see section A). We will assume that the constraint is of the form $z_2 \leqslant z_2^0$. There is a fixed ceiling on the amount of z_2 available in the period but, since inputs are assumed divisible, the firm *can* choose to use less if it wants to. To bring out the circumstances under which it *would* or would not choose to, we consider the following two cases:

(a) The firm faces a quota or ration on z_2 and pays the market price p_2 for units of z_2 bought, up to a maximum of z_2^0 units. The marginal opportunity cost of z_2 is p_2 for $z_2 \leqslant z_2^0$ and effectively infinite for $z_2 > z_2^0$. Short-run total cost is $p_1 z_1 + p_2 z_2$ and the short-run isocost lines have a slope (the negative of the ratio of marginal opportunity costs) of $-p_1/p_2$ for $z_2 < z_2^0$. An example of this case would be where the firm has a leasing agreement under which it may lease units of z_2 up to some stipulated maximum per period, and *it only pays for what it uses*. Since inputs are assumed divisible, this implies that it is free to *use and pay for less* z_2 than the maximum z_2^0.

(b) The firm has contracted to pay $p_2 z_2^0$ for the fixed input regardless of whether it uses less of it than z_2^0 or not. Equivalently, the firm may own z_2^0 units of z_2 and transactions costs or the absence of a market prevent the firm from selling those units of z_2 it does not want to use. Hence, unlike case (a), the *existence of a fixed input creates a fixed cost*. This is the essence of the difference between cases (a) and (b), and reflects the fact that a 'fixed input', i.e. one which is subject to a maximum level of use, *need not* imply a *fixed cost* – it all depends on the nature of the relevant contract into which the firm has entered. Here, the short-run total cost is $p_1 z_1 + p_2 z_2^0$, where $p_1 z_1$ is *total variable cost* and $p_2 z_2^0$ is *total fixed cost*. Since changes in z_2 below the capacity level z_2^0 cause no change in costs, the marginal opportunity cost of z_2 is zero for $z_2 < z_2^0$, and is effectively infinite for $z_2 > z_2^0$ (no more can be had at any price).

The derivation of the short-run cost curves for cases (a) and (b), and their relation to the long-run cost curve, are shown in Figs 6.8 and 6.9. In Fig. 6.8, the curve EP again represents the expansion path – the locus of points of tangency of price lines of slope $-p_1/p_2$ with isoquants. The cost/output pairs lying along EP are then plotted as the long-run total cost curve in Fig. 6.9. In the figures we show just three such points. Output y^1, corresponding to isoquant I_1, and the associated minimized cost C^1, output y^0, corresponding to isoquant I_0, and its minimized cost C^0, and output y^2 with cost C^2. We now consider the analysis for the short run.

Take first case (a). For $z_2 < z_2^0$, the marginal opportunity cost of z_2 is identical to that in the long run. For example, if the firm wished to produce output y^1 then the solution to its cost-minimizing problem is point z^1 in the figure (supply the details of the argument). Thus at such an output the firm would choose to use less than z_2^0, the maximum available. A similar result holds for all outputs up to and including y^0, corresponding to isoquant I^0. (Again, supply the argument.) Thus for case (a) the

Figure 6.8

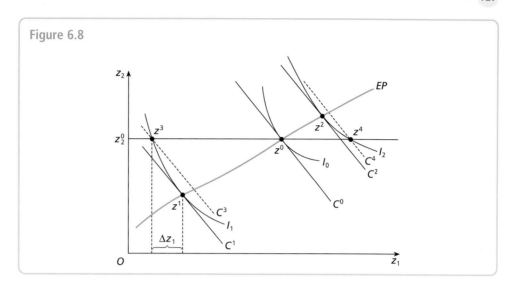

Figure 6.9

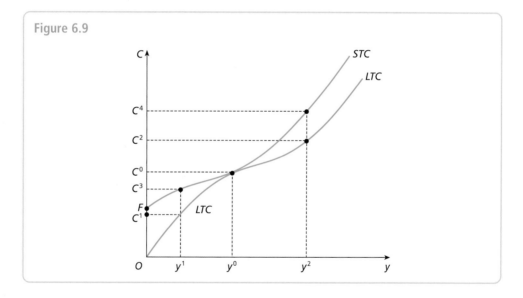

expansion path *coincides with EP* up to and including the point z^0 and over the corresponding range of outputs the short-run total cost curve coincides with the long-run total cost curve in this case.

For outputs greater than y^0, to move further along EP would require amounts of $z_2 > z_2^0$, which are unavailable to the firm. For example, output y^2 corresponding to isoquant I_2 would require an amount of z_2 which is the coordinate of point z^2 in the figure. To produce y^2, the best the firm can do is to choose point z^4, using the fixed input to capacity at z_2^0, and a greater amount of the variable input z_1, than at z^2.

It follows that at such an output the total production cost in the short run will be greater than in the long run. Point z^4 lies on the isocost line C^4 indicated in the diagram, and $C^4 > C^2$. Hence, for all outputs greater than y_0 in Fig. 6.9, the short-run total cost lies above the long-run total cost. The capacity constraint on z_2 is binding and causes a departure in the short run from the optimal input combination for producing each output level.

In case (b), recall that $p_2 z_2^0$ is a fixed cost and the marginal opportunity cost of z_2 is zero. Since z_2 is divisible, the portion of the expansion path EP to the left of point z^0 in Fig. 6.8 is still available to the firm, but the firm will *not choose* to be on it. The firm's *chosen* expansion path will now be the horizontal line $z_2^0 z^3 z^0 z^4$. To see this, suppose the firm were to choose point z^1 to produce output y^1 on isoquant I_1. By moving along I_1 to z^3, it reduces the amount of z_1 by Δz_1 and therefore saves costs equal to $p_1 \Delta z_1$. There is no corresponding increase in cost due to the increased use of z_2 because its marginal opportunity cost is zero: all costs associated with z_2 are fixed and do not vary with the level of use. Hence it always pays the firm to use z_2 to capacity even when it has the (technological) option of not doing so.

This argument can be repeated at all outputs up to y^0. For outputs above y^0 the earlier argument again holds – no more than z_2^0 can be used to produce any such output. Thus in case (b) the entire short-run expansion path is the horizontal line through z_2^0. (This conclusion may have to be qualified where this line intersects a ridge line. See Question 3, Exercise 6C.)

The implications of this for the STC curve in case (b) are easy to see. At all outputs below y^0 total costs, though minimized *given the capacity constraint*, are higher than in the long run. At a zero output the fixed cost $p_2 z_2^0$ must still be paid, and the intercept OF of the STC curve in Fig. 6.9 represents this. As output increases STC lies above LTC (compare C^3, the cost of input combination z^3, with C^1 in Fig. 6.8) but converges to it. At y^0 long-run and short-run costs are equal. This is because y^0 is the unique output level with the property that the fixed input level z_2^0 is actually the *optimal* long-run z_2-level for the output. For outputs above y^0 input combinations are again sub-optimal in the short run, STC lies above LTC and diverges steadily from it.

Thus we conclude that in case (a) given the input constraint $z_2 \leqslant z_2^0$, the short-run total cost curve coincides with the long-run total cost curve up to output y^0 (the unique output for which z_2^0 is in fact optimal) and then is the STC curve shown in Fig. 6.9. In case (b), on the other hand, the short-run total cost curve is the entire STC curve.

Short-run average and marginal cost

We can now derive the short-run average and marginal cost curves from Fig. 6.9 for case (b), leaving the simpler case (a) (in which there are no fixed costs) to the reader. The short-run average and marginal curves are derived in the same way as for the long-run curves in section B and are shown in Fig. 6.10 together with the long-run curves. SAC is the short-run average cost, SMC the short-run marginal cost curve. Notice that SMC cuts SAC from below at the output at which SAC is at minimum. SAC lies above LAC for output other than y^0 since short-run total cost exceeds long-run total cost for outputs other than y^0. Letting $S(y)$ be short-run cost we have $S(y) \geqslant C(y)$ and hence $S(y)/y \geqslant C(y)/y$, short-run average cost is never less than long-run average cost. SAC is tangent to LAC at y^0 because $S(y)$ is tangent to $C(y)$ at y^0. Differentiating $SAC = S(y)/y$ with respect to y gives

$$\frac{1}{(y)^2}\left[\frac{dS}{dy} \cdot y - S\right]$$

Figure 6.10

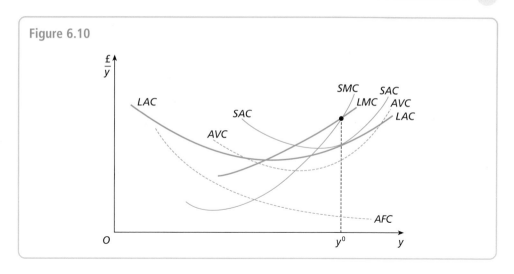

but at y^0, dS/dy equals dC/dy and $S = C$, so that the slope of *SAC* equals the slope of *LAC*. Note also that the tangency of S and C at y^0 implies that *SMC* equals *LMC* at y^0, since short- and long-run marginal costs are the slopes of the short-run and long-run total cost curves respectively.

In case (b) short-run cost is the sum of variable cost (*VC*) and fixed cost (*FC*):

$$S = VC + FC = p_1z_1 + p_2z_2^0 \qquad \text{[C.1]}$$

where z_1 varies with y. In Fig. 6.10 the dashed *AVC* curve plots *average variable cost* p_1z_1/y and the *AFC* curve *average fixed cost* ($p_2z_2^0/y$) which is a rectangular hyperbola. y/z_1 is the average product AP_1 of z_1 (see section 5D) and so

$$AVC = \frac{p_1z_1}{y} = \frac{p_1}{AP_1} \qquad \text{[C.2]}$$

By similar arguments to those used in the long-run case

$$SMC = \frac{p_1}{f_1} = \frac{p_1}{MP_1} \qquad \text{[C.3]}$$

The reader should compare the relationship between the short-run average and marginal cost curves shown in Fig. 6.10 with that between the average and marginal product curves of Chapter 5, Fig. 5.6. The general shapes of the former are the inverse of those of the latter, because of [C.2] and [C.3].

The envelope property

Fixing the z_2 constraint at different levels will generate different short-run cost curves, each of which, in case (b), will lie above the long-run curve except where they are tangent to it at the output for which the constrained level of z_2 is the long-run cost-minimizing level. If the expansion path is upward sloping as in Fig. 6.8 the short-run and long-run cost curves will touch at higher levels of output as the fixed level of z_2 is increased. This is illustrated in (a) of Fig. 6.11 where S^0, S^1, S^2 are short-run cost curves for z_2 constraints of $z_2^0 > z_2^1 > z_2^2$. As the constrained level of z_2 varies,

Figure 6.11

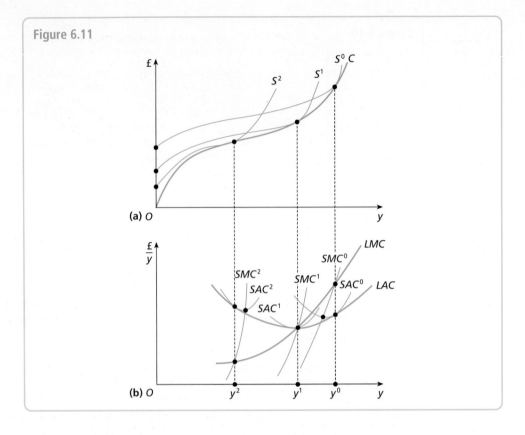

more short-run cost curves are generated and we can see that the long-run cost curve *C* is the lower boundary or *envelope* of the short-run curves, in that all of them lie above *C* except at the output at which they are tangent to it. In part (b) of the figure are shown the average and marginal curves derived from part (a). The SAC^0, SAC^1, SAC^2 and SMC^0, SMC^1, SMC^2 curves are the short-run average and marginal cost curves derived from S^0, S^1, S^2. Each of the *SAC* curves lies above the *LAC* curve except at the output for which $S = C$, where they are tangent to it. Hence the *LAC* curve is the envelope of the *SAC* curves. The *SMC* curves, however, *cut* the *LMC* curve at the output for which their respective *SAC* curves are tangent to *LAC*, and so the *LMC* curve is not the envelope of the *SMC* curves. Short-run marginal cost may be greater *or* less than long-run depending on the output and the level of the fixed input. When the fixed input is at the long-run cost-minimizing level for a particular output level *SMC* equals *LMC*. In the neighbourhood of this point for larger outputs *SMC* will exceed *LMC*, indicating that it will cost more in the short run to expand output than in the long run. On the other hand, at *smaller* outputs than that for which the fixed z_2 is optimal, short-run marginal costs are below long-run marginal costs. This is because output expansion over this range is improving the rate of utilization of the fixed input – the short-run input combinations are converging towards the long-run input combination (cf. Fig. 6.8).

This relationship between *SMC* and *LMC* is derived from that between the *STC* and *LTC* curves in the neighbourhood of the output level at which the fixed input is at its optimal long-run level. Since the *STC* curve is tangent to the *LTC* curve from above at y^0 the slope of the *STC* curve (*SMC*) must be less than that of the *LTC* curve (*LMC*) for $y < y^0$ and greater for $y > y^0$ for some neighbourhood of y^0:

$$\left.\frac{\partial SMC}{\partial y}\right|_{y=y^0} > \left.\frac{\partial LMC}{\partial y}\right|_{y=y^0} \qquad [C.4]$$

However, it is possible to construct *LTC* curves with the envelope property but having *SMC* > (<) *LMC* for some $y <$ (>) y^0 outside the immediate neighbourhood of y^0. (Show this.) The implications of the relationship between *SMC* and *LMC* for the firm's response to output price changes in the short and long runs is examined in the next chapter in Question 4, Exercise 7B.

Comparative statics in the short run

We have already considered the effect of variations in output on short-run cost and input use in deriving the firm's short-run cost curves. Let us now briefly examine the effect of changes in the price of the variable input on the firm's cost curves. In case (a) defined above, the firm's short-run expansion path is its long-run expansion path up to $y = y^0$ and $z_2 = z_2^0$ line thereafter. Hence changes in p_1 will cause the expansion path for $y \leqslant y^0$ to alter in the same way as the long-run path and so all the remarks relevant to the long-run case apply. For $y > y^0$ the expansion path is identical to the case (b) path, to which we now turn.

In case (b) the expansion path is the $z_2 = z_2^0$ line for all outputs. This path is the same for all levels of p_1 so that *the optimal short-run input combination is independent of p_1*. Variable cost is $p_1 z_1$ and average variable cost is $p_1 z_1/y$, so a given percentage change in p_1 will shift the *VC* and *AVC* curves upward in the same proportion. Since the optimal input bundles do not change when p_1 alters, $MP_1 = f_1(z_1, z_2)$ will also be unaffected and so $SMC = p_1/f_1$ will vary proportionately with p_1. Compare the analogous results for the long run where the effect of changes in p_1 on *LMC* could not be predicted without detailed knowledge of the production function.

Formal analysis

The results derived graphically for the case in which there is one variable and one fixed input also hold when there are more than two inputs. Denote the n vector of variable inputs $z_v = (z_{v1}, \ldots, z_{vn})$ and let p_v be the corresponding n vector of the prices of the variable inputs. Let the m vector of fixed inputs be $z_k = (z_{k1}, \ldots, z_{km})$ and p_k be the corresponding m vector of the prices of the fixed inputs. The firm has contracted to pay for z_{kj}^0 units of the jth fixed input but can use less than this if it wishes, i.e. we consider only case (b) here. z_k^0 is the m vector of constraints on the fixed inputs. The firm's short-run cost minimization problem is

$$\min_{z_v, z_k} \ p_v z_v + p_k z_k^0 \quad \text{s.t. } y = f(z_v, z_k)$$

$$z_{kj}^0 \geqslant z_{kj} \geqslant 0 \qquad j = 1, \ldots, m \qquad [C.5]$$

$$z_{vi} \geqslant 0 \qquad i = 1, \ldots, n$$

The Lagrangean for the problem is

$$L = p_v z_v + p_k z_k^0 + \lambda[y - f(z_v, z_k)] + \sum_j \mu_j(z_{kj} - z_{kj}^0) \qquad [C.6]$$

Assume that the production function is strictly quasi-concave and twice continuously differentiable and that at the solution to the problem all inputs are used. Then the following Kuhn–Tucker conditions are necessary and sufficient:

$$L_{vi} = p_i - \lambda f_{vi} = 0 \qquad i = 1, \ldots, n \tag{C.7}$$

$$L_{kj} = -\lambda f_{kj} + \mu_j = 0 \qquad j = 1, \ldots, m \tag{C.8}$$

$$L_\lambda = y - f(z_v, z_k) = 0 \tag{C.9}$$

$$L_{\mu j} = z_{kj} - z_{kj}^0 \leq 0, \qquad \mu_j \geq 0, \qquad \mu_j(z_{kj} - z_{kj}^0) = 0, \qquad j = 1, \ldots, m \tag{C.10}$$

The conditions [C.7] on the variable inputs are identical in form to those from the long-run problem [B.1] and have the same interpretation. The marginal rate of technical substitution between variable inputs will equal the ratio of their prices. The Lagrangean multiplier λ on the output constraint again gives the rate at which the objective function increases with y, only now λ is the short-run marginal cost rather than the long-run marginal cost.

μ_j is the Lagrange multiplier on the constraint on the amount of fixed input j and is the rate at which the objective function *falls* as the constraint is relaxed. (Note that z_{kj}^0 enters negatively in L whereas y enters positively.) It is the reduction in cost of producing y if the firm was given a free unit of the jth fixed input. From [C.8] we see that $\mu_j > 0$ only if the marginal product of the jth fixed input is positive at the solution. If the marginal product is zero then cost cannot be reduced by substituting the fixed input for variable inputs because output would fall below the required level. Using the Envelope Theorem (Appendix J) the effect on the firm's cost of being able to buy another unit of the jth fixed input at price p_{kj} is $p_{kj} - \mu_j$. Thus, if $p_{kj} < \mu_j$, the firm can reduce its cost by buying the additional unit of z_{kj} and reducing the amount of z_{vi} used.

The cost-minimizing variable and fixed-input vectors are $z_v(p, y, z_k^0)$ and $z_k(p, y, z_k^0)$, where $p = (p_v, p_k)$ is the $n + m$ vector of all input prices, and the *short-run or restricted cost function* is

$$S(p, y, z_k^0) = p_v z_v(p, y, z_k^0) + p_k z_k(p, y, z_k^0) \tag{C.11}$$

It possesses the same properties as the long-run cost function $C(p, y)$, as the reader should check (see Question 5). In particular Shephard's lemma holds for the variable inputs:

$$\frac{\partial S(p, y, z_k^0)}{\partial p_{vi}} = z_{vi}(p, y, z_k^0) \tag{C.12}$$

We can use Shephard's lemma to examine the relationship between the long- and short-run responses of input use to changes in input price. Let $z(p, y) = (z_v(p, y), z_k(p, y))$ be the $n + m$ input vector which solves the long-run cost-minimization problem at prices p for output y. Suppose that the fixed input vector z_k^0 in the short-run problem would be optimal in the long-run cost-minimization problem for output y^0 at some input price vector p^0 so that $z_k(p^0, y^0) = z_k^0$. Then at prices p^0 the solutions of the short- and long-run problems of minimizing the cost of producing y^0 are identical. To see this, note that $(z_v(p^0, y^0), z_k(p^0, y^0))$ solves the long-run problem if and only if, for all feasible (z_v, z_k^0) in $Z(y^0)$,

$$p_v^0 z_v(p^0, y^0) + p_k^0 z_k(p^0, y^0) \leq p_v^0 z_v + p_k^0 z_k^0 \tag{C.13}$$

But by assumption $z_k(p^0, y^0) = z_k^0$ and so [C.13] implies

$$p_v^0 z_v(p^0, y^0) + p_k^0 z_k^0 \leq p_v^0 z_v + p_k^0 z_k^0 \qquad [C.14]$$

so that $(z_v(p^0, y^0), z_k^0)$ also solves the short-run problem. Hence we have

$$z_v(p^0, y^0, z_k^0) = z_v(p^0, y^0) \qquad [C.15]$$

and

$$S(p^0, y^0, z_k^0) = C(p^0, y^0) \qquad [C.16]$$

At other prices p, the long- and short-run cost-minimizing z_v will not coincide and the definition of $(z_v(p, y^0), z_k(p, y^0))$ as the long-run cost-minimizing choice for output y^0 implies that

$$\begin{aligned} C(p, y^0) &= p_v z_v(p, y^0) + p_k z_k(p, y^0) \\ &\leq p_v z_v(p, y^0, z_k^0) + p_k z_k^0 = S(p, y^0, z_k^0) \end{aligned} \qquad [C.17]$$

In part (a) of Fig. 6.12, the short- and long-run cost function are plotted against one of the variable input prices, all other prices being held constant at p_{vj}^0 ($j = 1, \ldots, n$; $j \neq i$) or p_{kj}^0 ($j = 1, \ldots, m$) and output being held constant at y^0. $S(p, y^0, z_k^0)$ lies above $C(p, y^0)$ everywhere except at $p_{vi} = p_{vi}^0$ where p is then equal to p^0. In the neighbourhood of p_{vi}^0, $S(p, y^0, z_k^0)$ must be flatter than $C(p, y^0)$ for $p_{vi} < p_{vi}^0$, steeper than it for $p_{vi} > p_{vi}^0$ and tangent to it at $p_{vi} = p_{vi}^0$. But the slopes of S and C in part (a) are just their derivatives with respect to p_{vi} and Shephard's lemma holds for the variable inputs in both the short- and the long-run. Hence $S_{vi}(p, y^0, z_k^0) = z_{vi}(p, y^0, z_k^0)$ is smaller than,

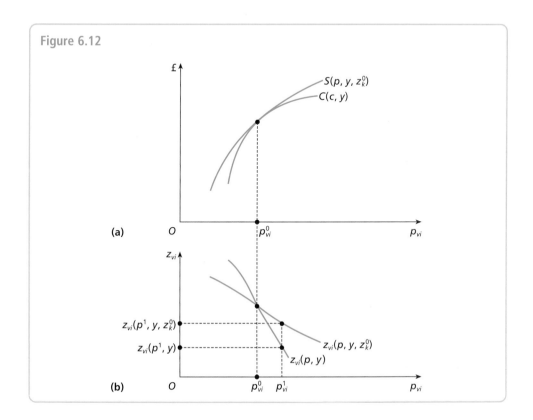

Figure 6.12

greater than or equal to $C_{vi}(p, y^0) = z_{vi}(p, y^0)$ as p_{vi} is less than, greater than or equal to p_{vi}^0. The vertical axis of part (b) of Fig. 6.12 plots the slopes of S and C with respect to p_{vi} against p_{vi}. Comparing, for example, the effects on $z_{vi}(p, y^0, z_k^0)$ and $z_{vi}(p, y^0)$ of an increase in p_{vi} from p_{vi}^0 to p_{vi}^1, we see that in the neighbourhood of p^0 the response of the cost-minimizing demand for z_{vi} to changes in its price is smaller in the short- than in the long-run problem:

$$\frac{\partial z_{vi}(p^0, y^0, z_k^0)}{\partial p_{vi}} < \frac{\partial z_{vi}(p^0, y^0)}{\partial p_{vi}} \tag{C.18}$$

This result illustrates the *Le Chatelier–Samuelson Principle* that imposing additional constraints on an optimization problem will reduce the responsiveness of choice variables to changes in exogenous variables. The two-input case is an extreme example: in the short run the cost-minimizing input mix is not affected by the input prices, whereas in the long-run problem we would expect that choices do vary with p.

A similar envelope argument can be used to confirm our earlier diagrammatic analysis of the relationship between short- and long-run curves. Instead of comparing the effect on short- and long-run cost of varying input prices while holding output constant we would compare the effects of varying output while holding prices constant. At p^0 the short- and long-run costs of producing y^0 are equal: $C(p^0, y^0) = S(p^0, y^0)$, but at other outputs

$$C(p^0, y) = p_v^0 z_v(p^0, y) + p_k^0 z_k(p^0, y) \leqslant p_v^0 z_v(p^0, y, z_k^0) + p_k^0 z_k^0 = S(p^0, y, z_k^0)$$

The short-run cost function lies above the long-run function at all outputs except at y_0 where it is tangent to it. Thus short-run marginal cost will equal long-run marginal cost at y^0 and increase more rapidly with output than long-run marginal cost in the neighbourhood of y^0.

EXERCISE 6C

1. Solve the short-run cost-minimization problem and draw the short-run cost curves for a firm with a multi-process fixed proportions technology. Why does the short-run marginal cost curve become vertical?

2. Repeat Question 1 for the case of a Cobb–Douglas production function. Does the *SMC* curve become vertical? Why, or why not?

3. What happens in Fig. 6.8 if part of the ridge line lies below the horizontal line at z_2^0? How will the short-run expansion path and cost curves differ?

4. Assume that the firm wishes to produce a given output next month, has already contracted to hire z_2^0 units of labour at a price of p_2 per unit and cannot fire workers without giving them a month's notice, i.e. without paying them for the time they would have worked during the month. Additional labour can, however, be hired for next month at a price of p_2, though the firm cannot resell the labour-hours it has already contracted for. Solve the short-run cost-minimization problem for a firm with one other freely variable input and draw the short-run cost curves. How do the results obtained differ from those in the text?

5. Show that the short-run cost function $S(p, y, z_k^0)$ derived from [C.5] satisfies properties (a) to (d) in section B.

D. Cost minimization with several plants

Many firms possess more than one plant capable of producing their product and hence face the problem of allocating a required total output among their plants so as to minimize the cost of producing that output. The problem can be solved in two stages. First, each plant solves the problem of producing a given output level at least cost in that plant, subject to the production function for that plant, by choosing a plant cost-minimizing input bundle. Each plant then has a cost function derived in the usual way. In the two-plant problem the plant cost function is

$$C_i = C_i(y^i) \qquad (i = 1, 2)$$

where C_i is total cost in plant i, y^i is the output in plant i (y^1 and y^2 are the same goods but produced in different plants) and the input prices have been omitted from the cost functions. C_i may be the short- or long-run cost function depending on the constraints on the adjustment of inputs. The second stage of the problem is

$$\min_{y_1, y_2} C = C_1(y^1) + C_2(y^2) \quad \text{s.t. (i)} \ y^1 + y^2 \geqslant y^0$$
$$\text{(ii)} \ y^i \geqslant 0 \qquad (i = 1, 2) \qquad \text{[D.1]}$$

The marginal cost in plant i is $C_i'(y^i)$ and we assume that the cost functions are strictly convex in y^i so that marginal cost is increasing with output: $C_i''(y^i) > 0, y^i \geqslant 0$. This means that $C_1 + C_2$ is convex in the output levels and thus the Kuhn–Tucker conditions are sufficient as well as necessary. The Lagrangean is

$$L = C_1(y^1) + C_2(y^2) + \lambda(y^0 - y^1 - y^2) \qquad \text{[D.2]}$$

and the Kuhn–Tucker conditions are

$$L_i = C_i'(y^i) - \lambda \geqslant 0, \qquad y^i \geqslant 0, \qquad y^i [C_i'(y^i) - \lambda] = 0, \qquad i = 1, 2 \qquad \text{[D.3]}$$
$$L_\lambda = y^0 - y^1 - y^2 \leqslant 0, \qquad \lambda \geqslant 0, \qquad \lambda(y^0 - y^1 - y^2) = 0 \qquad \text{[D.4]}$$

λ is the rate at which the firm's cost would increase if its output requirement y^0 was increased: it is the marginal cost of the multi-plant firm. At least one of the y^i must be positive to satisfy the output requirement constraint and for the positive y^i it must also be true that $\lambda = C_i'(y^i)$. Since marginal cost is positive so must λ be and so the output requirement constraint must bind at the solution. Unsurprisingly, a cost-minimizing firm with positive marginal cost will never produce more output than it requires.

There are two types of solution depending on whether only one or both plants are used when costs are minimized. If both plants are used then [D.3] implies

$$C_1'(y^1) = C_2'(y^2) = \lambda$$

and costs are minimized when output is allocated between the plants to equalize marginal costs in the two plants. Figure 6.13 illustrates this type of solution. The marginal cost curves C_1' and C_2' for the two plants are shown in parts (a) and (b) and the cost-minimizing output of plant i is y^{i*}, with $y^{1*} + y^{2*} = y^0$. If C_1' was not equal to C_2' at an allocation where both plants are used it would be possible to reduce cost by transferring output from the plant with the higher marginal cost to the plant with a lower marginal cost. For example, if $C_1' > C_2'$ then increasing y^2 by one unit and reducing y^1 by one unit would leave total output unchanged and reduce total cost by approximately $C_1' - C_2' > 0$.

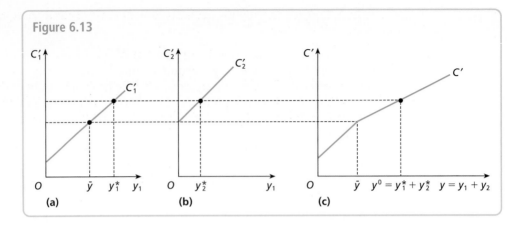

Figure 6.13

The other type of solution has only one of the plants in operation. Suppose that $C_2'(0) > C_1'(y^0)$. Then it is cost-minimizing to use only plant 1. Marginal costs are not equalized by transferring output from the high marginal cost plant 2 to the low marginal cost plant 1 because plant 2 output cannot be reduced below zero. In terms of [D.3] we have $C_2'(0) - \lambda = C_2'(0) - C_1'(y^0) > 0$ which implies from the complementary slackness condition that the optimal level of $y^{2\star} = 0$. In Fig. 6.13 the firm would produce a required output of less than $\bar{y}$ (defined by $C_2'(0) = C_1'(\bar{y})$) only in plant 1, leaving plant 2 idle.

Part (c) of Fig. 6.13 shows the firm's marginal cost of producing different total outputs, given that at each output it allocates output between the two plants so as to minimize total cost. For outputs of $\bar{y}$ or less only plant 1 is used and so the firm's marginal cost curve $C'(y)$ is just the marginal cost curve of plant 1. For outputs of more than $\bar{y}$, cost minimization requires that both plants are used and that plant marginal costs are equal. The firm's marginal cost curve is then the horizontal sum of the marginal cost curves of the two plants.

Least cost production with increasing returns: 'natural' monopoly

If plants all have identical strictly convex cost functions, least-cost production requires that each produces the same amount (so that marginal costs are equalized) whatever the total output required. When the cost functions are not convex this conclusion may not be valid and it may be most efficient, in the sense of producing a given output at least cost, to produce all the output in one of the identical plants. The fact that it is cheaper to produce output in one plant rather than in several obviously has implications for the number of firms in the market. When it is cost-minimizing to produce any output up to y^0 in one plant there is said to be 'natural' monopoly in that output. The implication is that with this type of technology one would expect to see only one firm producing the entire industry output. However, a satisfactory theory of the equilibrium number of firms in an industry must rest on more than the technology: the entry and output decisions of profit-maximizing firms depend on the revenues they anticipate from different decisions as well as on their costs. Hence the quotation marks. The reader should remember in what follows that the relationship between the properties of the cost function and the cost-minimizing number of firms or plants is not a complete explanation of monopoly, although it may be an important part of such an explanation.

The cost function for the identical plants is denoted $C(y)$ and there is 'natural' monopoly for $y \leqslant y^0$ when

$$C(y^1 + y^2) < C(y^1) + C(y^2) \qquad 0 \leqslant y^1 + y^2 \leqslant y^0 \qquad \text{[D.5]}$$

$C(y^1 + y^2)$ is the cost of producing $y^1 + y^2$ in a single plant, $C(y^i)$ the cost of producing y^i in a single plant. If [D.5] holds it is cheaper to produce a total output of $y^1 + y^2$ in a single plant rather than using two identical plants to produce separately outputs of y^1 and y^2. A cost function which satisfies [D.5] is *sub-additive* so that sub-additivity and 'natural' monopoly are merely different labels for the same type of cost function. We prefer sub-additivity since it is a more neutral term.

We can establish some relationships between sub-additivity and other properties of the cost function:

(a) We have already seen that if $C(y)$ is strictly convex ($C''(y) > 0$ for all $y \geqslant 0$) [D.5] cannot hold. (Just apply the discussion of [D.3] with identical cost functions ($C_1(y) = C_2(y)$) for the two plants and recall that total cost is not minimized if the plants have different marginal costs.) *Sub-additivity requires some degree of non-convexity in the cost function.*

(b) If there are economies of scale the average cost of production falls with output (see section B) and so

$$\frac{C(y^1 + y^2)}{y^1 + y^2} < \frac{C(y^i)}{y^i} \qquad i = 1, 2 \qquad \text{[D.6]}$$

must hold if $y^1 > 0$, $y^2 > 0$ (so that $y^i < y^1 + y^2$). Multiplying both sides of the inequalities by y^i and adding the two inequalities we have

$$\frac{y^1 C(y^1 + y^2)}{y^1 + y^2} + \frac{y^2 C(y^1 + y^2)}{y^1 + y^2} = C(y^1 + y^2) < C(y^1) + C(y^2) \qquad \text{[D.7]}$$

and so we have established that *economies of scale imply sub-additivity.*

(c) The converse does not hold and *sub-additivity over an output range does not imply economies of scale over that output range.* Figure 6.14 gives an example of a cost function with a U-shaped average cost curve. There is a fixed cost F which must be incurred to produce any output but which can be avoided if no output is produced. The cost function is discontinuous at $y = 0$ and so it is not everywhere convex despite the fact that marginal cost (the slope of $C(y)$) is increasing at all positive output levels. Average cost $C(y)/y$ is measured by the slope of a line from the origin to the cost function and up to output $\hat{y}$ average cost decreases with output (economies of scale) and beyond $\hat{y}$ average cost increases with y (diseconomies of scale). For positive outputs, marginal cost increases with output so that *if* production is carried on in two plants it is cost minimizing to produce a total output of y by producing $y/2$ in each plant. Hence with two-plant production total cost is $2C(y/2)$. It is clear from the diagram that for output less than $\bar{y}$ it is cheaper to produce in one plant only because of the saving on fixed costs. (If there were no fixed costs (so that $C(y)$ is shifted down by F to start at the origin), two plants would be more efficient than one because of the saving on variable costs achieved by equalizing marginal costs.) Note that over the range $\hat{y} \leqslant y \leqslant \bar{y}$ there are diseconomies of scale but it is cheaper to use one plant rather than two so that sub-additivity can occur even with diseconomies of scale.

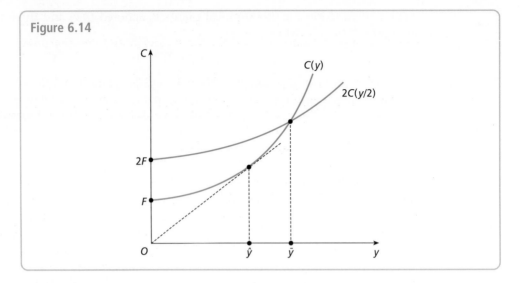

Figure 6.14

EXERCISE 6D

1. *Merit order*. Suppose that a power company has *n* plants each of which embodies a different fixed proportions process. Each plant has a maximum output rate which cannot be exceeded in the period because of constraints on the fixed input in each plant. Derive the short-run marginal cost curve for the firm and the merit order of plants which shows the order in which the plants are brought into production as the required output level increases.

2. *Cost minimization with U-shaped cost curves*. Suppose that the firm has two plants with identical cost functions $C(y) = F + V(y) = F + vy^\alpha$, ($F > 0$, $v > 0$), $C(0) = 0$.

   (a) Why may the cost-minimization conditions [D.3] and [D.4] fail to identify the least-cost allocation?

   (b) Over what output ranges are there economies of scale when $\alpha = 1$ and when $\alpha = 3$?

   (c) Over what output ranges is it cheaper to use one rather than two plants (sub-additivity) when $\alpha = 1$ and when $\alpha = 3$?

E. Multi-product cost functions

If the firm produces two outputs, y_1 and y_2, its problem is to minimize the cost of producing specified levels, y_1^0 and y_2^0 of its products. The production function constraint is written in the implicit form $g(y_1, y_2, z_1, \ldots, z_n) \leq 0$ of section 5E. If input prices are positive the firm will produce exactly the specified levels of outputs ($y_1 = y_1^0$, $y_2 = y_2^0$) and in a technically efficient way: $g(\ldots) = 0$. The cost-minimization problem therefore is

$$\min_{z_1, \ldots, z_n} \Sigma p_i z_i \quad \text{s.t. (i)} \ g(y_1^0, y_2^0, z_1, \ldots, z_n) = 0$$
$$\text{(ii)} \ z_i \geq 0 \quad i = 1, \ldots, n \qquad \text{[E.1]}$$

The Lagrange function is

$$L = \Sigma p_i z_i + \lambda g(y_1^0, y_2^0, z_1, \ldots, z_n)$$

and the first-order conditions on the inputs are, in an interior solution,

$$\frac{\partial L}{\partial z_i} = p_i + \lambda g_i = 0 \qquad i = 1, \ldots, n \qquad \text{[E.2]}$$

Writing the conditions as $p_i = -\lambda g_i$ and dividing the ith condition by the jth gives

$$\frac{p_i}{p_j} = \frac{g_i}{g_j} \qquad \text{[E.3]}$$

In section 5E it was demonstrated that g_i/g_j is the marginal rate of technical substitution between the two inputs so that the necessary condition for cost minimization in the multi-product case is identical with that in the single-product case.

The Lagrange multiplier λ has a somewhat different interpretation in the multi-product problem [E.1]. λ is attached to the production function constraint rather than to the output constraint as in the single output problem. It measures the rate at which the minimized cost of production is reduced if the production function constraint is relaxed slightly, i.e. if it is possible to produce the specified outputs with less of each input.

As in the single output case, the optimal input levels will be functions of input prices and the required output levels:

$$z_i^* = z_i(y_1, y_2; p)$$

and substitution in $\Sigma p_i z_i$ gives the multi-product cost function which shows the minimized cost of production as a function of the output levels and input prices:

$$C = \Sigma p_i z_i^* = C(y_1, y_2; p) \qquad \text{[E.4]}$$

The multi-product cost function possesses all the convenient properties (a)−(d) of the single-product cost function in section B. The arguments are very similar so we leave them to the reader.

Joint production and the cost function

Part of the explanation for the fact that multi-product firms are more common than single-product firms is that in some circumstances production of several different goods in the same plant or firm is less costly than if the same quantities of the different goods were produced in specialist single-product firms. The relationship between cost and output for multi-product cost functions is therefore of some interest in explaining the existence of multi-product firms. The marginal cost of good i is just the partial derivative of [E.4] with respect to good i: $C_i(y_1, y_2, p) = \partial C(y_1, y_2, p)/\partial y_i$. In section B there were said to be economies of scale if the elasticity of cost with respect to output was less than one. In the multi-product case we can examine the effect on cost of an equal proportionate increase in all outputs. Thus there are *multi-product economies of scale* if the elasticity of cost with respect to the scale of output, E_t^c, defined as

$$E_t^c = \frac{\partial C(ty_1, ty_2, p)}{\partial t} \cdot \frac{t}{C(ty_1, ty_2, p)} = \sum_i C_i y_i \cdot \frac{t}{C} \qquad \text{[E.5]}$$

is less than one. For given y, increases in the output scale parameter t imply equal proportional increases in all outputs, and so t can be thought of as a measure of size of the firm's output. The last term in [E.5] is the reciprocal of $C(ty_1, ty_2, p)/t$, which can be interpreted as a kind of average cost since it divides cost by a measure of output. It is known as the *ray average cost* since increases in t correspond to movements along a ray from the origin in output space. The term $\sum_i C_i y_i$ in [E.5] is the rate of change of cost as the firm increases its output scale and can be defined as *ray marginal cost*. [E.5] is therefore rather similar to the elasticity of cost with respect to output in the case of a single-product firm.

To see when joint production is less costly than specialist production, at some input price vector p define the *stand-alone cost* of y_1 as the minimized cost of producing y_1 when $y_2 = 0$:

$$C(y_1, 0, p) = C^1(y_1, p) \qquad \text{[E.6]}$$

and analogously for the stand-alone cost of good 2. Joint production is less costly than specialist production if

$$C(y_1, y_2, p) < C(y_1, 0, p) + C(0, y_2, p) \qquad \text{[E.7]}$$

Conversely, if the inequality in [E.7] is replaced with an equality the cost function is *output separable* and any output vector $y = (y_1, y_2)$ could be produced as cheaply in separate specialist firms as in a multi-product firm.

If [E.7] holds for all output vectors $0 \leqslant y \leqslant y^0$ the cost function is said to exhibit *economies of scope* over this range. Since input prices are assumed to be independent of the firm's decisions, whether [E.7] holds or not depends on the form of its production function. The cost of producing, say, good 1 is unaffected by the output of good 2 only if the inputs required to produce good 1 do not vary with the output of good 2, that is if the production function is separable. When y_1 and y_2 are joint products in the sense of section 5E the cost function is non-separable. Obvious examples in which it is cheaper to produce a pair of goods in one organization rather than in two range from beef and cow-hides to peak and off-peak electricity. (What about research and teaching in a university?)

In section D we introduced the concept of sub-additivity ('natural' monopoly) in the context of a single type of good, but the same issues arise when plants or firms can produce more than one type of good. We can extend the definition of sub-additivity to the multi-product case by saying that the cost function $C(y, p)$ is sub-additive if

$$C(y^1 + y^2, p) < C(y^1, p) + C(y^2, p) \qquad \text{[E.8]}$$

where $y^i = (y_1^i, y_2^i)$ is an output vector. Our definition of sub-additivity in section D is just a special case of this with, say, $y^i = (y_1^i, 0)$. When [E.8] holds for all $0 \leqslant y \leqslant y^0$ the cost function is *globally sub-additive* over this range and it is cheaper to organize production in a single firm or plant than in separate specialist production units.

The relationships between the economies of scope and scale and sub-additivity can turn out to be rather surprising. Intuition would suggest that if the cost function has multi-product economies of scale or economies of scope it would be cheaper to organize production in one unit than in separate production units. But this is not so: *a cost function with economies of scope and multi-product economies of scale need not be sub-additive.* Consider the following cost function (due to Sharkey, 1982):

$$C(y_1, y_2, p) = \begin{cases} a(p)y_2 + b(p)y_1^2/y_2 & \text{for } y_1 \leqslant ky_2 \\ a(p)y_1 + b(p)y_2^2/y_1 & \text{for } y_1 \geqslant ky_2 \end{cases} \qquad \text{[E.9]}$$

where $a(p)$, $b(p)$, k are positive coefficients. The reader should check that this function has both multi-product economies of scale and economies of scope. However, if $a = b = k = 1$ we have $C(3, 3, p) = 6$, $C(1, 2, p) = 2.5$, and $C(2, 1, p) = 2.5$ so that C is not globally sub-additive. The reason economies of scale and scope do not imply global sub-additivity is that output vectors used to define economies of scale and scope are highly restricted. With economies of scale one is examining the effects on cost of movements along rays from the origin in output space and with economies of scope one is comparing the cost of a vector (y_1, y_2) with the costs of $(y_1, 0)$ and $(0, y_2)$, i.e. with the costs of projections of the vector on to the y_1 and y_2 axes. Global sub-additivity, however, requires comparisons of the cost of (y_1, y_2) with the costs of all vectors which add up to (y_1, y_2), not just those on the ray from y_1, y_2 to the origin or those at $(y_1, 0)$ and $(0, y_2)$.

One condition on the cost function which implies sub-additivity is *cost complementarity*:

$$C(y^1 + y^2 + y^3, p) - C(y^1 + y^2, p) < C(y^1 + y^3, p) - C(y^1, p) \qquad \text{[E.10]}$$

for all output vectors $y^1 \geqslant 0$, $y^2 > 0$, $y^3 > 0$. If [E.10] holds, the incremental cost arising from increasing output by the vector y^3 is smaller the larger is the initial output vector. By considering special cases in which $y^3 = (\Delta y_1, 0)$ or $y^3 = (0, \Delta y_2)$, and $y^2 = (\Delta y_1, 0)$ or $y^2 = (0, \Delta y_2)$ and taking appropriate limits we can show that [E.10] is equivalent to increases in good j reducing the marginal cost of good i: $C_{ij} = \partial^2 C(y_1, y_2, p)/\partial y_i \partial y_j < 0$ $(i, j = 1, 2)$. It can be shown that *cost complementarity implies economies of scope and multi-product economies of scale* (see the exercises). More importantly *cost complementarity implies global sub-additivity*. To see this just use the definition [E.10] with $y^1 = (0, 0)$, so that $C(y^1, p) = C(0, 0, p) = 0$ and [E.10] becomes

$$C(y^2 + y^3, p) - C(y^2, p) < C(y^3, p)$$

which rearranges to give [E.8].

Sub-additivity has implications for the way in which cost-minimizing firms will organize production. It also suggests that attempts to allocate the total cost of producing several products among the products so as to yield a 'cost' of producing each particular product will be meaningless. Accounting conventions may apportion the total cost $C(y_1, y_2, p)$ between the two products by various procedures, but the resulting relationship between outputs and cost provides no information useful for decision-making. Any attempt, for example, to decentralize production by creating product divisions and instructing them to maximize the difference between their revenue and the 'cost' allocated to their product will lead to sub-optimization. Similarly, attempts to regulate the behaviour of public utilities on the basis of costs apportioned between different products may lead regulators astray. Sensible decisions require information about the effects of a change in, say, output 1 on the total costs of the firm, not on the 'costs' apportioned to that product by arbitrary conventions. We return to this question in the next chapter, but note here that apportioning cost between different products will be sensible only if the cost function is output separable.

EXERCISE 6E

1. *Concavity and sub-additivity.* Consider the cost function

$$C(y_1, y_2, p) = a_1(p)\sqrt{y_1} + a_2(p)\sqrt{y_2} + b(p)\sqrt{(y_1 y_2)}$$

with $a_1(p)$, $a_2(p)$, $b(p)$ equal to 1. Does it exhibit (a) concavity in output; (b) multi-product economies of scale; (c) economies of scope; (d) cost complementarity; (e) global sub-additivity?

2. Show that cost complementarity implies (a) economies of scale and (b) economies of scope.

CHAPTER 7

Supply and firm objectives

The discussion of the technological constraints on the firm in Chapter 5 required no mention of the firm's objectives and even for the derivation of the cost functions and curves of Chapter 6 all that was required was the assumption that the firm wished to produce each output level at least cost. Nothing was said about how that output level was determined. It is now necessary to make some assumptions about the objectives of the firm. We can then proceed to analyse the firm's output decision and its responses to changes in the environment. The assumption we adopt in sections A to D is that the firm wishes to maximize its profits. This assumption has not gone unchallenged, and the implications of some alternatives are considered in sections E and F.

The existence of adjustment costs means that the firm must make two kinds of decisions at any point in time: it must choose an output level that it will produce in the current period and it must *plan* the outputs to be produced in future periods. This plan of future outputs will imply a sequence of future input levels and this in turn will imply a programme of actions by the firm, to be implemented over time, beginning in the current period, to increase or decrease input levels to the planned future levels.

As in Chapter 6, we will not analyse this problem in its full generality but will instead consider a two-period approximation to it. At the start of period 0 the firm will choose (a) an output level for the current period (period 0) given the constraints on the adjustment of the fixed input and (b) a planned output level for period 1, given that all inputs are variable. Problem (a) is the short-run profit maximization problem which is analysed in section B and problem (b) the long-run profit maximization problem analysed in section A.

Sections A and B are concerned with the case of a single output y and two inputs z_1 and z_2. Section C extends the analysis to a multi-product firm. The firm is assumed to operate in competitive markets in the sense that it takes the prices of inputs and outputs as unaffected by its decisions. We discuss the implications of the firm's decisions affecting the prices it faces in Chapter 9 (monopoly), section 10B (monopsony) and Chapter 16 (oligopoly). When, as in this chapter, the firm treats prices as parameters, the maximum profit it can earn is a function of the prices it faces. In section D we discuss the properties of this maximum profit function and show that it is a useful tool for investigating the firm's behaviour.

Profit maximization requires that the only aspect of the firm that its owners care about is the income that the firm generates and that the owners can control its activities so that profits are indeed maximised. Both these assumptions can be questioned. We defer until Chapter 20 consideration of the extent to which the firm's owners can control the behaviour of its workers and managers to ensure that they act in the interest of the owners. But we do examine in this chapter two other possible assumptions about objectives and their implications for the firm's production decisions.

In section E, the firm is owned and run by a single individual who cares not only about the income she gets from the firm but also about the managerial effort she supplies to it. We show that, in the absence of a market in managerial effort, utility maximization by the owner leads to profit maximization by the firm only if her preferences are of a special type. In section F the firm is a partnership or workers' cooperative. It is owned by its partners or workers who supply labour and in exchange receive a share of its revenue after payment of all non-labour costs. These models show the importance of assumptions about objectives and throw additional light on the standard assumption of profit maximization.

A. Long-run profit maximization

The firm's long-run decision problem is to *plan* an output and input combination to maximize profit, π, where profit is revenue $R = py$ *minus* cost $\sum p_i z_i$, and p, p_i are the prices of y and z_i respectively. Formally, the problem is:

$$\max_{y, z_1, z_2} \pi = py - \sum p_i z_i \quad \text{s.t. } y \leqslant f(z_1, z_2)$$
$$y \geqslant 0, \quad z_1 \geqslant 0, \quad z_2 \geqslant 0 \tag{A.1}$$

This problem can be reformulated in two equivalent ways:

(a) For any output, profit cannot be maximized unless cost is minimized. Hence, we can make use of the earlier analysis of cost minimization, and work with the long-run cost function $C(p_1, p_2, y)$, derived there. The profit maximization problem can be expressed as:

$$\max_{y} py - C(p_1, p_2, y) \quad \text{s.t. } y \geqslant 0 \tag{A.2}$$

The firm chooses the output level which maximizes profit given its revenue function py and cost function C.

The two-stage optimization procedure (minimizing costs to derive the cost function and then maximizing the difference between the revenue and cost functions) has thus reduced the profit maximization problem to a single decision variable problem. As we will see below, this makes the analysis fairly easy.

(b) Alternatively, we can state the problem as follows: since prices are positive the profit-maximizing firm will never produce in an output-inefficient way. If $y < f(z_1, z_2)$ then either y can be increased holding z_1 and z_2 constant, or one or both of the inputs can be reduced with y constant, and so profit cannot be at a maximum. Hence the production constraint on a profit-maximizing firm can be written as $y = f(z_1, z_2)$. Since a choice of z_1 and z_2 determines y, there are only two independent decision variables: the two input levels. The firm's profit-maximization problem is therefore:

$$\max_{z_1, z_2} \pi = p \cdot f(z_1, z_2) - p_1 z_1 - p_2 z_2 \quad \text{s.t. } z_1 \geqslant 0, z_2 \geqslant 0 \tag{A.3}$$

We will use approach (b) in section 10A because it is useful when we wish to focus on the firm's input demands. In this section we use approach (a) to emphasize the firm's output decision.

Differentiating [A.2] with respect to y gives the first-order condition for y^* to provide a maximum of the profit function:

$$\frac{d\pi}{dy} = p - \frac{\partial C}{\partial y} \leqslant 0, \qquad y^* \geqslant 0, \qquad y^* \cdot \frac{d\pi}{dy} = 0 \qquad \text{[A.4]}$$

Since nothing has been assumed about the shape of the profit function, [A.4] is a necessary but not a sufficient condition for y^* to yield a maximum. [A.4] may be satisfied by a number of local maxima or minima as Fig. 7.1 illustrates. The total cost, revenue and profit functions are plotted in part (a) and the marginal cost, revenue and profit and average cost functions in part (b).

It is clear from Fig. 7.1(a) that y^* is the global profit maximizing output and that y^* satisfies [A.4]. But consider two other output levels: $y = y^1$ and $y = 0$. At $y = 0$. $d\pi/dy = p - \partial C/\partial y < 0$ so that [A.4] is satisfied and this is a local profit maximum since profit is larger (loss is smaller) than at neighbouring feasible outputs. At y^1, $d\pi/dy = 0$ but π is at a minimum. To distinguish between *interior* local maxima and minima (when $y > 0$) a second-order condition is required:

$$\frac{d^2\pi}{dy^2} = \frac{-\partial^2 C}{\partial y^2} < 0 \qquad \text{i.e.} \qquad \frac{\partial LMC}{\partial y} > 0 \qquad \text{[A.5]}$$

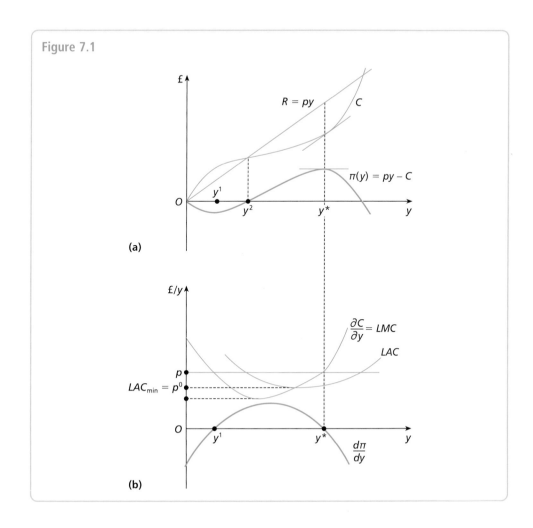

Figure 7.1

(a)

(b)

This condition is satisfied at y^* but not at y^1, and hence distinguishes between *interior* points ($y > 0$) which satisfy the necessary condition in [A.4] but which may be minima or maxima. Condition [A.5] is, however, *not applicable* at $y = 0$. The zero output position is a true *local* maximum because small permissible changes (i.e. increases) in y from $y = 0$ reduce profit (refer to Fig. 7.1(a)) even though *LMC* is falling at that point. We have multiple local optima and the global optimum can only be found by direct comparison of them: profit or loss at $y = 0$ must be compared with profit or loss at $y = y^*$. In the figure, y^* is clearly superior, but it is easy to redraw the curves in such a way that total cost is everywhere above total revenue and the interior point at which profit is maximized (loss is minimized) is inferior to $y = 0$. (Draw the diagram.)

In terms of the discussion of local and global optima in Appendix D, the problem has arisen here because the conditions of the local–global theorem are not satisfied. The theorem states that if the feasible set is convex and the objective function is quasi-concave *every* local optimum is a global optimum, and so all local optima must yield equal values of the objective function. Here the feasible set defined by $y \geqslant 0$ is convex but the objective function is *not* quasi-concave. To see this, take two points at which profit is equal, say $y = 0$ and $y = y^2$ in Fig. 7.1(a) (where profit is zero). The definition of quasi-concavity requires that, for *any* pair of points at which profit is the same, the profit yielded by an output on the straight line joining them must be at least as great as that yielded by the two points. But, clearly, at all outputs on the straight line joining $y = 0$ and $y = y^2$ profit is less than zero and so the profit function is *not* quasi-concave. We cannot then be sure that every local maximum will be a global maximum and, indeed, in the case shown in Fig. 7.1(a), one will not be.

The conditions of the local–global theorem are sufficient but not necessary. The reader is invited to redraw Fig. 7.1(a) in such a way that $y = 0$ and $y = y^*$ are equally good. (*Hint*: look for a point of tangency.) But this would be a special case and in general we cannot guarantee that a local optimum is a global optimum when the profit function is not quasi-concave.

Long-run supply function

When $y^* > 0$ conditions [A.4] and [A.5] can be given a familiar interpretation. Condition [A.4] states that for profit to be maximized at y^* it is necessary that a small change in output adds as much to costs as it does to revenue. Marginal revenue (which is equal to the price of the product in a competitive market) must equal marginal cost. Condition [A.5] requires that marginal cost be increasing with output at y^* so that the marginal cost curve cuts the price line (the competitive firm's marginal revenue curve) from below. The firm maximizes profit by moving along its marginal cost curve until marginal cost is equal to price.

As Fig. 7.1 shows, the firm responds to an increase in the price of its output by moving along its *LMC* curve provided price exceeds long-run average cost. The portion of *LMC* curve above the *LAC* is therefore the *long-run supply curve* of the competitive firm.

More formally, the first-order condition

$$\pi_y(y^*; p, p_1, p_2) = p - C_y(p_1, p_2, y^*) = 0 \qquad \text{[A.6]}$$

is an implicit function of y^*, p, p_1 and p_2 which can be solved to give the *long-run supply function of the competitive firm*:

$$y^* = y^*(p, p_1, p_2) \tag{A.7}$$

The fact that the firm increases y^* when p increases is clear from Fig. 7.1 but it is instructive to demonstrate this using the comparative static method of Appendix I.

Applying the Implicit Function Theorem to [A.6] gives

$$\frac{dy^*}{dp} = \frac{-\pi_{yp}}{\pi_{yy}} = \frac{1}{C_{yy}(p_1, p_2, y^*)} > 0 \tag{A.8}$$

(Remember that the second-order condition [A.5] requires that $\pi_{yy} = -C_{yy} < 0$.)

The firm's long-run supply decision will also depend on its cost conditions and as Fig. 7.1 indicates any change in input prices or its technology which increases its long-run marginal cost will reduce output supplied at any given output price: the long-run supply curve of the firm will have shifted upward.

Again applying the Implicit Function Theorem to [A.6] gives

$$\frac{dy^*}{dp_i} = \frac{-\pi_{yp_i}}{\pi_{yy}} = \frac{-C_{yp_i}(p_1, p_2, y^*)}{C_{yy}(p_1, p_2, y^*)} \tag{A.9}$$

where $C_{yp_i} = \partial C_y/\partial p_i$ is the effect of an increase in the price of input i on long-run marginal cost. Recalling from section 6B that C_{yp_i} is positive or negative as input i is normal or regressive we see that the *firm's output is reduced or increased by an increase in price of input i as i is normal or regressive*.

The firm's optimal y^* is zero if p is less than the minimum long-run average cost LAC_{min} at which it can produce. The firm earns its maximum profit (of zero) by setting $y^* = 0$ if $p < LAC_{min}$. In Fig. 7.1(b) an anticipated price of less than p^0 will cause the firm to plan to cease production next period since p^0 is the lowest price at which LAC can be covered.

The possibility that the optimal output can be zero means that our discussion of the firm's comparative static responses requires qualification. The firm's long run supply curve is the vertical axis (nothing is supplied) for $p < LAC_{min}$ and its LMC curve for $p > LAC_{min}$. If the firm has a U shaped LAC curve its supply curve will be discontinuous at $p^0 = LAC_{min}$. At $p^0 = LAC_{min}$ the firm would be indifferent between supplying $y^* = 0$ or the output at which LAC is minimized. Its long-run supply decision is then strictly speaking a correspondence rather than a function.

EXERCISE 7A

1. Show that the equilibrium conditions derived from problem [A.3] are equivalent to those from the two-stage approach to profit maximization.

2. *Returns to scale and the supply function.* Sketch the long-run supply function of a competitive firm with (a) diminishing returns to scale and (b) constant returns to scale. Why will the firm never plan to supply an output at which it has increasing returns to scale?

3. *Input prices and the supply function.* What is the effect of an increase in the price of input i on (a) LAC_{min} and (b) the output at which LAC is minimized?
   Sketch the effect of an increase in the price of input i on the firm's long run supply curve for (i) a normal input and (ii) a regressive input. (*Hint:* recall the analysis in section 6B.)

B. Short-run profit maximization

The firm's short-run problem is to choose output and input levels for the current period which maximize its current period profits, given that there are constraints on the adjustment of some of the inputs. Since inputs are chosen to minimize cost for any given output level the problem can be reduced to choosing current period output, y, to maximize the difference between revenue and short-run cost:

$$\max_{y} \pi = py - S(p_1, p_2, z_2^0, y) \quad \text{s.t. } y \geqslant 0 \qquad [\text{B.1}]$$

where the constraint on the adjustment of z_2 is assumed to be an upper limit on the use of z_2 and the firm must pay for z_2^0 units irrespective of use. (See section 6C on the firm's short-run cost function.)

The first- and second-order conditions for this problem are very similar in form and interpretation to [A.4] and [A.5]. The firm will either produce where $p = \partial S/\partial y = SMC$ and where the SMC curve cuts the horizontal price line from below; or the firm will produce nothing if price is less than short-run average opportunity cost (average variable cost) at all positive outputs.

In the short-run the maximized level of profit may be negative, even if p exceeds minimum AVC. In Fig. 7.2, for example, which is based on Fig. 6.10 the firm makes a loss if $p < SAC_{\min}$ since fixed costs ($p_2 z_2^0$) are not covered. If p is less than $AVC_{\min}$ the firm will set $y = 0$ since positive y implies that revenue would not cover variable cost, and so a loss would be made in addition to the loss on fixed costs. Conversely, if p exceeds $AVC_{\min}$ then revenue is made over and above variable costs, so that some of the fixed costs are recovered by producing and selling some output. The firm may still make a loss but this is lower than the loss at zero output, which is equal to the fixed cost.

The firm's *short-run supply curve*, which shows the output it wishes to produce given the prevailing constraints on the adjustment of its inputs, will be the SMC curve for $p \geqslant AVC_{\min}$ and the vertical axis at $y = 0$ for $p < AVC_{\min}$. The firm's short-run supply curve, therefore, is discontinuous when the minimum of the AVC curve does not occur at $y = 0$.

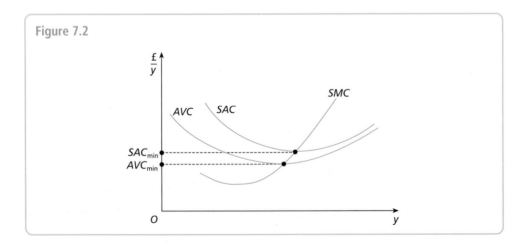

Figure 7.2

The relationship between long- and short-run profit maximization

We pointed out in the introduction to this chapter, and in section 6A, that the firm makes two kinds of decisions at the start of each period: (a) it chooses the actual output level for that period, given the constraints on the adjustment of its inputs; (b) it *plans* an output level for the next period, when all inputs are freely variable (provided the decision to change them is made at the start of the current period). The first decision is the short-run, and the second the long-run, problem. We will now investigate in more detail how the two types of decision are related.

Some new notation is needed to distinguish between actual and planned, and between actual and forecast, magnitudes:

y_a^t: actual output in period t

y_p^t: planned output in period t, decided upon in period $t - 1$

p_a^t: actual price of output in period t

p_f^t: forecast of price of output in period t made in period $t - 1$

Since all inputs are freely variable after the current period, plans and expectations need only be made one period ahead, so that as indicated y_p^t refers to a plan made at period $t - 1$ and p_f^t to the firm's forecast of p_a^t made at period $t - 1$. It is assumed for simplicity that input prices and technological conditions are constant over all periods and that they are correctly anticipated at all times, so that actual and expected cost curves coincide and are the same in each period. To make the analysis more concrete let us take z_2 to be a measure of *plant size*.

Initially, at the start of period 0 the firm has a given plant size (z_2^0) which it cannot vary in period 0. Its short-run cost curves are shown in Fig. 7.3 as SMC^0 and SAC^0. In period 0 the firm maximizes its profits by equating short-run marginal cost to the known, current price of y (p_a^0) and so produces y_a^0. At the same time the firm *plans* an output for period 1. Since the level of z_2 for period 1 can be varied if the decision to do so is made at the start of period 0, the relevant cost curves for planning the next period's output are the long-run curves LMC and LAC in Fig. 7.3. (Recall that these curves are derived from a cost-minimization problem in which all inputs are freely variable.) At the start of period 0 the firm *expects* the period 1 price

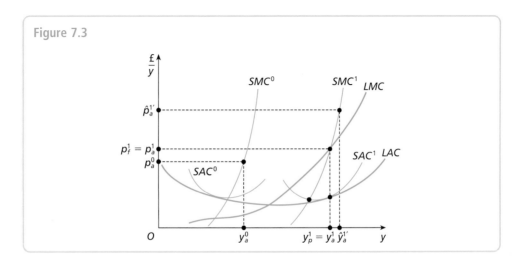

Figure 7.3

to be p_f^1 and so it *plans* to maximize period 1 profit by producing y_p^1, where $p_f^1 = LMC$. The planned period 1 output in turn implies that the period 1 level of z_2 is z_2^1. To ensure that z_2^1 is actually available at the start of period 1, the firm must, at the start of period 0, order and install the additional plant required. Hence the decisions taken in period 0 are (a) to set the actual output in period 0, on the basis of the actual price p_a^1 and actual plant size z_2^0; (b) to choose the plant size z_2^1 for period 1, on the basis of planned period 1 output, which in turn depends on the forecast period 1 price.

At the start of period 1 the firm's actual plant is z_2^1, giving rise to the short-run cost curves SMC^1, SAC^1. Suppose that the actual price is p_a^1. Period 1 profit is maximized by equating SMC^1 to the actual price. In this case the firm's forecast was correct and $p_a^1 = p_f^1$. This means that actual and planned period 1 output are equal: $y_a^1 = y_p^1$. Note that at this output level $SMC^1 = LMC$, indicating that the actual plant (z_2^1) is the optimal plant for producing that output level.

The firm will also plan in period 1 for an output for period 2, based on its forecast p_f^2 of the period 2 price, and this will imply a period 1 decision on the actual plant for period 2 (z_2^2). If the firm expects p_f^2 to equal p_a^1 then $y_p^2 = y_a^1$ and there is no need to adjust plant size ($z_2^2 = z_2^1$). The firm will then be in *long-run equilibrium*: it will be maximizing profit for the current period (1) and its current plant will be optimal for the next period (2), given the firm's forecast of the next period's price (and ignoring depreciation).

Suppose, however, that at time 0 the firm had made the wrong price forecast, i.e. the actual and forecast period 1 prices differ (e.g. actual period 1 price is $\hat{p}_a^1 > p_f^1$). The firm would find that its actual period 1 plant (z_2^1) was not optimal for the market price $\hat{p}_a^1$. In order to maximize period 1 profit, given z_2^1 and the corresponding SMC^1 curve, the firm will set $SMC^1 = \hat{p}_a^1$ and produce the output $\hat{y}_a^1$. At the same time it will plan to produce y_p^2, given its price forecast p_f^2, and it will adjust its plant if $p_f^2 \neq p_f^1$, i.e. if *its forecast* of the price has changed (rather than if $\hat{p}_a^1 \neq p_f^2$. Explain why.).

The output that the firm *plans* to produce in the next period, based on its forecast of the next period's price, determines the actual plant in the next period, but if the forecast is incorrect actual output next period will in general differ from that planned. The plan made commits the firm to a particular plant size next period, but *not* to a particular output level. When the firm chooses its current output at the start of a period it is *always* 'in the short-run': its plant size is fixed by the plan made in the previous period and is unalterable in the current period. Hence the firm will *always* produce where $p_a^t = SMC$ in order to maximize current period profit. If the past forecast was correct, then the current plant is optimal and the firm will be producing where $LMC = SMC^t = p_a^t = p_f^t$. If the past forecast was incorrect then the firm will not produce where $LMC = SMC^t$ and the existing plant will not be optimal. Short-run marginal cost and *actual* price determine *actual* output in the current period. Long-run marginal cost and the *forecast* price determine *planned* output and *actual* plant in the next period.

The relationship between forecast and actual, and planned and actual magnitudes can be represented in the following way:

$$p_f^{t+1} \to y_p^{t+1} \to z_2^{t+1} \to SMC^{t+1}$$
$$\searrow$$
$$y_a^{t+1}$$
$$\nearrow$$
$$p_a^{t+1} \dashrightarrow p_f^{t+2} \to y_p^{t+2} \to z_2^{t+2} \to \dots$$

This emphasizes that a model which attempts to predict the firm's *actual* behaviour must include a sub-model of the way in which the firm makes its price forecasts. In the diagram above, for example, the dashed arrow from actual price to the forecast of the next period's price indicates that the forecast may depend on the actual current price.

EXERCISE 7B

1. Adapt Fig. 7.3 to show that period $t + 1$ profit is larger if the firm's expectation of period $t + 1$ price is correct, than if it is incorrect.

2. Will the firm have a larger profit if its expectation of p_f^t is 10 per cent larger than p_a^{t+1}, or 10 per cent smaller?

3. Analyse the relationship between the short- and long-run decisions if the actual and forecast output prices are equal and constant, but the firm's forecast of the price of its variable input may differ from its actual price.

4. Assume that the firm has correctly forecast current price and believes that next period's price will be the same as this period's. Suppose that this forecast is incorrect and the actual price in period $t + 1$ is less than forecast, but that the firm correctly forecasts that the price in period $t + 2$ will remain at the actual level for period $t + 1$. Show that for *small* changes in the actual price the long-run response exceeds the short-run, i.e. that the long-run supply curve is *more* elastic than the short-run. Draw *SMC* and *LMC* curves and the corresponding total cost curves which will lead to the long-run supply elasticity being (a) more and (b) *less* than the short-run for *large* price changes.

C. The multi-product firm

In this and the next section we will not use the two-stage optimization procedure (deriving a cost function and then maximizing the difference between revenue and cost) of the previous sections. We will instead adopt the single-stage procedure of simultaneous choice of input and output levels. These two sections are also concerned with the firm's *long-run* decision or plan, it being assumed that there are no constraints on the adjustment of inputs. It is also assumed that the actual and forecast price are always equal and constant.

The notation of section 5D will be adopted in this section, so that the firm's decision variables are its *net* output levels $y = (y_1, \ldots, y_n)$. Recall from that section that if $y_i < 0$ good i is an input and so $p_i y_i$ will be negative and measure the outlay on good i by the firm. If $y_i > 0$ good i is an output so that $p_i y_i > 0$ is the revenue from the sale of i. Since profit π is the difference between revenues and costs the firm's profit is

$$\pi = \Sigma p_i y_i = py$$

The reader should also recall from section 5D that the firm's technologically feasible net output bundles can be described either by means of the implicit production function $g(y) \leq 0$, or the concept of the production set (*PS*). If all goods are divisible profit π will be a continuous function of the firm's net outputs and, if the *PS* is assumed to be non-empty, closed and bounded, the Existence Theorem of Appendix B applies.

When all prices are positive the firm will never choose a bundle y where $g(y) < 0$. (Readers should apply the argument of section A for the single-output, two-input case to convince themselves of this.) Hence the firm's decision problem is

$$\max_{y} \pi = py \quad \text{s.t. } g(y) = 0 \tag{C.1}$$

The Lagrange function for [C.1] is $\pi + \lambda g(y)$ and the first-order conditions are

$$p_i + \lambda g_i = 0 \quad i = 1, \ldots, n \tag{C.2}$$
$$g(y) = 0$$

Rearranging the condition on good i gives $p_i = -\lambda g_i$ and dividing by the similarly rearranged condition on good j gives

$$\frac{p_i}{p_j} = \frac{g_i}{g_j} \quad i = 1, \ldots, n; i \neq j \tag{C.3}$$

This general condition succinctly summarizes a number a familiar results for the three logically possible cases:

1. Both goods i and j are inputs. In this case g_i/g_j is the marginal rate of technical substitution between two inputs (see section 5D) and for profit maximization this must be equated to the ratio of the inputs' prices. This is the same condition as that required for cost minimization in section 6B, which is to be expected since cost minimization is a necessary condition for profit maximization.

2. When i is an input and j an output g_i/g_j is the marginal product of i in the production of good j: MP_i^j. Rearranging [C.3] yields

$$p_j = \frac{p_i}{MP_i^j}$$

But p_i/MP_i^j is the marginal cost of good j (see section 6B) so that [C.3] states that for profit maximization the output of a good should be set at the level at which its marginal cost is equal to its price, thus confirming the results of section A. This is illustrated in Fig. 7.4 where y_1 is the firm's sole input and y_2 its sole output. The shaded area is the PS, π_1 is an isoprofit line satisfying the equation $\pi_1 = p_1 y_1 + p_2 y_2$ or $y_2 = (\pi_1 - p_1 y_1)/p_2$, and π_2, π_3 are derived in a similar way. The profit-maximizing net output bundle is $y^* = (y_1^*, y_2^*)$ where the highest attainable isoprofit line, π_2, is tangent to the upper boundary of the firm's PS. The negative of the slope of the isoprofit line is p_1/p_2 and the negative of the slope of the boundary of the PS is the rate at which y_2 increases as y_1 decreases (the input 1 is *increased*) or the marginal product of the input 1 in production of output 2: MP_1^2. Hence condition 3 is satisfied at y^*: $p_1/p_2 = MP_1^2$, or $p_2 = p_1/MP_1^2$, so that price is equated to marginal cost. The firm's profit is $\pi_2 = p_1 y_1^* + p_2 y_2^* = py^*$ or, measured in terms of the output y_2 by the intercept of the iso-profit curve on the y_2 axis: π_2/p_2.

3. If both i and j are outputs g_i/g_j is the marginal rate of transformation between them (MRT_{ji}), so that when the firm produces more than one output it will maximize profit by producing where the MRT between two outputs is equal to the ratio of their prices. This is illustrated in Fig. 7.5 where the firm produces two outputs (y_1, y_2) from the single input, good 3. The three transformation curves show the varying combinations of the outputs that can be produced from different fixed input levels. The $g(y_1, y_2, y_3^1) = 0$ curve, for example, shows the combinations of goods 1 and 2 that can be produced in a technically efficient way when good 3

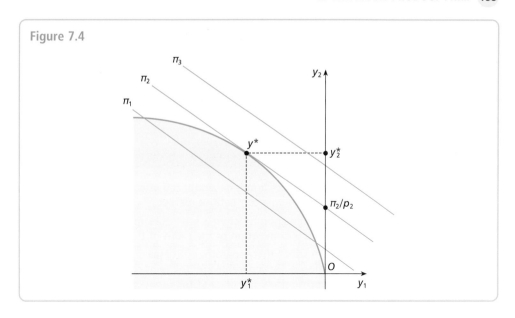

Figure 7.4

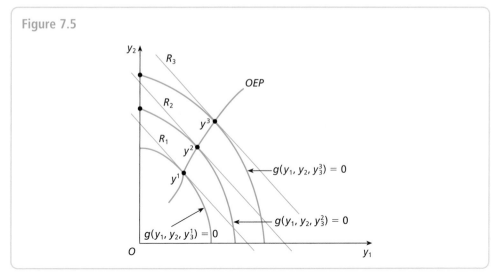

Figure 7.5

(the input) is fixed at y_3^1. As the input level is increased the transformation curve shifts outwards.

R_1, R_2 and R_3 can be called *isorevenue lines*. They show output bundles which will produce the same total revenue: $p_1 y_1 + p_2 y_2 = R_j$, $j = 1, 2, 3$ where R_j is a given constant, $R_1 < R_2 < R_3$. Thus the lines have the equation $y_2 = (R_j - p_1 y_1)/p_2$, $j = 1, 2, 3$.

For a given level of the input y_3, the firm's costs are given and so it maximizes profit by choosing an output combination which *maximizes revenue*. If, for example, $y_3 = y_3^1$ the firm will choose the output bundle y^1, *where the highest attainable isorevenue line R_1 is tangent to the transformation curve generated by $y_3 = y_3^1$*. If $y_3 = y_3^2$ or $y_3 = y_3^3$ the firm chooses y^2 or y^3 where the respective transformation curves are tangent to isorevenue lines. *OEP* is the *output expansion path*: the locus of points such as y^1, y^2, y^3, generated by the transformation curve shifting as the input level varies. The firm's profit varies as it moves out along *OEP* since its revenue is increasing (higher isorevenue curves are reached) and so is its cost (larger inputs are required to reach higher transformation curves). The firm will choose the point on *OEP* where the difference between revenue and cost is at a maximum. If for example this is y^2, the firm's profit is $p_1 y_1^2 + p_2 y_2^2 + p_3 y_3^2 = R_2 + p_3 y_3^2$ (where of course y_3^2 is negative since good 3 is an input).

EXERCISE 7C

1. Suppose that a multi-product firm is decentralized into autonomous product divisions, where each product is sold in a competitive market.

   (a) Show that if the production function is separable, maximization of the profit of each division will lead to maximization of the profit of the firm as a whole.

   (b) Conversely, demonstrate that separate profit maximization is not optimal if the production function is not separable and the joint cost is charged to the different divisions in proportion to (i) the price of the product; (ii) revenue from each product; (iii) the separate costs of each division.

   (c) Should a division which makes a loss under one of the above joint cost allocations be closed down?

   (d) If not, under what circumstances should a division be closed down?

D. The profit function and comparative statics

Using the terminology of section 6D, the net output vector y^* which solves the firm's profit maximization problem [C.1] is a function of the price vector p: $y^* = y(p)$ and so is the firm's maximized profit

$$\Pi = py^* = py(p) = \sum_i p_i y_i(p) = \Pi(p) \qquad \text{[D.1]}$$

The *profit function* $\Pi(p)$ has a number of properties which are useful in deriving predictions about the firm's response to price changes.

(a) $\Pi(p)$ is increasing in p_i if the firm supplies good i ($y_i(p) > 0$) and decreasing in p_i if good i is an input used by the firm ($y_i(p) < 0$)

We leave it to the reader to prove that firms are made better off by increases in the prices of goods that they sell and worse off by increases in the prices of goods that they buy. (Use the Envelope Theorem or see (d) below.)

(b) $\Pi(p)$ is linear homogeneous in p

This follows from the fact that if $y(p)$ is profit-maximizing at prices p then it is feasible [$y(p) \in PS$] and satisfies

$$py(p) \geqslant py \qquad \text{all } y \in PS \qquad \text{[D.2]}$$

which implies

$$tpy(p) \geqslant tpy \qquad \text{all } y \in PS, t > 0 \qquad \text{[D.3]}$$

Thus $y(p)$ is also optimal at prices tp and profit at prices tp is

$$\Pi(tp) = tpy(tp) = tpy(p) = t\Pi(p)$$

[D.3] also implies that the firm's optimal net output bundle is unaffected by equal proportionate changes in prices: *the net supply functions of the firm are homogeneous of degree 0 in prices*:

$$y_i(tp) = y_i(p) \tag{D.4}$$

(c) $\Pi(p)$ is convex in p

The proof is similar to that used to establish the concavity of the consumer's cost or expenditure function in section 3A. Consider three price vectors p^0, p^1 and $\bar{p} = tp^0 + (1 - t)p^1$ for $t \in [0, 1]$. Using the definition [D.2] of the output vector which is profit-maximizing at p implies

$$p^0 y(p^0) \geqslant p^0 y(\bar{p}) \quad \text{and} \quad p^1 y(p^1) \geqslant p^1 y(\bar{p})$$

which in turn implies

$$tp^0 y(p^0) \geqslant tp^0 y(\bar{p}) \quad \text{and} \quad (1 - t)p^1 y(p^1) \geqslant (1 - t)p^1 y(\bar{p}) \tag{D.5}$$

Using the definition of the profit function [D.1], adding the left-hand side of the first inequality in [D.5] to the left-hand side in the second and similarly for the right-hand sides, gives

$$t\Pi(p^0) + (1 - t)\Pi(p^1) \geqslant tp^0 y(\bar{p}) + (1 - t)p^1 y(\bar{p})$$
$$= [tp^0 + (1 - t)p^1]y(\bar{p}) = \bar{p}y(\bar{p}) = \Pi(\bar{p}) \tag{D.6}$$

which establishes the convexity of $\Pi(p)$.

(d) Hotelling's lemma: $\partial\Pi(p)/\partial p_i = y_i(p)$

We can prove this by adapting the argument of section 6B used to establish Shephard's lemma. Define the function

$$G(p, p^0) = \Pi(p) - py(p^0) \geqslant 0$$

which cannot be negative because $y(p^0)$ is profit-maximizing at p^0 and cannot yield a greater profit at p than $y(p)$ which is profit-maximizing at p and which yields profit $\Pi(p) = py(p)$. Since G is minimized with respect to p at $p = p^0$ (where $G(p^0, p^0) = 0$) its partial derivatives with respect to p_i must be zero:

$$\left.\frac{\partial G(p, p^0)}{\partial p_i}\right|_{p=p^0} = \left.\frac{\partial\Pi(p)}{\partial p_i}\right|_{p=p^0} - y_i(p^0) = 0 \tag{D.7}$$

and since $\Pi_i(p^0) = y_i(p^0)$ must be true for all p^0, Hotelling's lemma is established.

Suppose that the firm's technology ensures that the profit function is twice continuously differentiable. Hotelling's lemma can then be used to conclude that *cross-price effects on net supply functions are equal*. A function which is twice continuously differentiable has equal cross-partial derivatives so $\Pi_{ij}(p) = \Pi_{ji}(p)$ and using [D.7] we see that $\partial y_i(p)/\partial p_j = \partial y_j(p)/\partial p_i$. Convexity implies further restrictions on the second-order partial derivatives of $\Pi(p)$ and thus, using Hotelling's lemma, on the changes in the net supplies induced by price changes. In particular, convexity implies that the second-order partial derivatives of $\Pi(p)$ are non-negative and so

$$\frac{\partial y_i(p)}{\partial p_i} = \frac{\partial^2\Pi(p)}{\partial p_i^2} \geqslant 0 \tag{D.8}$$

or: *the firm's net supply of a good never decreases with its price.*

When good i is an output this result confirms the result derived in the special case of the single-output firm in section A where the supply curve of output was positively sloped. When good i is an input an increase in its price causes the firm to use less of it (if $y_i < 0$ then an increase in y_i corresponds to a reduction in the use of an input). Thus *the firm's demand curve for an input can never be positively sloped*. In section 6B we used Shephard's lemma to show that the demand for an input at given output level could not be increased by an increase in its price, i.e. the own price substitution effect was non-positive. The result derived here, using Hotelling's lemma, is much more powerful because it takes account both of the substitution effect and of the fact that a change in the input price will generally change the firm's maximizing output as well (the output effect), leading to a further change in the demand for the input.

If the firm's technology implies that the profit function is not twice continuously differentiable we can still use the definition [D.2] of the profit-maximizing net output vector $y(p)$ to make predictions about its response to price changes. Let p^0 and p^1 be two price vectors and $y(p^0)$ and $y(p^1)$ be the respective profit-maximizing net output vectors. Then from the definition [D.2]

$$p^0 y(p^0) - p^0 y(p^1) = p^0[y(p^0) - y(p^1)] = p^0 \Delta y \geq 0 \qquad [D.9]$$

and

$$p^1 y(p^1) - p^1 y(p^0) = p^1[y(p^1) - y(p^0)] = -p^1 \Delta y \geq 0 \qquad [D.10]$$

Adding [D.9] and [D.10] gives

$$p^0 \Delta y - p^1 \Delta y = (p^0 - p^1)\Delta y = \Delta p \Delta y \geq 0 \qquad [D.11]$$

which is the *fundamental inequality of profit maximization*.

[D.11] is a strong result because it requires only that the firm's profit maximization problem has a solution (not necessarily unique) for all p so that the profit function is well defined. It is not necessary that the profit function be differentiable. [D.11] says that the sum of the product of the price changes and the net supply changes $\sum \Delta p_i \Delta y_i$ must be non-negative and can be used to test the profit maximization hypothesis. If only one price changes, [D.11] reduces to

$$\Delta p_i \Delta y_i \geq 0 \qquad [D.12]$$

which confirms our earlier conclusion, reached via Hotelling's lemma and the convexity of $\Pi(p)$, that increases in the price of good i do not reduce the supply of good i if it is an output and do not increase the firm's demand for it if it is an input.

Corporation taxes

Suppose that the firm must pay a percentage tax on its profits. The net of tax profit is $(1 - t)py$ where t is the percentage rate of corporation tax. (Since in the long run the firm can always earn a zero profit by ceasing production, py can be safely considered to be non-negative.) If both sides of [D.2] are multiplied by $(1 - t)$ we get

$$(1 - t)py(p) > (1 - t)py$$

If $y(p)$ maximizes pre-tax profit it will also maximize post-tax profit. Hence the *rate of corporation tax will have no effect on the profit-maximizing firm's net supply decisions*.

The reader is warned that this result applies to a tax levied on what economists usually define as profit, namely the difference between revenue and *all opportunity*

Figure 7.6

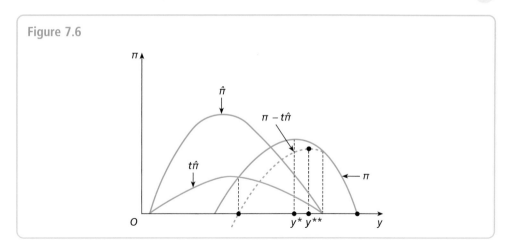

costs. Most of the taxes which are in practice called 'profits' taxes or corporation taxes, however, are taxes on the difference between revenue and the costs *allowed by the tax authorities.* If there is any difference between opportunity costs and the allowable costs a 'profits' tax *may* lead to a change in the firm's behaviour, as we see in Fig. 7.6.

Two kinds of divergence between opportunity and allowable costs are likely to be important. First, the funds invested in a firm by the owners will have an opportunity cost (the return which could have been earned in alternative uses of the funds), but unlike, say, interest charges on bank loans to the firm, this opportunity cost is not usually counted as an allowable cost in calculating the taxable profit. Second, in a period of rapid inflation the recorded cost of inputs used by the firm, which is the allowable cost of the inputs for tax purposes, will be less than their opportunity costs if there is any appreciable lag between purchase and use of the inputs. In either of these cases some of the opportunity costs will be disallowed for calculation of the taxable profit, which will therefore exceed the true profit.

It should also be noted that the tax authorities' definition of revenue may also differ from that of the economist and this will be a further reason why we would expect actual 'profits' taxes to alter the behaviour of firms.

Figure 7.6 illustrates our remark about the importance of the distinction between opportunity and allowable costs. $\hat{\pi}$ plots taxable profit, which differs from π because some opportunity costs are not recorded or are disallowed. If a tax is levied on taxable profits $\hat{\pi}$ the firm's tax bill is $t\hat{\pi}$, which is also plotted in Fig. 7.6. The firm's post-tax pure profit, which it wishes to maximize, is $(\pi - t\hat{\pi})$ which is drawn as the dashed line. The tax on taxable profit will therefore alter the firm's output from y^*, which maximizes pre-tax pure profit, to y^{**}, which maximizes post-tax pure profit $(\pi - t\hat{\pi})$. Similarly, changes in t will change the $(\pi - t\hat{\pi})$-maximizing output.

Lump-sum taxes and fixed costs

Let T be some lump-sum tax or fixed cost that the firm must pay whatever its output level. Then the firm's net profit is $py - T$ and if T is subtracted from both sides of [D.2] we have

$$py(p) - T > py - T$$

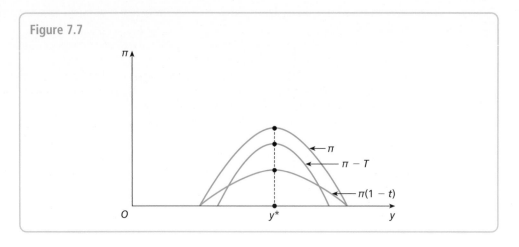

Figure 7.7

and if $y(p)$ maximizes profit before tax or the fixed cost it will maximize net profit after the tax or fixed cost. The *level of lump-sum taxes will have no effect on the firm's decisions*. This result is critically dependent on T being independent of py. Suppose, for example, that the firm had to pay a licence fee in order to operate. This licence fee is *not* a lump-sum tax or fixed cost because if the firm does not operate, i.e. $y = (0, \ldots, 0)$, it does not have to pay the fee. The fee therefore varies discontinuously with the firm's net output decision. If, for example, the firm's optimal bundle is $y^* > (0, \ldots, 0)$, raising T from $0 < T < py^*$ to $T > py^*$ will cause the firm to switch from y^* to $(0, \ldots, 0)$: it will go out of business.

These results are illustrated in Fig. 7.7 for a single-product firm. π is the non-negative part of the pre-tax profit curve in the figure. Pre-tax profit is maximized at y^*. A proportional profit tax of t will give rise to the post-tax profit curve which plots $(1 - t)\pi$. The proportional tax flattens the profit curve, as (except where $d\pi/dy = 0$) the slope of π_t is $(1 - t)d\pi/dy < d\pi/dy$. y^* also maximizes post-tax profit and so changes in t do not affect the output at which profit is maximized. Lump-sum taxes T shift the profit curve vertically downwards to $\pi - T$. Again, no change in post-tax profit-maximizing output is caused by changes in T, as long as optimal output remains positive.

EXERCISE 7D

1. Draw diagrams of the firm's PS in the single-input, single-output case to illustrate the circumstances under which

   (a) the profit-maximizing y is not unique,

   (b) the same y is optimal at different relative prices.

   What do the firm's net supply curves look like in these two cases?

2. Suppose that in the time between the firm's purchase and use of inputs *all* prices (including the price of its output) double. How, if at all, will recorded profit (revenue minus the purchase cost of the inputs) differ from actual or pure profit? Does a percentage tax on recorded profit lead to a rise or fall in the firm's output? (Assume that the firm realizes that the tax is levied on recorded profit and it correctly anticipates the rate of inflation.)

E. The entrepreneurial firm

We now consider the first of two alternatives to the model of profit maximization used in sections A to D. Because of the separation of ownership from control associated with large firms, which we examine in Chapter 20, it is sometimes argued that the profit maximization assumption is more plausible when applied to firms which are small enough to be run by their owners. Examples of such *entrepreneurial firms* are particularly common in industries, from hairdressing to craft potteries, where there are no significant economies of scale. It is argued that, since in the entrepreneurial firm the owner receives all the the firm's profit as income, she will seek to maximize profit in order to maximize her income. But this raises a number of questions, from the definition of profit to the nature of the owner's preferences over income and effort, which we address in this section.

In generating the firm's 'gross income' (defined as revenue less all costs *except that of her own services*), the entrepreneur must expend time and effort. If we regard the amount of effort as constant per unit time, then we can measure the entrepreneur's input in terms of, say, the number of hours per day, up to a maximum of 24, devoted to the firm. We expect that, at least over some range, the firm's gross income increases with the entrepreneurial input as she devotes more time to getting business and controlling costs, but at a diminishing rate. The curve $P(E)$ in Fig. 7.8 shows the relation between gross income per day measured on the vertical axis, and effort, measured in hours per day, along the horizontal (cf. the analysis of labour supply in section 4C).

The fact that $P(E)$ has a positive intercept indicates that even if the entrepreneur put no effort into her firm it would still generate an income for her. If the entrepreneur had to devote at least some effort to the firm in order to get a positive gross income, the intercept would be negative. The value of $P(0)$ does not affect the analysis, provided that over some range of E the firm produces a positive income for the entrepreneur.

Figure 7.8

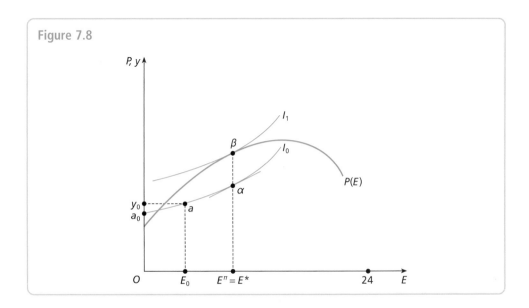

In defining gross income we did not make any allowance for the cost of the entrepreneur's own services, so that the curve $P(E)$ does not measure profit, which was defined in earlier chapters as revenue minus *all* opportunity costs. We therefore need a measure of the opportunity cost of the services the entrepreneur provides to the firm. By providing services to the firm the entrepreneur forgoes the opportunities of using them elsewhere to generate income or of having more time available for leisure. To measure the value of these forgone alternatives we must make some assumptions about her preferences as regards income and effort.

It is plausible that these preferences are similar to those of the labour suppliers examined in section 4C. Letting $u(E, y)$ be the entrepreneur's strictly quasi-concave utility function, we expect that she prefers less effort to more ($\partial u/\partial E = u_E < 0$) and more income to less ($\partial u/\partial y = u_y > 0$). Figure 7.8 shows one possible indifference map for the entrepreneur. The indifference curves are upward sloping because she must be compensated with additional income for additional effort. The slope of an indifference curve increases as she supplies more effort, indicating that additional effort becomes increasingly distasteful and must be compensated for by larger increases in income.

Suppose that the entrepreneur's best alternative to supplying effort to run the firm is the effort–income combination E_0, y_0 at a in Fig. 7.8. The indifference curve I_0 shows all effort–income combinations which yield the same utility as a.

$$u(E, y) = u(E_0 \, y_0) = u^0 \qquad \text{[E.1]}$$

I_0 shows the minimum income that she must be given to induce her to supply different levels of effort if she is to be no worse off than in her forgone alternative. The height of I_0 is a monetary measure of the opportunity cost of supplying effort to the firm and thereby forgoing the alternative a. Solving [E.1] for y, as a function of E and the utility level achieved in the alternative a, gives the opportunity cost A of effort as $A(E; u^0)$. Writing [E.1] as an implicit function and using the implicit function rule confirms that the marginal opportunity cost of effort is the slope of the indifference curve I_0:

$$\frac{\partial A(E; u^0)}{\partial E} = A_E(E; u^0) = \left.\frac{dy}{dE}\right|_{u=u^0} = -\frac{u_E}{u_y} \qquad \text{[E.2]}$$

Two points should be noted about the opportunity cost of effort. First, it depends on the preferences of the entrepreneur and is therefore unobservable and likely to differ for different individuals. Thus profit maximization may imply different effort levels for different entrepreneurial firms, even if the entrepreneurs confront the same $P(E)$ curve. Second, in general, the marginal opportunity cost of effort depends on the level of utility achieved in the forgone alternative. As we will see, this is crucial in answering the question of whether the entrepreneurial firm will in fact maximize profit.

Since the height of the indifference curve I_0 measures the opportunity cost of the effort the entrepreneur supplies to the firm, the firm's profit in Fig. 7.8 at each effort level is the vertical distance between the income curve $P(E)$ and I_0:

$$\Pi(E) = P(E) - A(E; u^0) \qquad \text{[E.3]}$$

Profit is maximized at the effort level E^π, where the slope of $P(E)$ at β is equal to the slope of I_0 at α:

$$P'(E^\pi) = A_E(E^\pi; u^0) \qquad \text{[E.4]}$$

But the entrepreneur chooses her effort level to maximize her utility $u(E, y)$, subject to the constraint $y = P(E)$. (As Question 1, Exercise 7E, asks you to demonstrate, the analysis is not substantively different if she has an endowed income $\bar{y}$, so that her income constraint is $y = P(E) + \bar{y}$.) Does utility maximizing effort E^* also maximize the firm's profit: is $E^* = E^\pi$? Substituting the constraint into the utility function, the entrepreneur's problem is

$$\max_{E} u(E, P(E)) \qquad [E.5]$$

and, assuming a non-corner solution, the optimal effort level E^* satisfies the first-order condition

$$u_E(E^*, P(E^*)) + u_y(E^*, P(E^*))P' = 0 \qquad [E.6]$$

which can be rearranged to get

$$P'(E^*) = -\frac{u_E(E^*, P(E^*))}{u_y(E^*, P(E^*))} \qquad [E.7]$$

The left-hand side of [E.7] is the slope of the $P(E)$ curve and the right-hand side is the slope of an indifference curve at the optimal point. In terms of Fig. 7.8, she maximizes utility by moving along $P(E)$ until she reaches the highest possible indifference curve. The optimum effort level E^* is where an indifference curve is tangent to $P(E)$. In Fig. 7.8 this is at β, where I_1 is tangent to $P(E)$ at the effort level $E^* = E^\pi$. In this case, utility maximization by the entrepreneur leads to profit maximization.

However, in general, the tangency of $P(E)$ with an indifference curve need not occur at E^π. From [E.4] and [E.2], the profit-maximizing effort level E^π is defined by the slope of P being equal to the slope of the forgone opportunity indifference curve I_0, whereas the utility-maximizing effort level E^* is defined by the slope of P being equal to the slope of an indifference curve which can be reached by moving along P. Thus E^* and E^π will coincide only if indifference curves are vertically parallel: their slope must depend only on the level of effort and not on the income level. In Fig. 7.8 the preferences of the entrepreneur satisfy this rather special requirement: the slope of I_1 is equal to the slope of I_0 at all levels of E. In section 3C we saw that this is the requirement that the utility function be *quasi-linear*. Since the slope of the indifference curves measures the marginal cost of effort, vertically parallel indifference curves mean that the marginal cost of effort depends only on effort. Thus an entrepreneur who, as she gets richer, supplies less effort even though the marginal return to effort is unchanged, is not a profit maximizer.

Entrepreneurial input market

Suppose that there is a competitive market on which it is possible to buy and sell entrepreneurial inputs at a given price w. The entrepreneur can choose to run her own business, employ someone else to run it, or become employed running a firm for someone else. Suppose also that she does not mind whether she is 'her own boss' or whether she works for someone else for the same income. In these circumstances the conclusion that profit maximization requires a special type of preferences is no longer valid. The reason is that, with an entrepreneurial input market, the opportunity cost of the entrepreneur's effort is not the sum of money required to induce her to work in the firm but rather the sum she could get if she sold her services on the market, rather than supplying them to her own firm.

The existence of the entrepreneurial input market enables the entrepreneur to separate the decisions on how much effort should be used in her firm and how much effort she should supply. Let E_f denote the level of entrepreneurial input used in the firm and E be the amount of effort that she supplies on the entrepreneurial input market.

The existence of the entrepreneurial input market means that the opportunity cost of effort used in the firm is wE_f: the sum the entrepreneur would have to pay someone to work for her. Thus the firm's profit is

$$\Pi(E_f) = P(E_f) - wE_f \qquad [E.8]$$

and her income is

$$y = \Pi(E_f) + wE \qquad [E.9]$$

The entrepreneur chooses E and E_f to solve

$$\max_{E, E_f} u(E, \Pi(E_f) + wE) \qquad [E.10]$$

The first-order conditions, assuming a non-corner solution, are

$$\frac{du}{dE} = u_E + u_y w = 0 \qquad [E.11]$$

$$\frac{du}{dE_f} = u_y[P'(E_f) - w] = 0 \qquad [E.12]$$

Rearranging [E.11] gives the condition for optimal own effort supply:

$$-u_E/u_y = w \qquad [E.13]$$

In supplying effort she acts just like the labour suppliers in section 4C, equating her marginal cost of effort to the marginal increase in income from selling extra effort. Since $u_y > 0$, [E.12] implies that the optimal entrepreneurial input into the firm satisfies

$$P'(E_f^*) = w \qquad [E.14]$$

so that the level of effort used in the firm is profit-maximizing. The entrepreneur's income is $y = \Pi(E_f) + wE$ and, because her utility $u(E, \Pi(E_f) + wE)$ depends on the level of effort employed in the firm only via its effect on the firm's profit, she will want to make the profit from the firm as large as possible.

The solution is illustrated in Fig. 7.9. $P(E_f)$ shows the gross income from the entrepreneur's firm as a function of managerial effort. The line OW has slope equal to the price of entrepreneurial effort w and measures the opportunity cost of effort wE_f used in the firm. The firm's profit is the vertical distance between OW and $P(E_f)$ and is maximized at E_f^*. If the entrepreneur decided to supply this amount of effort to her firm ($E = E_f^*$) she would have the income–effort combination β on $P(E_f)$. Consider the line W^*W^* which has slope w and is tangent to $P(E_f)$ at β. If she decides to put $E = E_f^*$ of her effort into her firm and also to sell some of her effort on the entrepreneurial labour market, she would move rightwards up the line W^*W^*. On the other hand, she could decide to reduce her effort, while keeping the amount of effort in the firm constant at E_f^* by buying effort from the market equal to $E_f^* - E$. She would then move leftwards down W^*W^*. Thus the line W^*W^* is the constraint along which she can transact in the managerial labour market, given that she has

Figure 7.9

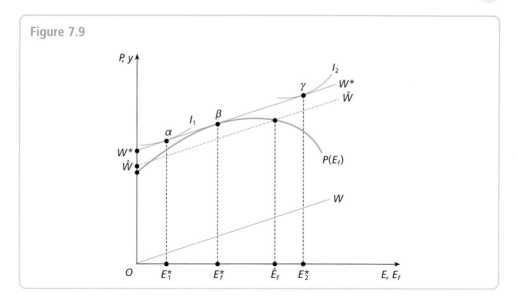

fixed the input into her firm at the profit-maximizing level E_f^*. She will choose a point on W^*W^* which gives her the largest utility. Notice that, if she had fixed E_f at some other level which did not maximize profit, the labour market opportunity line along which she could transact would lie below W^*W^*. For example, with $E_f = \hat{E}_f$, she would be on the market opportunity line $\hat{W}\hat{W}$. Since she can achieve a higher indifference curve on W^*W^* than on $\hat{W}\hat{W}$, she will wish to maximize the profit from her firm.

The entrepreneur's optimal position on W^*W^* depends on her preferences. There are three types of solution:

(a) An indifference curve like I_1 is tangent to W^*W^* at α. She supplies effort E_1^* and sets the level of effort used in the firm at $E_f = E_f^*$. This solution could be achieved by putting E_1^* of her effort into the firm and then buying in $E_f^* - E_1^*$ from the labour market. Equivalently, she could buy in all the effort required for her firm and sell E_1^* of her labour on the market. We have assumed that she is indifferent to whether she works in her own firm or for someone else, so the model serves only to predict the level of input into her firm and her total effort supply, not how she divides her effort between working for herself and for others.

(b) An indifference curve like I_2 is tangent to W^*W^* at γ. She sets $E_f = E_f^*$ and supplies E_2^* of her effort. This solution could be achieved by supplying E_2^* of her own effort to her firm and then selling $E_2^* - E_f^*$ of her effort on the market.

(c) An indifference curve (not shown) is tangent to W^*W^* at β. This solution could be achieved by her supplying all the effort required for her firm and neither buying nor selling labour in the market.

The crucial result of this analysis is the *separation* between the production decision of the entrepreneur in her role as owner of the firm and the decision of the entrepreneur in her role as effort supplier. (This separation appears again in Chapter 11 when we examine investment and consumption choices, which also involve a decision-maker who has *both production and exchange opportunities*.) The production decision (E_f) depends on the productive opportunities embodied in $P(E)$ and on the market price of effort w. The preferences of the entrepreneur as regards income and her effort have no influence on her production decision and affect only her effort supply.

The existence of the market in entrepreneurial effort establishes an objective opportunity cost of effort used in the firm and enables the entrepreneur to separate the production decision from the effort supply decision. Profit maximization is not a special case *if* there is a market in effort. Chapter 20 is devoted to analysis of the difficulties which must be overcome if such markets are to function effectively.

EXERCISE 7E

1. How is the entrepreneur's decision altered if she has an endowed income $\bar{y}$ which she gets irrespective of whether she supplies effort to her firm or elsewhere?

2. Show that if the entrepreneur has the *quasi-linear* utility function $u = g(E) + y$, with $g' < 0$, $g'' < 0$, her effort choice will always maximize profit.

3. Suppose that the entrepreneur's concave production function is $q = F(E, z)$, where z is an input bought at a constant price p_z and q is output sold at a constant price p. Assume there is no market for effort.

   (a) Derive the entrepreneurial firm's output supply and input demand functions.

   (b) Are the entrepreneur's input and output responses to changes in p and p_z different from those of the competitive firm examined in earlier chapters?

   (c) Describe the long-run equilibrium if there is free entry into the entrepreneur's industry.

4. What are the consequences of assuming that, although the entrepreneur dislikes supplying effort, other things being equal she prefers to work for herself rather than for someone else?

5. A physician has a number of private patients, whom he can arrange in order of fee per minute spent in attendance, from highest to lowest. He may also work in the state health service, at a given fee per unit time. Adapting Fig. 7.9 to this case, state necessary and sufficient conditions under which he would attend private patients *and* work for the state health service. Suppose that he is now forced to choose to work *either* privately *or* for the state health service. Analyse the determinants of his choice, indicating also the effects on his income and total supply of effort. Finally, suppose that a special tax is levied on his earnings from private practice. Analyse the consequences.

F. Labour-managed firms

In the standard model of the capitalist firm in earlier sections, workers are paid a fixed market-determined wage in exchange for their labour. The surplus of revenue over all payments to input suppliers accrues to the owners of the firm. However, there are many firms in which the workers own the firm, in the sense that they are rewarded for supplying labour by a share in the surplus of revenue over payments to all the non-labour inputs. Examples of such labour cooperatives or labour-managed firms (LMF) include kibbutzim in Israel, Basque industrial firms and partnerships of professionals such as lawyers. In this section we analyse the behaviour of such firms, and compare them with those of the standard capitalist firm, by outlining a model of the LMF first formulated by Ward (1958) and Vanek (1970).

Suppose that each worker supplies a fixed number of hours of labour to the firm, so that we can ignore complications arising from variable labour supply by individual workers. The firm's short-run decision variable is the number of workers N who should be employed. The amount of capital K used in the firm is fixed. The firm's production function is $q = f(N, \bar{K})$, with $f_N > 0$, $f_{NN} < 0$. Assume that it sells into a perfectly competitive market with given price p. Let F denote the fixed cost payable for the firm's capital stock $\bar{K}$. Each worker receives an income y given by

$$y = (pq - F)/N \qquad \text{[F.1]}$$

i.e. since the workers own the firm they share its profits. Since each employee works fixed hours, all of them will wish the firm to maximize this income per worker. So, it solves

$$\max_N y = [pf(N, \bar{K}) - F]/N \qquad \text{[F.2]}$$

giving the first-order condition

$$pf_N(N^*, \bar{K}) = [pf(N^*, \bar{K}) - F]/N^* = y^* \qquad \text{[F.3]}$$

to determine optimal employment N^*. The firm sets employment at a level that equates the marginal value product of labour to income per worker. Employment will be expanded as long as an additional worker adds more to revenue than she is paid. Unlike the capitalist firm, each worker is paid a profit share rather than an externally determined market wage.

The comparative statics effect of a change in the market price p is startling. If we differentiate through [F.3] totally and rearrange, we obtain

$$\frac{\partial N}{\partial p} = \frac{-(f_N - f/N)}{f_{NN}} < 0 \qquad \text{[F.4]}$$

since $f_{NN} < 0$ implies $f_N < f/N$. An increase in the market price reduces the firm's employment level, and hence its output! The reason is illustrated in Fig. 7.10. When

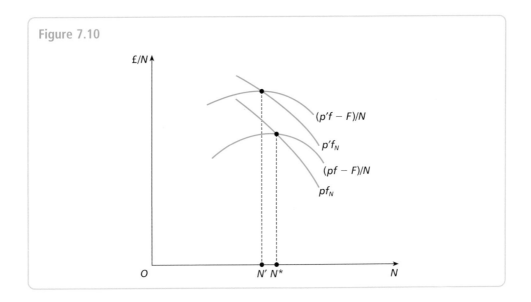

Figure 7.10

the market price rises from p to p', the marginal value product of labour curve, which is the labour demand curve of a capitalist firm, shifts up, but so also does the curve of income per worker. Because of the presence of the fixed cost, the latter curve shifts upwards by more than the former, and the result is that the equilibrium employment level, which, as [F.3] shows, is at the intersection of the two curves, falls. The cost of the marginal worker rises relative to the contribution to revenue she makes, and so a firm seeking to maximize income per worker would fire her!

Since this result follows directly from the formulation of the problem in [F.2], it is not surprising that criticism of the model has focused on the Ward–Vanek formulation of the firm's objective function. Suppose we were to formulate the objective of a capitalist firm as maximizing profit per unit of capital, which on the face of it does not seem at all unreasonable. Then the firm's demand for capital would have the same perverse characteristics as the LMF's demand for labour in the Ward–Vanek model. Why is the formulation of the maximand as the absolute amount of profit appropriate in one case, and profit per unit of input inappropriate in the other? The resolution of this point by Meade (1986) gives an interesting insight into the nature of the capitalist firm. The crucial issue is *discrimination*. The LMF in the Ward–Vanek model is a *non-discriminating* firm in the sense that a new worker receives the same income or profit share as existing workers. On the other hand, a capitalist firm *discriminates* among owners in the return it pays on capital: suppliers of new capital may well receive a lower rate of return than existing owners, and this creates an important difference in decisions on input levels.

To see this, consider the following simple example (based on Meade, 1986). The 10 original owners of a firm each put up £100 to provide an initial capital stock costing £1000 and yielding £2000 in profit. They have the opportunity to increase the profit of the company by £1600 if they install extra capital costing £1000. They turn to the stock market. The stock market rate of return is 20 per cent. That is, a firm with a profit of £3600 would be valued at £3600/1.2 = £3000. It follows that they can create 30 shares in the company, each worth £100, and sell 10 of them on the market to raise the required capital, dividing the remainder among themselves. The new shareholders will receive £1200 of the profit of the enlarged firm, to earn the market rate of return of 20 per cent. Each original owner is receiving £240 on his original investment of £100, a rate of return of 140 per cent. Clearly, it will pay the initial owners of the firm to expand capital, financed by issuing new shares, as long as the rate of return on the investment exceeds the market rate of return. In that case it makes sense to formulate the firm's maximand as the *absolute* difference between profit, discounted at the market rate of return, and the cost of the investment (this is simply the net present value of investment, extensively discussed in Chapter 11).

Suppose instead that there is a rule requiring *all* shareholders, old and new, to receive the same rate of return – the firm is non-discriminating in Meade's terminology. This implies that the £3600 profit of the enlarged firm would have to be divided equally between the suppliers of the initial £1000, and the suppliers of the next £1000: each £1 of capital subscribed now earns the same rate of return of 80 per cent. The initial shareholders now receive £1800 on this initial investment, which is less than the £2000 they receive if they do not bring in new shareholders. Thus they will not do so. This case corresponds to the Ward–Vanek LMF model.

This discussion suggests that the non-discriminating nature of the LMF is an important element in explaining its behaviour. For example, if new workers were hired at a market wage rate, rather than at a profit share equal to that of existing workers, then it is easy to show that employment will equate the marginal value product of labour to the wage rate and the perverse effects of changes in the output price disappear. (See Question 2 in the Exercises.)

Other critics of the Ward–Vanek model focus on the narrow specification of the objective function which neglects social and ideological aspects of labour cooperatives. An LMF may have wider goals, in particular a concern with employment as such, than can be captured by maximization of the income of the representative worker. For example, labour cooperatives often originate in an attempt to maintain employment in a firm that has gone bankrupt under conventional ownership.

To bring out the implications of such objectives, suppose that there is a given population of G workers available to be employed in an LMF. If one of these workers is unemployed, she receives an income of b (say, unemployment benefit). The LMF has a *social* objective, which is the maximization of the total income accruing to all G workers. As in the Ward–Vanek model, the income of an employed worker is $y = [pf(N, \bar{K}) - F]/N$. The firm's objective is now

$$\max_N Ny + (G - N)b \tag{F.5}$$

yielding the first-order condition

$$(y^* - b) + (pf_N - y^*) = 0 \tag{F.6}$$

$$\Rightarrow pf_N(N^*, \bar{K}) = b \quad \text{for } N^* < G \tag{F.7}$$

As long as an extra worker adds more to the firm's revenue than b, *total* income is increased by employing her. Moreover, differentiating through [F.7] now gives

$$\partial N^*/\partial p = -f_N/f_{NN} > 0 \tag{F.8}$$

and an increase in the market price increases employment in the firm. Figure 7.11 illustrates this model (and shows also a solution where, for a low $b = b'$, $N^* = G$ and so $pf_N > b$, in which case $\partial N^*/\partial p = 0$).

Since workers will supply labour to the LMF, rather than remain unemployed, if they receive an income of at least b from the firm, we can regard the 'curve' *bea* as a

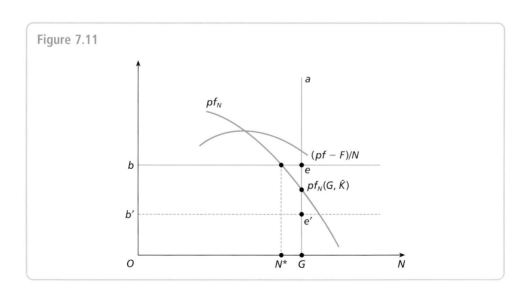

Figure 7.11

supply curve of labour. A conventional capitalist firm would also presumably be able to hire up to G workers by paying a wage of b and it would maximize profit by employing workers up to the point where $pf_N = b$. Thus the LMF with the social objective [F.5] employs the same number of workers as a profit-maximizing firm. However, if the supply curve was $b'e'a$ the workers would be better off with an LMF than working for a capitalist firm. With the supply curve $b'e'a$ both types of firm would use the same number of workers G. The LMF would pay them each an income of $pf_N(G, \bar{K})$. But since G workers would be forthcoming for b', the capitalist firm would only need to pay each of them $b' < pf_N(G, \bar{K})$. In this case the difference in objectives does make a difference because the LMF with the social objective does not attempt to exploit its monopsony power to keep the wage down to b'. Thus we have another example of the general lesson of this chapter: whether a firm will behave like a conventional profit maximizer will depend both on its objectives and on its environment.

There are many other non-standard models in which firms may not seek to maximize profit because their owners are interested in other aspects of the firm's behaviour or are unable to fully control them to ensure profit maximization. The exercises ask you to investigate the implications of the fact that the owners of firms are often consumers of their products. The sales maximization and expense preference models, proposed by Baumol (1959) and Williamson (1964) respectively, are two examples of what may happen when managers are imperfectly controlled by the firm's owners. (Chapter 20 examines why control may be imperfect.) 'Alternative' models of the firm are of interest in their own right and also deepen our understanding of the conventional theory by focusing attention on what is required for the firm to pursue profit maximization.

EXERCISE 7F

1. Derive the results for the Ward–Vanek model in the case in which labour is the only input, so that $\bar{K} = F = 0$.

2. Suppose there are N_I 'inside workers' who control the decisions of the firm. They share the firm's profit equally among themselves. All other workers are hired at the competitive market wage rate. Thus we have a 'discriminating LMF'. Analyse its employment choice and the effect on this of changes in the output price.

3. The Ward–Vanek model could be interpreted as maximizing the utility of the 'representative worker', where this utility is linear in income and defined on no other variable. Suppose instead that each of the N workers may work l hours, and that each possesses the identical quasi-linear utility function $v(y) - l$. Analyse the LMF's choice of N and l when it seeks to maximize the *utility* of the representative worker. What are the effects of a change in the output price in this case? (*Hint*: write the production function as $f(Nl, \bar{K})$.)

4. *Consumers as owners.* A firm is the only producer of a good x, which sells at a price p and costs $c(x)$ to produce. The ith shareholder in the firm receives the share θ_i of its profit $\pi = px - c(x)$, but may also consume its product. Individual i has the utility function $u^i(x_i, y_i)$ where x_i is consumption of the firm's product and y_i expenditure on all other goods and services (a composite commodity with a price of 1). Assume that all consumer-owners have preferences such that their income elasticity of demand for the firm's product is zero. The budget constraint of the consumer-owner is $\bar{y}_i + \theta_i \Pi \geq y_i + px_i$, where $\bar{y}_i$ is income other than from the firm.

(a) Show that, in their role as consumers, owner-consumers will act as if they each faced different prices $\hat{p}_i = p - \theta_i(p - c')$ where c' is the firm's marginal cost.

(b) Show that the ith consumer-owner will wish the firm to set a price satisfying

$$\frac{p - c'}{p} = \frac{(\theta_i - \delta_i)}{\theta_i} \frac{1}{e}$$

where $\delta_i = x_i/x$ is the ratio of i's consumption to the total output of the firm and e is the price elasticity of demand for the firm's product. (Compare this with the standard monopoly price marginal cost margin in Chapter 9, section B.) Interpret this result: When will i wish the firm to maximize profit? Will i ever wish the price to be greater than the profit-maximizing level, or less than marginal cost? When will owners be able to agree on what price the firm should set?

5. *Taxpayer-consumers and public sector firms.* Suppose that the firm in the previous question is a public sector firm and that the public sector budget constraint is $G = \Pi + t\bar{y}$, where G is fixed government expenditure, $\bar{y} = \Sigma_i \bar{y}_i$ is the total income of the individuals in the economy and t is the proportional income tax rate. Thus increases in Π reduce the rate of income tax. Taxpayer-consumers have the budget constraint $\bar{y}_i(1 - t) \geqslant y_i + px_i$. What price will the ith taxpayer-consumer wish the public sector firm to set? (*Hint*: show that the previous analysis can be used with $\theta_i = \bar{y}_i/\bar{y}$.)

6. *Consumer cooperatives.* Consider the firm in Question 4 being operated as a consumer cooperative in which all consumers are members. The profit is distributed to consumer-members by giving them a share equal to the ratio of their expenditure to the total revenue of the firm. Hence $\theta_i = px_i/px = x_i/x$ and consumers get a 'dividend' of $\Pi x_i/x$. Show that consumer-members (a) act as if they were faced with a price equal to average cost $c(x)/x$ and (b) do not care *what* price the firm sets. (c) Why do consumers not wish to see $p = c'$ even though $\theta_i = \delta_i$?

The theory of a competitive market

In preceding chapters we considered models of the optimal choices of consumers and firms. In these models, prices were always taken as parameters outside the control of the individual decision-taker. We now examine how these prices are determined by the interaction of the decisions of such 'price-taking' individuals. Since the interaction takes place through markets, we examine theories of markets whose participants act as price-takers, that is, of *competitive markets*. In later chapters we examine markets in which some of the decision-takers believe that their actions influence the price, and allow for this in making their decisions.

In Chapters 6 and 7 we drew a distinction between production and supply in the short run and in the long run. We maintain that distinction in market analysis, since supply conditions are an important determinant of the market outcome. We again think of demand and supply as rates of flow per unit time. The short run is the period over which firms have fixed capacity. In the long run all inputs are variable. For example, if it takes a year to plan and implement capacity changes then the short run is this year and the long run is next year. Since decisions for the long run are necessarily *planning* decisions, expectations must come into the picture. So should uncertainty, but we postpone consideration of it to later chapters of the book.

The chapter adopts a *partial equilibrium* approach: a single market is considered in isolation. This is not entirely satisfactory, since there may be interactions between markets. For example, we shall see that in aggregating firms' supply curves to obtain a market supply curve we may wish to take account of the effect of expansion of aggregate market output on the prices of inputs used by the firms. A general equilibrium analysis in which market interactions are fully taken into account is provided in Chapter 12. The justification for a partial equilibrium analysis is that it is simple and can give useful insights. Moreover, the key issues concerning the existence and stability of equilibrium can be introduced in a particularly simple context.

A. Short-run equilibrium

Let $x_i = D_i(p)$ be the ith consumer's demand for the commodity at price p and

$$x = \sum_i x_i = \sum_i D_i(p) = D(p) \qquad \text{[A.1]}$$

be the market demand function. The short-run supply function of firm j is

$$y_j = s_j(p, w) \qquad \text{[A.2]}$$

where y_j is the output of firm j and w is the price of the variable input.

It might appear that we could proceed to obtain a market supply function by aggregating the firms' supply functions as we did the consumers' demand functions in [A.1], but this is not in general the case. In deriving the *firm's* supply function in

Figure 8.1

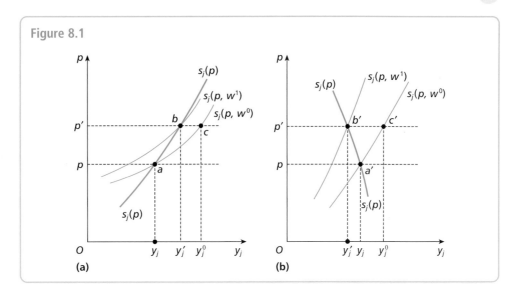

(a)   (b)

Chapter 6 we assumed input prices constant. This was a natural assumption to make, since any one firm in a competitive 'industry' (defined as the set of all producers of a given commodity) could be expected to be faced with perfectly elastic input supply curves. Then, as its output price is raised, the firm could expand its desired production and input levels without raising input prices. The assumption may not be appropriate for the industry as a whole, however: as the price at which they can sell their outputs rises for all firms, expansion in production and input demands may raise input prices because the increase in demand for inputs is no longer insignificant, and input supply functions have positive slopes to the industry as a whole.

Denote the total amount of the variable input used by the industry by $z(y)$ ($z'(y) > 0$). If

$$w = w(z(y)) \qquad\qquad [A.3]$$

with $w'(z) > 0$, there are *pecuniary external diseconomies*: an increase in the total output of firms in the industry increases the price of an input.

The consequences for the firm's actual supply are shown in Fig. 8.1. In the figure, price is assumed to rise from p to p'. The firm's initial supply ($\equiv SMC$) curve is in each case $s_j(p, w^0)$. If simultaneous expansion by all firms raises input prices from w^0 to w^1, the marginal cost curves and short-run supply curves of each firm must rise. Figure 8.1(a) shows one possible result of the expansion of firms in response to the higher price. The short-run supply curve has risen to $s_j(p, w^1)$ and so at price p' the firm will want to supply y_j' and not y_j^0. Hence the points on the firm's supply curve corresponding to p and p', when *all* firms expand, are a and b respectively and $s_j(p)$ is the locus of all such price–supply pairs. Clearly, the firm's *effective market supply curve* $s_j(p)$ will be less elastic than its *ceteris paribus* supply curve $s_j(p, w)$. They would coincide if input prices were not bid up by simultaneous expansion of output by all firms (and there were no technological externalities – see Question 2).

In (b) of the figure a more extreme case is shown. The increase in input prices causes a sufficient shift in the firm's *SMC* curve to make the post-adjustment output y_j' actually less than y_j, and so its effective market supply curve s_j has a negative slope. Thus, although the 'law of diminishing returns' ensures that each firm's *ceteris paribus* supply curve has a positive slope this is not sufficient to ensure that the firm's effective supply curve has a positive slope, if input prices increase with the expansion of outputs of all firms.

Denoting the effective industry supply function by $y(p)$ and substituting [A.3] in [A.2] gives the effective supply function of firm j:

$$y_j = s_j(p, w(z(y(p)))) = s_j(p) \qquad [\text{A.4}]$$

and summing gives the effective industry supply function

$$y = \sum_j y_j = \sum_j s_j(p) = s(p) \qquad [\text{A.5}]$$

Differentiating [A.4] with respect to the market price gives the effective supply response of firm j (after allowing for the effect of the increase in w induced by the change in output of all firms) as

$$\frac{dy_j}{dp} = s_{jp} + s_{jw} w'(z)z'(y)\frac{dy}{dp} = s_j'(p) \gtreqless 0 \qquad [\text{A.6}]$$

Since $s_{jp} = \partial s_j(p, w)/\partial p > 0$ and $s_{jw} = \partial s_j/\partial w < 0$ we see that the firm's effective supply could be increasing or decreasing in p.

The change in industry supply as a result of the increases in p is the sum of the effective changes in the firms' supplies and so from [A.5] and [A.6].

$$\frac{dy}{dp} = \sum_j \frac{dy_j}{dp} = \sum_j s_{jp} + w'z'\frac{dy}{dp}\sum_j s_{jw} \qquad [\text{A.7}]$$

Since $s_{jp} > 0$ and $w' > 0$, $z' > 0$, $s_{jw} < 0$, solving for dy/dp gives

$$\frac{dy}{dp} = \frac{\sum_j s_{jp}}{1 - w'z'\sum_j s_{jw}} > 0 \qquad [\text{A.8}]$$

Thus the effective industry supply curve is positively sloped despite the fact that some of the firms may have negatively sloped effective supply curves. The slope of the market supply function depends on the extent to which increases in input demands increase input prices and the consequent increases in marginal costs at all output levels. Note that at a market supply $s = s(p)$, i.e. a point on this supply function, each firm's marginal cost is exactly equal to p, given that all output adjustments have been completed. We define p as the *supply price* of the corresponding rates of output y_j since it is the price at which each firm would be content to supply – and to go on supplying – the output y_j. At any greater price firms would find it profitable to expand production; at any lower price, they would wish to contract.

Figure 8.2 shows a number of possible situations which might arise when we put the market supply function together with the demand function. In (a) we show a 'well-behaved' case. The price p^*, with demand x^* equal to supply y^*, is obviously an equilibrium, since sellers are receiving the price they require for the output they are producing, and this output is being taken off the market by buyers at that price. There is no reason either for sellers to change their output (since each $y_i^* = s_i(p^*)$ maximizes i's profit at price p^*) or for buyers to change the amount they buy.

Figure 8.2(b) represents a case which could arise when there is a certain kind of discontinuity in the supply curve $s(p)$. Recall from Chapter 7 that when price falls below average variable cost (AVC) a profit-maximizing firm will produce zero output.

Figure 8.2

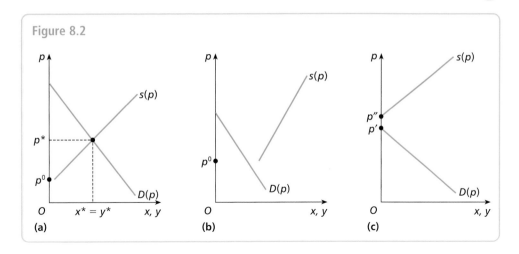

If all firms have identical $AVCs$, they will all produce zero output at the same price. Hence, at some critical price, shown as p^0 in the figure, supply may suddenly drop to zero. Thus there is a discontinuity in the short-run supply function at p^0. If it happens that the demand curve has the position shown, there is no equilibrium. Individual buyers would be prepared to offer individual sellers prices in excess of p^0 for some output but, if firms respond by starting up production, they flood the market and price must fall to a level below p^0. Discontinuities cause problems for the existence of equilibrium. Note, however, that continuity is sufficient but not necessary: if $D(p)$ were higher and intersected $s(p)$, as in part (a) of the figure, the discontinuity at p^0 would present no difficulty.

In (c) we show a third possibility. Suppose that firms do not all have the same AVC, but instead are evenly distributed over a range of $AVCs$, with the minimum point of the lowest AVC curve being equal to p''. If there are many sellers, and each seller is an insignificant part of the market, we can then take the $s(p)$ curve as continuous, with intercept at p''. However, at price $p' < p''$, demand is zero – no one would be prepared to pay p' or more for this good. It follows that equilibrium in this market implies a zero output and a price in the interval $[p', p'']$ – the highest price any buyer would pay is insufficient to cover the AVC of the firm with the lowest minimum AVC. We have a 'non-produced good' which firms would supply if the price were high enough, but which nobody wants to buy at such a price. The reader will find it instructive at this point to construct the *excess demand functions*

$$z(p) = D(p) - s(p) \tag{A.9}$$

in these three cases, and illustrate them in a price–excess demand graph of the type shown in Fig. 8.3.

Figure 8.2(b) suggests that a discontinuity in a supply or demand function – and thus in the excess demand function – may imply that there is no equilibrium. This is a matter of some concern, since our theory of the market predicts the market outcome to be the *equilibrium* outcome, and raises the question: what do we have to assume to *ensure* that the market has an equilibrium? In Chapter 11, we consider this question for the entire system of markets. To take the case of one market is to give only a provisional answer to the question since we ignore the interdependence

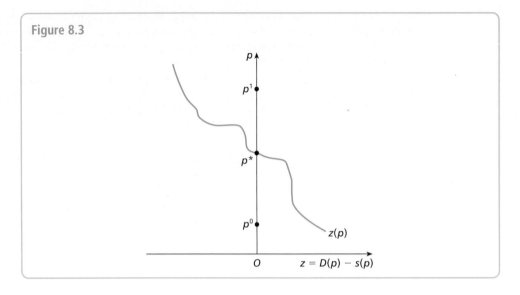

Figure 8.3

among markets. Nevertheless, it is instructive to consider the existence question in the simple context of one market.

Figure 8.2 shows that discontinuity is a problem. Is it then enough to assume that $z(p)$ is a continuous function of p? Clearly not. An equilibrium is a price $p* > 0$ such that $z(p*) = 0$. If $z(p) < 0$, or $z(p) > 0$, for all $p > 0$, then $z(p)$ may be continuous but we will not have an equilibrium. This suggests the following *existence theorem for a single market*. If

(a) the excess demand function $z(p)$ is continuous for $p \geqslant 0$,

(b) there exists a price $p^0 > 0$ such that $z(p^0) > 0$, and

(c) there exists a price $p^1 > 0$ such that $z(p^1) < 0$,

then there exists an equilibrium price $p* > 0$ such that $z(p*) = 0$.

The intuition is clear from Fig. 8.3. If the excess demand curve is continuous and passes from a point at which excess demand is positive to a point at which excess demand is negative, it *must* cross the price axis, giving an equilibrium price.

The significance of the equilibrium price is that it induces buyers to demand exactly the output that results from individual sellers' profit-maximizing decisions at that price. Plans are all mutually consistent and can be realized. We now turn to the equally important question of the stability of a market in the short-run.

EXERCISE 8A

1. *External pecuniary economies.* Derive the market and firm effective supply functions on the assumption that input prices fall as all firms expand output. What could account for this?

2. *Technological external diseconomies* exist when an increase in industry output increases all firms' costs. For example, owners of oil wells drilled into the same oil field may find that it is more expensive to produce any given output from their well when total output from the field is larger. Congestion of fishing grounds is another example. Suppose that, as the industry output expands, all firms' short-run *marginal* costs are increased. Apply the

analysis of pecuniary diseconomies to show that the effective supply of some firms may be negatively sloped but the effective industry supply curve will be positively sloped. (*Hint*: write the supply function of firm j as $y_j = s_j(p, a)$ where $a(y)$, $a' > 0$ is a shift parameter reflecting the external diseconomy: $s_{ja} < 0$.)

3. Suppose that (a) the market supply function $s(p)$ is continuous and non-decreasing in p with $s(p) > 0$ for $p > p^0$; (b) the demand function $D(p)$ is continuous, non-increasing in p, with $D(p) \to 0$ as $p \to \infty$ (because consumers have finite incomes) and $D(p^0) > 0$. Are these assumptions sufficient to ensure the existence of an equilibrium in the market?

4. The supply curve of labour $s(w)$ may be backward bending for some range of wage rates (recall section 4C). Does this mean that there may be no equilibrium in the market for labour even if the labour demand curve $D(w)$ is continuous and strictly decreasing in w?

5. *Incidence of taxes.* Consider a market in which a per unit tax t is levied so that $p_s = p_c - t$, where p_s is the price received by suppliers and p_c the price paid by consumers. The supply function is $s(p_s)$ and the demand function $D(p_c)$.

    (a) Show that the *economic incidence* of the tax (its effects on p_s, p_c and the quantity traded) are independent of the *legal incidence*, i.e. whether producers or consumers must pay the tax to the government.

    (b) Show that legal incidence does affect economic incidence if there is a binding maximum price in the market.

    (c) What happens if there is a binding minimum price?

B. Stability of equilibrium

Stability is an important characteristic of a market since predictions of the effects of changes in supply or demand conditions typically take the form of comparisons of the equilibrium before and after the change. Stability, like the question of existence considered in section A, is also relevant for analyses of welfare, which typically focus on properties of equilibria. Such analyses would have less point if one could not be sure that the market had an equilibrium to which it would tend.

A market is *stable* if, whenever the market price is not an equilibrium price, the price converges over time to an equilibrium price. The market is *locally stable* if it tends to an equilibrium when it starts off in a small neighbourhood of that equilibrium and *globally stable* when it tends to some equilibrium price whatever its initial disequilibrium price.

In general we are more interested in global stability and whether the market will eventually end up in some equilibrium. Local stability does not imply global stability but, if there is only one equilibrium, global stability implies local stability. If a market has multiple equilibria it may be locally stable in the neighbourhood of some equilibria and unstable in the neighbourhood of others. Global stability then implies that at least one of the multiple equilibria is locally stable, though others may be unstable. Even if all the equilibria were locally stable this would not imply that the market was globally stable.

Formally a market is stable if

$$\lim_{t \to \infty} p(t) = p^\star$$

where $p^\star$ is an equilibrium price, $t \geqslant 0$ is time, $p(t)$ is the time path of price and the initial price $p(0) \neq p^\star$.

The analysis of stability is concerned with a market's *disequilibrium* behaviour and requires a theory of how markets operate out of equilibrium. Any such theory rests on answers to three fundamental questions:

1. How do the market price or prices respond to non-zero excess demand?
2. How do buyers and sellers obtain information on the price or prices being offered and asked in the market?
3. At what point does trading actually take place, i.e. when do buyers and sellers enter into binding contracts?

These questions are important because answers to them may differ and differences in the answers lead to significant differences in the models of disequilibrium adjustment to which the theories give rise. In questions 1 and 2 we use the phrase 'price or prices' because at this stage we prefer to keep our options open. Some theories may provide for a single price to prevail throughout the market even out of equilibrium, whereas others allow there to be differences in prices offered by buyers and asked by sellers throughout the market. Whether or not a unique price will always prevail depends on the answers to questions 2 and 3.

To begin with we consider two continuous time models of market adjustment. The first, known as the *tâtonnement process* (tâtonnement can be interpreted as 'groping') was proposed by Walras. The second, which it can be argued is better suited to markets with production, was suggested by Marshall.

The tâtonnement process (TP)

The TP is an idealized model of how a market may operate out of equilibrium, in the sense that it may not *describe* the way a market works, but under certain conditions a market may operate *as if* its adjustment process were a TP. There is a central individual, who can be called the market 'umpire', and who has the role of a market coordinator. He announces to all decision-takers a single market price (the answer to question 2), which they take as a parameter in choosing their planned supplies or demands. They each inform the umpire of their choices and he aggregates them to find the excess demand at the announced price. He then revises the announced price by the following rule (the answer to question 1):

$$\frac{dp}{dt} = \lambda z(p(t)) \qquad \lambda > 0 \qquad\qquad \text{[B.1]}$$

that is, he changes the price at a rate proportionate to the excess demand. No trading takes place unless and until equilibrium is reached (the answer to question 3) at which time sellers deliver their planned supply and buyers take their planned demand. Notice that in this process there is no contact between buyers and sellers out of equilibrium – everything is mediated through the umpire.

Figure 8.4 shows three possible market excess demand functions. In (a), the excess demand curve has a negative slope. If, initially, the umpire announces the price $p^0 < p^*$, excess demand will be positive and he will revise the announced price upwards towards p^*; if the announced price were above p^* it would be revised downwards. Since these movements are always in the equilibrating direction, from *wherever* the process starts, equilibrium will be globally stable.

Figure 8.4

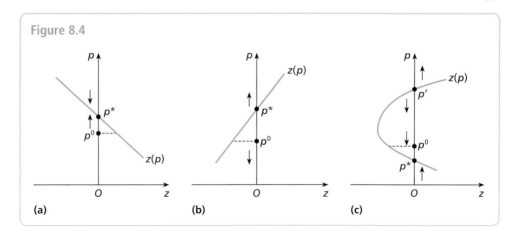

(a)   (b)   (c)

In (b), the excess demand curve has a positive slope. If the announced price is initially at p^0 the umpire will now *reduce* price, since $z < 0$, and hence the TP leads away from equilibrium. A similar result would occur if the initial price were above p^*. Hence in this market the equilibrium is globally unstable.

In (c) we have a somewhat more complex case. The excess demand curve is *backward bending*, having a negative slope over one range of prices and a positive slope over another. In this case, if the initial price were anywhere in the interval $0 \leqslant p < p'$, the TP would converge to the equilibrium p^*. If, however, the initial price was $p'' > p'$, the market would move away from equilibrium, since excess demand is positive for $p > p'$ and so price would be increased. Therefore the market is not globally stable, since an initial point sufficiently far from the equilibrium p^* would lead away from market equilibrium. The market has two equilibrium positions, one at p^* and one at p'; the former is locally but not globally stable, the latter is locally (and therefore globally) unstable.

From this discussion we can deduce the following *stability conditions*, i.e. sufficient conditions for the TP to be stable:

(a) equilibrium is globally stable if excess demand is positive whenever price is less than its equilibrium value and negative when price is above its equilibrium value;

(b) equilibrium is locally stable if the condition (a) holds for prices in a small neighbourhood of an equilibrium.

For a more formal analysis of stability we can use a *distance function*, which measures the distance between two points. Thus define

$$\delta(p(t), p^*) = (p(t) - p^*)^2 \qquad \text{[B.2]}$$

which measures the distance between an equilibrium price p^* and some other price $p(t)$. (Note that $\delta(p(t), p^*) > 0 \Leftrightarrow p(t) \neq p^*$.) A necessary condition for the time path of price $p(t)$ to converge to p^* is that $d\delta/dt < 0$, i.e. the distance between the price path and p^* is falling through time. Differentiating we have

$$\frac{d\delta}{dt} = 2(p(t) - p^*)\frac{dp}{dt} = 2(p(t) - p^*)\lambda z(p(t)) \qquad \text{[B.3]}$$

from [B.1]. Then clearly $d\delta/dt < 0$ if and only if $(p(t) - p^\star)$ and $z(p(t))$ have opposite signs, as in the stability condition. Note that this is true regardless of the value of λ: the 'speed of adjustment' parameter determines only how fast, and not whether, the TP converges to equilibrium.

Is the condition also *sufficient* for convergence, however? It may seem 'intuitively obvious' that it is, but consider the example of the function $y = a + 1/t$. Here we have $dy/dt < 0$, but $\lim_{t\to\infty} y = a$. So we have to provide a further argument to justify the claim that $\delta(p(t), p^\star)$ is *not* bounded away from zero under the TP.

We do this by establishing a contradiction. Suppose, without loss of generality, that $p(0) > p^\star$, and suppose that $\lim_{t\to\infty} p(t) = \bar{p}$ where $\bar{p} > p^\star$. The interval $[p(0), \bar{p}]$ is non-empty, closed and bounded and the function $d\delta/dt$ is continuous, so at some t we must have that $d\delta/dt$ takes on a maximum, by Weierstrass' Theorem (Appendix C). Call this maximum $s^\star$. Note that, since for $p(t) \neq p^\star$ we must have $d\delta/dt < 0$, then $s^\star < 0$ also. For any arbitrary $t = \bar{t}$, integrate to obtain:

$$\int_0^{\bar{t}} \frac{d\delta}{dt}\, dt = \delta(p(\bar{t}), p^\star) - \delta(p(0), p^\star) \tag{B.4}$$

and

$$\int_0^{\bar{t}} s^\star\, dt = s^\star \bar{t} \tag{B.5}$$

Then by definition of $s^\star$ we must have

$$\delta(p(\bar{t}), p^\star) - \delta(p(0), p^\star) \leqslant s^\star \bar{t} \tag{B.6}$$

or

$$\delta(p(\bar{t}), p^\star) \leqslant s^\star \bar{t} + \delta(p(0), p^\star) \tag{B.7}$$

By choosing $\bar{t}$ large enough, we can make the right-hand side of [B.7] negative, implying we must have on the left-hand side a negative value of the distance function, which is impossible. Thus we have the contradiction.

This proof makes precise the intuition that, if $p(t)$ is always moving closer to $p^\star$ whenever $p(t) \neq p^\star$, *it cannot tend to anything other than* $p^\star$.

Marshall's process

Marshall suggested the following alternative to Walras' TP. Suppose that when sellers bring their output to market they sell it for whatever it will fetch. Refer to Fig. 8.5. If supply is less than the *equilibrium supply* $y^\star$ then the price buyers will be prepared to pay if it is auctioned off to the highest bidders, the *demand* price, p_D^0, exceeds the *supply price*, p_s^0. Conversely, if supply exceeds equilibrium supply, auctioning off the available supply causes demand price to fall below supply price. Marshall argued that when demand price p_D exceeds supply price p_s sellers will expand supply, and conversely when p_D is less than p_s. This is because p_s equals each seller's marginal cost, and so $p_D > p_s$ implies output expansion increases profits, while when $p_D < p_s$ profits are increased by an output contraction. This suggests the adjustment rule:

$$\frac{dy}{dt} = \lambda(p_D(y) - p_s(y)) \tag{B.8}$$

Figure 8.5

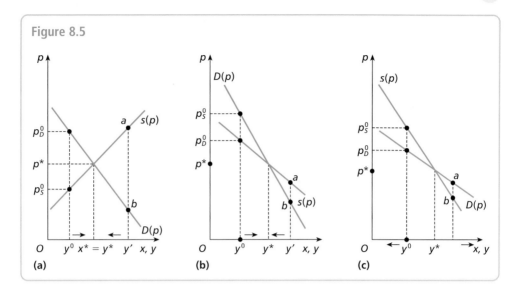

where $p_D(y)$ is the *inverse* demand function, giving demand price as a function of quantity supplied (= quantity traded at any t) and similarly, $p_s(y)$ is the *inverse* supply function (derived from the firm's marginal cost functions as before). Note that, at equilibrium quantity y^*, $p_D = p_s = p^*$.

Under what conditions is Marshall's process stable? If output expands when $p_D > p_s$ and contracts when $p_D < p_s$ then Fig. 8.5(a) suggests that, when the supply and demand curves have the usual slopes, the market is stable. Figure 8.5(b) and (c) show that, when the supply curve has a negative slope, the process is stable if the demand curve cuts the supply curve from above but *unstable* in the converse case. This is interesting, not only because backward bending supply curves are possible (recall section 3D), but also because the Walrasian TP has precisely the opposite outcomes in these cases. In Fig. 8.5(b), the corresponding excess demand function $z(p) = D(p) - s(p)$ increases with price and so the Walrasian TP would be unstable. In Fig. 8.5(c), $z(p)$ has a negative slope and so the Walrasian TP is stable. Thus although the two adjustment processes have the same outcomes in the 'standard case', it matters which we adopt in a 'non-standard' case.

To make the stability conditions for Marshall's process more precise, we again adopt a distance function approach. Define the distance function

$$\delta(y(t), y^*) = (y(t) - y^*)^2 \qquad \text{[B.9]}$$

Then

$$\frac{d\delta}{dt} = 2(y(t) - y^*)\frac{dy}{dt} = 2(y(t) - y^*)\lambda[p_D(t) - p_s(t)] \qquad \text{[B.10]}$$

using [B.8]. Then, for $d\delta/dt < 0$, we require $(y(t) - y^*)$ and $(p_D(t) - p_s(t))$ to have opposite signs, confirming the diagrammatic analysis. We can establish the sufficiency of this condition along similar lines to those used in the case of the TP process.

We have already noted that in 'non-standard' cases the Walrasian TP and Marshall's process have opposite implications for market stability – it matters whether we take price as adjusting to a difference in quantities, or quantity as adjusting to a difference in demand and supply prices. We can also compare the processes in terms of the answers to the three questions at the beginning of this section:

1. *Responsiveness of price to non-zero excess demand.* In the standard case of negatively sloped demand and positively sloped supply, both processes result in market price rising (falling) when there is positive (negative) excess demand. In the Walrasian case this happens directly through the TP; in the Marshallian case, it happens via the auction mechanism which establishes the demand price.

2. *Information on price(s).* In the TP, this is transmitted simultaneously to all buyers and sellers by the umpire; in Marshall's process, at each instant the auction mechanism rations off available output and the demand price is immediately made known. Buyers never need to know the supply price – sellers know their own marginal costs and so once the demand price is known an output change can result.

3. *When does trade take place?* In the TP, *only* at equilibrium; under Marshall's process, at every instant as available supply is auctioned off. Marshall's process has *trading out of equilibrium*, with an *efficient rationing rule*, so that available supply is auctioned off to the highest bidders. Alternatively, think of Marshall's process as consisting of a sequence of 'very short-run' or instantaneous equilibria, with a vertical supply curve at each of these equilibria, and the analysis then establishes conditions under which this sequence of instantaneous equilibria converges to a full equilibrium of supply and demand.

Which model is 'better' depends on which process captures more closely the way a particular market works. Walras' TP may seem unrealistic in its reliance on a central 'umpire' collecting buying and selling intentions and announcing an equilibrium price, but some markets, for example markets in stocks and shares, and minerals such as gold and silver, are highly organized with brokers who may function much as a Walrasian umpire.

There are two features of both models which are unsatisfactory in the light of observations of how many markets work. First, both processes are centralized: some device – the umpire or the auction mechanism – ensures that all buyers and sellers simultaneously face the same price. However, in many real markets, price formation is *decentralized*. Individual buyers meet, haggle and deal with individual sellers, and pressures of excess demand or supply exert their influence by causing sellers and buyers to bid prices up or down. If information on all the prices being offered and asked is fully and costlessly available throughout the market then this would be equivalent to a centralized adjustment process. But this is often not the case. Buyers and sellers have to seek each other out to find the prices at which they are prepared to trade, and this *search process* is costly.

Second, in neither model do buyers and sellers *form expectations* and act upon them. In the TP this possibility is simply excluded. In Marshall's process, sellers must make some forecast of future price in order to make decisions which determine their future supply, but this is not modelled explicitly, being subsumed in the adjustment rule [B.8]. In the rest of this section therefore we consider the explicit modelling of expectations in market adjustment processes.

Expectations and market stability

The concept of a *supply lag* is important in understanding the adjustment process in many markets and to bring out its implications we move from a continuous to a discrete treatment of time. It appears in its simplest form in the market for an agricultural good, say, potatoes. At some point in time a farmer decides on the acreage of potatoes to plant. Ignoring problems such as pests, disease and adverse weather, this determines the amount of potatoes she will put on the market some time later. Thus supply of potatoes at time t, q_s^t, depends on a decision taken at $t - 1$, where the time period is the length of time between planting and harvesting. We hypothesize that the acreage planted at $t - 1$ depends on the price the farmer expects to prevail at t. If all farmers behave like this the market supply function is given by

$$y_t = s(p_t^e) \qquad s' > 0 \qquad\qquad \text{[B.11]}$$

where p_t^e is the (assumed identical) price at t all farmers expect at $t - 1$. It is assumed that demand adjusts to price at t, and so the demand function is, as before,

$$x_t = D(p_t) \qquad\qquad \text{[B.12]}$$

To analyse the market we have to specify how price expectations are formed. The *naive expectations* hypothesis says that

$$p_t^e = p_{t-1} \qquad \text{all } t \qquad\qquad \text{[B.13]}$$

That is, farmers simply assume that the current price will continue to hold next period. This presents no problems if the market is in equilibrium over successive periods: the current period's equilibrium price is also next period's equilibrium price, so the farmers' naive price expectation is correct and supply and demand will be consistent:

$$D(p_t) = s(p_{t-1}^e) = s(p_t^\star) \qquad\qquad \text{[B.14]}$$

where $p_t^\star$ is the equilibrium price. Suppose, however, that between $t - 1$ and t there has been a demand shift, so that $p_{t-1}^\star$ is not the equilibrium price at t. The analysis of the subsequent disequilibrium behaviour in the market is illustrated in Fig. 8.6.

In (a), p_0 was the old equilibrium price but between $t = 0$ and $t = 1$ demand has shifted to $D(p)$. $y_1 = s(p_0)$ is the available supply at $t = 1$, and so when this is put on the market price rises to p_1, where $D(p_1) = y_1$. Farmers then expect p_1 to be

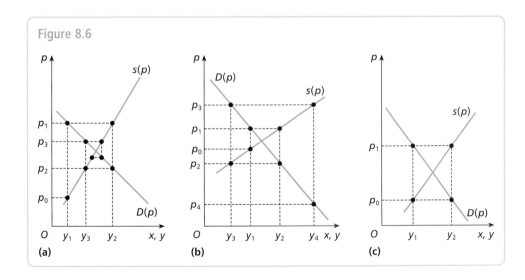

Figure 8.6

(a)

(b)

(c)

the market price at $t = 2$, so they plant their acreage accordingly and at $t = 2$ put $y_2 = s(p_1)$ on the market. This causes price to fall to p_2, inducing at $t = 3$ supply of y_3, and so on. We observe that the successive prices p_0, p_1, p_2, p_3 are converging on the new equilibrium, and so we conclude that the market is *stable*.

In (b) of the figure we have a *Cobweb cycle*. The process is the same as before: price is initially p_0, and so farmers supply $y_1 = s(p_0)$ at $t = 1$, causing price to rise to p_1. As a result farmers plant a larger acreage and at $t = 2$ put the supply $y_2 = s(p_1)$ on the market, causing price to fall to p_2, and so on. But now the sequence of prices $p_0, p_1, p_2, p_3, \ldots$ is moving away from equilibrium: the market is *unstable*. In (c) we show the remaining possibility, that price moves for ever between p_0 and p_1, and so, since it never converges to equilibrium, the market is *unstable*.

In Fig. 8.6 the supply and demand functions are linear. The difference between the stable and unstable cases is that, in the stable case (a), the demand curve is less steep (absolutely) than the supply curve, whereas in the unstable case (b) the converse is true. In (c) the slopes are exactly equal. More precisely, let the supply and demand functions be, respectively

$$y_t = a + bp_{t-1}, \qquad x_t = \alpha - \beta p_t \qquad \text{[B.15]}$$

Since at each t the market clears, $x_t = y_t$, we can use [B.15] to obtain the first-order linear difference equation

$$p_t = \frac{\alpha - a}{\beta} - \frac{b}{\beta} p_{t-1} \qquad \text{[B.16]}$$

For stability, the differences between successive prices (which are alternately positive and negative) should become successively smaller in *absolute value*. That is

$$-(p_{t+1} - p_t) < p_t - p_{t-1} \Rightarrow p_t - p_{t+1} < p_t - p_{t-1} \qquad \text{[B.17]}$$

(where, without loss of generality, we have assumed $p_{t+1} < p_t$ and so $p_{t-1} < p_t$). Then substituting from [B.16] gives

$$\left(\frac{\alpha - a}{\beta} - \frac{b}{\beta} p_{t-1} \right) - \left(\frac{\alpha - a}{\beta} - \frac{b}{\beta} p_t \right) < p_t - p_{t-1} \qquad \text{[B.18]}$$

and so

$$\frac{b}{\beta} (p_t - p_{t-1}) < p_t - p_{t-1} \qquad \text{[B.19]}$$

giving the stability condition

$$b < \beta \qquad \text{[B.20]}$$

Recall that b and β are the absolute values of the slopes of the supply and demand curves with respect to the *price* axes, and so [B.20] is the condition we derived from the diagram.

The naive expectations assumption is aptly named. Farmers believe that next period's price will be the same as the current period's, even though their belief is always shown to be wrong when the market is not in equilibrium. Further, in each period, the output which each farmer sells is not the profit maximizing output corresponding to the market price that actually prevails. To see this, note that the successive price–quantity pairs $(p_1, y_1), (p_2, y_2), \ldots$, in Fig. 8.6 are not on the market supply curve, implying that each seller's marginal cost is not equal to the market price at which the corresponding output is sold. Farmers always produce too little when market price is high, and too much when market price is low, relative to the quantities that maximize profit at those prices. Naive expectations lead to behaviour inconsistent with the farmers's objective of profit maximisation and we could call them irrational.

This reasoning led Muth (1962) to propose the theory of *rational expectations*. Suppose that it is possible to estimate accurately the market demand and supply functions (for simplicity we ignore the issue of random errors of estimation). Then, it would be possible to predict the equilibrium price in each period. Farmers would find it worth paying for such information because they can take more profitable production decisions. But then, if farmers' expectations consist of the actual market outcome, the market *will always be in equilibrium*. To see this, simply set $p_t^e = p_t^\star$ in the market supply function $s(p_t^e)$ and solve for the resulting equilibrium price from

$$D(p_t^\star, t) = s(p_t^\star) \qquad\qquad \text{[B.21]}$$

(where the time argument is included in the demand function to indicate that it may shift over time). This illustrates Muth's proposition: it is rational to take as one's expectation the predicted outcome of the market model. Here 'rational' means *profit maximizing*: no other farmer can increase profit by forming an expectation in any other way, given that all other farmers form their expectations this way (note the similarity to the concept of *Nash equilibrium* discussed in Chapter 15). This was certainly not true of the naive expectations assumption: if she believed that all other farmers simply extrapolated this period's price, the rational farmer would expand her potato acreage when current price is low and conversely.

The conclusion of the rational expectations hypothesis – that the market is always in equilibrium – implies that price fluctuations in the market are driven by shifts in the underlying supply and demand functions rather than by the expectations formation process as such. This is, at least in principle, a testable proposition. Certainly the rational expectations hypothesis is intellectually more appealing than the naive hypothesis, and we should note that forecasting and modelling markets are important areas of economic activity. Nevertheless, the hypothesis is a strong one and may not be appropriate for all markets.

EXERCISE 8B

1. Compare the stability properties of the Walrasian TP and Marshall's process when demand and supply curves both have positive slopes.

2. Do you think Cobweb cycles are most likely in the market for lettuce, coffee or lawyers?

3. *Correspondence principle: stability and comparative statics.* Consider a market with a continuous and differentiable supply function $s(p)$ and a continuous and differentiable demand function $D(p, a)$ where a is a shift parameter which increases demand: $D_a(p, a) > 0$. Assume that for each value of a there exists a p^0 and a p^1 such that $z(p, a) = D(p, a) - s(p) > 0$ for all $p \geqslant p^0$ and $z(p, a) < 0$ for all $p \leqslant p^1$. Thus there always exists an equilibrium price $p(a)$ satisfying $z(p, a) = 0$.

   (a) Show that an increase in a always increases the equilibrium price provided (i) the market adjustment process is the Walrasian TP and (ii) the initial equilibrium was stable.
       (*Hint*: differentiate the equilibrium condition totally with respect to a.)

   (b) What if the Marshallian adjustment process was used?

(c) Show that under the Walrasian TP an increase in a always increases the equilibrium price even if the initial equilibrium was unstable. (*Hint*: draw some diagrams and use the intermediate value theorem. Differentiating the equilibrium condition will give a misleading result.)

(d) Does the previous conclusion hold under the Marshallian adjustment process?

4. *Adaptive expectations.* Suppose that expectations are formed adaptively:
$p_t^e - p_{t-1}^e = k(p_{t-1} - p_{t-1}^e)$ $(0 < k < 1)$. Will the market converge to an equilibrium?

C. Long-run equilibrium

In Chapter 7 we saw that the *firm's* long-run supply curve is that part of its long-run marginal cost curve above its long-run average cost curve. There are several reasons why the market supply curve cannot be obtained simply by summing these supply curves:

(a) *External pecuniary effects.* As *all* firms vary output, input prices may change, causing each firm's cost curves to shift.

(b) *External technological effects.* Individual firms' cost curves shift as a result of expansion of scale by all firms leading to congestion or improvement in common facilities such as transport or communications.

(c) *Changes in the number of firms in the market.* As price rises firms which previously found it unprofitable to produce the commodity now find it profitable, and so invest in capacity and add to output. In a competitive market there are no barriers such as patents, legal restrictions, ownership of raw material sources, which impede the entry of new firms. A firm which at the going price just breaks even, with total revenue equal to long-run total cost (including the opportunity cost of capital and effort supplied by its owner(s)) is called a *marginal firm* at that price. One which makes an 'excess profit' (total revenue > total long-run opportunity costs) is called an *intra-marginal* firm, and one which would make a loss, but breaks even at a higher price, is called an *extra-marginal* firm. As price rises, marginal firms become intra-marginal and some extra-marginal firms enter.

It is therefore by no means assured that the long-run market supply curve will be positively sloped (see Questions 1, 2). However, in Fig. 8.7(c) we assume this to be the case. $S(p)$ shows how the rate of output varies with price when capacity is adjusted and the number of sellers may change. It should be noted that underlying this curve is a possibly complex set of adjustments, and the transition from one point on the curve to another is not so smooth and effortless as the curve suggests. It should be interpreted as showing the aggregate output which will be forthcoming at each price *after* all these adjustments have been made. Or, alternatively, it shows the price at which a given number of firms would remain in the industry, maintain their capacity and supply in aggregate a given rate of output. The p-coordinate of any point y is then the *long-run* supply price of that rate of output.

The long-run equilibrium is shown in Fig. 8.7(c) as the point (y^*, p^*). At this point firms are prepared to maintain the rate of supply y^*, and consumers are prepared to buy this output at price p^*. If, therefore, the short-run supply curve $s(p)$ was as shown in the figure, the short-run equilibrium we have earlier been examining would also be a long-run equilibrium. It would be maintained indefinitely in the absence of any change in demand, input prices or technology.

Figure 8.7

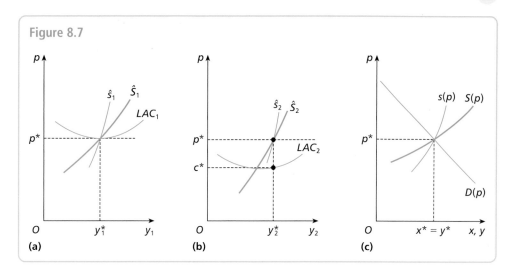

The other parts of the figure show the implications of the long-run equilibrium for two 'representative firms'. In (a), firm 1 is a marginal firm. At market price p^* it chooses a long-run profit-maximizing scale of output y_1^*, and at that output p^* is equal to its minimum long-run average cost. Firm 2, on the other hand, shown in (b) of the figure, is an intra-marginal firm; at its profit-maximizing scale of output y_2^*, its long-run average cost $c^* < p^*$, and it makes an excess profit equal to $(p^* - c^*)y_2^*$. However, such 'excess profits', which may be earned temporarily, will not persist indefinitely, but rather should be regarded as true opportunity costs to the firm in the long run.

The argument goes as follows: the fact that the intra-marginal firm's average costs are lower than those of a marginal firm must reflect the possession of some particularly efficient input, for example especially fertile soil or exceptionally skilful management. Since these generate excess profits, we expect other firms to compete for them, so that after a period long enough for contracts to lapse, the firm which currently enjoys the services of these super-productive inputs will have to pay them what they ask or lose them. The maximum these inputs can extract is the whole of the excess profit $(p^* - c^*)y_2^*$, and so what was a profit during the period when the contract was in force becomes a true opportunity cost to the firm after that time. Such excess profits are therefore called *quasi-rents*, to emphasize that they are not true long-run excess profits, but merely rents accruing to the contractual property rights in certain efficient input services, which become transformed into costs 'in the long run'. Once this transformation has taken place, the 'intra-marginal' firm's *LAC* curve will rise until its minimum point is equal to p^*. Hence in the long run *all* firms in the market will be marginal firms in the sense that they just break even.

Figure 8.7 illustrates the three conditions which must hold in long-run equilibrium:

1. Each firm in the market equates its long-run marginal cost to price, so that output maximizes profit.

2. For each firm price must equal long-run average cost (if necessary after quasi-rents have been transformed into opportunity costs) so that profits are zero and no entry or exit takes place.

3. Demand must equal supply.

Conditions (1) and (2) then imply that each firm produces at the minimum point of its long-run average cost curve, as Fig. 8.7(a) illustrates. This is a strong result on the efficiency of the competitive market equilibrium, since it implies that total market output is being produced at the lowest possible cost.

As with the short-run supply curve in Fig. 8.2(b), discontinuities in the long-run supply curve may imply that equilibrium does not exist. Suppose that

(a) all firms, whether currently in the market or not, have identical, U-shaped *LAC* curves as shown in Fig. 8.7(a);

(b) input prices do not vary with industry output.

Then, there could be a discontinuity in the long-run market supply curve at price p^* in Fig. 8.7. At any price below p^*, *all firms* would leave the market, and market supply will fall to zero, while at price p^* planned market supply is y_1^* multiplied by the number of firms which are capable of producing the good with the given *LAC* curve. This discontinuity could be avoided if there is some mechanism which selects potential suppliers in such a way as to ensure that any given market demand at price p^* is just met by the appropriate number of firms each producing at minimum long-run average cost. Then, the long-run market supply curve would be a horizontal line at price p^*: expansion of market output is brought about entirely by new entry rather than through output expansion by existing firms. Long-run equilibrium price cannot differ from p^*, and so is entirely *cost determined*. The level of demand determines only aggregate output and the equilibrium number of firms. Note that for a long-run market supply curve which is a continuous horizontal line we need the least-cost output of a firm (y_1^* in Fig. 8.7(a)) to be 'very small' relative to market demand, and the number of firms to be 'very large'.

More simply, if the technology of production is such that there is no range of outputs over which there are increasing returns to scale, then there is no discontinuity in market supply. For example, if all firms experience decreasing returns to scale at all outputs then long-run average and marginal cost curves will be everywhere upward sloping and their horizontal sum (taking into account any input price effects) will have an intercept on the price axis.

Alternatively, if we assume all firms have identical production functions with *constant* returns to scale, and face identical (constant) input prices, then the long-run market supply curve is again a horizontal straight line. Each firm's long-run marginal cost curve is a horizontal line and coincides with its long-run average cost curve, and these are at the same level for all firms. Then, the only possible equilibrium price is given by this common marginal = average cost so that price is again completely cost-determined. Demand again determines only the aggregate equilibrium market output. Note that, in such a market model, the equilibrium output of each firm, as well as the equilibrium number of firms producing in the market, are indeterminate.

Stability in the long-run

The analysis of the stability of long-run equilibrium in a competitive market must take into account the interaction between short- and long-run decisions of firms, the effects of new entry and the role of price expectations. We carry out the analysis for the case in which input prices increase with aggregate market output, and all firms have U-shaped cost curves. As shown in Fig. 8.8, the long-run market supply curve is upward sloping. It should be thought of as the locus of price–quantity points at which the long-run equilibrium conditions are satisfied: at each point, price = long-run

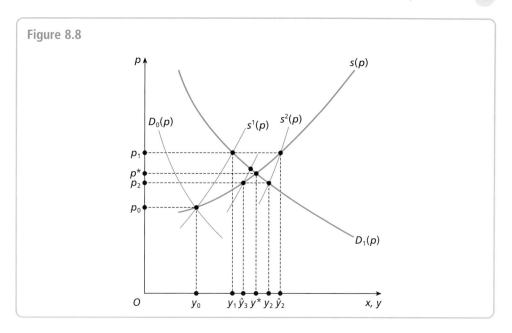

Figure 8.8

marginal cost for each firm in the market, and no further entry or exit will take place at a given price because firms are just breaking even at that price (given that the quasi-rents of intra-marginal firms have been transformed into opportunity costs). Thus corresponding to each point on the curve is a particular set of firms, each with a profit-maximizing capacity and output level. As price rises, output increases along the curve as a result of both output expansion by existing firms and entry of new firms. However, the *actual time path of price and output may not lie on the supply curve*. For that to happen, we again need the assumption of rational expectations, as we shall now see.

Suppose at year 0 the market is initially in long-run equilibrium at the price and output pair (p_0, y_0) in Fig. 8.8. In year 1 demand shifts to $D_1(p)$. In the short-run – year 1 – output can only expand along the short-run supply function $s^1(p)$, determined by the short-run marginal cost functions of the firms already in the market (together with any effects of increasing input prices as analysed in section A). Thus price in year 1 is established as p_1. Since p_0 corresponded to zero profits of the existing firms, p_1 must imply positive profits. The market is clearly not in long-run equilibrium. What happens next depends upon the assumption we make about price expectations formation.

Begin, as in the Cobweb model of section B, with the assumption of naive expectations: all firms, whether currently in the market or contemplating entry, expect price p_1 to prevail next year, in year 2. The existing firms expand capacity and new firms enter and install capacity to the extent that planned market output expands to $\hat{y}_2$, since this is the aggregate output corresponding to long-run profit maximization at price p_1. But of course, when period 2 arrives, $(p_1, \hat{y}_2)$ is not an equilibrium: price will have to fall to p_2, where demand equals short-run supply as indicated by the short-run supply curves $s^2(p)$. This is determined by the short-run marginal cost curves of all firms in the market – initial incumbents *and* new entrants in year 2. If all firms again assume, naively, that p_2 will prevail in year 3, then capacity will be contracted and some firms will leave the market until $\hat{y}_3$ will be the aggregate market supply that will be *planned* for year 3. And so on. Under naive expectations, price fluctuates around the equilibrium value $p*$ and, in the case illustrated in Fig. 8.8, eventually converges to it (in the absence of further demand change). The fact that capacity can only be adjusted 'in the long run' introduces the same kind of supply lag that we assumed for an agricultural market. The main difference is that here the short-run supply curve is positively sloped whereas in the Cobweb model it was in effect vertical. The role of the long-run supply curve in the present analysis is to show how *future planned* output varies with the *expected future* price. Although the ultimate effect of the demand shift is to move the market from one point on the long-run supply curve to another, the actual time path of price and output through the adjustment process lies along the demand curve and describes a diminishing sequence of jumps from one side of the equilibrium point to the other.

However, our previous criticisms of the naive expectations assumption apply equally here. It is irrational for a profit-maximizing firm to form its expectations in this way because then it is consistently sacrificing potential profits. Suppose instead that all firms have rational expectations, that is, they know the market model and use its prediction as their price expectation. Then, if the change in demand between periods 0 and 1 is unanticipated, the year 1 short-run equilibrium is at (p_1, y_1) as before, but now firms can predict the new long-run equilibrium price $p*$. This is the only price with the property that the planned outputs which maximize profits at that price can actually be realized, i.e. sold, on the market next period. Hence existing firms will expand capacity and new firms will enter so as to expand market output to $y*$, and the market moves to its long-run equilibrium in year 2. If the change in demand had been fully anticipated at year 0, then the same argument leads to the conclusion that the market would move to its new long-run equilibrium in year 1. In that case, the market adjusts smoothly along its long-run supply curve to changes in demand.

EXERCISE 8C

1. Explain the shapes of the market supply curves in the following cases:
   (a) Firms have identical constant returns to scale production functions and face identical constant input prices.
   (b) Firms have identical decreasing returns production functions and face identical constant input prices.
   (c) As in (a) but with input prices increasing as market output increases.

2. Take an industry in which firms have identical *decreasing returns* production functions with input prices that fall as market output expands. Show that market equilibrium is fully determinate and a competitive market structure can be sustained, even if the market supply curve has a negative slope. Contrast this with the case in which firms have identical *increasing returns* production functions and input prices are constant.

3. Analyse the long-run adjustment process in markets of types (a), (b) and (c) of Question 1, first on the assumption of naive expectations, and second on the assumption of rational expectations.

4. Assume that all firms, incumbents and potential entrants, have identical U-shaped long-run marginal and average cost curves. Analyse the process of adjustment from the initial equilibrium to a new equilibrium following an unexpected demand increase. (Assume constant input prices.) Explain why, under rational expectations, incumbent firms never change their long-run output and capacity.

D. Conclusions

The long-run market supply curve is a complex construction. Its slope and elasticity depend on: the nature of returns to scale in individual firms; the extent to which input prices vary with aggregate industry output; the existence of external technological economies and diseconomies of scale; and the flow of new entrants into the market. Moreover, the process of adjustment between points on the long-run supply curve, in response to demand shifts, may also be complex, and depends on the relation between short-run and long-run supply, on the one hand, and the nature of expectations on the other. The analysis of long-run competitive equilibrium must then be treated with some care. On the other hand, the analysis of existence and stability of short-run equilibrium is relatively straightforward and has served to introduce some ideas which will be greatly extended in Chapter 11 on general competitive equilibrium.

9 Monopoly

A. Introduction

The assumption that buyers and sellers act as price-takers which underlies the model of the competitive market is often not satisfied. Sellers perceive that the market price will vary with the amount of output they put on the market: buyers appreciate that an increase in their purchases will drive the price up. This chapter will be concerned with theories of the price-setting behaviour of *sellers*; parts of Chapter 10 will be concerned with analysis of cases in which *buyers* have influence over market price.

A market in which the seller perceives that market price varies with the amount it sells is non-competitive. We can classify non-competitive markets into two types depending on the nature of the *perceived interdependence* among sellers. In *monopoly* a seller does not perceive that a change in its behaviour will cause changes in the profits of other firms which lead them to alter their actions which in turn affect its profits. In *oligopoly* the firm does perceive such interdependence and takes account of it in deciding its output level. Oligopoly requires a different set of analytical tools and is dealt with in Chapter 16, after we present the necessary game theory in Chapter 15.

It is usual to define monopoly and oligopoly in terms of the size distribution of sellers in a market: monopoly is a 'single seller' of a good, and oligopoly is the case of a 'few sellers'. But consider the following cases:

(a) A public utility may be the only supplier of electricity, yet in its sales to domestic consumers, there may be a close competitive relation with the firms which sell oil, coal and gas. The relevant good here is 'energy' or 'heat', and the various 'monopolies' are in an oligopoly.

(b) A cement manufacturer may be one of, say, five sellers in the nationwide cement industry. However, because of high transport costs, it may be able to vary its price over some range to buyers in a region around its cement works, without affecting the demand of any of the other sellers, and the same may be true of them. Each enjoys a local monopoly. Thus what is apparently an oligopolistic market is really a collection of monopoly sub-markets.

(c) A restaurant is able to raise its prices relative to those of the other, say, forty restaurants in town, without losing all its customers to them; and is able to lower its prices relative to theirs, without taking all their customers. This is because of differences in quality, location, style of cooking, ambience. If its gains or losses of customers are spread evenly over all other restaurants, then there is unlikely to be a perceived interdependence among the restaurants. Each restaurant could be regarded as a monopoly (although possibly with a very elastic demand curve). On the other hand, if the customer changes are concentrated on just one or two close rivals (the only other *Chinese* restaurants in town) then the restaurant is in an oligopolistic market.

(d) An airline is the only firm on a route for which there are no close road or rail substitutes. Suppose that, because of the size of the market and the capacity of aircraft capable of making the flight, production takes place under increasing returns to scale, so that, in the terminology of section 6D, the firm has a 'natural' monopoly. Despite this, the firm may earn no more than a normal rate of return on its assets because in its pricing decisions it takes account not just of the market elasticity of demand and its cost conditions but the threat of potential competition from other airlines. Such perceived interdependence between the airline and potential rivals means that the market is better analysed using game theoretic models and we present an example of an entry game in section 15B.

The point of these examples is to show that the appropriate model to use depends not on the size distribution of firms in the market, but on the nature of the competitive relations between sellers. Indeed, the *appropriate definition of the 'market' depends on the nature of the competitive relations*, rather than the other way around.

B. Price and output determination under monopoly

The monopoly firm is assumed to maximize profit in a stable, known environment, with given technology and market conditions. We assume diminishing marginal productivity and so, in the presence of fixed inputs, the firm's average and marginal costs will at some point begin to rise with the rate of output per unit time. However, we no longer assume that diminishing returns to scale set in at some point: we leave the question open, and permit any one of increasing, constant, or diminishing returns to scale to exist over the range of outputs we are concerned with. The essential difference from the competitive model is the assumption that the firm faces a downward sloping demand curve. We write its demand function in the inverse form:

$$p = D(q) \qquad dp/dq < 0 \tag{B.1}$$

where p is price, q is output per unit time, and D is the demand function. We do not place restrictions on the second derivative of the function, but do require its first derivative to be negative.

The firm's total cost function is

$$C = C(q) \qquad C'(q) > 0 \tag{B.2}$$

where C is total cost per unit time. Marginal cost is always positive, but we do not place restrictions on the second derivative, the slope of the marginal cost curve. The profit function of the firm is

$$\pi(q) = pq - C(q) \tag{B.3}$$

where π is profit per unit time. We assume that the profit maximising output q^* is positive. Hence q^* satisfies the conditions

$$\pi'(q) = p + q\,dp/dq - C'(q) = 0 \tag{B.4}$$

$$\pi''(q) = 2dp/dq + q\,d^2p/dq^2 - C''(q) < 0 \tag{B.5}$$

where [B.4] is the first-order and [B.5] the second-order condition. The term $(p + qdp/dq)$ is the derivative of total revenue pq with respect to q (taking account of [B.1]), and is *marginal revenue*. Thus, [B.4] expresses the condition of equality of marginal cost with marginal revenue. The term $(2dp/dq + qd^2p/dq^2)$ is the derivative of marginal revenue with respect to output and so [B.5] is the condition that the slope of the marginal cost curve must exceed that of the marginal revenue curve at the optimal point. If marginal costs are increasing with output while, by assumption, marginal revenue is diminishing with output, [B.5] will necessarily be satisfied, since in that case

$$C''(q) > 0 > 2dp/dq + qd^2p/dq^2 \qquad [B.6]$$

However, unlike the competitive case, the second-order condition may also be satisfied if $C''(q) < 0$ (see Question 2, Exercise 9B).

More insight into this solution can be gained if we write marginal revenue, MR, as

$$MR = p(1 + (q/p)dp/dq) \qquad [B.7]$$

Given the definition of the elasticity of demand from Chapter 2:

$$e = p(dq/dp)/q < 0 \qquad [B.8]$$

we can write as the relationship between demand elasticity and marginal revenue:

$$MR = p(1 + 1/e) \qquad [B.9]$$

Clearly, $e < -1 \Rightarrow MR > 0$ while $e = -1 \Rightarrow MR = 0$, and $e > -1 \Rightarrow MR < 0$. Combining [B.9] with [B.4], we can write the condition for optimal output as

$$p(1 + 1/e) = C'(q) = MC \qquad [B.10]$$

This equation then establishes immediately the two propositions:

(a) the monopolist's chosen price always exceeds marginal cost since its price elasticity is finite;

(b) optimal output is always at a point on the demand curve at which $e < -1$ (given that $C'(q) > 0$).

Under competition each firm equates marginal cost to price. Hence the extent of the divergence of price from marginal cost under monopoly is often regarded as a measure of the degree of monopoly power enjoyed by the seller. From [B.10],

$$\frac{p - MC}{p} = \frac{-1}{e} \qquad -\infty < e < -1 \qquad [B.11]$$

The left-hand side, the price marginal cost difference expressed as a proportion of the price, is the *Lerner* index of monopoly power. Thus, as $e \rightarrow -\infty$ (the competitive case) monopoly power tends to zero.

The equilibrium position of the firm implied by its choice of output q^* satisfying the above conditions is illustrated in Fig. 9.1. In (a) of the figure, the demand curve is $D(q)$ and the corresponding marginal revenue curve is MR. Given the marginal and average cost curves $C'(q)$ and AC, profit-maximizing output is at q^*. Since this

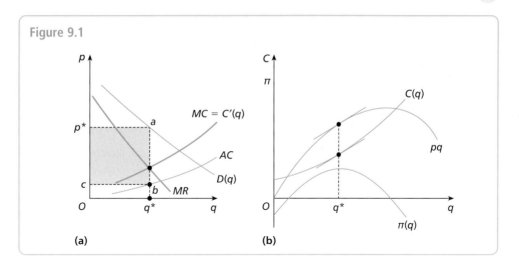

Figure 9.1

(a)　　　　(b)

must be sold at a market-clearing price, choice of q^* requires the price $p^* = D(q^*)$. We could therefore regard the equilibrium position as a choice either of profit-maximizing price p^* or of output q^*, since each implies the other. At output q^*, profit is the difference between total revenue p^*q^* and total cost $AC \cdot q^*$, and is shown by the area p^*abc in Fig. 9.1(a). In (b) of the figure, the same equilibrium position is shown in terms of total revenue and cost curves. The total revenue curve is denoted pq, and its slope at any point measures marginal revenue at that output. Its concave shape reflects the assumption of diminishing marginal revenue. The total cost curve is denoted $C(q)$, and its convex shape reflects the assumption of increasing marginal cost. The total profit function is the vertical difference between these two curves, and is shown as the curve $\pi(q)$ in the figure. The maximum of this curve occurs at the output q^*, which is also the point at which the tangents to the total revenue and total costs curves respectively are parallel, i.e. marginal revenue is equal to marginal cost.

The supernormal profit, i.e. profit in excess of all opportunity costs (including a market-determined rate of return on capital which enters into determination of the average and marginal cost curves), is given by the area $q^*(p^* - c)$. It can be imputed as a rent to whatever property right confers the monopoly power *and* prevents the new entry which would compete the profits away. It may be that this right is owned by an individual who leases it to the firm. If the supplier is rational and well-informed, she will bid up the price of the lease so as just to absorb the supernormal profit, and so the rent is transformed into an opportunity cost for the monopolist. This would be true, for example, if the monopolist rented a particularly favourable location. If the monopolist owns the property rights, then he can impute the profits as the return on this property right. Note that the identity of the owner of the right does not affect the price and output which will be set by the monopolist (since this is determined by the desire to maximize profit) but simply determines the division of the spoils. Note also that the term 'property right' is used here in its widest possible sense: it is meant to include the ownership not only of land, but also of such things as brand names, public reputations, mineral rights, franchises and patents.

EXERCISE 9B

1. The analysis in the text assumed implicitly that there were constraints on the firm's inputs, so that the short-run cost function of Chapter 6 was the relevant cost function for the firm's decisions. Extend the analysis to take account of the interaction of long-run and short-run decisions (cf. Chapter 7). Show that the firm will set output so that $SMC = MR$ in each period and will plan to produce next period where $SMC = LMC = MR$. (Assume no threat of entry exists.)

2. Using diagrams analogous to those in Figs 9.1(a) and (b), illustrate cases in which there are increasing returns to scale.

3. Show how a monopolist's price and output will be affected by:

   (a) an increase in demand;

   (b) a specific tax per unit of output;

   (c) a proportionate profit tax.

   Compare these comparative statics results with those for the competitive firm in Chapter 7.

4. What method could you use to induce the monopolist to produce at the output at which $C'(q)$ cuts $D(q)$ (i.e. at which price = marginal cost) in Fig. 9.1(a)? Describe four methods, and assess their advantages and disadvantages.

5. (a) Explain why it is meaningless to talk of 'the supply curve' of a monopolist.

   (b) Is it also meaningless to talk of 'the demand curve' of the monopoly for inputs it uses in production?

6. Suppose that the right to be a monopolist is auctioned off by the government (for example, the right to be the only petrol station on a stretch of motorway). What will be the monopoly price, output and profit if the right is given to the firm (a) making the highest money bid; (b) promising to sell petrol at the lowest price; (c) promising to pay the largest share of its revenue over to the government.

7. A monopoly produces two outputs which are interdependent in demand. Set up, solve and interpret a model of its profit-maximizing output choices.

8. A monopoly faces the inverse demand function $p = q^{-\alpha}$ and has the total cost function $C = cq$. Analyse the problem which may arise in modelling its profit-maximizing output choice. Under what condition would no such difficulty arise?

9. Explain why a monopolist with zero marginal cost would produce at an output at which $e = -1$. What is the value of the Lerner index at such a point?

C. Price discrimination

Price discrimination exists when different buyers are charged different prices for the same good. It is a practice which could not prevail in a competitive market because of *arbitrage*: those buying at lower prices would resell to those offered higher prices and so a seller would not gain from discrimination. Its presence therefore suggests imperfection of competition.

Third-degree price discrimination: market segmentation

Suppose that the monopolist can divide the market for his output into two sub-groups between which arbitrage can be prevented at zero cost. To concentrate on essentials assume that the costs of supplying the two sub-markets are identical, so that any price difference between the sub-markets will arise from discrimination, not differences in, say, transport or distribution costs.

The monopolist knows the demand, and therefore marginal revenue, curves, for each group. Let q_1 and q_2 be the quantities sold to the first and second groups respectively, so that total output $q = q_1 + q_2$. Take some *fixed* total output level, q_0, and consider the division of this between the two sub-markets in such a way as to maximize profit. Since the total production cost of q_0 is given, profit from the division of this between the two markets is maximized if revenue is maximized. But revenue is maximized only if q_1 and q_2 are chosen such that the marginal revenues in each sub-market are equal. To see this let MR_1 be the marginal revenue in sub-market 1, and MR_2 that in 2. Suppose $MR_1 > MR_2$. Then it would be possible to take one unit of output from market 2, and sell it in market 1, with a net gain in revenue of $MR_1 - MR_2 > 0$. As long as the marginal revenues were unequal such possibilities for increasing revenue, and therefore profit, would exist. Hence a necessary condition for a profit-maximizing allocation of any given total output between the two markets is that marginal revenues in the markets be equal.

In determining the optimal total output level, we are on familiar ground. If MR_1 ($= MR_2$) differed from marginal cost, it would be possible to vary output in such a way as to increase total profit: by increasing output when $MR_1 > MC$, and reducing it in the converse case. Hence a necessary condition for maximum profit is that $MC = MR_1 = MR_2$.

Now let e_1 and e_2 be the price elasticities of demand in the respective sub-markets. Then the basic relation given in [B.9] applies in this case, so that

$$MC = p_1(1 + 1/e_1) = p_2(1 + 1/e_2) \qquad \text{[C.1]}$$

From the second equality in [C.1] we have

$$\frac{p_1}{p_2} = \frac{1 + \dfrac{1}{e_2}}{1 + \dfrac{1}{e_1}} \qquad \text{[C.2]}$$

If $e_1 = e_2$, then clearly $p_1/p_2 = 1$, and there is no discrimination. There will be price discrimination as long as the elasticities are unequal at the profit-maximizing point. Moreover, if $e_1 < e_2$, then from [C.2] $p_1 < p_2$, and conversely. (Remember $e_i < 0$.) In maximizing profit the monopolist will set a higher price in the market with the less elastic demand.

The analysis is illustrated in Fig. 9.2. In (a) of the figure are the demand and marginal revenue curves for sub-market 1 and in (b) those for 2. The curve MR in (c) is the *horizontal sum* of the MR_1 and MR_2 curves. MR has the property that at any total output, q^0, the output levels q_1^0 and q_2^0 which have the same marginal revenues in the sub-markets as that at q^0, sum exactly to q^0, i.e. $q_1^0 + q_2^0 = q^0$. The horizontal summation therefore reflects the first condition derived above, that

Figure 9.2

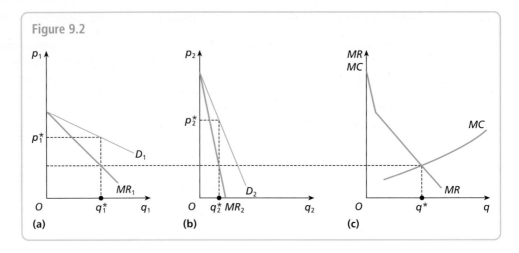

any total output must be divided between the sub-markets in such a way as to equalize their marginal revenues. The profit maximizing level of total output is shown at q^*, where $MC = MR$. q^* is optimally divided between the sub-markets at q_1^* and q_2^* where the sub-market outputs have marginal revenues equal to MC and by construction must sum to q^*. Demand for q_2 is less elastic than that for q_1 so that $p_2^* > p_1^*$.

First-degree discrimination

Under third-degree price discrimination the monopolist had some information he could use to partition buyers into sub-markets and prevent arbitrage between the sub-markets. This, as the name suggests, is in contrast to

(a) *first-degree price discrimination*, where the monopolist is able to identify the demand of each individual buyer and prevent arbitrage among all buyers;

(b) *second-degree price discrimination*, where the monopolist knows the demand characteristics of buyers in general, but does not know *which* buyer has *which* characteristics.

In first-degree price discrimination the monopolist can extract *all* the consumer surplus of each buyer. An interesting aspect of this case is that total output of the good is at the level at which each buyer pays a price equal to marginal cost and monopoly does not distort the allocation of resources. In the terminology of Chapter 13, we have a Pareto efficient outcome, although the monopolist expropriates *all* the gains from trade. Any objection to monopoly in this case therefore would have to be on grounds of equity – fairness of the income distribution – rather than efficiency.

In the second case, the obstacle to price discrimination is that, if one type of buyer is offered a more favourable price–quantity deal than other types, and the monopoly is not able to identify a buyer's type, then all buyers will take the most favourable deal. The solution for the monopolist is to offer alternative deals which satisfy a *self-selection constraint*: a given deal will be preferred to all others by, and only by, the type for which it is designed.

In the rest of this section we explore first- and second-degree price discrimination with a simple model. We assume:

(a) two types of buyer in the market, with n_1 buyers of the first type and n_2 buyers of the second;

(b) a buyer's type is determined by her preferences which for each type of buyer can be represented by the *quasi-linear* form

$$u_i = U_i(x_i) + y_i \qquad i = 1, 2 \tag{C.3}$$

where x_i is the monopolized good and y_i is a composite commodity representing all other goods;

(c) type 2 buyers have a stronger preference for the good in the sense that for any x

$$MRS^2_{xy} = u_{2x}/u_{2y} = U'_2(x) > U'_1(x) = u_{1x}/u_{1y} = MRS^1_{xy} > 0 \tag{C.4}$$

(d) $U_i(0) = 0$ and $U''_i(x) < 0$: buyers have diminishing marginal utility;

(e) the buyers have identical incomes M, and the price of the composite commodity is the same for all consumers and is set at unity. So if $x_1 = x_2 = 0$, then $y_1 = y_2 = M$;

(f) the monopolist produces at a constant marginal (= average) cost c.

Recall from Question 2, Exercise 3c, that a quasi-linear utility function implies that a consumer's indifference curves in the x, y plane are vertically parallel, and there is a zero income effect for good x. The consumer's choice problem is:

$$\max_{x_i, y_i} U_i(x_i) + y_i \quad \text{s.t.} \ px_i + y_i = M - F \tag{C.5}$$

p is the price the monopolist charges, and $F \geqslant 0$ is a *fixed charge* that the monopolist may set for the right to buy the good at price p (examples of such fixed charges are telephone rentals, entrance charges to amusement parks, subscription fees to a book or wine club).

First-order conditions include

$$U'_i - \lambda p = 0 \tag{C.6}$$

$$1 - \lambda = 0 \tag{C.7}$$

Hence $U'_i(x) = \lambda p = p$, yielding demand functions

$$x_i = U'^{-1}_i(p) = x_i(p) \tag{C.8}$$

$$y_i = M - F - px_i(p) \tag{C.9}$$

The indirect utility function is

$$v_i(p, F) = U_i(x_i(p)) + M - F - px_i(p) \tag{C.10}$$

Of particular interest are the derivatives

Figure 9.3

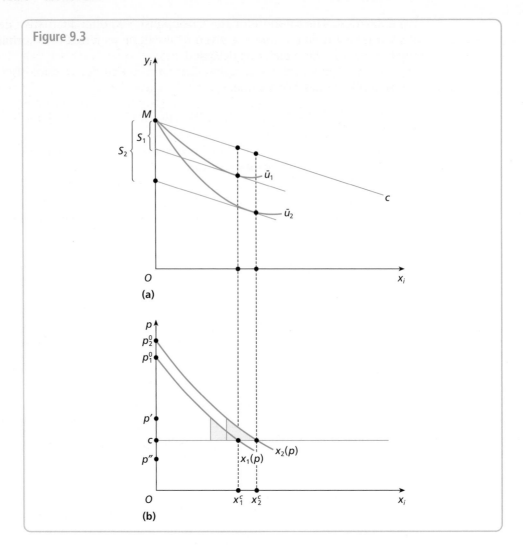

$$\frac{\partial v_i}{\partial p} = U_i' x_i' - (x_i + p x_i') = -x_i, \qquad \frac{\partial v_i}{\partial F} = -1 \qquad \text{[C.11]}$$

where the result for $\partial v_i/\partial p$ is simply Roy's identity. In Fig. 9.3(a), we show the 'reservation indifference curves' $\bar{u}_i$ for each of the two types of consumers. Since they have the same income M, they are at the same point when consuming no x, but assumption (c) implies that a type 2 indifference curve is steeper than that of a type 1 at every x (since $MRS_{xy}^i = -dy_i/dx_i = U_i'(x)$). The budget line marked c in the figure corresponds to $p = c$, so that x_i^c are the respective consumers' demands at that price. In (b) of the figure we show the demand curves derived from these reservation indifference curves. Because of the quasi-linearity assumption, these are both Hicksian and Marshallian demand curves, and the area under each between prices p_i^0 and $p = c$ gives the type's compensating variation, or maximum willingness to pay for the right to buy x at price c. These consumer surpluses are denoted by S_i, and correspond to the distances on the y axis shown in (a) of the figure.

We now show that under first-degree price discrimination the monopolist's optimal policy is to set a price for each type equal to c, and to set a fixed charge $F_i = S_i$ ($i = 1, 2$). The monopolist sells at marginal cost and sets separate fixed charges equal to the total willingness of each type to pay. This requires first that he knows the type of each buyer, and so can prevent a type 2 buyer taking advantage of the lower type 1 fixed charge. Second, he must be able to prevent arbitrage and stop a type 1 buyer reselling to a type 2 buyer at some price between c and $F_2/x_2^c + c$, which is the average price per unit a type 2 buyer pays in this solution.

The idea underlying this policy can be seen in Fig. 9.3(b). If the monopolist sets $p = c$ to both types and extracts the total surplus his profit is $S_1 + S_2$. If he sets a higher price, say $p' > c$, although he makes a profit on each unit he sells, the sum of these profits and the *remaining* consumer surpluses is less than $S_1 + S_2$ by the sum of the two shaded triangles. It pays him to expand output and lower price as long as $p > c$ because his own profit increases precisely by the difference $p - c$, which he can recover through the fixed charge. He will not set a price such as $p'' < c$, because the extra surplus he can recover falls short of the extra cost he incurs. And clearly it would never be worthwhile to set a fixed charge $F_i > S_i$ for any p, because then he sells nothing to type i.

We can derive this result more formally. The monopolist's total profit is

$$\pi = n_1[p_1 x_1(p_1) + F_1] + n_2[p_2 x_2(p_2) + F_2] - c[n_1 x_1(p_1) + n_2 x_2(p_2)] \qquad [C.12]$$

He must not offer a deal which is worse for each consumer than not buying the good at all. We can express this by the *reservation constraints*

$$v_i(p_i, F_i) \geq \bar{u}_i \qquad i = 1, 2 \qquad [C.13]$$

where, recall, $\bar{u}_i$ is the utility i obtains by buying none of good x. With β_i as the Lagrange multiplier on these constraints, optimal p_i and F_i are defined by (see Appendix H)

$$n_i(x_i + p_i x_i' - c x_i') + \beta_i \partial v_i / \partial p_i = 0 \qquad i = 1, 2 \qquad [C.14]$$

$$n_i + \beta_i \partial v_i / \partial F_i = 0 \qquad i = 1, 2 \qquad [C.15]$$

$$v_i(p_i, F_i) \geq \bar{u}_i, \qquad \beta_i \geq 0, \qquad \beta_i[v_i - \bar{u}_i] = 0 \qquad i = 1, 2 \qquad [C.16]$$

From [C.15] we see that non-zero n_i and $\partial v_i / \partial F_i$ imply $\beta_i > 0$ and so [C.16] implies $v_i = \bar{u}_i$. Both types of consumers receive only their reservation utilities. Then, using [C.11] and [C.15] we have $\beta_i = n_i$ and

$$n_i(x_i + p_i x_i' - c x_i') - n_i x_i = 0 \qquad [C.17]$$

implying

$$p_i = c \qquad [C.18]$$

The value of F_i then satisfies $v_i(c, F_i) = \bar{u}_i$ and so must be equal to consumer surplus S_i at price c.

We could interpret third-degree price discrimination (analysed in the first part of this section) as the case in which the monopolist can identify each buyer's type and prevent arbitrage between types, but for some reason cannot set fixed charges. He must set a constant price per unit to all buyers of a given type. (See Question 8, Exercise 9C.) Then, profit maximization implies a price to each type which is above marginal cost, as we saw earlier. Clearly, the monopolist's profits are lower than under first-degree price discrimination. Buyers are better off under third-degree price discrimination since, although they face a higher price and so consume less, they retain some consumer surplus and are on an indifference curve that must be higher than their reservation indifference curve (use Fig. 9.3).

Second-degree price discrimination

In the case of second-degree price discrimination, the monopolist is unable to determine the type of the buyer before she has purchased the good. In that case if he offered any buyer the option of either (c, S_1) or (c, S_2), every type 2 buyer (as well as every type 1 buyer) would choose (c, S_1). Can the monopolist do better than this by offering options chosen so that only a buyer of type i would want to choose the option designed for her type? In other words, can the monopolist do better by inducing buyers to reveal their type by 'self-selecting' the appropriate deal?

Assume that the monopolist knows the number of buyers of each type, n_i, and can specify in a contract *both* the quantity of output he will supply to a buyer *and* the total charge for that output. That is, a contract is a pair (x_i, F_i). This implies a price per unit $p_i = F_i/x_i$ and the contract could be equivalently expressed as some combination of a fixed charge and constant price per unit, as in a two-part tariff. The point is that the consumer is offered a *quantity* and a fixed charge, and not a *price* and a fixed charge. We shall see the reason for this at the end of the following analysis.

The monopolist's profit is

$$\pi = \sum_{i=1}^{2} n_i(F_i - cx_i) \qquad \text{[C.19]}$$

We again have the reservation constraints, since buyers always have the option of refusing a contract. These are now written in terms of direct utilities, to reflect the fact that quantities are being specified:

$$U_i(x_i) + M - F_i \geqslant \bar{u}_i \qquad i = 1, 2 \qquad \text{[C.20]}$$

where we use the fact that $y_i = M - F_i$. There are also *self-selection* constraints which ensure that each type chooses the appropriate deal. We write these as

$$U_1(x_1) - F_1 \geqslant U_1(x_2) - F_2 \qquad \text{[C.21]}$$

$$U_2(x_2) - F_2 \geqslant U_2(x_1) - F_1 \qquad \text{[C.22]}$$

(*M* cancels out in these expressions.)

If (x_i, F_i) satisfies these constraints, it will only be accepted by type i. (We assume, to be able to have a *closed* feasible set, that if a buyer is indifferent between the two deals she takes the one appropriate to her type.)

In principle we now solve for x_i, F_i by maximizing π subject to [C.20]–[C.22]. However, the first-order conditions for this would not be instructive. Instead, we first show that, in any optimal solution, (a) the *reservation* constraint for a *type 2 buyer*, and (b) the *self-selection* constraint for a *type 1 buyer* are non-binding. They

Figure 9.4

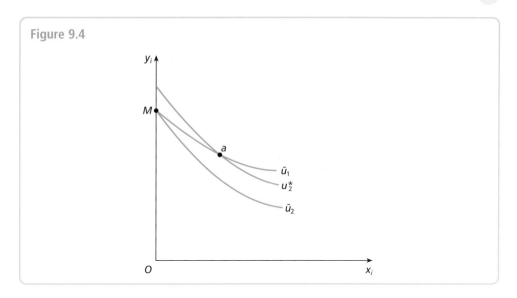

can be dropped from the problem thus simplifying the derivation of the optimal contract.

We show this in Fig. 9.4, which reproduces the reservation indifference curves from Fig. 9.3(a).

(a) *Type 2 buyers must be offered* (x_2, F_2) *such that* $u_2 > \bar{u}_2$. To see that, note that type 1 buyers must be offered a contract (x_1, F_1) that puts them on or above $\bar{u}_1$. But since $\bar{u}_1$ lies above $\bar{u}_2$, such a deal must always be better for type 2 buyers than any contract (x_2, F_2) that puts them on $\bar{u}_2$. So only a point above $\bar{u}_2$ can satisfy their self-selection constraint.

(b) *Type 1 buyers will always strictly prefer their deal to that offered to type 2 buyers, in an optimal solution.* Suppose the optimal deal offered to type 1 buyers is at a in Fig. 9.4 (it is not relevant to the present argument that a is on $\bar{u}_1$, but we show below that this must be so). Then the deal offered to type 2 buyers must lie on the type 2 indifference curve passing through a, labelled u_2^*. If it were below this, type 2 buyers would prefer a; if above, the monopolist is being needlessly generous to type 2 buyers because, at any given x_2, he could increase F_2 (move vertically downward in the figure) without violating either the reservation or self-selection constraints. (This incidentally established that the self-selection constraint for type 2 buyers is strictly binding, as we verify later.) Now if the deal offered to type 2 buyers were on u_2^* at a point to the left of a, it would be preferred to a by type 1 buyers and this violates the self-selection constraint on type 1. It is easy to show that point a itself could not be offered to both types of buyer in equilibrium (see Question 9, Exercise 9C). This leaves only points on u_2^* to the right of a as possible deals to be offered to type 2 buyers, and since these must be strictly below $\bar{u}_1$ the type 1 self-selection constraint is non-binding. This argument also establishes that at an optimum $x_2 > x_1$.

As a result of these arguments, the monopolist's problem is to find (x_1, F_1), (x_2, F_2) to maximize π in [C.19] subject only to [C.20] with $i = 1$, and [C.22]. Using β_1 and μ_2 for the Lagrange multipliers on [C.20] and [C.22], the first-order conditions are

$$-n_1 c + \beta_1 U_1'(x_1^\star) - \mu_2 U_2'(x_1^\star) = 0 \qquad \text{[C.23]}$$

$$-n_2 c + \mu_2 U_2'(x_2^\star) = 0 \qquad \text{[C.24]}$$

$$n_1 - \beta_1 + \mu_2 = 0 \qquad \text{[C.25]}$$

$$n_2 - \mu_2 = 0 \qquad \text{[C.26]}$$

$$U_1(x_1^\star) + M - F_1^\star - \bar{u}_1 \geq 0, \quad \beta_1 \geq 0, \quad \beta_1[U_1 + M - F_1^\star - \bar{u}_1] = 0 \qquad \text{[C.27]}$$

$$U_2(x_2^\star) - F_2^\star - U_2(x_1^\star) + F_1^\star \geq 0, \quad \mu_2 \geq 0, \quad \mu_2[U_2 - F_2^\star - U_2 + F_1^\star] = 0 \qquad \text{[C.28]}$$

From [C.26] and [C.28] we see that the type 2 self-selection constraint must bind, and from [C.25] and [C.27] that the type 1 reservation constraint must bind. Substituting for μ_2 in [C.24] gives

$$U_2'(x_2^\star) = c \qquad \text{[C.29]}$$

implying $x_2^\star = x_2^c$, so that type 2 consumption is exactly that under first-degree price discrimination. Then, substituting for β_1 and μ_2 in [C.23] gives

$$U_1'(x_1^\star) = \frac{n_1 c}{n_1 + n_2} + \frac{n_2}{n_1 + n_2} U_2'(x_1^\star) \qquad \text{(C.30)}$$

Recall that we established in Fig. 9.4 that we must have $x_2^\star > x_1^\star$, so that $U_2'(x_1^\star) > U_2'(x_2^\star) = c$, given diminishing marginal utility. Thus, writing $U_2'(x_1^\star) \equiv c + \delta$, where $\delta > 0$, we have

$$U_1'(x_1^\star) = c + \frac{n_2 \delta}{n_1 + n_2} \qquad \text{[C.31]}$$

implying that $x_1^\star < x_1^c$, so that type 1 buyers consume less than under first-degree price discrimination. The optimal values $F_1^\star$ and $F_2^\star$ then follow from solving the constraints as equalities with the optimal $x_i^\star$ inserted. We know that $F_1^\star$ will leave type 1 buyers with their reservation utilities, while $F_2^\star$ is such that type 2 buyers retain some consumer surplus. It follows that, compared with first-degree price discrimination, type 1 buyers are neither better nor worse off, type 2 buyers are better off, and the monopoly makes less profit.

The optimal second-degree price discrimination equilibrium is illustrated in Fig. 9.5. The contracts are $(x_1^\star, F_1^\star)$ and $(x_2^c, F_2^\star)$. The two most interesting aspects of the solution are first that $x_1^\star < x_1^c$, and second that $x_2^\star = x_2^c$. These can be rationalized as follows. At any x_1, the total net surplus can be expropriated from type 1 buyers since they can be held to their reservation constraint. Suppose x_1 were set at x_1^c. The contract for type 2 buyers would have to be a point on the indifference curve $\hat{u}_2$, as shown in Fig. 9.5. Now consider a small reduction in x_1 from x_1^c. Since at x_1^c net surplus is at a maximum, this results in a change in net surplus from type 1 buyers of just about zero. On the other hand, it permits a downward shift in the indifference curve on which type 2 buyers can be placed, and at any x_2 this results in a strictly positive gain in net surplus to the monopolist. Thus it pays to reduce x_1 below x_1^c. Of course, for further reductions in x_1 the monopolist will lose some net surplus from type 1 buyers, but this must be traded off against the gain in surplus from type 2 buyers, and the optimum, $x_1^\star$, just balances these at the margin.

Figure 9.5

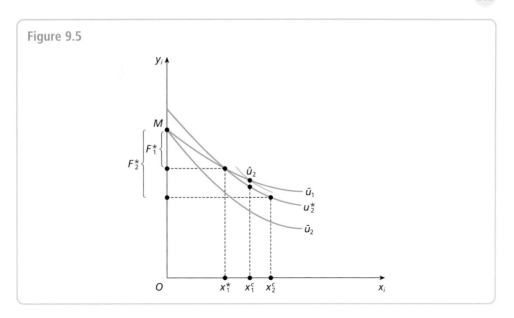

To see why $x_2^* = x_2^c$, note that it pays the monopolist to maximize the net surplus of type 2 buyers with respect to output, since this then maximizes the value of F_2 that can be set, subject to the constraint that type 2 buyers would not prefer the type 1 contract.

There is a qualification to the condition in [C.31]. Note that as n_1 falls, given n_2, x_1^* must also fall. It is then possible, for suitably small n_1, that [C.31] cannot be satisfied for any $x_1 > 0$, in which case F_1 is set sufficiently high that no type 1 buyers enter the market. The monopolist then knows that the only buyers in the market are of type 2, and so he can extract all their consumer surplus, with $F_2^* = S_2$. In terms of Fig. 9.5, u_2^* becomes $\bar{u}_2$. The intuitive explanation is that, when the proportion of type 1 buyers is sufficiently small, the loss in total profit from reducing x_1, and the corresponding extracted surplus, is small relative to the gain from being able to extract more surplus from type 2 buyers. The equilibrium position in Fig. 9.5 depends on the proportions of buyers of the two types as well as on the shapes of the indifference curves and the value of c.

The importance of the specification of quantities in the contract can be seen if we consider the *two-part tariffs* implied by the equilibrium in Fig. 9.5. If type 1 buyers took a contract in which they paid a fixed charge C_1^* and then a price per unit of $p_1^* = U_1'(x_1^*)$, then they would choose consumption x_1^* and pay precisely $C_1^* + p_1^* x_1^* = F_1^*$. Likewise, if type 2 buyers were set a fixed charge C_2^* and paid a price per unit $p_2^* = U_2'(x_2^c) = c$ then they would choose to consume x_2^c and pay in total $F_2^* = C_2^* + cx_2^c$. If the monopolist made these contracts available to all buyers and did not restrict the quantity that could be bought, Fig. 9.6 shows that the self-selection constraint would be violated. Type 2 buyers would clearly choose a type 1 contract, which would dominate the contract (x_2^c, F_2^*), although type 1 buyers still prefer their own contract. On the other hand, if the monopolist specified contracts of the form: a fixed charge C_1^* and a price per unit p^*, up to a maximum of x_1^* units of consumption; *or* a fixed charge C_2^* and a price of c for any amount of consumption, then the self-selection

Figure 9.6

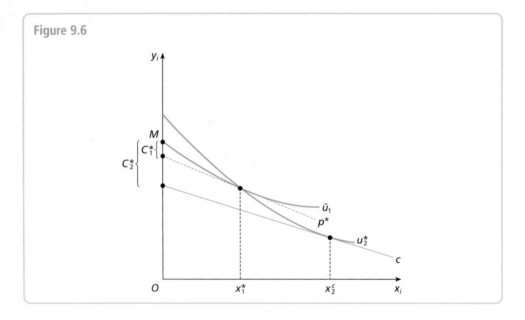

constraints would continue to hold. In fact, the tariffs or price schedules that firms with market power offer often do specify maximum consumption quantities as well as fixed and variable charges.

A note on terminology. *Linear pricing* refers to the case in which a buyer is charged a fixed price p per unit bought, so that her total expenditure is $E = px$, a linear function. A *two-part tariff* consists of a fixed charge C and a fixed price p per unit bought, so that total expenditure is the affine function $E = C + px$. In this case, the average price per unit, $p + C/x$, is a non-linear, decreasing function of the quantity bought. In Fig. 9.5, the implied unit price F_i^*/x_i^* to each type of buyer will not be the same, implying a kind of non-linearity in the way in which unit price varies with quantity bought. Thus this kind of price discrimination, as well as two-part tariffs, falls under the general heading of 'non-linear pricing'.

To summarize: if a seller can identify each buyer's type (her demand function), and prevent arbitrage between types, then he maximizes profit by offering a two-part tariff consisting of a unit price equal to marginal cost c, and a fixed charge which expropriates all the consumer surplus of the given type. If a seller cannot identify a buyer's type, he must offer optional contracts: a high demand type will choose a contract which offers a unit price equal to marginal cost and a fixed charge which leaves her with some consumer surplus; a low demand type will choose a contract which offers a higher price up to a quantity maximum (x_1^*) and a lower fixed charge which nevertheless appropriates all her consumer surplus. Alternatively, the contracts may simply specify a quantity supplied and a total charge for that quantity. The aim is to prevent high demand buyers pretending to be low demand buyers, and taking the contract the latter would be offered under first-degree price discrimination, by making the low demand buyers' contract less attractive to the high demand buyers. Finally, if a buyer's type can be identified and arbitrage between types can be prevented, but the seller is constrained to use linear pricing, we have third-degree price discrimination.

EXERCISE 9C

1. Academic journals charge different subscription rates to institutions (college libraries, etc.); individual academics; and students. Explain this in terms of the theory of price discrimination. What would you predict about the pattern of relative subscription rates across these groups? Some journals are owned by profit maximizing firms and others by learned societies. What difference, if any, would you expect this to make to (a) the level of their rates and (b) the pattern of price discrimination?

2. Why are spark plugs sold to car manufacturers as 'initial equipment', to be installed in new cars, at a price just about equal to average production cost, and sold to retailers and garages, for replacement purposes, at a price several times greater than average production cost?

3. Why are the fees charged by solicitors and estate agents, for services provided in buying and selling houses, expressed as percentages of the house price, even though the cost of the services involved is independent of the house price?

4. Why do firms sometimes offer quantity discounts ('one packet for 50p, two for 90p')?

5. A firm which monopolizes one good may sometimes insist that people wishing to buy that good must also buy their requirements of some other good, which would otherwise be competitively produced, from the monopolist. (Examples have included Kodak and IBM.) Why is this *full line force* profitable given that the monopolist can charge a monopoly price for the monopolized good?

6. *Multinational firm.* A monopolist sells its output in Japan and in the USA. It also has a factory in both countries. Its profit maximization problem is to choose the amounts produced and the amounts sold in each country.

   (a) Solve its problem diagrammatically.

   (b) Suppose that the dollar is devalued against the yen. What effect will this have on the firm's decisions if it is (i) Japanese owned, (ii) American owned?

7. In the model of second-degree discrimination impose the constraints that the fixed charges must be zero, hence obtaining the case of third-degree discrimination. Use the resulting first-order conditions to confirm the diagrammatic analysis of third-degree discrimination.

8. A monopolist has two sub-market demand functions $p_i = a_i - b_i q_i$ and the total cost function $C = c(q_1 + q_2)$ where $c > 0$ is a constant. Compare prices, outputs and profits for the cases in which he does and does not practise price discrimination. Give an expression for the maximum cost the monopolist would incur to be able to prevent arbitrage.

9. Show that, on the assumptions of this section, under second-degree price discrimination different types would be offered different contracts.

10. *Self-selection by quality difference.* Monopolists often produce high and low quality goods and set prices such that the price differential between the high and low quality exceeds the additional cost of the higher quality version. Examples include first and tourist class seats on airlines, hardcover and paperback books. Adopt the analysis of second-degree price discrimination to explain this practice.

D. Monopoly welfare loss

As we discuss more fully in Chapter 13, monopoly is a form of *market failure* in that it is *Pareto inefficient*: it would be possible to change the allocation of resources so as to make some individuals better off and none worse off. At the monopoly equilibrium, a consumer is willing to pay the market price p for an additional unit of the good which costs $MC < p$ to produce. Hence, assuming that the consumer and the monopolist are the only parties affected by the increase in production, it would be possible to increase production by one unit and make one of them better off and the other no worse off. (Section C and Chapter 13 consider some reasons why consumers and the monopolist do not contract to remove the inefficiency.)

The demonstration that monopoly is inefficient is instructive, but does not in itself serve as a useful guide to policy-making: we would like a measure of the overall welfare loss due to monopoly. If the welfare loss is small it may not be worthwhile devoting scarce resources to policies intended to eliminate it. Changes in the price set by a monopoly affect the utility of consumers and the profit of the owners. We need to weight the utilities of consumers and profit to get a measure of welfare. We can then determine the welfare-maximizing price, compare it with the monopoly equilibrium price and measure the welfare loss as the difference between welfare at the two prices.

The argument in the first paragraph that monopoly is inefficient suggests that under certain circumstances the welfare maximising price is equal to marginal cost. A formal demonstration that efficient resource allocation requires price equal to marginal cost is given in Chapter 13, but here we sketch a partial equilibrium justification for using marginal cost pricing as a welfare benchmark. We do so by examining the welfare significance of the monopolist's marginal cost and demand curves as shown in Fig. 9.7, where the monopoly price is p^* and the price where the demand curve cuts the marginal cost curve is p_0.

To focus on welfare losses due solely to the monopolist's exploitation of its power in the market in which it sells its output, assume that prices in the other markets in the economy are welfare-maximizing. To further simplify suppose that the monopolist uses a single input: labour. Let dx be a small increment in output of the good, and dL the increase in the amount of labour required to produce it, where

$$dx = MP_L dL$$

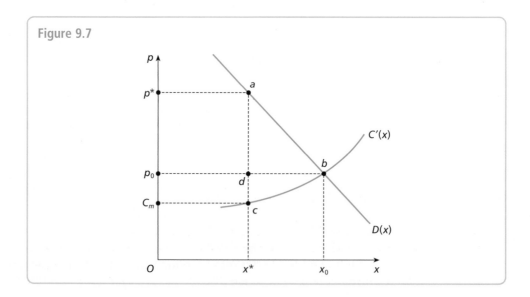

Figure 9.7

and MP_L is the marginal product of labour. If w is the wage rate the increment in cost is

$$dC = wdL$$

Since all other prices are welfare-maximizing, the marginal social value of an hour of leisure of workers equals the marginal value of the output of an hour of work time and both are equal to the the the wage rate w. Hence wdL is the social opportunity cost (in leisure or output elsewhere) of the extra labour employed by the monopolist. Expressed per unit of the increase in output of x gives (recall section 6B)

$$\frac{wdL}{dx} = \frac{w}{MP_L} = \frac{dC}{dx}$$

Thus, in Fig. 9.7, the marginal cost curve of the monopolist is also the marginal social cost of the monopolized good.

The demand curve in Fig. 9.7 is the aggregate Marshallian demand curve for the good. We saw in Chapter 3 that, if the income effect is zero, the area between an individual's Marshallian demand curve and two price lines measures her compensating variation: the largest amount of income she would be prepared to pay in exchange for the reduction in price. The area between the market demand and price lines is the *sum* of the corresponding areas under the individual consumers' demand curves. To take this sum as a measure of the benefits to consumers of the price reduction requires us to assume that £1's worth of benefit has the same social value regardless of which consumer it accrues to. Since changes in price also change the monopolist's profit we must also make an assumption about the social value of £1 of profit accruing to the owners of the firm. The simplest assumption is that it has the same value as £1 of consumer benefit or consumer surplus. Notice that this assumption implies that the distribution of income is optimal: it would not be possible to increase welfare by redistributing income among individuals.

If we are prepared to make these distributional value judgements and to make the positive assumption that income effects are zero, then the measure of the welfare loss due to monopoly is the wedge-shaped area abc in the figure. If price is reduced from the monopoly level p^* to the efficient level p_0, so that output expands from x^* to x_0, then consumers benefit by the area p^*abp_0. The increase in output changes the firm's revenue by dbx_0x^* minus p^*adp_0. The firm's cost also increases by cbx_0x^* which is the area under its marginal cost curve between x_0 and x^*. The sum of the gains to consumers and the change in the firm's profit is

$$p^*abp_0 + (dbx_0x^* - p^*adp_0) - cbx_0x^* = abc$$

We can write the monopoly welfare loss as

$$\int_{x^*}^{x_0} [D(x) - C'(x)]\, dx \simeq \frac{1}{2}[(p^* - p_0) + (p_0 - c_m)](x_0 - x^*) \qquad [\text{D.1}]$$

where $D(x)$ is the demand function and $C'(x)$ the marginal cost function. Knowledge of these functions is sufficient to estimate the welfare loss due to monopoly, provided that our normative and positive assumptions are satisfied.

Another intuition for abc as the welfare loss can be given by remembering that the price (the height of the demand curve) measures the amount of money that consumers are willing to pay for an additional unit of the good. Hence the area abx_0x^* underneath the demand curve between x_0 and x^* measures their willingness to pay for the additional output. The area cbx_0x^* under the marginal cost curve between x_0 and x^* measures the increase in cost of the additional output. Hence the difference between the area under the demand and the area under the marginal cost curve measures the net social loss due to the monopoly restricting output to x^* where marginal revenue equals marginal cost, compared with the welfare-maximizing output x_0 where price equals marginal cost.

Rent seeking and monopoly welfare loss

Attempts to estimate the monopoly welfare loss triangle typically suggest that the welfare loss is small – of the order of one to two percent of national income. There are two reasons why the triangle may understate the welfare loss. First, as Liebenstein (1966) have argued, the monopoly may not be minimizing production cost. Hence there is an additional welfare loss equal to the difference between the actual and minimized cost of production. Since a failure to minimize cost is inconsistent with profit maximization, a full analysis of the monopoly welfare loss requires models of non-profit-maximizing firms since they may also choose an output and price which differs from that chosen by a profit-maximizing monopolist. (See section 7E and Chapter 20.) We will not attempt such an analysis but note the possibility of excess costs of production as a further source of monopoly welfare loss.

Second, there may be welfare losses from *rent seeking*. Firms may expend resources to acquire monopoly power and the associated monopoly profits or rents. Firms may lobby politicians or officials to get protection from competition. They may hire consultants and lawyers to persuade politicians to pass favourable laws, or they may resort to bribery. Such rent-seeking activity can increase welfare losses if it uses resources which could have been employed in producing outputs elsewhere in the economy.

Suppose that a group of n identical firms are competing for the right to be a monopoly and to earn a monopoly profit of π. Firm i's rent-seeking cost is r_i. Its probability of being successful is increasing in r_i and decreasing in the rent-seeking costs of other firms. To fix ideas, assume that the probability of success in the rent-seeking competition is $r_i/\sum_j^n r_j$. The firm chooses r_i to maximize its expected net gain from rent seeking

$$\left(\frac{r_i}{\sum r_j}\right)\pi - r_i \qquad [\text{D.2}]$$

We assume that it takes the actions of its rivals as given so that there is no perceived interdependence among those competing for the rent. (Allowing for perceived interdependence among rivals again requires the game theoretic tools of Chapter 15.) The first-order condition is

$$\frac{\pi}{\sum r_j}\left[1 - \frac{r_i}{\sum r_j}\right] - 1 = 0 \qquad [\text{D.3}]$$

Since the competing firms are identical they will choose the same rent-seeking expenditure. Denote the identical optimal level of rent seeking by each firm by r^*. Substituting r^* in the first-order condition (so that, for example $\sum r_j = nr^*$) and rearranging gives the equilibrium level of rent seeking by each firm as

$$r^* = \frac{\pi}{n}\left(1 - \frac{1}{n}\right)$$ [D.4]

The total rent-seeking expenditure of the rival rent seekers

$$nr^* = \pi\left(1 - \frac{1}{n}\right)$$ [D.5]

which tends to the level of monopoly rent π as the number of rivals becomes large. Even with two firms, total rent-seeking expenditure will be half the profit the successful rent seeker expects to earn as a monopolist.

The welfare consequences of rent seeking depend on how much of the rent-seeking expenditure by firms is a transfer of income from rent seekers to those who can award the prize of a monopoly rent and how much reflects the cost of resources used up in the rent-seeking process. Payment of cash bribes to politicians or officials has relatively low resource costs. But if the bribery takes the form of helping them get elected via additional political advertisements or providing them with extra campaign staff, all the expenditure has a social cost.

This simple model of rent seeking is by no means complete: we have said nothing about how the number of rent seekers is determined. Nor have we explored the possibility that even pure bribes can have a social cost if the expectation of bribes induces officials to create additional monopolies. However, the model serves to alert us to the possibility that the welfare losses of monopoly may be greater than those measured by the simple welfare loss triangle.

EXERCISE 9D

1. *Welfare loss.* (a) Show that for a monopolist facing a linear demand curve and with constant marginal cost the welfare loss is equal to half of monopoly profit. (b) Retaining the assumption of constant marginal cost, suppose that the demand function has constant elasticity with respect to price: $q = kp^{-\alpha}$. Derive an exact expression for welfare loss as proportion of total expenditure on the monopolised good and show that it depends only on the elasticity of demand $-\alpha$. Using a spreadsheet investigate how the proportional welfare loss varies with the demand elasticity.

2. *X-efficiency.* (a) Suppose that a monopolist fails to minimise the cost of production and as a consequence marginal cost is greater at all output levels than if the firm had to operate in a competitive market. Draw a diagram to show the welfare loss taking account of such X-inefficiency. (b) What is the welfare loss if marginal cost is not affected but fixed costs are increased (for example because the firm has unnecessarily luxurious offices)? (c) Should the welfare loss from monopoly be reduced if the monopolist derives utility from hiring incompetent relatives who result in higher production cost? What if the higher cost results from the monopolist refusing to hire workers from particular ethnic groups?

Input markets

In this chapter we examine aspects of the markets for inputs. Although the explicit focus will usually be on labour markets, much of the analysis will have a wider application. Section A addresses competitive input markets and considers the demand for inputs by profit-maximizing firms who treat input prices as parameters. We do not examine the competitive supply of inputs since we have already covered this in Chapter 4 (supply of labour by utility-maximizing consumers). Non-competitive input markets are dealt with in section B, where there is a single buyer of the input (monopsony), and in section C, where we consider unions as monopoly sellers of labour. Section D examines a bilateral monopoly, in which a monopoly union bargains with a single buyer of labour, and sets out the efficient bargain model. This is an example of the cooperative game approach to bargaining which is set out in general terms in Chapter 15.

A. Demand for inputs

We concentrate on the demand for inputs by a profit-maximizing firm facing input prices which it regards as unalterable by its actions. There are assumed to be no adjustment costs involved in varying input levels or, in the terminology of earlier chapters, the firm's problem is *long-run*: there are no constraints on the adjustment of its inputs. Derivation of the short-run demand for inputs is left to the exercises. To keep the analysis simple it is further assumed that the firm produces a single output y from two inputs z_1, z_2 subject to the constraint $y \leqslant f(z_1, z_2)$, where f is a production function. Since a profit-maximizing firm never produces where $y < f(z_1, z_2)$, the production constraint can be treated as an equality: $y = f(z_1, z_2)$. The firm faces a demand curve for its output, $p = p(y)$. If $dp/dy = 0$ the demand curve is horizontal and the firm sells y in a competitive market. If $dp/dy < 0$ the demand curve is negatively sloped and the firm is a monopolist. The firm's total revenue is $R(y) = p(y)y$ and since the production constraint is an equality we can write $R(y) = R[f(z_1, z_2)]$. Since choice of z_1, z_2 determines costs and revenue the firm's output need not appear explicitly in its profit maximization problem

$$\max_{z_1 z_2} R[f(z_1, z_2)] - \sum_i p_i z_i \qquad \text{[A.1]}$$

where p_i is the price of z_i.

Assuming that both inputs are positive at the solution, necessary conditions for a maximum are

$$R'f_i - p_i = 0 \qquad i = 1, 2 \qquad \text{[A.2]}$$

where $R' = dR/dy$ is marginal revenue and f_i is the marginal product of z_i in the production of y. [A.2] can be rewritten as

$$MR \cdot MP_i = p_i \qquad i = 1, 2 \qquad\qquad [\text{A.3}]$$

The firm will adjust its input levels until the cost of an extra unit of input i, p_i, is equal to the extra revenue generated by the extra unit, $MR \cdot MP_i$. The increase in z_i increases y by MP_i (its marginal product) and a unit increase in output increases revenue by marginal revenue. $MR \cdot MP_i$ is usually called the *marginal revenue product* of z_i and written MRP_i. When the firm sells y in a competitive market

$$MR = \frac{dp}{dy} \cdot y + p = p$$

since dp/dy is zero. In this case the MRP_i is $p \cdot MP_i$ which is known as the *value of the marginal product* and written VMP_i. Given that dp/dy is non-positive we see that $VMP_i \geqslant MRP_i$.

Recalling from section 6B that p_i/MP_i is marginal cost, if we divide both sides of [A.3] by MP_i we get

$$MR = MC = \frac{p_i}{MP_i} \qquad i = 1, 2 \qquad\qquad [\text{A.4}]$$

and so we have the familiar conclusion that profit maximization requires that marginal revenue be equated to marginal cost.

Profit maximization also requires that the cost of any given output level be minimized. Dividing the profit-maximizing condition [A.3] on input 1 by the profit-maximizing condition on input 2 gives

$$\frac{MP_1}{MP_2} = \frac{p_1}{p_2}$$

which is just the requirement for cost minimization: the firm chooses an input combination where its isoquant is tangent to its isocost line (recall section 6B).

From the equilibrium conditions [A.2], the firm's demand for inputs depends on the prices of the inputs and the parameters of the production and output demand functions. Consider how the demand for an input varies with its price. Denote the initial price of z_1 by p_1^0. At this price, and given the price of z_2, the firm chooses the initial optimal combination (z_1^*, z_2^*). If z_2 is held constant at z_2^*, then $MRP_1 = R'[f(z_1, z_2^*)] \cdot f_1(z_1, z_2^*)$ varies only with z_1 in Fig. 10.1. This is the curve labelled $MRP_1(z_2^*)$, to indicate that its position depends on the given level of z_2. As z_1 varies with z_2 fixed, MRP_1 varies, first because more output is produced and this will reduce MR if the firm faces a negatively sloped demand curve in its output market; and second because MP_1 varies with z_1. Now over a range of values of z_1, MP_1 may *rise* with z_1 (see section 5C) and so it is possible that MRP_1 at first rises with z_1 (the increase in MP_1 offsetting any decrease in MR) and then falls (the MP_1 must eventually decline and so reinforce the nonpositive change in MR). The $MRP_1(z_2^*)$ curve in Fig. 10.1 reflects this possibility.

The firm chooses its profit-maximizing level of z_1 where $p_1^0 = MRP_1$. But MRP_1 equals p_1^0 *at both* z_1^2 and z_1^*. At z_1^2, however, the $MRP_1(z_2^*)$ curve cuts the p_1^0 line from below, indicating that an increase in z_1 above z_1^2 will lead to $MRP_1 > p_1$, i.e. an increase in z_1 will generate revenue in excess of its cost. Hence z_1^2 cannot be the optimum. At z_1^*, on the other hand, an increase in z_1 will lead to $MRP_1 < p_1$ so that profit is reduced and a reduction in z_1 loses more revenue than cost (since then $MRP_1 > p_1$). Hence the profit-maximizing level of z_1 must occur where MRP_1 is negatively sloped and cuts the p_1^0 line at z_1^*.

Figure 10.1

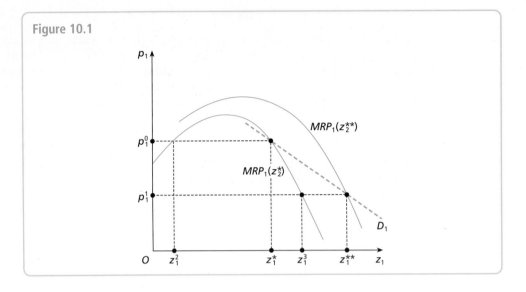

Now suppose that p_1 falls to p_1^1, so that the price line cuts $MRP_1(z_2^*)$ at z_1^3. Is this the new profit-maximizing level of z_1? The answer is no, because a change in p_1 will also cause a change in the optimal z_2, to z_2^{**}, so that the MRP_1 curve will shift to the right to $MRP_1(z_2^{**})$. The new optimal level for z_1 is z_1^{**} where $p_1^1 = MRP_1 (z_2^{**})$. The demand curve for z_1 is therefore the negatively sloped dashed line D_1: a fall in the price of an input leads to an increased demand for it by the firm.

If $MRP_1(z_2^{**})$ lies to the right of $MRP_1(z_2^*)$ the demand curve must be negatively sloped. We have merely asserted rather than proved that this is the case. We will support our conclusion that D_1 is negatively sloped by two direct arguments. For a firm selling y on a *competitive* market we have already proved that input demand functions are negatively sloped (section 7D) but the arguments used here also apply to the case of monopoly in the output market and have instructive similarities to the methods of sections 3B and 6B.

The first demonstration that the firm's demand curve for inputs is negatively sloped makes use of the properties of the *maximum profit function*. Since the optimal input demands depend on the input prices p_i

$$z_i^* = D_i(p_1, p_2) \qquad i = 1, 2 \qquad\qquad [A.5]$$

so does the firm's maximum profit:

$$\pi_{\max} = R(f(z_1^*, z_2^*)) - \Sigma p_i z_i^* = \pi^*(p_1, p_2) \qquad\qquad [A.6]$$

Differentiating $\pi^*(p_1, p_2)$ with respect to p_k gives

$$\frac{\partial \pi^*}{\partial p_k} = R'\left\{ f_1 \frac{\partial z_1^*}{\partial p_k} + f_2 \frac{\partial z_2^*}{\partial p_k} \right\} - \Sigma p_i \frac{\partial z_i^*}{\partial p_k} - z_k^* \qquad\qquad [A.7]$$

But from [A.2], $R'f_i = p_i$ and so rearranging [A.7] gives

$$\frac{\partial \pi^*}{\partial p_k} = \sum_i (R'f_i - p_i) \frac{\partial z_i^*}{\partial p_k} - z_k^* = -z_k^* = -D_k(p_1, p_2) \qquad\qquad [A.8]$$

This is yet another example of the Envelope Theorem (Appendix J) and shows that for all profit-maximizing firms Hotelling's lemma holds in respect of input prices, whether the firms operate in a competitive or monopolized output market (recall section 7D for the competitive firm). If we can also show that $\pi^*(p_1, p_2)$ is convex in input prices so that

$$\frac{\partial^2 \pi^*}{\partial p_k^2} = -\frac{\partial D_k}{\partial p_k} \geqslant 0 \qquad \text{[A.9]}$$

then we will have completed our first demonstration that input demand curves are (weakly) negatively sloped, i.e. $\partial D_k / \partial p_k \leqslant 0$.

To establish the convexity of $\pi^*(p_1, p_2)$, consider three input price vectors p^0, p^1 and $\bar{p} = tp^0 + (1 - t)p^1$ $(0 \leqslant t \leqslant 1)$ and the three corresponding profit-maximizing input vectors z^0, z^1 and $\bar{z}$. We have

$$\pi^*(p^0) = R(f(z^0)) - \Sigma p_i^0 z_i^0 \geqslant R(f(\bar{z})) - \Sigma p_i^0 \bar{z}_i \qquad \text{[A.10]}$$

and

$$\pi^*(p^1) = R(f(z^1)) - \Sigma p_i^1 z_i^1 \geqslant R(f(\bar{z})) - \Sigma p_i^1 \bar{z}_i \qquad \text{[A.11]}$$

Multiplying through [A.10] by t and [A.11] by $(1 - t)$ and then adding the corresponding sides of the two resulting inequalities gives

$$\begin{aligned}
t\pi^*(p^0) + (1 - t)\pi^*(p^1) &\geqslant t[R(f(\bar{z})) - \Sigma p_i^0 \bar{z}_i] + (1 - t)[R(f(\bar{z})) - \Sigma p_i^1 \bar{z}_i] \\
&= R(f(\bar{z})) - \Sigma[tp_i^0 + (1 - t)p_i^1]\bar{z}_i \\
&= R(f(\bar{z})) - \Sigma \bar{p}_i \bar{z}_i = \pi^*(\bar{p})
\end{aligned}$$

so that π^* is indeed convex in input prices and [A.9] holds.

Substitution and output effects

Our second demonstration of the negative slope of the firm's input demand curves requires a more detailed consideration of the effect of a change in the price of an input on the firm's behaviour. The firm's demand for z_1 changes as p_1 changes, first because a *different input combination* will now minimize the cost of any given output and second because a *different output level* will now be optimal. We can call these two effects the *substitution* and *output effects* of a change in p_1. In section 6B we showed that the substitution effect of an input price fall always leads to a rise in the use of the input whose price has fallen. We now use techniques similar to those used in deriving the Slutsky equation of section 3B, to decompose the total effect of a change in p_1 into the substitution and output effects.

From section 6B we know that the *cost-minimizing* z_1 depends on the input prices and the level of y:

$$\hat{z}_1 = h_1(p_1, p_2, y) \qquad \text{[A.12]}$$

where $\hat{z}_1$ denotes the cost-minimizing z_1. From the firms' profit maximization problem [A.1] we know that the *profit-maximizing* z_1 depends on p_1 and p_2, as shown in [A.5] and that the profit-maximizing output y^* will therefore also depend on p_1 and p_2 since choice of z_1, z_2 determines y:

$$y^* = f(z_1^*, z_2^*) = y^*(p_1, p_2) \qquad \text{[A.13]}$$

If we set y in [A.12] equal to $y*$ in [A.13]:

$$y = y*(p_1, p_2) \tag{A.14}$$

then, since profit maximization implies cost minimization, it must be true that

$$z_1^* = D_1(p_1, p_2) = \hat{z}_1 = h_1(p_1, p_2, y*(p_1, p_2)) \tag{A.15}$$

Now let p_1 vary but ensure that y in $h_1(p_1, p_2, y)$ varies to maintain the equalities in [A.14] and [A.15]. Hence h_1 will vary, first because with y constant a new cost-minimizing input combination is chosen and second because varying p_1 will change $y*$ and therefore y via [A.14]. Differentiating [A.15] with respect to p_1 gives

$$\frac{\partial D_1}{\partial p_1} = \frac{\partial h_1}{\partial p_1} + \frac{\partial h_1}{\partial y}\frac{\partial y}{\partial y*}\frac{\partial y*}{\partial p_1} \tag{A.16}$$

where the first term on the right-hand side of [A.16] shows how z_1 varies with p_1 when y is constant and so is the substitution effect. The second term is the rate at which z_1 varies indirectly with p_1 because of the effect of changes in p_1 on the optimal output level. This is the output effect. From section 6B we know that

$$\frac{\partial h_1}{\partial p_1} < 0$$

so let us consider the output effect. $\partial h_1/\partial y$ is the rate at which z_1 varies with y along the cost-minimizing expansion path and $\partial h_1/\partial y$ may be positive (z_1 is normal) or negative (z_1 is an inferior input). From [A.14], $\partial y/\partial y* = 1$. The last part of the second term is $\partial y*/\partial p_1$: the rate at which the profit-maximizing output varies with the price of input 1. Now, recalling equation [A.4] above, $y*$ is determined by the equality of marginal revenue with marginal cost. If a rise in p_1 shifts the marginal cost curve upwards then output must fall and, conversely, if the marginal cost curve falls as p_1 rises output will rise. Hence $\partial y*/\partial p_1$ is positive or negative as MC falls or rises with p_1, i.e. as $\partial MC/\partial p_1$ is negative or positive. But from section 8B, $\partial MC/\partial p_1$ is negative or positive as z_1 is inferior or normal. Hence

$$\frac{\partial h_1}{\partial y} \gtrless 0 \Leftrightarrow \frac{\partial MC}{\partial p_1} \gtrless 0 \Leftrightarrow \frac{\partial y*}{\partial p_1} \lessgtr 0$$

and therefore

$$\frac{\partial h_1}{\partial y}\frac{\partial y}{\partial y*}\frac{\partial y*}{\partial p_1} = \frac{\partial h_1}{\partial y}\frac{\partial y*}{\partial p_1} < 0 \tag{A.17}$$

The output effect of a rise in p_1 always reduces the demand for z_1, so reinforcing the substitution effect. We have therefore established by another route that

$$\frac{\partial D_1}{\partial p_1} = \frac{\partial h_1}{\partial p_1} + \frac{\partial h_1}{\partial y}\frac{\partial y*}{\partial p_1} < 0 \tag{A.18}$$

i.e. the input demand curve is negatively sloped, irrespective of whether the firm sells its output in a monopolized or competitive market.

From [A.18] we see that the slope of the firm's input demand curve depends on the magnitude of the substitution and output effects. The substitution effect in turn depends on the curvature of the firm's isoquants and, if the elasticity of substitution (section 6B) is taken as the measure of curvature, the substitution effect is larger the larger is the elasticity of substitution. The output effect is the product of two terms and is larger the greater is the response of the cost-minimizing level of z_1 to changes in output and the greater is the response of output to the change in input price. This latter influence depends on how much marginal cost varies with the price of the input: the bigger the shift in the marginal cost curve the bigger the change in the profit-maximizing output. If the firm is a monopolist in the output market the change in y also depends on the slope of the marginal revenue curve: the steeper this is the smaller will be the change in y as the marginal cost curve shifts. (Draw a diagram to show this.)

The market input demand curve

The market demand curve for a consumer good is derived by horizontally summing the individual demand curves. If an input is used only by firms which are monopolists in their respective output markets and these are unrelated in demand then the input market demand curve can be derived in the same way by horizontal summation of the individual firms' demand curves (see Question 4, Exercise 10A). Apart from this somewhat unlikely case the input market demand curve is *not* the horizontal sum of individual firms' demand curves. The reason can be seen if we examine an input used only in production of one type of good which is sold on a competitive market by the many firms producing it. Consider Fig. 10.2, in which the curve $\sum D_1^{j0}$ is the horizontal sum of the individual firms' demand curves for input 1 and, at the initial price p_1^0, $\sum z_1^{j0}$ is demanded. Each individual demand curve is like the dashed line D_1 in Fig. 10.1, which shows how each firm's *ceteris paribus* demand varies with p_1. It is assumed in drawing D_1 that the firm regards the price of output as unalterable by its actions, so that the D_1^{j0} curve of each firm is derived with the price of output held fixed. Hence the $\sum D_1^{j0}$ curve is also based on the assumption that the price of output is constant. But when the input price p_1 falls to p_1^1 all firms' average and marginal cost curves alter. In the long run, when the number of firms and the size of firms' plants can be varied, the change in total output is determined by the change in the firms' average cost curves (see Chapter 8). Average cost curves shift down when the price of the input falls (section 6B) and the long-run supply of the industry increases. The price of output will therefore fall, shifting the MRP_1, D_1^j

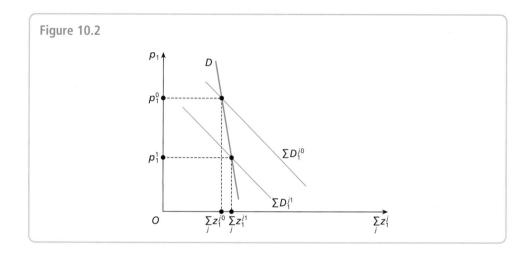

Figure 10.2

and $\sum D_1^j$ curves to the left. This is shown in Fig. 10.2, where $\sum D_1^{j1}$ is the new horizontal sum of the new individual D_1^{j1} curves and the amount of input demanded at p_1^1 is $\sum z_1^j$. We see that the market input demand curve is D, which is steeper than the $\sum_i D_1^j$ curves. (Compare the derivation of the market supply curves in Chapter 8.)

The market input demand curve is therefore determined by the demand conditions in the market for the output produced by the input, the change in firms' cost curves caused by the change in the input price and by the elasticity of substitution among the inputs.

EXERCISE 10A

1. The D curve in Fig. 10.2 is the long-run market demand curve for the input since it shows how demand varies when all inputs and the number of firms are freely variable. Construct the short-run market demand curve showing how demand varies with the price of the input when the other input is fixed and the number of firms does not alter. Would you expect this curve to be more or less elastic than that in Fig. 10.2?

2. Suppose that the fall in p_1 leads to a shift in the market demand curve for z_2. Under what circumstances will this change the price of z_2? What effect will this have on the market demand curve for z_1?

3. Explain why, when the buyers of an input are monopolists in markets unrelated to each other in demand, the input market demand curve can be obtained by horizontal summation of the individual firms' demand curves.

4. *Substitutes and complements.* Input i is a substitute (complement) for input k if an increase in p_k increases (reduces) the firm's profit-maximizing demand for input i. If i is a substitute for k does this imply that k must be a substitute for i? (Compare the definition of Marshallian substitutes and complements for the utility-maximizing consumer.)

B. Monopsony

Monopsony is defined as a market in which there is a single buyer of a commodity who confronts many sellers. Each of the sellers treats the market price of the good as a parameter and so there is a market supply curve for the good which is derived in the usual way from the supply curves of the individual suppliers. The single buyer of the good faces a market supply function relating total supply to the price he pays. This can be expressed (in the inverse form) as

$$p_1 = p_1(z_1) \qquad p_1' > 0 \qquad [\text{B.1}]$$

where [B.1] shows the price of the commodity which must be paid to generate a particular supply. Note that the buyer is assumed to face an upward-sloping supply curve; the price required is an increasing function of the amount supplied.

The market price of the monopsonized input is determined, given the supply function [B.1], by the buyer's demand for z_1. We assume that the monopsonist is a profit-maximizing firm, in which case the demand for z_1, and hence its price, is determined by the firm's profit-maximizing decision. In the two-input, single-output case the firm's problem is

$$\max_{z_1, z_2} R[f(z_1, z_2)] - p_1(z_1)z_1 - p_2 z_2 \qquad [\text{B.2}]$$

This is very similar to problem [A.1] except that p_1 depends on z_1 because of [B.1]. Input 2 is assumed to be bought on a market in which the firm treats p_2 as a parameter. The firm's output may be sold in a competitive or a monopolized market: monopsony need not imply monopoly. The firm may, for example, be the only employer of labour in a particular area but be selling its output in a market where it competes with many other firms, and labour may be relatively immobile.

Necessary conditions for a maximum of [B.2] are (when both z_1 and z_2 are positive at the optimum)

$$R'f_1 - (p_1 + p_1'z_1) = 0 \qquad \text{[B.3]}$$

$$R'f_2 - p_2 = 0 \qquad \text{[B.4]}$$

[B.4] is identical with [A.2], but [B.3] is not, because of the $p_1'z_1$ term. The firm will adjust its use of an input up to the point at which the additional revenue from a unit of the input equals the extra cost incurred. When the price of the input is independent of the number of units bought the cost of an extra unit is its price. But when the firm faces an upward sloping supply curve for the input it must pay a higher price for *all* units bought to ensure supply for an extra unit. This means that the cost of an extra unit of z_1 is the price paid for that unit *plus* the increased cost of the units already bought, which is the rise in p_1 times the amounts of z_1 bought: $p_1'z_1$. Hence writing MRP_i for the marginal revenue product of input i and MBC_i for the marginal cost of z_1 to the buyer (marginal buyer cost) the firm maximizes profits by setting

$$MRP_1 = MBC_1 > p_1 \qquad \text{[B.5]}$$

$$MRP_2 = MBC_2 = p_2 \qquad \text{[B.6]}$$

This equilibrium is illustrated for the monopsonized input in Fig. 10.3. S_1 is the supply curve of z_1 and MBC_1 plots the marginal buyer cost ($p_1 + p_1'z_1$) of the single buyer. $MRP_1(z_2^*)$ is the marginal revenue product curve for the input given the optimal level of z_2. The firm maximizes profit with respect to z_1 by equating MRP_1

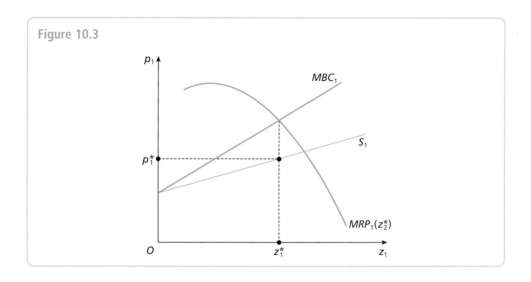

Figure 10.3

to MBC_1 at z_1^*. To generate this supply of z_1 the firm will set the monopsony price $p_1^* = p_1(z_1^*)$.

The analysis of the single buyer confronting many competitive sellers is rather similar to the analysis in Chapter 9 of the single seller confronting many competing buyers. In each case the firm realizes that it faces a curve relating price to quantity which summarizes the response of the competitive side of the market and the firm sets the quantity or price in the light of this interdependence of price and quantity. In each case the market price overstates the *marginal* profit contribution of the quantity and in each case this overstatement depends on the responsiveness of quantity to changes in price. Under monopoly the firm equates $MR = p[1 + (1/e)]$ to the marginal cost of output, and the less elastic is demand the greater is the difference between price and marginal cost. [B.5] can be rewritten in a similar way. Defining the elasticity of supply of z_1 with respect to price as

$$e_1^s = \frac{dz_1}{dp_1} \cdot \frac{p_1}{z_1} \qquad \text{[B.7]}$$

we see that

$$MBC_1 = p_1 + \frac{dp_1}{dz_1} \cdot z_1 = p_1 \left(1 + \frac{1}{e_1^s} \right) \qquad \text{[B.8]}$$

and so [B.5] becomes

$$MRP_1 = p_1 \left(1 + \frac{1}{e_1^s} \right) \qquad \text{[B.9]}$$

The less elastic is supply with respect to price the greater will be the difference between MRP_1 and the price of the input. In other words, the less responsive to price the input supply is, the greater the excess of the value of the marginal unit of the input over the price it receives. This could be regarded as a measure of the degree of 'monopsonistic exploitation'.

The effect of monopsony and output monopoly on the input market

When the output is produced from two or more inputs the analysis of the effect of both monopsony and output monopoly on the price of one of the inputs is complicated, because the use of the other input is likely to change as well, thus shifting the MRP_1 curve. If the output is produced by a single input this complication does not arise, and it is possible to show the implications of monopsony and output monopoly in a single simple diagram such as Fig. 10.4. Since there is a single input z_1 its marginal product depends only on z_1 and so the marginal revenue product MRP_1 and the value of the marginal product VMP_1 curves in Fig. 10.4 are fixed. S_1 and MBC_1 are supply and marginal buyer cost curves. There are four possible equilibria in this input market, where suppliers treat the price of z_1 as a parameter. If the firm also treats p_1 as given, i.e. if it acts as if it has no monopsony power and if it also treats output price as a parameter then VMP_1 is its demand curve for z_1 and the market price is p_1^0. If the firm uses its monopsony power but continues to treat output price as a parameter it will equate VMP_1 to MBC_1 and set the price p_1^1. If the firm monopolizes its output market but regards p_1 as a parameter its demand curve for z_1 is MRP_1 and the price of z_1 is p_1^2. Finally, if the firm exercises both monopoly and

Figure 10.4

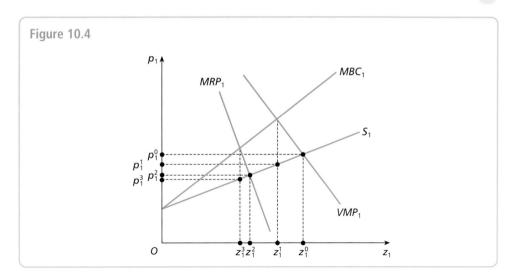

monopsony power it equates MRP_1 and MBC_1 and sets a price p_1^3. We see therefore that the price in an input market is reduced below the competitive level p_1^0 by both monopsony and monopoly power. The less elastic are the demand for output and the supply of input functions, the lower will be the price paid to suppliers of the input.

EXERCISE 10B

1. Under monopoly there is no supply curve for the monopolized output in the sense of a one to one correspondence between market price and quantity produced. Show that under monopsony there is no market demand curve for the monopsonized input.

2. Analyse the monopsonist's cost-minimization problem and the monopsonist's cost curves. (*Hint*: what does [B.1] imply about the isocost curves?) Show that at the monopsony equilibrium the input price ratio is not in general equal to the ratio of marginal products.

3. What is the effect of minimum wage legislation on the level of employment in (a) a competitive labour market, (b) a monopsonized labour market?

4. *Discriminating monopsony.* Suppose that a monopsony employer can segment its workers into two groups (men and women) and pay the two groups different wages. Show that it will pay a lower wage to the group with the less elastic supply function. What would be the effect on employment and wages of legislation which made it illegal to discriminate in this way?

5. Show that in the multi-input case, where the firm uses n inputs to produce its output and has monopsony power only in the market for input 1, that it is possible to use indifference curves in (p_1, z_1) space to analyze its behaviour in the markets for input 1. (*Hint*: maximize profit for given (p_1, z_1) and then use the envelope theorem.)

6. Show the welfare loss due to monopsony, and compare it with the welfare loss due to monopoly.

C. Unions as monopoly input suppliers

We define a union as any association of the suppliers of a particular type of labour which is formed with the aim of raising wages or improving working conditions. A union need not, of course, be described as such by its members: many professional associations (such as the British Medical Association and the Law Society) act as unions. Not all unions may be successful in raising the wages of their members above the competitive level. The union, like any would-be monopolist, must be able to control the supply of labour offered to firms. One method of doing this is to ensure that only union members can sell their labour in that particular market, a device known as the 'closed shop'. The closed shop may, by itself, reduce the supply of labour to the market if some potential workers dislike being union members as such. In general, however, the closed shop must be coupled with restrictions on the number of union members if all members are to be employed, since higher wages will increase the number of workers wishing to join the union, i.e. become employed at the higher wage.

If the union can act as a monopolist its behaviour will depend on the objective it pursues. It may be useful to distinguish between the objectives of the officials who run the union and those of the members. In the case of the firm, where conflicts of interest may exist between shareholders and managers, the extent to which the managers pursue the interests of the shareholders depends on the incentive system which relates managerial pay to profits and on the threat of product or capital market competition. Similar mechanisms may be at work in the case of the union. Officials' salaries can be related to the pay of members of the union. Unions which do not attend sufficiently closely to their members' interests may start to lose members to rival unions. Officials may be controlled directly through elections, but here the control mechanism may be much weaker than in a firm. Each union member has only one vote and so many members must cooperate to change the officials. Shareholders vote in proportion to the numbers of shares held and so a relatively small group of individual shareholders may exercise effective control.

It is by no means obvious that the political structure of a union will generate any well-defined preference ordering, let alone one which reflects the interests of its members. (See the discussion of the Arrow Impossibility Theorem in section 13F.) However, we will assume that such a preference ordering exists and can be represented by a utility function $U(w, z)$ where w is the wage paid to union members and z is the number of union members employed. (We assume that hours of work are fixed.) We illustrate the implications of different assumptions about union preferences by specifying three different forms for U.

The demand side of the labour market monopolized by the union is assumed to be competitive and the union is constrained to choose a wage and employment combination on the labour market demand curve D in Fig. 10.5. *MSR* is the corresponding 'marginal revenue to the seller' curve which shows the rate at which the total wage bill wz varies with z. S is the supply curve showing the minimum wage necessary to attract different numbers of workers into the industry. S plots the *reservation wage* or 'supply price' of workers. The competitive equilibrium in the absence of an effective union monopoly would be at ε with a wage rate of w_c.

The *economic rent* earned by a worker is the difference between the wage paid and the wage necessary to induce that worker to take a job in the industry. The total

Figure 10.5

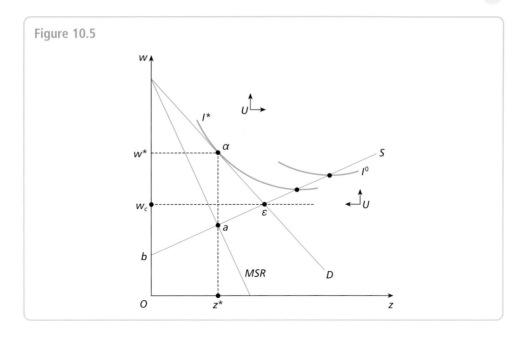

economic rent earned at any given wage is the difference between the total wages paid wz and the area under the labour supply curve up to the employment level. One possible objective for the union would be to maximize the total economic rent of the workers in the industry. In this case the union's utility function would be

$$U(w, z) = wz - \int_0^z \omega(\tilde{z}) \, d\tilde{z} \qquad [\text{C.1}]$$

where $\omega(z)$ is the *inverse supply function* of union members, showing the wage $\omega(z)$ necessary to induce a supply of z workers. If S is interpreted as a marginal cost curve we can see that the union's problem is identical to that of a profit-maximizing monopolist. Hence the union would restrict employment to where MSR cuts S by setting a wage w^*, yielding a total rent of αabw^* for its members.

Equivalently, we could consider the union's indifference curves in (w, z) space. They have slope

$$\left. \frac{dw}{dz} \right|_{dU=0} = -\frac{U_z}{U_w} = -\frac{w - \omega(z)}{z} \qquad [\text{C.2}]$$

Since $U_w = z > 0$ higher indifference curves are preferred to lower ones: the union is better off on I^0 than on I^*. To the left of the supply curve $w > \omega$ and so $U_z > 0$; to the right of S, where $w < \omega$, $U_z < 0$. Hence the indifference curves are $\cup$-shaped about the supply curve. The union is constrained by the market demand curve that it faces and chooses the wage employment combination (w^*, z^*) where its indifference curve I^* is tangent to D. (Where would the solution have been if the union takes the wage rate as a parameter which is unaffected by the employment level?)

An alternative union objective function is

$$U(w, z) = wz \qquad [\text{C.3}]$$

Figure 10.6

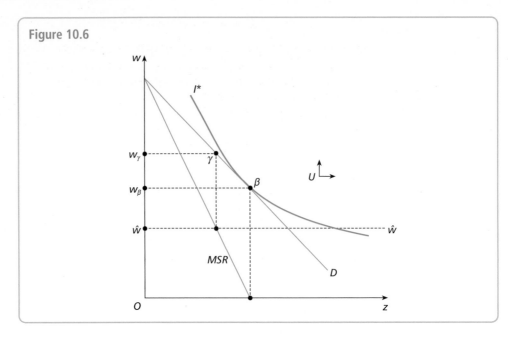

For example, the union officials may wish to maximize the total wage bill because union membership fees are proportional to the wage and the salaries of officials or other benefits (pleasant working conditions, union conferences in exotic locations) may increase with the union's income. Since $U_w = z > 0$, $U_z = w > 0$, the indifference curves corresponding to [C.3] are negatively sloped and are rectangular hyperbolas. Higher indifference curves are preferred to lower. In Fig. 10.6 the union maximizes wz by choosing the point β on D where the indifference curve I^* is tangent to D. At this point MSR is zero and the total seller revenue (the wage bill wz) is maximized.

We have so far ignored the possibility that the union may have unemployed members: at the wage set by the union not all of its members can find employment in the industry. Consider a union which has a total of z^0 members of whom z are employed at the wage w and who get a utility of $u(w)$ ($u' > 0$, $u'' < 0$). The $z^0 - z$ members who are not employed get unemployment pay of $\hat{w}$ yielding utility of $\hat{u}(\hat{w})$. u and $\hat{u}$ may be different utility functions to reflect the fact that members care about being employed or not as well as about the income they receive. Suppose that employed workers are chosen at random each period from the pool of union members, so that each member has a probability of z/z^0 of being employed and $(z^0 - z)/z^0$ of being unemployed. Assume that each member evaluates this *risky prospect* by its *expected utility*:

$$[u(w)z + \hat{u}(\hat{w})(z^0 - z)]/z^0 \tag{C.4}$$

(See Chapter 17 for a discussion of expected utility as a representation of preferences under uncertainty.) A union run in the interests of its members would aim to maximize [C.4], or since z^0 is constant, to maximize

$$U(w, z) = u(w)z + \hat{u}(\hat{w})(z^0 - z) = [u(w) - \hat{u}(\hat{w})]z + \hat{u}(\hat{w})z^0 \tag{C.5}$$

If we assume that union members are only interested in income and have a constant marginal utility of income we obtain the simple union utility function

$$U(w, z) = (w - \hat{w})z + \hat{w}z^0 \qquad [\text{C.6}]$$

(The union indifference curves are now rectangular hyperbolas with a horizontal axis at $\hat{w}$.) Since $\hat{w}$ and z^0 are constants, [C.5] is maximized by maximizing $(w - \hat{w})z$ and the union's optimization problem is now analogous to that of a monopolist with a constant 'marginal cost' of $\hat{w}$. In Fig. 10.6 the union would choose the point γ on D, determined by the intersection of its marginal revenue curve MSR and its 'marginal cost' curve at $\hat{w}$.

It is possible to construct many models of the above kinds, each of which may be appropriate to a particular union or industry. A model of the way in which the union's objectives are determined is necessary in order to be able to predict what objectives will be dominant in what circumstances. This will require a detailed specification of the political constitution of the union, including the frequency and type of elections, whether officials are elected or are appointed and controlled by elected representatives and so on. In addition, the theory could be extended to take account of inter-union conflict or cooperation: will unions compete for new members? In what circumstances will unions merge or collude? It would be interesting to approach these questions using the concepts of oligopoly theory developed in Chapter 16.

EXERCISE 10C

1. *Rent maximization.* Confirm formally that the rent-maximizing union will set a wage of w^* as shown in Fig. 10.5.

2. Sketch the indifference curves for the union utility functions [C.5] and [C.6] and the corresponding (w, z) points chosen by the union. What are the implications of assuming (a) that $\hat{u}(\hat{w}) < u(w)$ when $\hat{w} = w$ and (b) that $d\hat{u}(\hat{w})/d\hat{w} < du(w)/dw$ when $\hat{w} = w$?

D. Bilateral monopoly

Bilateral monopoly is a market situation in which a single seller confronts a single buyer. For definiteness and continuity, we consider a labour market in which supply is monopolized by a union and there is a single buyer of labour. z is the sole input in the production of an output $y = f(z)$. The revenue from sale of y is $R(f(z))$ and the MRP curve in Fig. 10.7 plots the marginal benefit to the buyer of z: $R'f' = MR \cdot MP$, using the notation of section A. The average revenue product curve ARP plots $R/z = py/z = pAP$ where AP is the average product of z: y/z.

The objective function of the firm is its profit function

$$\pi = R(f(z)) - wz = \pi(w, z) \qquad [\text{D.1}]$$

and its indifference curves in (w, z) space have slope

$$\left.\frac{dw}{dz}\right|_{d\pi=0} = -\frac{\pi_z}{\pi_w} = \frac{R'(f(z))f'(z) - w}{z} = \frac{MRP - w}{z} \qquad [\text{D.2}]$$

where $R'f' = MRP$ is the firm's marginal revenue product. For $w < MRP$ its indifference curves are positively sloped and for $w > MRP$ they are negatively sloped. Thus its indifference curves are $\cap$-shaped about the MRP curve. (Recall section B.) If the

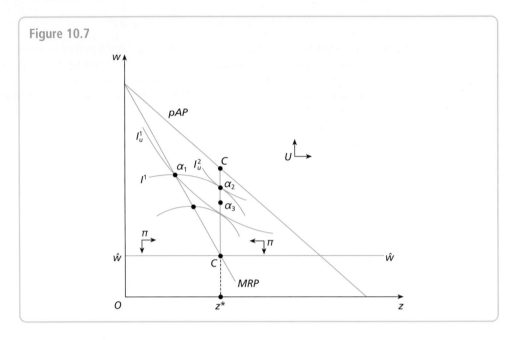

Figure 10.7

firm acted as a monopsonist facing competitive labour suppliers, it would announce a wage rate at which it is willing to hire workers and employment would be determined by the supply curves of the workers.

Suppose that the union has the simple objective function

$$U(w, z) = (w - \hat{w})z + \hat{w}z^0 \qquad [\text{D.3}]$$

examined in section C, where z^0 is the number of union members and $\hat{w}$ is the income or wage of those who are unemployed. The union's indifference curves are hyperbolas, rectangular to the $\hat{w}\hat{w}$ line, with slope

$$\frac{dw}{dz}\bigg|_{dU=0} = -\frac{w - \hat{w}}{z} \qquad [\text{D.4}]$$

If the union acted as a monopolist with respect to the labour supply of its members it would announce a wage rate at which its members would be willing to supply labour and employment would be determined by the demand curve for labour.

When a single buyer and a single seller of labour confront each other it seems implausible that either party will treat a wage rate announced by the other as parametric and passively adjust either their supply or demand. Both will realize that they possess market power in the sense that, by refusing to demand or supply labour at a wage announced by the other, they can prevent any gains from trade being achieved and thus impose costs on the other. The two parties must therefore agree on a wage and an employment level before production can occur.

We assume in this section that the agreement between the union and the firm is the outcome of a *cooperative game*. In such a game all the actions of the parties are controlled by a binding agreement between them specifying what each will do. The cooperative game approach to bargaining is concerned solely with the content of the agreement. It ignores the process of bargaining and negotiation by which agreements are reached. (We examine the alternative non-cooperative game approach, which does pay more attention to the bargaining process, in sections 15E and 15F.) We attempt to predict the agreement by requiring that it satisfy certain 'reasonable' conditions.

Two obvious conditions to impose are:

(a) *individual rationality*: any agreement should leave both parties at least as well off as they would be if there was no agreement;

(b) *efficiency*: there should be no other agreement which would make one of them better off and the other no worse off.

If an agreement satisfies these requirements it is an *efficient bargaining solution* to the cooperative bargaining game.

Applying these conditions provides a partial answer to the question of what agreement will be reached by the union and the firm. If there is no agreement and therefore no employment, the firm will have zero profit. Any agreement which yields a (w, z) combination on or below its average revenue product curve pAP will satisfy the individual rationality constraint for the firm. If the union achieves zero utility if there is no agreement, it will be no worse off with an agreement at any point on or above the line $\hat{w}\hat{w}$. Thus the set of individually rational agreements which make both parties no worse off is the triangle bounded by the vertical axis, $\hat{w}\hat{w}$ and pAP in Fig. 10.7.

Imposing the efficiency requirement further reduces the set of possible bargains. If the parties' indifference curves intersect at a point such as α_1 it is always possible to find another point or bargain which makes at least one of them better off and the other no worse off. Thus moving from the agreement α_1 where the indifference curves I^1 and I_u^1 intersect to the agreement α_2 will make the union better off since α_2 is on the higher indifference curve I_u^2. The firm is no worse off at α_2 since both point α_1 and α_2 are on I^1. A move from α_1 to α_3 would make both union and firm better off.

A necessary condition for efficiency is that the parties' indifference curves are tangent:

$$\left. \frac{dw}{dz} \right|_{d\pi=0} = -\frac{\pi_z}{\pi_w} = \frac{R'f' - w}{z} = \left. \frac{dw}{dz} \right|_{dU=0} = -\frac{w - \hat{w}}{z} \qquad [D.5]$$

which implies

$$R'f' = \hat{w} \qquad [D.6]$$

All agreements satisfying [D.6] are efficient. Notice that [D.6] depends only on the level of employment z (which enters into $R'f'$) and not on w. The locus of points where [D.6] is satisfied and the agreement is efficient is a vertical line at z^* where MRP cuts $\hat{w}\hat{w}$.

The set of agreements satisfying individual rationality and efficiency is the *contract curve*. In the current model the contract curve has a particularly simple form: it is the line CC in Fig. 10.7 between the pAP and $\hat{w}\hat{w}$ curves where indifference curves are tangent and the parties no worse off than if they do not agree.

The efficient bargain model predicts the level of employment z^* the parties will agree on but it is unable to predict the wage rate at which the workers will be employed. This is perhaps unsurprising: the parties can agree to choose an employment level which will maximize their potential gains from agreement: the difference between the firm's revenue $R(f(z))$ and the 'cost' of labour $\hat{w}z$ as perceived by the union. A change in z which increases $R - \hat{w}z$ can make both parties better off and they can therefore agree to it. However, for fixed z, changes in the wage rate have precisely opposite effects on their utilities:

$$\pi_w = -z, \qquad U_w = z$$

With z held constant changes in w merely make one party better off at the expense of the other. In Fig. 10.7 the firm will always prefer a bargain lower down CC and the union a bargain higher up CC.

One way to remove the indeterminacy of the bilateral monopoly model is to impose additional requirements on the agreement or solution of the cooperative bargaining game. We do this in section 15E.

EXERCISE 10D

1. Derive the contract curve if the union's objective function is given by [C.2] or [C.3].

2. *Non-linear union utility function.* Suppose that the union has the utility function $U(w, z) = [u(w) - \hat{u}(\hat{w})]z + \hat{u}(\hat{w})\hat{z}$, where $u' > 0$, $u'' < 0$.

   (a) Show that the contract curve has a positive slope.

   (b) Now suppose that the firm's production function is $y = f(z - l) = f(n)$ where z is total employment by the firm, l is the number of workers who contribute nothing to production (they spend all day playing cards) and n is the effective labour force employed by the firm. The firm's marginal revenue function is strictly concave in output: $R'' < 0$. For outputs in excess of $f(n^0)$ its marginal revenue is negative. When employed, workers are assumed not to mind whether they play cards or produce output and they get the same wage w. The agreement between the union and the firm now specifes w, z and l.

   (i) Show that the contract curve now has a horizontal segment for $z \geqslant n^0$. Interpret a bargain struck at a point on the horizontal segment.

   (ii) What effect would an increase in the demand for the firm's output have on the contract curve? What would happen to output, employment and the wage rate if the agreement was on the horizontal segment?

11 Capital markets

A. Introduction

The theory of the consumer developed in Chapter 2 related to choice of consumption goods in a single time period. It took no account of saving and dissaving, or lending and borrowing, which we would normally expect to be an important aspect of consumer behaviour. Moreover, we know that the operation of the capital market – the market for borrowing and lending – influences the economy in important ways, and so it is useful to develop a theory of the operation of that market.

In the theory of the firm, the process of change in equilibrium scale in the long run can be viewed in a different way from the approach in Chapter 6. The firm changes its scale by investing in new capacity, and so we could view the problem of determining long-run equilibrium output as the problem of choosing the most profitable amount of investment. Hence it is instructive to construct a theory of how such investment decisions are taken. Section B examines the problem of optimal intertemporal consumption, section C the investment decision and section D the capital market. Section E shows how the two-period model of previous sections may be generalized to many periods. Capital markets under uncertainty are considered in sections 21E and 21F.

B. Optimal consumption over time

Assume that time is divided into equal discrete intervals – say into years. Given the consumer's annual income, we assume that the atemporal theory applies, and the consumer allocates income optimally over goods. However, he also has a further choice, which is either to lend some of his income, or to borrow. Lending reduces current consumption, but increases future consumption, and conversely for borrowing. Thus, the analysis of borrowing and lending decisions is the analysis of the consumer's choice of a consumption pattern over time.

It is convenient initially to make the following assumptions:

(a) Within each period of time prices are given and the consumer spends his consumption budget optimally. We can therefore conduct the analysis entirely in terms of choices of the *total* consumption expenditure in each period, rather than of quantities of particular goods and services. (Recall the composite commodity theorem of section 3D)

(b) There are only two time periods: time 0 (the present) and time 1. We denote the individual's total consumption expenditures in the two periods by M_0 and M_1.

(c) The consumer faces a perfectly competitive capital market so that there is a given price for borrowing and lending, which is usually expressed as an interest rate, *r*. If £100 is borrowed at time 0 then £100$(1 + r)$ must be repaid at time 1 (*r* is defined as an *annual* interest rate). Thus $1 + r$ can be thought of as the price paid for borrowing, or received for lending £1. Since the capital market is perfect, all borrowers and lenders regard themselves as being able to borrow or lend as much as they like at the going rate of interest *r*.

Given these assumptions, we can construct a model of choice of consumption over time. The elements of the consumer's optimization problem are:

(a) The choice variables M_0 and M_1.

(b) The consumer preference ordering over combinations of current and future consumption expenditure (M_0, M_1) which satisfies all the assumptions made in section 2A. Preferences can be represented by the utility function $u(M_0, M_1)$ and indifference curves have the usual shape. Since the consumer prefers more expenditure in one period to less, other things being equal, the marginal utilities of current and future consumption are positive.

(c) The feasible set. The consumer is endowed with an income time-stream $(\bar{M}_0, \bar{M}_1)$, $\bar{M}_0, \bar{M}_1 \geq 0$. So that the problem is not trivial, we assume at least one of these is positive. Let *A* represent the amount the consumer borrows or lends in year 0, with $A > 0$ for borrowing, and $A < 0$ for lending. Then, the consumer's feasible consumptions are constrained by

$$0 \leq M_0 \leq \bar{M}_0 + A \tag{B.1}$$

$$0 \leq M_1 \leq \bar{M}_1 - (1 + r)A \tag{B.2}$$

The right-hand inequalities bind in [B.1] and [B.2] as a result of our non-satiation axiom and the optimal point is on a boundary of the feasible set. Solving for *A* in [B.2] and substituting into [B.1] gives

$$(M_0 - \bar{M}_0) + \frac{(M_1 - \bar{M}_1)}{1 + r} = 0 \tag{B.3}$$

or

$$M_0 + \frac{M_1}{1 + r} = \bar{M}_0 + \frac{\bar{M}_1}{1 + r} = V_0 \tag{B.4}$$

Equation [B.3] should be compared with the directly analogous consumer's budget constraint in section 2E. $(M_0 - \bar{M}_0)$ and $(M_1 - \bar{M}_1)$ are net demands for consumption in the two periods and $1/(1 + r)$ the relative price. Equation [B.4] is the consumer's *wealth constraint*. The value of the consumer's chosen consumption time-stream is equal to the value of his endowed income time-stream. The values are expressed in terms of income at time 0, i.e. they are *present values*. V_0 is the present value of the consumer's endowed income time-stream, or his wealth. By borrowing or lending the consumer may achieve a consumption time-stream which differs from his endowed time-stream, but in doing so is constrained by his wealth.

The assumption of a perfect capital market implies that *r* is taken as constant by the consumer. The wealth constraint can be graphed as a straight line such as V_0 in Fig. 11.1. The slope of this *wealth line* is

$$\frac{dM_1}{dM_0} = -(1 + r) \tag{B.5}$$

Figure 11.1

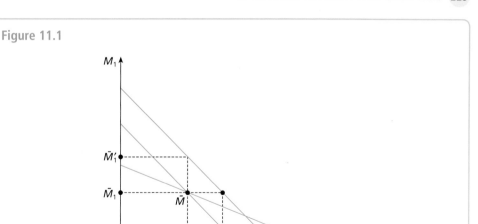

since [B.4] implies the equation $M_1 = (1 + r)V_0 - (1 + r)M_0$. Note that the wealth line *must* pass through the initial endowment point $\bar{M} = (\bar{M}_0, \bar{M}_1)$, since the point always satisfies [B.4]. The wealth line V_0 is the set of market exchange opportunities. By lending, the consumer can move leftwards from $\bar{M}$ along the line; by borrowing, he moves rightwards. Each point on V_0 represents simultaneously a consumption time-stream, an amount of borrowing or lending in year 0, and a corresponding repayment in year 1.

The absolute value of the slope of V_0 is determined by r. A reduction in r leads to a flatter line, such as V_0' in the figure. Note that this line must continue to pass through $\bar{M}$, since the initial endowment point continues to satisfy [B.4]. Hence, changes in r cause the line to rotate through $\bar{M}$. A change in an initial endowment, r remaining unchanged will change the intercept of V_0 but not the slope of the line, and so the line shifts parallel to itself, for example to V_0''. This line corresponds to, say, an increase in $\bar{M}_0$ to $\bar{M}_0'$, or an increase in $\bar{M}_1$ to $\bar{M}_1'$, or intermediate increases in both. The new wealth line must pass through the new initial endowment point.

Given our assumptions about preferences, we expect to obtain a tangency solution to the consumer's optimization problem such as that in Fig. 11.2 at M^*. (Why is it reasonable to assume that we would not have a corner solution?) The consumer's chosen consumption time-stream at (M_0^*, M_1^*) is achieved by borrowing an amount $M_0^* - \bar{M}_0$ in year 0, and repaying $\bar{M}_1 - M_1^* = (1 + r)(M_0^* - \bar{M}_0)$ in year 1. It is possible for the indifference curves, initial endowments, or interest rate to be such that the optimal point implies lending (M^* to the left of $\bar{M}$ on V_0), or neither borrowing nor lending (M^* coincides with $\bar{M}$). These cases are left to the reader.

At the optimum the slope of the indifference curve equals the slope of the wealth line. But the slope of the indifference curve is the negative of the ratio of marginal utilities, $-u_0/u_1$, where u_i is the marginal utility of period i consumption (see Chapter 2, section A). At the optimum, therefore, using [B.5],

$$\frac{u_0}{u_1} = 1 + r \qquad \text{[B.6]}$$

Figure 11.2

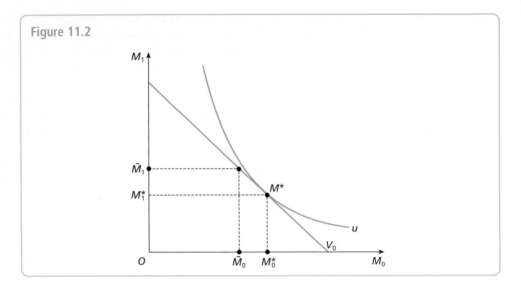

Now a £1 reduction in M_0 reduces u by the marginal utility u_0. There will exist an increase in M_1 which will make the consumer just as well off as before the £1 reduction in M_0. This compensating increase in M_1 is £$(1 + \rho)$ and is defined by

$$u_0(M_0, M_1) \equiv u_1(M_0, M_1)(1 + \rho) \qquad \text{[B.7]}$$

where the notation emphasizes that the marginal utilities u_0 and u_1 and hence ρ depend on the consumption time-stream. Raising M_1 by £1 increases u by the marginal utility u_1 so that increasing M_1 by £$(1 + \rho)$ will raise u by $u_1(1 + \rho)$ which just offsets the effect of the £1 reduction in M_0. Note that since $u_0 > 0$ and $u_1 > 0$ we must have $1 + \rho > 0$ (so that $\rho > -1$). ρ can be interpreted as the consumer's *subjective rate of interest* since it shows how much *extra* consumption in period 1 is required to compensate for the loss of £1 of current consumption. ρ may be negative if less than £1 extra of M_1 is required. It is subjective because it depends on the consumer's preferences, not on observable market phenomena. Since u_0 and u_1 will depend on M_0 and M_1 so must ρ: $\rho = \rho(M_0, M_1)$. Rearranging [B.7], we get

$$\frac{u_0}{u_1} \equiv 1 + \rho \qquad \text{[B.8]}$$

and we see that as the consumer moves along an indifference curve from left to right substituting M_0 for M_1, ρ will decline since the slope of the indifference curve becomes flatter, and current consumption relatively less valuable. ρ is also known as the consumer's *rate of time preference*. We can use [B.8] to write the optimum condition in [B.6] simply as

$$\rho = \rho(M_0, M_1) = r \qquad \text{[B.9]}$$

and this (or [B.6]) together with the constraint [B.4] provides two equations to determine the optimal M_0^*, M_1^*. The consumer is in equilibrium where his subjective rate of interest is equal to the market rate of interest. The consumer lends up to the point at which the market interest rate is just sufficient to compensate for the marginal reduction in current consumption. Alternatively, he borrows until he reaches the point at which the price he must pay (in terms of reduced consumption next period) is just sufficient to offset the value to him of the additional consumption this period.

EXERCISE 11B

1. (a) Explain in commonsense terms the inequalities in [B.1] and [B.2].
   (b) Draw diagrams analogous to Fig. 11.2, in which (i) the consumer lends at the optimum, and (ii) he neither borrows nor lends.
   (c) Explain why a corner solution (with M_0^* or $M_1^* = 0$) would be intuitively unreasonable.
   (d) Explain why a constant time preference rate would be intuitively unreasonable.
   (e) What would be implied by values of ρ equal, respectively, to -0.2, 0 and 0.2?

2. Derive the demand functions for present (period 0) and future (period 1) consumption as functions of wealth and the rate of interest, for a consumer who has the Cobb–Douglas utility function $u = M_0^\alpha M_1^{(1-\alpha)}$ $(0 < \alpha < 1)$.

3. *Discount factor.* The consumer's subjective discount factor δ is the rate at which the consumer is willing to give up period 0 consumption for period 1 consumption: $\delta \equiv u_1/u_0$. Is it always the case that $\delta < 1$? Recast the description of the consumer's optimum in terms of the discount factor.

4. *Imperfect capital market.* Suppose, because of transaction costs or taxation of interest income, that the interest rate at which the consumer can borrow exceeds that at which he can lend (though both are still invariant with the quantity borrowed or lent). Construct the feasible set in this case, and suggest the solution possibilities. Give, in terms of interest rates and the consumer's time preference rate, the condition which holds at the optimal solution for a consumer who neither borrows nor lends.

C. The optimal investment decision

A 'firm' can be regarded for the moment as a single decision-taker who has available some specific set of *productive investment opportunities*, i.e. some means of transforming current income into future income, by means of production rather than exchange. The investment and production decisions taken by the owner of the firm determine the cash flows she receives from the firm in each period. At the same time the owner has access to the capital market on which she can borrow or lend, and so her consumption expenditure in each period need not equal the cash flow generated by her investment and production decisions. (We assume that the firm is the only source of income for the owner.) The owner of a firm with investment opportunities must therefore solve both the *investment and production decision problem*, which determines the firm's cash flow, and the *consumption decision problem*, which determines how her consumption expenditures differ from the income she receives from the firm.

We make the same two-period and perfect capital market assumptions as in the case of the consumer. We also assume that the owner of the firm has a preference ordering over the consumption time-streams (M_0, M_1) representable by indifference curves in the usual way. The only new element in the analysis is the feasible set, which now depends on the technological possibilities of production and investment as well as the terms on which the owner can borrow or lend in the capital market.

Production and investment possibilities

The cash flow or dividend D_t $(t = 0, 1)$ received from the firm by the owner in each period is the firm's revenue less its expenditure. If labour is the only variable input, the expenditure in each period is the sum of the amount paid in wages and the outlay on purchases of additional physical capital, i.e. investment. Hence the cash flow is

$$D_0 = pf(L_0, K_0) - wL_0 - p_K(K_1 - K_0) = pf(L_0, K_0) - wL_0 - I \qquad [C.1]$$

$$D_1 = pf(L_1, K_1) - wL_1 \qquad [C.2]$$

where p, w and p_K are the competitive market prices of the firm's output, labour and physical capital; $f(L_t, K_t)$ is the firm's production function, L_t and K_t the labour and capital inputs, in period t. We assume that all prices and the form of the production function are constant over time. K_0 is the stock of physical capital inherited at the start of period 0 and $I = p_K(K_1 - K_0)$ is the expenditure by the firm in period 0 to increase its capital stock to K_1 for use in production in period 1. We assume that there is no depreciation of the capital stock. Note that there will be no investment in the second period since there is no third period, and also that if $K_1 < K_0$ the firm is disinvesting, i.e. selling off some of its capital to increase its cash flow in the first period (section E contains more general formulations, with many periods and depreciation).

In earlier chapters we defined the input variables in the production function as *flows* per period. Here we have a production function in which one of the inputs (L_t) is also a flow per period (so many hours of labour supplied by the workforce) but the other (K_t) is a stock (so many machines, say). The production function used here is compatible with our earlier approach because we can let $k_t = H(K_t)$ be the flow of capital services from a capital stock of size K_t. Then if the production function relating the output per period to the flow of labour and capital services per period is $y_t = \hat{f}(L_t, k_t)$, the production function used here is just $y_t = f(L_t, K_t) \equiv \hat{f}(L_t, H(K_t))$.

The firm will always choose the labour input to maximize the cash flow in each period for given levels of the capital stock, since choice of L_t affects only the cash flow of that period and the owner will always prefer a larger cash flow to a smaller in a period given that the other period's cash flow is unaffected. Given the optimal choice of the variable input L_t in each period and the fixed initial capital stock K_0, the cash flows in each period depend only on the capital stock K_1 chosen for period 1:

$$D_0 = pf(L_0^*, K_0) - wL_0^* - p_K(K_1 - K_0) = D_0(K_1) \qquad [C.3]$$

$$D_1 = pf(L_1^*, K_1) - wL_1^* = D_1(K_1) \qquad [C.4]$$

where L_t^* is the optimal level of the labour input in period t. Since both periods' cash flows depend on K_1 we can derive a relationship between D_0 and D_1 by varying K_1, i.e. by investing (or disinvesting). L_0^* does not depend on K_1, since the marginal cash flow from variations in L_0 is $p\partial f(L_0, K_0)/\partial L_0 - w$, which does not vary with K_1. Hence increasing K_1 reduces D_0 at the rate p_K. L_1^* will, however, depend on K_1 since the marginal period 1 cash flow from variations in L_1 is $p\partial f(L_1, K_1)/\partial L_1 - w$, which is affected by changes in K_1. Hence

$$\frac{dD_1}{dK_1} = p\frac{\partial f(L_1^*, K_1)}{\partial K_1} + \left(p\frac{\partial f(L_1^*, K_1)}{\partial L_1} - w\right)\frac{dL_1^*}{dK_1} = p\frac{\partial f(L_1^*, K_1)}{\partial K_1} \qquad [C.5]$$

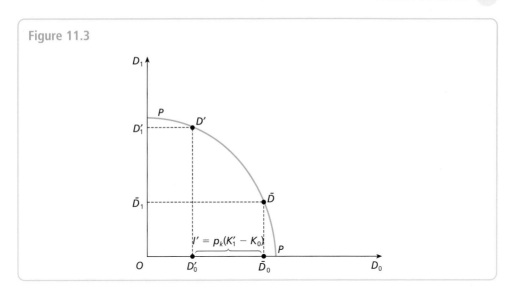

Figure 11.3

where we have used the fact that L_1^* maximizes D_1 for given K_1 and so the marginal period 1 cash flow from L_1 is zero at L_1^*. (This is yet another example of the Envelope Theorem of Appendix J.) Increasing K_1 will therefore reduce D_0 and increase D_1 (as long as the marginal product of capital is positive in period 1).

Figure 11.3 plots feasible combinations of cash flows that the owner of the firm can receive by varying her investment decision, i.e. by altering K_1 and so moving along the curve PP. $\bar{D} = (\bar{D}_0, \bar{D}_1)$ is assumed to be the cash flow time-stream the firm generates if it neither invests nor disinvests, so that $K_1 = K_0$ and $I = 0$. By increasing K_1 say to K_1' through investing $I' = p_K(K_1' - K_0)$, the cash flow of the first period is reduced to $D_0' = D_0 - I'$ and the next period's cash flow increased to D_1'. (The exercises at the end of this section ask you to investigate influences of the production function and p, w and p_K on the shape of curve PP.)

Borrowing and lending possibilities

The owner of the firm has access to a capital market on which she can borrow or lend at the interest rate r and so her consumption expenditure time-stream (M_0, M_1) may differ from the cash flow time stream (D_0, D_1) she receives from the firm.

Figure 11.4 combines wealth lines, similar to those of section B, with the curve PP from Fig. 11.3. It shows the feasible set when there are possibilities of altering the time pattern of consumption by both production and capital market activities, i.e. by moving along PP and along a wealth line (borrowing or lending).

By investing or disinvesting the owner of the firm can move along PP and achieve different combinations of cash flows. Given her investment decision (choice of D_0, D_1) the owner can then enter the capital market and trade (borrow or lend) to any point along the wealth line through her cash flow combination (D_0, D_1). For example if the owner does not invest or disinvest she will be at the point $\bar{D}$ on PP. She could then lend out some of her period 0 cash flow and move along the wealth line $\bar{V}$ to a point such as M' where she is better off (on a higher indifference curve than $\bar{u}$ through $\bar{D}$).

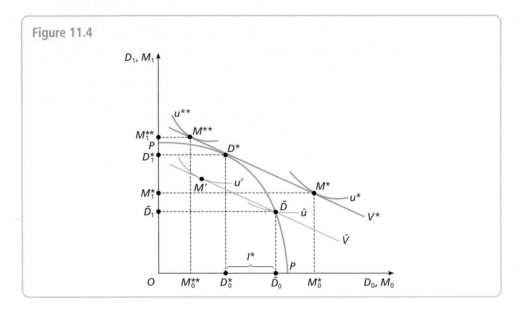

Figure 11.4

Higher wealth lines present the owner with better consumption possibilities than lower wealth lines since there will always be some point on the higher wealth line which is on a higher indifference curve than *all* the points on the lower wealth line. Hence the firm's optimal investment decision (choice of K_1 or equivalently choice of D_0, D_1) will be that which maximizes the owner's wealth. In Fig. 11.4 this is the cash flow combination D_0^*, D_1^* achieved by choosing a second period capital stock of K_1^* and investing $I^* = p_K(K_1^* - K_0)$ in the first period. V^* is the highest possible wealth line attainable by investment along PP and so by investing I^* the owner is put in the best possible position for engaging in borrowing or lending in the capital market.

Given the optimal wealth-maximizing investment and production decisions the owner chooses some combination of consumption expenditures in the two periods (M_0, M_1) along the maximum wealth line V^*.

In Fig. 11.4 are shown two possible final equilibrium positions. Given the pattern of preferences represented by indifference curve u^*, the overall optimum position is at $M^* = (M_0^*, M_1^*)$. We can think of the owner of the firm reaching this position in two steps: first, by investing I^* to get to D^*; and second, by *borrowing* the amount $M_0^* - D_0^*$, which implies that she will have to repay the amount $D_1^* - M_1^* = (1 + r)(M_0^* - D_0^*)$ out of cash flow in period 1. The first step is the solution to the *investment decision problem*, the second solves the *consumption decision problem*.

If, on the other hand, the pattern of preferences is represented by indifference curve u^{**}, then the overall optimal solution is at $M^{**} = (M_0^{**}, M_1^{**})$. This is again reached in two steps. First, the firm invests I^*; then the owner *lends* the amount $D_0^* - M_0^{**}$ on the capital market, implying that she will receive $M_1^{**} - D_1^* = (1 + r)(D_0^* - M_0^{**})$ in period 1, to add to period 1 cash flow. Thus, the solution to the investment decision problem is again to invest I^*, while the optimal consumption decision now involves further lending. There is a third kind of solution possibility, which would arise if an indifference curve happened to be tangent to V^* at D^*, in which case I^* would still solve the investment decision problem, with no lending or borrowing on the capital market and $D^* = M^*$.

Thus we have three types of solution to the firm's problem of choosing an optimal consumption time-stream, one involving borrowing, one involving lending, and the third involving neither. The important point, however, is that in each case the solution to the optimal investment decision is the same, and is *independent* of the pattern of preferences, which determines the solution to the consumption decision. Thus there is a *separation* between the investment and consumption decisions because of the existence of a perfect capital market. The investment decision requires information only on investment opportunities – the curve *PP* – and the market interest rate.

As the firm moves along *PP* and decreases D_0 by $-dD_0$, i.e. invests an increment $dI = -dD_0$, there is a corresponding increase in D_1 of dD_1, the gross return on the investment of dD_0, The net return is $dD_1 - dD_0$, and the *marginal rate of return* is the net return as a proportion of the additional investment:

$$i \equiv \frac{dD_1 - dD_0}{dD_0} \qquad [\text{C.6}]$$

Rearranging gives

$$\frac{dD_1}{dD_0} \equiv -(1 + i) \qquad [\text{C.7}]$$

i.e. the slope of *PP* is the negative of the marginal rate of return plus 1. As D_0 falls *PP* gets flatter and so i declines: the marginal rate of return on investment declines as investment increases. Since the solution point D^* is the point of tangency between *PP* and V^*

$$1 + r = 1 + i, \qquad \text{i.e. } r = i \qquad [\text{C.8}]$$

because $(1 + r)$ and $(1 + i)$ represent the absolute values of the slopes of V^* and *PP*. The firm invests up to the point at which the marginal rate of return equals the market interest rate. Up to that point, $i > r$, and so it pays the firm to invest, but after that point $r > i$, and it does not.

There is a second interpretation of the solution to the investment decision problem. Recall that point D^* corresponds to tangency between the highest possible wealth line, V^*, and the curve *PP*. We can interpret it as the solution to the optimization problem of maximizing the present value V of the income stream resulting from investment, subject to the constraint represented by the curve *PP*, which defines the feasible set of such income streams. Formally the problem is:

$$\max_{D_0, D_1} V = \frac{D_1}{1 + r} + D_0 \quad \text{s.t. } D_1 = P(D_0) \qquad [\text{C.9}]$$
$$0 \leqslant D_0$$

where the function P represents the curve *PP*. The solution implies (for $0 < D_0$) the necessary condition $dD_1/dD_0 \equiv -(1 + i) \equiv -(1 + r)$ at the optimal point (D_0^*, D_1^*). Thus the optimal investment decision is solved by maximizing the present value of the income stream generated by investment, or equivalently the owner's wealth, over the available set of income streams. *No information on preferences is necessary for wealth maximization.* Note also that the solution will determine the capital stock, labour and output produced by the firm in period 1.

Shareholder-owned firms

The above account was concerned with an owner-managed firm. A single decision-taker controlled the firm and chose an overall optimal consumption time-stream in the light of her own preferences (represented by indifference curves $u*$ or $u**$ in Fig. 11.4). The solution to the investment decision problem was independent of preferences, because the optimal finance decision was also taken. When the firm is owned by two or more shareholders, and production decisions are taken by a salaried manager, two kinds of problem may arise. First, the preferences of the shareholders are likely to differ, and so there appears to be the possibility of conflict. Second, how does the manager obtain information on shareholders' preferences to make decisions in accordance with them?

If shareholders are able to borrow and lend on the capital market at the same rate of interest both problems are solved. *If the capital market is perfect, then the manager of the firm acts in the best interests of the shareholders by choosing investment so as to maximize the present value of the firm's income stream.* We prove this proposition as follows.

The ith shareholder in the firm owns a proportion of the issued share capital, a_i, ($i = 1, 2, \ldots, n$), which entitles her to receive the share a_i in the income of the firm. Each shareholder wishes to choose a consumption time-stream which maximizes her utility, subject to her wealth constraint. But her endowed wealth depends at least in part on the income stream which accrues from ownership share in the firm, i.e.

$$V_i = V^0 + a_i D_0 + a_i \frac{D_1}{1 + r} = V^0 + a_i V$$

where V_i is the ith shareholder's wealth, V^0 that arising from sources other than the firm in question, and $V = D_0 + [D_1/(1 + r)]$ the present value of the firm's income stream. Given V^0, maximizing V is in the interest of *every* shareholder, regardless of her particular preferences, since it puts her on the highest possible wealth constraint. Thus the firm's manager can choose optimal investment as before to maximize the present value of the dividend stream. The only information he requires is the value of the market interest rate r. It is the *consumption decision* which changes for the shareholder-owned firm. There is now no single optimal solution to this, given $n(> 1)$ shareholders with differing preferences. The most straightforward solution is for the firm to distribute to shareholders their shares of the net income stream resulting from the optimal investment choice. Each shareholder then adopts their own borrowing or lending policies to maximize utility from current and future consumption.

The result is an implication of the separation between investment and consumption decisions described earlier. If the optimal investment decision can be taken independently of preferences, then the existence of a number of shareholders with diverse preferences over consumption does not create problems. Since all the shareholders can borrow or lend on the capital market at the same rate of interest, then each will be in equilibrium at the point at which her time preference rate equals the market interest rate. However diverse the general structure of their preferences, each values a marginal increment of future income at the same rate in terms of current income, i.e. at the rate measured by the market interest rate r. In taking investment decisions on behalf of shareholders, the managers of the firm can use the interest rate to evaluate gains in future income against sacrifices in current consumption. When the capital market is imperfect or incomplete, shareholders will disagree about the best investment policy because they will place different values on the benefits from the investment – the changes in their income streams. We return to this question in section 21F.

Present value and profit-maximizing models

We have outlined a model of the firm which chooses its variable input in each period and its capital stock for the next period so as to maximize the *present value of its cash flow*. In Chapter 7 we developed a model of the firm based on the assumption of *profit maximization*. We now show that these two models are equivalent.

The problem of maximizing the present value of the firm's cash flow is

$$\max_{L_0,L_1,K_1} V = D_0 + \frac{D_1}{(1+r)} \qquad \text{[C.10]}$$

where D_0 and D_1 are defined as in [C.1] and [C.2]. The first-order conditions are

$$\frac{\partial V}{\partial L_0} = \frac{\partial D_0}{\partial L_0} = p_0 f_L - w = 0 \qquad \text{[C.11]}$$

$$\frac{\partial V}{\partial L_1} = \frac{\partial D_1}{\partial L_1} \cdot \frac{1}{(1+r)} = \frac{1}{(1+r)}(p_1 f_L - w) = 0 \qquad \text{[C.12]}$$

$$\frac{\partial V}{\partial K_1} = \frac{\partial D_0}{\partial K_1} + \frac{\partial D_1}{\partial K_1}\frac{1}{(1+r)} = -p_K + \frac{1}{(1+r)}p_1 f_K = 0 \qquad \text{[C.13]}$$

where f_L, f_K are the marginal products of labour and capital and p_t is the price of output in period t and p_t may differ in the two periods. The variable labour input is chosen in each period so that $p_t = w/f_L$. Since (from section 6C) w/f_L is short-run marginal cost, the present-value-maximizing firm will always choose a variable input level (and hence output) where price is equal to short-run marginal cost, just like the profit-maximizing firm of section 8B.

From [C.13] the firm's investment decision (choice of K_1) satisfies

$$p_1 = \frac{p_K}{f_K}(1+r) = \frac{w}{f_L} \qquad \text{[C.14]}$$

An additional unit of capital bought in period 0 for use in period 1 costs p_K in cash flow forgone in period 0. Given the market rate of interest r, p_K forgone in period 0 is equivalent to $p_K(1 + r)$ forgone in period 1, since a loan of p_K in period 0 would have to be repaid at a cost of $p_K(1 + r)$ in period 1.

$p_K(1 + r)$ is the opportunity cost of an additional unit of physical capital in terms of period 1 cash flow. The middle term in [C.14] is the marginal cost in terms of period 1 cash flow of output in period 1 produced by installing more capital paid for in period 0. w/f_L is the marginal cost in terms of period 1 cash flow of producing output by hiring more labour (which must be paid for in that period). [C.14] expresses the requirement that when both inputs are variable, i.e. in *the long run*, the firm plans to produce where long-run marginal cost equals price and it chooses its fixed input on this basis. Actual output in period 1 is chosen by varying the labour input in period 1 so that short-run marginal cost is equal to price. If, as in this case, the firm accurately forecasts p_1, long-run marginal cost will also turn out to be equal to price. Thus maximizing the present value of the firm's cash flow and equating long-run marginal cost to price are equivalent formulations of the firm's investment decision.

We saw in Chapter 8 that for a competitive industry to be in long-run equilibrium every firm must have chosen the level of its fixed input so that price equals long-run marginal cost (so that it has no wish to alter its plant size) and every firm should just be breaking even, i.e. price equals long-run average cost (so that no firm wishes to enter or leave the industry). We can restate these requirements in the equivalent terms of the present-value-maximizing firm's investment decision.

Present value maximization requires that K_1 be chosen so that [C.14] holds and [C.14] can be rearranged to yield

$$r = \frac{p_1 f_K}{p_K} - 1 = \frac{p_1 f_K - p_K}{p_K} \qquad \text{[C.15]}$$

But the right-hand side of [C.15] is merely i, the marginal rate of return. (To see this use [C.1] and [C.2] to substitute for D_0 and D_1 in [C.6] which defines i.) Hence, as we noted in discussion of [C.8], optimal investment implies that $r = i$ and this is the equivalent of the condition that price equals long-run marginal cost.

There will be no incentive for firms to enter the industry if the present value of the cash flows generated by starting production is non-positive. Since it takes one period to install new plant the present value of the cash flow from entry is

$$\frac{D_1}{(1 + r)} - p_K K_1 \qquad \text{[C.16]}$$

since the new firm will not be producing any output in period 0. [C.16] is also the present value of the *additional* cash flow to an existing firm which decides to continue in production, i.e. to choose a positive K_1. [C.16] must therefore be non-negative for a firm which chooses to stay in the industry. Hence [C.16] must be zero if there is to be neither entry nor exit from the industry or

$$r = \frac{D_1 - p_K K_1}{p_K K_1} \qquad \text{[C.17]}$$

Now $D_1 - p_K K_1$ is the return from investing $p_K K_1$ in the industry so that $(D_1 - p_K K_1)/p_K K_1$ is the average rate of return, g. Hence if the industry is in long-run equilibrium the average rate of return being earned in the industry will be equal to the market rate of interest. This is an equivalent formulation of the price equals long-run average cost condition for long-run equilibrium in a competitive industry.

Thus in long-run competitive equilibrium the rate of return on capital to *all* firms is equal to the market interest rate. If $g > r$ then capital is moved into the industry in search of an excess profit, while if $g < r$ capital is moved out because a higher profit can be earned elsewhere, e.g. by lending on the market. Thus the equalization of gross profit rates with each other and with the market rate of interest is a long-run tendency of a competitive economy.

EXERCISE 11C

1. Examine the effects on the curve PP in Fig. 11.3 of
   (a) changes in the price of output, the capital good and labour;
   (b) the capital good depreciating at a constant percentage rate per period;
   (c) disinvestment being impossible.

2. How will the firm's investment and production decisions be affected by the changes in PP due to the factors listed in Question 1?

3. Show in Fig. 11.4 cases in which:
   (a) no investment would be undertaken;
   (b) D_1 would be maximized;
   and state necessary and sufficient conditions for each of these.

4. Show that at an optimal solution to the firm's problem, $i = r = \rho$, where ρ is the owner's rate of time preference.

5. Show that as long as the shareholder-owned firm makes the optimal investment choice (maximizes $D_0 + D_1/(1 + r)$, any borrowing or lending policy it then adopts leaves the shareholders' utility unaffected (provided of course that it distributes to shareholders all income flows resulting from investment, borrowing or lending). (*Hint*: consider the borrowing/lending policies which shareholders may then adopt in the perfect capital market.)

6. Show the effects on the firm's investment and production decisions of a tax on operating profit (revenue less variable costs) when
   (a) interest payments are tax deductible;
   (b) interest payments are not tax deductible.

7. Generalize the model of this section to the case in which the firm is a monopolist in the output market. Will the monopolist's average and marginal rates of return be equal to or exceed r?

8. What restrictions on the production function are necessary to ensure that PP is concave?

9. *Imperfect capital market*. Analyse the solutions to the optimal investment and consumption decisions when the interest rate at which the owner can borrow differs from that at which she can lend. State the implications for the separation of the two decisions discussed in this section. From that, suggest what difficulties confront a firm in which a salaried manager wishes to take decisions in the interests of n shareholders, where $n \geqslant 2$.

10. Suppose that the firm could sell its capital equipment at the end of period 1. How would this affect Figs 11.3 and 11.4?

11. *Net present value and internal rate of return*. The net present value of an investment project is

$$NPV(r) = \sum_{t=0}^{T} \frac{R_t}{(1 + r)^t}$$

where R_t is the change in the firm's cash flow in period t caused by the project.
   (a) Show that the firm should accept all projects for which $NPV(r) \geqslant 0$.
   (b) The *internal rate of return* on an investment project is defined as the rate of interest i at which the net present value is zero: $NPV(i) = 0$. It is often suggested that the rule of accepting all projects for which $i > r$ is equivalent to the NPV criterion. Explain the rationale for this.
   (c) Under what circumstances will the two criteria yield different decisions?
   (*Hints*: When would $NPV(i) = 0$ have multiple roots? Suppose investment projects are mutually exclusive?)

D. Capital market equilibrium under certainty

The interest rate is a price and, although the perfect capital market assumption implies that it can be taken as constant by each borrower and lender, its value will be determined by the overall interaction of the decisions of borrowers and lenders. The capital market is in equilibrium when supply, in the form of lending, equals demand, in the form of borrowing for investment and consumption. We derive the relation between the market interest rate and the borrowing or lending decisions of consumers and firms from the solutions to their intertemporal optimization problems. Aggregation of the relationships then leads to the determination of market equilibrium.

We first examine the consumer's demand functions for current M_0^* and future M_1^* consumption which will then yield his net demand for current funds $(M_0^* - \bar{M}_0)$ to finance his optimal consumption plans. To emphasize the formal similarities with the analysis of the consumer in Chapter 3, write the wealth constraint as

$$V_0 = \bar{M}_0 + \mu\bar{M}_1 \geqslant M_0 + \mu M_1 \qquad [D.1]$$

where $\mu \equiv 1/(1 + r)$ is the *discount factor*. Think of μ as the relative price of period 1 money in terms of period 0 money: £1 of period 1 money can be exchanged for £μ of period 0 funds. The Lagrangean for the consumer's problem of maximizing $u(M_0, M_1)$ subject to [D.1] (but assuming the non-negativity constraints on the M_t do not bind) is

$$u(M_0, M_1) + \lambda[\bar{M}_0 + \mu\bar{M}_1 - M_0 - \mu M_1] \qquad [D.2]$$

The resulting first-order conditions determine the consumer's demand for period t consumption

$$M_t^* = M_t^*(\mu, V_0) \qquad t = 0, 1 \qquad [D.3]$$

as functions of the relative price μ and the consumer's wealth V_0. Substituting them into the direct utility function yields the indirect utility function for the intertemporal consumption problem:

$$u^* = u^*(\mu, V_0) = u(M_0^*, M_1^*) \qquad [D.4]$$

To analyse the effect of changes in μ, and hence in r, on the demand for consumption we use the duality methods of sections 3A and 3B. Consider the problem of minimizing the wealth which must be given to a consumer to enable him to achieve a specified level of utility u:

$$\min_{M_0, M_1} M_0 + \mu M_1 \quad \text{s.t.} \quad u(M_0, M_1) \geqslant u \qquad [D.5]$$

(ignoring the non-negativity constraints on the M_t). The values of current and future consumption which solve the wealth minimization problem are the Hicksian constant utility demands h_t for consumption as functions of the relative price of period 1 and period 0 consumption and the required level of utility:

$$h_t = h_t(\mu, u) \qquad [D.6]$$

The minimized wealth is

$$m = m(\mu, u) = h_0(\mu, u) + \mu h_1(\mu, u) \qquad [D.7]$$

Applying the Envelope Theorem to [D.7] we have $\partial m/\partial \mu = h_1$, which is a version of Shephard's lemma. The methods of section 3A can be used to show that $m(\mu, u)$ is concave in μ so that the own substitution effect on period 1 consumption demand is negative: $\partial h_1/\partial \mu = \partial^2 m/\partial \mu^2 < 0$. It is also clear from Fig. 11.2 that, since an increase in μ leads to a flattening of the wealth line, the consumer moves around an indifference curve from left to right as μ increases, so that $\partial h_0/\partial \mu > 0$ and $\partial h_1/\partial \mu < 0$.

If we set the required utility level in the wealth minimization problem equal to u^* from the consumer's utility maximization problem, then recalling section 3B, the wealth-minimizing Hicksian consumption demands are equal to the utility-maximizing Marshallian consumption demands:

$$M_t^*(\mu, V_0) = h_t(\mu, u^*(\mu, V_0)) \qquad t = 0, 1 \qquad\qquad [\text{D.8}]$$

and the minimized wealth is equal to consumer's wealth in the utility-maximization problem: $m(\mu, u^*) = V_0$. Differentiating [D.8] with respect to V_0 gives the effect of increases in wealth on the Marshallian demand

$$\frac{\partial M_t^*}{\partial V_0} = \frac{\partial h_t}{\partial u}\frac{\partial u^*}{\partial V_0} = \frac{\partial h_t}{\partial u}\lambda \qquad\qquad [\text{D.9}]$$

(where we use the Envelope Theorem on [D.2] to get $\partial u^*/\partial V_0 = \lambda$). Differentiating [D.8] with respect to the relative price μ and using [D.9] gives

$$\begin{aligned}\frac{\partial M_t^*}{\partial \mu} &= \frac{\partial h_t}{\partial \mu} + \frac{\partial h_t}{\partial u}\frac{\partial u^*}{\partial \mu} = \frac{\partial h_t}{\partial \mu} + \frac{\partial h_t}{\partial u}\lambda(\bar{M}_1 - M_1^*) \\ &= \frac{\partial h_t}{\partial \mu} + \frac{\partial M_t^*}{\partial V_0}(\bar{M}_1 - M_1^*)\end{aligned} \qquad\qquad [\text{D.10}]$$

[D.10] is the Slutsky equation for the intertemporal consumption demand. As in section 3B, we can decompose the effect of an increase in the relative price μ on the Marshallian demand into a definitely signed substitution effect ($\partial h_0/\partial \mu > 0$ and $\partial h_1/\partial \mu < 0$) and a real wealth effect whose sign is ambiguous. The wealth effect is ambiguous both because the effect of an increase in wealth on demand is ambiguous (consumption in period t may be a normal or an inferior good) and because wealth may be increased or decreased by an increase in μ. For example, if the consumer is borrowing, $\bar{M}_1 - M_1^*$ is positive and an increase in μ makes him better off since he is in effect 'selling' period 1 consumption to finance an increase in period 0 consumption.

To find the effect of an increase in the rate of interest on consumption demands, remember that $\mu = 1/(1 + r)$ and multiply [D.10] by $d\mu/dr = -1/(1 + r)^2$ to get $\partial M_t^*/\partial r$ decomposed into a substitution effect and a wealth effect. Since increases in r steepen the wealth line $\partial h_0/\partial r < 0$ and $\partial h_1/\partial r > 0$.

In Fig. 11.5 the consumer has an initial endowment $(\bar{M}_0, \bar{M}_1)$. The line V_0 in (a) corresponds to interest rate r, and the consumer chooses current consumption of M_0^*. This implies lending $\bar{M}_0 - M_0^*$, shown as $A^*(< 0)$ in (b) of the figure. The line V_0' corresponds to interest rate r', and yields an equilibrium current consumption choice at M_0^{**}. This implies borrowing of the amount $M_0^{**} - \bar{M}_0$, shown as $A^{**}(> 0)$ in (b) of the figure. The curve A_c traces out the relation between the market interest rate and the consumer's lending ($A < 0$) or borrowing ($A > 0$). It can be thought of as corresponding to a sequence of equilibrium points in (a) of the figure, such as M^*

Figure 11.5

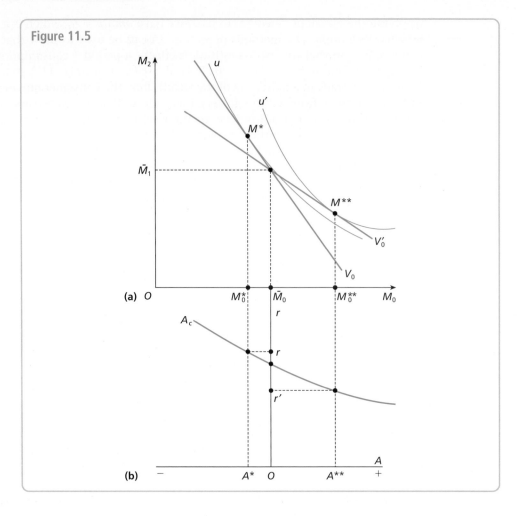

and M^{**} (compare the analysis of the offer curve in section 2E). Figure 11.5(b) shows an intuitively appealing case: at sufficiently high interest rates, the consumer is a lender. Given his preferences and initial endowment, a falling interest rate causes a decrease in his lending until, after a point at which he neither lends nor borrows, he begins to borrow. Borrowing then varies inversely with the interest rate. In what follows, we take the case shown in Fig. 11.5 as typical. (But see Question 1, Exercise 11D.)

The effect of changes in r on the intertemporal production and consumption plans of the sole owner of a firm can also be most easily derived by initially using μ as the relative price of period 1 consumption. Recalling the separation theorem from section C, the owner's decisions can be separated into first maximizing wealth via an intertemporal production plan and then maximizing utility subject to the resulting wealth constraint. The constraint on the owners's wealth maximization problem is $D_1 = P(D_0)$ ($P' < 0$, $P'' < 0$) and her wealth maximization problem is to choose D_0 to maximize

$$V = D_0 + \mu D_1 = D_0 + \mu P(D_0) = V(D_0, \mu) \qquad [\text{D.11}]$$

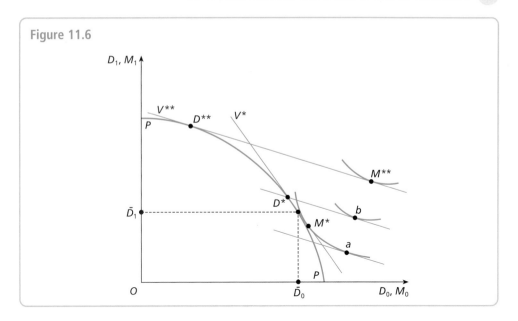

Figure 11.6

The first- and second-order conditions (assuming a non-corner solution) are

$$\partial V(D_0, \mu)/\partial D_0 = V_D = 1 + \mu P'(D_0) = 0 \qquad \text{[D.12]}$$

$$\partial^2 V(D_0, \mu)/\partial D_0^2 = V_{DD} = \mu P'' < 0 \qquad \text{[D.13]}$$

These determine the wealth-maximizing cash flows from the firm and imply a particular level of capital stock in period 1 and thus a particular level of investment in period 0.

The effect of an increase in μ on the optimal $D_0^\star$ is, using the comparative statics procedure of Appendix I,

$$\frac{\partial D_0^\star}{\partial \mu} = -\frac{\partial^2 V/\partial D_0 \partial \mu}{V_{DD}} = -\frac{\partial [1 + \mu P'(D_0^\star)]/\partial \mu}{V_{DD}} = -\frac{P'(D_0^\star)}{V_{DD}} < 0 \qquad \text{[D.14]}$$

Thus increases in μ reduce the period 0 cash flow from the firm, implying a larger period 1 capital stock and more investment in period 0. Since reductions in r are equivalent to increases in μ, reductions in the rate of interest reduce the period 0 cash flow and increase period 0 investment and period 1 capital stock. Thus in Fig. 11.6 a reduction in r (or increase in μ) flattens the wealth lines and shifts the optimal production plan from $D^\star$ to $D^{\star\star}$.

The effect of μ on the maximized value $V^\star$ of the wealth of the owner is found by using the Envelope Theorem on [D.11] to get

$$dV^\star/d\mu = \partial V(D_0^\star, \mu)/\partial \mu = V_\mu(D_0^\star, \mu) = P(D_0^\star) = D_1^\star > 0 \qquad \text{[D.15]}$$

Hence a reduction in r (which increases μ) leads to an increase in the owner's wealth. This is shown in Fig. 11.6 by the fact that the new wealth line $V^{\star\star}$ has a greater intercept on the horizontal axis than the original wealth line $V^\star$.

The owner's optimal consumption plan is found by maximizing $u(M_0, M_1)$ subject to the constraint $V^* \geqslant M_0 + \mu M_1$. The Marshallian period 0 consumption demand is $M_0^*(\mu, V^*)$ and so the effect of an increase in μ is

$$\frac{dM_0^*}{d\mu} = \frac{\partial M_0^*}{\partial \mu} + \frac{\partial M_0^*}{\partial V^*}\frac{dV^*}{d\mu} = \frac{\partial h_0}{\partial \mu} + \frac{\partial M_0^*}{\partial V^*}(D_1^* - M_1^*) + \frac{\partial M_0^*}{\partial V^*}D_1^* \qquad [\text{D.16}]$$

where we have used the Slutsky equation [D.10], with D_1^* instead of $\bar{M}_1$, to substitute for $\partial M_0^*/\partial \mu$. From [D.16] we see that the effect of an increase in μ on the period 0 consumption of the owner of the firm can be decomposed into three terms. The first term is the substitution effect which is always positive. The last two terms are the two wealth effects of μ. The first is the wealth effect with an unchanged cash flow from the firm and may be positive or negative depending on whether current consumption is a normal or inferior good and whether the owner is borrowing or lending, so that she is made better or worse off by an increase in μ. The second wealth effect arises because the change in μ alters the owner's cash flows from the firm as she changes her wealth-maximizing production plan. Her wealth always increases as a result of an increase in μ and so the sign of the second wealth effect depends only on whether period 0 consumption is normal or inferior. We will refer to this effect as the *production effect* on consumption.

Again by using $d\mu/dr = -1/(1 + r)^2$ we can translate these results into the effects of an increase in the rate of interest on the owner's consumption plan. In Fig. 11.6 the consumer is initially at M^* and a reduction in r (increase in μ) changes the optimal consumption plan to M^{**}. The substitution effect is from M^* to a, the usual wealth effect is from a to b and the production effect leads to the change from b to M^{**}. The effect of the reduction in r is to increase the firm's investment from $\bar{D}_0 - D_0^*$ to $\bar{D}_0 - D_0^{**}$ and to increase the owner's borrowing from $M_0^* - D_0^*$ to $M_0^{**} - D_0^{**}$. In this case the owner would have a negatively sloped net demand curve for current consumption. As the reader should check, it is easy to construct cases with a positive slope if the owner is a lender at sufficiently high interest rates.

When the firm is owned by more than one shareholder the analysis is essentially unchanged: a change in the rate of interest will change the firm's cash flows and the wealth of its owners. There will again be a substitution effect, a wealth effect and a production effect on the lending and borrowing decisions of the individual owners.

Assume that the consumers and owner/consumers have well behaved net demand functions for period 0 consumption:

$$A_j = A_j(r) \qquad dA_j(r)/dr < 0 \qquad j = 1, \ldots, J \qquad [\text{D.17}]$$

An equilibrium interest rate r^* satisfies

$$A(r^*) = \sum_{j=1}^{J} A_j(r^*) = 0 \qquad [\text{D.18}]$$

where borrowing ($A_j > 0$) equals lending ($A_j < 0$) in the aggregate, at interest rate r^*. The equilibrium is shown in Fig. 11.7, where $\sum_j A_j = 0$ holds at the interest rate r^*; the curve $A(r)$ is the horizontal sum of all individual curves showing lending and borrowing as functions of the interest rate. (Compare the excess demand functions in Chapters 8 and 12.)

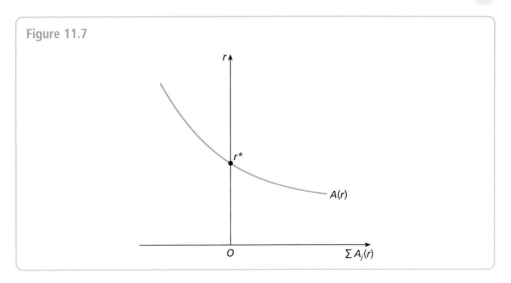

Figure 11.7

EXERCISE 11D

1. Construct cases in which

(a) a consumer never borrows;

(b) a consumer never lends;

(c) the curve A_c in Fig. 11.5(b) has a positive slope over some range.

By separating the effects of an interest rate change into substitution and wealth effects, formulate sufficient conditions under which the curve A_c will always have a negative slope.

2. Analyse the effects on a consumer's borrowing/lending behaviour of:

(a) a windfall gain in next-period income;

(b) the imposition of an income tax;

(c) the imposition of a tax on the returns to lending.

3. Analyse the effects on the market interest rate of:

(a) an increase in the price of output expected next period;

(b) an increase in next period's expected wage rate;

(c) a tax on returns to lending;

(d) a profits tax (with loan interest not deductible).

4. Analyse the implications for the market interest rate of the changes listed in Question 2 above.

5. Construct a case in which the owner of a firm increases his borrowing following a rise in the interest rate. Explain the relation between the strength of the wealth effect and the curvature of *PP* in this case.

E. Extension to many periods

The analysis of the preceding sections suggested that the equilibrium interest rate, levels of borrowing and lending and investment depend on consumers' preferences for consumption now as compared with consumption later, future production functions, and expectations about future prices and wage rates. At least in part, interest and investment are determined by the classical forces of 'productivity and thrift'. However, expectations about future prices and technology also play an important role which we investigate.

Suppose that there are $T > 2$ periods, indexed $t = 0, 1, \ldots T$. The consumer faces a sequence of budget constraints:

$$\sum_{j=1}^{m} p_{tj} x_{tj} + A_t \leq \sum_{j=1}^{m} p_{tj} \bar{x}_{tj} + A_{t-1}(1 + r_{t-1}) \qquad t = 0, \ldots T \qquad [\text{E.1}]$$

where p_{tj} is the price of good j *expected by the consumer* to prevail in year t, x_{tj} is planned consumption of good j in year t, A_t is bond purchase or sale in that year, $\bar{x}_{tj}$ the initial endowment of good j in year t, and r_{t-1} is the interest rate which is expected to prevail in year $t - 1$. Equation [E.1] says that in any year the consumer's expenditure plus net bond purchases cannot exceed the value of endowment of goods plus the net repayment of principal and interest on the consumer's bond purchase of the previous year. The difference from the constraints in equations [B.1] and [B.2] is that now we explicitly incorporate *goods*.

In year 0, $A_{-1}(1 + r_{-1})$ will be given, determined by past decisions, and we denote it by R_0. In year T, $A_T = 0$, since in effect the economy (or the consumer) ceases to exist after that time. Thus in year T:

$$\sum_{j} p_{Tj}(x_{Tj} - \bar{x}_{Tj})/(1 + r_{T-1}) = A_{T-1} \qquad [\text{E.2}]$$

from [E.1], where we have dropped the inequality on the premise that a boundary solution will always obtain. Substituting into the budget constraint for year $t - 1$ gives

$$\sum_{j} p_{T-1,j} x_{T-1,j} + \sum_{j} p_{Tj} \frac{(x_{Tj} - \bar{x}_{Tj})}{(1 + r_{T-1})} = \sum_{j} p_{T-1,j} \bar{x}_{T-1,j} + A_{T-2}(1 + r_{T-2}) \qquad [\text{E.3}]$$

and so solving for A_{T-2} gives

$$\sum_{j} p_{T-1,j}(x_{T-1,j} - \bar{x}_{T-1,j})/(1 + r_{T-2}) + \sum_{j} p_{Tj}(x_{T,j} - \bar{x}_{Tj})/(1 + r_{T-2})(1 + r_{T-1}) = A_{T-2} \qquad [\text{E.4}]$$

from which we could then substitute into the budget constraint for year $T - 2$, and so on. Continuing this process gives the *single wealth constraint*:

$$\sum_{j} p_{0j}(x_{0j} - \bar{x}_{0j}) + \sum_{j} p_{1j}(x_{1j} - \bar{x}_{1j})/(1 + r_0) + \ldots$$
$$\ldots + \sum_{j} p_{Tj}(x_{Tj} - \bar{x}_{Tj})/(1 + r_0)(1 + r_1) \ldots (1 + r_{T-1}) = R_0 \qquad [\text{E.5}]$$

This is the T-period counterpart of the wealth constraint in equation [B.3] written in terms of goods rather than generalized consumption. Now let us define

$$p'_{tj} = p_{tj}/(1 + r_0)(1 + r_1) \ldots (1 + r_{t-1}) \qquad t = 1, \ldots, T$$
$$= p_{tj} \qquad\qquad\qquad\qquad\qquad\qquad t = 0 \qquad [\text{E.6}]$$

as the present value, at year 0, of the price of good j in year t. Then [E.5] can be rewritten as

$$\sum_{j} \sum_{t} p'_{tj}(x_{tj} - \bar{x}_{tj}) = R_0 \qquad [\text{E.7}]$$

Finally, define the consumer's utility function on goods rather than general consumption expenditure time-streams, so that

$$u = u(x) \qquad\qquad [E.8]$$

where

$$x = (x_{01}, x_{02}, \dots, x_{TJ})$$

We can view the consumer's optimization problem as choosing values of the goods which maximize u subject to the wealth constraint in [E.7]. Provided the consumer knows the prices p_{tj} and interest rates $r_0, \dots, r_{T-1}$, this problem is formally no different from that of consumption choices within a time period. Thus, if we characterize a good not only by its physical characteristics but also by the date at which it is to be consumed, the earlier consumer analysis is directly applicable. In this case the equilibrium of the consumer determines not only a consumption pattern but also a pattern of lending and borrowing over time. But can we reasonably expect consumers to know future prices and interest rates? We shall consider this question further when we have generalized the model of the firm.

Let y_{tj} be the firm's net output of good j in year t with $y_{tj} < 0$ for an input in year t and $y_{tj} > 0$ for an output. I_t is the firm's acquisition of the single capital good in year t, K_t is the firm's capital stock in year t and the capital stock is increased by investment and reduced by depreciation according to

$$K_t = K_{t-1}(1 - \gamma) + I_{t-1} \qquad t = 1, 2, \dots, T \qquad [E.9]$$

$0 \le \gamma < 1$ is the proportion of capital stock which wears out in one year, i.e. the *depreciation rate*. The price of a unit of the investment good at time t is p_{tK} and the present value of this price at year 0 is

$$p'_{tK} = p_{tK}/(1 + r_0)(1 + r_1) \dots (1 + r_{t-1}) \qquad t = 1, 2, \dots, T - 1 \qquad [E.10]$$
$$p'_{0K} = p_{0K}$$

In each year the firm faces the implicit production function

$$g_t(y_t, K_t) = 0 \qquad t = 0, 1, \dots, T \qquad [E.11]$$

(where y_t is the vector of non-capital goods) which defines the feasible input–output combinations in year t. Since the firm operates in competitive input and output markets and takes all prices as given, we assume that diminishing returns set in at a fairly small scale. Its profit in year t is

$$\pi_t = \sum_j p_{tj} y_{tj}$$

(Remember that outputs are measured positively and inputs, apart from capital, negatively.) If the firm is acting in the best interests of its shareholders it will maximize their wealth by maximizing the present value of its cash flow:

$$V = \sum_t (\pi_t - p_{tK} I_t)/(1 + r_0)(1 + r_1) \dots (1 + r_{t-1}) = \sum_t \sum_j (p'_{tj} y_{tj} - p'_{tK} I_t) \qquad [E.12]$$

[E.12] is the present value of the firm's profits less the present value of its investment expenditures.

The constraints on the maximization of V are the production constraints in each period, the equations [E.9] governing the evolution of the capital stock and the firm's initial capital stock K_0. The Lagrangean for the problem is

$$\mathcal{L} = V + \sum_t \beta_t g_t(y_t, K_t) + \sum_t \alpha_t[K_{t-1}(1 - \gamma) + I_{t-1} - K_t] \qquad \text{[E.13]}$$

and the first-order conditions are

$$\partial\mathcal{L}/\partial y_{tj} = p'_{tj} + \beta_t g_{tj} = 0 \qquad\qquad t = 0, 1, \ldots, T; j = 1, \ldots, J \quad \text{[E.14]}$$

$$\partial\mathcal{L}/\partial K_t = \beta_t g_{tK} - \alpha_t + \alpha_{t+1}(1 - \gamma) = 0 \qquad t = 1, 2, \ldots, T \qquad\qquad \text{[E.15]}$$

$$\partial\mathcal{L}/\partial I_t = -p'_{tK} + \alpha_{t+1} = 0 \qquad\qquad t = 0, 1, \ldots, T - 1 \qquad\quad \text{[E.16]}$$

where $g_{tj} = \partial g_t/\partial y_{tj}$ and $g_{tK} = \partial g_t/\partial K_t$. (Notice that since there is no production after period T there is no point in making any investment in period T.) These conditions together with the constraints determine the firm's production plan from year 0 to year T, including its purchase of investment goods and the evolution of its capital stock. We can extract some insights from the conditions by recalling, from section 5D, that we can interpret $-g_{tK}/g_{tj} = \partial y_{tj}/\partial K_t$ as the marginal product MP_{Kjt} of capital in the production of good j when $y_{tj} > 0$, or as the marginal rate of technical substitution $MRTS_{Kjt}$ between capital and input j if $y_{tj} < 0$. If we take the condition on good j at time t and write it as $\beta_t = -p'_{tj}/g_{tj}$ and use [E.16] to substitute for α_t in [E.15] we get (assuming for definiteness that good j is an output at time t):

$$p'_{tj}MP_{Kjt} = p'_{t-1K} - p'_{tK}(1 - \gamma) \qquad\qquad \text{[E.17]}$$

Recalling the definition of the present value prices p'_{tj} and p'_{tK} from [E.6] and [E.10], we can multiply both sides of [E.17] by $(1 + r_0)(1 + r_1) \ldots (1 + r_{t-1})$ to get

$$p_{tj}MP_{Kjt} = (1 - r_{t-1})p_{t-1K} - p_{tK}(1 - \gamma) \qquad\qquad \text{[E.18]}$$

If we define the proportionate rate of growth θ in the price of the investment good between period $t - 1$ and period t we can write p_{tK} as $p_{t-1K}(1 + \theta)$ and rearrange [E.18]

$$p_{tj}MP_{Kjt} = p_{t-1K}(r_{r-1} + \gamma - \theta + \theta\gamma) \qquad\qquad \text{[E.19]}$$

If we finally assume that the rate of interest is constant and that γ and θ are both relatively small we have

$$p_{tj}MP_{Kjt} \simeq p_{t-1K}(r + \gamma - \theta) \qquad\qquad \text{[E.20]}$$

The left-hand side of [E.20] is the value of the marginal product of capital: the value of the extra output produced in period t by having an extra unit of capital at that date. (Notice that the value of the marginal product of capital is the same whichever output j is considered.) The right-hand side is the *rental price* of capital in period t. To acquire the use of an extra unit of capital for period t the firm can be thought of as buying an extra unit of the investment good in year $t - 1$ and then reselling what is left of the unit after one period. The cost to the firm of these transactions depends on (a) the interest r on the forgone cash flow used to purchase the investment good; (b) the loss of γ of the extra unit of the investment good from depreciation; and (c) the gain or loss to the firm from the change in the price of the investment good at the rate θ between the period $t - 1$ when the extra unit is bought and period t when it is resold.

The condition [E.20] is thus a generalization of the results in section C to allow for many goods, many periods and depreciation. We leave it to the reader to examine the case in which good j is an input by substituting $MRTS_{Kjt}$ for MP_{Kjt} in [E.20] and then dividing through to get the generalization of the minimum cost production condition that the marginal rate of technical substitution should be equal to the marginal costs of the inputs to the firm.

The analysis emphasizes the importance of the expectations of consumers and firms. We can envisage an extreme case, in which all consumers and firms expect the same prices, and at these prices, all planned supplies and demands are consistent, so that the expected prices are the true equilibrium prices. In that case, all consumers' lending/borrowing and consumption plans will be realized, as will firms' production and investment plans. Equivalently, we could imagine that at year 0 there are markets for the exchange of claims to specified goods at each future date and claims to wealth at each date. There would be a market for every j and every t, held at year 0. If so the prices p_j^t would actually be established at year 0, and consumers and firms would then spend the rest of time ($t = 1, 2, \dots$) honouring the commitments they made at year 0.

Neither of these cases appears to be an adequate description of the real world. Although some futures markets exist, most goods are traded on 'spot' markets, i.e. markets are held at every time t, including capital markets. Moreover, at any time, consumers may not know with certainty the tastes they will have at some future time, nor what their endowments of wealth will be. Similarly, firms may not know with certainty future technological possibilities. Expectations about future prices and interest rates may differ and the plans made by consumers and firms may be inconsistent, and so a given consumption or production plan may not be capable of realization at a given date. Firms and consumers are likely to be aware of this, and that awareness may influence the decisions they take at any date. Thus, decisions over time can be handled without any change in the formal structure of analysis *if* we rule out uncertainty about future prices, tastes, and technology. But this means ignoring what appears to be an important and pervasive aspect of economic activity. Hence, in sections 21E and 21F, we consider some elements of the economics of capital markets under uncertainty.

12 General equilibrium

A. Introduction

In previous chapters we have considered separately the constituent elements of the economy: households, firms, goods markets and factor markets. We now combine all these elements into a model of the equilibrium of the economy as a whole.

The first question, addressed in sections B and C, is the *existence* of equilibrium: does the model of the economy, consisting of a system of interrelated markets of the kind we have been studying, have an equilibrium solution? A proof of existence is necessary for the logical consistency of the model. We describe an economy by a general set of supply and demand relationships for goods and services and wish to examine the resource allocation which is determined when they hold simultaneously. But if there is no situation in which they can hold simultaneously, our model has failed to achieve its purpose.

In section D we examine the *stability* of the equilibrium. As in the models of single markets in section 8B, this is required to make predictions of the effects of changes in exogenous variables by comparison of equilibria. The *uniqueness* of equilibria is also important for comparative statics. We give one reasonably simple set of conditions which are sufficient for uniqueness.

In the general equilibrium model, consumers and firms are regarded as passive price takers. Given some price vector, they choose net demands and supplies and an equilibrium exists when those demands and supplies are consistent and can be realized. The rationale for price-taking behaviour is that, loosely, there are 'many' such buyers and sellers, so that the effect any one of them has on the market is imperceptible, and passive adaptation to prices somehow 'announced' seems plausible. We call the model based on this view of economic activity the *Walrasian general equilibrium model*, since it was first formulated by Walras. There is, however, an alternative view of economic activity, associated with Edgeworth and set out in section E. This sees buyers and sellers as active market participants, haggling and dealing, shopping around and bargaining, and an equilibrium is achieved only when everyone believes she has made the best deal possible. The question addressed in section F is: what is the relation between the equilibria that result from these two views of economic activity? The answer is both complex and interesting. In an economy with a small number of individuals, the set of possible equilibrium resource allocations following from the Edgeworthian view is much larger than the set of Walrasian equilibria. However, the latter set is always contained in the former. As the number of individuals increases, the set of Edgeworthian equilibria shrinks and converges to the set of Walrasian equilibria. This suggests that, though we may regard the Edgeworthian view of economic activity as more realistic and appealing than the Walrasian, for suitably large economies Walrasian equilibrium can be regarded as giving the outcome of either type of economy. The analysis also gives some insights into the efficiency of a competitive market equilibrium, a subject further developed in the next two chapters.

B. Walrasian equilibrium of a competitive economy

The economy is made up of households and firms trading n goods and services in markets. Let $\hat{x}_{hj}$ be the *net* demand for the jth good of the hth household, $h = 1, 2, \ldots, H$ and y_{ij} the *net* supply of the good by the ith firm, $i = 1, 2, \ldots, M$. Recall from the analysis in Chapters 2, 5 and 7 that household net supplies of, and firms' net demands for, goods are measured negatively.

Households possess *strictly* quasi-concave utility functions $u_h(\hat{x}^h)$ where $\hat{x}^h = (\hat{x}_{h1}, \hat{x}_{h2}, \ldots, \hat{x}_{hn})$, which they maximize subject to the budget constraints

$$\sum_{j=1}^{n} p_j \hat{x}_{hj} \leq M_h \qquad h = 1, 2, \ldots, H \qquad [\text{B.1}]$$

where we define household income M_h as follows. Household h is *endowed* with a given vector of shares in firms, $\beta_h = (\beta_{h1}, \ldots, \beta_{hF})$ with $1 \geq \beta_{hi} \geq 0$, all h, i. It must be the case that $\sum_h \beta_{hi} = 1$. Then

$$M_h = \sum_{i=1}^{F} \beta_{hi} \pi_i$$

where π_i is profit of the ith firm. Thus a household's income is the sum of its shares of firms' profits.

Firms maximize profit,

$$\pi_i = \sum_{j=1}^{n} p_j y_{ij} \qquad i = 1, 2, \ldots, F \qquad [\text{B.2}]$$

subject to the production possibilities which satisfy

$$f_i(y_i) \leq 0 \qquad i = 1, 2, \ldots, F \qquad [\text{B.3}]$$

where $y_i = (y_{i1}, y_{i2}, \ldots, y_{in})$. We assume that each production function, f_i, exhibits *strictly* diminishing returns: each firm's production set is strictly convex. This rules out the discontinuity in supply considered in Chapter 8.

From the analysis of Chapters 2 and 7, each household has net demand functions

$$\hat{x}_{hj} = D_{hj}(p_1, p_2, \ldots, p_n) \qquad h = 1, 2, \ldots, H \qquad j = 1, 2, \ldots, n \qquad [\text{B.4}]$$

and each firm has net supply functions

$$y_{ij} = S_{ij}(p_1, p_2, \ldots, p_n) \qquad i = 1, 2, \ldots, F \qquad j = 1, 2, \ldots, n \qquad [\text{B.5}]$$

with the properties:

(a) for a given vector of prices, each net demand or supply is unique;
(b) each net demand or supply varies continuously with prices (for all strictly positive prices);
(c) if all prices change in the same proportion, each net demand or supply is unchanged.

Figure 12.1

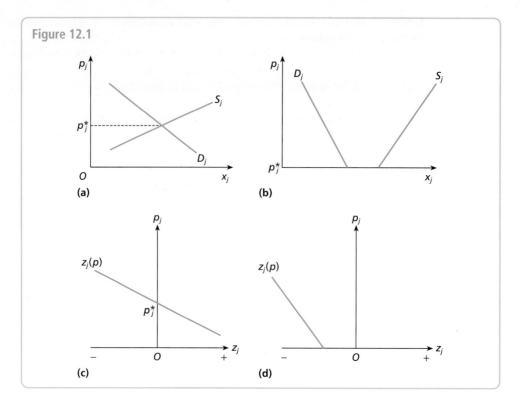

(a)

(b)

(c)

(d)

Now consider, for good j, the sum

$$z_j = \sum_{h=1}^{H} \hat{x}_{hj} - \sum_{i=1}^{F} y_{ij} \qquad j = 1, 2, \ldots, n \qquad \text{[B.6]}$$

which is the *excess demand* for good j, since it is the difference between demand and supply. Recalling the definitions of $\hat{x}_{hj}$ and y_{ij}, it is clear that, if market demand exceeds supply, z_j will be positive, while if supply exceeds demand, z_j will be negative. We can write

$$z_j = z_j(p_1, p_2, \ldots, p_n) \qquad j = 1, 2, \ldots, n \qquad \text{[B.7]}$$

and the three properties possessed by the individual D_{hj} and S_{ij} functions are also possessed by the functions z_j. From now on, the analysis will be conducted entirely in terms of excess demands rather than the underlying individual demands and supplies. Figure 12.1 illustrates the derivation of the excess demands.

In (a) we have the market demand and supply curves and in (c) the corresponding excess demand curve, which is given by taking the horizontal distance between the two curves in (a).

In (b), the market demand and supply curves generate the excess demand curve in (d). In (d), supply everywhere exceeds demand, and there is no positive price (such as p_j^* in (a)) at which excess demand is exactly zero. There is, however, an equilibrium at a zero price and negative excess demand, since once this price is achieved there is no tendency to change. This is the case of a free good. If it is possible to dispose of the excess supply costlessly, then we can incorporate the case into our model. There are strong reasons for doing so, since goods which may be free at some sets of relative prices may not be so for all; for example, increases in prices for substitutes for the good (or increases in prices for goods which use it as an input) could lead it to have a positive price.

An *equilibrium* of the economy is a vector of prices, $(p_1^*, p_2^*, \ldots, p_n^*)$, and a vector of excess demands, $(z_1^*, z_2^*, \ldots, z_n^*)$, which have the following properties:

1. The individual household net demands, $\hat{x}_{hj}^*$, corresponding to these z_j^* must be such that

$$u_h(\hat{x}^{h*}) \geq u_h(\hat{x}^h) \qquad \text{all } h \qquad [\text{B.8}]$$

    for all $\hat{x}^h$ satisfying

$$\sum_j p_j^* \hat{x}_{hj} \leq M_h$$

2. The individual firms' demands and supplies corresponding to these z_j^*, denoted y_{ij}^*, must be such that

$$\sum_j p_j^* y_{ij}^* \geq \sum_j p_j^* y_{ij} \qquad \text{all } i \qquad [\text{B.9}]$$

    for all y_{ij} in the production set. The y_{ij}^* are those values in the production set which maximize profits for the given prices p_j^*.

3. The equilibrium prices must satisfy:

$$p_j^* \geq 0 \qquad \text{all } j \qquad [\text{B.10}]$$

    since negative prices are not possible if goods can be disposed of at zero cost.

4. There must be an equilibrium in every market, which requires

$$\begin{aligned} z_j^* &= 0 \qquad \text{if } p_j^* > 0 \\ z_j^* &\leq 0 \qquad \text{if } p_j^* = 0 \end{aligned} \qquad j = 1, 2, \ldots, n \qquad [\text{B.11}]$$

The first line in [B.11] corresponds to the case shown in (a) and (c) of Fig. 12.1. The second corresponds to the case of free goods shown in (b) and (d). A more succinct way of writing [B.11] is

$$z_j^* \leq 0 \qquad p_j^* \geq 0 \qquad p_j^* z_j^* = 0 \qquad j = 1, 2, \ldots, n \qquad [\text{B.12}]$$

As Fig. 12.1 shows, this corresponds to the usual idea of a market equilibrium, with supply equal to demand, but it also takes account of the possibility of free goods.

Conditions [B.8], [B.9], [B.10] and [B.12] can be summarized: a general equilibrium is a set of non-negative prices, and a set of demands and supplies of households and firms, such that each demand or supply is optimal for the corresponding household or firm at those prices (so that no decision-taker wishes to change their plans) and the resulting excess demands are all non-positive (so that all decision-takers' plans are compatible and can be realized).

EXERCISE 12B

1. Solve the consumer's problem

$$\max u_h \quad \text{s.t.} \quad \sum_{j=1}^{n} p_j \hat{x}_{hj} \leq M_h$$

with

$$M_h = \sum_i \beta_{hi} \pi_i$$

Using the net supply functions given in [B.5], show that the consumer's net demands are functions of prices alone, as in [B.4], and that these demand functions are homogeneous of degree zero in prices.

2. What problem could arise with consumers' net demand functions as any price becomes zero? What axiom of consumer theory is involved here? How might it be changed to exclude this possibility?

3. Explain carefully why positive excess demand implies that some decision takers' optimal plans cannot be fulfilled but negative excess demand need not have the same implication. (What is the role of the 'free disposal' assumption?)

C. Existence of Walrasian equilibrium

For each good and market there is an excess demand function

$$z_j = z_j(p_1, p_2, \ldots, p_n) \qquad j = 1, 2, \ldots, n \qquad \text{[C.1]}$$

which defines a *mapping* from the set of price vectors into the set of excess demand vectors. The mapping is *continuous* for strictly positive prices and *homogeneous of degree zero*.

In proving that an equilibrium, in the sense defined in the previous section, exists for this economy, we make use of the Fixed Point Theorem set out in Appendix K. Our immediate task is to make assumptions and definitions which allow us to bring this theorem into operation.

First, consider the set of prices P, where an element of this set is a vector of prices $(p_1, p_2, \ldots, p_n)$. The set is bounded below by the condition that $p_j \geq 0$, but is not bounded above. To apply the Fixed Point Theorem, the set of prices must be bounded and closed. Hence, we adopt the following *normalization rule*. Given any price vector $(p_1, p_2, \ldots, p_n)$ in P we form a new price vector $(p_1', p_2', \ldots, p_n')$ by the normalization rule

$$p_j' = p_j \frac{1}{\sum p_j} = p_j \frac{1}{pe} \qquad j = 1, 2, \ldots, n \qquad \text{[C.2]}$$

where $e = (1, 1, \ldots, 1)$. $\sum p_j = pe$ is the cost of a bundle of goods consisting of one unit of each commodity and $1/pe$ is the number of bundles that can be bought for £1.

Notice that the normalization procedure is well-defined only if there is at least one price which is not zero. The definition of equilibrium does not rule out the possibility of an equilibrium in which all prices are zero. Such an economy would be of little interest since there would be no scarcity. Hence nothing is lost by restricting attention to price vectors in which at least one price is strictly positive.

The set of *normalized price vectors* P' defined by the normalization rule [C.2] is bounded, closed and convex. P' is bounded below since $p_j \geq 0$, all j, and all p' are positive multiples $(1/pe)$ of some p in P, thus $p'_j \geq 0$, all j. We can show that P' is also bounded above and hence bounded. From [C.2],

$$p'e = \sum_j p'_j = \sum_j p_j \frac{1}{pe} = 1 \qquad [C.3]$$

and since the normalized prices are non-negative this implies that $p'_j \leq 1$, all j. We have therefore established

$$0 \leq p'_j \leq 1 \qquad j = 1, 2, \ldots, n \qquad [C.4]$$

and P' is bounded. P' is also clearly closed. We leave the proof of the convexity of P' to Question 5, Exercise 12C.

The normalization procedure is illustrated for $n = 2$ in Fig. 12.2. The positive quadrant is the set P, since it corresponds to all pairs of non-negative price vectors (p_1, p_2). The line ab joins the price vectors $(0, 1)$ and $(1, 0)$, and so is the locus of price vectors satisfying the conditions in [C.3], [C.4] for $n = 2$. It has the equation

$$p_2 = 1 - p_1$$

Thus it represents in two dimensions the set of normalized price vectors P'.

To illustrate the normalization rule, note first that every price vector (p_1, p_2) must lie on some ray through the origin in Fig. 12.2 and each ray must intersect ab. Take, for example, the ray Oc in the figure. Given the price vector $p^0 = (p_1^0, p_2^0)$ on Oc and ab, any positive price vector along the ray can be written as

$$p = kp^0 \qquad k > 0 \qquad [C.5]$$

for some number k. $\bar{p}$ in the figure is such a vector for a value of k, say $\bar{k}$. Note that $p^0e = 1$. Now, applying the normalization rule to $\bar{p}$ gives the price vector

$$\left(\frac{\bar{p}_1}{\bar{p}e}, \frac{\bar{p}_2}{\bar{p}e} \right) = \left(\frac{\bar{k}p_1^0}{\bar{k}p^0e}, \frac{\bar{k}p_2^0}{\bar{k}p^0e} \right) = \left(\frac{p_1^0}{p^0e}, \frac{p_2^0}{p^0e} \right) = p^0 \qquad [C.6]$$

Figure 12.2

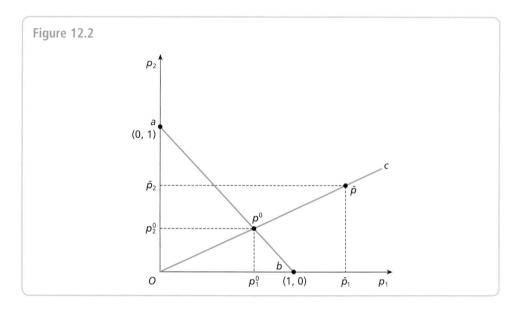

and this will be true for all values of k. The normalization rule collapses the price vectors along any ray in the figure to a single point on the line ab. It is easy to see that the set is bounded, closed and convex. [C.3] and [C.4] define the n-dimensional counterpart of the line ab.

Is it possible to restrict price vectors to the set P'? The zero-degree homogeneity property of the excess demand functions implies that

$$z_j = z_j(p_1, p_2, \ldots, p_n) = z_j(p_1', p_2', \ldots, p_n') \qquad \text{[C.7]}$$

provided that

$$p_j' = \lambda p_j \qquad \text{all } j, \qquad \lambda > 0 \qquad \text{[C.8]}$$

If we set $\lambda = 1/pe$, it follows that the normalized prices p_j' lead to the same excess demands and the initial vector of prices. Hence we are justified in replacing the set P with the 'more useful' set P'.

We consider now a problem which relates to the continuity of the mapping from prices to excess demands. It was asserted earlier that the excess demands are *continuous* functions of prices. This is true as long as all prices are positive, but a problem may arise when some prices are zero. For some households, this may mean that the prices of the goods and services they sell are positive, while those of the goods they buy are zero. It is therefore possible that their demands for these free goods are infinite, thus implying a discontinuity in the excess demand functions. In fact, the axiom of non-satiation as stated in Chapter 2 implies that this will be the case. (See also Question 2, Exercise 12B).

The possibility of discontinuity raises problems for the application of the fixed point theorem, since a condition in that theorem is that the mapping be continuous. We adopt the simple, but crude, solution of assuming that this problem does not arise: *there is always a finite excess demand for a good whose price is zero.* This could be ensured by a modification of the non-satiation axiom: satiation levels, beyond which increments of consumption yield zero utility, exist for all goods, but there is always at least one good which consumers buy at a positive price, and with which they are not satiated. The reason for this latter qualification will become clear when we derive *Walras' Law*, to which we now turn.

Recall that the $\hat{x}^h$ and y_i represent the *desired* or *planned* net demand and supply vectors of households and firms respectively. Then, each $\hat{x}^h$ must satisfy the budget constraint

$$\sum_j p_j \hat{x}_{hj} \leq M_h \qquad h = 1, 2, \ldots, H \qquad \text{[C.9]}$$

But as long as each household is non-satiated with at least one good for each price vector, its budget constraint will be satisfied as an equality, and so summing [C.9] over h gives

$$\sum_h \sum_j p_j \hat{x}_{hj} = \sum_j p_j \sum_h \hat{x}_{hj} = \sum_h M_h \qquad \text{[C.10]}$$

We have

$$\sum_h M_h = \sum_h \sum_i \beta_{hi} \pi_i = \sum_i \pi_i \qquad \text{[C.11]}$$

since $\sum_h \beta_{hi} = 1$. Then using [B.2] we can rewrite [C.10] as

$$\sum_j p_j \sum_h \hat{x}_{hj} - \sum_j p_j \sum_i y_{ij} = \sum_j p_j \left[\sum_h \hat{x}_{hj} - \sum_i y_{ij} \right] = \sum_j p_j z_j = 0 \qquad \text{[C.12]}$$

In other words, at *any price vector* the total value of excess demands is exactly zero. This result is known as Walras' Law, and plays an important role in what follows.

We now present a proof of the existence of general equilibrium. The proposition can be stated formally as follows: given the continuity and zero-degree homogeneity of the excess demand functions $z_j = z_j(p)$, $p \in P'$, and Walras' Law, there exists a price vector $p^* \in P'$, such that

$$z_j^* = z_j(p^*) \leqslant 0, \qquad p_j^* \geqslant 0, \qquad p_j^* z_j^* = 0 \qquad \text{all } j \qquad \text{[C.13]}$$

where the excess demands correspond to utility-maximizing choices by consumers and profit-maximizing choices by firms.

We prove this proposition for the general case with n goods, and then illustrate the proof in two dimensions.

First, the excess demand functions define a continuous mapping from the set of normalized price vectors, P', to the set of excess demand vectors,

$$Z = \{(z_1, z_2, \ldots, z_n) \mid z_j = z_j(p), p \in P', j = 1, 2, \ldots, n\} \qquad \text{[C.14]}$$

We write this mapping as

$$z : P' \to Z \qquad \text{[C.15]}$$

The strategy of the proof is to define a second continuous mapping, from the set Z of excess demands back into the set P'. Taking the composition of these two mappings, we then have a continuous mapping of the closed, bounded, convex set P' into itself, and so there exists a fixed point, i.e. a price vector p^* which, under the composite mapping, has itself as its image. By careful definition of the second mapping, we ensure that such a fixed point is also an equilibrium price vector. We shall then have proved that an equilibrium exists, on the stated assumptions.

Consider the mapping defined by the rule

$$p_j = \frac{\max[0, p_j' + k_j z_j(p')]}{\sum_j \max[0, p_j' + k_j z_j(p')]} \qquad \text{for all } p' \in P', \quad k_j > 0, \quad \text{all } j = 1, \ldots, n \quad \text{[C.16]}$$

This is explained as follows. Choose some initial price vector $p' \in P'$, and consider each corresponding excess demand $z_j(p')$ and the associated price p_j'. We define a new price, p_j, by the following rules:

1. If the excess demand $z_j(p')$ is positive, add to the initial price p_j' some multiple k_j of the excess demand.

2. If the excess demand $z_j(p')$ is zero, set the new price equal to the old price.

3. If the excess demand is negative, add to the old price p_j' some multiple k_j of the excess demand *unless* doing so would make the new price negative, in which case set it instead at zero.

4. Reapply the normalization rule, by summing the prices obtained by applying rules 1–3, and dividing each of them by this sum.

[C.16] defines the mapping

$$k : Z \to P' \qquad\qquad [\text{C.17}]$$

which, it can be shown, is continuous (see Question 3, Exercise 12C). Hence, the composite mapping

$$k \circ z : P' \to P' \qquad\qquad [\text{C.18}]$$

is continuous and maps the closed, bounded, convex set P' into itself. Given some initial $p' \in P'$, we find $z(p') \in Z$, and then $p = k[z(p')] \in P'$. But then, by the Brouwer Fixed Point Theorem, we know that there exists a price vector $p^* \in P'$ such that

$$p^* = k[z(p^*)] \qquad\qquad [\text{C.19}]$$

or, in terms of [C.16],

$$p_j^* = \frac{\max[0,\, p_j^* + k_j z_j(p^*)]}{\sum_j \max[0,\, p_j^* + k_j z_j(p^*)]} \qquad j = 1, \ldots, n \qquad [\text{C.20}]$$

We then have to prove that p^* is an equilibrium price vector. Consider first those goods, if any, for which the right-hand side of [C.20] is zero. Then, since $p_j^* = 0$ for these j, and $p_j^* + k_j z_j(p^*) \leq 0$, we must have (since $k_j > 0$)

$$z_j(p^*) \leq 0 \qquad \text{if } p_j^* = 0 \qquad\qquad [\text{C.21}]$$

These are the free goods. Denote the index set of the remaining goods, for which the right-hand side of [C.20] is positive, by N, i.e. $p_j^* > 0$ for $j \in N$. Multiply through [C.20] by $z_j(p^*)$ for each $j \in N$, to obtain

$$p_j^* z_j(p^*) = \frac{p_j^* z_j^*(p^*) + k_j[z_j(p^*)]^2}{\sum_j \max[0,\, p_j^* + k_j z_j(p^*)]} \qquad j \in N \qquad [\text{C.22}]$$

Now note that, from Walras' Law,

$$\sum_{j \in N} p_j^* z_j(p^*) = \sum_j p_j^* z_j(p^*) = 0$$

(since $p_j^* = 0$, $j \notin N$) and so summing through [C.22] over $j \in N$ and using this fact gives

$$\frac{\sum_{j \in N}(p_j^* z_j(p^*) + k_j[z_j(p^*)]^2)}{\sum_j \max[0,\, p_j^* + k_j z_j(p^*)]} = 0 \qquad\qquad [\text{C.23}]$$

We can cancel the denominator because it is just some positive number, and applying Walras' Law again gives

$$\sum_{j \in N} k_j[z_j(p^*)]^2 = 0 \qquad\qquad [\text{C.24}]$$

But, since $k_j > 0$, this can clearly hold only if $z_j(p^*) = 0$, so

$$z_j(p^*) = 0 \qquad \text{if } p_j^* > 0 \qquad\qquad [\text{C.25}]$$

We have thus established that the fixed point p^* is an equilibrium price vector since $z(p^*)$ is an excess demand vector satisfying the requirements [B.8] and [B.9], p^* is non-negative so [B.10] is satisfied and [C.21] and [C.25] together imply that [B.11] holds.

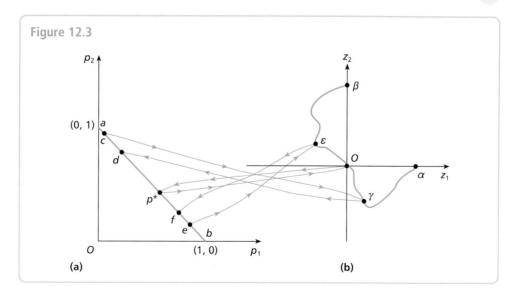

Figure 12.3

We now give a proof of the existence of an equilibrium price vector in two dimensions which, as well as being valid in its own right, allows us to illustrate the more general proof. In (a) of Fig. 12.3, the line *ab* again shows the set of normalized price vectors, and (b) of the figure shows the space of excess demand vectors (z_1, z_2). The point *a* in (a) is the price vector $(0, 1)$. Assume (since we are trying to prove the existence of an equilibrium) that this is not an equilibrium. Then the corresponding excess demand vector cannot be at the origin – the excess demand vector $(0, 0)$ – in (b) of the figure. From Walras' Law we must have

$$0 \cdot z_1 + 1 \cdot z_2 = 0 \qquad \text{[C.26]}$$

implying $z_2 = 0$ and $z_1 > 0$. This latter follows because if $z_1 \leqslant 0$, then point *a* satisfies the definition of an equilibrium, which we have ruled out by assumption. Thus, corresponding to the price vector $(0, 1)$ in Fig. 12.3(a) there must be an excess demand vector like point α in Fig. 12.3(b), with $z_1 > 0$ and $z_2 = 0$. By a similar argument, point *b* in Fig. 12.3(a) must map into a point such as β in Fig. 12.3(b). Now consider the set of excess demand vectors which will be obtained in (b) of the figure, as we choose successive price vectors along the line from *a* to *b* in (a) of the figure. Because of the continuity of the excess demand functions, the resulting excess demand vectors must lie along a continuous curve in the excess demand space, such as that shown joining α and β. Moreover, because of Walras' Law, the excess demands cannot *both* be in the positive quadrant (since then $p_1z_1 + p_2z_2 > 0$), or in the negative quadrant (since then $p_1z_1 + p_2z_2 < 0$). But then any continuous curve passing from α to β, and not passing through the positive or negative quadrants, *must* pass through the origin: that is, there must be a price vector which generates the excess demand vector $(0, 0)$, and so this is the equilibrium price vector.

The more general proof can then be illustrated as follows. Take some point such as *c* in Fig. 12.3(a), and assume that, under the mapping *z*, this yields point γ in (b). Then, under the mapping *k*, γ maps back into, say, point *d*, and so the composite mapping $k \circ z$ maps *c* into *d*. Similarly, point *e* maps into point ε and then back into *f*. Then, given that this mapping of the line *ab* into itself is continuous, there must, by Brouwer's Theorem, be a point such as p^* which maps into itself. But, by the way we have defined the mapping k from the set of excess demands back to the line, we know that p^* must, under the mapping z, yield the origin $(0, 0)$, and must therefore be an equilibrium price vector.

EXERCISE 12C

1. Summarize the roles played by the continuity and zero-degree homogeneity of the excess demand functions, and by Walras' Law, in the existence proofs of this section.

2. Why, in Fig. 12.3, is point d to the right of point c, and point f to the left of point e?

3. (a) Show that the mapping

$$p_j = \max(0, p'_j + k_j z_j)/\sum \max[0, p'_j + k_j z_j]$$

   for p'_j given, and z_j variable is continuous.

   (b) Suppose the z_j is a linear function of p'_j, with all prices but the jth held constant. Draw the graph of the mapping

$$p_j = \max(0, p'_j + k_j z(p'_j))$$

   in (p'_j, p_j) space.

4. Prove that the set P' of normalized price vectors is convex.

5. Illustrate the set of price vectors

$$p' = \left\{ (p_1, p_2, p_3) \mid 0 \leqslant p_j \leqslant 1, \sum_j p_j = 1, j = 1, 2, 3 \right\}$$

   in three dimensions.

6. Prove that, for at least one j, the numerator of the right-hand side of [C.16] is positive.

D. Stability of Walrasian equilibrium

It is not enough to know whether and under what conditions an equilibrium position of the system exists. We are also interested in whether the system will tend to return to an equilibrium when it is in disequilibrium. This is the problem of stability which was discussed, in connection with single markets, in Chapter 8.

The question of stability involves analysis of the movement of prices through successive disequilibrium positions over time. Assume that there exists at least one equilibrium price vector $p^* = (p_1^*, p_2^*, \dots, p_n^*)$, and at an initial moment of time $t = 0$, there exists a price vector $p(0) \neq p^*$. Time varies continuously, and the price vector is a vector-valued function of time, $p(t) = (p_1(t), p_2(t), \dots, p_n(t))$. The system is globally stable if

$$\lim_{t \to \infty} p(t) = p^* \qquad \text{[D.1]}$$

given any initial price vector $p(0)$.

To examine the question of stability we must have some hypothesis of the adjustment process which determines the time path of the price vector. Different adjustment processes have different dynamic behaviour, and so we have to discuss stability relative to a particular adjustment process. Here we shall consider the *tâtonnement process*, already considered in relation to a single market, in Chapter 8. For the multi-market economy, the tâtonnement process is as follows: there is an 'umpire', who announces a price vector at each instant of time, collects (instant-aneously) the information on the resulting offers and demands for every good in the economy, and decides whether or not to permit trading at those prices. She acts according to the following rules:

(a) She announces a new price vector, if and only if the previous price vector is not an equilibrium, in the sense of the preceding section.

(b) She permits trading only at equilibrium prices.

(c) The rate at which she changes each price is proportional to its excess demand:

$$\frac{dp_j(t)}{dt} = \dot{p}_j = \lambda_j z_j \quad j = 1, 2, \ldots, n \quad \lambda_j > 0 \qquad \text{[D.2]}$$

The assumption that this adjustment process works in continuous time is not restrictive. On the other hand, the assumption of no trading at disequilibrium prices is substantive rather than simplifying.

Walras' Law again holds for all price vectors, in and out of equilibrium. The rea-soning is as before: since, for any announced price vector, consumers' net demands satisfy their budget constraints, aggregating over households and firms yields Walras' Law. Since trading does not take place out of equilibrium, the fact that plans are in aggregate inconsistent, and all consumers' *ex ante* demands *could not* be satisfied simultaneously if trade *did* take place, has no bearing on Walras' Law.

The adjustment rule defined in [D.2] is a generalization of the rule for a single market, in Chapter 8. Goods in excess demand have their prices increased, and those in excess supply have their prices reduced. It, however, specifies nothing beyond that about how markets actually work and the criticisms of the tâtonnement process given in Chapter 8 apply equally here.

For a single market, it was shown in Chapter 8 that the adjustment process in [D.2], in the presence of a negatively sloped excess demand curve, always generated a time-path of prices which converged to equilibrium. But now each excess demand depends on *all* prices, and so a negative slope for each excess demand curve is no longer sufficient. Thus, suppose all markets except those for goods 1 and 2 are in equilibrium, but $z_1 > 0$. Raising p_1 will cause increased excess demands for substi-tutes of good 1 and lower excess demands for its complements, and so the attempt to reach equilibrium in the first market may bring about disequilibrium in others. Moreover, if goods 1 and 2 are complements, the extent of the excess supply in mar-ket 2 will also have increased. Examples can be constructed in which the adjustment process defined in [D.2] is unstable, and so it cannot be sufficient for stability.

There are, however, several related but distinct cases in which sufficient conditions for global stability of the system under the tâtonnement process can be formulated. The following analysis illustrates the approach.

Assume that there are only two goods, with excess demand functions $z_j(p_1, p_2)$, $j = 1, 2$. The prices are *not* normalized in the sense of the previous section, so that the set of price vectors is the entire positive quadrant. We assume that there exists an equilibrium price vector $p^* > 0$ such that

$$z_j(p_1^*, p_2^*) = 0 \quad j = 1, 2 \qquad \text{[D.3]}$$

(thus ruling out the possibility of a free good). We examine a central proposition of stability theory, in the context of this two-good economy:

Stability proposition: if all goods in the economy are *gross substitutes*, then the time path of prices, $p(t)$, determined by the tâtonnement adjustment process described in [D.2], converges to an equilibrium. That is, [D.2] implies

$$\lim_{t\to\infty} p(t) = p^* \qquad\qquad [D.4]$$

for any initial price vector $p(0)$. Thus, the economic system is globally stable.

Goods 1 and 2 are gross substitutes if

$$\frac{\partial z_1}{\partial p_2} > 0, \qquad \frac{\partial z_2}{\partial p_1} > 0 \qquad\qquad [D.5]$$

at all price vectors p. In Chapter 2 we referred to substitutes in consumption. Here the term 'gross substitute' has a rather wider meaning since we are concerned with *excess* demand, i.e. with both supply and demand responses to price changes, rather than just demand responses.

Now, it is very simple to prove the above stability proposition using the special features of this two-good economy, and this is set as an exercise. (See Question 1, Exercise 12D.) However, we shall work through the proof, which holds for an *n*-good economy, making use of the two-good assumption just to simplify the algebra and to permit diagrammatic illustration.

In proving the stability proposition, we need three subsidiary propositions (which are also of interest in their own right).

Proposition 1. Given gross substitutability, the equilibrium price vector $p^* = (p_1^*, p_2^*)$ is unique (up to a scalar multiple).

That is, we can show that if there are two price vectors say p^* and p^{**}, such that $z_j(p^*) = z_j(p^{**}) = 0$, all j, then gross substitutability implies that $p^{**} = \mu p^*$, for μ some positive number. We proceed by assuming the p^* and p^{**} are equilibrium price vectors, but that no such μ exists. We then show that this leads to a contradiction. Consider Fig. 12.4.

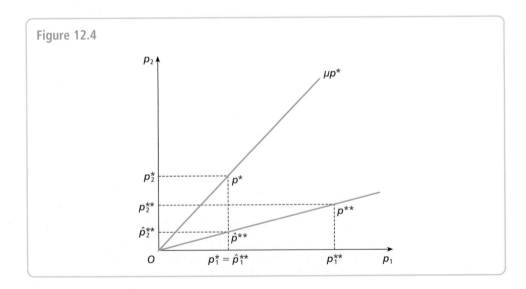

Figure 12.4

The line through p^*, denoted by μp^*, shows the set of all price vectors which are scalar multiples of p^*. Because of the zero-degree homogeneity of the excess demand functions we know that, if p^* is an equilibrium price vector, so must be μp^*, for any $\mu > 0$. If $p^{**} \neq \mu p^*$, then the line Op^{**} must be distinct from Op^*, as shown in the figure. Again, from the zero-degree homogeneity of excess demand functions, if p^{**} is an equilibrium price vector, so must be any point on the line Op^{**}, since such a point can be written as, say, $\hat{p}^{**} = \mu p^{**}$, for $1 > \mu > 0$. Consider in particular the point $\hat{p}^{**}$ shown in the figure. Comparing it with the vector p^*, we have

$$\hat{p}_1^{**} = p_1^* \tag{D.6}$$

$$\hat{p}_2^{**} < p_2^* \tag{D.7}$$

Now, since p^* is an equilibrium, we must have

$$z_1(p_1^*, p_2^*) = 0 = z_2(p_1^*, p_2^*) \tag{D.8}$$

But, given gross substitutability, [D.6] and [D.7] imply

$$\begin{aligned} z_1(\hat{p}_1^{**}, \hat{p}_2^{**}) &< 0 \\ z_2(\hat{p}_1^{**}, \hat{p}_2^{**}) &> 0 \end{aligned} \tag{D.9}$$

since $\hat{p}^{**}$ involves a lower price of good 2 than p^*. Hence, [D.9] implies that $\hat{p}^{**}$ is not an equilibrium, which in turn implies that $p^{**} = (1/\mu)p^{**}$ cannot be an equilibrium. Hence, an equilibrium price vector can only lie along μp^*.

Proposition 2. Gross substitutability, together with Walras' Law, implies that $p_1^* z_1(p_1, p_2) + p_2^* z_2(p_1, p_2) > 0$ for any *disequilibrium* price vector $p = (p_1, p_2)$.

In other words, we can show that the total value of disequilibrium excess demands, when valued at *equilibrium* prices, must always be strictly positive (the total value of equilibrium excess demands at equilibrium prices is of course zero, as is the total value of all excess demands when valued at the prices which generate them, from Walras' Law). First, we note again that, by the properties of the equilibrium

$$z_1(p_1^*, p_2^*) = 0 = z_2(p_1^*, p_2^*) \tag{D.10}$$

Now define a new price vector, say $\hat{p}$ (which, because of 1, will be a disequilibrium price vector) as follows:

$$\hat{p}_1 < p_1^*, \qquad \hat{p}_2 > p_2^* \tag{D.11}$$

Then, because of gross substitutability, we must have

$$z_1(\hat{p}_1, \hat{p}_2) > 0, \qquad z_2(\hat{p}_1, \hat{p}_2) < 0 \tag{D.12}$$

Then [D.11] and [D.12] together imply

$$(p_1^* - \hat{p}_1) \cdot z_1(\hat{p}_1, \hat{p}_2) + (p_2^* - \hat{p}_2) \cdot z_2(\hat{p}_1, \hat{p}_2) > 0 \tag{D.13}$$

since each term in the sum must be positive. Rearranging gives

$$p_1^* z_1 + p_2^* z_2 > \hat{p}_1 z_1 + \hat{p}_2 z_2 \tag{D.14}$$

But by Walras' Law the right-hand side of this expression is zero. Hence the proposition is proved, at least for the directions of change in [D.11]. It is left to the reader to prove that it will also hold for all price vectors $\hat{p} = (\hat{p}_1, \hat{p}_2)$ such that $\hat{p}_1/\hat{p}_2 \neq p_2^*/p_2^*$ (see Question 2, Exercise 12D).

Proposition 3. Given an equilibrium price vector p^*, it is possible on the assumptions made to define a *distance function* $D(p(t), p^*)$, such that $dD/dt < 0$ for all $p(t) \neq \mu p^*$, while $p(t) = \mu p^*$ implies $dD/dt = 0$.

A distance function assigns a real number D to each price vector $p(t)$, measuring its distance from an equilibrium vector p^*. Proposition 3 asserts that such a function can always be defined in the present case, and, given the tâtonnement process, Walras' Law, and the gross substitute assumption, its value falls monotonically through time. Moreover, it ceases to fall when $p(t)$ is either at the equilibrium vector p^*, or some scalar multiple of it, which must also be an equilibrium vector (given zero-degree homogeneity of the excess demand functions). In other words, the time-path of the price vector is getting steadily closer to an equilibrium price vector, and, if it reaches the equilibrium *price ray*, will cease to change.

To prove proposition 3, define the distance function

$$D(p(t), p^*) = \frac{1}{2\lambda_1}[p_1(t) - p_1^*]^2 + \frac{1}{2\lambda_2}[p_2(t) - p_2^*]^2 \qquad [\text{D.15}]$$

where λ_i is the speed of adjustment parameter (recall [D.2]). Differentiating with respect to t we get

$$\frac{dD}{dt} = \frac{1}{\lambda_1}[p_1(t) - p_1^*]\frac{dp_1}{dt} + \frac{1}{\lambda_2}[p_2(t) - p_2^*]\frac{dp_2}{dt} \qquad [\text{D.16}]$$

Substituting for dp_1/dt and dp_2/dt from [D.2] and rearranging gives

$$\frac{dD}{dt} = [p_1(t) - p_1^*]z_1(p_1, p_2) + [p_2(t) - p_2^*]z_2(p_1, p_2) \qquad [\text{D.17}]$$

$$= p_1z_1 + p_2z_2 - (p_1^*z_1 + p_2^*z_2) \qquad [\text{D.18}]$$

But, by Walras' Law, $p_1z_1 + p_2z_2 = 0$, while, from proposition 2 above, $p_1^*z_1 + p_2^*z_2 > 0$, and so

$$\frac{dD}{dt} = -(p_1^*z_1 + p_2^*z_2) < 0 \qquad [\text{D.19}]$$

If $p(t) = \mu p^*$, $\mu > 0$, then

$$p_1^*z_1(\mu p_1^*, \mu p_2^*) + p_2^*z_2(\mu p_1^*, \mu p_2^*) = p_1^*z_1(p_1^*, p_2^*) + p_2^*z_2(p_1^*, p_2^*) = 0 \qquad [\text{D.20}]$$

using the zero-degree homogeneity property, and Walras' Law. Hence,

$$\frac{dD}{dt}(\mu p^*, p^*) = -\{p_1^*z_1(p_1^*, p_2^*) + p_2^*z_2(p_1^*, p_2^*)\} = 0 \qquad [\text{D.21}]$$

These three propositions, and in particular proposition 3, allow us to prove the stability proposition given earlier.

Intuitively, we might think that proposition 3 provides us directly with the proof of stability, since if, as time passes, the distance between the price vector $p(t)$ and the equilibrium is steadily diminishing, we might feel that the time-path of price vectors must converge to p^*, while, because of [D.21], it would not overshoot. However, there is an awkward possibility, which is that the price vector time-path may converge to a limit other than p^*, so that, even though it is always getting closer to p^*, it does not converge to it. If this seems counter-intuitive, consider the function

$$y = \frac{1}{x} + a \qquad a, x > 0 \qquad\qquad [D.22]$$

As $x \to \infty$, y is becoming closer to zero – the distance between y and zero is decreasing monotonically – but $\lim_{x \to \infty} y = a \neq 0$, and so y does not converge to zero. We have to prove that in the present case no such possibility exists. This proof is somewhat technical, however, and its main idea was presented in a simpler context in Chapter 8. We do not, therefore, give it here. The interested reader is referred to Takayama (1985).

To summarize: given the assumptions underlying the form of the tâtonnement process, we have been able to find a set of conditions, namely the gross substitutability conditions, under which the system of interrelated markets will converge to an equilibrium, however far away from it the initial position is and whatever the speeds of adjustment λ_1, λ_2. Moreover, these conditions were also seen to imply uniqueness of the equilibrium price vector.

It would have been damaging to the theory if no such conditions could have been found. If equilibrium in that model was found never to be stable, then this would severely limit the model's analytical scope. For example, the model could not be used for comparative statics analysis.

The analysis of this section related to the tâtonnement process, which, as Chapter 8 has suggested, may not be a good description of real adjustment processes especially where *production* is involved. An essential feature is the 'no-trading out of equilibrium' assumption. If we permit trading at disequilibrium prices, then quantities which individuals and firms buy and sell in one 'round' of trading may differ from those expected, and the precise quantities which have been traded will affect trading in the next 'round'. Hence, the process of adjustment must take into account the time-paths of quantities traded, and not only the time-paths of prices. It is significant that many attempts to explain the persistence of disequilibrium phenomena such as inflation and unemployment begin by discarding the assumption of no trading out of equilibrium.

EXERCISE 12D

1. Show in a simple diagram that in a two-good economy, where the goods are gross substitutes, equilibrium is stable. (*Hint*: set $p_2 = 1$ and draw the excess demand functions as functions of p_1/p_2 only, beginning with the equilibrium value.)

2. Prove proposition 2 for the case in which $p_1 > p_1^*$ and $p_2 < p_2^*$, and show that this, together with the case considered in equation [D.1], establishes the proposition for all possible price vectors.

3. Discuss in detail the meaning of gross substitutability by

    (a) distinguishing between supply and demand effects in the excess demand functions;

    (b) distinguishing between income and substitution effects in consumer demand functions.

    If two goods are gross substitutes are they also necessarily Marshallian or Hicksian substitutes in consumption or Hicks–Allen substitutes?

E. Edgeworth exchange theory

The view of the market which has underlain the analysis so far is of individual decision-takers responding to a given market price by choosing optimal quantities, which then are aggregated into excess demands. Nothing has been said about *exchange activity* in the market.

We now examine a theory of markets which takes a more realistic view of the process. The theory formulated by Edgeworth begins by considering direct exchange between two individuals and proceeds to analyse a market in which many individuals shop around, bargain, make tentative deals, look for better ones, and then make contracts with each other when they think they have found the best deals they can. This theory has much more of the flavour of the marketplace about it but, more importantly, it gives significant insights, introduces powerful concepts, and leads to interesting generalizations of the theory we have considered so far.

We begin with two individuals 1 and 2. x_i, $\bar{x}_i$ and $\hat{x}_i$ denote individual i's consumption, endowment and net demand, respectively, of commodity x, $i = 1, 2$. $\bar{x} = \bar{x}_1 + \bar{x}_2$ is the total endowment of the commodity. In addition, each possesses some amount of a commodity y and y_i, $\bar{y}_i$ and $\hat{y}_i$ are respectively i's consumption, endowment and net demand for this.

The central tool of analysis in this theory is the Edgeworth (strictly, the Edgeworth–Bowley) box diagram, in conjunction with the consumers' indifference maps. Figure 12.5 shows an Edgeworth box. The length of the horizontal side of the box represents the total endowment $\bar{x}$ of commodity x, and the length of the vertical side of the box represents the total endowment of y. The usefulness of the diagram stems from the fact that a single point within it shows the four consumption values (x_1, y_1, x_2, y_2) and moreover these values satisfy the *feasibility conditions*

$$x_1 + x_2 = \bar{x}$$
$$y_1 + y_2 = \bar{y}$$

[E.1]

Figure 12.5

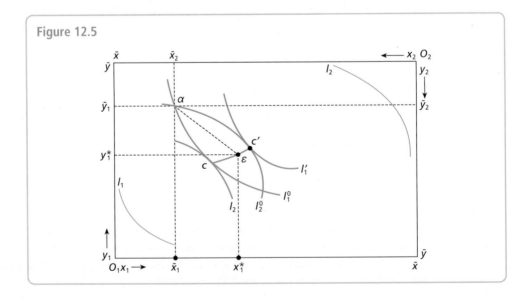

i.e. the sum of the consumptions of each good exactly exhausts the total endowment, and no more. This is because we measure 1's consumption of x rightwards from the origin O_1 at the bottom left-hand corner of the box, and her consumption of y vertically upwards from O_1; while 2's consumption of x is measured leftwards from the origin O_2 at the top right-hand corner of the box, and his consumption of y_2 is measured vertically downwards from O_2. Thus each point in the box has four consumption coordinates. We can draw 1's indifference curves with reference to origin O_1, and 2's with reference to origin O_2 – examples are I_1 and I_2 in the figure. The initial endowment point at α has the coordinates $(\bar{x}_1, \bar{y}_1, \bar{x}_2, \bar{y}_2)$.

The indifference curves of the consumers satisfy the assumptions of Chapter 2 and so are drawn convex to their respective origins. Before trading, the consumers are located at α on indifference curves I_1^0, I_2^0. Will trading take place, and if so, what will its outcome be? The answer is based upon two propositions which we call the *Edgeworth hypotheses* (*EH*):

1. The two individuals will always agree to an exchange which makes at least one of them better off and the other no worse off.

2. Neither individual will ever agree to an exchange which makes him or her worse off.

The first hypothesis rules out a failure to agree. Although the parties will haggle and bargain we assume that each is sufficiently rational as to end up making some exchange which makes him or her at least no worse off.

Given *EH*, exchange will take place in the situation shown in Fig. 12.5. For example, by moving along I_2^0, with 1 giving 2 y in exchange for x, i.e. with 1 buying x from 2, 1 is making herself better off and 2 is no worse off. Likewise, by moving along I_1^0, with 1 again buying x from 2, but not getting so much x for each payment of y, 2 is getting better off and 1 is no worse off. Clearly *both* can be better off if 1 buys x from 2 with payments falling between those implied by moving along I_2^0, and those implied by moving along I_1^0. Thus, by hypothesis 1, trade will take place. It is left to the reader to confirm that this will always be true when the initial endowment point occurs at an intersection of the indifference curves, i.e. at a point at which the consumers' marginal rates of substitution are unequal and when the set of points which are both below I_2^0 and above I_1^0 is non-empty (see Question 4, Exercise 12E).

We now have to determine the outcome of the exchange process. Consider the curve cc' in the figure. It has the property that it is the locus of *points of tangency of the indifference curves of the consumers in the area bounded above by I_2^0 and below by I_1^0*. Two such points of tangency at c and c' are shown as an illustration. Because of the strict convexity assumption, any given pair of indifference curves for the two consumers will have no more than one tangency point, and so no point off cc' in the area bounded by I_1^0 and I_2^0 can be a tangency point. *All* points off cc' must therefore be points of intersection. But given any point of intersection of indifference curves, it is always possible for one consumer to become better off (by sliding along an indifference curve) if not both (by moving into the lens-shaped area between the indifference curves), as point α has illustrated. Hence no point off cc' can be an outcome of the exchange process, since it does not satisfy hypothesis 1.

On the other hand, a point on cc' cannot be improved upon once reached. A move off cc' must make at least one consumer worse off, since a move in any direction off the curve leads to a lower indifference curve for at least one consumer. Once the exchange process reaches a point on cc', it will not move along this curve 'searching' for another point, because any move from one point to another along cc' makes one consumer worse off. Thus, *all* points along cc' satisfy hypothesis 1. Since hypothesis 2 rules out any outcome of the exchange process outside the area bounded by I_1^0 and I_2^0 it follows that *only* the points on cc' satisfy *both EH*. Therefore the curve cc' is the equilibrium we seek. Edgeworth called this the 'contract curve', because it shows the set of possible contracts for purchases/sales which the individuals will make.

Notice that the theory does not specify exactly how the consumers get from point α to a particular point on cc': we do not say anything specific about the nature of the bargaining process.

However, the two hypotheses are inexorable: if they are satisfied the bargainers must end up at a point on the contract curve and nowhere else and would not agree to change.

The theory predicts the equilibrium as one of a *set of points* rather than as a particular point. Economists accustomed to single-point solutions have tended to call this model 'indeterminate' because it results in a *set* of points. (Bargaining theory – see Chapter 15 – has developed to try to predict the point in the set at which the parties will arrive in terms of the dynamics of the bargaining process.) To this extent the conclusions of Edgeworth's theory may appear weaker than those of the earlier theory of markets, but it should be remembered that it started from a far more general, and in the two-person case rather more plausible, view of the market. The individuals are not acting as passive respondents to a given market price, but are actively bargaining and dealing until they have found an exchange which cannot be improved upon for both of them (though of course it could be improved upon for one at the expense of the other).

This exchange *implies a price*, as can be seen in Fig. 12.5. Suppose the process ends up at point ε. Then the line $\alpha\varepsilon$ defines a price ratio. Consumer 1 pays 2 the amount $\bar{y}_1 - y_1^*$ in exchange for $x_1^* - \bar{x}_1$ of x, and so the *implied* equilibrium price of x is $p^* = (\bar{y}_1 - y_1^*)/(x_1^* - \bar{x}_1)$. It follows that the equilibrium could be expressed in terms of a set of prices, defined by the slopes of the lines from α to the curve cc', and bounded above by the slope of αc and below by the slope of $\alpha c'$ (ignoring minus signs in each case).

We can prove that the assumptions of continuity and strict convexity ensure that an equilibrium always exists. Thus, note that any points on cc' can be generated by solving the problem

$$\max u_1(x_1, y_1) \quad \text{s.t.} \quad u_2(x_2, y_2) \geq u_2^0 \qquad \text{[E.2]}$$

and subject to the endowment constraints [E.1] and the non-negativity constraints $(x_i \geq 0, y_i \geq 0, i = 1, 2)$. u_2^0 is a utility value for 2 which varies between the values of utility corresponding to indifference curves I_2^0 and I_2 in Fig. 12.5. For each u_2^0, this problem has a non-empty, closed and bounded feasible set as well as a continuous objective function, and so by Weierstrass' Theorem a solution exists. Strict convexity of preferences ensures that the theorem on uniqueness of solutions also applies.

We therefore have a satisfactory equilibrium theory for this two-person exchange situation. However, markets in general contain more than two participants, and we would like to extend the analysis to a situation of exchange among $n > 2$ individuals. We are also interested in going beyond the simple comparison made earlier of the 'size' of the equilibrium solution here as compared with the (possibly) unique equilibrium of the Walrasian approach, to examine in some depth the relation between the two approaches. We can in fact achieve both of these in one step, introducing in the process some interesting new ideas. This is the subject of the next section.

EXERCISE 12E

1. (a) What is the implication of the two consumers being at different points in the Edgeworth box?

   (b) What would be implied if 1 was at a point south-west of 2? North-east of 2?

   (c) What is the interpretation of a single point on a vertical side of the box? A horizontal side?

   (d) Suppose you were faced with two 'ordinary' indifference curve diagrams for the two consumers, placed side by side on the page. How would you obtain the Edgeworth box from them?

   (e) Where would the initial endowment point be if all of good 1 were owned by consumer 1, and all of good 2 by consumer 2? If 1 owned all of both goods?

   (f) Under what conditions would the box be square? State as concisely as you can a sufficient condition on the initial endowment point for no trade to take place.

2. Under what circumstances would the contract curve lie along an edge of the box and what necessary conditions characterize these equilibrium outcomes?

3. Show that if we relax the assumption of *strict* convexity of indifference curves for both consumers the contract curve may widen into an area.

F. Exchange, equilibrium and the core

The concept of the *core* of a game is of direct relevance to the theory of markets. Here, we explain and apply the concept only as it relates to exchange situations, but it has a wider definition and field of application.

Consider the two-person exchange situation of the previous section. A way of looking at the situation is in terms of the possible coalitions of the participants in the situation ('players' in the 'exchange game'). There are three possible coalitions: those consisting of each player alone, and that consisting of both of them together.

An *allocation* is a specification of a quantity of each good received by each consumer, i.e. a value of the vector (x_1, y_1, x_2, y_2). Hence, if an allocation satisfies the conditions in [E.1], so that it is a feasible allocation, then it is a point in the Edgeworth box. An allocation is said to be *blocked* if a coalition can find a way of *improving upon* it (i.e. make at least one of its members better off and none worse off) by exchanging only among themselves (or, if the coalition has just one member, she does not trade at all but keeps what she has).

The *core* is defined as *the set of allocations which is not blocked by any coalition*, i.e. the set of allocations having the property that no coalition could do better by rejecting them and trading among themselves. The core in the two-person exchange situation is the contract curve. Refer again to Fig. 12.5. Any allocation outside the lens-shaped area bounded by the indifference curves I_1^0 and I_2^0 can be improved upon by the coalition containing the first consumer only, or that containing the second

Figure 12.6

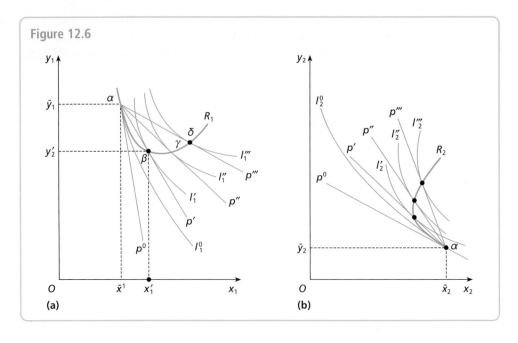

(a)   **(b)**

only, since one or the other would always prefer the initial endowment to such an allocation. Therefore all these allocations are blocked. But in addition, any allocation within the lens-shaped area but not on cc' can be improved upon by the coalition of the two consumers, since they can always find a feasible trade which makes at least one better off and the other no worse off and so these allocations are blocked. Finally, at an allocation on cc', no trade can be found which would make one better off without making the other worse off and so these allocations cannot be improved upon by any coalition – they are not blocked. The definition of the core is equivalent to *EH* and they yield the same sets of possible solutions to the exchange process. From now on we refer to the contract curve as the core (of this two-person exchange situation). The analysis of the previous section showed that in this case the core is not an empty set: the two-person exchange game has a non-empty core.

In a Walrasian economy there is some mechanism by which a price vector is announced and consumers respond by making optimal choices. An equilibrium occurs when excess demand is zero. We consider how this equilibrium relates to the core in the two-person exchange situation and then generalize to n persons. Recall from Chapter 2 the construction of the *offer curve* of an individual. Figure 12.6 repeats the construction for the two individuals. In (a) and (b), α is the initial endowment point, and I_1^0 and I_2^0 are the initial indifference curves. The line p^0 in (a) is defined to be tangent to I_1^0 at α, and similarly p^0 in (b) is tangent to I_2^0 at α (hence in general the two lines have different slopes). As successively lower values of p are announced in (a), we have a sequence of tangency points such as β, γ and δ. Each shows the amount of y consumer 1 would be prepared to give up, at the prevailing price, for the amount of x read off from the other coordinate. For example, at price p', the tangency at point β indicates that consumer 1 would give up $(\bar{y}_1 - y_1')$ units of y in exchange for $(x_1' - \bar{x}_1)$ units of x, with the ratio $(\bar{y}_1 - y_1')/(x_1' - \bar{x}_1)$ of course equal to p'. The locus of all such points of tangency, αR_1 in the figure, is 1's *offer curve*. It shows the trades that 1 would want to make at each market price. The offer

Figure 12.7

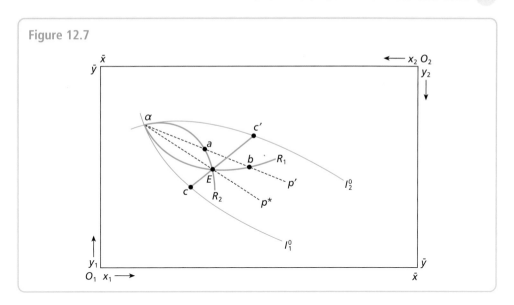

curve αR_2 in (b) of the figure is derived in a similar way. The two properties of the offer curves which are of central importance are:

(a) They must lie entirely above their respective initial indifference curves I_1^0 and I_2^0.

(b) A line drawn from α to a point on the offer curve represents a price line to which the consumer's indifference curve is tangent at that point.

The significance of offer curves is that they provide us with a means of finding a market equilibrium when we are using the Edgeworth box. In Fig. 12.7 we reproduce the Edgeworth box of the previous section and include the offer curves αR_1 and αR_2. Because of property (a) above, both must lie in the lens-shaped area bounded by I_1^0 and I_2^0. It is no accident that their intersection point lies on the contract curve cc', i.e. is a point in the core. In a competitive equilibrium a single price prevails; it must be tangent to an indifference curve of each consumer and it must be such that the chosen demands and supplies of each good are equal. These three conditions are all satisfied at and only at a point of intersection of the offer curves. Suppose the price corresponding to the line $\alpha p'$ is announced. Then consumer 2 would choose point a while consumer 1 would choose point b. Therefore this cannot be an equilibrium. At a price corresponding to the line $\alpha p^\star$, however, consumer 1 chooses point E, as does consumer 2, and so we have an equilibrium. Moreover, $\alpha p^\star$ is tangent to each consumer's indifference curve at E (by definition of the offer curves) and therefore they must be tangent to each other at this point. Since the intersection can only occur within the lens-shaped area, the market equilibrium is a point of tangency of indifference curves within this area and so must be on cc'. Hence, *the competitive equilibrium is in the core.*

When the two consumers act as price-takers in a market, passively responding to movements in the market price, they are guided to an equilibrium position which is one of a large number of allocations which they *may* have achieved if instead they had got together, bargained and haggled, and made a contract when they had exhausted all possible mutual gains from trade.

The consequences of assuming a competitive market mechanism with passive price adjustment is to collapse the whole set of possible exchange equilibria into a single point (or at most a finite number of points if the offer curves have multiple intersections). This greater precision of the competitive market theory is bought at a cost: the tâtonnement process by which equilibrium is brought about does not accord well with reality and neither does the assumption that in a market with only two participants we will in fact get passive price-taking behaviour. The weaker solution concept of the core seems a better model of two-person markets.

The answer to the question of what happens in economies with a larger number of consumers can be stated in two propositions:

1. Regardless of the number of consumers, the competitive market equilibrium is always in the core.
2. As the number of consumers increases, the set of allocations in the core shrinks until, in the limit, it contains only the competitive market equilibrium allocation(s).

The propositions imply that, for markets with large numbers of participants, the solution concepts are equivalent: whether we view a market as a collection of active, bargaining, wheeling-and-dealing individuals or as a collection of passive price-takers coordinated by a price adjustment mechanism, makes no difference in terms of the equilibrium outcome.

Suppose that there are n individuals each characterized by a preference ordering and initial endowment vector. There are $2^n - 1$ possible coalitions altogether (excluding the coalition with no members). An allocation assigns a quantity of x and y to each individual and it will be blocked if any subset of the n individuals can trade among themselves and do better than under the original allocation. This definition of 'blocking' is again equivalent to EH, suitably redefined for any number of consumers.

If people are going to be able to wheel and deal we have to allow them to make tentative contracts which they can break if they find another individual, or group, with whom they can make a better deal, i.e. they have to be free to *re-contract*. Thus, any consumer can set up a tentative trade with one or more others, so that she knows exactly what that would imply for her allocation, but can then drop out – blocking this allocation – if she can do better elsewhere.

More formally, let S denote a set of consumer subscripts or indexes. Then $i \in S$ means that consumer i belongs to the coalition whose subscripts are shown in the index set S. Given initial endowments $\bar{x}_i$ and $\bar{y}_i$ for each individual i, the total resources available to a coalition S are

$$\bar{x}_s = \sum_{i \in S} \bar{x}_i \qquad \bar{y}_s = \sum_{i \in S} \bar{y}_i \qquad \text{[F.1]}$$

i.e. the sum of endowments for members of that coalition. A *feasible* allocation for that coalition is a set of consumptions (x_i, y_i) for each member such that

$$\sum_{i \in S} x_i \leq \bar{x}_s$$

$$\sum_{i \in S} y_i \leq \bar{y}_s \qquad \text{[F.2]}$$

So if some particular allocation is blocked by some coalition the resulting allocation must be feasible for the coalition in the sense of [F.2].

We now prove proposition 1. Suppose we have a competitive market equilibrium allocation in which the ith consumer receives the bundle (x_i^*, y_i^*), which by definition of a competitive equilibrium is the bundle she prefers at the equilibrium price p^*. Since her budget constraint must be satisfied, we have for each i

$$p^*(x_i^* - \bar{x}_i) + y_i^* - \bar{y}_i = 0 \qquad \text{all } i \qquad \text{[F.3]}$$

where we take the price of y as 1 and p is the price of x in terms of y. Now we have to show that the market equilibrium is in the core, so that no coalition S can find a feasible allocation which makes at least one member better off and no one worse off. We assume that such a coalition does exist, and then show that this implies a contradiction.

Suppose there exists a coalition S such that for *each* individual $i \in S$ we have

$$(x_i', y_i') \gtrsim (x_i^*, y_i^*) \qquad \text{[F.4]}$$

and for at least one $i \in S$ we have

$$(x_i', y_i') > (x_i^*, y_i^*) \qquad \text{[F.5]}$$

where (x_i', y_i') is a feasible allocation for $i \in S$. Take an individual who is strictly better off. It must be the case that

$$p^*x_i' + y_i' > p^*x_i^* + y_i^* \qquad i \in S \qquad \text{[F.6]}$$

If this were not true she could have afforded (x_i', y_i') at the competitive equilibrium and so would have chosen it. By the same argument, for all other individuals in the coalition who satisfy [F.4], we must have

$$p^*x_i' + y_i' \geq p^*x_i^* + y_i^* \qquad i \in S \qquad \text{[F.7]}$$

Now, sum [F.6] and [F.7] over all the individuals in the coalition,

$$p^* \sum_{i \in S} x_i' + \sum_{i \in S} y_i' > p^* \sum_{i \in S} x_i^* + \sum_{i \in S} y_i^* \qquad \text{[F.8]}$$

But summing the budget constraints in [F.3] for $i \in S$ gives

$$p^* \sum_{i \in S} x_i^* + \sum_{i \in S} y_i^* = p^* \sum_{i \in S} \bar{x}_i + \sum_{i \in S} \bar{y}_i = p^*\bar{x}_s + \bar{y}_s \qquad \text{[F.9]}$$

and therefore substituting from [F.9] into [F.8] implies

$$p^* \sum_{i \in S} x_i' + \sum_{i \in S} y_i' > p^*\bar{x}_s + \bar{y}_s \qquad \text{[F.10]}$$

But from the definition of feasible allocations in [F.2] we have that for any feasible allocation

$$p^* \sum_{i \in S} x_i + \sum_{i \in S} y_i \leq p^*\bar{x}_s + \bar{y}_s \qquad \text{[F.11]}$$

(since multiplying the first line of [F.2] by $p^* > 0$ and then adding gives [F.11]). Hence the allocations (x_i', y_i') cannot be feasible for the coalition S, and so the assumption that such a coalition exists must be false.

Thus no coalition can do better than a competitive market equilibrium allocation, whatever the number of consumers in the market, and so *that allocation must be in the core*. Note that the only assumption used in the proof was the degree of consumer rationality implied by inequalities [F.6] and [F.7].

Proposition 1 also establishes that, under the conditions which guarantee exist-ence of a competitive equilibrium, the core is non-empty because it always contains the competitive equilibrium.

Turning to proposition 2, we prove this for a somewhat special case (which can be generalized). Assume there are two types of consumer with an equal number n of consumers of each type. We show that given any point in the core of the two-person economy that is not a Walrasian equilibrium, we can find a sufficiently large n such that this point is not in the core of the $2n$-person economy. The only points that cannot be 'knocked out' of the core in this way are the Walrasian equilibrium points. Thus, in the limit, as n grows indefinitely large, these are the only allocations remaining in the core.

From the point of view of the model, there are only two aspects of the consumer which are relevant. The first is her initial endowment and the second is her prefer-ence ordering or indifference map. Accordingly we use the term 'a consumer of type A' for a consumer with initial endowment $(\bar{x}_A, \bar{y}_A)$ and indifference curves $I_A^0, I_A', I_A'', \ldots$, and 'a consumer of type B' for one endowed with $(\bar{x}_B, \bar{y}_B)$ and with indifference curves $I_B^0, I_B', I_B'', \ldots$. There are n consumers of each type, denoted res-pectively by A_i and B_i, $i = 1, \ldots, n$. The total initial endowments available to this economy are therefore

$$\bar{x} = n\bar{x}_A + n\bar{x}_B$$
$$\bar{y} = n\bar{y}_A + n\bar{y}_B$$

[F.12]

We initially work through the analysis for the case in which $n = 2$. Then we prove the general results. The analysis proceeds in two steps. First, we establish the *equal treatment principle* which states that, at any core allocation, individuals of the *same* type must receive the *same* consumption allocations. We then show how, in moving from an economy with one individual of each type, to one with two individuals of each type, it is possible to block some of the allocations which are in the core of the $n = 1$ economy.

If $n = 2$, a feasible resource allocation requires

$$x_{A_1} + x_{A_2} + x_{B_1} + x_{B_2} \leqslant \bar{x} = 2\bar{x}_A + 2\bar{x}_B$$

[F.13]

$$y_{A_1} + y_{A_2} + y_{B_1} + y_{B_2} \leqslant \bar{y} = 2\bar{y}_A + 2\bar{y}_B$$

[F.14]

Now suppose A_1 and A_2 have different bundles under an allocation. Two cases are possible:

(a) The bundles put the consumers on the same indifference curve, such as I_A in Fig. 12.8, where point a_1 denotes A_1's bundle and a_2 denotes A_2's bundle. In this case it follows from the strict convexity assumption that A_1 and A_2 could gain by trading along the line a_1a_2, since points on this line have the property that they are feasible reallocations of the total amounts of goods held by the two at a_1 and a_2.

For example, suppose A_1 gave $(x'_{A_1} - x''_A)$ to A_2 in exchange for $(y''_A - y'_{A_1})$ where $x''_A = \frac{1}{2}(x'_{A_1} - x'_{A_2})$ and $y''_A = \frac{1}{2}(y'_{A_2} - y'_{A_1})$. This is clearly feasible since the total holdings of the two goods by the consumers are unchanged, while both are better off at point a. The strict convexity of indifference curves implies that a point such as a *always exists* whenever a_1 and a_2 are separate. Thus the coalition of A_1, A_2 and one or both of the Bs with whom they were initially contracting to achieve a_1 and a_2 can improve upon the initial allocation by A_1 and A_2 engaging

Figure 12.8

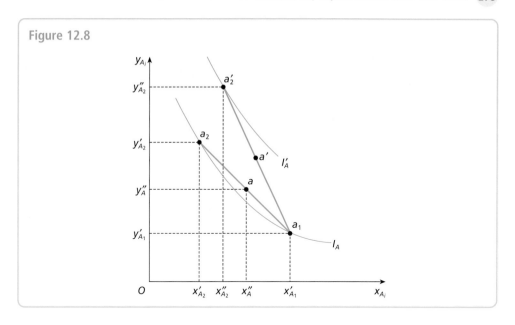

in further contracting to get to a. Both As are better off and the B or Bs with whom they contracted to get to a_1 and a_2 are no worse off. Thus the initial allocation cannot have been in the core.

(b) The bundles put A_1 and A_2 on different indifference curves. In this case the coalition $\{A_1, A_2\}$ may or may not be able to do better, but we can show that, if we take A_1 as being on a lower indifference curve than A_2, and B_1 being on *no higher* an indifference curve than B_2, then the coalition $\{A_1, B_1\}$ can certainly improve upon the initial allocation. In Fig. 12.8 suppose the initial allocation puts A_1 at a_1 and A_2 at a_2', where, as it happens, A_2 would not want to trade with A_1. The point a' is halfway along the line a_1a_2', and so has coordinates $\frac{1}{2}(x_{A_1}' + x_{A_2}'')$ and $\frac{1}{2}(y_{A_1}' + y_{A_2}'')$. It is clearly better than a_1 for A_1 and this will always be so by the convexity assumption.

B_1's initial allocation (x_{B_1}', y_{B_1}') may be indifferent to or worse than B_2's (x_{B_2}', y_{B_2}') but in either event simply by relabelling Fig. 12.8 and using the same argument B_1 would always prefer the bundle with $\frac{1}{2}(x_{B_1}' + x_{B_2}')$ of x and $\frac{1}{2}(y_{B_1}' + y_{B_2}')$ of y, that is the average of B_1 and B_2's initial allocation. But if we consider the total requirements of these bundles which both A_1 and B_1 prefer to the initial allocation, we have

$$\tfrac{1}{2}(x_{A_1}' + x_{A_2}'') + \tfrac{1}{2}(x_{B_1}' + x_{B_2}') = \bar{x}_A + \bar{x}_B \qquad [\text{F.15}]$$

$$\tfrac{1}{2}(y_{A_1}' + y_{A_2}'') + \tfrac{1}{2}(y_{B_1}' + y_{B_2}') = \bar{y}_A + \bar{y}_B \qquad [\text{F.16}]$$

given that the initial allocation was feasible (to see this multiply through by 2 and compare with [F.13] and [F.14]). Thus there exists a feasible allocation for the coalition $\{A_1, B_1\}$ which improves upon the initial allocation at which A_1 was worse off than A_2 and so the initial allocation cannot be in the core. (The alert reader may wonder what happens if, in the initial allocation, B_1 and B_2 are at the *same point*. See Question 5, Exercise 12F and show that this presents no obstacle.)

Figure 12.9

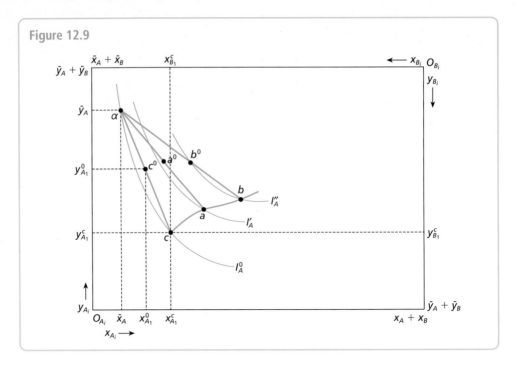

We now show how the core shrinks. Consider the Edgeworth box of Fig. 12.9. The indifference curves I_A^0, I_A', I_A'' describe the preferences of both A_1 and A_2 and the initial endowment point α is also the same for both. But suppose that the market contains initially *only* consumers A_1 and B_1. The curve *cab* is a portion of the contract curve (to keep the figure uncluttered, B_i indifference curves are not drawn). We assume that in this two-person market the equilibrium allocation is at point c where A has the allocation $(x_{A_1}^c, y_{A_1}^c)$ – in fact she has managed to emerge with no gains from trade. B_1's allocation at this point is $(x_{B_1}^c, y_{B_1}^c)$ and clearly these allocations are feasible, i.e.

$$x_{A_1}^c + x_{B_1}^c = \bar{x}_A + \bar{x}_B \qquad [\text{F.17}]$$

$$y_{A_1}^c + y_{B_1}^c = \bar{y}_A + \bar{y}_B \qquad [\text{F.18}]$$

Now suppose we expand the market by adding A_2 and B_2. A_2 'comes in' at point α, the A_i initial endowment point. Consider point c^0 in the figure which is halfway along the line αc. Because of strict convexity this point is preferred to c by A_1 and preferred to α by A_2. Moreover, it can be reached by A_1 and A_2, since if A_1 gives A_2 $\frac{1}{2}(x_{A_1}^c - \bar{x}_A)$ in exchange for $\frac{1}{2}(\bar{y}_A - y_{A_1}^c)$, they will clearly each be at the allocation $(x_{A_i}^0, y_{A_i}^0)$. Thus we have shown that point c cannot be in the core, since the coalition $\{A_1, A_2, B_1\}$ can improve upon it. It may be wondered why B_1 is included in this coalition, since A_1 and A_2 appeared to manage everything between themselves. The coalition $\{A_1, A_2\}$ alone can manage nothing better than their initial endowment point – recall that consumers with identical preferences and initial endowments can get no gains from trade. B_1 was necessary to get A_1 to point c, away from α; once this deal was done A_1 could then set up a mutually advantageous deal with A_2. The allocation as a whole therefore required the coalition $\{A_1, A_2, B_1\}$.

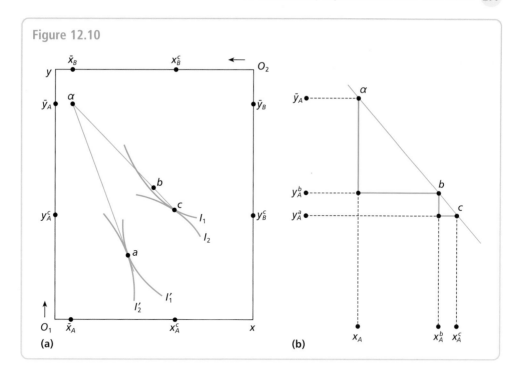

Figure 12.10

We cannot conclude from this that c^0 is in the core, since B_2 may propose an allocation which is better for some members of the coalition. Our purpose was to show that a point which was in the core of the two-person economy may not be in the core of the four-person economy – the introduction of new participants *widens* the possibilities for trade, and *narrows* the set of core allocations which the original traders will find themselves in.

In going from an (A_1, B_1) economy to an (A_1, A_2, B_1, B_2) economy there will be many points that are not Walrasian equilibria and which can not be excluded from the core. We now show that any such point *can* be excluded for some value of n.

First we show the equal treatment principle for any n. Just take A_1 in the earlier argument to be *the worst off* of the $n \geqslant 2$ A-types, and B_1 to be the worst off of the B-types (if there is one, otherwise an arbitrary B), and the argument is unchanged. Thus, in a core allocation, there cannot be a 'worse-off A-type or B-type' which implies equal treatment.

Next we show, in an extension of the $n = 2$ example, how any point that is not a Walrasian equilibrium can be knocked out of the core of the (A_1, B_1) economy. Figure 12.10(a) illustrates that, if a point in the two-person core, such as a, is a Walrasian equilibrium, the line connecting it to the initial endowment point cannot intersect either of the two indifference curves through the equilibrium point.

If a core allocation such as c is not a Walrasian equilibrium, there is *always* an intersection point, and so always a point such as b which lies above the relevant indifference curve for *either* A_1 or B_1. Figure 12.10(b) amplifies this. As shown, the A-type could do better than the core allocation c if there are trades which enable her to reach b. However, adding one other A-type, located at the initial endowment point α, to the $\{A, B\}$ coalition at c would not be enough – the A-type at c would give up too little x, and require too little y, to enable the A-type at α to reach b. Suppose that we have k A-types at c and m A-types at α where

$$k(x_A^c - x_A^b) = m(x_A^b - \bar{x}_A) \quad \text{or} \quad k/m = (x_A^b - \bar{x}_A)/(x_A^c - x_A^b) \qquad [\text{F.19}]$$

It follows at once from linearity that

$$k(y_A^b - y_A^c) = m(\bar{y}_A - y_A^b) \qquad [\text{F.20}]$$

Then the point b can be reached if we have an economy with $n = k + m$ individuals of each type, and the allocation among the coalition $\{A_1, \ldots, A_n, B_1, \ldots, B_k\}$ takes the following form. The k B-types exchange with k of the A-types to reach point c. Then, the k A-types exchange with the $m = n - k$ remaining A-types to reach b. For the first step, we must have

$$k[(x_A^c, y_A^c) + (x_B^c, y_B^c)] = k[(\bar{x}_A, \bar{y}_A) + (\bar{x}_B, \bar{y}_B)] \qquad [\text{F.21}]$$

and from the second stage we have, from [F.19] and [F.20],

$$(m + k)(x_A^b, y_A^b) = k(x_A^c, y_A^c) + m(\bar{x}_A, \bar{y}_A) \qquad [\text{F.22}]$$

Then substituting for $k(x_A^c, y_A^c)$ from [F.22] into [F.21] gives

$$(m + k)(x_A^b, y_A^b) + k(x_B^c, y_B^c) = (m + k)(\bar{x}_A, \bar{y}_A) + k(\bar{x}_B, \bar{y}_B) \qquad [\text{F.23}]$$

proving the feasibility of the allocation. Thus c cannot be in the core of the $2n$-person economy.

The fact that the Walrasian equilibrium allocation must be in the core shows that no group would ever wish to withdraw and trade among themselves. We have now shown that, for large economies, only allocations which are Walrasian equilibria are in the core. Although the Walrasian approach to markets seems less realistic than the Edgeworth approach, in the limit the outcomes are the same.

EXERCISE 12F

1. Suppose that in the analysis of Fig. 12.7 consumer 2 acts as a passive price-taker, while consumer 1 seeks to make herself as well off as possible given this fact. What is the nature of the resulting equilibrium? Is it in the core? How might it be driven into the core?

2. Explain why a consumption bundle which is preferred to a bundle chosen at price p^* must be more expensive at that price.

3. For the market consisting of $\{A_1, A_2, B_1, B_2\}$ spell out the proof that the competitive market equilibrium is in this core.

4. Prove that in the competitive market equilibrium in the four-person case consumers of the same type must have the same consumption bundle. What is the role played by *strict* convexity in this proof?

5. Suppose that B_1 and B_2 have identical consumption bundles but that A_1 has a bundle which makes him worse off than A_2. Show that the coalition $\{A_1, B_1\}$ can block this initial allocation.

6. Suppose that in an initial allocation A_1 and B_1 have agreed a deal which puts them at point c of Fig. 12.9 as have A_2 and B_2. Use the argument of this section to show that the coalition $\{A_1, A_2, B_1\}$ can block this allocation. (*Hint*: recall that A_2 can break his deal with B_2.)

13 Welfare economics

A. Introduction

The subject matter of welfare economics is the ethical appraisal of economic systems. In this chapter we are primarily interested in the optimality of the equilibrium allocation produced by a market mechanism, although many of the concepts, techniques and results we discuss can be applied to the analysis of other systems. The market economy examined consists of a large number of individual decision-takers, each pursuing their own self-interest, subject to the stimuli and constraints of the price mechanism. No one is concerned with the general welfare. Yet, is it possible that this kind of economic organization could bring about a 'good' resource allocation and, if so, under what circumstances?

The most widely used criterion for evaluating resource allocations is Pareto efficiency. In section B we discuss the value judgements underlying this welfare criterion and derive and illustrate a set of conditions which can be used to test whether an allocation is Pareto efficient or not. Pareto efficiency provides an incomplete welfare ordering since it cannot rank all pairs of allocations. In section C we therefore introduce the Bergsonian social welfare function (swf) as a useful means of representing stronger welfare preferences or value judgements which do produce complete welfare orderings of allocations. The use of an swf also brings out clearly the distinction between Pareto efficiency and Pareto optimality. We examine the Pareto efficiency and optimality of the equilibrium of a competitive market economy in section D. In section E we discuss the separation of efficiency and distributional considerations in a market economy. Finally, in section F we consider whether it is possible to find some reasonable procedure for deriving welfare criteria from the preferences of the individuals in the society. Chapter 14 continues our welfare analysis with an examination of the circumstances in which markets fail to be efficient and the implications for government action.

B. Pareto efficient resource allocation

An *allocation A* is a list which describes the use of resources in an economy: the consumption bundles of the consumers, the amounts of labour and other inputs they supply, the use of these inputs by the firms in the economy and the outputs produced. Welfare judgements require comparisons of pairs of allocations, in terms of whether one allocation is better than, or equally as good as, another. In this section we examine the simple and intuitively appealing Paretian welfare judgements and use them to derive a set of criteria for evaluating allocations.

Allocation A^1 is *Pareto superior* to allocation A^2 if A^1 is weakly preferred by all individuals and strictly preferred by some of them. In the two-person economy illustrated

Figure 13.1

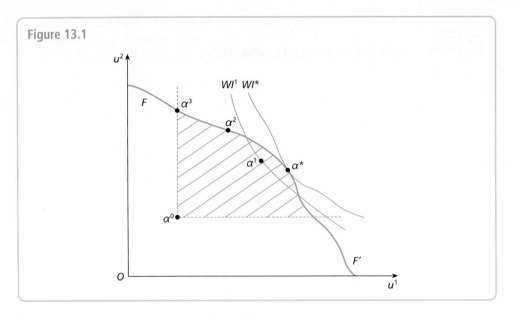

in Fig. 13.1, all allocations which generate utility combinations (like α^1, α^2, α^3 and $\alpha\star$) in the shaded area are Pareto superior to the allocation which generates α^0.

A *Pareto efficient* allocation has the property that there is no other feasible allocation which makes some individual better off and no individual worse off. More formally: an allocation is Pareto efficient if it maximizes u^1, the utility of individual 1, subject to the constraints that $u^h \geqslant \bar{u}^h$ for $h = 2, \ldots, H$ and to the constraints imposed by technology and the endowments of the economy. Note that an allocation is Pareto efficient if there is no feasible allocation which is Pareto superior to it.

Varying the minimum required utilities $\bar{u}^h$ alters the Pareto efficient allocation achieved. (Question 1 asks you to confirm that it does not matter which individual's utility is to be maximized in the definition of Pareto efficient allocation.) In Fig. 13.1 the *utility frontier FF'* is derived by maximizing u^1 subject to $u^2 \geqslant \bar{u}^2$ for different values of $\bar{u}^2$. Thus the allocations generating utility combinations on the utility frontier, such as α^2 or $\alpha\star$, are Pareto efficient, while allocations generating points inside the frontier, like α^0, are Pareto inefficient.

Paretian value judgements

Since the concepts of Pareto efficiency and Pareto superiority are widely used, it is important to realize that they embody a set of value judgements which are far from innocuous.

Process independence

In restricting attention to differences between allocations we have already incorporated the strong value judgement that the process by which a particular allocation is achieved does not matter. For example, no account is taken of whether the allocation mechanism which produces the allocation is one which leaves individuals to make their own decisions or one which tells them what they should do with their labour or what bundles they must consume. Many people would argue that a resource allocation mechanism, such as a market or a centrally planned economy, should not be judged solely by the allocations which it produces.

Individualism

Under the Paretian criteria the only aspect of an allocation which is relevant is its effect on the utilities of the individuals in the society. It does not matter *per se*, for example, whether a given output is produced in one large or many small firms, or whether the firms are privately or publicly owned. The organization of production is relevant for welfare purposes only in so far as it affects the utilities of individuals.

Non-paternalism

The fact that allocations are evaluated by reference to the individuals' own utility functions or preferences means that it is assumed that individuals are the best judges of their own welfare. This is also a strong value judgement and one which most people would not be willing to adopt in all circumstances. Many people would not wish to respect individual decision-takers' preferences in respect of heroin consumption, for example. Other examples sometimes put forward include soft drugs, alcohol, tobacco, health care, education and savings.

Benevolence

The Paretian criteria are also benevolent towards individuals since a *ceteris paribus* increase in the utility of one individual is judged to be an improvement. Benevolence seems a very weak and therefore uncontroversial value judgement but it is not universally accepted (see Question 1, Exercise 13C). It requires, for example, that an increase in the well-being of a very rich individual, with everyone else no better off, is considered an improvement, even if some individuals in the community are very poor.

Pareto efficiency conditions

We derive a set of conditions which a Pareto efficient allocation must satisfy by considering a simple economy in which there are two consumers, two goods, two inputs and two firms. The method generalizes in an obvious way to larger economies. Individual h has the utility function $u^h(x_{h1}, x_{h2}, z_h)$ where x_{hi} is h's consumption of commodity i and z_h is h's supply of an input. To simplify the exposition we assume that the individuals supply different types of input (perhaps skilled and unskilled labour) so an input can be numbered according to which individual supplies it. The individuals' *initial endowments* of the inputs are denoted $\bar{z}_h$. We assume non-satiation, so that the marginal utility of commodity i for individual h is always positive: $u_i^h > 0$ ($i = 1, 2$; $h = 1, 2$) and the marginal utility to h of supplying more of input h is always negative: $u_z^h < 0$.

Firm i produces the total output x_i of commodity i according to the production function

$$x_i = f^i(z_{i1}, z_{i2}) \qquad i = 1, 2 \qquad \text{[B.1]}$$

where z_{ih} is the quantity of input type h (supplied by individual h) used in producing good i. The marginal product of input h in producing good i is positive: $f_h^i = \partial f^i / \partial z_{ih} > 0$ $(i = 1, 2; h = 1, 2)$.

It is impossible for the total consumption of good i by individuals to exceed the output of firm i and for the total use of input h by the firms to exceed the supply by individual h:

$$x_i \geqslant \sum_{h=1}^{2} x_{hi} \qquad i = 1, 2 \qquad [\text{B.2}]$$

$$z_h \geqslant \sum_{i=1}^{2} z_{ih} \qquad h = 1, 2 \qquad [\text{B.3}]$$

Our assumptions that consumers are not satiated and that marginal products are positive means that these *material balance* requirements will bind as equalities in a Pareto efficient allocation. If [B.3] held as a strict inequality, input z_{1h} could be increased (without reducing u^h) thereby increasing the output of commodity 1 and permitting an increase in consumption by individual 1 and increasing u^1. Similarly, if [B.2] is a strict inequality the consumption of individual 1 can be increased without the need for any increase in inputs and this must increase u^1.

Feasible allocations must also satisfy the constraint that the supply of input h cannot exceed individual h's initial endowment; $\bar{z}_h \geqslant z_h$. We will assume that preferences are such that the inequality is always strict and the constraint never binds. If we interpret z_h as labour this is not implausible (recall our discussion of the individual's preferences concerning labour supply in section 4C).

We restrict our attention to non-corner Pareto efficient allocations in which both individuals consume both goods and supply inputs and both firms use both types of inputs.

A Pareto efficient allocation is the solution to the problem

$$\max_{x_{hi}, z_{ih}, x_i, z_h} u^1(x_{11}, x_{12}, z_1) \quad \text{s.t.} \quad u^2(x_{21}, x_{22}, z_2) \geqslant \bar{u}^2 \qquad [\text{B.4}]$$

and to [B.1], [B.2], [B.3].

The Lagrangean for the Pareto efficiency problem is

$$L = u^1(x_{11}, x_{12}, z_1) + \lambda[u^2(x_{21}, x_{22}, z_2) - \bar{u}^2] + \sum_i \rho_i \left[x_i - \sum_h x_{hi} \right]$$

$$+ \sum_h \omega_h \left[z_h - \sum_i z_{ih} \right] + \sum_i \mu_i [f^i(z_{i1}, z_{i2}) - x_i] \qquad [\text{B.5}]$$

The first-order conditions are

$$\partial L / \partial x_{1i} = u_i^1 - \rho_i = 0 \qquad \left. \begin{matrix} i = 1, 2 \\ \\ i = 1, 2 \end{matrix} \right\} \text{efficient consumption} \qquad \begin{matrix} [\text{B.6}] \\ \\ [\text{B.7}] \end{matrix}$$

$$\partial L / \partial x_{2i} = \lambda u_i^2 - \rho_i = 0$$

$$\partial L / \partial z_1 = u_z^1 + \omega_1 = 0 \qquad \qquad \qquad \qquad \qquad [\text{B.8}]$$

$$\left. \begin{matrix} \\ \end{matrix} \right\} \text{efficient input supply}$$

$$\partial L / \partial z_2 = \lambda u_z^2 + \omega_2 = 0 \qquad \qquad \qquad \qquad \qquad [\text{B.9}]$$

$$\partial L / \partial z_{ih} = \mu_i f_h^i - \omega_h = 0 \qquad i, h = 1, 2 \quad \text{efficient input use} \qquad [\text{B.10}]$$

$$\partial L / \partial x_i = \rho_i - \mu_i = 0 \qquad \qquad i = 1, 2 \quad \text{efficient output mix} \qquad [\text{B.11}]$$

together with the constraints [B.1], [B.2] and [B.3].

Efficient consumption

We can rearrange the conditions [B.6] and [B.7] to get

$$MRS_{21}^1 = \frac{u_1^1}{u_2^1} = \frac{p_1}{p_2} = \frac{u_1^2}{u_2^2} = MRS_{21}^2 \qquad \text{[B.12]}$$

([B.6] implies $u_1^1 = p_1$, $u_2^1 = p_2$ and [B.7] implies $\lambda u_1^2 = p_1$, $\lambda u_2^2 = p_2$. Dividing each condition on good 1 by the condition on good 2 for each individual gives [B.12].) An efficient allocation of a given total output x_1, x_2 between the two consumers therefore requires that consumers are given a bundle which equalizes their marginal rates of substitution (MRS_{21}^h) between the two goods. MRS_{21}^h measures the rate at which h is willing to substitute commodity 1 for commodity 2 – it is h's marginal valuation of commodity 1 in terms of commodity 2. Consumption cannot be efficient if the individuals have different marginal valuations of the goods. Thus suppose that the $MRS_{21}^1 = 5$ and $MRS_{21}^2 = 3$, so that individual 1 is willing to give up five units of commodity 2 to acquire one unit of commodity 1 whereas individual 2 is only willing to give up three units of commodity 2 in exchange for one unit of commodity 1. Then transferring four units of commodity 2 from individual 1 to individual 2 and 1 unit of commodity 1 from individual 2 to individual 1 will make both individuals better off. Hence the initial situation cannot have been Pareto efficient and equality of *MRS* is a necessary condition for a Pareto efficient allocation of goods among consumers.

Figure 13.2 is an Edgeworth box (see section 12E). The horizontal side of the box measures a fixed total output of good 1 and the vertical side measures a fixed total output of good 2. Individual 1's consumption of good 1 is measured horizontally from the origin at 0^1 and her consumption of good 2 vertically from 0^1. Similarly, individual 2's consumption is measured from the origin at 0^2. The assumption of non-satiation means that it cannot be efficient to have total consumption of any good less than the output of the good. Hence we restrict attention to consumption bundles for the individuals which add up to the total output of the two goods. In

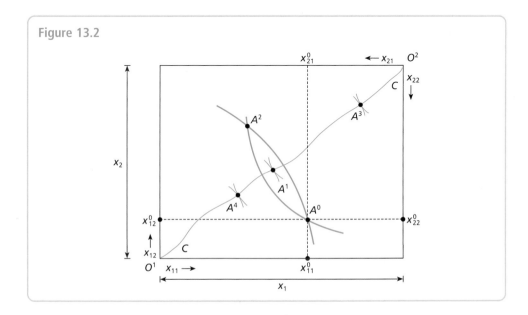

Figure 13.2

terms of the Edgeworth box this means that a single point defines the consumption bundle of both individuals. For example, the allocation A^0 has individual 1 getting the bundle (x_{11}^0, x_{12}^0) and individual 2 getting (x_{21}^0, x_{22}^0).

Since we are holding the individuals' labour supplies constant we can draw their indifference curves for the two commodities in the box. The individuals have strictly quasi-concave utility functions so that their indifference curves are convex to their respective origins. The allocation A^0 is not Pareto efficient since it is possible to transfer commodities between the individuals so as to make them both better off. For example the allocation A^1 is Pareto superior to A^0 since it puts both individuals on indifference curves further from their respective origins. Any allocation, except A^2, in the lens shaped area defined by the indifference curves through A^0 is Pareto superior to A^0. *No allocation in the box where the indifference curves cross can be Pareto efficient.* Allocations where the indifference curves are tangent as at A^1, A^3 or A^4 are efficient. Since the slopes of the indifference curves are just the negative of the marginal rates of substitution we have another demonstration of the necessity of [B.13] for Pareto efficiency.

The locus CC of points of tangency between the indifference curves is the set of all Pareto efficient allocations of the given total outputs measured by the sides of the box. In a simple pure exchange economy (refer back to section 12E), with consumers having a fixed endowment of consumption goods, the efficient consumption conditions are all that is required for Pareto efficiency. Each allocation or point in the box would generate a utility combination (u^1, u^2). The Pareto efficient allocations on the curve CC would generate utility combinations on a utility frontier like that in Fig. 13.1 and inefficient allocations off the curve would generate combinations inside the utility frontier. (The optimized value of u^1 in the Pareto efficiency problem is a function of the constraint parameter $\bar{u}^2$ and the graph of this function is the utility frontier.)

Efficient input supply

Combining the respective conditions on individual h's consumption of good i and supply of input z_h [B.6] and [B.8], [B.7] and [B.9] yields

$$-\frac{u_z^h}{u_i^h} = \frac{\omega_h}{\rho_i} \qquad \text{[B.13]}$$

From [B.10] and [B.11] we have

$$f_h^i = \omega_h/\mu_i = \omega_h/\rho_i$$

and thus efficiency implies:

$$MRS_{iz}^h = -\frac{u_z^h}{u_i^h} = \frac{\omega_h}{\rho_i} = f_h^i \qquad h, i = 1, 2 \qquad \text{[B.14]}$$

The left-hand side of [B.14] is h's marginal rate of substitution between his input supply and consumption of commodity i. It is the rate at which h must be compensated by being given more of commodity i if he increases his supply of z_h by one unit (remember that u_z^h is negative). The right-hand side of [B.14] is the marginal product of z_h in the production of commodity i. Pareto efficiency requires that the additional output produced by an extra unit of z_h is just equal to the marginal cost, in terms of good i, of z_h to h. If h can be compensated by two units of good i for supplying one

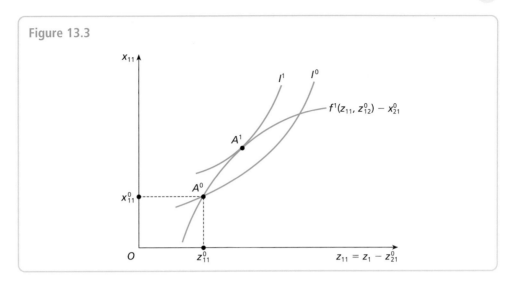

Figure 13.3

unit of z_h which can be used to increase output of good i by 3 units, then the allocation cannot be Pareto efficient.

Figure 13.3 illustrates the condition for efficient input supply by individual 1 (the reader should sketch the analogous figure for individual 2). All consumption levels except x_{11} and all input uses except z_{11} are held constant. The vertical axis plots the consumption of good 1 by individual 1: $x_{11} = x_1 - x_{21}^0$ and the horizontal axis plots the use of his input by firm 1: $z_{11} = z_1 - z_{21}^0$. With all other consumption and input use levels fixed, increases in z_{11} imply equal increases in z_1. Thus we can show the indifference curves of individual 1 in (z_{11}, x_{11}) space as I^0, I^1, etc. These curves are just the contours of $u^1(x_{11}, x_{12}^0, z_1) = u^1(x_1 - x_{21}^0, x_{12}^0, z_{11} + z_{21}^0)$. The curve $f^1 - x_{21}^0$ plots $f^1(z_{11}, z_{12}^0) - x_{21}^0$ against z_{11} and shows the effect of variations in z_{11} on the consumption of good 1 by individual 1. (Remember that with individual 2's consumption fixed, all increases in the output of good 1 are consumed by individual 1.)

Suppose the initial allocation is A^0 where consumption of good 1 by individual 1 is x_{11}^0 and the use of input by firm 1 is z_{11}^0. At A^0 the indifference curve I^0 cuts the curve $f^1 - x_{21}^0$. This allocation is clearly not efficient since by shifting to allocation A^1 (where all other consumption and input use variables are fixed at their initial levels) individual 1 achieves a higher utility level of I^1. Only when the indifference curves of individual 1 are tangent to the curve $f^1 - x_{21}^0$ is the allocation efficient. But the slope of the curve $f^1 - x_{21}^0$ is $\partial[f^1(z_{11}, z_{12}^0) - x_{21}^0]/\partial z_{11} = f_1^1$, the marginal product of input 1 in the production of good 1, and the slopes of the indifference curves in $(x_{11}, z_1 - z_{21}^0)$ space are just individual 1's marginal rate of substitution between commodity 1 and his input supply. Thus we have again established the input supply condition [B.14] as necessary for efficiency.

Efficient input use

Rearrangement of condition [B.10] on the use of a given total supply of inputs by the firms gives

$$MRTS_{21}^1 = \frac{f_1^1}{f_2^1} = \frac{\omega_1}{\omega_2} = \frac{f_1^2}{f_2^2} = MRTS_{21}^2 \qquad [B.15]$$

Figure 13.4

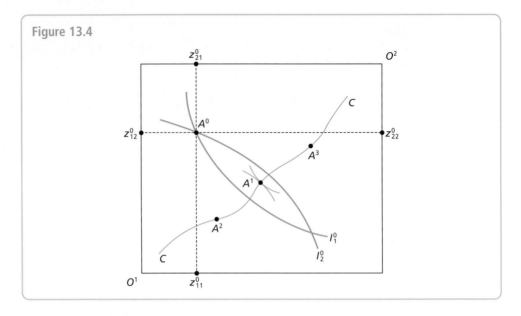

(just follow the same procedure used to derive [B.13]). Recalling section 5A, the ratio of the marginal products f_1^i/f_2^i is the marginal rate of technical substitution $MRTS_{21}^i$ of input 1 for input 2 in the production of good i. $MRTS_{21}^i$ is the rate at which input 1 can be substituted for input 2 without changing the output of good i. For example, if $MRTS_{21}^1 = 5$ then if firm 1 reduces its use of input 2 by five units and increases its use of input 1 by one unit the output of good 1 will be unchanged. Suppose also that $MRTS_{21}^2 = 3$. Consider the following feasible reallocation: increase z_{11} by one unit, reduce z_{21} by one unit, reduce z_{12} by four units, increase z_{22} by four units. The effect will be to increase the output of both goods and so the initial allocation cannot have been Pareto efficient. Equality of marginal rates of technical substitution across firms is necessary for efficiency.

We illustrate this condition with a production Edgeworth box. In Fig. 13.4 the fixed input supplies of the two individuals are measured by the lengths of the sides of the box. Firm 1's use of the inputs is measured from the origin O^1 and firm 2's from the origin O^2. Since it cannot be efficient for the total use of an input to be less than the supply we can restrict attention to allocations where $\sum_i z_{ih} = z_h$. Such allocations are defined by a point like A^0 in the box. We assume that the production functions are strictly quasi-concave so that the isoquants for firm 1 are the curves like I_1^0 and those for firm 2 are the curves like I_2^0. Since we have assumed that marginal products are positive, isoquants further away from the relevant origin correspond to larger outputs. Allocations, like A^0, where the isoquants for the two firms cross are not efficient since there always exist other feasible allocations, like A^1, which produce more of both outputs. Only allocations where the isoquants are tangent are efficient and, since the slope of an isoquant is the firm's marginal rate of technical substitution, this yields [B.15] as a necessary condition for efficient use of a given supply of inputs.

Efficient output mix

The last set of conditions are those necessary for the mix of outputs x_1, x_2 produced by the firms to be efficient, with the supply of inputs held constant. Making use of the fact that $\mu_i = \rho_i$ from [B.12] we can rearrange [B.11] to get

$$f_h^1 = \omega_h/\rho_1 \qquad f_h^2 = \omega_h/\rho_2 \qquad h = 1, 2 \qquad\qquad [B.16]$$

Dividing the condition on good 2 by the condition on good 1 gives the efficient output mix condition

$$MRT_{21} = \frac{f_1^2}{f_1^1} = \frac{f_2^2}{f_2^1} = \frac{\rho_1}{\rho_2} = \frac{u_1^1}{u_2^1} = \frac{u_1^2}{u_2^2} = MRS_{21} \qquad\qquad [B.17]$$

where the last equality follows from [B.12]. The second term in [B.17] is the ratio of the marginal product of input 1 in the production of goods 2 and 1. This ratio is the marginal rate of transformation between the two goods: the rate at which the output of good 2 falls as the output of good 1 is increased as input 1 is transferred from firm 2 to firm 1 with the total input supply held constant. (A one-unit increase in the output of good 1 requires $1/f_1^1$ units of input 1 to be transferred from firm 2 to firm 1. This will reduce the output of firm 2 by the marginal product of input 1 in firm 2 times the reduction in z_{21}: $f_1^2 \times (1/f_1^1)$.) Similarly, the second term is the rate at which the output of good 2 falls when output 1 is increased by shifting input 2 from firm 2 to firm 1. Note that the condition for efficient use of inputs [B.15] implies that the first two terms in [B.17] must be equal: the amount of good 2 forgone when good 1 output is increased is the same, however inputs are shifted from firm 2 to firm 1.

From [B.17], an optimal output mix requires that the marginal rate of transformation MRT_{21} between the two goods is equal to the consumers' marginal rate of substitution MRS_{21} between the goods. Suppose for example that $MRT_{21} = 3$ and $MRS_{21} = 4$. Then holding the total input supply constant it is possible to transfer inputs from firm 2 to firm 1 in such a way as to raise firm 1 output by 1 unit and reduce firm 2 output by 3 units. If we leave the consumption of individual 1 constant then the output change leads to an increase in individual 2's consumption of good 1 by 1 unit and a reduction in his consumption of good 2 of 3 units. Since individual 2 was willing to give up 4 units of good 2 to acquire 1 unit of good 1 the reallocation makes him better off and individual 1 no worse off. Hence the initial allocation in which $MRT_{21} \neq MRS_{21}$ cannot have been efficient.

Figure 13.5 illustrates the necessity of the efficient output condition. With a given supply of inputs the production possibility set for the economy is the set of all output combinations on or inside the production possibility curve *PP*. The production possibility set is generated from the production Edgeworth box whose sides measure the given input supplies. The efficient input allocations on the curve *CC* in Fig. 13.4 produce output combinations on *PP* in Fig. 13.5. Inefficient input allocations off the curve *CC* in Fig. 13.4 yield output combinations inside the production possibility curve in Fig. 13.5. The slope of *PP* is MRT_{21}, the rate at which x_2 is reduced as x_1 is increased.

Suppose that the input supplies are efficiently utilized so that the economy is on the curve *PP*, for example at A^0. The consumption Edgeworth box for this output has origins at O (corresponding to O^1 in Fig. 13.2) and at A^0 (corresponding to O^2 in Fig. 13.2). Assume that the allocation a^0 of the total output between consumers is also efficient, so that a^0 is on the locus C^0 of points of tangency of their indifference curves. Suppose, however, that the common slope of their indifference curves at a^0 is not equal to the slope of the production possibility curve at A^0, thus violating condition [B.17]. Since the indifference curves at a^0 have a steeper slope than *PP* at A^0, consider shifting inputs from firm 2 to firm 1, moving down *PP* to A^1. (What movement along *CC* in Fig. 13.4 does this imply?) This movement gives rise to a new consumption Edgeworth box with the same O^1 origin but with O^2 shifted to A^1. We give individual 2 the same consumption bundle as he had in the original Edgeworth box.

Figure 13.5

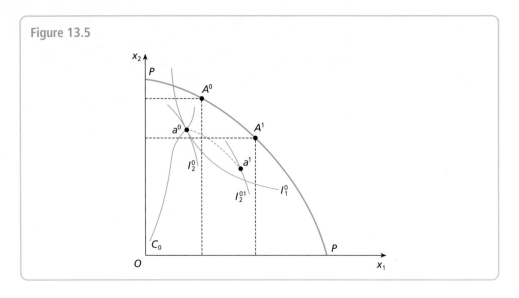

Thus the consumption allocation is now at a^1 where the distance from a^1 to A^1 is the same as the distance from a^0 to A^0 so that individual 2 has the same consumption bundle. Since he has the same consumption bundle he is on the same indifference curve: I_2^{01} is just I_2^0 measured from an origin at A^1 rather than an origin at A^0. Individual 2's utility is unaffected by the change in the output mix. Individual 1's consumption is still measured from O. He is better off at a^1 than at a^0 since a^1 lies above his indifference curve through a^0. Hence the change in the allocation from (A^0, a^0) to (A^1, a^1) is a Pareto improvement and the initial allocation was not Pareto efficient.

The curve $a^0 a^1$ plots the consumption bundle of consumer 1 traced out as the output mix changes with the consumption of consumer 2 held constant. It is the curve PP with consumer 2's constant consumption bundle subtracted and its slope is therefore the slope of the production possibility curve PP. If the slope of PP at A^0 was the same as the slope of the individuals' indifference curves at a^0 then the $a^0 a^1$ locus would be tangent to I_1^0 at a^0 and would lie inside it elsewhere. Hence it would be impossible to change the production mix so as to make a Pareto improvement because movements along $a^0 a^1$ would then make individual 1 worse off.

EXERCISE 13B

1. Show that the form of the Pareto efficiency conditions do not depend on which individual's utility is maximized.

2. (a) What assumptions about preferences and technology would ensure that the first order efficiency conditions are also sufficient?

    (b) Under what circumstances would endowment constraints bind?

    (c) How are the efficiency conditions changed at corner solutions?

    (d) What interpretation can you give to the Lagrange multipliers in the Pareto efficiency problem?

C. Welfare functions and the Pareto criterion

Pareto superiority is a powerful and intuitive criterion for ranking allocations but, even if we accept the value judgements it embodies, it suffers from the severe drawback that it does not yield a complete ordering of allocations. Some pairs of allocations are incomparable. For example in Fig. 13.1, although α^1, α^2, α^3 and α^* are all Pareto superior to α^0, they are not rankable by Pareto superiority. If two points are Pareto efficient, like α^2 and α^*, it is impossible to rank them by Pareto superiority since a Pareto efficient allocation has the property that there is no feasible allocation which is Pareto superior to it. Thus α^* cannot be Pareto superior to α^2 nor α^2 Pareto superior to α^*. Even more frustrating, as comparison of α^1 with α^2 or α^* shows, it is not the case that a Pareto efficient allocation must be Pareto superior to a particular inefficient allocation. The Pareto criteria do not even allow us to conclude that efficient allocations are necessarily better than inefficient ones.

What is required is a set of welfare judgements which provide complete, transitive and reflexive comparisons of allocations, i.e. a welfare preference ordering. (Compare the discussion of the consumer's preference ordering over consumption bundles in section 2A.) Such a welfare preference ordering can be used to rank all alternative allocations. An *optimal allocation* is a feasible allocation with the property that there is no other feasible allocation which is ranked higher by the welfare preference ordering. Recalling section 2A, if it is also the case that the welfare preference ordering is continuous, it can be conveniently represented by a *Bergsonian social welfare function (swf)* W. An optimal allocation is then defined as the allocation which maximizes W over the set of feasible allocations.

We are not, in this and the next two sections, concerned with *whose* welfare judgements are represented in the swf. Rather we examine the consequences of different welfare judgements for the form of the swf and hence for the nature of the optimal allocation. Note that, by letting the domain of the welfare function be the set of allocations, we have already made the *process independence* assumption discussed in section B. If we make the *individualistic* value judgement that the only aspects of the allocation which matter are the individuals' consumption bundles then the swf can be written, for the simple two-person economy of section B, as

$$W = W(x_{11}, x_{12}, z_1, x_{21}, x_{22}, z_2) \qquad \text{[C.1]}$$

If we make the non-paternalistic value judgement that individuals are the best judges of their own welfare [C.1] can be written

$$W = W(u^1(x_{11}, x_{12}, z_1), u^2(x_{21}, x_{22}, z_2)) = W(u^1, u^2) \qquad \text{[C.2]}$$

where u^h is the hth individual's utility function and represents her own preference ordering over her consumption bundles and labour supply. If it was felt that individuals were not the best judges of their own welfare, we could specify a swf in which the individuals' own utility functions were replaced with welfare functions $g^h(x_{h1}, x_{h2}, z_h)$ which represent paternalistic views on the effect of allocations on individuals.

The *benevolence* value judgement implies that the partial derivatives of W with respect to u^h or g^h are positive. Thus, in conjunction with non-paternalism, benevolence implies

$$\frac{\partial W(u^1, u^2)}{\partial u^h} = W_h > 0 \qquad h = 1, 2 \qquad \text{[C.3]}$$

Pareto optimality

A *Paretian* swf is a Bergson social welfare function embodying the value judgements of individualism, non-paternalism and benevolence, and a *Pareto optimal* allocation maximizes a Paretian swf subject to the production and material balance constraints. In Fig. 13.1 the feasible utility combinations are those on or inside the utility frontier *FF'*. The Paretian swf $W(u^1, u^2)$ gives rise to welfare indifference curves, such as WI^1 and WI^*, which have slope

$$\left. \frac{du^2}{du^1} \right|_{dW=0} = -\frac{W_1}{W_2} < 0 \qquad \text{[C.4]}$$

The assumption of benevolence implies that the welfare indifference curves are negatively sloped and that higher indifference curves correspond to greater welfare. The utility combination α^* on the utility frontier maximizes W over the set of feasible utility combinations. An allocation A^* which generates the utility combination α^* is a Pareto optimal allocation. (Note that there may be more than one allocation which will generate a given utility combination.) Different value judgements about the relative merits of the two individuals would be represented by a different welfare function and would give rise to different Pareto optimal resource allocations (see Question 1, Exercise 13C).

In the previous section we derived conditions for an allocation to be Pareto efficient. The reason for our interest in Pareto efficiency is that all Pareto optimal allocations must be Pareto efficient: *Pareto efficiency is necessary for Pareto optimality.* Thus consider any resource allocation $\bar{A}$ which is *not* Pareto efficient and which generates utility levels $\bar{u}^h$ for the individuals. Since the allocation is not Pareto efficient there exists a feasible allocation $\hat{A}$ which has $\hat{u}^h \geqslant \bar{u}^h$ for all h and $\hat{u}^h > \bar{u}^h$ for some h. Since *all* Paretian welfare functions satisfy [C.3] we must have $W(\hat{u}^1, \ldots, \hat{u}^H) > W(\bar{u}^1, \ldots, \bar{u}^H)$ and so $\bar{A}$ does not maximize W over the set of feasible allocations and is not Pareto optimal. In terms of Fig. 13.1: whatever the precise value judgements about the relative merits of individuals (the shape of the welfare indifference curves) a Pareto optimal allocation must generate a point on the utility frontier. Thus the conditions which define Pareto efficient allocations are relevant whatever the particular form of the Paretian swf. If an allocation violates these conditions we know that there is a feasible allocation which is better for *all* Paretian welfare functions. In Fig. 13.1 all Paretian swfs would have a lower value at α^0 than at α^1 or α^2.

We must, however, take care to remember that Pareto efficiency does not imply Pareto optimality. All the utility combinations of *FF'* are Pareto efficient but we cannot designate one of them as optimal until we have augmented the Paretian value judgements with explicit *interpersonal comparisons*. We must be willing to make judgements of the form that, in moving from α^2 to α^*, the reduction in individual 2's utility is more than offset by the increase in individual 1's utility, so that α^* is a 'better' allocation than α^2.

Compensation principle

The Hicks–Kaldor compensation test is an ingenious, but unsuccessful, attempt to extend the set of situations which can be compared without the need to specify value judgements concerning the relative merits of individuals, i.e. without the need to construct a Bergson swf. Let $v^h(y_{h\ell}, a_{h\ell})$ be the utility that individual h gets in situation ℓ, where $y_{h\ell}$ is h's income and $a_{h\ell}$ is a vector of attributes of the situation which h cares about. Depending on the context $a_{h\ell}$ might be anything from the price vector confronting the individual to the set of property rights regulating her behaviour. Recall section 3C and define CV_{12}^h as the compensating variation for a change from situation 1 to situation 2: the amount of money h would be willing to give up to be in situation 2 rather than in situation 1. It is defined implicitly by

$$v^h(y_{h2} - CV_{12}^h, a_2) = v^h(y_{h1}, a_1) \tag{C.5}$$

If she is better off in situation 2 than in situation 1 CV_{12}^h is positive and is the amount she would be willing to pay for the change. If she is worse off CV_{12}^h is negative and is the amount of money she must be paid to accept the move from situation 1 to situation 2.

The Hicks–Kaldor compensation test recommends a move from situation 1 to situation 2 if the gainers from the move could compensate the losers and still be better off. Formally, the move is recommended if

$$\sum_h CV_{12}^h > 0 \tag{C.6}$$

The criterion has the apparent merit that it does not seem to require any inter-personal value judgements: we do not have to say whether we feel that the utility gain to one individual is worth more than the utility loss to another. The individuals make this judgement themselves in the amounts they are willing to pay or must be paid to be as well off after the change as before it.

Many cost–benefit analyses of large public sector investment projects are based on the aggregation of compensating variations. It is therefore important to realize that, although the Hicks–Kaldor test is intuitively appealing and appears value-free, it has two fundamental flaws. Both arise from the fact that the compensation in the test is purely hypothetical. (If [C.6] holds *and* the losers *are* compensated by the gainers, then there is an actual Pareto improvement. Making the policy change and paying compensation leads to a Pareto superior allocation.)

The first problem is that the hypothetical nature of the compensation means that the need for interpersonal value judgements cannot be avoided. Consider a change which makes the rich better off and the poor worse off and which passes the com-pensation test because the rich could, but do not, compensate the poor and still be better off. Since some individuals' utilities have increased and other individuals' utilities have decreased, it is impossible to evaluate the change without making a judgement about the relative merits of the individuals and the existing distribution of income. If we do use the sum of hypothetical compensations as our welfare criterion we must implicitly place the same value on £1 of income no matter which individual receives it.

The second difficulty is illustrated in Fig. 13.6. Suppose that the initial situation generates the utility distribution α^1 and that the new situation yields α^2. In situation α^2 it is possible to redistribute income from individual 1 to individual 2 and by doing so to increase v^2 and reduce v^1. The curve f_2 through α^2 is a *utility feasibility* curve showing the utility distributions which are achievable from situation 2 by transferring income between the individuals. Since f_2 passes through a point like b_2, where individual 2 has the same utility as in the initial situation and individual 1 has more, it is possible for individual 1 to compensate individual 2 for the move to situation 2 and still be better off. There is potential Pareto improvement and the compensation test is passed.

Now consider reversing the argument. Suppose that initially the individuals are in situation 2 at α^2 and there is a move to situation 1 at α^1 where individual 1 is worse

Figure 13.6

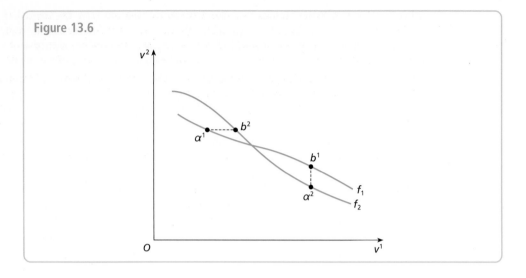

off and individual 2 is better off. Apply the compensation test by examining the utility feasibility curve f_1 through α^1 which shows the utility combinations reachable from α^1 by means of transfers of income between the parties. In this case it is possible to reach b_1 where individual 1 has the same utility as in situation 2 and individual 2 has greater utility. Thus the move from situation 2 to situation 1 also passes the compensation test! This is known as the *Scitovsky paradox*: the compensation test may lead to cycles because compensation is not actually paid.

The compensating variation for the move from situation 2 to situation 1 is defined by

$$v^h(y_{h2}, a_2) = v^h(y_{h1} - CV_{21}^h, a_1) \qquad \text{[C.7]}$$

It is only if $CV_{12}^h = -CV_{21}^h$ for all the individuals that we can be sure that there will be no paradox. Now CV_{21}^h, the compensating variation for the move from situation 2 to situation 1, is also the equivalent variation for the move from situation 1 to situation 2: the amount of money h must be paid in situation 1 to achieve the same utility as she would get in situation 2. As we saw in section 3C the compensating variation will equal the negative of the equivalent variation only if income effects are zero. Only if the individuals' valuations of the change in the situation are independent of their incomes can we be sure that there is no paradox.

EXERCISE 13C

1. *Pareto efficiency and Pareto optimality.*

   (a) Derive the first-order conditions for maximizing a Paretian social welfare function $W(u^1, \ldots, u^H)$ subject to the production function, material balance, endowment and non-negativity constraints. The optimality conditions will include terms $W_h = \partial W/\partial u^h$ reflecting the value judgements about the relative merits of individuals embedded in W.

   (b) Show that optimality implies efficiency by rearranging these optimality conditions to yield the efficiency conditions which do not involve any W_h terms.

2. *Rawlsian swf.* A Rawlsian judges allocations solely by their effect on the worst-off member of the society: $W = \min\{u^1, u^2, \ldots, u^H\}$. Sketch the welfare indifference curves of this swf. Are there any circumstances in which a Rawlsian would choose a point on the utility feasibility frontier which did not have equal utilities for all members of the society?

3. *Utilitarian swf.* A utilitarian judges allocations by their effect on the sum of utilities: $W = \sum_h u_h$. Sketch the welfare indifference curves for this swf. Under what circumstances would a utilitarian and a Rawlsian choose the same utility distribution on the utility possibility frontier?

4. Show that for all non-paternal swf the marginal rate of substitution between a pair of goods consumed by one individual is independent of the consumption of all other individuals.

5. *Scitovsky paradox.* Let a be a parameter measuring the coverage of laws restricting smoking in public places. Individual 1 is a non-smoker and prefers more restrictive laws, individual 2 is a smoker and prefers less restrictive laws. Suppose that changes in a do not change the income of the two individuals.

   (i) Draw an Edgeworth box to show the effect of increasing the coverage of the laws from a^1 to a^2.

   (ii) Sketch the indifference curves of the two individuals so that the compensation test is passed for a move from a^1 to a^2 and for a move from a^2 to a^1.

   (iii) Do you have to assume that a is a normal or inferior good for the individuals? (*Hint:* let the horizontal axis measure a, the vertical axis measure total income, and put the origins for the two individuals at the bottom left and top left corners of the box.)

6. *Gorman paradox and the Scitovsky compensation test.* Scitovsky proposed the following amendment to the compensation test: situation 2 is better than situation 1 if (a) $\sum_h CV^h_{12} > 0$ and (b) $\sum_h CV^h_{21} < 0$. Show that the Scitovsky criterion is not transitive. (*Hint:* use Fig. 13.2 with three situations and three intersecting utility feasibility curves.)

7. *Compensation tests and income distribution.* Let the direct utility of h be $v^h(y_h, p)$ where p is the price vector and y_h income, and the Paretian social welfare function be $W(v^1, v^2)$. Suppose that the price vector changes from p^0 to p^1. Show that evaluating the price change by using the Hicks–Kaldor test yields the same conclusion as using W if $W_1 v^1_y = W_2 v^2_y$ ($v^h_y = \partial v^h / \partial y_h$). Interpret this condition.

D. Pareto efficiency and competitive markets

In section B we derived a set of conditions which are necessary for an allocation to be Pareto efficient. Under certain standard assumptions they are also sufficient. The conditions can be used to investigate whether a particular institutional framework leads to an efficient allocation of resources. In this section we examine the circumstances in which the equilibrium resource allocation in a market economy is Pareto efficient.

Our main conclusion is summarized in the First Theorem of Welfare Economics (FTWE).

First Theorem of Welfare Economics (FTWE)

The First Theorem of Welfare Economics states that *if (a) there are markets for all commodities which enter into production and utility functions and (b) all markets are competitive, then the equilibrium of the economy is Pareto efficient.*

To bring out the intuition behind this result we first consider a competitive market version of the simple economy studied in section B and use the efficiency conditions derived there. We then present a more formal (though beautifully simple) demonstration which works, however elaborate our specification of the economy. Last, we consider briefly the role played by the requirements that markets be complete and competitive. Chapter 14 investigates these requirements in more detail.

Markets are competitive when consumers and producers believe that their decisions have no effect on prices. The simple economy of section B has two commodity markets and two input markets and each market has two demanders and one supplier. We sacrifice plausibility for simplicity by assuming that the agents regard prices as parameters. As the reader should check, our arguments carry through to the case in which competition is more plausible because there is a large number of traders on both sides of the market.

Individual h gets income from selling input z_h and from owning shares in the profits of the two firms in the economy and maximizes the utility function $u^h(x_{h1}, x_{h2}, z_h)$ subject to the budget constraint:

$$\sum_i p_i x_{hi} - w_h z_h - R^h = 0 \qquad h = 1, 2 \qquad \text{[D.1]}$$

where p_i is the price of commodity i, w_h the price of input h and R^h the non-wage income of h derived from share ownership. (Since consumers are non-satiated the budget constraint can be treated as an equality.) The proportion of firm i owned by individual h is β_{hi} and the profit of firm i is π_i, so that non-wage income is defined as

$$R^h = \sum_i \beta_{hi} \pi_i \qquad h = 1, 2 \qquad \text{[D.2]}$$

where $0 \leqslant \beta_{hi} \leqslant 1$ and $\sum_h \beta_{hi} = 1$ $(i = 1, 2)$. Firm i seeks to maximize its profit

$$\pi_i = p_i x_i - \sum_h z_{ih} \qquad i = 1, 2 \qquad \text{[D.3]}$$

subject to its production function $x_i = f^i(z_{i1}, z_{i2})$.

We show that the equilibrium of the economy is Pareto efficient by establishing that it satisfies the conditions derived in the previous section. Note first that, since infeasible decisions cannot form part of an equilibrium, it must satisfy the constraints [B.1] imposed by the firms' production functions. The equilibrium decisions must be compatible in that the demand for each commodity or input cannot exceed its supply (see Chapter 12) and so the material balance requirements [B.2] and [B.3] will also be satisfied.

Recall, from the analysis of consumers in Chapters 2 to 4 and of firms in Chapters 5 to 7, the conditions which the consumers' and firms' decisions will satisfy. (Alternatively, set up the Lagrangeans for the consumers' and firms' optimization problems, derive the first-order conditions and rearrange them to get the results used below. We will restrict attention for the moment, as in section B, to non-corner solutions.)

Consumption choices

For a given input supply, consumers choose consumption bundles where their indifference curves for the two goods are tangent to the budget line in goods space and so

$$MRS^1_{21} = \frac{u^1_1}{u^1_2} = \frac{p_1}{p_2} = \frac{u^2_1}{u^2_2} = MRS^2_{21} \qquad \text{[D.4]}$$

Thus the condition for efficient consumption [B.12] is satisfied. Each consumer equates the marginal rates of substitution between the two goods to the price ratio and, because in competitive markets they face the same prices, their marginal rates of substitution are equalized.

Supply of inputs

Individual h equates the marginal rate of substitution between supply of input h and consumption of good i to the ratio of the market prices of the input and good i:

$$MRS_{iz}^h = -\frac{u_z^h}{u_i^h} = \frac{w_h}{p_i} \qquad [D.5]$$

Firm i will maximize π_i by choosing z_{ih} to satisfy

$$p_i f_h^i = w_h \qquad h, i = 1, 2 \qquad [D.6]$$

so that the value of the extra output of good i produced by an additional unit of input h is equal to the cost of a unit of input h. Rearranging [D.6] we see that $f_h^i = w_h/p_i$ and from [D.5]

$$MRS_{iz}^h = -\frac{u_z^h}{u_i^h} = \frac{w_h}{p_i} = f_h^i \qquad [D.7]$$

The condition for efficient input supply [B.14] is satisfied because consumers and firms face the same relative prices for goods and inputs.

Input use

Profit maximization by firm i requires cost minimization and cost minimization requires that the firm choose an input mix where its isoquant is tangent to the isocost line. Alternatively, use [D.6] and divide the condition on z_1 by the condition on z_2 for both firms in turn to get

$$MRTS_{21}^1 = \frac{f_1^1}{f_2^1} = \frac{w_1}{w_2} = \frac{f_1^2}{f_2^2} = MRTS_{21}^2 \qquad [D.8]$$

The condition [B.15] for efficient input use is satisfied because the firms face the same relative prices for inputs.

Output mix

Using [D.6] and [D.4] we get

$$MRT_{21}^i = \frac{f_2^1}{f_1^1} = \frac{f_2^2}{f_1^2} = \frac{p_1}{p_2} = \frac{u_1^1}{u_2^1} = \frac{u_1^2}{u_2^2} = MRS_{21}^h \qquad [D.9]$$

(since $f_h^i = w_h/p_i$ from [D.6]) and so the marginal rate of transformation between outputs is equal to the consumers' marginal rates of substitution between the two goods, satisfying condition [B.17] for an efficient output mix.

We have thus shown that the equilibrium of this simple competitive economy satisfies the necessary conditions for Pareto efficiency. If the consumers' utility functions are strictly quasi-concave and the production functions convex, then the necessary conditions are also sufficient and the equilibrium will indeed be efficient.

This proof of the efficiency of competitive equilibrium readily generalizes to an economy with many consumers, goods, inputs and firms and brings out very clearly the role of prices in achieving an efficient equilibrium. The choices of the individuals are guided by the prices that they face and the fact that all decision-takers face the same relative prices means that in equilibrium they all place the same relative valuation on goods and inputs, so that no reallocation of goods or inputs can achieve a Pareto improvement. Put differently, all gains from mutually advantageous trade at the equilibrium prices have been exhausted.

The proof has one major and two minor limitations. The minor limitations are that we restrict attention to non-corner allocations and assume that utility and production functions are differentiable. It is possible to amend both the Pareto efficiency conditions and the proof that the competitive equilibrium is efficient to overcome these limitations, though the resulting analysis is cumbersome. The major limitation in our argument is that we have to assume that preferences and production possibilities are convex so that the efficiency conditions are sufficient as well as necessary. This is a substantive assumption and there are many circumstances in which it is not valid. We therefore turn next to a surprisingly simple demonstration of the efficiency of competitive equilibrium which does not require assumptions of convexity or differentiability and is not restricted to non-corner allocations.

A simple formal proof of FTWE

We change our notation to emphasize the generality of the argument and to bring out its relationship with the analysis of general equilibrium in Chapter 12. There are n commodities (both inputs and outputs). p_i is the price of commodity i and p is the price vector. $y^j = (y_{j1}, \ldots, y_{jn})$ is the net output vector of firm j($j = 1, \ldots, J$) (recall section 5D). If $y_{ji} > 0$ firm j supplies commodity i and if $y_{ji} < 0$ commodity i is an input used by firm j. Y^j is the production possibility set of firm j: the set of all technically feasible net output vectors for the firm. Firm j chooses y^j to maximize its profit

$$\pi_j = py^j \qquad [D.10]$$

subject to $y^j \in Y^j$. The total production of commodity i by all firms is $y_i = \sum_j y_{ji}$ and the aggregate output vector for the economy is $y = (y_1, \ldots, y_n) = \sum_j y^j$.

$x^h = (x_{h1}, \ldots, x_{hn})$ is the consumption and $\bar{x}^h = (\bar{x}_{h1}, \ldots, \bar{x}_{hn})$ is the endowment of individual h ($h = 1, \ldots, H$). If $x_{hi} < \bar{x}_{hi}$ then h is supplying commodity i. For example, if 'commodity' i is leisure time individual h sells $\bar{x}_{hi} - x_{hi}$ units of her time on the labour market to generate earned income of $p_i(\bar{x}_{hi} - x_{hi})$. Individual h has the utility function $u^h(x^h)$ (strictly we need only assume that h has a well-defined preference ordering over net demand vectors). u^h is maximized subject to the full budget constraint

$$px^h \le R^h = p\bar{x}^h + \sum_j \beta_{hj}\pi_j = p\bar{x}^h + \sum_j \beta_{hj}py^j \qquad [D.11]$$

where $0 \le \beta_{hj} \le 1$ is the proportion of firm j owned by h and $\sum_h \beta_{hj} = 1$ ($j = 1, \ldots, J$). R^h is the full income of individual h (recall sections 4C and 4D). We assume that all consumers are non-satiated so that [D.11] will be an equality at h's optimal consumption x^{h*}. The total consumption of commodity i summed over all consumers is $x_i = \sum_h x_{hi}$ and the total endowment of i is $\bar{x}_i = \sum_h \bar{x}_{hi}$. The aggregate consumption and endowment vectors are $x = (x_1, \ldots, x_n) = \sum_h x^h$ and $\bar{x} = (\bar{x}_1, \ldots, \bar{x}_n) = \sum_h \bar{x}^h$.

We assume that all n markets are competitive. Recall from section 12B that an equilibrium of such an economy is a price vector p^*, consumer demands x^{h*} and firm net outputs y^{j*} such that, for all markets, firms and consumers,

(a) *Market clearing:* $p_i^* \geq 0$, $x_i^* - \bar{x}_i - y_i^* \leq 0$, $p_i^*[x_i^* - \bar{x}_i - y_i^*] = 0$;

(b) *Firm optimization:* y^{j*} maximizes $p^* y^j$ over Y^j, so that $y^{j*} \in Y^j$ and

$$p^* y^{j*} \geq p^* y^j \quad \text{for all } y^j \in Y^j \tag{D.12}$$

(c) *Consumer optimization:* x^{h*} maximizes $u^h(x^h)$ subject to $p^* x^h = R^h - \sum_j \beta_{hj} p^* y^{j*}$ so that

$$u^h(x^h) \geq u^h(x^{h*}) \qquad \text{implies} \qquad p^* x^h \geq R^{h*} = p^* x^{h*} \tag{D.13}$$

$$u^h(x^h) > u^h(x^{h*}) \qquad \text{implies} \qquad p^* x^h > R^{h*} = p^* x^{h*} \tag{D.14}$$

According to [D.13], any consumption vector which gives the consumer at least as much utility as her optimal vector is at least as expensive as the optimal vector. (If such a bundle cost less than R^{h*} then since the consumer is not satiated there is a feasible bundle which yields more utility than x^{h*}.) Equation [D.14] states that the consumer cannot afford a consumption vector which yields a greater utility than x^{h*} (otherwise she would have chosen it).

Recall from section B the definition of a Pareto efficient allocation as an allocation which is feasible and which has no other feasible allocation which is superior to it. The competitive equilibrium allocation $A^* = (x^{1*}, \ldots, x^{H*}, y^{1*}, \ldots, y^{J*})$ is feasible (since demand cannot exceed supply in an equilibrium and $y^{j*} \in Y^j$ for all j.) We now establish that there is no other feasible allocation which is Pareto superior to A^*. The proof is by contradiction: assume that the allocation $\hat{A} = (\hat{x}^1, \ldots, \hat{x}^H, \hat{y}^1, \ldots, \hat{y}^J)$ is feasible and Pareto superior to A^*. If $\hat{A}$ is Pareto superior to A^* it must have

$$u^h(\hat{x}^h) \geq u^h(x^{h*}) \qquad h = 1, \ldots, H \tag{D.15}$$

with

$$u^h(\hat{x}^h) > u^h(x^{h*}) \qquad \text{for some } h \tag{D.16}$$

Consumers are optimizing at the competitive equilibrium so that [D.13] and [D.14] hold for $\hat{x}^h$. [D.15] and [D.13] imply

$$p^* \hat{x}^h \geq p^* x^{h*} = R^{h*} \qquad h = 1, \ldots, H \tag{D.17}$$

and [D.16] and [D.14] imply

$$p^* \hat{x}^h > p^* x^{h*} = R^{h*} \qquad \text{for some } h \tag{D.18}$$

Summing [D.17] and [D.18] over all h and writing $\hat{x} = \sum_h \hat{x}^h$, $y^* = \sum_j y^{j*}$ gives

$$p^* \hat{x} = \sum_h p^* \hat{x}^h > \sum_h R^{h*} = \sum_h p^* \bar{x}^h + \sum_h \left(\sum_j \beta_{hj} p^* y^{j*} \right)$$

$$= p^* \bar{x} + \sum_j \left(\sum_h \beta_{hj} p^* y^{j*} \right) = p^* \bar{x} + \sum_j p^* y^{j*} = p^* \bar{x} + p^* y^* \tag{D.19}$$

The penultimate step follows because $\sum_h \beta_{hj} = 1$. Now y^{j*} maximizes the profit of firm j at prices p^* and we have assumed that $\hat{y}^j$ is feasible so that [D.12] holds for $\hat{y}^j$:

$$p^* y^{j*} \geq p^* \hat{y}^j \qquad j = 1, \ldots, J \tag{D.20}$$

Summing [D.20] over all j and writing $\hat{y} = \sum_j \hat{y}^j$ gives

$$\sum_j p^* y^{j*} = p^* y^* \geqslant p^* \hat{y} = \sum_j p^* \hat{y}^j \qquad [D.21]$$

Using [D.21] with [D.19] yields

$$p^* \hat{x} > p^* \bar{x} + p^* y^* \geqslant p^* \bar{x} + p^* \hat{y} \qquad [D.22]$$

which implies

$$p^* \hat{x} - p^* \bar{x} - p^* \hat{y} = p^*[\hat{x} - \bar{x} - \hat{y}] > 0 \qquad [D.23]$$

Now $\hat{x} = (\hat{x}_1, \ldots, \hat{x}_n)$ is the aggregate consumption vector and $\hat{y} = (\hat{y}_1, \ldots, \hat{y}_n)$ the aggregate output vector for the allocation $\hat{A}$. Equation [D.23] requires that the inner product of the price vector p^* and the materials balance vector $\hat{x} - \bar{x} - \hat{y}$ is positive or writing [D.23] out in full:

$$\sum_i p_i^*[\hat{x}_i - \bar{x}_i - \hat{y}_i] > 0 \qquad [D.24]$$

Since the equilibrium prices are non-negative ($p_i^* \geqslant 0$, $i = 1, \ldots, n$), [D.24] implies that there is at least one commodity where

$$\hat{x}_i - \bar{x}_i - \hat{y}_i > 0 \qquad [D.25]$$

But this says that the consumption of commodity i exceeds its endowment plus production, which violates the material balance constraint and contradicts our assumption that $\hat{A}$ is feasible. We have established that all allocations which are Pareto superior to the competitive equilibrium allocation are infeasible. Thus the competitive equilibrium allocation A^* is Pareto efficient.

Some caveats

The reader should be careful not to be led astray about the welfare properties of markets by the generality of this proof of the FTWE. It is important to remember that the fact that the equilibrium of a complete set of competitive markets is Pareto efficient does *not* imply that any *particular* market economy achieves a Pareto optimal allocation.

First, the conditions of the theorem may not be satisfied and consequently the market economy may not be efficient and therefore cannot be optimal:

(a) Firms and consumers may not be price-takers. If some of the markets in the economy are monopolized or monopsonized some decision-takers will not take prices as parameters. Consequently, prices will not measure the marginal value of activities to all decision-takers. The efficiency conditions will be violated because different decision-takers will have different marginal values of activities.

(b) Markets may not be complete. The requirement that there be markets for all commodities or activities which matter to any individuals (in the sense of entering utility or production functions) is unlikely to be satisfied in a real-world economy. It is not difficult to think of commodities, for example clean air, for which there are no markets. The completeness requirement is even more demanding once intertemporal allocation is considered: there must exist a full set of futures markets for delivery of commodities at any period in the future. (If there is uncertainty there must also be markets for delivery of commodities in all possible states of the world – see Chapter 21.) If there are no market prices to guide decisions then individual marginal valuations of activities are likely to differ and the allocation will be inefficient.

(c) Markets may not be in equilibrium. Decisions taken in markets in disequilibrium have no single set of relative prices to guide them and so individuals' marginal valuations will differ and the allocation will then be inefficient.

We explore the implications of the fact that an economy does not satisfy the conditions of the FTWE in Chapters 14 and 21.

Second, even if the conditions of the FTWE are satisfied this merely ensures that the market allocation is Pareto efficient, not that it is Pareto optimal. The efficient allocation achieved by a market economy may be highly inequitable and therefore may not maximize welfare functions based on value judgements which favour equity. For example, in the simple economy considered earlier in this section, individual 1 may own none of the firms (and so have no non-wage income) and have only a small amount of labour of low marginal productivity to sell. In equilibrium individual 2 will end up with most of the consumption and individual 1 with very little. Indeed, allocations which leave some individuals starving can be Pareto efficient.

EXERCISE 13D

1. *Incomplete markets.* Suppose that in a competitive market economy with n commodities there is no market in one of the commodities so that there are only $n - 2$ relative prices. Show that the equilibrium in such an economy does not satisfy the efficiency conditions of section C.

2. *Non-competitive markets.* Consider a two-person, two-commodity pure exchange economy in which a Walrasian umpire announces a relative price, the two parties state their demand at the announced price and the umpire adjusts the price until an equilibrium is achieved. Individual 2 always states the demand which maximizes his utility at the announced price. Suppose that individual 1 knows the preferences of individual 2 (and so knows 2's demand at each relative price). Show that individual 1 can do better by dissembling: stating a demand which does not maximize her utility at the announced price. (*Hint*: use an Edgeworth box, sketch in the offer curves of non-dissemblers and show the Walrasian equilibrium. Show that there is a point on 2's offer curve that individual 1 prefers to the Walrasian equilibrium.)

E. Distribution and markets

Under certain circumstances it may be possible to resolve the conflict between efficiency and equity by intervening to redistribute the initial endowments of individuals and then letting the market allocate resources efficiently. Thus in the simple two-person economy considered earlier in this chapter suppose that the initial shareholdings of the two individuals led to an efficient but highly inequitable allocation in which individual 2 had a large utility and individual 1 had a small utility at α^2 on the utility frontier in Fig. 13.1. By transferring some of 2's shareholdings to individual 1 but then letting them trade in competitive markets we can shift them down FF' to the welfare optimum at α^*. In this way we can separate issues of efficiency from issues of distribution and fairness.

Second Theorem of Welfare Economics (STWE)

The Second Theorem of Welfare Economics states that, *if all consumers have convex preferences and all firms have convex production possibility sets, any Pareto efficient allocation can be achieved as the equilibrium of a complete set of competitive markets after a suitable redistribution of initial endowments.*

We have sacrificed a little rigour for ease of comprehension in this statement of the theorem and the reader is referred to the Appendix at the end of this chapter for a more precise version and a proof. We give a simple intuitive account here. Suppose that we wish to achieve a particular Pareto efficient allocation A^* in which individual $h = 1, \ldots, H$ has consumption x^{h*} and firm $j = 1, \ldots, J$ produces y^{j*}. From section B we know that at A^* all consumers will have the same marginal rates of substitution between all pairs of commodities. (We assume A^* is not a corner allocation.) Let $\dot{p}_i$ denote the consumers' marginal rates of substitution between commodity i and commodity 1:

$$\dot{p}_i \equiv MRS^h_{i1}(x^{h*}) \qquad i = 2, \ldots, n, \quad h = 1, \ldots, H \qquad [\text{E.1}]$$

and define

$$\dot{p}_1 \equiv 1 \qquad [\text{E.2}]$$

We can interpret $\dot{p} = (1, \dot{p}_2, \ldots, \dot{p}_n)$ as the set of relative prices, with commodity 1 as the numeraire, implicit in the Pareto efficient allocation A^*. Now redistribute the individuals' initial endowments of commodities and initial shareholdings until

$$\dot{p}x^{h*} = \dot{R}^h \equiv \dot{p}\dot{x}^h + \sum_j \dot{\beta}_{hj} \dot{p}y^{j*} \qquad h = 1, \ldots, H \qquad [\text{E.3}]$$

Here $\dot{x}^h$ is h's initial endowment after the redistribution, $\dot{\beta}_{hj}$ the post-redistribution shareholding in firm j and $\dot{p}y^{j*}$ is the profit firm j earns (valued in terms of the numeraire) if it produces the Pareto efficient net output y^{j*}.

There are two apparent problems with this redistribution. It may be objected that in some cases individuals' original initial endowments $\bar{x}^h$ consist only of labour time and that it is not possible to transfer such endowments since they are inseparable from the individual. It may also be objected that if firms have constant returns they will just break even at y^{j*} when facing price $\dot{p}$. Redistributing shareholdings will not affect budget constraints when firms earn zero profits. The answer to both of these apparent problems is to use transfers $\dot{T}^h$, with $\sum_h \dot{T}^h = 0$, measured in terms of the numeraire (which we choose to be a good which is transferable among individuals). If $\dot{T}^h > 0$ individual h must pay a tax of $\dot{T}^h$ units of good 1. If he has an initial holding of good 1 this merely reduces his holding of good 1. If $\dot{x}_{h1} \equiv \bar{x}_{h1} - \dot{T}^h < 0$, he must pay the tax by selling some of his holdings of other goods. If $\dot{T}^h < 0$, he receives a lump-sum subsidy by having his holding of good 1 increased. If we adopt this procedure the lump-sum transfers are chosen so that

$$\dot{p}x^{h*} = \dot{R}^h \equiv \dot{p}\bar{x}^h + \sum_j \beta_{hj} \dot{p}y^{j*} - \dot{T}^h = R^h - \dot{T}^h \qquad h = 1, 2, \ldots, H \qquad [\text{E.4}]$$

where R^h is the individual's full income at the original initial holdings. With $\dot{T}^h = \dot{p}(\bar{x} - \dot{x}^h) + \sum_j (\beta_{hj} - \dot{\beta}_{hj})\dot{p}y^{j*}$ the lump-sum transfer approach is equivalent to redistributing the initial holdings of all goods and shares. (Check that the transfers are feasible: $\sum_h \dot{T}^h = 0$.)

If [E.3] or [E.4] hold, the value of h's full income in terms of the numeraire is equal to the cost of the Pareto efficient commodity bundle x^{h*} at the prices $\dot{p}$. If h maximized $u^h(x^h)$ subject to the budget constraint $\dot{p}x^h \leq \dot{R}^h$ she would set her marginal rate of substitution between commodity i and 1 equal to the relative price $\dot{p}_i$. Her demand for good i at relative prices $\dot{p}$ would be equal to the amount of good i she receives in the Pareto efficient allocation A^*.

If firm j faced the relative prices $\dot{p}$ it would choose to produce y^{j*} in order to maximize its profits. Pareto efficiency requires that firms' marginal rates of transformation, marginal rates of technical substitution and marginal products are equal to the consumers' relevant marginal rates of substitution. Profit maximization requires firms' marginal rates of transformation, marginal rates of technical substitution and marginal products to be equal to the relevant relative commodity prices (recall the first part of section D). Since the relative prices $\dot{p}_i$ are equal by definition to consumers' marginal rates of substitution at the Pareto efficient commodity bundles, profits $\dot{p}y^j$ are maximized at the Pareto efficient y^{j*}. Thus the relative prices $\dot{p}$ lead to demand and supply decisions which are identical to those required for the Pareto efficient allocation A^*.

Pareto efficient allocations satisfy the material balance requirement that consumption does not exceed output plus endowments. The supply and demand decisions generated by $\dot{p}$ are therefore compatible and the market economy is in equilibrium at $\dot{p}$. Thus by suitable choice of endowments we have achieved the desired Pareto efficient allocation as the equilibrium of a competitive market economy.

Some caveats

Unfortunately for real-world policy-making, the conditions under which the STWE holds are unlikely to be satisfied and we will not usually be able to separate efficiency and distributional considerations. First, if in a real economy markets are neither complete nor competitive, redistributing initial endowments and then leaving markets to allocate resources need not lead to the desired efficient allocation. For example, the fact that a firm would produce its efficient net output vector *if* it took prices as parameters is irrelevant if it has market power and realizes that the prices it faces are affected by its production decisions.

Second, if preferences and technology are not convex the relative prices $\dot{p}$ may not support the desired efficient allocation as a competitive equilibrium. Figure 13.7 shows a consumer with non-convex preferences. The desired Pareto efficient allocation gives this consumer the consumption bundle x^{h*}. $\dot{p}_2$, the relative price of good 2 in terms of good 1 implied by this allocation, is shown by the negative of the inverse of the slope of the indifference curve I^{h*} at x^{h*}. By adjusting h's initial endowments we can give her a full income of $\dot{R}^h$ which at prices $\dot{p}$ is just sufficient to enable her to buy x^{h*}, but confronted with these prices h will demand x^{h0} rather than x^{h*}.

In Fig. 13.8 firm j has the non-convex production possibility set Y^j: over some range the marginal rate of transformation MRT_{21}^j is increasing. The desired Pareto efficient net output for the firm is y^{j*}. $\dot{p}_2$, the relative price of commodity 2 implicit in the desired efficient allocation, is equal to MRT_{21}^j at this point. The firm's profit contours in (y_{j1}, y_{j2}) space at prices $\dot{p}$ are straight lines with slope $-1/\dot{p}_2$. If the firm is confronted with price $\dot{p}$ it will produce at y^{j0} because it earns more profit here than at y^{j*}.

The last difficulty is that it may not be possible to make the kind of initial redistribution required by the theorem. It is essential that the redistributions are *lump*

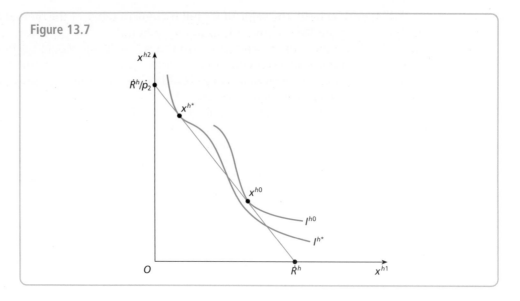

Figure 13.7

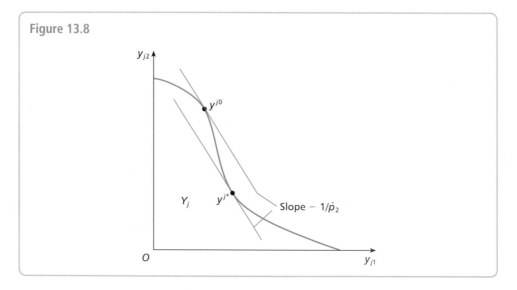

Figure 13.8

sum: the individuals should not be able to alter the amounts paid or received. The taxes should not affect their behaviour at the margin. If it is possible for an individual to alter the amount paid or received under the redistribution by changing their demands or supplies, the effective prices individuals face are not the market prices and will differ across individuals. If they do not adjust to the same set of relative prices $\dot{p}$ the efficiency conditions of section D will be violated. In the simple one-period economy considered above, shareholdings or initial endowments are exogenous and not affected by decisions taken by the individuals. In a more complete model such decisions would be endogenous. Individuals could accumulate shares by saving and alter their endowments by investment in human capital to raise their skill levels. Redistribution from individuals with large shareholdings or valuable initial endowments is effectively a tax on saving or human capital investment and is no longer a lump-sum tax. Further, the relative prices the individuals face would then vary depending on their shareholdings or skill levels and would also vary across individuals.

To see in more detail why non-lump-sum taxes violate the efficiency requirements of section B, consider the example of an income tax in the simple two-by-two economy of section D. Suppose that we redistribute from individual 1 to individual 2 by placing a tax at the proportional rate t on the income individual 1 earns by selling input z_1 and give the proceeds tw_1z_1 to individual 2. Consumer 1 now faces the budget constraint

$$\sum_i p_i x_{1i} - (1 - t) w_1 z_1 - \sum_j \beta_{1j} \pi^j = 0 \qquad [E.5]$$

and chooses a supply of input 1 and consumption bundle so that her marginal rate of substitution between the input and consumption of good i is equal to the relevant post-tax price ratio:

$$MRS_{1i}^1 = (1 - t) w_1 / p_i \qquad [E.6]$$

Firm i maximizes profit by equating the value of the marginal product of input 1 to its market price or

$$f_1^i = w_1 / p_i \qquad [E.7]$$

and we see that

$$MRS_{1i}^1 = (1 - t) w_1 / p_i < w_1 / p_i = f_1^i$$

which violates the condition on efficient input supply [B.7].

What goes wrong here is that the amount of tax paid by individual 1 (tw_1z_1) is affected by her decisions and consequently she will take account of the change in her tax bill as well as the market price when deciding how much of the input to supply. The other parties in the economy, however, take account only of the market prices and so marginal valuations of activities will diverge, leading to violation of the efficiency conditions of section B. Any tax or subsidy which results in different consumers or firms facing different relative prices will lead to inefficiency. We leave the reader to demonstrate that purchase taxes also violate the Pareto efficiency conditions derived in section B (see Question 1, Exercise 13E).

The ability of individuals to alter their tax bills by changing their behaviour is what makes a tax non-lump-sum and therefore a source of inefficiency. This ability is not just a question of varying the amount of taxed goods they buy and sell. Taxation may lead them to alter other kinds of behaviour. They can hire tax lawyers and accountants to reduce their tax bills or emigrate to other states which have lower tax rates. Such possibilities suggest the *First Rule of Public Finance* (FRPF): *there is no such thing as a lump-sum tax.*

If the FRPF is true the set of allocations which can be achieved by redistribution depends on the original distribution of endowments and does not include all Pareto efficient allocations achievable by lump-sum taxes. Figure 13.9 reproduces the utility possibility frontier FF' from Fig. 13.1. Given the original distribution of endowments a competitive market economy generates the utility distribution α^2 on FF' from an allocation satisfying the efficiency conditions of section B. If we wish to change the distribution and there are no lump sum taxes and subsidies to redistribute the

Figure 13.9

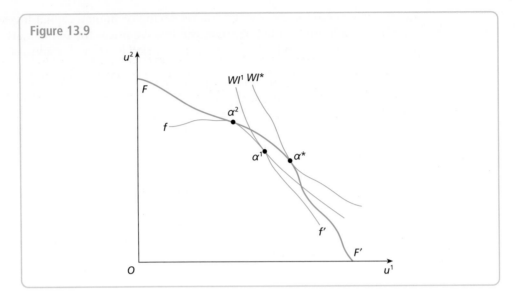

endowments of the two individuals, we are forced to redistribute via distorting taxes and subsidies which violate the section B Pareto efficiency conditions. The curve *ff'* is the *utility feasibility frontier* showing the utility combinations achievable from the original endowments by varying the level of non-lump-sum transfers. The distance between *ff'* and *FF'* is a measure of the *deadweight loss* arising from the fact that we have to use non-lump-sum taxes to redistribute endowments. Given the welfare judgements giving rise to the welfare indifference curves shown, the Pareto optimal utility distribution is α^1 on *ff'*. The distribution α^* on *FF'* is not reachable from α^2 because there are no feasible lump-sum taxes.

Figure 13.9 appears to contradict our argument in section B that Pareto efficiency is necessary for Pareto optimality since α^1 maximizes a Paretian welfare function but does not satisfy the section B conditions for Pareto efficiency. The contradiction disappears when we realize that in deriving the efficiency conditions in section B we assumed that it was possible to choose the allocation to maximize u^1 for given u^2 subject only to production function and material balance constraints. Here we are assuming that allocation must take place via markets and that our only means of influencing the allocation is by non-lump-sum taxes and subsidies. Thus there are additional constraints on the efficiency problem of maximizing u^1 for given u^2.

Imposing additional binding constraints gives rise to a *second-best problem* and changes both the solution to an optimization problem and the conditions characterizing it. We discuss the theory of the second best in section 14C and merely note here that when lump-sum taxes are infeasible the efficiency conditions of section B are no longer relevant in judging the efficiency of allocations. When there are no lump-sum taxes the problem of ensuring that an allocation is optimal is no longer trivial (we cannot leave the market to allocate resources and just redistribute via lump-sum taxes). We have to choose the least distorting means of redistributing, i.e. to solve the *optimal tax problem*. In terms of Fig. 13.9 we wish to find the set of taxes and other policies which minimizes the deadweight loss and gives rise to the utility feasibility curve which lies closest to *FF'* for the utility distribution we wish to achieve.

EXERCISE 13E

1. Show that purchase taxes violate the efficiency conditions of section B. Would levying an equal rate proportional purchase tax on all consumption goods violate the conditions?

2. Can you think of *any* lump-sum taxes? What about a fixed sum per head payable by all members of a population (a poll tax)?

F. Arrow's Impossibility Theorem

When we introduced the Bergson social welfare function in section B we were deliberately vague about the source of the preference ordering over alternative social states represented by the swf. One possibility is that it is derived from the preference orderings of the individuals in the society. To derive the social ordering of alternative social states from the individuals' orderings, a mechanism or procedure is necessary. For example, the procedure might be a voting scheme under which each individual is allowed to cast a vote for one of the alternative social states. Individuals' votes are determined by their preference orderings and the social states are then ordered by the total number of votes each state receives and the state with the most votes is chosen. Political systems are usually more complex than this procedure of direct democracy but ultimately they can be thought of as methods of making social choices by aggregating individuals' preference orderings into social orderings. The same is true of the rules or constitutions of many social organizations, such as clubs, committees, trade unions, joint-stock companies and workers' cooperatives. We can give our analysis wide applicability by defining a 'social state' very generally as being whatever set of variables enters into the individual preference orderings of the particular social group we are considering. So, for an economy this could be the allocation of resources; for a joint-stock company it could be the level of dividends or whether to accept a takeover bid; and for the members of a social club it could be the price of beer or the membership fee. The individual preference orderings reflect their views of the social state and are not simply preferences over, say, their own consumption bundles. They are thus the individuals' *ethical preferences*.

Arrow was concerned with the following problem. Suppose that we lay down criteria we would like the social choice procedure to satisfy. What types of procedures satisfy these criteria? Arrow proves that there is no procedure which can simultaneously satisfy four apparently reasonable criteria.

The Impossibility Theorem

Arrow called the procedure or constitution by which a social ordering is derived from individual preference orderings a social welfare function. Arrow's social welfare function (SWF) is not the same as Bergson's social welfare function (swf) introduced in section B. An SWF is a procedure for aggregating individual preference orderings into a social ordering of alternative social states. Applying an SWF to a given set of individual preference orderings yields a social ordering of alternatives which, under certain continuity assumptions, can be represented by an swf. Thus, the concept of an SWF is more fundamental and more general: SWFs generate swfs. Changes in the individual preference orders with a *given* SWF change the social ordering (and thus the swf). A different SWF applied to a given set of individual preference orderings will produce a different social ordering (and thus a different swf). An swf is a function on the set of social states and associates a real number with each social state so as to reflect an ordering of those states. An SWF is a function (strictly functional) on the set of individuals' preference orderings and associates a social preference ordering with each possible configuration of the individuals' preference orderings.

The first requirement of an SWF is that it produces a social preference ordering from the orderings of the individual members of the group. It is easy to find an example of an SWF which does not do this, and the presentation of this example is a useful means of introducing the notation used throughout the analysis. Consider a group of three individuals, labelled 1, 2, 3. There are also three possible social states, a, b, c. It is assumed that preferences over states are *strict* – no individual is indifferent between any two states. These assumptions are purely simplifying. A particular preference ordering for individual $i = 1, 2, 3$ is written $(a, b, c)_i$, which means that i prefers a to b and b to c. This implies the three pairwise orderings $(a, b)_i$, $(a, c)_i$, and $(b, c)_i$. A particular *social* preference ordering is denoted $[a, b, c]$, which means that a is socially preferred to b and b to c. This implies the three pairwise social orderings $[a, b]$, $[b, c]$ and $[a, c]$.

Consider now an SWF consisting of the simple *majority voting* rule in this three-person, three-state society. The individual preference orderings are assumed to be $(a, b, c)_1$, $(b, c, a)_2$, and $(c, a, b)_3$. The individuals vote on each pair of alternatives, and the social ordering is to be determined by the majority outcomes of the votes. We assume that individuals vote in accordance with their preference orderings, i.e. there is no 'strategic voting'.

Taking first the pair (a, b), from the above preference orderings we have

$$(a, b)_1 \quad \text{and} \quad (b, a)_2 \quad \text{and} \quad (a, b)_3 \Rightarrow [a, b]$$

i.e. 2 is outvoted by 1 and 3. Taking the pair (b, c) we have

$$(b, c)_1 \quad \text{and} \quad (b, c)_2 \quad \text{and} \quad (c, b)_3 \Rightarrow [b, c]$$

i.e. 3 is outvoted by 1 and 2. Finally, taking the pair (a, c) we have

$$(a, c)_1 \quad \text{and} \quad (c, a)_2 \quad \text{and} \quad (c, a)_3 \Rightarrow [c, a]$$

i.e. 1 is outvoted by 2 and 3. The result of the voting is that a is socially preferred to b and b is socially preferred to c but c is socially preferred to a. This is intransitive and so rules out the existence of a social ordering over the three states. Thus the majority voting SWF does not produce a social ordering (and so a Bergson swf).

A natural response to the 'paradox of majority voting' is to design an SWF which does yield transitive social choices. However, we would want it to possess some desirable attributes as well as resulting in a social ordering. Arrow suggested four *minimal* and apparently rather mild properties that the SWF should possess (the presentation here follows closely that of Sen (1970)):

1. *U: the condition of unrestricted domain.* The majority voting rule failed for one pattern of individual preference orderings but gives a social ordering for $(a, b, c)_i$, all i. We would presumably want an SWF to 'work' *whatever* the pattern of individual preferences. Thus, within the brackets $(\cdot)_i$ we would wish to allow any of the six possible permutations of the three alternatives a, b, c. Each of these can be

combined with any of the six possible permutations for each of the others. Thus there are $6^3 = 216$ possible patterns of individual preferences. The *SWF* must 'work' for them all. In other words the domain of the function which maps a set of individual preferences $\{(\cdot)_1, (\cdot)_2, (\cdot)_3\}$ into a social preference ordering $[\cdot]$ is unrestricted.

2. *D: non-dictatorship.* A dictator is defined as someone whose choice between all pairs of alternatives is *decisive*, i.e. determines the social choice regardless of the preferences of all other members of the group. Thus for example if, given $(a, b, c)_1$, we had [a, b], [a, c] and [b, c] regardless of the preferences of 2 and 3, then 1 would be a dictator. It seems a plausible reflection of the values of liberal democracies that this be ruled out in the SWF.

3. *P: Pareto principle.* We have earlier emphasized the reasonableness of the Paretian value judgement, which here takes the form: suppose $(a, b)_i$ for all i; then [a, b]. If *everyone* prefers a to b then a should be preferred to b in the social ordering.

4. *I: independence of irrelevant alternatives.* This is a condition whose appeal is *technical* rather than *ethical*. Suppose we have [a, b]. Now let the individual orderings $(\cdot)_i$ change in a way which *leaves unchanged* each i's preferences between a and b. Then [a, b] should continue to hold. Thus a change only of c's position in the individual preference orderings would not of itself change the social ordering of a and b (c is the irrelevant alternative in a pairwise choice between a and b).

Although one may be able to think of further desirable properties of a constitution or SWF, one could hardly be content with fewer. And though these conditions form a minimal set, Arrow proved the general impossibility theorem: *no SWF exists which satisfies the four conditions, U, P, I and D, and which can produce a transitive preference ordering over social states.*

Thus any attempt to draw up a constitution which transforms individual into social preference orderings and satisfies these four reasonable conditions is doomed to failure. Moreover, any process which does yield a social ordering must violate at least one of the conditions.

Proof of Arrow's Theorem

The proof of the theorem will be given here for our three-person, three-state society.

First we define the concepts of an *almost decisive individual or group* and a *decisive individual or group.* Suppose we have that $(a, b)_1$, $(b, a)_2$ and $(b, a)_3$, but the SWF produces [a, b]. 1's preference becomes the social preference despite strict opposition by 2 and 3. 1 is then called *almost decisive* for the pair (a, b), and we use the notation $A(a, b)$ to denote this. Suppose, alternatively, we have $(a, b)_1$ and [a, b] *whatever* the preferences of the other two. Then 1 is called *decisive* for (a, b) and we denote this by $D(a, b)$. Clearly, $D(a, b) \Rightarrow A(a, b)$ since if 1 is decisive whatever the others' preferences he is decisive if they are strictly opposed to his own. The ideas of almost decisive and decisive could be applied to a group – the group's pairwise ordering becomes the social ordering despite strict opposition, or whatever the orderings, of the rest of society. The notation $A(\cdot)$ and $D(\cdot)$ will, in what follows, always refer to 1's decisiveness, however (nothing is lost by this since the numbering of the individuals is arbitrary).

We now prove Arrow's Theorem, in two steps. First we prove that, if 1 is almost decisive for any one pair of alternatives, then under an SWF satisfying conditions *U*,

I and *P* and producing a transitive social preference ordering he must be a dictator. We then prove that if the SWF does satisfy *U*, *I* and *P* there must be an individual (whom we can number 1) who is almost decisive over at least one pair of alternatives, and therefore, by the first step, is a dictator. Thus the requirements that an SWF produces a transitive preference ordering and that it satisfies Arrow's four conditions are mutually inconsistent.

To prove the first step, suppose $A(a, b)$. Then:

1. If the pattern of preferences is such that $(a, b, c)_1$, $(b, a)_i$, $(b, c)_i$, $i = 2, 3$:

    (a) the fact that 1 is almost decisive over (a, b) implies $[a, b]$;

    (b) the Pareto principle *P* implies $[b, c]$;

    (c) therefore transitivity of the social preference ordering implies $[a, c]$. Nothing was specified about 2 and 3's preferences over the pair (a, c), and yet we have $[a, c]$. Moreover, condition *I* says that if 2 and 3's stated preferences above were changed to $(a, b)_i$ and $(c, b)_i$, $i = 2, 3$, the social ordering $[a, c]$ cannot change. Thus $[a, c]$ has been obtained independently of the orderings of this pair by 2 and 3, so that 1 must be decisive over (a, c). We have therefore:

$$A(a, b) \Rightarrow D(a, c) \qquad\qquad \text{[F.1]}$$

   1 is decisive over the pair (a, c) if he is almost decisive over (a, b).

2. If the preference pattern is such that $(c, a, b)_1$, $(c, a)_i$, $(b, a)_i$, $i = 2, 3$:

    (a) $P \Rightarrow [c, a]$

    (b) $A(a, b) \Rightarrow [a, b]$

    (c) transitivity implies $[c, b]$

   Again, 1 is decisive over (c, b) since $[c, b]$ must follow whatever the preferences of 2 and 3 (*I* rules out a change if we were to have $(a, c)_i$ or $(a, b)_i$, $i = 2, 3$). Thus:

$$A(a, b) \Rightarrow D(c, b) \qquad\qquad \text{[F.2]}$$

3. Suppose now that 1 is almost decisive over (a, c), i.e. $A(a, c)$. Then given the preference pattern $(b, a, c)_1$, $(c, a)_i$, $(b, a)_i$, $i = 2, 3$:

    (a) $P \Rightarrow [b, a]$

    (b) $A(a, c) \Rightarrow [a, c]$

    (c) transitivity $\Rightarrow [b, c]$

   By exactly similar reasoning as before therefore, we have

$$A(a, c) \Rightarrow D(b, c) \qquad\qquad \text{[F.3]}$$

4. Suppose now that $A(b, c)$. Then given the preference pattern $(b, c, a)_1$, $(c, a)_i$, $(c, a)_i$, $i = 2, 3$:

    (a) $P \Rightarrow [c, a]$

    (b) $A(b, c) \Rightarrow [b, c]$

    (c) transitivity $\Rightarrow [b, a]$

   and so, by the usual reasoning:

$$A(b, c) \Rightarrow D(b, a) \qquad\qquad \text{[F.4]}$$

5. Suppose that $A(b, a)$. Given $(c, b, a)_1$, $(a, b)_i$, $(c, b)_i$, $i = 2, 3$:

   (a) $P \Rightarrow [c, b]$

   (b) $A(b, a) \Rightarrow [b, a]$

   (c) transitivity $\Rightarrow [c, a]$

   and so in the usual way:

$$A(b, a) \Rightarrow D(c, a) \qquad [\text{F.5}]$$

6. Suppose $A(c, b)$. Given $(a, c, b)_1$, $(a, c)_i$, $(b, c)_i$, $i = 2, 3$:

   (a) $P \Rightarrow [a, c]$

   (b) $A(c, b) \Rightarrow [c, b]$

   (c) transitivity $\Rightarrow [a, b]$

   and so:

$$A(c, b) \Rightarrow D(a, b) \qquad [\text{F.6}]$$

This first step in the proof is now virtually complete. Recall that by definition $D(\cdot) \Rightarrow A(\cdot)$ for any pair of alternatives. Therefore, putting together [F.1], [F.3]–[F.5] gives the chain of implications

$$\underbrace{A(a, b) \Rightarrow D(a, c)}_{[\text{F.1}]} \Rightarrow \underbrace{A(a, c) \Rightarrow D(b, c)}_{[\text{F.3}]} \Rightarrow \underbrace{A(b, c) \Rightarrow D(b, a)}_{[\text{F.4}]} \Rightarrow \underbrace{A(b, a) \Rightarrow D(c, a)}_{[\text{F.5}]}$$

while putting together [F.2] and [F.6] gives the chain

$$\underbrace{A(a, b) \Rightarrow D(c, b)}_{[\text{F.2}]} \Rightarrow \underbrace{A(c, b) \Rightarrow D(a, b)}_{[\text{F.6}]}$$

But these chains of implications mean that, if 1 is almost decisive over one pair, *he is decisive over all six pairs of choices* and is therefore a dictator. In other words, if the design of the SWF meets the conditions *U*, *P* and *I*, and allows one individual to override the opposition of all others on just *one* pairwise choice, then it effectively allows him to have his way on *all* pairwise choices whatever the preferences of the others. This might perhaps be taken as a salutary warning not to allow an almost decisive individual in design of the SWF, if it were not for the second part of the proof, which shows that there is *always* such an individual for any SWF with properties *U*, *P* and *I*.

First, note that taking any pair of alternatives, say (a, b), the set of all three individuals {1, 2, 3} must be decisive for this pair since by *P*, if $(a, b)_i$, $i = 1, 2, 3$, then $[a, b]$. Thus for every pair of alternatives at least one decisive set of individuals exists, namely {1, 2, 3}. It may be that for some pairs a smaller decisive set of individuals exists, e.g. if $(b, c)_i \Rightarrow [b, c]$ for $i = 1, 2$, then {1, 2} is a decisive set for this pair. Moreover, any decisive set must be almost decisive. What we have to prove is that for some pair there exists an almost decisive set containing just one individual.

The proof proceeds by contradiction: suppose any almost decisive set has more than one member. Given that for each pair of alternatives there is at least one almost decisive set, we take the almost decisive set with fewest elements – it must contain either two or three individuals. For concreteness suppose it is the set {1, 2}, and let $(a, b)_i$, $i = 1, 2$. *Because of condition U*, we are free to assume the following pattern of preferences: $(a, b, c)_1$, $(c, a, b)_2$, and $(b, c, a)_3$. Since $\{1, 2\}$ is almost decisive for (a, b) we must have $[a, b]$. Only individual 2 prefers c to b, and so if $[c, b]$, he would be an almost decisive individual which is ruled out by assumption. Therefore we can take it that $[b, c]$ (strictly, b and c could be socially indifferent but this turns out not to matter). Therefore the transitivity of the social ordering implies $[a, c]$. But looking again at the individual orderings we see that $(a, c)_1$, $(c, a)_2$, $(c, a)_3$, and so individual 1 is almost decisive over (a, c). But this contradicts the assertion that there is no almost decisive individual, which is therefore false.

Consequences of the theorem

The method of proof of the theorem was to show that an SWF producing a transitive social preference ordering and satisfying conditions U, P and I must allow for the existence of a dictator. It would be wrong however to interpret this as implying that 'dictatorship is inevitable' or indeed that there is any *particular* difficulty in defining an SWF which meets condition D. Rather it is the *full set* of requirements, including that of a transitive social ordering, which has been proved to be *mutually* incompatible. The impossibility result can be made to disappear by relaxing an appropriately chosen requirement. For example, the consequence of dropping U, the unrestricted domain condition, was discussed earlier (see also Question 2, Exercise 13F). It might be argued that in a given social group it is unreasonable to allow all possible logical combinations of individual orderings. The nature of social relationships may be such as to suggest certain patterns of orderings, and SWFs may exist satisfying conditions P, I and D for such patterns.

Alternatively, it has been suggested that the requirement that the SWF produce a *transitive* social preference ordering is unnecessarily stringent (see Sen, 1970, ch. 4). If what we want is a definite choice of an alternative out of a given set, then transitivity is sufficient but not necessary. A somewhat weaker condition of *acyclicity*, which, in terms of the social ordering, means that if $[a, b]$ and $[b, c]$ then we do not have $[c, a]$, is all that is required for social choice. Moreover, Sen shows that SWFs exist which satisfy conditions U, P, I, D and yield acyclic orderings.

Each of Arrow's conditions has been closely examined to see if more scope can be found for the possibility of the existence of an SWF. The reader is referred to Sen (1970) for an exhaustive treatment of the literature.

EXERCISE 13F

1. Construct examples where three individuals' preference orderings over three social states are all different, but the majority voting rule yields a transitive social preference ordering.

2. Suppose, in the second step in the proof of Arrow's Theorem, that the smallest almost decisive set was $\{1, 2, 3\}$. Show that the proof carries through nevertheless. (*Hint*: partition the set into $\{1\}$, $\{2, 3\}$, assume $(a, b, c)_1$, $(c, a, b)_i$, $i = 2, 3$, and show that, if 1 is not almost decisive over (a, c), $\{1, 2\}$ must be almost decisive over (b, c).)

3. Explain the difference between transitivity and acyclicity. Why is the latter a weaker requirement?

Appendix: Second Theorem of Welfare Economics

STWE: If individuals have strictly increasing, strictly convex preferences and firms have convex production possibility sets then any Pareto efficient allocation in which all individuals have strictly positive consumption of all goods can be achieved as the competitive equilibrium generated by some distribution of initial endowments.

Proof

We use the same notation as in the formal proof of FTWE. Suppose that A^* is a Pareto efficient allocation. We wish to show that this implies that there is a vector $p^* = (p_1^*, \ldots, p_n^*)$ such that $p^*, x^{1*}, \ldots, x^{H*}, y^{1*}, \ldots, y^{J*}$ is a competitive equilibrium for a suitable choice of initial endowments $\bar{x} = (\bar{x}^1, \ldots, \bar{x}^H)$ and shareholdings $(\beta^1, \ldots, \beta^H)$ where $\beta^h = (\beta_{h1}, \ldots, \beta_{hJ})$. Thus we must show that the conditions (a), (b) and (c) in section D (page 297) defining a competitive equilibrium are satisfied.

The proof requires the *Minkowski Theorem on Separating Hyperplanes*. A hyperplane is the n dimensional analogue of a line in two dimensions or a plane in three dimensions. A hyperplane H in n-dimensional space is the set of vectors x which satisfy $\sum_i p_i x_i = K$ for constants $p_i \neq 0$ $(i = 1, \ldots, n)$ and $K : H = \{x : px = K, p \neq 0\}$. Consider two convex sets B and C where the interior of B is not empty and C does not contain any points in the interior of B. The Minkowski theorem states that it is always possible to find a hyperplane which separates the two sets, i.e. that there exists a $p \neq 0$ and K such that

$$px \geqslant K \qquad \text{all } x \text{ in } B \qquad\qquad [1]$$

$$px \leqslant K \qquad \text{all } x \text{ in } C \qquad\qquad [2]$$

Readers should draw some two-dimensional diagrams to illustrate the result. In two dimensions the theorem asserts that it is always possible to draw a straight line with the property that all points in one of the sets are on or above the line and all points in the other are on or below the line. Notice that B and C can have boundary points in common (Fig. 13.10).

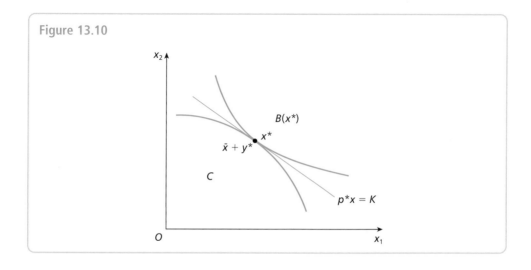

Figure 13.10

Condition (a)

We first use the separation theorem to establish that we can find a vector p^* which satisfies condition (a) of the definition of competitive equilibrium. Recall from section 2A the definition of the better set $B^h(x^{h*})$ as the set of consumption vectors which consumer h regards as being at least as good as x^{h*}. The assumption that preferences are convex means that $B^h(x^{h*})$ is convex. Let $B(x^*)$ be the sum of the sets $B^h(x^{h*})$ over all consumers. Since it is the sum of convex sets it is also convex. $B(x^*)$ is the set of aggregate consumption bundles $\sum_h x^h$ which can be allocated among the consumers in such a way as to make them all at least as well off as they are at x^{h*}. Non-satiation implies that any $x > x^*$ is in the interior of $B(x^*)$ since x can always be allocated so that $x^h > x^{h*}$. Thus $B(x^*)$ has a non-empty interior.

The aggregate production possibility set Y is the sum of the production possibility sets of the firms and is the set of feasible aggregate net outputs. Since all production possibility sets Y^j are convex the aggregate production possibility set is also convex. The other means of providing for consumption is the aggregated initial endowment vector $\bar{x}$. Define C as the set of feasible aggregate consumption bundles: $C = \{x : x \leqslant \bar{x} + y, y \in Y)$ which is also convex. No $x \in C$ can be in the interior of B. If it was then it would be possible to allocate x so as to make at least one individual better off than at x^{h*} and no individual worse off and since x is feasible the allocation A^* where consumer h gets x^{h*} cannot have been Pareto efficient. Hence the conditions for the separation theorem are satisfied and there exists a vector p^* and a constant K such that [1] and [2] hold. The assumption that preferences are strictly increasing implies that an efficient allocation will not waste any of the commodities: $x^* = \bar{x} + y^*$ and so x^* is in C. x^* is in $B(x^*)$ (on its boundary) so we must have $p^*x^* \geqslant K$ and since it is also in C we have $K \geqslant p^*x^*$ and so

$$p^*x^* = K \tag{3}$$

Applying [1] with $K = p^*x^*$ gives

$$p^*x - p^*x^* = p^*[x - x^*] = \sum_i p_i^*[x_i - x_i^*] \geqslant 0 \qquad \text{all } x \in B \tag{4}$$

In particular, [4] holds for all $x \geqslant x^*$ (since all such x are in B) which implies that $p_i^* \geqslant 0$ for all i. (If $p_s^* < 0$ for some s choose an $x \geqslant x^*$ where $x_s > x_s^*$ and $x_i = x_i^*$ for all other i which violates the inequality.)

Thus we have established that $p^* \geqslant 0$ which is the first part of condition (a). Since a Pareto efficient allocation is feasible, the second part is also satisfied: $x_i^* - \bar{x}_i - y_i^* \leqslant 0$, all i. The assumption that utility is strictly increasing in all commodities implies that the efficient allocation has $x_i^* = \bar{x}_i + y_i^*$ and so the third part is satisfied: $p_i^*[x_i^* - \bar{x}_i - y_i^*] = 0$.

Condition (b)

Condition B requires that $p^*y^{j*} \geqslant p^*y^j$ for all $y^j \in Y^j$. Since $x^* = \bar{x} + y^*$, [2] and [3] give

$$p^*x^* = K = p^*[\bar{x} + y^*] \geqslant p^*[\bar{x} + y] \qquad \text{all } y \in Y \tag{5}$$

Subtracting $p^*\bar{x}$ from both sides of the last inequality gives

$$p^*y^* = \sum_j p^*y^{j*} \geqslant \sum_j p^*y^j = p^*y \qquad \text{all } y \in Y \tag{6}$$

The sum of the firms' profits $\sum_j py^j$ cannot be maximized unless each firm's profit is maximized which establishes condition (b).

Condition (c)

Suppose that the initial endowments $\bar{x}$ and shareholdings β are chosen so that each individual h has an income such that h can purchase x^{h*} at prices p^*:

$$R^h = p^* \bar{x}^h + \sum_j \beta_{hj} p^* y^{j*} = p^* x^{h*} \qquad [7]$$

Such a distribution of endowments is always possible since summing [7] over all h gives $p^* \bar{x} + p^* y^* = p^* x^*$ which must hold since it is a rearrangement of the last part of condition (a) which we have already established. Condition (c) requires that x^{h*} maximizes u^h subject to $p^* x^h \leq R^h = p^* \bar{x}^h + \sum_j \beta_{hj} p^* y^{j*}$ for all h. We show that it does by demonstrating that the equivalent requirements [D.12] and [D.13] are satisfied. Consider $\hat{x} = (\hat{x}^1, x^{2*}, \ldots, x^{H*})$ where $u^1(\hat{x}^1) \geq u^1(x^{1*})$. Since $\hat{x} \in B(x^*)$ we have from [4]

$$p^* \hat{x} = p^* \hat{x}^1 + p^* \sum_{h=2}^{H} x^{h*} \geq p^* x^{1*} + p^* \sum_{h=2}^{H} x^{h*} = p^* x^* \qquad [8]$$

and so

$$u^1(\hat{x}^1) \geq u^1(x^{1*}) \qquad \text{implies} \qquad p^* \hat{x}^1 \geq p^* x^{1*} \qquad [9]$$

Repeating the argument for $h = 2, \ldots, H$ shows that [D.12] holds. Now suppose that $u^1(\hat{x}^1) > u^1(x^{1*})$. [9] tells us that $p^* \hat{x}^1 \geq p^* x^{1*}$. Assume that $p^* \hat{x}^1 = p^* x^{1*}$. Since we have shown that $p^* \geq 0$ and assumed that $x^{1*} > 0$ we have $p^* \hat{x}^1 = p^* x^{1*} > 0$. Now choose some number $0 < \theta < 1$ with $u^1(\theta \hat{x}^1) > u^1(x^{1*})$ which is always possible given that u^h is continuous. But the same argument that established [9] for $\hat{x}^1$ can be applied to the bundle $\theta \hat{x}^1$ and so

$$p^* \theta \hat{x}^1 \geq p^* x^{1*} = p^* \hat{x}^1$$

which is impossible since $0 < \theta < 1$. Thus, since [9] is true and we have just proved that $p^* \hat{x}^1 \neq p^* x^{1*}$, it must be the case that

$$u^1(\hat{x}^1) > u^1(x^{1*}) \qquad \text{implies} \qquad p^* \hat{x}^1 > p^* x^{1*} \qquad [10]$$

The same arguments show that [10] holds for all other $h = 2, \ldots, H$ and so we have now proved that, for all h, x^{h*} does maximize $u^h(x^h)$ subject to $p^* x^h \leq R^h = p^* \bar{x}^h + \sum_j \beta_{hj} p^* y^{j*}$. QED

It is possible to weaken the conditions on preferences and the requirement that $x^{h*} > 0$ for all h. (See Takayama, 1985, ch. 2C.)

Market failure and government failure

In the previous chapter it was shown that the resource allocation at the equilibrium of a competitive market system is Pareto efficient. We now consider the circumstances under which markets may fail to allocate resources efficiently and whether and how government action can correct this market failure.

The conventional approach to market failure is to list the situations in which resource misallocation may occur: monopoly, interdependence of economic agents external to the market mechanism, public goods, common access resources and so on. However, a deeper analysis of these *instances* of market failure suggests that underlying them all is a common set of fundamental *causes* relating to property rights, information and transactions costs. For example, the existence of a single seller is not in itself *sufficient* to lead to a market outcome in which there are unexploited gains from trade, i.e. in which there is market failure. Examination of the causes of market failure gives insight into the market mechanism as well as a better understanding of particular instances of market failure and the means of their correction. Accordingly, in section A we consider the causes of market failure and, in section B, the specific instances of resource misallocation.

The observation that markets may fail has been a major factor in supporting microeconomic activity by governments. In the last two sections of the chapter we consider the theory of the second best, which is concerned with government policy in an economy characterized by market failure, and the concept of 'government failure', which stems from the observation that it is misleading to assume an omniscient and altruistic central policy-maker if we wish to analyse government action.

A. The causes of market failure

A market is an institution in which individuals or firms exchange not just commodities, but the *rights* to use them in particular ways for particular lengths of time. For example, when a consumer buys a motor car, he buys not just a physical asset but the rights to use that asset in certain specified ways. He acquires the right to drive on public highways, at certain speeds, carrying specified numbers of passengers. He may have the rights to park on the public highway without payment, to prevent other individuals using the car without his consent, and so on. When an employer hires a worker she buys the right to direct the worker to perform certain tasks at certain times for a specified period. These rights, which define the uses to which the assets may be put, are known as *property rights*. Markets are institutions which organize the *exchange of control* of commodities, where the nature of the control is defined by the property rights attached to the commodity.

We saw in the previous chapter that, if marginal rates of substitution between two goods are not equal for two consumers, allocation would be inefficient: it would be possible by rearranging consumption vectors to make at least one individual better off and no-one worse off. In such a situation there is the possibility of mutually advantageous trade between the two individuals. Thus if $MRS_{21}^1 = 5$ and $MRS_{21}^2 = 3$, a contract whereby individual 1 sold one unit of x_1 to individual 2 in exchange for four units of x_2 would make both individuals better off. Alternatively, an arbitrager could make contracts with both individuals whereby the arbitrager traded $3\frac{1}{2}$ units of x_2 for one unit of x_1 with individual 1 and one unit of x_1 for $4\frac{1}{2}$ units of x_2 with individual 2. As a result both individuals would be better off and the arbitrager would make a profit of one unit of x_2.

The example is an illustration of a general rule which follows from the very definition of Pareto efficiency. If there is inefficiency it is possible, by exchange or production, to make at least one person better off without making anyone else worse off. Inefficiency implies the existence of potentially mutually advantageous trades or profitable production decisions. Hence the question of why a particular resource allocation mechanism is inefficient can be rephrased as the question of why such advantageous or profitable exchanges or production decisions do not occur. Given that individuals would wish to make themselves better off by trade or production, inefficiency can only persist: (a) if individuals do not have sufficient control over commodities (including productive assets) to effect profitable or advantageous exchanges and production; (b) if transaction and information costs exceed the gains from trade; or (c) if the individuals cannot agree on how to share the gains from their mutually advantageous exchange.

Insufficient control: imperfect excludability and non-transferability

An individual's control over commodities is defined by the system of property rights, and a system of property rights can be incomplete because of *imperfect excludability* or because of *non-transferability*.

Imperfect excludability arises when effective control of a commodity is not conferred on a single individual but rather on a (possibly very large) group of individuals. Control of a commodity or asset means the ability to determine who shall use it, in what circumstances, for what length of time and under what terms. When control is vested in a group, an individual who wishes to acquire that control must enter into contracts with all the individuals in the group, and this may be so difficult or costly (for reasons examined below) that no individual can acquire exclusive control. Consider the example of the level of traffic on a public road which, as the name suggests, is an asset 'owned' by all, in the sense that everyone with a valid driving licence, insurance certificate and roadworthy vehicle has the right to drive on the road. An individual who wishes to acquire control of the level of traffic on the road would have to enter into contracts with every actual or potential road user, whereby the road user agreed, in return for some suitable consideration, to limit his use of the road in some specified fashion. The difficulties of this procedure indicate why there is no market for the control of the use of public roads. Commodities or assets with this characteristic are described variously as *non-exclusive, common-property* or *free access* resources because all the joint owners (which may be every individual in the economy) have the right to use them in particular ways. Further possible examples are common grazing lands, ocean fishing grounds, beaches, public parks and rivers.

Control may also be defined in terms of the ability to *exclude* any individuals, i.e. to determine who shall *not* use the commodity. The first requirement for excludability, as we have seen, is one of law: the property rights attached to a commodity must allow one group of individuals to prevent all individuals outside the group from using the commodity. The legal *right* to exclude must also be supported by the *ability* to enforce that right. In many cases enforcement of the right to exclude is simple and inexpensive. The consumer who purchases a loaf of bread has a very good chance, in a reasonably law-abiding society, of getting it home and consuming it without incurring significant costs of excluding others from consuming it. The supermarket which sells the loaf has a more difficult task of preventing consumers from removing goods they have not paid for, and it has to incur the expense of hiring checkout and security staff. Cinemas, theatres and football grounds have to install box offices and turnstiles, print tickets and employ staff to ensure that all who enjoy the entertainment provided have paid and that those who have paid for low-priced seats do not occupy high-priced seats. In addition to attempting to prevent unauthorized use of their property, individuals may also have to devote resources to the detection and punishment if unauthorized use does occur. The costs of preventing, detecting and punishing unauthorized use are *exclusion costs*. They depend on the legal and social framework of the economy and on the state of technology. For example if the maximum punishments for unauthorized use of some assets are reduced, more resources must be devoted to prevention and detection. Inventions such as barbed wire or better burglar alarms reduce exclusion costs.

Potentially advantageous trades or exchanges may not take place because of imperfect excludability. It may be impossible for an individual to acquire effective control or exclusive use of the good or asset in question, either because of the lack of a legal right to exclude, or because high exclusion costs more than outweigh the gains from trade. Similarly, potentially beneficial production may not occur if individuals making production decisions cannot exclude other individuals from the benefits of the decision. Farmers will have little incentive to plant crops if the law permits anybody to harvest the crops without the consent of the farmer. The lack of exclusion dissipates the benefits of the increased output among many individuals and hence reduces any single individual's incentives to bear the costs necessary to produce the extra output.

Non-transferability arises when the legal right to exclude is vested in a single individual and exclusion costs are low, but the owner of the asset or good does not have the unrestricted legal right to *transfer* use or ownership to any individual on any terms. Lack of transferability may take the extreme form of a complete absence of the right to transfer any of the property rights associated with the good or asset on any terms to anybody. For example, squatters who occupy land or property without the consent of the owner of the land may have the right to uninterrupted use and enjoyment of the property, but they do not have the right to sell it; tenants may hold property on leases which do not permit sub-letting; land may be entailed, i.e. owned by an individual in the sense that he can exclude others, but he cannot sell the land to anyone. Less extreme is the case of labour: individuals own their labour and can sell it for limited periods, but the law does not permit permanent transfer of control over labour: slavery is illegal. Milder forms of reduced transferability exist when individuals are constrained in the terms on which they can conclude an exchange, as for example when maximum or minimum prices are fixed by law; or when the hours during which trades may take place are prescribed; or when trade must be carried on in specified locations. There may also be restrictions on *which* individuals may trade: those aged under 18 years cannot buy alcohol from licensed premises, but they can consume it; gunsmiths cannot sell arms to people who do not have a firearms licence; taxis cannot ply for hire unless licensed by the local authority. Thus, restrictions on the terms of exchange may prevent or inhibit trades which the parties perceive to be mutually advantageous.

Information and transaction costs

Exchange requires information: the identity and location of potential buyers and sellers must be known; the terms on which they are prepared to trade must be ascertained; and the quality of goods or services to be exchanged and the property rights attached to them must be checked. Acquiring such information may be costly. Individuals may have to incur *search* costs to find trading partners and *observation* costs to discover the quality of what is being exchanged. There will be costs of negotiating and specifying the terms of exchanges and of enforcing them. Such information and transaction costs may be so great that potentially advantageous contracts are not made or contracts may be incomplete, leaving some potential gains unexploited. We have already noted the importance of such costs in our discussion of the boundaries of markets and firms in Chapter 5 and we consider further implications of imperfect information in Chapters 20 and 21.

Bargaining problems

Mutually advantageous trades may not be concluded because of the failure of the trading parties to agree upon terms. For example, in Chapter 13, Fig. 13.2, *any* bargain by which individual 1 exchanges some of good x_1 for some of individual 2's x_2, such that there is a movement from A^0 to a point on C between the indifference curves through A^0, will make both individuals better off. There is an infinite number of such bargains; they differ in the final utility levels achieved by the individuals. Individual 1 will obviously prefer to trade at a low price of x_2 in terms of x_1 since she is buying x_2 with her x_1; individual 2 prefers to trade at a higher price. Both will gain from the trade but the division of the gains from trade depends on the precise terms of the bargain. This may lead to lengthy and costly bargaining and in some cases the parties may not be able to reach agreement at all, especially if they do not have the same information about potential gains from trade.

Failure to agree stems in part from the *multiplicity* of possible terms. If the only alternatives open to the parties were to trade at some fixed terms or not at all, then there is nothing for them to bargain about: if the prescribed terms make both parties better off they will trade; if the terms make either party worse off they will not trade. Both parties treat the prescribed terms as parameters which cannot be altered by their actions. At the equilibrium of a competitive market there is a single price which is taken as given by every trader. There is no scope for bargaining and no failure to conclude mutually advantageous trades because of lack of agreement on terms. In equilibrium, no seller will ask and no buyer would pay a price exceeding the market price, because any buyer confronted with a higher price will buy from another seller at the market price. Similarly, no seller will offer, or buyer ask for, a price below the market price because sellers all know they can sell at the market price to other buyers.

B. Instances of market failure

We now examine some of the ways in which market failure manifests itself, relate them to the underlying causes of market failure and examine some government interventions which may increase efficiency.

Monopoly

As we have seen in Chapter 9, a monopolist maximizes profit by producing an output at which marginal revenue equals marginal cost. The monopolist's equilibrium is shown in Fig. 14.1, where q_m and p_m are the monopoly output and price, and we have assumed constant average and marginal costs for simplicity. The market is Pareto inefficient. The consumers would be prepared to pay up to p_m for an additional unit of output, and the cost of an additional unit is the monopolist's marginal cost MC. Since $MR = MC$ and $p_m > MR$ it follows that $p_m > MC$: consumers are willing to pay more for an extra unit than its cost of production. If consumers actually paid something less than p_m but more than MC for the additional unit, *while continuing to pay $p_m q_m$ for the units already produced*, both monopolist and consumers would be better off: the monopolist's profit increases, while consumers obtain extra consumption at a price which is less than its value to them.

The Pareto efficient output is at the point where consumers' willingness to pay for an extra unit, measured by the height of the demand curve, is equal to the cost of the extra unit. This is the output $q*$ where the demand curve cuts the marginal cost curve. Since the monopoly price and output are inefficient there are potential gains to consumers and monopolist if output is increased from q_m to the level $q*$. One contract between monopolist and consumers which would lead to the efficient output is for the monopolist to agree to sell output $q*$ at a price $p*$ equal to marginal cost. Since profit on sales would fall by $(p_m - p*)q_m$ the consumers would have to agree to pay a lump sum of at least this magnitude. They could do so and still be better off

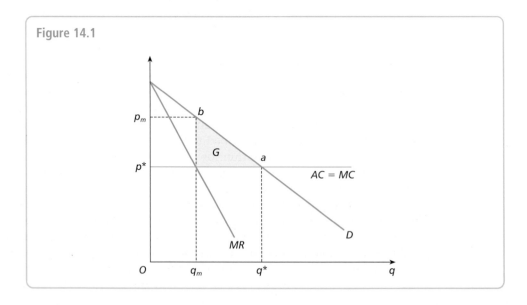

Figure 14.1

since the gain to them of a fall in price is measured by the area $p_m bap^*$. (Recall the discussion of consumer's surplus in Chapter 3.) This area exceeds $(p_m - p^*)q_m$ by G, which is the gain available for division between the monopolist and consumers. (In section 9D we showed that, if certain value judgements were made, G is a measure of welfare loss.)

Why does inefficiency persist under monopoly? The answer must be that, for the reasons outlined in section A, consumers and the producer fail to conclude a mutually satisfactory bargain. They may not be able to agree on the division of the gain from the increase in output. There may be very high costs associated with locating and organizing consumers, who may not be able to agree on how the burden of the lump-sum payment should be shared out. It may be impossible to prevent consumers who do not contribute to the lump-sum payment from enjoying the benefits (lower price) from the contract with the monopolists. (This type of failure through inability to exclude is known as the *free-rider problem*.) The monopolist therefore may be forced to make individual contracts with consumers. If the monopolist cannot prevent resale, it will have to set the same price in each contract. We then have the standard, inefficient monopoly in which the monopolist confronts a downward sloping demand curve and sets $MR = MC$. Consumers will treat prices as a parameter, since an individual consumer cannot persuade the monopolist to lower the price, because of the monopolist's inability to prevent resale.

Externality

An externality is said to exist if some of the variables which affect one decision-taker's utility or profit are under the control of another decision-taker. For example, a brewery sited downstream from a chemical works which pumps effluent into the stream will find that the cost of producing beer depends on its choice of output level and input combinations *and* on the amount of effluent which has to be removed from the water before it can be used in beer production. In this case the externality is *detrimental*, but in other cases there may be *beneficial externalities*, as for example when a bee-keeper is located next to an apple grower. The bees will cross-pollinate the apple trees, benefiting the orchard owner, and feed off the apple blossom, benefiting the bee-keeper. This is also an example of a *reciprocal externality*: the bee-keeper's output of honey depends on the number of apple trees; the output of apples depends on the number of beehives. In addition to such producer–producer externalities there may be consumer–consumer externalities (my utility depends on, among other things, your use of your personal stereo), producer–consumer externalities (residential area sited downwind of a smoky or odorous factory) and consumer–producer externalities (hikers damaging crops).

To see why externalities may lead to inefficiency, consider our first example of the upstream chemical factory and the downstream brewery. The chemical factory will set the level of its output to maximize its profits and will not take account of the effects of the resulting pollution on the profits of the brewery. But the brewery would be willing to pay the chemical works to reduce the amount of effluent. Such a reduction in effluent will reduce the chemical works' profits, perhaps because the firm's output of chemicals and the effluents are produced in fixed proportions and a reduction in effluent therefore requires a reduction in output of chemicals. If the reduction in the brewery's costs exceeds the reduction in the chemical factory's profit there are potential gains from trade and the initial level of effluent cannot have been efficient. This observation leads to a possible solution to the externality problem first analysed by Coase (1960).

The Coase Theorem

Let x denote the amount of effluent. If the chemical firm produces its saleable output of chemicals and the effluent in fixed proportions we can write its profit as a function of the amount of effluent produced: $B(x)$. The damage (reduced brewery profits) inflicted downstream by the pollution is $D(x)$. Fig. 14.2 plots the marginal benefit $B'(x)$ and marginal damage $D'(x)$ from pollution. Assuming that the profits of the two firms measure the social value of their outputs and that the effluent does not impose costs on any other individual, the efficient level of pollution maximizes the total profits of the two firms. The efficient level of pollution is x^* satisfying

$$B'(x^*) - D'(x^*) = 0 \qquad\qquad\qquad [\text{B.1}]$$

(We ignore corner solutions and assume that B is concave and D is convex in x so that [B.1] is also sufficient for efficiency. When is the efficient amount of pollution zero?)

Consider two alternative legal situations, perhaps determined by which firm first set up in business on the stream.

(a) *Permissive.* The chemical works has the legal right to discharge as much effluent as it wishes into the stream. It therefore controls x and would choose a level of x^1 where $B' = 0$. Here the level of pollution is inefficiently large because its effects on the brewery are ignored by the chemical firm.

(b) *Restrictive.* The chemical works has no legal right to discharge effluent and the brewery can obtain a court order to prevent it doing so. In this case the brewery controls the level of pollution and chooses a level $x^2 = 0$ where its costs from the effluent are minimized. A zero level of pollution is also inefficient (given our assumptions about $B(x)$ and $D(x)$) since the brewery ignores the effect of its choice on the profit of the chemical works.

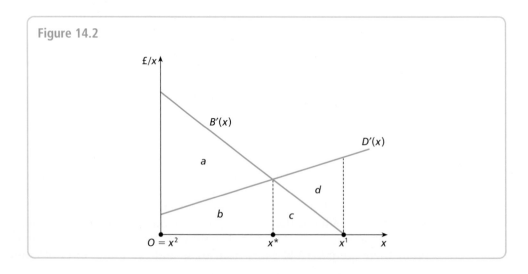

Figure 14.2

Since x^1 and x^2 are inefficient there are potential gains from trade, i.e. from a contract between the two firms to control the level of pollution. Suppose the legal regime is permissive and consider a reduction in pollution from x^1 to x^*. The reduction in the chemical firm's profit is c (the area under $B'(x)$ from x^1 to x^*) and the reduction in the brewery's costs is $c + d$ (the area under $D'(x)$ from x^1 to x^*). A contract whereby the brewery paid the chemical firm $c + \theta d$ ($0 < \theta < 1$) in exchange for a reduction in pollution from x^1 to x^* would achieve an efficient allocation of resources and make both firms better off. The brewery's profits would increase by $(c + d) - (c + \theta d) = (1 - \theta)d$ and the chemical firm's profits by $-c + (c + \theta d) = \theta d$. The contract would generate a combined gain from trade of d.

If the legal regime is restrictive a contract whereby the chemical works paid the brewery $\theta a + b$ in exchange for an increase in effluent from zero to x^* would lead to an efficient level of pollution and make both parties better off. The payment to the brewery would more than compensate for the increase in costs b and the chemical works increase in profit $a + b$ would more than cover the payment to the brewery. The contract would split the gains from trade a between the two firms.

This is a simple example of a general result known as the *Coase Theorem: bargaining can achieve an efficient allocation of resources whatever the initial assignment of property rights*. If the affected parties can contract with each other the externality will be internalized and the party who has the legal right to control the level of pollution will take account of its effects on the other. The initial assignment of rights *does* affect the distribution of income. Under a permissive law an efficient bargain increases the polluter's profit by θd and under a restrictive regime an efficient bargain increases it by θa.

Despite the scope for private bargaining inefficiencies arising from externalities persist for a variety of reasons. In 'small number' externality situations, there may be failure to agree on the division of the gains from a move to a more efficient allocation. In 'large number' externality cases (as when a factory pollutes over a large area) the absence of contracting between polluter and victims may arise from any of the reasons mentioned at the end of our discussion of monopoly. The free-rider problem, for example, is likely to be important, because it will be difficult for the polluter to control the pollution level for a particular victim. Reductions in pollution will tend to benefit all victims in the area. Hence individual victims will have a reduced incentive to contract individually with the polluter, since they will benefit from contracts made between the polluter and other victims to which they are not party. Similarly, a contract between the polluter and a voluntary association of victims: it will be difficult to exclude those who do not pay for a reduction in pollution from benefiting. In addition, the legal situation may not be well defined, so that it is not clear whether the polluter has the legal right to pollute, or his victims the legal right to protection from his pollution. Establishing through the courts who has the ownership of 'the right to pollute' may be very costly. Even if the market in pollution is established it may not be competitive. A single polluter confronting many victims may act like a monopolist with respect to changes in the level of pollution. There is, therefore, interest in public intervention as a solution to the externality problem.

Pigovian taxes

If the parties cannot internalize the externality via a Coasian bargain it may be possible to mitigate the inefficiency by government action. Pigou suggested that externalities could be internalized by a suitable set of taxes or subsidies. Suppose the legal regime is permissive, so that a polluter would choose an inefficiently high level of pollution. Placing a tax of t per unit on the output of pollution would give the polluter a profit function of $B(x) - tx$ and the level of pollution chosen would satisfy $B'(x) - t = 0$. If the Pigovian tax rate was set at the marginal damage imposed by the polluter's efficient pollution level: $t = D'(x^*)$, the polluter would be led to choose the efficient amount of pollution where

$$B'(x^*) = t = D'(x^*) \qquad\qquad [\text{B.2}]$$

By making the polluter pay the marginal damage imposed by pollution the tax internalizes the externality.

Apart from the obvious difficulties of obtaining the information necessary to calculate the correct rate of tax, there are potential problems with Pigovian taxes. If the parties can bargain about the level of the externality a Pigovian tax on the polluter will not lead to efficiency. Thus in Fig. 14.3 the effect of the tax is to shift the polluter's marginal benefit curve down from $B'(x)$ to $B'(x) - t$ and the polluter will maximize after tax profit by choosing x^*. But suppose that the chemical works and the brewery can still negotiate. At x^* the brewery suffers positive marginal damage from pollution whereas the marginal after tax benefit to the polluter is zero. A bargain to reduce x to x^0 could make both of them better off (the reader should supply the argument). Such a bargain reduces the government's tax revenue by $t(x^* - x^0)$ which is larger than the private gain from the bargain. The new allocation at x^0 is Pareto inefficient: it would be possible to increase tax revenue and make both firms better off if x was increased from x^0 to x^*. If private bargaining is possible efficiency can be achieved without Pigovian taxes. One justification for such taxes might be that they lead to a 'better' distribution of income since, compared with the outcome of Coasian bargains under a permissive regime, they make the victims of pollution better off and the polluters worse off. If this justification is accepted and an efficient allocation is to be achieved by Pigovian taxes, it is necessary to ensure that private bargains do not occur.

A tax on polluters could be combined with a subsidy to those who suffer from an externality to compensate them for the damage imposed. If such a subsidy is paid it

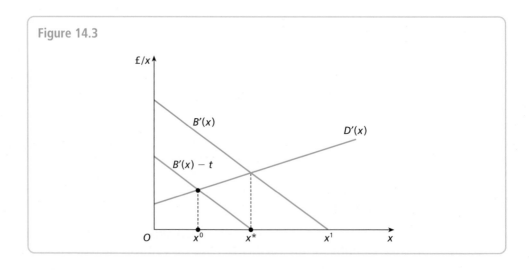

Figure 14.3

may remove any incentive for private bargaining between the parties. Thus suppose that out of the proceeds of the Pigovian tax the brewery was paid a subsidy equal to the damage it suffers from the effluent. Since the brewery's profit is now unaffected by the amount of effluent it has no incentive to bargain with the chemical works to reduce x (its marginal post-subsidy damage curve is the horizontal axis). The combination of a Pigovian tax and a compensatory subsidy leads to efficiency, even if the parties could make Coasian bargains, *provided that the brewery can do nothing to alter the damage that it suffers.*

The magnitude of the effects of most externalities can be influenced by the actions of *both* parties, not just the party who ostensibly causes the externality. For example, victims of noise pollution can fit sound insulation or move to less noisy areas. The brewery might be able to use a different production process which required less water or sink a well to get less polluted water. In such cases efficiency requires that both parties mitigate the damage. We leave it to the exercises to demonstrate that efficient mitigation by both parties can be achieved by a Coasian bargain. Instead we will demonstrate that paying compensation to the brewery when it can influence the costs imposed by the effluent leads to inefficiency. Suppose the damage function is $D(x, z)$ where z is expenditure by the brewery to reduce the damage imposed: $D_z < 0$. Let $S(D)$ be the compensatory subsidy paid to the brewery. The brewery will choose z to maximize $S(D) - D - z$ and so z will satisfy the Kuhn–Tucker condition

$$S'(D)D_z - D_z - 1 = D_z(x, z)[S'(D) - 1] - 1 \leqslant 0 \qquad z \geqslant 0 \qquad \text{[B.3]}$$

But efficiency requires that $B(x) - D(x, z) - z$ is maximized, which implies

$$-D_z(x, z) - 1 = 0 \qquad \text{[B.4]}$$

(We assume $-D_z(x, 0) > 1$ if $x > 0$ so that it is always efficient for the brewery to undertake cost reducing expenditure if there is any effluent in the stream.) Comparing [B.3] and [B.4] we see that paying full compensation ($S = D$) to the brewery eliminates its incentive to reduce the damage it suffers: since $S'(D) = 1$ the brewery sets $z = 0$. In general if the compensation varies with the amount of damage suffered ($S'(D) > 0$) there will be a less than efficient level of mitigation expenditure.

Common property resources

A common property resource is an asset whose services are used in production or consumption and which is not owned by any one individual. Examples include ocean fisheries (anyone may fish outside territorial waters), common grazing land (anyone satisfying certain requirements, such as residence in a particular area, may graze as many cattle as they wish on the land) and public roads (any motorist with a valid driving licence may drive a roadworthy insured vehicle on public roads). We suggested earlier that common ownership can cause inefficiency and we will now show this a little more rigorously. Take the case of a lake in which all members of a community have the right to fish. For simplicity assume that the total catch (the 'output' of fish from the lake) depends only on the total time spent fishing by all individuals:

$$q = f(L) = f(\Sigma L_i) \qquad \text{[B.5]}$$

Figure 14.4

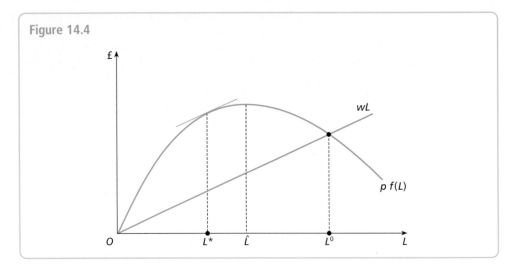

where q is the total catch, L_i is time spent fishing by the ith individual and $L = \sum L_i$ is total time spent fishing. $f(L)$ is strictly concave in L and reaches a maximum at $\hat{L}$ (see Fig. 14.4). The ith individual's catch q_i is

$$q_i = (L_i/L)f(L) \qquad [\text{B.6}]$$

The assumptions underlying [B.6] are that everyone is equally skilful, can fish anywhere in the lake, and the fish can swim anywhere in the lake. Hence the proportion of the total catch made by i is simply the proportion of total fishing effort accounted for by i's labour input: $q_i/q = L_i/L$. Alternatively, output per unit of labour input is q/L and so L_i hours spent fishing yield a catch of L_iq/L.

Assume that variations in total fish output from the lake have no effect on the price of fish p and that variations in the total labour input to fishing in the lake have no effect on the wage rate w. The individuals each wish to maximize their individual profit

$$\pi_i = pq_i - wL_i$$

where π_i is i's profit. Hence each sets L_i so that

$$\frac{d\pi_i}{dL_i} = \frac{d}{dL_i}\left(\frac{pL_if(L)}{L} - wL_i\right)$$

$$= p[q/L + (L_i/L)(f' - q/L)] - w = 0 \qquad [\text{B.7}]$$

When [B.7] is satisfied each individual is maximizing profit and is earning a positive profit. Write profit π_i as

$$pq_i - wL_i = (pq/L - w)L_i$$

which is positive, for $L_i > 0$, if and only if

$$pq/L - w > 0$$

Now by our assumption that marginal product is declining ($f'' < 0$) marginal product f' is less than average product q/L. Hence, from [B.7],

$$pq/L - w = p(L_i/L)(q/L - f') > 0$$

and positive profits are made.

Positive profits will attract more individuals to the lake since there are no restrictions on entry to a free access resource. Entry will continue until each individual provides a very small share of the total labour input and π_i tends to zero with L_i/L. The full equilibrium will be characterized by an arbitrarily large number of individuals, each earning zero profit, and hence total industry profits are zero:

$$pq - wL = 0 \qquad \text{[B.8]}$$

This is illustrated in Fig. 14.4 where $pq = pf(L)$ shows the total value of fish produced and wL the cost of the labour employed. The free access equilibrium is at L^0 where $pq = wL$ and [B.8] is satisfied.

At the equilibrium total labour input L^0 a reduction in total fishing effort, say to $\hat{L}$, would increase total output. The wage rate is low enough for [B.8] to hold where the marginal product is negative. The outcome is inefficient as long as the output of fish has a positive value and labour devoted to fishing has an opportunity cost. To examine the efficiency of cases where marginal product is positive at equilibrium we have to make some assumptions about the marginal social value of fish and the marginal social cost of labour. Assume that they are measured by the market prices of fish (p) and labour (w). Hence the net social benefit from fishing in the lake is

$$pq - wL$$

which is maximized when

$$pf' - w = 0 \qquad \text{[B.9]}$$

In terms of Fig. 14.4 the efficient level of L is L^*, where the vertical distance between the pq and wL curves is greatest. Notice that by comparing [B.9] and [B.7] L^* is always less than L^0 since $f' < q/L$: free access always leads to overfishing if there are diminishing returns. The intersection of wL and $pf(L)$ in the figure always occurs at a value of L greater than that at which their slopes are equal.

The efficient outcome could be achieved if all the individuals with fishing rights can agree to reduce their total labour to L^*. Such an agreement may not be very likely if there are a large number of individuals with fishing rights or if it is difficult to police the agreement. Any individual will always find it profitable to break the agreement. The marginal profit from extra L_i is (see [B.7])

$$p[q/L + (L_i/L)(f' - q/L)] - w \qquad \text{[B.10]}$$

and at L^* we have $pf' = w$ from [B.9]. Substituting for w in [B.10] and rearranging gives

$$d\pi_i/dL_i = p(q/L - f')(1 - L_i/L) > 0$$

and so there will always be an incentive for an individual to increase labour input. One solution is to divide the lake among the individual fishermen and give each of them exclusive fishing rights to part of the lake. These rights will, however, require policing and enforcing and this may be costly. An alternative solution, which might not require so large an expenditure on exclusion, would be to vest ownership of the lake in one individual. Since, on our assumptions, total profit from fish production from the lake is the net social benefit, maximization of profit then leads to the efficient labour input (*provided the final fish market remains competitive*).

Unrestricted access can lead to overly intensive use, but it may also cause other kinds of inefficiency because it weakens the incentive to individual decision-takers to invest in improvements to the productivity of the resource, or to pay regard to the possibility of extinction of the fish stock through overfishing. Since a single individual cannot prevent others from using the resource, the benefits from investment or voluntary restraint will be spread over all other users, rather than being appropriated by him or herself. As a result it will not pay any single decision-taker to undertake the investment (for example improving the fish stock), or to restrict his or her catch, even though the total benefits to all users exceed the cost. Even if the share of the benefits accruing to a single individual exceeds the cost of the investment, it may not be undertaken if each individual believes that he or she will benefit from the investment of other users. Because of non-excludability, investment by other users is a substitute for investment by any particular individual and, if all individuals realize this, no investment may occur.

There is inefficiency in this case because no market can exist in the absence of well-defined and easily enforceable rights to exclude by any *single* individual. There is nothing, in other words, which can be exchanged and no means by which individuals can capture or be made to bear *all* the results of their actions.

Public goods

The defining characteristic of a public good is that it is *non-rival*: consumption of it by one individual does not actually or potentially reduce the amount available to be consumed by another individual. Examples include radio and television broadcasts and national defence. Any individual can listen to or watch the output of a broadcasting station, without preventing any other individual who possesses a radio or television receiver from consuming the same output. Any individual can increase their consumption of television broadcasts up to the total number of hours broadcast, without reducing any other individual's actual or potential consumption. Broadcasts are an example of an *optional* public good in that one can choose to consume any amount of the output produced, including zero. Defence, which is the protection of civil and property rights against external threats, is a *non-optional* public good. All inhabitants of the country consume the total quantity provided: if one inhabitant is defended, all will be.

In the case of non-optional public goods, if we denote the total quantity produced by q and the quantity consumed by the ith individual by $q_i (i = 1, \ldots, n)$,

$$q_1 = q_2 = \ldots = q_n = q \qquad [\text{B.11}]$$

By contrast, a private good has the characteristic that, with a given output, an increase in one individual's consumption of a private good reduces the amount *available for consumption* by other individuals. Note that an increase in one individual's consumption of a private good need not reduce the level of consumption by any other individual, but only the amount *available* to be consumed by others if the given output exceeds total consumption. For a private good, the relationship between individual consumption x_i and output x is

$$x_1 + x_2 + \ldots + x_n \leqslant x \qquad [\text{B.12}]$$

Efficiency with public goods

We derive the necessary conditions for Pareto efficiency from a diagrammatic analysis of a two-person, two-good economy. (See Question 6, Exercise 14B for a more general case.) The preferences of consumer i are represented by the *quasi-linear* utility function

$$u^i(x_i, q) = B_i(q) + x_i, \qquad B_i' > 0, \qquad B_i'' < 0, \qquad i = 1, 2 \qquad [\text{B.13}]$$

where q is the consumption of the non-optional public good by consumer i and x_i is consumption of the private good. The marginal rate of substitution of consumer i

$$MRS_{xq}^i = u_q^i/u_x^i = B_i'(q_i)$$

is the marginal valuation of the public good by i in terms of the private good. Notice that the assumption that preferences are representable by a quasi-linear utility function means that the marginal valuation of the public good is independent of the amount of the private good consumed. (Think of the private good as a composite good or as expenditure on all other goods and services.)

The production possibilities for the economy are shown in Fig. 14.5(a). The production possibility frontier PP is a straight line so that $MRT_{xq} = c$, indicating that the public good has a constant marginal cost in terms of forgone private good output.

We derive the efficiency conditions by maximizing u^1 subject to individual 2 getting at least a specified level of utility $\bar{u}^2$ and subject to the technological and material balance constraints. The feasible output combinations are those on or below PP and satisfying the material balance constraints [B.11] and [B.12]. Since

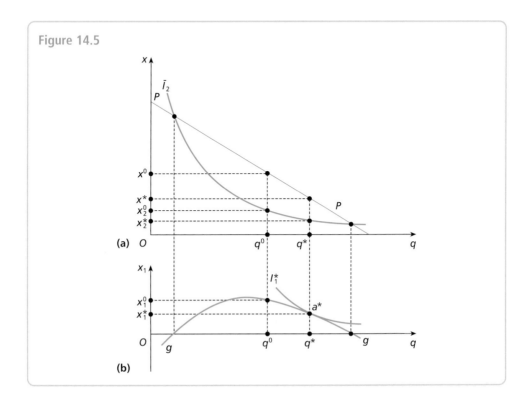

Figure 14.5

consumer 1 is non-satiated the constraint on u^2 and the materials balance constraint on the private good will bind as equalities in an efficient allocation. The indifference curve $\bar{I}_2$ in Fig. 14.5(a) shows combinations of x_2 and q which satisfy the utility constraint $u^2(x_2, q) = \bar{u}^2$. The vertical distance between PP and $\bar{I}_2$ shows, for any level of q, the maximum amount of the private good which can be consumed by individual 1 given the technology of economy (which determines the maximum output of x for given q) and the constraint that $u^2 = \bar{u}^2$. For example, when $q = q^0$, the maximum amount of the private good available for individual 1 is $x_1^0 = x^0 - x_2^0$. Thus, since individual 1 will also be able to consume the output of the public good, her consumption bundle is (x_1^0, q^0) when the output of the public good is q^0.

The curve g in Fig. 14.5(b) plots the vertical distance between PP and $\bar{I}_2$ and shows the feasible consumption bundles of individual 1 given that individual 2 has utility $\bar{u}^2$. Individual 1's utility is maximized at $a*$ on g where her indifference curve is tangent to g. Since the slope of g is the slope of PP minus the slope of $\bar{I}_2$: $-(MRT_{xq} - MRS_{xq}^2)$, and the slope of I_1^* is $- MRS_{xq}^1$, the efficient allocation is characterized by

$$MRS_{xq}^1 + MRS_{xq}^2 = MRT_{xq} \qquad \text{[B.14]}$$

or, given our simple specification of preferences and technology,

$$B_1'(q) + B_2'(q) = c \qquad \text{[B.15]}$$

Because q is a public or non-rival good an increase in q by one unit increases all individuals' consumption of the public good by one unit. Hence the marginal value of the additional unit of the public good in terms of the private good is the *sum* of all the individuals' marginal valuations of the public good. Efficiency requires that the amount of the private good the individuals would in total be willing to give up to acquire an extra unit of the public good ($\sum_i MRS_{xq}^i$) must be equal to the amount by which production of the private good must be reduced to raise the output of the public good by one unit (MRT_{xq}).

A market economy is unlikely to satisfy the efficiency conditions for the supply of public goods for two reasons. First, like some private goods, many public goods are non-excludable. Defence and many aspects of police services are obvious examples. If it is not possible to exclude non-payers from consuming a public good, firms will find it difficult to collect revenue from consumers to cover the cost of producing the public good. If any consumers free-ride because they cannot be excluded, the prices that firms charge for supplying public goods will not be an adequate measure of the marginal benefit of the good and there will be a less than efficient supply of the good.

Some public goods are excludable or can be produced in excludable form at relatively low cost. For example, television broadcasts can be scrambled in transmission so that they can be watched only by consumers who have a descrambler fitted to their television set and use of the descrambler can be charged for by the broadcasters. The second, and more fundamental, reason the market may fail to provide an efficient quantity of public goods, even when they are excludable, arises from the defining characteristic of public goods: non-rivalry.

Suppose that a good is excludable, transferable, there are low information costs, many producers and many consumers. If the good is private the resulting market equilibrium allocation will be efficient. Competition among producers will ensure that all consumers face the same price, which will be equal to the marginal cost of the good in each of the firms. Consumers will compete for a given output of the good and, since the opportunity cost of a unit sold to one consumer is the sale of that unit at the market price to some other consumer, no consumer will be offered or be able to force a sale at less than the market price.

By contrast, if the good is public, even though excludable, the opportunity cost of a unit sold to one customer *when output q is given* is zero. Because the good is public, an additional unit consumed by one individual does not reduce the amount available for consumption by any other individual. This means that no consumer is competing against any other consumer for the units *he* consumes. *The market is not competitive* despite the large numbers of buyers and sellers. If a consumer realizes that the marginal cost of his own consumption is zero, he may offer to the producer a very low payment for the right to consume the producer's output. If all consumers act in this way the amount offered by consumers will be insufficient to cover the costs of production and a zero output will result. In a competitive market for a private good, consumers realize that they cannot affect the market price and hence they adjust their consumption until their marginal valuation of the private good is equal to its price. Hence all consumers' marginal valuations are equal to the price, and in a competitive market price is equal to marginal cost, and the efficiency conditions for private goods will be satisfied. In a market for public goods, consumers' marginal valuations of any given quantity will generally differ. Hence they should each face a different price equal to their own marginal valuation of the public good and the producer should expand production up to the point at which the sum of the prices paid by consumers equals the marginal cost of the public good. If the producer sets the same price to all consumers and the public good is optional the equilibrium uniform price will leave some consumers demanding more than the amount produced and some consuming less. (If they all demand more than is produced the producer can increase profit by raising price, holding output constant. If they all consume less than is produced, the producer can increase profit by reducing output, holding price constant.) Such an equilibrium is inefficient since those with low marginal valuations will consume less than the amount supplied and the marginal cost of consumption by such consumers is zero since the good is public. If the public good is non-optional but excludable, consumers will decide whether to pay to consume the quantity supplied or to do without. In equilibrium some will decide not to purchase the good (if they all purchase, the producer can raise the price holding supply constant and increase profit). Hence the equilibrium is inefficient because some consumers do not consume a good on which they place a positive value and which could be supplied to them without increasing the producer's costs.

Lindahl equilibrium

The state can finance the cost of producing a public good by compulsory taxation. Suppose that individual i is required to pay a per unit tax t_i to finance the public good:

$$u^i = B_i(q) + \bar{x}_i - t_i q = U^i(q, t_i) \qquad \text{[B.16]}$$

where $\bar{x}_i$ is i's endowment or income. Suppose also that the tax prices satisfy

$$t_1 + t_2 = c \qquad \text{[B.17]}$$

so that the cost of the public good is covered. Under the *Lindahl process* a planner announces a set of tax prices satisfying [B.17]. Consumers then say how much of the public good they would each like to consume at the announced tax prices. If these demands are not equal, the planner announces a new set of tax prices. The adjustment rule for the tax prices is that the tax price to the consumer who announced the larger demand is increased and the tax price to the consumer with the smaller demand is reduced. The process reaches the *Lindahl equilibrium* when the consumers agree about the amount of the public good they would demand at the announced tax prices.

The Lindahl equilibrium is efficient *provided that consumers honestly reveal their demands at each tax price.* If consumer *i* treats t_i as a parameter the utility-maximizing demand is $q_i = D_i(t_i)$ which maximizes [B.16] and satisfies

$$\partial U^i / \partial q_i = U_q^i = B_i'(q) - t_i = 0 \Rightarrow q_i = B'^{-1}(t_i) \equiv D_i(t_i) \qquad [B.18]$$

If both consumers are honest and announce $D_i(t_i)$ the Lindahl process leads to a level of the public good $q = D_1(t_1) = D_2(t_2)$ where, from [B.18] and [B.17],

$$\sum_i B_i'(q) = \sum_i t_i = c \qquad [B.19]$$

so that the efficiency condition [B.15] is satisfied at the Lindahl equilibrium.

Figure 14.6 illustrates. The vertical axis from O to c measures the constant marginal cost of the public good. t_1 is measured upwards from O and $t_2 = c - t_1$ downwards from c. The indifference curves such as I_1^0, I_1^* show combinations of the public good and tax price t_1 among which consumer 1 is indifferent. Since $U_q^i = B_1'(q) - t_i$ and $\partial U / \partial t_i = U_t^i = -q$, the slope of the indifference curves for individual 1

$$\left. \frac{dt_1}{dq} \right|_{dU^1 = 0} = \frac{U_q^1}{U_t^1} = \frac{B_1'(q) - t_1}{q}$$

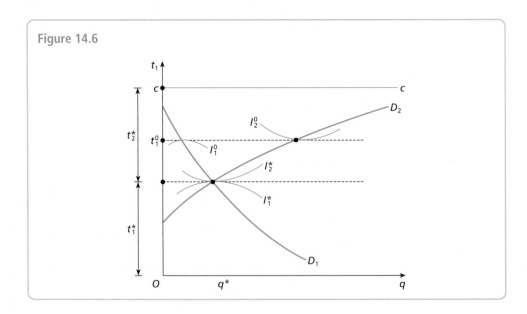

Figure 14.6

is positive for small q and negative for large q. Higher indifference curves correspond to lower utility levels for individual 1 since lower tax prices are preferred to higher. The reader should check that the same reasoning explains the shape of the indifference curves of individual 2 who is better off on higher indifference curves. Since utility-maximizing demands at a given t_i satisfy [B.18], the demand function $D_i(t_i)$ for individual i is the locus of points where an indifference curve is tangent to the horizontal tax price line. Note that the height of D_1 at a given q is the tax price at which that level of q is demanded by individual 1. Since $t_1 = B_1'(q)$ the marginal value of q to individual 1 is given by the height of the demand curve. (Similarly, the vertical distance from D_2 to cc measures consumer 2's marginal valuation of the public good.) The value of a discrete change in the public good to consumer 1, gross of any change in her tax bill, is measured by the area under D_1 between the two levels of q since $B_1(q') - B_1(q'')$ is just the integral of $B_1'(q)$ from q'' to q'. (How is the value to consumer 2 of the same change measured?)

The Lindahl equilibrium is at q^* where the demand curves intersect and the individuals demand the same level of public good at the announced tax prices t_1^* and t_2^*. At the tax price $t_1^0 > t_1^*$ the demand of individual 2 exceeds the demand of individual 1 and the planner would reduce t_1 and increase $t_2 = c - t_1$. At the Lindahl equilibrium the height of D_1 plus the height of D_2 (measured from the cc line) is equal to c and so the sum of the marginal valuations of the public good equals its marginal cost and the efficiency condition is satisfied.

The Lindahl process does not lead to efficiency if any of the individuals lie about their true demands at the announced tax prices. Unfortunately, the process gives them an incentive to misrepresent their demands. Suppose that individual 2 is honest and always reports $D_2(t_2)$. Individual 1 realizes as a consequence that she can control the amount of the public good through her reported demand. She realizes that the Lindahl equilibrium is at the intersection of the announced demand curves. Hence she can choose a particular q by reporting a demand curve $\hat{D}_1(t_1)$ which cuts D_2 at that level of q. Individual 1's problem is therefore to choose the best point for her on D_2 and then to report a $\hat{D}_1$ which generates the point as the Lindahl equilibrium. The tax price for individual 1 increases along D_2 with the level of the public good that she chooses. Her tax price for a supply of the public good of q is

$$t_1 = c - t_2 = c - B_2'(q) = t_1(q) \tag{B.20}$$

since she knows that individual 2 is honest and reports a demand which satisfies [B.18]. Since individual 1 realizes that her tax price varies with q according to [B.20], she chooses q (and hence her announced demand schedule) to maximize

$$B_1(q) + \bar{x}_1 - t_1(q)q = B_1(q) + \bar{x}_1 - [c - B_2'(q)]q \tag{B.21}$$

Her utility-maximizing q is $\hat{q}$ which satisfies

$$B_1'(\hat{q}) - t_1(\hat{q}) - q\,dt_1/dq = B_1'(\hat{q}) - [c - B_2'(\hat{q})] + \hat{q}B_2''(\hat{q}) = 0 \tag{B.22}$$

rather than [B.18]. Since $dt/dq = -B_2'' > 0$, comparison of [B.18] and [B.22] indicates that individual 1 will underestimate her demand and the equilibrium of the Lindahl process satisfies [B.22] so that

$$B_1'(\hat{q}) + B_2'(\hat{q}) = c + \hat{q}B_2''(\hat{q}) < c \tag{B.23}$$

and the supply of the public good is inefficiently small.

Figure 14.7

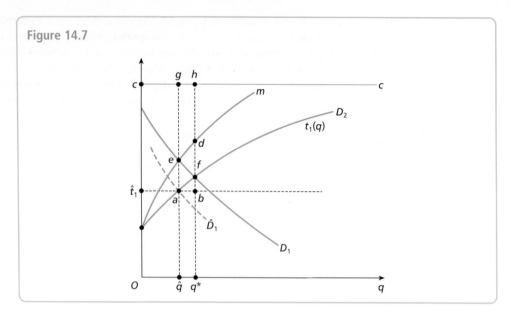

Figure 14.7 illustrates the incentive for individual 1 to understate her demand for the public good. The height of D_2 from the Oq line shows the tax price individual 1 will have to pay for each level of q : $t_1(q)$. It can be thought of as the inverse 'supply' curve confronting individual 1 under the Lindahl process. It measures the per unit or average cost of q to individual 1. To obtain a larger supply of the public good she must pay a higher tax price by moving up the $t_1(q)$ curve. Consequently, the marginal cost of the public good to her exceeds the tax price. The curve $m(q)$ plots the marginal cost of the public good to individual 1: $t_1(q) + qdt_1/dq$. (Compare the analysis of the monopsonist in section 10B.) Individual 1 chooses the level of q where the marginal value of the public good to her (the height of her true demand curve D_1) is equal to its marginal cost to her $m(q)$. She chooses $\hat{q}$ and a tax price of $\hat{t}_1$. To ensure that this is achieved by the Lindahl equilibrium she reports a demand curve like $\hat{D}_1$ which cuts D_2 at $\hat{q}$.

Compared with the efficient allocation at (t_1^*, q^*) which results from honest demand reporting, her tax bill is reduced by the area under her marginal tax cost curve m between q^* and $\hat{q}$: $edq^*\hat{q}$. This more than offsets the reduction in her consumption of the public good which has a value to her of the area under D_1 between q^* and $\hat{q}$: $efq^*\hat{q}$. She obtains a net gain from misreporting her demand of $edfa$. The cost saving on the public good is $(q^* - \hat{q})c$ or $ghq^*\hat{q}$ but the reduction in benefit is $efq^*\hat{q}$ to individual 1 and $afhg$ to individual 2. Thus the overall welfare loss from individual 1's strategic behaviour is efa.

A preference revelation mechanism

The Lindahl process creates an incentive for individuals to misrepresent their demand for the public good because they realize that the tax price they face depends on their announced demand. There is inefficiency because each individual neglects the effect of their announcement on the tax bills and consumption of the public good by the other individuals. The *Clark–Groves–Vickrey (CGV) preference revelation mechanism* uses a two-part tax to pay for the public good and to internalize any potential externalities arising from the fact that each individual's announced demand changes the supply of the public good and thus affects all individuals.

The CGV mechanism asks individuals to report their marginal valuations $\hat{B}'_i(q)$ of different amounts of the public good (their inverse demand curves) and the supply of the public good is determined by equating the summed marginal valuations to the marginal cost of the public good: $\sum_i \hat{B}'_i(q) = c$. The first part of the CGV tax is a per unit tax price t_i (with $\sum_i t_i = c$) which is fixed and cannot be altered by individual i's announcement. The second part of the tax on individual i is determined by calculating q_{-i}, the amount of the public good which would be supplied if i announced a constant marginal valuation equal to her tax price: $\sum_{j \neq i} \hat{B}'_j(q_{-i}) + t_i = c$. With i's announcement $\hat{B}'_i$ the supply of the public good changes to q satisfying $\sum_j \hat{B}'_j(q) = c$. The second part of the CGV tax on i is the change in reported benefits to all other individuals less their payments of per unit taxes:

$$T_i(q) = \sum_{j \neq i} [\hat{B}_j(q_{-1}) - \hat{B}_j(q)] - \sum_{j \neq i} t_j[q_{-i} - q] \qquad [\text{B.24}]$$

(The calculation is possible because $\hat{B}_j(q_{-i}) - \hat{B}_j(q)$ is the area under individual j's reported demand curve or marginal valuation schedule between q_{-i} and q.)

Under the CGV tax individual i has utility

$$B_i(q) + \bar{x}_i - t_i q - T_i(q) \qquad [\text{B.25}]$$

She chooses q (by her announcement of a marginal valuation schedule $\hat{B}'_i$) to maximize [B.25] and so q satisfies

$$B'_i(q) - t_i - \frac{dT_i(q)}{dq} = B'_i(q) - t_i + \sum_{j \neq i} \hat{B}'_j(q) - \sum_{j \neq i} t_j$$

$$= B'_i(q) + \sum_{j \neq i} \hat{B}'_j(q) - c = 0 \qquad [\text{B.26}]$$

(remember that $\sum_j t_j = c$). Thus i chooses a level of the public good which is efficient given the announced marginal valuations of the other individuals: i cannot do better than announcing her true marginal valuation, whatever the announcements of other individuals. The CGV mechanism is a *dominant strategy mechanism* since it makes correct revelation of preferences a dominant strategy for all individuals. Since all are motivated to reveal their true marginal valuations the mechanism leads to an efficient supply of the public good (replace the $\hat{B}'_j$ in [B.26] by B'_j).

Notice two features of the CGV process. First, unlike the Lindahl process, the per unit taxes do not adjust in response to the individuals' announcement and the t_j can therefore be set arbitrarily, subject only to $\sum_j t_j = c$. Second, the fact that the per unit taxes cover the cost of the public good means that the CGV two-part tax produces a surplus of $\sum_j T_j$. If the surplus is given back to the individuals the CGV mechanism will not induce correct revelation of preferences because each individual will take account of the effect of their announcement on their share of the surplus as well as on the CGV taxes. For example, if each of the m individuals is given $S_i = (\sum_j T_j)/n$, each will choose their announcement to maximize $B_i(q) + \bar{x}_i - t_i q - T_i(q) + S_i$ and, since S_i varies with q, [B.26] will not be satisfied and i will not report preferences honestly. Correct revelation requires that the surplus is wasted from the point of view of the individuals consuming the public good. (The surplus could be given away to another community which does not consume the public good.) If the surplus is not 'wasted' there will be distorted revelation of preferences and an inefficient supply of the public good. Fortunately, it can be shown that the potential surplus becomes relatively small as the number of individuals becomes large and so the amount of waste or inefficiency in public good supply becomes small.

The CGV mechanism is illustrated in Fig. 14.7. Suppose that the tax prices are $\hat{t}_i$. Given the tax prices $q_{-1} = \hat{q}$, where B'_2 (the vertical distance from D_2 to cc) plus $\hat{t}_1$ is equal to c. If the supply of the public good is increased to q^* from $\hat{q}$ individual 2 will have a gross benefit equal to $af\,hg$ and will pay extra per unit taxes of $\hat{t}_2(q^* - \hat{q}) = abhg$. Thus $T_1(q^*)$ is abf: (the area above the $\hat{t}_1$ line and below D_2). In order to increase q from $\hat{q}$ to q^* individual 1 must pay additional taxes of $\hat{t}_1(q^* - \hat{q}) + T_1(q^*)$ = $afq^*\hat{q}$ which is the area under D_2 between $\hat{q}$ and q^*. But $afq^*\hat{q}$ is the social cost of the increase in q: the difference between the resource cost of the additional public good output ($q^*\hat{q}hg$) and its gross value to individual 2 ($af\,hg$). The CGV mechanism confronts individual 1 with a marginal cost of the public good equal to the height of the D_2 curve and she will choose a public good output of q^* where her true marginal valuation cuts her marginal cost curve under the mechanism. The CGV mechanism makes each individual bear the social cost of changes in the public good supply resulting from their announcement.

EXERCISE 14B

1. *Correction of monopoly.* Which of the following types of government intervention will lead a monopoly to produce an efficient output level: (a) profits tax; (b) sales tax; (c) per unit subsidy; (d) maximum price control; (e) auctioning off the right to be a monopolist to the highest bidder; (f) auctioning off the right to be a monopolist to the firm which promises to sell at the lowest price.

2. *Monopoly price discrimination and welfare.* Consider the three types of price discrimination described in section 9C. Are the resulting allocations Pareto inefficient? If so, why do such inefficiencies persist under price discrimination?

3. *Monopoly and quality.* Suppose that a monopolist can vary the quality of the good produced, that all consumers must be provided with the same quality, that higher quality is more costly for the monopolist and that all consumers are willing to pay more for a higher quality. Will the monopolist supply an efficient quality if the good can only be sold for a constant per unit price? Would more sophisticated contracts between the monopolist and the consumers lead to an efficient choice of quality?

4. *Accidents as externalities.* Society consists of two individuals, P and D. If an accident occurs it imposes a loss of £L on P. The probability of an accident is $\pi(x)$ ($\pi' < 0$, $\pi'' > 0$) where x is expenditure on care by D. Both individuals care only about expected costs falling on them.

   (a) What is the efficient level of care x^*?

   (b) Suppose that the individuals cannot bargain about P's level of care before an accident occurs. Which of the following legal regimes leads to efficient care: (i) D has no legal liability for damage to P; (ii) D is strictly liable, irrespective of x, for damages to P; (iii) D is liable only if negligent, i.e. only if x is less than some specified due care level x^0.

   (c) How are the answers to (b) affected if the accident is bilateral: the accident probability is $\pi(x, y)$, a decreasing convex function of the care expenditure of P(y) and of D(x)?

5. *Government policy towards common property resources.* Which of the following interventions can lead to efficiency in the case of common property fishing grounds:

(a) tax on fish caught; (b) tax on labour input; (c) vesting sole ownership in a single firm with monopoly power in the output market.

6. *Congestion.* Reformulate the diagrammatic analysis of free access resources in terms of average and marginal revenue product and cost curves. Derive the lake's supply curve of fish as a function of the relative price of fish in terms of labour (p/w) under free access and under private ownership by a single individual. Show that the same diagram can be used, with suitable relabelling, to analyse the problem of congestion on public roads. What price should be charged for the use of congested public roads to induce an efficient use by motorists?

7. *Efficiency with public goods.* Derive the efficiency conditions for an economy with many consumers, many private goods and one non-optional public good. How would the conditions differ if the public good was optional?

8. *Market supply of public goods.* Discuss the merits of the following methods of financing the production of television broadcasts: (a) sale of advertising; (b) annual licence fee paid for the right to own a television set; (c) metered descramblers fitted to television sets; (d) voluntary subscription.

9. *Preference revelation.* The Clark–Groves–Vickrey mechanism will induce correct revelation of preferences for indivisible public goods such as flood control programmes or measures to reduce atmospheric pollution. Denote by v_i the benefit to individual i of the indivisible good or project, net of the taxes levied to finance it. The project is undertaken if $\sum_i \hat{v}_i > 0$ where $\hat{v}_i$ is i's announced net valuation of the project. In addition to the taxes levied to pay for the project, i must also pay a tax T_i equal to the absolute value of the sum of the announced valuations of all other individuals $|\sum_{j \neq i} \hat{v}_j|$ if i's announced net valuation changes the decision on whether the project is accepted or not.

   (a) Show the correct preference revelation is a dominant strategy, provided that the tax surplus $\sum_i T_i$ is wasted.

   (b) Consider a four-person community where $(v_1, v_2, v_3, v_4) = (10, 15, -18, -3)$ and show that individuals 3 and 4 have an incentive to collude and agree to misrepresent their preferences. Is this vulnerability to collusion likely to be serious if (i) there are many individuals; (ii) individuals' announcements are known only to the individual and the government.

10. *Compensation mechanism for externalities.* Varian (1994) has suggested the following mechanism to solve the externality problem when the regulator does not know the damage imposed by the upstream polluting chemical works on the downstream brewery. The chemical works tells the regulator the subsidy s per unit of pollution which the brewery should receive from the regulator. The brewery tells the regulator the tax t the chemical works should pay to the regulator. The regulator imposes t and s on the firms and in addition imposes a penalty of $\alpha(s - t)^2$ on the chemical works. Hence, the profit of the chemical works is $B(x) - tx - \alpha(s - t)^2$ and the profit of the brewery is $\pi^0 + sx - D(x)$ where π^0 is independent of the level of pollution x. Show that at the sub-game perfect Nash equilibrium (see section 15B) of the game induced by the mechanism there is an efficient level of pollution and the payments by and to the regulator sum to zero. (*Hint:* work backwards by examining the chemical works' choice of x at given t, s and then consider the firms' choices of t and s allowing for their effect on x.)

C. The theory of the second best

The theory of the second best concerns government policy formation in an economy in which there is market failure. We can distinguish three broad aims of government microeconomic policy:

(a) The correction of market failure: for example, the nationalization or regulation of monopolies, correction of externalities, provision of public goods.

(b) Overriding individuals' choices because they are based on 'inappropriate' preferences which one does not wish to respect. For example, it might be thought that individuals do not take proper account of the consequences of consumption of certain types of good or service, such as heroin, education or classical music. Pareto efficiency respects individuals' preferences, so that intervention can be justified on such paternalistic grounds even if the allocation is Pareto efficient.

(c) The achievement of a desirable distribution of real income.

The theory of the second best in general ignores the second of these aims and is concerned with the formulation of policies designed to correct market failure and change income distribution.

An economic policy is a rule for associating with each member of a given set of economic agents (consumers and firms) values of the elements of a given set of policy instruments. For example, a policy to correct the external detriment created by a firm which pollutes specifies the amount of the tax (the instrument) to be charged to the polluter (the economic agent), with a zero tax to all other consumers and firms in the economy.

If the policy-maker has full information about preferences and technology and if there are no restrictions on the two sets involved in policy formulation – the set of economic agents to whom the instruments can be applied and the set of instruments – then the policy-maker can achieve a 'first-best' resource allocation which cannot be improved upon. In terms of Chapter 13, Fig. 13.1, the economy can be moved to a point such as α^* on the utility frontier from a point such as α^1 below it (at which there is market failure) or from a point such as α^2 also on it (which has an 'undesirable' welfare distribution). If the sets are unrestricted, lump-sum redistribution is possible and so, as we saw in section 13E, income distribution goals can be achieved without losses of allocative efficiency – the economy can be moved around the welfare frontier. Likewise any specific instance of market failure can be corrected if the two sets are unrestricted. For example, a monopolist can be forced to price at marginal cost (or can be subsidized to do so) and lump-sum redistributions used to correct any undesirable effects on income distribution.

A *second-best* policy problem arises when the policy-maker has imperfect information about preferences or technology or there are non-trivial restrictions on the set of policy instruments or the set of agents whose behaviour can be influenced. In this section we discuss second-best policy under full information. In finding the optimal policy for correcting some form of market failure, the crucial first step is specifying the set of policy instruments and the set of economic agents to whom they can be applied. The specifications may affect both the methods of analysis and the policy prescriptions.

Suppose the government has nationalized a monopoly and can directly determine its pricing policy (nationalization is an element in the set of instruments). However, for some reason it has not nationalized a second monopoly whose output is a close substitute to that of the first (this in itself may seem illogical if we ignore the political realities of market economies). If the government can directly influence the behaviour of the private monopolist, for example by paying a subsidy per unit of output, it can ensure that its output is set where price equals marginal cost. If the government also equates price to marginal cost in the nationalized monopoly, we have the 'first-best' outcome with all consumers' marginal rates of substitution between the two outputs equal to the marginal rate of transformation (ratio of marginal costs). If, on the other hand, the government cannot tax or subsidize the private monopolist directly, or alter its behaviour in any way except through the demand interdependence with the nationalized monopoly, we have to exclude the private monopoly from the set of economic agents for whom values of policy instruments can be directly prescribed. The second-best policy problem is to choose a price for the nationalized monopoly when this is the only instrument determining the resource allocation in both monopolies. Given the restriction on instruments, the optimal second-best policy for the nationalized monopoly differs from the first best. (See Question 1, Exercise 14C.)

The first type of policy, where the monopolist can be directly influenced, is clearly more powerful than the second, which can be called 'piecemeal second-best policy'. The question of which is the more appropriate approach to adopt cannot be resolved at the purely logical level (illogical though it may appear that a government uses only a piecemeal policy) but requires a specification of the constraints on agents and instruments which are *actually* in force. Such 'illogicalities' in government policies do exist, at least in part because policies are carried out by a range of different agencies with differing goals and among which communication and coordination are imperfect.

We illustrate these ideas about the theory of the second best with a specific example. Suppose that a public agency is planning to construct a road bridge across an estuary, on which a toll will be charged. The demand curve in Fig. 14.8 shows the estimated relation between the toll, p, and the number of trips per day across the bridge. Assume that demand is constant over time – there is neither long-term growth nor seasonal variation. Trips across the bridge take place at a constant rate throughout the day – there are no 'peak load' problems. The *LMC* curve in the figure reflects the assumption that total costs per day increase proportionately with the capacity of the bridge. The optimal solution in an economy without market failure would be to set a toll of $p^* = LMC$ and construct a bridge of capacity x^* – this is the 'marginal cost price solution'.

Figure 14.8

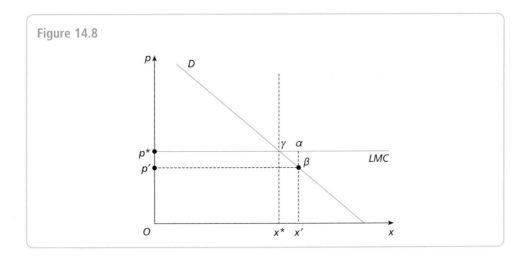

Figure 14.9

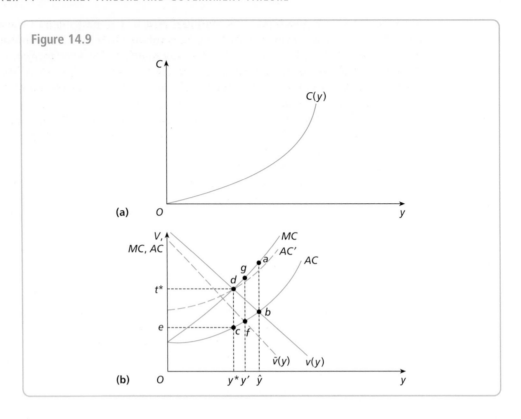

Suppose now that there is market failure in the economy. There is already a road around the estuary, *on which no toll is charged* and which is severely congested. The nature of the market failure here is similar to that of the fishery problem analysed in the previous section – overutilization of a common access resource. Figure 14.9(a) shows how the total costs per day to the users of the estuary road increase with the number of trips. The costs include not only petrol and vehicle wear and tear costs, but also maintenance costs of the roadway and the cost of the time of motorists. The curvature of the total cost function $C(y)$ indicates that, as traffic flow y increases, so journey time lengthens and so time and petrol costs increase more than propor-tionately. In (b) of the figure, the marginal and average cost curves corresponding to $C(y)$ are shown, with MC everywhere above AC.

Let v denote the 'full price' a motorist is willing to pay to make a trip on the road, i.e. to cover the cost in terms of petrol, vehicle wear and tear and time, *plus* any toll which may be charged. Then $v(y)$ shows the demand curve for trips on the road – the lower the full price the greater the number of trips. At any level of y, say $\hat{y}$, the marginal trip along the road has a value to the motorist who makes it of $v(\hat{y})$.

In the absence of a toll each motorist would take as the cost of making a trip along the road the *average cost, AC*, since this is the actual cost incurred by each motorist who makes the trip. Hence, $\hat{y}$ is the resulting equilibrium number of trips – the value of the marginal trip is just equal to the cost to the motorist who makes it, at b in the figure. However, at this equilibrium the social cost of the marginal trip is MC at a: in costing a trip at the *average* cost the marginal user is ignoring the extra costs imposed through longer journey times on all other users. There is resource misallocation. The Pareto efficient solution would be to impose a toll of $et^* = cd$ in the figure, resulting in the *perceived* average cost curve AC' and an equilibrium at y^*, where marginal cost MC is equal to marginal value $v(y^*)$. This solution is ruled out by the absence of a pricing mechanism in the market for trips along the road. The *marginal welfare loss* – the excess of social cost over value of the marginal trip – is given by $MC - v(\hat{y}) = ab$.

The bridge is a substitute for the estuary road. Assume that the equilibrium for the road shown in Fig. 14.9(b) is that which would obtain if the bridge were built at capacity x^* and a toll of p^* charged. We can now show that the optimal second-best solution *given the restriction that no toll can be charged on the road* involves a departure from marginal cost pricing on the bridge. Thus suppose the bridge toll were reduced from p^* to p', and capacity increased from x^* to x'. In terms of the bridge alone there is an apparent resource misallocation since the value of the extra resources absorbed by the bridge – area $x^*\gamma\alpha x'$ – exceeds the value of the extra trips to those who make them – area $x^*\gamma\beta x'$. At toll p' the *marginal* welfare loss on the bridge is $p^* - p' = \alpha\beta$. However, the reduction in the bridge toll will cause a fall in the demand for road trips, say to $\bar{v}(y)$ in Fig. 14.9(b). As a result there is a reduction in net welfare losses ('congestion costs') on the estuary road which may more than offset the welfare losses on the bridge, since the marginal welfare loss on the road fg exceeds the marginal welfare loss on the bridge $\alpha\beta$. The savings in social costs on the road could be used to meet the excess of the value of resources absorbed by the additional bridge trips over their value to those who make them, and there would still be a net gain. Thus the toll of p^* on the bridge cannot be Pareto efficient. The necessary condition for the (second-best) Pareto efficient bridge toll p^0 is

$$(p^* - p^0)\frac{\partial x}{\partial p} = (-)(MC - v(y))\frac{\partial y}{\partial p} \qquad [\text{C.1}]$$

or: marginal welfare loss on bridge equals marginal welfare gain on road. Only if these two marginal welfare changes, the first imposed by the extra trip made across the bridge, the second saved on the marginal trip not made on the road, as a result of the bridge toll reduction, are equal, will it not be possible to change the bridge toll further and achieve a net welfare gain.

In [C.1] the first-best solution $p^* = p^0$ arises if

(a) $MC = v(y)$, i.e. no marginal welfare loss on the road, or

(b) $\partial y/\partial p = 0$, i.e. a change in the bridge toll has no effect on road demand.

The former will only be satisfied if resource allocation on the road can be optimized directly, which is ruled out by assumption.

We have a characteristic solution to 'piecemeal second-best' problems: even when the policy-maker is able to implement the first-best solution ($p = p^*$) in one sector (the bridge) the solution will not in general be correct (Pareto efficient) when that sector is interdependent with another in which the first-best condition ($MC = v(y)$) does not hold and *cannot directly be achieved*.

The second-best solution is in general inferior to the first-best solution, and so we may be led to question the logic of the policy constraints which leave the bridge toll as the only instrument. The illogicality stems from an apparent inconsistency in the way in which transport policy is formulated and applied, and raises the issue of 'government failure' which is the subject of the next section.

EXERCISE 14C

1. *Monopoly.* Monopoly i has the demand function $x_i = D_i(p_1, p_2)$ and cost function $c(x_i)$ ($i = 1, 2$) where x_i is the level of its output and p_i its price. Monopoly 1 is in the public sector and monopoly 2 is a private sector profit-maximizing firm. The only policy instrument available to influence the behaviour of the private sector firm is the price charged for the output of the public sector firm. Assume that social welfare can be represented as the sum of consumer surplus and profits in the two industries.

(a) Show that the optimal second-best price of the public sector firm satisfies

$$m_1 e_{11} + m_2 e_{22} r R_2 / R_1 = 0$$

where $m_i = (p_i - c_i')/p_i$ is the proportionate deviation of price from marginal cost in firm i, $e_{ii} = D_{ii} p_i / D_i$ is the own price elasticity of demand for firm i's output, $R_i = p_i D_i$ is expenditure on firm i's output and $r = (dp_2/dp_1)(p_1/p_2)$ is the *response elasticity* of firm 2's price to changes in the price set by the public firm. (*Hint*: work backwards from the above expression by writing it out in full and cancelling as many terms as possible; then differentiate the welfare function with respect to p_1; compare the two expressions.)

(b) Show that if the products of the two firms are substitutes and the demand curve of firm 2 is linear firm 1 should price above marginal cost. (*Hint*: use simple comparative static analysis on the private sector firm's profit-maximizing price.)

D. Government action and government failure

Types of government action

The possibility of market failure raises the question of action by the political authorities in an economy as a means of rectifying departures from the Pareto efficiency conditions. Governments can alter resource allocations in a variety of ways. First, they can legislate to modify the system of property rights governing the exchange of goods and services. Common access resources can be transformed into private property by vesting the right to exclusive use and disposal in a single individual, as, for example, in the Acts by which the commons were enclosed in England. The ability to exclude can be strengthened by changes in the criminal law. The terms on which exchanges can be made may be restricted by legislation. Regulatory bodies can be established to mitigate the market power of monopolies by limiting their prices or profits. Minimum levels of consumption of goods, such as education, generating beneficial externalities, may be laid down. Public bodies may be set up to regulate common access resources, as an alternative to vesting ownership in private individuals.

Second, the prices at which exchanges take place may be varied by the imposition of taxes or subsidies to reduce the production and consumption of commodities which give rise to detrimental externalities and to increase those of commodities causing beneficial externalities. Effluent taxes equal to the marginal damage caused by firms' discharge of effluent may be levied so that private and social costs of effluent discharge are equated. Subsidies may be paid to increase the output of monopolized goods.

Third, the state may intervene in the allocation mechanism directly by producing goods and services itself. Monopolies may be nationalized and their outputs sold at marginal cost. Education and health care may be produced at zero price to encourage its consumption. The government will provide police and legal services to determine and enforce individual property rights.

Government failure

Government action will not necessarily lead to Pareto efficiency, even of the second best. It must first be established that the government will be both willing and able to act in the required way. We need a *positive* theory of government decision-making in the same way that prediction of consumer or firm behaviour requires a positive theory of consumer or firm decision-making. Two propositions have been advanced in support of the argument that, to put it no higher, it is not obvious that government intervention in the economy will fully correct for market failure.

First, the policies pursued by the state result from the actions and interactions of voters, politicians, civil servants, bureaucrats and managers and workers in public firms. We cannot assume that any of these individuals are completely altruistic in the sense that they are motivated solely by the desire to achieve a Pareto efficient resource allocation. Voters may be concerned about the effect of policies on their tax bills; politicians about their chances of re-election; managers of public firms may prefer not to devote a large amount of time and effort to producing output at least cost; bureaucrats may adopt the size of their bureau's budgeted expenditure on its staff as a measure of their status.

Second, *information is required* for policy-making and control, both in deciding what policy should be adopted, and in ensuring that it has in fact been implemented and the desired result achieved. But information is not a free good: it is often dispersed over many individuals and it is costly to acquire and to transmit.

These two factors – non-altruism and information costs – mean that in order to predict the ways in which government will intervene in the economy we must examine the institutions in the public sector. The institutions will constrain the actions of individuals in the public sector and provide incentives for particular sorts of behaviour and the production, processing and transmission of particular kinds of information. An analysis of the way in which institutional frameworks structure the rewards and penalties for different types of individual behaviour is required to decide whether a particular institutional setting will induce efficient behaviour.

A comparative institutions approach to policy-making

A demonstration of the ways in which one particular institutional framework may fail to satisfy the marginal conditions for Pareto efficiency does not provide a conclusive argument in favour of adopting an alternative framework. Market failure does not imply the necessity for government action, and likewise government failure does not imply that the scope of market allocation should be extended. Since both institutional frameworks may fail to satisfy the Pareto efficiency conditions, a move from one to the other is justified on such grounds only if one institutional framework is more efficient than the other. This will depend on the particular cases being considered: what is required is a comparison of the way different institutions allocate resources in each case.

As an illustration of the kind of analysis which might be conducted, consider again the case of the proposed construction of a bridge which we now assume *can only be built in one size*, with high costs of construction and low constant marginal

Figure 14.10

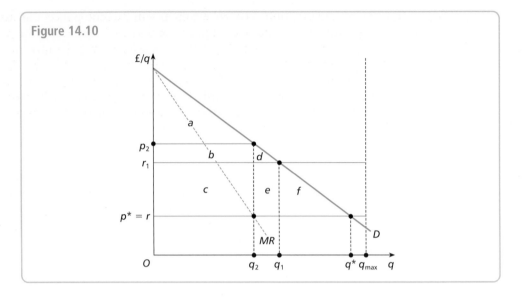

running costs. In Fig. 14.10, D is the demand curve for trips across the bridge, MR the corresponding marginal revenue curve, the marginal cost of trips across the bridge is r, the capacity of the bridge is q_{max} trips per year and the annuitized construction cost of the bridge is K. Two interdependent decisions must be made: (a) If the bridge is built, what is the optimal number of trips per annum across it (or alternatively what toll should be charged)? (b) Should the bridge be built at all? Assume that the rest of the economy is efficient. A consumer's marginal valuation of a trip is equal to the price paid for it. Efficient use of the bridge requires that each consumer's marginal valuation be equal to the marginal cost of extra trips. Hence the efficient price $p*$ is equal to r and there should be $q*$ trips across the bridge. There is spare capacity in that $q* < q_{max}$ and consumers could be induced to use the bridge fully by a reduction in p. This, however, would be inefficient since their marginal valuation of these additional trips is less than the extra cost incurred.

The second decision, whether to build the bridge, is made by comparing the total cost of providing the bridge with the total benefit to consumers *at its actual rate of use*. If the bridge is used efficiently at $q*$ the total benefit to consumers is the total amount they would be prepared to pay for $q*$. This willingness to pay $W(q*)$ is measured by the area under the demand curve up to $q*$:

$$W(q*) = a + b + c + d + e + f + p*q* \qquad \text{[D.1]}$$

The total cost of supplying $q*$ is the construction cost plus the running costs:

$$C(q*) = K + rq* \qquad \text{[D.2]}$$

The difference between the benefit [D.1] and the cost [D.2] is the net social benefit when the bridge is used optimally:

$$W - C = a + b + c + d + e + f - K \qquad \text{[D.3]}$$

where we have used the fact that $p* = r$. The bridge should be built or not as [D.3] is positive or negative.

Now let us compare the ways in which the two decisions, on construction and use of the bridge, would be made by a private monopolist and by a public sector decision-taker. Assuming that the monopoly wishes to maximize profits it will, if the bridge is built, set $MR = r$ and charge a price p_2 so that $q_2 < q^*$ trips are made. It will base its decision on whether to build the bridge or not on a comparison of the construction cost with the excess of revenue ($p_2 q_2$) over the running costs $r q_2$. It will build the bridge if the profit from doing so, and operating it at its most profitable level q_2 is positive, i.e. if

$$(p_2 - r)q_2 - K = b + c - K > 0 \qquad [D.4]$$

Private monopoly will always lead to an inefficient use of the bridge ($q_2 < q^*$) if exclusion and other problems prevent the kind of contract between the monopolist and consumers discussed in section B. In addition the monopolist may not build a bridge when it would be optimal to do so. Note that, if the number of trips across the bridge is q_2, consumers' willingness to pay is $a + b + c$ and

$$W(q_2) - C(q_2) = a + b + c - K \qquad [D.5]$$

may be positive when [D.4] is negative. Hence the monopolist may fail to build a bridge when it would be efficient to do so even at an inefficient price which restricts use below q^*. These inefficiencies arise because the feasible set of contracts between monopolist and consumers does not permit consumers to bribe the monopolist to act optimally.

The inefficiencies resulting from monopoly would not arise with an ideally functioning public sector: the decision to build would be made by reference to consumers' willingness to pay rather than their actual payments (the revenue from the bridge). The toll would be set at its efficient level p^* and the resulting losses

$$C(q^*) - p^* q^* = K + r q^* - p^* q^* = K \qquad [D.6]$$

(i.e. the construction costs) could be financed out of general taxation. We cannot, however, conclude that efficiency dictates that the bridge ought to be supplied by the state until we have examined how public supply would *actually* operate. There are a number of reasons for supposing that public sector decision-making about the construction and use of the bridges may not be efficient either. For example:

(a) The political authorities may not use the sign of [D.3] as the criterion for building the bridge. They may instead be motivated by the effect of the bridge on their chances of retaining office. The bridge may, for example, be situated in a marginal constituency, and even if the benefits were less than the costs, the benefits will accrue to the voters in the constituency and may be substantial enough to secure their votes. The construction cost will be spread across all taxpayers in all constituencies and may therefore not hit other taxpayers hard enough to influence their votes adversely. The same circumstances may lead to an inefficiently low price being charged for use of the bridge.

(b) A decision to build the bridge must be based on an estimate of the demand curve for the bridge made before the bridge is actually built. This problem faces both the monopolist and the public sector decision-makers. It is not clear which institutional setting will lead to more accurate estimates. A private firm bears the cost of any erroneous demand estimates. An erroneous decision to build will result in irreversible losses. A mistaken decision not to build, however, may not be so easily identified and in any case may be rectified later. Managers in a private firm, particularly if risk-averse, may therefore underestimate rather than over-estimate demand, thus further increasing the possibility of an inefficient decision not to build. In the case of public supply, losses do not necessarily indicate a mistaken decision to build since a loss would be incurred in any case if $p = r$. A mistaken decision to build could only be identified by a deliberate *ex post* comparison of the estimated demand with the actual demand. Since the public sector decision-makers have no incentive to audit past decisions, and *individual* taxpayers only a very diluted one, mistakes may not be discovered. Given the factors mentioned under point (a), this may lead to a tendency to build the bridge when it would not be warranted by an objective comparison of costs and benefits.

(c) A publicly supplied bridge may have a higher than minimum construction cost because of the lack of incentives for public officials to ensure that costs are minimized. If we denote the construction cost under public supply by K_1, the net benefits from the bridge under public supply and efficient pricing can be written

$$a + b + c + d + e + f - K_1 \qquad [D.7]$$

Under private supply the net social benefits are

$$W(q_2) - C(q_2) = a + b + c - K \qquad [D.8]$$

and hence public supply may be less efficient than private supply if [D.7] is less than [D.8], or

$$K_1 - K > d + e + f \qquad [D.9]$$

Private supply leads to a loss in net social benefit due to inefficient pricing of $d + e + f$, against which must be set the loss in net social benefit under public supply, due to non-minimized construction costs, of $K_1 - K$.

(d) Similarly, a publicly operated bridge may have marginal running costs of r_1 rather than the minimum marginal running cost of r under a profit-maximizing (and hence cost-minimizing) private supplier. If the public bridge is priced at actual marginal running cost so that $p = p_1 = r_1$ then net social benefit is

$$W(q_1) - r_1 q_1 - K = a + b + d - K \qquad [D.10]$$

(Why is p_1 the optimal price under public supply *in these circumstances*?) Comparing [D.10] and [D.8], we see that public operation is preferable if

$$d > c \qquad [D.11]$$

The choice is between private supply at q_2 and public supply of q_1 with higher running costs. c is the additional running costs incurred on output up to q_2 with public operation. This must be compared with the net gain resulting from the higher output of a public bridge compared with private operation. The benefit to consumers of the additional $q_1 - q_2$ units is the area under the demand curve between these two points and the cost of producing it is $r_1(q_1 - q_2)$. The net gain from the increased output is therefore d. [D.11] will hold provided the public managers of the bridge are not 'too inefficient'. If they are very ineffici-ent then we may have $q_2 > q_1$ and a larger output under monopoly than with public operation.

EXERCISE 14D

1. *Majority voting.* Suppose that the cost of a public good is $C(q)$, that there are n individuals (n is odd) and that each pays $C(q)/n$ in taxes to cover the cost of the public good. The benefit individual i receives from the public good is $B_i(q)$. The level of q is determined by majority voting. Let q_i^* be the level of q which is optimal for individual i. Label the individuals so that $q_1^* < q_2^* < \ldots < q_n^*$.

   (a) Show that the amount of the public good is that preferred by individual $M = (n + 1)/2$ (the median voter).

   (b) Does the amount preferred by the median voter satisfy the efficiency condition of section B?

2. *Bureaucracy.* A good is provided by a public sector bureaucracy with expenditure of $E(q) = C(q) + w$, where C is the minimum cost of producing q ($C' > 0$, $C'' > 0$) and w is wasteful expenditure. The benefit from the good (summed over all consumers) is $B(q)$ ($B'(0) > 0$, $B'' < 0$). The bureaucracy wishes to maximize its total budget allocation A but must cover its expenditure. Supervising politicians do not know the $C(q)$ function but can observe actual expenditure. The bureau is able to persuade them to provide it with a budget allocation of $A = kB(q)$ ($0 < k \leqslant 1$) by telling them that it will cost A to provide q.

   (a) Characterize the efficient allocation.

   (b) What output will the bureau produce? Is it efficient? Will the bureau choose $w > 0$?

3. *Regulated monopoly.* A profit-maximizing private sector monopoly faces the demand function $D(p)$ for its output x and has the cost function $C(x)$. The firm is subject to mark-up regulation and not permitted to charge a price which exceeds its actual expenditure per unit of output: $p \leqslant (1 + k)[C(x) + w]/x$ ($k > 0$) where w is wasteful expenditure. (The regulators do not know the cost function and can only observe actual expenditure by the firm.) Assume that welfare is measured by the sum of consumer and producer surplus.

   (a) What is the welfare-maximizing price?

   (b) What levels of p and w will a profit-maximizing firm choose when subject to mark-up regulation?

   (c) Is it possible for welfare to be greater when the firm is unregulated than when it is subject to mark-up regulation?

A. Introduction

In a game, two or more decision-takers know that their decisions are *strategically interdependent*: the outcome of decisions taken by one decision-taker depends on the decisions of the other(s). To work out the consequences of their actions each player must formulate expectations about how the other player(s) will act. Game theory is concerned with the analysis of such decision problems. It provides a deeper and more satisfactory analysis of subjects, such as oligopoly and bargaining theory, that have long engaged economists, and has opened up important new areas, such as the theory of auctions and of signalling and screening mechanisms.

   In the first part of this chapter we use three examples based on a simple market to illustrate the main elements of games and the way in which they can be analysed. In all three examples, two firms, A and B, are the only actual or potential suppliers in the market. Their outputs q_A, q_B are perfect substitutes, they have identical, constant, marginal costs of £1 per unit and zero fixed costs. The market demand function is $p = 41 - q$, where $q = q_A + q_B$ is total output. The combined joint profit of the firms depends only on their total output and not on how a given total output is produced. As the reader should check, the total output that maximizes their joint profit, given by $40q - q^2$, is 20 units. The firms cannot make legally binding agreements about their decisions because such collusion is illegal.

   The three examples differ in certain key elements which give rise to different games with different solutions.

Prisoner's Dilemma game

Each firm has a fixed maximum production capacity of 12 units. Each will only know what output the other firm has actually produced after it has made its own output decision and the resulting total output is put on the market to determine the market clearing price. We suppose that each firm considers only two output levels: 10 and 12 units. The first is the output each would produce under a collusive agreement to maximize joint profits, with equal market shares. The second is the output which is optimal for a firm if it reneges on the agreement to maximize joint profits and produce 10 units. The reader should check that 12 is the value of q_i that maximizes $[41 - (q_j + q_i)]q_i - q_i$ subject to the constraint that $q_i \leqslant 12$, and for any $q_j \leqslant 12$.

   (The game's name comes from a classic story in which two partners in a crime have been arrested and must decide whether to stay silent or confess. If they are both silent they get light jail sentences, if both confess they get moderate jail sentences, and if one confesses and the other does not, the one who confesses is set free and the other gets a very heavy sentence.)

Stackelberg game

Now suppose that there are no capacity constraints and that firm A will produce its output today and firm B will produce tomorrow after observing the output of firm A. Firm A must put all its output up for sale once it has been produced. The outputs of the two firms will be sold on the market simultaneously tomorrow. The game is named after the German economist who first formulated it as a model of oligopoly. It is sometimes known as the Leader–Follower game.

Entry game

Firm A is a monopolist with enough production capacity to supply the entire market demand at any price at or above £1. Firm B is a potential entrant who must decide whether to enter the market by building production capacity today and, if it does enter, how much to produce tomorrow. Firm A, after observing whether firm B has entered, will decide tomorrow how much to produce. Neither firm will know how much the other has produced until the total supply is placed on the market and the price determined.

An abstract game is formally described by the key elements which determine its *solution*. A solution of a game is a prediction of how the decision-takers will play the game. Many different situations have the same key elements and can be modelled by the same abstract game. By focusing on the key elements and analysing the abstract game defined by them, game theory provides a solution for a wide range of situations, all of which correspond to the same game.

These key elements are:

- The set of *players*: the decision-takers. In the above examples the players are the two firms.
- The set of *actions* available to each player. In the first two examples they are output levels; in the third the incumbent firm must choose an output, the entrant, whether to enter and, if so, what output to produce.
- The *timing* of the players' choices of actions. In the first example, the firms make simultaneous choices; in the second, one player chooses an output and then the other chooses. In the third example, the entrant chooses to enter or not and then the two players simultaneously choose their outputs.
- The *payoffs* to each player resulting from all possible plays of the game. In the above examples the payoffs are the profits the firms receive from the output pairs they could produce. More generally, the players may have the von Neumann–Morgenstern cardinal utility functions described in Chapter 17 (indeed, von Neumann and Morgenstern developed their utility theory in the course of their pioneering work on game theory).
- The set of *strategies* available to each player in the game. A *pure strategy* is a complete specification of the action to be taken at each point in the game at which the player has to make a choice. The set of all possible pure strategies for a player is the set of all possible combinations of that player's actions. In games such as the Prisoner's Dilemma, where the players simultaneously choose one action, the set of strategies coincides with the set of actions. In games like the Stackelberg game, where decisions are sequential, a strategy will consist of contingent instructions of the form 'If situation S_1 has occurred, do a_1; if situation S_2 has occurred do a_2...'. A strategy must specify the action to be taken in all conceivable

situations in which the player would have to make a decision. A *mixed strategy* is a probability distribution over pure strategies: it specifies a probability with which each pure strategy will be played. Initially we consider only pure strategies. We discuss mixed strategies in section D below. The choice of a strategy by each player fully determines how the game will be played, so that each player's payoff is a function of the vector or *profile* of all players' strategies.

- The *information* each player possesses, first about the game itself, and second, about what has happened in the course of playing the game. In a game of *complete information*, every player knows everything there is to know about the game, including the characteristics, such as cost functions, of the other players. The Prisoner's Dilemma, Stackelberg and Entry games are examples of games of complete information. There is *perfect information* if, when a player has to choose an action, she knows what actions, if any, have already been chosen up to that point by the other players (she is assumed always to be able to recall her own previous actions). The Stackelberg game is a game of perfect information since firm *B* knows the output of *A* when it is its turn to choose an output level. The Prisoners' Dilemma game has *imperfect information* since neither player knows the output of the other when taking its decision. It is usual to make the *common knowledge assumption*: every player knows that the other players know the characteristics of the game, knows that they know she knows, and so on *ad infinitum*.

- The feasibility of *binding commitments* to choose certain actions in certain circumstances in the course of the game. In a *cooperative game* it is possible for all players to make binding commitments about the actions to be taken in all possible circumstances, i.e. all players can commit themselves to choosing a particular strategy. A *non-cooperative game* is one in which it is not possible to commit to strategies. The Prisoner's Dilemma, Stackelberg and Entry games are assumed to be non-cooperative. In a sense the terminology is unfortunate. An important type of cooperative game is a bargaining game, but there may be little that looks cooperative, in the usual sense, about the behaviour of the bargaining parties. We shall also see that non-cooperative games may produce solutions that look collusive or cooperative, in that the payoffs to the players are the same as at the solution of a cooperative game in which they could commit themselves to strategies.

In the next section we use the three basic examples of games to illustrate different ways of describing the key elements of games, and to derive three solution concepts: strict dominance, Nash equilibrium and sub-game perfect equilibrium. In section C we examine games of incomplete and imperfect information and the Bayes–Nash and perfect Bayesian equilibrium concepts, and present two examples of such games: the finitely repeated prisoner's dilemma, and a 'herding' model. In section D we give a short exposition of mixed strategies. The last three sections examine cooperative and non-cooperative models of bargaining.

B. Game representation and solutions

There are two main ways of representing games. The *extensive form* uses a graphical device known as a game tree to illustrate the actions available to the players and the sequence in which they have to be chosen. The *strategic form*, also often called the *normal form*, collapses the extensive form into a matrix, which shows the payoffs

Figure 15.1

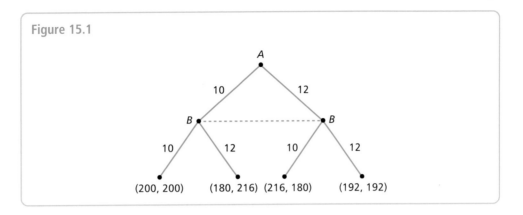

corresponding to the possible strategy choices of the two players. Both representations are too cumbersome for more complex games with many players or strategies. Their main use is to illustrate game-theoretic ideas in a simple context.

The Prisoner's Dilemma

The two firms in the market could agree verbally to produce 10 units each, thus producing the monopoly output of 20, and sharing the resulting profit of 400 equally between them. But because we assume that they cannot make binding commitments, there is nothing to stop one or both firms reneging on such an agreement and producing some other amount. To fix ideas, suppose that the only other action considered by each firm is to produce its capacity output of 12 units. Thus each firm has the action set {10, 12}.

Figure 15.1 shows the extensive form of the game in which the firms produce and put their outputs onto the market simultaneously. The letter A by the first node means that firm A must decide whether to produce 10 units, and so move down the left branch, or 12 units, and move down the right branch. The letter B beside the nodes then reached shows that firm B must then take its decision. The dashed line joining the two B-nodes indicates that firm B does not know, when it has to take its decision, what the choice of firm A is. The two nodes are in the same *information set* for firm B. (The device of the information set is useful to represent simultaneous choices: we could equivalently have firm B 'choosing first', with firm A then having an information set containing two nodes.) At its information set, B can choose 10 or 12, and the end-node reached will also depend on the decision taken by firm A. Note that, at each node in a given information set, a player must have exactly the same set of choices available; otherwise she would know which node she was at, and the nodes could not then be in the same information set.

There are four possible outcomes, each corresponding to a particular path through the tree. The profit function for firm $i = A, B$ (recalling the demand function, and that unit cost is £1) is

$$v_i = (41 - q_A - q_B)q_i - q_i \qquad [\text{B.1}]$$

The reader should confirm that the four possible output pairs (10, 10), (10, 12), (12, 10) and (12, 12) generate the profit pairs for the two firms, with A's written first, shown at the outcome nodes of the tree. What will the firms choose?

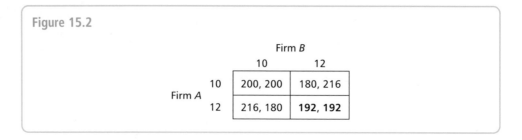

Figure 15.2

First consider B's decision. B does not know what A has chosen, but, whichever node in its information set B is at, it does better by choosing 12, since $216 > 200$ and $192 > 180$. The same is true for A. If it chooses 12 rather than 10, it will get 216 rather than 200 if B chooses 10, and 192 rather than 180 if B chooses 12. It therefore seems reasonable to regard (12, 12) as the solution of the Prisoner's Dilemma game.

The answer may be seen even more easily using the strategic form of the game. Since the firms simultaneously choose one of two output levels, we can take an output level as a strategy. The payoff matrix in Fig. 15.2 shows the profit pairs resulting from each possible strategy pair or play of the game. In the figure, firm A chooses the row and firm B the column. The numbers in the cells of the matrix are the resulting profits v_A, v_B.

Regardless of what firm B chooses, firm A does better by choosing 12. Likewise for firm B. Setting output at 12 is a *dominant strategy* for each firm. If firm A expects B to stick to a verbal agreement to maximize joint profits by producing 10 units, A does better by reneging on the agreement and choosing 12. But if A reasons that B will also choose 12 because B follows the same argument, A still does better by choosing 12. The same logic applies to firm B.

The matrix shows why the Prisoner's Dilemma game has received so much attention in economics. The most striking feature of this outcome is that both players would be better off if they played (10, 10), which maximizes their combined profits, but in the absence of a binding agreement the dominant strategy solution is (12, 12).

The Stackelberg game

The Stackelberg game differs from the Prisoners' Dilemma game in that firm A commits to producing some output level simply by producing it today. Firm B must then take firm A's action as given when deciding how much to produce tomorrow. As we shall see, being the leader (A) creates an advantage. The other, less important difference concerns the firms' possible output levels. For reasons we shall shortly make clear, suppose firm A considers the output choices of 20 units and $13\frac{1}{3}$ units, while firm B considers the outputs 10 and $13\frac{1}{3}$, so that the action sets are $\{20, 13\frac{1}{3}\}$ and $\{10, 13\frac{1}{3}\}$, respectively.

Figure 15.3 gives the extensive form for the game. Firm A can choose 20 or $13\frac{1}{3}$. Since firm B observes the choice by firm A, its information sets when it is its turn to move consist only of single nodes. The game is one of perfect information. Using the profit function in [B.1], the reader should confirm that the profit pairs shown at each end-node correspond (after rounding) to the output pairs by which the end-node is reached.

Figure 15.3

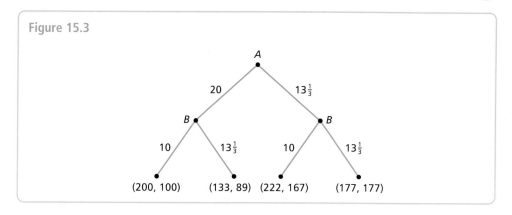

To derive the strategic form of the game requires a little more work than in the Prisoner's Dilemma game. Recall that a strategy must specify what the player will do at each point in the game at which it is her turn to move. In other words, it must be a 'set of instructions' of the form: 'If my opponent does a, I do b, whereas if she does c, I do d', and so on. In the game, firm A moves first and its choices are not contingent on the actions of firm B. Firm A's strategies are thus to choose 20 or $13\frac{1}{3}$ once and for all. We denote firm A's strategies by s_1^A and s_2^A respectively.

Firm B will know what action A has chosen and each of B's strategies must therefore consist of instructions on what to do for each of A's actions. Since A has two actions, each strategy for B must specify two courses of action, and, since B has the same two choices whatever A has chosen, there are four possible strategies for B. (If A could have chosen five output levels and if B could choose three output levels, then B would have three possible actions contingent on each of A's five choices, making for $3^5 = 243$ possible strategies. Strategy sets can thus become large, even in apparently simple games.) In the current case, B's four possible strategies are:

s_1^B: if A chooses 20, choose 10; if A chooses $13\frac{1}{3}$, choose 10

s_2^B: if A chooses 20, choose 10; if A chooses $13\frac{1}{3}$, choose $13\frac{1}{3}$

s_3^B: if A chooses 20, choose $13\frac{1}{3}$; if A chooses $13\frac{1}{3}$, choose 10

s_4^B: if A chooses 20, choose $13\frac{1}{3}$; if A chooses $13\frac{1}{3}$, choose $13\frac{1}{3}$

The set of strategies gives a complete specification of how B may play the game. The description can be shortened to

$$s_1^B = (10, 10); \quad s_2^B = (10, 13\tfrac{1}{3}); \quad s_3^B = (13\tfrac{1}{3}, 10); \quad s_4^B = (13\tfrac{1}{3}, 13\tfrac{1}{3})$$

as long as it is understood that the first number in each pair is B's choice if A chooses 20, and the second is B's choice if A chooses $13\frac{1}{3}$. The payoff matrix for the strategic form is shown in Fig. 15.4. (We sometimes round payoffs to the nearest whole number to avoid clutter but this has no effect on the analysis.)

Thus, when firm A chooses s_1^A, an output of 20, firm B's strategy s_1^B specifies playing 10, yielding payoffs (200, 100), whereas when A chooses s_2^A, an output of $13\frac{1}{3}$, s_1^B also specifies choosing 10, thus yielding (222, 167). The reader should similarly explain the other entries in the matrix.

What outcome would we predict in the game? From the extensive form the answer seems clear. If A produces 20, the best that B can do is to produce 10, giving

Figure 15.4

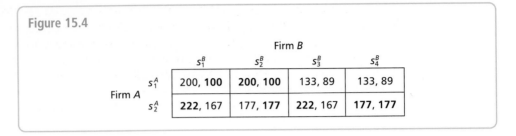

A a payoff of 200. On the other hand, if A produces $13\frac{1}{3}$, B does best by also producing $13\frac{1}{3}$, since a profit of 177 is better than 167. In that case A has a payoff of 177. We argue that A will predict that B will follow with 10 if it leads with 20 and $13\frac{1}{3}$ if it leads with $13\frac{1}{3}$. Hence A will do best choosing to lead with 20.

In the strategic form the outcome seems less obvious. Unlike the Prisoner's Dilemma game, A does not have a dominant strategy, and so we cannot find an equilibrium in dominant strategies. Instead we introduce the concept of a *Nash equilibrium*. Let $v^A(s_i^A, s_j^B)$ and $v^B(s_i^A, s_j^B)$ be the payoffs to A and B when A chooses strategy s_i^A and B chooses strategy s_j^B ($i = 1, 2; j = 1, \ldots, 4$). A strategy pair (s_N^A, s_N^B) is a *Nash equilibrium* of the two-player game if and only if

$$v^A(s_N^A, s_N^B) \geq v^A(s_i^A, s_N^B) \qquad i = 1, 2 \qquad\qquad \text{[B.2]}$$

and

$$v^B(s_N^A, s_N^B) \geq v^B(s_N^A, s_j^B) \qquad j = 1, \ldots, 4 \qquad\qquad \text{[B.3]}$$

A strategy for player A is a *best reply* to a given strategy of player B, if it gives A at least as high a payoff as any of her other strategies. [B.2] shows that s_N^A is A's best reply to s_N^B, and [B.3] that s_N^B is B's best reply to s_N^A. Hence a strategy pair (s_N^A, s_N^B) is a *Nash equilibrium* when s_N^A and s_N^B are *mutual best replies*.

To find a Nash equilibrium in the payoff matrix in Fig. 15.4, first scan the cells of the matrix to find the cases in which the first entry, the payoff to firm A, is the *highest value in its column*. The answers are shown in bold in the matrix. Thus s_1^A is the best reply to s_2^B and s_2^A is the best reply to the rest of B's strategies. Next, scan the matrix to find the cases in which the second entry, the payoff to firm B, is the *highest value in its row*. Again the answers are shown in bold: s_1^B and s_2^B are best replies to s_1^A, whereas s_2^B and s_4^B are best replies to s_2^A. Cells (s_1^A, s_2^B) and (s_2^A, s_4^B), corresponding to the strategy pairs, have *both* entries in bold, meaning that they are mutual best replies, and therefore Nash equilibria. If B plays s_2^B, A's highest profit from the cells in that column results from playing s_1^A, whereas if A plays s_1^A, B's best reply in that row is s_2^B. Similarly, if B plays s_4^B, A's best reply is s_2^A, whereas if A plays s_2^A, B's best reply is s_4^B. Thus, the strategic form shows that the game has two Nash equilibria, something not readily apparent from the extensive form. Note that, although (s_1^A, s_1^B) yields exactly the same payoffs as (s_1^A, s_2^B), it is not a Nash equilibrium. If firm A expects firm B to play s_1^B, its best reply is s_2^A, not s_1^A.

What play of the game do the two Nash equilibria in the Stackelberg game represent? In (s_1^A, s_2^B), firm A chooses 20 and B chooses 10, which is the play that it seems reasonable to expect from inspection of the extensive form in Fig. 15.3. Firm A realizes that, when B is faced with an output of 20, the best that B can do is produce an output of 10, and so the best A can do for itself is indeed to produce 20.

In the other Nash equilibrium (s_2^A, s_4^B), firm A produces $13\frac{1}{3}$, and firm B's best reply is also to produce $13\frac{1}{3}$. But why should A produce $13\frac{1}{3}$ in the first place? The answer is given by looking at B's strategy s_4^B, in which firm B will produce $13\frac{1}{3}$ if firm A produces 20. We can interpret s_4^B as a *threat* to deter firm A from producing 20. If firm B produces $13\frac{1}{3}$ rather than 10 when A produces 20 it will reduce A's payoff from 200 to 133. If firm A believes the threat, then indeed its best reply is to produce $13\frac{1}{3}$ rather than 20. But it is not reasonable for A to believe the threat. If firm A does produce 20 today then B hurts itself if it produces $13\frac{1}{3}$, rather than 10, tomorrow. Since A has already produced 20 units, B's choice can have no effect on A's output. It seems plausible therefore that A would not regard B's threat as credible and would produce 20. The extensive form of the game suggests that only one of the two Nash equilibria identified in the strategic form is a reasonable play of the game. The lack of plausibility of one of the Nash equilibria is not as apparent in the strategic form representation because the timing of moves is less obvious. After discussing the third of our simple games, we will investigate the way in which the Nash equilibrium concept can be refined and strengthened to rule out implausible Nash equilibria, in which one player makes threats which are not credible.

The Entry game

Firm A is an incumbent monopolist and firm B the potential entrant. To simplify the calculations we assume that firm B will produce output of $13\frac{1}{3}$ if it enters, so that firm B's actions are to enter and produce $13\frac{1}{3}$ or not to enter. This simplification does not alter the solution of the game. If, following entry by firm B, both firms could simultaneously choose any output level, then the only Nash equilibrium is the output pair $(13\frac{1}{3}, 13\frac{1}{3})$. (See Question 3, Exercise 15B.) Hence we can assume that firm B, if it enters, in effect 'offers' the incumbent A the Nash equilibrium of the post-entry output game. We also assume firm A considers only three possible output levels: the 'accommodating' output level $13\frac{1}{3}$, the monopoly output 20, and the 'warlike' output $27\frac{2}{3}$. The reason the latter is warlike is that if B does enter and produces $13\frac{1}{3}$, the total output is 41, which reduces market price to zero. Hence the firms make losses of £$27\frac{2}{3}$ and £$13\frac{1}{3}$ respectively (recall costs are £1 per unit), and entry for firm B is highly unprofitable. Thus we can interpret output of $27\frac{2}{3}$ as instigating a price war, the threat of which is intended to deter entry.

The extensive form of the entry game is shown in Fig. 15.5. Like the Stackelberg game, but unlike the Prisoner's Dilemma game, in the current specification it is a game of perfect information, since A chooses from its action set $\{13\frac{1}{3}, 20, 27\frac{2}{3}\}$ after B has made its choice from $\{0, 13\frac{1}{3}\}$, where we interpret '0' as the decision not to enter.

The reasonable play of the game seems clear from the extensive form. If B enters with $13\frac{1}{3}$, A's best reply is the accommodating output $13\frac{1}{3}$, which yields positive profit for B. The alternative for B is not to enter and to earn a zero profit. Hence B will enter and A will accommodate.

Now consider the strategic form. Since B chooses an output once and for all, we can equate its strategies with its two possible outputs: $s_1^B = 0$; $s_2^B = 13\frac{1}{3}$. On the other hand, A has $3^2 = 9$ possible strategies, since with each of the three output levels it could produce if B does enter, it can combine each of the three output levels if B does not enter.

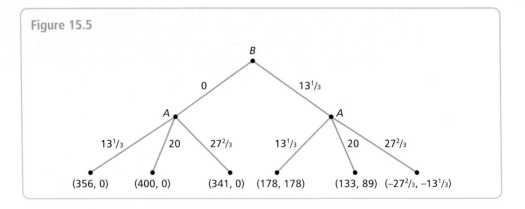

Figure 15.5

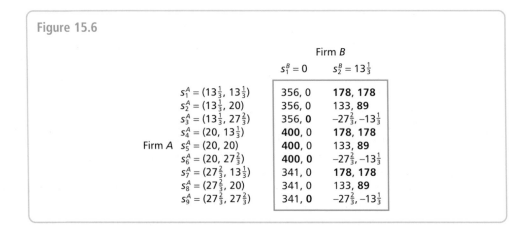

Figure 15.6

The payoff matrix is shown in Fig. 15.6 where, for example, $s_2^A = (13\frac{1}{3}, 20)$ means that A responds to B's choice of 0 (non-entry) with $13\frac{1}{3}$ and to B's choice of entry at output $13\frac{1}{3}$ with output of 20.

The highest payoff for A in each column, and the highest payoff for B in each row, are again highlighted. We find the Nash equilibria by searching for cells with a first entry that is highest in its column and a second entry that is highest in its row, i.e. with *both* payoffs in bold. There are four Nash equilibria: (s_4^A, s_2^B), (s_1^A, s_2^B), (s_7^A, s_2^B) and (s_6^A, s_1^B). The first, (s_4^A, s_2^B), corresponds to what appeared in the extensive form to be a reasonable play of the game: B enters, A accommodates. The two equilibria (s_1^A, s_2^B), (s_7^A, s_2^B) have the same accommodating reply by A to entry by B as in the first equilibrium, but A responds by producing non-monopoly outputs if B does not enter. This seems very implausible behaviour. The last Nash equilibrium (s_6^A, s_1^B) has B staying out of the market and A producing the monopoly output. Again, as in the Stackelberg game, we can interpret A's strategy s_6^A as a threat: if B does enter, A will initiate a price war by producing $27\frac{2}{3}$. If B believes the threat, then its best reply is to stay out of the market, but again we doubt that it is reasonable for B to believe that A would carry out the threat. If B does enter, A gains nothing, but rather loses a lot by forcing a price war. The threat of the price war is not credible. Nevertheless, (s_6^A, s_1^B) is a Nash equilibrium.

There are four possible Nash equilibria of the game. As in the Stackelberg game, only one of them seems plausible. Rather than making ad hoc decisions to drop the implausible equilibria in each specific game, we next examine the concept of sub-game perfection, which yields a definition of equilibrium which rules them out generally.

Sub-game perfect equilibrium

We found a solution of the Prisoner's Dilemma game by using the equilibrium concept of strict dominance, and solutions of the Stackelberg and Entry games by applying the concept of Nash equilibrium. Since a strictly dominating strategy is a best reply to *any* strategy choice of the other player, it is a best reply to her strictly dominating strategy. Hence any equilibrium in strictly dominating strategies is also a Nash equilibrium and we can restrict attention to Nash equilibria.

Some of the Nash equilibria in the Stackelberg and Entry games did not seem plausible. They involved strategies based on threats that did not appear credible, in the sense that the firm making the threat would have been made worse off if it carried out the threat. The concept of *Sub-game Perfect Equilibrium* (SPE) was proposed by Reinhard Selten to identify Nash equilibria which do not embody non-credible threats. Since SPE solutions are always also Nash equilibria, the SPE concept is a *refinement* of Nash equilibrium. The use of the concept increases the predictive power of the theory since the number of possible equilibria is reduced. For example, as we will see in the Entry game, whereas we were only able to say that there are Nash equilibria in which entry occurs and others where it does not, we will be able to find a unique solution using the SPE concept. We shall also see in the analysis of non-cooperative bargaining games in section 15F that there can be a unique SPE solution even when there are infinitely many Nash equilibria.

To define the SPE concept formally we use the idea of a sub-game. A sub-game of a game G is a game that begins at a single node (other than an end-node) of G and contains all the information sets that can be reached from that node. A game is defined to be a sub-game of itself, and so we use the term *proper* sub-game to denote a sub-game that is not identical to the whole game (the terminology comes from set theory). The distinction between a node and an information set is crucial for the definition of sub-games. In games of imperfect information, at least one information set for at least one player contains more than one decision node. By contrast, in games of perfect information each player knows the previous actions of the other player or players when it is her turn to move, and so all information sets consist of a single decision node. Thus games of perfect information will always have proper sub-games, whereas games of imperfect information may not.

We illustrate the concept of the subgame using the extensive forms of our three example games (the strategic form of a game is useless for this purpose):

1. The Prisoner's Dilemma (Fig. 15.1) has no proper sub-games: the only sub-game is the game itself. The game is one of imperfect information and the nodes at which B chooses lie in the same information set. The only single decision node and hence the only starting point for a sub-game is at the start of the game. In games with no proper sub-games, we will see that the sets of SPE and Nash equilibria are identical.

2. The Stackelberg game (Fig. 15.3) has three sub-games: the game itself and the two proper sub-games that begin at B's decision nodes. The two proper sub-games are very simple, each consisting just of B's choice between 10 and $13\frac{1}{3}$.

3. The Entry game (Fig. 15.5) also has three sub-games: the game itself and the two proper sub-games beginning at A's decision nodes. The two proper sub-games are again very simple, since, in each, A has to choose among $13\frac{1}{3}$, 20 and $27\frac{2}{3}$. (Question 5, Exercise 15B, examines the entry game with a richer sub-game structure but the same solution.)

We can now define a sub-game perfect equilibrium of a game G as a list of strategies, one for each player, which yield a Nash equilibrium *in every sub-game of G*. Since G is a sub-game of itself, the SPE must also be a Nash equilibrium of the whole game and hence must be in the set of Nash equilibria. However, it need not be the case that all the Nash equilibria are also sub-game perfect. In the Prisoner's Dilemma, the SPE and the Nash equilibrium coincide, but in the Stackelberg and Entry games we can show that applying the SPE concept gets rid of the Nash equilibria that we regarded as implausible.

In the case of finite games, that is games which contain a finite number of information sets, we find the SPE strategies by *backward induction*. We begin with the last proper sub-games, find their Nash equilibria and replace the sub-games by their Nash equilibrium payoffs. We then find the Nash equilibria of the next-to-last subgames, replace them with their equilibrium payoffs, and so on back to the start of the game.

Consider the Stackelberg game in Fig. 15.3. The last proper sub-games are the two games beginning at B's decision nodes. The Nash equilibria of the sub-games are simply B's best choices. In the left-hand sub-game (resulting from A's previous choice of 20), B's best choice is 10. In the right-hand sub-game (resulting from A's previous choice of $13\frac{1}{3}$), B's best choice is $13\frac{1}{3}$. We can now form the new sub-game shown in Fig. 15.7, in which A chooses either 20 or $13\frac{1}{3}$.

In the sub-game, A chooses in the expectation that in the resulting sub-game the outcome will be the Nash equilibrium. A will choose 20 which yields a sub-game with a higher payoff than the sub-game resulting from choice of $13\frac{1}{3}$. Hence the SPE yields the output pair (20, 10) and is identical to the Nash equilibrium which we earlier suggested was the most plausible. In the sub-game following A's choice of 20, B's threatened response of $13\frac{1}{3}$ is not a Nash equilibrium. Thus the Nash equilibrium (s_2^A, s_4^B) of the entire game which includes the threat is ruled out as an SPE solution. The unique SPE strategy pair is (s_1^A, s_2^B).

In the Entry game of Fig. 15.5 the last proper sub-games are at A's decision nodes. The Nash equilibria of the proper sub-games are simply A's best choices: 20 in the

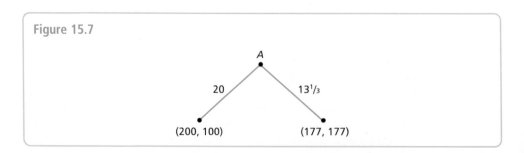

Figure 15.7

A

20      $13^1/_3$

(200, 100)   (177, 177)

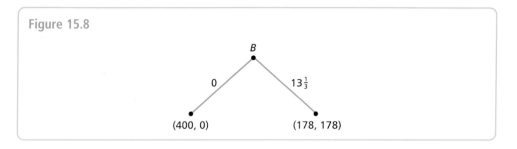

Figure 15.8

left-hand sub-game arising if B does not enter, and $13\frac{1}{3}$ in the right-hand sub-game arising if B does enter. Replacing the subgames by the corresponding payoffs gives the game in Fig. 15.8. B's best choice here is $13\frac{1}{3}$. Thus the unique SPE strategy profile is (s_4^A, s_2^B). The Nash equilibrium profile (s_6^A, s_1^B) is not an SPE profile because it does not yield a Nash equilibrium in the right-hand sub-game in Fig. 15.5 following B's decision to enter. The other two Nash equilibrium profiles (s_1^{1A}, s_2^B), (s_7^A, s_2^B) are also not sub-game perfect because they do not yield Nash equilibria – the best choice – in the left-hand sub-game following B's decision not to enter.

Repeated games

In a repeated game a given *constituent game* is played more than once. For example, in the Prisoner's Dilemma game the two firms could choose their outputs simult-aneously every day with demand and cost conditions the same on all days. If v_{it} is the payoff player i receives at the tth repetition of the constituent game, for $t = 1, \ldots, T$, and r is the per-period interest rate, assumed constant and the same for both players, then player i's payoff in the repeated game is

$$v_i = \sum_{t=1}^{T} \delta^{t-1} v_{it} \qquad [B.4]$$

where $\delta \equiv 1/(1 + r)$ is the discount factor. The payoff in the repeated game is the present value of the payoffs in the constituent games.

Figure 15.9 illustrates the extensive form for the repeated game in which the constituent Prisoner's Dilemma game is played twice. At each end-node of the first play of the constituent game is the game tree for the second play of the constituent game. There are 16 possible end-nodes for the repeated game. A strategy for the repeated game specifies an action for each player at each of her decision nodes. Thus player A's strategy must specify a choice at the first node, labelled $A1$, together with a choice at each of the four end-nodes of the first constituent game, or beginning nodes of the second, labelled $A2$. Likewise for player B. In deriving the payoffs at the end of the repeated game, we have assumed $\delta = 0.9$, or an interest rate of about 10%.

We derive the equilibrium outcome of the repeated Prisoner's Dilemma game using only the extensive form (Question 7, Exercise 15B, analyses the strategic form). Play-ing 12 in each constituent game for each player is a Nash equilibrium. It is also an SPE. The last proper sub-games begin at the nodes labelled $A2$, since the players are assumed to observe the outcomes at the end of the first period, and can therefore deduce what strategy pair was played. Replacing the sub-games with their Nash equilibrium pay-offs results in Fig. 15.10. The only sub-game is now the game starting at $A1$, which

Figure 15.9

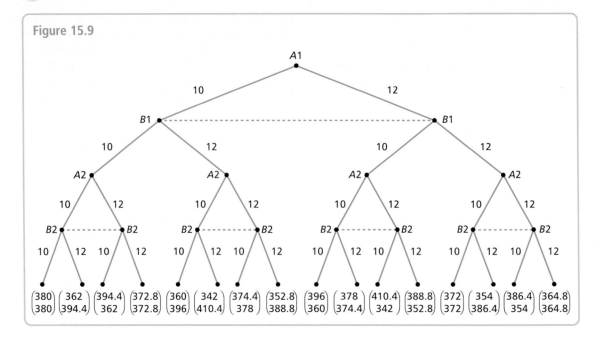

Figure 15.10

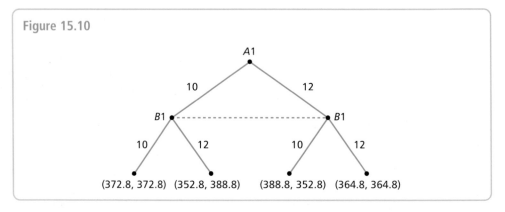

is a Prisoner's Dilemma game with the same structure as, but different payoffs from, the constituent Prisoner's Dilemma game of Fig. 15.1. The dominant actions are (12, 12). Thus in the repeated game consisting of two plays of the Prisoner's Dilemma, the equilibrium strategies are the repeated choice of the output levels that are the equilibrium of the *one-shot game*, i.e. the constituent game played only once.

After the first round of the constituent game, the players can work out from their own output and the market price what output the other firm produced. This raises the possibility of enforcing the 'cooperative' joint profit-maximizing choices of (10, 10) in each round of the game. For example, one firm could say to the other: 'Let's cooperate by producing 10 each in the first period. If you honour the agreement I will play 10 in the second round, but if you break the agreement I will produce 12 in the second round.' If, as a result, the firms choose (10, 10) in both rounds they each get discounted payoffs of $200 + \delta200 = 380$ rather than the SPE payoff of $192 + \delta192 = 364.8$.

But the cooperative strategy is not part of the SPE. In the second period, the sub-game is identical to the one-shot Prisoner's Dilemma. Each player can predict that (12, 12) will be played in the second period. But then the promised reward in the second period for cooperation in the first period is not credible since firm A knows that firm B will choose the 'punishment' output irrespective of whether A cooperated or not in the first period. Firm B will reason in the same way. Hence the best action for each firm is to produce 12 in the first period.

The cooperative strategy will unravel in similar fashion for any *finite* number of repetitions of the Prisoner's Dilemma. There must always be a last period, in which (12, 12) will be played. Hence the reward for playing cooperatively in the next-to-last round is not credible and so the choice in the next-to-last round will also be (12, 12). Since (12, 12) will be played in the next-to-last period the reward for cooperation in the second-to-last round is also not credible and the outcome will be (12, 12), which implies that (12, 12) will be the outcome in the third-to-last round, and so on back to the first round of the game.

The *infinitely repeated* Prisoner's Dilemma, in which the constituent game is played an infinite number of times, has dramatically different solutions. There is no last period and so no last sub-game, implying that backward induction arguments cannot be used. The concept of sub-game perfect equilibrium can, however, still be applied since the sub-games of the game beginning at $t = 1$ are well-defined. With T infinite, the sub-games beginning at $t = 2, 3, \ldots$ are identical to each other as well as to the game beginning at $t = 1$, and consist of infinitely many repetitions of the same constituent game.

Unsurprisingly, one SPE of the infinitely repeated game consists of the repeated play of the one-shot Nash equilibrium choice (12, 12). If, in each sub-game beginning at period $t = 1, 2, \ldots$, firm A expects firm B to produce 12 in periods $t, t + 1, t + 2, \ldots$, then its best reply is also always to produce 12, and likewise for firm B. Thus both players always choosing 12 from t onwards is a Nash equilibrium in the sub-game starting at $t = 1, 2, \ldots$. Thus the strategy profile in which both players choose 12 in all periods is an SPE.

However, unlike the finitely repeated Prisoner's Dilemma game, there are many SPEs. One of particular interest is the *cooperative equilibrium*. Suppose firm $i = A, B$ adopts the following *trigger strategy*: in each period it produces 10, unless the other firm has produced 12 in the previous period, in which case i will punish the other firm by producing 12 in *every period thereafter*. If firm B expects firm A to play the trigger strategy, is firm B's best reply also to play the trigger strategy? If firm B produces 12 in some period t, it has an immediate gain of 16, which is the difference between its period t payoff of 216 from (10, 12) and of 200 from (10, 10). In *every* subsequent period $t + 1, t + 2, \ldots$, firm B will lose 8. This is the difference between the period payoff of 200 from (10, 10) and of 192 from (12, 12), which will be the equilibrium in the sub-game following a deviation. The present value of 8 per period for ever, starting in one period's time, is $8/r$. Thus it is better not to deviate if the one-period gain at t is less than the discounted loss from $t + 1$ onwards: $16 < 8/r$. Thus for $r < 0.5$ it is better not to deviate. The same argument applies to firm A. Hence for interest rates less than 50% the trigger strategies are mutually best replies and so constitute a Nash equilibrium.

Do trigger strategies also constitute a sub-game perfect equilibrium, when $r < 0.5$? In any sub-game beginning in a period after the players have chosen (10, 10), we have just shown that it is a Nash equilibrium to play the trigger strategies. Consider the sub-game following a period in which one of the firms has deviated by playing 12. In the following sub-game the punishment equilibrium (12, 12) is a Nash equilibrium, as we also showed earlier. Thus trigger strategies are a Nash equilibrium in all possible sub-games, and so are sub-game perfect.

The analysis of the possible equilibria in infinitely repeated games is of considerable importance for oligopoly theory, which is the subject of the next chapter. We therefore do not pursue this topic further here, except for setting the analysis of the infinitely repeated Stackelberg game as an exercise (see Question 8, Exercise 15B).

Justifications for Nash equilibrium

There are two main arguments for using the Nash equilibrium as a solution concept. The first is based on the concept of rational behaviour. A rational player is one who chooses her best strategy. A rational player who believes that her opponent is just as rational as she is will, by a process of logical deduction, come to the conclusion that her Nash equilibrium strategy is the best one to play. As we noted at the beginning of the chapter, a player must form an expectation of how the other player will choose, in order to work out the consequences of her own choices. Suppose that in the Prisoner's Dilemma game A were to begin with the expectation that B will choose 10. Then her best reply is to play 12. However, if she believes that B can reason similarly, A will conclude that B will also play 12. Hence the expectation that B will choose 10 is not consistent with A's belief about what a rational player would do. As A therefore expects B, as a rational player, to choose 12, her best reply is also 12. B will apply the same reasoning and will still want to choose 12. Thus there is no need for A to revise her expectation about how B will play. Similarly for B's expectations about how A will play. This is the key aspect of a pair of strategies which possess the mutually best reply property defining the Nash equilibrium. If A expects B to play his Nash equilibrium strategy, A's best reply is her own Nash equilibrium strategy. Believing that B, as a rational player, will also have reasoned in the same way, A has no reason to change her expectation about B's choice. Furthermore, suppose the players have verbally agreed to play their Nash equilibrium strategies. Then, even though it is not a binding commitment, neither has an incentive to deviate when they choose their actions. *Only* the Nash equilibrium strategy profile has this self-enforcing property.

However, we saw also, in the Stackelberg and Entry games, that there can be Nash equilibria which it would not be sensible or rational to play. Thus we could say that this argument of rationality justifies restricting one's attention to the set of Nash equilibria but does not necessarily justify choosing a particular member of this set. Refinements of Nash equilibrium, such as the SPE, can be thought of as attempting to extend the application of the idea of rational play to such situations.

Of course, in a particular game, if a player has reason to believe that the other player does not reason in the same way as herself, then she may choose a strategy which is not part of a Nash equilibrium. For example, much of the pleasure, and pain, of playing board games such as chess, or card games such as bridge and poker, comes precisely from establishing who is the best player. If you believe that the person you are playing against in a game of chess is weaker than you, you might risk moves which you would not try against a stronger player. Game theory generally assumes that players possess unbounded abilities to remember past events, process information and reason rationally. Games with players with *bounded rationality*, that is of limited ability to remember, reason and process information, are beginning to be studied, though the players are still assumed to be equal in ability.

The second justification for Nash equilibrium as a solution concept is based on learning rather than rationality. Over time, players learn about the features of certain kinds of games, for example the Prisoner's Dilemma, and what the outcomes of different strategies are. For example, someone on first encountering a Prisoner's Dilemma game may play the collectively rational or cooperative strategy (10 in our example). Over time they would come to realize that the individually rational or dominant strategy (12) gives them higher payoffs. The Nash equilibrium concept will yield better predictions as players learn. An interesting area of game theory – the theory of evolutionary games – has developed to explore the question of how and whether experience of playing games over time could lead to Nash equilibria emerging as individuals learn the 'right' way to play the game. Ultimately, the only answer to the question of whether concepts such Nash equilibrium yield useful predictions is whether observed decisions and outcomes are consistent with their predictions.

EXERCISE 15B

1. *The Original Prisoner's Dilemma.* Two prisoners suspected of being accomplices in a crime are being interrogated in separate rooms. Each is told that if he confesses while the other does not, he will be set free, and that if the other confesses while he does not, he will get 5 years in jail. If they both confess, they will each get 2 years in jail; and if neither confesses, each will get 1 year. Set up the payoff matrix of the game, and show that the solution is the same as the market game discussed in the text. Explain why the game is said to illustrate the conflict between the pursuit of individual self-interest and the interest of society as a whole.

2. For the Stackelberg game discussed in the text, derive firm *B*'s reaction function, showing its profit-maximizing output for each output of firm *A*. Then solve the problem of maximizing firm *A*'s profit subject to this reaction function as a constraint. Explain why this procedure yields a Nash equilibrium of this game.

3. Show that $(13\frac{1}{3}, 13\frac{1}{3})$ is the Nash equilibrium of the market game in which each firm simultaneously chooses an output level.

4. Show that, in a game with no proper sub-games, a Nash equilibrium is always an SPE.

5. In the Entry game, suppose that, if it enters in the first period, firm B chooses its output simultaneously with firm *A* in the second period. Show the extensive form of this game. Is it a game of perfect information? Find the SPE and show that it is the same as that of the game discussed in the text.

6. *Selten's Chain Store Paradox.* A company has a chain of five stores in five different cities, in each of which it currently has a monopoly. In each city it is faced by a different potential entrant, and entry will take place sequentially. The incumbent may in each city either fight entry, in which case it will incur a payoff of −1, or accept entry, in which case it will have a payoff of zero. Its monopoly profit is 2 in each city. It receives the advice that it should fight entry, at least initially, since the loss it may incur in the first few markets will be more than compensated by deterring entry subsequently. Use the method of backward induction to show that this is not an SPE, and that the only SPE is to accept entry in every market.

7. Construct the strategic form of the repeated Prisoner's Dilemma game discussed in the text, and find its Nash equilibrium.

8. Are there trigger strategies that would support a cooperative equilibrium as an SPE in an infinitely repeated version of the Stackelberg game?

C. Games of imperfect and incomplete information

In a game of perfect information, every information set consists of a single node: each player knows which actions have previously been chosen by the other players whenever it is her turn to act. If at least one information set contains more than one node, the game is one of *imperfect* information. The Prisoner's Dilemma game is one of imperfect information, since the players choose simultaneously. The Stackelberg game has perfect information since the follower B observes the action of the leader A before making his choice. The Entry game in section B is a game of perfect information, but it has more plausible versions which are games of imperfect information: for example, firm B enters (by constructing production capacity which would be observed by firm A) and then the two firms choose their outputs simultaneously.

When a player is at an information set containing more than one node, her best action will usually depend on precisely which node she is at. We can think of the reasoning underlying the equilibrium concepts of Nash equilibrium and SPE as allowing the player to decide, with probability 1, where she must be, i.e. what the other player must have chosen or be choosing. In games of *incomplete* information, such reasoning is not sufficient, and the players' probability beliefs become an essential feature of the game.

The Stackelberg and Entry games of imperfect information we considered were games of complete information, because all the elements of the game – payoff functions, action sets – were common knowledge. A game of *incomplete information* arises when some elements of the game are not common knowledge. In most games of incomplete information it is assumed that it is the payoff function of at least one player which is not known with certainty by the other player(s), though in general it could be that some other aspect of the game's structure, for example a player's set of possible actions, or whether or not the player is rational, are not known with certainty by the other(s). We develop the theory of games of incomplete information by first extending the example of the Stackelberg game.

Stackelberg game with incomplete information

Assume that in the Stackelberg game firm B could have a cost per unit of either £2 or £0. B is one of two *types* defined by its unit cost. Firm B knows its own type (unit cost) for sure, and that it does so is common knowledge. However, the leader A does not know the unit cost of firm B. Instead, A has probability beliefs about B's costs. Firm A attaches probability $\pi \in (0, 1)$ to B having a unit cost of £2 and probability $1 - \pi$ to B having unit cost £0.

Firm A's payoff from any strategy depends on the strategy of firm B, and the strategy of firm B depends on its type. Hence the payoff to firm A from any given strategy is uncertain. The rational way for A to proceed is to assign a probability to each possible type of firm B and then choose the strategy which maximizes its expected profit (in the terminology of Chapter 17 we are assuming that A is *risk neutral*). Such games are known as *Bayesian games*.

The players are rational and use all the information available in calculating the probabilities of the types of other players. Before the game is played they have initial or prior probability beliefs about the type of the other players. During the course of the game, a player may acquire additional information and we assume she will update her probability beliefs using Bayes' Rule (see Appendix L). In the above simple extension to the basic Stackelberg game, there is no updating by firm A of its probability beliefs, since it moves before firm B and so cannot use information on B's choice to revise its probability beliefs about B's type. However, as we shall see, it is easy to incorporate updating into the game.

The analysis of Bayesian games uses an approach suggested by Harsanyi, which transforms a game of incomplete information into a game of imperfect information. We introduce a fictitious player, Nature, who does not possess a payoff function and does not play strategically. Nature has the first move and its only decision is to choose player B's type – cost level – according to the given probability distribution. Firm A moves next and has an information set consisting of two nodes, since it does not know which choice was made by Nature. Since Nature does not play strategically, firm A cannot use strategic reasoning to work out which node it is at. Rather, it can only assign the given probabilities, π and $1 - \pi$, to each node, and play accordingly. With probability π it is playing the game against type $B2$, and with probability $1 - \pi$ it is playing against type $B0$.

We can find one equilibrium of the simple Stackelberg Bayesian game by examining the profit-maximizing choice of B given that it is high cost, type $B2$, and its profit-maximizing choice given that it is low cost, type $B0$. Firm A believes that firm B is a rational profit-maximizer and so believes that B will choose the output level which maximizes B's profit *given its type*. A can also work out what profit it will earn at any of its output levels given the subsequent choice of B. Hence A's probability beliefs about B's type will imply a probability distribution of profit for A, and A will choose its output level to maximize its expected profit.

Firm B observes q_A. If it has unit cost of £2 its best reply to q_A is found by solving

$$\max_{q_B} (41 - q_A - q_B)q_B - 2q_B$$

yielding

$$q_{B2} = \frac{39 - q_A}{2} \tag{C.1}$$

If B has a unit cost of £0, it chooses q_B to solve

$$\max_{q_B} (41 - q_A - q_B)q_B$$

and its best reply to q_A if it has low cost is

$$q_{B0} = \frac{41 - q_A}{2} \tag{C.2}$$

[C.1] and [C.2] are *reaction functions*, which give each type of B its best response as a function of A's choice.

Firm A knows that the probability of B responding to q_A with q_{B2} is π and with q_{B0} is $1 - \pi$. Hence firm A chooses q_A to solve

$$\max_{q_A} \bar{v}_A = \pi[(41 - q_A - q_{B2})q_A - q_A] + (1 - \pi)[(41 - q_A - q_{B0})q_A - q_A]$$
$$= [40 - q_A - (\pi q_{B2} + (1 - \pi)q_{B0})]q_A \tag{C.3}$$

Substituting from [C.1] and [C.2], obtaining the first-order condition on q_A and solving gives

$$q_A^{BN} = 19\tfrac{1}{2} + \pi \qquad\qquad\qquad\text{[C.4]}$$

where the superscript BN indicates the *Bayes–Nash equilibrium* quantities. Thus A's optimal output depends on its probability belief about the type – the cost level – of firm B. Suppose that $\pi = \tfrac{3}{4}$. Then

$$q_A^{BN} = 20\tfrac{1}{4} \qquad\qquad\qquad\text{[C.5]}$$

and, from [C.1] and [C.2],

$$q_{B2}^{BN} = 9\tfrac{3}{8} \qquad\qquad\qquad\text{[C.6]}$$

$$q_{B0}^{BN} = 10\tfrac{3}{8} \qquad\qquad\qquad\text{[C.7]}$$

The incomplete information version of the Stackelberg game has a Bayes–Nash equilibrium in which

- for *each type* of firm B, its output is a best reply to the output of firm A;
- firm A's output is a best reply to the probability distribution of outputs of firm B, given its probability beliefs about firm B's type.

Note that in a Bayes–Nash equilibrium the action for firm B is type-dependent, rather than a unique value. The equilibrium gives an action for firm B as a function of its type.

Next we show how additional Bayesian elements can be introduced. Suppose that, initially, firm A's type is also uncertain, in that it may have a unit cost of £1 or £0. When Nature makes its choice of firm A's type, both firms observe Nature's choice. Firm A's cost is common knowledge, so firm B will know what type of firm A it is playing against. But it is possible that learning its own type gives information to firm A about the type of firm B. For example, the two firms' cost levels may be positively correlated, so if firm A learns it is the higher cost type, with unit cost of £1, it uses Bayes' Rule to revise its probability belief about firm B's type. The converse holds if firm A learns that it has a unit cost of £0.

Suppose that the joint probabilities with which Nature chooses firm types are those shown in Fig. 15.11. The probability that firms A and B are high cost (£1 and £2, respectively) is 0.6, the probability that firm A is high cost and firm B low cost (£1 and £0) is 0.05, and so on. The last column gives the marginal probabilities of firm A's types and the bottom row those of firm B's types. The information in the table is common knowledge. Thus, before it learns its type, firm A knows that the probability that firm B is high cost is 0.75 and the probability that it is low cost is

Figure 15.11

		Firm B		
		£2	£0	
Firm A	£1	0.6	0.05	0.65
	£0	0.15	0.2	0.35
		0.75	0.25	

0.25. When firm A learns its type, it can revise the probabilities of firm B being high or low cost, using Bayes' Rule, as follows:

$$\pi(B2|A1) = 0.92$$
$$\pi(B0|A1) = 0.08$$
$$\pi(B2|A0) = 0.43$$
$$\pi(B0|A0) = 0.57$$

For example, the probability that firm B has a unit cost of £2 conditional on firm A having a unit cost of £1 is $\pi(B2|A1) = \pi(B2)\pi(A1|B2)/\pi(A1)$, and since $\pi(A1|B2) = \pi(A1 \text{ and } B2)/\pi(A1)$, we have $\pi(B2|A1) = [(0.75)(0.6)/(0.75)]/(0.65)$.

Thus if firm A learns that it has a unit cost of £1 it can be almost certain that firm B has a unit cost of £2, whereas if A has a cost of zero, matters are more evenly balanced. Note that, because we assumed that firm A's cost is common knowledge so that firm B does not acquire any additional information when it learns its own type, B does not revise its beliefs about firm A's type.

We now recalculate the Bayes–Nash equilibrium we found earlier to reflect the change in the information firm A possesses. Firm A's action now depends on its type since this affects its probability beliefs about B's type. If firm A has unit cost of £1, it solves

$$\max_{q_{A1}} \bar{v}_{A1} = [40 - q_{A1} - \pi(B2|A1)q_{B2} - \pi(B0|A1)q_{B0}]q_{A1} \qquad [\text{C.8}]$$

instead of [C.3], whereas if it has unit cost of £0, it solves

$$\max_{q_{A0}} \bar{v}_{A0} = [41 - q_{A0} - \pi(B2|A0)q_{B2} - \pi(B0|A0)q_{B0}]q_{A0} \qquad [\text{C.9}]$$

where in each case we substitute for q_{B2} and q_{B0} from [C.1] and [C.2] before carrying out the maximization. Thus we have the Bayes–Nash equilibrium in which the equilibrium actions of *both* players are functions of their types:

- If firm A has unit cost of £1, $q_{A1} = 20.4$, $q_{B2} = 9.3$, $q_{B0} = 10.3$
- If firm A has unit cost of £0, $q_{A0} = 20.9$, $q_{B2} = 9$, $q_{B0} = 10$

We can generalize from this example to give a definition of a Bayesian game and a Bayes–Nash equilibrium. A Bayesian game consists of

- a set of players – the two firms in the example;
- a set of possible types for each player – defined in the example by the possible cost levels;
- a strategy set for *each* type of *each* player;
- a payoff function defined for *each* type of *each* player – in the example the profit functions at the different cost levels;
- probability beliefs of *each* player over the set of possible types of *all other* players. In the first example, B knew A's type and A assigned probabilities π and $1 - \pi$ to B's types. In the second example, B again knew A's type but A was able to use her knowledge of the matrix of joint probabilities shown in Fig. 15.11 to calculate a probability distribution for B's types conditional on her own type.

A *Bayes–Nash equilibrium* specifies an action for each type of each player, which gives a best reply to the actions of all the possible types of each other player.

In section B we saw that, in the Stackelberg game of complete information, the Nash equilibrium suggested by consideration of the extensive form was not the only Nash equilibrium. We can similarly show that the Bayes–Nash equilibrium we have just derived is not unique.

Thus consider the following strategies for each type of firm B:

- Type $B2$ (unit cost is £2): if A has a cost of £1, produce 12.69; if £0, produce 12.523.
- Type $B0$ (unit cost is £0): if A has a cost of £1, produce 13.69; if £0, produce 13.523.

Firm $A1$'s best reply to these type-dependent strategies is found by solving

$$\max_{q_{A1}} \bar{v}_{A1} = [40 - q_{A1} - \pi(B2|A1)12.69 - \pi(B0|A1)13.69]q_{A1} \qquad [\text{C.10}]$$

giving an output for $A1$ of 13.62. Firm $A0$'s best reply solves

$$\max_{q_{A0}} \bar{v}_{A0} = [41 - q_{A1} - \pi(B2|A0)12.523 - \pi(B0|A0)13.253]q_{A1} \qquad [\text{C.11}]$$

giving an output for firm $A0$ of 13.95. Inserting these outputs into the firm B reaction functions in [C.1] and [C.2] shows that 12.69 and 12.523 are the best replies of $B2$ and 13.69 and 13.523 are the best replies of $B0$, to the respective types of firm A. The strategies of both types of A and both types of B are mutually best replies and constitute a Bayes–Nash equilibrium. The difference between this and the other equilibrium we found is that here A does not insert B's *reaction functions* into its maximization problems, as we did in [C.8] and [C.9], but simply finds its best replies to the given outputs of the B-types.

As in the earlier Stackelberg complete information game in section B, the strategy of either type of B can be interpreted as a threat which will punish A by lower profits if $A1$ does not choose $q_A = 13.62$ and $A0$ $q_A = 13.95$. If firm A believes the threat contained in each type of firm B's strategy, then indeed its best reply is to produce whichever of these outputs corresponds to its type. But why should A believe the threat? If $A1$ produces an output of 20.4 on day 1, its decision is unalterable on day 2 when firm B takes its decision, and firm B would not find it profitable to carry out its threat, and similarly for $A0$. The threat is not credible. Thus the Bayes–Nash equilibrium concept suffers from the same limitation as the Nash equilibrium concept. It may allow non-credible threats to form part of an equilibrium.

In the case of Nash equilibrium in the game of complete information, the refinement of sub-game perfect equilibrium eliminated non-credible threats. Similarly, the concept of *Perfect Bayesian Equilibrium* (PBE) eliminates equilibria based on non-credible threats in games of incomplete information. However, more is involved than a simple application of sub-game perfection. Recall that sub-game perfection was defined in terms of proper sub-games, beginning at an information set consisting of a single node. In Bayesian games such information sets may be rare or non-existent. We cannot therefore apply a definition of equilibrium based on information sets containing only one node. Nevertheless, the key idea, that, when it is a player's turn to move, her actions should constitute a Nash equilibrium for the remainder of the game – the *continuation game* – carries over.

The PBE concept can be defined, informally, as follows:

- At any information set, the player who has to choose an action must assign a probability distribution over the nodes in that information set, reflecting her beliefs about which node has been reached.

- The probability beliefs reflect, where necessary, the results of Bayesian updating, based on the hypothesis that equilibrium strategies have been used up to that point.

- The action taken by the player at each information set must be part of an optimal strategy for the continuation game *starting from that information set*, given her beliefs and the other players' subsequent actions, which correspond to their equilibrium strategies.

The best way to understand the definition is to work through some examples. We begin with the above Stackelberg game. Consider either type of firm B's information set at the point at which it is its turn to choose an output, that is, *after* firm A has chosen *its* output. B's optimal action for this continuation game is to choose its best reply, as given by [C.1] or [C.2]. Then, at firm A's information set, A's optimal action is to solve the problems in [C.8] and [C.9], depending on its type. Thus we have eliminated the Bayes–Nash equilibrium based on non-credible threats and have only the reasonable equilibrium as a PBE. Notice that, if firm B did not observe Nature's choice of firm A's type, it should, under the PBE requirement, use Bayes' Rule to update its probability beliefs on A's type when it has observed A's choice of output and it is its turn to move. If it observes the output 20.4, it should set to 1 the probability that firm A is of type A_2; and if it observes 20.9, it should set this probability to zero. These are the appropriate probability beliefs for firm B along the equilibrium path, since they correspond to the equilibrium strategies of each type of A.

Finitely repeated Prisoner's Dilemma

To examine the PBE concept further, we use an example in which the Prisoner's Dilemma game is repeated a finite number of times. When there is complete information, as in section B, the only sub-game perfect equilibrium of the finitely repeated game consists of the repeated play of the single-period equilibrium. We now present a repeated Prisoner's Dilemma model with incomplete information, based on Kreps *et al.* (1982), to show that there is a PBE which is not the repeated play of the single-period equilibrium.

We introduce incomplete information and drop the unrealistic assumption that both players know the other's type. The finitely repeated Prisoner's Dilemma game is repeated four times, which keeps the calculations relatively simple but is sufficient to bring out the main ideas. Suppose that firm B could, with probability π, be a 'naive' type of player, who always employs a *tit-for-tat* strategy, such that

- in the first period of the game, $t = 1$, B chooses the cooperative action, output level $q_B = 10$;

- in every subsequent period, B chooses the output level the other firm has chosen in the previous period. So, if firm A has cooperated in period $t - 1$ with $q_A = 10$, B chooses $q_B = 10$ in period t, whereas if A has reneged by choosing $q_A = 12$ in period $t - 1$, B chooses $q_B = 12$ in t, for $t = 2, 3, 4$.

Although tit-for-tat is a popular strategy in experiments using Prisoner's Dilemma games, it is not a Nash equilibrium strategy for B.

With probability $(1 - \pi)$, firm B is a rational player, as envisaged in the earlier analysis. Firm A is always rational. At the start of the game, Nature chooses whether B's type is rational, denoted by B_R, or naive, denoted by B_N. Firm B knows its type, but A initially knows only the prior probabilities π and $1 - \pi$. We assume that if B should at any point choose an action that would *not* have been chosen by B_N then A *will immediately revise* π *to zero*. All this is common knowledge.

The point of the model is two-fold. First, it demonstrates that there can be a PBE in which the rational type of firm B_R would for the first two periods play as if it were naive. For these first two periods it is in B_R's interest to maintain A's belief that with probability π it is a tit-for-tat player. If we think of 'reputation' as the probability belief π held by firm A, then we could say that for the first two periods the rational B maintains a reputation for being naive. Second, the model shows that, with (possibly even a small amount of) incomplete information (a low π), the equilibrium of a finitely repeated Prisoner's Dilemma game can have at least some periods in which the players behave cooperatively.

It is convenient, in view of the arithmetic we are going to have to do, to transform the payoffs in the game, shown earlier in Fig. 15.2, by subtracting from all of them the payoff (192) that each receives in the one-period Nash equilibrium. This is just a normalization and does not change anything essential. We also simplify by assuming no discounting ($\delta = 1$). The payoff matrix for the revised constituent game is shown in Fig. 15.12.

This constituent game is played four times. Figure 15.13 shows time paths of choices for A and for each type of B for a PBE in which the rational type of firm B seeks to maintain a reputation for being naive by playing cooperatively for the first two periods.

The equilibrium path for A, shown in the first row, has it playing cooperatively for the first three periods, and only in the last period does it renege. The rational B plays cooperatively for the first two periods, then reneges in the last two, as shown in the second row. Finally, the naive B plays cooperatively in every period. We now derive the conditions under which these time paths of choices result from a PBE.

Figure 15.12

		Firm B	
		10	12
Firm A	10	8, 8	−12, 24
	12	24, −12	0, 0

Figure 15.13

	$t = 1$	$t = 2$	$t = 3$	$t = 4$
A	10	10	10	12
B_R	10	10	12	12
B_N	10	10	10	10

Period 4

In the last period there is a one-shot game, and both A and the rational B_R choose 12 units of output, the Nash Equilibrium. The naive B_N produces 10 in response to A having produced 10 in period 3.

Period 3

In period $t = 3$, B_R plays 12 because it knows that the Nash equilibrium in period 4 is (12, 12). There is no point in maintaining its reputation for being naive in period 3, so it does better by revealing its type. The naive B_N plays tit-for-tat, responding to A's 10 in period 2 by playing 10 in period 3.

   A will choose 10 in period 3 if it is worth taking the chance that B is naive, in order to have it produce 10, rather than 12, in period 4. Thus if, in period 3, A produces 10, its payoff (refer to Fig. 15.12) in $t = 3$ is $\pi 8 + (1 - \pi)(-12) = 20\pi - 12$, since with probability π the output pair is (10, 10), and with probability $(1 - \pi)$ it is (10, 12). In $t = 4$, the payoff is $\pi 24 + (1 - \pi)0$, since with probability π the output pair is (12, 10), and with probability $(1 - \pi)$ it is (12, 12). Thus its overall payoff in the continuation game beginning at $t = 3$ (recalling that there is no discounting) is

$$V_A^3(10, 12) = [\pi 8 + (1 - \pi)(-12)] + [\pi 24 + (1 - \pi)0] = 44\pi - 12 \quad [C.12]$$

We now have to consider whether A could gain by deviating from this strategy.

Deviation 3.1.

In period 4 we know that A cannot do better than to choose 12, given the strategies of the two B types. Hence the only deviation from A's path shown in Fig. 15.13 that is worth considering is to play 12 in period 3 and 12 in period 4. If it does play 12 in period 3, its period 3 payoff is $\pi 24 + (1 - \pi)(0) = 24\pi$, since with probability π the period 3 output pair is (12, 10), and with probability $(1 - \pi)$ it is (12, 12). Playing 12 in period 4 leads to a period 4 payoff of 0 for sure since both the tit-for-tat player B_N and the rational B_R would also choose 12. Thus A's overall payoff from period 3 onwards in the continuation game beginning at $t = 3$, if it plays 12 in period 3, would be $24\pi + 0$. Thus A will not deviate in period 3 from the path shown in Fig. 15.13 if and only if

$$V_A^3(10, 12) = 44\pi - 12 \geqslant V_A^3(12, 12) = 24\pi$$

which is equivalent to

$$\pi \geqslant \frac{12}{20} = \frac{3}{5} \quad [C.13]$$

Period 2

On the equilibrium path shown in Fig. 15.13, if A produces 10 in period 2 its payoff in period 2 is 8 for sure, given that both types of B behave as shown. Thus its overall payoff in the continuation game beginning in period 2 is

$$V_A^2(10, 10, 12) = 8 + V_A^3(10, 12) = 8 + 44\pi - 12 = 44\pi - 4 \quad [C.14]$$

We now have to find conditions under which it would not pay A to deviate in period 2. It could deviate in one of three ways.

Deviation 2.1.

Produce 12 in period 2, 10 in period 3, 12 in period 4. Its payoff from this would be 24 in period 2 (both B types choose 10), but -12 in period 3, since B_N would then also choose 12, and finally 24π in period 4, since B_N would respond with 10 in that period. Its payoff in this deviation is therefore

$$V_A^2(12, 10, 12) = 24 + (-12) + 24\pi = 24\pi + 12 \qquad \text{[C.15]}$$

Thus it pays A not to choose this deviation if and only if

$$V_A^2(10, 10, 12) = 44\pi - 4 \geqslant V_A^2(12, 10, 12) = 24\pi + 12$$

or

$$\pi \geqslant \frac{16}{20} = \frac{4}{5} \qquad \text{[C.16]}$$

Deviation 2.2.

Produce 12 in period 2, 12 in period 3, 12 in period 4. Its payoff would again be 24 in period 2, but 0 in period 3, and also 0 in period 4, since B_N would respond with 12 in both periods. Thus its payoff in this deviation is 24 for sure, and it pays A not to choose this deviation if and only if

$$V_A^2(10, 10, 12) = 44\pi - 4 \geqslant V_A^2(12, 12, 12) = 24$$

which is equivalent to

$$\pi \geqslant \frac{20}{44} = \frac{5}{11} \qquad \text{[C.17]}$$

Deviation 2.3.

Produce 10 in period 2, 12 in period 3, 12 in period 4. Its payoff would then be 8 in period 2, $\pi 24 + (1 - \pi)0$ in period 3, and 0 for sure in period 4. Thus it will not choose this deviation if and only if

$$V_A^2(10, 10, 12) = 44\pi - 4 \geqslant V_A^2(10, 12, 12) = 8 + [\pi 24 + (1 - \pi)0] + 0$$
$$= 8 + 24\pi$$

which is equivalent to

$$\pi \geqslant \frac{12}{20} = \frac{3}{5} \qquad \text{[C.18]}$$

Note that this deviation is in essence equivalent to deviation 3.1 and so yields the same non-deviation condition.

The important thing to note about period 2 is that the rational B chooses to play cooperatively rather than rationally, so the reputation effect is in operation. We must show this is an equilibrium, in that B_R will not wish to deviate from Fig. 15.13 in period 2, given that it does not pay A to deviate from the path shown in the table. B_R's payoff in the continuation game beginning at $t = 2$ is 8 in period 2, plus 24 in period 3, plus 0 in period 4, or $V_B^2(10, 12, 12) = 32$. Consider now what it would gain from deviating by producing 12 in period 2 (we know it could not do better by also deviating by producing 10 in period 3). B would have a payoff of 24 in period 2, but then 0 in periods 3 and 4, since A would revise the probability that B is naive down to zero and produce 12 in period 3. Thus B_R does better by 'investing in its reputation' for being naive in period 2: $V_B^2(10, 12, 12) = 32 \geqslant V_B^2(12, 12, 12) = 24$. As long as A plays as envisaged in Fig. 15.13, which requires that $\pi \geqslant \frac{4}{5}$, B_R will not deviate in period 2 either.

Period 1

If A plays as shown in Fig. 15.13, it earns 8 in each of the first two periods (both types of B choose 10), $\pi 8 + (1 - \pi)(-12)$ in period 3 and $\pi 24 + (1 - \pi)0$ in period 4 and its continuation payoff is

$$V_A^1(10, 10, 10, 12) = 8 + V_A^2(10, 10, 12) = 4 + 44\pi \qquad [\text{C.19}]$$

We now consider what it could earn by deviating.

Deviation 1.1.

Produce 12 in periods 1, 2, 3 and 4. This gives A 24 in period 1. If B_R produces 10 in period 2, it will have revealed its type, since B_N always responds to 12 in period $t - 1$ with 12 in period t. It cannot pay B_R to do this, because it makes a sacrifice of -12 in period 2, and then gets zero thereafter because A knows it is rational. Thus in deviation 1.1 B_R would respond with 12 in each period, as does B_N, and A's payoff from this deviation is 24. It will not find this deviation worthwhile if and only if

$$V_A^1(10, 10, 10, 12) = 4 + 44\pi \geqslant V_A^1(12, 12, 12, 12) = 24$$

or

$$\pi \geqslant \frac{20}{44} = \frac{5}{11} \qquad [\text{C.20}]$$

Deviation 1.2.

Produce 12 in periods 1 and 2, 10 in 3 and 12 in period 4. This gives it 24 in period 1, 0 in period 2 (because, as just explained, both types of B respond with 12 in period 2), -12 in period 3 and $(1 - \pi)0 + \pi 24$ in period 4 (B_N responds with 10 in period 4 to A's 10 in period 3). Hence

$$V_A^1(12, 12, 10, 12) = 12 + 24\pi$$

The deviation will not pay if and only if

$$V_A^1(10, 10, 10, 12) = 4 + 44\pi \geqslant V_A^1(12, 12, 10, 12) \geqslant 12 + 24\pi$$

or

$$\pi \geqslant \frac{8}{20} = \frac{2}{5} \qquad [\text{C.21}]$$

Deviation 1.3.

Produce 12 in period 1, 10 in periods 2, 3 and 12 in period 4. The payoffs are 24 in period 1, -12 in period 2 (B_R mimics B_N by choosing 12 in period 2), $\pi 8 + (1 - \pi)(-12)$ in period 3, and $\pi 24$ in period 4. Hence

$$V_A^1(12, 10, 10, 12) = 24 - 12 + 8\pi - 12 + 12\pi + 24\pi = 44\pi$$

The deviation will therefore not pay if and only if

$$V_A^1(10, 10, 10, 12) = 4 + 44\pi \geqslant V_A^1(12, 10, 10, 12) = 44\pi$$

which is satisfied for all π.

Deviation 1.4.

Produce 12 in period 1, 10 in period 2, 12 in periods 3 and 4. The reader is invited to show that this has a payoff of $12 + 24\pi$ and so the non-deviation condition $V_A^1(10, 10, 10, 12) \geqslant V_A^1(12, 10, 10, 12)$ implies

$$\pi \geqslant \frac{2}{5} \qquad \text{[C.22]}$$

Deviation 1.5.

Produce 12 in period 1, 12 in period 2, 10 in period 3, 12 in period 4. The reader is invited to show that this also has a payoff of $12 + 24\pi$ and so also implies the same non-deviation restriction on the probability distribution of types [C.22].

We should also consider possible deviations involving A producing 10 in period 1 and then the output paths given in deviations 2.1–2.3 above. However, a moment's thought shows that we would be adding 8 to the total payoff of these deviations in each case, and since the payoff on the equilibrium path has also increased by 8, the conditions for non-deviation remain unchanged.

Comparing all the non-deviation conditions, we see that the tightest condition is [C.16], required to rule out deviation 2.1 by A. Thus, if the prior probability that B is a naive, tit-for-tat player is higher than 0.8, A has no incentive to deviate from the output path shown in the table given that both types of B follow their output paths. Does B_R have an incentive to deviate? Its total payoff from that output path is $8 + 8 + 24 + 0 = 40$. If it deviated in the first period it would earn 24 then but zero thereafter, since A would then know its type and would always choose 12. Thus as long as A would not deviate, B_R would not do so either. Given that A follows the path in Fig. 15.13, then B_N would also follow its path in the figure. Hence if $\pi \geqslant 0.8$, the output paths in Fig. 15.13 are a PBE.

In this example, the critical probability that B could be a tit-for-tat player is quite high. Question 3, Exercise 15C, shows that with different payoffs the critical probability becomes very small as the number of finite repetitions is made sufficiently large.

Herding

To conclude the section, we sketch a simple model of *herding*. Herding may arise when a number of individuals take decisions sequentially, given the private information they possess and their observations of the decisions taken by the individuals before them. We show that it can be a PBE for decision-takers to herd, that is to follow the decisions of those before them, even when the private information that they themselves possess suggests they should do otherwise. Such behaviour is held to be responsible for, for example, fashions and fads in consumer choices, and panics and bubbles on stock and foreign exchange markets.

There are n individuals who are identical, except in the exogenously given order in which they take a decision to undertake a specific action or not. Each individual i has as her private information the value of a random variable θ_i. The θ_i are identically and independently uniformly distributed on the interval $[-1, 1]$, with expected value of zero. The payoff to taking the action for each individual is the sum $\sum_{j=1}^{n} \theta_j$, and an individual i will take the action if and only if

$$E_i \left[\sum_{j=1}^{n} \theta_j \right] \geq 0 \qquad [C.23]$$

where $E_i[\sum_{j=1}^{n} \theta_j]$ is i's expected value of the payoff, given her private information on θ_i and her observations of the decisions of individuals $1, 2, \ldots, i-1$.

The first person to take the decision has only her own information, θ_1, and her expectation of all the other values of θ, which is zero. Thus she decides to act if

$$E_1 \left[\sum_{i=1}^{n} \theta_i \right] = \theta_1 \geq 0 \qquad [C.24]$$

Suppose that [C.24] holds. Then the second person to decide observes that the first has taken the action and so can infer that $\theta_1 \geq 0$. Since θ_1 is uniformly distributed, she can calculate the conditional expected value of θ_1 as $\frac{1}{2}$. Thus, given that individual 1 has taken the action, individual 2 will take the action if

$$E_2 \left[\sum_{i=1}^{n} \theta_i \right] = \theta_2 + \tfrac{1}{2} \geq 0 \qquad [C.25]$$

or, equivalently, if

$$\theta_2 \geq -\tfrac{1}{2} \qquad [C.26]$$

(Remember that her expectations of the values of θ_j ($j = 3, 4, \ldots, n$) of the remaining decision-takers are also zero since the θ are independently distributed and she does not observe the actions of later decision-takers when making her decision.) Individual 2's information could be that say $\theta = -\frac{3}{8}$, and the sum of θ_1 and θ_2 could be negative. But nevertheless in a PBE of this game she would take the action if [C.26] is satisfied.

Suppose that [C.26] holds. Now individual 3 observes that both 1 and 2 have taken the action, so she calculates that θ_2 is uniformly distributed between $-\frac{1}{2}$ and 1 and so has a conditional expected value of $\frac{1}{4}$. Then individual 3 takes the action if

$$E_3 \left[\sum_{i=1}^{n} \theta_i \right] = \theta_3 + \tfrac{1}{2} + \tfrac{1}{4} \geq 0 \qquad [C.27]$$

that is, if

$$\theta_3 \geq -\tfrac{3}{4} \qquad [C.28]$$

Thus she could have a very negative value of θ_3 but would still take the action. In this sequence of realizations of the random variables, the private information of each successive decision-taker is becoming of less importance. Everyone could be taking the action even though its total value is strongly negative.

Herding can be volatile, however. Suppose that $\theta_3 < -\frac{3}{4}$, so that individual 3 does not take the action. Individual 4 can calculate that the conditional expected value of $\theta_3 = [-\frac{3}{4} + (-1)]/2 = -\frac{7}{8}$. Then she in turn will not take the action if

$$E_4\left[\sum_{i=1}^{n} \theta_i\right] = \theta_4 + \tfrac{1}{2} + \tfrac{1}{4} - \tfrac{7}{8} < 0$$

that is, if

$$\theta_4 < \tfrac{1}{8} \qquad\qquad \text{[C.29]}$$

so that she could have a (small) positive value and still reject the action. If she did, individual 5 would reject if

$$E_5\left[\sum_{i=1}^{n} \theta_i\right] = \theta_5 + \tfrac{1}{2} + \tfrac{1}{4} - \tfrac{7}{8} - \tfrac{7}{16} < 0$$

that is, if

$$\theta_5 < \tfrac{9}{16} \qquad\qquad \text{[C.30]}$$

Observation of the decisions of others is a poor substitute for observation of their information, because so much information is filtered out in the decision process.

EXERCISE 15C

1. In the example of the Stackelberg Bayesian game, assume that firm B does not observe firm A's type, but knows the information in Fig. 15.11 and observes its own type. Find the PBE of the game.

2. In the Entry game, suppose that the entrant's costs are not observed by the incumbent monopolist, whose costs are common knowledge. Formulate the game as a Bayesian game and discuss its Bayes–Nash and Perfect Bayesian Equilibria.

3. A and B play the following Prisoner's Dilemma game where C denotes the cooperative action and R is the action that would be chosen in the Nash equilibrium of the one-shot game.

		B	
		C	R
A	C	1, 1	$-1, \frac{3}{2}$
	R	$\frac{3}{2}, -1$	0, 0

(a) If the game is played four times, find the minimum probability π that B is a tit-for-tat player, such that in a PBE a rational B would play C in the first two periods.

(b) Let the number of repetitions be $n > 4$, and show that, as n increases, the minimum value of π such that the rational B will play tit-for-tat for the first k periods, with k depending on π but not on n, will decrease.

D. Mixed strategies

So far we have limited our attention to games in which players were restricted to pure strategies: they had to choose a strategy for sure. Unfortunately not all games have a Nash equilibrium, refined or not, in pure strategies. One example is the oligopoly price-setting game we examine in section 16B. Another example is the simple one-shot simultaneous play game shown in Fig. 15.14. Each player has two pure strategies: *l* (*left*) and *r* (*right*) for player A, and *u* (*up*) and *d* (*down*) for player B.

If the players choose pure strategies there is no Nash equilibrium. The pair (*r*, *u*) is not a Nash equilibrium: player A's best response to *u* is *r*. But (*r*, *u*) is not an equilibrium since player B's best response to *r* is *d*. Similarly (*r*, *d*) is not a Nash equilibrium since player A's best response to *d* is *l*. Finally (*l*, *d*) is also not a Nash equilibrium since player B's best response to *l* is *u*. None of the four possible pure strategy combinations is a Nash equilibrium. (The reader should check that if the payoff to player B from the strategy pair (*l*, *u*) was changed to 6 there would be a Nash equilibrium at (*l*, *d*).)

Now suppose that the players can choose the probability with which to play each of their pure strategies. For example, if player A decides to play *l* and *r* with equal probabilities, she could toss a fair coin. If she decided to play *l* with probability 2/13 she could shuffle and cut a pack of cards and play *l* if the Ace or King turned up and *r* otherwise. Whatever the probabilities, we assume that a suitable randomizing device is available. Denote the probability that player A chooses *l* by *x*, so that she chooses *r* with probability (1 − *x*). Similarly *y* is the probability that player B chooses *u*. A mixed strategy for player A is a choice of *x* which determines the probability with which she plays her *l* and *r* pure strategies. Similarly, a mixed strategy for player B is a choice of the probability *y* with which he plays *u*. Games in mixed strategies includes games in pure strategies as special cases where *x* and *y* are restricted to be 0 or 1.

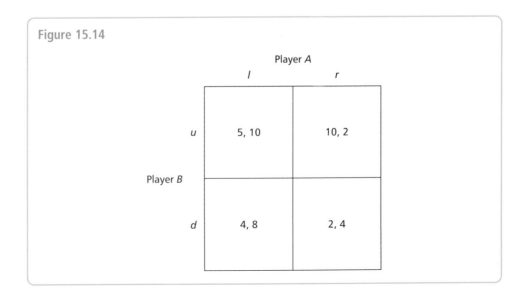

Figure 15.14

Player A

		l	*r*
	u	5, 10	10, 2
Player B			
	d	4, 8	2, 4

Given the chosen probabilities the *expected payoffs* V^i to the players are

$$V^A(x, y) = 5xy + 4x(1 - y) + 10(1 - x)y + 2(1 - x)(1 - y)$$
$$V^B(x, y) = 10xy + 8x(1 - y) + 2(1 - x)y + 4(1 - x)(1 - y)$$

A *mixed strategy Nash equilibrium* is a pair of mixed strategies (x^*, y^*) with the property that $V^A(x^*, y^*) \geqslant V^A(x, y^*)$ for all $x \in [0, 1]$ and $V^B(x^*, y^*) \geqslant V^B(x^*, y)$ for all $y \in [0, 1]$. The mixed strategies must be best responses to each other.

The partial derivative of V^A with respect to x is

$$V_x^A(x, y) = 5y + 4(1 - y) - 10y - (1 - y)2 = 2 - 7y$$

which is positive, zero or negative as y is less than, equal to or greater than 2/7. Thus player A's best response to $y < 2/7$ is to set $x = 1$, and to $y > 2/7$ is to set $x = 0$. If $y = 2/7$ player A would get the same expected payoff from choosing any $x \in [0, 1]$. Figure 15.15 plots player A's best mixed strategy response to y.

The partial derivative of V^B with respect to y is

$$V_y^B(x, y) = 10x - 8x + 2(1 - x) - 4(1 - x) = 4x - 2$$

Player B's best response to x less than $\frac{1}{2}$ is $y = 0$, to x greater than $\frac{1}{2}$ is $y = 1$. If $x = \frac{1}{2}$ player B would be indifferent among all $y \in [0, 1]$. His best mixed strategy response to x is also shown in Fig. 15.15.

It is apparent from Fig. 15.15 that there is an equilibrium in mixed strategies for this one-shot game at $(x^*, y^*) = (\frac{1}{2}, \frac{2}{7})$. This pair of mixed strategies are best responses to each other: if player A chooses to play her pure strategy l with probability $\frac{1}{2}$ then player B cannot do better than to play u with probability 2/7. But, faced with player B choosing u with probability 2/7, player A cannot do better than to play l with probability $\frac{1}{2}$.

Figure 15.15

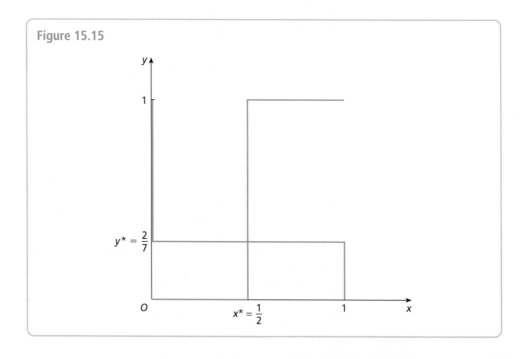

It is possible to show that a Nash equilibrium in mixed strategies exists for *all* games in which the players have a finite number of pure strategies and for a wide class of games in which they have a continuum of strategies.

The alert reader will notice that faced with $y = 2/7$ player A gets the same expected payoff whatever her choice of x. In order to predict that she will actually choose $x^* = \frac{1}{2}$ we would have to extend our specification of the model beyond that shown in the payoff matrix. For example, we could assume that other things being equal players prefer to make choices which sustain an equilibrium. In some circumstances it may be appropriate to think of populations of players of each type. A proportion of type A players always choose l and the rest always choose r. Similarly, a proportion of type B players always choose u and the rest always choose d. If we also specify some kind of evolutionary process which adjusts the proportions of both types of players when there is disequilibrium, the mixed strategy equilibrium has some plausible appeal as a stable state in the evolutionary process. Which story we use to justify predicting that the mixed strategy equilibrium strategies will actually be chosen depends on the context.

EXERCISE 15D

1. *Matching pennies.* The players simultaneously place a £1 coin on the table. If both coins show heads, or if both show tails, then player A wins both coins. If the coins do not match, player B wins both coins. Show that the game has no pure strategy Nash equilibrium. Find the mixed strategy equilibrium. What is the equilibrium if A wins the two displayed coins plus another coin of the same value from B if the coins match, but B wins only the two displayed coins if they do not match?

2. *Scissors, paper, stone.* Two players simultaneously play for a prize of £1 by making hand signals indicating scissors, paper or stone. A player displaying scissors beats a player displaying paper, paper beats stone, and stone beats scissors. Find the equilibrium.

3. *Coordination game.* Two firms make complementary products and have a choice of two locations. If they both choose location 1, firm A has profits of 10 and firm B has profits of 5. If they both choose location 2, firm A's profit will be 5 and firm B's profit will be 10. If they choose different locations they both earn zero profit because both will suffer from reduced demand since consumers will have higher travel costs to buy both goods. They choose their locations simultaneously and cannot communicate or make binding commitments. Find the Nash equilibria.

E. Cooperative bargaining games

In this section we continue the examination of the cooperative game approach to modelling bargaining we introduced in section 10D in the context of union–firm bargaining. We adopt a more general framework to emphasize that the same concepts can be applied in very different contexts. We consider two individuals who can make an agreement in some set of possible agreements P. In section 10D, P was a set of employment and wage combinations. When two individuals are negotiating over the sale of a house, P might be a set of multi-dimensional vectors, whose elements denote the price to be paid, the date of the sale, the form of payments, and which of the fixtures and fittings are to be included in the sale. If the parties fail to agree the outcome is the disagreement event d. In the bilateral monopoly of section 10D the disagreement event is zero employment and no payment by the firm to the workers.

The bargainers have preferences over P and d which are represented by the cardinal utility functions u_i $(i = A, B)$. In the analysis of the consumer in Chapters 2 to 4 preferences satisfied a set of axioms which ensured that they were representable by ordinal utility functions, unique up to order-preserving transformations. We now place stronger restrictions on preferences. If u_i and v_i both represent individual i's preferences then v_i must be a positive linear transformation of u_i: $v_i = \alpha_i + \beta_i u_i$ with $\beta_i > 0$. (See Chapter 17 for a full discussion of cardinal utility.)

The *utility payoff* set U is the set of possible utility combinations which can be produced by an agreement a in P. Formally,

$$U = \{u_A(a), u_B(a) \,|\, a \in P\}$$

The *disagreement utilities* are $\bar{u}_i = u_i(d)$ and the *disagreement point* is $\bar{u} = (\bar{u}_A, \bar{u}_B)$. We assume that the bargainers care only about the outcome of bargaining and not about the procedure or process by which agreement is reached. Thus their attitude to agreements is fully reflected in their utilities. As far as they are concerned the bargaining situation is completely described by U and $\bar{u}$. We therefore attempt to predict the outcome of the cooperative bargaining game as though the parties bargained directly over utility levels, rather than over the terms of an agreement which implies particular utility levels. In many bargaining situations an agreement in terms of utility levels will imply a unique agreement in P.

A number of not very demanding requirements are placed on the utility payoff set (which implies restrictions on P, d and the individuals' preferences). It is assumed that (a) U is closed, bounded and convex; (b) $\bar{u} \in U$; (c) that there is a $u = (u_A, u_B) \in U$ such that $u_i > \bar{u}_i$ $(i = A, B)$. The closedness requirement will be satisfied if P is closed, which it will be for most bargaining situations. Boundedness is also not demanding since it means that all elements in P yield a finite utility to both individuals. Convexity is also not restrictive. For example, it is satisfied by the bilateral monopoly model in section 10D. It will always be satisfied if it is possible for the parties to choose the outcome in P by an agreed randomization rule. (See Question 1, Exercise 15E.) The assumption (b) that $\bar{u}$ is in U merely means that the parties can agree to give themselves what they would get if there is no agreement, i.e. they can agree to disagree. Finally, (c) is necessary to ensure that the game is interesting: if there is no agreement which makes both parties strictly better off than not agreeing they would have no incentive to cooperate.

A *bargaining problem* or *cooperative bargaining game* is a utility payoff set U and a disagreement point $\bar{u}$ satisfying the above assumptions. A *bargaining solution* is a rule which can be applied to all bargaining problems to pick a unique point in U as the outcome. Formally, a bargaining solution is a function s from the set $(U, \bar{u})$ to a point $(s_A, s_B) = (s_A(U, \bar{u}), s_B(U, \bar{u}))$ in U.

There are a large number of such functions. For example the rule 'maximize u_A subject to $u \in U$ and to $u_B = \bar{u}_B$' is a bargaining solution, though not an appealing one in many situations. It implies that the first party has all the bargaining strength or ability. An even more objectionable feature is apparent if we apply it to the union–firm model of section 10D. Labelling the union, say, as the first party is essentially arbitrary. Changing the labelling, so that the firm is the first party, would lead to a different outcome (with lower w). Thus the agreement would be dependent on arbitrary features of the model.

Nash bargaining solution

Nash argued that a bargaining solution ought to satisfy four reasonable requirements and then showed that there was only one rule – the Nash bargaining solution
– satisfying those requirements. The Nash bargaining solution is a solution concept
for *cooperative* bargaining games. It is to be distinguished from the Nash equilibrium
of earlier sections of this chapter, which is a solution concept used in *non-cooperative*
games. In general, the outcomes derived by applying the two solution concepts will
not coincide.

Nash's axioms, or reasonable requirements that the solution to a cooperative
bargaining game should satisfy, are:

1. *Efficiency* (**E**). There should be no feasible bargain which makes at least one party
   better off and the other no worse off than at the outcome chosen by the solution. Formally, there must be no $u \in U$ such that $u_i \geqslant s_i(U, \bar{u})$ for $i = A, B$ and
   $u_i > s_i(U, \bar{u})$ for $i = A$ or B. In terms of part (a) of Fig. 15.16, the solution outcomes
   must lie on the upper right boundaries of the utility payoff sets U and V.

2. *Linear invariance* (**LI**). Consider two bargaining games $(U, \bar{u})$ and $(V, \bar{v})$ where the
   second game is derived from the first by transforming the players' utility functions from u_i to $v_i = \alpha_i + \beta_i u_i$ ($\beta_i > 0$). The two games have exactly the same set
   of potential bargains P and disagreement point d and the players' preferences are
   the same. The only difference between the games is the numerical representation
   of their preferences. It seems reasonable to require that the only effect of the
   relabelling of the utility functions should be to relabel the solution outcome in
   exactly the same way: $s_i(V, \bar{v}) = \alpha_i + \beta_i s_i(U, \bar{u})$.

The invariance requirement implies that the solution outcome in P should not be
affected by the numerical representation of the parties' preferences if the underlying
preferences are unchanged. This is illustrated in part (a) of Fig. 15.16 where individual A's utility is transformed from u_A to $v_A = \alpha_A + u_A$. The transformation alters
U to V and $\bar{u}$ to $\bar{v}$. The solution outcome to the new game $(V, \bar{v})$ is now $s(V, \bar{v})$ but
this corresponds to the same agreement in P in part (b) of the figure.

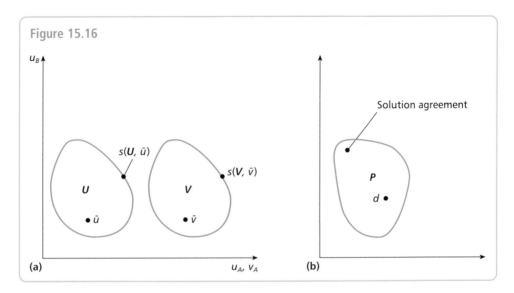

Figure 15.16

Figure 15.17

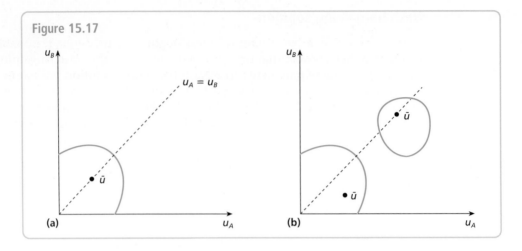

(a)

(b)

A bargaining game is *symmetric* if (a) $\bar{u}_A = \bar{u}_B$, so that the disagreement point lies on the 45° line in (u_A, u_B) space; and (b) U is symmetric about the 45° line. Thus the game illustrated in Fig. 15.16 is not symmetric. In Fig. 15.17 only the game in part (a) is symmetric. Note that if $\bar{u}_A \neq \bar{u}_B$ we can always transform u_A to $u_A^* = \alpha_A + u_A$ with $\alpha_A = \bar{u}_B - \bar{u}_A$ to yield a game with the disagreement point on the 45° line. From the invariance requirement, this transformation will not affect the solution outcome in any essential way. Thus the restrictive part of the symmetry definition is that U be symmetrical about the 45° line. We can now state the third of Nash's requirements:

3. *Symmetry* (**S**). If the bargaining game is symmetric the solution outcome must lie on the 45° line: $s_A(U, \bar{u}) = s_B(U, \bar{u})$.

The bargaining game will be symmetric if the two players have identical preferences and are in identical circumstances. It seems reasonable to require that the bargaining solution would then give them the same utility. The symmetry requirement rules out any effect of bargaining ability on the solution. Any difference in utilities between the parties at the solution must arise from differences in their circumstances or their preferences.

4. *Independence of irrelevant alternatives* (**IIA**). Consider two bargaining games: $(U, \bar{u})$ and $(U^*, \bar{u})$ where $U^* \subset U$. (The games have the same disagreement point but U^* is contained in U.) If the solution outcome $s(U, \bar{u})$ to $(U, \bar{u})$ is in U^* then $s(U^*, \bar{u}) = s(U, \bar{u})$: the two games must have the same solution outcome.

IIA is illustrated in Fig. 15.18 where U^* is equal to U less the shaded area. **IIA** requires that the bargaining outcome is unchanged if an agreement which the parties do not make is no longer feasible. This seems reasonable if we have in mind a process of bargaining by which the parties gradually narrow down the set of potential agreement until only one remains. On the other hand, we might believe that it is plausible that the outcome ought to depend on the worst (except for disagreement) or best possible outcome for each player because these somehow reflect 'bargaining power'. The **IIA** axiom rules out solutions based on these types of intuition.

Now consider the optimization problem

$$\max_{u_A, u_B} N(u_A, u_B) = (u_A - \bar{u}_A)(u_B - \bar{u}_B) \quad \text{s.t.} \quad u_i \geq \bar{u}_i \quad i = A, B \qquad \text{[E.1]}$$
$$(u_A, u_B) \in U$$

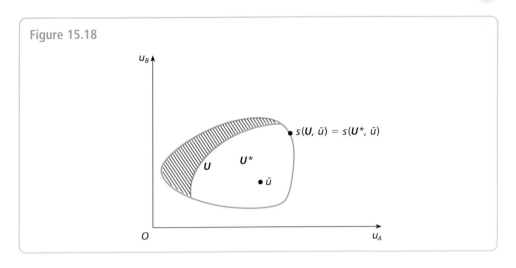

Figure 15.18

derived from the bargaining game $(U, \bar{u})$. The objective function in [E.1] is the *Nash product*. It is continuous and strictly quasi-concave. The assumptions about the bargaining game imply that the feasible set in [E.1] is non-empty, closed, bounded and convex. Hence (see Appendices C, D, E) the solution to the optimization problem [E.1] exists and is unique. Denote the optimal values of u_A and u_B which solve [E.1] as $s_A^N(U, \bar{u})$ and $s_B^N(U, \bar{u})$. The *Nash bargaining solution* to the bargaining game $(U, \bar{u})$ is $s^N(U, \bar{u}) = (s_A^N(U, \bar{u}), s_B^N(U, \bar{u}))$.

The solution is illustrated in Fig. 15.19. The contours of the Nash product $N(u_A, u_B)$ are rectangular hyperbolas asymptotic to axes with an origin at the disagreement point $\bar{u}$. At s^N the contour is tangent to the upper right boundary of U. (Note the constraint $u \geqslant \bar{u}$ ensures that we can ignore points in the other quadrants centred at $\bar{u}$.) Thus the Nash bargaining solution satisfies *E*. It is also clear that it satisfies *IIA*, as the reader should check by sketching in new bargaining games $(U^*, \bar{u})$ with $U^* \subset U$ and $s^N \in U^*$. Since the disagreement point is unchanged, the contours of N are not affected, so that s^N will maximize N over U^*. The symmetry requirement *S* is also satisfied by the Nash bargaining solution. If $\bar{u}_A = \bar{u}_B$ the contours of N will be symmetrical about the 45° line. If U is also symmetrical about the 45° line, the solution s^N will also be on the 45° line and *S* is satisfied. (Sketch some diagrams to show this.)

We can show also that *LI* holds for the Nash solution. Let $v_i = \alpha_i + \beta_i u_i$ $(\beta_i > 0)$ so that

$$N(v_A, v_B) = [(\alpha_A + \beta_A u_A) - (\alpha_A + \beta_A \bar{u}_A)][(\alpha_B + \beta_B u_B) - (\alpha_B + \beta_B \bar{u}_B)]$$
$$= [\beta_A u_A - \beta_A \bar{u}_A][\beta_B u_B - \beta_B \bar{u}_B]$$
$$= \beta_A \beta_B N(u_A, u_B) \qquad \text{[E.2]}$$

The solution to the problem of maximizing the Nash product $N(v_A, v_B)$ subject to $v \in V, v \geqslant \bar{v}$ is $s^N(V, \bar{v})$. Since $s^N(U, \bar{u})$ solves [E.1]:

$$N(s_A^N(U, \bar{u}), s_B^N(U, \bar{u})) \geqslant N(u_A, u_B) \qquad \text{all } (u_A, u_B) \in U \qquad \text{[E.3]}$$

and [E.2] and [E.3] imply

Figure 15.19

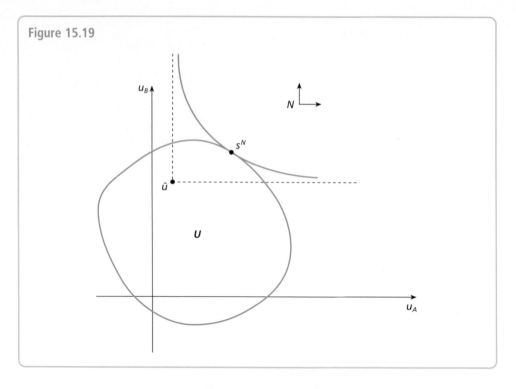

$$N(\alpha_A + \beta_A s_A^N(U, \bar{u}), \alpha_B + \beta_B s_B^N(U, \bar{u})) = \beta_A \beta_B N(s_A^N(U, \bar{u}), s_B^N(U, \bar{u}))$$
$$\geqslant \beta_A \beta_B N(u_A, u_B)$$
$$= N(\alpha_A + \beta_A u_A, \alpha_B + \beta_B u_B) = N(v_A, v_B)$$

Hence $s_i^N(V, \bar{v}) = \alpha_i + \beta_i s_i^N(U, \bar{u})$ ($i = 1, 2$) as required for **LI**.

The Nash bargaining solution is simple to apply and, since it satisfies the four axioms, it has some appealing properties. More interestingly, Nash proved that *the Nash bargaining solution $s^N(U, \bar{u})$ is the only bargaining solution satisfying the four requirements E, LI, S and IIA.*

Proof

To prove the theorem we assume that some bargaining solution $s(U, \bar{u})$ satisfies the four axioms when applied to bargaining games $(U, \bar{u})$ and show that this implies that it is the Nash solution: $s(U, \bar{u}) = s^N(U, \bar{u})$. Suppose that for any bargaining game $(U, \bar{u})$ we apply linear transformations $v_i = \alpha_i + \beta_i u_i$ ($\beta_i > 0$) to both individuals' utility functions to get the transformed game $(V, \bar{v})$. Since $s(\cdot)$ satisfies **LI** it must be true that

$$s_i(V, \bar{v}) = \alpha_i + \beta_i s_i(U, \bar{u}) \qquad i = A, B \qquad \text{[E.4]}$$

But remember that the Nash solution also satisfies **LI**, so that

$$s_i^N(V, \bar{v}) = \alpha_i + \beta_i s_i^N(U, \bar{u}) \qquad i = A, B \qquad \text{[E.5]}$$

Hence **LI**, [E.4] and [E.5] imply that proving that '$s(U, \bar{u}) = s^N(U, \bar{u})$ when $s(\cdot)$ satisfies **LI, E, S** and **IIA**' is equivalent to proving that '$s(V, \bar{v}) = s^N(V, \bar{v})$ when $s(\cdot)$ satisfies **E, S** and **IIA**'. The latter is easier to prove if we make the cunning choice of linear transformations:

$$\beta_i = \frac{1}{s_i^N(U, \bar{u}) - \bar{u}_i} \qquad \alpha_i = -\frac{\bar{u}_i}{s_i^N(U, \bar{u}) - \bar{u}_i} = -\beta_i \bar{u}_i \qquad \text{[E.6]}$$

Figure 15.20

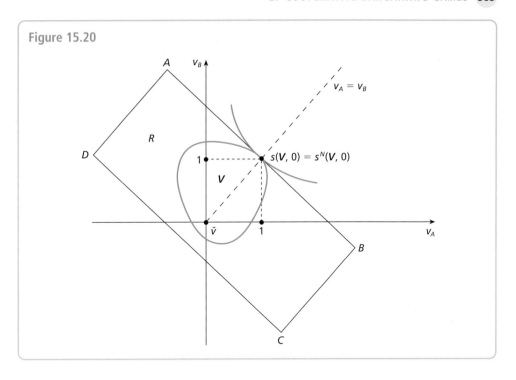

where s_A^N, s_B^N is the Nash solution of the original game. These transformations ensure that the disagreement point of the new game is the origin:

$$\bar{v}_i = \alpha_i + \beta_i \bar{u}_i = 0 \qquad i = A, B$$

Since the Nash solution satisfies **LI**, the Nash solution of the transformed game $(V, \bar{v}) = (V, 0)$ is

$$(s_A^N(V, 0), s_B^N(V, 0)) = (\alpha_A + \beta_A s_A^N(U, \bar{u}), \alpha_B + \beta_B s_B^N(U, \bar{u}) = (1, 1) \qquad [\text{E.7}]$$

See Fig. 15.20, where V is the utility payoff set of the transformed game, with disagreement point at the origin and Nash bargaining solution $s^N(V, 0)$ on the 45° line at (1, 1). (The original game is not shown.)

We can now establish the theorem by showing that, if $s(\cdot)$ satisfies **E**, **S** and **IIA**, applying it to the transformed game yields the Nash solution: $s(V, 0) = s^N(V, 0) = (1, 1)$. The Nash product for the transformed game is

$$N(v_A, v_B) = (v_A - \bar{v}_A)(v_B - \bar{v}_B) = v_A v_B \qquad [\text{E.8}]$$

The line AB in Fig. 15.20 is tangent to the contour of the Nash product $v_A v_B$ at the Nash solution $s^N(V, 0)$ to the transformed game. All points in V except $s^N(V, 0)$ must lie below AB, otherwise $v_A v_B$ would not be maximized over the convex set V at $s^N(V, 0)$. (V must be convex since it is a linear transformation of the convex set U.) Since the slope of the contour of the Nash product $v_A v_B$ at the Nash solution is $dv_B/dv_A = -v_B/v_A = -1$, the line AB also has slope -1. We construct another bargaining game $(R, 0)$ with disagreement point at the origin. The utility payoff set for the new game R is the rectangle $ABCD$ which is symmetrical about the 45° line. Since U is bounded, V must also be bounded and so we can always construct a rectangle like $ABCD$ which contains the transformed game V.

Now we apply $s(\cdot)$ to the bargaining game $(R, 0)$ to get the solution outcome $s(R, 0)$. Since $s(\cdot)$ satisfies **E** the solution outcome must be on AB which is the upper right boundary of R. $s(\cdot)$ also satisfies **S**, so that the outcome must also be on the 45° line. Hence **E** and **S** imply that

$$s(R, 0) = (1, 1) = s^N(V, 0) \qquad\qquad [E.9]$$

But V is a subset of R, has the same disagreement point at the origin and contains the solution outcome $s(R, 0)$. Therefore, since $s(\cdot)$ satisfies **IIA**, we have

$$s(V, 0) = s(R, 0) = s^N(V, 0) \qquad\qquad [E.10]$$

which completes the proof.

It is remarkable that imposing four reasonable requirements on the agreement results in a unique and analytically tractable solution to the cooperative bargaining game. However, there are several difficulties with the axiomatic approach.

First, there are other, equally appealing, solutions, which satisfy different sets of axioms. For example, consider the *Kalai–Smorodinsky solution*. Denote the maximum utility that player i can get in U by $\hat{u}_i$. The Kalai–Smorodinsky solution is the intersection of the upper right boundary of U with a straight line connecting the disagreement point $\bar{u}$ to $\hat{u} = (\hat{u}_A, \hat{u}_B)$. The solution satisfies **E**, **S** and **LI** but can differ from the Nash solution (see Fig. 15.21). We could think of $\hat{u}$ as possibly reflecting the parties' bargaining strength, in that an increase in $\hat{u}_i$ might plausibly be expected to make i less willing to accept a given agreement. As the reader should check by sketching some examples, an increase in $\hat{u}_i$ will increase the payoff received by i in the Kalai–Smorodinsky solution, but may have no effect on the Nash solution.

Second, it is usually possible to construct examples of cooperative bargaining games in which the outcome produced by a particular bargaining solution is not intuitively appealing. (Question 2, Exercise 15E, gives an example for the Nash solution.)

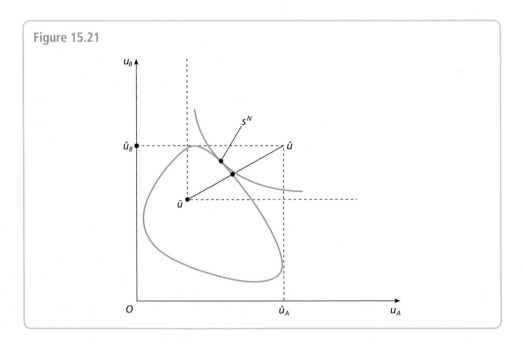

Figure 15.21

Third, we would usually think of an agreement between parties as resulting from a bargaining process in which offers are exchanged, rejected or modified until agreement is reached or the parties give up trying to reach agreement. The cooperative game approach leaves the process of bargaining unexamined. In particular it has nothing to say about why bargaining may not always lead to agreement. In order to model disagreement, we need to widen the set of actions being examined to include the bargaining strategies (what offers to make in what circumstances, what offers to accept or reject) that the parties adopt, as well as the actions they eventually agree upon. Since they cannot make binding agreements about their choice of bargaining strategies, we should use the tools and concepts of non-cooperative game theory for a more complete account of bargaining. The next two sections examine this approach.

EXERCISE 15E

1. Show that, no matter what form of **P**, the utility payoff set **U** will be convex and contain $\bar{u}$ if the parties can choose a point in **P** by an agreed randomization rule which determines the probability with which each point in **P** is chosen.

2. *Divide a dollar.* Two individuals have initial wealth y_i. A mischievous dead relative has left a total of $1 to be shared between them provided they agree on how the $1 should be divided. If the sum of their agreed shares in the dollar is less than 1 the balance will be given to a charity. If the sum of their agreed shares is greater than 1 or if they fail to agree, they will each receive nothing and the dollar will be given to the charity. Both individuals are entirely selfish and derive no utility from the money received by the charity. Suppose that the individuals have identical utility functions $u_i = \ln x_i$ where x_i is i's wealth including her payout under the terms of the will.

   (a) Draw diagrams to show the set of outcomes **P** and the disagreement outcome in income space and the utility payoff set. Show the effect of linear transformations of the utility functions.

   (b) What is the Nash solution?

   (c) Is more of the $1 given to the richer or the poorer of the individuals?

3. *Union–firm bilateral monopoly.* Show that the union–firm model of section 10D satisfies the definition of a bargaining game and derive the Nash bargaining solution.

4. *Asymmetric Nash bargaining solution.* If the solution must satisfy **E, LI** and **IIA**, the bargaining solution maximizes the *asymmetric Nash product* $[u_A - \bar{u}_A]^\alpha [u_B - \bar{u}_B]^{(1-\alpha)}$ for some value of the parameter $0 < \alpha < 1$. α can be interpreted as relative bargaining power. Derive the asymmetric Nash solution to the union–firm bargaining problem. Show that (a) if $\alpha = \frac{1}{2}$ the asymmetric solution is identical with the Nash solution; (b) for all $0 < \alpha < 1$ the asymmetric solution has the same employment level as the symmetric Nash solution but the wage may be greater or smaller than w^* depending on α.

F. Bargaining as a non-cooperative game

In this section we attempt to predict the outcome of bargaining between two individuals by drawing on the techniques and concepts of non-cooperative game theory. As we suggested at the end of section E, it may be fruitful to model the individuals as choosing negotiation or bargaining strategies which specify their offers and counter-offers. We can then look for an equilibrium pair of strategies and examine the agreement generated by the equilibrium strategies. Since individuals will not make binding agreements about their negotiation strategies, we seek a non-cooperative equilibrium in bargaining strategies. By contrast, in section E we derived the Nash bargaining solution for cooperative games by concentrating on the properties of agreements and made no attempt to analyse the bargaining strategies which may lead to them.

The equilibrium of a non-cooperative bargaining game depends on the exogenously given rules of the game which specify the types, sequences and timing of offers and responses to offers the parties are allowed to make, the information available to them when they make offers and responses and whether bargaining takes place over a finite or infinite time horizon. In this section we consider the Rubinstein (1982) bargaining model and show how a unique equilibrium can be derived by using the concept of sub-game perfection introduced in section B. We will also indicate how the solution depends on particular features of the specification of the bargaining game and the implications of alternative assumptions.

In the Rubinstein model individuals bargain over the division of a pie (or sum of money or some other divisible object which yields utility). The units of measurement are chosen so that the size of the pie is 1. At date 0 player A makes a proposal or offer that she should get x_0 in [0, 1] and individual B should get $1 - x_0$. B may accept the offer, in which case the game is over, or reject it. If B rejects the offer then, in period 1, he makes a proposal that he should get y_1 and A get $1 - y_1$. If A accepts this offer the game terminates in period 1. If A rejects B's period 1 offer, she makes a further proposal x_2 to B in period 2, which B may again accept, terminating the game, or reject. The game will continue with players making alternating offers until one of them accepts an offer.

When the game terminates in period t, with acceptance of an offer by one of the parties which gives s to A and $1 - s$ to B, their utilities are

$$u_a = \delta_a^t s, \qquad u_b = \delta_b^t (1 - s) \qquad\qquad [\text{F.1}]$$

where $0 < \delta_i < 1$ is individual i's discount factor. Both individuals are impatient: pie received at a later date is less valuable than the same amount of pie received earlier. This cost from delaying settlement provides an incentive to settle and determines the equilibrium of the model.

Both players know the discount factor of the other (and know that the other knows that they know). At each date both players also know the full history of the game (the offers made and rejected) up to that date. Thus the game is one of complete information.

Before the game begins individual A formulates a bargaining strategy σ_a which is a complete specification of what offers she will make in even numbered periods 0, 2, 4, . . . and what offer from individual B she will accept in odd numbered periods 1, 3, 5, ... We can describe A's strategy by $\sigma_a = (x_0, r_{1a}, x_2, r_{3a}, \dots)$ where x_t is A's offer in even periods and r_{ta} her rejection rule: in an odd-numbered period t she turns down any proposal by B which gives her less than r_{ta}. B's strategy σ_b is analogously defined: $\sigma_b = (r_{0b}, y_1, r_{2b}, y_3, \dots)$. The strategies specify offer or accept/reject decisions in period t which depend on the whole history of the game up to period t, i.e. on the whole sequence of offers and counter-offers in periods 0 to $t - 1$. (Thus x_t, r_{ta}, y_t, r_{tb} should be written as functions of the history of the game up to $t - 1$.) Despite the fact that the strategies could be extremely complex, Rubinstein proved that the players' equilibrium strategies are simple and result in the game finishing in the first period with player A making an offer which is accepted by B.

Constant strategy equilibria

The game structure is essentially stationary in that, if the game has not terminated by period t, it has the same structure as the game at period $t - 2$: the size of pie is unchanged, the possible offers and accept/reject rules are the same at t and $t - 2$ and the parties' preferences concerning pie at the current date and in the future are the same. A has a *constant strategy* if she always makes the same proposal $\bar{x}$ when it is her turn to make offers and if she always rejects proposals from B unless they give her at least $\bar{r}_a$. We write constant strategies as $\bar{\sigma}_a = (\bar{x}, \bar{r}_a)$. B's constant strategies $\bar{\sigma}_b = (\bar{y}, \bar{r}_b)$ are similarly defined. The stationarity of the game suggests that we can restrict ourselves to looking for constant strategy equilibria. (In the last sub-section we prove that this restriction is justified because the only sensible equilibrium involves constant strategies.)

One obvious equilibrium concept for this non-cooperative game is the *Nash equilibrium*. A Nash equilibrium is a pair of strategies (σ_a^*, σ_b^*) such that σ_a^* is the best reply for A to σ_b^* and vice versa. (Remember that the Nash equilibrium is a concept which is defined only for non-cooperative games and should not be confused with the Nash bargaining solution of section E which is defined only for cooperative bargaining games.) Unfortunately, there are many Nash equilibria in the current non-cooperative bargaining game, even though we restrict the players to constant strategies.

For example, consider *intransigent* constant strategies defined by $\bar{\sigma}_a = (\bar{x}, \bar{x})$ and $\bar{\sigma}_b = (\bar{y}, \bar{y})$. Here player A always proposes $\bar{x}$ in periods 0, 2, 4, . . . , and accepts any proposal y where $(1 - y) \geq \bar{x}$ in periods 1, 3, 5, ... In effect, A insists in getting at least $\bar{x}$ of the pie whenever the game terminates. Similarly, B always proposes $\bar{y}$ in periods 1, 3, 5, . . . , and accepts any proposal x where $(1 - x) \geq \bar{y}$ in periods 0, 2, 4, ...

A pair of intransigent strategies need not constitute a Nash equilibrium: if $\bar{x} + \bar{y} > 1$ then one party always rejects the other's proposal and if $\bar{x} + \bar{y} < 1$ then either party would be better off increasing their intransigent demand. However, any pair of *reciprocal* intransigent strategies with $\sigma_a = (\bar{x}, \bar{x})$, $\bar{\sigma}_b = (1 - \bar{x}, 1 - \bar{x})$ is a Nash equilibrium. This pair of strategies results in the game terminating in period 0 when B accepts A's proposal, yielding A a utility of $\bar{x}$ and B a utility of $(1 - \bar{x}) = \bar{r}_b = \bar{y}$.

To see that reciprocal intransigent strategies are a Nash equilibrium, consider whether A can do better by choosing another strategy, given that B will continue to choose his intransigent strategy. For example, consider the reciprocal intransigent strategies $\bar{x} = 0.6$, $\bar{r}_a = 0.6$ and $\bar{y} = 0.4$, $\bar{r}_b = 0.4$. Suppose that, at date 0, A makes an offer which yields B only 0.3. Since he sticks to his intransigent strategy, B rejects this proposal because $0.3 < \bar{r}_b = 0.4$. Given that B sticks to his intransigent strategy in all periods, the game can only terminate when A makes an offer acceptable to B (which requires $(1 - x) = y \geq 0.4$, i.e. $x \leq 0.6$) or when A accepts the offer from B (giving her a slice of pie $(1 - 0.4) = 0.6$). Thus by demanding more than 0.6 in period 0, A, at best, merely postpones receipt of the same amount of pie by at least one period, yielding utility of at most $0.6\delta_a < 0.6$. Hence, *given that B sticks to his intransigent strategy*, A cannot do better by deviating from her intransigent strategy in period 0.

Similar arguments apply to any other deviation by A or by B from any reciprocal intransigent strategy. Since neither can do better by unilaterally deviating from *any* reciprocal intransigent strategies, the Nash equilibrium is clearly not unique: *all* reciprocal intransigent strategies are Nash equilibria.

Reciprocal instransigent strategies are not intuitively appealing Nash equilibria. They require that A believes that B sticks to his intransigent strategy in the face of a deviation by A (and vice versa). But B's intransigence is not credible: faced with a deviation by A he could do better if he does not stick to his intransigent strategy. Thus suppose that the reciprocal instransigent strategies are $\bar{x} = 0.6$, $\bar{r}_a = 0.6$, $\bar{y} = 0.4$, $\bar{r}_b = 0.4$ and that B's discount factor is $\delta_b = 0.7$. B's intransigent strategy requires him to refuse all offers from A which give him less than 0.4 and to make an offer of 0.4 whenever it is his turn to do so. Suppose that, at date 0, A proposes $x = 0.7$, which would give B a slice of pie of 0.3 in period 0. In all other periods 1, 2, . . . , A's strategy is the same as her intransigent strategy. If B sticks with his intransigent strategy he will reject the proposal. The game will then terminate when A accepts B's proposal of $y = \bar{y} = 0.4$ in period 1. By sticking to his intransigent strategy in period 0, B will get a slice of pie of size 0.4 in period 1 which gives him a discounted utility of

$$\delta_b \bar{y} = (0.7)(0.4) = 0.28 < 0.3$$

Thus he does worse by sticking to his intransigent strategy than by accepting A's proposal which would give him 0.3 of the pie in period 0. B's threat to reject A's offer is therefore not credible.

More generally, B's threat to stick to his intransigent strategy $(\bar{y}, \bar{y})$ is not credible against a proposal by A of $\bar{x} + \varepsilon$, where $0 < \varepsilon < (1 - \delta_b)\bar{y}$. B would always prefer to deviate from his intransigent strategy to accept the proposal since $\bar{y} - \varepsilon > \delta_b\bar{y}$. Similar reasoning establishes that A's threat to stick to her intransigent strategy, whatever proposals are made by B, is also not credible.

Recall from section B that strategies constitute a *sub-game perfect equilibrium* (SPE) if they constitute Nash equilibria at every stage or sub-game reached in the game. SPE strategies therefore cannot involve incredible threats because such threats require behaviour which is not a best reply to the other player's actions. We have just shown that, since all reciprocal intransigent strategies involve incredible threats, *no* reciprocal intransigent strategy pair can be an SPE. We will now demonstrate that there is in fact a unique constant strategy SPE for the Rubinstein bargaining game and that in it neither player is intransigent: $\bar{x} \neq \bar{r}_a$, $\bar{y} \neq \bar{r}_b$.

We seek $\sigma_a = (\bar{x}, \bar{r}_a)$, $\sigma_b = (\bar{y}, \bar{r}_b)$ which are best replies to each other and such that player i's refusal to accept less than $\bar{r}_i$ is credible. If B turns down an offer of $(1 - x)$, then given A's constant strategy, the best he can do is to make a proposal next period which gives A the least she will accept: $\bar{r}_a$. Since A will accept this proposal, B will get $(1 - \bar{r}_a)$ next period. It is therefore credible for B to reject $(1 - x)$ if $(1 - x) \leq \delta_b(1 - \bar{r}_a)$. Thus B's credible rejection criterion must satisfy $\bar{r}_b \leq \delta_b(1 - \bar{r}_a)$. It cannot be optimal for him to set $\bar{r}_b < \delta_b(1 - \bar{r}_a)$ since he would be worse off rejecting, rather than accepting, a proposal x such that $\bar{r}_b < (1 - x) < \delta_b(1 - \bar{r}_a)$. Hence, given A's strategy $(\bar{x}, \bar{r}_a)$, B's optimal credible rejection criterion is

$$\bar{r}_b = \delta_b(1 - \bar{r}_a) \tag{F.2}$$

Similar reasoning for A gives her optimal credible rejection criterion

$$\bar{r}_a = \delta_a(1 - \bar{r}_b) \tag{F.3}$$

Since player i will accept $\bar{r}_i$ it is not optimal for the other player to make a larger offer and so the offer must satisfy

$$(1 - \bar{x}) = \bar{r}_b \qquad\qquad\qquad\qquad [F.4]$$

$$(1 - \bar{y}) = \bar{r}_a \qquad\qquad\qquad\qquad [F.5]$$

An SPE must satisfy [F.2] to [F.5] and, since there is only one set of $(\bar{x}, \bar{r}_a, \bar{y}, \bar{r}_b)$ satisfying these four equations, [F.2] to [F.5] define the unique SPE in constant strategies. Solving [F.2] and [F.3] for $\bar{r}_a$ and $\bar{r}_b$ and substituting in [F.4] and [F.5], the unique SPE in constant strategies is

$$x^* = \frac{1 - \delta_b}{1 - \delta_a \delta_b}, \qquad r_a^* = \frac{\delta_a(1 - \delta_b)}{1 - \delta_a \delta_b} = \delta_a x^* \qquad [F.6]$$

$$y^* = \frac{1 - \delta_a}{1 - \delta_a \delta_b}, \qquad r_b^* = \frac{\delta_b(1 - \delta_a)}{1 - \delta_a \delta_b} = \delta_b y^*$$

The game will terminate in period 0 when player A proposes x^*, which player B accepts since $(1 - x^*) = r_b^*$. The utilities of the players at this SPE are

$$u_a^* = x^* = (1 - \delta_b)/(1 - \delta_a \delta_b), \qquad u_b^* = r_b^* = \delta_b(1 - \delta_a)/(1 - \delta_a \delta_b) \qquad [F.7]$$

Notice that B's utility is not equal to his proposal but to his rejection criterion, since he accepts A's just-acceptable offer and never gets to make a proposal.

Specification of the model

The solution to the Rubinstein bargaining model depends on the parties' discount rates because the fact that they value future consumption less than current consumption means that delay in settlement is costly. It is this which gives them an incentive to agree rather than to continue bargaining. The assumption on preferences, that consumption is discounted at a constant proportional rate, is quite strong. However, though it is necessary to get the particularly elegant form of the solution in [F.6], much weaker restrictions on preferences over future consumption will still yield a unique SPE solution with constant strategies.

Some of the assumptions about the exogenously given structure of the bargaining game are less innocuous. For example, the assumption that the parties make alternating offers, rather than one party making offers, is crucial. If only player A made proposals which player B could only accept or reject then the unique SPE has A getting all the pie. (See Question 2, Exercise 15F.) In the alternating offers game, the fact that B can credibly threaten to turn down some offers from A and make a counter-proposal limits A's ability to extract all the pie.

The alternating offers assumption is also important in that it gives a *first-mover advantage* to A. If the players are identical in that they have the same discount rate: $\delta_a = \delta_b = \delta$, the SPE utilities are

$$u_a^* = \frac{1 - \delta}{1 - \delta^2} = \frac{1 - \delta}{(1 - \delta)(1 + \delta)} = \frac{1}{(1 + \delta)}, \qquad u_b^* = \frac{\delta}{(1 + \delta)}$$

Thus even if the parties have identical preferences they do not receive equal utility in the SPE. The first mover A gets a larger share of the pie and the first-mover advantage increases as the common discount factor becomes smaller, i.e. as the players discount the future more heavily. Since in many bargaining situations the order of play is arbitrary, the first-mover advantage is a drawback of the model.

To see the intuition underlying the first-mover advantage, note that, if the game lasted one period only and A moved first, she could get all the pie, since B could not credibly threaten to turn down any offer. In the infinite horizon game, A's first-mover advantage is constrained by B's credible threat to turn down her proposal and to make a counter-proposal. But B's threat is limited, first by the fact that he has to defer receipt of the pie to exercise his threat, and second by A's ability to credibly turn down *his* proposal. Referring to [F.6] we see that A's advantage from moving first is larger the smaller is B's discount factor and the greater is A's. Indeed, as δ_a approaches 1 with δ_b held constant, A's share approaches 1.

Intuition suggests, correctly, that if the reduction in utility from deferring consumption by one period becomes smaller, so that delay becomes less important, the first-mover advantage should disappear. Imagine that the period (initially a day) is split into n shorter periods. Let δ_i continue to be the daily discount factor and let δ_{in} denote the discount factor for a period of $(1/n)$th of a day. If player i is to have the same attitude to pie in one day's time it must be true that $(\delta_{in})^n = \delta_i$ or $\delta_{in} = (\delta_i)^{1/n}$. Inserting δ_{in} in [F.6] gives the SPE strategies as functions of the length of period $(1/n)$. Taking the limit as $n \to \infty$ (see Question 3, Exercise 15F), the shares of the players tend to

$$x^\star = \frac{\log \delta_b}{\log \delta_a + \log \delta_b}, \quad y^\star = \frac{\log \delta_a}{\log \delta_a + \log \delta_b} \qquad [\text{F.8}]$$

If the parties have identical preferences (one-day discount factors), the SPE yields an intuitively appealing equal division of the pie. A now has no first-mover advantage because delay for one period imposes a vanishingly small cost.

Although we have emphasized that the Nash bargaining solution is applicable only to cooperative games, it is interesting to note the relationship between [F.8] and the division of the pie produced by the asymmetric Nash bargaining solution in the corresponding cooperative bargaining game (see Question 4, Exercise 15E). The asymmetric Nash solution to the cooperative bargaining game in which A and B seek to divide a pie of size 1 is found by maximizing the asymmetric Nash product

$$x^\alpha y^{(1-\alpha)}$$

subject to $0 \leqslant x = (1 - y) \leqslant 1$, where $0 < \alpha < 1$ is usually interpreted as a measure of A's bargaining power. The amounts of pie given to the parties at the asymmetric Nash solutions are

$$x^\star = \alpha, \quad y^\star = 1 - \alpha \qquad [\text{F.9}]$$

Comparing [F.9] and [F.8], we see that if $\alpha = \log \delta_b / (\log \delta_a + \log \delta_b)$, the shares implied by the asymmetric Nash bargaining solution to the cooperative game and the limit of the Rubinstein solution to the non-cooperative bargaining game are identical.

Proof that the unique SPE has constant strategies

Our analysis above assumed that we need only examine constant strategies in seeking an SPE. We found a unique SPE [F.6] in constant strategies. We now demonstrate that this is the only SPE even when the players are not restricted to constant strategies. The proof is in two stages. We show that (a) the utilities the players will get in any SPE must be the same as they would get in the unique SPE in constant strategies and (b) these constant strategies are the only means of achieving these payoffs in an SPE.

(a) Each SPE gives a player some piece of pie. An SPE has the characteristic that its strategies also lead to an SPE for sub-games starting in any subsequent period. The sub-game starting in period 2 has exactly the same structure as the game starting in period 0. The pie has the same size, the same player (A) will make the offer, the players' possible choices are the same. They have the same attitude to delays in consumption of pie: at dates 0 and 2 player i is indifferent between consuming s now and $s\delta_i^t$ in t periods time and in period 2 she places utility s on consumption of s in period 2. Thus at date 2 the highest utility that player A can get from any SPE of the sub-game starting in period 2 is equal to the highest utility she could get from any SPE of the game starting in period 0. Let us call this M. Consider player B's proposal in period 1. Since A will accept any period 1 proposal which gives her at least $\delta_a M$, B cannot do worse in any SPE than he gets by making the proposal $1 - \delta_a M$ in period 1.

Consider player A's proposal in period 0. Since B can always reject a proposal and then make the acceptable proposal $1 - \delta_a M$ in period 1, the best that A can do in period 0 is to make a proposal giving B the share $\delta_b(1 - \delta_a M)$ and herself $1 - \delta_b(1 - \delta_a M)$. But by definition M is the highest utility that A can get from any SPE. Hence $M = 1 - \delta_b(1 - \delta_a M)$ or

$$M = (1 - \delta_b)/(1 - \delta_a \delta_b) \qquad [\text{F}.10]$$

Next we define m as the lowest utility that A can obtain from any SPE and apply similar reasoning. At date 1 B knows that A can get at least m in period 2 and so B cannot do better than make a proposal giving A the share $\delta_a m$ and himself $1 - \delta_a m$. At date 0, A realizes that B will accept any proposal which gives him at least $\delta_b(1 - \delta_a m)$ and so A can assure herself of at least $1 - \delta_b(1 - \delta_a m)$ in any SPE of a game starting at period 0. But this is the definition of m and so $m = 1 - \delta_b(1 - \delta_a m)$ or

$$m = (1 - \delta_b)/(1 - \delta_a \delta_b) \qquad [\text{F}.11]$$

Since, from [F.10] and [F.11], the best that A can get from any SPE is equal to the least she can get from any SPE, we see that A gets the same utility $(1 - \delta_b)/(1 - \delta_a \delta_b)$ from all SPEs. B must therefore also get the same utility $\delta_b(1 - \delta_b)/(1 - \delta_a \delta_b)$ in all SPEs. Note that these are the utilities [F.7] at the unique SPE in constant strategies.

(b) Now we establish that the only pair of SPE strategies which give the players these unique utility payoffs is the constant strategy pair [F.6]. Suppose that there is an SPE in which the first offer by A is rejected, in which case there must be a settlement reached t periods later. But such a settlement must give the players consumption levels at date t which yield the required SPE utilities when discounted back to period 0. Thus each player's consumption of pie at date t must exceed their consumption at date 0. But this is impossible since their total consumption at date 0 was just equal to the total pie. Thus there can be no SPE in which the first offer is rejected. If the first period offer is to be accepted and to yield the unique SPE utilities, A must offer the x^* and B adopt the rejection rule r_b^* defined in [F.6] in period 0. But what about their offers and rejection rules in periods 1, 2, . . . ? An SPE must lay down strategies which constitute an SPE at all sub-games starting in periods 1, 2, ... In an even-numbered period it is A's turn to make the offer and, if the strategies in this sub-game are to be SPEs, they must also have the offer in the first period of the sub-game being accepted. Hence an SPE strategy for the game staring at period 0 must say that x^* and r_b^* would be chosen in all even-numbered periods.

In odd-numbered periods it is B's turn to make the offer. The sub-games starting in odd-numbered periods must also be SPEs. We can apply the argument in (a) above to show that, in an alternating offer game in which B moves first, the SPE utilities must be

$$u_a^* = \delta_a(1 - \delta_b)/(1 - \delta_a\delta_b), \qquad u_b^* = (1 - \delta_a)/(1 - \delta_a\delta_b)$$

Now just adapt the argument of the previous paragraph to show that all sub-games starting in odd-numbered periods must terminate in the first period with B offering y^* and A using the rejection rule r_a^* and that this gives the required SPE utilities.

Hence we have established that the only SPE strategies which yield the parties the required SPE utilities have them choosing x^*, r_b^* in all even-numbered periods and r_a^*, y^* in all odd-numbered periods. Thus the only SPE strategies are the constant strategies [F.6].

EXERCISE 15F

1. *Finite horizon bargaining game.* Consider an alternating offer bargaining game which has the same structure as the one described in the text except that there is a finite number T of bargaining periods. If agreement is not reached by the end of period T the game terminates with neither player getting any pie. Show that the unique SPE of this game tends to the SPE of the finite horizon bargaining game as $T \to \infty$. (*Hint*: work backwards from period T. What is the unique SPE of the single period game starting at date T? Given this, what is the SPE of the two-period game starting at $T - 1$? Carry on back to period 0. Now take the limit.)

2. *One-sided offers.* Suppose preferences are the same as those in the text but that only A makes offers in each period and B's actions are limited to accepting or refusing them. What is the sub-game perfect equilibrium if (a) there is only one period; (b) there is a finite number of periods; (c) the number of periods is infinite?

3. Prove the assertion in the text that as the length of periods tends to zero the solution tends to [F8]. (*Hint*: use L'Hôpital's Rule; recall that $dz^{f(n)}/dn = z^{f(n)}f'(n) \log z$.)

G. Delay and disagreement in bargaining

Bargainers do not always settle immediately, even though delay is costly, and they sometimes fail to reach any agreement, even though there are bargains which would make both of them better off. The bargaining models of sections E and F do not provide any insight into these two common phenomena. The models cannot explain, for example, why strikes occur, why international trade negotiations can take years and why some litigants fail to reach an out-of-court settlement to avoid the expense of a trial. Models which use cooperative game concepts, as in section E, seek to predict the terms of agreement by requiring them to satisfy certain axioms. Such models *assume* that the parties will always agree and so cannot be used to explain disagreement. The Rubinstein non-cooperative game model of section F does not assume that agreement will occur, but it *predicts* that the parties will always make a bargain, and do so in the first period.

What is required is an explanation of why rational players fail to realize potential gains from trade. We present a non-cooperative model in which the parties have different information and consequently may fail to agree or do so only after a costly delay.

The model is based on Fudenberg and Tirole (1983). A seller S and a buyer B negotiate about the sale of an asset by S to B. Both B and S know that the asset has no value to S if she does not sell it to B. The value of the asset to the buyer is $b > 0$. If b were known to both parties the situation would be similar to those considered in previous sections where the parties bargain over splitting the known gain from trade b (a pie of known size) by agreeing on a price p which gives S a gain of p and B a gain of $b - p$.

Instead we assume that B may have either a high valuation ($b = h$) or a low valuation ($b = \ell$) of the asset with

$$h > \ell > 0 \qquad\qquad [\text{G.1}]$$

Whatever the buyer's valuation there are always potential gains from trade. The seller does not know which type of buyer she faces but she does know that the probability of the buyer being type h is π.

The bargaining framework differs from the infinite horizon, alternating offers game of section F. There is a finite number of periods and only the seller makes proposals concerning p. The buyer can only accept or reject the proposed price. The fact that there is a finite number of periods enables us to apply backward induction reasoning to determine the parties' optimal bargaining strategies. The assumption that only the seller makes proposals about p means that the game is a form of monopoly. As we will see, the seller's incomplete information about the buyer's valuation of the asset reduces her ability to exploit her monopoly position. (Question 6, Exercise 15G, extends the analysis to allow both parties to make proposals.)

One period of bargaining

If there is only one bargaining period the solution is straightforward. B's optimal strategy depends on his type: he accepts the offer if $b \geqslant p$ and rejects it if $b < p$. The seller knows that this is B's strategy and so realizes that the probability of the offer being accepted is 1 if $p \leqslant \ell$ (since then both type B's would accept), π for $\ell < p \leqslant h$, and 0 if $p > h$. Setting $p < \ell$ cannot be optimal for S, since such an offer is certain to be accepted and S could do better by setting $p = \ell$, which is also certain to be accepted. Setting $p > h$ also is not optimal for S, since there will be no sale and she would do better by setting $p = \ell$ and getting ℓ for sure. Finally, $\ell < p < h$ cannot be optimal either, since raising p to h does not affect the sale probability. Thus the seller either sets a price of ℓ or h. She prefers the alternative which yields the greater expected value and so chooses $p = h$ if $\pi h > \ell$.

There is a critical probability

$$\bar{\pi} \equiv \ell/h \qquad\qquad [\text{G.2}]$$

such that if $\pi > \bar{\pi}$ the seller is *strong* and sets a high price and if $\pi < \bar{\pi}$ the seller is *weak* and chooses the low price.

When S chooses the high price she gets an expected payoff of πh. The high price gives both types of buyer a zero surplus: the type ℓ because he does not buy at the price h and the type h because the price paid is equal to his valuation of the asset. Thus the expected combined surplus of the seller and buyers is πh. If the seller sets a low price she would get a surplus of ℓ, the type ℓ buyer would have a zero surplus and the type h buyer would get a surplus of $h - \ell$. The combined surplus if the low price is set is $\ell + \pi(h - \ell) = \pi h + (1 - \pi)\ell > \pi h$. One-period bargaining with the uninformed seller setting the price may therefore result in the total surplus of the parties not being maximized. (See Question 2, Exercise 15G.)

With a single period the analysis is similar to monopoly: the seller faces a downward sloping 'demand' curve in that the expected quantity sold declines with the price she sets. (The analogy is even closer if there is a continuous distribution of buyer types – see Question 1, Exercise 15G.) Her market power from being able to make a single take it or leave it offer is tempered by her lack of knowledge of the type of buyer she confronts. If she sets a price of h, the buyer's behaviour – his response to her offer – will provide her with information on his type since it is only optimal for a type h to accept her offer. This information is, however, of no use to the seller in a one-period model: she makes her only decision – a binding offer to sell at price p – before she observes the potentially informative decision of the buyer.

Two periods of bargaining

With more than one period the game becomes much more complicated because both parties will realize that B's responses to offers convey information. Assume that there are two periods and that both parties apply the same discount factor δ to second-period income.

At date 0 the seller makes an offer p_0. The buyer, who may be type h or ℓ, decides to accept or reject the period 0 offer. The period 0 decision rule of a type b buyer is described by the probability $a_0(p_0, b)$ that he accepts the offer p_0. For example, if a type ℓ buyer decides that he will accept all offers with $p_0 \leq \ell$ and reject all $p_0 > \ell$, his decision rule is $a_0(p_0, \ell) = 1$ for $p_0 \leq \ell$, $a_0(p_0, \ell) = 0$ for $p_0 > \ell$.

If her period 0 offer is rejected the seller makes another offer in period 1: p_1. B's response to the period 1 offer is again described by the probability with which he chooses to accept it: $a_1(p_1, b)$. Neither buyer nor seller can make binding commitments to take specified actions: for example in period 0 the seller cannot commit never to reduce her period 1 offer below h. (Question 5, Exercise 15G, examines the implications of commitment.)

The seller formulates her strategy to maximize her expected discounted income given her probability beliefs about the type of buyer she faces. At date 0 she attaches probability π to B being type h. At date 1 she has acquired information from B's response to her period 0 offer. If her offer p_0 was accepted, the information is of no value because the game has terminated, but if it was rejected she can use the additional information to revise her probability beliefs about the type of buyer she faces. Assume that she uses Bayes' Rule (Appendix L) to update her beliefs. Denote S's updated probability that the buyer is type h given that the period 0 offer was rejected by $\pi_1 = \pi_1(p_0)$. The notation $\pi_1(p_0)$ indicates that the information conveyed by a rejection may vary with the offer rejected.

The equilibrium concept we use is the *perfect Bayesian equilibrium* (PBE) (section C). A pair of strategies is a PBE if they constitute best replies to the other player's strategy in all sub-games, given that in each sub-game each player will use the past behaviour of the other and their knowledge of the other's strategy to update their probability beliefs using Bayes' Rule.

For a PBE the strategies of the players must be equilibrium strategies for any sub-game. The seller, by her initial offer p_0, can force the game into the sub-game starting with B's response to that particular initial offer. She chooses which sub-game will be played and will, in equilibrium, choose the sub-game which maximizes her expected discounted payoff. We therefore characterize the PBE by first working out the equilibrium strategies for the sub-games starting with a given p_0. The equilibrium for the whole game starting with S's choice of p_0 is then found by looking for the p_0 which maximizes her expected discounted payoff. We will only consider the case in which the seller would be strong in a one-period game: her prior probability belief π exceeds the critical value $\bar{\pi}$ defined by [G.2]. (Question 3, Exercise 15G, examines the weak seller case in which $\pi < \bar{\pi}$.)

The type ℓ buyer's optimal strategy is simple: in any period always refuse any price higher than ℓ and accept in any period any offer which is less than or equal to ℓ. (Buyers realize that it cannot be optimal for S to set p_1 less than ℓ in period 1 and so the type ℓ buyer cannot gain by rejecting $p_0 \leqslant \ell$ in the hope of getting a lower price in period 1.) Thus the type ℓ buyer's decisions rules are

$$a_t(p_t, \ell) = 1 \text{ for } p_t \leqslant \ell, \qquad a_t(p_t, \ell) = 0 \text{ for } p_t > \ell \qquad t = 0, 1 \qquad [\text{G.3}]$$

The type h buyer's strategy in period 1 is also simple: since his is the last move in the game, he just compares S's offer p_1 with his valuation of the asset and accepts if $p_1 \leqslant h$:

$$a_1(p_1, h) = 1 \text{ for } p_1 \leqslant h, \qquad a_1(p_1, h) = 0 \text{ for } p_1 > h \qquad [\text{G.4}]$$

In the last period of the game the seller is in essentially the same position as in the one-period game *except that her probability beliefs may have been changed by the buyer's rejection of her first period offer*. We can apply the same kind of argument as in the one-period model to conclude that S will set $p_1 = \ell$ or $p_1 = h$. We can therefore describe her decision rule in period 1 by the probability

$$\lambda = Pr[p_1 = \ell]$$

Given her updated probability belief following the buyer's rejection of her first-period offer p_0, the seller's optimal second-period decision rule is

$$
\begin{aligned}
\lambda &= 0 & &\text{if } \pi_1(p_0) > \bar{\pi} \\
\lambda &= 1 & &\text{if } \pi_1(p_0) < \bar{\pi} \\
\lambda &\in [0, 1] & &\text{if } \pi_1(p_0) = \bar{\pi} \qquad [\text{G.5}]
\end{aligned}
$$

We must now find a period 0 acceptance rule for the type h buyer which together with the strategies [G.3], [G.4] and [G.5] yields equilibria of the sub-games starting from a given first-period offer. First, consider the sub-game starting with a first-period offer of $p_0 = \ell$. The type h's optimal response is clearly to accept this offer since he cannot do better by waiting even if the seller's second-period strategy [G.5] resulted in $p_1 = \ell$ for sure:

$$h - \ell > \delta(h - \ell)$$

Thus he will set $a_0(\ell, h) = 1$. This acceptance rule and the decision rules [G.3], [G.4], [G.5] generate an equilibrium in the sub-game starting at $p_0 = \ell$. If the seller sets $p_0 = \ell$, the game will end after one period since both types of buyer will accept the offer, and the seller will get an income of ℓ.

Next, consider sub-games starting with S setting $p_0 > \ell$. The type ℓ buyer, following [G.3], will reject this offer whatever he believed about the period 1 offer. If the type h buyer was sure that $p_1 = \ell$, he would accept $p_0 > \ell$ if and only if

$$h - p_0 \geqslant \delta(h - \ell)$$

or, equivalently, if and only if

$$p_0 \leqslant \tilde{p}_0 \equiv (1 - \delta)h + \delta\ell \qquad \text{[G.6]}$$

Over the range of sub-games starting with $p_0 \in (\ell, \tilde{p}_0]$ the acceptance rule $a_0(p_0, h) = 1$ and the decision rules [G.3], [G.4] and [G.5] constitute an equilibrium. If the offer $p_0 \leqslant \tilde{p}_0$ is rejected the seller knows that such behaviour is optimal only for the type ℓ buyer and will revise her probability belief to $\pi_1(p_0) = 0$. Hence, from [G.4], she will set $p_1 = \ell$ and the asset will be bought by the type ℓ in the second period. If the seller faced the type h buyer the offer $p_0 \leqslant \tilde{p}_0$ would be accepted in the first period, since the type h buyer gains nothing by delaying acceptance.

The seller's expected proceeds from choosing an initial price in the range $(\ell, \tilde{p}_0]$, is $\pi p_0 + \delta(1 - \pi)\ell$ which is increasing in p_0. (Remember that when the buyer chooses p_0 she must use the prior probability π since she only acquires information from observing the buyer's response to her initial offer.) If the seller's optimal initial offer is in the range $(\ell, \tilde{p}_0]$ it must be equal to $\tilde{p}_0$ and will yield her an expected discounted income

$$v(\tilde{p}_0) = \pi\tilde{p}_0 + \delta(1 - \pi)\ell = \pi[(1 - \delta)h + \delta\ell] + \delta(1 - \pi)\ell = \pi h(1 - \delta) + \pi\ell \quad \text{[G.7]}$$

Since the seller is strong ($\pi > \bar{\pi} = \ell/h$) we see that

$$v(\tilde{p}_0) > \bar{\pi}h(1 - \delta) + \delta\ell = \ell \qquad \text{[G.8]}$$

A strong seller would do better to choose $\tilde{p}_0$ rather than ℓ as the first-period price. Hence the only possible candidate for a PBE with $p_0 \in (\ell, \tilde{p}_0]$ has the seller setting the first-period price $\tilde{p}_0$ and getting a payoff of $\pi h(1 - \delta) + \delta\ell$.

Now consider sub-games starting with an initial price in the range $(\tilde{p}_0, h]$. We will show that there is a constant acceptance probability $0 < a_0(p_0, h) = \bar{a}_0 < 1$ for the type h which yields an equilibrium for this range of sub-games. First, note that if the type h set his acceptance probability for p_0 in this range at $a_0(p_0, h) = 1$ there would not be an equilibrium. If type h was certain to accept such a p_0 the seller would be sure that she faced type ℓ if p_0 was rejected and, since $\pi_1(p_0) = 0$, [G.5] would lead her to set $p_1 = \ell$. But, from [G.6],

$$h - p_0 < h - \tilde{p}_0 = \delta(h - \ell)$$

so that the type h buyer would be better off rejecting the first-period offer and waiting to receive the offer ℓ in the next period. Thus $a_0 = 1$ cannot be part of a sub-game equilibrium in this range of p_0 since it is not optimal against the strategy [G.5] given the Bayesian updating by S.

Nor can there be an equilibrium if $a_0 = 0$ for all $p_0 \in (\tilde{p}_0, h]$. If the type h refuses the price p_0 then, since both types refuse it, the seller gains no information from having her initial price refused: $\pi_1(p_0) = \pi$. Since $\pi > \bar{\pi}$ she will set $p_1 = h$ (see [G.5]) and the type h would do better by accepting a first-period offer $p_0 < h$.

If the type h follows the strictly mixed strategy $0 < a_0(p_0, h) = \bar{a}_0 < 1$ he would get an expected payoff

$$(h - p_0)\bar{a}_0 + \delta[\lambda(h - \ell) + (1 - \lambda)(h - h)](1 - \bar{a}_0) = (h - p_0)\bar{a}_0 + \delta\lambda(h - \ell)(1 - \bar{a}_0)$$

The marginal value of increase in $\bar{a}_0$ to him is $(h - p_0) - \delta\lambda(h - \ell)$. If this is positive he will set $\bar{a}_0 = 1$ and if it is negative he will set $\bar{a}_0 = 0$. Hence he is willing to play the strictly mixed strategy only if $h - p_0 - \delta\lambda(h - \ell) = 0$ or

$$\lambda = (h - p_0)/\delta(h - \ell) \qquad \text{[G.9]}$$

Now [G.9] implies that, when $p_0 \in (\tilde{p}_0, h)$, the seller also must be willing to play a strictly mixed strategy $0 < \lambda < 1$ in the second period. From [G.5] this in turn implies that $\pi_1(p_0) = \bar{\pi}$ or, using Bayes' Rule

$$\frac{[1 - a_0(p_0, h)]\pi}{[1 - a_0(p_0, h)]\pi + [1 - a_0(p_0, \ell)](1 - \pi)} = \frac{[1 - a_0(p_0, h)]\pi}{[1 - a_0(p_0, h)]\pi + (1 - \pi)} = \bar{\pi} \quad [G.10]$$

Hence, if over the range $p_0 \in (\tilde{p}_0, h]$ the type h buyer has a first-period acceptance probability of

$$a_0 = \bar{a}_0 = (\pi - \bar{\pi})/\pi(1 - \bar{\pi}) \qquad (G.11)$$

which satisfies [G.10], the seller would be willing to follow a mixed strategy in the second period satisfying [G.9]. Thus the strategies defined by [G.3], [G.4], [G.5], [G.9] and [G.11] (or [G.10]) are an equilibrium for the sub-games starting with $p_0 \in (\tilde{p}_0, h]$.

The expected payoff to S from the sub-game equilibria with $p_0 \in (\tilde{p}_0, h]$ is

$$\pi \bar{a}_0 p_0 + \delta\{(1 - \lambda)\pi(1 - \bar{a}_0)h + \lambda[\pi(1 - \bar{a}_0) + (1 - \pi)]\ell\}$$

which is increasing in p_0. (The reader should check this by substituting for λ from [G.9] and differentiating with respect to p_0.) Hence *if* the seller's optimal first-period offer is in the range $p_0 \in (\tilde{p}_0, h]$ it will be h, yielding an expected discounted income of

$$v(h) = \pi \bar{a}_0 h + \delta\pi(1 - \bar{a}_0)h = \pi h[\bar{a}_0 + \delta(1 - \bar{a}_0)] \qquad [G.12]$$

An initial price $\tilde{p}_0$ is best for S over the range $p_0 \in [\ell, \tilde{p}_0]$ and $p_0 = h$ is best over the range $(\tilde{p}_0, h]$. Comparing [G.6] and [G.12], we see that the seller's optimal initial price will depend on the values of the parameters (h, ℓ, π, δ). Thus there are two types of equilibrium:

1. *High price equilibrium.* S follows the high price strategy h in period 0 and sets $p_1 = h$ in period 1. There is a probability $\pi(1 - \bar{a}_0)$ that agreement is reached in period 0, a probability $\pi \bar{a}_0$ that agreement is delayed until period 1 and a probability $(1 - \pi)$ that there is no agreement at all. Thus adding an extra period to the bargaining game has, in this case, reduced the efficiency of the outcome: although the probability of no trade is the same, there is a positive probability of delay in reaching agreement. Both types of buyer still get a zero surplus and the expected discounted surplus of the seller is reduced because of the positive probability of delay.

    The conclusion that the seller is worse off in the two-period game is somewhat surprising since she can get the same high price in both periods as she does in the one-period game. The explanation is that setting a price of h in both periods is an equilibrium strategy only if the type h buyer follows a strictly mixed strategy in the first period, so that there is positive probability that the type h does not buy until the second period.

2. *Intermediate price equilibrium.* Here S follows the intermediate initial price strategy of $p_0 = \tilde{p}_0$ and sets $p_1 = \ell$. Since the type h accepts $\tilde{p}_0$ and the type ℓ rejects it, there is a probability $(1 - \pi)$ that agreement is not reached until the second period. With this equilibrium there is a positive probability of delay in reaching agreement and the seller makes a concession over time in that the price she sets is lower in the second period than in the first. Thus we have one possible explanation for two commonly observed features of real-world bargaining.

The addition of one period to the one-period model makes a considerable difference to the outcome. Remember that we have assumed that the seller is strong, so that in a one-period game she would set a price of h and with probability $(1 - \pi)$ there would be no trade. Here trade is only delayed if the seller faces a type ℓ buyer. The extra period provides an opportunity for the seller to acquire information. If her first-period offer is rejected she revises her probability belief and reduces her offer, since she is now sure that she faces the type ℓ buyer. This opportunity is not available if there is only one period.

The seller is again worse off in the two-period game than in the one-period game, despite the opportunity for acting on information produced in the first period. In the one-period model the seller gets πh which exceeds her payoff from the intermediate price strategy [G.7]: $\pi h > v(\tilde{p}_0) = \pi h(1 - \delta) + \delta \ell$. The seller would do better with two periods if the type h used his acceptance rule from the one-period game with both periods. S would then set a high price in period 0 and reduce the price to ℓ to sell to the type ℓ in period 1 if there was no sale in period 0. However, the type h buyer will reject $p_0 = h$ in period 0 if he knew that $p_1 = \ell$. The seller must reduce p_0 to $\tilde{p}_0$ to induce the type h to buy in period 0, so that she can be sure that she faces a type ℓ buyer if her first period offer is refused.

The type h faces a lower price and is made better off by $h - \tilde{p}_0$. The type ℓ buyer faces the second-period price ℓ and is no worse off by the addition of the extra period. Since the probability of a type h buyer is π, the effect on the expected combined surplus of buyers and seller of adding an extra period in the intermediate price case is

$$(h - \tilde{p}_0)\pi + [\pi\tilde{p}_0 + \delta(1 - \pi)\ell] - h\pi = \delta(1 - \pi)\ell > 0$$

Thus the total expected gain from trade is increased, in contrast with the high price equilibrium case.

The values of the parameters (π, h, ℓ, δ) will determine which equilibrium yields the seller the highest expected discount payoff and therefore which one is chosen. For example, if π is close to 1 then $v(h) > v(\tilde{p}_0)$. As [G.11] indicates, the equilibrium probability that the type h buyer accepts a first-period price of h tends to 1 as π tends to 1, so that $v(h)$ tends to h. Although $v(\tilde{p}_0)$ also increases with π it can never exceed $h(1 - \delta)$.

The intermediate price equilibrium will occur if the discount factor δ is small. A small δ makes the intermediate price strategy more attractive for the seller because it increases the intermediate first-period price $\tilde{p}_0$ and reduces the significance of the fact that the seller will set a low price in the second period. $v(\tilde{p}_0)$ tends to πh as δ tends to 0, whereas $v(h)$ tends to $\pi h \bar{a}_0$.

Conclusion

The non-cooperative game studied in this section provides an example of how rational individuals may fail to reach agreements or do so only after a delay, despite the fact that their joint gains are maximized by immediate agreement. The model gives a rigorous demonstration of the way in which differences in the information available to the parties can affect both the likelihood of trade and the terms on which trade takes place, a point to which we will return in Chapter 20. However, the non-cooperative approach is still far from providing a complete and useful theory of bargaining.

The equilibrium of the simple two-period game of this section is surprisingly complex because actions can convey information. A further consequence of actions providing information is that predictions of models with incomplete information are often strongly dependent on fine, and apparently arbitrary, details of the bargaining process. Details, such as whether the parties make simultaneous or sequential moves, or whether one or both can make offers, matter because they affect the way in which actions transmit information. The difference in the results between the one- and two-period bargaining model in this section arises because in a two-period model the action of the better informed party (acceptance or rejection of the first-period offer) conveys information to the less well-informed party. There are equally dramatic consequences if it is assumed that the better informed party is the one who makes the offers (see Question 6, Exercise 15G). Unfortunately, it is often arbitrary to adopt one set of assumptions about the bargaining process, and therefore the structure of the game, rather than another. For example, in a model of union–firm bargaining it is plausible that the firm is better informed about its revenue from employing union members than the union (see Question 4, Exercise 15G). We should therefore reflect this in the specification of what the parties know at the start of the game. But there is no obvious reason why we should assume that it is the union, or the firm, which makes the offers to which the other party responds. The predictions of the model will, however, depend on the identity of the party making the offer, since offers by the firm may reveal its information about demand conditions to the union. Until we can resolve such issues the theory of non-cooperative bargaining will consist of a set of interesting but essentially ad hoc models.

EXERCISE 15G

1. *Continuum of buyer types.* Suppose that, in the one-period game, b is uniformly distributed over the interval $[\ell, h]$. What price will S propose and what is the probability that trade will take place? What is the expected gain from trade and how is it split between S and B?

2. *Efficiency.* Is the outcome of bargaining in the one-period model inefficient in the sense that there exists an alternative allocation mechanism which could make seller and buyers better off and which does not require a regulator with better information than the seller?

3. *Equilibrium with weak seller.* Show that the PBE for the two-period game with a weak seller ($\pi < \bar{\pi}$) has the seller setting $p_0 = \ell$.

4. *Union–firm bargaining with asymmetric information.* Refer to section 10D and use the results of this section to examine the outcome of union and firm bargaining when the union makes the offers but only knows that the firm's revenue function is either $hR(f(z))$ with probability q or $\ell R(f(z))$ with probability $(1-q)$.

5. *Commitment.* Suppose that S could commit herself at period 0 to the prices she offers in period 0 and period 1. What prices will she set?

6. *Offers by the informed player.* In the following variations on the game in the text, both players make offers. Derive and compare the PBEs. (a) In period 0 the seller makes an offer and the buyer accepts or rejects. If B rejects then in period 1 he makes an offer and S accepts or rejects. (b) In period 0, B makes an offer and S accepts or rejects. If S rejects p_0 she makes a proposal p_1 which B may accept or reject. (*Hint:* remember that B's action in period 0 may convey information.)

A. Introduction

There is oligopoly when a firm believes that the outcome of its decisions depends significantly on the decisions taken by one or more other identifiable sellers. It is usual to define oligopoly as a market with 'few sellers' (and indeed the word 'oligopoly' means this) but a definition in terms of the number of sellers in a market is not without ambiguity. Since the essence of the situation is the nature of the competitive relationships between sellers, it is best to make this the basis of the definition. Nevertheless, loosely and intuitively we always think of oligopoly as 'competition among the few'.

We assume that a firm in this situation of close interdependence of decision-taking will seek to maximize profit. The problem it faces is to assign a profit outcome to each decision alternative (e.g. production plan), in order to rank them and find the optimum. Each firm is necessarily involved in reasoning: 'if I choose A, and he chooses B, then I get X, whereas if I choose C, and he chooses D, then I get Y...', and so on. In this example, the competitor's reactions, B, D, ..., could take one of a number of forms, and so the firm in question must try to reason out what the response will be. Before it can come to a ranking of alternative decisions, it must take some view of the actions of each of its competitors. The theory of oligopoly is concerned with understanding and predicting the decisions of sellers in such situations of 'strategic interdependence', i.e. of interactions of reasoning and decision-taking among sellers.

A natural way to proceed would seem to be to formulate a particular hypothesis about the nature of the reactions which each firm expects and use this to find an equilibrium solution. The hypothesis allows us to say that each decision-taker will associate with her decision A some specific response B, and with her decision C some specific response D, and so on. Then, by using the basic analytical framework of cost and demand curves, we arrive at a prediction of the market equilibrium. However, there are several hypotheses about reaction patterns which are possible, each with a different associated equilibrium solution. We then have several possible theories with different solutions. This in itself need not be a serious cause for concern, since we could use empirical evidence to distinguish among the various hypotheses.

The application of game theory to oligopoly theory has however led to a fundamental reinterpretation of these models. The game-theoretic approach does not allow choice of an arbitrary, even if plausible, pattern of reactions. Rather, beliefs about the actions of a competitor have to be shown to follow from rational calculation by the firm concerned. Though, as we see below, several of the traditional oligopoly models still hold a central place, the game-theoretic approach has led to a more careful definition of the types of market situation for which they can be expected to hold, and a deeper understanding of the models themselves.

A further criticism of the 'reaction pattern' approach is that it ignores the possibility of explicit communication and cooperation among sellers. It assumes that the sellers remain 'at arm's length', guessing at each other's likely reactions, whereas an obvious possibility is that they would at least consult and quite conceivably cooperate. To quote a famous passage from Adam Smith's *Wealth of Nations*: 'People of the same trade seldom meet together, even for merriment or diversion, but the conversation ends in a conspiracy against the public, or in some contrivance to raise prices. It is impossible indeed to prevent such meetings, by any law which either could be executed, or would be consistent with liberty and justice' (vol. 1, p. 117, Everyman edition). The modern phenomenon of the expense account lunch or the trade association conference fits Smith's description of a meeting 'for merriment or diversion' quite accurately. Admitting the possibilities of communication and cooperation changes the focus of the analysis. Instead of constructing hypotheses about expected reaction patterns and examining their consequences, we are interested in answers to the questions:

(a) Under what conditions will the sellers agree to cooperate in their decisions?

(b) If they agree to cooperate, what price and output policies will result?

(c) Will their cooperative agreement be *stable*, in the sense of being maintained over time in the face of changing circumstances, and, in particular, are there forces making for a breakdown of the agreement?

Whether profit-maximizing firms will agree to cooperate depends crucially on the number of times the market situation is repeated. The traditional oligopoly models implicitly treat the market situation as a *one-shot game*: the firms produce and sell outputs just once. In this case it is very difficult to rationalize collusive behaviour. If on the other hand we view the market situation as being repeated (possibly infinitely) many times, it becomes quite easy to explain collusive behaviour, and the difficulty becomes that of explaining the prices and quantities that will be chosen.

In this chapter we use the game theory concepts developed in the previous chapter to analyse a small number of the more important oligopoly models. In section B firms play a one-shot duopoly game and we use the notion of a Nash equilibrium in pure and mixed strategies to consider four alternative models suggested by Cournot, Stackelberg, Bertrand and Edgeworth. In sections C and D firms interact repeatedly, leading us to apply the theory of dynamic games (subgame perfection, the Folk Theorem and renegotiation proofness) to examine whether collusive outcomes can be sustained by threats of future retaliation.

B. One-shot games

In this chapter we work in terms of a very specific model. The advantage is that the central results can be shown very simply and clearly. The disadvantage is that it is not always clear how or whether these results generalize.

We assume there are just two firms, with total cost functions

$$C_i = c_i q_i \qquad i = 1, 2 \qquad c_i > 0 \tag{B.1}$$

so that the firms have constant marginal costs. The goods produced by the firms may or may not be identical. If they are identical then we assume $c_1 = c_2 = c$. The inverse demand function for output of firm i is

$$p_i = \alpha_i - \beta_i q_i - \gamma q_j \qquad i, j = 1, 2 \qquad i \neq j \qquad\qquad \text{[B.2]}$$

where $\gamma > 0$. The goods are therefore substitutes: an expansion of firm j's output (corresponding to a fall in its price) pushes down the demand and revenue functions of firm i. The symmetry of cross-partials $\partial p_i / \partial q_j$ is useful, but recall from Chapter 3 that we would not in general expect it to exist for Marshallian demand functions, so [B.2] is a substantive restriction on the nature of demands for these goods. We assume $\alpha_i > c_i$ so that the markets are active.

If the firms' outputs are perfect substitutes, then

$$\alpha_1 = \alpha_2 = \alpha \qquad \text{and} \qquad \gamma = \beta_1 = \beta_2 \qquad\qquad \text{[B.3]}$$

and so the outputs must sell at identical prices determined by the sum of the firms' outputs – we have in effect only one demand function, $p = \alpha - \gamma(q_1 + q_2)$. The firms' profit functions, as functions of outputs, are

$$\pi_i(q_1, q_2) = p_i q_i - c_i q_i = (\alpha_i - c_i - \gamma q_j)q_i - \beta_i q_i^2 \qquad i, j = 1, 2 \qquad i \neq j \quad \text{[B.4]}$$

If the firms' outputs are not perfect substitutes, we can use the inverse demand functions in [B.2] to get the demand functions

$$q_i = q_i(p_1, p_2) = a_i - b_i p_i - \phi p_j \qquad i, j = 1, 2 \qquad i \neq j \qquad\qquad \text{[B.5]}$$

where a_i, b_i and ϕ are all positive. (See Question 1, Exercise 16B for the definition of these parameters and the implied restrictions on the α_i, β_i and γ.) Note that the individual demand functions cannot be expressed in this way if the outputs are perfect substitutes. We can also think of profit as a function of prices

$$\pi_i(q_1(p_1, p_2), q_2(p_1, p_2)) \qquad i = 1, 2 \qquad\qquad \text{[B.6]}$$

Note, finally, from [B.4] that the profit function π_i is strictly concave in q_i *for given* q_j, with a maximum at

$$q_i = \frac{\alpha_i - c_i - \gamma q_j}{2\beta_i} \qquad i, j = 1, 2 \qquad i \neq j \qquad\qquad \text{[B.7]}$$

while it is linear and decreasing in q_j for *given* q_i. Its Hessian determinant is

$$\begin{vmatrix} -2\beta_i & -\gamma \\ -\gamma & 0 \end{vmatrix} = -\gamma^2 < 0 \qquad\qquad \text{[B.8]}$$

which implies that the function is *not jointly concave in* q_i *and* q_j (see Appendix I). However, it can be shown that the function is strictly quasi-concave (see Question 7, Exercise 16B).

We now consider some oligopoly models in the context of this rather well behaved example.

1. The Cournot model

Assume the market operates as follows. Each firm must decide, without consulting the other, what output it will produce. The firms simultaneously put their outputs on the market. Prices then move to the levels that clear the market, and the firms receive the resulting profits. What outputs will they choose?

Figure 16.1

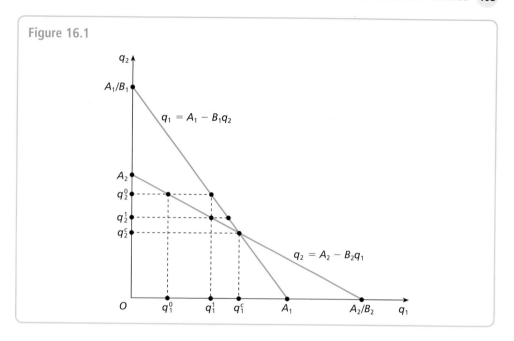

First, note that [B.7] gives each firm important information. Given any output q_j that firm i expects the other to produce, its *best response* is to produce the q_i given by [B.7]. Accordingly [B.7] defines the firms' *best response functions*,

$$q_i = A_i - B_i q_j \qquad i, j = 1, 2 \qquad i \neq j \qquad [\text{B.9}]$$

where $A_i \equiv (\alpha_i - c_i)/2\beta_i$; $B_i \equiv \gamma/2\beta_i$.

Examples of these functions are graphed in Fig. 16.1. The slopes are negative because increases in output q_j reduce firm i's profit-maximizing output.

The intersection point of these two best response functions gives

$$q_i^c = \frac{A_i - A_j B_i}{1 - B_i B_j} \qquad i, j = 1, 2 \qquad i \neq j \qquad [\text{B.10}]$$

by solving simultaneously the two equations defined by [B.9]. When the outputs are homogeneous, we have, using [B.3] in [B.10],

$$q_1^c = q_2^c = (\alpha - c)/3\gamma \qquad [\text{B.11}]$$

where $-\gamma$ is the slope of the inverse market demand function.

In his original analysis of this model over 150 years ago, the French economist Augustin Cournot proposed this intersection point as the equilibrium outcome in the market. His argument went as follows. Suppose firm 1 puts output q_1^0 (in Fig. 16.1) onto the market. Then firm 2 will react by producing its profit-maximizing output q_2^0. But if firm 2 does this, firm 1 will change its output to q_1^1, which maximizes its profit when $q_2 = q_2^0$. This in turn induces firm 2 to change its output to q_2^1. And so on. Since each firm reacts to the other's output by producing at a point on its best response function (or, in Cournot's terminology, *reaction curve*) the only possible equilibrium in the market, at which no further output changes will take place, is at the intersection point (q_1^c, q_2^c). Here, neither firm wants to change its output given the other's output choice.

This argument is not very convincing. Notice that it is inconsistent with the one-shot assumption since it requires that outputs are being chosen sequentially over a (possibly infinite) number of time periods. Each firm behaves myopically. Each expects that the other will keep its output constant, and this expectation about the other's reaction is held to, even though it is continually falsified. In section C we will see that rational firms may be able to do much better than the Cournot solution in multi-period situations. If the game is played only once, Cournot's process of sequential reactions to actual output choices cannot be used to rationalize the equilibrium at (q_1^c, q_2^c).

The game-theoretic treatment of the model provides a different rationale for the same equilibrium outcome. Each firm is assumed rationally to think through the consequences of its choices, in the knowledge that the other firm knows the situation and is also rationally thinking things through. The outputs that the firms produce are the *Nash equilibrium* output choices. The output pair (q_1^*, q_2^*) is a Nash equilibrium if

$$\pi_1(q_1^*, q_2^*) \geq \pi_1(q_1, q_2^*) \quad \text{and} \quad \pi_2(q_1^*, q_2^*) \geq \pi_2(q_1^*, q_2) \qquad \text{[B.12]}$$

for all feasible outputs q_1, q_2. That is, q_i^* must maximize i's profit given that firm j is producing q_j^* $(i, j = 1, 2, i \neq j)$. But clearly, the output pair (q_1^c, q_2^c) satisfies this definition and is moreover the only output pair that does so in this model. Thus the Nash equilibrium of this game is the Cournot equilibrium output pair, since it must be at the intersection of the firms' best response functions.

As we saw in Chapter 15, the argument underlying the use of the Nash equilibrium concept as the solution concept for games of this type is as follows. Suppose firm 2 thinks that firm 1 will produce output q_1^0 in Fig. 16.1. It can then calculate that q_2^0 is its best output on that assumption. But *it then realizes that firm 1 can also work that out*, and that if 1 thinks 2 will choose q_2^0, 1 will then want to produce q_1^1. So 2 would be irrational to persist in believing that 1 will choose q_1^0. Such an argument applies at *every* point except (q_1^c, q_2^c). If 2 believes 1 will choose q_1^c, its best response is q_2^c, and if it thinks that 1 has also figured that out, it will not want to change its choice because q_1^c is 1's best response to q_2^c. The Nash equilibrium pair has the property that, if i *knows* j will choose q_j^* $(= q_j^c)$, it will still wish to choose q_i^* $(= q_i^c)$. The firms are then led to make this choice of outputs by going through the above reasoning process. The argument for applying the Nash equilibrium concept is that any non-Nash equilibrium point is open to the criticism that it would not be chosen by a player who believes that its opponent is as rational and well-informed as it is itself.

We can compare the Cournot–Nash equilibrium with two other possible output pairs. The first, denoted $(\hat{q}_1, \hat{q}_2)$ corresponds to the 'perfectly competitive' solution[1] where price equals marginal cost:

$$p_i = \alpha_i - \beta_i \hat{q}_i - \gamma \hat{q}_j = c_i \qquad i, j = 1, 2 \qquad i \neq j \qquad \text{[B.13]}$$

The second, denoted (q_1^m, q_2^m), corresponds to the joint profit maximization or monopoly solution, and solves

$$\max_{q_1, q_2} \pi_1(q_1, q_2) + \pi_2(q_1, q_2) \qquad \text{[B.14]}$$

with first-order conditions

$$\alpha_i - c_i - 2\gamma q_j - 2\beta_i q_i = 0 \qquad i, j = 1, 2 \qquad i \neq j \qquad \text{[B.15]}$$

Table 16.1

Equilibrium outputs	Product differentiation	Homogeneous outputs
Cournot–Nash	$q_i^c = \dfrac{2\beta_j(\alpha_i - c_i) - \gamma(\alpha_j - c_j)}{4\beta_1\beta_2 - \gamma^2}$	$q_i^c = \dfrac{\alpha - c}{3\gamma}$
Perfect competition	$\hat{q}_i = \dfrac{\beta_j(\alpha_i - c_i) - \gamma(\alpha_j - c_j)}{\beta_1\beta_2 - \gamma^2}$	$\hat{q}_1 + \hat{q}_2 = \dfrac{\alpha - c}{\gamma}$
Monopoly	$q_i^m = \dfrac{\beta_j(\alpha_i - c_i) - \gamma(\alpha_j - c_j)}{2(\beta_1\beta_2 - \gamma^2)}$	$q_1^m + q_2^m = \dfrac{\alpha - c}{2\gamma}$
Stackelberg		
(Firm 1 is leader Firm 2 is follower)	$q_1^s = \dfrac{2\beta_2(\alpha_1 - c_1) - \gamma(\alpha_2 - c_2)}{4\beta_1\beta_2 - \gamma^2}$	$q_1^s = \dfrac{\alpha - c}{2\gamma}$
	$q_2^s = \dfrac{2\beta_1(\alpha_2 - c_2) - \gamma(\alpha_1 - c_1) - \gamma A_2}{4\beta_1\beta_2 - 2\gamma^2}$	$q_2^s = \dfrac{\alpha - c}{4\gamma}$

Table 16.1 shows the output solutions for each of these cases, for both differentiated and homogeneous outputs. Note that, because they have identical constant marginal costs, the firms' individual outputs are indeterminate in the competitive and monopolistic homogeneous output cases. It is left as an exercise (Question 2, Exercise 16B) to show that in the differentiated case

$$q_i^m < q_i^c < \hat{q}_i \qquad\qquad [\text{B.16}]$$

Thus outputs are lower and prices higher at the Cournot solution than under competition, and so the firms earn positive profits; but prices and profits are not as high as when outputs are set to maximize joint profits. This is easily seen (for the sum of outputs) in the homogeneous case, since

$$(\alpha - c)/2\gamma < 2(\alpha - c)/3\gamma < (\alpha - c)/\gamma$$

If the firms want to maximize profits, why do they not collude and agree to set outputs q_i^m? The answer is that, *in this one-shot game*, they will only do so if they can make a *binding commitment* to keep the agreed outputs. Otherwise, the attempt will fail because (q_1^m, q_2^m) is not a Nash equilibrium output pair.

Thus suppose the managers of the two firms meet, possibly for merriment and diversion, and agree to produce outputs q_i^m (or, for that matter, *any* outputs *other than* (q_1^c, q_2^c)). When they return to their firms and set about drawing up their production plans, the following thought will, if they are rational, occur to each of them. If the other firm is going to produce q_j^m, then i's best response is not q_i^m but rather $q_i^R = A_i - B_i q_j^m$. It is an exercise to show that $q_i^R > q_i^m$. The R stands for renege – firm i is going to renege or cheat on the agreement, by producing a larger output than agreed, and thereby earning a still larger profit. But, then, i will realize that j has also worked this out, and so producing q_j^m is even less of a good idea. The same process of reasoning described earlier will lead the two firms back to the Cournot–Nash equilibrium output pair.

How might they make a binding commitment? One possibility would be to draw up a legally binding contract, which provides for penalties of at least $\pi_i^R = \pi_i(q_i^R, q_j^m) - \pi_i(q_i^m, q_j^m)$ if i reneges. However, in many countries such an agreement would be illegal, so unenforceable, and therefore not binding. It is the possibility of punishing reneging by market sanctions, such as a price war, that makes the distinction between a one-shot and a repeated game important, as we shall see in section C. In a one-shot game there is no next period in which to hold a price war. If they cannot find a way of making a binding commitment, the firms will not be able to agree to a more profitable output pair than (q_1^c, q_2^c).

2. The Stackelberg model

Suppose that, instead of the firms making simultaneous output choices, firm 1 announces its output first and, once that announcement is made, the output cannot be changed. This makes firm 1 the *market leader*, and defines a model analysed by the German economist H. von Stackelberg. Firm 1 reasons that firm 2 will make the best response to its own announced output. There would be no point in firm 2's choosing its Cournot output, say, because firm 1 cannot then change its output from that announced. Thus, somehow, firm 1 is able to make a credible, binding commitment to an output level. What is firm 1's optimal output?

For any q_1, firm 2 will choose q_2 on its best response function. Thus firm 1 chooses q_1 to maximize its profit subject to this constraint, i.e. it solves

$$\max_{q_1, q_2} \pi_1(q_1, q_2) \quad \text{s.t.} \quad q_2 = A_2 - B_2 q_1 \qquad \text{[B.17]}$$

The first-order conditions

$$\alpha_1 - c_1 - \gamma q_2 - 2\beta_1 q_1 - \lambda B_2 = 0 \qquad \text{[B.18]}$$

$$-\gamma q_1 - \lambda = 0 \qquad \text{[B.19]}$$

$$q_2 = A_2 - B_2 q_1 \qquad \text{[B.20]}$$

yield firm 1's Stackelberg output as

$$q_1^s = [2\beta_2(\alpha_1 - c_1) - \gamma(\alpha_2 - c_2)]/(4\beta_1\beta_2 - 2\gamma^2) \qquad \text{[B.21]}$$

A comparison with the first row of Table 16.1 shows that $q_1^s > q_1^c$. Since this represents a rightward shift along firm 2's best response function, we must have $q_2^s < q_2^c$. In the homogeneous case

$$q_1^s = (\alpha - c)/2\gamma \qquad \text{[B.22]}$$

giving the interesting (but special to the chosen functional form) result that $q_1^s = q_1^m + q_2^m$. Since $q_2^s > 0$, this tells us that again total profits are not maximized. Indeed, total profits are even lower than at the Cournot–Nash equilibrium, though firm 1's profit is greater, reflecting its *first-mover advantage*.

Figure 16.2 illustrates the Stackelberg outcome. The curves shown are the contours of firm 1's profit function $\pi_1(q_1, q_2)$. Firm 1's profits increase as we move *downwards* in the figure, i.e. lower contours correspond to higher profits. Its best response function passes through the peaks of these contours because, for any q_2, firm 1 finds the profit-maximizing q_1. The Stackelberg equilibrium is a point of tangency of a profit contour with 2's best response function, since [B.17] requires firm 1 to find the point on this function which is on the lowest possible profit contour. Note that the slope of a profit contour is

$$\frac{dq_2}{dq_1} = (\alpha_1 - c_1 - \gamma q_2 - 2\beta_1 q_1)/\gamma q_1$$

Figure 16.2

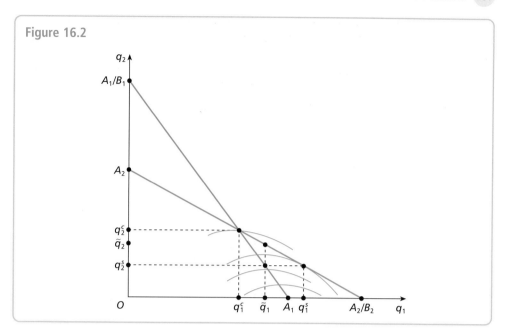

and [B.18] and [B.19] then yield the condition

$$\frac{dq_2}{dq_1} = -B_2$$

Since the slope of firm 2's best response curve is $-B_2$, this implies the type of tangency point shown in Fig. 16.2.

The Stackelberg solution is also a Nash equilibrium of the game defined by the assumption that firm 1 credibly commits to an output level before firm 2 chooses its output level. If firm 2 knows for sure that firm 1 will choose output q_1^s, then it will still want to choose output q_2^s; and if firm 1 knows for sure that firm 2 will make its best response to 1's announcement, it will want to precommit to q_1^s and not some other level of output.

One might be tempted to argue at this point: but what about output $\tilde{q}_1$ in Fig. 16.2. Surely, if firm 1 knew firm 2 would produce q_2^s, then $\tilde{q}_1$, on 1's best response function, yields higher profit than q_1^s. The answer is that this is a different game. If firm 1 can revise its output choice when it knows firm 2's output then $\tilde{q}_1$ would be the best response to q_2^s, but in that case we are back in the Cournot game and the outcome will be (q_1^c, q_2^c). Firm 1 would never *precommit* to $\tilde{q}_1$, because then firm 2 would choose its best response to this, at $\tilde{q}_2$. Thus the Stackelberg outcome only makes sense *as equilibrium* when the leader is credibly committed to producing his announced output.

3. The Bertrand model

Up until now we have assumed that the firms choose outputs, with prices then being determined by the inverse demand functions [B.2]. In many oligopolistic markets firms appear to set prices, then sell what the market demands. In a monopoly it makes no difference whether we carry out the analysis in terms of prices or quantities as the choice variables. In his critical review of the book in which Cournot set out his oligopoly model, Bertrand showed that in the case of oligopoly it is crucial whether firms are assumed to choose prices or quantities.

Suppose that the firms choose *prices* simultaneously and independently then sell the outputs generated by the demand functions in [B.5]. For the moment assume that products are differentiated. What prices will they choose?

We again proceed by finding the Nash equilibrium of this game. First we require the *best price-response functions*, since a Nash equilibrium will be at their intersection. Thus for *given p_j*, we solve

$$\max_{p_i} \pi_i = (p_i - c_i)q_i(p_i, p_j) = (p_i - c_i)(a_i - b_i p_i + \phi p_j)$$
$$i, j = 1, 2 \qquad i \neq j \qquad\qquad [\text{B.23}]$$

giving the best price-response function

$$p_i = \frac{a_i + c_i b_i}{2b_i} + \frac{\phi p_j}{2b_i} = \hat{A}_i + \hat{B}_i p_j \qquad i, j = 1, 2 \qquad i \neq j \qquad [\text{B.24}]$$

where $\hat{A}_i \equiv (a_i + c_i b_i)/2b_i$, $\hat{B}_i \equiv \phi/2b_i$. The best price-response functions are linear with *positive* slopes. As shown in Fig. 16.3, they intersect at the point (p_1^B, p_2^B), where

$$p_i^B = \frac{\hat{A}_i + \hat{A}_j \hat{B}_i}{1 - \hat{B}_i \hat{B}_j} \qquad i, j = 1, 2 \qquad i \neq j \qquad\qquad [\text{B.25}]$$

The Nash equilibrium in the Bertrand model is the pair of prices (p_1^B, p_2^B). The rationalization of the equilibrium is on the same lines as in the Cournot model. No other pair of price choices has the property of mutual consistency. If player i begins by assuming that j will choose $p_j^0 \neq p_j^B$, and reasons things through, i must conclude that j will *not* choose p_j^0, given that j has thought things through also.

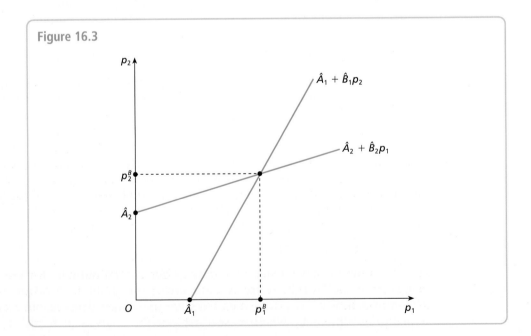

Figure 16.3

It is an exercise (Question 5, Exercise 16B) to show that the best price response functions in [B.24] do intersect, and that they imply prices p_i^B which are greater than marginal cost c_i' but less than the prices at the Cournot equilibrium. Thus, in the case of differentiated products, Bertrand prices and outputs are 'more competitive' than Cournot prices and outputs, but still generate excess profits.

It is in the case of homogeneous products that the consequences of the Bertrand analysis are the most striking. We can show that in this market the Nash equilibrium is at $p_1^B = p_2^B = c$, the competitive market outcome. Suppose i expects j to set $p_j^0 > c$. Then i's best response is to set $p_i^0 = p_j^0 - \varepsilon > c$ ($\varepsilon > 0$), since this captures the entire market and for small enough ε gives i the highest profit possible. But i will then realize that j will have realized this, and so would plan $p_j^1 = p_i^0 - \varepsilon > c$, in which case i should set $p_i^1 = p_j^1 - \varepsilon > c$, and so on. Clearly, in the end i cannot rationally believe that j will set $p_j > c$. But neither firm would set $p_j < c$, because this leads to losses. Thus $p_1 = p_2 = c$ is the only mutually consistent price pair in this market, and so it is the Nash equilibrium.

Bertrand intended this to be a *reductio ad absurdum*, to demonstrate the weakness of Cournot's approach. But both results are applications of the standard Nash equilibrium solution concept and there is nothing inherently unattractive about the idea that firms choose prices. The Bertrand outcome is a striking prediction from a model that is in many respects reasonable. If we feel that the competitive outcome in a homogeneous market with two firms is somehow implausible, a leading candidate for revision is the one-shot game assumption.

It is possible that the extreme nature of Bertrand's result led to its relative neglect in economics until recently – the 'standard' oligopoly model was that of Cournot. Bertrand's model seemed to deprive oligopoly theory of much of its interest: in the homogeneous goods case, the move from one firm to two leads directly from monopoly to perfect competition! We next turn to a model which seeks to explore this further, with even more problematic results.

4. The Edgeworth model

Suppose that in the Bertrand homogeneous output model each firm has an exogenously given upper bound on capacity output, $\bar{q}_i$. In choosing prices the firms have to take account of the constraints $q_i \leqslant \bar{q}_i$ ($i = 1, 2$).

For simplicity we assume

$$\bar{q}_1 = \bar{q}_2 = \bar{q}$$

To simplify the notation we assume that the firms' identical marginal production cost is zero: $c = 0$. (As the reader could check, all of the results below hold in the case in which $c > 0$.) Coupled with the assumption that the firms' capacities are exogenously determined, so that any costs of acquiring the capacity $\bar{q}$ are fixed, the assumption that $c = 0$ implies that profit maximization is equivalent to revenue maximization.

Although the Edgeworth model is a capacity constrained price setting model, the best output response functions from the capacity constrained quantity setting game have an important role in the analysis. Because demand is homogeneous the inverse market demand function is given by $p = \alpha - \gamma(q_1 + q_2)$ and the best output response function for firm i is derived from the problem

Figure 16.4

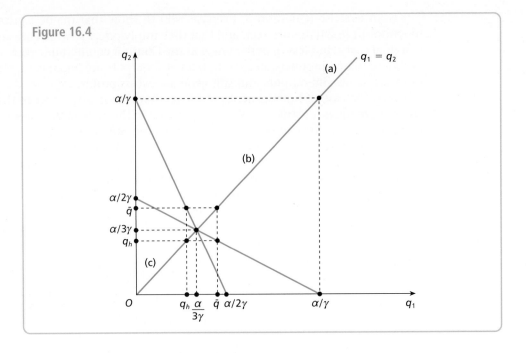

$$\max_{q_i} \alpha q_i - \gamma(q_1 + q_2)q_i \quad \text{s.t.} \quad q_i \leq \bar{q} \qquad [\text{B.26}]$$

as

$$q_i = (\alpha/2\gamma) - q_j/2 \quad \text{for } q_i < \bar{q} \quad \text{and} \quad q_i = \bar{q} \text{ otherwise} \qquad [\text{B.27}]$$

The best output response functions are graphed in Fig. 16.4. The Cournot–Nash outputs are $q_i^c = \alpha/3\gamma$. (Just use Table 16.1 and remember that $c = 0$.) The Cournot–Nash outputs lie on the 45° line, as do the output capacities $(\bar{q}, \bar{q})$.

Depending on the level of the exogenous capacity constraint parameter $\bar{q}$ there are three types of solution to the price-setting game. The three cases are:

(a) $\bar{q} \geq \alpha/\gamma$: each firm has enough capacity to supply the entire market at a price equal to the marginal production cost of zero;

(b) $(\alpha/3\gamma) < \bar{q} < \alpha/\gamma$: firm capacity is smaller than in case (a) but larger than the Cournot–Nash equilibrium output;

(c) $0 < \bar{q} \leq (\alpha/3\gamma)$: firm capacity is equal to or smaller than the Cournot–Nash output.

In case (a) the Nash equilibrium solution of the capacity constrained price-setting game is $p_1 = p_2 = 0$ which is the Bertrand solution when marginal production cost is zero. The capacity constraints have no effect on the solution because either firm can supply the entire demand at a price equal to marginal production cost.

The interesting cases are (b) and (c). Before we can analyse these we need to make two further assumptions. The first is *equal sharing*: if firms charge the same price they will each sell half the total quantity demanded at that price. The second is *efficient rationing*: if firm j sets a lower price than firm i and sells to its capacity $\bar{q}$, then firm i will face the residual demand curve $p_i = (\alpha - \gamma\bar{q}) - \gamma q_i$ shown by the segment $\hat{\alpha}(\alpha/\gamma)$

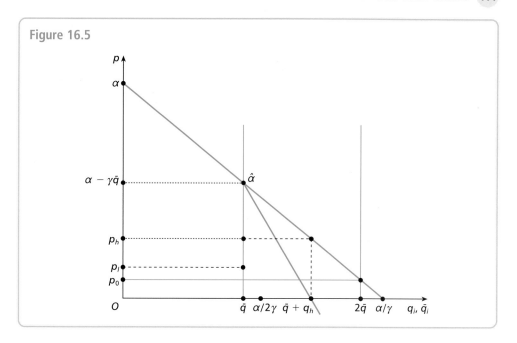

Figure 16.5

in Fig. 16.5. Rationing is efficient because it is as if j's $\bar{q}$ units of output were sold to those consumers who value them most highly, thus removing the upper segment $\alpha\hat{\alpha}$ of the market demand curve and leaving firm i with the remainder. The efficient rationing assumption is rather strong since it is possible to think of other plausible means of allocating firm j's output. For example, it could be allocated randomly to consumers, or to those who are first in line. As we note below, the form of rationing has a significant effect on the model's results.

The price p_0 at which demand is equal to the combined capacities of the firm is:

$$p_0 = \alpha - 2\gamma\bar{q}$$

Figure 16.5 illustrates for case (b). In cases (b) and (c) neither firm will ever choose a price below p_0. (If $\bar{q} > \alpha/2\gamma$ it would not be possible to set such a price.) If firm j has set $p_j \geqslant p_0$ then firm i can sell $\bar{q}$ units at all prices $p_i \leqslant p_0$. Hence $p_i < p_0$ is not an optimal response to $p_j \geqslant p_0$ because raising p_i to p_0 would increase revenue. If firm j has set $p_j < p_0$ firm i will be able to sell $\bar{q}$ units at $p_i = p_0$ and so $p_i < p_0$ is not an optimal response to $p_j < p_0$. Thus $p_i < p_0$ is a *dominated strategy* for firm i: it is not a best response to *any* strategy (p_j) of firm j.

The other significant feature of p_0 is that if firm j sets a price greater than p_0 the best response of firm i is not to set the same price. The equal sharing assumption implies that if $p_i = p_j > p_0$ firm i gets only half the market demand, which from the definition of p_0 is less than its capacity. By undercutting firm j slightly firm i can sell an output equal to its capacity and thereby earn more revenue than sharing the market. Thus a Nash equilibrium can never have $p_i > p_0$.

Now we consider case (b) and show that the best price response functions $p_i^\star(p_j)$ are those graphed in Fig. 16.6. Since the response functions do not intersect there is no pair of prices which are best responses to each other: case (b) does not have a Nash equilibrium when firms' strategies are to choose a single price (i.e. if they are restricted to pure strategies in the terminology of Chapter 15).

Figure 16.6

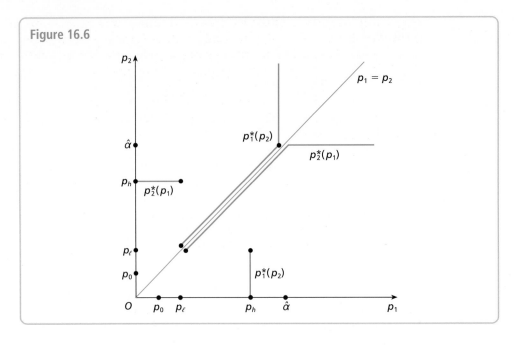

First note that a single firm faced with the demand function $\alpha - \gamma q$ would maximize revenue (and therefore profit since $c = 0$) by choosing either a quantity of $\alpha/2\gamma$, if this output was feasible, or an output equal to capacity if, as in Fig. 16.5, $\bar{q} < \alpha/2\gamma$. Consider the sub-case in which $\bar{q} < \alpha/2\gamma$ and denote the price at which demand equals the capacity of a single firm by

$$\hat{\alpha} = \alpha - \gamma\bar{q}$$

(See Fig. 16.5.) Then $\hat{\alpha}$ is the best response by firm i to firm j setting any price greater than $\hat{\alpha}$: firm i gets all the demand because it has the lower price and $\hat{\alpha}$ is its capacity constrained revenue-maximizing price given $p_j > \hat{\alpha}$. If firm j sets $p_j = \hat{\alpha}$ firm i's best response is to set a very slightly lower price $p_i = \hat{\alpha} - \varepsilon$. (If it sets $p_i > \hat{\alpha}$ it sells nothing and we showed above that it does better undercutting rather than equalling $p_j = \hat{\alpha} > p_0$.) Thus the best response function of firm 2 graphed in Fig. 16.6 as $p_2^*(p_1)$ is horizontal at $\hat{\alpha}$ for $p_1 > \hat{\alpha}$ and lies ε below the 45° line at $p_1 = \hat{\alpha}$. Similarly, firm 1's best response curve $p_1^*(p_2)$ is vertical at $\hat{\alpha}$ for $p_2 > \hat{\alpha}$ and lies ε to the left of the 45° line at $p_2 = \hat{\alpha}$.

In the other sub-case where $\alpha/2\gamma \leq \bar{q}$ the best response curve for firm 2 is horizontal at the unconstrained revenue-maximizing price $\frac{1}{2}\alpha$ for $p_1 > \frac{1}{2}\alpha$ and ε below the 45° line at $\frac{1}{2}\alpha$. The best response by firm i to $p_j \in [\hat{\alpha}, \frac{1}{2}\alpha]$ is to set p_i just slightly less than p_j. (If it sets a higher price it gets no revenue and we have already established that setting the same price cannot be a best response.) Thus in both sub-cases the best response functions do not intersect at any price greater than or equal to the price $\hat{\alpha}$ at which demand is equal to the capacity of a single firm. Bertrand price competition rules out any equilibrium with prices of $\hat{\alpha}$ or greater.

Before we can consider best responses to prices below $\hat{\alpha}$, we must define two other price levels p_h and p_ℓ which play a crucial role in the argument. Denote by p_h the price that firm i would set given that firm j sets a lower price and produces its capacity output. In these circumstances the efficient rationing assumption implies that firm i will face the residual demand curve $\hat{\alpha}(\alpha/\gamma)$ and residual marginal revenue curve $\hat{\alpha}(\bar{q} + q_h)$ in Fig. 16.5. It would set the price p_h at which the quantity sold was q_h. (q_h is also the best quantity response to firm j's choice of $\bar{q}$. Thus in terms of Fig. 16.4, q_h is the point on firm i's best response function for $q_j = \bar{q}$.) Define p_ℓ by

$$p_\ell\bar{q} = p_h q_h \qquad [B.28]$$

The firm would be indifferent between selling its capacity output at p_ℓ and selling q_h at p_h. The reader should check that $p_h > p_\ell > p_0$ as in Fig. 16.5.

We can now show that firm i's best response to $p_j \in [\hat{\alpha}, p_h]$ is to undercut p_j slightly: $p_i = p_j - \varepsilon$. If firm i responds to $p_j \in [\hat{\alpha}, p_h]$ by setting $p_i^+ > p_j$ it must have $p_i^+ > p_h$. It faces the residual demand curve and sells $q_i^+ < \bar{q}$, which yields revenue $p_i^+ q_i^+ < p_h q_h$. (Remember, p_h maximizes its revenue if it faces the residual demand curve.) If firm i instead sets $p_i^- = p_j - \varepsilon > p_\ell$ it sells $\bar{q}$. For small enough ε this is better than setting the same price as firm j and getting half the market demand, which, since $p_i^- > p_0$, is less than $2\bar{q}$. Because $p_i^- > p_\ell$, [B.28] implies

$$p_i^-\bar{q} > p_\ell\bar{q} = p_h q_h > p_i^+ q_i^+$$

Hence firm i's best response to $p_j \in [\hat{\alpha}, p_h]$ is to undercut p_j slightly.

If firm j sets $p_j \in (p_h, p_\ell)$ firm i's best response is again to undercut it slightly. Its best price greater than p_j is p_h. By setting $p_i = p_j - \varepsilon > p_\ell$ firm i sells its capacity output, yielding greater revenue than a price of p_h:

$$(p_j - \varepsilon)\bar{q} > p_\ell\bar{q} = p_h q_h$$

Thus over the range $[\hat{\alpha}, p_\ell)$ firm 2's best response function lies ε below the 45° line and firm 1's is ε to the left of it.

Firm i's best response to $p_j \in [p_\ell, 0]$ is to set $p_i = p_h$. We know that matching firm j's price $p_j > p_0$ is never optimal for firm i and setting a price ε less than p_j yields smaller revenue than choosing p_h since now

$$(p_j - \varepsilon)\bar{q} < p_\ell\bar{q} = p_h q_h$$

Over the range $[p_\ell, 0]$ firm 2's best response function is the horizontal line at $p_2 = p_h$ and firm 1's is the vertical line at $p_1 = p_h$.

Notice in Fig. 16.6 that because the best price response curves are discontinuous at p_ℓ they never intersect and there is no pair of prices which are best responses to each other. Edgeworth viewed this market as a process taking place over successive time periods and argued that prices would cycle endlessly without reaching an equilibrium. No matter where the process started it would eventually lead to prices cycling over the range $[p_\ell, p_h]$. From p_h a process of competitive undercutting would drive price down to p_ℓ, there would then be a jump back to p_h and the undercutting process would start again. However, here we view the market as a one-shot game, with each firm reasoning through the 'process' in an attempt to formulate an optimal response to the other firm's price. We cannot then predict what decisions they will take because there is no Nash equilibrium in pure strategies.

This pessimistic result arises because we required the equilibrium to be a pair of prices which were best responses to each other. In game-theoretic terms, the players were assumed to be restricted to *pure strategies*: they had to choose a definite price (strategy) in response to a definite price (strategy) of the other player. The solution to this analytical difficulty is to introduce the concept of a *mixed strategy* (see Chapter 15). A mixed strategy is a probability distribution over pure strategies, specifying the probability with which each pure strategy will be chosen. (Note that the concept includes pure strategies as a special case: by setting the probabilities attached to all pure strategies except one equal to zero a player can choose one of the pure strategies for sure.) It can be shown that for the type of game we are analysing there must always exist a mixed strategy Nash equilibrium: a pair of probability distributions over pure strategies which are best responses to each other.

Before we find the mixed strategy equilibrium in case (b) we shall analyse case (c) in which the exogenously given fixed capacities are at or below the Cournot–Nash equilibrium output levels. The same argument as in case (b) establishes that there cannot be any equilibrium with price above p_h. Remember that p_h is the optimal price for firm i given that firm j will sell $q_j = \bar{q}$. The reader should check that in case (c) the capacity constraint binds at p_h so that $q_h = \bar{q}$ and

$$p_h = \hat{\alpha} - \gamma\bar{q} = (\alpha - \gamma\bar{q}) - \gamma\bar{q} = \alpha - 2\gamma\bar{q} = p_0$$

Thus $p_i = p_0$ is the best response to any price set by firm j which results in j selling its capacity. But this means that $p_i = p_0$ is also the best response to $p_j = p_0$. Hence we have a Nash equilibrium in prices with $p_1 = p_2 = p_0$ and both firms selling their capacity outputs. Thus the Edgeworth non-existence of an equilibrium in pure strategies occurs only in case (b).

In terms of Fig. 16.4, the best unconstrained output response by firm 1 to firm 2 setting $q_2 = \bar{q}$ is at the intersection of the horizontal line at $q_2 = \bar{q}$ with its best output response curve. But this would violate firm 1's capacity constraint and firm 1 maximizes its profit, given $q_1 = \bar{q}$, making q_1 as large as possible: it moves along the horizontal line at $q_2 = \bar{q}$ until it reaches the capacity constraint. Thus when the firms' capacities are less than their Cournot–Nash equilibrium outputs the solution is at the intersection of the capacity constraints. Notice that if the capacity constraints were equal to the Cournot–Nash equilibrium outputs the Bertrand capacity constrained price-setting game yields the same result as the unconstrained Cournot quantity-setting game.

Mixed strategy equilibrium in Edgeworth's duopoly model

We saw earlier that for the case in which the exogenously fixed capacity output $\bar{q}$ lies between α/γ (demand at zero price) and $\alpha/3\gamma$ (Cournot–Nash output q_i^c) Edgeworth's model has no Nash equilibrium price pair. Since in this model the firms' strategies are prices, this is equivalent to saying that the model has no pure strategy Nash equilibrium. We now show that it does have an equilibrium in mixed strategies, by actually calculating the probability distributions over prices that define this equilibrium. There is also a simple characterization of the equilibrium expected payoff to each firm.

Figure 16.7 gives an alternative way of finding the interval $[p_\ell, p_h]$ which, as we will show, is the only set of prices chosen with positive probability in the mixed strategy equilibrium. The curve $R(p)$ is given by

$$R(p) = pq(p) = p(\alpha - p)/\gamma = (\alpha p - p^2)/\gamma$$

where $q(p) = (\alpha - p)/\gamma$ is the demand function for total output $q = q_1 + q_2$. This is the revenue function a monopolist would face. Now if a firm is the higher priced firm, it faces the revenue function $R_h(p)$ defined by

$$R_h(p) = p(q(p) - \bar{q}) = [(\alpha p - p^2)/\gamma] - p\bar{q} \qquad \text{[B.29]}$$

Figure 16.7

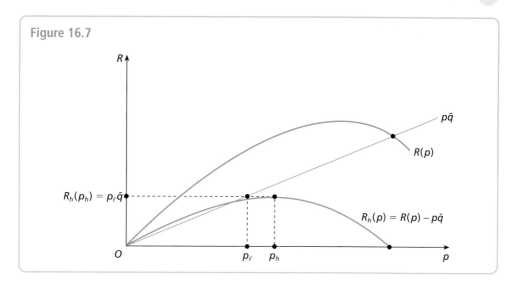

since it receives the residual demand, after the lower-priced firm has sold its capacity output (recall the 'efficient rationing' assumption). We saw earlier that p_h maximizes $R_h(p)$ and so satisfies

$$(\alpha/\gamma) - 2p/\gamma - \bar{q} = 0 \Rightarrow p_h = (\alpha - \gamma\bar{q})/2 \qquad [\text{B.30}]$$

We then have from [B.29] and [B.30] after some rearrangement

$$R_h(p_h) = \frac{1}{\gamma}\left(\frac{\alpha - \gamma\bar{q}}{2}\right)^2 \qquad [\text{B.31}]$$

In the figure, p_h is shown as the price which maximizes $R_h(p)$. Then, p_ℓ is found as the price which equates $p\bar{q}$ with $R_h(p_h)$, as in [B.28].

A mixed strategy for firm i is a distribution function $\psi_i(p)$ such that $\psi_i(\hat{p})$ is the probability that i chooses a price less than or equal to $\hat{p}$. A mixed strategy equilibrium is a pair of distribution functions (ψ_1, ψ_2) which are best replies to each other. We will show that there is a mixed strategy equilibrium in which the distribution functions are identical and increasing in $p \in [p_\ell, p_h]$. Thus the probability density functions ψ_i' are positive over this interval.

If firm i chooses the mixed strategy $\psi_i(p)$, then ignoring some technical issues (for which see Kreps and Scheinkman (1983)), when j sets price p it will be the lower price firm with probability $1 - \psi_i(p)$ and the higher price firm with probability $\psi_i(p)$. Thus j's expected revenue if it sets price p is

$$ER_j(p) = [1 - \psi_i(p)]p\bar{q} + \psi_i(p)R_h(p) \qquad [\text{B.32}]$$

Now we are looking for an equilibrium in which all prices in the interval $[p_\ell, p_h]$ may be chosen by firm i. But this requires that all prices in the interval yield j the same expected revenue when firm i chooses the distribution function $\psi_i(p)$. If there was a price which yielded a unique global maximum over this interval firm j would choose it for sure. Any price which yields a smaller expected revenue than some other price in the interval would never be chosen. Thus all prices p must yield the same expected revenue to j if the requirement that all prices in the interval have a positive probability of being chosen ($\psi_j'(p) > 0$) is to be satisfied.

By choosing p_ℓ, j can get expected revenue of

$$ER_j(p_\ell) = [1 - \psi_i(p_\ell)]p_\ell\bar{q} + \psi_i(p_\ell)R_h(p_\ell) = p_\ell\bar{q}$$

since $\psi_i(p_\ell) = 0$. Thus firm i's distribution function ψ_i must be such that for all $p \in [p_\ell, p_h]$ firm j gets an expected revenue of $p_\ell\bar{q}$:

$$ER_j(p) = p_\ell\bar{q} = [1 - \psi_i(p)]p\bar{q} + \psi_i(p)R_h(p) \qquad p \in [p_\ell, p_h] \qquad [B.33]$$

Solving this for $\psi_i(p)$ gives

$$\psi_i(p) = (p\bar{q} - p_\ell\bar{q})/[p\bar{q} - R_h(p)] \qquad p \in [p_\ell, p_h] \qquad [B.34]$$

To see that this indeed gives a strictly increasing distribution function, note that

(a) if $p = p_\ell$, then $\psi_i(p_\ell) = 0$

(b) if $p = p_h$, then $\psi_i(p_h) = 1$ (since $R_h(p_h) = p_\ell\bar{q}$)

(c) for $p_\ell < p < p_h$, $\psi_i(p) > 0$ (since then $p\bar{q} > R_h(p)$, as can be confirmed from Fig. 16.7)

(d) $\psi_i' > 0$ if and only if (differentiating through [B.34] and cancelling terms),

$$[p_\ell\bar{q} - R_h(p)] + R_h' \cdot [p - p_\ell] > 0 \qquad [B.35]$$

which Fig. 16.7 readily confirms will hold.

If firm i chose the strictly increasing distribution function given by [B.34] then firm j would be willing to randomize over its price and would, in particular, be willing to choose the same distribution function as firm i. Thus we have a symmetric mixed strategy Nash equilibrium in which the distribution function [B.34] is a best reply to itself.

Prices vs. quantities and the Kreps–Scheinkman model

Whether firms are assumed to choose prices or quantities is of considerable importance. Bertrand thought it obvious that firms should be regarded as price-setters and indeed thought that Cournot's specification in terms of quantity choice was simply an analytical mistake. One prevalent modern view seems to be that no such judgment need be made, and that it is an empirical matter to decide which type of model better fits a particular market. In the market being analysed, do firms set outputs and then allow price to adjust to whatever level allows them to be sold, or do they set prices and then produce to meet whatever demands arise? The answer determines which type of model to use. A second strand in the literature considers the question of the *endogenous* choice of strategy variable. An important paper somewhat in this spirit is that of Kreps and Scheinkman (1983). This paper could be thought of as an extension of the Edgeworth model just considered, in that it allows the firms' capacity levels to be *endogenously chosen*. In doing so the paper makes an interesting reconciliation between the Cournot and Bertrand models. It is shown that if firms first choose capacity outputs and then, with these capacities fixed, play a price-setting game of the kind just analysed as the Edgeworth model, then the equilibrium of the model takes the following form. The equilibrium capacities at the first stage correspond to the Cournot–Nash equilibrium outputs for the market, $\bar{q} = q_i^c$. The second stage price game consists of the firms setting their prices at the level at which demand equals the sum of Cournot–Nash outputs. Thus we have the Cournot–Nash equilibrium in a market in which firms set prices, subject to precommitted capacity levels.

Unfortunately, this striking result is not robust to variations in the assumption on the form of rationing by the lower priced firm in this model. As Davidson and Deneckere (1985) show, if some other assumption is made than that referred to above as the 'efficient rationing assumption', which defines the residual demand function for the higher-priced firm as $p_i = (\alpha - \gamma \bar{q}) - \gamma q_i$, then the Kreps–Scheinkman result no longer holds. The choice between prices or quantities as strategy variables matters.

EXERCISE 16B

1. Given the inverse demand functions in [B.2], show that the parameters of the demand function in [B.5] are:

$$a_i = \frac{\beta_j \alpha_i - \gamma \alpha_j}{\beta_1 \beta_2 - \gamma^2}; \qquad b_i \equiv \frac{\beta_j}{\beta_1 \beta_2 - \gamma^2}; \qquad \phi \equiv \frac{\gamma}{\beta_1 \beta_2 - \gamma^2} \qquad i, j = 1, 2 \qquad i \neq j$$

   for the case where outputs are not homogeneous. Why is it necessary to assume that $\beta_j \alpha_i > \gamma \alpha_j$ and $\beta_1 \beta_2 > \gamma^2$?

2. Use Table 16.1 to prove [B.16] in the case of non-homogeneous outputs.

3. Explain why, in Table 16.1, the *individual* outputs q_i^m and $\hat{q}_i$ are indeterminate, when firms' outputs are homogeneous.

4. Show that q_i^R and q_i^m as defined in the text satisfy $q_i^R > q_i^m$.

5. Confirm the construction of Fig. 16.4, and hence the unique Bertrand equilibrium (p_1^B, p_2^B), by showing that $\hat{A}_i > 0$, $1 > \hat{B}_i > 0$, $i = 1, 2$. (*Hint*: use the facts and assumptions in Question 1.)

6. Show that (p_1^B, p_2^B) imply positive profits, but a more competitive outcome than (q_1^c, q_2^c), in the model of this section with non-homogeneous outputs.

7. Show that the profit functions in [B.4] are strictly quasi-concave. (*Hint*: use the expression for dq_2/dq_1 given in the discussion of the Stackelberg model.)

8. Show that in case (a) of the Edgeworth model the Nash equilibrium of the price-setting game has each firm setting a price of zero. Draw the best price response functions and confirm they intersect at the origin.

C. Oligopoly as a repeated game

We retain the basic duopoly model set out at the beginning of the previous section, but now the firms choose prices or outputs in each of a sequence of time periods. The game played in each period is the *constituent game*, and it is common knowledge to the firms that they are engaged in a sequence of repetitions of this game. They formulate strategies for the repeated game, not just for the one-period constituent game in isolation from any other period.

   In such a context it is possible to rationalize collusive behaviour in the absence of binding (legally enforceable) agreements. If the firms agree, explicitly or tacitly, to collude in one period, and if one firm then deviates from that agreement, the other can punish it by instigating a price war (output expansion) or carrying out some other retaliatory action in the next period. The threat of anticipated future punishment may make it rational for each firm to adhere to the agreement. The firms can make an agreement in the belief that it will be sustained by self interest: it is *self-enforcing*.

This simple and appealing idea must however be subjected to further analysis. First, the gains from deviation will be realized immediately, whereas the losses from punishment will occur in the future. Will it always be the case that sufficiently large future losses can be threatened to offset the gains from immediate deviation? This depends on the mechanism by which punishment is inflicted, the rate at which firms discount future profits, and the length of time for which the deviant can gain from breaking the agreement before punishment begins. A second issue is the credibility of the threat of punishment. Typically, inflicting punishment through the market – for example by a price war – hurts the punisher as well as the deviant. The threat of punishment will be an effective deterrent only if potential deviants believe that it will actually be carried out. These questions are the central concern in the models we consider in this section and the next.

We first need to consider whether the constituent game is repeated a finite number of times or infinitely often. If there is a known last period of the game, backward induction shows that the above intuitive argument for collusion may break down. The equilibrium repeated game strategy may then simply consist of repeated plays of the one-shot Nash equilibrium. For example, consider the differentiated product model of the previous section in which firms choose prices. In the last period of the repeated game, the usual argument establishes that firms choose the (unique) Bertrand–Nash equilibrium prices. There is no next period in which to punish deviation and collusive prices are not a Nash equilibrium of this one-shot game.

In the next to last period, the firms could agree to collude, but it is not possible to support this with credible threats of punishment in the last period. For the *sub-game of the repeated game* consisting of the last period one-shot game, the only Nash equilibrium is the Bertrand equilibrium. In the next to last period both firms realize that this is the case. So the threat of punishment by setting a price in the last period other than the Nash equilibrium price is not credible and cannot sustain collusion in the next to last period. But if collusion cannot be sustained the Nash equilibrium in the next to last period is the Bertrand price equilibrium. This in turn implies that the threat of setting non-Bertrand prices in the next to last or the last period cannot sustain collusion in the second to last period game and Bertrand equilibrium prices are the only Nash equilibrium in the second to last period. The argument extends, period by period, right back to the first. Thus the only credible Nash equilibrium of the finitely repeated game has the firms choosing the Nash equilibrium of the one-shot game in every period.

If the game is repeated forever, there is no last period in which to start the backwards induction process. The repeated game will look exactly the same from whatever point in time it is considered. In this case, as we shall see, collusion can be rationalized as a Nash equilibrium of the repeated game.

In the remainder of this chapter we assume an infinitely repeated market game. Although individuals have finite lives, firms as institutions have potentially infinite lives, and the individuals within them who take decisions realise this. Moreover, it can be shown that, if a repeated game has a finite, but uncertain, number of periods, then collusion may be sustainable. If, in a given period, there is some probability that there *will* be a next period, then there will be an expected value of loss from punishment which might sustain collusion. In effect, the *probability* of a future can be incorporated into the time discount factor.[2]

We take the model of the previous section in both the differentiated and homogeneous product cases. The time period is denoted $t = 0, 1, \ldots, \infty$, and choices of prices or outputs are made in each period. We assume that the firms face the same interest rate $r > 0$, and wish to maximize the present value of profit.

$$V_i = \sum_{t=0}^{\infty} \delta^t \pi_i^t \qquad \text{[C.1]}$$

where $\delta \equiv (1 + r)^{-1}$ is each firm's discount factor and π_i^t is i's profit in period t. In the discounting formula we assume that profits accrue at the beginning of each period, which is also when decisions are taken.

Before considering firms' strategies for the repeated game, we need to extend our previous analysis of the constituent game. It will be useful for illustrative purposes to have numerical versions of the models defined earlier in [B.1]–[B.5]. We assume:

$$\alpha_1 = \alpha_2 = 10 \qquad c_1 = c_2 = 1$$

Differentiated products case: $\quad \beta_1 = \beta_2 = 1 \qquad \gamma = 0.5$

Homogeneous products case: $\quad \gamma = 1$

Thus the firms have identical cost and demand functions. We are interested in the Nash equilibria of the one-shot game for both quantity and price choices, as well as in the joint profit maximizing solution. Table 16.2 gives the values of prices, outputs and profits at these various solutions for this numerical example. The numbers of course confirm the earlier algebraic results. Note that in the homogeneous products case, since individual outputs are indeterminate in the Bertrand–Nash and joint profit maximization (monopoly) cases, only total outputs are given. In the former case individual profits are necessarily zero since $p^B = c$, whereas in the latter case individual profits are *a priori* indeterminate and the total profit is given.

Table 16.2

	Differentiated products	Homogeneous products
Cournot–Nash	$q_i^c = 3.6$; $p_i^c = 4.6$; $\pi_i^c = 12.96$	$q_i^c = 3$; $p^c = 4$; $\pi_i^c = 9$
Bertrand–Nash	$q_i^B = 4$; $p_i^B = 4$; $\pi_i^B = 12$	$q^B = 9$; $p^B = 1$; $\pi_i^B = 0$
Joint profit maximization	$q_i^m = 3$; $p_i^m = 5.5$; $\pi_i^m = 13.5$	$q^m = 4.5$; $p^m = 5.5$; $\pi^m = 20.25$

If we assume that the firms collude, the joint profit maximizing allocation is a natural one to focus upon, because it gives the maximum gain they can make from their cooperation. However, we should not think of it as the only possible collusive outcome, in the absence of a well-defined model that would predict it to be so. Moreover, it is not difficult to construct models in which the Cournot–Nash equilibrium output yields a higher profit for one of the firms than it would obtain from the output it would produce at the joint profit maximizing equilibrium (see Question 1, Exercise 16C). Such a firm would not then agree to move from the former to the latter unless *side-payments*, or lump-sum redistributions of profit between the two firms, are feasible. If they are, the firms maximize their gains from collusion by producing outputs q_i^m in the differentiated products case and q^m in the homogeneous products case to generate a total profit π^m, and then making whatever side-payment from one to the other is necessary to achieve agreement. The relationship between their actual profits π_i^L after side-payments is

$$\pi_2^L = \pi^m - \pi_1^L \qquad \text{[C.2]}$$

Suppose, however, that side-payments are not feasible. For example, in many countries collusion is illegal, and lump-sum side-payments would be strong evidence of collusion. An alternative way to transfer profit is to vary outputs away from the levels q_i^m, with each firm retaining the profit it makes from sale of its own output. Two questions then arise: how should the firms do this? And, is it costly to them in the sense that total joint profits are lower than in the case where side-payments are feasible?

In the homogeneous product case, the answers to both questions are immediate. If the firms keep total output at the level q^m, so that price remains at p^m, then redistributing profit by output variation is equivalent to lump-sum redistribution. Since firms' marginal costs are constant and identical at c, total profit does not depend on how the firms allocate a given total output between themselves:

$$\pi_i = (p^m - c)q_i \quad \text{and} \quad q_1 + q_2 = q^m \Rightarrow \Sigma \pi_i = (p^m - c)q^m = \pi^m \qquad \text{[C.3]}$$

This would not be true if the firms had non-constant marginal costs (whether or not they are identical), or constant but unequal marginal costs. In these cases, reallocation of outputs away from the joint profit maximum, increasing one firm's output and profit and reducing the other's, also reduces total profit because it violates the condition that total output be produced at minimum cost, a necessary condition for joint profit maximization. For example, if the firms have unequal constant marginal costs then under joint profit maximization the lower cost firm should produce the entire output. (Question 2, Exercise 16C asks you to examine these cases further.)

In the differentiated products model, if side-payments are not possible the firms will do the best they can by reallocating outputs and profits so that, for any given profit level of firm i, firm j's profit is maximized. Formally, they solve the problem

$$\max_{q_1 q_2} \pi_2(q_1, q_2) \quad \text{s.t.} \quad \pi_2(q_1, q_2) \geq \pi_1^0 \qquad \text{[C.4]}$$

where π_1^0 varies over the interval $[0, \hat{\pi}_1]$, with $\hat{\pi}_1$ the level at which the value of π_2 obtained at the solution to [C.4] is zero. This restriction is imposed because neither firm would accept a negative profit if zero output and profit are always an option. The properties of the π_i functions discussed in section B ensure that solution values $(q_1^\star, q_2^\star)$ for this problem exist and are unique for each π_1^0. Since the solution is a function of the value of the constraint constant π_1^0, the maximized value of firm 2's profit, $\pi_2^\star$, is also a function of π_1^0. That is

$$\pi_2^\star = \pi_2(q_1^\star(\pi_1^0), q_2^\star(\pi_1^0)) \equiv P(\pi_1^0) \qquad \text{[C.5]}$$

For $\pi_1 \in [0, \hat{\pi}_1]$, the set of profit pairs $(\pi_1, P(\pi_1))$ then defines the duopolist's *profit frontier*, giving the maximum level of one firm's profit for each level of the other's over a particular range. Since this frontier will play an important role in what follows we now examine it more closely.

The Lagrange function for the problem in [C.4] is

$$L(q_1, q_2, \lambda) = \pi_2(q_1, q_2) + \lambda[\pi_1(q_1, q_2) - \pi_1^0] \qquad \text{[C.6]}$$

and the first-order conditions are

$$\pi_{2k}(q_1^\star, q_2^\star) + \lambda^\star \pi_{1k}(q_1^\star, q_2^\star) = 0 \qquad k = 1, 2 \qquad \text{[C.7]}$$

$$\pi_1(q_1^\star, q_2^\star) = \pi_1^0 \qquad \text{[C.8]}$$

where $\pi_{ik} = \partial\pi_i/\partial q_k$. Consider first the interpretation of λ^*. From the Envelope Theorem (Appendix J),

$$\frac{\partial \pi_2^*}{\partial \pi_1^0} = \frac{\partial L}{\partial \pi_1^0} = -\lambda^* = P'(\pi_1^0) \qquad \text{[C.9]}$$

so that $-\lambda^*$ is the slope of the profit frontier. Note that in [C.6] setting $\lambda = 1$ gives the problem of maximizing the firms' joint profits, considered earlier in [B.14] (since addition of a constant π_1^0 to this problem makes no difference to its solution). Thus we can guess that the joint profit maximizing pair (π_1^m, π_2^m) is the point on the profit frontier at which its slope is -1. This can be confirmed by setting $\lambda^* = 1$ in conditions [C.7] and noting that they are then identical to [B.15] and so will give the same output pair. Thus for $\lambda = 1$, $\pi_1^0 = \pi_1^m$.

Next, taking conditions [C.7] and eliminating λ^* gives the usual kind of tangency condition

$$\frac{\pi_{21}(q_1^*, q_2^*)}{\pi_{22}(q_1^*, q_2^*)} = \frac{\pi_{11}(q_1^*, q_2^*)}{\pi_{12}(q_1^*, q_2^*)} \qquad \text{[C.10]}$$

since $-\pi_{i1}/\pi_{i2} = dq_2/dq_1$ is the slope of firm i's profit contour. The condition defines the set of pairs (q_1^*, q_2^*) at the points of tangency of the firms' profit contours, as Fig. 16.8(a) illustrates. This figure is drawn for the numerical values of the parameters given earlier, so that

$$p_i = 10 - q_i - 0.5q_j \qquad C_i = q_i \qquad i = 1, 2 \qquad i \neq j$$

are the underlying demand and cost functions.

In Fig. 16.8(b) the profit frontier is derived[3] from the locus of tangency points in Fig. 16.8(a). The tangent line L to the frontier at the joint profit maximizing point $\pi^m = (\pi_1^m, \pi_2^m)$ has slope -1 and corresponds to $\lambda^* = 1$. The symmetry and concavity of both curves in Fig. 16.8 are due to the specific example chosen. There would be

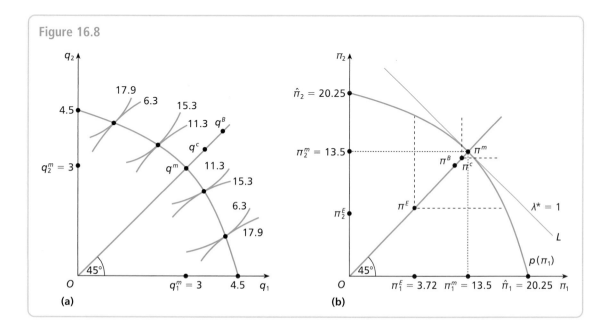

Figure 16.8

Figure 16.9

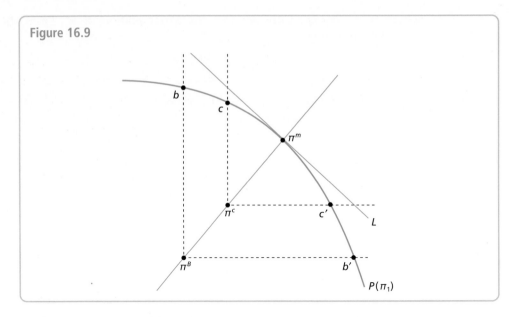

asymmetry if the firms had different profit functions, while the profit frontier in Fig. 16.8(b) can be made non-concave by choosing other, quite reasonable, functional forms for the demand or cost functions. The proof that for the functional forms used in this chapter the profit frontier is always concave is set as an exercise (see Question 3, Exercise 16C).

For comparison, the one-shot Nash equilibria in Table 16.3 are also shown in Fig. 16.8. Because of the symmetry in the example, the output and profit pairs lie on the 45° lines in the respective figures. The non-collusive equilibria lie inside the profit frontier and so are dominated by the allocations lying on the profit frontier north-east of them, as Fig. 16.9 illustrates in more detail. The Cournot–Nash equilibrium is dominated by all points on the arc cc', and the Bertrand–Nash by all points on the arc bb'. The figure illustrates the firms' *incentive to collude*.

We can now answer the two questions put earlier. If the firms wish to achieve a profit allocation other than π^m, and if side-payments are possible, they can move along the line L, since this has the equation $\pi_2 = \pi^m - \pi_1$ (its slope is -1). If side-payments are not possible then profit reallocation *is* costly, since the best the firms can do is to move along the curve $P(\pi_1)$, which must result in lower *total* profit than π^m.

Since in this example the firms have identical constant costs, the source of the loss in aggregate profit is the movement of outputs away from the values which equalize marginal revenues of the two outputs, where these marginal revenues take account of the effect of one output on the demand for the other. (Use condition [B.15] to show that this is a necessary condition for joint profit maximization.) The advantage of collusion is that it can internalize the 'external effect' that each firm's output has on the revenue of the other. Even if internalization is not complete (as it is under joint profit maximization), Fig. 16.8 shows that it can still achieve profit pairs which give higher profits to both firms than in the non-collusive equilibria.

We have established an incentive to collude, but will collusion be sustainable? We now consider some models which explore this question.

Punishment by Cournot–Nash competition

Suppose that the firms agree to produce an output pair $(q_1^\star, q_2^\star)$ that puts them at a point on the profit frontier $P(\pi_1)$ somewhere on the arc cc' in Fig. 16.9. Assume further that if instead they behaved non-collusively, then in each period of the repeated game they would be at the Cournot–Nash equilibrium, i.e. they are quantity-setters. To sustain their collusive agreement, the firms also agree on the following *trigger strategies*: for any $t = 0, 1, \ldots$, if firm i produces $q_i^\star$ in period t, then firm j will produce $q_j^\star$ in period $t + 1$; however, if i reneges by producing $q_i^R \neq q_i^\star$ in t, then j will produce its Cournot–Nash equilibrium output q_j^c in period $t + 1$ and *every succeeding period*. A deviation by one firm triggers a permanent switch by the other to its Cournot–Nash equilibrium output.

Suppose that at $t = 0$ firm i considers reneging on the agreement. Since it expects j to produce $q_j^\star$, its best reneging output is $q_i^R = A_i - B_i q_j^\star$, i.e. its best response to $q_j^\star$. Let $\pi_i^R = \pi_i(q_i^R, q_j^\star)$. Then its immediate gain is $\pi_i^R - \pi_i^\star$, which is positive because $q_i^\star$ is not the best response to $q_j^\star$. However, under the trigger strategy, firm i will then be faced with q_j^c in every future period. Its best response to q_j^c is q_i^c, yielding profit π_i^c. Thus relative to the case in which it does not renege at $t = 0$, i will lose an infinite profit stream of $(\pi_i^\star - \pi_i^c)$ with a present value of $(\pi_i^\star - \pi_i^c)/r$, and so it will *not* pay i to renege at $t = 0$ if

$$\pi_i^R - \pi_i^\star \leq (\pi_i^\star - \pi_i^c)/r \qquad [\text{C.11}]$$

or equivalently if

$$r \leq (\pi_i^\star - \pi_i^c)/(\pi_i^R - \pi_i^\star) \qquad [\text{C.12}]$$

Since the repeated game is the same regardless of the t at which it begins, if [C.11] is satisfied at one t it is satisfied at all and so the trigger strategies will support the outputs $(q_1^\star, q_2^\star)$ forever.

[C.11] says that i will not renege if its immediate profit gain is outweighed by the present value of future losses of profit. [C.12] expresses the condition in terms of an upper bound on the interest rate. Given the demand and cost parameters that determine the relations among π_i^c, π_i^R and $\pi_i^\star$, collusion will be sustainable provided the firms do not discount the future 'too heavily', thus weakening the force of the future punishment.

Since $r > 0$, [C.12] requires that $\pi_i^\star > \pi_i^c$. Thus, in terms of Fig. 16.9, any profit pair along cc' (or indeed in the convex set defined by $\pi^c cc'$), such that this inequality is satisfied, is sustainable at *some* interest rate. For example, consider the joint profit maximizing point $\pi^m = (13.5, 13.5)$. Firm j's best response output to $q_i^m = 3$ is $q_j^R = 3.75$, yielding a profit $\pi_j^R = 14.06$. Thus applying [C.12] we have

$$r \leq (13.5 - 12.96)/(14.06 - 13.5) = 0.96 \qquad [\text{C.13}]$$

Collusion at the joint profit maximum could be sustained in this market at any interest rate below 96% per period.

Returning to the general case, if [C.12] is satisfied then the trigger strategies sustaining collusion represent a Nash equilibrium of the repeated game. If i believes j will play its trigger strategy, then i's best response is to play its trigger strategy. Thus, the *equilibrium output path* will be $(q_1^\star, q_2^\star)$ in every period. Are the threats underlying these trigger strategies – of playing the one-shot Nash equilibrium forever following a deviation – credible?

Collusion supported by trigger strategies embodying punishment by Cournot–Nash competition is a *sub-game perfect equilibrium* (as defined in Chapter 15), and in that sense the threat of punishment is credible. Thus suppose that firm i observed that j has reneged at period t. Its trigger strategy prescribes that it should produce q_i^c in every period from $t + 1$ onward. Firm j's best response to q_i^c is to produce its Cournot–Nash output q_j^c. But choice of the output pair (q_i^c, q_j^c) in every period is a Nash equilibrium of this sub-game – the outputs are mutually best responses – and so the punishment strategies satisfy the requirement of sub-game perfection.

Nonetheless we may still doubt the reasonableness of these trigger strategies. Eternal punishment seems excessively grim, and we may feel that a punishment which 'fits the crime' would be a more plausible outcome. Punishment also hurts the punisher, in the sense that the Cournot–Nash output is less profitable for firm i than some collusive outputs. We might then expect firm j to propose to i that it should 'forgive and forget' and revert to cooperation. But if *ex ante* such *renegotiation* of the trigger strategies were anticipated to be successful, the credibility of the threat of punishment would be undermined. An alternative criterion of credibility of punishment strategies has therefore been proposed by Farrell and Maskin, that of *renegotiation-proofness*. We consider it at the end of this section.

Another difficulty with punishment by Cournot–Nash competition is that it may not be very severe if the Cournot–Nash profit is close to the collusive profit frontier as in Fig. 16.8(b). Since $r > 0$, condition [C.12] requires that $\pi_i > \pi_i^c$ if π_i is to be sustained. In Fig. 16.8(b), only the relatively small set of points on and below the profit frontier and within the dashed lines drawn from π^c are sustainable at some $r > 0$. The set of r-values for which any given collusive allocation is sustainable would be widened if a more severe punishment than π^c could be inflicted. We now turn to punishment strategies which dramatically expand the possibilities of collusion.

The Folk Theorem

It is part of the conventional wisdom of game theory that threats of *minimax punishments* can sustain any *individually rational* collusive allocation as a Nash equilibrium of an infinitely repeated game. Since it is not possible to assign authorship of the result, it is known as the Folk Theorem.

A *minimax punishment* is the worst one firm can do to the other given that the firm being punished is making its best response to the action of the punisher. Supposing for definiteness that firm 1 is punishing firm 2, the output pair (q_1^x, q_2^x) has firm 1 minimaxing firm 2 if it solves

$$\min_{q_1} \max_{q_2} \pi_2(q_1, q_2) \qquad [\text{C.14}]$$

In the differentiated products case (see Question 4, Exercise 16C, for the homogeneous product case) firm 2's best response is $q_2 = A_2 - B_2q_1$. Substituting this into firm 2's profit function takes care of the 'max' part of [C.14], so that [C.14] is equivalent to

$$\min_{q_1} \pi_2(q_1, A_2 - B_2q_1) \qquad [\text{C.15}]$$

Using the Envelope Theorem the effect of an increase in firm 1's output on firm 2's profit, given that firm 2 makes its best profit-maximizing response, is

$$d\pi_2/dq_1 = \pi_{21} + \pi_{22}(dq_2/dq_1) = \pi_{21} = -\gamma q_2 \qquad [\text{C.16}]$$

Thus, since firm 2 cannot be forced to continue to produce if it would earn negative profits, firm 1 will wish to increase its output until firm 2's profit is zero. Solving $\pi_2(q_1, A_2 - B_2q_1) = 0$ gives

$$q_1^x = (\alpha_2 - c_2)/\gamma \qquad q_2^x = 0 \qquad\qquad \text{[C.17]}$$

There are two potential difficulties for firm 1 with this minimax punishment. The first is that it may not be feasible. With $q_2 = 0$, the maximum amount that firm 1 can sell (by setting $p_1 = 0$) is

$$q_1^n = \alpha_1/\beta_1$$

which could be less than q_1^x. In the specific numerical example we are considering in fact $q_1^x = 18 > q_1^m = 10$. When the model's parameters are such that $q_1^x > q_1^n$ firm 1 will minimize firm 2's profit by producing its largest saleable output q_1^0 which satisfies

$$p^1 = \alpha_1 - \beta_1 q_1^0 - \gamma[A_2 - B_2 q_1^0] = 0 \qquad\qquad \text{[C.18]}$$

But this raises the second difficulty: choosing q_1^0 and a price of zero leaves firm 1 with a loss. This difficulty can arise even if $q_1^x < q_1^n$. With $q_2 = 0$ and $q_1 = q_1^x$, firm 1 earns non-negative profits only if

$$p_1 - c_1 = \alpha_1 - \beta_1 q_1^x - c_1 \geq 0 \qquad\qquad \text{[C.19]}$$

As the reader should check, by using [C.17] to substitute for q_1^x and referring back to Question 1 in section B, this condition need not be satisfied in the general linear differentiated products model. (It is obviously not in our numerical example.) If [C.19] does not hold and firm 1 wishes to break even while minimaxing firm 2, it must choose the output q_1^E satisfying

$$p_1 - c_1 = \alpha_1 - \beta_1 q_1^E - \gamma[A_2 - B_2 q_1^E] - c_1 = 0 \qquad\qquad \text{[C.20]}$$

Note that in this case the firm being punished (firm 2) will be earning positive profits whereas the minimaxing firm 1 just breaks even.

Thus there may be different feasible minimaxing outputs for the punishing firm depending on the parameters of the model and the loss we assume that the punishing firm can bear.

The definition of an *individually rational profit allocation* is straightforward. Let $\pi_i^x(= 0)$ be i's profit when it is being minimaxed by q_j^x, and $\pi_i^E(> 0)$ that when it is being minimaxed by q_j^E. Then an individually rational profit allocation for firm i is any allocation which yields it a profit $\pi_i > \pi_i^x$ in the first case and $\pi_i > \pi_i^E$ in the second. Thus, use our numerical example and refer to Fig. 16.8(b). If when i is minimaxed it earns $\pi_i^x = 0$, then the set of individually rational profit pairs consists of all the points on and below the profit frontier and within the axes. If on the other hand i's minimax profit is $\pi_i^E > 0$, as shown in the figure, then the individually rational profit pairs are all the points within the dotted lines drawn through π^E and on or below the profit frontier.

The Folk Theorem states that: *trigger strategies incorporating the punishment of being minimaxed forever can support all individually rational profit allocations as a Nash equilibrium for some set of values of the interest rate.* Thus, as compared with punishment by Cournot–Nash competition, minimax punishments considerably expand the set of possible collusive outcomes (or equivalently, the set of interest rates at which a particular collusive outcome can be sustained).

The proof is similar to the Cournot–Nash punishment threat case. Let $(\pi_1^\star, \pi_2^\star)$ be an individually rational profit pair which it is desired to sustain, and let $\pi_i^R \geq \pi_i^\star$ again denote the one-period profit i can make by reneging and making its best response to j's collusive output. The trigger strategies are: j will adhere to the agreement as long as i did in the previous period, but if i reneges in one period, j switches to the output (q_j^x or q_j^E) that minimaxes i, in *every* subsequent period. It suffices to take the case in which i's minimax profit is π_i^x.

Consider $t = 0$. If i reneges it gains $\pi_i^R - \pi_i^\star$ now, but loses the infinite future stream $\pi_i^\star - \pi_i^x$. This is strictly positive since $\pi_i^\star$ is individually rational. It will not renege if

$$\pi_i^R - \pi_i^\star \leq (\pi_i^\star - \pi_i^x)/r \qquad [C.21]$$

If $\pi_i^\star = \pi_i^c$ then the left-hand side is zero and the theorem certainly holds for *all* $r > 0$. If $\pi_i^\star \neq \pi_i^c$ then we have the condition

$$r \leq (\pi_i^\star - \pi_i^x)/(\pi_i^R - \pi_i^\star) \qquad [C.22]$$

Since the right-hand side is certainly positive, there always exists a range of interest rates for which this condition holds. Moreover, $\pi_i^x < \pi_i^c$ and so, comparing [C.22] and [C.12], the set of interest rates for which collusion can be sustained is clearly larger when minimax punishments are used.

The trigger strategies constitute a Nash equilibrium: if i believes j will play its trigger strategy then, given that condition [C.22] is satisfied, its best response is to play its trigger strategy and the result will be the collusive outcome $(\pi_1^\star, \pi_2^\star)$ in every period. However, the minimax trigger strategies do not constitute a sub-game perfect equilibrium. To see this, suppose i has reneged at t, and consider the sub-game beginning at $t + 1$ ($t = 0, 1, \ldots$). If j minimaxes i by producing q_j^x, i makes its best response q_i^x, but q_j^x is *not* j's best response to q_i^x (recall the only outputs that are mutually best responses are (q_1^c, q_2^c)). Therefore the output pair (q_i^x, q_j^x) is not a Nash equilibrium of the sub-game beginning at $t + 1$, in the contingency that i *has* reneged at t.

Thus punishment by Cournot–Nash competition may not be very severe but is at least credible in the sense of sub-game perfection, whereas punishment by minimaxing may be sufficiently severe but is not credible.

The carrot-and-stick approach

Abreu developed a simple but ingenious idea which allows more severe punishment than Cournot–Nash competition, but which also gives sub-game perfect strategies. Moreover, it dispenses with the assumption of eternal punishment, replacing it with the appealing idea that collusion would be resumed once a short sharp punishment for deviation has been inflicted. Collusion is sustained by the 'stick' of a profit-reducing output expansion to punish deviation and the 'carrot' of subsequent reversion to the collusive outputs, which plays the important role of inducing firms to accept the loss of profit required by the punishment phase.

We again denote the output and profit pairs that the firms choose as their collusive allocation by $(q_1^\star, q_2^\star)$ and $(\pi_1^\star, \pi_2^\star)$, respectively. These may or may not be on the profit frontier. The strategies defined by Abreu are as follows: the firms produce the agreed output pair in each period as long as this was done in the previous period; if firm $i = 1, 2$ deviates in period t, the firms are to produce *punishment outputs* (q_1^P, q_2^P) in period $t + 1$, which in general depend on $q_i^\star$ and on which firm has deviated at t. Given the symmetry of our model, we can however consider only punishment outputs that do *not* depend upon which firm deviated at t.

If the firms produce punishment outputs at $t + 1$ then they revert to (q_1^*, q_2^*) at $t + 2$ and continue with these outputs unless one of them deviates ... ; if firm $j = 1$, 2 deviates from its punishment output at $t + 1$, the punishment outputs (q_1^P, q_2^P) are again to be produced at $t + 2$ ... ; and so on. Deviation in the punishment phase (by *either* firm) results in *reimposition of punishment*, while acceptance of punishment (which is costly to both firms) results in reversion to collusion.

Denote punishment profits $\pi_i(q_1^P, q_2^P)$ by π_i^P. As before, we can consider the gains and losses to firm i from reneging on the agreed output q_i^* at $t = 0, 1, \ldots$ Its immediate profit gain is $\pi_i^R - \pi_i^*$, where again $\pi_i^R = \pi_i(q_i^R, q_j^*)$ is the profit it makes from producing q_i^R, its best response to q_j^*. Assume that in the following period *both* firms *do* produce the punishment outputs so that i earns π_i^P (we will later justify this assumption of non-deviation during the punishment phase). If reneging at t is profitable, so will be reneging at $t + 2$, because the game is identical at every possible starting point. Thus firm i will renege at $t + 2$ and earn π_i^R, and then be punished at $t = 3$ and earn π_i^P and so on. The profit stream from reneging is the alternating infinite stream $\{\pi_i^R, \pi_i^P, \pi_i^R, \pi_i^P, \ldots\}$, while that from not reneging is the constant infinite stream π_i^*, each of these streams beginning at t. Hence firm i will not renege at t if

$$\pi_i^R - \pi_i^* \leq \delta(\pi_i^* - \pi_i^P) + \delta^2(\pi_i^* - \pi_i^R) + \delta^3(\pi_i^* - \pi_i^P) + \ldots \qquad i = 1, 2 \quad \text{[C.23]}$$

where the left-hand side is the immediate gain from reneging and the right-hand side is the discounted value at t of the difference in profit streams from not reneging and reneging. Notice there is no guarantee that this right-hand side is even positive, let alone that it exceeds the left-hand side, since the $\pi_i^* - \pi_i^R$ terms are all negative. Now,

$$\sum_{t \in E} \delta^t = (1 - \delta^2)^{-1} \qquad E = \{0, 2, 4, \ldots\}$$

and

$$\sum_{t \in D} \delta^t = \delta(1 - \delta^2)^{-1} \qquad D = \{1, 3, 5, \ldots\}$$

so we can rearrange [C.23] to obtain the condition,

$$\pi_i^R - \pi_i^* \leq \delta(\pi_i^* - \pi_i^P) \qquad i = 1, 2 \qquad \text{[C.24]}$$

or

$$r \leq \frac{\pi_i^* - \pi_i^P}{\pi_i^R - \pi_i^*} - 1 \qquad i = 1, 2 \qquad \text{[C.25]}$$

Thus, since $r > 0$, a *necessary* (but not sufficient) condition for a collusive profit π_i^* to be sustainable (*given* that there is no deviation in the punishment phase) is that

$$\pi_i^R - \pi_i^* \leq \pi_i^* - \pi_i^P \qquad i = 1, 2 \qquad \text{[C.26]}$$

That is, that there exist sufficiently large outputs q_i^P to generate sufficiently small profit π_i^P that the one-period gain from reneging can be offset by a one-period punishment. Whether this will hold depends on the market structure – the demand and cost functions – which determine the relationships among these profit values. If condition [C.25] is satisfied then it is clearly in the firms' interests to choose π_i^P so as to equate the right-hand side with r, since the larger is π_i^P, the smaller the loss of profit in the punishment phase. On the other hand, for the smallest possible π_i^P feasible in the market, [C.25] defines the highest interest rate for which collusion is sustainable.

All this assumes that there is no defection in the punishment phase. Consider the sub-game beginning at $t = 1, 2, \ldots$, when a firm has reneged at $t - 1$. Firm $i = 1, 2$ is to produce q_i^P and earn π_i^P. If it does this, *and* condition [C.25] is satisfied, so that collusion from $t + 1$ onward will be maintained, then it earns the profit stream consisting of π_i^P at t and π_i^* from $t + 1$ onward. This has a discounted value at t of $\pi_i^P + (\pi_i^*/r)$. Let q_i^{RP} denote i's best response output to q_j^P and $\pi_i^{RP} = \pi^i(q_i^{RP}, q_j^P)$ the profit it will make if it reneges in the punishment phase in period t. If it reneges at t, under the strategy described above punishment is reimposed at $t + 1$. But if it *pays* to renege at t it will pay to renege also at $t + 1$, and in every future period when punishment is reimposed. Thus associated with the decision to renege in the punishment phase is the infinite stream of profit consisting of π_i^{RP} forever. This has a discounted value at t of $\pi_i^{RP} + (\pi_i^{RP}/r)$. Thus, for i to keep to the agreement in the punishment phase and *not* renege we require

$$\pi_i^P + (\pi_i^*/r) \geqslant \pi_i^{RP} + (\pi_i^{RP}/r) \qquad i = 1, 2 \qquad [\text{C.27}]$$

or

$$\pi_i^{RP} - \pi_i^P \leqslant (\pi_i^* - \pi_i^{RP})/r \qquad i = 1, 2 \qquad [\text{C.28}]$$

Thus the one period gain from reneging in the punishment phase must be more than offset by the present value of loss of profit resulting from having the punishment phase continually reimposed rather than restoring collusion. We can express this in terms of the interest rate

$$r \leqslant \frac{\pi_i^* - \pi_i^{RP}}{\pi_i^{RP} - \pi_i^P} \qquad i = 1, 2 \qquad [\text{C.29}]$$

If conditions [C.25] and [C.29] are then *simultaneously* satisfied, the profit pair (π_1^*, π_2^*) is sustainable by the strategies described. Note that the two conditions are mutually reinforcing and must hold simultaneously. [C.25] ensures that it never pays to deviate *given* that punishment *will* be inflicted; [C.29] guarantees that punishment will be inflicted (even though it hurts the punisher) given that in the period following punishment collusion will be reinstated and maintained.

We can show that the strategies are sub-game perfect equilibrium strategies, so that the threats inherent in them are credible on this criterion. There are four kinds of sub-game:

1. The game itself, beginning at $t = 0$. In this, if i expects j to adhere to the specified strategy then, given that conditions [C.25] and [C.29] are satisfied, its best response is also to adhere, and so the strategies are a Nash equilibrium for the entire game.

2. A (proper) sub-game beginning at $t = 1, 2, \ldots$, in which nobody has reneged at $t - 1$. Since this game is identical to the game at $t = 0$, the strategies are a Nash equilibrium for these sub-games.

3. A (proper) sub-game beginning at $t = 1, 2, \ldots$, in which one firm reneged at $t - 1$. Given conditions [C.28] and [C.29], i's best response to q_j^P at $t + 1, \ldots$, is itself to produce q_i^P at t and q_i^* at $t + 1, \ldots$. Thus the strategies induce a Nash equilibrium in these sub-games.

4. A (proper) sub-game beginning at $t = 2, \ldots$, in which one firm reneged at $t - 2$ and (q_1^P, q_2^P) was produced at $t - 1$. Since this game is identical to the game beginning at $t = 0$, we again have a Nash equilibrium.

Thus, since the strategies induce Nash equilibria in all possible sub-games they are sub-game perfect equilibrium strategies.

We can illustrate the strategies using the numerical example on which Fig. 16.8(b) is based and consider whether the joint profit maximizing profit pair (π_1^m, π_2^m) can be sustained. The symmetry in this example greatly simplifies calculations.

Table 16.3 sets out the results. We take three possible interest rates: 2%, 5% and 25% respectively. These could be thought of as showing the implications of different period lengths: since a reasonable *annual* interest rate is 25%, the first case corresponds roughly to a period of a month, the second to a period of one quarter and the third to one year. The length of the period determines the duration of punishment as well as the length of time for which a firm can make profits from reneging before retaliation takes place.

Table 16.3

	$r = 0.02$	$r = 0.05$	$r = 0.25$
$\pi_i^P = \pi_i^* - (1 + r)[\pi_i^R - \pi_i^*]$	12.9263	12.9094	12.7969
$q^P = (q + [81 - 6\pi_i^P]^{1/2})/3$	3.6184	3.6274	3.6847
$q_i^{RP} = 4.5 - 0.25q^P$	3.5954	3.5032	3.5788
$\pi_i^{RP} = (q - 0.5q^P)q_i^{RP} - (q_i^{RP})^2$	12.9270	12.9107	12.8077
$(\pi_i^* - \pi_i^{RP})/(\pi_i^{RP} - \pi_i^P)$	$\dfrac{13.5 - 12.9270}{12.9270 - 12.9263}$	$\dfrac{13.5 - 12.9107}{12.9107 - 12.9094}$	$\dfrac{13.5 - 12.8077}{12.8077 - 12.7969}$

Given the assumed interest rate, the first line of the table uses [C.25] as an equality to calculate the *minimum* required punishment profit π_i^P – recall from Table 16.2 that $q_i^m = 3$, $\pi_i^m = 13.5$, and so π_i^R is given by $q_i^R = A_i - B_i q_i^m$. We next calculate the punishment outputs required to generate π_i^P. For simplicity we assume *symmetric punishments*: the firms are assumed to produce the same outputs q^P in the punishment phase. Solving $\pi_i^P = (\alpha - c - \gamma q^P)q^P - (q^P)^2$ for q^P yields two roots but we take that root which exceeds $q_i^m = 3$. The output that i will choose in the punishment phase if it reneges, q_i^{RP}, is found from the best response function, $q_i^{RP} = A_i - B_i q^P$. This gives i's profit from reneging in the punishment phase, $\pi_i^{RP} = \pi_i(q_i^{RP}, q^P)$. The last line of the table gives the value of the right-hand side of [C.29]. If the implied value is greater than r, then the joint profit maximizing allocation is sustainable by the punishment output q^P. In each case in the table this is true by a very substantial margin. In fact, for any value of r up to about 2.8, i.e. an interest rate of 280%, this allocation is sustainable in this example.

The reason for the ease with which collusion can be sustained in this example should be clear from the last line of the table: the gain in profit from reneging on the punishment output is very small relative to the difference between the profit from colluding and that earned by reneging on punishment. Figure 16.10 illustrates the various output pairs in this example. The (symmetric) collusive output pair (3, 3) is of course below the Cournot–Nash equilibrium pair (3.6, 3.6). Suppose firm 2 reneges by producing its best response output 3.75. From Table 16.3 we see that the most profitable symmetric punishment pair (which gives π_i^P satisfying [C.25] as an equality) is (for $r = 0.25$) (3.68, 3.68). This represents more severe punishment than Cournot–Nash competition. If either firm reneges on the punishment output, it will produce $q_i^{RP} = 3.58$. But we know from condition [C.29] that it is more profitable for

Figure 16.10

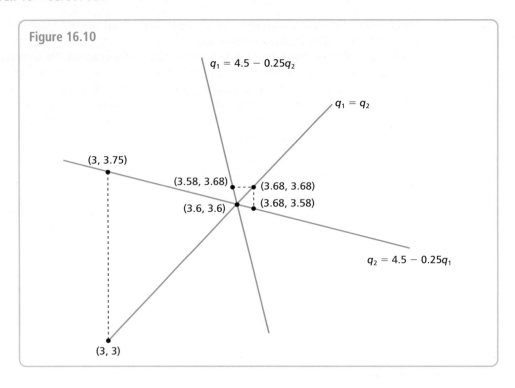

each firm to accept the lower profit π_i^P in the punishment period and then return to the collusive profit than to have punishment reimposed.

Note that in the punishment phase not only does the punisher have an incentive to bear the costs of inflicting the punishment, but the firm being punished has an incentive to accept or 'cooperate in' its punishment – *both* firms produce their punishment outputs q^P. Moreover, if firm 2 reneges at t, and then 1 does not inflict the punishment at $t + 1$ the strategies call for 2 to punish 1 at $t + 2$: thus the cheat punishes the non-cheat for not punishing him for cheating! Nevertheless, as long as our criterion of credibility is sub-game perfection, the threats underlying the strategies are credible and the equilibrium output path, when [C.25] and [C.29] are satisfied, will be the agreed outputs $(q_1^\star, q_2^\star)$ $(= (q_1^m, q_2^m)$ in our example) in every period.

Whether any given profit pair can be sustained by Abreu's punishment strategies depends on the cost and demand functions and the interest rate, since the former determine the profit functions and the latter the present value of future losses from reneging. A further analysis of the carrot-and-stick approach by Fudenberg and Maskin (1986) shows that any individually rational profit pair can be sustained for some range of interest rates as a sub-game perfect equilibrium. They base the punishment outputs on *mutual minimaxing* by the two firms: *each* firm produces the output it would use to minimax the other. The resulting profit for the deviating firm is therefore in general worse than it would be in the case envisaged in the original Folk Theorem. Consequently there always exists a duration of the period of punishment such that any individually rational profit allocation can be sustained by credible threats of this type of punishment, for some set of interest rates. However, punishment by mutual minimaxing is only guaranteed to work in the case of two firms. Whereas all the propositions on sustainability of collusion we have so far considered generalize to more than two firms, the Fudenberg–Maskin result does not. For example, in the case of three firms, there may not in general exist output levels q_1^x, q_2^x, q_3^x, such that q_i^x and q_j^x simultaneously minimax firm k ($i, j, k = 1, 2, 3, i \neq j, j \neq k, i \neq k$).

Renegotiation proof strategies

The criterion of the credibility of threats of punishment we have applied so far is sub-game perfection. The underlying idea of the trigger strategies considered so far is that the firms agree on a collusive equilibrium (q_1^*, q_2^*), agree also on trigger strategies (say of Abreu's type), and then spend the rest of the time independently implementing those strategies. It is *as if* they conclude a contract, which is self-enforcing because of the sub-game perfect punishment threats it contains, and which is never renegotiated. Since the initial 'contract' was self-enforcing rather than legally binding the parties cannot include in it a tacit agreement not to renegotiate by introducing a suitable punishment for proposing renegotiation: any renegotiation proposal can also cover the punishment for making the proposal. It is impossible for the parties to commit themselves not to renegotiate: if such commitment is possible they would presumably have committed themselves to the collusive solution at the start, without the need for elaborate punishment strategies. Suppose then that firm i has reneged at time t. Firm j now faces the prospect of punishing i in the knowledge that, if it does not, under the agreed (Abreu) strategy firm i will punish firm j next period. What is then to stop i suggesting to j that instead of going through this self-lacerating process they renegotiate the agreement and simply start colluding again? Certainly, at this point renegotiating to a collusive outcome is better for both i and j. But if this is anticipated *ex ante* the Abreu strategies no longer embody credible threats.

The requirement that strategies be credible in the sense that they are renegotiation proof reduces the set of possible equilibrium allocations to a subset of those that can be supported as sub-game perfect equilibria – it represents a further refinement of Nash equilibrium. Suppose the firms wish to support a profit pair (π_1^*, π_2^*). If firm i is called upon to punish firm j after a deviation, then it must be in its interest to do so rather than allow itself to be 'negotiated back' to the profit pair (π_1^*, π_2^*). This will be assured if i's profit in the punishment phase, π_i^P, satisfies

$$\pi_i^P \geqslant \pi_i^* \qquad \text{[C.30]}$$

But in addition, for the punishment to be credible, the punishment pair (π_1^P, π_2^P) must itself be renegotiation proof. Thus an allocation (π_1^*, π_2^*) is *weakly renegotiation proof* if there is a weakly renegotiation proof profit pair (π_1^P, π_2^P) which

(a) satisfies conditions [C.25] and [C.29] so that the punishment strategy is sub-game perfect;

(b) satisfies condition [C.30] so that i can never do worse by carrying out the punishment than by reverting to the initial equilibrium.

For punishment of j to be effective we must have $\pi_j^P < \pi_j^*$. This, and [C.30], implies that (π_1^P, π_2^P) is *Pareto undominated* by (π_1^*, π_2^*) and conversely. Figure 16.11 shows

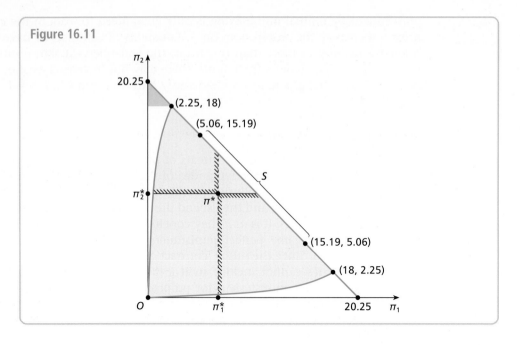

Figure 16.11

the profit frontier for the homogeneous output numerical example. Pairs which are Pareto undominated relative to the allocation (π_1^*, π_2^*), and so could be used as punishments, are the points north-west and south-east of π^*.

In Fig. 16.11, for any point in the shaded area (excluding the boundary curves) there is a weakly renegotiation proof set of profit allocations which are mutually Pareto undominated and support each other as punishments. Question 6, Exercise 16C, examines the derivation of the sets. Any point in the shaded area, but excluding the boundary curves, is a weakly renegotiation proof equilibrium. The reason a point on the boundary curve, such as (2.25, 18) is not weakly renegotiation proof is that a deviation by one firm (in this case firm 1) could not be punished adequately by any profit pair in the shaded triangle north-west of (2.25, 18).

If the credibility requirement is strengthened to *strong renegotiation proofness* the set of equilibrium outcomes shrinks quite dramatically. A profit pair is strongly renegotiation proof if it is weakly renegotiation proof *and* can be supported by punishment outputs which are Pareto undominated, i.e. maximize joint profits. In Fig. 16.11 the set of strongly renegotiation proof equilibrium payoffs lies along the profit frontier and is denoted as the set S. The set S does not include its endpoints. For example, the point (15.19, 5.06) in Fig. 16.11 is not strongly renegotiation proof because a deviation by firm 2 could not be adequately punished by a rightward move along the profit frontier. Any point below the frontier is Pareto dominated by a point on the frontier, while the points in S can support each other as punishments. (Question 6, Exercise 16C, asks you to derive S.) The rationale for strong renegotiation proofness is straightforward: if the firms are able to renegotiate at any time, we would expect them to prefer an output pair which yields both of them higher profits, and so a Pareto dominated punishment output pair would not be immune to renegotiation.

EXERCISE 16C

1. Two firms produce homogeneous outputs with cost functions

$$C_1 = q_1^2 \qquad C_2 = 2q_2^2$$

and the inverse market demand function

$$p = 100 - (q_1 + q_2)$$

Show that at the Cournot–Nash equilibrium firm 2 makes higher profit than at the joint profit maximizing equilibrium. Explain why this is so.

2. In the example of Question 1, derive the profit frontier, and explain why total profits fall as the firms redistribute profit between themselves by redistributing output. Then go through the same exercise replacing the cost functions of Question 1 by

$$C_1 = q_1 \qquad C_2 = 2q_2$$

3. Prove that for the functional forms assumed in this chapter the profit frontier is concave. Construct the profit frontier for the homogeneous output example of this section.

4. Derive the minimaxing output for firm j in the case of homogeneous products.

5. Explain why, in the example of this section, a price-setting duopoly could sustain a wider set of collusive allocations than does a quantity-setting duopoly, by sub-game perfect equilibrium trigger strategies involving punishment by Bertrand–Nash competition. Consider both differentiated and homogeneous outputs.

6. Take the numerical example for the homogeneous output case in this section, and derive the sets of weakly and strongly renegotiation proof profit pairs illustrated in Fig. 16.11.

D. Entry

In the absence of competition, or the threat of it, from other sellers, a monopolist will earn excess profits. The excess profits will be an attraction for other sellers. Monopoly power might therefore sow the seeds of its own destruction, and we expect a rational monopolist to take this into account. We now analyse some implications of the possibility of new entry for the behaviour of the monopolist. Since this involves the analysis of the interaction between two firms, it is appropriate to include it in a chapter on oligopoly.

The first question is, do *barriers to entry* exist? We distinguish between an *absolute entry barrier*, which rules out, over some time horizon, all new entry whatsoever; and a *relative entry barrier*, which places a new entrant at a disadvantage, but not an insurmountable one. An absolute entry barrier may arise out of some legal impediment, such as a patent or statutory monopoly right, or out of the exclusive ownership of some resource which is indispensable for production. In that case, we interpret the monopoly profits, which will continue for as long as the absolute barrier exists, as rents accruing to the monopoly's holding of the legal rights or privileges.

Relative entry barriers may arise out of: capital market imperfections; specific cost advantages; and consumer loyalty. Capital market imperfections imply that different borrowers pay different interest rates, and also that the interest rate increases with the amount borrowed. This means that an entrant may have to pay a higher interest rate than the well-established monopolist, particularly if the lenders regard the entry as a risky proposition. It takes on particular force if there are significant economies of scale in production of the monopolized good. If the entrant sets up production on a scale smaller than that at which long-run average costs are at a minimum, then it will incur average costs which exceed those of the monopolist (assuming the latter *is* producing at minimum long-run average costs). On the other hand, if it enters on a scale large enough to achieve minimum average costs, the capital expenditure required may be very large, and may again involve it in higher interest costs than those incurred by the monopolist. Indeed, if there is capital rationing in the capital market, then the entrant may not be able to obtain the amount of funds it would require to set up on the optimal scale. If, on the other hand, the capital market were perfect, then both the monopolist and potential entrants would borrow at the same interest rate, and the entrants could borrow as much as they wished at the going rate, so the scale of capital expenditure required would be irrelevant.

'Specific cost advantage' is a cover-all term for things like superior location, availability of marketing outlets, advantageous input supplies, information, expertise and contacts, which are enjoyed by an established firm and make its costs lower, other things being equal, than those of a firm new to the market.

Consumer loyalty, built up and reinforced by advertising, and strengthened perhaps by innate conservatism and risk aversion of buyers, may impose on an entrant higher costs of advertising, packaging, sales promotion and product quality. In order to get its product known and accepted it will have to spend more on these than the established monopolist, at least in the initial stages.

Each of these relative entry barriers can be converted into a cost, and incorporated into the long-run cost curve of the entrant, which would then lie above that of the monopolist. A consequence would be that, since entry takes place only as long as the *entrant* anticipates excess profits, positive monopoly profits are not a sufficient condition for new entry. Then, any excess profits which remain to the monopolist could be imputed as rents to the factors which create the relative entry barrier.

Note that a relative entry barrier depends on the characteristics of *both* the monopoly and the potential entrant. In general, we might expect different potential entrants to have different long-run average costs of producing the good supplied by the monopolist. For example, a large firm, well established in a market which is closely related to the monopolized one, may have little difficulty in raising cheap capital, may possess information about the market, and may be able to use its reputation in its existing markets to overcome consumer resistance in the new one. Indeed, a great deal of the 'new entry' which takes place is in the form of diversification and integration by already established firms. Thus it is not possible to gauge the extent of relative entry barriers by reference to the characteristics of the monopoly alone; it is also necessary to take account of the characteristics of potential entrants.

Limit pricing

The monopolist could adopt a pricing policy which makes new entry unattractive: it may set a *limit price*. An effective limit price would be one which was equal to the monopolist's own long-run average cost, since no excess profit would be made and so no signals would go out to other sellers that opportunities exist for excess profit. However, we assume that the monopolist wishes *to maximize* profit, *subject to the constraint* that no other seller will find it profitable to enter the market. The question then is whether there exists a limit price which yields positive excess profits to the monopolist, and, if so, how is it determined? We now show that *provided the monopolist adopts or threatens to adopt the appropriate post-entry response* and that *this is believed by the potential entrant*, a limit price exists which yields positive excess profits. This is true even in the absence of relative entry barriers, while the existence of such barriers would increase the profitability of the limit-pricing strategy.

Assume:

(a) the monopolist knows the long-run average cost curve on which a potential entrant will operate (possibly, though not necessarily, because it is identical with its own);

(b) it also knows the market demand curve;

(c) the entrant's output would be undifferentiated from its own, so that both firms' outputs must sell at the same price;

(d) economies of scale exist over a significant range of the entrant's long-run average cost curve.

Figure 16.12 sets out the analysis. D is the market demand curve for the monopolist's output, and AC_E is the potential entrant's long-run average cost curve (incorporating assumption (d)). The entry-excluding price which maximizes the monopolist's profit is p_m^*, implying an output of q_m^*. It is always assumed that the entrant's costs are such as to make the highest possible limit price less than the price which maximizes the monopolist's short-run profits, otherwise the problem is trivial. p_m^* is the optimal limit price.

The reasoning is as follows: consider the demand curve D', which is found by shifting D leftward and parallel to itself until it is just tangent to the entrant's average cost curve. This tangency point is labelled a. The price p_m^* is found as the point at which D' cuts the vertical axis. Suppose that *the entrant is made to believe that, if it enters the market, the existing seller will maintain its output at q_m^**, so that total market output will be q_m^* *plus* the entrant's output. Then, it will perceive that price must fall along the portion bD of the market demand curve, to an extent dependent on its own output. In other words, the line p_m^*D' is, in effect, the entrant's perceived

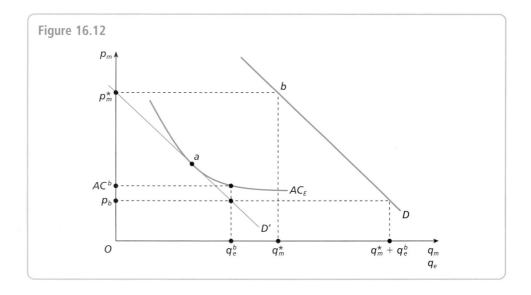

Figure 16.12

demand curve, since it shows the price at which it can sell the various amounts of outputs it may want to put on to the market. But since this demand curve lies nowhere above the entrant's long-run cost curve, it will see that it cannot earn excess profits, and so there appears to be no incentive to enter. A policy of setting the price p_m^* and output q_m^*, together with the 'declared intention' of maintaining this output in the event of entry taking place and allowing the entrant's output to 'spoil the market', appears to offer to the monopolist maximum profit consistent with complete exclusion of new entry.

The central aspect of the analysis is the entrant's belief that the monopolist will continue to produce the output q_m^* in the event of entry. It is in fact this output, rather than the price as such, which is the crucial feature of the entry-excluding strategy – the price p_m^* simply follows from the need to sell this output on the market – and the theory could perhaps be more aptly described as one of 'limit output'.

Credible threats and entry deterrence

Our analysis of the limit price did not specify how the entrant could be made to believe that the monopolist would in fact maintain the output q_m^*. This is a severe limitation, because it is not hard to construct an argument that suggests the potential entrant would not believe the threat. The entrant could reason that if it enters, say, at a scale q_e^b, total output $q_m^* + q_e^b$ would drive price down to p_b which is assumed below the incumbent monopoly's minimum average cost (not shown in the figure). Then, both firms make losses for as long as the monopoly produces q_m^*. The entrant may believe that, once entry has taken place, the incumbent will realize that such continued losses are pointless, and the firms will move to an equilibrium in which both make positive profits. So, the entrant moves into the market. The monopoly's threat has not been credible.

The weakness of the limit pricing analysis is that it ignores the question of the *strategic interdependence* between the incumbent firm and the potential entrant. The two firms are involved in a *game*, and the theory of games tells us that the credibility of threats cannot simply be assumed, but instead must be explicitly analysed. In the rest of this section we examine some aspects of the game-theoretic approach to entry into a monopolized market.

Figure 16.13 shows two *game trees*, (a) corresponding to a 'strong monopolist' M_s, and (b) to a 'weak monopolist' M_w. Each tree should be read as follows. The circled E indicates that the entrant must make a choice of moves, and it may choose to move *in* or to stay *out*. The incumbent monopoly must decide what to do given the entrant's choice. If this has been *in*, then the monopolist must decide whether to *fight* (as in the above limit pricing analysis) or to *accept* the entry. The resulting profit payoffs to the two firms are shown in the brackets, with the monopolist's above and the entrant's below. If the entrant stays out, then the monopolist simply has a payoff consisting of its maximum monopoly profit. The difference between the two game trees is in the pattern of payoffs.

Consider how E will reason in case (a), where it is playing against M_s. If it chooses *in*, then M_s will certainly choose *fight*, because its payoff at 5 is greater than its payoff if it accommodates to the new entry, at 4. Thus E will believe any threat M_s may make that it will *fight*, and choose *out*. In other words, a threat is *credible* if it is clearly in a player's interest to carry it out when called upon to do so, and this is why we call case (a) the 'strong monopolist' case.

Figure 16.13

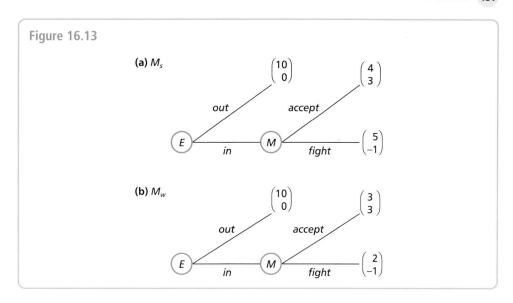

In (b), such a threat is clearly not credible. If E chooses *in*, M_w does better by accepting rather than fighting, a payoff of 3 as opposed to 2, and so E will enter the market because its payoff from the sequence (*in*, *accept*) is greater than that from staying out. Note that we must assume that M_w will act rationally following E's choice of *in* – as the game is constructed, *accept* is really the best thing for him to do in that case.

The difference between the 'weak' and 'strong' monopolist clearly lies in the relation between the payoffs to fighting and accepting entry. The payoffs to fighting entry could be thought of as being determined by the relative costs of the incumbent and entrant – the strong monopolist has the benefit of higher entry barriers, or some other advantage which makes a price war less damaging. We construct these payoffs in a particular example below. The payoffs to both firms following acceptance of entry depend on the exact nature of the *duopoly equilibrium*. For the moment we simply assume that the firms can predict the payoffs to which this will give rise.

This simple game analysis suggests another weakness of the previous limit pricing theory. There is no need for the incumbent monopolist to forgo short-run profits by setting the limit price p_m^*. If a potential entrant appears, then the strong monopolist can go on earning those profits because, if the potential entrant is rational and well-informed, it knows that it is not worth entering, while the weak monopolist knows that if an entrant appears the days of high profit are over in any case. Note also that the game analysis suggests that we would never actually observe *contested entry*, i.e. entry followed by a defensive fight, whether successful or unsuccessful. Since such fights are observed, we may question whether the players are assumed to have too much information.

If we assume that the entrant is imperfectly informed about the monopolist's true cost structure in relation to its own, then it is easy to explain contested entry. In terms of the game analysis, we could interpret this imperfect information as implying that the entrant does not know for sure which type of monopolist it faces, M_s or M_w, but that it can assign prior probabilities to these. Let us assume the entrant is *risk neutral*; that is, it evaluates any risky decision in terms of the expected value of the profit associated with it. We can calculate a critical probability $\hat{\gamma}$ that the entrant may assign to the event that it faces M_s, such that if the probability it actually assigns is $\gamma < \hat{\gamma}$ it will enter the market.

Thus, if γ is the probability that the monopolist is strong, and if the entrant moves into the market, it receives a payoff of -2 with probability γ and a payoff of 3 with probability $1 - \gamma$, since M_s will fight and M_w will accept. The expected value of profit for the choice of *in* is therefore $-2\gamma + 3(1 - \gamma) = 3 - 5\gamma$. Since the entrant is risk neutral it will enter if this is positive and stay out if this is negative, and so the critical value $\hat{\gamma}$ satisfies

$$3 - 5\hat{\gamma} = 0 \Rightarrow \hat{\gamma} = 0.6$$

If the entrant believes that the probability that the monopolist is strong is anything below 0.6 it will enter. Then, if it is wrong, we will observe contested entry and the subsequent exit of the would-be entrant. The greater the positive payoff from sharing the market with a weak monopolist relative to the negative payoff from running into a strong monopolist, the larger is $\hat{\gamma}$ and the greater the range of prior probability beliefs of the entrant that are consistent with entry.

Let us now concentrate on the case that the monopolist is known to be weak. It seems impossible to deny the logic of the argument that any threat to resist entry in this case is simply not credible, since once entry has taken place the incumbent does better by not fighting. One rationale for the intuitive feeling that this somehow is too simple is that it may pay even the weak monopolist to fight entry on one occasion, if this will establish a reputation for combativeness and so discourage entry at any time in the future. This changes the specification of the game, from a *one-shot game* to a *repeated game*, the *constituent game* of which we can take as given in Fig. 16.13(b).

Much depends on the firm's *discount rate*, that is, the rate at which it discounts future profits to a present value. Even more important is whether the game is to be repeated a *finite* or *infinite* number of times. To emphasize the latter point, we assume that the firm does not discount the future, and we take Selten's (1978) Chain Store Paradox. The paradox is that, even though it appears in the monopoly's interest to fight entry, it will accept entry from the very beginning.

Suppose a supermarket chain has stores in ten cities, in each of which it enjoys a local monopoly. In each city there is a local potential entrant, and the situation in each city is represented in Fig. 16.13(b). The potential entrants act sequentially, so we number cities from 1 to 10 in the order in which entry will be attempted. Consider city 1. We might feel that the monopoly ought to fight any entrant into that market, because, although it sacrifices a payoff of 1 as compared with the accept strategy, if this then deters entry in the remaining nine cities, it will gain $90 - 27 = 63$. But consider the last market to be defended, in city 10. Since there is no subsequent threat of entry to be deterred, the earlier logic of the one-shot game holds and the monopoly does better by accepting entry. All participants in the game, including the other nine potential entrants, can work this out. Take now city 9. Since the monopoly's decision in city 10 is to accept entry, it gains nothing in city 9 by fighting – the entrant in city 10 would not be deterred because it knows that, once it enters, it is in the monopolist's interest to accept. Thus in city 9 the entrant will move in and the monopoly's best choice is to accept. But this argument can then be repeated for each market right back to city 1. Thus entry takes place in all markets.

Another way of interpreting this argument is the following. Everyone knows that the monopolist is weak. If it were to fight entry in the first city this would not change anyone's knowledge that in fact it is a weak monopolist: the entrant in city 10 would still believe that its entry will be accepted, and so will the entrant in city 9, and so on down the line. The incumbent will simply then be faced with a sequence of entries, each of which it would do better to accept than fight.

Again, this conclusion rests on the completeness of the information available to all the entrants. We could relax this by supposing that each entrant is uncertain whether the incumbent monopoly is weak or strong, with prior probabilities attached to these events. It can then be shown that under some conditions it *will* pay the weak monopolist to fight entry at earlier stages in the sequence, in order to create a reputation for being strong. It can exploit the uncertainty in the entrants' mind about his true type. In the later stages it will accept entry because the benefits of deterring future entry fall relative to the costs of fighting entry. (See the analysis of the Kreps–Wilson Reputation game in Chapter 15.)

Capacity as credible precommitment

In the case of the one-shot game the problem for the weak monopolist is the lack of credibility of its threat to fight entry – its bluff can too easily be called. A way to avoid this problem would be to find some means of *credible precommitment* to fighting, so that the entrant would expect entry to be contested. One possibility might be for the monopolist to appoint a manager to take the firm's decisions, and to draw up a binding contract under which the manager is paid as a function of the firm's market share – perhaps with a sharp fall in pay for anything less than 100 per cent of the market! The manager then has a powerful incentive to fight entry, and, provided the owner of the firm can credibly commit not to interfere with management, the entrant will not enter. (This is an example of a case in which a principal can do better by appointing an agent with different preferences from his own.)

A different type of precommitment underlies *the Spence–Dixit model of entry-deterrence*. Suppose that the incumbent is able to commit to a particular level of capacity before entry takes place. For this to represent a credible commitment, we must assume that, once installed, the capacity cannot be sold off at the market price for capacity – it represents a *sunk cost*. For the model it is also important to assume that, if the potential entrant comes into the market, the incumbent can expand capacity at the same time as the entrant. Thus there is an asymmetry in the costs to the incumbent of expanding and contracting capacity. A second asymmetry is that the entrant must incur a fixed cost upon entry, although there is a constant marginal cost per unit of capacity output. This implies a falling average total cost curve with respect to the entrant's output, and so captures the idea of economies of scale for the entrant. The incumbent incurred its fixed cost in the past and so this is no longer relevant to its decisions. The importance of this model is that it brings out clearly the way in which the incumbent can use capacity precommitment either to forestall entry completely, or to improve its profitability should entry take place. For concreteness we analyse the model in the form of a specific numerical example, but in Exercise 16D a number of questions explore the effects of varying the assumptions.

The inverse market demand function is given by

$$p = 100 - q \qquad\qquad [\text{D.1}]$$

where q is total market output. The incumbent is denoted firm 1, the entrant firm 2, and their outputs are q_1 and q_2 respectively. Capacity is denoted k_i, $i = 1, 2$, and each firm can install capacity at a constant cost of 30 per unit. Increases in output below capacity have a zero marginal cost, but output cannot exceed capacity at any cost. The entrant, if it decides to enter, has to pay a fixed cost F. Thus the firms' cost functions and capacity constraints are

$$C_1 = 30k_1 \qquad q_1 \leqslant k_1; \qquad C_2 = F + 30k_2 \qquad q_2 \leqslant k_2 \qquad \text{[D.2]}$$

We consider first the situation in which firms choose capacities simultaneously, and assume that their choices are a *Cournot–Nash equilibrium*. The firms' choices must be *mutually best responses*: firm 1's output and capacity must maximize its profit given firm 2's output and capacity, which in turn must maximize firm 2's profit given firm 1's choices. We find the equilibrium by deriving each firm's *reaction function*. For given q_2, solve for firm 1 the problem

$$\max_{k_1, q_1} \pi_1 = [100 - (q_1 + q_2)]q_1 - 30k_1 \quad \text{s.t.} \quad q_1 \leqslant k_1 \qquad \text{[D.3]}$$

giving the solution

$$q_1 = k_1 = 35 - 0.5q_2 \qquad \text{[D.4]}$$

which is 1's reaction function showing its optimal decision as a function of the given q_2. Likewise for firm 2 solve

$$\max_{k_2, q_2} \pi_2 = [100 - (q_1 + q_2)]q_2 - 30k_2 - F \quad \text{s.t.} \quad q_2 \leqslant k_2 \qquad \text{[D.5]}$$

giving

$$q_2 = k_2 = 35 - 0.5q_1 \qquad \text{[D.6]}$$

Note that it never pays to set output below capacity, and that the reaction functions are symmetrical, despite the presence of the fixed cost to firm 2.

The Cournot–Nash equilibrium is the pair of capacities k_i^c which satisfy the reaction functions simultaneously, so that we have

$$k_1^c = k_2^c = 23.33 \qquad \text{[D.7]}$$

Then, market price is $(100 - 46.66) = 53.33$, and profits are

$$\pi_1^c = 544.44 \qquad \pi_2^c = 544.44 - F \qquad \text{[D.8]}$$

The reaction functions [D.4] and [D.6] are labelled R_1 and R_2 in Fig. 16.14 (ignore $\bar{R}_1$ for the moment) and the above Cournot–Nash equilibrium is also illustrated. The intercept of R_1 on the q_1 axis is firm 1's monopoly output, since it corresponds to $k_2 = q_2 = 0$. As we move along R_1 leftwards firm 1's profit is falling since q_2 is increasing; and similarly as we move along R_2 rightwards firm 2's profit is falling since q_1 is increasing. Finally, note that, if $F \geqslant 544.44$, the potential entrant cannot make a profit at the post-entry equilibrium, and so will not enter. Thus entry-deterrence would be irrelevant and the incumbent could set monopoly output and price. In what follows therefore we assume throughout that $F < 544.44$.

Now we introduce the possibility that firm 1 can commit itself to a capacity level *before* the entrant appears. We emphasize the assumption that it cannot reduce its costs by reducing capacity *after* the entrant appears – committing itself to a capacity

Figure 16.14

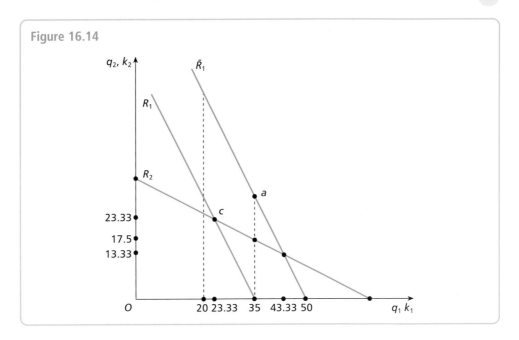

implies that it then has a fixed cost of $30k_1$ and zero variable costs. In this case we find its output reaction function for a *given* commitment to capacity, $\bar{k}_1$ by solving

$$\max_{q_1} \pi_1 = [100 - (q_1 + q_2)]q_1 \quad \text{s.t.} \quad q_1 \leqslant \bar{k}_1 \qquad [\text{D.9}]$$

yielding

$$q_1 = 50 - 0.5q_2 \quad \text{when} \quad q_1 < \bar{k}_1$$
$$q_1 = \bar{k}_1 \text{ otherwise} \qquad [\text{D.10}]$$

This is illustrated as $\bar{R}_1$ in Fig. 16.14, for three assumed values of $\bar{k}_1$, at $\bar{k}_1 = 20$, $\bar{k}_1 = 35$, and $\bar{k}_1 = 50$. Note that, if $\bar{k}_1 = 50$, the reaction function $\bar{R}_1$ intersects firm 2's reaction function at the point (43.33, 13.33). The significance of this point is that, if firm 1 had installed a capacity of 50 (or *any* $k_1 \geqslant 43.33$), then when the entrant appears and chooses a capacity and output, while firm 1 simply chooses an output (the marginal cost of which is *zero* up to 50), then this intersection point would be the Cournot–Nash equilibrium of this game, since it is the point at which the firms are making mutually best responses. On the other hand, if firm 1 had initially installed capacity $\bar{k}_1 < 43.33$, this point would not be feasible in the post-entry game.

We now examine firm 1's optimal choice of a prior capacity $\bar{k}_1$. First, we show that it will never choose $\bar{k}_1 < 23.33$, or $\bar{k}_1 > 43.33$. Thus, the two reaction function intersection points define an interval [23.33, 43.33] within which firm 1 will choose its capacity.

Note first that, if it chooses $\bar{k}_1 > 43.33$, the post-entry equilibrium will be at $q_1 = 43.33$. But then any excess of capacity over 43.33 is wasted, and, since it costs 30 per unit to install, will not be chosen.

The argument that the incumbent will not choose $\bar{k}_1 < 23.33$ rests on the assumption that it can always increase its capacity in the post-entry period, just as the entrant is installing its own. It follows that choice of $\bar{k}_1 < 23.33$ is not a credible threat to the entrant. If the entrant chooses $k_2^c = 23.33$, firm 1's best response is to expand capacity to 23.33 (moving along its *lower* reaction curve since it is having to buy capacity) and so setting $\bar{k}_1 < 23.33$ is pointless. The incumbent can commit to a minimum level of capacity $\bar{k}_1$ but cannot commit not to install additional capacity after entry.

The incumbent therefore will choose its most profitable minimum capacity commitment in the interval [23.33, 43.33]. Its level will depend on the value of the entrant's fixed cost. We can distinguish two cases:

1. At $k_2 = 13.33$, the entrant would make a profit. Since at the point (43.33, 13.33), we have $\pi_2 = 177.69 - F$, this case corresponds to

$$0 < F < 177.69$$

   It then follows that for any $\bar{k}_1$ in the interval [23.33, 43.33] the entrant can make a profit (recall the entrant's profit increases as we move leftward along R_2) and so entry cannot be deterred. All the incumbent can do is to choose $\bar{k}_1$ so as to make the post-entry situation as profitable to itself as possible. Now for any $\bar{k}_1$ it chooses, the entrant will choose a point on R_2. Thus, the incumbent can find its optimal capacity and output by using [D.6] to substitute for q_2 in its profit function and solving

$$\max_{q_1, \bar{k}_1} [100 - (q_1 + 35 - 0.5q_1)]q_1 - 30\bar{k}_1 \quad \text{s.t.} \quad q_1 \le \bar{k}_1 \qquad \text{[D.11]}$$

   This yields $q_1^\star = \bar{k}_1^\star = 35$. If the incumbent commits to this capacity level, the entrant's most profitable output and capacity are $q_2^\star = k_2^\star = 17.5$. Thus market price will be 57.5 and the firms' profits will be

$$\pi_1^s = 962.5; \qquad \pi_2^s = 481.25 - F \qquad \text{[D.12]}$$

   This solution, in which the incumbent in effect maximizes its profit subject to the entrant's reaction function as a constraint, is known as the *Stackelberg leadership solution*. It is entirely an accident of the parameter values in this example that this solution happens to be at the incumbent's monopoly output level of 35. In general, the Stackelberg solution could be above or below the monopoly output. It is, however, not an accident that $q_1^\star = \bar{k}_1^\star$: it would not pay the incumbent to install capacity it would not use. The incumbent would never expand capacity post-entry, while the assumption that capacity, once installed, cannot be sold off makes it impossible for the incumbent to move back along R_1 in response to any higher capacity choice than 17.5 by the entrant. The fact that capital cost is a sunk cost enables the incumbent credibly to commit to an output and capacity of 35. In effect this precommitment makes the reaction function of firm 1 the portion of $\bar{R}_1$ from 100 to a, and the vertical dashed line from a to 35. Then, (35, 17.5) is an intersection of the reaction functions and hence a Cournot–Nash equilibrium.

2. The other possibility is that the entrant's fixed cost lies in the interval

$$177.69 \le F < 544.44$$

   implying that its profits become zero at some point on R_2 between (23.33, 23.33) and (43.33, 13.33). We can think of this point as being fixed by its q_1-coordinate. Then we can solve for this q_1-coordinate, as a function of F, by noting that it satisfies the condition

$$\pi_2 = [100 - (q_1 + q_2)]q_2 - 30q_2 - F = 0 \qquad \text{[D.13]}$$

Substituting the firm 2 reaction function $q_2 = 35 - 0.5q_1$ into this condition yields the function

$$\hat{q}_1 = 70 - 2F^{1/2} \qquad \text{for } 177.69 \leqslant F < 544.44 \qquad \text{[D.14]}$$

(strictly, [D.13] gives a quadratic and therefore two solutions for $\hat{q}_1$, but only the root given in [D.14] is feasible). The significance of $\hat{q}_1$ is that, if the incumbent sets $\bar{k}_1 \geqslant \hat{q}_1$, then entry will be deterred, since the entrant's best response to this will yield it no profit, given the level of its fixed cost. Again, the irreversibility of the investment makes this precommitment a credible means of deterring entry. Is it a profit-maximizing strategy for the incumbent to choose $k_1 = \hat{q}_1$ and deter entry? We can distinguish two sub-cases:

(a) $23.33 < \hat{q}_1 \leqslant 35$, corresponding to $306.25 \leqslant F < 544.44$.

   In this case, by setting $\bar{k}_1 = q_1 = 35$ the incumbent deters entry and maximizes monopoly profit.

(b) $35 < \hat{q}_1 \leqslant 43.33$, corresponding to $177.69 \leqslant F < 306.25$.

   The optimal capacity choice in this case requires a comparison of the profit to be made by permitting entry, on the one hand, or by setting $\bar{k}_1 = \hat{q}_1$ and so preventing entry, on the other. We already saw that, if entry is going to take place, the best output for the monopolist is its Stackelberg output of 35, yielding post-entry profit of 962.5. On the other hand, if the incumbent preserves its monopoly at any output over the interval [35, 43.33], its profit lies in the interval [1155.61, 1225]. Clearly then it pays always to deter entry and to set $\bar{k}_1 = \hat{q}_1$ (again, note that as long as capacity is costly we would never have $\bar{k}_1 > \hat{q}_1$, since such excess capacity is unnecessary).

   In general, a third sub-case is possible. Over an upper part of the interval [35, 43.33] it might have been the case that the monopoly's profit from setting $\bar{k}_1 = \hat{q}_1$ was below that from setting $\bar{k}_1$ at the Stackelberg point. Then the latter would be optimal. For the parameter values in this example, however, that never happens.

In Table 16.4 we summarize the various cases just analysed. They are defined in terms of the entrant's fixed cost. Only in the lowest range of F-values does entry take place, while in the simultaneous game entry occurs for $F < 544.44$. Even when entry occurs, we see that the incumbent's output and profit are both higher than in the simultaneous game, in which the Cournot–Nash equilibrium gave the incumbent a profit of 544.44. By being able to precommit to capacity the incumbent has a higher reaction function in the post-entry game and so secures a more favourable equilibrium. In the other cases precommitment allows the incumbent actually to prevent entry and earn even higher profit, and in one range the incumbent can earn monopoly profit.

Table 16.4 Possible equilibrium in capacity precommitment game

Fixed cost	Entrant chooses	Incumbent chooses	Incumbent profit
$0 < F < 177.69$	In, $k_2 = 17.5$	$q_1 = \bar{k}_1 = 35$	962.5
$177.69 \leqslant F < 306.25$	Out, $k_2 = 0$	$q_1 = \bar{k}_1 = 70 - 2F^{1/2}$	(1155.44, 1225]
$306.25 \leqslant F < 544.44$	Out, $k_2 = 0$	$q_1 = \bar{k}_1 = 35$	1225
$544.44 \leqslant F$	Out, $k_2 = 0$	$q_1 = \bar{k}_1 = 35$	1225

EXERCISE 16D

1. Show that the qualitative nature of the analysis of the capacity precommitment (Spence–Dixit) model is unaffected if we assume a constant positive marginal cost of output for each firm.

2. In the example of the Spence–Dixit model given in this section, take the entrant's fixed cost $F = 300$, and analyse the implications of taking different possible values of the marginal capacity cost c (in the example it was set at 30).

3. In the Spence–Dixit model, what would be the consequence of assuming that the incumbent *could* sell off units of capacity, post-entry, but at a price less than the cost of installing new capacity?

4. What happens in the Spence–Dixit model if the entrant has zero fixed cost?

E. Conclusions

Firms in an oligopoly have an incentive to collude because by doing so they can in general earn higher profit than that resulting from a non-cooperative one-shot game equilibrium. In an infinitely repeated game there are punishment strategies, the threat of which can support collusion. Such threats must, however, be credible. The weakest criterion of credibility is sub-game perfection. We saw that both Friedman's formulation of punishment by Cournot–Nash competition, and Abreu's stick-and-carrot strategies, satisfy that criterion. The latter have the added attraction that they provide for reversion to cooperation once punishment has been meted out. In the case of Cournot–Nash competition, punishment certainly does hurt the punisher, and in the stick-and-carrot case some punishment may do so. This may undermine the credibility of the threats, if the firms can reopen negotiations at any time. Consequently the credibility requirement is tightened by imposing the renegotiation proofness condition. Punishment is inflicted by moving to an allocation which is better for the punisher and worse for the cheat than the initially agreed-upon allocation. In its strong form, this condition implies that the set of equilibrium profit allocations is a subset of the points on the market profit frontier.

The theories surveyed in this chapter provide testable hypotheses concerning the conditions under which we would observe collusion: the conditions involve measurable parameters of the firms' cost and demand functions and the interest rates the firms face. A drawback is that there still remains a wide set of possible equilibrium allocations: theories concerning how equilibria may be supported by threats do not predict a unique market equilibrium. Further hypotheses are required to predict which allocation in the set of sustainable allocations will actually be the market outcome. This is still an open question in oligopoly theory.

Most of the field of economics known as industrial organization is taken up by the theoretical and empirical study of oligopolistic markets. Here we have considered just some of the central themes in this literature: hypotheses about equilibrium resource allocation for homogeneous and differentiated products when the market is viewed as a one-shot game; and the conditions under which firms may make and sustain cooperative agreements when there is repeated market interaction between the firms.

Notes

1. With just two firms of course perfect competition would not be feasible especially if outputs are not homogeneous. This 'price = marginal cost' allocation is simply a useful benchmark against which to assess the various duopoly outcomes, since it corresponds to the allocatively efficient outcome.

2. It can be shown that collusion can also be sustained in finitely repeated games if there are multiple Nash equilibria of the constituent game, or if each firm believes there is some probability, however small, that the other firm is of the type that would choose the collectively rational strategy – collude – rather than the individually rational strategy, cheat. See the references at the end of the book.

3. In actually deriving the profit frontier it is more useful to approach the solution to the problem in [C.4] as follows. For $\lambda \in (0, 1)$ solve the *unconstrained* problem, with parameter λ

$$\max_{q_1 q_2} \lambda \pi^1(q_1, q_2) + (1 - \lambda)\pi^2(q_1, q_2)$$

The solutions (q_1^*, q_2^*) are functions of λ. Varying λ over the interval $[0.25, 0.75]$ then generates numerically the solution pairs in Fig. 16.8(a).

Choice under uncertainty

A. Introduction

The analysis in the preceding chapters has assumed that all decisions are taken in conditions of certainty. Any decision would result in one and only one outcome. When a firm chooses a set of input quantities, there is only one level of output which will result, and it knows the profit which it will receive from the sale of each output, no matter how far in the future production and sale will take place. Likewise, in planning their purchases of goods and services, and borrowing or lending decisions, households are assumed to know with certainty the expenditure and utility associated with each consumption vector.

But uncertainty is pervasive. There is *technological uncertainty*, when the firm is not able to predict for sure the output level which would result from a given set of input quantities. Machines may break down; crops may be affected by the weather. There is *market uncertainty* when a single household or firm is not able to predict for sure the prices at which it will buy or sell. Market uncertainty is associated with disequilibrium and change: if an economy were permanently in long-run static equilibrium, then firms and households would expect to trade at equilibrium prices, which, by experience, become known. If, however, changes are taking place through time which change equilibrium positions, the individual agents in the markets cannot know the new equilibria in advance, and can only form expectations of prices which they know may be wrong.

Extension of the theory to take account of uncertainty has two main aims. It should first tell us something about the usefulness and validity of the concepts and propositions already derived. What becomes of the conclusions about the working of a decentralized price mechanism, for example? Can we still establish existence and optimality of competitive equilibrium? Are the predictions about households' and firms' responses to changes in parameters affected qualitatively? The answers are important positively and normatively. Second, many important aspects of economic activity cannot be adequately analysed without explicit recognition of uncertainty. For example, the joint stock limited liability company, the basic institutional form of the firm in capitalist economies, has no real rationale in a world of certainty, and neither has the stock market. Insurance, futures markets and speculation cannot be understood expect in the context of uncertainty. Relaxation of the certainty assumption gives new insights into many other areas, for example investment decisions.

As with models of an economy with certainty, we begin with the optimization problem of a single decision-taker. The optimization problem under uncertainty has the same basic structure as under certainty: objects of choice; objective function; and constraints defining a feasible set of choice objects. The main interest centres on the first two of these, and, in particular, the construction of a set of axioms which allows us to define a preference ordering, representable by a utility function, over the objects of choice.

B. A formalization of 'uncertainty'

Uncertainty arises because the consequence of a decision is not a single sure outcome but rather a number of possible outcomes. Our first task in developing a theory of choice under uncertainty is to set out a precise formalization of the decision-taking situation. We can begin by distinguishing three kinds of variables which play a part in an economic system. These are:

(a) The choice variables of the decision-taker which are directly under his control. Such variables are not only endogenous to the model of the economic system, but are also endogenous to the model of the individual economic agent. Examples in earlier chapters include firms' output levels and consumers' purchases.

(b) Variables whose values are determined by the operation of the economic system, i.e. by the interaction of the choices of individual economic agents, and which are regarded as parameters by them. Prices are an example in a competitive economy. Such *determined variables* are endogenous to the model of the economic system, but exogenous to the model of the individual economic agent.

(c) *Environmental variables*, whose values are determined by some mechanism outside the economic system and which can be regarded as parameters of the economic system. They influence its outcome, but are not in turn affected by it. The weather is an example, at least for some problems, though, in the light of such events as global warming, even this could be seen as endogenous in some models.

Suppose that the economy operates over only two periods, period 1 (the present) and period 2 (the future). In period 1, the environmental variables take on specific values which are known to all economic agents. We assume that the economy produces a resource allocation and a set of relative prices. If there were complete independence between the decisions made in period 1 and those to be made in period 2, then the state of knowledge at period 1 about the environmental variables at period 2 is irrelevant. In this case, decisions for period 2 can be left until period 2, and do not affect decision-taking at period 1. We assume that this kind of *temporal separability* of decision-taking does not exist. At period 1, economic agents will have to choose values of variables such as investment (purchase of durable goods) and financial assets (bonds and shares), which affect what they will be able to do in period 2. Agents' *plans* for the values of variables they will choose at period 2, influenced by their *expectations* about the values of variables outside their control at period 2 – determined variables such as prices, and environmental variables like the weather – will condition their choices at period 1. We therefore need a theoretical framework to analyse the formation of plans and expectations, and their influence on current choices.

We proceed as follows: suppose there exists a vector of environmental variables $(e_1, e_2, \ldots, e_n)$, where each environmental variable is capable of taking on a finite number of values in period 2. Let E_j denote the set of values which can be taken by environmental variable e_j ($j = 1, 2, \ldots, n$). For example, e_1 could be the average temperature over period 2, measured to the nearest degree centigrade, and E_1 could be the set $\{e_1 \mid 50°C \geqslant e_1 \geqslant -80°C\}$, which has a finite number of elements (since the temperature is measured in units of 1°C). Define a *state of the world* as a specific combination of the values of the environmental variables, i.e. as a specific value of the vector $(e_1, e_2, \ldots, e_n)$. Since each element of the vector can take only a finite number of values the number S of states of the world is also finite, though possibly very large. We index the states of the world by a number $s = 1, 2, \ldots, S$ and use the index to label the value of the choice variables or determined variables in each state of the world. Thus, for example, we can use y_s to denote the level of income the individual gets in state s.

Three fundamental properties of the set of states of the world should be clear:

(a) The set is *exhaustive*, in that it contains *all* the states of the world which could possibly obtain at period 2.

(b) Members of the set are *mutually exclusive*, in that the occurrence of any one rules out the occurrence of any other.

(c) The states of the world are *outside the control* of any decision-taker, so that the occurrence of any one of them cannot be influenced by the choice of any economic agent, or indeed by any coalition of agents.

The definition and properties of 'states of the world' are basic to all subsequent analysis. They can be regarded as an attempt to eliminate the elements of doubt, apprehension, and muddle which are part of the every-day meaning of the word 'uncertainty', and to give the situation a precise formalization, for purposes of the theory. Three further assumptions which can be made are:

(a) All decision-takers have in their minds the same sets of states of the world – they classify the possible combinations of environmental variables in the same way.

(b) When period 2 arrives, all decision-takers will be able to recognize which state of the world exists, and will all agree on it.

(c) At period 1, each decision-taker is able to assign a probability to the event that a particular state of the world will occur at period 2. The probabilities may differ for different decision-takers, but all probability assignments satisfy the basic probability laws. The probability associated with the sth state by decision-taker i, denoted π_s^i, lies on the interval $1 \geqslant \pi_s^i \geqslant 0$, with $\pi_s^i = 1$ implying that i regards state s as certain to occur, and $\pi_s^i = 0$ implying that he regards state s as certain *not* to occur. The probability of one or another of several states occurring is the sum of their probabilities (with the probability of their simultaneous occurrence being zero), and, in particular, one of the S states *must* occur, i.e. $\sum_{s=1}^{S} \pi_s^i = 1$.

Each of these assumptions is quite strong, and plays an important part in what follows. The first is necessary if we are to portray decision-takers as making agreements in *state-contingent* terms: in order for one to agree with another that 'if state 1 occurs I will do A, in return for your doing B if state 2 occurs', it is necessary that they should understand each other's references to states.

The second assumption is also required for the formation and discharge of agreements framed in state-contingent terms. If parties to an agreement would differ about which state of the world exists *ex post*, they are unlikely to agree *ex ante* on some exchange which is contingent on states of the world. The assumption also rules out problems which might arise from differences in the information which different decision-takers may possess. Suppose, for example, that individual I cannot tell whether it is state 1 or state 2 which actually prevails at period 2, while individual J does know. Then I is unlikely to conclude an agreement with J under which, say, I gains and J loses if state 1 occurs, while J gains and I loses if state 2 occurs, because of course I could be exploited by J.

C. Choice under uncertainty

We now consider the question of optimal choice under uncertainty. First, we need to define the objects of choice, and then we can consider the question of the decision-taker's preference ordering over these choice objects. We present what is usually called the von Neumann–Morgenstern Theory of Expected Utility.

Initially, we assume that there is a single good, which is measured in units of account, and which can be thought of as 'income'. Let y_s ($s = 1, 2, \ldots, S$) denote an amount of income which the decision-taker will have if and only if state s occurs (in this section we shall be concerned only with a single decision-taker and so do not need to burden ourselves with a notation which distinguishes among decision-takers). Assume that the individual assigns a probability π_s to state of the world s, and denote the vector of probabilities by $\pi = [\pi_1, \pi_2, \ldots, \pi_S]$, while $y = [y_1, y_2, \ldots, y_S]$ is the corresponding vector of state-contingent incomes. Define a *prospect*, P, as a given income vector with an associated probability vector,

$$P = (\pi, y) = (\pi_1, \ldots, \pi_S, y_1, \ldots, y_S) \qquad \text{[C.1]}$$

Changing the probability vector π, or the income vector y (or both) produces a different prospect. Another term for a prospect would be a *probability distribution of incomes*.

The choice objects of our theory are prospects such as P. Any decision has as its *only* and *entire* consequence some prospect P, and so choice between alternative actions or decisions is equivalent to choice between alternative prospects. A preference ordering over decisions can only be derived from a preference ordering over their associated prospects.

For example, consider the decision of a market gardener to insure or not against loss of income through sickness or poor weather such as severe frost. Decision A is the decision *not* to insure, decision B is to insure. Associated with A is a prospect, $P^A = (\pi, y^A)$ where y^A is an income vector, the components of which vary across states of the world. In the subset of states in which he is sick, income will take on one value; in the subset of states in which there is frost, income takes on another value; in the subset in which he is sick and there is frost, there will be a third value; and when he is not sick and there is no frost, there will be a fourth (and presumably the highest) value. Associated with B is a *certain prospect* (assuming that compensation for loss of income through sickness or frost is complete) $P^B = (\pi, y^B)$, where each element of y^B is equal to what income would be in the absence of sickness and frost, *minus* the insurance premium, which must be paid in all states of the world. The choice between A and B, i.e. the decision whether or not to insure, depends on whether P^A is or is not preferred to P^B. To analyse choice under uncertainty therefore requires us to construct a theory of the preference ordering over prospects.

If certain assumptions (axioms) concerning a decision-taker's preferences are satisfied, then we are able to represent those preferences – the criterion by which he takes his choices – in a simple and appealing way. A test of the appropriateness of the assumptions would be to show that we can correctly predict choices not yet observed, on the basis of observation of choice already made. It should be emphasized that our theory is a device for permitting such predictions, rather than for describing whatever thought process a decision-taker goes through when making choices. The objects of choice consist of a set of prospects, which we can denote by $\{P^1, P^2, \ldots, P^n\}$. The five axioms are described next.

Axiom 1: Ordering of prospects

Given any two prospects, the decision-taker prefers one to the other, or is indifferent between them, and these relations of preference and indifference are *transitive*. In the notation of Chapter 2, for any two prospects P^j, P^k, exactly one of the statements $P^j > P^k$, $P^j < P^k$, $P^j \sim P^k$, is true, while

$$P^j > P^k \quad \text{and} \quad P^k > P^l \Rightarrow P^j > P^l \qquad [\text{C.2}]$$

and similarly for the indifference relation $\sim$. This axiom means that the preference ordering over prospects has the same desirable properties of completeness and consistency which were attributed to the preferences ordering over bundles of goods in Chapter 2.

Before stating the second axiom, we need to introduce the concept of a *standard prospect*. Given the set of prospects under consideration we can take all the income values which appear in them, regardless of the state and the prospect to which they belong, as defining a set of values of the variable, income. Since there is a finite number of states and prospects, there is a finite number of such income values (*at most, nS* of them). There will be a greatest and a smallest income value. Denote these values by y_u and y_L respectively. It follows that all income values lie on the interval $[y_L, y_u]$, and we can construct the theory so as to apply to this entire interval on the real line. Define a standard prospect, P_0, as a prospect involving only the two outcomes y_u and y_L, with probabilities v and $1 - v$ respectively, where $1 \geqslant v \geqslant 0$. A specific standard prospect, P_0^1, can be written as

$$P_0^1 = (v^1, y_u, y_L) \qquad [\text{C.3}]$$

(where, for convenience, we do not bother to write the second probability $1 - v^1$). We obtain a second standard prospect, P_0^{11}, by changing v^1, the probability of getting the better outcome, to v^{11}, so that

$$P_0^{11} = (v^{11}, y_u, y_L) \qquad [\text{C.4}]$$

We can then state the second axiom.

Axiom 2: Preference increasing with probability

Given any two standard prospects P_0^1 and P_0^{11},

$$P_0^1 > P_0^{11} \Leftrightarrow v^1 > v^{11} \qquad [\text{C.5}]$$

$$P_0^1 \sim P_0^{11} \Leftrightarrow v^1 = v^{11} \qquad [\text{C.6}]$$

The decision-taker always prefers the standard prospect which gives the better chance of getting the higher-valued outcome, while two standard prospects with the same chance of getting the better outcome would be regarded as equivalent.

Axiom 3: Equivalent standard prospects

Given any certain income value y^1 such that $y_u \geqslant y^1 \geqslant y_L$, there exists one and only one value v^1 such that

$$y^1 \sim P_0^1 = (v^1, y_u, y_L) \qquad \text{[C.7]}$$

where P_0^1 will be called the *equivalent standard prospect* for y^1.

We can take a value of income in the given interval and always find a probability of getting the better outcome in the standard prospect such that the decision-taker would be indifferent between getting the income for certain, and having the standard prospect. This is true for two values of income, namely y_u and y_L. We must have

$$y_u \sim P_0^u = (1, y_u, y_L) \qquad \text{[C.8]}$$

$$y_L \sim P_0^L = (0, y_u, y_L) \qquad \text{[C.9]}$$

since P_0^u and P_0^L correspond to the *certain* receipt of y_u and y_L respectively. Axiom 3 asserts that we could choose any income between y_u and y_L and always find a unique v value to define an equivalent standard prospect. But then [C.7] defines a *function* from the income domain $y_u \geqslant y^1 \geqslant y_L$ to the range of probability values $1 \geqslant v \geqslant 0$. We could write the function as $v(y^1)$. On the plausible assumption that more income is preferred to less, axiom 2 implies that the value of v must increase as y^1 increases, in order to maintain indifference between y^1 and the standard prospect. Hence $v(y^1)$ is an increasing function. *Given* y_u and y_L, axiom 3 implies that the function is uniquely defined. However, the values of y_u and y_L are essentially arbitrary and can be changed without affecting the basic nature of the theory. For example, if we define a new standard prospect, P_0^1, by choosing a better outcome $y_u^1 > y_u$, then we could apply axiom 3 to find the v values in P_0^1 corresponding to each y value, and we would expect them to be different – in particular, we would now have $u(y_u) < 1$. Similarly, we could choose y_L^1, to define a new standard prospect, and again we would expect to obtain a different relationship between v and y. Thus the function $v(y)$ cannot be unique in a general sense, but only relative to a specific choice of outcomes for the standard prospect. We return to this point later, when we take up again the properties of the function $v(y)$.

To describe the fourth axiom we need to introduce yet another type of prospect, known as a *compound prospect*. In general, a compound prospect P_c is one which has, for at least one of its outcomes, another prospect, rather than a single value of income. A commonplace example of a compound prospect is a so-called 'accumulator' bet which one may place on horse-racing. If one places a 'double', one puts a stake t on a horse in race 1, and specifies that, if it wins, the gross payout $t + W_1$ will be used as a stake on a horse in race 2. The possible outcomes of the prospect are therefore to lose the original stake, t, with probability π_1, or to gain a further gamble, on the second race, with probability $1 - \pi_1$. This second gamble, or prospect, has the possible outcomes of losing the stake with probability π_2, and winning the net payout on the 'double', W_2. Hence, the 'double', as a compound prospect, can be written

$$P_c^d = [\pi_1, y - t, (\pi_2, y - t, y + W_2)] = (\pi_1, y - t, P^1) \qquad \text{[C.10]}$$

where $P^1 = (\pi_2, y + W_1 - t - W_1, y + W_2)$ is the gamble on the second race, W_1 is the payout on winning the first race and y is income without the bet. (As with the notation for the standard prospect, whenever a prospect involves only two outcomes, only the probability of the first outcome will be written, since the probability of the second is simply 1 *minus* the probability of the first.)

How should a rational decision-taker evaluate a compound prospect? Take our accumulator bet, the 'double', as an example. The punter may lose in one of two mutually exclusive ways: losing on the first race, with probability π_1; and losing on the second race, with probability π_2, given that he has won on the first race, with probability $1 - \pi_1$. Applying standard probability laws, the overall probability that he will lose on the second race is $\pi_2(1 - \pi_1)$ (probability of joint event 'win on first race *and* lose on second'. Where the separate probabilities are independent), and so the probability that he will lose on either the first or second race is $\pi_1 + \pi_2(1 - \pi_1)$ $= \hat{\pi}$. The probability that he will win the net payout W_2 is the probability of winning the second race *and* winning the first, i.e. $(1 - \pi_1)(1 - \pi_2) = (1 - \hat{\pi})$. If the punter loses, his income loss is $-t$, the loss of the stake money. Looking at the net income difference brought about by the bet, he ends up *either* with having lost the stake t, with probability $\hat{\pi}$, or having won the payout W_2, with probability $1 - \hat{\pi}$. We can define the *simple* prospect P^d, which summarizes the *overall* net income represented by the *compound* prospect P^d_c, as

$$P^d = (\hat{\pi}, y - t, y + W_2) \qquad [\text{C.11}]$$

We could argue that P^d is *equivalent* to P^d_c, in that a rational gambler, working out the final possible income positions, and their associated probabilities, would conclude that the compound prospect 'boils down' to this simple prospect. However this is not quite the same as saying that any decision-taker would be *indifferent* between the compound prospect P^d_c and its *rational equivalent* P^d. We might feel that a rational individual *ought* to be indifferent between the two, but it is not hard to find punters who prefer to go for a double even when exactly the same payouts are available with separate bets on the two races (Question 4, Exercise 17C, asks you to discuss this further).

Now let us generalize from this example and consider the compound prospect which has *standard prospects* as its outcomes. Such compound prospects have

$$P^1_c = [\pi^1, (v^1, y_u, y_L), (v^2, y_u, y_L), \ldots, (v^S, y_u, y_L)]$$
$$= (\pi^1, P^1_0, P^2_0, \ldots, P^S_0) \qquad [\text{C.12}]$$

where π^1 is a vector of probabilities, $\pi^1 = [\pi^1_1, \pi^1_2, \ldots, \pi^1_S]$, and v^s $(s = 1, 2, \ldots, S)$ is the probability of getting the better outcome y_u in the sth standard prospect. Thus, π^1_s is the probability of getting the sth standard prospect which has probability v^s of getting y_u. The compound prospect P^1_c has S different ways of getting either y_u or y_L. The probability of getting y_u overall is

$$\bar{v} = \pi^1_1 v^1 + \pi^1_2 v^2 + \ldots + \pi^1_s v^s + \ldots + \pi^1_S v^S = \sum_{s=1}^{S} \pi^1_s v^s \qquad [\text{C.13}]$$

y_u may be won by winning prospect P^s_0 with probability π^1_s and then winning y_u with probability v^s, so that the probability of winning y_u in *this particular* way is $\pi^1_s v^s$. Hence the probability of winning y_u in one of these S mutually exclusive ways is $\bar{v} = \sum_{s=1}^{S} \pi^1_s v^s$. The overall probability of winning y_L is $1 - \bar{v}$. Thus, we can define as the *rational equivalent* of P^1_c in [C.12] the standard prospect

$$P^1_0 = (\bar{v}, y_u, y_L) \qquad [\text{C.14}]$$

since P^1_0 yields y_u with probability $\bar{v}$, and y_L with probability $1 - \bar{v}$. We can now state the fourth axiom.

Axiom 4: Rational equivalence

Given any compound prospect P_c^1, having as outcomes only standard prospects (as in [C.12]), and given its rational equivalent P_0^1 (as in [C.14]), then $P_c^1 \sim P_0^1$.

Axiom 4 asserts that the decision-taker does indeed rationally evaluate the probabilities of ultimately obtaining the two outcomes, and is not affected by the two-stage nature of the gamble – we could perhaps say that he does not suffer from '*risk illusion*'. Clearly, the axiom incorporates a strong assumption about the rationality and computational ability of the individual decision-taker.

Axiom 3 stated that for any income value y^1 we can find an equivalent standard prospect P_0^1 by suitable choice of a value v^1. Take now any one of the prospects $P^1, P^2, \ldots P^n$, which form the original set of objects of choice for the decision-taker, with:

$$P^j = (\pi, y^j) \qquad j = 1, 2, \ldots, n \qquad \text{[C.15]}$$

where π is the vector of probabilities and $y^j = [y_1^j, y_2^j, \ldots, y_S^j]$ is the vector of state-contingent incomes. Applying axiom 3, we can find for each $y_s^j (s = 1, 2, \ldots, S)$ the equivalent standard prospect P_0^{js} such that

$$y_s^j \sim P_0^{js} = (v^{js}, y_u, y_L) \qquad \text{[C.16]}$$

where, consistent with our earlier notation, we have

$$v^{js} = v(y_s^j) \qquad j = 1, 2, \ldots, n \qquad s = 1, 2, \ldots, S \qquad \text{[C.17]}$$

Now consider the *compound prospect*, P_c^j, which is formed from P^j by replacing each component of the income vector by its equivalent standard prospect, i.e.

$$P_c^j = (\pi, (P_0^{j1}, P_0^{j2}, \ldots, P_0^{jS})) \qquad \text{[C.18]}$$

where each P_0^{js} ($s = 1, 2, \ldots, S$) satisfies [C.16]. Thus, whereas the outcomes in P^j are amounts of income, the outcomes in P_c^j are the equivalent standard prospects. Then the fifth and final axiom can be stated.

Axiom 5: Context independence

$$P^j \sim P_c^j \qquad \text{all } j = 1, 2, \ldots, n$$

In words: the decision-taker is indifferent between a given prospect and a compound prospect formed by replacing each value of income by its equivalent standard prospect. For example, suppose that the decision-taker is in turn indifferent between (a) £70 for certain, and a 50–50 chance of £200 or £10, and (b) £100 for certain, and a 75–25 chance of £200 or £10. Axiom 5 asserts that he would then be indifferent between a 50–50 chance of £70 or £100, on the one hand, and a 50–50 chance of obtaining one of two further gambles: (a) a 50–50 chance of £200 or £10, and (b) a 75–25 chance of £200 or £10, on the other. The fact that values of income, and their equivalent standard prospects, may be included in prospects, does not change their basic relation of indifference (which is what the term 'context independence' tries to convey). We could represent this example as

$$([0.5 \ 0.5], [£70 \ £100]) \sim ([0.5 \ 0.5][(0.5, £200, £10)(0.75, £200, £10)]) \qquad \text{[C.19]}$$

Thus equivalent standard prospects can be substituted for incomes, without changing the place of a prospect in the preference ordering.

We now show that the five axioms lead to an appealing way of representing the decision-taker's preference ordering. Axiom 5 implies that given any set of prospects $\{P^1, P^2, \ldots, P^n\}$ we can replace each by the corresponding compound prospects $P_c^1, P_c^2, \ldots, P_c^n$, where each P_c^j ($j = 1, 2, \ldots, n$) satisfies [C.18]. In other words, we can express each of the 'primary' prospects as a compound prospect involving *only* various chances of obtaining standard prospects. This is an important step, since it puts the individual prospects on to a common basis of comparison – *they become simply different ways of winning one or other of the same two outcomes*. Moreover, axiom 4 tells us that each of the P_c^j will be indifferent to its rational equivalent, i.e. a standard prospect involving only outcomes y_u and y_L, with probabilities derived in a straightforward way from those appearing in the P_c^j. Thus, we can write

$$P^j \sim P_c^j \sim P_0^j \tag{C.20}$$

or, more fully,

$$(\pi, y^j) \sim (\pi, [P_0^{j1}, P_0^{j2}, \ldots, P_0^{jS}]) \sim (\bar{v}^j, y_u, y_L) \tag{C.21}$$

where $P_0^{js} = (v^{js}, y_u, y_L)$, and

$$\bar{v}^j = \sum_{s=1}^{S} \pi_s v^{js} = \sum_{s=1}^{S} \pi_s v(y_s^j) \tag{C.22}$$

Now, from axiom 2, we have that $P_0^j > P_0^k$, if and only if $\bar{v}^j > \bar{v}^k$, and that $P_0^j \sim P_0^k$ if and only if $\bar{v}^j = \bar{v}^k$. It follows that the rational equivalent standard prospects P_0^1, $P_0^2, \ldots, P_0^n$ can be completely ordered by the values of $\bar{v}$ which appear in them. The preferred rational equivalent standard prospect will be that with the highest $\bar{v}$ value. Thus the decision-taker chooses among the prospects P_0^j in such a way as *to maximize the value of $\bar{v}$*. He acts *as if* his intention is to make $\bar{v}$ as large as possible. But, from axiom 1, the preference ordering over all prospects (including standard prospects) is transitive, so that

$$P^j \sim P_0^j \quad \text{and} \quad P^k \sim P_0^k \quad \text{and} \quad P_0^j > P_0^k \Rightarrow P^j > P^k \tag{C.23}$$

Thus, because of [C.20], the preference ordering over the rational equivalent standard prospects P_0^j, represented by the values of the $\bar{v}^j$, is identical to the preference ordering over the initial prospects, P^j ($j = 1, 2, \ldots, n$). It follows that choice among the initial prospects can be modelled as if the decision-taker maximizes $\bar{v}$.

The axioms provide a procedure for predicting the choices among prospects of a decision-taker to whom they apply. We might proceed as follows: by a large number (in principle an infinity) of paired comparisons between certain income values on the interval $[y_u, y_L]$, and standard prospects P_0, we could find the function $v(y)$. We could then take two prospects, say P^1 and P^2, and, by inserting the values of the incomes y_s^1, y_s^2 ($s = 1, 2, \ldots, S$) into this function, we obtain the values $v_s^1 = v(y_s^1)$, $v_s^2 = v(y_s^2)$. Then we can calculate $\bar{v}^1 = \Sigma_s \pi_s v_s^1$, and $\bar{v}^2 = \Sigma_s \pi_s v_s^2$ and predict that the prospects with the higher of these two values will be chosen.

In theoretical analysis we do not know the specific functions $v(y)$. Rather, we have to use certain general properties of this function. In the next section, we consider the most important properties in some detail. We conclude this section with a note on terminology. It is usual to call the function $v(y)$ a utility function, since it is a real-valued numerical representation of a preference ordering. It should be clear from the way in which this function is derived that 'utility' is not to be interpreted as a quantity of satisfaction, well-being or other psychic sensation but simply as a name for the numbers which result when we carry out a series of paired comparisons.

We refer to the value $\bar{v}^j = \sum_{s=1}^{S} \pi_s v_s^j$ as the *expected utility* of prospect P^j, and we can interpret the axioms to mean that the decision-taker chooses among projects as if to maximize expected utility. The theory based on the axioms is often called the Expected Utility Theory of Choice under Uncertainty.

We have set out the axioms underlying the Expected Utility Theory. In the next section, we discuss some properties which can be attributed to the utility function $v(y)$.

EXERCISE 17C

1. Ms A has a utility function given by $v = \sqrt{y}$, where y is income. She is asked to enter a business venture, which involves a 50–50 chance of an income of £900, or £400, and so the expected value of income from the venture is £650.

   (a) If asked to pay a 'fair price' of £650 in order to take part in the venture, would she accept?

   (b) What is the largest sum of money she would be prepared to pay to take part in the venture?

   (*Hint*: find the *certainty equivalent* of the prospect defined by the venture, i.e. the income which, if received for certain, has a utility equal to the expected utility of the prospect. Don't worry, for the moment, that the v-values in this question do not lie between 0 and 1. This is discussed in the next section.)

2. Now suppose Ms A has the utility function (a) $v = ay$ where $a > 0$, or (b) $v = y^2$. How would your answers to question 1 change?

3. *St Petersburg Paradox.* Suppose we define the following gamble: we toss a coin, and if it lands heads, you receive £2, and if it lands tails, we toss it again; if on the second toss it lands heads, you receive £4 (= £2^2), and if it lands tails, we toss it again; if on the third toss it lands heads, you receive £8 (= £2^3), and if it lands tails, we toss it again ... and so on *ad infinitum*. Thus on the nth toss, a head wins you £2^n, while a tail leads to a further toss. Now, assuming the coin is fair, the probability of a head on the first toss is $\frac{1}{2}$; the probability of a head on the second toss (the sequence, a tail then a head) is $(\frac{1}{2})^2$; and the probability of a sequence of $n - 1$ tails and then a head on the nth toss is $(\frac{1}{2})^n$. Therefore, the expected value of the game is:

$$E = (\tfrac{1}{2})£2 + (\tfrac{1}{2})^2 £4 + (\tfrac{1}{2})^2 £8 + \ldots + (\tfrac{1}{2})^n £2^n + \ldots$$
$$= 1 + 1 + 1 + \ldots$$

   which is infinite, assuming nothing prevents us playing the game for ever. It has been noticed, however, that the maximum amount one would pay to take part in the game is, for most people, finite. Discuss possible explanations of this, and, in particular, what it might imply about the utility function $v(y)$.

4. Consider an accumulator bet on horse racing, known as a treble: the punter specifies three horses in successive races, and places a stake on the horse in the first race; if it wins, the winnings become the stake on the horse in the second race; if this wins, the winnings become the stake on the horse in the third race. Write down the 'treble' in the notation for prospects, assuming the punter assigns probabilities to the events of each horse winning its race. Now derive the rational equivalent of this prospect. How many outcomes does it have? Suppose that the punter also has the option of making three separate bets on each of the races, the bet on the second race being laid after the result of the first is known, and the bet on the third race being made after the result of the second is known. Describe this option as a prospect, and compare it with the treble. Discuss possible reasons for a punter preferring the treble.

5. Choose someone with enough patience, and try to construct their utility function for incomes over the range £0–£100 a week, in the manner suggested by the section. Note the problems you encounter, and relate them to the axioms set out above.

D. Properties of the utility function

The axioms set out in the previous section imply certain properties of the utility function $v(y)$. It increases with income, y; it is uniquely defined *relative to* the values y_u and y_L; and it is bounded above by the value 1 and below by the value 0. Moreover, as we shall see, the fact that the decision-taker can be assumed to act as if he maximized expected utility implies a further important property of the function. But there are certain properties of the function which we would like it to have but which are not implied by the axioms set out so far, and so further assumptions have to be made to endow it with them. We shall consider these assumptions first and then look at the properties already implied by the axioms of the previous section.

For the kinds of analysis we wish to carry out, it is useful if the utility function is differentiable at least twice in its entire domain, that is, if the derivatives $v'(y)$ and $v''(y)$ exist for all y in the interval $[y_L, y_u]$. Thus we make the assumption that the utility function is at least twice differentiable, at all income levels in the given domain. Call $v'(y)$ the *marginal utility of income*. $v''(y)$ is the rate at which marginal utility of income changes with income. Note that the differentiability assumption implies that the utility function is continuous.

The second assumption concerns the attitude of the decision-taker towards risk. Suppose he is confronted with a prospect $P = (\pi, y_1, y_2)$. The expected value of the outcomes is $\bar{y} = \pi y_1 + (1 - \pi)y_2$. Define the *certainty equivalent* of the prospect, y_c, as that value of income which satisfies

$$y_c \sim P \tag{D.1}$$

or equivalently

$$v(y_c) = \bar{v} = \pi v(y_1) + (1 - \pi)v(y_2) \tag{D.2}$$

y_c is the amount of income which, if received for certain, would be regarded by the decision-taker as just as good as the prospect P. [D.1] says that y_c is indifferent to P, and [D.2] that its utility must equal the expected utility of P, which, in the light of the analysis in the previous section, is an equivalent statement.

Consider the three possible relationships between the certainty equivalent, y_c, and the expected value of the outcomes, $\bar{y}$.

(a) $y_c = \bar{y}$. The decision-taker values the prospect at its expected value. For example, offered a bet that if a fair coin lands heads he will receive £6, and if it lands tails he must pay £4, he would certainly accept the bet. When his original income is y the choice is between the prospect $P^1 = (0.5, y + £6, y - £4)$, and the prospect $P^2 = (1, y, y)$ since to refuse the bet is to accept the certainty of no income gain. The expected value of the prospect P^2 is $\bar{y}^2 = y$, while that of P^1 is $\bar{y}^1 = £1 + y$. But since certainty equivalents equal expected values, and $v(y + 1) > v(y)$, he must prefer P^1 and so will take the bet. Indeed, he would be prepared to pay anything up to £1 for the opportunity to engage in the bet, since the expected value of his winnings, £1 *minus* what he pays, will still be positive. In general terms in this case

$$\pi v(y_1) + (1 - \pi)v(y_2) = \bar{v} = v(y_c) = v(\bar{y}) \tag{D.3}$$

where $\bar{y} = \pi y_1 + (1 - \pi)y_2$. A preference ordering over alternative prospects can then be based entirely on the expected values of the outcomes of the prospects, with higher expected value always being preferred to lower.

(b) $y_c < \bar{y}$. The decision-taker values the prospect at less than its expected value. For example, given the above example of the prospect $P^1 = (0.5,\, y + £6,\, y - £4)$ we can no longer be sure that it will be accepted in preference to the prospect $P^2 = (1,\, y,\, y)$, and the decision-taker would certainly pay less than £1 for the opportunity to take it. In general terms,

$$\pi v(y_1) + (1 - \pi)v(y_2) = \bar{v} = v(y_c) < v(\bar{y}) \qquad [D.4]$$

In this case a preference ordering over alternative prospects could *not* be based on the expected values of outcomes, since they overstate the values of the prospects. To predict the rankings we would need to know the utility function or the certainty equivalents.

(c) $y_c > \bar{y}$. The decision-taker values the prospect at more than its expected value. In our previous example, he would certainly accept the prospect P^1, since $y_c > \bar{y} > y$, while he would actually be prepared to pay more than $\bar{y} - y = £1$ for the opportunity to take the gamble. In general terms,

$$\pi v(y_1) + (1 - \pi)v(y_2) = \bar{v} = v(y_c) > v(\bar{y}) \qquad [D.5]$$

Again, a preference ordering over prospects could not be based on the expected values of outcomes, since these now *understate* the values of the prospects. To predict the ranking we would again need to know the utility function or the certainty equivalents.

The three cases provide a way of classifying attitudes to risk, based on a comparison of the certainty equivalent and expected value. In the first case, where prospects are valued at their expected values, the decision-taker is *risk neutral*; in the second, where prospects are valued at less than their expected values, he is *risk-averse*; and in the third case he is *risk-attracted*. As we shall see later, there are strong arguments for regarding risk-aversion as typical.

We consider now the implications of these three cases for the utility function $v(y)$. First recall (Appendix B) the definitions of convex and concave functions. Given some function $f(y)$, defined on a convex set Y, the function is concave if and only if

$$f(\bar{y}) \geqslant kf(y_1) + (1 - k)f(y_2) \qquad 0 \leqslant k \leqslant 1 \qquad y_1, y_2 \in Y \qquad [D.6]$$

where $\bar{y} = ky_1 + (1 - k)y_2$. A linear function satisfies [D.6] as an equality, while a *strictly* concave function satisfies it as a strict inequality. But in equations [D.3], [D.4] and [D.5], if we replace k by the probability π (defined on precisely the same interval), and replace f by v, we see that case (a), risk neutrality, corresponds to a linear utility function (at least over the range $[y_1, y_2]$), while case (b), risk aversion, corresponds to a strictly concave utility function (over the range $[y_1, y_2]$), Moreover, the function $f(y)$ is strictly convex if $-f(y)$ is strictly concave, and so case (c), risk attraction, corresponds to a strictly convex utility function. Figure 17.1 illustrates these propositions. In (a) of the figure, the utility function $v(y)$ is strictly concave. Corresponding to the income levels y_1, y_2 are the utility values $v(y_1)$, $v(y_2)$, at points a and b respectively. Given a value of π, the expected value $\bar{y} = \pi y_1 + (1 - \pi)y_2$ will lie somewhere between y_1 and y_2. Consider the straight line ab, whose end points are at the values $v(y_1)$ and $v(y_2)$ respectively. The expected utility of the prospect $P = (\pi, y_1, y_2)$ is at point c, on the line ab directly above the expected value of

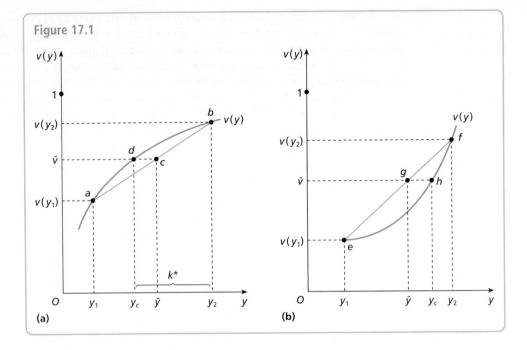

Figure 17.1

the prospect, $\bar{y} = \pi y_1 + (1 - \pi)y_2$. Thus, since the slope of the straight line ab is $[v(y_2) - v(y_1)]/(y_2 - y_1)$, letting $f(y)$ denote its height at y, we have

$$f(y) = v(y_1) + \frac{[v(y_2) - v(y_1)](y - y_1)}{y_2 - y_1} \qquad [\text{D.7}]$$

In particular the height of the line at c above $\bar{y} = \pi y_1 + (1 - \pi)y_2$ is

$$f(y) = v(y_1) + \frac{[v(y_2) - v(y_1)][\pi y_1 + (1 - \pi)y_2 - y_1]}{y_2 - y_1}$$

$$= v(y_1) + \frac{[v(y_2) - v(y_1)](1 - \pi)(y_2 - y_1)}{y_2 - y_1}$$

$$= v(y_1) + [v(y_2) - v(y_1)](1 - \pi)$$

$$= \pi v(y_1) + (1 - \pi)v(y_2) = \bar{v} \qquad [\text{D.8}]$$

which gives $\bar{v}$ as point c in the figure.

We can now find the certainty equivalent of the prospect P, the income which satisfies

$$v(y_c) = \bar{v} \qquad [\text{D.9}]$$

It is given by y_c in the figure since, at point d, the utility of y, received for certain, is equal to the expected utility of the prospect. Thus, we see the equivalence between the inequality $y_c < \bar{y}$, and the strict concavity of the utility function. Each can represent the assumption of risk aversion.

In (b) of the figure, $v(y)$ is strictly convex. $\bar{y}$ again shows the expected value of income, for a particular choice of π, and the expected utility $\bar{v}$ is given by g in the figure. Now, however, the certainty equivalent is $y_c > \bar{y}$, since $v(y_c) = \bar{v}$ at h. Thus, risk attraction is equivalent to a strictly convex utility function, or to a certainty equivalent in excess of the expected value of income.

Risk neutrality could be illustrated in either part of the figure. Take (a), and suppose that the utility function *is* the line drawn between a and b. Then $\bar{v} = v(\bar{y})$ (whereas in the strictly concave case $v(\bar{y}) > \bar{v}$), and $\bar{y}$ is the certainty equivalent of the prospect P. Hence, risk neutrality corresponds to the case of a linear utility function.

Risk premium

The risk averse individual in Fig. 17.1(a) will prefer to have a certain income of $\bar{y}$ rather than the risky prospect $P = (\pi, y_1, y_2)$, where $\bar{y}$ is the mean of the risky incomes y_1 and y_2. The risky prospect is costly to the risk averse individual in that it reduces expected utility compared with the certain prospect of $\bar{y}$. A monetary measure of the cost of risk can be obtained by asking the individual how much of his certain income he would be willing to give up rather than face the risky prospect. (Recall the discussion of the compensating variation in section 3C.) This sum of money r is the *risk premium* or the *cost of risk* and is defined by

$$v(\bar{y} - r) = \pi v(y_1) + (1 - \pi)v(y_2) = \bar{v} \qquad [\text{D.10}]$$

since the individual is indifferent between the risky prospect P with expected income $\bar{y}$ and the certain income $\bar{y} - r$.

Comparing [D.10] which defines the risk premium, with [D.9] which defines the certainty equivalent income y_c we see that

$$v(y_c) = \bar{v} = v(\bar{y} - r)$$

and we can equivalently define the risk premium for the prospect P by

$$r = \bar{y} - y_c \qquad [\text{D.11}]$$

In Fig. 17.1(a) the risk premium is the horizontal distance cd and shows how much the individual would be willing to pay rather than face a risky prospect with an expected income equal to his certain income $\bar{y}$.

If the individual is risk attracted, as in Fig. 17.1(b), he would have a larger expected utility with the risky prospect than with the certain income $\bar{y}$. The risk premium would be negative because he would be willing to pay to have P rather than the certainty of $\bar{y}$. Hence in Fig. 17.1(b), $r = \bar{y} - y_c < 0$.

A *fair bet* is one which leaves expected income unchanged, as for example if a gambler wins £5 if a coin turns up heads and loses £5 if it turns up tails. If an individual has a certain income of $\bar{y}$ then the prospect $P = (\pi, y_1, y_2)$ which yields an expected income of $\bar{y}$ is a fair bet since $\pi(y_1 - \bar{y}) + (1 - \pi)(y_2 - \bar{y}) = 0$. We can therefore equivalently define a risk averter as an individual who would refuse a fair bet since he will prefer $\bar{y}$ to P, i.e. $v(\bar{y}) > \bar{v}$. Similarly, risk preferers are made better off by fair bets and risk neutral individuals are indifferent to such bets.

There is yet another way to describe the decision-taker's attitude to risk. The differentiability assumption allows us to express convexity and concavity in terms of derivatives of the utility function. Thus marginal utility $v'(y)$ is the slope at a point of the curve $v(y)$ in Fig. 17.1, while the second derivative, $v''(y)$, is determined by the curvature. Thus, strict concavity over the range of y values implies that, at every point, $v''(y) < 0$, i.e. there is diminishing marginal utility of income. Similarly, strict convexity implies $v''(y) > 0$ or increasing marginal utility of income, and linearity implies $v''(y) = 0$ or constant marginal utility of income. A decision-taker is risk averse, risk attracted or risk neutral, as his marginal utility of income is decreasing, increasing or constant.

The different but equivalent characterizations of attitudes to risk are summarized in Table 17.1.

Table 17.1

	Risk aversion	Risk neutrality	Risk preference
Certainty equivalence	$y_c < \bar{y}$	$y_c = \bar{y}$	$y_c > \bar{y}$
Risk premium	$r > 0$	$r = 0$	$r < 0$
Fair bets	Reject	Indifferent	Accept
Utility function	Strictly concave	Linear	Strictly convex
	$v'' < 0$	$v'' = 0$	$v'' > 0$

Nothing in the axioms of section B implies a particular shape for the utility function or attitude to risk for individuals in general. The usual assumption is that decision-takers are risk averse and so have strictly concave utility functions. Part of the reason for the assumption is empirical: most people behave in ways consistent with risk aversion rather than risk neutrality or risk preference. Offered a 50–50 chance of winning, say, £5000, or losing £5000, most people would reject the gamble. Another common example of risk averse behaviour is the purchase of insurance at a premium which is higher than would be actuarially fair (see section 19B).

Figure 17.1 raises the question: is it valid to ascribe a particular shape to the utility function $v(y)$ representing the preferences of a given individual who satisfies the axioms of section B; or, equivalently, to place restrictions on the sign of the second derivative $v''(y)$? Recall the discussion of the ordinal utility function in Chapter 2. We argued there that the utility function was unique only up to a positive monotonic transformation. It could not be specified as 'convex' or 'concave', since functions of both kinds could be permissible representations of the preferences satisfying the axioms stated in the chapter. Indeed, this provided the motivation for the introduction of the concepts of quasi-concavity and quasi-convexity. If $v(y)$ *were* an ordinal utility function, we could not place a sign restriction on its second derivative. For example, if $v = \sqrt{y}$ were a permissible ordinal utility function, with $v''(y) = -\frac{1}{4}y^{-3/2} < 0$, so would be $g = v^2$, or $g = v^4$, which have zero and positive second derivatives, respectively. The implicit assumption in the preceding discussion of attitudes to risk that it is meaningful to place sign restrictions on $v''(y)$ hints that the utility function $v(y)$ is not an ordinal utility function.

The utility function $v(y)$ is *not a unique* representation of the decision-taker's preferences. By changing one or both of the outcomes in the standard prospect we would obtain, for each certain income y, a different probability v at which the decision-taker would be indifferent between the certain income and the standard prospect. Figure 17.2 illustrates. In (a) of the figure, we assume first that $v(y)$ is measured against a standard prospect containing y_L and y_u, and then we replace y_L by $y'_L < y_L$. We then obtain the new utility function, denoted $g(y)$, for which we must

Figure 17.2

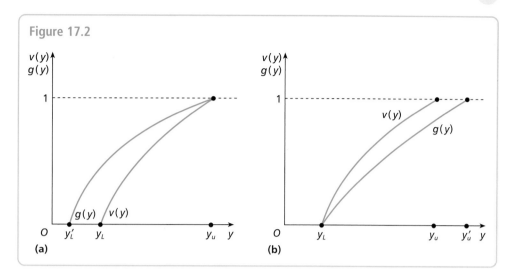

have $g(y_L') = 0$, $g(y_u) = 1$ and $g(y) > v(y)$ for $y_L < y < y_u$ (explain why). Thus $g(y)$ and $v(y)$ must bear the general relationship to each other shown in the figure. In (b) of the figure, we assume $v(y)$ is as before, while $g(y)$ is obtained by replacing y_u with y_u' in the standard prospect. Here, we must have $g(y_L) = 0$, $g(y_u') = 1$ and $g(y) < v(y)$ for $y_L < y < y_u$ (explain why), and so the general relationship between the two functions is as shown in the figure.

Although the utility function representing preferences satisfying the axioms of expected utility cannot be unique, the relationship among all possible utility functions, of which $v(y)$ and $g(y)$ are examples, is much more restricted than among the ordinal utility functions which represent consumer preferences under certainty. We can show that any two utility functions $v(y)$ and $g(y)$ for a particular decision-taker whose preferences conform to our axioms must satisfy the linear relationship:

$$g(y) = a + bv(y) \qquad b > 0 \qquad\qquad [D.12]$$

As the level of certain income varies, the utility numbers obtained by use of one standard prospect must vary linearly with those obtained by use of a different standard prospect. Figure 17.3 illustrates. A given income level, y, implies a pair of values (v, g) (such as at α), and, as the income value varies, through y^1 to y^3, the pair of utility values varies along the line through β to γ. The restriction on the class of permissible utility functions is strong. The utility function $v(y)$ is unique up to a *positive linear* transformation (cf. the ordinal utility function's property of uniqueness up to a *positive monotonic* transformation). The restriction justifies attaching significance to the sign of $v''(y)$, since, if $g(y)$ must satisfy [D.12], $g''(y)$ must have the same sign (see Question 4, Exercise 17D).

The property of uniqueness up to a linear transformation is implied by the axioms. Take three income values $y^1 < y^2 < y^3$, and let π be the probability that

$$y^2 \sim (\pi, y^1, y^3) \qquad\qquad [D.13]$$

The decision-taker is indifferent between y^2 for certain and a prospect with y^1 and y^3. (The axioms imply that such a π always exists.) Then

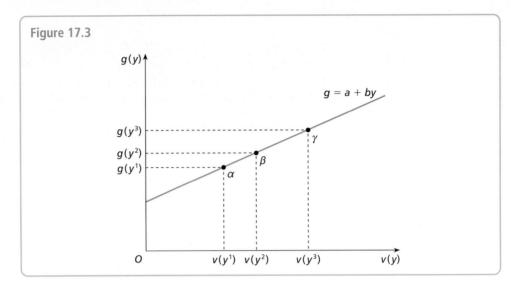

Figure 17.3

$$v(y^2) = \pi v(y^1) + (1 - \pi)v(y^3) \qquad\qquad \text{[D.14]}$$

$$g(y^2) = \pi g(y^1) + (1 - \pi)g(y^3) \qquad\qquad \text{[D.15]}$$

for any two permissible utility functions $v(y)$ and $g(y)$. Given that the decision-taker conforms to our axioms, [D.14] and [D.15] are equivalent ways of expressing [D.13]. Writing [D.14] and [D.15] in vector notation gives

$$[v^2, g^2] = \pi[v^1, g^1] + (1 - \pi)[v^3, g^3] \qquad 0 \le \pi \le 1 \qquad\qquad \text{[D.16]}$$

where $v^2 = v(y^2)$, $g^2 = g(y^2)$, and so on. But [D.16] states that the pair of utility values (v^2, g^2) lie on the line joining the pair (v^1, g^1) with the pair (v^3, g^3), since it is equivalent to the standard expression for a convex combination of two vectors. Hence any two permissible functions $v(y)$ and $g(y)$ must be linearly related.

Uniqueness up to a positive *linear* transformation implies that the utility function $v(y)$ is a *cardinal* rather than an ordinal measure of utility. The von Neumann–Morgenstern axioms provide a measure of utility comparable to measures of temperature – the Fahrenheit and Centigrade scales are similarly linearly related. If the theory holds, utility is cardinally measurable. This does *not* mean that we have succeeded in 'measuring utility' as if utility were a physical magnitude in the same sense as weight or height. Nothing has been said about the 'amount' of intrinsic pleasure which the decision-taker receives from various amounts of income. The basis of the theory is still the ordering relation of preference or indifference, and the decision-taker's ability to compare and rank is the only aspect of his psychology in which we are interested. What we have shown is that, if his preferences satisfy a number of conditions of rationality and consistency, then he can be represented as acting *as if* he maximized the expected value of a numerical function which must therefore be cardinal. The label 'utility' attached, perhaps unfortunately, to the function implies nothing about the measurability of sensations of pleasure or satisfaction.

Measures of risk aversion

The risk premium r (cost of risk) defined in [D.10] depends on the individual's attitude to risk and the prospect she is confronted with. It will be larger the greater is the risk and the more risk averse the individual. We can make this explicit by a method of approximating the risk premium which shows how it depends on a measure of risk and on a measure of the individual's attitude to risk.

Suppose that an individual has a certain income $\bar{y}$. We offer her a bet which pays off z_s in state s where the probability of state s is π_s. Assume that the bet is fair: $Ez_s = \sum \pi_s z_s = 0$ and all the payoffs z_s (negative or positive) are small. Her income in state s with the bet is $y_s = \bar{y} + z_s$. Her expected income if she accepts the bet is unchanged since $\sum \pi_s y_s = \sum \pi_s(\bar{y} + z_s) = \bar{y} + \sum \pi_s z_s = \bar{y}$ but her expected utility will be reduced if she is risk averse. The risk premium for the bet is defined, as in the two-state case in [D.10], by

$$v(\bar{y} - r) = \sum \pi_s v(y_s) = \sum \pi_s v(\bar{y} + z_s) \qquad [D.17]$$

We can approximate $v(\bar{y} + z_s)$ by a second-order Taylor series expansion about $\bar{y}$:

$$v(y_s) = v(\bar{y} + z_s) \simeq v(\bar{y}) + v'(\bar{y})z_s + \tfrac{1}{2}v''(\bar{y})z_s^2 \qquad [D.18]$$

Similarly, we can approximate $v(\bar{y} - r)$ by a first-order expansion

$$v(\bar{y} - r) \simeq v(\bar{y}) - v'(\bar{y})r \qquad [D.19]$$

(Provided the z_s are small the risk premium r will also be small and the approximations will not be too inaccurate.) Multiplying both sides of [D.18] by the probabilities π_s and summing over all s gives

$$\sum \pi_s v(y_s) \simeq \sum \pi_s v(\bar{y}) + \sum \pi_s v'(\bar{y})z_s + \tfrac{1}{2}\sum \pi_s v''(\bar{y})z_s^2$$
$$= v(\bar{y}) \sum \pi_s + v'(\bar{y}) \sum \pi_s z_s + \tfrac{1}{2}v''(\bar{y}) \sum \pi_s z_s^2 \qquad [D.20]$$

Since the π_s are probabilities, $\sum \pi_s = 1$. The bet is fair and so $Ez_s = \sum \pi_s z_s = 0$. The variance of the z_s is $\sigma_z^2 = \sum \pi_s(z_s - Ez_s)^2 = \sum \pi_s z_s^2$. Thus [D.20] reduces to

$$\sum \pi_s v(y_s) \simeq v(\bar{y}) + \tfrac{1}{2}v''(\bar{y})\sigma_z^2 \qquad [D.21]$$

From the definition of the risk premium in [D.17] the right-hand sides of [D.19] and [D.21] must be approximately equal

$$v(\bar{y}) - v'(\bar{y})r \simeq v(\bar{y}) + \tfrac{1}{2}v''(\bar{y})\sigma_z^2$$

and rearranging gives an approximation to the cost of risk (the risk premium) as

$$r \simeq -\frac{1}{2}\frac{v''(\bar{y})}{v'(\bar{y})}\sigma_z^2 = \tfrac{1}{2}A(\bar{y})\sigma_z^2 \qquad [D.22]$$

[D.22] shows that the approximate risk premium depends on preferences (the first and second derivatives of the utility function) and the variance of the bet. The first term $-v''(\bar{y})/v'(\bar{y}) \equiv A(\bar{y})$ in the approximation is known as the *Pratt–Arrow coefficient of absolute risk aversion* and is a useful measure of attitude to risk.

If the individual is risk averse ($v'' < 0$) A is positive. A depends on the individual's income and may increase or decrease as income varies. Larger As lead to a larger risk premium. Although $A(y)$ appears as part of an approximation to the risk premium its usefulness does not depend on the accuracy of the approximation. As we see in the next chapter, making assumptions about $A(y)$ enables us to predict how the decision-taker will respond to changes in her uncertain environment even when the risks or bets are large and [D.22] would not be a useful approximation.

Risk aversion is related to the concavity of the utility function but using v'' as a measure of attitudes to risk is only valid if we are interested in very crude distinctions, i.e. between risk aversion ($v'' < 0$), risk neutrality ($v'' = 0$) and risk preference ($v'' > 0$). As the discussion of the permissible ways in which we can numerically represent preferences in risky situations showed, the utility function for a decision-maker with given preferences is unique only up to positive linear transformations. Statements about v'' being negative, positive or zero convey information about preferences but statements about v'' being larger or smaller at some given level of income do not. We could make the second derivative of the utility function as large or small as we like by choosing some other, equivalent representation of preferences. If $v(y)$ represents preferences so will $g(y) = a + bv(y)$ if $b > 0$ and so $g''(y) = bv''(y)$ could be made greater or less than v'' by suitable choice of b. Part of the usefulness of the coefficient of absolute risk aversion is that it is *not* affected by such linear transformations. It has the same value whatever acceptable numerical representation of preferences is used. If $g = a + bv(y)$ then

$$A(y) = \frac{-g''(y)}{g'(y)} = \frac{-bv''(y)}{bv'(y)} = \frac{-v''(y)}{v'(y)} \qquad \text{[D.23]}$$

The coefficient of absolute risk aversion conveys information about the decision-taker's preferences (i.e. attitude to risk), not about particular numerical representations of them. Only differences in attitude to risk (as income varies or across different decision-takers) will affect A.

$A(y)$ was introduced in deriving an approximation to the cost of risk r. r is measured in monetary units (income) and is the absolute amount of money the decision-maker would give up rather than face a risky prospect. It is often useful to have a measure of the risk premium or cost of risk which does not depend on the monetary units. One obvious measure is the relative cost of risk or relative risk premium which is the risk premium as a proportion of mean income: $r/\bar{y}$. We can derive an approximation for the relative risk premium which relates it to a measure of the individual's attitude to risk and a measure of the riskiness of the prospect. (We leave the steps in the argument to the exercises since they are very similar to those for the absolute risk premium.) The relative or proportional risk premium is approximately

$$\frac{r}{\bar{y}} \simeq -\frac{1}{2} \frac{v''(\bar{y})\bar{y}}{v'(\bar{y})} \left[\frac{\sigma_z}{\bar{y}} \right]^2 = \frac{1}{2} R(\bar{y}) \left[\frac{\sigma_z}{\bar{y}} \right]^2 \qquad \text{[D.24]}$$

where $\sigma_z/\bar{y}$ is the *coefficient of variation* for the prospect and $R(y) \equiv -v''(y)y/v'(y)$ is the *Pratt–Arrow coefficient of relative risk aversion*. Note that $R(y)$ is the negative of the *elasticity of marginal utility of income* and measures the responsiveness of marginal utility to changes in income in a way which is independent of the particular utility function used to represent preferences and of the units in which income is measured.

$R(y)$ is useful in circumstances in which [D.24] would not be a sensible approximation and it is not affected by the particular utility function used to represent preferences. Since $R = Ay$ assumptions about R frequently place restrictions on A and vice versa.

EXERCISE 17D

1. Someone is offered a 50–50 chance of winning £21 or losing £20, and she rejects it. Which of the following reasons for her rejection are consistent with the expected utility theory:

   (a) She never gambles, because she believes gambling to be morally wrong.

   (b) She is sure she will lose, because she is always unlucky at gambling.

   (c) The £20 she might lose is worth more to her than the £21 she might win.

   (d) She cannot afford to risk £20.

   (e) She has better ways of risking £20.

   (f) She does not have £20.

2. Under the expected utility formulation of this chapter, the utility number associated with a given income is independent of the state of the world in which that income is to be received. Give reasonably plausible examples which suggest that the utility of income could depend on the state of the world in which it will be received. What part of the axiom system implicitly ruled out such dependence?

3. It has been observed that an individual will, in insuring himself against loss, pay a premium greater than the expected value of his loss; and, at the same time accept a gamble whose expected value is negative (for example by buying a premium bond). Explain why this appears to contradict the assumption of risk aversion. Suggest ways in which the observation of such behaviour could be made consistent with the analysis.

4. Given the relation between utility functions: $g(y) = a + bv(y)$, $a, b > 0$, use the definition of concave functions to prove that, if v is concave, so must be g. Extend this to show that any function $\bar{v}(y)$, which is a linear combination of concave functions, v_s, of the form

$$\bar{v}(y) = \sum_{s=1}^{S} \pi_s v_s(y_s) \qquad 1 > \pi_s > 0 \qquad \sum_s \pi_s = 1$$

   is itself a concave function.

5. Give an explanation of why, in Fig. 17.2(a), $g(y)$ lies above $v(y)$, and in Fig. 17.2(b), $g(y)$ lies below $v(y)$, in terms of the choice between each income value and each of the standard prospects.

6. In Alexander Pushkin's short story 'Queen of Spades', Herrman explains his refusal to gamble by the statement: 'I am not in a position to sacrifice the essential in the hope of acquiring the superfluous.' Rationalize this in terms of expected utility theory.

7. Construct a numerical example to show that, if the utility function $v(y)$ were an *ordinal* function, i.e. unique up to a positive monotonic transformation, then two permissible utility functions could be found, such that with one of them prospect P^1 is preferred to prospect P^2, and with the other the converse is true.

8. Show that the risk premium and the certainty equivalent income are not affected by whether $v(y)$ or $g(y)$ is used to represent the individual's preferences if $g(y) = a + bv(y)$ with $b > 0$.

9. Suppose that two individuals have utility functions $v(y)$ and $g(y)$ and $g(y) = f(v(y))$ is an increasing concave transformation ($f' > 0$, $f'' < 0$) of v. Show that the individual with the utility function $g(y)$ has greater absolute and relative risk aversion. Use the approximation [D.22] to show that she will also have a larger risk premium.

10. Consider the following utility functions:

    (a) $v = a - b\exp(-Ay)$

    (b) $v = a + by^{(1-R)}/(1 - R)$

    (c) $v = a + b\ln y$

where the parameters b, A and $R \neq 1$ are all positive and ln denotes the natural logarithm. Show that (a) has a constant absolute risk aversion of A, that (b) has constant relative risk aversion of R and that (c) has constant relative risk aversion of 1. Show that these are the *only* utility functions with these properties. (*Hint:* integrate $-v''(y)/v'(y) = A$ twice to get (a) and proceed similarly for constant relative risk aversion.)

11. Consider the *quadratic utility function* $v = a + by + cy^2$. (a) For what range of incomes and for what restrictions on the parameters a, b and c is it a sensible specification for an individual who is risk averse? (b) Show that with the utility function the individual is only interested in the mean and variance of the state distribution of income. (c) Sketch the indifference curves in mean, variance space.

E. Risk aversion and indifference curves

As we saw in earlier chapters it is often helpful to be able to represent the decision-taker's preferences by an indifference map. Under uncertainty the decision-taker's objective function is expected utility and with two possible states

$$V = \pi_1 v(y_1) + \pi_2 v(y_2) \qquad \text{[E.1]}$$

where y_s is income in state $s = 1, 2$ and π_s the probability she assigns to state s. A risk-averse individual has a strictly concave $v(y_s)$ and V is strictly concave in (y_1, y_2) (see Question 4, Exercise 17D). A contour of the expected utility function in state-contingent income space is the set of (y_1, y_2) combinations yielding the same expected utility:

$$V^0 = \pi_1 v(y_1) + \pi_2 v(y_2) \qquad \text{[E.2]}$$

Figure 17.4 illustrates, in state-contingent income space, the same situations as shown in Fig. 17.1(a) in section D. State 1 and 2 incomes are plotted along the horizontal and vertical axes respectively and the curve I^0 is a typical indifference

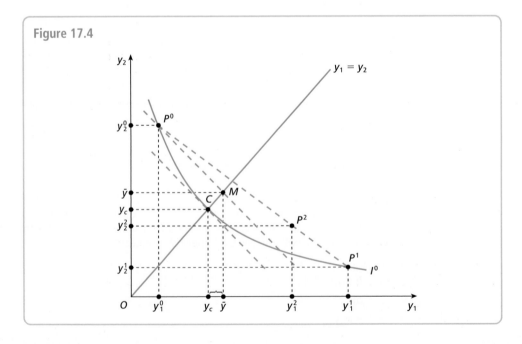

Figure 17.4

curve showing combinations of (y_1, y_2) which yield the same expected utility V^0 (where $V^0 = \bar{v}$ in Fig. 17.1(a)). We denote the particular levels of state s income in the prospect P in Fig. 17.1(a) by y_s^0 (so that, for example, y_1 in Fig. 17.1(a) is now y_1^0 in Fig. 17.4). The decision-taker faces the same prospect as in Fig. 17.1(a) and is thus at P^0 in Fig. 17.4 where $y_1 = y_1^0$, $y_2 = y_2^0$.

The indifference curve is very similar to those in the theory of the consumer. Differentiate [E.2] to obtain

$$\frac{dV}{dy_1} = \pi_1 v'(y_1) + \pi_2 v'(y_2)\frac{dy_2}{dy_1} = 0$$

Rearranging this gives the slope of the indifference curve:

$$\frac{dy_2}{dy_1} = -\frac{\pi_1 v'(y_1)}{\pi_2 v'(y_2)} \qquad [E.3]$$

which is negative since probabilities and marginal utilities are positive. With given state probabilities, an increase in income in state 1 is required to compensate for a reduction in state 2 income. If $y_1 = y_2$ the individual has a certain income and is on the 45° line where the marginal utilities of state contingent income are equal: $v'(y_1) = v'(y_2)$. The slope of I^0 at the 45° line is

$$\frac{dy_2}{dy_1} = \frac{-\pi_1}{\pi_2} \qquad [E.4]$$

The individual's probability beliefs are reflected in Fig. 17.4 by the slope of the indifference curve at the 45° line.

The indifference curve is convex to the origin if the decision-maker is risk averse. Expected utility is a strictly concave function and thus must also be strictly quasi concave. (The convexity of the indifference curves of a risk averse decision-maker can also be established by differentiating [E.3] with respect to y_1, as in Question 1, Exercise 17E.)

We can also use Fig. 17.4 to illustrate the certainty equivalent income y_c and the risk premium r. The 45° line in Fig. 17.4 is known as the *certainty line* since along it the individual will have the same income whatever the state. The certainty equivalent income is the certain income which the individual would regard as equivalent to the risky prospect P^0. Since a certain income must be on the 45° line and all state contingent combinations regarded as equivalent to P^0 lie on the indifference curve I^0 through P^0, the certainty equivalent income is given by the intersection of I^0 and the 45° line at C where $y_1 = y_2 = y_c$. The individual would be indifferent between y_c in each state (i.e. for sure) and the risky prospect P^0. Combinations of y_1, y_2 which have the same expected value or mean satisfy

$$\pi_1 y_1 + \pi_2 y_2 = \bar{y} \qquad [E.5]$$

Differentiating [E.5] gives

$$\pi_1 + \pi_2 \frac{dy_2}{dy_1} = 0$$

and the slope of the *iso-expected income line* in y_1, y_2 space is

$$\frac{dy_2}{dy_1} = \frac{-\pi_1}{\pi_2} \qquad [E.6]$$

Iso-expected income lines are negatively sloped straight lines. All combinations of y_1, y_2 with the same expected value or mean will lie on a straight line with a slope of $-\pi_1/\pi_2$. To find expected income from a risky prospect, draw an iso-expected income line through the prospect to the 45° line. In Fig. 17.4 the mean income from the prospect P^0 is at the intersection M of the dashed iso-expected income line P^0M through P^0 and the 45° line. At M income in both states is equal to the mean income from the prospect, i.e. $\bar{y} = \pi_1 y_1^0 + \pi_2 y_2^0$. Note that from [E.4] and [E.6] the slopes of the line through P^0M and the line tangent to I^0 at C are equal.

The risk premium for the prospect can now be shown in Fig. 17.4. Since $r = \bar{y} - y_c$ (recall [D.11]) the risk premium is just the vertical or horizontal distance between M and C on the 45° line.

The figure also demonstrates another aspect of risk aversion: a preference for *diversification*. Suppose the individual had the two prospects P^0 and P^1 available. Since they are on the same indifference curve she is indifferent between them. Now a prospect P^2, which is formed by a fraction k ($0 < k < 1$) of prospect P^1 and a fraction $(1 - k)$ of prospect P^0, will give the state-contingent income vector

$$y^2 = (y_1^2, y_2^2) = ky^1 + (1 - k)y^0 = (ky_1^1 + (1 - k)y_1^0, ky_2^1 + (1 - k)y_2^0)$$

which lies on the straight line P^0P^1. Such a prospect could be regarded as a mixed portfolio of the initial prospects P^0, P^1. It is obvious from the figure that the diversified portfolio P^2 gives a larger expected utility than a portfolio consisting only of P^0 or only of P^1. P^2 will be on a higher indifference curve than P^0 and P^1. This is true for any pair of initial prospects which have the same initial expected utility and for any diversified portfolio formed from them, i.e. for all $k \in (0, 1)$.

Although the similarity of Fig. 17.4 to many of the diagrams of consumer theory is frequently instructive there are some important differences. Consider the interpretation of a point such as P^0 or P^1 in Fig. 17.4 and a point representing a consumption vector in the theory of the consumer under certainty. In the latter, all the components of the vector are available *ex post* as well as *ex ante* – the consumer would end up consuming the entire vector she chose. Under uncertainty, one and only one state of the world can occur, and *ex post* the decision-taker receives only one element of the vector. The choice of a point in (y_1, y_2) space is an *ex ante* choice of claims to income, made before the state of the world is known. Only one income claim is 'valid' or 'enforceable' when the uncertainty is resolved, namely the claim for income in that state which actually occurs. The points in (y_1, y_2) space are vectors of *state-contingent income claims*. The term 'state-contingent' emphasizes that a particular element y_s of the vector is only available to the decision-maker if state s occurs.

Indifference curves and the coefficients of risk aversion

In Fig. 17.5 the decision-taker initially has the certain prospect P^0. His preferences are represented by the utility function $v_a(y)$ and his indifference curve through P^0 is I_a^0. The set of prospects which he regards as at least as good as the certain prospect P^0 is the area on or above I_a^0. We define an increase in risk aversion as a reduced willingness to accept risks, i.e. the set of prospects he regards as at least as good as the certain prospect becomes smaller. In terms of Fig. 17.5 his preferences would now give rise to an indifference curve like I_b^0 so that the set of prospects at least as good as P^0 is smaller. Prospects like P^1 and P^2 which were previously better than P^0 are now worse. Since the individual's preferences have changed so must the utility function

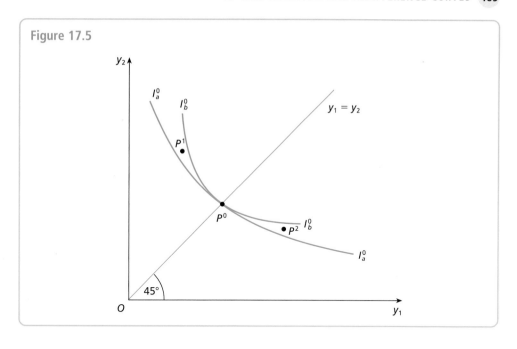

Figure 17.5

which represents them. His preferences are now represented by $v_b(y)$ which is *not* just a linear transformation of $v_a(y)$.

In section D we justified the usefulness of the coefficient of absolute risk aversion by showing that it could be linked to the risk premium and was independent of the particular utility function used to represent preferences. We now provide a further justification by showing that an increase in $A(y)$ implies that the individual is more risk averse in the sense that the set of prospects at least as good as the certain prospect is smaller. We do so by showing that an increase in $A(y)$ is equivalent to the indifference curves becoming more 'bowed in' near the 45° line, as in Fig. 17.5.

An indifference curve implicitly defines y_2 as a function of y_1:

$$y_2 = I(y_1) \qquad \text{[E.7]}$$

where $I(y_1)$ is the amount of y_2 necessary to yield a given expected utility for the specified amount of y_1. The slope of the indifference curve [E.3] can be written

$$\frac{dI(y_1)}{dy_1} = -\frac{\pi_1 v'(y_1)}{\pi_2 v'(y_2)} = -\frac{\pi_1 v'(y_1)}{\pi_2 v'(I(y_1))} \qquad \text{[E.8]}$$

The rate of change of the slope of an indifference curve is found by differentiating [E.8] with respect to y_1:

$$\frac{d^2 I(y_1)}{dy_1^2} = \frac{-\pi_1}{\pi_2 v'(y_2)^2}\left[v''(y_1)v'(I(y_1)) - v'(y_1)v''(I(y_1))\frac{dI}{dy_1} \right] \qquad \text{[E.9]}$$

At the 45° line $y_2 = I(y_1) = y_1$ and so $v''(y_2) = v''(I(y_1)) = v''(y_1)$, $v'(y_2) = v'(I(y_1)) = v'(y_1)$ and $dI(y_1)/dy_1 = -\pi_1/\pi_2$. Hence, on the 45° line [E.9] is

$$\frac{d^2 I(y_1)}{dy_1^2} = \frac{-v''(y)}{v'(y)}\left[1 + \frac{\pi_1}{\pi_2} \right]\frac{\pi_1}{\pi_2} = A(y)\frac{\pi_1}{\pi_2}\left[1 + \frac{\pi_1}{\pi_2} \right] \qquad \text{[E.10]}$$

Consider the slopes of I_a^0 and I_b^0 at P^0. Since $y_1 = y_2$ the slope of both indifference curves at P^0 is $-\pi_1/\pi_2$ (recall [E.4]) and we have $dI_b^0/dy_1 = dI_a^0/dy_1$. On the other hand,

$$\frac{d^2 I_b^0}{dy_1^2} > \frac{d^2 I_a^0}{dy_1^2} \qquad \text{[E.11]}$$

Since I_b^0 lies above I_a^0 to the right or left of P^0, its slope is becoming less negative more rapidly. Since the probabilities are not affected by the change in preferences we can use [E.10] to show that [E.11] is equivalent to

$$A_a(y) \equiv \frac{-v_a''(y)}{v_a'(y)} < \frac{-v_b''(y)}{v_b'(y)} \equiv A_b(y) \qquad \text{[E.12]}$$

We have thus established that, if an individual's coefficient of absolute risk aversion increases, his indifference curves become more 'bowed in' near the 45° line and he will be less willing to accept risky prospects.

Even with given preferences the individual's attitude to risk may vary with income. We now consider how assumptions about the relationship between attitude to risk, measured by the coefficients of risk aversion, and income manifest themselves in the shape of the indifference map. In Fig. 17.6 the horizontal distance from P^0 to the 45° line shows the absolute risk $|y_1^0 - y_2^0|$ associated with the prospect P^0. The prospect P^1 has larger incomes in both states but the difference between y_1^1 and y_2^1 is the same as in prospect P^0 and the line $P^1 P^0$ is parallel to the 45° line. The individual's attitude to risk is shown by her willingness to accept a reduction in y_2 in return for an increase in y_1, i.e. her willingness to accept an increase in absolute risk $|y_1 - y_2|$. This willingness is shown by the slope of her indifference curves at P^0 and P^1. If I^0 and I^1 have the same slope at P^0 and P^1 then her attitude to risk is unaffected by the increase in income of Δy in both states.

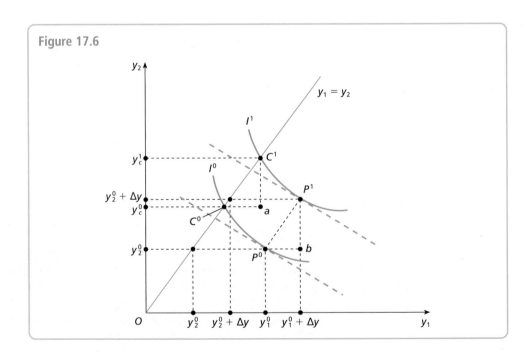

Figure 17.6

Along a line like P^1P^0 which is parallel to the 45° line, $|y_1 - y_2|$ is constant and $y_2 = y_1 - k$, where $k = y_1 - y_2$ is the constant difference in incomes. Thus the slope of the indifference curves along such a line is

$$\frac{dy_2}{dy_1} = \frac{-\pi_1 v'(y_1)}{\pi_2 v'(y_2)} = \frac{-\pi_1 v'(y_1)}{\pi_2 v'(y_1 - k)} \qquad [\text{E.13}]$$

Differentiation of [E.13] with respect to y_1 shows how the slopes of indifference curves alter as the individual's incomes in both states increase at the same rate:

$$\frac{d}{dy_1} \left[\frac{-\pi_1 v'(y_1)}{\pi_2 v'(y_1 - k)} \right] = \frac{-\pi_1}{\pi_2} \frac{1}{v'(y_1 - k)^2} [v''(y_1) v'(y_1 - k) - v'(y_1) v''(y_1 - k)]$$

$$= \frac{\pi_1 v'(y_1)}{\pi_2 v'(y_2)} \left[\frac{-v''(y_1)}{v'(y_1)} + \frac{v''(y_2)}{v'(y_2)} \right]$$

$$= \frac{\pi_1}{\pi_2} \frac{v'(y_1)}{v'(y_2)} [A(y_1) - A(y_2)] \qquad [\text{E.14}]$$

Since probabilities and marginal utilities are positive, the sign of [E.14] depends on the change in the coefficient of absolute risk aversion between y_1 and y_2. If A does not vary with income then [E.14] is zero and the slopes of the indifference curves at P^0 and P^1 are the same. Thus a constant coefficient of absolute risk aversion implies a constant marginal willingness to accept an increase in absolute risk as income increases in both states. An increased willingness to accept an increase in absolute risk would imply that the indifference curves became steeper along P^0P^1. A steeper indifference curve indicates that a given reduction in y_2 can be compensated by a smaller increase in y_1. An increased willingness to accept absolute risk would also imply a smaller coefficient of absolute risk aversion at higher incomes: $A(y_1) < A(y_2)$ when $y_1 > y_2$. If $A(y_1) < A(y_2)$ then [E.14] is negative and the slopes of the indifference curves become more negative and steeper as income in both states is increased by equal amounts as the individual moves along P^0P^1.

The risk premium $r = \bar{y} - y_c$ also shows the individual's attitude to risk and assumptions about the effect of increases in income on A or on the indifference map can also be made in terms of the effect of increases in income on r. The change in the risk premium caused by the increase in income in both states of Δy (i.e. the movement from P^0 to P^1) is

$$r^1 - r^0 = (\bar{y}^0 + \Delta y - y_c^1) - (\bar{y}^0 - y_c^0) = \Delta y - (y_c^1 - y_c^0) \qquad [\text{E.15}]$$

where y_c^1, y_c^0 are the certainty equivalent incomes for P^1, P^0 and the mean income at P^1 is the mean income at P^0 plus Δy (the increase in income in both states). If the slopes of the indifference curves are unaffected by equal changes in y_1 and y_2 then the 45° distance between I^0 and I^1 is the same at all points along I^0. In particular the distance along the 45° line from I^0 to I^1 (C^0C^1) is the same as the distance along P^0P^1. But the intersection of I^0 and the 45° line at C^0 defines the certainty equivalent income y_c^0 for P^0 and similarly for the intersection of I^1 and the 45° line at C^1. Since P^0P^1 and C^0C^1 are parallel and equal, the distance aC^1 is equal to bP^1. But $bP^1 = \Delta y$ (the increase in mean income) and $aC^1 = y_c^1 - y_c^0$ (the increase in certainty equivalent income). Hence [E.15] is zero and the risk premium is unaffected by equal increases in state incomes if the individual has constant absolute risk aversion or, equivalently, her indifference curves have a constant slope along lines parallel to the

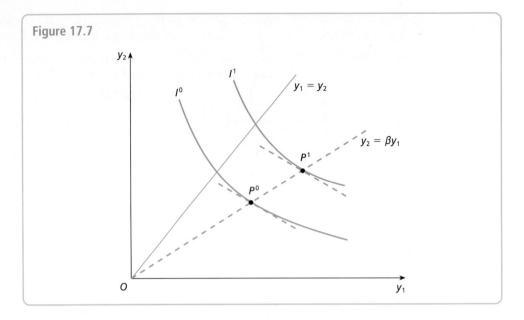

Figure 17.7

45° line. It is left to the reader to show that decreasing absolute risk aversion is equivalent to the risk premium decreasing with equal increases in all state incomes.

Assumptions about the coefficient of relative risk aversion $R(y) = A(y)y = -v''(y)y/v'(y)$ will also have implications for the shape of the indifference map and vice versa. A measure of relative risk in the case of prospects with two states is the ratio of the larger income to the smaller (y_1^0/y_2^0 in Fig. 17.7 where $y_1^0/y_2^0 > 1$ at P^0). Relative risk is constant along a ray from the origin. Thus prospect P^1 in Fig. 17.7 has the same relative risk as P^0 although income in both states is proportionally larger than at P^0: $y_s^1 = \lambda y_s^0$ and $y_1^1/y_2^1 = \lambda y_1^0/\lambda y_2^0 = y_1^0/y_2^0 = 1/\beta$. The individual's attitude to the risky prospects is indicated by her willingness to reduce y_2 in exchange for increases in y_1, i.e. by the slopes of I^0 and I^1 at P^0 and P^1. Along the line P^0P^1 y_2 is proportional to $y_1 : y_2 = \beta y_1$ and thus the slope of indifference curves along P^0P^1 is

$$\frac{-\pi_1 v'(y_1)}{\pi_2 v'(y_2)} = \frac{-\pi_1 v'(y_1)}{\pi_2 v'(\beta y_1)}$$

The slope of the indifference curves along P^0P^1 changes at the rate

$$\frac{d}{dy_1}\left[\frac{-\pi_1 v'(y_1)}{\pi_2 v'(\beta y_1)}\right] = \frac{-\pi_1}{\pi_2}\frac{1}{v'(y_2)^2}[v''(y_1)v'(\beta y_1) - v'(y_1)v''(\beta y_1)\beta]$$

$$= \frac{-\pi_1}{\pi_2}\frac{v'(y_1)v'(y_2)}{v'(y_2)^2}\left[\frac{v''(y_1)}{v'(y_1)} - \frac{v''(y_2)}{v'(y_2)}\frac{y_2}{y_1}\right]$$

$$= \frac{\pi_1}{\pi_2}\frac{v'(y_1)}{v'(y_2)}\frac{1}{y_1}[R(y_1) - R(y_2)] \qquad [\text{E.16}]$$

Hence if the individual has constant relative risk aversion ($R(y_1) = R(y_2)$) her indifference curves have a constant slope along P^0P^1, i.e. along rays from the origin. The relationship between R, the indifference curves and the relative risk premium $r/\bar{y}$ is analogous to those for absolute risk aversion and reinforces the basic message: attitudes to risk can be characterized in a variety of equivalent ways. Which characterization is most appropriate will depend on the particular issues being discussed.

EXERCISE 17E

1. Show that if the individual has a concave utility function indifference curves must be convex towards the origin. What do the indifference curves of risk attracted individuals look like? (*Hint*: differentiate [E.3] with respect to y_1, remembering that y_2 varies with y_1 to keep the individual on the same indifference curve.)

2. *Risk neutrality.* Show that a risk neutral individual has indifference curves which are straight lines with slope $-\pi_1/\pi_2$.

3. What is the effect on the indifference curve in Fig. 17.4 of an increase in the probability of state 1?

4. Suppose that the individual has decreasing absolute risk aversion. What would her indifference curves look like? (*Hint*: would the locus of y_1, y_2 combinations along which the indifference curves had the same slope be flatter or steeper than the 45° line?)

5. Use the particular forms of the utility function of Question 10, Exercise 17D to confirm the implications of constant absolute or constant relative risk aversion for the shape of the indifference curves.

6. Suppose that the utility function $m(y)$ is an increasing concave transformation of the utility function $v(y)$: $m(y) = g(v(y))$, $g' > 0$, $g'' < 0$. What effect does the transformation have on the indifference curves in state-contingent income space? Show that the certainty equivalent income falls and the risk premium increases. Show that an individual with $m(y)$ is more risk averse than an individual with $v(y)$ in the sense that the coefficient of risk aversion is greater at all income levels: $A^m(y) = -m''/m' > A^v = -v''/v'$.

7. *Infinite risk aversion.* An individual is infinitely risk averse if he is only concerned about the worst possible outcome of a risky prospect: $\min_s\{y_1, y_2, \ldots, y_s\}$ and ignores all other outcomes and the state probabilities.

   (a) What do his indifference curves look like?

   (b) Apply the transformation $f(u) = -u^{-\alpha}$ to a concave utility function $u(y)$, $\alpha > 0$. Check that the transformation is concave and thus that the utility function $g(y) = f(u(y))$ has greater risk aversion than $u(y)$.

   (c) Show that in the limit as $\alpha \to \infty$ the individual becomes infinitely risk averse in that his ordering of prospects by their expected utility $\sum \pi_s g(y_s)$ is equivalent to ordering them by $\min_s\{y_1, \ldots, y_s\}$.

8. *Decreasing risk aversion.* Show that individuals who have decreasing risk aversion $A'(y) < 0$ must have $v''' > 0$.

F. Measures of risk

In the previous section we examined different methods of characterizing *attitude to risk*. In this section we consider how to describe the *riskiness of the decision-taker's situation* in ways which are intuitively appealing and analytically tractable. One intuitive criterion for judging whether a measure of risk is useful is that an increase in the riskiness of the distribution of state contingent incomes measured in this way should make risk-averse individuals worse off, have no effect on risk-neutral individuals and make risk-attracted individuals better off. The fact that risk-neutral individuals only care about the expected value of their income implies that the measure of risk that we use should indicate that the 'riskiness' of the state distribution of incomes has increased if mean income is unchanged but risk-averse individuals are made worse off and risk lovers better off.

Range

When there are only two states of the world it is possible to describe the amount of risk facing an individual by the absolute or relative range of incomes: i.e. by $|y_2 - y_1|$ or y_2/y_1. These absolute or relative distances from the 45° certainty line where $y_1 = y_2$ are crude measures of risk in that they ignore the probabilities of the states. When there are more than two states the absolute or relative difference between the largest and smallest state-contingent incomes are even more suspect because they take no account of states in which income is less than the maximum and greater than the minimum. As an illustration of the weaknesses of the measures consider the two prospects in the next subsection where the prospect P^b has the same mean and a greater absolute and relative range of incomes than the prospect P^a. With the risk-averse utility function $v(y) = \sqrt{y}$, the prospect P^b yields greater expected utility than P^a.

Variance

The variance seems an obvious measure of risk: it takes account of all the state contingent incomes and their probabilities and we have seen that it arises naturally in deriving the risk premium. But consider a risk-averse individual with utility function $v(y) = \sqrt{y}$ and the prospects

$$P^a = \{0.75;\ 10,\ 100\} \qquad P^b = \{0.99;\ 22.727,\ 1000\}$$
$$Ey^a = 32.5 \qquad Ey^b = 32.5$$
$$\text{Var}(y^a) = 1518.75 \qquad \text{Var}(y^b) = 9455.11$$
$$Ev(y^a) = 4.872 \qquad Ev(y^b) = 5.036$$

In this case the prospect with the greater variance yields a greater expected utility.

The reason the variance is not usually a satisfactory measure of risk becomes clear if we consider an individual with state s income $y_s = \bar{y} + z_s$ where $Ey_s = \bar{y}$ so that z_s is the deviation of income about its mean and $Ez_s = 0$. Writing $v(y_s)$ as a Taylor series expansion around $\bar{y}$ gives

$$v(y_s) = v(\bar{y}) + v'(\bar{y})z_s + v''(\bar{y})z_s^2\frac{1}{2!} + v'''(\bar{y})z_s^3\frac{1}{3!} + \dots$$

and taking expectations

$$Ev(y_s) = v(\bar{y}) + v''(\bar{y})\frac{1}{2!}Ez_s^2 + \sum_{n=3}^{\infty} v^n(\bar{y})\frac{1}{n!}Ez_s^n \qquad \text{[F.1]}$$

where v^n is the nth derivative of the utility function. As [F.1] shows expected utility depends on the mean of the distribution of state contingent incomes $\bar{y}$, the second moment about the mean (the variance Ez_s^2) and all the higher moments about the mean (Ez_s^n, $n = 3, 4, \dots$) which are related to other aspects of the distribution such as skewness, kurtosis and so on. In general, all the moments of the distribution matter to the decision-taker. The use of the variance to measure the riskiness of distributions is valid only if *preferences or the set of distributions being compared* are restricted, so the higher moments of the distribution either do not matter to the decision-taker or are determined by mean and variance.

The required restriction on *preferences* is that the utility function be quadratic ($v(y_s) = a + by_s + cy_s^2$), so that in [F.1] all the derivatives are zero except for $v'' = 2c$

and expected utility can be written as $Ev(y_s) = a + b\bar{y} + c(\bar{y}^2 + \sigma^2)$. (See Question 11, Exercise 17D.) Since $c < (>) 0$ for a risk averter (risk lover), increases in the variance σ^2 with mean constant satisfy our requirement for a sensible measure of risk.

To describe the restrictions on the *set of distributions* necessary and sufficient for the variance to be a satisfactory measure of risk it is convenient to assume that the income from different prospects is a continuously, rather than discretely, distributed random variable. The distribution function of the random income y^i from the ith prospect is $F_i(y^i)$ and the probability density is $f_i(y^i) = dF_i/dy^i$. The restriction that justifies the use of the variance as a measure of risk for a set of prospects is that *the prospects should have distributions which differ only by scale and location parameters*.

Suppose that the prospect P^0, with random income y^0, and the prospect P^i, with random income y^i, are members of such a set. Then there exist parameters α_i and β_i such that y^i has the same distribution as $\alpha_i + \beta_i y^0$:

$$y^i \overset{d}{\sim} \alpha_i + \beta_i y^0 \qquad \text{[F.2]}$$

where $\overset{d}{\sim}$ is read as 'is identically distributed to'. Note that this does *not* require that y^i is a linear function of y^0, although if $y^i = \alpha_i + \beta_i y^0$ does hold [F.2] will also be true. Thus suppose y^0 is the outcome of rolling a fair six-sided die with faces numbered 1 to 6 and y^i is the outcome of rolling a different six-sided die with faces numbered 2, 4, 6, ..., 12. Then y^0 and y^i are independently distributed random variables and satisfy [F.2] but it will not always be the case that the *realized* value of y^i is twice the *realized* value of y^0. On the other hand, if we define y^i to be the random variable $2y^0$ [F.2] will also be satisfied, although now y^0 and y^i will exhibit perfect positive correlation.

Now [F.2] requires that

$$F_i(y) = \Pr[y^i \leqslant y] = \Pr[\alpha_i + \beta_i y^0 \leqslant y] = \Pr[y^0 \leqslant (y - \alpha_i)/\beta_i]$$
$$= F_0((y - \alpha_i)/\beta_i) \qquad \text{[F.3]}$$

Denote the mean and standard deviation of the ith member of the set by μ_i and σ_i and construct the standardized variable z from y^0:

$$\tilde{z} = (y^0 - \mu_0)/\sigma_0 \qquad \text{[F.4]}$$

which has the distribution function

$$G(z) = \Pr[\tilde{z} \leqslant z] = \Pr[(y^0 - \mu_0)/\sigma_0 \leqslant z] = \Pr[y^0 \leqslant \mu_0 + \sigma_0 z]$$
$$= F_0(\mu_0 + \sigma_0 z) \qquad \text{[F.5]}$$

with probability density $g(z)$, zero mean and unit variance. Using [F.4] to substitute for $y^0 = \mu_0 + \sigma_0 z$ we can rewrite [F.2] as

$$y^i \overset{d}{\sim} \alpha_i + \beta_i \mu_0 + \beta_i \sigma_0 z = \mu_i + \sigma_i z \qquad \text{[F.6]}$$

since $\mu_i = \alpha_i + \beta_i \mu_0$ and $\sigma_i = \beta_i \sigma_0$.

We can then use [F.6] to write the expected utility of the individual as

$$\int v(y^i) f_i(y^i)\, dy^i = \int v(\mu_i + \sigma_i z) g(z)\, dz = V(\mu_i, \sigma_i) \qquad \text{[F.7]}$$

Thus the decision-taker's ordering of prospects which differ only in location and scale parameters depends on their mean and standard deviation (or mean and variance).

Increases in the mean of y^i increase expected utility:

$$\partial V/\partial \mu_i = \int v'(\mu_i + \sigma_i z)g(z)\,dz = Ev'(\mu_i + \sigma_i z) > 0 \qquad [\text{F.8}]$$

since marginal utility is always positive. Less obviously, but more importantly for our present purposes, increases in the standard deviation reduce expected utility:

$$\begin{aligned}
\partial V/\partial \sigma_i &= \int v'(\mu_i + \sigma_i z)zg(z)\,dz = Ev'(\mu_i + \sigma_i z)z \\
&= Ev'(\mu_i + \sigma_i z)Ez + \text{Cov}(v'(\mu_i + \sigma_i z),\, z) \\
&= \text{Cov}(v'(\mu_i + \sigma_i z),\, z) < 0 \qquad\qquad\qquad [\text{F.9}]
\end{aligned}$$

(Remember from [F.4] that $Ez = E(y^0 - \mu_0)/\sigma_0 = 0$ by construction and that since $\text{Cov}(\mu_i + \sigma_i z,\, z) > 0$ larger values of z are associated with larger values of $\mu_i + \sigma_i z$ and hence lower values of $v'(\mu_i + \sigma_i z)$ when $v'' < 0$.)

[F.9] shows that risk-averse individuals choosing among prospects which differ only in scale and location parameters will prefer prospects with smaller standard deviations (or variances) for a given mean. Hence over such sets of prospects we can use the variance or standard deviation as a measure of risk. Notice that we did *not* have to place restrictions on the distribution function F_0, other than the assumed existence of mean and variance. Any set of distribution functions of random variables defined by [F.2] can be ranked on the basis of mean and variance. In particular, it is not true that we have to restrict attention to normally distributed variables to use variance as a measure of risk, though normal distributions do of course satisfy the required restrictions.

Stochastic dominance

The concept of stochastic dominance is useful in its own right and because it leads to the most general measure of riskiness – the mean-preserving spread – which we consider in the next subsection. We illustrate the concepts for the case in which the individual's random income is continuously distributed. The concepts of stochastic dominance and mean-preserving spreads also apply to discrete distributions but their exposition is messier.

By assuming that there are minimum and maximum possible incomes which are the same for all distributions and by suitably defining the units in which income is measured, we can restrict attention to situations in which the random income y lies in the interval $[0, 1]$. Thus if income Y always lies in the interval $[Y_{\min}, Y_{\max}]$ we can define a new income variable $y = (Y - Y_{\min})/(Y_{\max} - Y_{\min})$. Note that $y = 0$ does not mean that the individual actually has no income but that her income measured in the original units is at its minimum level $Y_{\min}$. The distribution and density function for income y are $F^i(y)$ and $f^i(y)$, where the superscript i indicates a particular distribution i.

Examples of such distributions are in Figs 17.8 and 17.9. In part (a) of Fig. 17.8 the distribution function $F^2(y)$ always lies below $F^1(y)$ indicating that the probability of getting an income of no more than y with distribution F^2 is smaller than with distribution F^1 for all incomes. In Fig. 17.8, F^2 stochastically dominates F^1. Formally:

Distribution function F^2 has first-degree stochastic dominance over distribution function F^1 if and only if

$$F^2(y) \leqslant F^1(y),\ \text{all } y \in [0, 1] \text{ with } F^2(y) < F^1(y),\ \text{some } y \in [0, 1] \qquad [\text{F.10}]$$

We indicate the relationship of first-degree stochastic dominance by $F^2 >_{\text{FSD}} F^1$.

Figure 17.8

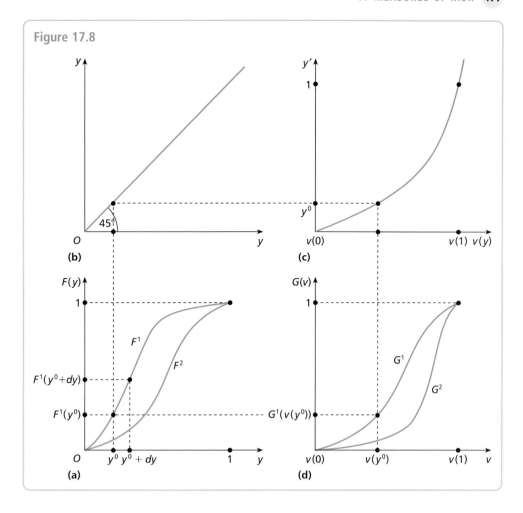

Figure 17.9

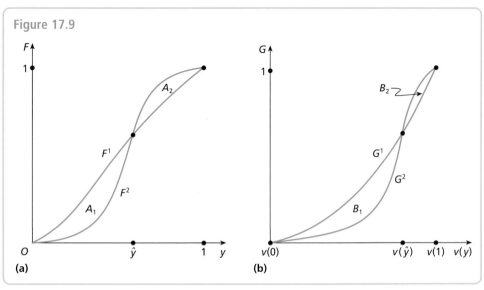

By contrast, in Fig. 17.9 the distribution functions cross at $\hat{y}$ and for incomes above $\hat{y}$ the probability of getting an income no more than y is smaller with distribution F^1. Neither distribution has first-degree stochastic dominance over the other.

Preferences over income y are represented by the cardinal function $v(y)$ and we can always find a linear transformation of the utility function so that $v(0) = 0$ and $v(1) = 1$. Figure 17.8 shows how the distribution function $F^1(y)$ over income in part (a) implies a distribution function over utility levels $G^1(v)$ in part (d) of the figure. An income y in part (a) maps, via the 45° line in part (b) and the utility function graphed in part (c), into the utility level $v(y)$ on the horizontal axis in part (d).

Since utility is increasing in income, the probability $F^1(y)$ of getting at most an income y is equal to the probability of getting a utility of at most $v(y)$:

$$G^1(v) = \Pr[\tilde{v} \leqslant v] = \Pr[v(\tilde{y}) \leqslant v(y)] = \Pr[\tilde{y} \leqslant y] = F^1(y)$$

and so $F^1(y)$ maps horizontally into $G^1(y)$. Similarly, we get the distribution function of utility G^2 from the distribution function of income $F^2(y)$. Since F^2 has first-order stochastic dominance over F^1, and utility is increasing in income, $G^2(v(y)) = F^2(y)$ must also have first-order stochastic dominance over $G^1(v(y)) = F^1(y)$:

$$F^2(y) >_{\text{FSD}} F^1(y) \text{ and } v'(y) > 0 \Rightarrow G^2(v(y)) >_{\text{FSD}} G^1(v(y)) \qquad [\text{F.11}]$$

If distribution 2 has first-order stochastic dominance over distribution 1, then we can show that it must have a higher expected value. In terms of the distributions over income,

$$F^2(y) >_{\text{FSD}} F^1(y) \Rightarrow E_2 y > E_1 y \qquad [\text{F.12}]$$

where the notation $E_i y$ indicates that the expectation of income is taken with respect to distribution i.

To get some intuition for [F.12], consider the area between the horizontal lines at $F^1(y^0)$ and $F^1(y^0 + dy)$ and the graph of F^1 in part (a) of Fig. 17.8. For small dy we can replace $F^1(y^0 + dy)$ by the first-order approximation $F^1(y^0) + f^1(y^0)dy$ so that the area is approximately

$$y^0[F^1(y^0 + dy) - F^1(y^0)] \simeq y^0 f^1(y^0)dy$$

where $f^1(y) = dF^1(y)/dy$ is the probability density. Adding up (integrating) all such areas over the range of y shows that the area above the graph of $F^1(y)$ and below the horizontal line at $F(t) = 1$ is the expected value of income with distribution 1

$$E_1 y = \int_0^1 y f^1(y)\, dy$$

Similarly for the area above the graph of F^2. Since F^2 always lies below F^1, the area above F^2 is larger than the area above F^1 and so distribution 2 has a larger expected value of income.

Slightly more formally, take the expression for expected income and integrate by parts:

$$E_i y = \int_0^1 y f^i(y)\, dy = [1F^1(1) - 0F^1(0)] - \int_0^1 1F^i(y)\, dy = 1 - \int_0^1 F^i(y)\, dy$$

$$= \int_0^1 [1 - F^i(y)]\, dy \qquad [\text{F.13}]$$

which is just the area above the graph of F^i. [Recall that the formula for the derivative of a product of two functions is $d[h(y)m(y)]/dy = h'm + hm'$ which implies $hm' = d[h(y)m(y)]/dy - h'm$. Integrating both sides gives the formula for integration by parts. In our case $h = y$, $m = F^i$.] Then

$$E_2y - E_1y = \int_0^1 [1 - F^2]\,dy - \int_0^1 [1 - F^1]\,dy = \int_0^1 [F^1 - F^2]\,dy > 0$$

because, by first-degree stochastic dominance, $F^2(y) \leqslant F^1(y)$ with $F^2(y) < F^1(y)$ for some y.

The statement in [F.12] applies to *any* distribution functions of *any* random variables. In particular, it applies when we replace F^i and y with G^i and v. Hence, combining [F.11] and [F.12] shows that, if $F^2(y)$ has first-order stochastic dominance over $F^1(y)$, then all decision-takers who prefer more income to less will get greater expected utility from distribution 2 than from distribution 1. We have established the *FSD Theorem*.

FSD Theorem. $F^2(y) >_{\text{FSD}} F^1(y)$ and $v'(y) > 0 \Rightarrow E_2u > E_1u.$

For an explicit proof, take the expression for expected utility and integrate by parts:

$$E_iv = \int_0^1 v(y)f^i(y)\,dy = [v(1)F^i(1) - v(0)F^i(0)] - \int_0^1 v'(y)F^i(y)\,dy$$

$$= v(1) - \int_0^1 v'(y)F^i(y)\,dy$$

(Notice that we integrate with respect to income y, not utility, so that we do not get expected utility expressed in terms of the area above the graph of G^i in part (d) of Fig. 17.8.) Hence

$$E_2v - E_1v = v(1) - \int_0^1 v'(y)F^2(y)\,dy - v(1) + \int_0^1 v'(y)F^1(y)\,dy$$

$$= \int_0^1 v'(y)[F^1(y) - F^2(y)]\,dy > 0 \qquad\qquad \text{[F.14]}$$

Since distribution 2 has first-order stochastic dominance over distribution 1, the term in the square brackets in the integrand is always non-negative and is positive over some range of y. If marginal utility is positive, the product of the two terms in the integrand is always non-negative and is somewhere positive. Hence the integral over the entire range of y is positive and so first-order stochastic dominance implies higher expected utility.

Although $F^2 >_{\text{FSD}} F^1$ implies that distribution 2 has higher mean than distribution 1, it is not this fact alone which ensures that distribution 2 is preferred to distribution 1 by all decision-takers who prefer more income to less. An increase in expected income is sufficient to make risk-neutral individuals better off but the assumption on the utility function in the FSD Theorem is much weaker and covers both risk lovers and risk-averse as well as risk-neutral individuals. The reason why all individuals with positive marginal utility prefer a stochastically dominant distribution is that, for any given income level, the probability of getting less than that income is reduced.

The FSD Theorem places weak restrictions on preferences and strong restrictions on distributions. If we want to find larger sets of distributions which we can rank in terms of expected utility we have to place stronger restrictions on preferences. Consider Fig. 17.9 where the distribution functions cross so that the distributions cannot be ranked in terms of first-degree stochastic dominance. Suppose that in part (a) the area A_1 is greater that area A_2. Then the total area above F^2 is greater than the total area above F^1 and expected income is greater with distribution 2 than with distribution 1.

Part (a) of Fig. 17.9 is an example of second-degree stochastic dominance. Define

$$T^i(y) \equiv \int_0^y F^i(\tilde{y})\, d\tilde{y}$$

so that $T^i(y)$ is the area under the distribution function up to income y. A distribution $F^2(y)$ has second-degree stochastic dominance over distribution $F^1(y)$ if and only if

$$T^1(y) \geqslant T^2(y) \text{ for all } y \in [0, 1], \text{ with } T^1(y) > T^2(y) \text{ for some } y \qquad \text{[F.15]}$$

If [F.15] holds then we write $F^2 >_{SSD} F^1$.

Note that

$$E_i y = \int_0^1 [1 - F^i(y)] = 1 - T^i(1)$$

so that if $T^1(1) = T^2(1)$ the means of the two distributions are equal and if $T^1(1) > T^2(1)$ distribution 2 has a larger mean income.

[F.15] does not restrict the number of times the distribution functions may cross. If they never cross then $F^2 >_{FSD} F^1$, so that first-order stochastic dominance implies second-order stochastic dominance. If the distribution functions do cross, [F.15] requires that F^2 lies below F^1 before F^2 lies above F^1. Part (a) of Fig. 17.9 is an example of second-degree stochastic dominance in which there is a single crossing.

Unless we make stronger assumptions about the preference function $v(y)$, in particular whether it is concave, linear, or convex, we know that increases in expected income do not imply increases in expected utility. In terms of Fig. 17.9, area A_1 being greater than area A_2 in part (a) does not imply that in part (b) area B_1 is greater than area B_2. Hence we cannot conclude that the expected utility (the area above the distribution function for utility) is greater with distribution G^2 than G^1 merely because expected income (the area above the distribution function for income) is greater with distribution F^2 than with F^1.

Although the vertical distances between $F^1(y)$ and $F^2(y)$ in part (a) are the same as the vertical distances between $G^1(v(y))$ and $G^2(v(y))$ in part (b) the horizontal differences are not since one measures income and the other measures utility. The utility distances in part (b) depend not just on income differences but also on the form of the utility function. If utility is concave in income then utility distances become compressed as income increases, so that the area B_2 is smaller relative to B_1 than is A_2 relative to A_1 Since area A_2 is smaller than area A_1 this suggests that area B_2 is smaller than B_1 and hence that expected utility is greater with distribution 2 than with distribution 1.

The above argument provides the intuition, though not the proof, for the second-degree stochastic dominance theorem.

SSD Theorem. $\quad T^2(y) >_{SSD} T^1(1)$ and $v' > 0$, $v'' < 0 \Rightarrow E_2 v > E_1 v$.

To prove the theorem we use [F.13] and integrate by parts again:

$$E_2v - E_1v = \int_0^1 v'(y)[F^1(y) - F^2(y)]\,dy$$

$$= v'(1)[T^1(1) - T^2(1)] - v'(0)[T^1(0) - T^2(0)] - \int_0^1 v''(y)[T^1(y) - T^2(y)]\,dy$$

$$= v'(1)[T^1(1) - T^2(1)] - \int_0^1 v''(y)[T^1(y) - T^2(y)]\,dy > 0$$

Second-degree stochastic dominance of F^2 over F^1 implies that the square bracketed parts of the first term on the last line are non-negative, which, together with the assumption that marginal utility is positive, ensures that the first term is positive or zero. Second-degree stochastic dominance implies that the square bracketed part of the second term is non-negative everywhere and positive somewhere. Hence, because of the assumption of diminishing marginal utility of income, the integral is negative, ensuring that the last line is positive.

Mean-preserving spread

A distribution F^1 is a mean-preserving spread of another distribution F^2 if it has the same mean and is obtained from F^2 by shifting the probability weight from the centre to the tails of the distribution. Figure 17.10 is an example of a simple mean-preserving spread where the F^1 is the uniform distribution and F^2 has the same mean but is obtained from F^1 by shifting probability weight in the two extreme ranges towards the centre. Note that Fig. 17.10 is similar to part (a) of Fig. 17.9 in that the distribution function F^2 lies below F^1 up to the crossing point at $\hat{y}$ and above it thereafter. However, in Fig. 17.9 the area above F^2 is greater than the area under F^1 so that distribution 2 has a greater mean. In Fig. 17.10 the areas above F^1 and F^2 are equal and so the two distributions have the same mean.

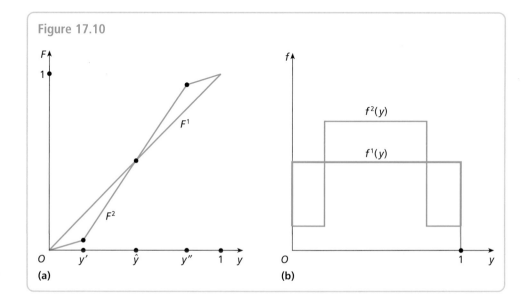

Figure 17.10

Formally:

$F^1(y)$ is a mean-preserving spread of $F^2(y)$ if and only if

$$T^1(y) - T^2(y) \geq 0 \qquad \text{all } y \in [0, 1], \text{ with } T^1(y) - T^2(y) > 0 \text{ some } y \in [0, 1] \qquad \text{[F.16]}$$

$$T^1(1) - T^2(1) = 0 \qquad \text{[F.17]}$$

Comparing [F.16] and [F.17] with [F.15] we see that if $F^1(y)$ is a mean-preserving spread of $F^2(y)$ then $F^2(y)$ has second-degree stochastic dominance over $F^1(y)$. Hence from the SSD Theorem all risk-averse inviduals prefer F^2 to F^1: all risk averters are made worse off by a mean-preserving spread. From the proof of the SSO Theorem we can also see that all risk lovers ($v'' > 0$) prefer F^1 to F^2.

Mean-preserving Spread Theorem. All risk averters prefer F^2 to F^1 (and all risk lovers prefer F^1 to F^2) if and only if F^1 is a mean-preserving spread of F^2.

The concept of risk embodied in the mean-preserving spread is a property of the distribution function. The concept of risk aversion is a property of individual preferences and is embodied in the utility function. The mean-preserving spread theorem shows that the two concepts are intimately connected.

The first part of the theorem (all risk averters are made worse off by a mean-preserving spread) is a direct consequence of the second-degree stochastic dominance theorem. The second part (if all risk averters prefer F^2 to F^1 then F^1 is a mean-preserving spread of F^2) is much less obvious. Since its proof is correspondingly harder we do not present here but stress the implication: if we wish to measure risk in such a way that all risk-averse individuals, whatever the precise form of their utility function $v(y)$, are made worse off by an increase in risk, then we are restricted to using the mean-preserving spread as our concept of the riskiness of a distribution.

The mean-preserving spread is only a partial measure of risk: there are many pairs of distributions which do not satisfy the definition [F.16], [F.17] (or its equivalent for discrete distributions) and which therefore cannot be ranked as more or less risky in the sense that one is a mean-preserving spread of the other. The concept of a mean-preserving spread is, however, useful because only very weak restrictions on preferences (risk aversion) are required for the statistical relationship (F^1 is a mean-preserving spread of F^2) to imply a preference relationship (F^2 is preferred to F^1).

It is often useful to be able to say that some marginal change in a parameter describing the decision-taker's environment has led to a mean-preserving spread in the distribution. Thus suppose that the distribution function for income is written as $F(y; \beta)$ where β is the parameter in question. Then *an increase in β is a mean-preserving increase in risk if and only if*

$$\int_0^y F_\beta(\tilde{y}; \beta) \, d\tilde{y} = T_\beta(y; \beta) \geq 0 \text{ for } y \in [0, 1], \, T_\beta(y; \beta) > 0 \text{ some } y \qquad \text{[F.18]}$$

$$\int_0^1 F_\beta(\tilde{y}; \beta) \, d\tilde{y} = T_\beta(1; \beta) = 0 \qquad \text{[F.19]}$$

where $F_\beta(y; \beta) = \partial F(y; \beta)/\partial \beta$ is the rate at which the distribution function of y shifts as β varies. As β varies expected utility alters at the rate $\int v(y) f_\beta(y; \beta) \, dy$. It is possible to show that [F.18] and [F.19] are equivalent to $\int v(y) f_\beta(y; \beta) \, dy < 0$ for all concave $v(y)$ where $f_\beta = \partial f(y; \beta)/\partial \beta$ is the shift in the probability density function as β varies. Thus mean-preserving increases in risk reduce the expected utility of risk averters.

EXERCISE 17F

1. Prove that a mean-preserving increase in risk increases the variance of the distribution of y. (*Hint*: the variance is the expected value of $g(y) = (y - \bar{y})^2$. Is $g(y)$ convex or concave in y?)

2. *Mean-preserving spread for discrete distributions.* Consider two discrete prospects P^a, P^b which assign probabilities π^a_s, π^b_s to income y_s. P^a and P^b differ by a mean-preserving spread if (1) they differ only in the probabilities attached to four values of y: $y_1 < y_2 < y_3 < y_4$ and (2) the differences in the probabilities of these states $\Delta_s = \pi^a_s - \pi^b_s$ satisfies (a) $\Delta_1 = -\Delta_2 \geqslant 0$, $\Delta_4 = -\Delta_3 \geqslant 0$ and (b) $\sum \Delta_s y_s = 0$. Here (a) means that P^a has more weight in the tails that P^b and (b) ensures that the prospects have the same mean. Show that the example in the text where a risk averter preferred the prospect with the greater variance does not satisfy the conditions for a mean-preserving spread. Construct another prospect P^c which differs from P^a by a mean-preserving spread. Check that P^c has a greater variance than P^a and is worse than P^a for risk averters with $u = \sqrt{y}$ and $u = \log y$.

3. *Mean-preserving spreads and location and scale parameters.* Suppose that y^i and y^j are members of a set of random variables which differ only in location and scale parameters. Show that, if $\mu_i = \mu_j$, y^j is a mean-preserving spread of y^i if and only if $\sigma_j > \sigma_i$.

4. *Sandmo increase in risk.* From a random variable y construct another random variable $y(\gamma) = \gamma(y - \bar{y}) + \bar{y}$ where $\bar{y}$ is the mean of y and $\gamma \geqslant 0$ is a parameter which can be used to measure risk. Show that the random variables $y(\gamma)$ form a set which differ only in scale and location parameters. If $F(y)$ is the distribution function of y show that the distribution function of $y(\gamma)$ is $F([y - (1 - \gamma)\bar{y}]/\gamma)$ and hence that an increase in γ is a mean-preserving spread. Show directly, without use of the properties of mean-preserving spreads, that, if $y(\gamma)$ is income, an increase in γ reduces the expected utility $Ev(y(\gamma))$ of risk-averse individuals.

G. Comparative statics under uncertainty

In previous chapters we have investigated how differences in preferences and changes in the environment confronting decision-takers affect behaviour. We now examine how changes in the amount of risk and differences in attitudes to risk affect behaviour. We start with a fairly general model of decision-taking under uncertainty and then use and extend the methods to investigate an interesting example: precautionary saving.

Mean-preserving spreads and behaviour

Suppose that the income of a decision-taker depends on her action a and on a random variable e:

$$y = y(a, e)$$

Many of the models developed in later chapters take this form, as does the precautionary saving example we investigate below. The distribution function of e is $F(e; \beta)$ where β is a parameter which shifts the distribution of e. For any given choice of a her income is random and her preferences over income are representable by the cardinal utility function $v(y)$. She chooses her action to maximize her expected utility. We can write her utility as depending on her action and the random variable

$$u(a, e) = v(y(a, e)) \qquad \text{[G.1]}$$

and her expected utility as

$$\bar{u} = \bar{u}(a; \beta) = Eu(a, e) = \int u(a, e) f(e; \beta) \, de = \int v(y(a, e)) f(e; \beta) \, de \qquad \text{[G.2]}$$

We assume that $u(a, e)$ is concave in her action:

$$u_{aa} = v''(y) y_a y_a + v'(y) y_{aa} < 0$$

Note that concavity of the income function with respect to the action ($y_{aa} < 0$) is sufficient for $u_{aa} < 0$ but it is not necessary.

Given $u_{aa} < 0$, the optimal action $a^*(\beta)$ satisfies the first- and second-order conditions

$$\bar{u}_a(a; \beta) = \int u_a(a, e) f(e; \beta) \, de = 0 \qquad \text{[G.3]}$$

$$\bar{u}_{aa}(a; \beta) = \int u_{aa}(a, e) f(e; \beta) \, de < 0 \qquad$$

Total differentiation of [G.3] with respect to β gives

$$\frac{da^*}{d\beta} = -\frac{\bar{u}_{a\beta}}{\bar{u}_{aa}} \qquad \text{[G.4]}$$

where

$$\bar{u}_{a\beta}(a; \beta) = \int u_a(a, e) f_\beta(e; \beta) \, de \qquad \text{[G.5]}$$

For a given value of a, $u_a(a, e)$ is a function of the random variable e and we can write $u_a(a, e) = h(e)$ and rewrite [G.5] as

$$\bar{u}_{a\beta}(a; \beta) = \int h(e) f_\beta(e; \beta) \, de \qquad \text{[G.6]}$$

Provided that the random variable e lies in some finite interval, we can always transform it so that it lies between 0 and 1. For example, if the minimum value of e is $e_{min} < 0$, we can redefine the random variable as $e^1 = e - e_{min}$ which is always non-negative and has density function $f^1(e^1; \beta) = f(e^1 + e_{min}; \beta)$. The income function is then $y^1(a, e^1) = y(a, e^1 + e_{min})$. The redefinitions have no substantive effect on the model and in particular do not alter the optimal action. They do mean that we can examine the effects of a mean-preserving spread on the optimal action. Since, without loss of generality, we can always assume that $e \in [0, 1]$, we can define a mean-preserving increase in the riskiness of e as an increase in the parameter β which satisfies the definitions [F.18] and [F.19] (with e replacing y in the definition).

A mean-preserving increase in the riskiness of e reduces the expected value of a function $h(e)$ of e if h is concave and increases it if h is a convex. Hence we have established

$$\frac{da^*}{d\beta} < 0 \text{ or } > 0 \text{ as } h''(e) = u_{aee}(a, e) < 0 \text{ or } > 0 \qquad \text{[G.7]}$$

The condition [G.7] refers to the third derivative of the function $u(a, e)$ which gives utility as a function of the action a and the state of the world, not to the third derivative of the utility of income function $v(y)$. Since $u(a, s) = v(y(a, s))$, repeated application of the function of a function rule for differentiation shows that, provided the utility function $v(y)$ and the income function $y(a, s)$ are suitably differentiable,

$$u_{aee} = v'''y_a y_e y_e + v''y_{ae}y_e + v''y_a y_{ee} + v'y_{aee} \qquad [G.8]$$

Assumptions about the individual's preferences over income or their risk aversion will not in general be sufficient to sign u_{aee} which depends both on preferences over income and on the way in which actions and the state of the world affect income. For example (see Question 8, Exercise 17E), a risk-averse individual whose absolute risk aversion $A(y) = -v''/v'$ is decreasing in income must have a utility of income function with $v' > 0$, $v'' < 0$ and $v''' > 0$. But the assumptions that $y(a, e)$ is concave in a and that there is decreasing absolute risk aversion are not enough to determine how the individual will change their decision in the face of a mean-preserving increase in risk. In some models, further restrictions are also plausible and enable us to sign u_{aee} and hence to make definite comparative static predictions.

Increases in risk aversion and behaviour

We expect individuals with the same income function $y(a, e)$ and facing the same distribution of the random variable e but with different degrees of risk aversion to choose different actions a. Suppose one individual has the utility of income function $v(y)$ and a second has $m(y) = g(v(y))$ where g is an increasing concave transformation of v: $g'(v) > 0$, $g''(v) < 0$. The second individual is more risk averse than the first in the sense that she has greater absolute risk aversion at all levels of income: $A^m(y) > A^v(y)$. (See Question 6, Exercise 17E.)

Suppose that $v(y(a, e))$ is strictly concave in the decision variable a, so that a_v^*, the optimal level of a for the first individual, is defined by the first-order condition

$$Ev'(y(a_v^*, e))y_a(a_v^*, e) = 0 \qquad [G.9]$$

Does the assumption that the second individual is more risk averse than the first individual imply anything about whether her optimal decision level a_m^* is greater or smaller than a_v^*? The expected marginal utility from the decision variable for the second individual at the optimal level for the first individual is

$$Em'(y(a_v^*, e))y_a(a_v^*, e) = Eg'(v)v'(y(a_v^*, e))y_a(a_v^*, e) \qquad [G.10]$$

Using [G.9] and the fact that the expected value of the product of two random variables x and z is $Exz = ExEz + \text{Cov}(x, z)$, we have

$$Eg'(v)v'(y(a_v^*, e))y_a(a_v^*, e) = Eg'(v)Ev'(y(a_v^*, e))y_a(a_v^*, e) + \text{Cov}(g', v'y_a)$$
$$= \text{Cov}(g'(v(y(a_v^*, e)), v'(y(a_v^*, e))y_a(a_v^*, e))$$

so that

$$a_m^* \lessgtr a_v^* \quad \text{if and only if} \quad \text{Cov}(g', v'y_a) \lessgtr 0 \qquad [G.11]$$

As with the effect of a mean-preserving spread on behaviour, the effect of greater risk aversion depends both on preferences and on the income function. In particular we require assumptions about the effect of the random variable e on the marginal effect of the decision variable a on income. If an increase in e increases income, g' will decline with e because $g'' < 0$, and so will v'. Similarly, if an increase in e reduces income, both g' and v' will increase. Hence g' and v' have a positive covariance provided only that income is monotonic in e. But we are interested in the covariance of g' and the product $v'y_a$. If the effect of e on y_a is of the opposite sign to its effect on y then the sign of the effect of e on their product requires assumptions about the magnitude of v', y_e and y_{ae}.

In some instances, as with the model of the competitive firm under price uncertainty in Chapter 18, we can make plausible assumptions which enable us say something about the effect of absolute risk aversion on behaviour. In other cases, for example precautionary savings examined in the next section, we must make further assumptions about preferences.

Prudence and precautionary savings

We examined saving (lending and borrowing) decisions under certainty in section 11B. When an individual chooses how much they wish to lend (save out of current income), they may face uncertainty in that they do not know for sure what real (allowing for inflation) rate of interest will be paid or what their future income will be. We focus here on the implications of uncertain future income and leave the analysis of uncertainty in the returns to saving to section 21E where we consider the stock market.

The individual has a certain current income y_0, and can borrow or lend at a certain rate of interest i but faces an uncertain future income y_1 from employment. The individual's preferences over consumption in period t are representable by the same concave cardinal utility function in each period: $v(c_t)$, $t = 0, 1$. Current consumption is $c_0 = y_0 - a$ and future consumption is $c_1 = y_1 + (1 + i)a$ where a is saving out of current income. For any given realization of the random future income y_1 total utility over the two periods is

$$u(a, y_1) = v(y_0 - a) + v(y_1 + (1 + i)a) \qquad [\text{G.12}]$$

and expected utility is

$$\bar{u}(a; \beta) = E[v(y_0 - a) + v(y_1 + (1 + i)a)] = v(y_0 - a) + Ev(y_1 + (1 + i)a) \qquad [\text{G.13}]$$

β is a parameter, increases in which create mean-preserving spreads in uncertain future income y_1.

The first-order condition for optimal saving is

$$\bar{u}_a(a; \beta) = -v'(y_0 - a) + (1 + i)Ev'(y_1 + (1 + i)a) = 0 \qquad [\text{G.14}]$$

As the reader should check, the assumption that v is concave means that the condition is necessary and sufficient. Note that random future income y_1 plays exactly the same role in $u(a, y_1)$ in [G.12] and [G.13] as e plays in [G.1] and [G.2]. Applying [G.7], a mean-preserving increase in the riskiness of future income reduces or increases saving as $u_{ay_1y_1}$ is negative or positive. Differentiating [G.12] with respect to a and then twice with respect to y_1 gives

$$u_{ay_1y_1}(a, y_1) = (1 + i)v'''(y_1 + (1 + i)a) \qquad [\text{G.15}]$$

Hence the effect of a mean-preserving spread in future income on saving out of current income depends on the third derivative of the utility function.

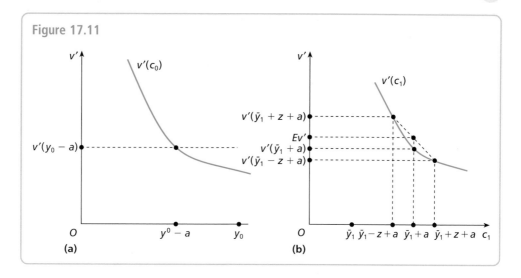

Figure 17.11

We can gain some intuition for this result and also prepare for an analysis of the effects of attitudes to risk on saving by considering Fig. 17.11. Part (a) of the figure plots marginal utility from current consumption and part (b) plots marginal utility from future consumption. The marginal utility curves are negatively sloped to reflect the concavity assumptionon that marginal utility declines with consumption: $v''(c_t) < 0$. We consider the case in which the interest rate is zero: $i = 0$ but the simplification makes no difference to the results.

First consider the case in which future income is certain but less than current income: $y_1 = \bar{y}_1 < y_0$, where $\bar{y}_1$ is certain future income. The first-order condition [G.14] simplifies to $v'(c_0) = v'(c_1)$. Since the utility functions for current and future consumption are identical the individual saves out of current income to equalise current and future consumption: $c_0^\star = c_1^\star$ which implies that $a^\star = (y_0 - \bar{y}_1)/2$. The motivation for saving under certainty is often referred to as *consumption smoothing* but it is perhaps more accurate to think of it as smoothing marginal utility across periods. If the individual had different marginal utility functions for current and future consumption, optimal saving would still imply equalizing marginal utility across periods, but consumption would not be equalized.

Now suppose that future income takes on two possible values: $\bar{y}_1 + z$ and $\bar{y}_1 - z$ with equal probability so that $Ez = 0$ and $Ey_1 = \bar{y}_1$. There has been a mean-preserving increase in risk. If saving is unchanged the individual has future consumption of $\bar{y}_1 + z + a^\star$ or $\bar{y}_1 - z + a^\star$ with equal probability. Expected marginal utility from future consumption at the previously optimal saving level is now

$$\frac{1}{2}v'(\bar{y}_1 + z + a^\star) + \frac{1}{2}v'(\bar{y}_1 - z + a^\star)$$

whereas it was $v'(\bar{y}_1 + a^\star)$. Hence the individual will want to increase saving if and only if

$$\frac{1}{2}v'(\bar{y}_1 + z + a^\star) + \frac{1}{2}v'(\bar{y}_1 - z + a^\star) > v'(\bar{y}_1 + a^\star) \qquad \text{[G.16]}$$

Recalling the definition of concave and convex functions, [G.16] is true only if $v'(c_1)$ is convex: $v''' > 0$. In Fig. 17.11 the slope of the marginal utility curve is declining with c_1 but at a declining rate so that $v''' > 0$ and saving will be greater under uncertainty than under certainty.

Imposing a mean-preserving risk on the future income of a saver who previously had a certain future income will increase saving if and only if $v''' > 0$. The increase in saving due to future income uncertainty is known as *precautionary saving*. Only individuals with convex marginal utility will have a precautionary motive for saving. Risk aversion is equivalent to concavity of the utility function v but it has no implications for the concavity or convexity of the marginal utility function v'. However, assumptions about how absolute risk aversion $A(c) = -v''/v'$ varies with consumption can determine the sign of v''' and, as Question 8 of Exercise 17E showed, individuals with decreasing absolute risk aversion must have $v''' > 0$. Hence decreasing absolute risk aversion implies a precautionary motive for saving. Mean-preserving increases in the riskiness of future income lead to an increase in saving out of current income: the consumption function plotting current consumption against current income is shifted down and to the right.

Figure 17.12 illustrates the importance of the shape of the individual's marginal utility function for decisions about saving. Individual 1 has marginal utility function $v'(c)$ and individual 2 has $m'(c)$. When there is no uncertainty the two marginal utility curves lead to the same optimal amount of future consumption $c_v^* = c_m^* = c^*$. Since the two curves have different shapes the marginal utility curves for current consumption will also have different shapes so that the level of saving may not be equal. However, our interest is in the *change* in saving of the two individuals caused by the introduction of uncertainty in future income, not in a comparison of the absolute level of their savings. The two marginal utility curves touch at c^* so that the two individuals have the same initial future consumption under certainty.

Now we impose a mean-preserving spread in future income on the two individuals. Income may be greater or smaller by an amount z with equal probability,

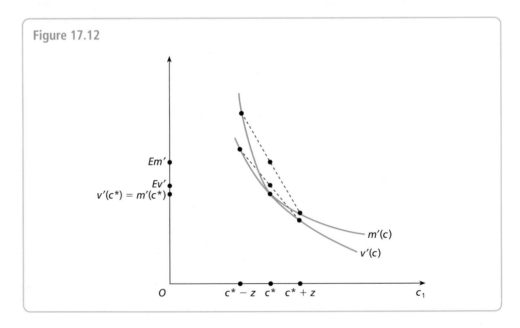

Figure 17.12

so that, with unchanged saving, future consumption is either $c^* + z$ or $c^* - z$ with equal probability. Individual 2 has a more convex or 'bowed in' marginal utility curve and hence the expected value of her marginal utility is greater than the expected value of marginal utility for individual 1. Hence individual 2 has a larger expected benefit from additional saving to increase future consumption. Her saving will increase by more as a result of the introduction of uncertainty in future income. Her precautionary saving motive is greater.

We could compare the curvature of the two marginal utility curves by comparing v''' and m'''. But preferences over consumption can also be represented by any positive linear transformation. Hence individual 1's preferences could also be represented by $\hat{v}(y) = k_0 + k_1 v(c)$ where $k_1 > 0$. By choosing a large or small enough k_1 we can always pick a representation of individual 1's preferences such that the third derivative of the utility function is larger or smaller than the third derivative of individual 2's utility function. We faced the same issue in section E when considering whether we could use the size of the second derivative of the utility function to compare degrees of risk aversion. We found there that $A = -v''/v'$ was a good measure of risk aversion and was not affected by linear transformations of the utility function. We will therefore use

$$P^v = -\frac{v'''}{v''} \qquad \text{[G.17]}$$

and $P^m = -m'''/m''$ to measure the curvature of the marginal utility functions and refer to P as a measure of *prudence*.

As the reader should check, prudence is unaffected by the particular numerical representation of preferences. We say an individual is prudent if $P > 0$. P^v has the same sign as v''' and so is positive if and only if imposing a mean-preserving increase in risk leads to an increase in saving. Hence prudent individuals have positive precautionary saving.

We found in section E that risk-averse individuals had a positive coefficient of absolute risk aversion and that the coefficient of absolute risk aversion was closely related to the risk premium: the amount of money the individual would be willing to give up to purchase a certain income. We can extend the analogy between prudence and absolute risk aversion by considering the *precautionary premium* which is the reduction in future income which would have the same effect on saving as the introduction of uncertainty. We can show that the precautionary premium is a useful measure of how sensitive the individual's decisions are to risk and that it is related to prudence.

For simplicity assume that $i = 0$ and consider the first order condition for optimal saving [G.14] which equates expected future marginal utility and current marginal utility:

$$v'(y_0 - a^\star) = Ev'(\bar{y}_1 + \tilde{z} + a^\star) \qquad \text{[G.18]}$$

where $E\tilde{z} = 0$. Suppose that $y_0 = \bar{y}_1$ so that the only motive for saving is precautionary and if there was no risk ($\tilde{z} = 0$) there would be no saving. The *action certainty equivalent* future income y_1^a is the certain future income at which the individual would save the same amount as under uncertainty. It satisfies

$$v'(y_1^a + a^\star) = Ev'(\bar{y}_1 + \tilde{z} + a^\star) \qquad \text{[G.19]}$$

By analogy with the risk premium (section 17D) we can define the *precautionary premium* ψ as the reduction in certain future income which leads to the same level of saving as with uncertain future income: $\psi = \bar{y}_1 - y_1^a$ so that

$$v'(\bar{y}_1 - \psi + a^*) = Ev'(\bar{y}_1 + \tilde{z} + a^*) \qquad [\text{G.20}]$$

The larger is ψ the greater the amount of precautionary saving.

We derived the expression [D.22] for the risk premium by applying first and second order approximations to [D.17]. By applying first and second order approximations to [G.20] in the same way we can show that for small risks

$$\psi(\bar{y}_1); \qquad P(\bar{y}_1)\tfrac{1}{2}\sigma_z^2 \qquad [\text{G.21}]$$

Hence the change in the individual's action (saving) caused by the introduction of uncertainty depends on her preferences, as measured by prudence, and the risk, as measured by the variance.

EXERCISE 17G

1. What must be assumed about the utility function $v(y)$ if an individual has decreasing prudence: $dP(y)/dy < 0$?

2. Do the utility functions in Question 10, Exercise 17D exhibit increasing, constant or decreasing prudence?

3. Use the model in the text of precautionary saving to investigate the effect on saving of (a) an increase in current income y_0; (b) an increase in future mean income $\bar{y}_1$; (c) an increase in the rate of interest i. Use the result in (b) to show that the effect of an increase in the rate of interest can be decomposed into a definitely signed substitution effect and an ambiguously signed "income" effect. (d) Show that the effect of i on savings depends on the individual's absolute and relative risk aversion and that if relative risk aversion is less than 1 saving is increased by an increase in the rate of interest.

4. *Sandmo risk and saving.* Write the individual's uncertain income as $\bar{y}_1 + \beta(y_1 - \bar{y}_1) = \bar{y}_1 + \beta z$. Under what circumstances will a Sandmo increase in risk (an increase in β) increase saving?

Production under uncertainty

A. Introduction

In this chapter we show how the techniques and concepts developed in Chapter 17 can be used to analyse behaviour under uncertainty in economies with production. We set out a model of a firm operating under market and technological uncertainty in section B, examine the firm's input and output choices and compare them with production decisions which would be taken under certainty. A futures market is introduced in section C and its effects on the firm's production decisions are considered.

B. Competitive firm under uncertainty

Firms face two types of uncertainty. There may be *technological uncertainty* in that the amount of output produced from a given input combination is uncertain. The output of wheat depends on the weather as well as the amounts of seed, fertilizer, labour and other inputs chosen by the farmer. Machines may fail or factories burn down. The firm faces *market uncertainty* if the prices at which it transacts in input or output markets are uncertain.

Uncertainty in market prices may arise because of random changes in demand (perhaps because of random variations in preferences, consumer incomes or the prices of related goods). Much price uncertainty can also be linked to supply randomness and so production uncertainty may lead to market uncertainty. If the output of wheat is affected by the weather (production uncertainty) there will be an uncertain price of wheat because of the random fluctuations in supply. A firm will typically be subject to both types of uncertainty but it is easier initially to consider their effects separately.

Price uncertainty

A firm produces a good x which it sells on a competitive market at the random market price p_s. The firm chooses its output before it knows what the state of the world (the price p_s) will be. The firm's random revenue is $p_s x$. Its cost of production is $c(x)$ and profit is $p_s x - c(x)$. We assume that the firm is owned by a single individual who wishes to maximize expected utility. The income of the owner is

$$y_s = p_s x - c(x) + B \qquad \text{[B.1]}$$

where B is the other, non-random, income of the owner.

In the models of the competitive firm in earlier chapters we did not need to enquire too closely into the ownership of the firm. Provided that the owners of a firm preferred more income to less, they would all agree that the firm should aim to maximize its certain profit and thus the income of each of the owners. Under uncertainty, profit, the income of the owner or owners, is random. A given decision (output level) will yield a prospect or vector of state contingent incomes. Individuals with different preferences (attitudes to risk) may not agree on the ranking of the prospects resulting from different output decisions. For the moment we avoid these problems by assuming a single owner who is entitled to all of the firm's profit. The owner (or the firm) has a utility function $v(y_s)$ with $v'(y_s) > 0$ and $v''(y_s) \leq 0$. We usually assume that the firm is risk averse ($v'' < 0$) but the risk-neutral case is also of interest if only to distinguish the effects of uncertainty (random p_s) and of preferences (risk aversion) on behaviour when contrasting our results with those of models based on the assumption of certainty.

The firm chooses output to maximize

$$V = Ev(y_s) = Ev(p_s x - c(x) + B) \tag{B.2}$$

If the optimal output is positive it will satisfy the first-order condition

$$V_x = Ev'(p_s x - c(x) + B)\frac{dy_s}{dx} = Ev'(p_s x - c(x) + B)[p_s - c'(x)] = 0 \tag{B.3}$$

where $c'(x)$ is marginal cost. The second-order condition is

$$V_{xx} = Ev''(p_s x - c(x) + B)[p_s - c']^2 - Ev'(p_s x - c(x) + B)c''(x) < 0 \tag{B.4}$$

Comparison with the certainty case

The first- and second-order conditions for the choice of output differ from those under certainty in several respects. Suppose that the firm knew that when it came to sell its output it would face a certain price p. The firm would wish to maximize

$$v(px - c(x) + B) \tag{B.5}$$

and since larger income is preferred to smaller ($v' > 0$) it would make its choice to maximize the certain profit $px - c(x)$. The first- and second-order conditions for maximizing [B.5] are

$$v'(px - c + B)[p - c'(x)] = 0 \tag{B.6}$$

$$v''(px - c + B)[p - c']^2 - v'(px - c + B)c''(x) < 0 \tag{B.7}$$

But notice that $v' > 0$ for all x and so [B.6] is equivalent to

$$p - c'(x) = 0 \tag{B.8}$$

Since [B.8] holds, $(p - c')^2$ is zero and the first term in [B.7] must be zero. Hence [B.7] is satisfied if and only if

$$-c'' < 0 \tag{B.9}$$

Thus the competitive firm under certainty produces where the certain price equals marginal cost and marginal cost is increasing. (See section 8A.)

In Fig. 18.1 the firm faces an upward sloping marginal cost curve and would produce at $x(p_1)$ if it knew for sure that the price would be p_1. Similarly, for $x(p_2)$ and $x(\bar{p})$. The firm's income at a given output will depend on the price it receives for its output. Since $p_1 > \bar{p} > p_2$ income will also be greater with p_1 than with $\bar{p}$ and with $\bar{p}$ rather than p_2 for a given x. Figure 18.2 plots income against output at the different prices.

Figure 18.1

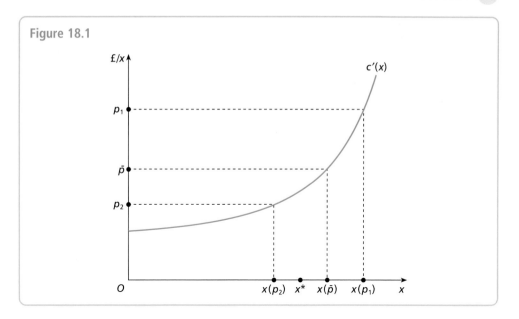

Figure 18.2

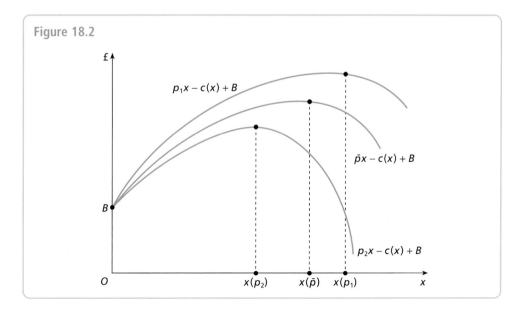

Under uncertainty the firm chooses an output *ex ante* before the state, and there-fore the price, is known by taking account of the marginal effect of output on income in *all* states of the world. *Ex post*, when the price p_s is known (the state is revealed) the output which was chosen *ex ante* will in general not maximize income in that state: $p_s \neq c'(x)$. For example, in Figs 18.1 and 18.2 where p_1, p_2 are the prices in the two possible states the firm will not choose to produce $x(p_1)$ or $x(p_2)$. Letting π_s be the probability of p_s, [B.3] in the two-state case is

$$\pi_1 v'(y_1)[p_1 - c'(x^*)] + \pi_2 v'(y_2)[p_2 - c'(x^*)] = 0 \qquad [\text{B.10}]$$

This cannot hold with $x = x(p_1)$ or $x = x(p_2)$ if $0 < \pi_s < 1$. At $x(p_1)$, $p_2 < p_1 = c'(x)$ so that the first term in [B.10] is zero and the second negative. The firm should therefore reduce output below $x(p_1)$. (Why should it not increase it?) Similarly, at $x(p_2)$, $p_1 > p_2 = c'(x(p_2))$ and the first term in [B.10] is positive and the second zero. The firm should raise output above $x(p_2)$.

The other main difference between the certainty and uncertainty cases is that under uncertainty the firm need not face increasing marginal cost ($c'' > 0$) in order for the second-order conditions to be satisfied. In [B.4] the first term must be negative if the firm is risk averse ($v'' < 0$) since $(p_s - c')^2$ is non-negative and, provided not all p_s are identical (i.e. that there *is* uncertainty), $(p_s - c')^2 > 0$ for some states. Hence even if $c'' < 0$, so that the marginal cost curve is downward sloping, the second-order condition could still be satisfied.

The risk-neutral firm

If the firm is risk neutral v can be written as $a + by_s$ ($b > 0$) and its objective is to maximize

$$Ev(y_s) = a + bEy_s$$

which is equivalent to maximizing

$$Ey_s = E(p_s x - c(x) + B) = \bar{p}x - c(x) + B \tag{B.11}$$

where $\bar{p} = Ep_s$ is the mean price. Differentiating [B.11] with respect to x or just using the fact that v' is a positive constant in [B.3] shows that the choice of x will satisfy

$$\bar{p} - c'(x) = 0 \tag{B.12}$$

and the risk-neutral firm will behave *as if* it faced a certain price equal to the mean price $\bar{p}$. In Fig. 18.1 it will produce $x(\bar{p})$. (Note that because $v'' = 0$ the second-order condition [B.4] does require $c'' > 0$.)

The risk-averse firm

How does attitude to risk affect the firm's choice of output? Does a risk-averse firm facing a random price produce a larger or smaller output than a risk-neutral firm? We can show that risk-averse firms produce a smaller output than if they were risk neutral.

The first-order condition [B.3] can be written as

$$Ev'(y_s)[p_s - c'] = Ev'(y_s)E[p_s - c'] + \mathrm{Cov}(v'(y_s), p_s - c')$$
$$= Ev'(y_s)[\bar{p} - c'] + \mathrm{Cov}(v'(y_s), p_s) = 0 \tag{B.13}$$

A higher p_s means that $y_s = p_s x - c + B$ is larger and, since $v'' < 0$ for a risk-averse firm, so that higher y_s reduces $v'(y_s)$, p_s and $v'(y_s)$ have a negative covariance. Hence for [B.13] to be satisfied $Ev'(y_s)(\bar{p} - c')$ must be positive and since $Ev'(y_s) > 0$ we must have

$$c'(x) < \bar{p} = c'(x(\bar{p})) \tag{B.14}$$

for a risk-averse firm. Since $c'' > 0$ (otherwise the risk-neutral firm would not satisfy the second-order conditions) [B.12] implies

$$x < x(\bar{p}) \tag{B.15}$$

The risk-averse firm chooses a smaller output than the risk-neutral firm.

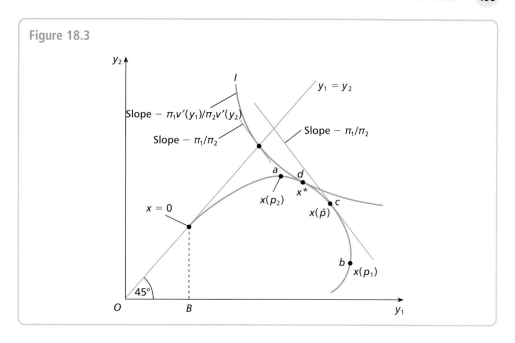

Figure 18.3

Figure 18.3 illustrates this in the two-state case. Since the firm's choice of output determines its state-contingent income $y_s = p_s x - c(x) + B$, we can plot the combinations (y_1, y_2) available to the firm as it varies its output. With zero output the firm has an income of B in both states and is on the 45° line where $y_1 = y_2 = B$. For outputs $0 \leqslant x < x(p_2)$, increases in x raise income in both states (see Fig. 18.2) and the state-contingent income possibility frontier is positively sloped. At $x = x(p_2)$ income in state 2 is maximized and further increases in x reduce y_2. For $x(p_2) \leqslant x < x(p_1)$, y_1 increases with x and y_2 falls and the frontier is negatively sloped. At $x = x(p_1)$, y_1 is at a maximum and for $x \geqslant x(p_1)$, y_1 and y_2 decline as x increases. The frontier is thus positively sloped for $x > x(p_1)$. Since the firm prefers more income in a state to less, the economically relevant section of the frontier is the negatively sloped segment ab (outputs between $x(p_2)$ and $x(p_1)$).

Increases in output alter state-contingent income at the rate

$$\frac{dy_s}{dx} = p_s - c'(x) \qquad \text{[B.16]}$$

so that the slope of the state-contingent income possibility frontier is

$$\frac{dy_2}{dy_1} = \frac{p_2 - c'(x)}{p_1 - c'(x)} \qquad \text{[B.17]}$$

(The reader should check by differentiation that as x increases this expression is at first positive, then zero, then negative and finally positive again.)

In Fig. 18.3 the risk-neutral firm chooses point c where expected income is maximized by output $x(\bar{p})$. At $x(\bar{p})$ the iso-expected income line with slope $-\pi_1/\pi_2$ (recall section 17E) is tangent to the state-contingent income possibility frontier. The risk-averse firm chooses d where its indifference curve I is tangent to the frontier. The indifference curves of the risk-averse firm have slope of $-\pi_1/\pi_2$ at the 45° line but flatten as y_1 increases and y_2 falls. Hence the tangency point d *must* be to the left of *c* on the frontier and the risk-averse firm chooses a smaller output than the risk-neutral firm.

Comparative statics

Effects of lump-sum income changes

We saw in section 7B that lump-sum taxes or changes in fixed costs had no effect on the decisions made by a competitive firm under certainty. The firm responds only if there are changes in price or marginal cost, since only these affect the marginal benefits or costs of its action (see [B.8] above). Under uncertainty the risk-averse firm may alter its behaviour in response to changes in lump-sum taxes or fixed costs. The reason, as [B.3] shows, is that the marginal value of output depends on the marginal utility of income in each state as well as prices and marginal cost. Changes in the lump-sum *B* component of income change the marginal utility of income $v'(y_s)$ in all states and may lead the firm to adjust its output.

Figure 18.4 shows the effect of an increase in *B* of ΔB. The state-contingent income possibility frontier is shifted out by such an increase. For a given output, income in both states increases by ΔB and each point on the frontier is shifted out along a line parallel to the 45° line. The slope of the frontier for any given output is not affected by *B* (see [B.17]). The firm again chooses an output at which an indifference curve is tangent to the frontier. If the indifference curves have the same slope along lines parallel with the 45° line then, since the slope of the frontier is the same at d^0 and d^1, I^1 will be tangent to the new frontier at d^1. The firm will choose d^1 and its output is not altered by an increase in lump-sum income: $x^{0*} = x^{1*}$. From section 17E, the firm has indifference curves with constant slope along $d^0 d^1$ if it has constant absolute risk aversion. Constant absolute risk aversion implies that changes in lump-sum income have no effect on output.

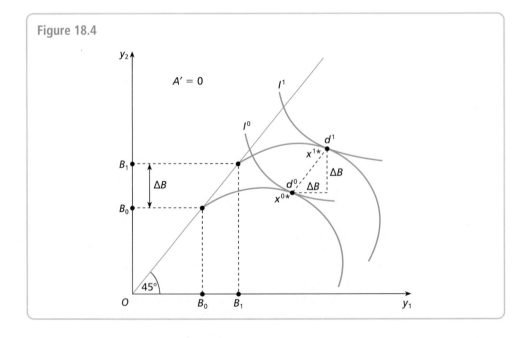

Figure 18.4

The firm's response to a change in B can also be shown to depend on its absolute risk aversion when there are more than two states and diagrammatic methods cannot be used. The firm will increase, decrease or leave its output unchanged when lump-sum income increases if the marginal value of output V_x is increased, decreased or unaffected. Totally differentiating the first-order condition [B.3] with respect to B gives (see Question 1, Exercise 18B)

$$\frac{\partial x}{\partial B} = \frac{-V_{xB}}{V_{xx}} \gtreqless 0 \Leftrightarrow A' \lesseqgtr 0 \qquad [\text{B.18}]$$

where the effect of B on the marginal value of output to the firm is

$$V_{xB} = Ev''(y_s)[p_s - c'(x)] \qquad [\text{B.19}]$$

The intuition behind [B.18] is that increases in output increase the riskiness of income (since $p_s x$ is now more variable) and if the firm is less risk averse at higher income levels it will raise its output when lump-sum income is increased. The cost of the risks associated with any given output will be reduced because the firm is wealthier and the firm will therefore be willing to expand its output in order to increase its expected income.

Increase in mean price

Under certainty the firm produces a larger output if the price of its output increases. Its supply curve is its marginal cost curve. When the firm faces an uncertain price the closest analogy to an increase in the certain price is an increase in the mean price. The price in state s can be written as

$$p_s = \bar{p} + e_s \qquad [\text{B.20}]$$

where $\bar{p}$ is the mean price Ep_s and $Ee_s = Ep_s - \bar{p} = 0$. Income in state s can be written

$$y_s = (\bar{p} + e_s)x - c(x) + B \qquad [\text{B.21}]$$

and the first-order condition as

$$V_x = Ev'((\bar{p} + e_s)x - c(x) + B)[\bar{p} + e_s - c'(x)] = 0 \qquad [\text{B.22}]$$

Output increases, is constant or decreases with $\bar{p}$ as the increase in $\bar{p}$ raises, does not alter or reduces the marginal value of output (V_x). Partially differentiating V_x with respect to $\bar{p}$ gives

$$V_{x\bar{p}} = Ev''(y_s)[\bar{p} + e_s - c'(x)]x + Ev'(y_s) \qquad [\text{B.23}]$$

The second term in [B.23] is positive since $v' > 0$ and so a risk-neutral firm $(v'' = 0)$ will increase output as mean price increases. The first term is just V_{xB} ([B.19]) multiplied by output x and with state-contingent prices written as $\bar{p} + e_s$ instead of p_s. The results we derived ([B.18]) concerning V_{xB} and A' apply to the first term in [B.21] since $x > 0$.

Totally differentiating the first-order condition [B.22] with respect to $\bar{p}$, rearranging and substituting from [B.17] gives the effect of an increase in mean price on output

$$\frac{\partial x}{\partial \bar{p}} = \frac{-V_{x\bar{p}}}{V_{xx}} = -\frac{V_{xB}}{V_{xx}}x - \frac{Ev'(y_s)}{V_{xx}} = \frac{\partial x}{\partial B}x - \frac{Ev'(y_s)}{V_{xx}} \qquad [\text{B.24}]$$

Figure 18.5

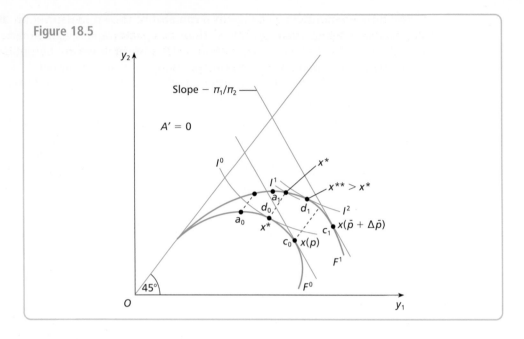

This result is a Slutsky equation which decomposes the effect of the increase in $\bar{p}$ into an ambiguous income effect $x\,\partial x/\partial B$ and a positive substitution effect $-Ev'/V''$. The marginal value of output depends on its effect on the firm's mean income and the amount of risk the firm is exposed to. Increasing the mean price always increases mean income and this substitution effect works to increase output whatever the firm's attitude to risk. Increasing the mean price also makes the firm better off at a given output level and if the firm is more willing to bear risk when its income is increased ($A' < 0$) the risk cost of additional output is reduced. If $A' > 0$ the negative income effect will at least partially offset the positive substitution effect, but output may still increase.

Figure 18.5 illustrates the effect of an increase in $\bar{p}$. The state-contingent income possibility frontier is shifted out as income in each state is increased by $x\,\Delta\bar{p}$ at each level of x. Each point on the initial frontier F^0 is shifted up parallel with the 45° line, but since the shift is proportional to output, the frontier is shifted out by more at larger levels of x. In the economically relevant negative segment the frontier will thus shift out and become flatter (remember that output increases around the frontier from B on the 45° line where $x = 0$). The reader can check this assertion by writing the slope of the frontier ([B.15]) as $(\bar{p} + e_2 - c')/(\bar{p} + e_1 - c')$ and differentiating with respect to $\bar{p}$. Notice that at $x(\bar{p} + e_2)$ state 2 income is not maximized when state 2 price is increased to $\bar{p} + \Delta\bar{p} + e_2$. Hence at $x(\bar{p} + e_2)$ the new frontier F^1 is positively sloped. At the now higher state 2 price a larger output will maximize y_2. The maximum state 2 income on F^1 at a^1 is thus not 45° above a^0.

The flattening of F^1 means that expected income is maximized at a larger output $(x(\bar{p} + \Delta\bar{p}) > x(\bar{p}))$ since the tangency of the constant expected income line is now further round F^1 than F^0.

The indifference curves in Fig. 18.5 show constant absolute risk aversion and have the same slope along lines parallel with the 45° line. At the initially optimal output

x^* the indifference curve I' now cuts the new frontier F^1 which has become flatter along a line parallel to the 45° line. The optimal point on F^1 is d^1 and output is larger at d^1 than d^0. Only if I' had been flatter than I^0 at x^* ($A' > 0$) could output have been reduced by the increase in mean price.

Increased uncertainty

Instead of a rightward shift in the price distribution suppose that the distribution becomes riskier in the sense of a mean-preserving spread. Recalling section 17F we know that a mean-preserving spread in a random variable decreases the expected value of a concave function of that variable. Thus a mean-preserving spread in the price distribution makes the owner of the firm worse off if utility is concave in price. Now $v = v(p_s x - c(x) + B)$ and so

$$\partial^2 v/\partial p^2 = v''(y_s)x^2 \qquad [B.25]$$

Hence a mean-preserving spread in the price distribution makes risk-averse firms worse off. Risk-averse firms always gain from price stability (see the exercises for further analysis).

The effect of increased uncertainty on the firm's output depends on whether the marginal value of output [B.3] is increased or reduced by an increase in uncertainty. The marginal value of output V_x is the expected value of $v'(p_s x - c(x) + B)[p_s - c'(x)]$. Hence V_x is increased or decreased by a mean-preserving spread in price as $v'(y_s)[p_s - c']$ is concave or convex in p_s. Partially differentiating $v'(y_s)[p_s - c']$ twice with respect to p_s gives

$$v'''(y_s)x^2[p_s - c'] + 2v''(y_s)x \qquad [B.26]$$

If the firm is risk neutral [B.26] is zero so that V_x and therefore x is unaffected by a mean-preserving spread in prices. Since risk-neutral firms are only concerned with the expected price it is not surprising that a mean-preserving spread in prices has no effect on their behaviour. If the firm is risk averse the second term in [B.26] is negative. However, the first term is ambiguous. Even if we make stronger assumptions about preferences and thus sign v''', $p_s - c'$ is negative in some states and positive in others.

[B.26] does, however, confirm our earlier conclusion that a risk-averse firm facing a certain price of $\bar{p}$ will reduce its output in response to the introduction of a *small* mean-preserving spread in prices. (Initially $p_s = \bar{p} = c'(x)$ in all states and the first term in [B.26] is zero.)

In order to make more definite predictions about the effect of increased uncertainty it is necessary to consider less general definitions of increased uncertainty than the mean-preserving spread. One simple parameterization is to take the initial prices p_s and define new prices p_s'

$$p_s' = \beta[p_s - \bar{p}] + \bar{p} \qquad [B.27]$$

Starting from $\beta = 1$ (when $p_s' = p_s$) an increase in β is a *Sandmo increase in price risk*. (See Question 4, Exercise 18F.) Substituting p_s' for p_s with $\beta = 1$ in the first-order condition [B.3] and then partially differentiating with respect to β gives the effect of an increase in Sandmo price risk on the marginal value of output:

$$V_{x\beta} = Ev''(y_s)(p_s - \bar{p})(p_s - c')x + Ev'(y_s)(p_s - \bar{p}) \qquad [B.28]$$

Adding and subtracting c' to the first term, rearranging and using [B.19], gives

$$V_{xy} = xEv''(y_s)(p_s - c')^2 - x(\bar{p} - c')Ev''(y_s)(p_s - c') + Ev'(y_s)(p_s - \bar{p})$$
$$= xEv''(y_s)(p_s - c')^2 - x(\bar{p} - c')V_{xB} + Ev'(y_s)(p_s - \bar{p}) \qquad [B.29]$$

The first term in [B.29] is negative since $v'' < 0$. The third term can be written as $Ev'E(p_s - \bar{p}) + \text{Cov}(v', p_s) = \text{Cov}(v', p_s)$ (remember $Ep_s = \bar{p}$). $\text{Cov}(v', p_s)$ is negative since larger p_s imply larger y_s and smaller $v'(y_s)$. Since $\bar{p} > c'(x)$ for risk-averse firms, the second term is negative if V_{xB} is positive, i.e. if $A' < 0$ (see [B.18]). Hence diminishing or constant absolute risk aversion implies that the firm will reduce its output if there is a Sandmo increase in risk. The rationale is that an increase in risk makes the risk-averse firm worse off. If it has diminishing absolute risk aversion it will now be more averse to risk and will want to reduce its exposure to risk by reducing its output. The first and third terms in [B.29] are akin to substitution effects: with a more risky distribution of prices the risk cost of any given output level is increased and so a risk-averse firm will reduce its output level.

Technological uncertainty

We now examine the firm's behaviour when it faces technological uncertainty: its output is determined both by its choice and by random factors over which it has no control. Assume that the firm uses a single input z to produce its output and has the stochastic production function

$$x_s = f_s(z) \qquad [B.30]$$

The firm sets its input level z before it knows the state of the world and the output depends on the state once z is chosen. For example, the farmer's output of wheat will depend on the amount of seed sown and the weather during the growing season. Assume that the input always has a positive but declining marginal product ($f_s'(z) > 0, f_s'' < 0$).

The production function [B.30] is very general and two highly restrictive specifications of $f_s(z)$ are often encountered in the literature as a means of deriving unambiguous conclusions. The firm faces *additive uncertainty* if the production function is

$$x_s = f(z) + e_s \qquad [B.31]$$

where e_s is a random increment to output in state s with $Ee_s = 0$. There is *multiplicative uncertainty* if

$$x_s = f(z)e_s \qquad [B.32]$$

where $Ee_s = 1$ and $e_s > 0$. With additive uncertainty the input's marginal product is the same in all states ($f_s' = f'(z)$), while total output varies across states and so the marginal and total products are uncorrelated. Under multiplicative uncertainty, marginal product depends on the state ($f_s' = f'(z)e_s$) and marginal and total product are positively correlated across states. Under more general specifications, marginal and total product may be negatively or positively correlated.

The firm buys the input on a competitive input market at the certain price w and sells its output on a competitive market at the certain price p. Income in state s is

$$y_s = pf_s(z) - wz + B \qquad [B.33]$$

where B is non-random income of the owner of the firm. The input is chosen, before the state of the world is known, to maximize $V = Ev(y_s)$ and satisfies the first-order condition

$$V_z = Ev'(pf_s(z) - wz + B)[pf_s'(z) - w] = 0 \qquad \text{[B.34]}$$

(The reader should check that the second-order condition is satisfied.)

We compare the behaviour of risk-averse and risk-neutral firms by writing [B.34] as

$$V_z = Ev'(y_s)[pEf_s' - w] + \text{Cov}(v'(y_s), pf_s') = 0 \qquad \text{[B.35]}$$

With a risk-neutral firm v' is constant, so that $\text{Cov}(v', pf_s') = 0$, and [B.35] implies

$$pEf_s'(z) - w = 0$$

The risk-neutral firm acts as if its marginal product were certain and equal to Ef_s'. If the firm is risk averse it will choose its input level to satisfy

$$pEf_s'(z) - w = -\frac{\text{Cov}(v'(y_s), pf_s')}{Ev'(y_s)} \qquad \text{[B.36]}$$

We noted above that, in general, marginal product f_s' and total product f_s can be negatively or positively correlated. If they are positively correlated, f_s' and y_s are also positively correlated and $\text{Cov}(v', pf_s')$ is negative. Hence the right-hand side of [B.36] is positive and, since $f_s'' < 0$, the risk-averse firm will choose a smaller input and thus produce less than the risk-neutral firm (for which the right-hand side of [B.36] is always zero). If $\text{Cov}(\cdot)$ is zero (as in the case of additive uncertainty) the risk-averse firm chooses the same input level as the risk-neutral firm and if marginal and total product are negatively correlated it chooses a larger input level.

The comparative static responses of the firm to changes in input or output prices and the degree of uncertainty can be analysed with the same techniques used in the previous subsection. We leave this to the exercises and turn to the firm which faces both price and technological uncertainty.

Price and technological uncertainty

With output price uncertain the firm's income is

$$y_s = p_s f_s(z) - wz + B \qquad \text{[B.37]}$$

and the expected utility-maximizing choice of z satisfies

$$\begin{aligned} V_z &= Ev'(y_s)[p_s f_s'(z) - w] \\ &= Ev'(y_s)[\bar{p}Ef_s' - w + \text{Cov}(p_s, f_s')] + \text{Cov}(v'(y_s), p_s f_s') = 0 \end{aligned} \qquad \text{[B.38]}$$

Rearranging gives

$$\bar{p}Ef_s'(z) - w = -\text{Cov}(p_s, f_s') - \frac{\text{Cov}(v'(y_s), p_s f_s')}{Ev'(y_s)} \qquad \text{[B.39]}$$

If there was certainty with the price $p = \bar{p}$ and the non-stochastic production function $f(z) = Ef_s(z)$, the firm would choose an input level z_c^* where

$$\bar{p}Ef_s'(z_c^*) - w = 0 \qquad \text{[B.40]}$$

When there is only price uncertainty or technological uncertainty the risk-neutral firm acts as if the random variables it faces were fixed at their mean values: there is *certainty equivalence*. Comparing [B.39] and [B.40] we now see that, with *both* types of uncertainty present, certainty equivalence fails to hold even for the risk-neutral firm. With risk neutrality the second term on the right-hand side of [B.39] is zero since v' does not vary with y_s. The first covariance term, however, may be positive or zero and the risk-neutral firm's input choice z_n^* may be greater or smaller than under certainty.

Consider two simple special cases. In case (a) the demand function in the market for the firm's output is non-random so that p_s varies across states only because total supply is random. Further, the random output fluctuations of firms are independent and all firms' outputs are very small in relation to total supply so that fluctuations in individual firm output have negligible effects on market price. Then each firm's marginal product will be uncorrelated with the market price and certainty equivalence will hold: $z_n^* = z_c^*$.

In case (b) the market demand function is again non-random but there is multiplicative uncertainty and all firms are affected by the same random factors (e.g. rainfall) so that their outputs are positively correlated. Since high output from one firm tends to be associated with high output from all other firms there will be negative correlation between each firm's output and the market price. Under multiplicative uncertainty, output and marginal product are positively correlated and so the covariance of price and marginal product is negative. The risk-neutral firm will therefore choose an input level z_n^* such that

$$\bar{p}Ef'(z_n^*)e_s - w = \bar{p}f'(z_n^*)Ee_s - w = \bar{p}f'(z_n^*) - w > 0 \qquad [B.41]$$

($Ee_s = 1$ under multiplicative uncertainty.) Since $f'' < 0$, the risk-neutral firm chooses a smaller input level under uncertainty than under certainty: $z_n^* < z_c^*$.

The difference between the behaviour of risk-averse and risk-neutral firms depends on the second covariance term in [B.38] and, since y_s depends on p_s and f_s, we need strong assumptions to compare the input choice z_a^* of a risk-averse and z_n^* of a risk-neutral firm. What is required are assumptions which sign the correlation between revenue $p_s f_s$ (which determines y_s) and the marginal revenue product $p_s f_s'$. Thus in case (a) above, although p_s is not correlated with f_s or f_s', $p_s f_s$ and $p_s f_s'$ are positively correlated and $\text{Cov}(v'(p_s f_s - wz + B), p_s f_s')$ is negative, so that $z_a^* < z_n^* = z_c^*$. In case (b), revenue in state s is $p_s f e_s$, marginal revenue product is $p_s f_s' e_s$ and these are positively correlated, so that $z_a^* < z_n^* < z_c^*$.

As a final example consider case (c) in which the market demand curve is non-stochastic and has constant elasticity ε. There are N identical firms with perfectly correlated outputs and facing additive production uncertainty. Since $f_s' = f'$ does not vary across the states of the world the correlation between $p_s f_s$ and $p_s f_s'$ depends on the correlation of $p_s f_s$ and p_s. The price in state s is determined by the market clearing condition that total output Nf_s is equal to demand. If the demand is elastic ($\varepsilon < -1$) larger total output (and therefore lower price) is associated with larger total revenue $Np_s f_s$. (Recall the discussion of monopoly in Chapter 9.) Since each firm gets $1/N$ of total revenue the correlation between $p_s f_s$ and p_s is negative if and only if demand is elastic. Hence we have established that $\text{Cov}(v'(y_s), p_s f_s')$ is positive or negative as demand is elastic or inelastic and so

$$z_a^* \gtreqless z_n^* = z_c \Leftrightarrow \varepsilon \gtreqless -1 \qquad [B.42]$$

The risk-averse firm is concerned about the riskiness of its income. It suffers from income risk because it faces market and technological uncertainty. In some circumstances market and technological uncertainty tend to offset each other. Because the market demand curve is downward sloping, high output tends to be associated with low price and vice versa. Thus the riskiness of the firm's income may be less than the riskiness of the distribution of prices or output levels. In case (c) price and output risk are exactly offsetting if the market demand curve has unit elasticity. The firm faces a random output price and random output but its income is certain since $p_s f_s$ is constant. The risk-averse firm then makes the same decisions as it would under certainty.

EXERCISE 18B

1. Use the method outlined in section 17E to establish that output increases when lump-sum income increases if and only if the firm has diminishing absolute risk aversion. (*Hint:* first consider states in which $p_s \geqslant p^0 = c'(x^*)$ so that $y_s \geqslant y^0 = p^0 x^* - c(x^*) + B$ and $v''(y_s)[p_s - c'(x^*)] \geqslant -A(y^0)v'(y_s)[p_s - c'(x^*)]$. Then show that this holds with strict inequality for states in which $p_s < p^0$, and use the first-order condition [B.3] to establish $Ev''(y_s)[p_s - c'(x^*)] > 0$.)

2. Show that the variance of the firm's income is increased by an increase in its output. Hence show that a risk-averse firm with a quadratic utility function will produce less than a risk-neutral firm.

3. *Price stabilization and the timing of decisions.* Suppose that the firm is able to choose output when it knows the state of the world, i.e. its output price.

   (a) What output will it choose in state s?

   (b) What is its expected utility given that it chooses its output optimally in each state when the price is revealed?

   (c) Is the firm better off by choosing its output before or after the state of the world is revealed?

   (d) Show that, depending on its supply elasticity and its degree of relative risk aversion, the firm may be better or worse off as a result of a mean-preserving contraction in the distribution of prices.

4. Show that $v''' < 0$ ensures that the firm has diminishing absolute risk aversion.

5. Show that, if the firm is risk neutral, increases in w reduce its demand for labour when it faces technological uncertainty. Show that if it is risk averse the effect of an increase in w can be decomposed into an income effect of ambiguous sign and a negative substitution effect.

6. *Price, output and revenue risk.* Measure the riskiness of a random variable by the variance of its log. Show that, if the market demand function is non-stochastic with constant elasticity ε, the riskiness of total revenue (expenditure on the good) is less than the riskiness of total output if $\varepsilon < -\frac{1}{2}$ and vanishes when $\varepsilon = -1$.

C. Production with futures markets

Risk-averse firms faced with technological or market uncertainty can attempt to reduce the uncertainty in their incomes in a variety of ways. They can adopt more flexible production methods, so that when the state of the world is revealed they have a wider set of opportunities or smaller penalties for having taken *ex ante* decisions which are *ex post* 'incorrect'. For example, they can install dual-fired electricity generators which can use oil or coal if they face uncertain fuel prices. They can spread the risks of plant breakdown by buying several smaller machines rather than one large one. They can diversify by producing a mixture of products. They can also enter into contracts to reduce their risks by insuring assets against fire or by selling part of their output on futures markets for a certain price rather than on spot markets for an uncertain price.

As these examples indicate, technological means can be used to reduce technological and market risk and market means can be used to reduce market and technological risk. We will demonstrate another feature of firms' attempts to reduce risk: devices to reduce risk also alter other decisions, leading to changes in the firm's output or input levels. Thus technological or market innovations which make it easier for firms to shed risk are likely to have significant repercussions in input and output markets.

We take the example of futures markets (Question 2, Exercise 18C considers the implications of insurance). The firm is subject to market and technological uncertainty as before but it now has the opportunity to trade in the futures market. In this market individuals buy and sell promises to deliver a unit of the commodity at a specified date and place. The contracts are made *before* and delivery is made *after* the state of the world is known. The contracts are *not* state contingent: the seller of the contract promises to deliver one unit of the good whatever the state of the world.

The price of a one-unit futures contract is p_f and the buyer of such a contract is entitled to take delivery of one unit of the good from the seller at the specified date when the state of the world is known. At that date the spot market for the good will open and the spot price p_s will be determined by the total demand from consumers and the total supply in state s in the usual way. The total supply of the good to the spot market is the total amount produced. That part of producers' output which was sold on the futures market and delivered to the purchasers of futures contracts is then sold on the spot market by the holders of the futures contracts. The rest of the producers' output is sold directly on the spot market.

The state s income of a firm producing the good is

$$y_s = p_s(f_s(z) - x_f) + p_f x_f - wz + B \qquad [\text{C.1}]$$

where $f_s(z)$ is its output in state s from input level z and x_f is the amount of output sold on the futures market at the certain futures price p_f. The firm now takes two decisions: its input z and its trade in futures contracts x_f. The first-order conditions for these decisions are

$$V_z = Ev'(y_s)[p_s f_s'(z) - w] = 0 \qquad [\text{C.2}]$$

$$V_{x_f} = Ev'(y_s)(p_f - p_s) = Ev'(y_s)E[p_f - p_s] + \text{Cov}(v'(y_s), p_f - p_s)$$
$$= Ev'(y_s)[p_f - \bar{p}] - \text{Cov}(v'(y_s), p_s) = 0 \qquad [\text{C.3}]$$

The condition on z is identical to [B.38] but, as we will see, this does not mean that the futures market has no effect on the firm's input choice.

The condition on x_f is derived from the decision problem of a producer, but by fixing $z = 0$ it can also serve for those speculative traders in the futures markets who are not producers. [C.3] shows that, if there are competitive risk-neutral traders in the futures markets and there are no transaction costs, the equilibrium futures price must equal the expected spot price. (The Cov term in [C.3] is zero for a risk-neutral futures trader so that p_f must equal $\bar{p}$ if [C.3] is to be zero. Alternatively, if $p_f \neq \bar{p}$ it would be possible to make arbitrarily large expected profits by buying (if $p_f < \bar{p}$) or selling (if $p_f > \bar{p}$) futures contracts.) If there are transactions costs then the risk-neutral traders must earn a gross expected profit and so the futures price at which they buy must be less than the expected spot price at which they will sell – a situation known as *normal backwardation*. There is *contango* when the futures price is greater than the expected spot price. (Question 1, Exercise 18C considers the circumstances required for contango.)

Suppose initially that there is no technological uncertainty. If $p_f = \bar{p}$ the first term in [C.3] is zero and hence so is $\mathrm{Cov}(v'(y_s), p_s)$. But if the firm is risk averse the only way in which $\mathrm{Cov}(v(y_s), p_s)$ can be zero is if y_s is constant across all states. As inspection of [C.1] shows this requires that $x_f = f(z)$. Thus with no production uncertainty and $p_f = \bar{p}$, the risk-averse producer sells all output on the futures market and gets rid of all risk. In these circumstances the futures market provides fair insurance against price risks and the risk-averse producer will take full advantage of it and achieve a certain income. Having achieved a certain income by selling all planned output forward, the producer can then choose the input or output level which maximizes certain income $p_f f(z) - wz + B$. The input decision is identical to that of a risk-neutral producer facing the mean spot price $\bar{p}$ or of a producer facing a certain spot price of $\bar{p} = p_f$.

If $p_f < \bar{p}$, sales on the futures market still provide insurance against spot price risk but the insurance is now unfair: sales on the futures market reduce the firm's expected income as well as its risks. The firm will therefore not wish to shed all risks and its futures contract sales will be less than output $f(z)$. The $\mathrm{Cov}(v'(y_s), p_s)$ term must now be negative since $p_f < \bar{p}$ implies the first term in [C.3] is negative. The negativity of $\mathrm{Cov}(v'(y_s), p_s)$ requires that income is positively correlated with p_s and so the firm sells less than its output on the futures market and retains some exposure to price risk. Recalling our discussion of the risk-averse firm under price uncertainty in section B, the firm will choose a smaller output or input level than if it were risk neutral.

Now suppose that the firm is subject to production risk as well as price risk so that the firm cannot shed all its risk by trading in futures. If $p_f = \bar{p}$, the firm will choose to set x_f so that $\mathrm{Cov}(v'(y_s), p_s)$ is zero. The covariance term depends on the correlation between y_s and p_s, i.e. between $p_s[f_s(z) - x_f]$ and p_s. The correlation is a decreasing function of futures sales (why?). By making x_f large enough the correlation can be made negative and by making x_f sufficiently negative (purchase of futures contracts rather than sales) it can be made positive. When $x_f = 0$ the $\mathrm{Cov}(v'(y_s), p_s)$ depends on the correlation of the firm's spot revenue $p_s f_s$ and the spot price p_s. This in turn will depend on the elasticity of spot market demand and the correlation between the firm's output and the total supply of all other firms. In case (c) considered in section B where there is perfect correlation of outputs the correlation between revenue and price depends only on the spot market demand elasticity. If we further assume that $\varepsilon = -1$ the firm's revenue and the spot price are not correlated and the $\mathrm{Cov}(v'(y_s), p_s)$ term is zero at $x_f = 0$. In this very special case the firm will not trade in the futures market. The fact that $\varepsilon = -1$ means that its income is the same in all states and it has no uncertainty and hence no rationale for trading in the futures market. If demand is inelastic higher prices imply greater revenue and so $\mathrm{Cov}(v'(y_s), p_s) < 0$. Hence [C.3] is positive at $x_f = 0$ and the firm will wish to sell futures to shed some of its risk because its income is highest and v' lowest in states in which the spot price is high and vice versa. Hence by selling futures the firm can shift income from states when v' is low to states when v' is high.

The implications of the futures market for the firm's production decision with technological uncertainty depend on the precise form of its production function and highly specific assumptions are necessary to derive strong conclusions. Suppose that $p_f = \bar{p}$ so that $\text{Cov}(v', p_s)$ must be zero from [C.3]. Now examine the condition on the firm's input choice as written in [B.34]. If there is additive uncertainty f_s' is constant across all states and $\text{Cov}(v'(y_s), p_s) = 0$ implies $\text{Cov}(v'(y_s), p_s f_s') = 0$. Hence, since $\text{Cov}(p_s, f_s')$ is also zero the condition on the input reduces to $\bar{p}Ef_s' = w$. Thus with futures markets and additive uncertainty the risk-averse firm behaves as though it were risk neutral. The existence of the futures market removes the effect of price risks on its behaviour and the fact that its marginal product is non-random removes the influence of technological risk on its production decision.

In this case we see that the futures market leads the firm to increase its input and thus its output in all states of the world. If this is true for all other firms as well, the introduction of the futures market will increase total output in all states and thus reduce the spot price in all states. The particular result depends on the highly specific assumptions ($p_f = \bar{p}$ and additive uncertainty) we made but the general lesson is clear: futures markets can have significant implications for the equilibrium prices and quantities traded in spot markets. Indeed the lesson is applicable to any other means, such as insurance, which firms can adopt to shed some of their risks. Such devices alter the state distribution of income generated by the firm's decisions and will lead to changes in these decisions.

EXERCISE 18C

1. *Contango*. Contango occurs when the expected spot price is less than the futures price and buyers of futures contracts make an expected loss. (a) Why is this situation not an equilibrium if there are risk-neutral traders? (b) In what circumstances will contango arise? (*Hint*: examine the $\text{Cov}(v', p_s)$ term in [C.3] and the definition of y_s.)

2. *Insurance and production*. Suppose that there are two states of the world, 'wet' and 'fine', and that the firm's output for given input is greater in the fine state than in the wet state but that the price of its output is greater in the wet state. Assume that there is no futures market but that the firm could buy insurance against the wet state at an actuarially fair price. How does the existence of such insurance affect (a) the firm's choice of input level, (b) its expected utility?

Insurance, risk spreading and pooling

A. Introduction

In this chapter we continue to apply the tools developed in Chapter 17 for modelling behaviour under uncertainty by examining some of the ways in which individuals can relieve themselves of risk. We begin with an analysis of the demand for insurance in section B. In section C we consider an individual facing two sources of risk but with an incomplete insurance market which only provides cover against one of the risks. Sections D and E consider two other methods of dealing with uncertainty which are closely related to insurance: risk spreading and pooling. Sections F and G introduce two types of information asymmetry which were first investigated in the context of insurance. In section F there is adverse selection when the insured has better information about the probability of the event she wishes to insure against than the insurer. Section G considers moral hazard where the insured can take more or less care to reduce the probability of an accident but the insurer cannot observe her level of care. We show how insurance contracts are adapted to mitigate the effects of information asymmetry. Section H examines the implications of signalling when the better informed party to a contract can convey their information to the less well informed by actions whose cost depends on the better informed party's type.

B. The insurance decision

A risk-averse individual has a concave utility function and so has different marginal utilities of income across the states of the world if his income is not the same in all states. The individual may therefore be willing to give up income in states where income is high and thus marginal utility is low in exchange for an increase in income in states where income is low and thus marginal utility is high. Whether such exchanges would be made depends on the probabilities the individual attaches to the different states and on the terms at which the exchanges can be made. In this section we examine insurance markets as a means of transferring income between states.

Suppose there are only two states of the world and that in state 1 the individual has an initial income of y and in state 2 she has an income of $y - L$. State 2 could be thought of as the occurrence of an accident which imposes a financial loss. In Fig. 19.1 the individual is initially at a. We assume that the individual can affect neither the loss L nor the probability of the loss. (This is implicit in identifying a state by the amount of initial income.) Relaxing the assumption leads to *moral hazard* problems which we examine in section G.

An insurance company is willing to sell insurance cover against the accident at a premium rate of p ($0 < p < 1$). The decision-taker pays £qp to the insurer in exchange for the insurer's promise to pay her £q if and only if an accident occurs. q is the

Figure 19.1

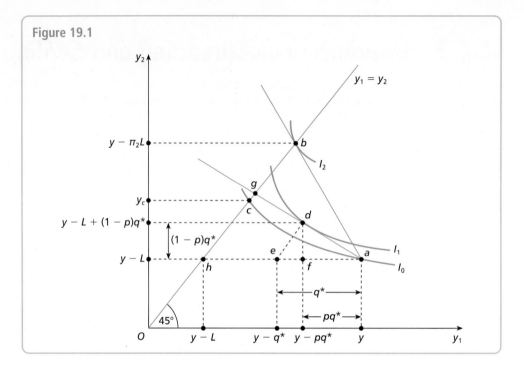

amount of *insurance cover*. With such an insurance contract the decision-taker's state-contingent incomes are

$$y_1 = y - pq \tag{B.1}$$

$$y_2 = y - L - pq + q = y - L + (1 - p)q \tag{B.2}$$

(Remember that the decision-taker must pay the premium pq before the state of the world is known. Thus her income is reduced by pq in both states.)

Increases in the amount of cover q reduce state 1 income and increase state 2 incomes so that insurance transfers income between states. Use [B.1] to write $q = (y - y_1)/p$ and substitute in [B.2] to get

$$y_2 = y - L + \frac{(1 - p)}{p}(y - y_1) \tag{B.3}$$

We can interpret this as a budget constraint in state-contingent income space since it shows the combinations of state-contingent incomes available by varying the amount of insurance cover. The interpretation is even clearer if we rearrange [B.3] to get

$$(1 - p)y_1 + py_2 = (1 - p)y + p(y - L) \tag{B.4}$$

$(1 - p)$ and p can be thought of as the prices of a claim to £1 of income in states 1 and 2. The left-hand side of [B.4] is then expenditure on state-contingent claims and the right-hand side the value of the insured's initial endowment of state-contingent income.

Differentiation of [B.3] with respect to y_1 gives the slope of the budget line

$$\frac{dy_2}{dy_1} = -\frac{(1 - p)}{p} \tag{B.5}$$

which is the rate at which the decision-taker can exchange state 1 and state 2 income by means of an insurance contract. If the premium rate p is not affected by the amount of cover bought the budget constraint is a straight line through the initial state-contingent income point at a (since the decision-taker can always choose not to buy any insurance cover).

An insurance contract has an *actuarially fair premium* if it does not alter the insured individual's expected income. (Compare the definition of a fair bet in section 17E.) The insured individual pays pq before the state of the world is known and receives q if there is an accident, i.e. if state 2 occurs. Let π_s be the probability the decision-taker attaches to state s. From [B.1] and [B.2], expected income with insurance is

$$\pi_1[y - pq] + \pi_2[y - L + (1 - p)q] = y - \pi_2 L - q[\pi_1 p - \pi_2(1 - p)]$$
$$= y - \pi_2 L - q[p - \pi_2] \qquad \text{[B.6]}$$

(remember $\pi_1 = 1 - \pi_2$). The insurance contract will not alter the expected income of the insured if $p = \pi_2$ and so π_2 is the fair premium rate and $\pi_2 q$ the fair premium. Insurance companies typically include a loading in their premia to cover their administration and other costs, so that $p > \pi_2$ and the contract is actuarially unfair (see Question 1, Exercise 19B). We assume that both the insurer and the insured know the insured's accident probability or *risk class*. If the insured knows her risk class but the insurer does not, problems of *adverse selection* arise. We discuss adverse selection models in section F.

In Fig. 19.1 the line ba has slope $-\pi_1/\pi_2$ and all state-contingent income combinations along it have an expected value equal to the decision-taker's expected income without insurance: $y - \pi_2 L$. The line gda with slope $-(1 - p)/p$ is the budget constraint and shows the state-contingent income combinations available through insurance. The budget line gda is flatter than the constant expected income line ba (the absolute value of its slope is smaller) and so $(1 - p)/p < \pi_1/\pi_2$. Since $\pi_1 = 1 - \pi_2$ we have $p > \pi_2$ and the insurance premium is unfair to the insured.

The decision-taker chooses the insurance cover q to maximize expected utility

$$V = \pi_1 v(y_1) + \pi_2 v(y_2) = \pi_1 v(y - pq) + \pi_2 v(y - L + (1 - p)q)$$
$$= V(q; y, L, p, \pi_2) \qquad \text{[B.7]}$$

Assuming that some insurance cover is purchased, the optimal cover q^* satisfies the first-order condition

$$\frac{\partial V}{\partial q} = V_q = -\pi_1 v'(y - pq^*)p + \pi_2 v'(y - L + (1 - p)q^*)(1 - p) = 0 \qquad \text{[B.8]}$$

The second-order condition

$$\frac{\partial^2 V}{\partial q^2} = V_{qq} = \pi_1 v''(y - pq^*)p^2 + \pi_2 v''(y - L + (1 - p)q^*)(1 - p)^2 < 0 \qquad \text{[B.9]}$$

is satisfied because of the concavity of v ($v'' < 0$).

Rearrange [B.8] to get

$$\frac{-\pi_1 v'(y_1)}{\pi_2 v'(y_2)} = \frac{-(1 - p)}{p} \qquad \text{[B.10]}$$

The left-hand side of [B.10] is the slope of the indifference curve (recall section 17E) and the right-hand side the slope of the insurance budget line. As in the consumer theory of Chapter 2 we have a tangency solution where the marginal rate of substitution between state-contingent incomes is equal to the slope of the budget line.

Another rearrangement of [B.8] gives

$$[\pi_1 v'(y_1) + \pi_2 v'(y_2)]p = \pi_2 v'(y_2) \tag{B.11}$$

The left-hand side of [B.11] is the marginal cost in expected utility terms of an additional £1 of cover. The £1 of cover reduces income in both states by £p and $\sum \pi_s v'(y_s) = Ev'(y_s)$ is expected marginal utility of income. If the decision-taker had an additional £1 of income in all states, i.e. for sure, her expected utility would increase by $Ev'(y_s)$. The right-hand side of [B.11] is the marginal benefit of an additional £1 of cover which increases income in state 2 by £1.

If the premium is unfair $p > \pi_2$ and so $1 - p < 1 - \pi_2 = \pi_1$. Hence if [B.10] holds $v'(y_1) < v'(y_2)$ and, since the utility function is concave, $y_1 > y_2$. Using [B.1] and [B.2] we have

$$y_1 - y_2 = y - pq^\star - (y - L + (1 - p)q^\star)$$
$$= y - pq^\star - y + L - (1 - p)q^\star = L - q^\star > 0 \tag{B.12}$$

Thus if the decision-taker faces an unfair premium she buys less than complete cover against her potential accident loss. As in Fig. 19.1, she will choose a state-contingent income vector at d which leaves her still bearing some of the accident loss.

We have assumed that the individual's utility depends only on income and not directly on the state of the world. But an insured individual may dislike having an accident or being burgled or having her house burn down even if she had full cover against financial loss so that her wealth or income was unaffected. Thus her state-dependent utility functions would have $v_1(y) > v_2(y)$. But [B.8] indicates that what matters for her insurance decision is whether marginal utility of income is state dependent: $v_1'(y) \neq v_2'(y)$. Introspection suggests that it is much less clear whether marginal utility of income is reduced or increased by having an accident, being burgled, etc. One would feel worse off after an accident even if income was unaffected, but is the value of an additional £1 of income greater or smaller? We will therefore continue to assume that utility and thus marginal utility is state independent and leave to Question 2, Exercise 19B considerations of the implications of state-dependent marginal utility.

Returning to Fig. 19.1, the distance ah is the difference between the state-contingent incomes without insurance (L). The amount of insurance bought when the decision-taker chooses a contract which puts her at d can also be shown in the diagram. The contract moves the decision-taker from a to d, reducing state 1 income by $pq^\star$ (equals af) and raising state 2 income by $(1 - p)q^\star$ (equals df). The line de is parallel to the 45° line and so $ef = df = (1 - p)q^\star$. Hence the distance ae which is the sum of af and ef is $pq^\star + (1 - p)q^\star = q^\star$. The decision-taker chooses the contract d which provides cover $q^\star$ and is left bearing $L - q^\star$ (equals eh) of the risk.

With fair insurance ($p = \pi_2$) the budget line would be ba and the decision-taker would choose the contract b where her state-contingent incomes are equal and she takes out full cover insurance $q = L$. (Remember that the slope of the indifference curve at the 45° certainty line is $-\pi_1/\pi_2$.)

If the decision-taker was not offered a variable cover contract but was forced to choose between full cover or no cover, she might still prefer to be fully insured and on the 45° line rather than be completely uninsured at a. In Fig. 19.1, although the decision-taker would prefer the variable cover contract d, she would still accept the full cover contract g (paying pL in exchange for full cover L) rather than be completely uninsured at a. Indeed she would accept any full cover contract which moved her from a to the certainty line at or above c. She will accept a full cover contract provided it does not reduce her certain income below the certainty equivalent income y_c for the uninsured contingent income vector $(y, y - L)$.

Demand for insurance

Given her attitude to risk, the decision-taker's optimal cover or demand for insurance depends on the exogenous variables which determine the position of her budget constraint (y, L and p) and the shape of her indifference curves (π_2). Solving [B.8] for the optimal cover as a function of these parameters we get her demand function for insurance

$$q^* = D(y, L, p, \pi_2) \qquad \text{[B.13]}$$

We now consider how the demand varies as the exogenous variables alter.

Income

Suppose that the individual's income in both states is increased by Δy. This will shift the initial position in Fig. 19.2 from a to a'. Since the premium rate p is unchanged the slope of the new insurance budget line $a'g'$ is the same as the old budget line ag. The decision-taker chooses d on ag with cover of q, equal to ae. The new equilibrium is at d' where I' is tangent to $a'g'$. The points e, d, e' and d' all lie on the same line parallel to the 45°. Thus, by similar triangles, $a'e'$ equals ae and the new cover q' is identical to the initial level before the change in income. It would be possible to draw indifference curves which are tangent to $a'g'$ to the left (d'') or right (d''') and the demand for cover could be increased (to $a'e''$) or reduced (to $a'e'''$).

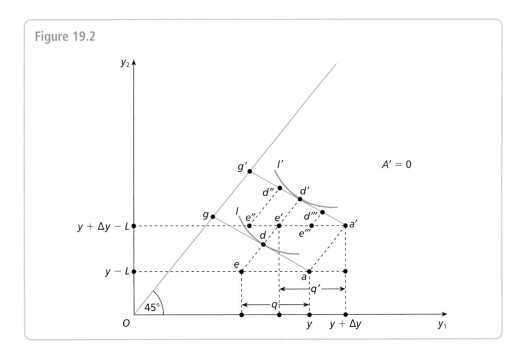

Figure 19.2

Without further restrictions on preferences it is not possible to say whether the demand for insurance increases or decreases as income increases. If the indifference curves become steeper along lines parallel to the 45° line (i.e. as income in both states increases by the same amount) then the demand for insurance will fall since any point of tangency must be to the right of d'. Conversely, if the curves become flatter along a line parallel to the 45° line. But the indifference curves are steeper, flatter or have a constant slope along such lines depending on whether the coefficient of absolute risk aversion $A = -v''/v'$ is decreasing, increasing or constant (see section 17E). Hence

$$\frac{\partial D}{\partial y} \gtreqless 0 \Leftrightarrow A' \gtreqless 0 \qquad \text{[B.14]}$$

This result can be derived using the standard method of comparative statics (see Appendix I). The first-order condition [B.8] is an implicit function relating q^* to the parameters. Using the Implicit Function Theorem,

$$\frac{\partial D}{\partial y} = \frac{\partial q^*}{\partial y} = \frac{-V_{qy}}{V_{qq}} \qquad \text{[B.15]}$$

where $V_{qy} = \partial^2 V/\partial q \partial y$ is the marginal effect of income on the marginal value of insurance cover. Since $V_{qq} < 0$ by the second-order condition [B.9], q^* increases or decreases with y, as increases in y raise or lower the marginal value of q (i.e. as V_{qy} is positive or negative). Differentiating [B.8] partially with respect to y gives

$$\begin{aligned} V_{qy} &= -\pi_1 v''(y - pq^*)p + \pi_2 v''(y - L + (1 - p)q^*)(1 - p) \\ &= -\pi_1 v''(y_1)p + \pi_2 v''(y_2)(1 - p) \end{aligned} \qquad \text{[B.16]}$$

Since the first term is positive ($v'' < 0$) and the second is negative, [B.16] could be negative or positive. If we rearrange the first-order condition [B.8] to get

$$\pi_1 p = \pi_2 v'(y_2)(1 - p)/v'(y_1)$$

and substitute it in [B.16] we have, after rearrangement,

$$V_{qy} = (1 - p)\pi_2 v'(y_2)\left[\frac{-v''(y_1)}{v'(y_1)} + \frac{v''(y_2)}{v'(y_2)}\right]$$

$$= (1 - p)\pi_2 v'(y_2)[A(y_1) - A(y_2)] \qquad \text{[B.17]}$$

The sign of V_{qy}, and thus $\partial D/\partial y$, depends on the sign of $A(y_1) - A(y_2)$. The decision-taker faces an unfair premium and takes out less than full cover, so that $y_1 > y_2$. Hence we have again established [B.14]: the demand for insurance increases or decreases with income as the insured has increasing or decreasing absolute risk aversion. If the decision-taker has diminishing absolute risk aversion she is more willing to take risks and less willing to buy insurance as income increases.

Premium rate

Next we consider the effect of increases in the premium rate on the amount of cover bought to see whether the demand curve for insurance is negatively sloped. Figure 19.3 illustrates the effect of an increase in p. The budget constraint pivots through a and becomes flatter since increases in p reduce $(1 - p)/p$. The point d'

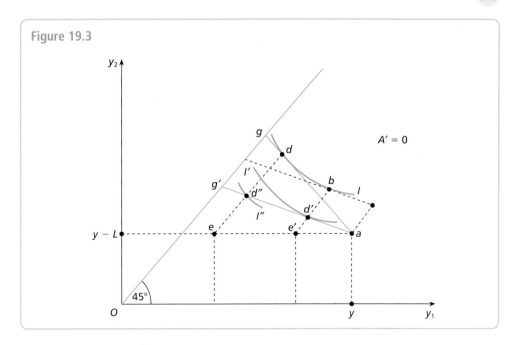

Figure 19.3

chosen on the new lower budget line ag' corresponds to a smaller amount of cover (ae') compared with the point d on the initial budget line ag where cover bought was ae. Again it is obvious that with different preferences (indifference curves) the amount of cover could have been smaller or larger than ae.

As in consumer theory, we can decompose the effect of the premium rate change into a substitution effect and an ambiguously signed income effect. The substitution effect is found by shifting a hypothetical budget line parallel with ag' until it is tangent to the initial indifference curve I at b. Since the premium rate has increased, the relative price of state 2 income has increased, and the decision-taker substitutes away from the 'good' (state 2 income) whose relative price has increased. The amount of cover bought at b is ae' which must be less than ae because b is to the right of d. The income effect is the change from b to d' induced by the reduction in real income with p held constant. In Fig. 19.3 we have assumed that the decision-taker has constant absolute risk aversion ($A' = 0$) and so the indifference curves I and I' have the same slope along lines such as $e'd'b$ which are parallel to the 45° line. Hence the income effect is zero and the demand for insurance falls as p increases. Alternatively, the indifference curve at d'' must be steeper than ag' if A is constant and so d' must be to the right of d''.

If the decision-taker had decreasing absolute risk aversion the indifference curve at d' would be flatter than at b and the income effect would at least partially offset the substitution effect.

More formally, differentiate the first-order condition [B.8] with respect to p to get

$$V_{qp} = -\pi_1 v'(y_1) - \pi_2 v'(y_2) + \pi_1 v''(y_1)pq^* - \pi_2 v''(y_2)(1 - p)q^*$$

and using [B.16]

$$V_{qp} = -[\pi_1 v'(y_1) + \pi_2 v'(y_2)] - V_{qy}q^* \qquad [\text{B.18}]$$

The first term is negative but V_{qy} may be positive, negative or zero depending on whether the coefficient of absolute risk aversion is increasing, decreasing or constant. Dividing [B.18] through by $-V_{qq}$ and using [B.15] gives

$$\frac{\partial D}{\partial p} = -\frac{V_{qp}}{V_{qq}} = \frac{Ev'(y_s)}{V_{qq}} - \frac{\partial D}{\partial y}q^* \qquad [\text{B.19}]$$

which is very similar to the Slutsky equation in consumer theory. The first term is the substitution effect and is negative ($V_{qq} < 0$). The second term is the income effect which is not signable without further assumptions about preferences, i.e. about the coefficient of absolute risk aversion.

We leave it to the reader to investigate the effects of increases in the loss L and the accident probability on the demand for insurance.

EXERCISE 19B

1. *Insurance loading.* (a) What is the effect in Fig. 19.1 if the insurer sets a premium at the rate $p = k\pi_2$ with $k > 1$ being the loading factor which enables the insurer to cover administrative costs. (b) Suppose that the insurer's administrative cost function is $k_0 + kq$ ($k_0 \geq 0$, $k > 0$). What will the breakeven set of contracts look like in Fig. 19.1?

2. *State-dependent marginal utility.* Suppose that the individual's utility functions are state dependent with $v_2(y) = a + bv_1(y)$, with $a < 0$ and $b > 0$. What is the effect on the demand for insurance of increases in a and b? Under what circumstances will full cover be bought even though $p > \pi_2$?

3. *Risk premium.* Show that the maximum amount the individual would pay for full cover is the actuarially fair premium $\pi_2 L$ plus the risk premium $r \equiv \bar{y} - y_c$.

4. *Demand for insurance.* Show that demand for insurance is increased by *ceteris paribus* increases in (a) the accident probability and (b) the accident loss. (c) What is the effect of an increase in the accident probability if allowance is made for the effect on the premium: $p = k\pi_2$ ($k > 1$)?

5. *Insurance with continuous loss distribution.* Suppose that the accident loss L is continuously distributed on $[0, L_1]$ with density function $f(L)$. The insurance contract gives cover of q in exchange for a premium payment of $P(q)$ ($dP/dq > 0$) and pays the insured L if $L \leq q$ and q if $L > q$. The insured's expected utility is

$$V(q; y) = \int_0^q v(y - P(q))f(L)\, dL + \int_q^{L_1} v(y - L - P(q) + q)f(L)\, dL$$

What is the first-order condition for the amount of cover q? Show that the amount of cover decreases with income y if the insured has diminishing absolute risk aversion. (*Hint*: rewrite $V_{qy}(q^*; y)$ by substituting $-Av'$ for v'' and use the fact that income is never more than $y - P$ so that $A \geq A(y - P)$ to obtain the inequality $V_{qy} < A(y - P)V_q(q^*; y) = 0$.)

C. Incomplete insurance markets

So far we have assumed that there is only one source of income risk and that it is possible to buy insurance against it. But some types of income risk will not be insurable because it will be too costly for the insurer to verify a claim from the insured that some component of their income has been reduced. For example, a waiter whose income is the sum of a weekly salary from a restaurant and cash tips from customers may be able buy insurance against the loss of salary if ill and unable to work but no sensible insurer would be willing to insure him against fluctuations in income from tips.

Consider an individual who faces two sources of income risk, one insurable, the other not. If the insurable loss occurs, the individual's income is reduced by L, whereas if the uninsurable risk occurs she loses D. It is possible that both losses occur, in which case she loses $D + L$. She can buy insurance against the occurrence of the loss L at a premium rate of p for cover of q but no insurance is available against D. Thus her incomes in the four possible states of the world are

s	1	2	3	4	
y_s	$x - pq$	$x - pq - D$	$x - L + (1 - p)q$	$x - L - D + (1 - p)q$	[C.1]

[C.1] shows that the incompleteness of insurance markets means she cannot exchange income between pairs of individual states by varying her cover. Because only L is insurable, she is only able to transfer income between proper *subsets* of states. By increasing cover q against L she can transfer income from states 1 *and* 2 to states 3 *and* 4.

The individual cannot in general be better off if she can only insure against L than when she can insure against both losses. The missing insurance market cannot increase her welfare, since with complete insurance markets she always has the option of not insuring against D. On the other hand, it is not necessarily the case that she is strictly worse off. Thus suppose that $L = D$, and that the losses are mutually exclusive and one of them is certain to occur, so that the probability of states 1 and 4 are zero. Then, if she does not buy any insurance, she will have a certain income: $y_2 = y_3$. Even if fair insurance is available on one or both risks, she will not buy it. In the case of perfect negative correlation of risks each risk is a perfect hedge for the other.

The example is obviously special: in general we expect the individual to be worse off when her insurance possibilities are restricted. More interesting is the effect of the uninsurable or *background* risk on her demand for insurance against the other risk. As we will see, the absence of some markets will alter the individual's behaviour in the markets which do exist.

Denoting the probability of state s by f_s, the probabilities of the insurable loss L and the background risk D are

$$\pi = f_3 + f_4 \qquad \tau = f_2 + f_4 \qquad \qquad [C.2]$$

To focus on the implications of the uninsurability of D, we assume that fair insurance is available against L so that $p = \pi$. The individual is strictly risk averse with utility function $u(y)$, $u' > 0$, $u'' < 0$. She chooses her cover against L to solve

$$\max_q Eu(y_s) = f_1 u(x - \pi q) + f_2 u(x - \pi q - D) + f_3 u(x - L + (1 - \pi)q)$$
$$+ f_4 u(x - L - D + (1 - \pi)q) \qquad \text{s.t.} \quad q \geqslant 0 \qquad [C.3]$$

The Kuhn–Tucker condition is

$$\frac{dEu}{dq} = -\pi[f_1 u'(y_1^*) + f_2 u'(y_2^*)] + (1 - \pi)[f_3 u'(y_3^*) + f_4 u'(y_4^*)] \leqslant 0$$

$$q^* \geqslant 0 \qquad q^* \frac{dEu}{dq} = 0 \qquad \qquad [C.4]$$

where y_s^* is state s income at the optimal cover q^*.

Because of the missing insurance market, marginal utilities $u'(y_s)$ are not equalized across states as they would be with a full set of insurance markets with fair premia. Risk bearing is inefficient compared with the first best allocation. Only expected marginal utilities *averaged across subsets of states* can be equalized. Letting

$$\varphi \equiv f_1/(f_1 + f_2) \qquad \psi \equiv f_3/(f_3 + f_4) \qquad [\text{C.5}]$$

we can write the first part of [C.4] as

$$\psi u'(y_3^*) + (1 - \psi)u'(y_4^*) \leqslant \varphi u'(y_1^*) + (1 - \varphi)u'(y_2^*) \qquad [\text{C.6}]$$

Thus if the optimal level of cover is positive, so that [C.6] is an equality, the individual equates the expected marginal utility conditional on loss L (the left-hand side of [C.6]) to the expected marginal utility of income conditional on L not occurring.

We can get some insight into the implications of incomplete markets for the demand for insurance by considering some special cases of the joint distribution of risks.

(a) *Perfect negative correlation of identical risks*: $f_1 = f_4 = 0$, $L = D$. This is the case considered informally above. Here $\varphi = 0 = (1 - \psi)$, $(1 - \varphi) = 1 = \psi$ and the Kuhn–Tucker conditions are

$$u'(y_3^*) \leqslant u'(y_2^*) \qquad q^* \geqslant 0 \qquad q^*[u'(y_3^*) - u'(y_2^*)] = 0 \qquad [\text{C.7}]$$

But if $q^* > 0$, then (see [C.1]) $y_2^* < y_3^*$, implying $u'(y_3^*) > u'(y_2^*)$. Thus we must have $q^* = 0$, as we suggested above.

(b) *Perfect negative correlation, non-identical risks*: $f_1 = f_4 = 0$, $L \neq D$. The risks are perfectly negatively correlated, but losses are unequal. [C.7] still defines the optimal cover, but now incomes before insurance are unequal. If $q^* > 0$, [C.7] implies that $y_2^* = y_3^*$, and so

$$q^* = L - D \qquad [\text{C.8}]$$

A necessary and sufficient condition for $q^* > 0$ is therefore that $L > D$. Because the two losses are perfectly negatively correlated, the *uncertain component* of income is only $L - D$, since before insurance $y_3 = y_2 - (L - D)$. The individual will get 'full insurance' by buying cover equal to the uncertain component of his income at the fair premium π. ($L - D$ occurs with probability $f_3 = \pi$.) The perfect negative correlation provides a partial hedge against the larger insurable loss L, so that the individual need only buy partial cover against the insurable loss. Our basic point that missing markets alter behaviour in the remaining markets is illustrated: the demand for insurance against L is reduced.

If the uninsurable loss D exceeds the insurable loss: $D > L$, the individual will not wish to buy cover against L to transfer income from state 2 to state 3. To the contrary: with $D > L$, income in state 2 is now smaller than in state 3 when $q = 0$. If possible, the individual would like to be able to gamble at fair odds on the occurrence of the loss L: to set $q < 0$.

Figure 19.4 illustrates cases (a) and (b). With y_2 measured on the horizontal axis and y_3 on the vertical axis, increases in cover against L will move the individual up and to the left in the figure. When $D = L$, she is initially at a point, such as A, on the 45° line where $y_2 = y_3$. Since insurance is available at a fair premium, the slope of the insurance budget constraint $(-f_2/f_3)$ is equal to the slope of her indifference curve at the 45° line $(-f_2 u'(y_2)/f_3 u'(y_3))$ and she will buy no insurance

Figure 19.4

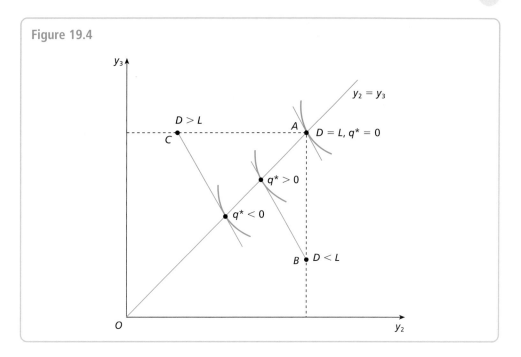

against L. When $L > D$, the individual is initially at a point, such as B, below the 45° line. If faced with a fair premium for cover against L she will buy sufficient cover ($q^* = L - D$) to give her a certain income on the 45° line. Finally, if $D > L$, she is initially above the 45° line and would like to sell insurance or gamble at fair odds, to move down to the 45° line. In these cases the missing market affects the individual's insurance decision but does not make her worse off.

(c) *Perfect positive correlation*: $f_2 = f_3 = 0$. Either both losses occur or neither does. Since $\pi = f_4$, and $\varphi = 1$, $\psi = 0$, [C.6] becomes simply

$$u'(y_4^*) \leq u'(y_1^*) \tag{C.9}$$

Without insurance, income in state 1 is larger than in state 4, so that the individual will wish to buy insurance to transfer income from state 1, where marginal utility is initially high, to state 4, where marginal utility is initially low. She will wish to buy sufficient insurance to equalize marginal utilities and therefore incomes across states:

$$q^* = L + D \tag{C.10}$$

Again, the missing market will make no difference to the individual's expected utility: she can achieve the first best if she can overinsure against L by an amount D to offset the risk of the uninsurable loss. However, if insurance is restricted to the actual loss L, she will set $q^* = L$ and be left with the risk of loss D. She will then certainly be worse off because the insurance market is incomplete. Figure 19.5 illustrates. Note that insurers would still break even if they charge a premium of $\pi = f_4$ for insurance cover of $L + D$, and so, in a competitive market of the kind described in section B, we would expect to observe over-insurance in equilibrium.

Figure 19.5

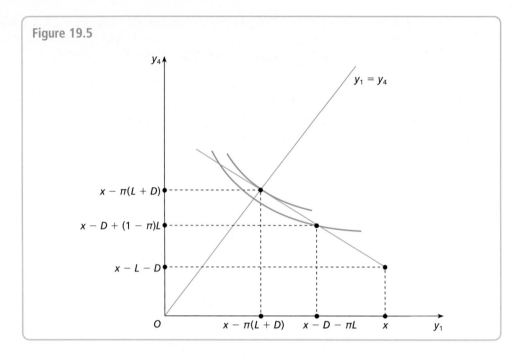

(d) *Independent risks*: $f_1 = (1 - \tau)(1 - \pi)$; $f_2 = \tau(1 - \pi)$; $f_3 = (1 - \tau)\pi$; $f_4 = \tau\pi$. Here the occurrence of loss D is statistically independent of loss L. From [C.5], [C.6] becomes

$$(1 - \tau)[u'(y_3^*) - u'(y_1^*)] \leq \tau[u'(y_2^*) - u'(y_4^*)] \qquad [C.11]$$

Reference to [C.1] shows that with no cover $y_1 > y_3$ and $y_2 > y_4$, so that the left-hand side of [C.11] is greater than the right-hand side. Hence the optimal level of cover is positive. In fact at the fair premium $p = \pi$, the individual buys full cover against the insurable loss: setting $q^* = L$ implies

$$y_1^* = y_3^* = x - \pi L; \qquad y_2^* = y_4^* = x - D - \pi L \qquad [C.12]$$

so that [C.11] is satisfied as an equality. Under independent risks, the individual is left with income uncertainty arising only from the uninsurable risk D. She is strictly worse off than if there was also insurance against D, but her choice in the insurance market that does exist is unaffected by the missing market.

The four cases exhaust the simple possibilities. In general the individual is worse off under missing insurance markets because marginal expected utilities cannot be equalized across all states. As [C.4] shows, behaviour will be affected by the absence of other insurance markets in a way that depends on the joint distribution of losses and the preferences of the individual. As a further illustration, consider the effect of a 'small' uninsurable risk on the demand for the insurance against the other risk. Suppose that initially $D = 0$, and that there is a premium $p \geq \pi$ for cover against the insurable risk. Assume that initially, even if the premium is unfair, she buys some cover against the occurrence of L. Thus her decision is characterized by

$$\frac{dEu}{dq} = -p[f_1 u'(y_1^*) + f_2 u'(y_2^*)] + (1 - p)[f_3 u'(y_3^*) + f_4 u'(y_4^*)] = 0 \qquad [C.13]$$

which is just [C.5] with p replacing π. Recalling the comparative static methodology (Appendix I), the qualitative effect of a small uninsurable risk on the optimal cover q^* depends on the sign of the partial derivative of [C.13] with respect to D at $D = 0$:

$$\partial(dEu/dq)/\partial D = pf_2u''(y_2) - (1 - p)f_4u''(y_4) \qquad \text{[C.14]}$$

Since at $D = 0$ we have $y_1 = y_2$ and $y_3 = y_4$, we can use [C.13] to substitute for p in [C.14]. Rearrangement yields the conclusion

$$\left.\frac{dq^*}{dD}\right|_{D=0} \gtreqless 0 \Leftrightarrow \frac{f_4}{(f_3 + f_4)}A(y_4^*) \gtreqless \frac{f_2}{(f_1 + f_2)}A(y_2^*) \qquad \text{[C.15]}$$

where $A(y)$ is the coefficient of absolute risk aversion.

The effect of introducing a small uninsurable risk on the demand for insurance against the insurable risk depends on the risk aversion of the insured and the correlation of the insurable and uninsurable risks. The terms multiplying the coefficients of risk aversion are the conditional probabilities of D, given that L has occurred $(f_4/(f_3 + f_4))$, and that L has not occurred $(f_2/(f_1 + f_2))$. The losses are positively correlated if the former exceeds the latter. If the premium for cover against L was fair, the individual would have taken out full cover so that $y_2^* = y_4^*$. The effect of the small uninsurable risk would then be entirely dependent on whether it was positively or negatively correlated with insurable risk. If it was positively correlated the demand for insurance against the insurable risk would be increased. The intuition is that 'on average' the uninsured loss occurs more often when the insured risk has occurred and so, by buying insurance against L, the insured is 'on average' buying cover against D also. Conversely, if the risks are negatively correlated, the demand for insurance is reduced because 'on average' the occurrence of D reduces the difference between the insured's incomes and therefore the need to transfer income from sets of states which have high income 'on average' to sets of states which have low income 'on average'. When insurance against L has an unfair premium, the insured will initially buy incomplete cover against L. Then the effect of the small uninsurable risk also depends on her preferences. If we make the plausible assumption that the insured has decreasing absolute risk aversion, initially she will have $A(y_2^*) < A(y_4^*)$. Now she will certainly wish to over-insure if the risks are positively correlated or independent and may wish to do so even if they are negatively correlated.

These results with a small uninsurable risk but a general joint probability distribution confirm the previous analysis, where we allowed for non-negligible uninsurable risks but made extreme assumptions about correlations. Further results in this area require more precise specifications of preferences or the distributions. Interested readers can consult the references at the end of the book.

EXERCISE 19C

1. Examine the effect of a small uninsurable fair risk on the insured's expected utility. Show that the correlation between the risks is again crucial. Relate these results to the analysis of the value of small risky prospects in the analysis of risk spreading in section 19D. [*Hint*: don't forget the Envelope Theorem.]

D. Risk spreading: the Arrow-Lind Theorem

The analysis of insurance in section C assumed that the risk-averse insured could contract with a risk-neutral insurer and so shed some risk. If the insurance was provided by a risk-averse insurer the premium charged would reflect the risk aversion of the insurer as well as the probability of the event being insured against. In this section we investigate the effect on the premium of sharing the insured risk among an increasing number of insurers. We show that, in the absence of administrative costs, as the number of risk-averse insurers sharing the risk increases, the premium paid by the insured will tend to the expected cost of the accident or event insured against, i.e. to the actuarially fair premium. Thus even in an economy in which all individuals are risk averse it is possible to insure on terms which are not affected by the risk aversion of insurers: it is 'as if' there is indeed a risk-neutral agent in the economy. We could think of an insurance syndicate owned equally by risk-averse individuals. If there are many individuals in the insurance syndicate they will be willing to make insurance contracts solely on the basis of expected costs and benefits without any allowance for the cost of bearing risk.

The result we derive is known as the *Arrow–Lind Theorem* and has a wider relevance than insurance contracts and to emphasize this we adopt a more general approach. We consider how much the n members of a syndicate would be willing to pay to acquire a risky project in which they all share equally in any gains or losses. To simplify the exposition we assume that the syndicate members have identical preferences, probability beliefs and incomes. The income of a representative member of the syndicate in state s is

$$y_s + kz_s - p \qquad \text{[D.1]}$$

where y_s is her original income in state s, z_s is the payoff from the risky prospect in state s and $k = 1/n$ is the fraction of the prospect received by each of the n members of the syndicate. p is the amount paid by each member for the right to share in the risky prospect. Alternatively, the syndicate pays P for the prospect and shares the cost equally among the members so that $P = np$. It is assumed that the payoffs z_s from the prospect and the syndicate members' initial incomes y_s are statistically independent:

$$\text{Cov}(y_s, z_s) = 0 \qquad \text{[D.2]}$$

The assumption is crucial and its consequences are discussed below. One special case in which it would hold is if income without the project is certain, so that y_s is constant across states.

The maximum price each member of the syndicate would be willing to pay for her share in the prospect is defined implicitly by

$$Ev(y_s + kz_s - p) = Ev(y_s) \qquad \text{[D.3]}$$

The expected value of the individual's share in the prospect is kEz_s. The difference between the expected value of the prospect to the syndicate member kEz_s and the price p she would be willing to pay for her share of the risky prospect is the *risk loading*:

$$\ell = kEz_s - p \qquad \text{[D.4]}$$

The risk loading is the excess of expected return over the price paid which is necessary to induce the syndicate member to accept the prospect.

The prospect payoff in state s can always be expressed as the sum of the expected value of the prospect and a random deviation e_s about the expected value:

$$z_s = Ez_s + e_s \qquad Ee_s = 0 \qquad [D.5]$$

Using [D.4] and [D.5] to substitute for p and z_s in [D.3] gives

$$Ev(y_s + kz_s - p) = Ev(y_s + kz_s - kEz_s + \ell) = Ev(y_s + ke_s + \ell) = Ev(y_s) \quad [D.6]$$

The last equality in [D.6] shows that we can also interpret the risk loading as the compensation required to make the individual accept the risky but fair bet which pays $ke_s = kz_s - kEz_s$ in state s (remember that $Eke_s = kEe_s = 0$). The risk loading depends on the share of the risky prospect borne by each syndicate member:

$$\ell = \ell(k) = \ell(1/n)$$

The *risk premium* r introduced in section 17D is the amount the individual would be willing to pay in order to be relieved of a fair but risky prospect. Thus if the syndicate member was forced to pay kEz_s for a share kz_s of the risky prospect she would be willing to pay r, defined by

$$Ev(y_s + kz_s - kEz_s) = Ev(y_s + ke_s) = Ev(y_s - r) \qquad [D.7]$$

to be relieved of the risky transaction.

Comparing [D.6] and [D.7] we see that the relationship between the risk loading and the risk premium is analogous to the relationship between the compensating and equivalent variations of section 3C. Both convey information about the individual's attitude to risk but the risk loading is the more appropriate measure when syndicate members cannot be forced to accept risky prospects and will not accept a risky prospect which reduces their expected utility.

The maximum amount that the syndicate would pay for the risky prospect is

$$P = np = n[kEz_s - \ell(k)] = nkEz_s - n\ell(k) = Ez_s - n\ell(1/n) \qquad [D.8]$$

If $n\ell(1/n)$ tends to zero as n becomes large then a large syndicate will be willing to pay the expected value of the risky prospect for the right to undertake it, i.e. to contract as though all members of the syndicate were risk neutral.

The effect of the member's share k on her risk loading is found by using the Implicit Function Theorem on the last equation in [D.6]

$$\frac{d\ell(k)}{dk} = \frac{-Ev'(y_s + ke_s + \ell)e_s}{Ev'(y_s + ke_s + \ell)} = \frac{-Ev'Ee_s - \text{Cov}(v', e_s)}{Ev'(y_s + ke_s + \ell)}$$

$$= \frac{-\text{Cov}(v'(y_s + ke_s + \ell), e_s)}{Ev'(y_s + ke_s + \ell)} > 0 \qquad [D.9]$$

where we have used the fact that $Ee_s = 0$ (see [D.5]) and the assumption [D.2] that the returns on the risky prospect are statistically independent of the syndicate member's initial income. Because $z_s = Ez_s + e_s$ is not correlated with y_s then neither is e_s and so the only source of correlation between v' and e_s is the fact that increases in e_s increase income in state s and so reduce marginal utility in state s. Hence $\text{Cov}(v', e_s)$ is negative and [D.9] is positive.

We see from [D.9] that increasing the number of members in the syndicate reduces the risk loading since increases in n reduce each member's share $k = 1/n$. It is also clear from [D.6] that

$$\lim_{n\to\infty} \ell(1/n) = \lim_{k\to 0} \ell(k) = 0 \qquad [D.10]$$

but we have to establish the stronger result that the *total* risk loading tends to zero as n becomes large:

$$\lim_{n\to\infty} n\ell(1/n) = \lim_{k\to 0} \frac{\ell(k)}{k} = 0 \qquad [D.11]$$

We show that [D.11] is true by examining $\ell(k)/k$ as $k \to 0$. Since both the numerator and denominator of $\ell(k)/k$ have the limit of 0 as $k \to 0$ we use L'Hôpital's Rule and investigate

$$\lim_{k\to 0} \frac{\ell(k)}{k} = \lim_{k\to 0} \frac{d\ell(k)/dk}{dk/dk} = \lim_{k\to 0} d\ell(k)/dk \qquad [D.12]$$

From [D.9]

$$\lim_{k\to 0} d\ell(k)/dk = \lim_{k\to 0} \frac{-\text{Cov}(v'(y_s + ke_s + \ell), e_s)}{Ev'(y_s + ke_s + \ell)}$$

$$= \frac{-\text{Cov}(v'(y_s), e_s)}{Ev'(y_s)} = 0 \qquad [D.13]$$

where we use the fact that $\lim_{k\to 0} \ell = 0$ (from [D.10]) and the assumption that z_s and y_s (and thus e_s and y_s) are statistically independent.

We have demonstrated that [D.11] holds and so large syndicates of risk-averse members will be willing to contract as though they were all risk neutral, i.e. that $P \to Ez_s$ as $n \to \infty$. The total risk loading $n\ell(1/n)$ in [D.8] tends to zero as the syndicate size increases because the risk loading of each member $\ell(1/n)$ decreases faster than the rate at which the syndicate size n is increasing.

To see this intuitively, note that $\ell(1/n)$ depends on the riskiness of the contract for the individual member and measure riskiness by the variance of the prospect payoffs for each member:

$$\text{Var}(kz_s) = \text{Var}(ke_s) = k^2\text{Var}(e_s) = \text{Var}(e_s)/n^2$$

Thus the riskiness of the prospect for each member falls at a rate proportional to n^2. Hence riskiness and thus $\ell(1/n)$ decreases at a rate greater than n and so $n\ell(1/n)$ falls as n increases.

Small bets and risk aversion

Yet another way of seeing why risk-averse individuals would be willing to act as if they were risk neutral is to write the individual's expected utility with the prospect as $Ev(y_s + kz_s)$. The prospect represents a bet of size k to the individual. If

$$\frac{dEv(y_s + kz_s)}{dk}\bigg|_{k=0} = Ev'(y_s + kz_s)z_s|_{k=0}$$

$$= Ev'(y_s)Ez_s + \text{Cov}(v'(y_s), z_s) \qquad [D.14]$$

is positive she will be willing to accept a small enough bet. Since z_s and y_s are independent by the assumption [D.2], the covariance term in [D.14] is zero and the individual would be willing to accept the small bet if and only if $Ez_s > 0$. Thus even risk-averse individuals will be willing to accept a risky bet provided it is (a) better than fair, (b) small enough and (c) independent of their income.

As we noted earlier and as [D.13] and [D.14] show, the assumption [D.2] that the payoffs to the risky prospect are statistically independent of the initial income of each individual member is crucial. If the y_s and e_s are positively correlated then $v'(y_s)$ and e_s are negatively correlated and $-\text{Cov}(v'(y_s), e_s) > 0$. Thus even if the syndicate is large the members are not willing to contract as if they were risk neutral. The price P the syndicate is willing to pay for the prospect is always less than the expected value of the prospect Ez_s. The positive correlation of y_s and e_s means that when the prospective payoff is above average ($e_s > 0$) the syndicate member's income is likely to be higher (and marginal utility lower) than when the payoff is below average ($e_s < 0$). Above average returns will have a smaller impact on utility than below-average returns and the prospect will be valued at less than its expected payoff.

Application 1: Insurance

An insurance contract under which the insured is paid specified sums in the different states of the world in exchange for a premium is a risky prospect for a syndicate of insurers. In this interpretation the project payoffs z_s are negative or zero and are the amounts that the insurance syndicate agrees to pay the insured in state s. P is negative and $-P$ is the smallest premium the syndicate would be willing to accept to assume the risk. If insurance syndicates are large and the risks they insure are statistically independent of their members' initial incomes, the premium charged for insurance will reflect the expected cost of risks covered and will not depend on the risk aversion of the members of the insurance syndicate. If there is also competition among actual or potential syndicates the insured will pay an actuarially fair price for cover.

If [D.2] does not hold, even large syndicates will not contract on actuarially fair terms. If the payouts under the insurance contracts are negatively correlated with the incomes of syndicate members the syndicate will require a premium which exceeds the expected payout since on average they would be paying out in states of the world when their incomes are below average and their marginal utility of income is above average. Thus a syndicate of Los Angeles residents would require a larger premium for insuring earthquake damage in California than an English syndicate.

Application 2: Behaviour of firms

Suppose that z_s is the change in the dividend paid by a firm to its shareholders as the result of a decision. (The decision may be to invest in new plant, to increase output, to enter another industry, and so on.) The value of the decision to the shareholders is P: they would be willing to pay this total amount for the change in dividends. Managers of the firm who wish to act in the interest of the shareholders will only accept prospects for which $P > 0$. Suppose that there are many shareholders all of whom own a small proportion of the shares and that the change in dividends is statistically independent of the shareholders' income from other sources. Then, since $P \to Ez_s$, the managers should act as if the firm was risk neutral, accepting projects for which $Ez_s > 0$ and rejecting those with negative expected payoffs. Thus in some circumstances it may be sensible to model the behaviour of firms on the assumption that they are owned by a single risk-neutral individual. But in many cases project payoffs are positively correlated with the owners' incomes, since both are likely to be correlated with the overall level of activity in the economy. Firms will then only accept projects for which

$$Ez_s > -\text{Cov}(v'(y_s), z_s)/Ev'(y_s) > 0$$

i.e. they will require a risk loading despite the fact that projects are spread over many shareholders.

Application 3: The Arrow–Lind Theorem and public sector projects

The result that a large syndicate of risk-averse individuals will be willing to act as though they were all risk neutral was first derived formally in the context of public sector investment criteria by Arrow and Lind (1970) and is known as the *Arrow–Lind Theorem*. Now the z_s are interpreted as the payoffs from a public sector project. The payoffs are assumed to be captured by the state and then to be distributed to the members of the society via the tax system. If the project payoffs are independent of the members' incomes and the population is sufficiently large the value of the project to the community is Ez_s. The government should be risk neutral in assessing projects even if all members of the population are risk averse.

The requirement that project returns are independent of members' incomes is perhaps even stronger than in the case of private sector decisions. For example: in the absence of lump-sum taxes the government may have to distribute the payoffs from the project via changes in income taxes. Tax rates will be lower when z_s is positive and higher when z_s is negative. But then the taxpayer's gain from the project will be larger the greater is his income since his tax bill is larger the greater is his income. Hence even if the taxpayer's before-tax income is independent of the project payoffs his post-tax income will be positively correlated with the project payoff.

EXERCISE 19D

1. An investment project will yield £10,000 or −£9000 with equal probability. An individual has a certain income of £10,000 and utility function $v(y) = \ln y$.

    (a) Show that the individual would turn down the project.

    (b) Suppose that it is possible for a syndicate of n individuals (with the same preferences and certain income as the first individual) to undertake the project. How large must n be before they would be willing to accept the project?

    (c) What is the size of syndicate which maximizes the expected utility of syndicate members if the project is accepted?

    (d) If there are N individuals in the community (all identical to the first individual) and all individuals count equally in the social welfare function, what is the socially optimal size of the syndicate?

    (e) If the first individual owned the project and could not sell shares in it but could give away a proportion λ of the project, how much would he give away?

    (f) If he could sell shares, how much of the project would he sell? Is it better to permit the owner to sell shares or to restrict him to giving away part of the project?

E. Risk pooling and diversification

In the previous section we saw that as a risk was spread over an increasing number of individuals in a syndicate the total cost of risk to the syndicate tended to zero and the price the syndicate was willing to pay for the risky prospect tended to the expected value of the prospect. The spreading of the given risk over a larger number of individuals was clearly beneficial. In this section we consider two other means of reducing the costs of risk: risk pooling and diversification. Risk pooling occurs when individuals who each have a risky prospect agree to share the total realized income from all their prospects. There is diversification when a single decision-taker chooses to accept several small prospects rather than a single larger prospect. As we will see, the same kind of argument can be used to justify both the pooling and diversification of risks.

Risk pooling: two individuals

We first illustrate the gains from risk pooling with a simple example involving two individuals, each with a prospect with two outcomes. We then show that the general principle applies in more general settings, with more individuals and more complex prospects. Consider two risk-averse individuals A and B whose incomes are identical independent risky prospects $P = \{\pi, y', y''\}$. Each individual has the probability π of income y' and probability $(1 - \pi)$ of income y''. Let $v(y)$ be the utility function of A (it does not matter which individual we consider). The expected utility of A is

$$V(1) = \pi v(y') + (1 - \pi)v(y'') \qquad \text{[E.1]}$$

Suppose that A and B decide to form a syndicate and pool their incomes. They pay their realized income into the pool and each gets half of the total income of the pool. Since the two prospects are identical and independent there are now four possible outcomes for each individual:

Realized income of individual		Probability of this event	Pooled income per individual
A	B		
y'	y'	π^2	y'
y'	y''	$\pi(1 - \pi)$	$(y' + y'')/2$
y''	y'	$(1 - \pi)\pi$	$(y' + y'')/2$
y''	y''	$(1 - \pi)^2$	y''

The events (y', y'') and (y'', y') have the same outcome after pooling of incomes, so that the expected utility of A under the pooling scheme is

$$V(2) = \pi^2 v(y') + 2\pi(1 - \pi)v((y' + y'')/2) + (1 - \pi)^2 v(y'') \qquad \text{[E.2]}$$

We can show that $V(2) > V(1)$ so the pooling scheme makes A better off. Subtract [E.1] from [E.2]

$$V(2) - V(1) = (\pi^2 - \pi)v(y') + [(1 - \pi)^2 - (1 - \pi)]v(y'') + 2\pi(1 - \pi)v((y' + y'')/2)$$
$$= \pi(\pi - 1)v(y') + (1 - \pi)(1 - \pi - 1)v(y'') + 2\pi(1 - \pi)v((y' + y'')/2)$$

which can be rearranged to get

$$V(2) - V(1) = 2\pi(1 - \pi)[v(\tfrac{1}{2}y' + \tfrac{1}{2}y'') - \tfrac{1}{2}v(y') - \tfrac{1}{2}v(y'')] \qquad \text{[E.3]}$$

Since A is risk averse, $v(y)$ is concave and the square-bracketed term in [E.3] must be positive (recall the definition of a concave function). The same argument applies to B and so the pooling scheme makes both individuals better off.

Pooling does not alter the expected incomes of the individuals but it does reduce the riskiness of the income prospect they face. The risky distribution of income is more concentrated around its mean because when one individual has a high income the other is equally likely to have a high or low income and the pooled income per person is less variable.

Risk pooling: n individuals

If more individuals with identical and independently distributed incomes are added to the pool the number of possible outcomes for each member of the pool increases rapidly. (A pool with n members each with a prospect with k income levels has k^n possible outcomes.) The expected utility of members of the pool continues to increase as more members are added. We can demonstrate the gains from pooling by using the properties of the risk measures introduced in section 17F.

Suppose there are n individuals with identically and independently distributed random incomes. The random income of individual i without pooling is y^i and by choosing suitable units we can restrict y^i to the interval [0, 1]. The random income is continuously distributed on [0, 1] and has the distribution function $F(y^i)$. We now prove the following proposition:

The optimal pooling arrangement when n risk-averse individuals have identically and independently distributed incomes is an equal shares pool in which each gets 1/n of the realized total income of the pool.

With an equal shares pooling scheme the n members put their realized incomes y^i into the pool and share out the total realized income equally. The random pooled income of each member can be written as

$$w(n) \equiv \frac{1}{n}\sum_i^n y^i = y^n + \sum_i^{n-1}(y^i - y^n)\frac{1}{n} \qquad \text{[E.4]}$$

Suppose that another pooling scheme is adopted which gives some individual member of the pool the share k_i of the income of the jth member of the pool, where $k_i \neq (1/n)$ for some i. The random income of such a member would be

$$w(k) = \sum_i^n k_i y^i = \sum_i^{n-1} k_i y^i + \left(1 - \sum_i^{n-1} k_i\right) y^n = y^n + \sum_i^{n-1} k_i (y^i - y^n)$$

$$= w(n) + \sum_i^{n-1}\left(k_i - \frac{1}{n}\right)(y^i - y^n) \qquad \text{[E.5]}$$

where we have substituted for y^n from [E.4]. Thus the income of a member of the alternative pooling scheme can be expressed as the sum of the random income under the equal shares pooling scheme and a weighted sum of a further $(n-1)$ random variables. Consider one of the random terms $y^i - y^n$ which is the difference between the random incomes of the ith and nth members of the pool. Define S_{in} to be the sum of the realizations of all the $n-2$ random incomes except y^i and y^n so that $w(n) = (S_{in} + y^i + y^n)/n$. The probability that $y^i - y^n = y$ given that the realized value of $w(n) = w$ is

$$\Pr[y^i - y^n = y \mid S_{in} + y^i + y^n = nw] = \Pr[y^i - y^n = y \mid y^i + y^n = nw - S_{in}]$$
$$= \frac{\Pr[y^i - y^n = y \text{ and } y^i + y^n = nw - S_{in}]}{\Pr[y^i + y^n = nw - S_{in}]} \qquad [\text{E.6}]$$

But $y^i - y^n = y$ and $y^i + y^n = nw - S_{in}$ imply that

$$y^i = (y + nw - S_{in})/2 \quad \text{and} \quad y^n = (nw - S_{in} - y)/2$$

and so

$$\Pr[y^i - y^n = y \mid y^i + y^n = nw - S_{in}]$$
$$= \Pr[y^i = (y + nw - S_{in})/2] \Pr[y^n = (nw - S_{in} - y)/2] / \Pr[y^i + y^n = nw - S_{in}] \qquad [\text{E.7}]$$

since y^i and y^n are independently distributed. Now consider the probability that $y^i - y^n = -y$ given that $w(n) = w$:

$$\Pr[y^i - y^n = -y \mid y^i + y^n = -nw - S_{in}] = \Pr[y^n - y^i = y \mid y^n + y^i = nw - S_{in}]$$
$$= \Pr[y^n = (y + nw - S_{in})/2] \Pr[y^i = (nw - S_{in} - y)/2] / \Pr[y^n + y^i = nw - S_{in}] \qquad [\text{E.8}]$$

Since y^i and y^n are identically distributed, [E.8] and [E.7] are equal and the events that $y^i - y^n = y$ and $y^i - y^n = -y$ given values of $w(n)$ have the same probability. Hence the expected value of $y^i - y^n$ given $w(n)$ is zero and, from [E.5], $w(k)$ is the sum of $w(n)$ and $n - 1$ random variables which have a zero mean for given $w(n)$. $w(k)$ is therefore riskier than $w(n)$ in the sense that it has the same distribution as $w(n)$ plus noise. As we saw in section 17E this implies that all risk averters would prefer $w(n)$ to $w(k)$ and we have proved the proposition that the equal shares pooling scheme is optimal.

The proposition is interesting in its own right but it has the important corollary that *increasing the number of members increases their expected utility*. To see this note that a scheme in which an n member pool decides to give the first $n - 1$ members $1/(n - 1)$ of their total realized income and the nth member just y^n is identical to an $n - 1$ member pool with an optimal equal shares scheme for its members. We have proved that such a sharing rule is worse than an equal shares scheme in which all n individuals get a share of $1/n$. Hence the expected utility of pool members is increased by increases in the size n of the pool.

This result is much stronger than our earlier demonstration that equal pooling by two individuals makes them both better off. It holds for any situation in which prospects are identically and independently distributed and it proves that equal shares is the optimal pooling scheme, rather than just being better than no pooling. Indeed the requirement that prospects are independently distributed can be weakened. An equal-shares pooling is optimal if the distribution function $F(y^1, \ldots, y^n)$ is symmetrical with equal means for the incomes. Nor need any restrictions be placed on the preferences of the pool members apart from risk aversion: it is not necessary to assume that pool members have the same specific attitudes to risk.

Risk pooling with non-identical distributions

The general result that pooling increases expected utility continues to hold when incomes are not identically distributed although the optimal scheme is not usually equal shares. Suppose two individuals have random incomes independently distributed according to the distribution functions $F_i(y^i)$ where the means of the distributions are identical but otherwise F_1 and F_2 differ. Consider a sharing scheme under which individual 1 gets $(1 - k)$ of his realized income and k of the realized income of individual 2:

$$y(k) = (1 - k)y^1 + ky^2 = y^1 + k(y^2 - y^1) \qquad (0 < k < 1) \qquad [E.9]$$

The distribution function of his income $y(k)$ under the scheme is

$$\Pr[y(k) \leqslant y] = \Pr\left[y^1 \leqslant \frac{y - ky^2}{1 - k}\right] = G(y; k) = \int_0^1 F_1\left[\frac{y - ky^2}{1 - k}\right] f_2(y^2)\, dy^2 \qquad [E.10]$$

We wish to show that the individual is better off with some pooling rather than with none, i.e. that he would prefer the distribution function $G(y; k)$ to the distribution function $G(y; 0) = F_1(y^1)$. We do so by showing that at $k = 0$ an increase in k is a mean-preserving reduction in risk. Since the means of y^1 and y^2 are equal by assumption, we have to prove (see section 17F):

$$\int_0^w G_k(y; 0)\, dy = T_k(w; 0) \leqslant 0 \qquad \text{for } 0 \leqslant w \leqslant 1 \qquad [E.11]$$

where $G_k(y; 0)$ is $\partial G(y; k)/\partial k$ evaluated at $k = 0$. Differentiation of [E.10] with respect to k gives

$$G_k(y; 0) = \int_0^1 f_1(y) f_2(y^2)(y - y^2)\, dy^2 = f_1(y)y \int_0^1 f_2(y^2)\, dy^2 - \int_0^1 y^2 f_2(y^2)\, dy^2$$

$$= f_1(y)(y - \bar{y}^2) = f_1(y)(y - \bar{y}) \qquad [E.12]$$

where $\bar{y} = \bar{y}^2$ is the mean of y^2 (and therefore of y^1 and $y(k)$). Substituting [E.12] into [D.11] gives

$$T_k(w; 0) = \int_0^w f_1(y)(y - \bar{y})\, dy = \int_0^w f_1(y)y\, dy - F_1(w)\bar{y} \leqslant 0 \qquad [E.13]$$

with a strict equality holding when $0 < w < 1$. (Dividing through the last expression in [E.13] by $F_1(w)$ gives the difference between the mean of y^1 conditional on $y^1 \leqslant w \leqslant 1$ and the mean of y^1 conditional on $y^1 \leqslant 1$ which must be negative for $0 < w < 1$.)

[E.13] establishes that by introducing some degree of pooling ($k > 0$) individual 1 will get a mean-preserving decrease in risk and thus be made better off. Individual 2 gets $ky^1 + (1 - k)y^2$ under the pooling scheme and the same type of argument can be applied to demonstrate she is also made better off by the introduction of pooling. (Define $k' = (1 - k)$ and reverse the roles of the distributions in [E.10] to [E.13].) The two individuals may have different risk-aversion preferences and F_1, F_2 also differ, so they are likely to disagree on what degree of pooling is optimal. Since they are both made better off by the introduction of pooling there are potential gains from trade to motivate them to strike a bargain. Such bargains may require departure from the simple pooling scheme defined by [E.9]. For example, if individual 1 would prefer more pooling than individual 2 he could induce individual 2 to accept more pooling by proposing a scheme in which individual i received

$$y(k_{i1}, k_{i2}) = k_{i1}y^1 + k_{i2}y^2 \qquad \Sigma_i k_{i1} = \Sigma_i k_{i2} = 1 \qquad [E.14]$$

By setting the shares so that $k_{11} + k_{12} < 1$ individual 1 could arrange to increase the mean income of individual 2 as compensation for an increase in the degree of pooling. Individual 1 would be accepting some decrease in his mean income in exchange for a distribution he perceived as less risky.

The demonstration that some degree of pooling increases expected utility for two individuals also applies to increasing the number of individuals in the pool. We just interpret y^1 as the income of individual 1 under an n-member pooling scheme, $F_1(y^1)$ as its distribution function and $F_2(y^2)$ as the distribution function of the income of some individual who is not a member of the n person pool. Then the argument above establishes that both individual 1 and the new member are made better off by admitting the new member. Successively reinterpreting y^1 and F_1 to apply to all the other members of the n-person pool shows that there exists a sharing scheme which makes all n existing members and the new member better off. Hence expected utility increases as the size of the pool grows even if the individual members' incomes are not identically distributed.

The only circumstances in which pooling is not beneficial to both individuals is when y^1 and y^2 are perfectly positively correlated, i.e. $y^2 = a + by^1$ (where $b > 0$ and $a = (1 - b)\bar{y}$ because the mean of y^1 and y^2 are both equal to $\bar{y}$). Let $y^i(k)$ be the income of individual i under a pooling scheme where

$$y^1(k) = (1 - k)y^1 + ky^2 = [1 - (1 - b)k]y^1 + ka \qquad [\text{E.15}]$$

$$y^2(k) = ky^1 + (1 - k)y^2 = [k + (1 - k)b]y^1 + (1 - k)a \qquad [\text{E.16}]$$

The distribution of $y^i(k)$ differs from the distribution of y^1 only in location and scale parameters since $y^i(k)$ is a linear function of y^1. In section 17F we showed that in choosing between distributions which differ only in location and scale parameters all risk-averse individuals would prefer the distribution with the smallest variance if the means of the distribution were equal. Since the mean of $y^i(k)$ is $\bar{y}$ for all k, the two individuals will be interested only in the variances of $y^1(k)$ and $y^2(k)$. But

$$d\,\text{Var}(y^1(k))/dk = d[1 - (1 - b)k]^2\text{Var}(y^1)/dk$$
$$= -2(1 - b)[1 - (1 - b)k]\text{Var}(y^1) \qquad [\text{E.17}]$$

$$d\,\text{Var}(y^2(k))/dk = d[k + (1 - k)b]^2\text{Var}(y^1)/dk$$
$$= 2(1 - b)[k + (1 - k)b]\text{Var}(y^1) \qquad [\text{E.18}]$$

If $b = 1$ both derivatives are zero and the variances of both individuals' incomes are unaffected by k and there is no gain from pooling. If $b \neq 1$ the derivatives are always of opposite sign since $-[1 - (1 - b)k]$ and $[k + (1 - k)b]$ are always of opposite sign if $b > 0$. Hence the two individuals would never be able to agree on k, i.e. on a pooling scheme. If $b > 1$ individual 1 has an unpooled income with a smaller variance than individual 2 and will never agree to share it with her. There are no gains from trade to be exploited.

If the individuals' incomes are perfectly *negatively* correlated so that $y^2 = a + by^1$, with $b < 0$ and $a = (1 - b)\bar{y}$, there are gains from pooling. At $k = 0$ both [E.17] and [E.18] are negative indicating that some pooling will reduce the variance of both individuals' incomes and thus increase their expected utility. The variance of $y^1(k)$ is minimized by $k = 1/(1 - b) > 0$ and of $y^2(k)$ by $k = -b/(1 - b) > 0$. If $b = -1$ they will agree on an equal shares pooling scheme which gives them both a certain income of $\bar{y}$. With b negative but not equal to -1 the optimal pooling scheme will usually require some departure from simple proportional sharing.

Diversification

The results above provide a formal justification for the old adage 'Don't put all your eggs in one basket'. As an example suppose that an individual wishes to invest w in risky securities. Each security i has a random rate of return h_i so that £1 invested in the ith security yields $£(1 + h_i)$ and all securities have the same expected yield. Let k_i be the proportion of the portfolio invested in security i. The random payoff from the portfolio is

$$y(k) = \Sigma w k_i (1 + h_i) = \Sigma k_i y^i \qquad [\text{E.19}]$$

where $y^i = w(1 + h_i)$ is the payoff from investing all the portfolio in security i. Comparing [E.19] and [E.9] we see that we can immediately apply all the results on pooling schemes to the individual's choice of a portfolio. If returns are independently but not identically distributed he should invest in all securities ($k_i > 0$). If the distribution of returns $F(h_1, \ldots, h_n)$ is symmetrical or if the returns are identically and independently distributed he should invest equally in all securities ($k_i = 1/n$). If two securities are perfectly positively correlated (but independently distributed from the other securities) he should include the security with the smaller variance in his portfolio. If there are two perfectly negatively correlated securities the portfolio should consist only of those two securities in the proportion necessary to yield a zero portfolio variance and a certain income.

EXERCISE 19D

1. Suppose there are n securities with identically and independently distributed rates of return and that an investor has y to invest in a portolio. Show (a) that dividing y equally among all the securities minimizes the variance of the portfolio and (b) that the portfolio variance tends to zero as $n \to \infty$.

F. Asymmetric information in insurance markets: adverse selection

In section B we assumed that both parties to the insurance contract – insurer and insured – had the same information. In particular both knew the probability that the insured would suffer a loss and make a claim under the policy. Further, we assumed that the probability of loss was exogenous and not affected by the actions of the insured individual. We now relax both assumptions to consider the implications of two types of *asymmetric information* where one party to a transaction has information not available to the other. *Adverse selection* arises when the insured has better information about her accident probability than the insurer. *Moral hazard* occurs when the actions of the insured can alter the accident probability and those actions are not observable to the insurer. This section is concerned with adverse selection and the next with moral hazard.

To focus on the implications of asymmetric information, we assume that there are no administrative and legal costs of supplying insurance contracts. Insurance is provided by competitive risk-neutral insurers. Both buyers and sellers of insurance act as price-takers and there is free entry and exit for firms.

The competitive market assumptions imply:

1. *Zero expected profit in equilibrium.* If positive expected profit were being made on insurance contracts, entry and increased supply of insurance would take place, driving down revenue – premium income – to equality with the expected costs of insurers.

2. *Better breakeven contracts always offered.* If it is possible to offer an insurance contract which at least breaks even and would be preferred by buyers to contracts currently being offered, firms will do so.

We examine adverse selection using the simple two-state model of insurance of section B. We make one change in terminology: an insurance contract is defined by premium P and an amount of cover q. The insured pays P to the insurer and, if she suffers a loss, the insurer pays her q.

Suppose that there are two types of individuals: high-risk types, for whom the probability of loss is π_h, and low-risk types, for whom the accident probability is $\pi_\ell < \pi_h$. Both types are otherwise identical: they have the same concave utility function $v(\cdot)$, the same endowed income y and suffer the same loss L. The accident probability of an individual is exogenously determined and is known to the individual. The proportion of the population who are low (or good) risks is λ. Insurers also know v, y, L, π_h, π_ℓ and λ. We examine the implications for the market equilibrium of insurers' ability or inability to determine whether any *particular* buyer of insurance is a high- or low-risk type.

Under *full information* an insurer can costlessly ascertain an individual's type. Thus he can offer two contracts (P_h, q_h) and (P_ℓ, q_ℓ) designed for the high- and low-risk types respectively. Competition will ensure that the only contracts sold at the market equilibrium are those which *maximize the expected utilities of each type* and *break even*. Type i will be charged its appropriate fair premium $P_i = \pi_i q_i$, so that the state-contingent incomes of a type i are

$$y_1 = y - P_i = y - \pi_i q_i \qquad \text{[F.1]}$$

$$y_2 = y - L - P_i + q_i = y - L + (1 - \pi_i)q_i \qquad \text{[F.2]}$$

and her expected utility is

$$V^i = V^i(P_i, q_i) = (1 - \pi_i)v(y - P_i) + \pi_i v(y - L - P_i + q_i) \qquad \text{[F.3]}$$

At the market equilibrium, the type i will be offered the contract which mazimizes [F.3], subject to the contract breaking even $(P_i = \pi_i q_i)$. Substituting $\pi_i q_i$ for P_i in [F.3], the equilibrium contract for type i is defined by the first-order condition

$$dV^i/dq_i = -(1 - \pi_i)v'(y_1)\pi_i + \pi_i v'(y_2)(1 - \pi_i) = 0 \qquad \text{[F.4]}$$

Since the marginal utility of income does not depend directly on the state, only on income, [F.4] implies that $y_1 = y_2$. As in section B, the optimal fair insurance contract has full cover: $q_i^* = L$ and both types have a certain income equal to their expected income $\bar{y}_i = y - \pi_i L$.

Figure 19.6 illustrates the full information *separating equilibrium* in which the different types buy different contracts. Recall that the slope of an indifference curve in (y_1, y_2) space for a type i individual is

$$\frac{dy_2}{dy_1} = -\frac{(1 - \pi_i)}{\pi_i}\frac{v'(y_1)}{v'(y_2)} \qquad \text{[F.5]}$$

Figure 19.6

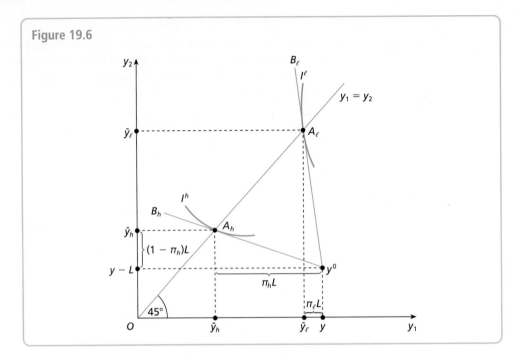

and that expected income of the insured and thus the expected profit of the insurer is constant along lines with slope $-(1 - \pi_i)/\pi_i$. Thus the equilibrium contract for a type i insured is at A_i on the 45° line, where her indifference curve I^i is tangent to the constant expected income line $B_i y^0$ through her endowment point $y^0 = (y, y - L)$.

Now suppose that it is impossible for an insurer to ascertain a buyer's type. The full information separating equilibrium is no longer feasible. Low and high risks get the same cover $q_i^* = L$ but the high risks pay a higher premium $P_h = \pi_h L > P_\ell = \pi_\ell L$. High-risk types will choose the contract for low risks if the insurer is unable to observe the risk type of an insured. But then the contract designed for low risks no longer breaks even since $P_\ell < \pi_h L$. This is the problem of *adverse selection*: the selection of contracts by insureds with better information than the insurer is adverse to the seller.

An equilibrium must either be a *separating equilibrium* in which the two risk types buy different contracts, or a *pooling equilibrium* in which both types buy the same contract. Under full information there was a separating equilibrium. We now consider whether either kind of equilibrium exists in a market with adverse selection.

Consider first the possibility that there is an equilibrium with a *pooling contract* bought by both types. Since the proportion of low-risk types is λ, the *pooled probability* that a randomly drawn individual will suffer the loss is

$$\bar{\pi} = \lambda \pi_\ell + (1 - \lambda)\pi_h \qquad \text{[F.8]}$$

In Fig. 19.7 the line $\bar{B}y^0$ has slope $-(1 - \bar{\pi})/\bar{\pi}$. Any contract along $\bar{B}y^0$ would break even for an insurer if it was bought by a randomly drawn individual or, equivalently, if the proportion of buyers who were low risk was λ. Since $\pi_h > \bar{\pi} > \pi_\ell$, the best contract for the low- and high-risk types along $\bar{B}y^0$ would be at a and b respectively. However, the pair of contracts (a, b) connot be an equilibrium. Insurers would realize that only high-risk types would buy contract b and that it would therefore

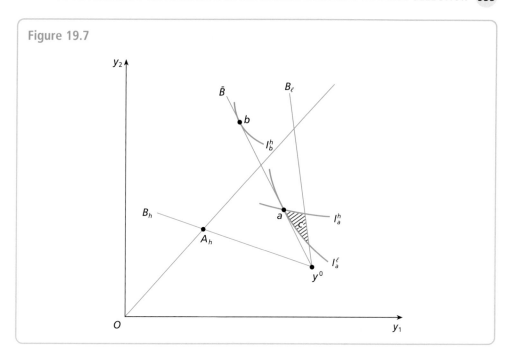

Figure 19.7

make a loss. Any individual asking for contract b, when a is available, reveals herself as high risk. She would not be sold b but the contract designed for high risks A_h. This would be true for all contracts on $\bar{B}y^0$ with more cover than at a. Since high risks prefer a to A_h, they will buy the contract a, the contract which maximizes the expected utility of the low-risk types along $\bar{B}y^0$. Thus the probability that a is sold to a low-risk individual is λ and the pooling contract a breaks even.

We have established that *if* there is a pooling equilibrium it will be the contract a. But we now show that *no* pooling contract bought by both types can be an equilibrium in a competitive insurance market. Refer to Fig. 19.7 and recall from [F.5] that at any point (y_1, y_2) the indifference curve of a low-risk type will be steeper negatively than the indifference curve of a high-risk type. Now consider any contract, such as c, in the shaded area. Since c is below the high-risk type indifference curve I_a^h through a it will not be bought by high risks: they prefer the pooling contract a. But c is above the low-risk type indifference curve I_a^ℓ through a and it will be bought by low risks, who prefer it to the pooling contract a. Finally, c is below the break-even line B_ℓ for contracts sold to low-risk types and therefore makes an expected profit if sold only to them. Thus, in a competitive market, c would be offered and would draw the low-risk types away from the pooling contract. The pooling contract would then make a loss, since it would be bought only by high-risk types. There cannot be a competitive equilibrium with a pooling contract.

If there is a competitive equilibrium it must have separating contracts designed for high- and low-risk types. Since each insured will have a choice between the two contracts (P_ℓ, q_ℓ) and (P_h, q_h), there will not be an equilibrium unless each insured buys the contract designed for her type. Formally, this *self-selection constraint* is expressed by the two inequalities:

$$V^i(P_i, q_i) \geqslant V^i(P_j, q_j) \qquad i, j = h, \ell \qquad i \neq j \qquad \text{[F.9]}$$

The constraints require that an individual of type i must achieve at least as high expected utility from the contract (P_i, q_i) designed for her type as from the contract designed for type j (P_j, q_j). Note that we express these constraints as weak inequalities to ensure a closed feasible set. We assume that, if indifferent between the two types of contract, an individual chooses the contract designed for her type.

It can be shown (see Question 1) that the self-selection constraint for a low-risk individual is non-binding. Intuitively, the problem is to prevent high-risk types from acting as though they were low risk, not the other way round. Thus [F.9] reduces to a single constraint with $i = h$ and $j = \ell$. Competition leads insurers to find the best breakeven contract for each type, with high risks (weakly) preferring their contract $(\pi_h q_h, q_h)$ to the contract $(\pi_\ell q_\ell, \pi_\ell)$.

A simple solution to this problem can be found if we write out the self-selection constraint in full:

$$(1 - \pi_h)v(y - \pi_h q_h) + \pi_h v(y - L + (1 - \pi_h)q_h)$$
$$\geq (1 - \pi_h)v(y - \pi_\ell q_\ell) + \pi_h v(y - L + (1 - \pi_\ell)q_\ell) \qquad \text{[F.10]}$$

The greater the left-hand side of the inequality, the greater can be the right-hand side. For $q_h < L$, $q_\ell < L$, the left-hand side is increasing in q_h and the right-hand side is increasing in q_ℓ. For $q_\ell < L$, the low-risk buyer's expected utility $V^\ell(\pi_\ell q_\ell, q_\ell)$ is also increasing in q_ℓ. Hence insurers will offer a contract to high risks which maximizes the left-hand side of [F.10]. But the best breakeven contract for high risks has full cover: $q_h^* = L$. Thus the separating contract designed for high risks under adverse selection is the one they had under full information: full insurance at the fair premium.

The separating contract for low risks is $(\pi_\ell \hat{q}_\ell, \hat{q}_\ell)$, which gives them the greatest expected utility, subject to [F.10] being satisfied with $q_h = L$:

$$v(y - \pi_h L) = (1 - \pi_h)v(y - \pi_\ell \hat{q}_\ell) + \pi_h v(y - L + (1 - \pi_\ell)\hat{q}_\ell) \qquad \text{[F.11]}$$

To induce high-risk types to select the contract designed for them, the contract offered to low risks must be made sufficiently unattractive to high-risk types. Cover must be less than the full extent of the loss, since with $q_\ell = L$, high-risk types would prefer the contract designed for low risks: the inequality [F.10] would be strictly reversed. The separating contracts make the low-risk types worse off, and the high risks no better off, than they were under full information. The existence of high-risk types, and the inability of insurers to observe the type of a buyer, imposes an externality on the low-risk types.

Figure 19.8 illustrates the separating pair of contracts (A_h, d). The high risks choose the full cover contract A_h. The best contract available to low risks which breaks even and is not bought by high risks is at d, where the high-risk indifference curve I^h through A_h intersects the breakeven line $B_\ell y^0$ for low-risk types. Any contract above I^h on $B_\ell y^0$ would be bought by high risks and would then make a loss. Any contract below I^h on $B_\ell y^0$ would not maximize the expected utility of the low-risk type. Question 2 asks you to analyse the comparative static effects of changes in endowments, preferences and probabilities of this solution, while Question 3 takes you through a more formal derivation of the results.

If there is a separating equilibrium, it must be the pair of contracts (A_h, d) shown in Fig. 19.8. The contracts break even, separate and there are no other contracts which also separate, break even and would be bought by insureds in preference to (A_h, d). But might there be a *pooling* contract which at least breaks even and would attract both types away from the separating pair (A_h, d)? The answer to the question,

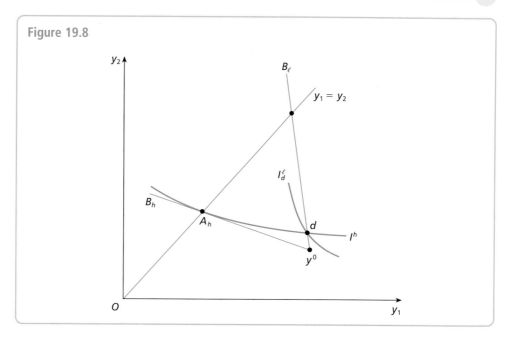

Figure 19.8

and therefore the existence of a competitive equilibrium, depends crucially on the proportion λ of low-risk types in the population.

For a pooling contract (P, q) to drive the best possible separating contracts (A_h, d) off the market it must at least break even:

$$P \geqslant \bar{\pi}q \qquad \text{[F.12]}$$

and attract the low-risk types away from d:

$$(1 - \pi_\ell)v(y - P) + \pi_\ell v(y - L - P + q)$$
$$\geqslant (1 - \pi_\ell)v(y - \pi_\ell \hat{q}_\ell) + \pi_\ell v(y - L + (1 - \pi_\ell)\hat{q}_\ell) \qquad \text{[F.13]}$$

In terms of Fig. 19.9, the breakeven requirement on (P, q) is that it lies on or below the pooled breakeven line $\bar{B}y^0$. The requirement [F.13] that (P, q) attract low risks from d is that it lies on or above the low-risk indifference curve I_d^ℓ through d. (Note that any contract satisfying both [F.12] and [F.13] will also attract all the high risks away from A_h.)

In Fig. 19.9 all the pooling contracts in the shaded area on or above I_d^ℓ and on or below $\bar{B}y^0$ satisfy [F.12] and [F.13]. Any contract in the shaded area drives the separating contracts off the market. For this *not* to be possible, the breakeven line for pooling contracts must be below the low-risk indifference curve through d. The slope of the pooling contracts breakeven line is $-(1 - \bar{\pi})/\bar{\pi}$. It will get flatter, and eventually lie below I_d^ℓ, as λ falls and thus $\bar{\pi} = \lambda\pi_\ell + (1 - \lambda)\pi_h$ increases. There will exist a critical proportion $\lambda^\star$ of low risks in the population, generating the pooling contracts breakeven line $\bar{B}^\star y^0$, such that if $\lambda < \lambda^\star$ the separating contracts are not driven from the market.

We conclude that if $\lambda \in (\lambda^\star, 1)$ there will be a pooling contract which breaks even and attracts the low risks from their separating contract at d. There will not be a separating equilibrium. But we have already established that no pooling contract can be an equilibrium. Hence, for $\lambda \in (\lambda^\star, 1)$ *no competitive equilibrium exists.*

Figure 19.9

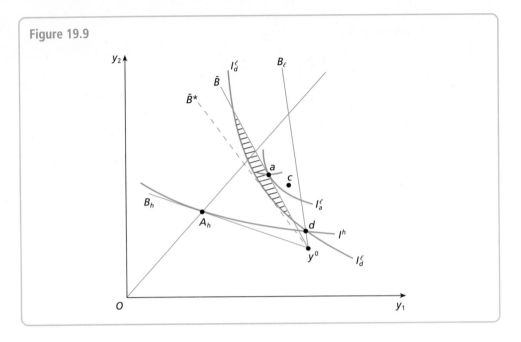

On the other hand, for $\lambda \in (0, \lambda^*)$ there is no pooling contract which satisfies both [F.12] and [F.13]. The separating contracts cannot then be driven from the market and constitute the competitive equilibrium.

At the separating contract d the low-risk buyers are *rationed*: they would be willing to buy more cover at a fair premium. But no insurer will offer such a contract because it would also be bought by high risks. Indeed the low risks are willing to pay more than the fair premium for extra cover, though not unboundedly more. Whether a pooling contract can satisfy their demand for extra cover, and thus undermine the separating contracts, depends on how high the premium is, which in turn depends on the mix of high and low risks. If the proportion of low risks $\lambda > \lambda^*$, then the fair premium on pooled contracts would be low enough, though above the fair premium for low risks, to make the purchase of extra cover attractive to low risks.

To summarize: under adverse selection a competitive equilibrium will not exist if the proportion of low risks is large enough. If the competitive equilibrium does exist, it involves two contracts: high-risk individuals take out full cover at a fair premium; low-risk individuals pay a fair premium for less than full cover.

Welfare implications of adverse selection

Suppose that there is a separating equilibrium in the insurance market. The inability of insurers to ascertain the risk class of insureds means that, compared with a situation of full information, low-risk types are worse off at the competitive equilibrium. High-risk types are not better off; nor are insurers, who always break even on contracts. Compared with full information, the market allocation under adverse selection is Pareto inefficient.

But in evaluating the efficiency of a market allocation, we should be careful to compare the allocation with what is feasible. The full information allocation, in which both types get full cover at fair premia, is not feasible via the market because

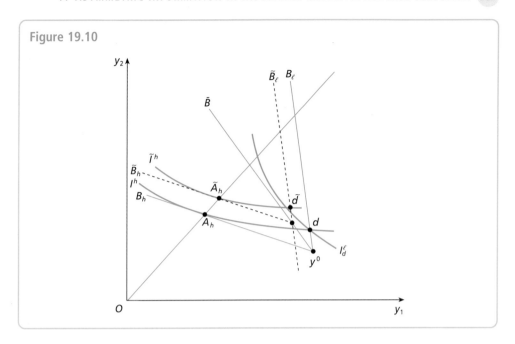

Figure 19.10

we assumed that firms cannot observe the risk type of insureds. Any firm which could discover the risk class of insureds could offer a contract to low risks which attracts them away from their separating contract, prevent high risks from buying it and make a profit. Given the incentive for firms to discover the risk class of insureds, it seems sensible to rest our welfare analysis on the assumption that a policy-maker will not be able to discover the risk class of insureds if firms cannot. The relevant welfare comparison is between the market allocation and the allocation which could be achieved by a policy-maker with no better information than firms.

We can show that the market allocation may be *constrained* or *restricted Pareto inefficient*: a policy-maker subject to the same information constraints as firms could achieve a Pareto improvement compared with the separating equilibrium allocation. Refer to Fig. 19.10 in which there is a separating equilibrium at (A_h, d). To make the diagrammatic analysis clearer, we assume that there are equal numbers of low- and high-risk types: $\lambda = \frac{1}{2}$. Suppose that the policy maker places a tax T on all policies sold to low-risk types. The effect is to shift the breakeven line for policies sold to low-risk types from B_ℓ to $\tilde{B}_\ell$ since firms must make a profit on low-risk policies to pay for the tax. All policies along $\tilde{B}_\ell$ will just break even after the tax. The amount of the tax is measured by the horizontal (or vertical) distance between the intercepts of B_ℓ and $\tilde{B}_\ell$ on the 45° line. At any contract, such as $(\tilde{P}_\ell, \tilde{q}_\ell)$ at $\tilde{d}$ on $\tilde{B}_\ell$, the insurers set a premium at which they just break even after tax if the policy is bought by a low-risk type:

$$\tilde{P}_\ell = \pi_\ell \tilde{q}_\ell + T$$

Suppose that the proceeds of the tax are paid as a subsidy on contracts sold to high-risk types. Since there are equal numbers of the two types, the subsidy per high-risk contract is T. Insurers can now offer a full cover contract $\tilde{A}_h$ to high risks at a reduced premium

$$\tilde{P}_h = P_h - T = \pi_h L - T$$

and still break even. Because high risks now get the improved contract $\tilde{A}_h$, it is possible to improve the contract offered to low risks without violating the self-selection constraint that the high risks prefer $\tilde{A}_h$ to the contract designed for low risks. The best contract for low risks which breaks even after the tax, and does not attract high risks, is now $\tilde{d}$. The contract $\tilde{d}$ is more expensive for the low risks than d because of the tax and because it provides more cover than d. However, they are better off at $\tilde{d}$ since it lies above the low-risk indifference curve I_d^{ℓ} through d.

The *cross-subsidization* separating equilibrium $(\tilde{A}_h, \tilde{d})$ makes both types better off, breaks even, and is feasible since it does not require information on the risk class of individual insureds. Hence the initial separating equilibrium was not constrained Pareto efficient. Notice that our assumptions about the nature of competition in the insurance market mean that such cross-subsidization is not possible without taxation and subsidy. Suppose all firms offer $(\tilde{A}_h, \tilde{d})$, using the profit on $\tilde{d}$ sold to low risks to cover the loss on $\tilde{A}_h$ sold to high risks. But a firm could earn positive profit by just offering the profitable contract $\tilde{d}$, which would only be bought by low risks if all other firms offered the breakeven cross-subsidizing pair $(\tilde{A}_h, \tilde{d})$.

Anticipatory equilibrium

One analytical response to the possibility of the non-existence of competitive equilibrium is to drop the assumption that insurance markets are competitive. A monopolized insurance market would not be vulnerable to the undermining of potential equilibria by competing contracts. In section B we derived the demand for cover as a function of the premium and the accident probability. It would be possible to model the expected profit-maximizing policies offered by a monopoly insurer faced with such demand functions and to investigate the implication of the insurer not being able to observe the risk type of insureds.

Alternatively we could argue that the definition of competitive equilibrium adopted is inappropriate. It implicitly assumes that insurers are extremely myopic. They fail to anticipate that one of the consequences of offering new types of contract may be that existing contracts are withdrawn, with repercussions on the profitability of the new contracts. Wilson (1977) has suggested that a more appropriate equilibrium concept for insurance markets is the *anticipatory equilibrium*. A set of contracts C is an anticipatory equilibrium if all the contracts in C break even and there is no other set of contracts C' which would break even after any contracts in C made unprofitable by the introduction of C' are withdrawn from the market.

The definition of an equilibrium we used to show the possible non-existence of equilibrium is akin to a Nash equilibrium (see section 15B). Our concept of competition implies that *better breakeven contracts are always offered*. If one firm could offer a contract or set of contracts which will at least break even, given the set of contracts offered by all other firms, it would do so. By contrast, Wilson argued that each firm will anticipate that other firms may react to any new contract it introduces, and the competitive unravelling of potential equilibria does not occur.

Thus consider Fig. 19.9. The separating contracts (A_h, d) are not an anticipatory equilibrium. A firm could introduce a pooling contract, say a, which attracts all the low risks from d and all the high risks from A_h. Such a pooling contract would still break even after the contracts (A_h, d) are withdrawn. a is not a Nash equilibrium because a firm would be willing to offer c given that all other firms continue to offer a: c would attract only low risks and would make a profit. But a is an anticipatory equilibrium. If c is offered it will attract all the low risks from a, which then would only be bought by high risks and would make a loss. a would be withdrawn from the market after the introduction of c. But then all the high risks would also buy c and it would make a loss because it lies above the breakeven line for pooling contracts. Firms will anticipate that contracts like c will be unprofitable when a is withdrawn and they will not offer it. Hence a is an anticipatory pooling equilibrium. Notice that it still involves only partial coverage.

We leave it for the reader to demonstrate that, if the proportion of low-risk types $\lambda < \lambda^*$, the separating contracts are an anticipatory equilibrium. The implication of adopting the anticipatory equilibrium concept is that an equilibrium always exists: pooling for $\lambda \in [\lambda^*, 1)$ and separating for $\lambda \in (0, \lambda^*)$.

An explicit specification of the nature of competition in insurance markets is essential to make sensible comparisons of alternative models. The specifications should spell out clearly the timing of actions by insurers and insureds and the information available when they take those actions. Dynamics are also important. The contract that an insured chooses in one period may convey information about her risk class. Insureds' current choice of policy will be influenced by its effect on the policies they will be offered in the future. In short: it is likely to be useful to put the analysis of adverse selection in a model resting on solid game theoretic foundations. This is not an easy task. Interested readers should follow up the references at the end of the book.

EXERCISE 19F

1. Show that the self-selection constraint [F.9] is not binding for low risks.

2. Illustrate the comparative static properties of the separating equilibrium contracts by sketching the effects of changes in the loss, the accident probabilities and the degree of risk aversion of insureds.

3. Use [F.11] to confirm your diagrammatic comparative static analysis in Question 2.

4. In the analysis of the separating equilibrium, why is it necessary to make the implicit assumption that an insurer can observe the total amount of cover bought by an insured from all insurers?

5. Why is it usual for insurers to include a term in the insurance contract to the effect that if an insured takes out insurance against the same event with another company the insurer will reduce the cover provided *pro rata*?

6. If insureds become more risk averse does this make it more or less likely that a pooling contract can undermine separating contracts? [*Hint*: what does an increase in risk aversion imply about the curvature of the indifference curves?]

7. Notice in Fig. 19.10 that the cross-subsidy insurance lines $\tilde{B}_h$ and $\tilde{B}_c$ intersect on the breakeven pooling contract line $\bar{B}$. Why must this always be true whatever the amount of the tax on the low-risk contract and whatever the proportion of low risks in the population?

8. *Cross-subsidy market separating equilibrium.* Suppose that the relevant definition of equilibrium is the anticipatory equilibrium. Show that the equilibrium will always exist and will be a separating equilibrium, possibly with cross-subsidization. Does this imply that the market equilibrium is now always constrained Pareto efficient? [*Hints*: (i) show first that a pooling contract cannot be an anticipatory equilibrium if cross-subsidy is permitted; (ii) trace out the loci of separating cross-subsidy contracts as the amount of cross-subsidy varies and show that the locus runs from d (no cross-subsidy) to the intersection of the 45° line with the breakeven pooling contract line.]

G. Asymmetric information in insurance markets: moral hazard

Many of the risks that people face can be changed by their actions. The risk of loss from burglary can be reduced by installing security systems; from premature death by reducing smoking; from car accidents by driving more slowly; from fire by installing smoke detectors, and so on. Such actions are often costly to individuals. The availability of insurance against risks may affect incentives to incur such costs, since it reduces the benefits from risk reduction. This response to insurance is known as *moral hazard*. In this section we use a simple model to clarify the nature of the problem and its consequences for the equilibrium contracts offered in insurance markets.

Our model is again an extension of the basic model of section B. We assume that insurance is supplied by competitive, risk-neutral insurers, with no administration costs. Individuals have the same preferences and endowments as in the previous section. We now assume that the probability π of loss L is endogenous: it depends on which of two levels of expenditure on care a_1, a_0, with $a_1 > a_0$, the individual undertakes. Without any loss in generality we can set $a_0 = 0$. We denote the probability of loss when $a = 0$ by π_0 and when $a = a_1$ by π_1 with $0 < \pi_0 < \pi_2 < 1$. An individual who buys cover q at a premium of P and spends a on care will have incomes of

$$y_1 = y - a - P \quad\quad\quad [G.1]$$

$$y_2 = y - a - P - L + q \quad\quad\quad [G.2]$$

depending on whether there is a loss (y_2) or not (y_1).

Under full information, the insurer can observe the insured's expenditure on care a. In a competitive insurance market the equilibrium contract will maximize expected utility at a premium which is fair given the amount of care taken by the individual. The premium will be $P = \pi(a^*)q$, where $a^* \in \{0, a_1\}$ is amount of care taken under the expected utility maximizing contract. We find the contract by substituting $\pi(a_i)q$ for P in [G.1] and [G.2] and solving the following problem for each a_i in turn, $i = 0, 1$:

$$\max_q V^i(P, q) = (1 - \pi_i)v(y - a_i - \pi_i q) + \pi_i v (y - a_i - L + (1 - \pi_i)q) \quad [G.3]$$

Since the premium is fair, given the amount of care, the optimal contract has full cover: $q^* = L$.

Let $V^{i*} = v(y - \pi_i L - a_i)$ denote the maximized value of expected utility for $a = a_i$. Assume that $V^{1*} > V^{0*}$, so that the equilibrium contract will be $(\pi_1 L, L)$ with the individual setting $a = a_1$ and buying full cover for a premium of $\pi_1 L$. The insurer breaks even since it can check that the insured has incurred the expenditure a_1. Since

$$V^{1*} - V^{0*} = v(y - \pi_1 L - a_1) - v(y - \pi_0 L) > 0 \quad\quad\quad [G.4]$$

we must have

$$y - a_1 - \pi_1 L - (y - \pi_0 L) > 0 \quad\quad\quad [G.5]$$

because marginal utility is positive, [G.5] implies

$$(\pi_0 - \pi_1)L > a_1 \quad\quad \text{or} \quad\quad \pi_1 L + a_1 < \pi_0 L \quad\quad\quad [G.6]$$

Figure 19.11

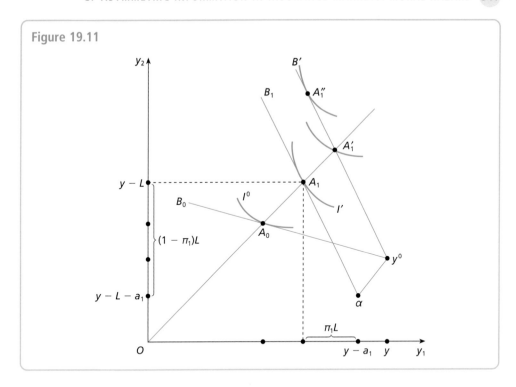

Thus a necessary and sufficient condition for it to be worth spending a_1 to get full cover at a lower premium is that the resulting reduction in the premium (equal to the reduction in the expected loss) exceeds the cost of care. The incremental benefit of care exceeds its incremental cost.

Figure 19.11 illustrates the full information equilibrium. The breakeven insurance budget line $B_0 y^0$, when the individual chooses $a_0 = 0$, has slope $-(1 - \pi_0)/\pi_0$. By spending a_1, rather than $a_0 = 0$, the individual's uninsured income combination shifts from $y^0 = (y, y - L)$ to $\alpha = (y - a_1, y - L - a_1)$. The line $y^0 \alpha$ is parallel to the 45° line. Because the insurer can observe that the individual has chosen a_1, it is willing to offer any contract along the breakeven line $B_1 \alpha$ with slope $-(1 - \pi_1)/\pi_1$.

The slope of the individual's indifference curves depends on the accident probability

$$\frac{dy_2}{dy_1} = -\frac{(1 - \pi_i)}{\pi_i} \frac{v'(y_1)}{v'(y_2)} \qquad [\text{G.7}]$$

Given the care level, and thus the accident probability, the optimal contract provides full cover at A_i on the 45° line. In the figure A_1 gives a larger certain income than A_0. As [G.6] shows the optimal contract depends on the size of the loss, a_1 and the resulting change in the accident probabilities. Note that the individual's degree of risk aversion does not affect the equilibrium. (Explain why.)

Now assume that there is asymmetry of information: the insurer cannot observe the value of a chosen by an individual insured. Suppose that the insurer was extremely naive, assumed that an individual *had* spent a_1, and offered the contract $(\pi_1 L, L)$. Then, from Fig. 19.11 we can see that the individual would set $a_0 = 0$, accept the full cover contract at the premium $\pi_1 L$ and end up at A_1'. The contract would make a loss for the insurer, since the expected payment on the contract exceeds the premium: $\pi_0 L > \pi_1 L$. If the insured were able to choose his cover, he would over-insure, choose the contract A_1'' and the naive insurer would have an even greater expected loss on the contract. Note that the moral hazard problem does not arise if the full information solution has $a^\star = 0$. The insurer can offer the contract $(\pi_0 L, L)$ which breaks even and the market equilibrium is the same as under full information. This case is uninteresting, so we henceforth confine our attention to cases in which, if there were full information, the insured would set $a^\star = a_1$.

If care is not observable, the insurance contract must be *incentive compatible*: the individual's choice of care must be consistent with the terms of the contract. Since the insurance market is competitive the insurer must design a contract which is optimal for the insured, otherwise he will not buy it. The contract must also break even. If it makes a profit it cannot maximize the insured's expected utility: it would be possible to reduce the premium or increase the cover. The optimal contract under information asymmetry may have $a = a_1$ or $a = 0$, even though the full information solution is $a = a_1$.

Suppose first that the insurer wishes to design a contract which is optimal given that the insured chooses a_1. The insurer sets the terms of the contract to solve the problem

$$\max_q V^1(P, q) = V^1(\pi_1 q, q)$$

$$= (1 - \pi_1)v(y - a_1 - \pi_1 q) + \pi_1 v(y - a_1 - L + (1 - \pi_1)q) \quad [\text{G.8}]$$

$$\text{s.t.} \quad V^1(\pi_1 q, q) \geq V^0(\pi_1 q, q) \quad [\text{G.9}]$$

where $V^0(\pi_1 q, q) = (1 - \pi_0)v(y - \pi_1 q) + \pi_0 v(y - L + (1 - \pi_1)q)$. Note that the requirement that the contract breaks even allows us to substitute $\pi_1 q$ for P and to reduce the problem to one with a single choice variable q.

[G.9] is the incentive compatibility constraint and requires that the level of cover must be set so that the insured weakly prefers to choose a_1 rather than a_0. ('Weakly' because we want to ensure that the feasible set is closed.)

As we have already noted, the insured will choose $a = 0$ if offered a full cover contract. At $q = L$ the right-hand side of [G.9] will exceed the left-hand side:

$$v(y - a_1 - \pi_1 L) < v(y - \pi_1 L) \quad [\text{G.10}]$$

Thus the solution must have partial cover $q < L$. Formally, the Kuhn–Tucker conditions are (see Appendix H)

$$\frac{dV^1}{dq} + \hat{\lambda}\left[\frac{dV^1}{dq} - \frac{dV^0}{dq}\right] = 0 \quad [\text{G.11}]$$

$$\hat{V}^1 - \hat{V}^0 \geq 0 \qquad \hat{\lambda} \geq 0 \qquad \hat{\lambda}[\hat{V}^1 - \hat{V}^0] = 0 \quad [\text{G.12}]$$

where $\hat{V}^i$ is the value of V^i at the solution. Suppose that the incentive compatibility constraint [G.9] was satisfied as a strict inequality at the solution. Then $\hat{\lambda} = 0$ and, from [G.11], we would have $dV^1/dq = 0$. But, since the premium is fair, the unconstrained optimal cover would be $q = L$, which would violate the incentive compatibility constraint (see [G.10]). The solution must have $\hat{\lambda} > 0$ and $\hat{V}^1 = \hat{V}^0$. We can use $\hat{V}^1 = \hat{V}^0$ and [G.11] to calculate the optimal level of partial cover $\hat{q}$. The optimal $\hat{q}$ must be such that, if the insured buys the contract $(\pi_1 \hat{q}, \hat{q})$, he is indifferent between spending a_1 and spending nothing on care *with the same contract*.

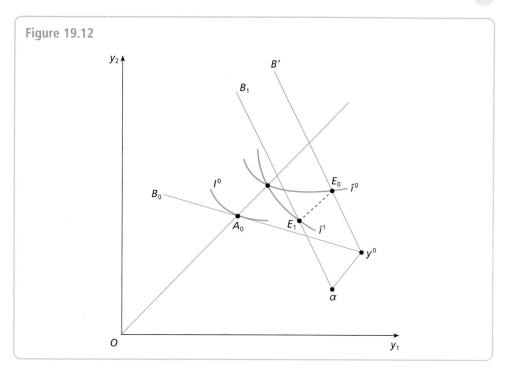

Figure 19.12

Figure 19.12 illustrates. The part cover optimal insurance contract provides sufficient cover $\hat{q}$ at a premium $\pi_1\hat{q}$ to take the individual from α to E_1 if he sets $a = a_1$. If he sets $a = 0$ and accepts the contract $(\pi_1\hat{q}, \hat{q})$, he can get from y^0 to E_0. (The line E_0E_1 is parallel to $y^0\alpha$ and to the 45° line.) $\hat{I}^1$ and $\hat{I}^0$ are the indifference curves corresponding to accepting the contract and then setting $a = a_1$ ($\pi = \pi_1$) and $a = a_0 = 0$ ($\pi = \pi_0$) respectively. The fact that the indifference curves through E_1 and E_0 intersect on the 45° line means that E_1 and E_0 yield the same certainty equivalent income. The individual gets the same expected utility from the contract $(\pi_1\hat{q}, \hat{q})$ whichever level of expenditure on care he chooses, and so he spends a_1 and the insurer breaks even.

The other possible equilibrium contract is the best possible breakeven contract which induces $a = 0$. This is the full cover contract at a premium $\pi_0 L$, which places the individual at A_0 and yields utility $v(y - \pi_0 L)$.

The contract which induces expenditure a_1 is the equilibrium contract if

$$\hat{V}^1 - v(y - \pi_0 L) = (1 - \pi_1)[v(y - \pi_1\hat{q} - a_1) - v(y - \pi_0 L)]$$
$$+ \pi_1[v(y - L - a_1 + (1 - \pi_1)\hat{q}) - v(y - \pi_0 L)] \geqslant 0 \qquad [\text{G.13}]$$

Using the mean value theorem we can write [D.13] as

$$(1 - \pi_1)v'(\tilde{y}_1)[\pi_0 L - \pi_1\hat{q} - a_1] + \pi_1 v'(\tilde{y}_2)[\pi_0 L + (1 - \pi_1)\hat{q} - L - a_1] \geqslant 0 \qquad [\text{G.14}]$$

where $\tilde{y}_1$ is suitably chosen between $(y - \pi_0 L)$ and $(y - \pi_1\hat{q} - a_1)$ and $\tilde{y}_2$ is suitably chosen between $(y - \pi_0 L)$ and $(y - L - a_1 + (1 - \pi_1)\hat{q})$. Our earlier assumption [G.6] ensures that

$$\pi_0 L - \pi_1\hat{q} - a_1 > 0 \qquad [\text{G.15}]$$

since $\hat{q} < L$, so that the first term in [G.14] is positive. However, the second term in [G.14] is positive only if

$$\pi_0 L - \pi_1 \hat{q} - a_1 > L - \hat{q} \qquad \text{[G.16]}$$

which is *not* implied by [G.6].

In terms of Fig. 19.12, the contract inducing a_1 is better than the full-cover contract with $a = 0$ at A_0 only if the indifference curve tangent to $B_0 y^0$ at A_0 cuts the $B' y^0$ line below E_0. In Fig. 19.12 this would clearly be so, but, as the reader should check, it is possible to construct cases in which the intersection is above E_0.

Notice now that whether the optimal contract is the one inducing a_1 depends on the shape of the indifference curves, i.e. on the degree of risk aversion. (Why is it more likely that the optimal contract will be that inducing a_1 the less risk averse the insured?)

Under moral hazard, when the insurer cannot observe the actions of the insured which affect the risk of loss, the equilibrium is one of two types. In one equilibrium the insured chooses to take no care and have full cover at a fair premium based on his higher accident probability. In the other, the individual may be offered part cover at a fair premium. The incomplete cover motivates the insured to take care to reduce the probability of loss by making him bear some of the consequences of the accident. The competitive equilibrium is unusual in that it involves rationing: the insurer fixes the quantity of cover it is willing to provide despite the fact that the insured would be willing to buy more cover at a fair premium. The reason the insurer does not meet the demand is that it knows that if the cover is increased the insured will accept the increased cover *and* reduce his care.

In the more general case in which the accident probability varies continuously with expenditure on care, the equilibrium is likely to have the insured taking less care than he would under full information and having less than full cover. (See questions 1 and 2). We explore the outcome in more depth in the analysis of the principal–agent problem in Chapter 20.

Pareto efficiency and moral hazard

Under full information the fact that the premium is linked to the level of care means that the insurance market induces an efficient level of care from the individual and provides efficient risk shifting from the risk-averse insured to the risk-neutral insurer. The social benefits of greater care are the reduction in expected accident costs, since under full cover insurance they fall on the risk-neutral insurer. The market is competitive and care is observable, so that the insurer passes the benefits of care on to the insured as a reduction in the premium for full cover. Thus the insured takes account of the social benefits of greater care in his care decision.

With asymmetric information the insured is worse off than when the insurer has full information. He either has full cover but a lower income than under full information, or the same expected income but incomplete cover, so that his certainty-equivalent income is reduced. The insurer breaks even under both information regimes. We conclude that the equilibrium under moral hazard is inefficient compared with the full information allocation. However, as we argued in the previous section, the relevant question is whether there are other allocations which are Pareto superior to the market allocation and feasible for a policy maker, given that the level of care is not observable.

In many cases a policy-maker will be able to improve on the market equilibrium under moral hazard, even though the equilibrium contract is designed to be optimal for the insured given asymmetric information. The policy-maker will not usually have better information about individuals, but will have instruments to change the behaviour of the parties which are not available to private contractors. Taxation is an obvious example. It is possible to reduce the amount of tobacco consumption of each individual smoker, without being able to observe any individual's consumption levels, by placing a tax on the sale of cigarettes by tobacco companies. Similarly, subsidies for the production of goods which reduce accident probabilities can increase care levels without the need for observation of individual behaviour.

We can use our simple insurance market model to show that such subsidy policies can lead to a Pareto improvement, despite the fact that the subsidy must be paid for out of taxation and despite the fact that the market provides insureds with privately optimal contracts designed to mitigate the effects of moral hazard.

Suppose that there are a large number of identical insureds whose individual levels of expenditure on care are not observable and that the initial moral hazard equilibrium has part cover insurance contracts which induce care of a_1. Thus the moral hazard costs take the form of the insureds' incomplete cover against the loss. A subsidy to expenditure on care at the rate of s is introduced. (Imagine that the government subsidized the production of burglar alarms or locks.) The net cost to an individual of reducing his probability of loss from π_0 to π_1 falls from a_1 to $(1 - s)a_1$. To finance the subsidy the government places a lump-sum tax on each individual of $T = sa_1$. This tax is paid *whatever the individual's expenditure on care*. (As we will see, the post-tax equilibrium will have all individuals spending the same amount on care.)

Figure 19.13 illustrates the effect of the lump-sum tax and the care subsidy on the market equilibrium shown in Fig. 19.12. If the individual spends nothing on care, he must still pay the lump-sum tax and his initial income combination with no insurance is $y^{00} = (y - T, y - L - T)$. If he decides to spend a gross amount a_1 on care to reduce his accident probability to π_1, his initial income combination is

$$\alpha = (y - T - (1 - s)a_1, y - L - T - (1 - s)a_1)$$
$$= (y - a_1, y - L - a_1) \qquad \text{[G.17]}$$

since $T = sa_1$. The net effect of the lump-sum tax and the care subsidy is that when gross expenditure on care is a_1 the initial position is the same as if there were no tax or subsidy.

The pre-subsidy equilibrium in the figure was at E_1 where the insured had part cover and spent a_1 on care. With the part cover contract he was indifferent between spending a_1 to get E_1 and spending $a_0 = 0$ to get E_0. After the introduction of the lump-sum tax the insured would be at E' on the indifference curve I_0' if he set $a = a_0$. He is now strictly worse off taking no care with the part cover policy than if he spends a gross amount a_1 on care. Hence the insurer can increase the amount of cover in the part cover policy until the insured is again indifferent between spending a_1 gross on care and spending nothing on care. The new optimal contract puts the insured at F_1 on the fair premium line $B_1\alpha$ if he spends a_1 gross on care. If he spends nothing on care, the same contract puts him at F_0 on $B''y^{00}$. Since the indifference curves through F_1 and F_0 intersect on the 45° line he is again indifferent between high and low care and chooses a_1.

Figure 19.13

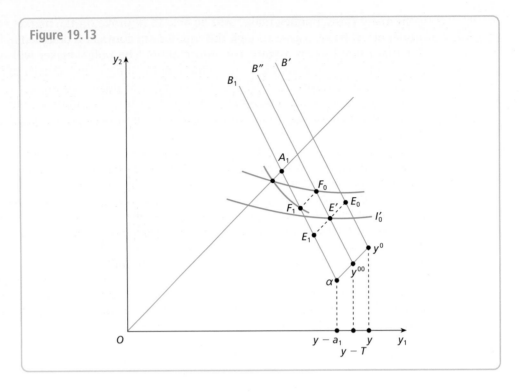

This feasible tax and subsidy policy makes insureds better off and the insurer no worse off. Thus the market equilibrium with moral hazard was restricted Pareto inefficient. In terms of the formal analysis of the insurer's problem, of choosing an insurance contract to maximize the expected utility of the insured subject to the incentive constraints, the tax and subsidy policy relaxes the incentive compatibility constraint at a given level of cover. As the reader should check, the right-hand side of [G.9] is reduced, and the left-hand side unaffected, by the tax and subsidy.

In our simple model with two levels of care expenditure, it is possible to achieve the same allocation as under full information. By setting $s = 1$ and $T = a_1$ the initial position without insurance will be at α whether the insured takes care or not. All contracts along $B_1 \alpha$ will then yield the same expected utility whatever his care level. The full information allocation at A_1 with full cover is feasible despite the presence of asymmetric information.

In general, when the expenditure level and associated loss probability vary continuously, the efficiency gains from intervening in a private insurance market by feasible tax and subsidy policies will be less dramatic. It will not usually be the case that the full information allocation can be achieved. But the basic point remains valid: the fact that the policy-maker can alter relative prices by taxes and subsidies, so as to influence unobservable individual behaviour, means that the market allocation is not restricted Pareto efficient. However, as Question 3 shows, even though the policy-maker does not need better information on individual behaviour than insurers, calculation of optimal taxes and subsidies will not be an easy task as it requires considerable amounts of information about preferences, endowments and technologies.

EXERCISE 19G

1. *Choice of care.* Retain the basic structure of the model in the section but now suppose that the loss probability varies continuously with care: $\pi = \pi(a)$, $\pi' < 0$, $\pi'' > 0$. (a) Model the insured's choice of care for a given insurance contract (P, q). (b) Investigate its comparative static properties: how does optimal care vary with the y, L, P, q? What restrictions must be placed on preferences and the probability function for it to be true that increases in cover reduce care?

2. *Optimal cover.* Use the model of question 1 to show that when the insurer cannot observe a she will offer the insured a premium function $P = P(q)$ with $P' > \pi$. Show that the optimal cover will be greater than zero.

3. *Market inefficiency.* Show that the equilibrium contract in Question 2 is restricted inefficient: a subsidy on care, funded by a lump-sum tax, can increase the expected utility of insureds. [*Hint*: solve for the equilibrium contract as a function of s and T, evaluate the derivative of the equilibrium expected utility of the insured with respect to s at $s = 0$, making plentiful use of the Envelope Theorem and remembering that $sa = T$.]

4. *Two-tier policy.* Now assume that insurance is provided only by the government (which cannot observe care). Show that it may be possible to achieve the full efficient information allocation by a suitable insurance and tax-subsidy policy. [*Hint*: there is now only a single breakeven constraint on tax policy and the insurance contract.]

H. Signalling

In the insurance model of section F, we saw that when there is adverse selection low-risk types are left worse off than under full information. This is one example of a common phenomenon: sellers of high-quality products suffer if the potential buyers cannot distinguish between high and low quality prior to purchase. (In the insurance market insurers are, in effect, buying risks from insureds.) In his classic analysis of the implications of asymmetrical information about product quality, Akerlof (1970) considered another example: the used car market.

Suppose that cars are either high quality (reliable), or low-quality 'lemons' (unreliable) and that quality does not change over time. The quality of a particular car (new or old) cannot be determined by inspection: it has to be owned and used before its reliability can be ascertained. The value of a lemon to an owner is θ_1, whilst the value of a high-quality car is $\theta_2 > \theta_1$. Risk-neutral potential buyers know that the proportion of lemons is π. The market price for new cars will reflect the *average* quality of new cars, since buyers will realize that they run the risk π of buying a lemon. Thus the price of new cars will be $\bar\theta = \pi\theta_1 + (1 - \pi)\theta_2$. The market price of a used car must be less than the price of a new car, otherwise all owners of lemons would sell them and buy a new car, with probability $(1 - \pi)$ of getting a high-quality car. Since the price of used cars must be less than $\bar\theta$, no owner of a good car will sell it on the used car market: its value to him exceeds the price he would get for it. Hence only lemons will be sold on the used car market and, since buyers will realize this, the price of used cars is θ_1. Thus we have one possible explanation for the fact that the price difference between new and used cars is greater than can be accounted for by any depreciation in quality over time.

Many used cars are in fact sold by dealers, who are able, at a cost, to make an accurate estimate of the quality of the car by inspection, road testing and so on.

When they sell the car, they attach guarantees or warranties, which not only provide insurance for the buyer, but also act as a *signal* of the car's quality. If the dealer sold lemons, these guarantees would be more expensive for the dealer to honour than if he sold high-quality cars. Because there is a negative correlation between the cost of the guarantee and the quality of the car, it is rational for a dealer to offer a comprehensive guarantee only if the car is indeed high quality. Thus one way in which the seller of a high-quality commodity can credibly convey information about quality to a buyer is to signal: engage in activity which would not be rational for a low-quality seller.

We develop this idea further using a simple version of the job-market signalling model of Spence (1974). Suppose that a worker A may either have a low productivity of θ_1 or a high productivity of $\theta_2 > \theta_1$, and that a risk-neutral employer P cannot determine the worker's productivity before hiring him. P knows that the probability that A is type θ_1 is π. We assume that P will always break even on the contract she offers A. This may be because of competition from other potential employers. (We shall have more to say below about the implications of competition among employers.) Thus if P knew A's type she would offer him an income or wage equal to his productivity: $y_i = \theta_i$. If she does not know his type she offers him the pooling wage $y = \bar{\theta} = \pi\theta_1 + (1 - \pi)\theta_2$.

A has a costly activity $s \geqslant 0$ which he can undertake. In the Spence model s is the educational level achieved by A. The cost of achieving a given s is smaller for the more productive type, so that s can be a signal to P of A's unobservable type. We assume that s has a constant marginal cost of c_i to a θ_i type, with $c_1 > c_2$. To simplify the analysis further, we also assume that s is a *pure signal*: it has no effect on the agent's productivity and has no direct effect on A's utility. This is obviously unrealistic: it implies, for example, that not only does obtaining a degree in economics have no effect on one's productivity, but also that it is not even enjoyable for its own sake. (As Question 5 shows, relaxing this assumption does not alter the basic results.)

A's utility function is his wage less his signalling cost: $u_i(y, s) = y - c_i s$. The indifference curves of a θ_i type in (s, y) space are positively sloped straight lines with slope $dy/ds = c_i$. Fig. 19.14 illustrates.

Since P can observe A's signal s, she can offer him a wage schedule $y(s)$ which relates the wage to the signal. The wage schedule offered will depend on P's beliefs about the relationship between the signal and productivity. But the wage schedule will also affect A's decision about s. In an *informationally consistent equilibrium* (ICE) the employer offers a wage schedule which induces each type of A to choose a level of s which is consistent with P's beliefs about the relationship between s and θ.

Suppose that the wage schedule is a simple step function: for $s < s^*$, the wage is θ_1 and for $s \geqslant s^*$, the wage is θ_2. This will be an *ICE* if it induces the θ_1 type to choose $s < s^*$ and the θ_2 type to set $s \geqslant s^*$. If A sets $s < s^*$, he will choose $s = 0$, since any higher $s \in (0, s^*)$ merely increases his signalling cost without increasing his wage. Similarly if A chooses $s \geqslant s^*$, he will optimally set $s = s^*$.

It will be rational for the low productivity type to set $s = 0$ if

$$\theta_1 \geqslant \theta_2 - c_1 s^* \Rightarrow s^* \geqslant (\theta_2 - \theta_1)/c_1 \equiv s_0 \qquad [\text{H.1}]$$

(As always in these sorts of models, we avoid tedious complications by assuming that, if the better informed party is indifferent between two choices, he will make the one which reveals his type.) In Fig. 19.14, the type θ_1 is better off at $(0, \theta_1)$ than at any point along the horizontal line at θ_2 to the right of (s_0, θ_2).

Figure 19.14

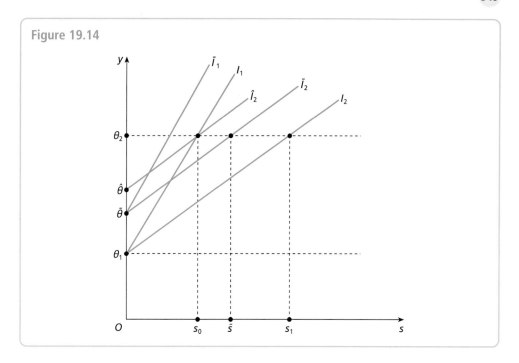

A high-productivity type will choose to set $s = s^*$ and get the wage θ_2, rather than set $s = 0$ and receive θ_1, provided

$$\theta_1 \leqslant \theta_2 - c_2 s^* \Rightarrow s^* \leqslant (\theta_2 - \theta_1)/c_2 \equiv s_1 \qquad [\text{H.2}]$$

Thus in Fig. 19.14 both the points $(0, \theta_1)$ and (s_1, θ_2) are on the indifference curve I_2 of the θ_2 type, who will be strictly better off with any contract (s, θ_2) with $s < s_1$ than with the contract $(0, \theta_1)$.

Since $c_1 > c_2$, [H.1] and [H.2] imply that $s_1 > s_0$. Hence if $s^* \in [s_0, s_1]$, the step function wage schedule constitutes a *fully revealing separating ICE* in which each type reveals his productivity and the employer's beliefs about the relationship between the signal and productivity are confirmed. There are an infinity of such equilibria. All of them yield the same utility to the θ_1 type, who always sets $s = 0$ and has utility $u_1 = \theta_1$, and to P who always breaks even. However, the θ_2 type prefers the equilibrium with $s^* = s_0$ since he spends least on signalling at this equilibrium. Thus fully revealing separating *ICE* are Pareto inefficient if $s^* > s_0$.

There is also a *pooling ICE* in which both types are paid the same wage of $\bar{\theta}$ and do not signal. Suppose the employer believes that

- if $s > s_1$, A is high productivity for sure;
- if $s \leqslant s_1$, A is low productivity with probability π and high productivity with probability $(1 - \pi)$.

If P then offers a wage of θ_2 if $s > s_1$ and a wage of $\bar{\theta}$ if $s \leqslant s_1$, both types will set $s = 0$, she will break even *ex ante* and never have her beliefs contradicted.

Since P breaks even in all *ICE* she is indifferent whether the equilibrium is pooling or separating. The type θ_1 is better off in the pooling equilibrium than in any separating equilibrium: his wage is $\bar{\theta}$ rather than θ_1. The high-productivity type may be better or worse off in the pooling equilibrium. Thus see Fig. 19.14 and notice that, if in the separating equilibrium, the level of s^* required to qualify for the wage θ_2 exceeds $\bar{s}$, the high-productivity type will prefer the pooling equilibrium, where he has the contract $(0, \bar{\theta})$. A contract (s^*, θ_2) with $s^* \in (\bar{s}, s_1)$ will put him on an indifference curve below $\bar{I}_2$. His wage is higher in such a separating equilibrium, but not sufficiently so to offset the increase in his signalling costs compared with the pooling equilibrium, where he set $s = 0$.

Clearly the larger are s^* and $\bar{\theta}$, the more likely it is that the separating equilibrium will be Pareto inefficient compared with the pooling equilibrium. Indeed, there will be a critical level of $\bar{\theta}$ at which the pooling equilibrium is Pareto superior to the least inefficient separating equilibrium where $s^* = s_0$. Referring to Fig. 19.14 again, we see that if $\bar{\theta} \geqslant \hat{\theta}$, the pooling equilibrium is Pareto superior to the separating equilibrium with $s^* = s_0$. We can calculate the critical pooling wage $\hat{\theta}$ and the critical proportion of low-productivity types $\hat{\pi}$ at which the two equilibria are equivalent. The high-productivity type is indifferent between the separating equilibrium with $s^* = s_0$ and the pooling equilibrium when

$$\pi\theta_1 + (1 - \pi)\theta_2 = \theta_2 - c_2 s_0 \qquad [\text{H.3}]$$

Substituting for s_0 from [H.1] and rearranging gives the critical probability of the low-productivity type as

$$\hat{\pi} = c_2/c_1 \qquad [\text{H.4}]$$

Thus, somewhat surprisingly, whether the pooling equilibrium is Pareto superior to all separating equilibria depends only on the relative signalling costs and is unaffected by the relative productivities of the two types. The reason is that changes in either of the productivity levels have precisely offsetting effects on the two sides of [H.3].

If $\pi < \hat{\pi}$, so that the pooling equilibrium is Pareto superior to all separating equilibria, both types of agent would be made better off by the simple and feasible policy of banning signalling. If $\pi > \hat{\pi}$ the welfare implications are less clear. It is then possible that the high-productivity types are better off in the separating equilibrium. The low-productivity types are worse off. The expected effect of a move from pooling to separating is to reduce the utility of the average agent since

$$\pi\theta_1 + (1 - \pi)[\theta_2 - c_2 s^*] = \bar{\theta} - (1 - \pi)c_2 s^* < \bar{\theta} \qquad [\text{H.5}]$$

Expected *per capita* output is reduced by the expected cost of signalling. If we placed an equal weight on the utility of both types we would conclude that equilibria with any signalling are not welfare maximizing.

This is to be expected: signalling is assumed only to convey information in this model, it does not increase productivity. The private gain to high-productivity types from signalling exceeds the (zero) social gain and signalling is merely a costly means of redistributing income from low-productivity types to high-productivity types. The same general conclusion holds in models in which signalling is also productive: the private benefits from signalling will reflect both the increased productivity and the information conveyed, but only the former is socially beneficial.

Although signalling equilibria reduce *per capita* output net of signalling costs it is not clear that there are feasible policies which are a Pareto improvement on signalling equilibra when signalling would make the high-productivity types better off. If high- and low-productivity types can be identified, it would be possible to compensate the high-productivity types by a transfer from the low-productivity types and leave both types better off. But how are they to be identified in the absence of signalling? Unless we assume that a policy-maker has better information about individuals than their potential employers, there is no feasible Pareto improvement on a signalling equilibrium when high-productivity types prefer the screening equilibrium.

Competition and signalling

The labour market signalling model outlined above raises many fascinating issues and has generated a large literature. Some of this literature has arisen out of a feature of the model about which we have so far been deliberately vague: the nature of competition in markets when signalling is possible. The reader will have noticed significant similarities between the model and the analysis of adverse selection in section F. Indeed, with relatively minor amendments, it is possible to make the two models formally equivalent: only the interpretation of the notation differs. Thus we could interpret the amount of insurance cover demanded by insureds as a signal: for given premium rates low-risk types will rationally demand less cover than high-risk types. Thus the amount of cover demanded can be used as a signal to convey information to the insurer about the risk class of the insured.

In our analysis of adverse selection, we noted that pooling could never be a Nash equilibrium and that there might not be a Nash separating equilibrium if the proportion of low-risk insureds was sufficiently large. In this section we have used the relatively undemanding concept of informationally consistent equilibrium: we were interested only in wage schedules which did not lead to behaviour which contradicted the beliefs on which the schedule was based. It is easy to show that informationally consistent equilibria may not be Nash equilibria: given the *ICE* wage schedules of all other employers, there may be another *ICE* schedule which makes positive profits for the employer offering it.

First, consider the pooling contract $(0, \bar{\theta})$ in Fig. 19.14. Whatever the position of $\bar{\theta} \in (\theta_1, \theta_2)$ (whatever the proportion of high-productivity types in the population of agents) it will always be possible for an employer to offer a contract which would attract high-productivity types but not low-productivity types. Since the indifference curves of a low-productivity type are always steeper than those of a high-productivity type, an employer can always offer a contract which lies above the $\bar{I}_2$ indifference curve and below the $\bar{I}_1$ indifference curve through the pooling contract. The contract would offer a wage greater than $\bar{\theta}$, but less than θ_2, if s was at least some specified level, and it would make a profit for the employer. Thus no pooling contract is a Nash equilibrium.

Next, consider the separating equilibrium wage schedule. If $s^* > s_0$ the schedule is not a Nash equilibrium: some other employer could attract high-productivity types by offering a wage less than θ_2 to individuals who signalled at the level s_0. Thus, if there is a Nash separating equilibrium, it must offer the contracts $(0, \theta_1)$ and (s_0, θ_2). But as reference to Fig. 19.14 shows, if the pooling wage exceeds $\hat{\theta}$, the separating contracts are not a Nash equilibrium, since some employer could offer a wage less than the pooling wage for a zero signal, attract both types and make a profit. Thus, if the proportion of high-productivity types exceeds $(1 - \hat{\theta})$ (defined by [H.4]), there is no Nash separating equilibrium with signalling, and therefore no Nash equilibrium.

Since the responses to this analytical difficulty are the same as for adverse selection models, we refer the reader to our remarks at the conclusion of section F and the references at the end of the book.

EXERCISE 19H

1. Suppose that P's beliefs are of the following form:

   if $s < s*$ then A is θ_1 for sure

   if $s \geq s*$ then A is θ_1 with probability π and θ_2 with probability $(1 - \pi)$.

   What are the *ICE*?

2. What would be the consequences of assuming that costs are positively related to productivity: $c_1 < c_2$?

3. Suppose that the θ_i type has a reservation wage of $r_i \geq 0$, with $r_2 > r_1 = 0$. Show that 'lemon' like results can arise in the pooling *ICE*. Suppose that $r_2 < \theta_2$ and consider the possible outcomes in the separating *ICE*. What are the utility gains and losses from signalling?

4. *Monopsony*. Suppose that P faces no competition in the market for A's services, so that she can set $y_i < \theta_i$ if she can identify A's type, and $y < \bar{\theta}$ if she cannot. Suppose that the θ_i type has a disutility of work or reservation wage of $r_i \geq 0$, with $r_2 > r_1 = 0$. Under what conditions would P prefer the pooling equilibrium to the separating equilibrium?

5. *Productive signals*. What are the separating and pooling *ICE* in the following cases?

   (a) The productivity of a θ_i type is $\theta_i s^\alpha$ with $\alpha \in (0, 1)$ and the marginal costs of signalling are $c_i = 1/\theta_i$ ($i = 1, 2$).

   (b) Assume that there is a continuum of types θ uniformly distributed over $[1, 2]$, the productivity of type θ is θs^α with $\alpha = 0$ and that the marginal signalling cost and type θ is $1/\theta$.

   (c) As in (b) but now $\alpha \in (0, 1)$.

Agency, contract theory and the firm

In the previous chapter we illustrated some of the implications of asymmetrical information by reference to the insurance market. We extend the analysis in this chapter by presenting more general models of contracting under asymmetrical information. Although the models and lessons are general we set them in the context of the theory of the firm. We start in section A by setting out some issues about the existence, internal organization and contractual structure of firms which we have ignored in earlier chapters. Then, in section B, we use a simple principal–agent model of hidden action (moral hazard in the insurance terminology) to consider how contracts between managers and owners can mitigate some of the problems posed by the separation of ownership from control. Section C generalizes the model. In section D we examine situations where the manager has information not possessed by the owners. We show that in these circumstances the optimal contract between the manager/agent and the owner/principal will induce the agent to report private information truthfully, though at a cost to the less well informed principal. We illustrate the power of this Revelation Principle with two further examples of hidden information models (adverse selection in the insurance terminology): financing of investment and public procurement.

A. Critique of the classical theory of the firm

There appear to be many features of real firms which have no counterparts in the traditional theory outlined in sections 7A to 7D.

(a) *Ownership*. A firm may be owned by a single individual or by a small group, with each owner liable for the debts of the firm to the complete extent of his wealth. Alternatively, the firm may be owned by any number from a few to several thousands of people, with liability limited to the value of their ownership shares, exchangeable on a stock market. Part or all of the shares may be held by other firms, or financial organizations such as pension funds and insurance companies.

(b) *Control*. Where the firm is owned by one individual or a small group, it is likely that overall control will be exercised by someone with a significant ownership share. Where the ownership is dispersed over many individuals, overall control is exercised by a 'board of directors', acting in principle as fiduciary representatives of the owners, and comprising employees of the firm (senior executives) and 'outside directors'. Where the firm is partly owned by another firm or financial organization, some members of this group will often represent it on the board. If ownership is total, then control will usually be exercised by having the senior executives directly responsible to executives of the owning firm.

(c) *Organization*. A hierarchical structure will exist between the people who directly carry out the basic activities of production, selling output and buying inputs, on the one hand, and the people exercising overall control, on the other. This is intended to fulfil a number of functions: to translate broad policy objectives formulated by controllers into specific plans; to coordinate the separate activities at lower levels and ensure consistency of plans; to monitor performance, transmit information on this up to controllers and implement incentive systems; and to provide information with which overall policy objectives can be formulated. The larger the scale and greater the diversity of the basic production and selling activities of the organization, the more extended and complex this hierarchical structure will be.

(d) *Information*. The operations of the firm will generate information (reports from salespeople on demand conditions, performance of production processes, etc.) and also activities will be undertaken to acquire it (market research, technological research and development). This information must be transmitted to the points in the firm at which it is required for decision-taking. The information will rarely be complete, so that decisions will be taken under varying degrees of uncertainty.

(e) *Conflict*. Objectives, plans and decisions will generally be formulated or taken by more than one individual. Conflicts may arise between these individuals, for one or both of two reasons: because of lack of objective information, beliefs may differ about possible outcomes of decisions and their relative likelihood; or preference orderings of the individuals over the outcomes of the decision may differ. The latter source of conflict is in turn due to the fact that a given outcome of a decision may benefit different decision-takers in different ways, so that conflict would be avoided only if they subordinated their own self-interest to some common objective, possibly that of the firm's shareholders. Moreover, although the direct participants in decision-taking are more often than not the executives of a firm, there will usually be other groups who can influence certain decisions by their behaviour. For example, workers can refuse to work if they dislike decisions about wages, hours and conditions of work; shareholders can sell their shares if profits are low, and so on.

The description of the firm implicit in the profit maximization theory seems to include little of this. Nothing is said about control or organization structures and a very restricted view is taken of the nature of ownership. It seems to be assumed that whatever these may be, the firm will act in the best interests of its owners, i.e. the recipients of the 'residual income', and that there is no organizational problem in translating this objective into decisions. Moreover, no conflict is seen to exist: all decisions are taken in a way consistent with the objective of the firm. In all its decisions the firm has complete information, and there is no uncertainty. Thus, the theory clearly does not seem to take into account many features of reality.

However, any theory must abstract from or ignore *some* aspects of reality. The classical theory is designed to provide a foundation for models of the firm which allow us to derive relationships between output supply and input demand decisions, on the one hand, and changes in parameters such as output and input prices, taxes, and technological coefficients on the other. This can be done most tractably by taking a fairly abstract 'black box' model of the firm, and the real test of the value of this abstraction is the evaluation of how well it predicts the decisions firms take.

There is no body of well-founded empirical evidence to support the view that, *in respect of the class of decisions with which it is concerned*, the classical theory gives false or misleading predictions. On the contrary the classical theory has proved its usefulness in many applications.

The more important criticism is that the classical theory cannot help us analyse issues that arise out of the nature of the firm itself and which are of interest and importance quite independently of whether they affect qualitatively the forms of the firm's output supply and input demand relationships. The most important are:

(a) the consequences of the separation of ownership from control;

(b) the firm's capital structure, i.e. the appropriate mix of debt and equity;

(c) the internal structure and organization of the firm – why hierarchy, and what is the most efficient 'architecture' for the structure of decision-taking within the firm?

(d) the 'boundaries' of the firm and the nature of the firm itself – if transactions costs are saved by integrating activities within a firm, why is the entire economy not one large firm?

(e) the firm's 'internal labour market'.

The classical theory of the firm says nothing about these issues because it takes for granted the answers to the questions they pose. It would be wrong, however, to suppose that microeconomic theory has nothing to say on them. There has been a great deal of valuable work on these issues by economists working within the 'neoclassical' tradition, and they are still at the forefront of current research. In the remainder of this chapter, we consider the main approaches to the first two of these issues, based on principal–agent theory and contract theory.

B. Agency theory and the separation of ownership from control

The classical theory of the firm is based upon the idea of a central individual who: owns the firm's assets, which he finances by saving and borrowing; receives as his income the profits of the business; employs the inputs; bears the risks; and controls the firm. A different view of the nature of capitalism has become general, receiving impetus from the ever-increasing size of firms and concentration of economic activity. Though owner-controlled firms may still form the majority of business units, the bulk of economic activity is controlled by large corporations, the distinguishing characteristic of which is a divorce of ownership from control. The owners of the firm are the shareholders, who may number thousands, and each of them has a very small proportion of the total equity of the company. They bear the risks, in the sense that fluctuations in the profits of the company imply fluctuations in their income – dividends – from it. They also supply the risk capital for new investment, either by buying new issues of shares, or, more usually, by forgoing profits which are ploughed back into the business. On the other hand, by diversifying their shareholdings across a number of companies (or having experts do this for them, in unit trusts or investment trusts), they reduce the riskiness of the overall portfolio. As a consequence shareholders take only a very limited interest in the running of any one company. Dissatisfied shareholders vote with their feet: they sell their shares, thus reducing the company's share price. This may represent an effective control on management, first because managers may like a high stock market valuation (share price × number of shares issued) for its own sake, but probably more importantly because a valuation which is low relative to the earning power of the assets of the company raises the threat of takeover by another company and the senior managers being fired. Hence there is some constraint on managers to take account of shareholders' interests.

In principle, the directors of a firm are the stewards for the shareholders, oversee-ing the operations of the company on their behalf. However, boards of directors are usually dominated by the senior executives of the company. The senior executives of the company rather than shareholders effectively control the firm (subject to the organizational problems which they themselves may have in ensuring that their decisions are actually implemented).

Initial attempts to model such *managerial capitalism* argued that, if managers' and shareholders' interests are in conflict, the divorce of ownership from control *permits* managers to pursue their own interests rather than those of shareholders, to an extent determined by the sanctions possessed by shareholders. The second step was to argue that the interests of managers and shareholders *do* conflict. It was suggested that managers derive their satisfactions from: their salaries; amounts of additional perquisites such as expense accounts, company cars, subsidized food and drink (which also have tax advantages); status, prestige, power and security. Although these things may depend on a profit performance which keeps shareholders happy, they do not necessarily vary directly with profit, but rather may vary with other dimensions of the firm's performance. The third step was the proposition that people take decisions in their own self-interest. Managers will therefore choose output and input levels, and investment plans, in the light of their effects on the determinants of their own satisfactions, taking account of shareholders's interests only insofar as they represent an externally imposed constraint.

Early models of managerial capitalism (by Baumol, Marris and Williamson) took the form of simple constrained maximization problems. The managers' objectives are characterized by a single maximand such as sales revenue (Baumol) or growth (Marris), or by a utility function defined on variables which more directly reflect managerial preferences, such as expenditures on staff, salaries and 'perks' (Williamson). The interests and influence of shareholders are expressed by a mini-mum profit constraint, rationalized as the amount required to avoid takeover, and allowing the firm to make less than maximum profit. The models provide a range of predictions about equilibrium choices and comparative statics responses which differ from those of the model of profit maximization, and also, in the case of Williamson's model provide an explanation of 'managerial slack' or 'X-inefficiency' (Liebenstein's term).

These models themselves beg a number of questions. Their central weakness is the absence of any explicit analysis of the role of information and of the behaviour of the owner(s) of the firm – the simple assumption of a given profit constraint dis-guises many important issues. A central implication of the separation of ownership from control is the *asymmetry of information* it creates between manager and owner. If an owner knew as much as the manager about the profit-making possibilities of the firm, the owner could threaten to punish observed deviations from profit-maximizing behaviour and so ensure that they did not take place. On the other hand, if an owner perceives that the manager's information is superior to her own, then she can try to devise a contract which takes account of this asymmetry of information and provides the manager with an incentive to take at least some account of the owner's objectives. For example, senior managers of large corporations are often given options to buy stock which encourage them to increase the value of the firm's shares. In addition, a large proportion of a senior manager's pay often consists of a profit-related bonus payment. We require an explicit analysis of the situation of asymmetric information to determine whether we can expect such incentive schemes to eliminate entirely the effects of the separation of ownership from control.

Relevant models are provided by *principal–agent theory*, which gives a general analysis of the following situation. A principal, P, employs an agent, A, to carry out some activity on her behalf. A must choose some action a which determines an outcome $x = x(a, \theta)$. θ is a random variable with known distribution. In models of *moral hazard*, A must choose a before θ is known. P observes the outcome x, but cannot observe either a or θ and so is unable to ensure that A chooses the value of a that P would prefer. Her problem is then to design a contract that rewards A according to the outcome x, taking into account any tendency A might have to choose a value of a which is non-optimal for P.

In models of *adverse selection*, A knows θ before a is chosen, whereas again P cannot observe a or θ. But P knows that A knows θ, and so faces the problem of designing a contract which induces A to reveal the true value of θ. If we identify P as the owner of the firm and A as the manager, principal–agent theory provides models to analyse explicitly the consequences of the separation of ownership from control. In the remainder of this section we show how a simple principal–agent model can clarify the issues raised by the separation of ownership from control in firms. Since principal–agent theory has many applications outside the theory of the firm, we devote the following two sections to a quite detailed analysis of the general moral hazard and adverse selection models.

A moral hazard model of managerial contracts

Suppose that the owner of a firm, denoted by P, delegates management of the firm to a professional manager, A. This may be because P does not possess the types of skills necessary to run the firm or because she prefers to use her labour in other activities. Since P does not supply any effort to her firm, she will only be concerned with the income it yields her.

Let a be the *manager's* effort supply and y his pay. I_0 is the manager's *reservation indifference curve* shown in Figure 20.1. If we measure the manager's pay, y, as well as profit, on the vertical axis, I_0 shows the set of (a, y) pairs such that the manager is indifferent between working for the firm and taking his next best employment opportunity. The manager's utility function is quasi-linear: $u(a, y) = v(y) - a$, where $v' > 0$, $v'' < 0$ so that the manager is averse to income risk.

A's reservation utility level v^0 is the utility A derives from his next best employment. All effort–income combinations along the reservation indifference curve I_0 yield v^0 to A. We assume that P can hold A down to his reservation utility level. Thus the height of I_0 measures the cost of A's effort to P: the minimum amount A must be paid to induce him to supply effort for P. Setting

$$v(y) - a = v^0 \tag{B.1}$$

and solving for y in terms of a, we can write

$$y = v^{-1}(v^0 + a) = y(a) \tag{B.2}$$

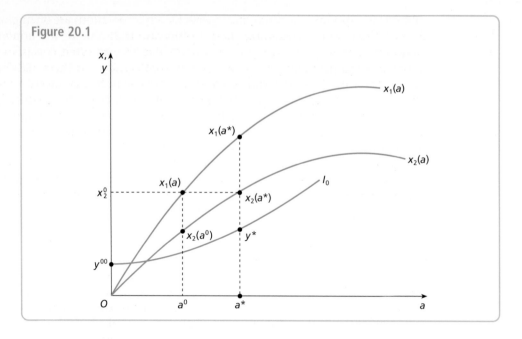

Figure 20.1

The graph of this function is the curve I_0 in Fig. 20.1. Differentiating through [B.2] we have

$$dy/da = 1/v'(y) \qquad [B.3]$$

as the slope of I_0, or the *marginal cost* to the owner of the manager's effort, at any a.

P's income from the firm is the profit of the firm: the difference between the gross profit and the amount she must pay A to supply effort.

Let $x(a)$ denote the function giving gross profit x as a function of managerial effort. If the owner:

1. knows the $x(a)$ and $y(a)$ functions, and
2. observes the gross profit outcome x, or a itself,

then no problem arises out of the separation of ownership from control. If a is the effort level she wants from the manager, she can engage A on a contract which specifies the payment $y^* = y(a^*)$ conditional on the profit outcome being $x(a^*)$ (or equivalently on A putting in effort a^*), and which penalizes him if any outcome other than $x(a^*)$ results. Under this contract A does best by supplying a^*, since any lower a can be costlessly detected and results in lower utility than $v(y^*) - a^* = v^0$.

When can the separation of ownership from control present difficulties to P? It seems natural to suppose that P will always be able to observe the gross profit outcome x. As long as there is a one-to-one relationship between x and a, the owner can always *infer* the value of a and apply the penalty clause for a deviation. We can begin to construct a model in which the separation of ownership from control could cause a problem if we assume:

1. P can never observe A's choice of a directly: a is always A's *private information*;
2. there is *uncertainty*: a number of possible values of x can result from a given choice of a.

These assumptions define a moral hazard type of principal–agent model. The implication of assumption (2) is that P cannot infer the value of a unambiguously from her observation of x. Figure 20.1 illustrates this. For each a, suppose that the outcome x lies either on the curve $x_1(a)$ with probability π, or $x_2(a)$ with probability $1 - \pi$. Then if P observed the outcome x_2^0, she would not be able to tell if it corresponded to an input of $a^\star$ and bad luck, or an input of a^0 and good luck.

Nevertheless, in this case P is able to write a contract enforcing choice of $a^\star$ or any a-value she desires. If A supplies any $a < a^\star$, P is certain to observe a value of x other than $x_1(a^\star)$ or $x_2(a^\star)$, unless A chooses a^0. If A chooses a^0 then with probability $(1 - \pi)$ P will observe $x_2(a^0) < x_2(a^\star)$, and with probability π she will observe $x_1(a^0) = x_2(a^\star)$. P then offers A the following contract. If she observes $x_1(a^\star)$ or $x_2(a^\star)$ she will pay $y^\star$. However, if she observes $x_2(a^0)$ she pays y^0, where y^0 satisfies

$$\pi v(y^\star) + (1 - \pi)v(y^0) - a^0 < v^0 \qquad \text{[B.4]}$$

Finally, if she observes any other x, she pays $y < y^{00}$ (See Figure 20.1.).

Faced with this contract A does best by supplying $a^\star$. [B.4] ensures that he does worse by supplying the lower effort level a^0 and running the risk that the adverse state of the world will reveal his lack of effort (but see also Question 2).

P is able to enforce a desired effort level $a^\star$ in this case because some outcomes have zero probability if $a^\star$ is chosen and positive probability if some other a-value is chosen. Provided she can impose a large enough penalty (find a y^0 to satisfy [B.4]) she can always make $a \neq a^\star$ not worthwhile for A. (Note that $a^\star$ may not actually be optimal for P in the above situation, but whatever a is optimal can be enforced in the same way.)

To formulate an agency problem which does not permit this type of solution, we make the *probabilities of the outcomes*, rather than the values of the outcomes, functions of A's effort level a. Suppose there are just two possible gross profit outcomes, x_1 and x_2, with $x_1 > x_2$, and two possible effort levels A can choose, a_h and a_ℓ. We assume $\pi_h > \pi_\ell$, so that higher effort makes a higher profit outcome more likely. We assume that P seeks to maximize the expected value of profit, net of any payment she makes to A:

$$\bar{z}_j = \pi_j(x_1 - y_1) + (1 - \pi_j)(x_2 - y_2) \qquad j = h, \ell \qquad \text{[B.5]}$$

where π_j corresponds to A's choice of a_j. Here we permit the payment to A to depend on the profit outcome. Note that $\bar{z}_j = \bar{x}_j - \bar{y}_j$ where $\bar{x}_j$ is the expected value of gross profit and $\bar{y}_j$ is the expected payment to A. Thus it is in P's interest to minimize $\bar{y}_j$.

To induce A to accept the contract, P must ensure that A's *reservation expected utility constraint*

$$\pi_j v(y_1) + (1 - \pi_j)v(y_2) - a_j \geqslant \bar{v}^0 \qquad i = h, \ell \qquad \text{[B.6]}$$

is satisfied for each choice of a_j. $\bar{v}^0$ is interpreted as the *expected* utility A would receive in his next best employment.

We begin by assuming that as a benchmark case P can observe A's choice of a_j. Then she can write a contract forcing A to choose whichever a_i is better for her, and it remains only to find the payments P should make. Suppose P wants A to choose a_h. Then she finds y_1 and y_2 by solving

$$\max \bar{z}_h \quad \text{s.t.} \quad \pi_h v(y_1) + (1 - \pi_h)v(y_2) - a_h \geqslant \bar{v}^0 \qquad \text{[B.7]}$$

with first-order conditions

$$-\pi_h + \lambda\pi_h v'(y_1^*) = 0 \tag{B.8}$$

$$-(1 - \pi_h) + \lambda(1 - \pi_h)v'(y_2^*) = 0 \tag{B.9}$$

$$\pi_h v(y_1^*) + (1 - \pi_h)v(y_2^*) - a_h = \bar{v}^0 \tag{B.10}$$

[B.8] and [B.9] yield

$$v'(y_1^*) = v'(y_2^*) = 1/\lambda \tag{B.11}$$

which in turn implies that $y_1^* = y_2^*$. Note also that $\lambda > 0$, so A's reservation constraint must bind. Thus P holds A down to his minimum utility level, and compensates him for supplying a_h by paying him $y^* = y_1^* = y_2^*$. The result, that A receives a *certain* payment independently of the value of the gross profit outcome x_j follows from the assumption that P is *risk neutral* – she maximizes the expected value of her net profit. Thus in this full information case all the risk is borne by the risk neutral individual. There is *efficient risk sharing*. (See the discussion of section 21B.) P minimizes A's expected payment $\bar{y}_h$ by leaving him with no risk. If his income was uncertain, he would require a higher expected value of payment to compensate for the risk.

We could now solve for the optimal payments when P wants A to choose the lower effort level a_ℓ, in exactly the same way. By comparing P's value of $\bar{z}$ at each of the two solutions, we could then find which a-level is better overall for P. However, we leave this as an exercise and *assume* that P would always want A to choose a_h.

Now suppose P cannot observe a. Then, since she cannot infer from the occurrence of an x-value which a has been chosen by A, she cannot write a (legally enforceable) contract forcing A to choose a_h. If she offers A the above payment, y^*, A can obviously make himself better off by choosing a_ℓ rather than a_h: his utility would be $v(y^*) - a_\ell$ for sure, and, from [B.10], $a_\ell < a_h$ must imply $v(y^*) - a_\ell > \bar{v}^0$. P can *predict ex ante* that under this contract A will choose a_ℓ, but she cannot *prove ex post* that he has done so.

It follows that, if P wants A to choose a_h, she must offer him a contract which gives him an incentive to do so – the contract must be *incentive compatible* with choice of a_h. We still wish to find y_1 and y_2 that maximize $\bar{z}_h$ and still satisfy A's reservation constraint [B.6] for $i = h$. However, to ensure it is in A's interest actually to choose a_h we need to add to the problem in [B.7] the *incentive compatibility constraint*

$$\pi_h v(y_1) + (1 - \pi_h)v(y_2) - a_h \geqslant \pi_\ell v(y_1) + (1 - \pi_\ell)v(y_2) - a_\ell \tag{B.12}$$

[B.12] requires that a pair of payments (y_1, y_2) must be chosen in such a way that A will *prefer* to choose a_h. (Note: to give a closed feasible set we assume that, if A is indifferent between a_h and a_ℓ for given (y_1, y_2), he chooses a_h.)

Before solving this problem formally, note that [B.12] implies we *cannot* have $y_1 = y_2$, since $a_\ell < a_h$. In other words A is now going to have to carry some risk – his payment will vary with the gross profit outcome x. Adding [B.12] as a constraint to [B.7] yields the first-order conditions

$$\frac{1}{v'(\hat{y}_1)} = \lambda + \mu\frac{(\pi_h - \pi_\ell)}{\pi_h} \tag{B.13}$$

$$\frac{1}{v'(\hat{y}_2)} = \lambda - \mu\frac{(\pi_h - \pi_\ell)}{(1 - \pi_h)} \tag{B.14}$$

$$\pi_h v(\hat{y}_1) + (1 - \pi_h)v(\hat{y}_2) - a_h = \bar{v}^0 \tag{B.15}$$

$$\pi_h v(\hat{y}_1) + (1 - \pi_h)v(\hat{y}_2) - a_h = \pi_\ell v(\hat{y}_1) + (1 - \pi_\ell)v(\hat{y}_2) - a_\ell \tag{B.16}$$

where $\hat{y}_1, \hat{y}_2$ are the optimal payments. It can be shown (see Question 5, Exercise 20B) that we must have $\lambda > 0$, $\mu > 0$, and so both constraints bind. Consider first [B.13] and [B.14]. Since $\pi_h > \pi_\ell$ (higher a increases the probability of the better outcome x_1), we must have

$$\frac{1}{v'(\hat{y}_1)} > \lambda > \frac{1}{v'(\hat{y}_2)} \tag{B.17}$$

or, since $v' > 0$,

$$v'(\hat{y}_1) < v'(\hat{y}_2) \tag{B.18}$$

Then, given $v'' < 0$ (diminishing marginal utility of income), we must have $\hat{y}_1 > \hat{y}_2$. In the light of [B.15] therefore

$$\hat{y}_1 > y^* > \hat{y}_2 \tag{B.19}$$

Thus, compared with the situation in which P can observe a, the payment to A now varies with the gross profit outcome: A receives less if x_2 occurs, and more if x_1 occurs, than in the full information contract. The reason for introducing this 'tilt' in the payment schedule is to give A an incentive to choose a_h rather than a_ℓ: by doing so A increases the probability that he will receive the higher payment.

We obtain further insight by rearranging [B.16] to obtain

$$(\pi_h - \pi_\ell)[v(\hat{y}_1) - v(\hat{y}_2)] = a_h - a_\ell \tag{B.20}$$

The right-hand side is the cost to A of increasing his effort level from a_ℓ to a_h. The left-hand side is the benefit: the probability of obtaining the higher outcome increases from π_ℓ to π_h and his utility increases from $v(\hat{y}_2)$ to $v(\hat{y}_1)$. The pair $(\hat{y}_1, \hat{y}_2)$ must then be chosen to satisfy

$$v(\hat{y}_1) - v(\hat{y}_2) = (a_h - a_\ell)/[\pi_h - \pi_\ell] \tag{B.21}$$

where the right-hand side of this equation is determined by exogenous parameters of the problem. That is, $\hat{y}_1$ and $\hat{y}_2$ must be chosen to give A a sufficiently large expected utility increase to compensate for the increase in effort level. Note, in fact, that [B.21] and the reservation constraint [B.15] are sufficient to determine the values of the two unknowns $\hat{y}_1, \hat{y}_2$. It is unnecessary (in this case) to use [B.13] and [B.14]. (See Question 6, Exercise 20B.)

We can illustrate in Fig. 20.2 the two types of solution which arise depending on whether P can or cannot observe A's effort level. Figure 20.2 is an Edgeworth Box. The horizontal side of the box has length x_1 and the vertical side has length x_2. The payment by P to A if the profit outcome is x_1 is y_1 and is measured rightward from the origin O_A. Similarly, payment to A when the outcome is x_2 is measured up the vertical axis. Thus any point in the box measured from O_A shows the contract payments (y_1, y_2) to A and, measured from O_P, the net profits $(x_1 - y_1, x_2 - y_2)$ of the owner. The 45° line gives the points where $y_1 = y_2$ and A has a certain income: the payment he receives is the same whatever the profit outcome.

Indifference curves of A in Fig. 20.2, such as I_h^0 and I_ℓ^α, show combinations of y_1 and y_2 which give A the same expected utility for a given level of effort and so satisfy the equation

$$\pi_i v(y_1) + (1 - \pi_i)v(y_2) - a_i = \text{constant} \tag{B.22}$$

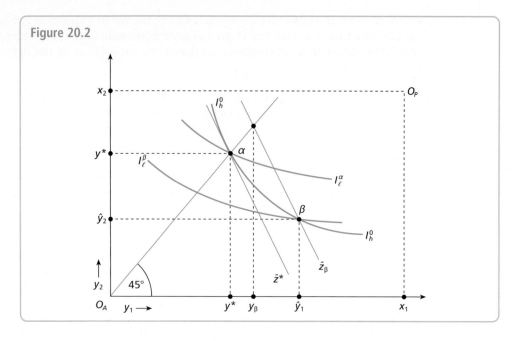

Figure 20.2

Applying the implicit function rule to [B.22] gives the slope of the indifference curves in y_1, y_2 space as

$$dy_2/dy_1 = -\pi_i v'(y_1)/(1 - \pi_i)v'(y_2) \qquad [B.23]$$

Note that the slope of the indifference curves depends on the probability of the high profit outcome. Since high effort implies a greater probability of the large profit x_1 ($\pi_h > \pi_\ell$), the indifference curves of A are steeper at any point if he chooses a high effort level than if he chooses a low effort level. (Compare I_h^0 and I_ℓ^α at α or I_h^0 and I_ℓ^β at β.) Intuitively, he will require a smaller increase in y_1 to compensate him for a given reduction in y_2 the greater the probability that he attaches to getting y_1.

P cares only about her expected income from the firm and so her indifference curves in the box show combinations of y_1 and y_2 which satisfy

$$\pi_i(x_1 - y_1) + (1 - \pi_i)(x_2 - y_2) = \text{constant} \qquad [B.24]$$

The slope of her indifference curves is

$$dy_2/dy_1 = -\pi_i/(1 - \pi_i) \qquad [B.25]$$

At the 45° line, incomes and therefore marginal utilities are equal, and so, from [B.23], the slope of A's indifference curve is also given by [B.25]. Thus the straight line $\bar{z}^*$ tangent to I_h^0 at α on the 45° line has slope

$$dy_2/dy_1 = -\pi_h/(1 - \pi_h) \qquad [B.26]$$

and is an indifference curve for P given that A has chosen a_h. P prefers to be on indifference curves further from her origin O_P since she then has a greater expected income. Note that along P's indifference curves her expected income is constant, and so expected payments to A are also constant along her indifference curves.

When the owner can observe A's effort the optimal contract is α. The indifference curve I_h^0 shows combinations of y_1 and y_2 which give A his reservation expected utility *if* he supplies high effort a_h:

$$\pi_h v(y_1) + (1 - \pi_h)v(y_2) - a_h = v^0$$

The contract α where I_h^0 crosses the 45° line therefore satisfies the condition [B.10] that A should get his reservation expected utility when he supplies high effort, and the condition [B.11] that $y_1 = y_2 = y^*$, so that he bears none of the risk.

Now consider the case in which P cannot observe A's effort level and therefore must now provide an incentive compatible contract, which makes A choose a_h rather than a_ℓ, even though his choice is not verifiable. If the contract is α then A will choose a_ℓ rather than a_h since he gets the same certain income and his effort is smaller. When the contract is α and A chooses a_ℓ he is on the flatter indifference curve I_ℓ^α. To induce him to supply high effort the contract must give him a larger payment if there is a larger profit. Since we have seen that the reservation expected utility constraint will also bind, the optimal contract under asymmetric information must be on I_h^0 and below the 45° line so that $y_1 > y_2$. At contracts further to the right below the 45° line along I_h^0, the expected utility that A gets from supplying low effort gets smaller. For example, compare the low effort indifference curves I_ℓ^β and I_ℓ^α – A has a smaller expected utility, given that he chooses a_ℓ, at β than at α because he is on a lower indifference curve. However, he is indifferent between the contracts α and β if he chooses a_h. By moving the contract down I_h^0, the owner will eventually find a contract where A's expected utility from choosing a_ℓ has fallen sufficiently that A is indifferent between a_h and a_ℓ.

We assume that β is in fact the optimal contract under asymmetric information. The precise location of β will depend on the cost of additional effort $(a_h - a_\ell)$ to A, and the slopes of his indifference curve, which in turn depend on the probabilities π_h and π_ℓ and his marginal utility of income v'. However the diagram can be used to bring out one important implication: his possession of private information about his choice of a makes A no better off and P strictly worse off, than in the case in which P can observe a. Thus there is an *agency cost*, or cost of asymmetric information, to the less well informed party P which confers no benefit on the better informed party A.

The agency cost is the difference in P's expected income from her optimal full information contract α and her optimal asymmetrical information contract β:

$$\pi_h(x_1 - y^*) + (1 - \pi_h)(x_2 - y^*) - \pi_h(x_1 - \hat{y}_1) - (1 - \pi_h)(x_2 - \hat{y}_2)$$
$$= \pi_h \hat{y}_1 + (1 - \pi_h)\hat{y}_2 - y^* \qquad [B.27]$$

In order to induce A to choose a_h when she cannot observe a, P must offer A a risky contract which gives him greater payment when profit is high. But, since A dislikes risk, the contract must also increase his expected income to compensate for the increased risk and to ensure that he gets his reservation expected utility. The agency cost to P is the increase in A's expected income necessary to induce him to accept the incentive compatible contract β. This is [B.27]. In Fig. 20.2, the agency cost is measured by the distance between P's indifference curves $\bar{z}^*$ and z_β at the 45° line: $y_\beta - y^*$.

What does the analysis of this section tell us about the implications of the separation of ownership from control? First, the nature of the owner's information is crucial. For there to be a potential problem, P must be unable to observe or infer

A's choice of decision variable – there must be asymmetry of information. However, such asymmetry of information is not sufficient for agency costs to arise. If some outcomes have zero probability of being observed when A does what he should do, and positive probability of being observed when he does not, then provided that P can impose sufficiently large penalties, she can always ensure that A acts in her best interests. A genuine agency problem arises when there is no chance that P will have clear evidence that A has not acted in her best interest. In this case, she should offer A a contract which will provide him with an incentive to make his choices conform more closely to P's interests. In the model of this section, the contract took an intuitively appealing form: the payment to A increases with the profit outcome of the business. When there is a separation of ownership from control, incentive contracts can be constructed to minimize the cost of asymmetric information or 'agency cost', but will not eliminate it entirely.

Structure of the optimal contract

The two-outcome, two-action model just considered was sufficient to bring out the central result of the standard moral hazard principal–agent model: the optimal contract under asymmetric information trades off efficient risk sharing against the provision of incentives. In the two-outcome world the agent receives a lower payment if there is a bad outcome and a higher payment if there is a good outcome. This is intuitive, and seems to conform with real contracts, for example profit-related bonuses for managers of firms.

However, the two-outcome, two-action model is too simple to explain the finer details of optimal contracts. Fortunately, this requires only a small extension of the model to three outcomes and two actions. The three profit outcomes have $x_1 > x_2 > x_3$. Let π_i^j denote the probability of outcome $j = 1, 2, 3$, if action a_i ($i = h, \ell$) is chosen by the manager, with $\sum_j \pi_i^j = 1$. We assume that the manager's effort is productive in the sense that a higher level of effort leads to an increase in expected profit:

$$\sum_{j=1}^{3} \pi_h^j x_j - \sum_{j=1}^{3} \pi_\ell^j x_j = \sum_{j=1}^{3} (\pi_h^j - \pi_\ell^j) x_j > 0 \qquad [\text{B.28}]$$

The rest of the model is as before.

It is straightforward to show that, under symmetric information, optimal risk-sharing again requires an equal payment to the manager in each state, i.e. $y_j = y^*$ ($j = 1, 2, 3$). P's problem under asymmetric information, assuming she wishes to implement a_h, is now

$$\max_{y_1, y_2, y_3} \bar{z}_h = \sum_{j=1}^{3} \pi_h^j (x_j - y_j) \qquad [\text{B.29}]$$

subject to the participation and incentive compatibility constraints

$$\sum_{j=1}^{3} \pi_h^j u(y_j) - a_h \geqslant 0 \qquad [\text{B.30}]$$

$$\sum_{j=1}^{3} \pi_h^j u(y_j) - a_h \geqslant \sum_{j=1}^{3} \pi_\ell^j u(y_j) - a_\ell \qquad [\text{B.31}]$$

The first-order conditions are

$$-\pi_h^j + \lambda\pi_h^j u'(\hat{y}_j) + \mu(\pi_h^j - \pi_\ell^j)u'(\hat{y}_j) = 0 \qquad j = 1, 2, 3 \qquad [\text{B.32}]$$

together with the constraints satisfied as equalities. λ and μ are the Lagrange multipliers on the participation constraint [B.30] and the incentive compatibility constraint [B.31]. We can rewrite the first-order conditions as

$$\frac{1}{u'(\hat{y}_j)} = \lambda + \mu\left(\frac{\pi_h^j - \pi_\ell^j}{\pi_h^j}\right) \qquad j = 1, 2, 3 \qquad [\text{B.33}]$$

Let

$$\phi(y) \equiv \frac{1}{u'(y)} \qquad\qquad [\text{B.34}]$$

$\phi(y)$ is monotonically increasing in y because $u'(y)$ is monotonically decreasing in y. Hence we invert $\phi(y)$ and write the first-order conditions as

$$\hat{y}_j = \phi^{-1}\left(\lambda + \mu\left(\frac{\pi_h^j - \pi_\ell^j}{\pi_h^j}\right)\right) \qquad i = 1, 2, 3 \qquad [\text{B.35}]$$

The optimal payment varies positively (and in general non-linearly) with the value of $\lambda + \mu(\pi_h^j - \pi_\ell^j)/\pi_h^j$. Since, as before, we can show that $\lambda, \mu > 0$, the optimal payment is higher, the larger is $(\pi_h^j - \pi_\ell^j)/\pi_h^j$. We can interpret $(\pi_h^j - \pi_\ell^j)/\pi_h^j$ as a measure of the productivity of high effort compared with low effort in terms of its effect on the probability of outcome j. Thus, for example, A would get a higher reward if x_1 occurs than if x_2 occurs if and only if the productivity of his effort was greater in terms of its effect on the probability of x_1 than on the probability of x_2.

The relationship between x_j and $\hat{y}_j$ depends on how $(\pi_h^j - \pi_\ell^j)/\pi_h^j$ varies across the outcomes. Although P would not want A to supply high effort unless expected profit is thereby increased, [B.35] is consistent with higher effort having effects on the probability distribution of outcomes which lead the payment function to have counter-intuitive shapes. To illustrate, parts (a), (b), (c) and (d) of Fig. 20.3 show payment functions corresponding to the following numerical examples

(a) $(\pi_h^1, \pi_h^2, \pi_h^3) = (0.5, 0.4, 0.1)$ $\qquad$ $(\pi_\ell^1, \pi_\ell^2, \pi_\ell^3) = (\tfrac{1}{3}, \tfrac{1}{3}, \tfrac{1}{3})$

(b) $(\pi_h^1, \pi_h^2, \pi_h^3) = (0.45, 0.45, 0.1)$ $\qquad$ $(\pi_\ell^1, \pi_\ell^2, \pi_\ell^3) = (\tfrac{1}{3}, \tfrac{1}{3}, \tfrac{1}{3})$

(c) $(\pi_h^1, \pi_h^2, \pi_h^3) = (0.4, 0.5, 0.1)$ $\qquad$ $(\pi_\ell^1, \pi_\ell^2, \pi_\ell^3) = (\tfrac{1}{3}, \tfrac{1}{3}, \tfrac{1}{3})$

(d) $(\pi_h^1, \pi_h^2, \pi_h^3) = (0.5, 0.2, 0.3)$ $\qquad$ $(\pi_\ell^1, \pi_\ell^2, \pi_\ell^3) = (\tfrac{1}{3}, \tfrac{1}{3}, \tfrac{1}{3})$

Only the first example is consistent with a profit-sharing contract in which the manager's payment increases monotonically (though not linearly) with profit. The last two examples show that the agent's payment may have to fall even if profit rises. The principal wants to induce the agent to choose the higher effort level at the least cost to herself, in terms of expected value of income forgone. It would be inefficient to give the manager a big bonus for achieving the highest profit outcome, if increasing a makes little difference to the probability with which this outcome occurs. Similarly, A should not be punished for occurrence of the worst state if its probability is relatively insensitive to his action. Rewards and punishments should reflect the *incremental effects* of changes in the effort level.

Figure 20.3

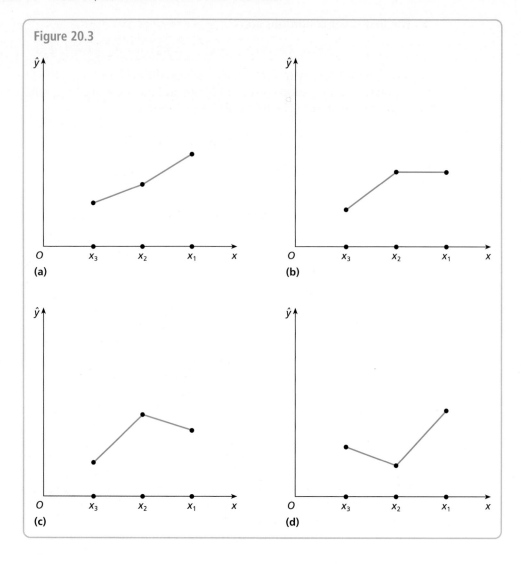

An alternative intuition for the relationship between the profit outcomes x_j and A's reward y_j can be given in terms of the information provided by the profit outcomes about A's effort level. Let $\pi(i)$ denote the prior probability that A supplies a_i (ignore for the moment that we know that the contract induces A to choose a). Let $\pi(i|x_j)$ be the posterior probability that A supplied effort a_i given that we observe the outcome x_j. Applying Bayes' Rule

$$\pi(i|x_j) = \frac{\pi(i)\pi(x_j|a_h)}{\pi(a_h)\pi(x_j|a_h) + \pi(a_\ell)\pi(x_j|a_\ell)} = \frac{\pi(i)\pi_h^j}{\pi(a_h)\pi_h^j + \pi(a_\ell)\pi_\ell^j} \qquad \text{[B.36]}$$

The odds that A supplied high effort given that we observe the outcome x_j are

$$\frac{\pi(h|y_j)}{\pi(l|y_j)} = \frac{\pi(h)\pi_h^j}{\pi(l)\pi_\ell^j} \qquad \text{[B.37]}$$

Hence, for example, the odds that A supplied high effort if we observe the outcome x_1 are greater than the odds that he supplied high effort if we observe the outcome x_2 if and only if

$$\frac{\pi(h)\pi_h^1}{\pi(l)\pi_\ell^1} > \frac{\pi(h)\pi_h^2}{\pi(l)\pi_\ell^2}$$

or

$$\frac{\pi_h^1}{\pi_\ell^1} > \frac{\pi_h^2}{\pi_\ell^2} \tag{B.38}$$

But, as the reader should check, [B.38] is equivalent to

$$\frac{\pi_h^1 - \pi_\ell^1}{\pi_h^1} > \frac{\pi_h^2 - \pi_\ell^2}{\pi_h^2} \tag{B.39}$$

and to A getting a greater reward if the outcome is x_1 than if it is x_2. Thus the reward is greater for the outcome which provides more reassurance that A has supplied high rather than low effort.

In general, the plausible assumption that higher effort increases expected profit does not imply that managerial rewards should increase when profit is higher. To reconcile the theory with real-life contracts we can, as in the next section, make stronger assumptions about the effects of effort on the distribution of outcomes.

EXERCISE 20B

1. Suppose that the optimal contract must maximize A's expected utility subject to a constraint on P's expected net profit. Derive the results for this case and compare them with those given in this section.

2. In equation [B.4], we define the payment y^0 as that which will induce A to choose $a = a^*$ rather than $a = a^0$. Will it always be possible to find such a y^0? If not, what kind of contract must P devise?

3. Solve the problem in [B.7] for the case in which P wants A to choose a_ℓ rather than a_h. Is there in this case a problem for P when she cannot observe A's choice of a?

4. Suppose that, instead of maximizing expected net profit, P seeks to maximize expected utility

$$\bar{U} = \pi U(x_1 - y_1) + (1 - \pi)U(x_2 - y_2)$$

where U is a cardinal utility function with $U' > 0$, $U'' < 0$. Show that in general A will not receive a payment that is independent of x even when P can observe choice of a.

5. Show that, in conditions [B.13]–[B.16], we must have $\lambda > 0$, $\mu > 0$, i.e. [B.6] and [B.12] cannot be satisfied as inequalities.

6. *Comparative statics of contracts.* Use the fact that P's optimal contract under asymmetric information is completely characterized by [B.15] and [B.16], to investigate the way in which changes in model parameters affect the optimal contract. In particular, what factors tend to increase agency costs?

C. The moral hazard principal–agent model

The simple models considered in the previous section are sufficient to bring out the main elements of the moral hazard agency problem. In this section we consider the issues that arise when we generalize the model. In particular, we are concerned with the question of the so-called first-order condition approach. First, we restate the problem more generally than before.

The agent A chooses the value of a variable a which is costly to him and which determines the output x of a production process. The output accrues to the principal P, who then pays A. Output x and the payment y to A are measured in the same units. The production and utility functions and A's reservation utility are common knowledge. P always observes the output *ex post* but she cannot observe A's choice of a. If the production process were non-stochastic there would be no agency problem: P could always infer a from the observation of x and write a contract which induces A to choose the value of a which is optimal for P. We are concerned only with situations in which the outcome of the activity is uncertain: $x = x(a, \theta)$, where θ is the random state of the world (for example the weather) which affects the output for a given action. The technology $x(a, \theta)$ and the probability distribution of states imply a distribution function $F(x, a)$ and probability density $dF/dx = f(x, a)$ of outcomes contingent on a. Changes in a alter the distribution of outcomes.

P observes x, so if she could also observe θ, she would be able to infer a and there would be no interesting problem. We therefore assume that θ is not observed by P.

Even this is not sufficient to create a genuine agency problem. If changes in a shift the support of the probability distribution of outcomes, and if P can impose sufficiently large punishments (small enough y), then again she can force A to choose whatever a she wishes.

Consider Fig. 20.4, where increases in a shift the whole distribution to the right. Thus with $a = a^*$, the probability density is $f(x, a^*)$ with support $[x_0(a^*), x_1(a^*)]$, and with $a = a' < a^*$, it is $f(x, a')$ with support $[x_0(a'), x_1(a')]$. Suppose that P wished A to choose a^*. Both P and A know that, if A chooses a', there is a probability $F(x_0(a^*), a') > 0$ (the shaded area in Fig. 20.4) that the output will be in the range $[x_0(a'), x_0(a^*)]$. Hence if P can impose a large enough punishment when she observes any x in this range, she can ensure that A prefers to choose a^* rather than $a' < a^*$. This is true

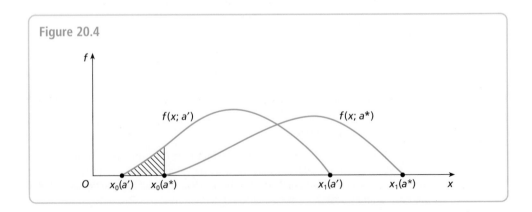

Figure 20.4

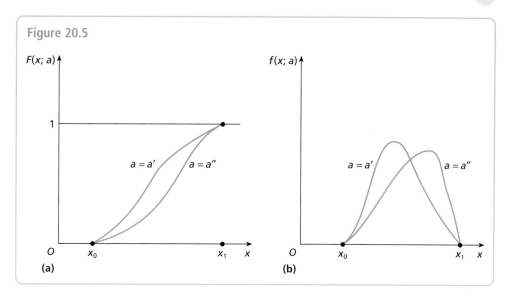

Figure 20.5

for any $a < a^\star$, so that P can ensure that A will not choose any a smaller than $a^\star$. Since a is costly for A, he will not wish to set $a > a^\star$, and so P can force A to choose whatever feasible $a^\star$ she wishes. We will therefore assume that a has no effect on the support of the distribution, which is always the interval $[x_0, x_1]$.

Unlike the two-action models in section B, we assume that a can take on any value in the interval $[a_0, a_1]$. For an interesting problem, increases in a must be of value to P, as well as being costly to A. In terms of the output function $x(a, \theta)$, this implies that the marginal product of a is positive: $x_a > 0$. It is more convenient to work with the distribution of outputs contingent on a. The assumption equivalent to positivity of marginal product is that increases in a reduce the probability of getting an output less than any specified level. In terms of the distribution function, $F(x, a)$ is decreasing in a: $F_a(x, a) < 0$.

The distribution $F(x, a'')$ *stochastically dominates* the distribution $F(x, a')$ if $F(x, a'') \leqslant F(x, a')$ for $x \in [x_0, x_1]$, with the inequality being strict over some part of the support. Thus if $F_a < 0$, increasing a gives a distribution of outcomes which stochastically dominates the initial distribution. In Fig. 20.5 $a'' > a'$ and the distribution $F(x, a'')$ stochastically dominates $F(x, a')$. Note that the support of the distribution is not affected by increases in a.

We can show that P will be made better off by increases in a if and only if $F_a < 0$. Let $u(x - y)$, $u' > 0$, $u'' \leqslant 0$, be P's utility function and integrate her expected utility, at given y and a, by parts to obtain

$$\int_{x_0}^{x_1} u(x - y)f(x, a)\, dx = [u(x - y)F(x, a)]_{x_0}^{x_1} - \int_{x_0}^{x_1} u'(x - y)F(x, a)\, dx$$

$$= u(x_1 - y) - \int_{x_0}^{x_1} u'(x - y)F(x, a)\, dx \qquad [\text{C.1}]$$

since $F(x_0, a) = 0$, $F(x_1, a) = 1$, at all a. Differentiating P's expected utility [C.1] with respect to a at given y gives the marginal value of a to P as

$$-\int_{x_0}^{x_1} u'(x - y)F_a(x, a)\, dx \qquad\qquad [\text{C.2}]$$

which is positive if $F_a < 0$, since $u' > 0$ at all x. We henceforth assume that increases in a have the stochastic dominance property $F_a < 0$. In fact, as Rogerson (1985) shows, MLRC – discussed below – implies stochastic dominance, so we do not need to assume it explicitly if MLRC holds.

In models based on optimization, we often assume that objective functions are concave in the choice variable to ensure that first-order conditions are necessary and sufficient for an optimum. In principal–agent problems this may be accomplished by placing further restrictions on $F(x, a)$. The first of these is the *convex distribution function condition* (CDFC): $F_{aa} \geqslant 0$, which has the interpretation of stochastically decreasing marginal returns to increases in a. The distribution function becomes more favourable to P as a increases but does so at a decreasing rate.

P's payment to A can only be a function of what she can observe. On our assumptions P can only observe the output x, so that the payment function or contract is $y = y(x)$. A's utility function is additively separable in income and a: $V = v(y) - a$, $v' > 0$, $v'' < 0$. (Question 1, Exercise 20C, shows that if A is risk neutral the fact that a is not observed does not matter: P can design a contract which yields her the same utility as under full information.) P's income after paying A is $z(x) = x - y(x)$ and her utility is $u(z)$.

Integrating P and A's expected utility functions by parts for a given, differentiable, payment function $y(x)$, yields

$$\text{E}u = u(z(x_1)) - \int_{x_0}^{x_1} u'(z(x))z'(x)F(x, a)\, dx \qquad\qquad [\text{C.3}]$$

$$\text{E}V = v(y(x_1)) - \int_{x_0}^{x_1} v'(y(x))y'(x)F(x, a)\, dx - a \qquad\qquad [\text{C.4}]$$

where $z'(x) = 1 - y'(x)$. Differentiating the expected utilities of P and A twice with respect to a, for a given payment schedule $y(x)$, gives

$$\frac{\partial^2 \text{E}u}{\partial a^2} = -\int_{x_0}^{x_1} u'z'F_{aa}(x, a)\, dx, \qquad \frac{\partial^2 \text{E}V}{\partial a^2} = -\int_{x_0}^{x_1} v'y'F_{aa}\, dx \qquad\qquad [\text{C.5}]$$

If the payment function satisfies $0 \leqslant y' \leqslant 1$, both P's and A's incomes are non-decreasing with x (remember $z' = 1 - y'$). But then CDFC ($F_{aa} \geqslant 0$) implies that P's and A's expected utilities are concave in a. In this case, the problem of maximizing P's expected utility, or A's expected utility, or any positively weighted sum of their expected utilities, over $[a_0, a_1]$ will be well behaved. In particular, there will be a global maximum, satisfying standard first-order conditions.

To ensure that the payment function will indeed have $0 \leqslant y' \leqslant 1$ a further condition must be imposed on $F(x, a)$. The *likelihood ratio* is $f_a(x, a)/f(x, a)$.[2] The *monotone likelihood ratio condition* (MLRC) is the requirement that f_a/f is non-decreasing in x. The reason why *MLRC* is required for a non-decreasing payment function will become clear when we have derived the first-order conditions characterizing the optimal contract when P cannot observe a. First, however, it is useful to investigate the optimal contract $y^*(x)$ under full information.

Full information first best

P wishes to solve the problem

$$\max_{a,y(x)} \int_{x_0}^{x_1} u(x-y)f(x,a)\,dx \quad \text{s.t.} \quad \int_{x_0}^{x_1} v(y)f(x,a)\,dx - a \geqslant V^0 \qquad \text{[C.6]}$$

$$a \in [a_0, a_1] \qquad x \geqslant y \geqslant 0$$

Although [C.6] is a problem in dynamic optimization (*P* is choosing a function $y(x)$), the rate of change of the state variable *y* does not enter either the objective function or the constraints. Consequently, the problem is equivalent to choosing *y* at each *x* to maximize the Lagrangean for [C.6]. Hence, assuming an interior solution, the first order conditions are

$$-u'(x-y^*(x)) + \lambda^*v'(y^*(x)) = 0 \qquad \text{[C.7]}$$

$$\int_{x_0}^{x_1} u(x-y^*(x))f_a(x,a^*)\,dx + \lambda^*\left[\int_{x_0}^{x_1} v(y^*(x))f_a(x,a^*)\,dx - 1\right] = 0 \qquad \text{[C.8]}$$

$$\int_{x_0}^{x_1} v(y^*(x))f(x,a^*)\,dx - a^* - V^0 = 0 \qquad \text{[C.9]}$$

The fact that $u' > 0$ implies that the participation constraint binds and so $\lambda^* > 0$ in [C.7]. Since *P* can observe *a* and control it directly via the contract, she has no need to use the payment schedule $y(x)$ to control *a* indirectly. Thus the payment schedule can be used solely to distribute the risks arising from the uncertain output. Taking a pair of output levels $x, \tilde{x} \in [x_0, x_1]$ and eliminating λ^* from [C.7] we have

$$\frac{u'(x-y^*(x))}{u'(\tilde{x}-y^*(\tilde{x}))} = \frac{v'(y^*(x))}{v'(y^*(\tilde{x}))} \qquad \text{[C.10]}$$

which gives the familiar result that the optimal risk-sharing arrangement equalizes *P*'s and *A*'s marginal rates of substitution between incomes in any two outcomes. If *P* is risk neutral, u' is a constant, so that the left-hand side of [C.10] is unity, which implies that $y^*(x) = y^*(\tilde{x})$ and *A* is guaranteed a certain income. All risk is shifted to the risk-neutral party.

To investigate the form of the optimal payment function $y^*(x)$ further, assume that it is differentiable and differentiate through [C.7] with respect to *x* (remembering that $\lambda^* = u'/v'$ does not vary with *x*). Rearranging the resulting equation, we obtain

$$\frac{-u''}{u'} = -\left[\frac{u''}{u'} + \frac{v''}{v'}\right]\frac{dy^*}{dx} \qquad \text{[C.11]}$$

Recalling the definition of the Pratt–Arrow coefficient of absolute risk aversion, and denoting this by r_A for *A* and r_P for *P*, [C.11] implies

$$\frac{dy^*}{dx} = \frac{r_P}{r_P + r_A} \in [0, 1] \qquad \text{[C.12]}$$

The shape of the first best full information payment function for any given *a* depends on how the risk aversion coefficients vary relative to each other. Since we have assumed that *A* is strictly risk averse, [C.12] implies that $dy^*/dx < 1$. If *CDFC* is satisfied, [C.5] implies that both expected utilities are concave in *a* and the first-order conditions [C.7]–[C.9] are necessary and sufficient for an optimum. Note that we do not need *MLRC* in the full information problem. To place further restrictions on $y^*(x)$ we would need to make further assumptions about preferences.

The interpretation of the condition [C.8] on a is standard: the optimal a equates the marginal expected value product of a for P with its expected marginal cost to P. The term in the brackets is the net marginal cost of additional a to A, after allowing for the fact that additional a both has a disutility to him and increases the probability of high x and therefore high payments. A would prefer to supply less a than the optimal a^*, given the payment schedule, but because P can observe a, he is not able to reduce a. λ^* is the shadow price on A's utility, so that the second term in [C.8] can be intepreted as the marginal cost of increased a for P.

Hidden action

We now assume that P cannot observe A's action a. She can of course infer it. Given the common knowledge assumption, P knows that, for any payment function $y(x)$, A will choose an a which maximizes

$$EV(y(x)) = \int_{x_0}^{x_1} v(y)f(x, a)\, dx - a \qquad \text{[C.13]}$$

Since P knows A's preferences and $f(\cdot)$ she can always calculate what value of a will be chosen by A for any given payment function. It is not discovering or inferring the value of a chosen by A that is important, but whether a is *verifiable*: observable or inferable by third parties. The courts do not permit P to sue A for breach of contract and use the argument that A must have breached a promise to supply a specified $a = \tilde{a}$ because $\tilde{a}$ did not maximize A's expected utility! Instead P must choose a payment function $y(x)$ given that A will optimize for himself relative to it. This is the incentive compatibility condition: P must design a contract which makes it in A's interest to choose the level of a which P requires.

P's second-best problem with hidden action is

$$\max_{a,y(x)} Eu \quad \text{s.t.} \quad EV \geqslant V^0 \qquad a \text{ maximizes } EV \qquad \text{(I.C.)}$$
$$a \in [a_0, a_1], \qquad x \geqslant y \geqslant 0 \qquad \text{[C.14]}$$

The additional constraint (I.C.) is the incentive compatibility condition. (Compare [C.6].) To make any progress we need to make I.C. analytically tractable.

Under the *first-order condition approach* the I.C. constraint is replaced by the first-order condition for A's choice of a:

$$\partial EV/\partial a = 0 \qquad \text{[C.15]}$$

and this constraint is included in the Lagrangean for P's problem in the usual way with a Lagrange multiplier attached. Although a natural way to proceed, this approach may not be valid. [C.15] imposes the constraint that P's choice of a in [C.14] must yield a *stationary value* of A's expected utility EV, which does not imply that P's choice of a yields a *global maximum* of EV. The first-order condition [C.15] is sufficient, as well as necessary, for a global maximum only if EV is concave in a. If EV is not concave in a, then, for a given payment schedule $y(x)$, there may be values of a which satisfy [C.15] but which would not be chosen by A. But then, in solving P's problem [C.14], with [C.15] replacing I.C., one of the 'wrong' a values, which A will not choose because it does not maximize EV, could yield higher expected utility for P than one of the 'right' a values which A will actually choose given the payment function.

Fortunately *CDFC* and *MLRC* imply that the first-order condition approach is valid. Let us replace the equality constraint [C.15] with the weak inequality

$$\partial EV / \partial a \geq 0 \qquad \text{[C.16]}$$

(It will turn out to be the case that [C.16] always binds as an equality.) Forming the Lagrangean (with the multiplier μ attached to [C.16]) the first-order conditions for an interior solution to [C.14] are

$$\frac{u'(x - \hat{y}(x))}{v'(\hat{y}(x))} = \hat{\lambda} + \hat{\mu} \frac{f_a(x, \hat{a})}{f(x, \hat{a})} \qquad \text{[C.17]}$$

$$\frac{\partial Eu}{\partial a} + \hat{\lambda} \frac{\partial EV}{\partial a} + \hat{\mu} \frac{\partial^2 EV}{\partial a^2} = 0 \qquad \text{[C.18]}$$

$$EV - V^0 \geq 0 \qquad \hat{\lambda} \geq 0 \qquad \hat{\lambda}[\hat{\mu}EV - V^0] = 0 \qquad \text{[C.19]}$$

$$\frac{\partial EV}{\partial a} \geq 0 \qquad \hat{\mu} \geq 0 \qquad \hat{\mu} \frac{\partial EV}{\partial a} = 0 \qquad \text{[C.20]}$$

We first demonstrate that $\hat{\mu} > 0$, so that, from the complementary slackness condition [C.20], [C.16] binds as an equality and imposing it is equivalent to imposing [C.15]. Suppose that $\hat{\mu} = 0$. But then [C.17] gives the same kind of payment function as [C.7] yields for the full information case. In particular, the payment function will be monotonically increasing (recall the discussion of [C.12]). Since the payment function is monotonically increasing, we know that the principal's utility is increasing in a: $\partial Eu / \partial a > 0$. (Differentiate [C.4] with respect to a and remember that $F_a < 0$.) Note also that, since u' and v' are positive, [C.17] implies that $\hat{\lambda} > 0$ if $\hat{\mu} = 0$. Then, in [C.18], if $\hat{\mu} = 0$, the last term is zero and the second term must be non-negative. But if [C.18] holds this implies that the first term is non-positive: $\partial Eu / \partial a \leq 0$, which establishes a contradiction with our conclusion that $\partial Eu / \partial a > 0$. Thus we must have $\hat{\mu} > 0$ and [C.16] binds as an equality: $\partial EV / \partial a = 0$.

Next consider [C.17]. Since $u'' \leq 0$ and $v'' < 0$, the left-hand side of [C.17] is increasing in x if and only if the payment function $\hat{y}(x)$ is increasing in x. (v' would then be non-decreasing and u' decreasing with x.) But the left-hand side can only be increasing with x if the right-hand side is also. The multipliers $\hat{\lambda}$ and $\hat{\mu}$ do not vary with x, so that the left-hand side of [C.17] is increasing in x if and only if the likelihood ratio f_a/f is increasing in x. Hence *MLRC* implies that $\hat{y}(x)$ is increasing in x, and this coupled with *CDFC* implies that EV is concave in a, thus validating the first-order condition approach.

There must be some values of x for which $f_a < 0$, otherwise the area under $f > 0$ will exceed 1. Hence, since u', v' and $\hat{\mu}$ are positive, [C.17] implies that $\hat{\lambda} > 0$. The participation constraint will also bind at the solution and so A is no better off than at the full information first-best (f.i.f.b.), outcome, while P is strictly worse off.

To consider the shape of $\hat{y}(x)$ further, differentiate [C.17] through with respect to x and rearrange to get

$$\frac{d\hat{y}}{dx} = \frac{r_P}{r_P + r_A} + \beta \frac{\partial}{\partial x}\left[\frac{f_a}{f}\right] \qquad \text{[C.21]}$$

where $\beta = \hat{\mu} v' / (r_P + r_A) u' > 0$ and r_P and r_A are again the Pratt–Arrow coefficients of absolute risk aversion. Thus the slope of the second-best payment function depends not only on the risk aversion of P and A, but also on the way in which the likelihood ratio f_a/f varies with x. For example, with a risk-neutral principal ($r_P = 0$) and an agent with constant absolute risk aversion, P would certainly not make a constant payment to A, as in the f.i.f.b. solution, since MLRC implies that $\partial (f_a/f)/\partial x \geqslant 0$. This is to be expected: a constant payment has terrible incentive properties – if A receives a payment which is unaffected by the outcome x he will choose the lowest possible a.

MLRC implies that $\hat{y}(x)$ is monotone increasing in x (recall we assume that y is always in the interior of its interval constraint). Let

$$X^- = \{x \in [x_0, x_1] \,|\, f_a(x, \hat{a}) < 0\}$$
$$X^+ = \{x \in [x_0, x_1] \,|\, f_a(x, \hat{a}) > 0\}$$

MLRC implies that if $x' \in X^-$ and $x'' \in X^+$ then $x'' > x'$. Loosely, X^- corresponds to 'smaller' values of output and X^+ to 'larger' values of output. We can show that the need to provide incentives introduces a 'tilt' in the payment function. Relative to a pure risk-sharing rule, $\hat{y}(x)$ pays less to A when $x \in X^-$ and more when $x \in X^+$. Thus A is penalized for worse outcomes and rewarded for better outcomes, to provide an incentive to increase a.

Thus, first assume that P is risk neutral, so that in the f.i.f.b. solution A would receive a certain payment y^*. Consider the payment function that satisfies

$$\frac{u'(x - y_\lambda)}{v'(y_\lambda)} = \hat{\lambda} \qquad\qquad [C.22]$$

where $\hat{\lambda}$ is the same as in [C.17]. Since P is risk neutral, u' is constant and the payment function satisfying [C.22] is a constant: y_λ is the same for all x. The constant payment y_λ optimally shares risk given that $a = \hat{a}$. In the first best A supplies more effort ($a^* > \hat{a}$) (see Question 3) and would require a larger certain income $y^* > y_\lambda$ to satisfy the participation constraint. Part (a) of Fig. 20.6 illustrates. Now rewrite [C.17] as

$$f(x, \hat{a})[u'(x - \hat{y}(x)) - \hat{\lambda} v'(\hat{y}(x))] = \hat{\mu} v' f_a \qquad\qquad [C.23]$$

Note that when $y = y_\lambda$ the left-hand side of [C.23] is zero. However, when $x \in X^-$, the right-hand side is negative, and so, since u' is constant and v' decreases with y, we must have on the left-hand side $\hat{y}(x) < y_\lambda$. (Substitute for $\hat{\lambda}$ from [C.22].) Conversely when $x \in X^+$, the right-hand side is positive, and we must have on the left-hand side $\hat{y}(x) > y_\lambda$. Hence the payment function is as shown in Fig. 20.6(a).

If P is risk averse both y^* and y_λ will be monotone increasing, and since $\hat{a} < a^*$, we expect that $y_\lambda(x) < y^*(x)$ at any given x. Applying the same reasoning as before to [C.23], we again conclude that for $x \in X^-$ we have $\hat{y}(x) < y_\lambda(x)$, and for $x \in X^+$, $\hat{y}(x) > y_\lambda(x)$, as Fig. 20.6(b) illustrates.

The condition [C.23] is also useful in understanding the nature of the solution. The left-hand side of [C.23] can be interpreted as the expected marginal cost to P of distorting y away from its optimal risk-sharing level for any given x. The right-hand side can be thought of as the marginal benefit of such a distortion, resulting from the increase in a that A is induced to make. By, in effect, transferring payments from outcomes whose probability is reduced by extra a to outcomes whose probability is

Figure 20.6

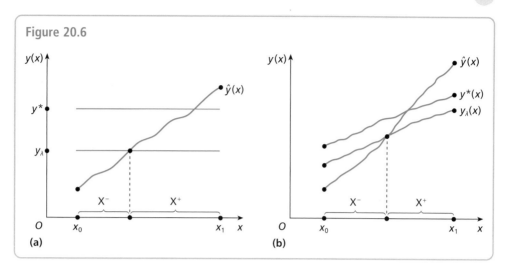

(a)

(b)

increased, A's marginal benefit from additional a is increased, leading him to choose larger a.

Imperfect information about a

Even though P cannot observe a directly she may be able to observe some variable m which provides information about a. Let the joint probability density of x and m for given a be $h(x, m, a)$. For example, m might be the output of another firm, which depends on θ and other random variables not observed by P. Or m might be an imperfect observation of a, with observation error distributed independently of the state variable θ in the production function. (The weather is not correlated with the observation error.) In this case the distribution function of observation errors will induce a distribution function of observations m for given a and the joint distribution of m and x will be of the form $h(x, m, a) = f(x, a)g(m, a)$.

It is not immediately obvious that the optimal second-best payment function should depend on m as well as x. It is clearly to P's advantage to get information about a from m and to use this to control A's actions more closely. However, including m in the payment schedule will make it more risky. Even if P is risk neutral, A is not and he will have to be compensated for the additional risk by an increase in his expected income. Thus it is not apparent that the beneficial incentive effects of including m in the payment schedule will outweigh the additional risk costs. We can in fact show that P will *always* wish to include m in the payment function, no matter how risk averse A is, provided that it does convey some information, no matter how imperfect, about A's action.

The principal's problem is to design a payment function $y(x, m)$ to maximize her expected utility subject to the participation and incentive compatibility constraints. The only difference is that now the expectations in [C.14] are taken with respect to the joint distribution of x and m and the payment function relates y to x and m. Assuming that the first-order condition approach is valid, we can derive a set of conditions similar to those from problem [C.14]. The main difference, as the reader should check, is that now [C.17] is replaced by

$$\frac{u'(x - \hat{y})}{v'(\hat{y})} = \hat{\lambda} + \hat{\mu} \frac{h_a(x, m, \hat{a})}{h(x, m, \hat{a})} \qquad \text{[C.24]}$$

In general, [C.24] defines the optimal payment to the agent as function of the output x and m if the right-hand side of [C.24] varies with both x and m. A's risk aversion determines whether m is included in the payment function only if A is risk neutral, in which case there is no real agency problem, or if A is infinitely risk averse, in which case the agency problem is insoluble since A will never accept any risky contract. Our assumptions on A's preferences rule out these extreme and uninteresting cases, so that A's risk aversion will only affect the precise form of $\hat{y}(x, m)$ and not determine whether the payment varies with m. Only when h_a/h does not vary with m will P make her payment to A depend only on output.

In the example above in which m is an imperfect observation of a, so that $h = f(x, a)g(m, a)$, [C.24] becomes

$$\frac{u'(x - \hat{y})}{v'(\hat{y})} = \hat{\lambda} + \hat{\mu} \left[\frac{f_a(x, \hat{a})}{f(x, \hat{a})} + \frac{g_a(m, a)}{g(m, a)} \right] \qquad \text{[C.25]}$$

(note that $h_a/h = \partial \ln h/\partial a$). Thus a payment to A is larger, for a given output, if g_a is positive than if g_a is negative. If the likelihood ratio for the observation g_a/g is increasing in m, we can apply the same kind of arguments as before, to conclude that it is sensible for P to reward A for a larger m because this suggests that a was larger.

P will not include the imperfect observation in the contract if g_a/g does not vary with m, which implies $g_a/g = k(a)$ or

$$g_a = k(a)g \qquad \text{[C.26]}$$

Integrating over the support of m gives

$$0 = \int g_a(m, a) \, dm = k(a) \int g(m, a) \, dm = k(a) \qquad \text{[C.27]}$$

(The first and last equation in [C.27] both make use of the fact that the area under the density function for m must be unity for all levels of a.) But then [C.26] and [C.27] together imply that $g_a = 0$. In this case, changes in a have no effect on the derived distribution of m and so do not affect the probability of any given observation. Hence an observation of m would convey no information about a. P would not then wish to include m in the payment function, since it can only increase the risks borne by A without any offsetting incentive effects.

More generally, the right-hand side of [C.24] will not vary with m if the joint density of x and m satisfies the *sufficient statistic condition*

$$h(x, m, a) = h^1(x, a)h^2(x, m) \qquad \text{[C.28]}$$

in which case $h_a/h = h_a^1(x, a)/h^1(x, a)$. We can think of P attempting to infer a from a sample observation of the random variables x and m. [C.28] implies that m provides no information about a that is not contained in observing x.

To get some intuition for [C.28] suppose, for the moment, that P wishes to infer the value of a and that x, m and a can take on only a finite number of values. Let $Q(a_k)$ be the principal's prior probability that $a = a_k$. Applying Bayes' Rule (Appendix L), after observing $x = x_i$ and $m = m_j$, her posterior beliefs, if [C.28] holds, will be

$$P_k(x_i, m_j) = \frac{h^1(x_i, a_k)h^2(x_i, m_j)Q(a_k)}{\sum_\ell h^1(x_i, a_\ell)h^2(x_i, m_j)Q(a_\ell)} = \frac{h^1(x_i, a_k)Q(a_k)}{\sum_\ell h^1(x_i, a_\ell)Q(a_\ell)} \qquad [C.29]$$

Thus, if the sufficient statistic condition holds, P's posterior probability for a depends only on her observation of x and observing m provides no additional information about a.

P's problem is not actually inferring a: since she knows A's utility function and the probability distribution she can work out exactly what value of a has been chosen. Her problem is to design a contract to induce A to choose a particular a at least cost to her. However, having more information is of value to P because it enables her to design a more discriminating contract. When she relies only on observations of x to determine y she makes A's income riskier for a given level of a. When m also conveys information about a, P can reduce the risk of supplying any given a. For example, suppose that the probability of a large m is greater if a is large than if a is small. Then, when A does supply high a but x is small, he is less likely to be punished with a small y if the payment function is increasing in m than if y did not vary with m. Thus, including m in the payment function will enable P to induce any given level of a at less cost to herself: A is bearing less risk for given a and therefore needs a smaller expected income to satisfy his participation constraint.

Conclusion

The assumption that $MLRC$ holds is crucial in determining the form of $\hat{y}(x)$. Without it we could not even draw the apparently obvious conclusion that A ought to receive a higher income when output is higher. If $d(f_a/f)/dx$ were sufficiently negative over some part of the interval $[x_0, x_1]$, [C.21] shows that $d\hat{y}/dx$ could also be negative – payment to A would fall as x increased. A deeper problem is that, if $MLRC$ or $CDFC$ are not satisfied, the first-order approach may not be valid. (As Question 5 asks you to show, even with a simple and well behaved stochastic production function, it is necessary to make very strong assumptions about the distribution of the state of the world to ensure that the derived distribution $f(x, a)$ satisfies $MLRC$.) It is then necessary to reformulate the problem as one with a finite number of outcomes and actions (as in section B of this chapter). Grossman and Hart (1983) use this method to circumvent the difficulties with the first-order condition approach, and show that in general the payment function is not monotonically increasing if $MLRC$ does not hold. Even in the apparently more tractable finite outcome, finite action model, intuitive results on the form of $\hat{y}(x)$ are only available if one makes assumptions which validate the first-order condition approach.

A further problem is that actual incentive contracts are often quite simple in structure, and usually linear. For example, a manager may be paid a flat-rate salary plus a fixed proportion of profit, or a salesman paid a constant commission rate, or an author a fixed proportion of revenues. The incentive contracts derived from the agency model examined above, on the other hand, may be quite complex, non-linear, and not even monotone increasing in output. Although the basic agency model provides many insights into incentive contracts, much work is still required if it is to explain the detail of incentive contracts. The interested reader should consult Holmstrom and Milgrom (1987) who have provided one explanation for linear incentive contracts.

EXERCISE 20C

1. *Risk-neutral agent.* Show that, when the agent is risk neutral, P can achieve the same solution when A's action is hidden as when it is observable. [*Hint*: what is the first-best full information contract and what would happen if P offered it to A when she cannot observe a?]

2. Assume that P and A each have decreasing absolute risk aversion, with utility of income functions $u = (x - y - d_P)^{k_P}$, $v = (y + d_A)^{k_A}$ where $d_i \geq 0$, $k_i \in (0, 1)$, $i = P, A$. Analyse the form of the f.i.f.b. payment function $y^*(x)$.

3. *First- and second-best effort.* Show that in the second-best solution A chooses a smaller a than in the f.i.f.b.

4. *Holmstrom's example.* Let $u = x - y(x)$; $f(x, a) = (1/a) \exp(-x/a)$; $V = 2y^{1/2} - a$. Does an increase in a lead to a stochastically dominant distribution? Does $f(x, a)$ satisfy CDFC and MLRC? Find the first- and second-best optimal payment functions and compare them.

5. Consider the simple additive stochastic production function $x(a, \theta) = g(a) + \theta$. What assumptions are required on $g(\cdot)$ and the distribution of θ to ensure that the distribution of x satisfies stochastic dominance, CDFD and MLRC?

6. *Linear incentive scheme.* Suppose that the stochastic production function is $x = ka + \theta$, where $k > 0$ is the marginal product of effort by A and θ is normally distributed with mean μ and variance σ^2. P cannot observe a but she can observe a random variable m which is normally distributed with mean zero and variance φ^2. The correlation between m and θ is ρ. If $\rho \neq 0$, m conveys imperfect information about a since it conveys information about θ and P can also observe x. The payment function is linear: $y(x, m) = \delta_0 + \delta_1 x + \delta_2 m$. The utility functions of P and A are $u = -\exp(-\beta(x - y))$ and $V = -\exp(\alpha(x - \frac{1}{2}a^2))$. Show that the optimal payment function has

$$\delta_1 = \frac{k^2 + \beta\sigma^2(1 - \rho^2)}{k^2 + (\alpha + \beta)\sigma^2(1 - \rho^2)} \qquad \delta_2 = \frac{\sigma\rho[\beta - (\alpha + \beta)\delta_1]}{\varphi(\alpha + \beta)}$$

and give an intuitive account of these results. [*Hint*: show first that the assumptions of normality and constant absolute risk aversion imply that P's and A's preferences can be represented by $E(x - y) - \frac{1}{2}\beta \mathrm{Var}(x - y)$ and $E(y - \frac{1}{2}a^2) - \frac{1}{2}\alpha \mathrm{Var}(y)$; then find A's optimal effort for given payment function parameters; then find P's optimal values of δ_0, δ_1, δ_2, a subject to A's participation and incentive compatibility constraints.]

7. *Imperfect observation of effort.* Suppose that in the owner–manager problem of section B the owner can make an imperfect observation of the manager's effort level, but only if the profit is small. For example, the 'manager' may operate a machine which has a probability of breakdown which is high or low depending on the amount of maintenance effort he supplies. If the machine breaks down, the owner calls in an engineer to repair it and gets a report from the engineer stating whether the manager has supplied high or low effort. Let r_ℓ be the conditional probability that the report indicates low effort when effort was low, and r_h be the conditional probability that the report indicates low effort when effort was actually high. Assume that $1 > r_\ell > r_h > 0$, so that the report is informative but imperfect. Show that P will make the manager's income depend on the profit and the imperfect report. [*Hint*: remember that the participation and incentive compatibility constraints bind and investigate the implications of introducing a small punishment (reduction in the low profit income) if the report indicates low effort.]

D. The adverse selection principal–agent model

We give a reasonably general formulation of the adverse selection agency model. The agent chooses an action $a \geqslant 0$ which is costly to him. To sharpen the results and simplify the analysis, we assume that A's utility function is separable in income and action, with the quasi-linear form

$$V = v(y) - a \qquad \text{[D.1]}$$

where y is A's income under the contract. His utility of income function $v(y)$ has $v' > 0$, $v'' \leqslant 0$. (This formulation permits A to have other income, say $\tilde{y}$, provided that it is certain and not affected by his action. We would then just write $\tilde{v}$ as the utility of income function and define $v(y) \equiv \tilde{v}(\tilde{y} + y))$. The outcome of A's action is x, which is measured in terms of money and accrues to P, whose utility function is

$$u = x - y \qquad \text{[D.2]}$$

(The outcome could be interpreted as the profit accruing to P as the owner of a firm whose manager A is paid a salary y.) P is risk neutral (nothing of interest is gained by assuming P to be risk averse) and her utility depends on output less the payment y she makes to A under the terms of the contract.

The technology is

$$x = x(a, \theta) \qquad x_a > 0, \qquad x_{aa} < 0 \qquad x_\theta > 0 \qquad x_{a\theta} > 0 \qquad \text{[D.3]}$$

which shows how output depends on the agent's action a for a value of θ. We assume positive but diminishing marginal productivity. We also assume that if the agent sets $a = 0$ there is no output: $x(0, \theta) = 0$. The parameter θ, which determines total and marginal productivity, is known to A at the time P offers him a contract. It is often referred to as A's *type*, an interpretation which is natural in many applications. (For example, in the adverse selection insurance model the insured's type is his accident probability.) We assume that $\theta \in \{\theta_1, \theta_2\}$, with $\theta_2 > \theta_1$. Though apparently very drastic, the assumption that there are only two types permits us to derive virtually all the central results for hidden information models with minimal mathematical complications. Note that marginal and total productivity increase with θ.

The specification and notation for the the adverse selection model set out in the previous paragraph may remind the reader of the simple moral hazard model of the optimal managerial contract in section B. There are, however, some crucial differences in timing and information between the two specifications which enable us to interpret one as a model of adverse selection and the other as a model of moral hazard. In the moral hazard model of section B it was assumed that A (the manager) took his decision on a before the random variable θ was realized and P (the owner) could observe only the outcome x, not the action or the random variable. P's problem was to design a contract to induce A to choose an action a which was optimal for the principal. The contract could only make A's reward y depend on the outcome x. In the adverse selection model in this section, P observes the outcome y and the action a taken by A and can therefore write a contract making A's reward depend on y and a. However, P does not observe the random variable θ which is known to A before he takes his decision a. θ affects the cost to A of his actions and hence the cost to P of getting A to choose a particular action. Thus P's problem is now to design a contract which enables her to get A to choose the desired action at minimum expected cost to P.

Full information, first-best contracts

Under *full information*, P can observe A's action a and knows the value of θ, A's type. P also knows the functions [D.1] and [D.3], defining A's preferences and the technology, and A's *reservation utility* V^0. The reservation utility of A is assumed to be the same for both types, so that types differ only in their productivity, not in their preferences or forgone opportunities. P can derive the full information, first-best (f.i.f.b.) contract by solving for each i

$$\max_{x_i, y_i, a_i} x_i - y_i \quad \text{s.t.} \quad v(y_i) - a_i \geq V^0 \qquad \text{[D.4]}$$
$$x_i = x(a_i, \theta_i)$$

The first-order conditions for each i imply

$$x_a(a_i^\star, \theta_i) = 1/v'(y_i^\star) \qquad \text{[D.5]}$$
$$v(y_i^\star) - a_i = V^0 \qquad \text{[D.6]}$$

The reservation utility or *participation constraint* must bind, as in [D.6], because P has positive marginal utility and would be made better off by a feasible reduction in the payment to A. Since A is held down to his reservation utility level, his income must increase at the rate $1/v'$ as a_i increases. Thus $1/v'$ is also the marginal cost of a to P and [D.5] requires P to choose a_i so as to equate the marginal cost of a to its marginal product given A's type θ_i.

Figure 20.7 illustrates. A's reservation indifference curve I^0 shows the combinations of income and action which yield him V^0. I^0 thus represents a *cost function* to P, since to induce A to supply any value of a she must pay him at least as much as the y coordinate of I^0 at that level of a. The slope of I^0 is $1/v'(y)$. The curves $x(a, \theta_1)$ and $x(a, \theta_2)$ are total output curves embodying the assumptions in [D.3]. For $\theta = \theta_i$, P requires A to set a at the level $a_i^\star$. This maximizes the vertical difference between the

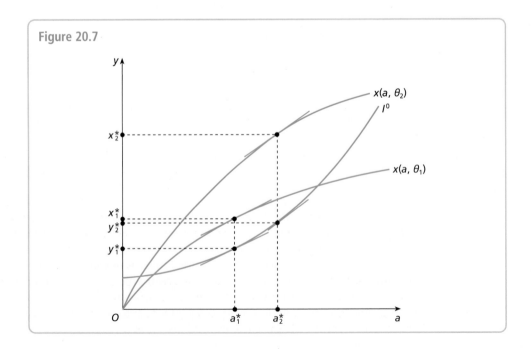

Figure 20.7

relevant output curve and I^0, giving the equality of slopes condition ([D.5]). We note that, because θ_2 is the more productive type, $a_2^* > a_1^*$ and $y_2^* > y_1^*$. Both types of A are equally well off, since the increase in income just compensates for the increase in a.

The subsequent analysis is easier if we reformulate the model and express its results in a different, but equivalent, way. Since x is monotonic in a for given θ, we can equivalently represent the technology by the amount of a required to produce x for a given θ. Thus inverting the output function $x = x(a, \theta)$, we obtain

$$a = \psi(x, \theta) \qquad \psi_x > 0 \qquad \psi_\theta < 0 \qquad \psi_{xx} > 0 \qquad \psi_{x\theta} < 0 \qquad \text{[D.7]}$$

which we can interpret as an 'input requirement function'. (The reader should use the implicit function rule on $x - x(a, \theta) = 0$ to check that our assumptions in [D.3] imply that $\psi(x, \theta)$ has the stated properties.) Substituting ψ for a in A's utility function gives

$$V = V(x, y, \theta) = v(y) - \psi(x, \theta) \qquad \text{[D.8]}$$

Using [D.8] we can rewrite P's problem [D.4] for each type i as

$$\max_{x_i, y_i} x_i - y_i \quad \text{s.t.} \quad v(y_i) - \psi(x_i, \theta_i) \geqslant V^0 \qquad \text{[D.9]}$$

The reformulation simply eliminates one variable and one constraint from the problem. The first-order conditions for [D.9] imply

$$\psi_x(x_i^*, \theta_i) = v'(y_i^*) \qquad \text{[D.10]}$$

$$v(y_i^*) - \psi(x_i^*, \theta_i) = V^0 \qquad \text{[D.11]}$$

Since $\psi_x(x, \theta) = 1/x_a(a, \theta)$ (use the implicit function rule on [D.3]), it is clear that [D.10] and [D.5] say the same thing.

The diagrammatic analysis looks very different however. Given his type, A's preferences are now expressed in terms of income y and output x. We can show his indifference curves in (x, y) space for given θ. From [D.8], the slope of the (x, y) indifference curves of type i are

$$\frac{dy_i}{dx_i} = \frac{\psi_x(x, \theta_i)}{v'(y_i)} = \frac{1}{x_a(a, \theta_i)v'(y_i)} \qquad \text{[D.12]}$$

In Fig. 20.8 the reservation indifference curves I_i^0 of the two types show combinations of income and outcome (implying a particular effort level) which yield each type the same reservation utility V^0. The two curves are obviously positively sloped, since, as output increases, A supplies more effort and must be compensated by more income. Higher indifference curves for a given type correspond to higher utility since A is better off with more y for given x (and therefore for given a). The slopes of the (x, y) indifference curves of each type increase with x at fixed y because of the assumption of diminishing marginal productivity: at high output levels increases in x require larger increases in a than at low output levels, and thus larger compensating increases in income. Note from [D.12] that increases in y for a given level of x steepen the indifference curves of a given type if A is risk averse ($v'' < 0$), since then v' declines with y. Indifference curves of a given type have the same slope along a vertical line if A is risk neutral, since then v' is constant.

Our assumption on the technology that $x_{a\theta}(a, \theta) > 0$ means that $x_a(a, \theta_1) < x_a(a, \theta_2)$ since $\theta_1 < \theta_2$. From [D.12] we see that this implies that, at a given income–output

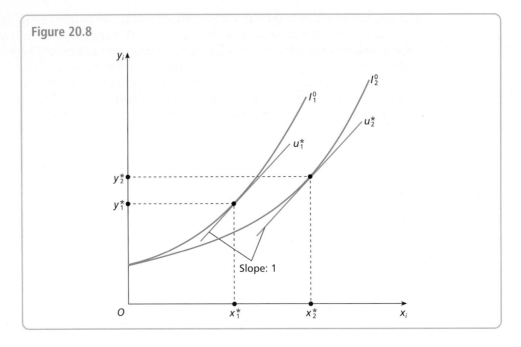

Figure 20.8

combination, the (x, y) indifference curves of the θ_1 type are steeper than those of the θ_2 type. Thus I_1^0 is steeper than I_2^0. The two types require the same increase in income to compensate them for a given increase in a (so their (a, y) indifference curves are identical), but the type θ_1 must make a larger increase in a to generate a given increase in x. Hence the (x, y) indifference curves of the less productive type must be steeper than those of the more productive type: any given increase in output requires a greater increase in a from the less productive type than from the more productive type. The (x, y) indifference curve of the θ_1 type for any given utility level must lie to the left of that of the θ_2 type for the same utility and be steeper at any fixed level of y, because a given (a, y) translates into a smaller x *and* a smaller marginal productivity for a θ_1 type.

In short, our assumptions on preferences and technology imply that the *single-crossing condition*

$$\frac{\partial}{\partial \theta}\left[\frac{dy_i}{dx_i}\right] = \frac{\psi_{x\theta}(x, \theta_i)}{v'(y_i)} < 0 \qquad \text{[D.13]}$$

holds. Note that we hold (x, y) constant under the differentiation, so that [D.13] says that the indifference curves of more productive types are flatter than those of less productive types at given points in Fig. 20.8. Thus a pair of indifference curves for different types can cross only once. The single crossing condition is important at several points in the analysis below.

In Fig. 20.8 the set of feasible contracts are those on or above the reservation indifference curves (so that they are acceptable to the different types) and on or below the 45° line (not shown) where the payment to A is less than the output. The solution points (x_i^*, y_i^*) in Fig. 20.8 satisfy conditions [D.10] and [D.11]. The slope of a contour of P's utility function is $dy/dx = 1$. [D.10] can be interpreted in the usual way as giving a point of tangency between P's and A's indifference curves, as illustrated in the figure, where the lines u_i^* have unit slopes. The contracts for both types are efficient: it would be impossible to vary their terms without making either A or P worse off. Clearly P would prefer that A is type $\theta_2 : u_2^*$ lies below u_1^*, indicating a greater utility for P, who prefers to make a smaller payment to A for a given output.

Hidden knowledge and the Revelation Principle

We now suppose that there is asymmetric information with P unable to observe A's type. Everything else is common knowledge, including the fact that A knows his type. Since P knows that A knows θ, suppose that she asks him to tell her his type and then offers the f.i.f.b. contract (x_i^*, y_i^*) appropriate for A's reported type. Whatever A's true type, it is in his interest always to tell P that he is type θ_1, if he expects subsequently to be given the f.i.f.b. contract which is best for P given A's reported type. If A is in fact type θ_2, and reports that he is type θ_1, he expects to get the contract (x_1^*, y_1^*) which lies above his true reservation indifference curve I_2^0 and he would have a utility greater than V^0. Although (x_1^*, y_1^*) pays less than (x_2^*, y_2^*), it requires less output, and the implied reduction in a more than compensates for the reduction in y. Thus a θ_2 type would lie and claim to be type θ_1. If A was a type θ_1 he would not claim to be type θ_2, since then he would be given (x_2^*, y_2^*) which lies below his reservation indifference curve I_1^0. Hence if P behaves naively and tries to implement the f.i.f.b. contract on the basis of A's reported type, she will always be told that A is a low-productivity type. The f.i.f.b. contracts are not incentive compatible: they do not induce A to act to fulfil the expectations on which P offered them.

A natural, intuitive way to proceed would be to formulate constraints which require the contracts for each type to be designed to give A an incentive to reveal his type truthfully to P. The *Revelation Principle* confirms that this intuition is correct. Suppose that P designs an *indirect* allocation mechanism α under which P asks A to choose some message m from a set M_α to transmit to P. The mechanism specifies a rule $R_\alpha(m)$ which governs what contract $(x, y) = (R_{\alpha x}(m), R_{\alpha y}(m))$ P will offer in response to m. Thus the mechanism is defined by the set M_α and the rule $R_\alpha(m)$. A will choose the message to maximize his utility $V(x, y, \theta)$. His optimal message $m_\alpha(\theta)$ will depend on the allocation mechanism α and his type θ and will satisfy

$$V(R_{\alpha x}(m_\alpha(\theta)), R_{\alpha y}(m_\alpha(\theta)), \theta) \geqslant V(R_{\alpha x}(m), R_{\alpha y}(m), \theta) \qquad \text{all } m \in M_\alpha \qquad [\text{D.14}]$$

Now consider the following *direct* mechanism $\delta(\alpha)$ under which P asks A to report his type, that is to transmit a message $\hat{\theta} \in \Theta$, where Θ is the set of A's possible types. When she receives the message from A that he is type $\hat{\theta}$, P then gives A the contract $R_{\alpha x}(m_\alpha(\hat{\theta})), R_{\alpha y}(m_\alpha(\hat{\theta}))$. That is, she calculates the message – $m_\alpha(\hat{\theta})$ – which A would have sent under the indirect mechanism α if A's type was $\hat{\theta}$ and then applies the contract selection rule R_α from the indirect mechanism α to this message. The direct mechanism $\delta(\alpha)$ will thus yield A the utility $V(R_{\alpha x}(m_\alpha(\hat{\theta})), R_{\alpha y}(m_\alpha(\hat{\theta})), \theta)$. Under the $\delta(\alpha)$ mechanism A's report of his type will determine the message which P uses in choosing the contract. But, from [D.14], A will want P to use the message $m_\alpha(\theta)$ rather than any other message m he could get P to calculate by sending a false report of his type. To ensure that she does calculate $m_\alpha(\theta)$ he must report his true type θ to her: $\hat{\theta} = \theta$. As a consequence P chooses exactly the same contract as under the indirect mechanism α. Thus the direct mechanism $\delta(\alpha)$ is equivalent to the indirect mechanism α and induces A to tell the truth.

Since α was an arbitrary mechanism, we have established that *any* resource allocation (contract) which can be achieved by an indirect mechanism can also be

Figure 20.9

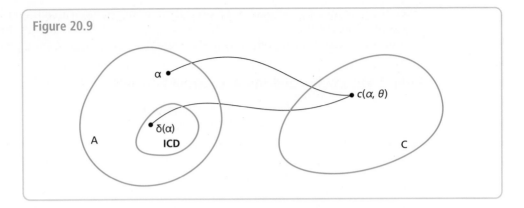

achieved by some equivalent direct mechanism which induces truth telling i.e. is incentive compatible. Hence P's search for an optimal mechanism can be confined to incentive compatible direct mechanisms. This is the Revelation Principle.

Figure 20.9 illustrates. Each mechanism or contract selection procedure α in the set of mechanisms **A** on the left yields, given the agent's type θ, a resource allocation or contract $c(\alpha; \theta)$ in the set of feasible allocations **C** on the right. The set **ICD** of incentive compatible direct mechanisms is a subset of the set of mechanisms. According to the Revelation Principle *any* contract or allocation $c(\alpha, \theta)$ in **C** which is produced by a mechanism α which is not in **ICD** can also be produced by a mechanism $\delta(\alpha)$ in **ICD**.

The Revelation Principle is useful because it enables us to restrict attention to a subset of all possible procedures for selecting contracts. Further, the subset is one which it is possible to model reasonably simply by imposing incentive compatibility constraints on the contracts. The principal's problem of selecting optimal contracts under hidden knowledge is then a relatively straightforward constrained optimization problem.

The contract offered to the agent when he reports a type must yield him at least as much utility from telling the truth as from lying:

$$v(y_i) - \psi(x_i, \theta_i) \geqslant v(y_j) - \psi(x_j, \theta_i) \qquad i, j = 1, 2 \qquad i \neq j \qquad [\text{D.15}]$$

The left-hand side is the utility a θ_i type agent gets from reporting his type truthfully and getting the contract designed for the θ_i type. The right-hand side is the utility a type θ_i would get by claiming to be type θ_j and getting the contract designed for such agents. Note that we assume that the agent only lies if he has a positive incentive to do so. P does not even need to ask A to report his type; she can just offer a pair of contracts satisfying [D.15] and the agent will reveal his type by his choice of contract. For this reason incentive compatibility constraints are sometimes also referred to as *self-selection* constraints.

When she designs the contracts P takes a decision under uncertainty: she does not know what type she faces. After she has designed the contracts which induce A to reveal his type correctly, she will be fully informed but by then she is committed to the contracts. She cannot renegotiate them after she knows A's type. We assume that P has a prior probability π that A is type θ_1 and $(1 - \pi)$ that he is type θ_2. The contract she designs for the θ_1 type will be accepted with probability π and the contract for the θ_2 type with probability $(1 - \pi)$.

We assume that she designs the contracts to maximize her expected net income

$$\pi(x_1 - y_1) + (1 - \pi)(x_2 - y_2) \qquad \text{[D.16]}$$

The optimal contracts under asymmetric information are found by maximizing [D.16] subject to the incentive compatibility constraints [D.15] and the reservation or participation constraints

$$v(y_i) - \psi(x_i, \theta_i) \geqslant V^0 \qquad i = 1, 2 \qquad \text{[D.17]}$$

We should also impose the technical feasibility constraints $x_i \geqslant y_i$ but we will assume that the solution satisfies them strictly. (Question 4 investigates the implications of binding technical feasibility constraints.)

We can simplify the analysis by noting that two of the four constraints in [D.15] and [D.17] do not bind at the optimum. We have seen that P could not expect a θ_2 type to tell the truth if offered a contract on his reservation indifference curve: he could always do better by pretending to be type θ_1. The type θ_1 cannot be offered a contract which lies below his reservation indifference curve I_1^0 in Fig. 20.8 and all contracts on or above I_1^0 are better for the type θ_2 than a contract on his reservation indifference curve I_2^0. Thus to induce the type θ_2 to reveal his type by his choice of contract, the optimum contract for him must give him more than his reservation utility. He will therefore obtain a *rent*, over and above his reservation utility, by virtue of his monopoly of his private information that he is more productive. The participation constraint in [D.17] on the type θ_2 cannot bind at the optimum (see Question 3, Exercise 20D, for a more formal argument.)

Second, the incentive compatibility constraint for the type θ_1 in [D.15] will be non-binding at the optimum. (See Question 3.) In Fig. 20.10 suppose that the contracts a and b, which are assumed to satisfy both incentive compatibility constraints, were optimal. The incentive compatibility constraint on the type θ_1 is binding: he is indifferent between a and b, where b is the contract designed for the type θ_2. Consider the contracts a and c which also satisfy incentive compatibility for both types, but now the incentive compatibility constraint on type θ_1 is no longer binding. The type θ_2 now gets c, which has a smaller income for the same output. This does not violate the participation constraint on the type θ_2, since we know that, if the original contracts a and b were optimal, the type θ_2 was above his reservation indifference

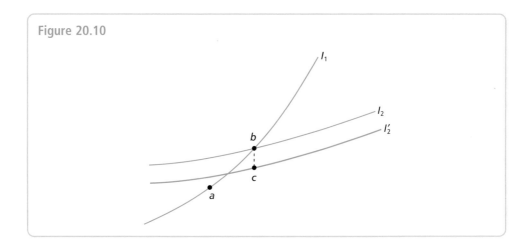

Figure 20.10

curve. For a small enough reduction in y_2, c will also satisfy the type θ_2 participation constraint and I'_2 will lie above the type θ_2 reservation indifference curve. Since output is unchanged, P must prefer the feasible contracts a and c to a and b because she pays less to the type θ_2. A pair of contracts, like a and b, where the incentive compatibility constraint on the type θ_1 binds, cannot be optimal.

Dropping the redundant constraints, the Lagrangean for the simplified problem is

$$L = \pi(x_1 - y_1) + (1 - \pi)(x_2 - y_2) + \lambda_1[v(y_1) - \psi(x_1, \theta_1) - V^0]$$
$$+ \mu_2[v(y_2) - \psi(x_2, \theta_2) - v(y_1) + \psi(x_1, \theta_2)] \qquad [D.17]$$

(Because the participation constraint on the θ_2 type and the incentive compatibility constraint on the θ_1 type are non-binding at the solution, we have, in effect, set the relevant Lagrange multipliers λ_2 and μ_1 equal to zero, so they do not appear in [D.17].) The Kuhn–Tucker conditions are

$$L_{x_1} = \pi - \hat{\lambda}_1\psi_x(\hat{x}_1, \theta_1) + \hat{\mu}_2\psi_x(\hat{x}_1, \theta_2) = 0 \qquad [D.18]$$

$$L_{y_1} = -\pi + \hat{\lambda}_1 v'(\hat{y}_1) - \hat{\mu}_2 v'(\hat{y}_1) = 0 \qquad [D.19]$$

$$L_{x_2} = (1 - \pi) - \hat{\mu}_2\psi_x(\hat{x}_2, \theta_2) = 0 \qquad [D.20]$$

$$L_{y_2} = -(1 - \pi) + \hat{\mu}_2 v'(\hat{y}_2) = 0 \qquad [D.21]$$

$$L_{\lambda_1} = v(\hat{y}_1) - \psi((\hat{x}_1, \theta_1) - V^0 \geqslant 0 \qquad \hat{\lambda}_1 \geqslant 0 \qquad \hat{\lambda}_1 L_{\lambda_1} = 0 \qquad [D.22]$$

$$L_{\mu_2} = v(\hat{y}_2) - \psi(\hat{x}_2, \theta_2) - v(\hat{y}_1) + \psi((\hat{x}_1, \theta_2) \geqslant 0 \qquad \hat{\mu}_2 \geqslant 0 \qquad \hat{\mu}L_{\mu_2} = 0 \qquad [D.23]$$

The solution determined by these conditions is shown in Fig. 20.11. The main characteristics of the optimal second-best asymmetrical information contracts $(\hat{x}_i, \hat{y}_i)$, $i = 1, 2$, are:

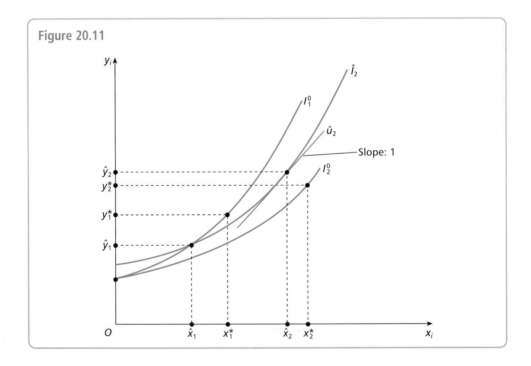

Figure 20.11

(a) The incentive compatibility constraint [D.23] is strictly binding. In Fig. 20.11 $(\hat{x}_1, \hat{y}_1)$ and $(\hat{x}_2, \hat{y}_2)$ lie on the same type θ_2 indifference curve $\hat{I}_2$, which, as we have already argued, lies above the reservation indifference curve I_2^0 of the type θ_2. To see this, note that in [D.21], $(1 - \pi) > 0$, and $v' > 0$, and so the incentive compatibility constraint must bind. The facts that $(\hat{x}_1, \hat{y}_1)$ and $(\hat{x}_2, \hat{y}_2)$ lie on $\hat{I}_2$ and that the θ_1 type strictly prefers $(\hat{x}_1, \hat{y}_1)$, together with the single crossing condition, imply that the contracts satisfy

$$\hat{x}_1 < \hat{x}_2 \qquad \hat{y}_1 < \hat{y}_2 \qquad\qquad \text{[D.24]}$$

(b) The θ_1 type reservation constraint is binding: $(\hat{x}_1, \hat{y}_1)$ is on I_1^0. From [D.19] we have $\hat{\lambda}_1 = \hat{\mu}_2 + \pi/v'(\hat{y}_1) > 0$, so that, from [D.23], the constraint must bind. Thus low productivity types gain no rents from their private information.

(c) At $(\hat{x}_2, \hat{y}_2)$ the slope of the type θ_2 indifference curve is unity, just as in the f.i.f.b. solution. (Use [D.21] to substitute for $\hat{\mu}_2$ in [D.20] to get $\psi_x(\hat{x}_2, \theta_2)/v'(\hat{y}_2) = 1$.) However, if $v'' < 0$, the asymmetrical information θ_2 contract differs from the full information contract in that

$$x_2^* > \hat{x}_2 \qquad y_2^* < \hat{y}_2 \qquad\qquad \text{[D.25]}$$

The θ_2 type is induced to reveal his true type by being offered a contract with lower output (and hence less a) and a higher income than the f.i.f.b. contract. Even so he is just indifferent between lying and telling the truth. The contract for the more productive type is efficient: at $(\hat{x}_2, \hat{y}_2)$ his indifference curve $\hat{I}_2$ is tangent to P's indifference curve $\hat{u}_2$ and any change in the contract would make one of them worse off. The result, that the first-order condition for the more productive type has the same *form* as his f.i.f.b. contract, is known as the '*no distortion at the top*' result. Remember though that actual θ_2 contracts may be very different under full and asymmetric information.

(d) Although θ_1 types obtain the same utility under full and asymmetric information, they have a different contract:

$$\hat{x}_1 < x_1^* \qquad \hat{y}_1 < y_1^* \qquad\qquad \text{[D.26]}$$

To see how this follows from the first-order conditions, recall that the f.i.f.b. contract for type θ_1 has the slope of the reservation indifference curve I_1^0 equal to the slope (unity) of P's indifference curve. Since we know that the optimal second-best contract is also on I_1^0, [D.26] is equivalent to the slope of I_1^0 being less than unity:

$$\psi_x(\hat{x}_1, \theta_1)/v'(\hat{y}_1) < 1 \qquad\qquad \text{[D.27]}$$

(refer to Fig. 20.11). From [D.18] and [D.19] we have

$$\frac{\psi_x(\hat{x}_1, \theta_1)}{v'(\hat{y}_1)} = \frac{\pi + \hat{\mu}_2\psi_x(x_1, \theta_2)}{\pi + \hat{\mu}_2 v'(\hat{y}_1)} \qquad\qquad \text{[D.28]}$$

and so [D.27] holds if and only if the right-hand side of [D.28] is less than 1. This in turn is equivalent to

$$\psi_x(\hat{x}_1, \theta_2)/v'(\hat{y}_1) < 1 \qquad\qquad \text{[D.29]}$$

The left-hand side of [D.29] is the slope of $\hat{I}_2$ at $(\hat{x}_1, \hat{y}_1)$. But from [D.24] and the curvature of the indifference curves we know that $\hat{I}_2$ is flatter at $(\hat{x}_1, \hat{y}_1)$ than at $(\hat{x}_2, \hat{y}_2)$, where its slope is 1. Hence [D.26] holds.

Figure 20.12

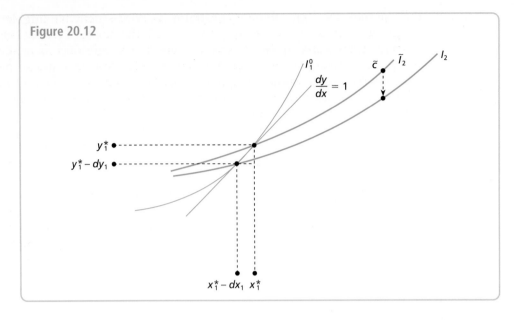

The intuition underlying the result is a nice application of second-best reasoning. Consider Fig. 20.12 and suppose that P had solved the problem of inducing the θ_2 type to reveal his type by offering him $\tilde{c} = (\tilde{x}_2, \tilde{y}_2)$ which puts this type on the indifference curve $\tilde{I}_2$, which passes through (x_1^*, y_1^*). Since the θ_1 type also reveals his type truthfully, the contracts $(\tilde{x}_2, \tilde{y}_2)$ and (x_1^*, y_1^*) are incentive compatible and satisfy the participation constraints. However, they are not optimal for P. At (x_1^*, y_1^*) the θ_1 type is willing to accept small reductions dx_1, dy_1 provided $dx_1 = dy_1$. Since his indifference curve has a slope of 1 at (x_1^*, y_1^*),

$$dV = v'(y_1^*)dy_1 - \psi_x(x_1^*, \theta_1)dx_1 = 0 \qquad \text{[D.30]}$$

Such reductions would also make no difference to P's utility $(x_1 - y_1)$ from the contract for θ_1 types. But the change in the type θ_1 contract reduces the utility that the type θ_2 would get from the type θ_1 contract:

$$dV = v'(y_1^*)dy_1 - \psi_x(x_1^*, \theta_2)dx_1 < 0 \qquad \text{[D.31]}$$

since $dx_1 = dy_1 < 0$ and $\psi_x(x_1^*, \theta_2) < \psi_x(x_1^*, \theta_1)$. The type θ_1 contract is now less attractive to the type θ_2, so that P can also adjust the type θ_2 contract in her favour without violating the incentive compatibility constraint for the type θ_2. For example, she could hold x_2 fixed and reduce y_2, increasing her expected utility by $(1 - \pi)dy_2$.

Thus it pays to introduce a distortion into the type θ_1 allocation to relax the incentive compatibility constraint on the type θ_2 and reduce his rent. The second-best contracts achieve an optimal tradeoff between the inefficiency on the type θ_1 contract and the need to pay the type θ_2 a rent to induce truthful revelation of his type. Note that the terms of this tradeoff depend on P's beliefs about the relative likelihood of facing the two types. The smaller is π, the greater the extent of the departure from (x_1^*, y_1^*) in order to reduce the deviation from (x_2^*, y_2^*).

This also provides intuition for the 'no distortion at the top' result. The inefficiency of the θ_1 type contract arises because P can thereby reduce the rent of the θ_2 type, who must be made indifferent between the two contracts. But the type θ_2

contract does not have to be inefficient to relax the incentive compatibility constraint on a more productive type, because θ_2 is the most productive type of agent. Thus P can place the type θ_2 on $\hat{I}_2$ at *any* point to the right of $(\hat{x}_1, \hat{y}_1)$ and still satisfy the incentive compatibility constraint. Thus she is free to choose the contract on $\hat{I}_2$ which maximizes her utility. Hence the type θ_2 contract at $(\hat{x}_2, \hat{y}_2)$ is efficient.

As a result of the information asymmetry P is strictly worse off *ex ante*, in terms of expected utility, and also *ex post*, in terms of the utility achieved from the contract with each type of agent. The low-productivity type agent is unaffected, but the high-productivity agent earns a positive rent. The principal incurs an agency cost, or cost of delegating decision making, which is minimized when the optimal second-best contracts are adopted.

There are many applications of the type of reasoning we have set out in this section. We have already considered one in the analysis of monopoly price discrimination in section C, Chapter 9. The monopoly was the principal and the agents of different types were the consumers with different preferences. Reinterpreting x as the purchases of the monopolist's output, y as the amount paid by the consumers, and making the minor change that P's objective function (profit) is concave in x, we can see that the results obtained earlier are identical to those of this section. For example, the consumer with the greater marginal valuation of the product does not have all his surplus extracted and consumes an efficient quantity: 'no distortion at the top'. The next two subsections provide two further examples of the power of the Revelation Principle in providing a rationale for debt contracts to finance investment and in deriving an optimal mechanism for government procurement when a supplier has unobservable cost. Whatever the particular context, the Revelation Principle means that hidden information principal–agent models have a common structure: the principal will design optimal contracts, subject to the constraints that the agent accepts a contract and in doing so reveals his information.

Costly state verification and debt contracts

In this subsection we illustrate the analytical power of the Revelation Principle and the truth-telling incentive compatibility constraints by examining the contract which will be written between an entrepreneur, who requires funds to finance a risky project, and an investor, who has imperfect information about the project's realized payoff. We will show that, out of the many possible contract forms, the optimal contract is a debt contract: in return for her initial investment the investor is paid a fixed sum from the project proceeds unless the proceeds are less than the fixed sum, in which case the investor gets all the proceeds.

The model is a simplified version of Gale and Hellwig (1985). A risk-neutral entrepreneur, E, seeks finance for an investment project with an uncertain return $x \in [x_0, x_1]$, with continuous distribution function $F(x)$, and a capital cost K. The entrepreneur has no initial funds to finance K and must acquire them from the capital market. The capital market is competitive with prevailing interest rate r, which defines the opportunity cost of funds a risk-neutral investor, I, may put into E's project. I knows that there will be asymmetric information *ex post*, in that E will know the realized value of x but may misreport it to I. However, I may audit the outcome at a cost α after receiving a report of the payoff from E. Auditing reveals the true value of x. The contract between the parties specifies the payment z to be made to I in return for funding the capital cost K. E gets the residual payoff from the investment: $y = x - z$. The payment z to I can be contingent on the reported value of the payoff if there is no audit or the true value if there is an audit. The contract also specifies what type of payoff reports by E will lead to an audit.

Since the capital market is competitive the contract will maximise E's expected payoff. The constraints on the contract are (a) the investor must get an expected return, net of any auditing cost, which covers her opportunity cost $(1 + r)K$; (b) the payment to the investor cannot exceed the project payoff: $z \leqslant x$ so that z must lie on or below the 45° line in Fig. 20.13; and (c) by the Revelation Principle, it must be in E's interest to report the project payoff proceeds truthfully: the contract must be incentive compatible.

Two assumptions ensure that the contract choice problem is not trivial. First, the lowest possible project payoff x_0 does not cover I's opportunity cost $(1 + r)K$. If it did, the optimal contract would be very simple since E could just repay $z = (1 + r)K$ whatever the realized value of x, I would not be exposed to any risk, and the information asymmetry would have no effect. Second, we assume that the expected project payoffs $\bar{x}$ satisfy $\bar{x} \geqslant \alpha + (1 + r)K$, which ensures that there always exists a contract which is better for E than no contract.

The optimal contract is a debt contract of the following form. For reports $x' \geqslant x^*$, no auditing takes place and I receives a fixed payment $z = x^*$ (leaving E with $y = x - x^*$), while, for reports $x' < x^*$, I audits and receives the payment $z = x$ (leaving E with $y = 0$). The debt contract is illustrated in Fig. 20.13. Over the interval $[x_0, x^*)$, z lies on the 45° line, while for $x \in [x^*, x_1]$ z is equal to the constant value x^*. E receives $x - z$. We now show why this contract is optimal and how x^* is determined.

First we consider the implications of the truth-telling constraint. It is intuitive that I would only wish to audit when she gets a report that the project has done badly and that consequently she will have to accept a low payment under the contract. Assume that there is a value $x^* \in [x_0, x_1]$, such that reports in $[x_0, x^*)$ lead to an audit

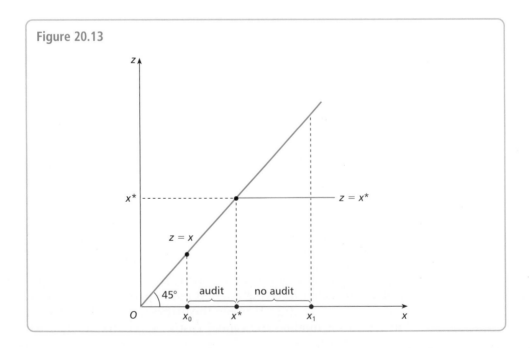

Figure 20.13

and reports in $[x^*, x_1]$ do not. It can be proved that the optimal contract will indeed have this form.

Now take x^* as given for the moment and consider why the payment must be constant for all reports in the no audit range $[x^*, x_1]$. Let $z^n(x)$ denote the payment to I from E reporting x if there is no audit of the report ($x \in [x^*, x_1]$). Let $\hat{x}$ denote the report in $[x^*, x_1]$ which minimizes the payment and $\hat{z} = z^n(\hat{x})$ be the minimum payment, so that

$$z^n(x) \geqslant z^n(\hat{x}) = \hat{z} \qquad x \in [x^*, x_1] \qquad \text{[D.32]}$$

If he is not audited E gets $x - z^n(x')$ from reporting $x' \in [x^*, x_1]$ and so will tell the truth only if

$$x - z^n(x) \geqslant x - z^n(\hat{x}) \Leftrightarrow z^n(x) \leqslant z^n(\hat{x}) \qquad \text{[D.33]}$$

But the weak inequalities in [D.32] and [D.33] can only both be satisfied if

$$z^n(x) = z^n(\hat{x}) = \hat{z} \qquad x \in [x^*, x_1] \qquad \text{[D.34]}$$

so that the payment is constant at $\hat{z}$ for all reports in the audit interval. Intuitively, if I does not audit, the only way E can be made indifferent between lying and telling the truth when the true value is $x \in [x^*, x_1]$ is if he has to pay the same amount $\hat{z}$ to I regardless of his report.

We also want to ensure that if the true value is in the audit range $[x_0, x^*)$ then E will not report that it is in the no audit range $[x^*, x_1]$. Let $z^a(x)$ be the payment to I if there is an audit and the true value is x. Then there is no incentive to misreport that $x \in [x^*, x_1]$ to escape audit if

$$x - z^a(x) \geqslant x - \hat{z} \Leftrightarrow z^a(x) \leqslant \hat{z} \qquad \text{[D.35]}$$

The debt contract illustrated in Fig. 20.13 satisfies the incentive compatibility constraints [D.34] and [D.35]. But so do contracts which are not debt contracts, as shown by the two examples in Fig. 20.14. Both of the contracts have $z^a(x) < x$ for some $x \in [x_0, x^*)$ and the one in Fig. 20.14(a) also has $x^* > \hat{z}_1$. We now show that the

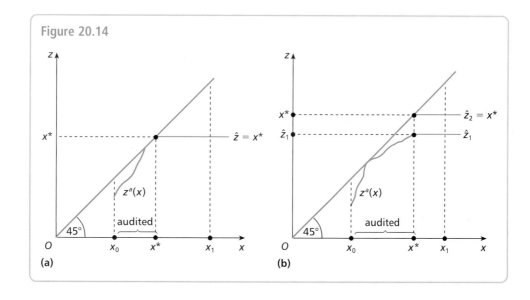

Figure 20.14

optimal contract will have $z^a(x) = x$ and $\hat{z} = x^*$ so that neither contract in Fig. 20.14 is optimal.

To be optimal, a contract must satisfy I's participation constraint for given x^*:

$$\bar{z}_I = \int_{x_0}^{x^*} [z^a(x) - \alpha]\, dF + \int_{x^*}^{x_1} \hat{z}\, dF \geqslant (1 + r)K \qquad \text{[D.36]}$$

The first part of the middle term is the expected value of payments net of auditing costs over the audited interval; the second, equal to $\hat{z}[1 - F(x^*)]$, is the expected value of payments over the non-audited interval. The last term is the opportunity cost of I's capital. The net expected surplus available to be shared between the two is the mean return less expected auditing costs:

$$\bar{z}_E + \bar{z}_I = \int_{x_0}^{x^*} (x - \alpha)\, dF + \int_{x^*}^{x_1} x\, dF = \bar{x} - \alpha F(x^*) \qquad \text{[D.37]}$$

where $\bar{z}_E$ is the expected income of E. If the participation constraint is satisfied as equality, $\bar{z}_I = (1 + r)K$ and so

$$\bar{z}_E = \bar{x} - \alpha F(x^*) - \bar{z}_I = \bar{x} - \alpha F(x^*) - (1 + r)K \qquad \text{[D.38]}$$

Notice that, when the participation constraint binds, which it will do in the optimal contract, the auditing costs are borne by E even though they are paid by I.

We now show that contracts which satisfy incentive compatibility but which are not debt contracts cannot be optimal. Suppose that E offers I a payment function, as in Fig. 20.14(a), which has $z^a(x) < x$ for some points in the audited interval. The contract satisfies incentive compatibility and the feasibility constraint $z \leqslant x$. Suppose also that the contract satisfies the participation constraint [D.36]. Now create a new contract by setting $z^a(x) = x$ over the audited interval in Fig. 20.14(a). The new contract is now a debt contract which satisfies the feasibility constraint and incentive compatibility. Since x^* was held constant I is better off since she gets higher payments in some states, the same payments in all others, and auditing costs are unchanged. Hence her participation constraint [D.36] is now satisfied as a strict inequality: $\bar{z}_I > (1 + r)K$.

Now consider part (b) of Fig. 20.14 where again we assume that the initial contract satisfies the participation constraint as an equality. The initial contract in Fig. 20.14(b) has $z^a(x) < x$ for some points in the audited interval and also has $x^* > \hat{z}_1$. Now create a new contract by increasing the payment $\hat{z}$ in the no audit range so that $x^* = \hat{z}_2$ and increase the payments in the audit range so that $z^a(x) = x$. Hence the new contract is a debt contract and since the payments to I have increased, and x^* and hence auditing costs are unchanged, the participation constraint is now satisfied as a strict inequality.

Thus by changing the payment schedules we can always transform a contract which satisfies incentive compatibility, feasibility and the participation constraint into a debt contract which satisfies the participation constraint as a strict inequality. We can then reduce x^* so that the participation constraint is satisfied as an equality again. I is now just as well off as before. As we can see from [D.38] the auditing costs are borne by E and, since x^* has been reduced, the expected auditing costs have fallen, making E better off. Thus contracts which are not debt contracts cannot be optimal since we can transform them into debt contracts, adjust x^*, and make E better off.

The alert reader will have noticed a possible problem with the argument in the last paragraph: reductions in x^* with a debt contract can increase z_I. The reason is that although a reduction in x^* reduces the payments to I it also reduces the expected auditing cost paid by I. Thus with a debt contract I's expected receipts net of auditing costs are

$$\bar{z}_I = \int_{x_0}^{x^*} (x - \alpha)\, dF + x^*[1 - F(x^*)] = \bar{z}_I(x^*) \tag{D.39}$$

and

$$\frac{d\bar{z}_I}{dx^*} = (x^* - \alpha)f(x^*)[1 - F(x^*)] - x^*f(x^*) = 1 - F(x^*) - \alpha f(x^*) \tag{D.40}$$

which can be negative or positive. Fortunately, we can show that there exists a smaller x^* which makes the participation constraint bind again. Refer to Fig. 20.15 where we plot the expected receipts for I from the debt contract $\bar{z}_I(x^*)$ against x^*. Non-debt contracts like those shown in Fig. 20.14 have $\bar{z}_I < \bar{z}_I(x^*)$ and are represented by points like c below the debt contract curve. The shape of the debt contract net receipts curve is determined by the distribution function $F(x)$. $\bar{z}_I(x^*)$ is continuous since we assumed that $F(x)$ is continuous and it satisfies $\bar{z}_I(x_0) = x_0$, $\bar{z}_I(x_1) = \bar{x} - a$. Notice that our initial assumption that $\bar{x} > \alpha + (1 + r)K$ means that there are values of x^* such that the participation constraint is satisfied as a strict inequality: $\bar{z}_I(x^*) > (1 + r)K$.

By changing a non-debt contract like c, which has $x^* = x_1^*$ and which just satisfies the participation constraint, into a debt contract with x^* held constant I's net receipts are increased to $\bar{z}_I(x_1^*)$. At x_1^* marginal reductions in x^* increase $\bar{z}_I(x^*)$ but, because $\bar{z}_I(x^*)$ is continuous and we assumed that $x_0 < (1 + r)K$, there will always

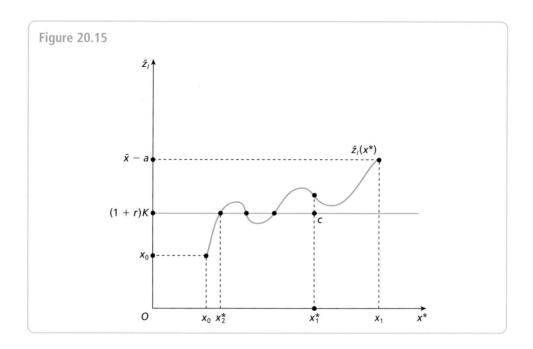

Figure 20.15

exist a level of x^*, less than x_1^*, satisfying the participation constraint as an equality. There are three such values in the example in Fig. 20.15. The optimal debt contract will have the lowest level of x^* satisfying the participation constraint. In Fig. 20.15 the optimal contract has $x^* = x_2^*$.

It is possible to relax some of the assumptions in the model without affecting the result that a debt contract is optimal. For example, we could allow the entrepreneur to have some initial assets or have the distribution of returns depend on the level of investment. The incentive compatibility constraints continue to play a powerful role in limiting the set of contracts to be considered.

Regulation with unobservable costs

The modern approach to regulation of firms with market power, typified by the model of Laffont and Tirole (1987) that we will present, sees the problem as one of asymmetric information. If the state-appointed regulator knows everything the monopoly knows, then she can simply instruct the firm to implement the welfare-maximizing policy. Typically, however, the firm will possess information not available to the regulator, for example on its technology and the effort it undertakes to keep costs down. Such information asymmetry creates the regulation problem.

To focus on the essentials we use a model which is perhaps more appropriately thought of as public procurement by the state for its citizens than regulation of a monopoly selling to consumers. (A more conventional monopoly regulation model is examined in Question 6, Exercise 20D.) Assume that a private firm is to undertake a project of a fixed size, say the construction of a hospital for the state health service. The cost of construction, c, will be known to everyone *ex post*, but *ex ante* it will be determined by two factors that are private information for the firm: its technology which determines its innate (exogenous) productivity, and the effort the management makes to keep costs down. Suppose there are two firm types – L low cost and H high cost – and their total production costs are is

$$c_i = \theta_i - a_i \qquad i = L, H \qquad \text{[D.41]}$$

where θ_i reflects the exogenous productivity of the firm, with $\theta_L < \theta_H$. a_i is the effort the firm expends to keep production costs down. Cost reducing effort itself is costly to the firm and the effort cost function is $\psi(a)$, with $\psi'(a) > 0$, $\psi''(a) > 0$. Note that the effort cost function is the same for each firm type.

The firm receives a total payment y_i from the regulator. It is convenient to define the firm's surplus of revenue over production cost as $s_i = y_i - c_i$ and to write the total payment as $s_i + c_i$. The firm wishes to maximize its net profit or rent $r_i = s_i - \psi(a_i) = y_i - c_i - \psi(a_i)$.

The project yields a fixed public benefit u. The total payment to the firm, $s_i + c_i$, is financed by distortionary taxation, with £1 of taxation having a social opportunity cost of £$(1 + \lambda)$ for $\lambda > 0$. If she knows she is faced with a firm of type i, the regulator would want to maximize the social welfare function

$$u - (1 + \lambda)(s_i + c_i) + s_i - \psi(a_i) \qquad \text{[D.42]}$$

by choice of s_i and a_i. The first two terms give the net benefits to consumer and taxpayers, taking account of the marginal social cost of public funds, whereas the last two terms give the monopoly's net profit which is included as part of social welfare.

The firm will only undertake the project if it is assured of non-negative profit, and so the participation constraints are

$$s_i - \psi(a_i) \geqslant 0 \qquad i = L, H \qquad [\text{D.43}]$$

If we rewrite the welfare function as

$$u - \lambda s_i - (1 + \lambda)(\theta_i - a_i) - \psi(a_i) \qquad [\text{D.44}]$$

we see that, with the cost of production and effort level held constant, the regulator wishes to minimize s_i, which is equivalent, when c_i and a_i are held constant, to minimizing the firm's rent. This is the goal of *rent extraction*. Note that if $\lambda = 0$ the regulator would be indifferent to the level of taxation and the firm's surplus, and, as we shall see, the regulation problem would disappear. If $\lambda > 0$ the regulator will want to give the monopoly no more than required to satisfy its participation constraint as an equality. The reason is that an increase in the firm's rent of £1 (which has a marginal social value of £1) has a marginal social cost of £$(1 + \lambda)$ if it is paid for by taxation.

Substituting from [D.43] for s_i and carrying out the unconstrained maximization of [D.44] with respect to a_i gives

$$\psi'(a_i^\star) = 1 \qquad [\text{D.45}]$$

The optimal effort level equates the marginal cost of cost-reducing effort with its marginal benefit, which is 1. The firm's surplus over production cost is then just enough to cover the cost of optimal effort

$$s_i^\star = \psi(a_i^\star) \qquad [\text{D.46}]$$

Overall the firm breaks even and all rent is extracted. Each type has the same effort level and surplus over production cost, though the high-cost type's cost level and corresponding gross payment is higher by the amount $\theta_H - \theta_L$.

It is useful, for the time when we examine the regulator's problem when she does not observe the firm's type, to define the regulatory regime in terms of s_i and c_i, rather than s_i and a_i. Note that the firm's indifference curves in the (c_i, s_i) space are (recall [D.41]) defined by

$$s_i - \psi(\theta_i - c_i) = r_i^0 \qquad i = L, H \qquad [\text{D.47}]$$

for a given rent level r_i^0. For $r_i = 0$, the reservation level, the reservation indifference curves for the two types are shown in Fig. 20.16. The reservation indifference curve for type H must lie above the reservation indifference curve for type L, since the type H must supply greater effort to achieve any surplus–production cost combination.

The slopes and curvatures of the indifference curves can be readily confirmed by applying the Implicit Function Theorem to [D.47] to obtain

$$\frac{ds_i}{dc_i} = -\psi' < 0 \qquad \frac{d^2 s_i}{dc_i^2} = \psi'' > 0 \qquad \frac{\partial}{\partial \theta}\left[\frac{ds_i}{dc_i}\right] = -\psi'' < 0 \qquad [\text{D.48}]$$

From the last of these derivatives we see that increasing θ at any given point (c_i, s_i) makes the slope of the indifference curve 'more negative', i.e. steeper. Hence, the low cost type's indifference curve will be flatter than that of the higher cost type at any given point. This is the *single-crossing condition*. Note also that the slopes of the indifference curves depend only on c_i and not on s_i, implying that each type's indifference curves are parallel along any vertical line.

Figure 20.16

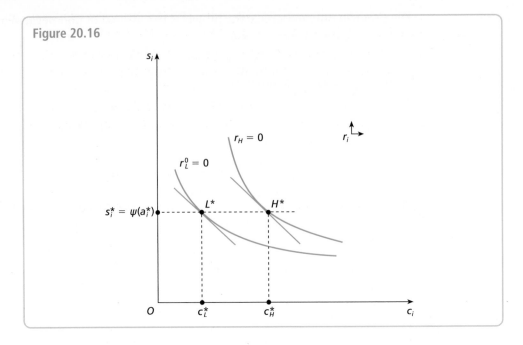

The solution to the full information case derived above is shown in Fig. 20.16. For each type $\psi'(a_i^*) = 1$, and so the regulator offers the contracts at L^*, H^* on the reservation indifference curves where $ds_i/dc_i = -1$.

In the more interesting case in which the regulator does not know the firm's type, we assume she has prior probabilities π_i that the firm is of type $i = L, H$, with $\pi_H + \pi_L = 1$, and she seeks to maximize

$$\sum \pi_i[u - \lambda s_i - (1 + \lambda)c_i - \psi(\theta_i - c_i)] = u - \sum \pi_i[\lambda s_i - (1 + \lambda)c_i - \psi(\theta_i - c_i)] \quad [\text{D.46}]$$

by choice of s_L, s_H, c_L, c_H. From the general analysis of the adverse selection problem, we know that the participation constraint of the low-cost firm will not be binding at the optimum: since type L is the type with the incentive to lie if the full information contracts L^*, H^* are offered it will have to be paid a rent to induce it to reveal its type. We also know that the incentive compatibility constraint for the high cost type will not be binding. Thus the constraints on the problem are

$$s_H - \psi(\theta_H - c_H) = 0 \quad [\text{D.47}]$$

$$s_L - \psi(\theta_L - c_L) = s_H - \psi(\theta_L - c_H) \quad [\text{D.48}]$$

First-order conditions on s_L, s_H, c_L, c_H are

$$-\lambda \pi_L + \mu = 0 \quad [\text{D.49}]$$

$$-\lambda \pi_H + \gamma - \mu = 0 \quad [\text{D.50}]$$

$$-\pi_L[(1 + \lambda) - \psi'(\theta_L - c_L^*)] + \mu \psi'(\theta_L - c_L^*) = 0 \quad [\text{D.51}]$$

$$-\pi_H[(1 + \lambda) - \psi'(\theta_H - \hat{c}_H)] + \gamma \psi'(\theta_H - \hat{c}_H) - \mu \psi'(\theta_L - \hat{c}_H) = 0 \quad [\text{D.52}]$$

where μ, γ are the Lagrange multipliers on the participation and incentive compatibility constraints.

The basic nature of the results defined by the first-order conditions and the constraints is familiar from the analysis of the general problem:

1. *No distortion at the top.* The low-cost firm has the same effort and production cost levels as in the full information case. Substituting for μ from [D.49] into [D.51] and rearranging gives $\psi'(\theta_L - c_L^*) = 1$, which is the same as [D.45].

2. *The high cost firm's effort level is lower, and production cost higher, than in the full information case:* $\hat{c}_H > c_H^*$, $\hat{a} = \theta_H - \hat{c}_H < a^*$. Substituting for γ from [D.50] into [D.52] and rearranging gives

$$\psi'(\theta_H - \hat{c}_H) = 1 - \frac{\lambda}{(1+\lambda)} \frac{\pi_L}{\pi_H} [\psi'(\theta_H - \hat{c}_H) - \psi'(\theta_L - \hat{c}_H)] < 1 \qquad [\text{D.53}]$$

The final inequality in [D.53] follows from the assumptions that $\theta_H > \theta_L$ and $\psi'' > 0$, which imply

$$\psi'(\theta_H - \hat{c}_H) - \psi'(\theta_L - \hat{c}_H) > 0 \qquad [\text{D.54}]$$

so that the second part of the middle term is positive. Hence the marginal cost of effort for the high cost type is less than its marginal benefit: $\psi'(\theta_H - \hat{c}_H) < 1$.

Figure 20.17 illustrates the solution. The low-cost firm is indifferent between point $\hat{L}$, offering the first-best cost (effort) level but a positive rent, and point $\hat{H}$, which the high-cost firm receives. $\hat{H}$ lies to the right of the first-best point H^* on the high-cost-type reservation indifference curve, because it is optimal to distort the high-cost firm's cost level away from the first-best level in order to reduce the rent that has to be paid to the low-cost firm. Since the type H has a lower effort than in the first-best, it also receives a lower surplus over production cost (and again zero rent). Welfare is less than in the first-best case because type H supplies too little effort and type L receives a rent and so distortionary taxation is higher.

Figure 20.17

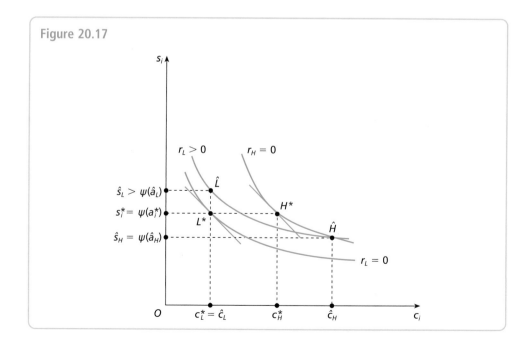

From [D.53] we see that the type H contract will have a lower marginal cost of effort and hence a lower effort level, the smaller is π_H. The optimal pair of contracts trade off the welfare loss from too low effort by type H against the cost of the rent earned by type L who supplies the first-best amount of effort. The smaller is the probability that the firm is type H, the relatively less important is the distortion in the type H contract. As π_H becomes smaller the required type H effort level becomes smaller, $\hat{H}$ shifts further round the type H reservation indifference curve and $\hat{L}$ moves vertically downwards and closer to L^*. The reader should also work through the reasons for the effects of an increase in the distortionary cost of taxation (λ) or an increase in the innate productivity of type $L(\theta_L)$.

Note finally that, if $\lambda = 0$, we see from [D.49] and [D.50] that $\mu = \gamma = 0$ and the above conditions reduce to those for the full information first best – the problem of asymmetric information disappears. If the regulator is indifferent to the size of the surplus earned by the monopolist, she could simply offer the firm a fixed payment larger than the type H cost of production plus first-best effort. Regardless of its type, the firm would then maximize its profit by minimizing costs, and thus would choose the first-best effort level.

Modelling regulation as a one-shot game is unrealistic. Monopolies produce over many periods. In the current example the government may wish to procure the building of two (identical) hospitals in succession. In a repeated regulation game different types of equilibria become possible, including equilibria where the high-cost firm may misrepresent its type and so receive a rent, as well as pooling equilibria, in which both types receive the same contract. As Laffont and Tirole (1987) show the details of the analysis are quite intricate. Here we give a general intuition for a two-round version of the procurement game set out above.

The regulator wishes to commission the production of a hospital in each of two successive periods. The low-cost firm realizes that, if it reveals its type in the first period, the regulator can force it down to its reservation indifference curve in the second and it will receive no second-period rent. This 'ratchet effect', a term first introduced in the analysis of Soviet-type central planning systems, could be avoided if the regulator is able to commit not to use the information gained in the first period in formulating the contract for the second. It can be shown that, if she can commit, she should optimally offer the second-best separating contracts just discussed in each of the two periods (see Question 8, Exercise 20D). The regulator does better by *not* using the information about the firm's type acquired in the first period. The reason is that a firm which realizes that the regulator will use the information has an incentive to lie in the first period, and so the contracts $\hat{L}$, $\hat{H}$ just derived are no longer an equilibrium of the game.

Suppose that it is not possible for a regulator to commit herself not to use information gained in the first period. Any promise not to use information gained in the first period will not be credible. Everyone knows that, when the regulator formulates contracts for the second period, she will do so on the basis of her probability beliefs about the firm's type, which will be based on information gained in the first period. The firm will therefore take this into account when choosing a contract in the first period, and hence so must the regulator when devising the first-period contracts.

Four kinds of equilibria are possible. First, suppose it does not cost the regulator very much to offer the low-cost firm a higher rent in the first period to compensate it for revealing its type and receiving a zero rent in the second. The size of the

Figure 20.18

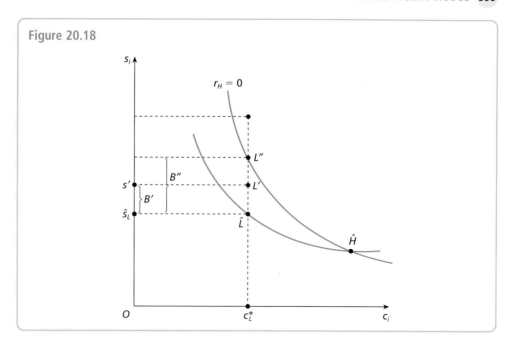

additional rent will depend in part on the firm's discount factor. If it discounts the future very heavily (or the second period is far into the future), the rent it would get in the second period from lying in the first will be heavily discounted. We would then have the equilibrium shown in Fig. 20.18. The high-cost type receives the contract $\hat{H}$ in each period. The low-cost type is indifferent between $\hat{L}$ and $\hat{H}$ if there was only one period: the amount B', which is equal to the present value of the rent he would get in the second period if he chose $\hat{H}$ in the first, ensures that he is indifferent between L' and $\hat{H}$. Thus the low-cost type produces at cost c_L^* in both periods and receives a rent of s' in each period. The high-cost firm strictly prefers $\hat{H}$ in both periods to L'. Thus there is a separating equilibrium, with the high-cost firm receiving no rent.

Next, suppose that the payment made to the low-cost firm to compensate it for no rent in the second period must be B'', putting it at L'' in Fig. 20.18. The low-cost firm is still indifferent between L'' and $\hat{H}$, but now the high-cost firm is also indifferent between the two contracts. However, given our assumption that when indifferent between contracts the firm chooses the one appropriate for its type, there is still a separating equilibrium, with the high-cost firm receiving no rent.

Now suppose that the payment to the low-cost firm has to be higher than B''. Then the high-cost firm would strictly prefer the following 'take the money and run' strategy, to telling the truth. In the first period, it claims to be low cost, puts in high effort to achieve the low-cost firm's cost level, and receives the rent. In the second period, when it would have again to put in high effort and receive no rent, it leaves the market. To deter this strategy and to achieve separation, the regulator must also pay the high-cost firm a rent, equal to the present value of the profit it earns through this strategy, to induce truth-telling.

Finally, it may be the case that the expected value of the rents the regulator must pay to both firms to induce truth-telling is larger than the expected value of the rent she would pay if she offered a single pooling contract (s, c). This could be the case if the future rents from lying in the first period are not discounted very highly by the firm. The optimal pooling contract solves the problem

$$\max_{s, c} \Sigma \pi_i[u - \lambda s - (1 + \lambda)c - \psi(\theta_i - c)] \qquad [D.55]$$

subject to the participation constraints

$$s - \psi(\theta_i - c) \geqslant 0 \qquad i = L, H$$

Remember that, at given c, $\theta_H - c > \theta_L - c$, which implies $\psi(\theta_H - c) > \psi(\theta_L - c)$, so that to achieve a given cost level the high-cost type must expend more effort than the low-cost type. It follows that, at an s-value at which the participation constraint for the high-cost type just binds, that constraint for the low-cost type will be non-binding. The low-cost type will receive a rent, though not, this time, to induce it to reveal its type since the contract is a pooling contract. We can set $s = \psi(\theta_H - c)$ and solve the problem

$$\max_{c} \Sigma \pi_i[u - \lambda\psi(\theta_H - c) - (1 + \lambda)c - \psi(\theta_i - c)] \qquad [D.56]$$

The first-order condition can be written

$$\Sigma \pi_i\psi'(\theta_i - \bar{c}) = 1 + \lambda[1 - \psi'(\theta_H - \bar{c})] \qquad [D.57]$$

which we will show implies that the optimal cost level $\bar{c}$ lies strictly between the first-best cost levels c_L^* and c_H^*. Consider the two alternative cases where $\bar{c}$ lies outside this range.

(a) $c_H^* \leqslant \bar{c}$. Recall that $\psi'(\theta_H - c^*) = 1$ and that $\psi'' > 0$. Thus $\psi'(\theta_L - \bar{c}) < \psi'(\theta_H - \bar{c}) \leqslant 1$. Therefore the left-hand side of [D.57] is strictly less than 1. But the right-hand side of [D.57] is strictly greater than 1. Hence $c_H^* \leqslant \bar{c}$ cannot be true.

(b) $c_L^* \geqslant \bar{c}$. This implies $1 \leqslant \psi'(\theta_L - \bar{c}) < \psi'(\theta_H - \bar{c})$ so that the left-hand side of [D.57] is strictly greater than 1. But the right-hand side of [D.57] is strictly greater than 1. Hence $c_L^* \geqslant \bar{c}$ cannot be true.

The result that the optimal pooling contract has $c_H^* < \bar{c} < c_H^*$ is intuitive: to set the uniform cost level below c_L^* would require a high effort level from the high-cost firm, and, given the convexity of the effort cost function, a high transfer s. The closer $\bar{c}$ is to c_H^*, the lower the effort cost of the high-cost firm and the smaller the transfer. However, setting $\bar{c}$ above c_H^*, although it involves low effort cost levels, is also costly since these high costs have to be covered by taxpayers. Thus $c_L^* < \bar{c} < c_H^*$.

We have already seen that in this pooling equilibrium the high-cost type will receive no rent while the low-cost type does receive a rent. Since the cost level for the high-cost type is lower than in the first-best, its effort level will be higher, while the converse is true for the low-cost type.

Even in this very simple model of the regulatory problem, extension to two periods produces a diversity of possible equilibria, resulting from the fact that firms recognize the effect of their choices in the first period on the contracts they will be offered in the second.

EXERCISE 20D

1. Confirm and explain the single crossing condition in [D.13].

2. Confirm that, if and only if A is risk neutral, his (x, y) indifference curves are parallel along vertical lines (vertical displacements of each other). Show that if he is risk averse the slopes increase with y for given x.

3. Show that at the optimum under asymmetrical information: (i) the participation constraint of the high productivity type is non-binding; (ii) the incentive compatibility constraint on the low productivity type is non-binding; (iii) $\hat{x}_2 = x_2^*$ if the agent is risk neutral. (iv) $\hat{\lambda}_1 > \mu_2$. Interpret this result.

4. We assume that the feasibility constraints $x_i > y_i$ on the contracts could be ignored. Under what circumstances would they matter and what would be the implication for the optimal contract under asymmetric information? [*Hint*: what happens to the optimal contracts as π increases?]

5. *Many types of agent.* Repeat the analysis of the asymmetrical information case with three agent types and show that the contracts with both of the less productive types will be inefficient but that there is still 'no distortion at the top'.

6. *Regulation of monopoly.* A monopoly has the cost function $\theta_i x$ where θ_i is constant marginal and average cost and x is output. The monopolist may have either high costs (θ_1) or low costs: $\theta_2 < \theta_1$. The regulator cannot observe the monopolist's type. Consumers' gross benefit from the product is $B(x)$ and their demand for the product is determined by $B'(x) = p$ where p is its price. The regulator can control the output of the monopoly. (Having decided on a particular output she just sets the price at $p = B'(x)$.) She can also make a transfer $T \geqslant 0$ to the monopolist. The transfer must be financed by distorting taxation elsewhere in the economy and has net social cost of $kT (k > 0)$. The regulator's welfare function is $B(x_i) - \theta_i x_i - kT_i$. She believes that the probability that the monopoly is high cost is π. The monopoly's objective function is just operating profit plus the transfer and it will close down if this is negative. What is the optimal regulatory regime (x_1, T_1, x_2, T_2) and what prices will result? What is the optimal regime if transfers have no social costs ($k = 0$)?

7. Under what conditions would the regulator wish to offer contracts which ensure that the high-cost type never produces and the low-cost type has the first-best contract?

8. Show that, in the two-period regulation game, if the regulator can commit to her period 2 contracts the optimal policy is to offer the optimal one-period contracts in both periods.

General equilibrium under uncertainty and incomplete markets

A. Introduction

In Chapter 19 we considered insurance markets as a means by which individuals can make transfers of income contingent on events (for example, having or not having an accident). If there are no information asymmetries, making contracts contingent on events is equivalent to making contracts contingent on states of the world. In this chapter we extend our examination of the ways in which other markets, including the capital market, can facilitate the exchange of income across states of the world. We start in section B with idealized simple markets in state-contingent income claims, where individuals trade amounts of income payable if and only if some specified future state of the world is realized. If these markets in *Arrow securities* are competitive, and *complete* – in the sense that a market exists for income payable in each and every possible state of the world – then we can apply standard tools to establish the existence and Pareto efficiency of equilibria.

Income is valuable only because it finances the purchase of goods and services for consumption. Underlying the demand for income in a given state is the demand for goods in that state. Commodity demands in each state of the world can be derived in the usual way since the consumer has well-defined preferences and a budget constraint. Section C examines markets in *state-contingent commodities*, where goods are distinguished not only by their physical characteristics but also by the state of the world in which they will be consumed. Beer tomorrow if the weather is sunny and hot is a different commodity from beer tomorrow if it is rainy and cold.

Suppose that it is possible to contract for a unit of each good to be delivered if and only if some specified future state of the world is realised, and such contracts can be made for every possible state. It is then possible to exchange any good to be delivered in one state for any good to be delivered in another and the model is formally identical to the standard model of consumption and exchange under certainty. We have simply extended the definition of a good or commodity by adding a subscript to denote the state in which the good will be delivered.

The model provides useful building blocks for the analysis of allocation across states and over time. But real-world economies do not possess such markets and individuals do not enter into contracts at the beginning of their lives and spend the rest of their time fulfilling them. The costs of writing and enforcing contracts which specify every possible future contingency, in order to define the 'state of the world', are greater than the benefits that would be derived from such a contract.

In section D we model an economy which looks more like the real world, in that it does not require the existence of $S \times J$ markets for the exchange of claims to J types of commodities in S states. In the economy, S markets for future state-contingent income claims are held at the present moment. Then when one of the S states of the world is realized the contracts are carried out and the individuals trade on N spot markets for goods. With only one further assumption, the equilibrium of such an economy with S state-contingent income markets plus J spot markets is equivalent to the equilibrium of an economy with a complete set of $S \times J$ markets in state-contingent commodities. But the required assumption is a very strong one: all economic agents must be able to predict correctly the prices that will be established at each possible equilibrium of the system of spot markets that will be held. If this assumption of *rational expectations* is not fulfilled, then the economy may not be Pareto efficient. Thus we have a further source of market failure, in addition to those considered in Chapter 13.

Markets in Arrow securities do not exist, and so we investigate whether other markets in state-contingent income claims, namely insurance and capital markets, provide the equivalent set of exchange possibilities. We saw in Chapter 19 that the existence of moral hazard and adverse selection may place severe restrictions on the set of exchange possibilities on insurance markets. In section E we show that, if there are fewer capital market assets with linearly independent vectors of returns than there are states of the world, then this market will also not in general provide a complete set of exchange possibilities. Hence an intertemporal economy with uncertainty does not satisfy the conditions for the First Theorem of Welfare Economics and may be Pareto inefficient. We can add asymmetrical information and an insufficiency of asset return vectors to the list of reasons for market failure. But comparison of the allocations which are achievable in such a world with those which can be achieved when there are no restrictions on transfers of state-contingent income claims may not be sensible. Hence in sections E and F we examine the welfare properties of the market equilibria using the benchmark of *constrained Pareto efficiency*.

Finally, in section F, we consider an important problem which arises when there is an incomplete set of markets in state-contingent income claims: what is the objective function of the shareholder-owned firm? As we saw in Chapter 11, under certainty when there are perfect capital markets, the manager of a firm acts in the best interests of its shareholders by maximizing the firm's market value using the market interest rate to discount future returns. When the capital market is perfect, maximization of the net present value of the firm's income stream maximizes the wealth of the shareholders. Even if they have different preferences over intertemporal consumption they will all prefer a larger wealth to a smaller. All shareholders apply the market interest rate in valuing their future income streams. Thus there is a well-defined, observable price at which the manager can evaluate future income streams on their behalf. But if the capital market is imperfect, for example because the borrowing rate differs from the lending rate, some owners will discount future income at the lending rate and others at the borrowing rate. There is now no longer a single price at which every shareholder discounts future income. The issue of what objectives the firm should pursue in the interest of its owners is even more acute in the case of uncertainty. If the capital market provides a complete set of exchange possibilities for state-contingent incomes, then prices can be defined at which a manager can evaluate future uncertain income streams on behalf of shareholders – the separation result holds. On the other hand, if the capital market is incomplete, this is no longer the case. Thus there is a problem, not yet satisfactorily resolved, in defining the objectives of the modern corporation under uncertainty.

B. Complete markets in state-contingent income claims

The insurance contract examined in Chapter 19 is a means by which the individual can transfer income from one state to another. The premium implicitly defined the prices of claims to income contingent on the accident and no accident states of the world. The risk-averse individual was able to contract with a risk-neutral party (the insurance company) and shed some of the risk. Here we first consider the exchange of risks between a pair of risk-averse individuals and consider on what terms they will make contracts for the exchange of income contingent on the state of the world. We then examine markets in state-contingent income claims and show that, if the set of such markets is *complete*, in a sense to be defined, the allocation of risks is Pareto efficient.

Contracts in state-contingent income claims

There are two individuals with $\hat{y}_{is}$ being the initial endowment of individual $i = a, b$ in state $s = 1, 2$ and y_{is} the amount of income actually consumed in state s by individual i. The individuals have expected utility functions

$$Ev_{is}(y_{is}) = \pi_{i1}v_{i1}(y_{i1}) + \pi_{i2}v_{i2}(y_{i2}) \tag{B.1}$$

where the individuals may have different probability beliefs and utility functions as well as different endowments. We also allow for the possibility that the utility of a given income depends on the state of the world in which it is received. Both individuals are risk averse and have indifference curves in state-contingent income space which are convex to the origin. Because this is a pure exchange economy the total amount of income available to the two individuals in each state of the world is fixed and is equal to the sum of their initial endowments in each state:

$$\sum_i \hat{y}_{is} = \hat{y}_s \tag{B.2}$$

We assume that the individuals can make contracts in state-contingent income claims, under which one individual promises to give the other a specified amount of income if and only if state 1 occurs, in exchange for the other individual promising to give her a specified amount of income if and only if state 2 occurs. Such contracts transfer income across states of the world for each individual, although, since this is a pure exchange economy, the total amount of income in the economy in each state is not altered. We are interested in the set of equilibrium contracts for such an economy.

Since the marginal utility of income is positive an equilibrium contract cannot waste income in any state and must satisfy

$$\sum_i y_{is} = \sum_i \hat{y}_{is} = \hat{y}_s \tag{B.3}$$

Figure 21.1 depicts the economy as an Edgeworth box. The horizontal side of the box measures the total initial endowment of income of the two individuals in state $1 : \hat{y}_1$. The vertical side measures the total endowment of the economy in state $2 : \hat{y}_2$. The origin for individual a is O_a in the south-west corner of the box and the north-east corner O_b is the origin for individual b. Individual a's state 1 income is measured rightward from the origin O_a and her state 2 income vertically upward from O_a.

Figure 21.1

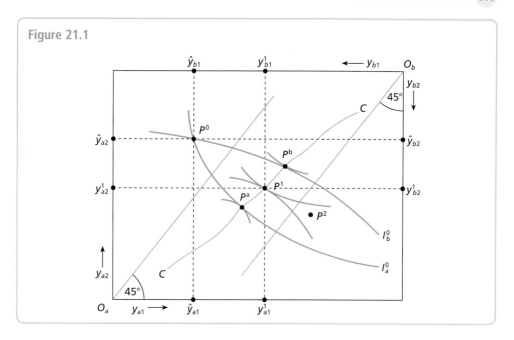

Individual b's state 1 income is measured leftwards from his origin O_b and his state 2 income vertically downward from O_b. A point in the box gives the amounts of income for each individual in the two states. For example the point P^0 shows the initial endowments. Since P^0 does not lie on either of the 45° lines from the two origins both individuals have *individual risk* in that their individual incomes vary across the states of the world.

The Edgeworth box has unequal sides and so the economy exhibits *social risk*: the total income of the economy differs in the two states. In Fig. 21.1 the total income of the economy is larger in state 1 than in state 2 since the box has horizontal sides which are longer than the vertical sides. Social risk is often referred to as *non-diversifiable risk* since there exists no set of contracts which can result in both of the individuals having a certain income. If there is social risk at least one of the individuals must face private or individual risk, but it is possible for there to be individual risk with no social risk.

A contract under which the individuals exchange promises or state-contingent income claims will move them from the endowment point P^0 in the box to some other point such as P^1. In this contract, a promises to give b $\hat{y}_{a2} - y_{a2}^1$ units of income if state 2 occurs and b promises to give a $\hat{y}_{b1} - y_{b1}^1 = y_{a1}^1 - \hat{y}_{a1}$ if state 1 occurs.

The equilibrium contracts will be in the *core*, which in this simple two-person economy is the set of contracts which satisfy the requirements that (a) both individuals are at least as well off with the contract as they would be without the contract and (b) there is no other contract which makes one party better off and the other party no worse off. Requirement (b) means that an equilibrium contract must be a point of tangency of the indifference curves of the two individuals such as P^1. Points such as P^2 which are not on the curve CC where the indifference curves are tangent are not equilibria since by moving to the curve (for example to P^1) both individuals can be made better off. The requirement (a) that both individuals are made no worse off by the contract means that the equilibrium contract will be on the segment P^aP^b of CC. The P^aP^b segment is the *contract curve* for the economy with the initial endowment P^0.

Efficient allocation of risk

There are no public goods, no utility interdependencies to create externalities and no restrictions on contracting. In these circumstances the contract the two individuals make will be Pareto efficient: there will be no other feasible allocation which can make one better off without making the other worse off. The set of Pareto efficient allocations is thus of added interest because it will include the allocation achieved by the equilibrium contract made by the two individuals.

To characterize the set of efficient allocations of state-contingent incomes we examine the conditions necessary to maximize a simple welfare function which is a weighted sum of the expected utilities of the two individuals:

$$W = Ev_{as} + \lambda Ev_{bs} \qquad \text{[B.4]}$$

where λ is a positive constant reflecting judgements about the worth of the two individuals. The optimal allocation solves the problem

$$\max_{y_{is}} Ev_{as}(y_{as}) + \lambda Ev_{bs}(y_{bs}) \quad \text{s.t.} \quad \hat{y}_s - \sum_i y_{is} \geq 0 \qquad \text{all } s$$

$$y_{is} \geq 0 \qquad \text{all } i, s \qquad \text{[B.5]}$$

The optimal allocation maximizes W subject to constraints on the availability of income in each state [B.3] and the non-negativity constraints. Since $\lambda > 0$ the optimal allocation is also a Pareto efficient allocation of risk and specifying λ is equivalent to choosing a point on the expected utility possibility frontier generated by maximizing Ev_{as} subject to b receiving some minimum level of Ev_{bs} and to the resource constraints. The particular combination of expected utilities generated by the contract written by the individuals will be on the segment of the expected utility possibility frontier which gives each individual at least as great an expected utility as they have at their endowment allocation P^0. The contract chosen by the individuals will also be the solution to the optimal allocation problem for a suitable choice of λ.

The Lagrangean for the problem [B.5] is

$$Ev_{as}(y_{as}) + \lambda Ev_{bs}(y_{bs}) + \sum_s \delta_s \left[\hat{y}_s - \sum_i y_{is} \right] \qquad \text{[B.6]}$$

and, assuming for simplicity that the non-negativity constraints do not bind, the efficient allocation is characterized by first-order conditions on the state-contingent incomes of the form:

$$\pi_{as} v'_{as}(y_{as}) - \delta_s = 0 \qquad \text{all } s$$
$$\lambda \pi_{bs} v'_{bs}(y_{bs}) - \delta_s = 0 \qquad \text{all } s$$

which can be rearranged to give

$$\pi_{as} v'_{as}(y_{as}) = \lambda \pi_{bs} v'_{bs}(y_{bs}) \qquad \text{all } s \qquad \text{[B.7]}$$

From Fig. 21.1 the efficient allocation of risk must be on the curve CC defined by the tangency of the individuals' indifference curves. Dividing the [B.7] condition for state 1 by the [B.7] condition for state 2 gives

$$\frac{\pi_{a1}v_{a1}'(y_{a1})}{\pi_{a2}v_{a2}'(y_{a2})} = \frac{\pi_{b1}v_{b1}'(y_{b1})}{\pi_{b2}v_{b2}'(y_{b2})} \qquad [B.8]$$

where the two sides are the negatives of the slopes of the indifference curves.

The efficient allocation of risk depends on the individuals' preferences, their probability beliefs and their endowments. In terms of Fig. 21.1, preferences and probability beliefs determine the shapes of the indifference curves and the endowments determine the dimensions of the Edgeworth box. Efficiency requires that the individuals have the same marginal rates of substitution between state-contingent incomes.

The optimal income of i in state s is

$$y_{is}^\star = y_{is}^\star(\hat{y}_s, \pi, \lambda) \qquad [B.9]$$

where π is a vector of the individuals' probability beliefs. Note that i's optimal income in any state s does not depend on the total endowment in any other state t. Only the total income in state s influences the optimal income of the individuals in that state. Suppose instead that $y_{is}^\star$ did depend on the total income in some other state t. Differentiate [B.7] with respect to $\hat{y}_t$ to get

$$\pi_{as}v_{as}''\partial y_{as}^\star/\partial\hat{y}_t = -\lambda\pi_{bs}v_{bs}''\partial y_{as}^\star/\partial\hat{y}_t \qquad [B.10]$$

since $y_{bs}^\star = \hat{y}_s - y_{as}^\star$. Rearranging [B.10] we have

$$[\pi_{as}v_{as}'' + \lambda\pi_{bs}v_{bs}'']\partial y_{as}^\star/\partial\hat{y}_t = 0 \qquad [B.11]$$

But the sum of the terms in the square brackets is negative since the individuals are risk averse and so $\partial y_{as}^\star/\partial\hat{y}_t$ must be zero if [B.11] is to be satisfied. The allocations in each state depend only on the total income in that state because the expected utility functions are separable in the state-contingent incomes. Separability also implies that both individuals will receive a larger allocation if the total income available in a state increases. Further consequences of separability are that $y_{as}^\star$ is decreasing in λ and increasing in π_{as}. We leave demonstration of these results to the exercises and examine the efficient risk allocation in a number of special cases.

Identical probability beliefs

If $\pi_{as} = \pi_{bs}$ for all states it is apparent from [B.7] that the efficient allocation does not depend on the probabilities assigned to the states. In a pure exchange economy the total income in each state ($\hat{y}_s$) is fixed. The only concern is with distributing the fixed $\hat{y}_s$ between the individuals before the state is known. Since the individuals agree on the probability of the state their relative valuation of additional income in a particular state depends only on their marginal utilities of income and not on their probability beliefs.

Risk neutrality

Suppose that b is risk neutral and his constant marginal utility of state s income is the same for all states (so that $v_{bs}'(y_{bs}) = k$ for all s). [B.7] or [B.8] would imply that the efficient allocation now satisfies

$$\frac{\pi_{a1}v_{a1}'(y_{a1})}{\pi_{a2}v_{a2}'(y_{a2})} = \frac{\pi_{b1}}{\pi_{b2}} \qquad [B.12]$$

Recall that risk-neutral individuals have linear indifference curves and compare Fig. 21.1 with the diagrams in Chapter 19 where we examined the insurance decision. There, the insured chose a state-contingent allocation where his indifference curve was tangent to a budget line generated by the terms on which the insurer was willing to offer insurance. The slope of the budget line was $-(1 - p)/p$ where p was the premium per £1 of cover. [B.12] shows that the allocation of risk between a risk-neutral insurer and risk-averse insured is efficient provided that the insurer offers a premium which is actuarially fair *given the probability beliefs of the insurer*: $p = \pi_{b2}$. Such a premium will not be actuarially fair from the insured's point of view if his probability beliefs differ from those of the insurer.

When probability beliefs differ or marginal utility is state dependent, efficiency with one risk-neutral individual does not require that the risk-neutral individual assumes all the risk leaving the risk-averse party with a certain income. [B.7] implies that the efficient allocation of risk will satisfy

$$v'_{as}(y_{as}) = \lambda k \pi_{bs}/\pi_{as} \qquad [B.13]$$

when b is risk neutral. If the two individuals have the same probability beliefs then

$$v'_{as}(y_{as}) = \lambda k \qquad [B.14]$$

Since the right-hand side of [B.14] does not depend on s, the efficient allocation gives the risk-averse a the same marginal utility of income in all states. If the marginal utility of income of a is state dependent, so that, for example, $v'_{a1}(y_{a1}) > v'_{a2}(y_{a2})$ when $y_{a1} = y_{a2}$, [B.14] implies that a's income should be greater in state 1 than in state 2. If a's marginal utility of income is state independent then [B.14] becomes

$$v'(y_{as}) = \lambda k \qquad [B.15]$$

and a has the same income in all states of the world – all risk has been shifted to the risk-neutral party b.

Absolute risk aversion and linear sharing rules

The optimal allocations [B.9] are *sharing rules* which determine how a given total state-contingent income is to be shared between the individuals. The sharing rules depend on the risk aversion of the individuals and in general will differ across states of the world. However, under some assumptions about preferences and probability beliefs the sharing rules are linear functions of the total income in a state:

$$y_{is} = \alpha_i + \beta_i \hat{y}_s \qquad i = a, b. \qquad [B.16]$$

where the α_i and β_i terms do not vary with the state of the world. (Show that this sharing rule must satisfy $\Sigma \alpha_i = 0$ and $\Sigma \beta_i = 1$.)

The assumptions about preferences which are necessary for the sharing rules to be of the form [B.16] are that the individuals' coefficients of absolute risk aversion are inversely related to a linear function of income:

$$-v''_i(y_{is})/v'_i(y_{is}) = (\rho_i + \tau_i y_{is})^{-1} \qquad [B.17]$$

Utility functions which exhibit this property are said to have *Hyperbolic Absolute Risk Aversion* (HARA). Equivalently, we can use the inverse of the coefficient of absolute risk aversion to define the same class of utility functions:

$$-v'_i(y_{is})/v''_i(y_{is}) = \rho_i + \tau_i y_{is} \qquad [B.18]$$

Since $-v_i'(y_{is})/v_i''(y_{is})$ is the inverse of a measure of risk aversion it is usually referred to as the *risk tolerance* of an individual and if [B.18] holds there is *Linear Risk Tolerance* (LRT). The LRT class includes a number of well-known utility functions as special cases:

Quadratic	$v_i(y_{is}) = -\rho_i^2 + 2\rho_i y_{is} - y_{is}^2$	$(\tau_i = -1)$
Exponential	$v_i(y_{is}) = -\exp(-y_{is}/\rho_i)$	$(\tau_i = 0)$
Logarithmic	$v_i(y_{is}) = \ln(\rho_i + y_{is})$	$(\tau_i = 1)$
Power	$v_i(y_{is}) = \dfrac{1}{(\tau_i - 1)}(\rho_i + \tau_i y_{is})^{(1-1/\tau_i)}$	

Exponential functions have constant absolute risk aversion (recall Question 10, Exercise 17E) so that by setting $\rho_i = 0$ in the last two cases we see that the LRT class includes all utility functions which have either constant absolute risk aversion or constant relative risk aversion. Since the quadratic is just a special case of the power function it is possible to show that all members of the LRT class must take on one of the last three forms (see Question 4).

We first show that there are linear sharing rules only if the utility functions have LRT. If the sharing rules are linear, the conditions [B.7] defining the optimal rules can be written

$$\pi_{as}v_{as}'(\alpha_a + \beta_a \hat{y}_s) = \lambda \pi_{bs}v_{bs}'(\alpha_b + \beta_b \hat{y}_s)$$
$$= \lambda \pi_{bs}v_{bs}'(-\alpha_a + (1 - \beta_a)\hat{y}_s) \qquad [\text{B.19}]$$

(remember that $\sum \alpha_i = 0$, $\sum \beta_i = 1$). Now we have already shown that the optimal y_{is}^* are not affected by the total income of any other state. This implies that the α_i and β_i do not depend on the total income in *any* state since if α_i or β_i varied with $\hat{y}_s$ the optimal $y_{it}^* = \alpha_i + \beta_i y_t$ of all other states would also vary. Hence variations in $\hat{y}_s$ do not affect the α_i and β_i and so, since [B.18] must continue to hold when $\hat{y}_s$ varies,

$$\pi_{as}v_{as}''\beta_a = \lambda \pi_{bs}v_{bs}''[1 - \beta_a] \qquad [\text{B.20}]$$

If the optimal allocations are to follow the linear sharing rules for all values of the distributional weight λ, the α_i and β_i coefficients must vary with λ in order that [B.19] continues to hold. Differentiating [B.19] with respect to λ gives

$$\pi_{as}v_{as}''[\alpha_{a\lambda} + \beta_{a\lambda}\hat{y}_s] = \pi_{bs}v_{bs}' - \lambda \pi_{bs}v_{bs}''[\alpha_{a\lambda} + \beta_{a\lambda}\hat{y}_s] \qquad [\text{B.21}]$$

where $\alpha_{a\lambda} = \partial\alpha_a/\partial\lambda$, $\beta_{a\lambda} = \partial\beta_a/\partial\lambda$ cannot both be zero. Substituting $\pi_{as}v_{as}'/\lambda$ for $\pi_{bs}v_{bs}'$ (from [B.7]), $\pi_{as}v_{as}''\beta_a/(1 - \beta_a)$ for $\lambda\pi_{bs}v_{bs}''$ (from [B.20]) in [B.21], dividing through by π_{as} and collecting terms yields

$$v_{as}''[\alpha_{a\lambda} + \beta_{a\lambda}\hat{y}_s]/(1 - \beta_a) = v_{as}'/\lambda \qquad [\text{B.22}]$$

Rearranging [B.22] and using $\hat{y}_s = (y_{as} - \alpha_a)/\beta_a$ from the linearity of the sharing rules we have

$$-\frac{v_{as}'}{v_{as}''} = -\frac{\lambda[\alpha_{a\lambda} + \beta_{a\lambda}\hat{y}_s]}{(1 - \beta_a)} = -\frac{\lambda[\alpha_{a\lambda} + \beta_{a\lambda}(y_{as} - \alpha_a)/\beta_a]}{(1 - \beta_a)}$$

$$= \frac{\lambda[\beta_{a\lambda}\alpha_a - \alpha_{a\lambda}\beta_a]}{(1 - \beta_a)\beta_a} - \frac{\lambda\beta_{a\lambda}}{(1 - \beta_a)\beta_a}y_{as} \qquad [\text{B.23}]$$

Since we have already established that α_a and β_a (and thus $\alpha_{a\lambda}$ and $\beta_{a\lambda}$) do not vary with $\hat{y}_s$ (and thus do not vary with y_{as}) we have now shown that neither the first term in [B.23] nor the coefficient on y_{as} in [B.23] vary with y_{as}. Hence, if sharing rules are linear then a must have linear risk tolerance. A similar argument shows that b must also have linear risk tolerance: use [B.7] to substitute $\lambda\pi_{bs}v'_{bs}$ for $\pi_{as}v'_{as}$ in [B.21]. Thus *LRT is necessary for linear sharing rules to be optimal.*

The *sufficiency* of LRT for linear sharing rules to be optimal is demonstrated by showing that each of the three possible types of LRT utility functions yield linear sharing rules. We will indicate how this is done for one of the LRT functions and leave the reader to complete the demonstration for the remaining types (see Question 5, Exercise 21B). If the utility functions of both individuals are power functions the optimality condition [B.7] is

$$\pi_{as}[\rho_a + \tau_a y_{as}]^{-1/\tau_a} = \lambda\pi_{bs}[\rho_b + \tau_b y_{bs}]^{-1/\tau_b}$$
$$= \lambda\pi_{bs}[\rho_b + \tau_b(\hat{y}_s - y_{as})]^{-1/\tau_b} \quad [\text{B.24}]$$

Now divide through by $\pi_{as}\tau_a$, invert both sides and raise them to the power τ_a, subtract ρ_a and divide by τ_a to get

$$y_{as} = \frac{\varphi}{\tau_a}[\rho_b + \tau_b(\hat{y}_s - y_{as})]^{\tau_a/\tau_b} - \frac{\rho_a}{\tau_a} \quad [\text{B.25}]$$

where $\varphi = (\pi_{as}/\lambda\pi_{bs})^{\tau_a}$. [B.25] defines a sharing rule like [B.16] if and only if (a) $\tau_a = \tau_b$ (so that y_{as} is linearly related to $\hat{y}_s$) and (b) $\pi_{as} = \pi_{bs}$ so that the linear relationship is the same for all states. As the reader should check if these two conditions are satisfied we can solve [B.25] for y_{as} to give the optimal state-independent linear sharing rule:

$$y_{as} = \frac{\varphi\rho_b - \rho_a}{(1 + \varphi)\tau} + \frac{\varphi}{(1 + \varphi)}\hat{y}_s \quad [\text{B.26}]$$

Notice that we had to assume not only that both individuals had LRT preferences but also that they had the same type of LRT preferences. The rule would not be linear if b had an exponential utility function and a had a power utility function. (Check this by writing down the optimality condition [B.7] in this case and showing that it is impossible to manipulate the condition to express y_{as} as a state independent linear function of $\hat{y}_s$.)

Similar reasoning can be applied for the logarithmic and the exponential functions to establish:

Pareto efficient sharing rules are linear in total income and state independent if (a) all individuals have utility functions in the same LRT class where $-v''_i/v''_i = \rho_i + \tau y_{is}$ and (b) individuals' probability beliefs are identical.

Markets in state-contingent income claims

We conclude the analysis of trade in state-contingent income claims by outlining how competitive markets in such claims would work and considering when markets in state-contingent income claims yield Pareto efficient risk bearing. There are n individuals who have endowments of state-contingent incomes $\hat{y}_{is}$, utility functions $v_{is}(y_{is})$ and probability beliefs π_{is}. Suppose that there is a complete set of contingent income claim markets where it is possible to buy or sell promises to deliver £1 conditional on the occurrence of a specified state s. Such claims are usually called Arrow securities. The price of a claim to a unit of income in state s is p_s.

The ith individual chooses a vector of state-contingent incomes $y_i = (y_{i1}, \ldots, y_{iS})$ to solve

$$\max_{y_{is}} \sum_s \pi_{is} v(y_{is}) \quad \text{s.t.} \quad \sum_s p_s(\hat{y}_{is} - y_{is}) \geq 0 \quad y_i \geq 0 \qquad \text{[B.27]}$$

The Lagrangean for the problem is

$$\sum_s \pi_{is} v_{is}(y_{is}) + \theta_i \sum_s p_s(\hat{y}_{is} - y_{is}) \qquad \text{[B.28]}$$

and with a non-corner solution the condition on y_{is} is

$$\pi_{is} v'_{is}(y_{is}) - \theta_i p_s = 0 \quad s = 1, \ldots, S \qquad \text{[B.29]}$$

Rearranging a pair of these conditions for state s and t gives

$$-\frac{\pi_{is} v'_{is}(y_{is})}{\pi_{it} v'_{it}(y_{it})} = -\frac{p_s}{p_t} \qquad \text{[B.30]}$$

This condition is very similar to the tangency condition for the consumer's consumption choice under certainty in section 13B. The left-hand side is the marginal rate of substitution between state-contingent incomes and the right-hand side is the ratio of prices to claims in states s and t. We leave it to the reader to explore the analogy further (see Question 8, Exercise 21B).

[B.30] is also very similar to the tangency condition for the choice of insurance cover examined in Chapter 19. If there are insurance markets in which it is possible to insure against the occurrence of any state it is possible to achieve the same results as explicit markets in state-contingent claims. Both types of market would enable the individual to transfer income from one state to another.

The individuals' optimization problems [B.27] yield sets of demand functions $D_{is}(p, \hat{y}_i)$ for state-contingent incomes and the aggregate demand for income in each state

$$D_s(p, \hat{y}) = \sum_i D_{is}(p, \hat{y}_i) \qquad \text{[B.31]}$$

It is possible to use the methods of Chapter 12 to show that our assumptions about preferences ensure that there exists an equilibrium in the markets for state-contingent income claims. Hence there is a price vector p^* such that demand equals supply in each market:

$$D_s(p^*, \hat{y}) = \sum_i \hat{y}_{is} = \hat{y}_s \quad s = 1, \ldots, S \qquad \text{[B.32]}$$

We will briefly examine the efficiency of markets in state-contingent claims using the methods of Chapter 13 and show that the First Theorem of Welfare Economics applies.

A Pareto efficient allocation of state-contingent incomes maximizes the expected utility of one of the individuals (say the first) subject to the other $n - 1$ individuals achieving some minimum expected utility level $\bar{v}_i$ and subject to the feasibility constraints $\sum_i y_{is} \leq \sum_i \hat{y}_{is} = \hat{y}_s$ and $y_{is} \geq 0$. The Lagrangean for the problem is

$$\sum_s \pi_{1s} v_{1s}(y_{1s}) + \sum_{i=2}^n \lambda_i \left[\sum_s \pi_{is} v_{is}(y_{is}) - \bar{v}_i \right] + \sum_s \delta_s \left[\hat{y}_s - \sum_i y_{is} \right] \qquad [\text{B.33}]$$

In a non-corner solution, typical conditions on the state-contingent incomes of individual 1 and the ith individual are

$$\pi_{1s} v'_{1s}(y_{1s}) - \delta_s = 0 \qquad [\text{B.34}]$$

$$\lambda_i \pi_{is} v'_{is}(y_{is}) - \delta_s = 0 \qquad [\text{B.35}]$$

Rearranging gives

$$\pi_{1s} v'_{1s}(y_{1s}) = \lambda_i \pi_{is} v'_{is}(y_{is}) \qquad [\text{B.36}]$$

The conditions are very similar to those derived earlier in this section when we were examining the optimal allocation with a pair of individuals. This is to be expected since if an allocation maximizes the weighted sum of the individual's expected utilities it must be Pareto efficient. The main difference between the current set of efficiency conditions and the optimality conditions derived earlier is that in the optimality problem λ was a fixed positive constant whereas in the efficiency problem the λ_i are variable Lagrangean multipliers. It is apparent from the similarity between the two-person optimality problem and the n-person efficiency problem that our earlier discussion of the form of the optimal sharing rules applies to efficient sharing rules in the n person case.

We can quickly establish that, if there is a complete set of competitive state-contingent income claim markets in the sense that there is a market for income in each state, then the equilibrium of the markets is Pareto efficient. Since all individuals face the same price vector for state-contingent claims, they all choose vectors of claims which satisfy [B.29]. Hence taking [B.29] for individual 1 and some other individual i and rearranging gives

$$\pi_{1s} v'_{1s}(y_{1s}) = (\theta_1/\theta_i) \pi_{is} v'_{is}(y_{is}) \qquad [\text{B.37}]$$

so that the market equilibrium satisfies [B.36] for some set of $\bar{v}_i$ such that $\lambda_i = \theta_1/\theta_i$. Alternatively, we could use the efficiency conditions for a pair of states to show that efficiency requires that all individuals have equal marginal rates of substitution between incomes in those states (see [B.8]). Since all individuals face the same prices [B.30] implies that they must all have the same marginal rates of substitution and thus the market equilibrium is efficient.

The fact that the equilibrium of a complete set of markets for state-contingent income claims is Pareto efficient is not suprising. It is merely an application of the First Theorem of Welfare Economics. The interesting issue is whether there are in reality complete markets in which trade in state-contingent incomes can take place. There are few explicit examples of such markets but transactions in other types of market may lead to state-contingent income transfers and so be equivalent to state-contingent claim markets. Two possibilities are insurance markets and stock markets.

In Chapter 19 we examined insurance contracts in a simple two-state example and showed how they could be viewed as devices for transferring income between states and how the premium could be used to define prices for state-contingent income transfers. Insurance markets are, however, not equivalent to a full set of state-contingent income claim markets because in many instances insurers cannot verify that particular states of the world have occurred. As a result, most insurance contracts make *outcome*-contingent transfers of income, where the outcome depends on actions of the insured as well as the state of the world. For example, a house contents insurance policy will provide for payments to the insured if water pipes burst, not if there is sub-zero temperature. The outcome of burst pipes depends both on the state (temperature) and on the action of the insured (the amount of lagging put on her pipes). Outcome-contingent insurance may alter actions (reduce the amount of lagging) as well as transferring income across states. We investigated such potential *moral hazard* problems in Chapter 19.

EXERCISE 21B

1. Will the contract curve always lie between the individuals' 45° lines?

2. *Contract curve and linear risk tolerance.*

   (a) Show that the contract curve will be a straight line if both individuals have identical probability beliefs and the same type of linear risk tolerance.

   (b) What is the shape of the contract curve if both individuals have (i) constant absolute risk aversion, (ii) constant and equal relative risk aversion.

   (c) What is its shape if one of them is risk neutral and the other has LRT preferences?

3. What is the effect on a's optimal share in state s of (a) an increase in the distributional weight λ on b's expected utility in the welfare function, (b) an increase in the probability a assigns to state s?

4. Show that the exponential, logarithmic and power functions are the only types of utility function which have LRT or HARA. (*Hint*: use the fact that $-v_{is}''/v_{is}' = d \ln v_{is}'/dy_{is}$ and integrate [B.17] to get

   $$\log v_{is}' = K + (-1/\tau_i)[\log(\rho_i + \tau_i y_{is})] = K + \log(\rho_i + \tau_i y_{is})^{-1/\tau_i}$$

   where K is the constant of integration.)

5. *Linear sharing rules: exponential and logarithmic utility.* Show that (a) if both individuals have exponential utility functions the sharing rule is

   $$y_{as}^* = \frac{1}{(\omega_a + \omega_b)} \log\left[\frac{\omega_a}{\hat{\lambda}\omega_b}\right] + \frac{\omega_b}{(\omega_a + \omega_b)}\hat{y}_s$$

   (b) if both individuals have logarithmic utility functions the sharing rule is

   $$y_{as}^* = \frac{1}{(1+\hat{\lambda})}[\rho_b - \hat{\lambda}\rho_a] + \frac{1}{(1+\hat{\lambda})}\hat{y}_s$$

   where $\hat{\lambda} = \lambda\pi_{bs}/\pi_{as}$ and in (a) $\omega_i = 1/\rho_i$ is the ith individual's constant coefficient of absolute risk aversion. Hence conclude that if they also have identical probability beliefs the sharing rules are linear and state independent.

6. *Increases in risk aversion and optimal shares.* Suppose that both individuals have exponential utility functions and thus constant absolute risk aversion. Show that an increase in a's coefficient of risk aversion will increase a's share if and only if a's coefficient of *relative* risk aversion is less than one. What is the rationale for the result? (*Hint*: what happens to a's marginal utility if the coefficient of absolute risk aversion increases?)

7. *Paternalism and probabilities.* The Pareto efficiency and optimality criteria rest on a number of value judgements including non-paternalism: individuals are the best judges of their own

welfare. If individuals are expected utility maximizers, both their utility functions and their probability beliefs must be respected.

(a) Is the value judgement less reasonable for probabilities than for utility functions?

(b) Suppose that in the two-person optimality problem both individuals had the same but mistaken probability beliefs and that the planner knows the true state probabilities. How would the optimal allocation differ if the planner used the correct probability beliefs to calculate the expected utilities rather than respecting the mistaken beliefs of the two individuals?

(c) How would it differ if only one of them had mistaken beliefs?

8. Assuming that there are competitive state-contingent income claim markets for the only two states, illustrate the individual's choice of state-contingent income claims. What is the effect of increases in (a) p_1 and (b) his endowment in state 1. (c) Why is it impossible for an expected utility maximizer to have a positively sloped demand curve for income in any state? (*Hint*: her preferences are additively separable in y_{is}.)

9. *Non-verifiable states*. Consider the two-person, two-state economy described at the beginning of this section and suppose that one of the individuals cannot observe which state has occurred. Use an Edgeworth box to illustrate your answers to the following questions. (a) What does this imply about her endowments and utility function? (b) What would happen if she wrote a state-contingent contract with the other individual? (c) What allocations would be in the core of the economy?

10. *Public and private value of information*. Continuing with the model in Question 8, suppose that, before the state of the world is revealed and before the market in state-contingent income claims opens, one of the individuals is given a perfect forecasting device which will tell her what the state of the world will be.

(a) What effect will this have on her transactions in the state-contingent income markets and thus on her income in each state? (Assume her transactions are small relative to the market and so do not alter the price of state-contingent income claims.)

(b) What effect will it have on her expected utility?

(c) How much would she be willing to pay to acquire such a device?

(d) What would be the effect if the forecasts of the device were made public before the markets open?

(e) What is the social value of such a device?

C. State-contingent commodities

In the previous section we analysed exchange under uncertainty in economies in which there was only one good (income) in each state of the world. We now examine exchange economies in which there are many (J) commodities. We start by considering a rather artificial economy in which there is a complete set of $S \times J$ state-contingent commodity markets. *Ex ante* and *ex post* efficiency are then defined. Where there is a single state-contingent composite commodity (income) the distinction between the two concepts of efficiency has little relevance. However, if there is more than one good, as in this section, the distinction is useful. We show that a complete set of state-contingent commodity markets is both *ex ante* and *ex post* efficient. We then consider what happens if there are only J spot commodity markets and S markets in contingent income claims and show that such an economy is *ex post* efficient, but is *ex ante* efficient only under the strong conditions that consumers correctly forecast the prices of all commodities in each state of the world.

Complete state-contingent commodity markets

Assume for the moment that it is possible to make contracts under which, *before* the state of the world is known, the seller will deliver to the buyer one unit of good j if and only if state s occurs. In return the buyer pays the seller the price p_{sj}^c before the state is known. Markets in state-contingent commodities differ from both spot and futures markets for commodities. In a spot market the seller contracts *after* the state of the world is known to deliver immediately one unit of a commodity j to the buyer. The price of one unit of commodity j is p_{sj}, which is the amount of money paid by the buyer in state s in exchange for one unit of commodity j. At the time the contract is made there is no uncertainty because the state of the world is known. The spot price of commodity j may differ in different states because of the effect of the state on the demands for the commodity. In a futures market the seller contracts *before* the state of the world is known to deliver one unit of commodity j to the buyer at some future date when the state of the world will have been revealed. In exchange for this promise the buyer pays the seller p_{fj} which is the futures price of commodity j. Although the contract is made before the state is known it is not state contingent because the commodity is to be delivered whatever state of the world is realized.

If there are S state-contingent markets for good j it would be possible to mimic a futures contract which delivers one unit of commodity j in all states by S separate contracts which each deliver one unit of j if and only if the specified state s occurs. The artificial futures contract would have a price of $p_{fj} = \Sigma_s p_{sj}^c$. Notice, however, that it is impossible to mimic the S separate state-contingent contracts for j by the single futures contract for j.

Let $x_{is} = (x_{is1}, \ldots, x_{isJ})$ be the vector of J commodities which individual i consumes in state $s = 1, \ldots, S$. x_{is} is similar to the consumption vectors of Chapters 2 to 4. The individual's vector of initial endowments of commodities in state s is $\hat{x}_{is} = (\hat{x}_{is1}, \ldots, \hat{x}_{isJ})$. The preferences of the ith individual are represented by the expected utility from the x_{is} vectors

$$V_i = Eu_{is}(x_{is}) = \Sigma_s \pi_{is} u_{is}(x_{is1}, \ldots, x_{isJ}) \qquad [C.1]$$

An axiom system for this representation could be constructed along the lines of Chapter 17 by substituting the commodity vectors x_{is} for the incomes y_{is}. No formal change in the axioms is required, provided the properties of the preference ordering over consumption vectors which are certain are first specified. (Thus, recall that in Chapter 17 we assumed that more income was preferred to less. When we replace the scalar income by a commodity vector the assumption has to be replaced by that of a complete transitive preference ordering over commodity vectors, with more of any commodity being preferred to less.) We assume that the utility functions u_{is} in [C.1] are differentiable, strictly quasi-concave, increasing in all their arguments and unique up to a positive linear transformation.

We assume that the markets in state-contingent commodity contracts are competitive and that there are $S \times J$ such markets. Thus it is possible to contract before the state is known for the delivery of any commodity conditional on the occurrence of any state. The ith individual chooses state-contingent consumption vectors, before the state is known, to maximize [C.1] subject to the budget constraint

$$\Sigma_s \Sigma_j p_{sj}^c (\hat{x}_{isj} - x_{isj}) \geqslant 0 \qquad [C.2]$$

Forming the Lagrangean

$$\sum_s \pi_{is} u_{is}(x_{is1}, \ldots, x_{isJ}) + \theta_i \sum_s \sum_j p^c_{sj}(\hat{x}_{isj} - x_{isj}) \qquad [C.3]$$

we derive the first-order conditions for a non-corner solution:

$$\pi_{is} u_{isj}(x_{is}) - \theta_i p^c_{sj} = 0 \qquad j = 1, \ldots, J, \qquad s = 1, \ldots, S \qquad [C.4]$$

where $u_{isj} = \partial u_{is}(x_{is})/\partial x_{isj}$ is the marginal utility from good j in state s.

Rearranging suitable pairs of conditions [C.4] we get the tangency conditions between goods within a given state

$$\frac{u_{isj}}{u_{isk}} = \frac{p^c_{sj}}{p^c_{sk}} \qquad [C.5]$$

and between states for a given good

$$\frac{\pi_{is} u_{isj}}{\pi_{it} u_{itj}} = \frac{p^c_{sj}}{p^c_{tj}} \qquad [C.6]$$

Note that the within-state conditions [C.5] do not depend on probability beliefs, whereas the between-state conditions [C.6] do.

The individuals' optimization problems yield their demand functions $D_{isj}(p, \hat{x}_i)$ which have all the properties of the demand functions derived in Chapter 2. We could easily apply the techniques of Chapter 12 to show that the equilibrium of the set of state-contingent markets exists. Provided that the $S \times J$ state-contingent commodity markets are competitive and there are no externalities or public goods we can use the methods of Chapter 13 to show that the equilibrium of this set of markets is Pareto efficient.

Ex ante and *ex post* Pareto efficiency

To develop the conditions for *ex ante* Pareto efficiency we formulate a welfare problem in which the state-contingent consumption vectors x_{is} are chosen *before* the state of the world is known. The aim is to maximize a welfare function which is a weighted sum of the *expected* utilities of the individuals: $\sum_i \lambda_i V_i$. The constraints on the problem are that total consumption of good j in state s cannot exceed the total endowment:

$$\hat{x}_{sj} = \sum_i \hat{x}_{isj} \geqslant \sum_i x_{isj} = x_{sj} \qquad [C.7]$$

Since the welfare weights λ_i are all positive any allocation which is optimal (i.e. maximizes $\sum_i \lambda_i V_i$) must also be Pareto efficient. The Lagrangean is

$$\sum_i \lambda_i \sum_s \pi_{is} u_{is}(x_{is}) + \sum_s \sum_j \beta_{sj}[\hat{x}_{sj} - x_{sj}] \qquad [C.8]$$

and rearranging the first-order conditions on the x_{isj}

$$\lambda_i \pi_{is} u_{isj}(x_{is}) - \beta_{sj} = 0 \qquad \text{all } i, s, j \qquad [C.9]$$

gives the condition for *within-state efficiency*

$$\frac{u_{isj}}{u_{isk}} = \frac{u_{\ell sj}}{u_{\ell sk}} \qquad \text{all } i \neq \ell, \qquad j \neq k, \qquad \text{all } s \qquad [C.10]$$

and *between-state efficiency*

$$\frac{\pi_{is}u_{isj}}{\pi_{it}u_{itj}} = \frac{\pi_{\ell s}u_{\ell sj}}{\pi_{\ell t}u_{\ell tj}} \qquad \text{all } i \neq \ell \qquad s \neq t \qquad \text{all } j \qquad \text{[C.11]}$$

Ex ante Pareto efficiency requires that all individuals have the same marginal rate of substitution between all pairs of goods given that state s has occurred [C.10] and the same marginal rate of substitution between states [C.11]. An allocation which satisfies [C.10] and [C.11] is *ex ante efficient*. Note that individuals' probability beliefs are only relevant for between-state efficiency.

Suppose that the planner had waited until the state of the world was known before deciding on the consumption vectors the individuals should receive in that state. The *ex post* welfare problem would be to maximize a weighted sum of utilities in that state s ($\sum_i \lambda_i u_{is}$) subject to the resource constraints $\hat{x}_{sj} \geq x_{sj}$ ($j = 1, \ldots, J$) in state s. The Lagrangean for the *ex post* welfare problem in state s is

$$\sum_i \lambda_i u_{is}(x_{is}) + \sum_j \beta_j^0 [\hat{x}_{sj} - x_{sj}] \qquad \text{[C.12]}$$

The first order *ex post* efficiency conditions are

$$\lambda_i u_{isj}(x_{is}) - \beta_j^0 = 0 \qquad \text{all } i, j \qquad \text{[C.13]}$$

which can be rearranged to yield the same kind of within state tangency conditions as [C.10].

An allocation which is *ex ante* efficient must also be *ex post* efficient in all states. If it was not *ex post* efficient in some state s it would be possible to reallocate the consumption vectors in state s so as to increase the utility u_{is} of some individual i in that state without reducing the utility of any other individual in that state. With the allocations (and therefore the utilities) in the other states unchanged the expected utility of i would have been increased by the state s reallocation and no other individual would have any change in their expected utility.

However, *ex post* efficiency does not imply *ex ante* efficiency. It is clearly possible that consumers' marginal rates of substitution between all pairs of goods are equalized within each state, but that the marginal rate of substitution between a good in one state and a good in another, for one consumer, may be unequal to the corresponding marginal rate of substitution for another consumer. The fact that consumers cannot find Pareto-improving trades of goods within a state does not imply that they cannot find Pareto-improving trades of goods between states. For example, suppose that, in state 1, consumer 1 has a very low income and consumer 2 a very high income, and conversely in state 2. Suppose that their marginal rates of substitution between all pairs of goods are equalized within states. However, goods will tend to have high marginal utilities in state 1 for consumer 1, and low marginal utilities in state 2, and conversely for consumer 2. Both consumers could then be made better off *ex ante* if consumer 1 promises to give consumer 2 some quantities of goods in the event state 2 occurs, in exchange for some quantities of goods in the event state 1 occurs.

We leave to the reader the demonstration that the equilibrium of a full set of competitive contingent commodity claim markets is *ex ante* Pareto efficient and therefore also *ex post* efficient. Just use the fact that all individuals face the same relative prices and so are led to equate their marginal rates of substitution as required for efficiency (see [C.5], [C.6] and [C.10], [C.11]. (Or, more rigorously, apply the methods of Chapter 13.)

The requirement that there is a full set of $S \times J$ state-contingent commodity markets is very stringent (and would be even more so if we introduced time into the model). It is not satisfied in reality because of the difficulties of writing enforceable contracts contingent on all relevant states of the world, i.e. all states which affect preferences, endowments and technology. We therefore now consider whether a smaller set of markets can yield a Pareto efficient allocation.

Efficiency of incomplete state-contingent markets

Suppose that instead of $S \times J$ markets for delivery of commodities in different states there were only S markets for the delivery of state-contingent income plus J spot markets. Thus before the state of the world is known individuals can enter into contracts for the delivery of income contingent on the occurrence of a specified state. When the state of the world is revealed the state-contingent income contracts are executed and individuals then buy and sell commodities in the J spot markets. The spot prices of the commodities are likely to differ across the states of the world because of the effect of the state on utility functions, endowments and the distribution of income among the individuals resulting from their trades in state-contingent income.

To decide on their transactions in the state-contingent income markets, individuals must decide what commodity bundles they would consume in each state of the world, and thus what the marginal utility of additional income would be in the different states. To do this they must forecast what the prices of commodities will be in the different states of the world. Let p_{isj} be individual i's forecast of what the price of commodity j will be if state s occurs. Individual i believes that if state s occurs the state s budget constraint on commodity choice in state s will be

$$\sum_j p_{isj} x_{isj} \leq \sum_j p_{isj} \hat{x}_{isj} + q_{is} = \hat{y}_{is}^a + q_{is} = y_{is}^a \qquad [C.14]$$

The left-hand side of [C.14] is the cost of the consumption vector x_{is} at the prices individual i forecasts. It cannot exceed y_{is}^a, which is the total amount of income that i expects to have in state s. y_{is}^a is the sum of the value of i's commodity endowment at the forecast prices ($\sum_j p_{isj} \hat{x}_{isj} = \hat{y}_{is}^a$) and q_{is}, which is the amount of income i has contracted to receive (if $q_{is} > 0$) or deliver (if $q_{is} < 0$).

Given the anticipated budget constraint, the individual plans to choose x_{is} to maximize $u_{is}(x_{is})$ if state s occurs. (Given that state s has occurred, V_i is maximized by maximizing utility in that state.) The Lagrangean for the anticipated state s problem is

$$u_{is}(x_{is}) + \theta_{is}^a [y_{is}^a - \sum_j p_{isj} x_{isj}] \qquad [C.15]$$

and the anticipated x_{isj} satisfy

$$u_{isj}(x_{is}) - \theta_{is}^a p_{isj} = 0 \qquad j = 1, \ldots, J \qquad [C.16]$$

The anticipated demand by i for commodity j in state s is $D_{isj}(p_{is}, y_{is}^a)$ and anticipated indirect utility in state s is

$$v_{is}^a = u_{is}(D_{is}(p_{is}, y_{is}^a)) = v_{is}(p_{is}, y_{is}^a) \qquad [C.17]$$

Given the anticipated price vector p_{is} and anticipated income y_{is} the anticipated marginal utility of income in state s is

$$\partial v_{is}/\partial y_{is}^a = v_{isy}(p_{is}, y_{is}^a) = \theta_{is}^a \qquad [\text{C.18}]$$

(remember the interpretation of the Lagrangean multiplier on the budget constraint in Chapter 2).

Given the anticipated decisions on x_{is}, if state s occurs individual i's expected utility before the state of the world is revealed is

$$V_i^a = \Sigma_s \pi_{is} v_{is}^a(p_{is}, y_{is}^a) \qquad [\text{C.19}]$$

By transacting in the state-contingent income claim markets before the state of the world is known i can alter the state distribution of the y_{is}^a. The price of a unit of income delivered if and only if state s occurs is p_{ys}. The anticipated value of the individual's endowments of commodities in state s is $\hat{y}_{is}^a$ and the total anticipated purchasing power i has available to redistribute across the states is $\Sigma_s p_{ys} \hat{y}_{is}^a$. The budget constraint on the transactions in these claims is

$$\Sigma_s p_{ys}[\hat{y}_{is}^a - y_{is}^a] = \Sigma_s p_{ys} q_{is} \geqslant 0 \qquad [\text{C.20}]$$

The individual chooses the y_{is}^a (and thus the trades q_{is}) to maximize [C.19] subject to [C.20]. The Lagrangean is

$$\Sigma_s \pi_{is} v_{is}^a(p_{is}, y_{is}^a) + \theta_i \Sigma_s p_{ys}[\hat{y}_{is}^a - y_{is}^a] \qquad [\text{C.21}]$$

and the choice of y_{is}^a satisfies

$$\pi_{is} v_{isy}(p_{is}, y_{is}^a) - \theta_i p_{sy} = \pi_{is}\theta_{is}^a - \theta_i p_{sy} = 0 \qquad [\text{C.22}]$$

(remember i's anticipated marginal utility of income is θ_{is}^a, from [C.18]).

After the individual has transacted in the state-contingent income claim markets on the basis of anticipations of the commodity prices in each state (p_{is}) the state of the world is revealed. The contracts for delivery of state-contingent income are then executed and the commodity markets in state s generate the actual commodity prices p_s in state s. The individual will then face the actual state s budget constraint

$$\Sigma_j p_{sj} x_{isj} \leqslant \Sigma_j p_{sj} \hat{x}_{isj} + q_{is} = \hat{y}_{is} + q_{is} = y_{is} \qquad [\text{C.23}]$$

which is similar to [C.14] except that actual prices p_{sj} replace the anticipated prices p_{isj}. Given [C.13] the individual maximizes $u_{is}(x_{is})$. The Lagrangean is

$$u_{is}(x_{is}) + \theta_{is}[y_{is} - \Sigma_j p_{sj} x_{isj}] \qquad [\text{C.24}]$$

and the actual x_{isj} satisfy

$$u_{isj}(x_{is}) - \theta_{is} p_{sj} = 0 \qquad j = 1, \dots, J \qquad [\text{C.25}]$$

plus the budget constraint. The actual state s demands are $D_{isj}(p_s, y_{is})$ and actual state s indirect utility $u_{is}(D_{is}) = v_{is}(p_s, y_{is})$. (In Chapter 17 and section B of this chapter we implicitly assumed that the spot price vector p_s is the same in all states so that we could write the indirect utility function as depending only upon the individual's income.) The actual marginal utility of income in state s is

$$\partial v_{is}/\partial y_{is} = v_{isy}(p_s, y_{is}) = \theta_{is} \qquad [\text{C.26}]$$

The fact that there are J spot commodity markets, which open once the state of the world is revealed, means that the actual allocation generated by those markets satisfies the within-state efficiency condition [C.10] and is *ex post* efficient. [C.25] implies that, once the state of the world is revealed and individuals face the same set of actual commodity prices in state s, they will all equate their marginal rates of substitution within the state to the same commodity price ratios. The individuals' price anticipations have no bearing on the *ex post* efficiency of incomplete markets since their actual trades in commodities are determined by the actual prices which are realised once the state is revealed.

The allocation will be *ex ante* efficient as well as *ex post* efficient if and only if the between-state efficiency condition [C.11] is satisfied. Suppose that *all individuals have correct price expectations*: $p_{is} = p_s$ for all s and i. Then their anticipated and actual state s incomes are equal ($y_{is}^a = y_{is}$) and so are their anticipated and actual demands ($D_{is}(p_{is}, y_{is}^a) = D_{is}(p_s, y_{is})$). Hence, their anticipated and actual marginal utilities of income in state s are also equal:

$$u_{isj}(D_{is}(p_{is}, y_{is}^a))/p_{isj} = \theta_{is}^a = \theta_{is} = u_{isj}(D_{is}(p_s, y_{is}))/p_{sj} \qquad \text{[C.27]}$$

(from [C.16], [C.17] and [C.25], [C.26]). Using [C.27] to substitute for θ_{is}^a in [C.22] gives

$$\pi_{is} u_{isj} = \theta_i p_{sy} p_{sj} \qquad \text{[C.28]}$$

and so the marginal rate of substitution across states is

$$-\frac{\pi_{is} u_{isj}}{\pi_{it} u_{itj}} = -\frac{p_{sy} p_{sj}}{p_{ty} p_{tj}} \qquad \text{[C.29]}$$

Since the right-hand side of [C.29] does not vary with i, all the individuals must have the same marginal rate of substitution across states and both conditions for *ex ante* efficiency are satisfied.

When the individuals correctly anticipate the price p_{sj} of commodity j in state s we can interpret $p_{sy} p_{sj}$ as a compound contingent commodity price. The individual can mimic the workings of a complete set of state-contingent commodity prices by transacting in the contingent income market and correctly anticipating the spot commodity prices in state s. Each individual believes correctly that an increase in consumption of good j in state s by one unit can be achieved by entering into a contract on the state s contingent income market to deliver an extra p_{sj} units of income in state s. Such a contract will cost $p_{sy} p_{sj}$.

When there are no markets in state-contingent income claims the individuals maximize their utility by trading in the spot commodity markets once the state of the world is known. Provided there are no externalities or public goods and that there are spot markets for all the commodities the resulting allocation will be *ex post* efficient. The conclusion is unaffected by whether the individuals have correct probability beliefs and whether they can make correct price forecasts of the spot prices, because they can make no decisions before the state of the world is revealed. Because each has separate budget constraints in each of the S states, the individuals' marginal rates of substitution of income between any pair of states may differ. There are therefore potential gains from being able to trade income across states to equalize marginal rates of substitution of incomes. However, even if there are markets in state-contingent income claims, so that marginal rates of substitution of incomes are equalized, this does not imply that the equilibrium will be *ex ante* efficient. The *ex ante* efficiency conditions involve the marginal rates of substitution of commodities, not incomes, across states. Only if the individuals have correct price expectations will the existence of state-contingent income claim markets lead to *ex ante* efficient commodity allocations.

Valuation of price changes under uncertainty

We have just considered the consumption decisions of individuals under uncertainty. If there are no markets in state-contingent commodities the consumer takes her consumption decisions after the state of the world is revealed. Given her direct utility function $u_s(x_s)$, the commodity price vector p_s and her income y_s, we can model her choice of consumption vector x_s *within* a state using the techniques developed in Chapters 2 to 4. Her demands are $D_s(p_s, y_s)$ and she has indirect utility $v_s(p_s, y_s)$. *Before* the state of the world is revealed her *ex ante* expected utility is $V = \sum_s \pi_s v_s(p_s, y_s)$. It is apparent that changes in the price vectors p_s will affect V and, since many government policies alter the price vectors which individuals face, it is of interest to consider how such changes can be valued and whether the consumer surplus measures examined in Chapter 3 can be used under conditions of uncertainty. Since the individual's valuation of prices and income depends on her preferences over consumption bundles we must first examine the relationship between her direct and indirect utility functions and her attitudes to price and income risks. We then define the compensating variation benefit measure under uncertainty and consider its relationship to the compensating variation under certainty discussed in Chapter 3. Finally, we use the measure to consider whether price stability makes consumers better off.

We noted earlier that the axioms of Chapter 17, which ensured that we could represent the individual's preferences under uncertainty by the expected utility of income, would also imply that we could represent her preferences by the expected value of her direct utility function. We assumed that the direct utility function has all the properties discussed in Chapters 2 and 3, such as quasi-concavity and differentiability. However, the direct utility function used in the analysis of consumer behaviour in earlier chapters was only required to be an ordinal representation of preferences, whereas the expected utility framework requires that the utility function is cardinal. This means that, when two commodity bundles are compared, the size as well as the sign of the difference in utility is relevant and so it is meaningful to consider whether the direct utility function is concave, convex or linear in the commodity bundles.

The concavity or otherwise of the direct utility function has implications for the properties of the indirect utility function and thus the individual's valuations of different price and income combinations. In considering the consumer's choice under conditions of certainty, we showed that the effects of changes in income and prices on her indirect utility function could be signed unambiguously, but because her direct utility function was only required to be unique up to a positive monotonic transformation, no meaning could be attached to the sign of the second derivatives of her direct or indirect utility functions. Some other ordinal representation of her preferences could always be found that had second derivatives of different sign. However, when the direct utility function is cardinal, it is meaningful to sign the second derivatives of the direct and indirect utility functions, since the signs are unaffected by a positive linear transformation of the direct utility function.

We are primarily concerned with the individual consumer and so do not index utility functions by consumer. Consider a consumer in some state with direct cardinal utility function $u_s(x_s)$, facing the price vector p_s with income y_s. Her utility maximizing demand vector is $D_s(p_s, y_s)$ and her indirect utility function is $v_s(p_s, y_s) = u_s(D_s(p_s, y_s))$. We know from Chapters 2 and 3 that v_s is increasing in y_s and decreasing in p_{sj}:

$$v_{sy}(p_s, y_s) > 0 \qquad\qquad\text{[C.30]}$$

$$v_{sj}(p_s, y_s) = -v_{sy}(p_s, y_s)D_{sj}(p_s, y_s) < 0 \qquad\qquad\text{[C.31]}$$

([C.31] is Roy's identity again).

Suppose that the direct utility function is strictly concave in x_s

$$u_s(kx_s^1 + (1 - k)x_s^2) > ku_s(x_s^1) + (1 + k)u_s(x_s^2) \qquad 0 < k < 1 \qquad\text{[C.32]}$$

We now show that the *indirect utility function is strictly concave in income if and only if the direct utility function is strictly concave*. Holding p_s fixed, let y_s^1 and y_s^2 be two different incomes and $\bar{y}_s = ky_s^1 + (1 - k)y_s^2$. The corresponding optimal bundles are $D_s(p_s, y_s^1)$, $D_s(p_s, y_s^2)$ and $D_s(p_s, \bar{y}_s)$. Let $\bar{x}_s = kD_s(p_s, y_s^1) + (1 - k)D_s(p_s, y_s^2)$. This weighted average of the bundles which are optimal at incomes y_s^1 and y_s^2 is certainly affordable by the consumer when her income is $\bar{y}_s$ since

$$p_s\bar{x}_s = p_s kD(p_s, y_s^1) + p_s(1 - k)D_s(p_s, y_s^2) = ky_s^1 + (1 - k)y_s^2 = \bar{y}_s \qquad\text{[C.33]}$$

But since $D_s(p_s, \bar{y}_s)$ is the optimal bundle at prices p_s and income $\bar{y}_s$ the consumer is at least as well off with $D_s(p_s, \bar{y}_s)$ as $\bar{x}_s$:

$$v_s(p_s, \bar{y}_s) = u_s(D_s(p_s, \bar{y}_s)) \geq u_s(\bar{x}_s) \qquad\qquad\text{[C.34]}$$

The strict concavity of u_s implies

$$u_s(\bar{x}_s) > ku_s(D_s(p_s, y_s^1)) + (1 - k)u_s(D_s(p_s, y_s^2))$$
$$= kv_s(p_s, y_s^1) + (1 - k)v_s(p_s, y_s^2) \qquad\qquad\text{[C.35]}$$

and putting [C.34] and [C.35] together we have established the strict concavity in income of the indirect utility function:

$$v_s(p_s, \bar{y}_s) > kv_s(p_s, y_s^1) + (1 - k)v_s(p_s, y_s^2) \qquad\qquad\text{[C.36]}$$

Thus aversion to income risk ($v_{syy} < 0$) arises from the strict concavity of the direct utility function. Because there are diminishing returns to scale in the production of utility from commodities the marginal value of income falls as income increases.

If the indifference curves in commodity space have the usual shape, the direct utility function is quasi-concave. Quasi-concavity does not, however, imply the concavity of the cardinal direct utility function. If the direct utility function is strictly quasi-concave then the indirect utility function is strictly quasi-convex in prices. Thus if p_s^1 and p_s^2 are two price vectors yielding the same utility $v_s(p_s^1, y_s) = v_s(p_s^2, y_s) = v^0$ then

$$v_s(\bar{p}_s, y_s) < kv_s(p_s^1, y_s) + (1 - k)v_s(p_s^2, y_s) = v^0 \qquad 0 < k < 1 \qquad\text{[C.37]}$$

where $\bar{p}_s = kp_s^1 + (1 - k)p_s^2$.

The implication of the strict quasi-convexity in prices of the indirect utility function is that, *if* two price vectors yield the same utility, the consumer would prefer to face the prospect of p_s^1 or p_s^2 with probabilities k and $(1 - k)$ respectively rather than the certain price vector $\bar{p}_s$ equal to their mean. However, if the price vectors do not yield the same utility, the strict quasi-convexity in p_s of $v_s(p_s, y_s)$ does not imply that the consumer has a preference for price risks. The reason is that, in general, price changes imply changes in utility or real income and the consumer's attitude to price risks also depends on her attitude to income risks. For example, suppose $p_s^2 = 2p_s^1$ with income unchanged. Then the risky prospect of (p_s^1, y_s) or $(p_s^2, y_s) = (2p_s^1, y_s)$ is equivalent to the risky prospect of (p_s^1, y_s) or $(p_s^1, y_s/2)$ and so attitudes to price risks cannot be separated from attitudes to income risk.

We examine this in more detail by considering whether the indirect utility function is concave or convex in a single price, holding all other prices and income constant, that is by investigating the sign of $\partial^2 v_s(p_s, y_s)/\partial p_{sj}^2 = v_{sjj}$. Differentiating Roy's identity [C.31] with respect to p_{sj} gives

$$v_{sjj} = -v_{syj}D_{sj} - v_{sy}D_{sjj} \qquad [C.38]$$

Because the order of differentiation is irrelevant we can write the v_{syj} term as v_{sjy} and using Roy's identity again

$$v_{syj} = v_{sjy} = \partial(-v_{sy}D_{sj})/\partial y = -v_{syy}D_{sj} - v_{sy}D_{sjy} \qquad [C.39]$$

Substituting [C.39] in [C.38] and collecting terms gives

$$v_{sjj} = v_{syy}D_{sj} + v_{sy}[D_{sjy}D_{sj} - D_{sjj}] \qquad [C.40]$$

Now the first term in [C.40] is negative if the indirect utility function is concave in y_s. The term in brackets is just the negative of the own substitution effect (recall the Slutsky equation in Chapter 3) and must be positive.

We can use [C.40] to show even more clearly the link between attitude to income risks and price risks. Divide [C.40] by $-v_{sy}$, multiply by p_{sj}, divide and multiply the first term on the right-hand side by y_s to get

$$v_{sjj} \gtreqless 0 \Leftrightarrow R_s w_{sj} + \sigma_{sjj} \gtreqless 0 \qquad [C.41]$$

where R_s is the coefficient of relative risk aversion $(-y_s v_{syy}/v_{sy})$, w_{sj} is the proportion of income spent on commodity $j (p_{sj}D_{sj}/y_s)$ and σ_{sjj} is the constant utility own price elasticity of demand for commodity j.

Thus the indirect utility function is more likely to be convex in p_{sj}, the smaller the proportion of income spent on the commodity j, the smaller the aversion to income risk and the more price elastic the constant utility demand.

Consumer surplus benefit measures under uncertainty

Suppose that the price vector in each state changes from p_s^1 to p_s^2. In many circumstances it would be useful to have a monetary measure of the gain or loss to the consumer of such a change. An obvious approach is to adapt the concepts of Chapter 3 where we investigate measures of the gain or loss from price changes under certainty and ask how much income the consumer would pay or have to receive as compensation for the change. We will consider the compensating variation measure of the benefit to the consumer of price changes. (The analysis of the equivalent variation measure is very similar and we leave it to the reader.)

There are two possible concepts of compensating variation depending on whether the compensation is paid after or before the state of the world is known. The *ex post compensating variation* $CV_s(p_s^1, p_s^2, y_s)$ is defined by

$$v_s(p_s^1, y_s) = v_s(p_s^2, y_s - CV_s) \qquad [C.42]$$

and is the amount of income the consumer would be willing to give up if state s occurs, in order to be faced with the price vector p_s^2 rather than p_s^1. ([C.42] is identical to the definition of the compensating variation under certainty examined in section 3C.) CV_s is an appropriate measure of the benefit to the consumer if the decision to change the price vector is made once the state of the world is revealed. The advantage of the *ex post* measure is that, as we saw in section 3C, it may be possible to estimate it using information on the consumer's demand function in the state.

Unfortunately, if the decision to change prices is taken before the state of the world is revealed the *ex post* CV_s is not the correct measure of the benefit. When the decision being evaluated is taken before s is known, the relevant measure is the *ex ante compensating variation* $CV_a(p^1, p^2, y)$ defined by

$$\sum \pi_s v_s(p_s^1, y_s) = \sum \pi_s v_s(p_s^2, y_s - CV_a) \qquad [\text{C.43}]$$

CV_a is the amount the consumer would be willing to pay for certain, before s is known, to face the prospect of the price vectors $p_1^2, \ldots, p_s^2$ rather than the prospect of the price vectors $p_1^1, \ldots, p_s^1$. The difficulty with CV_a is that it depends on attributes of the consumer's preferences – her attitude to risk – which are not revealed by her demand functions for commodities within any given state. The commodity demand functions depend only on the shapes of the consumer's indifference curves and not on the cardinal utility function which represents her preferences. For example, the direct utility functions $u(x_s)$ and $g(x_s) = \ln u(x_s)$ yield the same commodity demands $D_s(p_s, y_s)$ but imply very different attitudes to risk and hence *ex ante* compensating variations. The indirect utility function generated by $g(x_s)$ is $g^*(p_s, y_s) = g(D_s(p_s, y_s)) = \ln v_s(p_s, y_s)$ and the *ex ante* compensating variation is CV_a^g, defined by

$$\sum \pi_s \ln v_s(p_s^1, y_s) = \sum \pi_s \ln v_s(p_s^2, y_s - CV_a^g) \qquad [\text{C.44}]$$

and comparing [C.44] and [C.43] we see that CV_a and CV_a^g will generally differ. (The reader should check that the CV_s defined by [C.42] is not affected by taking logs of both sides and so the *ex post* compensating variation is not affected by attitudes to risk.)

Since CV_s may be measurable using information on state s demand it is of interest to investigate when it is possible to measure the *ex ante* compensating variation as the expected value of the *ex post* compensating variations. Taking the definitions of CV_s and CV_a it is always true that

$$\sum \pi_s v_s(p_s^2, y_s - CV_s) = \sum \pi_s v_s(p_s^2, y_s - CV_a) \qquad [\text{C.45}]$$

but when does [C.45] imply that $\sum \pi_s CV_s = CV_a$ or when does

$$\sum \pi_s v_s(p_s^2, y_s - CV_s) = \sum \pi_s v_s(p_s^2, y_s - \sum \pi_s CV_s) \qquad [\text{C.46}]$$

hold? [C.46] requires that the consumer would be indifferent between a certain reduction in her income of $\sum \pi_s CV_s$ and a random reduction of CV_s with probability π_s. But this must mean that she places the same value on an additional £1 of income whatever the state: her marginal utility of income must be the same in all states.

More formally, differentiate both sides of [C.46] with respect to p_{tj} holding all other prices in all other states constant. There is no effect on the left-hand side of [C.46] since $v_s(p_s^2, y_s - CV_s)$ is unaffected if $t \neq s$ and the definition of CV_t means that CV_t adjusts to keep $v_t(p_t^2, y_t - CV_t)$ constant. Thus the derivative of the right-hand side of [C.46] with respect to p_{tj} must also be zero. This derivative is

$$-[\sum_s \pi_s v_{sy}(p_s^2, y_s - \sum \pi_s CV_s)]\pi_t \frac{\partial CV_t}{\partial p_{tj}} + \pi_t v_{tj}(p_s^2, y_t - \sum_s \pi_s CV_s)$$

$$= [\sum_s \pi_s v_{sy}(p_s^2, y_s - \sum \pi_s CV_s)]\pi_t D_{tj} - v_{ty}(p_t^2, y_t - \sum_s \pi_s CV_s)\pi_t D_{tj}$$

where we have used $\partial CV_t / \partial p_{tj} = -D_{tj}$ (use the implicit function rule on [C.42]) and Roy's identity. If this is to be zero for all t and j we must have $v_{ty} = \sum \pi_s v_{sy}(p_s^2, y_s - \sum \pi_s CV_s)$ for all t, so that the marginal utility of income is the same in all states.

The requirement that $v_{sy}(p_s^2, y_s - \sum \pi_s CV_s)$ is the same in all states for all price changes is highly restrictive. It implies that the consumer is risk neutral towards income risks, $v_{syy} = 0$. Further, the marginal utility of income must not vary directly with the state so that $v_{sy}(p, y) = v_{ty}(p, y)$ when prices and incomes are the same in states s and t. This in turn implies that the marginal utility from commodities $[u_{sj}(x)]$ must be state independent (remember that $v_{sy} = u_{sj}/p_{sj}$) and so demand functions must be state independent $D_s(p, y) = D_t(p, y)]$.

Finally, even if v_{sy} is not directly dependent on s and is constant in y, the use of the expected *ex post* compensating variation will only be valid when the prices which vary across states in situation 2 are those which do not affect the marginal utility of income. Thus the expected *ex post* measure cannot be used when all prices vary across states since it is impossible for the marginal utility of income to be constant with respect to all prices and income. (Doubling all prices and income must halve the marginal utility of income since the amount purchased for £1 is halved.) From [C.39] we see that the requirement that v_{sy} is not affected by p_{sj} ($v_{syj} = 0$), coupled with the requirement that $v_{syy} = 0$, implies that good j must have a zero income elasticity of demand. In section 3C, we saw that, if the income elasticity of demand for a good was zero, then the compensating variation would coincide with the Marshallian and equivalent variation measures and could be estimated from the Marshallian demand curve. Now we have seen that a zero income elasticity is necessary for the expected *ex post* compensating variation to be a valid measure of the gains from *ex ante* price changes.

Price stabilization

Intervention in markets, particularly agricultural and resource markets, is often justified on the grounds, among others, that consumers benefit from price stability. We can use the previous results to examine the assertion. Assume that the direct utility functions are state independent so that consumers care only about the commodity vector or, equivalently, about the prices and their income. Suppose also that income is constant and that only the price of commodity 1 varies across states. Expected utility is $V = \sum_s \pi_s v(p_s, y)$.

From section 17F we know that a mean-preserving spread in a variable will reduce (increase) the expected value of a concave (convex) function of that variable. A price stabilization scheme which is a mean preserving contraction of the distribution of the price of good 1 will therefore increase expected utility if and only if $v(p, y)$ is concave in the price of good 1. But from [C.41] the plausible assumption that the consumer is averse to income risks does not imply that she is also averse to price risks. If the commodity accounts for a small proportion of her budget or she is not very risk averse, it is likely that she will lose from a reduction in the dispersion of prices.

Figure 21.2 illustrates, in a simple case in which the prices of all goods except good 1 are the same in all states, that there are two equiprobable states or values for p_{s1} initially and the scheme stabilizes p_{s1} at its mean value $\bar{p}_1$. To simplify the analysis further, assume that there are no income effects on the demand for good 1. Thus the consumer's Marshallian and Hicksian demand curves for good 1 are identical. Recalling section 3C on the gains from price changes under certainty, if state 1 occurs the consumer's gain from facing the price $\bar{p}_1$ rather than p_{11} is the area ΔCS_1. If state 2 occurs the consumer's loss from facing $\bar{p}_1$ rather than p_{21} is the area ΔCS_2. If the consumer's marginal utility of income is constant then, combined with the assumption that the income effect D_{s1y} is zero, this implies that the marginal utility

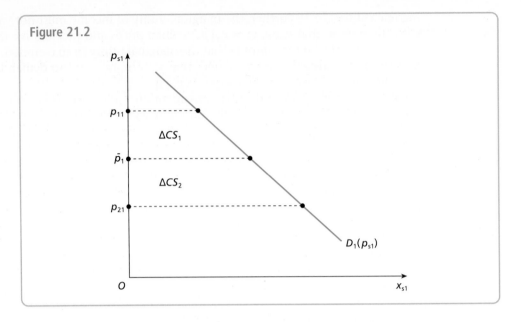

Figure 21.2

of income is independent of p_{s1} (see [C.39]). Hence the change in her expected utility from the stabilization scheme is

$$\tfrac{1}{2}[\Delta CS_1 v_{1y} - \Delta CS_2 v_{2y}] = \tfrac{1}{2}[\Delta CS_1 - \Delta CS_2]v_{sy} < 0 \qquad\qquad [\text{C.47}]$$

Thus risk-neutral consumers lose with stabilization.

If the consumer was averse to income risk so that $v_{syy} < 0$ she could be made better off by stabilization. The state 1 gain from stabilization occurs when p_1 is high and therefore marginal utility of income is high (because real income is low). The state 2 loss occurs when p_2 is low and thus the marginal utility of income is low. Hence although $\Delta CS_1 < \Delta CS_2$ it is possible that $\Delta CS_1 v_{1y} > \Delta CS_2 v_{2y}$ and the consumer would gain from price stability.

EXERCISE 21C

1. The indirect utility function is homogeneous of degree zero in prices and income: $v_s(kp_s, ky_s) = k^0 v_s(p_s, y_s) = v_s(p_s, y_s)$. What does this imply about the homogeneity of the marginal utility of income?

2. If the marginal utility of income is state independent and does not vary with the subset of prices which are varied, what does the concavity of $u(x_s)$ imply about the relationship between CV_a and $\sum \pi_s CV_s$?

3. Use the indirect utility function and Roy's identity to show that constant marginal utility of income is neither necessary nor sufficient for a good to have a zero income elasticity of demand.

4. *Stabilization and the timing of consumption decisions.* Suppose that the consumer must decide on the consumption of good 1 before the state and its price are known. Her direct utility function, income and all other prices do not vary across states. Thus when state s occurs the consumer has $y - p_{s1} x_{s1}$ to spend on all goods. Show that the consumer is made better off by a mean preserving contraction in the distribution of p_{s1} if she is averse to income risks. (*Hint*: derive her indirect utility function and show that it is concave in p_{s1} if it is concave in y.)

D. Efficiency with production

In this section we investigate whether the equilibrium of a competitive market economy with production under uncertainty is efficient. One way of proceeding would be to consider a very general formulation with many consumers, firms and commodities. We could derive the *ex ante* Pareto efficiency conditions and they would be very similar to those obtained earlier. Marginal rates of substitution within and between states must be equalized (as in section C) and in addition these must be equal to marginal rates of transformation within and between states. We could also show that if there is a complete set of competitive markets in state-contingent commodities the competitive equilibrium would be efficient – all producers and consumers face the same relative prices and so are led to equate their marginal rates of substitution and transformation (see Question 1, Exercise 21D). Rather than repeat the earlier analysis with minor modifications we will examine a more relevant issue: the *constrained efficiency* of an economy in which there is *not* a complete set of state-contingent commodity markets. In the absence of complete state-contingent markets it is not surprising that the equilibrium of a market economy does not satisfy the conditions for full Pareto efficiency. However, comparing the allocation achieved by an actual set of markets with the allocation achievable by a planner with the ability to control all state-contingent consumption and production vectors may not be very useful. It seems more sensible to impose the same restrictions on the planner as we implicitly impose on the market allocation and to consider whether the market economy is efficient relative to the set of allocations which could be achieved with the given set of markets.

In the absence of state-contingent markets, producers and consumers make their decisions on the basis of their expectations of what will happen when the state of the world is revealed. The allocation achieved by the market economy depends on these expectations. We will assume that consumers and producers have *rational expectations* and consider circumstances in which rational expectations equilibria are constrained Pareto efficient.

Rational expectations equilibrium

To focus on essentials we adapt the simple production model of section 18B. Producers are identical and have perfectly correlated production functions:

$$x_s = f_s(z) \tag{D.1}$$

where x_s is the output of the consumption good in state s and z is effort supplied before the state of the world is known. Since producers are identical we can simplify the notation by assuming that there is a single producer who behaves competitively and takes market prices as unalterable by her decisions. The single competitive producer has the utility function

$$v_s(y_s, z) \qquad v_{sy} > 0, \qquad v_{syy} \leqslant 0, \qquad v_{sz} < 0, \qquad v_{szz} < 0 \tag{D.2}$$

where y_s is her income. The producer's utility function is concave in income and her effort and she prefers less effort to more if income is held constant. The producer does not consume any of the good she produces and sells her entire output on the spot commodity market at price p_s to achieve the state-contingent income

$$y_s = p_s x_s + \hat{y}_s \qquad \text{[D.3]}$$

where $\hat{y}_s$ is her endowment of income in state s. y_s is her expenditure on all other goods and services (which have constant relative price and are treated as a single composite commodity).

In choosing z to maximize her expected utility the producer must form some expectations about the spot prices in each state of the world. Denoting her anticipated price in state s by p_s^a, her choice of effort z^* satisfies

$$Ev_{sy}(y_s, z^*) \, p_s^a f_s'(z^*) + Ev_{sz}(y_s, z^*) = 0 \qquad \text{[D.4]}$$

and depends on her vector of endowed incomes $\hat{y} = (\hat{y}_1, \ldots, \hat{y}_S)$, price expectations $p^a = (p_1^a, \ldots, p_S^a)$ and probability beliefs $\pi = (\pi_1, \ldots, \pi_S)$:

$$z^* = z^*(\hat{y}, p^a, \pi) \qquad \text{[D.5]}$$

The supply of the consumption good to the spot market in state s is $f_s(z^*)$.

Consumers are also identical and, again to economize on notation, there is assumed to be a single consumer who behaves competitively and takes prices as unalterable by his decisions. The consumer has the direct cardinal utility function $u_s^c(y_s^c, x_s^c)$ where x_s^c is his consumption of the commodity produced by the firm and y_s^c is his expenditure on all other goods and services. The consumer makes his consumption decision in state s, maximizing his utility u_s^c subject to his state s budget constraint

$$y_s^c + p_s x_s^c \leq \hat{y}_s^c \qquad \text{[D.6]}$$

where $\hat{y}_s^c$ is his endowment of income in state s. His demand for the producer's output of the consumption good in state s is $D_s(p_s, \hat{y}_s^c)$ and his state s indirect utility function is

$$v_s^c(p_s, \hat{y}_s^c) = u_s^c(\hat{y}_s^c - p_s D_s, D_s) \qquad \text{[D.7]}$$

Notice that, as the consumer does not have to make any decisions before the state of the world is revealed, his demand does not depend on his probability beliefs or price expectations.

The price p_s for the consumption good in state s is determined, after the state of the world is known, by the spot market clearing condition

$$f_s(z^*(\hat{y}, p^a, \pi)) - D_s(p_s, \hat{y}_s^c) = 0 \qquad s = 1, \ldots, S \qquad \text{[D.8]}$$

The vector of equilibrium spot prices p which satisfy the market clearing conditions [D.8] depends among other things on the producer's input choice and thus on her price expectations p^a.

The producer has *rational expectations* if her beliefs about the distribution of prices across the states of the world is correct: $p^a = p$. When she has rational expectations [D.8] becomes

$$f_s(z^*(\hat{y}, p_1, \ldots, p_S, \pi)) - D_s(p_s, \hat{y}_s^c) = 0 \qquad s = 1, \ldots, S \qquad \text{[D.9]}$$

and the S endogenous spot prices are determined as functions of the exogenous variables

$$p_s = p(s, \hat{y}, \hat{y}^c, \pi) \qquad \text{[D.10]}$$

from the S market clearing conditions in [D.9].

It would be possible to examine the comparative static properties of the equilibrium by totally differentiating the S equations in [D.9] and applying Cramer's Rule. The result would be complicated because changes in an exogenous variable in one state of the world would lead to changes in all spot prices. For example, an increase in consumer income in state 1 will shift the demand curve in state 1 and change p_1. The change in p_1 would alter the producer's input choice and thus the output in all states and so prices in all states would change. The fact that the producer has rational expectations means that the equilibria in the spot markets are interdependent.

When the producer has rational expectations her choice of input $z^*(\hat{y}, p, \pi)$ leads to a state distribution of output $f_s(z^*)$ which, together with the consumer's state distribution of demands, generates a state distribution of prices which is identical with the price distribution on which she based her input decision. The producer would never have any need to revise her production decision or her price expectations.

The economy is in a *rational expectations equilibrium* (REE) if the optimal plans of agents are compatible in each state (the market clears) and generate a state distribution of prices which is compatible with the distribution they anticipated in making their optimal plans. The economy must be in equilibrium both with respect to decisions and with respect to expectations.

Constrained Pareto efficiency

We now show that the rational expectations equilibrium of this simple competitive economy is *not* constrained Pareto efficient. It is not difficult to show that the competitive allocation is not Pareto efficient compared with a situation in which a policy-maker can make state-contingent income transfers and so improve the efficiency of risk bearing in the economy. However, if such transfers are feasible for a policy-maker, it is not obvious why the individuals do not organize a market in state-contingent income claims. We assume that the fact that there is no market in state-contingent income claims implies that it is impossible to make state-contingent income transfers.

The policy-maker can influence the economy in two ways. The first is by a non-state-contingent income transfer T from consumer to producer which is paid whatever the state of the world. The consumer's income is $\hat{y}_s^c - T$ and the producer's non-production income is $\hat{y}_s + T$. The ability to make such lump-sum transfers means it is possible to move along the expected utility possibility frontier to take account of distributional considerations. Second, the policy-maker can directly control the input choice of the producer. The assumption is less strong than it appears since any allocation achievable by choosing T and z can also be achieved by choosing T and controlling z indirectly via a purchase tax. (See Question 2, Exercise 21D.) The argument is simpler when conducted in terms of the policy-maker choosing z directly.

We use the simple welfare function

$$W = Ev(\hat{y}_s + T + p_s f_s(z), z) + \lambda Ev_s^c(p_s, \hat{y}_s^c - T) \qquad \text{[D.11]}$$

which is to be maximized by choice of T and z. The prices of the commodity in each state are determined by the market clearing conditions

$$f_s(z) - D_s(p_s, \hat{y}_s^c - T) = 0 \qquad s = 1, \ldots, S \qquad \text{[D.12]}$$

Note that [D.12] is much simpler than the corresponding conditions [D.8] which are relevant when z is chosen by the producer rather than by a policy-maker. In particular, the price in one state does not enter the market clearing condition in any other state. (This is the reason why it is easier to conduct the argument with z directly controlled rather than indirectly controlled via a purchase tax.) Each market clearing equation in [D.12] can be solved separately for the equilibrium price $p_s(z, \hat{y}_s^c - T)$ as a function of the policy variables. Totally differentiating [D.12] with respect to z and T gives the effect of the policy variables on the price in each state:

$$\partial p_s(z, \hat{y}_s^c - T)/\partial T = p_{sT} = D_{sy}/D_{sp} \tag{D.13}$$

$$\partial p_s(z, \hat{y}_s^c - T)/\partial z = p_{sz} = f_s'/D_{sp} < 0 \tag{D.14}$$

where $D_{sy} = \partial D_s/\partial \hat{y}_s^c$ is the effect of income on demand and could be positive or negative, $D_{sp} = \partial D_s/\partial p_s < 0$ is the price effect (the demand curve is assumed to be negatively sloped to ensure that the market is stable) and $f_s' > 0$ is the marginal product of z if state s occurs.

Remembering that T alters prices as well as incomes and that the market clears in each state so that $f_s = D_s$ and making use of Roy's identity [$v_{sp}^c = -v_{sy}^c D_s$], the welfare-maximizing transfer from consumer to producer satisfies

$$\frac{\partial W}{\partial T} = E(v_{sy} + v_{sy}f_s p_{sT}) - \lambda E(v_{sy}^c + v_{sy}^c D_s p_{sT}) = E[(v_{sy} - \lambda v_{sy}^c)(1 + D_s p_{sT})]$$

$$= E\left[(v_{sy} - \lambda v_{sy}^c)\frac{h_{sp}}{D_{sp}}\right] = 0 \tag{D.15}$$

(We get the last step by using [D.13] and recalling the Slutsky equation so that we can write

$$1 + D_s p_{sT} = (D_{sp} + D_s D_{sy})/D_{sp} = h_{sp}/D_{sp} > 0 \tag{D.16}$$

where $h_{sp} < 0$ is the substitution effect of a change in the price of the commodity in state s.)

Again using Roy's identity and $f_s = D_s$, the marginal social value of the input is

$$\frac{\partial W}{\partial z} = Ev_{sy}p_s^a f_s' + Ev_{sz} + E[(v_{sy} - \lambda v_{sy}^c)D_s p_{sz}] \tag{D.17}$$

When the level of z is chosen by the producer the first two terms in [D.17] sum to zero since they are the effects of the input on Ev_s which are taken account of by the producer when she chooses z (recall [D.4]). If the producer is given a transfer T and then is allowed to choose z to maximize Ev_s there will be an REE with $z = z^*(\hat{y}_s + T, p, \pi)$. This REE level of z is constrained Pareto efficient only if it makes [D.17] zero. From [D.4] the first two terms in [D.17] sum to zero at the privately optimal z^* chosen by the producer who has rational expectations ($p^a = p$). Thus the REE is constrained Pareto efficient only if

$$E[(v_{sy} - \lambda v_{sy}^c)D_s p_{sz}] = E(v_{sy} - \lambda v_{sy}^c)(p_s f_s'/\varepsilon_s) = 0 \tag{D.18}$$

holds at REE. (We have used [D.14] and the definition $\varepsilon_s = p_s D_{sp}/D_s$ of the price elasticity of demand for the producer's output in state s to substitute for $D_s p_{sz}$.)

Unfortunately, [D.18] holds at an REE only under rather restrictive assumptions about preferences or technology. Suppose that there is no risk in the economy, which would require that there is no production uncertainty and that producers and consumers have incomes and preferences which are not state dependent. Omitting the now redundant subscript s, [D.15] would then simplify to

$$(v_y - \lambda v_y^c)h_p/D_p = 0$$

which would imply (since $h_p/D_p > 0$) that $v_y = \lambda v_y^c$ and this would in turn imply that [D.18] is

$$(v_y - \lambda v_y^c)(pf'/\varepsilon) = 0$$

at the privately optimal z^*. The condition can always be satisfied by an unregulated market for some choice of λ. Choice of the welfare weight λ amounts to choosing a particular Pareto efficient allocation. Hence, with no uncertainty there are only two commodities in the economy y and x and the single competitive market for x is sufficient to ensure efficiency. This is just a simple example of the Second Theorem of Welfare Economics (see Chapter 13): lump-sum income transfers can be used to shift the economy around the utility possibility frontier and the market left to guide production and consumption decisions efficiently.

When there is uncertainty but the single-spot commodity market is supplemented by S markets for the exchange of state-contingent incomes and consumers and producers have correct expectations about the commodity price for each state, the equilibrium will be Pareto efficient. (See Question 1, Exercise 21D.) We could show that if all producers and consumers face the same prices for state-contingent income claims they will achieve an efficient allocation of risk where their marginal rates of substitution for state-contingent incomes are equal for all pairs of states

$$\frac{\pi_s v_{sy}}{\pi_\ell v_{\ell y}} = \frac{\pi_s v_{sy}^c}{\pi_\ell v_{\ell y}^c}$$

which implies that $v_{sy} = (v_{\ell y}/v_{\ell y}^c)v_{sy}^c$. Thus by setting T so that $\lambda = -\mu/\mu^c$ the first term in the expectation in [D.18] is zero for all states and [D.18] must hold at the privately optimal z^*. If there is a complete set of state-contingent income markets, it can be shown that the equilibrium achieves full Pareto efficiency: the policy-maker could not do better even if able to directly control consumption, production and make state-contingent income transfers, rather than just being able to make a non-contingent transfer T. For some value of λ the market will maximize the welfare function.

When there is uncertainty and there are no state-contingent income markets, restrictions on preferences and technology are necessary for an REE to be constrained Pareto efficient. If the marginal utility of income of the producer and consumer do not vary across states ($v_{sy} = v_y$, $v_{sy}^c = v_y^c$ for all s) then for some value of the distributional weight λ we will have $v_{sy} - \lambda v_{sy}^c = 0$ for all s and [D.18] will hold at an REE. We can give two sets of circumstances in which marginal utilities of income are constant across states. First suppose that the utility functions do not depend directly on the state of the world and that producers are risk neutral. Then, even though prices and thus the producer's income vary across the states, her marginal utility of income is constant. Suppose also that the consumer's income is constant across states. Then his marginal utility of income is $v_y^c(p_s, \hat{y}^c - T)$ which varies across states because p_s varies with s. Suppose that $\partial v_y^c/\partial p = v_{yp}^c = 0$. Then the consumer's marginal utility of income will also be constant across states and by varying T the policy-maker can ensure that $v_y - \lambda v_y^c = 0$ and that the REE is constrained Pareto efficient. The requirement that the marginal utility of income be unaffected by prices imposes severe restrictions on preferences, however.

Second, suppose that preferences and the endowed incomes of producer and consumer are state independent. If the consumer has unitary demand elasticity ($\varepsilon = -1$) for the producer's output, variations in p_s have no effect on his expenditure on x. Thus the producer's revenue is constant across states and so is her income and thus her marginal utility of income. To ensure that the consumer's marginal utility of income is constant across states we again require that $v_{yp}^c = 0$. We leave it to the reader to show (see Question 3, Exercise 21D) that the requirements that the consumer has unitary demand elasticity and $v_{yp}^c = 0$ are simultaneously satisfied if and only if the indirect utility function has the form

$$v_s^c = -k_0 \log p_s + k_1 g(\hat{y}_s^c - T) \qquad [\text{D.19}]$$

where k_0, k_1 are positive constants and $g(\cdot)$ is increasing in its argument.

The absence of state-contingent income markets means that there is inefficient risk bearing in the economy. The policy-maker cannot achieve fully efficient risk bearing because policy instruments are not state specific. It is not possible to transfer income between pairs of states so as to equate the individual marginal rates of substitution. However, even if the policy-maker can only alter the marginal utility of income in all states simultaneously for the individuals, it is possible to improve on the inefficient allocation achieved as a result of the individuals' decisions in non-state-contingent income markets. Any policy which can change the state distribution of spot prices by altering the individuals' behaviour is capable of improving the efficiency of risk bearing by changing the state distribution of marginal utilities, either directly by changing income or indirectly if the marginal utility of income depends on the spot prices of commodities. The inefficiency of the competitive market equilibrium arises in part because the market is competitive and so individuals do not take account of the effect of their supply or demand decisions on spot prices and thus on marginal utilities.

Futures markets

A futures market is a means of transferring the risks of price fluctuations between traders with different attitudes to risks or different probability beliefs. This raises the possibility that when there are futures markets a market economy will achieve an efficient allocation of risks despite the absence of markets in state-contingent income claims. We investigate the possibility using the simple economy just outlined.

The income of the producer in state s is

$$y_s = \hat{y}_s + p_s[x_s - x_f] + p_f x_f = \hat{y}_s + p_s[f_s(z) - x_f] + p_f x_f \qquad [\text{D.20}]$$

where x_f is the amount of output sold forward by the producer at a price of p_f before the state is known. The producer chooses her input level and her forward sale to maximize her expected utility. The first-order condition on the forward sale is

$$E v_{sy}(y_s)(p_f - p_s) = 0 \qquad [\text{D.21}]$$

and the input choice satisfies [D.4]. Notice that we have continued to assume that the producer has rational expectations and acts competitively. The input choice $z^*(\hat{y}_s, p, p_f, \pi)$ and the sale on the futures market $x_f(\hat{y}, p, p_f, \pi)$ depend on the vector of expected spot prices and the actual futures price.

The consumer also trades on the futures market. Before the state of the world and therefore the spot price is known, the consumer makes his decision to buy x_f^c claims on the futures market. His decision is based on correct, or rational expectations of the situation he will face in any given state s. In state s the consumer will maximize his utility function $u_s^c(y_s^c, x_s^c)$ subject to his period s budget constraint

$$y_s^c + p_s x_s^c \le \hat{y}_s^c + (p_s - p_f)x_f^c \qquad [D.22]$$

where x_f^c is his purchase of the commodity on the futures market and x_s^c is his consumption of the commodity. The right-hand side of [D.22] can be interpreted as the consumer's state s income, which consists of his endowed income plus his profit on his speculative purchase of the futures contracts. Alternatively, rearrange [D.22] to give

$$y_s^c + p_s(x_s^c - x_f^c) \le \hat{y}_s^c - p_f x_f^c$$

which has the interpretation that in state s the consumer takes delivery of the x_f^c units he bought forward and then buys additional units $(x_s^c - x_f^c)$ at price p_s out of the income $(\hat{y}_s^c - p_f x_f^c)$ he has left after making the earlier futures market purchase.

The consumer's state s demand for the producer's output is $D_s(p_s, \hat{y}_s^c + (p_s - p_f)x_f^c)$ and his indirect utility function in period s is $v_s^c(p_s, \hat{y}_s^c + (p_s - p_f)x_f^c)$. His expected utility before the state of the world is revealed is $E v_s^c(p_s, \hat{y}_s^c + (p_s - p_f)x_f^c)$. The consumer chooses his forward purchase to maximize $E v_s^c$ given his correct expectations about the spot prices. His demand on the futures market is $D_f(\hat{y}^c, p, p_f, \pi)$ which satisfies the first-order condition

$$E v_{sy}^c(p_s - p_f) = 0 \qquad [D.23]$$

The rational expectations equilibrium is characterized by a vector of spot prices p and a futures price p_f such that (a) the demand equals the supply in the futures market and in the spot market in each state and (b) the resulting state distribution of spot prices is the one used by consumers and producers in their decisions determining the demand and supply in the markets. The futures market clears when

$$x_f(\hat{y}, p, p_f, \pi) - D_f(\hat{y}^c, p, p_f, \pi) = 0 \qquad [D.24]$$

In state s the producer delivers x_f of his output to the consumer who has bought the futures contracts and sells the rest on the spot market so that the net supply to the spot market is $f_s(z) - x_f$. The consumer has a net demand for the good equal to his optimal consumption less the amount he has bought forward: $D_s - D_f$. Since [D.24] must hold at an equilibrium, the condition for demand and supply to be in equilibrium in each spot market reduces to

$$f_s(z^*(\hat{y}, p, p_f, \pi)) - D_s(p_s, \hat{y}_s^c + (p_s - p_f)D_f(\hat{y}^c, p, p_f, \pi)) = 0$$
$$s = 1, \ldots, S \qquad [D.25]$$

Although the condition is similar to the condition for spot market equilibrium in the economy without futures markets, the equilibrium spot price distribution will in general be different if there is a futures market. The existence of the futures market enables the producer to reduce the riskiness of any given input choice by selling futures and the change in risk will lead her to change her input choice. The consumer's demand for the commodity at any given spot price will also be different in each state because his income in each state is increased or reduced by his profit or loss on his futures purchase.

Our concern is the efficiency of the rational expectations equilibrium with a futures market and we consider first a situation in which there are only two states of the world. The producer's sale of futures satisfies (see [D.21])

$$\pi_1 v_{1y}(p_f - p_1) + \pi_2 v_{2y}(p_f - p_2) = 0$$

while the consumer's purchase of futures satisfies (see [D.23])

$$\pi_1 v_{1y}^c(p_1 - p_f) + \pi_2 v_{2y}^c(p_2 - p_f) = 0$$

Rearranging these we get

$$\left.\frac{dy_2}{dy_1}\right|_{Ev} = -\frac{\pi_1 v_{1y}}{\pi_2 v_{2y}} = \frac{p_f - p_2}{p_f - p_1} = -\frac{\pi_1 v_{1y}^c}{\pi_2 v_{2y}^c} = \left.\frac{dy_2}{dy_1}\right|_{Ev^c} \qquad [D.26]$$

so that the producer's and consumer's marginal rates of substitution for state 1 and state 2 income are equal and thus there is an efficient sharing of risk. Since there is efficient risk bearing the arguments in the first part of this section imply that there will also be efficiency in production (see also Question 1, Exercise 21D).

When there are two states of the world the spot and futures markets are together equivalent to a market in state-contingent income claims. By buying or selling futures it is possible to transfer income from one state to the other. Label the states so that $p_1 > p_f > p_2$ (why is p_f bounded by the state prices?). Consider a trader who buys a futures claim for one unit of the commodity, takes delivery of the unit when state s is realized and sells it for the spot price p_s. His state 1 income will increase by $p_1 - p_f$ and his state 2 income will fall by $p_2 - p_f$. This is equivalent to being able to sell a claim to income contingent on state 2 and using the proceeds to buy a claim to state 1 income. We can interpret the ratio $(p_f - p_2)/(p_1 - p_f)$ as the price of a claim to £1 of state 1 income relative to the price of a claim to £1 of state 2 income. For example, if p_1 increases with p_2 and p_f is constant the opportunity cost, in terms of forgone state 2 income, of increasing state 1 income by buying futures is reduced and the relative price of state 1 income is reduced.

Unfortunately, the equivalence of a spot and a futures market to a state-contingent income market breaks down when there are more than two states of the world. With S states of the world there are $S - 1$ conditions like [D.26] to be satisfied for efficient risk bearing. Since each individual's marginal utilities of income in each state are constrained only by a single equation like [D.21] or [D.23] there is no guarantee that marginal rates of substitution will be equalized across states. Thus, as is the case without a futures market, the equilibrium will in general not even be constrained Pareto efficient. We can show that a policy-maker who could control production and make lump-sum non-state-contingent transfers would choose a level of the input which differs from that chosen by the producer. The demonstration is, however, rather more complicated than when there is no futures market because the futures market demand and supply functions depend on the spot price distribution and the spot market demand functions depend on the price of futures and the consumer's futures purchase. It is no longer possible to derive the change in a spot price by examining the change in supply and demand functions in that spot market. We will therefore leave the derivation to the exercises (see Question 4, Exercise 21D). The intuition behind the result is, however, unchanged: policy can be used to change the spot price distribution in a way which leads to a more efficient bearing of risk despite the fact the individuals can use the futures market to exchange some risk.

The analysis of the two-state case suggests that efficient risk bearing can be achieved if there are $S - 1$ commodities (in addition to the composite commodity) each with their own spot and futures markets. Assume there are three states of the world and two commodities x_1 and x_2 in addition to the composite commodity y. The producer can allocate effort between production of the two commodities and the output of each is $x_{is} = f_{is}(z_i)$ where z_i is the amount of effort devoted to the production of commodity i. Assume that there is a futures market for each commodity in which the price of one unit of commodity i for future delivery is p_{fi}. When the state of the world is revealed the spot price of commodity i (p_{is}) is determined by the state s demand functions of the consumer and the supply f_{is}. The consumer's state s demand function for commodity i is $D_{is}(p_{1s}, p_{2s}, \hat{y}^c_s + \Sigma_i(p_{is} - p_{fi})D_{fi})$ derived by maximizing his state s utility function $u^c_s(y_s, x^c_{1s}, x^c_{2s})$ subject to his state s budget constraint $y_s + \Sigma_i p_{is} x^c_{is} \leq \hat{y}^c_s + \Sigma_i(p_{is} - p_{fi})D_{fi}$. His indirect utility function is $v^c_s(p_{1s}, p_{2s}, \hat{y}^c_s + \Sigma_i(p_{is} - p_{fi})D_{fi})$. His forward purchases of the two commodities maximize Ev^c_s and satisfy

$$\pi_1 v^c_{1y}(p_{i1} - p_{fi}) + \pi_2 v^c_{2y}(p_{i2} - p_{fi}) + \pi_3 v^c_{3y}(p_{i3} - p_{fi}) = 0 \qquad i = 1, 2 \quad \text{[D.27]}$$

The producer has state s income $\hat{y}_s + \Sigma_i p_{is}(f_{is} - x_{fi}) + \Sigma_i p_{fi} x_{fi}$ and his sales of commodity i forward satisfy

$$\pi_1 v_{1y}(p_{fi} - p_{i1}) + \pi_2 v_{2y}(p_{fi} - p_{i2}) + \pi_3 v_{3y}(p_{fi} - p_{i3}) = 0 \qquad i = 1, 2 \quad \text{[D.28]}$$

Dividing the first two terms in [D.28] by $-\pi_3 v_{3y}$, rearranging and writing ρ_{is} for $p_{fi} - p_{is}$ yields

$$\begin{bmatrix} \rho_{11} & \rho_{12} \\ \rho_{21} & \rho_{22} \end{bmatrix} \begin{bmatrix} \dfrac{-\pi_1 v_{1y}}{\pi_3 v_{3y}} \\ \dfrac{-\pi_2 v_{2y}}{\pi_3 v_{3y}} \end{bmatrix} = \begin{bmatrix} \rho_{13} \\ \rho_{23} \end{bmatrix} \qquad \text{[D.29]}$$

Provided that the inverse of the first matrix on the left-hand side exists we can solve for the marginal rates of substitution as functions of all of the spot and futures prices. Letting m denote the vector of marginal rates of substitution, ρ the 2×2 matrix on the left-hand side and ρ_3 the vector on the right-hand side we get $m = \rho^{-1}\rho_3$. We can repeat the procedure for the consumer and solve for his vector of marginal rates of substitution $m^c = \rho^{-1}\rho_3$. Thus the consumer and producer must have the same marginal rates of substitution for state-contingent income across all pairs of states and risk bearing is efficient. The economy would be fully Pareto efficient.

Two requirements are necessary for futures and spot markets to be equivalent to a full set of state-contingent income claim markets. The first requirement is that the inverse of ρ exists. If the inverse did not exist $\rho_{11}/\rho_{12} - \rho_{21}/\rho_{22}$ (the determinant of ρ) would be zero and hence $\rho_{11}/\rho_{12} = \rho_{21}/\rho_{22}$. But ρ_{11}/ρ_{21} is the 'price' of state 1 income in terms of state 2 income when a trade on the futures market for commodity 1 is made and ρ_{21}/ρ_{22} is the 'price' of state 1 income in terms of state 2 income when a trade is made on the futures market for commodity 2. When these 'prices' are identical the existence of two futures markets does not give the individual any greater freedom to make state-contingent income transfers than when there is only one futures market. Whatever pattern of futures markets trades is made it is impossible to vary income in state 1 without making a proportional change in state 2 income. Thus, for example, it is impossible to increase state 1 income while reducing state 3 income and holding state 2 income constant. When the futures and spot market prices do not span the space of state-contingent incomes there is inefficient risk bearing.

The second requirement is that there must be as many commodities traded on spot and futures markets as there are marginal rates of substitution, i.e. $S - 1$. If there had been, say, four states and only two commodities traded it would still have been possible to have solved for any two of the three marginal rates of substitution of, say, the producer using the first two first-order conditions on transactions in the futures market. However, the components of the vector on the right-hand side of [D.29] would have been of the form $-(\rho_{i3} + \rho_{i4}\pi_4 v_{4y}/\pi_3 v_{3y})$. Since these depend on preferences as well as spot and futures prices the solutions for m and m^c would not in general be the same and so marginal rates of substitution would differ. In general, we would expect that the number of states vastly exceeds the number of commodities, so an economy with futures markets as well as spot commodity markets will have risk bearing that is not fully Pareto efficient. We can adapt our earlier arguments to show that it will not even be constrained Pareto efficient.

EXERCISE 21D

1. *Efficiency under full information.* Derive the necessary conditions for Pareto efficiency of the economy in this section and show that in addition to the usual efficient risk bearing conditions (like [D.26]) the Pareto efficient input choice satisfies $\lambda Eu_{sx}^c f_s'(z) + Ev_{sz} = 0$. Interpret this production condition. Now show that if there are complete state-contingent income claim markets and either (a) the individuals have rational expectations about spot prices for the commodity or (b) there is a contingent claim market for the commodity, then the market equilibrium is Pareto efficient.

2. *Purchase tax policy.* Show that it is possible to achieve a restricted Pareto efficient level of z by means of a purchase tax t on the producer's output with the proceeds of the purchase tax $H_s = tf_s$ being returned to the producer as a lump-sum payment in each state. (*Hint*: the producer's income in state s is $\hat{y}_s + T + H_s + (p_s - t)f_s(z)$. Show that her input choice satisfies

   $$Ev_{sy}(\hat{y}_s + T + H_s + (p_s - t)f_s(z^*),z^*)(p_s - t)f_s'(z^*) + Ev_{sz}(\hat{y}_s + T + H_s + (p_s - t)f_s(z^*),z^*) = 0$$

   What level of t must be set so that satisfaction of this equation implies that [D.17] is equal to zero?)

3. *Restrictions on consumer preferences.* Prove the assertion in the text that $\varepsilon = -1$ and $v_{yp}^c = 0$ hold if and only if the indirect utility function has the form [D.19].

4. *Inefficiency with a futures market.* Prove the assertion in the text that when there are three states, two goods y and x and a spot and futures market for x then the rational expectations equilibrium is not constrained Pareto efficient. (*Hint*: assume that the policy-maker can make a non-state-contingent transfer T and control z directly. Write down the four market clearing conditions for the spot and futures markets and totally differentiate them with respect to T and z and solve for the effects of T and z on the spot and futures prices. Then examine the derivative of the welfare function with respect to z at the level which would be chosen by the producer and show that the derivative will not in general be zero.)

E. The stock market

Under certainty, the capital market is a market in fixed interest debt. When we introduce uncertainty we have to deal with the market in securities with uncertain returns, normally referred to as the stock market.

On stock markets, individuals exchange claims to shares in the profits of companies. (The formulation is broad enough to cover fixed interest securities, as we will see below.) In this section we take the production and investment decisions of firms which determine the state distribution of their profits as given. The only characteristics of firms which are of interest to shareholders are their profits in different states of the world. We consider how individuals choose optimal portfolios of securities or shareholdings and how these are related to their attitude to risk. By varying their portfolios individuals can alter their state distribution of income or wealth. We consider to what extent a stock market can replicate the workings of a market in state-contingent claims. We examine the circumstances in which the stock market leads to a Pareto efficient allocation of state-contingent incomes or risks.

The stock market as a market in state-contingent income claims

We assume that there is only one period and use the terms 'wealth' and 'income' interchangeably. Before the state of the world is known, individuals choose their portfolios by exchanging shares on the stock market. After all exchanges have been completed the state of the world is revealed and the firms pay out their profit to their owners. The profit of firm j in state s is Y_{js} and a decision-taker who owns the proportion a_j of firm j will receive a payment of $a_j Y_{js}$ from the firm. Let $\hat{a}_j$ denote the individual's initial holding in firm j. Shareholdings are the only source of income for shareholders. The stock market is assumed to be competitive and no individual owns a large proportion of the shares in any single firm. The stock market value of firm j is M_j, which is the number of shares in firm j times the price of a share. The budget constraint on an individual is

$$\Sigma a_j M_j = \Sigma \hat{a}_j M_j = w \qquad \text{[E.1]}$$

where w is the value of her initial portfolio or wealth. Given her choice of portfolio the individual's income in state s is

$$y_s = \Sigma a_j Y_{js} \qquad \text{[E.2]}$$

By varying the a_j subject to [E.1] the individual can alter her state distribution of income. We assume initially that a_j cannot be negative. (The consequences of allowing $a_j < 0$ (known as *short sales*) are examined below.) Let $m_j = w/M_j$ be the maximum shareholding in firm j that the individual could achieve by selling all her shares in other firms and buying shares only in firm j. The proportion of the individual's initial wealth w invested in firm j is $k_j = a_j M_j/w = a_j/m_j$. Given the prohibition on short sales, the k_j are constrained by $k_j \geqslant 0$ as well as $\Sigma k_j = 1$. The individual's *portfolio* can be defined as the vector $k = (k_1, \ldots, k_J)$ of the proportions of wealth invested in different firms.

We can write [E.2] as

$$y_s = \Sigma k_j m_j Y_{js} \qquad \text{[E.3]}$$

Figure 21.3

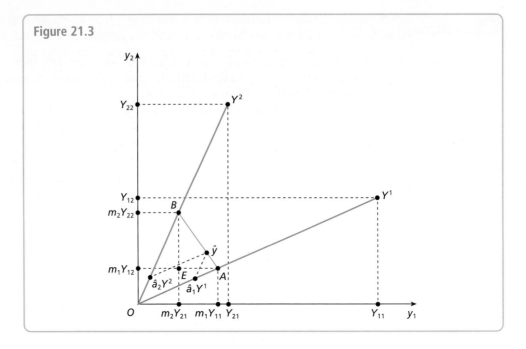

so that the set of feasible state-contingent income vectors achievable by trade on the stock market without short sales is a convex combination of the vectors achievable by investing all wealth in each type of share.

Figure 21.3 illustrates for the two-firm, two-state case. The points Y^1 and Y^2 are the state-contingent profit vectors of firms 1 and 2. The individual has an initial shareholding $(\hat{a}_1, \hat{a}_2)$ in the two firms. The initial shareholding entitles her to the income vector $\hat{a}_1 Y^1$ from firm 1 and $\hat{a}_2 Y^2$ from firm 2. (The ratio of the distance $O\hat{a}_1 Y^1$ to the distance OY^1 is the fraction of the profit of firm 1 to which the individual is entitled by her initial shareholding.) Using the parallelogram rule to sum the vectors $\hat{a}_1 Y^1$ and $\hat{a}_2 Y^2$ we see that her initial state distribution of income is $\hat{y}$. If she puts all her wealth into purchase of firm 1 shares she gets the state-contingent income vector $m_1 Y^1 = (m_1 Y_{11}, m_1 Y_{12})$ at A and if she puts all her wealth into purchase of shares in firm 2 she gets $m_2 Y^2 = (m_2 Y_{21}, m_2 Y_{22})$ at B. Since all feasible state-contingent income combinations are convex combinations of $m_1 Y^1$ and $m_2 Y^2$ her budget constraint in state-contingent income space is the line AB. Since her initial portfolio is obviously feasible $\hat{y}$ also lies on AB.

The slope of AB shows the rate at which the individual can exchange state 1 income for state 2 income by altering the composition of her portfolio. The stock market values of the firms M_j and the state-contingent profits Y_{js} determine implicit prices for state-contingent income claims and the ratio of these implicit prices is the slope of AB. From Fig. 21.3 the slope of AB is $-BE/AE$ or

$$\frac{dy_2}{dy_1} = \frac{m_2 Y_{22} - m_1 Y_{12}}{m_2 Y_{21} - m_1 Y_{11}} = \frac{\dfrac{Y_{22}}{M_2} - \dfrac{Y_{12}}{M_1}}{\dfrac{Y_{21}}{M_2} - \dfrac{Y_{11}}{M_1}} \qquad [E.4]$$

If the investor sells £1 of shares in firm 1 and buys £1 of shares in firm 2 the proportion of firm 1 she owns will fall by $1/M_1$ and the proportion of firm 2 owned will increase by $1/M_2$. The transactions increase her state s income from firm 2 by Y_{2s}/M_2 and reduce her state s income from firm 1 by Y_{1s}/M_1. Her state 2 income will therefore change by $Y_{22}/M_2 - Y_{12}/M_1$ and her state 1 income by $Y_{21}/M_2 - Y_{11}/M_1$.

Short sales

When short sales are not permitted the individual's portfolio is constrained by $a_j \geqslant 0$ or $k_j \geqslant 0$, as well as [E.1] or $\Sigma k_j = 1$. The feasible set of state-contingent income claims in Fig. 21.3 is the area OAB. When short sales are possible the individual can sell shares which she does not own and use the proceeds to buy shares in other companies. Thus suppose that she has sold her initial endowment of shares in firm 2 and bought shares in firm 1 and is at point A in Fig. 21.4. She then sells shares equal to the proportion OD/OY^2 of firm 2's outstanding shares and promises to deliver the certificates when the state of the world is known. When the state of the world is revealed she enters the market for firm 2 shares. Since the state of the world is known firm 2's profit is determined and the price of OD/OY^2 of firm 2 is just Y_{21} times OD/OY^2 if state 1 has occurred and Y_{22} times OD/OY^2 if state 2 has occurred. Hence she pays $FD = EF'$ for the shares she has sold if state 1 has occurred and $OF = CF'$ if state 2 has occurred. This sequence of transactions in firm 2 shares is equivalent to her having the negative holding D. The proceeds from selling firm 2 shares are used to buy more firm 1 securities to increase her ownership of firm 1 to OC/OY^1. Her state-contingent income vector is then the sum of OD and OC at OE.

Thus by selling shares in firm 2 which she does not own and redeeming her promise to deliver these shares by buying them in the market once the state of the

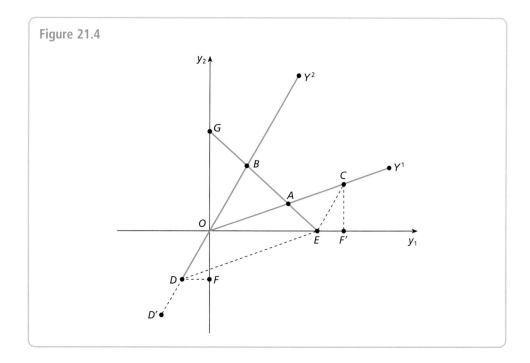

Figure 21.4

world is known, the individual can extend her budget line rightwards from A to the y_1 axis. A similar argument applies to short sales of firm 1 shares. Hence short sales extend the set of feasible state-contingent income vectors achievable via the stock market to the area OGE. The implicit market in state-contingent income claims generated by the stock market is thus equivalent to an explicit market in claims to state 1 and 2 income.

The argument generalizes to more than two states and if short sales are permitted the implicit budget line in state-contingent income space is defined by [E.3] without the restriction that k_j or $a_j \geq 0$.

The equivalence between stock markets and state-contingent income claims markets just demonstrated rests on several important assumptions. *First*, the implied shareholdings must not exceed the total shares of the firm. In Fig. 21.4 it is necessary for the individual to purchase OC/OY^1 of firm 1. If OC was greater than OY^1 this would not be possible. When the individual initially owns a small proportion of any firm the assumption is not restrictive. *Second*, purchasers of the shares sold short must be sure that the short seller will deliver once the state of the world is known, otherwise they will not be willing to pay the market price for the shares. Thus they must be able to be sure that they are not dealing with someone who has foolishly or fraudulently sold OD'/OY^2 of firm 2 since if state 2 occurs she will not be able to deliver all the shares in firm 2. (What state-contingent income vector is achieved by such a foolish or fraudulent short seller?) *Third*, and perhaps most demanding, if there are S states of the world there must be S firms with linearly independent profit vectors. Thus, in Fig. 21.4, if only firm 1 existed the budget line would collapse to the single point A and there would be no means of exchanging income in one state for income in another. Similarly, if firm 2 had profits in each state which were always a constant fraction of firm 1's, the point OY^2 would lie on the ray OY^1 and the budget constraint would again be a single point. (Where would m_2Y^2 be in relation to m_1Y^1?) The *spanning* requirement that there be S firms with linearly independent profit vectors is very strong given the large number of different states of the world. However, it may be possible to mimic a complete market in state-contingent income claims even if the spanning requirement is not satisfied by opening additional markets in certain derivative assets (options) based on the shares of the firms (see Question 6, Exercise 21E).

Portfolio choice

We illustrate the individual's choice of a portfolio of securities with the simple case in which there are only two states and two securities. Then we consider a more general case in which there are many securities and many states and show that it may be possible to reduce this case to the two-asset case.

First, it is useful to define the *rate of return* of a security j as

$$h_{js} = (Y_{js}/M_j) - 1 \qquad [E.5]$$

Recall that £z buys z/M_j shares in firm j and entitles the purchaser to income $z(Y_{js}/M_j)$ from firm j in state s. [E.5] is just the excess of the income gained in state s over the income forgone (£z) to purchase the shares, all divided by the amount invested (£z).

There is assumed to be a riskless asset which has a certain rate of return of h_0. (Question 2, Exercise 21E, investigates the circumstances in which a riskless asset

Figure 21.5

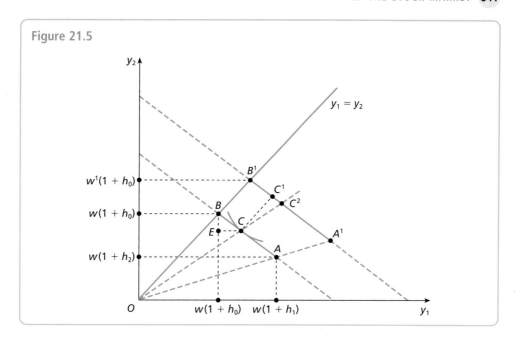

can be constructed from two risky assets.) The other asset is risky and has a rate of return of h_s. (We can drop the firm subscript since there is only one risky asset.) The amount invested in the risky asset is D so that the realized income of the individual in state s is

$$y_s = (w - D)(1 + h_0) + D(1 + h_s) = w(1 + h_0) + D(h_s - h_0) \qquad \text{[E.6]}$$

Figure 21.5 illustrates the state-contingent income possibilities. The budget constraint is a straight line with slope $(h_2 - h_0)/(h_1 - h_0)$. (Apply [E.4], together with the definition [E.5] of the rate of return, with firm 2 having certain profit so that $h_{21} = h_{22} = h_0$ and firm 1 having risky profits so that $h_{11} = h_1$ and $h_{12} = h_2$. Alternatively, use [E.6] to solve for D in terms of y_1, substitute for D in the expression for y_2 and differentiate y_2 with respect to y_1.) The solid portion of the budget line AB shows combinations of state-contingent incomes attainable when $0 \leqslant D \leqslant w$. Increasing the investment in the risky asset moves the individual down the budget line from B (where $D = 0$) towards A (where $D = w$). At point C the amount of investment in the risky asset is proportional to the distance BC since by Pythagoras's Theorem

$$BC = [(BE)^2 + (EC)^2]^{1/2} = [D^2(h_2 - h_0)^2 + D^2(h_1 - h_0)^2]^{1/2} = \psi D \qquad \text{[E.7]}$$

where $\psi = [(h_2 - h_0)^2 + (h_1 - h_0)^2]^{1/2}$.

If short sales of the risky asset ($D < 0$) are feasible the budget line extends above B. Short sales of the safe asset ($D > w$) extend the budget line below A. Short sales can be interpreted in more familiar terms as lending or borrowing. When $D > w$ the individual is borrowing (at an interest rate of h_0) to finance purchases of the risky asset with the repayment of $(D - w)(1 + h_0)$ being financed from the proceeds of the risky security $D(1 + h_s)$. When $D < 0$ the individual is lending D at an interest rate of h_0 financed from the proceeds of short sales of the risky asset. When the state of the world is revealed and her debtors repay $D(1 + h_0)$, she will purchase the risky security at a cost of $D(1 + h_s)$ to make good her short sale contract.

The portfolio problem is to choose D to maximize

$$V(D; w, h_0, \pi, h) = Ev(y_s) = \sum \pi_s v(y_s) \tag{E.8}$$

and the first-order condition in the case where the restrictions, if any, on short sales are not binding, is

$$V_D(D^*; w, h_0, \pi, h) = Ev'(y_s)(h_s - h_0) = \sum \pi_s v'(y_s)(h_s - h_0) = 0 \tag{E.9}$$

(The reader should check that V is concave in D so that [E.9] is sufficient as well as necessary for an optimum.)

We can investigate the circumstances in which the optimal D is positive by writing [E.9] as

$$Ev'(y_s)(h_s - h_0) = Ev'(y_s)(Eh_s - h_0) + \text{Cov}(v'(y_s), h_s) = 0 \tag{E.10}$$

Since $Ev'(y_s) > 0$, the covariance term in [E.10] must be negative if $Eh_s > h_0$ and positive if $Eh_s < h_0$. Since $v'' < 0$, the covariance of v' and h_s is negative only if y_s and h_s have positive covariance. Reference to [E.6] shows that y_s increases with h_s only if $D > 0$. Hence $Eh_s > h_0$ implies that $D^* > 0$. When $Eh_s < h_0$ the investor will set $D^* < 0$ if short sales of the risky asset (lending) are feasible.

There are only two states, so that [E.9] can be rearranged to give

$$-\frac{\pi_1 v'(y_1)}{\pi_2 v'(y_2)} = \frac{h_2 - h_0}{h_1 - h_0} \tag{E.11}$$

where the indifference curve of the investor is tangent to a budget line as at C in Fig. 21.5.

The simple two-asset, two-state portfolio problem is very similar to the insurance problem in section 19B, as comparison of Figs 21.5 and 19.1 and the first-order conditions [E.11] above and [B.10] in section 19B make clear. Insurance permits the insured to exchange income in one state for income in another state and so does the securities market. If the insured can buy insurance against losses in any state and if the investor is faced with a full set of linearly independent securities, the insurance and securities markets are each equivalent to a full set of contingent claim markets and hence equivalent to each other. The individual would be able to achieve the same state distribution of incomes by trading in either market. For example, if the two states are wet and fine weather she could buy what is known as 'pluvius' insurance whereby she receives compensation from the insurance company if the weather is wet. She can achieve the same kind of state-contingent transfer by an appropriate mix of the safe asset and the shares of a firm which has a higher rate of return in wet weather (an umbrella manufacturer?).

In view of the similarity of the simple portfolio problem with the insurance problem we leave the detailed derivation of the comparative static properties of portfolio choice to the exercises. We will investigate the effect of wealth changes on the demand for the risky asset since the results are relevant in more complex models of portfolio choice and also for the assessment of the efficiency of securities markets.

Wealth effects on the demand for a risky asset

In Fig. 21.5 an increase in initial wealth from w to w^1 shifts the budget line to $B^1 A^1$. If the demand for the risky asset is unchanged the new portfolio is at C^1 where $B^1 C^1 = BC = \psi D^*$. If the *share* of wealth $k^{*1} = D^{*1}/w^1$ invested in the risky asset is unaffected by the increase in w the new portfolio must be at C^2 where $k^{*1} = D^{*1}/w^1 = B^1C^2/B^1A^1 = BC/BA = D^*/w = k^*$. Since the slope of the budget line is unchanged the effect on the demand for the risky asset depends only on what happens to the slopes of the indifference curves as the investor moves from BA to B^1A^1. Recall from section 17E that the slope of the indifference curves is constant along lines (like CC^1) parallel to the 45° line if the investor has constant absolute risk aversion and is constant along rays from the origin (line OCC^2) if she has constant relative risk aversion. Thus the investor invests a constant amount in the risky asset if she has constant absolute risk aversion and a constant proportion in the risky asset if she has constant relative risk aversion.

More generally, even when there are many states we can establish that

$$\frac{\partial D^*}{\partial w} \gtreqless 0 \quad \text{if and only if} \quad \frac{dA(y)}{dy} \lesseqgtr 0 \qquad [E.12]$$

$$\frac{\partial(k^*)}{\partial w} \gtreqless 0 \quad \text{if and only if} \quad \frac{dR(y)}{dy} \lesseqgtr 0 \qquad [E.13]$$

where $A(y) = -v''/v'$ is absolute risk aversion and $R(y) = -v''y/v' = yA(y)$ is relative risk aversion. The method of proof is instructive. An increase in w increases the demand for the risky asset if and only if it increases the marginal value of the asset to the investor, i.e.

$$V_{Dw}(D^*; w, h_0, \pi, h) = Ev''(y_s)(h_s - h_0)(1 + h_0) \qquad [E.14]$$

must be positive. Assume that absolute risk aversion is decreasing and consider those states of the world where $h_s \geqslant h_0$ so that $y_s = w(1 + h_0) + D(h_s - h_0) \geqslant w(1 + h_0)$ and

$$A(y_s) = -v''(y_s)/v'(y_s) \leqslant A(w(1 + h_0)) \equiv A^c \qquad [E.15]$$

Hence multiplying both sides by $-\pi_s v'(y_s)(h_s - h_0) \leqslant 0$ gives

$$\pi_s v''(y_s)(h_s - h_0) \geqslant -A^c \pi_s v'(y_s)(h_s - h_0) \qquad [E.16]$$

Now consider the states where $h_s < h_0$ and $y_s < w(1 + h_0)$ so that

$$A(y_s) = -v''(y_s)/v'(y_s) \geqslant A(w(1 + h_0)) \equiv A^c$$

Multiply both sides by $-\pi_s y'(y_s)(h_s - h_0) > 0$ (remember $h_s < h_0$) to get

$$\pi_s v''(y_s)(h_s - h_0) \geqslant -A^c \pi_s v'(y_s)(h_s - h_0) \qquad [E.17]$$

Adding up [E.16] and [E.17] over all states and multiplying by $(1 + h_0)$ gives

$$(1 + h_0)\Sigma \pi_s v''(y_s)(h_s - h_0) \geqslant -(1 + h_0)A^c \sum \pi_s v'(y_s)(h_s - h_0) = 0 \qquad [E.18]$$

where the last equation follows from the first-order condition [E.9]. Since the left-hand side of [E.18] is just [E.14] we have shown that if and only if there is diminishing absolute risk aversion ($A' < 0$) the demand for the risky asset increases as initial income increases. The argument can be repeated for the other cases to establish [E.12] and adapted slightly to give [E.13].

Portfolio choice: general case

In the general case there are J risky securities with rates of return h_{js} ($j = 1, \ldots, J$), one security with a certain rate of return h_0 and S states of the world. Letting D_j be the amount invested in the jth risky security the investor's state s income is

$$y_s = (w - \Sigma D_j)(1 + h_0) + \Sigma D_j(1 + h_{js}) = w(1 + h_0) + \Sigma D_j(h_{js} - h_0) \quad \text{[E.19]}$$

The first-order conditions for the choice of D_j are

$$Ev'(y_s)(h_{js} - h_0) = 0 \qquad j = 1, \ldots, J \qquad \text{[E.20]}$$

which is analogous to [E.9].

The investor's portfolio choice is said to have the *separation property* if the mix of *risky* assets in her optimal portfolio is independent of her initial wealth. It is then possible to model many aspects of the individual's choice as if she were choosing between two assets: the safe asset and the single risky asset defined by the optimal mix of risky assets. Let $D = \Sigma D_j$ be the total amount invested in risky securities and $\delta_j = D_j/D$ be the proportion of the investment in risky securities which is invested in security j. Choosing D and the δ_j is clearly equivalent to choosing D_j, with y_s now given by

$$y_s = w(1 + h_0) + D\Sigma \delta_j(h_{js} - h_0) = w(1 + h_0) + D(\Sigma \delta_j h_{js} - h_0) \qquad \text{[E.21]}$$

If the separation property holds we could model the portfolio choice problem as the investor first constructing a single risky asset or *mutual fund* with a rate of return $h_s(\delta) = \Sigma \delta_j h_{js}$ and then deciding how to allocate her initial wealth between the safe asset with rate of return h_0 and the risky mutual fund asset with rate of return $h_s(\delta)$.

If the investor's choice is to exhibit the separation property it is necessary to restrict her preferences or the state distribution of returns on the risky assets. Recalling the discussion of linear risk tolerance in section B, we can state the Portfolio Separation Theorem.

Portfolio Separation Theorem. *The investor's optimal mix of risky assets is independent of initial wealth for all state distributions of returns if and only if there is linear risk tolerance (hyperbolic absolute risk aversion):* $-v'(y)/v''(y) = \rho + \tau y$.

The proof that LRT is necessary for separation would take up too much space and interested readers should consult Cass and Stiglitz (1970). We will demonstrate the sufficiency of one type of LRT for separation and leave the others to the exercises. Recall from section B that if $\tau = 0$ the utility function is exponential: $v(y) = -e^{-y/\rho}$ and exhibits constant LRT and absolute risk aversion (equal to $1/\rho$).

With these preferences the individual chooses D and the δ_j (subject to $\Sigma \delta_j = 1$) to maximize

$$Ev(y_s) = -Ee^{-[w(1+h_0)+D(\Sigma \delta_j h_{js} - h_0)]/\rho}$$
$$= -e^{-w(1+h_0)/\rho} Ee^{-D(\Sigma \delta_j h_{js} - h_0)/\rho} \qquad \text{[E.22]}$$

but since $e^{-w(1+h_0)/\rho}$ does not vary with the choice variables D and δ_j, maximization of [E.22] is equivalent to maximization of

$$-Ee^{-D(\Sigma \delta_j h_{js} - h_0)/\rho} \qquad \text{[E.23]}$$

Since [E.23] does not depend on w neither will its derivatives with respect to the choice variables and so the optimal value of D and the δ_j do not depend on w. Thus with this type of LRT preferences, the individual always puts the same absolute amount into risky assets and does not alter the proportions in which they are held. (As the exercises show, with the other LRT preferences the δ_j will also not vary with w but D will.)

Pareto efficiency and incomplete stock markets

We showed in section B that, if there is a set of competitive markets in which it is possible to trade claims for the delivery of income contingent on the occurrence of any of the S states of the world, the market equilibrium would be Pareto efficient. Stock markets trade securities which are bundles of claims to state-contingent incomes (the profit vectors of the J firms). We showed in the first part of this section that if there were S firms with linearly independent profit vectors (the spanning requirement) and no restrictions on short sales the stock market is equivalent to a complete set of state-contingent income claim markets. Hence if the spanning requirement is satisfied and there are no restrictions on short sales the equilibrium of the markets in the shares of the firms is Pareto efficient. Since the spanning requirement is very strong it is of interest to enquire about the Pareto efficiency of incomplete stock markets when there are fewer than S firms with linearly independent profit vectors.

Unfortunately, it can be shown that severe restrictions must be placed on the preferences and probability beliefs of investors if the equilibrium of an incomplete stock market is to be Pareto efficient:

Incomplete stock markets are Pareto efficient if and only if all investors have (a) LRT preferences: $-v_i'/v_i'' = \rho_i + \tau y_{is}$ and (b) identical probability beliefs.

The proof of this proposition is long and we will limit ourselves to sketching the necessity of (a) and (b) and leave the full proof to the references and the exercises. The chain of argument for (a) is as follows: (i) Pareto efficiency requires that y_{is} (the ith individual's income in state s) does not vary with the total income Y_t of the economy in any other state t (invariance); (ii) invariance implies that individual i owns the same proportion of all firms (equiproportionality); (iii) equiproportionality implies that y_{is} is a linear function of total income Y_s in state s, i.e. that the Pareto efficient sharing rule is linear (linearity); (iv) if linear sharing rules are Pareto efficient individuals must have LRT preferences.

The state-contingent income of the ith investor in state s under a stock market is

$$y_{is} = a_{i0}Y_0 + \Sigma_j a_{ij}Y_{js} \qquad \text{[E.24]}$$

(compare [E.3]). We assume that there is a certain asset, i.e. a firm with a certain profit vector which pays out Y_0 in all states of the world. Y_{js} is the total payout by the jth risky firm in state s. The proportion of each firm owned by the ith investor is a_{i0} for the firm with the certain payout and a_{ij} for the jth risky firm. The investor's demand for a share in the jth firm depends on her probability beliefs ($\pi_i = (\pi_{i1}, \ldots, \pi_{iS})$), her initial endowment of shares ($\hat{a}_i = (\hat{a}_{i0}, \ldots, \hat{a}_{iJ})$), the vector of prices of the firms ($M = (M_1, \ldots, M_J)$) and the $S \times (J + 1)$ matrix Y of the firms' payouts.

Section B showed that a Pareto efficient allocation has the invariance characteristic that each individual's income (y_{is}) in state s does not depend on the total income $Y_t = \Sigma_j Y_{jt}$ available in any other state of the world. Suppose that Y changes so that the profit of firm 1 increases by £q in one of the states s and the profit of firm J falls by £q in the same state s but there are no other changes in Y. The change in Y would leave total income in state $s(Y_s)$ and all the other states unchanged. Hence, if the stockmarket equilibrium always yields Pareto efficient allocations, such a change in Y must leave the state-contingent incomes of all investors unchanged. But their state-contingent incomes depend on their choice of shareholdings. Thus the Pareto efficiency requirement that state-contingent incomes are unaffected places restrictions on the choices made and hence on the preferences of the investors. The invariance of state-contingent incomes means that

$$dy_{is}/dq = a'_{i0}Y_0 + \sum a'_{ij}Y_{js} + a_{i1} - a_{ij} = 0 \qquad \text{[E.25]}$$

$$dy_{it}/dq = a'_{i0}Y_0 + \sum a'_{ij}Y_{jt} = 0 \qquad t \neq s \qquad \text{[E.26]}$$

where a'_{ij} is the change in i's demand for shares in the jth firm caused by the change in Y. (Note that in general a change in Y will lead to changes in demands for all firms' shares and to a new equilibrium set of prices M and so a'_{ij} reflects changes in M as well as the direct effect of the change in Y.) Although the state-contingent firm profits $(Y_0, Y_{1t}, \ldots, Y_{Jt})$ in some state t might lead to [E.26] holding for $a'_{ij} \neq 0$, the only way in which [E.26] can hold for all states $t \neq s$ and all Y is if $a'_{ij} = 0$ $(j = 0, 1, \ldots, J)$. But this implies that [E.25] is reduced to $a_{i1} = a_{ij}$. Repetition of the argument with firm 2, 3, $\ldots$, $J - 1$ replacing firm 1 establishes that if the stock market equilibrium allocation is to be Pareto efficient it must be the case that the investor's expected utility maximizing demands satisfy equiproportionality:

$$a_{ij} = a_i \qquad j = 1, \ldots, J \qquad i = 1, \ldots, n \qquad \text{[E.27]}$$

If the investor's income in each state is to be unaffected by changes in Y which do not alter the total income in any state she must always choose a portfolio in which she owns the same fraction of each risky firm. Her state-contingent income is

$$y_{is} = a_{i0}Y_0 + \sum a_i Y_{js} = a_{i0}Y_0 + a_i(Y_s - Y_0)$$
$$= \alpha_i + \beta_i Y_s \qquad \text{[E.28]}$$

where $\alpha_i = (a_{i0} - a_i)Y_0$, $\beta_i = a_i$ and $Y_s = Y_0 + \sum_j Y_{js}$ is total income in state s.

[E.28] is a linear sharing rule since a_i is independent of the state of the world and β_i is independent of Y_s. (If $\beta_i = a_i$ varied with Y_s then y_{it} for $t \neq s$ would also vary with Y_s and the allocation would not be Pareto efficient.) But from section B if linear sharing rules are Pareto efficient then individuals must have linear risk tolerance.

In fact [E.28] places even stronger restrictions on preferences. The amount invested in the jth risky firm by the ith investor is

$$D_{ij} = a_{ij}M_j = a_i M_j \qquad \text{[E.29]}$$

the total amount she invests in risky firms is

$$D_i = \sum_r D_{ir} = \sum a_{ij}M_r = a_i \sum M_r \qquad \text{[E.30]}$$

and so the proportion of D_i invested in the jth risky firm is

$$\delta_{ij} = D_{ij}/\sum_r D_{ir} = M_j/\sum M_r = \delta_j \qquad \text{[E.31]}$$

Hence all investors must make the same choice of δ_{ij} (although the total amount they invest in risky assets can differ). They must have the same type of LRT preferences and the same probability beliefs. This completes our sketch proof of the necessity of the proposition.

Conditions (a) and (b) are very restrictive, suggesting that incomplete stock markets will not usually yield Pareto efficient risk bearing. But is the concept of Pareto efficiency used a sensible criterion in these circumstances? The stock market is assumed to be incomplete in that the spanning condition is not satisfied: there are fewer linearly independent securities than states of the world and this restricts the individuals' abilities to transfer income across states. We compared the outcome of the stock market with a set of efficiency conditions derived in section B from an optimization problem in which there were no restrictions on state-contingent income transfers. A rigorous welfare analysis must involve consideration of why markets are incomplete and what prevents private individuals from making a full set of state-contingent transfers.

EXERCISE 21E

1. Consider the slope of the budget line AB in Fig. 21.5. What is the effect on AB of (a) a reduction in the individual's initial holding of firm j ($j = a, b$) shares; (b) an increase in the market price of firm j; (c) an increase in the profits of firm 1 in state s ($s = 1, 2$)?

2. Assume that there are two risky securities and two states of the world. Show that it is always possible to construct an asset which has a certain payoff, i.e. one which has the same yield in all states of the world if the spanning requirement is satisfied and short sales are permitted. When is it possible to construct a certain asset if short sales are not permitted?

3. Suppose that there is a safe asset, a single risky asset and two states of the world. Use a diagram to investigate the effects on the investor's demand for the risky asset of increases in (a) wealth; (b) the expected return on the risky asset; (c) the return on the safe asset; (d) the probability of the high rate of return state; (e) a mean preserving spread in the rate of return on the risky asset.

4. *Taxation and risk-taking.* Use the model in Question 3 to investigate whether increases in (a) a proportional tax on wealth $[(w - D)(1 + h_0) + D(1 + h_s)]$; (b) a proportional tax on the income from the portfolio $[(w - D)h_0 + Dh_s]$ increases or reduces investment in the risky asset.

5. *LRT with two assets.* We can use the model in Question 3 to examine the implications of LRT for the investor's response to wealth changes. As the investor's wealth varies the optimal D varies and traces a locus of state-contingent incomes in (y_1, y_2) space analogous to the income consumption curve in the consumer model in Chapter 2. Show that this locus is a straight line if and only if the investor has LRT preferences.

6. *LRT with many assets: separation.* Show that if the investor has a power or a logarithmic utility function the proportions of wealth invested in the risky assets are independent of her initial wealth. (*Hint:* it is best to work with choice variables c and δ_j where c is the amount invested in the safe asset and δ_j is the proportion of the remaining funds $w' \equiv (w - c)$ invested in the jth risky asset.)

7. *Options and spanning.* Suppose that there is only one firm with state-contingent profit vector (Y_1, Y_2) with $Y_1 > Y_2$. The spanning requirement is clearly not satisfied by a market in the firm's shares. Suppose that a market in call options on the firm's shares is introduced. The option entitles its holder to purchase one of the N shares in the firm at a fixed specified price once the state of the world is revealed and the firm declares its dividend Y_s. If the specified price p^0 satisfies $Y_1/N \geqslant p^0 > Y_2/N$ holders of an option to buy 1 share will exercise it if and only if the firm declares a dividend of Y_1. (a) Show that the original market in the firm's shares plus the derivative market in options together satisfy the spanning requirement. (b) Under what circumstances will markets in shares and options satisfy the spanning requirement?

8. *LRT and stock market efficiency.* Show that if all individuals have LRT preferences $-v_i'/v_i'' = \rho_i + \tau y_{is}$ and identical probability beliefs the stock market allocation is Pareto efficient (*Hint:* show that the conditions imply that the $\delta_{ij} = \delta_j$ for all individuals and are independent of wealth so that y_{is} is a linear function of the total income in state s.)

F. Incomplete stock markets

In this section we examine an economy in which it is possible to transfer income between states by production decisions and by transactions on stock markets. Firms carry out production activities and issue shares, which are traded on the stock market, and are the means by which individuals can exchange claims on incomes across states of the world. When there are as many linearly independent firm profit vectors as there are states of the world, and short sales are possible, then individuals have a full set of exchange possibilities between all states. As we saw in section E, trading in the shares of the firms is then equivalent to being able to trade a full set of Arrow securities. The prices of firms' shares imply a set of prices for income claims contingent on each state and, by valuing production plans at these implicit prices, managers are able to take production (investment) decisions in the best interests of all shareholders. Managers can choose the production plan which yields the most valuable vector of state-contingent profits and, since the firm's stock market value will be just the value of the profit vector at the implicit prices, managers act in the shareholders' interests by maximizing the stock market value of the firm.

In this section we assume that the stock market is incomplete in that there are fewer firms than states. The consequences are far-reaching. Not only may resource allocations be inefficient but the very possibility that firms *can* take decisions in their shareholders' interests is brought into question. The problem of defining the objectives of a firm under uncertainty when markets are incomplete is as yet unresolved, leaving an important gap at the centre of microeconomic theory.

We assume an economy with two individuals, two firms, two periods and three states of the world. At date 0, individuals have given endowments of shares in firms' outputs. Current output at date 0 is divided between current consumption and investment, the latter undertaken by firms. The investment produces an uncertain output at date 1. The date 1 outputs of each firm are distributed to individuals proportionately to their shareholdings. The single good or output can be thought of as income. We thus focus on the allocation of resources to investment and to consumption across states of the world, rather than the determination of relative prices of different goods.

Individual i's consumption is x_{i0} at date 0 and x_{is} in state $s = 1, 2, 3$ at date 1. Individuals always consume their entire income in each state and at each date. Here x_{i0}, x_{is} are also i's income at date 0 and at date 1, state s. Shareholdings are the only source of income. Her share in the output of firm $j = 1, 2$ at date 1, *in every state*, is $a_{ij} \in [0, 1]$ with $\Sigma_i a_{ij} = 1$. At date 0 she has the given share endowments $\hat{a}_{ij}$, and trade takes place on the stock market at that date to determine the final shareholdings a_{ij}. At date 0 each firm has a given output $\hat{Y}_{j0}$, of which it invests Y_{j0}, distributing the rest $(\hat{Y}_{j0} - Y_{j0})$ to individuals in proportion to their initial share holdings $\hat{a}_{ij}$. It obtains output $Y_{js} = f_{js}(Y_{j0})$ at date 1 in state $s = 1, 2, 3$. The stochastic production functions are twice differentiable and strictly concave. A firm's state contingent outputs at date 1 are *joint products*: the investment decision Y_{j0} at date 0 determines an entire state distribution of outputs $\{f_{j1}(Y_{j0}), f_{j2}(Y_{j0}), f_{j3}(Y_{j0})\}$ at date 1. The firm cannot alter the output in one state without altering output in all other states.

The *basic constraints* of the economy are

$$\Sigma_i x_{i0} + \Sigma_j Y_{j0} \leq \Sigma_j \hat{Y}_{j0} \tag{F.1}$$

$$\Sigma_i x_{is} \leq \Sigma_j f_{js}(Y_{j0}) \qquad s = 1, 2, 3 \tag{F.2}$$

At date 0, the total consumption of individuals plus the total investment of firms cannot exceed the total initial endowment. In each state at date 1, total consumption cannot exceed total output. In the stock market economy in which there are fewer firms than states, individual i's consumptions are constrained by the fact that she receives the same proportion θ_{ij} of firm j's outputs in each state, and not all the allocations which satisfy [F.1] and [F.2] are in fact feasible.

As a benchmark, we first examine the conditions for Pareto efficient allocation relative only to the basic constraints. Individual i's expected utility is

$$\bar{v}_i = v_{i0}(x_{i0}) + \Sigma_s \pi_s v_{is}(x_{is}) \qquad i = 1, 2 \qquad \text{[F.3]}$$

where we assume that utility is additively separable over time and that consumers are risk averse. π_s is the probability of state $s = 1, 2, 3$. (Note that we assume that both individuals agree on the state probabilities.) The Lagrangean for the Pareto efficiency problem of maximizing individual 1's expected utility, subject to the basic constraints and to individual 2 getting at least an expected utility of $\bar{v}_2^0$, is

$$L = \bar{v}_1 + \rho[\bar{v}_2^0 - \bar{v}_2] + \lambda_0[\Sigma_j \hat{Y}_{j0} - \Sigma_i x_{i0} - \Sigma_j Y_{j0}]$$
$$+ \Sigma_s \lambda_s[\Sigma_j f_{js}(Y_{j0}) - \Sigma_i x_{is}] \qquad \text{[F.4]}$$

The first-order conditions for the Pareto efficiency problem are

$$\frac{v'_{i0}}{\pi_s v'_{is}} = \frac{\lambda_0}{\lambda_s} \qquad i = 1, 2 \qquad s = 1, 2, 3 \qquad \text{[F.5]}$$

$$\Sigma_s \lambda_s f'_{js} = \lambda_0 \qquad j = 1, 2 \qquad \text{[F.6]}$$

plus the basic constraints [F.1] and [F.2] satisfied as equalities. Here v'_{i0} is the marginal utility of income at date 0 for consumer i, v'_{is} is her marginal utility of income at date 1 in state s and $f'_{js} = df_{js}(Y_{j0})/dY_{j0}$ is the marginal product of investment in firm j at date 0 in terms of state s output at date 1.

The left-hand side of [F.5] is consumer i's marginal rate of substitution between the good at date 0 and the good conditional on the occurrence of state s at date 1. As usual, efficiency in consumption requires that individuals' marginal rates of substitution must be equalized. Note that [F.5] also implies that marginal rates of substitution between income in different states at date 1 must also be equalized.

We choose the good at date 0 to be the numeraire and define $p_s \equiv \lambda_s/\lambda_0$ as the shadow price of a unit of the good contingent on state s. Then [F.5] requires that both consumers' marginal rates of substitution between date 0 consumption and state s, date 1, consumption should be equal to the shadow price p_s. We can also rewrite [F.6] as

$$\Sigma_s p_s f'_{js} = 1 \qquad j = 1, 2 \qquad \text{[F.7]}$$

The left-hand side of [F.7] is the *marginal value product* of investment Y_{j0} by firm j at date 0, and the right-hand side is its marginal cost. Thus investment is efficient when it has the same marginal value product in each firm and marginal value product is equal to marginal cost.

The efficient allocation could be decentralized as a competitive market equilibrium *if* consumers and firms faced the prices p_s. If each firm $j = 1, 2$ solved the problem of maximizing its profit P_j at the prices p_s:

$$\max_{Y_{j0}} P_j = \Sigma_s p_s f_{js}(Y_{j0}) + \hat{Y}_{j0} - Y_{j0} \qquad \text{[F.8]}$$

and each consumer $i = 1, 2$ solved the utility maximization problem

$$\max_{x_{i0}, x_{i1}, x_{i2}, x_{i3}} v_i \quad \text{s.t.} \quad x_{i0} + \Sigma_s p_s x_{is} \leq \Sigma_j a_{ij} P_j \qquad \text{[F.9]}$$

the efficiency conditions [F.6] and [F.7] would be satisfied. But to establish the prices p_s of state-contingent income claims, we need markets where, actually or effectively, claims to income contingent on each state of the world can be traded. We assume that there are no markets in Arrow securities, and, with three states of the world and two firms, the stock market is not equivalent to a complete set of Arrow-security markets. Hence an allocation which is Pareto efficient relative only to the basic constraints cannot in general be decentralized in this incomplete stock market economy: the equilibrium of the incomplete stock market economy cannot satisfy the Pareto efficiency conditions [F.6] and [F.7].

We now consider the characteristics of allocations that *are* feasible in an economy in which individual consumptions are determined by shareholdings in firms. We assume that at date 0 firms choose investments Y_{j0}, and pay the remaining output to shareholders. Trade in shares then takes place, with shareholders having full knowledge of the future state distributions of outputs of the firms. Then, at date 1, in whatever state is realized, consumers receive their chosen shares in the firm's outputs. The economy is still subject to the basic constraints but individual consumptions are now determined by shareholdings:

$$x_{i0} = \Sigma_j \hat{a}_{ij}(\hat{Y}_{j0} - Y_{j0}) \qquad i = 1, 2 \qquad \text{[F.10]}$$

$$\Sigma_i \hat{a}_{ij} = 1 \qquad j = 1, 2 \qquad \text{[F.11]}$$

$$x_{is} = \Sigma_j a_{ij} f_{js}(Y_{j0}) \qquad i = 1, 2 \qquad s = 1, 2, 3 \qquad \text{[F.12]}$$

$$\Sigma_i a_{ij} = 1 \qquad j = 1, 2 \qquad \text{[F.13]}$$

Summing over i in [F.10] and [F.12] shows that any allocations feasible under these constraints also satisfy the basic constraints [F.1] and [F.2]. The converse is not true – not all allocations that satisfy [F.1] and [F.2] can be attained by shareholding fixed across states of the world. For example, if the date 1 state output vectors of the two firms were (5, 10, 5) and (15, 20, 5), an allocation which gives a consumer a date 1 state-contingent consumption vector (10, 10, 5) is not feasible via shareholdings.

The conclusion that an economy with an incomplete set of markets is not efficient, compared with the allocation which could be achieved if it was possible to make unrestricted state-contingent income transfers, may not be relevant for policy purposes. The reasons for incompleteness of markets are also likely to prevent a planner choosing an allocation satisfying the Pareto efficiency conditions [F.5] and [F.6]. It seems more sensible to ask the question first posed by Diamond (1967): given the constraints on the means by which consumptions are allocated in an incomplete stock market economy, is the incomplete stock market equilibrium allocation Pareto efficient *relative to these constraints*? To answer the question, we must first characterize the *constrained Pareto efficient allocation* and then compare it with the equilibrium of the incomplete stock market economy.

The conditions for constrained Pareto efficiency are derived by choosing the shareholdings and investments that maximize $\bar{v}_1$ for given $\bar{v}_2$ subject to the constraints [F.10] to [F.13]. We can simplify somewhat by noting that the initial shareholdings $\hat{a}_{ij}$ do not affect date 1 consumptions. Choosing the $\hat{a}_{ij}$ is equivalent to choosing the date 0 consumptions. We therefore derive the constrained Pareto efficiency conditions by choosing the date 0 consumptions and investments (subject to [F.1]) and the shareholdings a_{ij}.

Substituting for x_{is} from [F.12] in $\bar{v}_i$, we form the Lagrangean

$$L = \bar{v}_1 + \rho(\bar{v}_2^0 - \bar{v}_2) + \lambda_0[\Sigma_j \hat{Y}_{j0} - \Sigma_i x_{i0} - \Sigma_j Y_{j0}] + \Sigma_j \lambda_j[\Sigma_i a_{ij} - 1] \qquad [F.14]$$

From the resulting first-order conditions we obtain

$$\frac{\Sigma_s \pi_s f_{js}(Y_{j0})v_{1s}'}{v_{10}'} = \frac{\lambda_j}{\lambda_0} = \frac{\Sigma_s f_{js}(Y_{js})v_{2s}'}{v_{20}'} \qquad j = 1, 2 \qquad [F.15]$$

$$\Sigma_s \Sigma_i a_{ij}\delta_{is}f_{sj}' = 1 \qquad j = 1, 2 \qquad [F.16]$$

where $\delta_{is} \equiv \pi_s v_{is}'/v_{i0}'$ is defined as i's *discount factor* on consumption contingent on state s. δ_{is} represents i's marginal rate of substitution between certain consumption at date 0 and consumption contingent on state s at date 1: the amount of certain date 0 consumption she would be willing to give up in exchange for a unit of consumption at date 1 in state s. Note that δ_{is} depends on i's preferences, the income levels in state s and at date 0 and the probability that state s will occur.

Condition [F.16] requires that the discounted marginal productivity of investment is equal to its marginal cost. The discount factor to be applied to value an additional unit of output from firm j in state s is $\Sigma_i a_{ij}\delta_{ij}$ – a weighted average of the shareholders' discount rates, where the weights are the individual's shareholdings. Thus a larger shareholder's preferences should carry more weight in the evaluation of the firm's investment plans. In this type of economy investment is analogous to a public good, in that all shareholders benefit from the resulting output in each state, to an extent determined by their shareholdings. Thus [F.16] is similar to the condition determining the optimal supply of a public good: marginal benefits are summed over individuals (see section 14B).

In condition [F.15] $\Sigma_s \pi_s f_{js}(Y_{j0})v_{is}'$ is the marginal expected utility to individual i of an increase in her share of firm j's output at date 1. A share in a company is a joint product in that it yields a distribution of consumption across states at date 1. Condition [F.15] has the interpretation that, in an incomplete stock market economy, constrained Pareto efficiency requires that marginal rates of substitution between current consumption and the joint product of a shareholding in firm j be equalized across individuals.

We can also write [F.15] as

$$\Sigma_s \delta_{1s}f_{js}(Y_{j0}) = \lambda_j/\lambda_0 = \Sigma_s \delta_{2s}f_{js}(Y_{j0}) \qquad j = 1, 2 \qquad [F.17]$$

so that, at a constrained Pareto efficient allocation, each consumer must assign the same discounted value to the distribution of firm j's output across states at date 1.

We next consider whether the equilibrium of the incomplete stock market economy satisfies conditions [F.15] and [F.16]. The firms choose their investments Y_{j0} and distribute what is left of their date 0 output to their shareholders in proportion to their initial shareholdings. The individuals, acting as price takers, then trade shares on the stock market at date 0. The total stock market value of firm j is M_j: the amount that will have to be paid to own 100 per cent of the shares of firm j. The individuals know the firms' investment plans, and thus the state distribution of outputs, when they trade shares on the stock market at date 0.

The budget constraints relating to the consumers' transactions on the stock market are

$$x_{i0} + \Sigma_j a_{ij}v_j \leq \Sigma_j \hat{a}_{ij}(\hat{Y}_{j0} - Y_{j0}) + \Sigma_j \hat{a}_{ij}M_j \qquad i = 1, 2 \qquad [F.18]$$

The right-hand side of [F.18] is the consumer's initial wealth: the current output received from the distribution of uninvested date 0 output plus the value of the initial endowment of shares. Consumers choose current consumption x_{i0} and share-holdings a_{ij} to maximize expected utility

$$v_i = v_i(x_{i0}) + \Sigma_s \pi_s v(\Sigma_j a_{ij} f_{js}(Y_{j0})) \qquad i = 1, 2 \qquad [\text{F.19}]$$

subject to the budget constraint [F.18]. The first-order conditions are

$$v_{i0}' - \mu_i = 0 \qquad [\text{F.20}]$$

$$\Sigma_s \pi_s v_{is}' f_{js}(Y_{j0}) - \mu_i M_j = 0 \qquad j = 1, 2 \qquad [\text{F.21}]$$

μ_i is the Lagrange multiplier on the wealth constraint and can be interpreted as the marginal expected utility of wealth. From [F.20] and [F.21] we obtain

$$\Sigma_s \delta_{1s} f_{js}(Y_{j0}) = M_j = \Sigma_s \delta_{2s} f_{js}(Y_{j0}) \qquad j = 1, 2 \qquad [\text{F.22}]$$

Thus, *given* the investment plans of firms, trading shares on a competitive stock market leads to a constrained efficient allocation of current consumption and share-holdings which satisfies [F.15] or [F.17]. In section E we concluded that in a pure exchange economy an incomplete stock market would not in general be Pareto efficient, in the sense of equating consumers' marginal rates of substitution between states, but left open whether this was an appropriate criterion. As the reader should be able to show, our results here imply that the equilibrium of the incomplete stock market pure exchange economy is *constrained* Pareto efficient.

The key issue is the constrained efficiency of the firms' investment choices. Suppose that the managers of the firms wished to act in the shareholders' interests by choosing the constrained efficient level of investment defined by [F.16]. This requires information on the equilibrium shareholdings a_{ij} and the discount factors δ_{is}. But, if firms choose investment and then shareholders trade, how are firms to know the equilibrium shareholdings? And how are firms to know shareholders' discount factors?

The first obstacle is not unduly severe if the second can be overcome. We could define a tâtonnement process under which firms announce investments which satisfy [F.16] for some arbitrary shareholdings. Given the investment announcement, notional trades take place on the stock market to establish planned shareholdings, though no exchange of shares actually takes place. Firms then choose investments to satisfy [F.16] given the planned shareholdings, planned shareholdings are changed in response to the new investment announcement, firms then remaximize given the new shareholdings, and so on. The process terminates, and shares are actually exchanged, when shareholders do not change their planned holdings in response to the announced investment. Drèze (1974) showed that the process will indeed converge to an equilibrium, provided that firms know the consumers' discount factors.

It is this second difficulty that is fundamental. How are firms to discover the discount factors δ_{is}? The firms do not know the utility functions of the shareholders. Assume they know the investment plans and the implied state-contingent outputs and can observe the market value of all firms. They also know that shareholders will choose optimal shareholdings to satisfy [F.22]. But this set of four equations is insufficient to determine the six unknown δ_{is}. Hence, because the number of firms is less than the number of states, shareholders' discount rates cannot be inferred, and it is impossible to prove that investment satisfies [F.16].

Note that multiplying [F.22] by a_{ij} and summing over i gives

$$\Sigma_i \Sigma_s a_{ij} \delta_{is} f_{js}(Y_{j0}) = M_j \qquad [\text{F.23}]$$

This suggests that, since managers can observe M_j, they can set Y_{j0} at its constrained efficient level satisfying [F.16] by maximizing $M_j - Y_{j0} + \hat{Y}_{j0}$, i.e. by maximizing the net value of the firm. Unfortunately, this is not so since it implies

$$dM_j/dY_{j0} - 1 = \Sigma_i \Sigma_s a_{ij} \delta_{is} f'_{js} + \Sigma_i \Sigma_s a_{ij} f_{js}(d\delta_{is}/dY_{j0}) - 1 = 0 \qquad [\text{F.24}]$$

This is *not* the same as the constrained efficiency condition [F.16]. Changes in the level of investment alter the state distribution of individuals' consumptions and hence will also alter their discount factors, so that $d\delta_{is}/dY_{j0}$ is not zero.

There is in general no way round the difficulty that shareholders' discount factors are unobservable. The managers of firms lack the information to make constrained efficient investment decisions, even if they wished to. This raises the question of what investment criterion firms will actually use. If shareholders agree on an investment plan this would presumably be the one the firm would adopt. To see if shareholders could agree, consider the effect of an increase in investment Y_{j0} on shareholder i.

Changing the firm's investment will affect the shareholder in two ways: directly by changing her consumption at date 0 and in each state at date 1, and indirectly by altering the prices of both firms. (The envelope theorem tells us that we can ignore the effects of the induced change in her shareholdings because they have a marginal value of zero to her.) Taking the Lagrangean for the shareholder's problem of maximizing [F.19] subject to [F.18]; and using [F.20], the marginal effect of an increase in Y_{j0} on shareholder i is

$$\frac{dv_i}{dY_{j0}} = a_{ij}\left[\Sigma_s \delta_{is} f'_{js} - \frac{dM_j}{dY_{j0}}\right] + \hat{a}_{ij}\left[\frac{dM_j}{dY_{j0}} - 1\right] + (\hat{a}_{ik} - a_{ik})\frac{dM_k}{dY_{j0}} \qquad [\text{F.25}]$$

(Notice that, if the manager of the firm chose Y_{j0} to maximize an unweighted sum of the individuals' utilities, they would sum [F.25] over all individuals and set the result equal to zero. As the reader should check, this would yield [F.16] again.)

Two conclusions follow from [F.25]. First, the level of investment preferred by shareholders will differ: they will not be able to agree on the optimal investment plan of the firm. Second, the obvious policy of choosing Y_{j0} to maximize the net value ($M_j - Y_{j0} + \hat{Y}_{j0}$) of firm j is in general not optimal for any shareholder! If the firm does maximize its net stock market value, so that the second term in [F.25] is zero, this does not imply that the remaining two terms are also zero. Changes in the state distribution of firm j's outputs will alter the value individuals place on firm k's state distribution of outputs as well and therefore change its stock market value. As the third term in [F.25] indicates, shareholder i will gain or lose depending on whether she is a net seller or buyer of firm k shares and on whether their price increases or decreases. Nor does net value maximization imply that the first term in [F.25] is zero. Using [F.22], net value maximization implies

$$dM_j/dY_{j0} = \Sigma_s a_{ij} \delta_{ij} f'_{js} + \Sigma_s a_{ij} f_{js}(d\delta_{is}/dY_{j0}) = 1$$

and using this to substitute for dM_j/dY_{j0} we see that the first term in [F.25] is not zero because changes in investment alter the discount factors.

There is *full spanning* when there are as many firms with linearly independent output vectors as there are states. The stock market is then equivalent to a full set of markets in Arrow securities. Implicit in the firms' stock market prices would be prices p_s for one unit of output contingent on each state of the world. The net stock market value of firm j would be given by [F.7] and each shareholder would choose shareholdings (or equivalently, state-contingent consumptions) such that $\delta_{is} = p_s$. In a complete competitive stock market economy, changes in the supply of state-contingent outputs by any firm would have no effect on the implicit prices p_s of output in state s and therefore have no effect on the discount factors $\delta_{is} = p_s$. But with δ_{is} unaffected by Y_{j0}, maximization of the net stock market value of firm j would imply that the level of investment was constrained Pareto efficient, since, from [F.24], [F.16] would be satisfied. Indeed, as we noted earlier, investment and consumption would be fully Pareto efficient, since [F.5] and [F.6] would also be satisfied.

In a complete stock market economy, changes in investment by firm j would have no effect on the stock market value of other firms. Hence the last term in [F.25] would be zero. Since the shareholders' discount factors are also unaffected by Y_{j0}, maximization of the net stock market value of the firm would also imply, from [F.22], that the first term in [F.25] is zero. All shareholders would agree that the firm should follow this policy.

When the stock market is incomplete because there are fewer firms than states, the simple net value maximization rule is in general no longer valid: shareholders will have different views on the best investment policy because their marginal valuations of income in different states have not been equalized by trading in a complete set of markets. Not only will shareholders have different discount factors, but the firms will not be able to infer them from observable stock market values and state-contingent outputs.

One solution to the analytical problems posed by incomplete stock markets is to place restrictions on the stochastic production functions $f_{js}(Y_{j0})$ which make it unnecessary to know shareholders' discount factors in determining the firm's investment policy. For example, in Diamond (1967), it is assumed that there is *multiplicative uncertainty*, so that the production functions can be written

$$Y_{js} = f_{js}(Y_{j0}) = \beta_{js} f_j(Y_{j0}) \qquad j = 1, 2 \qquad [F.26]$$

Thus firm j's outputs across states of the world are in fixed proportions. Increased investment leads to the same proportionate increases in output in each state. Diamond also assumes implicitly that there are many firms with production functions identical to firm j. (Notice that, since all these j-type firms have the same proportionate state output vectors, the stock market is still incomplete.) Hence, when firm j increases its investment, and therefore the 'scale' $f_j(Y_{j0})$ of its state-contingent outputs, there is no change in the price individuals are willing to pay for a 'unit' of stock which yields the state-contingent output $(\beta_{j1}, \beta_{j2}, \beta_{j3})$. Hence the stock market value M_j increases in proportion to the number of 'units' it can sell which is just $f_j(Y_{j0})$ and so

$$M_j = \alpha_j f_j(Y_{j0}) \qquad [F.27]$$

Here α_j is the implicit price of the 'unit' of stock.

With multiplicative uncertainty, [F.22] can be written

$$f_j(Y_{j0})\Sigma_s \delta_{is}\beta_{js} = M_j \qquad [F.28]$$

and so we see that

$$\alpha_j = \Sigma_s \delta_{is}\beta_{js} \qquad [F.29]$$

which implies that the right-hand side of [F.29] is unaffected by changes in firm j's investment. If the firm followed the policy of maximizing net stock market value, its investment level would satisfy

$$dM_j/dY_{j0} - 1 = \alpha_j f'_{js} - 1 = 0 \qquad \text{[F.30]}$$

But, using [F.29], multiplying by a_{ij} and summing over i, [F.30] implies that the condition [F.16] for constrained investment efficiency is satisfied. This policy will also maximize the expected utility of every shareholder: the last term in [F.25] is zero since changes in Y_{j0} do not affect the stock market value of the other firms in the economy; the middle term is zero because net stock market value is maximized; and [F.29] and [F.30] imply that the first term is zero.

Thus under multiplicative uncertainty there is *unanimity* among shareholders even though their discount factors differ. Moreover, the firm can ensure that it acts in the interests of its shareholders by basing its investment decision solely on observable variables. It does not need information about shareholders' preferences. And its decision is constrained efficient.

The assumption of multiplicative uncertainty is actually stronger than necessary to achieve this result. It can be shown, for example (see Question 1), that, if one of the outputs Y_{js} is a linear combination of the other two, then unanimity among shareholders will hold. As in [F.30], stock market information alone can be used to find the firm's optimal investment and the stock market equilibrium will be constrained Pareto efficient.

In general, if firms' output vectors lie in a linear subspace of dimension at most equal to the number of firms, then shareholders will be unanimous in their evaluation of investments. The intuition is that changes in the state distribution of outputs by one firm have no effect on the value of other firms or on consumer discount factors. Firms will not then need to know the discount factors and individual shareholdings of all their shareholders to find the investment plan (maximization of net stock market value) that is in their best interests.

If we do not make this *partial spanning* assumption, there are two alternatives. First, one may assume that, at each step in the tâtonnement process described earlier, shareholders truthfully reveal their discount rates (see, for example, Drèze (1974, 1984) and Grossman and Hart (1979)). It is difficult to believe that the mechanisms by which shareholders' preferences are actually brought to bear on managers meet the requirements of this process. The second alternative is to accept that, under incomplete markets, managers cannot take decisions in the interests of all their shareholders and try to construct models which explain their investment decisions. Among other things, this is likely to imply that resource allocations in an incomplete stock market economy are not constrained Pareto efficient in Diamond's sense. Unfortunately, no model of this type has achieved general acceptance. The issue of the behaviour of the firm in incomplete markets is still an open and important question.

EXERCISE 21F

1. Assume that, in the notation of this section, $Y_{j3} = k_{j1}Y_{j1} + k_{j2}Y_{j2}$ for constants k_{j1} and k_{j2} not both zero. Interpret this condition and show that it implies that shareholders will be unanimous in respect of firm j's investment decision.

2. Review the possible reasons why markets could be incomplete.

A The structure of an optimization problem

Optimization is the act of choosing the 'best' alternative out of whatever alternatives are available. It is a description of how decisions (choices among alternatives) are or should be taken. All optimization problems consist of three elements, as follows.

1. Choice variables

These are the variables whose optimal values have to be determined. For example:

(a) A firm wants to know at what level to set output in order to achieve maximum profit. Output is the choice variable.

(b) A firm wants to know what amounts of labour, machine time and raw materials to use so as to produce a given output level at minimum cost. Choice variables are labour, machine time, raw materials.

(c) A consumer wants to buy that bundle of commodities which she can afford and which makes her feel best off. Here the choice variables are quantities of commodities.

2. The objective function

This gives a mathematical specification of the relationship between the choice variables and some variable whose value we wish to *maximize* or *minimize*. In the three examples just discussed, the objective functions would relate:

(a) profit to the level of output;

(b) cost to the amounts of labour, machine time and raw materials;

(c) an index of the consumer's satisfaction to the quantities of the commodities she may buy.

In (a) and (c) the functions are to be maximized, and in (b) minimized, with respect to the relevant choice variables.

3. The feasible set

An essential part of any optimization problem is a specification of what alternatives are available to the decision-taker. The available set of alternatives is called the 'feasible set'.

There are three ways in which the feasible set may be specified:

(a) By direct enumeration, i.e. by a statement which says: the alternatives are *A*, *B*, *C*, ... Clearly, if the choice set contains one alternative, the optimization problem is trivial, and, if none, it is insoluble.

(b) By one or more inequalities which *directly* define a set of alternative values of the choice variable(s).

(c) By one or more *functions* or equations which define a set of alternative values.

Examples of the last two can be found in the problems discussed earlier. Thus, in problem (a), we would rule out negative outputs, but would expect any positive outputs to be possible. Hence we would say that output must be greater than or equal to zero, i.e. $y \geq 0$, where y is output. The feasible set is here directly defined by a *weak inequality*.

In the second problem, only those combinations of inputs which yield the desired output level can be considered. In this case the feasible set is generally defined by a function. Thus, suppose we have the *production function*: $y = f(L, M, R)$ where y is output, L, M, R are labour, machine time and raw materials respectively. Now let y^0 be the required output level. Then the equation:

$$y^0 = f(L, M, R) \qquad\qquad [A.1]$$

defines a set of values of L, M, R which are feasible. In addition, note that it may be possible for equation [A.1] to be satisfied by negative values of one or more of the choice variables, implying that such negative values may be chosen. We would not regard negative values of these variables as making sense and so we wish to exclude them. Thus, we would add the direct constraints:

$$L \geq 0 \qquad R \geq 0 \qquad M \geq 0 \qquad\qquad [A.2]$$

which, in conjunction with [A.1], define the feasible set.

In the example of the consumer's problem it is impossible to consume negative amounts of goods. Then, if we let $x_1, \ldots, x_n$ represent the quantities of the goods which the consumer could buy, we have the n inequalities:

$$x_1 \geq 0 \qquad x_2 \geq 0 \qquad x_3 \geq 0 \qquad \ldots \qquad x_n \geq 0 \qquad\qquad [A.3]$$

There is another limitation on the feasible set in the problem. Each good has a price. Let these prices be $p_1, p_2, \ldots, p_n$, for $x_1, \ldots, x_n$ respectively. The consumer's total expenditure for some set of quantities of the goods will be:

$$p_1 x_1 + p_2 x_2 + \ldots + p_n x_n = \sum_{i=1}^{n} p_i x_i \qquad\qquad [A.4]$$

The consumer will have a given income, M, which consumption expenditure cannot exceed. Hence the feasible set is given by the constraint

$$p_1 x_1 + p_2 x_2 + \ldots + p_n x_n \leq M \qquad\qquad [A.5]$$

together with the inequalities in [A.4].

To summarize: an optimization problem consists of choice variables, an objective function, and a feasible set. The problem is to choose the preferred alternative in the feasible set, and in general we can represent this as the problem of finding the maximum or minimum of the objective function with respect to the choice variables, subject to constraints. For this reason, optimization is taken to be synonymous with constrained maximization or minimization.

EXERCISE A

1. Describe the choice variables, objective functions and feasible sets in the following optimization problems:

   (a) You may go from college to home on foot, by bus or by train. You know with certainty how long it takes by each mode, and what it will cost. The problem is to choose the 'best' way of going home.

   (b) You want to go on a diet which will involves as few calories as possible, subject to a certain minimum, and which will ensure that you consume at least minimum amounts of vitamins. You also cannot exceed your weekly food expenditure budget. You know the price, calorie count and vitamin content of one unit of every foodstuff. There also exists a calorie-free but expensive all-vitamin tablet. How do you choose the 'best' diet?

   (c) A consumer may shop at market A, which is very close to his home, or take a bus ride and shop at market B, where prices are relatively lower. The problem is to choose whether to shop at market A, market B, or both.

2. Draw graphs of the feasible sets defined by the following constraints:

   (a) $x_2 + 2x_1 \leqslant 4$

   (b) $x_2 + 3x_1 < 6$
   $x_1 \geqslant 0 \qquad x_2 \geqslant 0$

   (c) $x_2 + 2x_1 \leqslant 4$
   $x_2 + 4x_1 \leqslant 6$
   $x_1 \geqslant 0 \qquad x_2 \geqslant 0$

   (d) $x_2 + 2x_1 = 4$
   $x_2 + 3x_1 = 7$

   (e) $x_2 + 2x_1 = 4$
   $x_2 + 3x_1 = 7$
   $x_1 \geqslant 0 \qquad x_2 \geqslant 0$

   (f) $x_2 - 2x_1^2 \leqslant 0$
   $x_2 \geqslant 0 \qquad x_1 \geqslant 0$

   (g) $x_2 + x_1^2 = 4$

   (h) $x_2 + x_1^2 = 4$
   $x_1 \geqslant 0 \qquad x_2 \geqslant 0$

   (i) $x_2 + x_1^2 \leqslant 4$
   $x_2 + 3x_1 \leqslant 6$
   $x_1 \geqslant 0 \qquad x_2 \geqslant 0$

   (j) $x_2 + x_1^2 = 4$
   $x_2 + 3x_1 = 6$

Solutions to optimization problems

A *solution* to an optimization problem is the vector of values of the choice variables which is in the feasible set and which yields a maximum or minimum of the objective function over the feasible set. We present the objective function as

$$f(x_1, x_2, \ldots, x_n) = f(x) \tag{B.1}$$

where x is the n-component vector of choice variables. For convenience, we assume that the problem is always to *maximize f*. This is not restrictive. Suppose the problem is to minimize some function $h(x)$. Then, this is equivalent to the problem of maximizing $f(x) = -h(x)$, since a solution to the latter problem solves the former. Making use of this, all the statements made in the Appendices about maximization problems can be applied directly to problems of minimization.

We denote the feasible set of x vectors by S. A solution to the problem is a vector of choice variables, x^*, having the property

$$f(x^*) \geqslant f(x) \qquad \text{all } x \in S \tag{B.2}$$

which is another way of saying that x^* maximizes f over the set S. By definition of the problem, we are interested in finding such a vector x^*.

There are certain important general questions we can ask about the solution to any optimization problem, as follows.

1. Existence

How can we be sure, in advance of trying to solve a particular problem, that a solution to it actually exists? We have no grounds for supposing that every problem *must* have a solution. In economic theory, we spend a great deal of time analysing solutions to optimization problems. We therefore have to take care that theories provide for their existence, otherwise the analysis is internally inconsistent.

2. Local and global solutions

A *global* solution is one which satisfies the condition [B.2]; at that point, the objective function takes on a value which is not exceeded at any other point within the feasible set. It is therefore the solution we seek. A local solution satisfies the condition:

$$f(x^{**}) \geqslant f(x) \qquad \text{all } x \in N^{**} \subset S \tag{B.3}$$

where N^{**} is a set of points in a *neighbourhood* of x^{**}. Figure B.1 illustrates the difference. We assume only one choice variable, so that the vector becomes the scalar

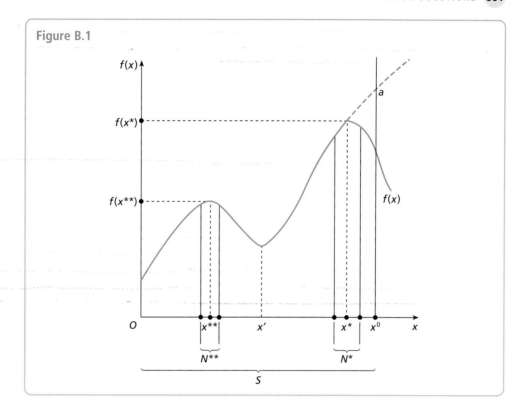

Figure B.1

x. The feasible set is defined only by the direct inequalities: $x \geqslant 0$, $x \leqslant x^0$. The objective function $f(x)$ has two peaks, one at x^* and the other at x^{**}. Neighbourhoods of these points are shown as N^* and N^{**} respectively. Clearly, both points satisfy [B.3], but only x^* satisfies [B.2]. Thus, x^* is a global maximum, while x^{**} is not.

The difficulty is that *all the methods we have for finding solutions to optimization problems locate only local maxima*. We are therefore interested in the question: under what conditions will every local maximum we locate also be a global maximum? From Fig. B.1 we see that this must have something to do with the shape of the objective function; we explore this question in more detail below.

3. Uniqueness

More than one global maximum may exist (e.g. suppose the first peak in Fig. B.1 is as high as the second, or that the function has a horizontal segment over the set N^* of values of x). Economists tend to assume unique solutions, and so it is of interest to consider conditions under which this is the case.

4. Interior solutions

We take the distinction between an interior and a boundary point of a set as understood for the moment. Thus, in Fig. B.1, the points $x = 0$ and $x = x^0$ are boundary points, while all other points in the set are interior points. Then an *interior solution* is an interior point which satisfies condition [B.2], while a *boundary solution* is a boundary point which satisfies [B.2]. In Fig. B.1, x^* is an interior solution. If, however, the function f took the shape indicated by the dotted line in the diagram, then there would be a boundary solution at x^0. The importance of the distinction relates to the question of the consequences of a change in a constraint (which in general changes the location of a boundary of the feasible set – refer back to Question 2, Exercise A). For a small change in a constraint, an interior solution is not affected – the optimal point is unchanged. But a boundary solution may be affected – for example, in the case in which x^0 in Fig. B.1 is optimal, a shift of the boundary would change the solution. Much of microeconomics is concerned with predictions of behaviour derived from an analysis of the change in optimal solutions following from a change in a constraint. It is therefore of importance to know whether a solution will be at a boundary or interior point.

We can also frame this question in terms of *binding* and *non-binding* constraints. A constraint is binding if there is a boundary solution which lies on the part of the boundary defined by that constraint. A constraint is non-binding if there is an interior solution, or if the boundary solution lies on a part of the boundary defined by another constraint. For example, in Fig. B.1, when the solution is at x^*, both constraints $x \geq 0$ and $x \leq x^0$ are non-binding while, in the case in which the solution is at x^0, the former constraint only is non-binding. We can always find a sufficiently small change in a non-binding constraint to leave the solution unaffected.

5. Location

Given that a solution exists, we would like to find it. In theoretical models we work with general functions, usually specifying little more than the signs of their first and second derivatives. As a result, the problem is not to *compute* solutions but rather to *describe* their essential general characteristics in the analytically most useful way, in terms of certain conditions they have to satisfy.

To illustrate: take the case of unconstrained maximization, and suppose that in Fig. B.1 no constraints on the feasible values of x exist. Then, at the value x^*, the derivative $f'(x^*) = 0$, and we can show that this must be true at all local maxima. However, it is also true that $f'(x') = 0$, but the function takes on a local minimum at x'. Hence, the condition that the first derivative be zero is satisfied at all local maxima but at other points also and so is necessary but not sufficient. We further note that, as x increases through x^*, the derivative $f'(x^*)$ passes from positive to negative values, i.e. is decreasing, and that this is only true at a local maximum. It follows that a sufficient condition for a local maximum is that $f'(x^*) = 0$ *and* $f''(x^*) < 0$, since these are only satisfied at local maxima.[1] Note that the conditions are defined only for *local* maxima, since, as the diagram makes clear, they cannot discriminate between points x^* and x^{**}. To describe an optimal point in terms of necessary and sufficient conditions is to 'locate' that point in terms of its general characteristics rather than its numerical value. Surprisingly we are often able to say a great deal on the basis of such a general description.

In discussing these questions concerning solutions to optimization problems, we make use of certain very general properties of objective functions and feasible sets. We shall first set out these properties, and then proceed to answer the questions.

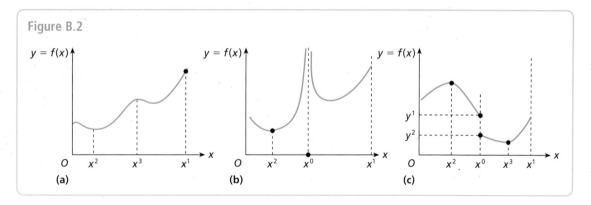

Figure B.2

(a)   (b)   (c)

1. Continuity of the objective function

A function $y = f(x)$ is continuous if there are no breaks in its graph, or crudely, if it can be drawn without taking the pen from the paper. In Fig. B.2 the functions drawn in (b) and (c) are not continuous, while that in (a) is continuous. In (b) $f(x)$ becomes arbitrarily large at x^0 (tends to infinity) and in part (c) $f(x)$ jumps from y^1 to y^2 at x^0. When there is more than one variable in the objective function the intuitive idea of continuity is still valid: there should be no jumps or breaks in the graph of the function.

2. Concavity of the objective function

In Fig. B.3 we show graphs of four kinds of function. A function with the curvature shown in (a) of the figure would generally be called *concave*, that in (c) *convex*, whereas that in (b) is linear and that in (d) neither convex nor concave. If we wanted to find a non-geometrical way of defining the concave function we could use the function's second derivative $f''(x)$. As we draw successive tangents to the curve in (a) of the figure, at increasing values of x, these tangents have flatter and flatter positive slopes and then steeper and steeper negative ones, implying that the first derivative of the function, $f'(x)$, is decreasing. Thus we could express concavity by the condition $f''(x) < 0$. By a similar argument, convexity could be expressed by the condition $f''(x) > 0$. There is, however, a drawback to this. A function is not differentiable at a point where it has a kink and so the definition cannot be applied (draw an example).

To overcome this drawback we define concave and convex functions in terms of a general property they possess. Note that in (a) of the figure, if we take any two points such as x^0 and x^1, and join the corresponding function values $f(x^0)$ and $f(x^1)$ by a straight line (a *chord* to the function), then the graph of the function between these values lies everywhere above the line. For the convex function, the graph lies entirely below the line. In the linear case the graph of the function coincides with the line while in (d) of the figure it moves from above to below it.

In order to express this geometric idea algebraically, we note two points:

1. We can express any x-value lying between x^0 and x^1 as the weighted sum $\bar{x} = kx^0 + (1 - k)x^1$, where k is between 0 and 1. For example $k = \frac{1}{2}$ gives us the x-value lying mid-way between x^0 and x^1. The value $\bar{x}$ is called the *convex combination* of the points x^0 and x^1.

Figure B.3

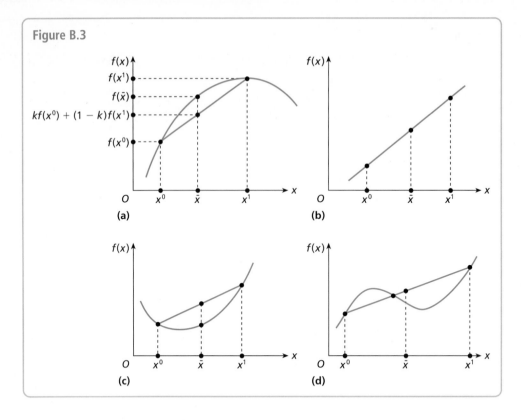

2. If we take the weighted sum of the two function values $f(x^0)$ and $f(x^1)$ using the *same* value of k, which we denote by $\bar{f} = kf(x^0) + (1 - k)f(x^1)$, then this value is found as the co-ordinate of the point on the chord directly above $\bar{x}$. For example, for $k = \frac{1}{2}$, $\bar{f}$ would lie at a point on the chord directly above $\bar{x} = \frac{1}{2}x^0 + \frac{1}{2}x^1$.[2]

For a concave function a point on the curve at any $\bar{x}$ between x^0 and x^1 lies above the chord joining $f(x^0)$ and $f(x^1)$. It therefore follows from point 2 that in this case $f(\bar{x}) > \bar{f}$, for all x lying between x^0 and x^1. For a convex function we have $f(\bar{x}) < \bar{f}$ at each $\bar{x}$ between x^0 and x^1. When the function is linear $f(\bar{x}) = \bar{f}$, as Fig. B.3(b) shows.

Some important propositions which are true when objective functions are shaped as in Fig. B.3(a) are also true when they are linear or have linear segments. It is useful therefore to define *concave functions* as functions which have the property

$$f(\bar{x}) \geqslant \bar{f} \qquad \text{[B.4]}$$

where $\bar{x} = kx^0 + (1 - k)x^1$, and $\bar{f} = kf(x^0) + (1 - k)f(x^1)$, $0 \leqslant k \leqslant 1$, so that linear functions, or functions with linear segments, may also be regarded as concave. A function which satisfies [B.4] as a strict inequality is called *strictly* concave Fig. B.3(a) is an example. Likewise a *convex function* satisfies:

$$f(\bar{x}) \leqslant \bar{f} \qquad \text{[B.5]}$$

with a *strictly* convex function satisfying [B.5] as a strict inequality. Note that [B.4] and [B.5] taken together imply that a linear function is *both* convex and concave, though neither strictly convex nor strictly concave.

3. Quasi-concave functions

Given a function $y = f(x_1, x_2, \ldots, x_n) = f(x)$ and some number c, the equation

$$f(x) = c \qquad \text{[B.6]}$$

defines a set of values of the vector x having the property that they all yield the same value c of the function. In other words, they are solutions to the equation in [B.6]. A contour on a map is a set of points of equal height. We say that [B.6] defines a *contour of the function f(x)* and call the set of x-values which satisfy [B.6] a *contour set*. For many purposes we are mainly interested in the *properties of contours of the objective function*.

Consider the contour

$$f(x_1, x_2) = c \qquad \text{[B.7]}$$

The advantage of taking the two-variable case is that we can graph the contour set satisfying [B.7] in two dimensions. In Fig. B.4 we present two examples. All the points on a contour line c are vectors x which satisfy an equation for a contour such as [B.7], and so belong to a given contour set. The diagram illustrates one important property of a contour of a function, namely continuity. Continuity can be thought of intuitively as the absence of breaks, gaps or jumps in the graph. Continuity of a function and of its contours are closely related: continuity of the function implies continuity of its contours.

To explore further the properties of contours, we go beyond continuity and assume that the function $f(x_1, x_2)$ is differentiable.

From the Implicit Function Theorem we have that, given $f_2 \neq 0$, we can solve [B.7] for x_2 as a function of x_1, $x_2(x_1)$, and so substituting into [B.7] and differentiating with respect to x_1 gives

$$\frac{df(x_1, x_2(x_1))}{dx_1} = f_1 + f_2\frac{dx_2}{dx_1} = 0 \qquad \text{[B.8]}$$

Figure B.4

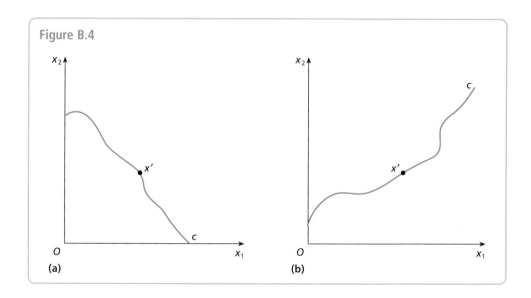

Rearranging then gives

$$\frac{dx_2}{dx_1} = -\frac{f_1}{f_2} \qquad\qquad [\text{B.9}]$$

Thus [B.9] shows that we can evaluate the slope of the contour at a point such as x' in Fig. B.4(a) directly from the values of the partial derivatives of the function at that point. Equation [B.9] also allows us to determine the direction of slope of the contour from the signs of the derivatives of the function. If the derivatives have the same sign, the slope of the contour must be negative as in (a) of Fig. B.4, while, if they have opposite signs, the contour must have a positive slope, as in (b) of the figure.

In optimization theory the continuity of its contours is an important general property which any given function may or may not possess. A second important property is the *concavity* of contours. Consider first functions whose derivatives f_1 and f_2 are positive; it follows that given two vectors x' and x, $x > x' \Rightarrow f(x) > f(x')$. Figure B.5 illustrates concavity of contours for such a function. The property can be described as follows: choose two points, such as x' and x'' in the figure, which lie on the same contour: $f(x') = f(x'') = c$. Choose any point on the straight line joining x' and x'', such as $\bar{x}$ in the figure. Then, the contour is concave if:

$$f(\bar{x}) \geqslant f(x') = f(x'') = c \qquad\qquad [\text{B.10}]$$

A convex combination of any two points on a concave contour yields at least as high a value of the function and so lies on the same or a higher contour. A function $f(x)$ is *quasi-concave* if

$$f(x') \geqslant f(x'') \text{ implies } f(k(x') + (1-k)x'') \geqslant f(x'') \qquad 0 \leqslant k \leqslant 1 \qquad [\text{B.11}]$$

When $f(x') = f(x'')$ [B.11] implies [B.10] so that quasi-concave functions have concave contours. The functions whose contours are shown in (a) and (b) of Fig. B.5 are quasi-concave,[3] whereas that in (c) is not. To see this, note that, in (a) and (b), part

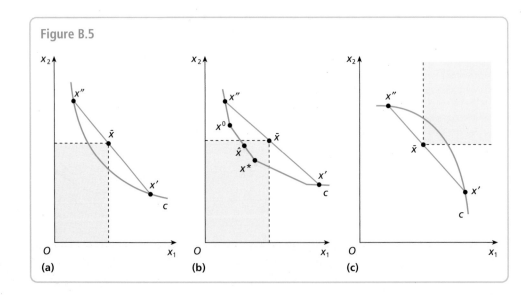

Figure B.5

of each contour passes through the shaded area south-west of $\bar{x}$, implying that some points on the contour have smaller values of both x_1 and x_2 than at $\bar{x}$. Since decreasing x_1 and x_2 must reduce the value of the function (since $f_1, f_2 > 0$), it follows that the value of the function must be smaller on the contour than at $\bar{x}$, and so [B.10] is satisfied. In (c) this is not the case; part of the contour lies in the area north-east of $\bar{x}$, and so contains points at which both x_1 and x_2 are greater than at x. Hence, the value of the function is greater along the contour.

A further distinction can be drawn by considering (a) and (b) of the figure. In (a), it is clear that, for *any* two points on the contour, the line joining them will always lie wholly above the contour, implying that the value of the function at a point such as $\bar{x}$ will always be strictly greater than that on the contour. Such a function is called *strictly quasi-concave*. This is not, however, true for the contour in (b). For example, if we take points x_0 and x^* on the contour, then a point such as $\hat{x}$ on the line joining them also lies on the contour, and so:

$$f(\hat{x}) = f(x^*) = f(x_0) = c \qquad \text{[B.12]}$$

Hence, a function possessing such contours, though quasi-concave, is not *strictly* quasi-concave.

A function $h(x)$ is said to be *quasi-convex*, if $f(x) = -h(x)$ is quasi-concave. The reader should draw a contour of a quasi-convex function, on the assumption that all its partial derivatives are strictly positive. The reader should show that, if the function $g(x_1, x_2)$ is quasi-convex, then the set of points satisfying: $g(x_1, x_2) \leqslant b$ is a convex set.

Note that changing the value of the constant c will change the contour of the function. Given $f_1, f_2 > 0$, increasing c will shift the contours in Fig. B.5 rightward, since, for any given value of x_2, a greater value of x_1 will be required to satisfy the equation defining the contour (and conversely). It follows that in an optimization problem the higher the contour attained, the greater the value of the objective function, so that *we can regard the aim of maximizing the objective function as equivalent to getting onto the highest possible contour.*

Properties of the feasible set

There are four important properties of point sets which are of interest in optimization theory:

1. Non-emptiness

A set is non-empty if it contains at least one element, the empty set being the set with no elements. Recall that the feasible set in a problem is the set of points or vectors x which satisfy the constraints. An empty feasible set implies that no such points exist: the constraints are such as to rule out any solution. If the constraints can be satisfied by at least one point, the feasible set is non-empty.

2. Closedness

A set is closed if *all* the points on its boundaries are elements of the set. Thus the set of numbers x on the interval $0 \leqslant x \leqslant 1$ is closed, while those sets defined on the intervals $0 < x \leqslant 1$ and $0 \leqslant x < 1$ are not. There is a close relationship between the existence of *weak* inequalities in the constraints of a problem, and the closedness of the feasible set (see Question 5, Exercise B).

3. Boundedness

A set is bounded when it is not possible to go off to infinity in any direction while remaining within the set. In other words, it will always be possible to enclose a bounded set within a sphere of sufficiently large finite size. Thus the set of numbers x on the interval $0 < x < 1$ is bounded, while the set $x \geq 0$ is unbounded. Note that boundedness and closedness are quite distinct: the set defined by $0 < x < 1$ is bounded but not closed; the set of values $x \geq 0$ is unbounded and closed.

4. Convexity

A set is convex if *every* pair of points in it can be joined by a straight line which lies entirely within the set. If two points in the set can be found such that the line joining them lies at least in part outside the set, then the set is non-convex. More formally, a set X is convex if x, x' are any two points in X and $\bar{x} = kx + (1 - k)x' \in X$, $0 \leq k \leq 1$. In Fig. B.6, (a) shows a number of convex sets, and (b) a number of non-convex sets. If, when *any* two boundary points of a convex set are joined with a line, the whole of the line except its end points is in the interior of the set, then the set is *strictly convex*. If two points can be found such that the line joining them coincides at least in part with the boundary, then the set is not strictly convex. In Fig. B.6(a), the sets B and C are strictly convex, while A is not.

   Recall that the *intersection* of two sets A and B, written $A \cap B$, is the set of points that are in *both* A and B. The intersection of convex sets is itself a convex set. To prove this, let x, x' be in both A and B, which are convex sets. Then the point $\bar{x} = kx + (1 - k)x'$, $0 \leq k \leq 1$, is in A *and* B, because both sets are convex, and so is in $A \cap B$. But since x and x' are any two points in $A \cap B$ this gives the result. The argument extends easily to any number of convex sets.

Figure B.6

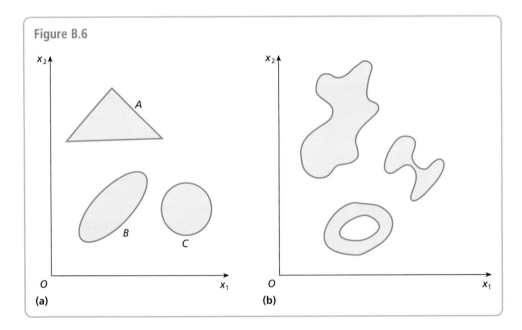

(a)

(b)

EXERCISE B

1. (a) Prove that any global maximum must also be a local maximum.

   (b) Prove that, if for a given problem more than one global maximum exists, the value of the objective function must be the same at each.

   (c) Show that a linear function is both convex and concave, but neither strictly convex nor strictly concave.

2. For each of the cases:

   (a) $f_1, f_2 < 0$ (b) $f_1 > 0, f_2 < 0$ (c) $f_1 < 0, f_2 > 0$

   where f_1 and f_2 are the partial derivatives of the function $f(x_1, x_2)$, define and draw contours of quasi-concave, strictly quasi-concave and non-quasi-concave functions. Indicate in each case the direction in which higher contours are attained.

3. Given some point x' on a contour of the function $f(x)$, define the 'better set' B' as that set of points which have the property: $f(x) \geq f(x')$. Can you frame definitions of quasi-concavity and of strict quasi-concavity of the function in terms of a property of this set B'?

4. Using the definitions in equations [B.4] and [B.10] or [B.11], show that a concave function is always quasi-concave. To prove that the converse need not hold, sketch or describe in three dimensions a quasi-concave non-concave function.

5. Take each of the feasible sets of Question 2, Appendix A, and state whether it is non-empty, closed, bounded and convex.

6. Explain why a set may be unbounded but closed, or bounded but not closed.

7. Recall from [B.9] the expression for the slope of a contour. The curvature of the contour is determined by the second derivative d^2x_2/dx_1^2. The function is strictly quasi-concave if $d^2x_2/dx_1^2 > 0$. Show by differentiating through [B.9] that this requires

$$\frac{1}{f_2^3}\{f_1^2 f_{22} - 2f_1 f_2 f_{12} + f_2^2 f_{11}\} < 0$$

Notes

1. These conditions are sufficient, but not necessary, because a maximum may occur at a point x^* at which $f''(x^*) = 0$, so that proper necessary and sufficient conditions have to be stated in terms of higher order derivatives.

2. The fact that $\bar{f}$ lies on the chord vertically above $\bar{x}$ stems from the essential property of straight lines. Thus, given two points (x_1, y_1) and (x_2, y_2), the points on the straight line joining them are given by:

$$(\bar{x}, \bar{y}) = k(x_1, y_1) + (1 - k)(x_2, y_2)$$
$$= (kx_1 + (1 - k)x_2, ky_1 + (1 - k)y_2) \qquad \text{for } 0 \leq k \leq 1$$

   In the present discussion we have $y_1 = f(x_1)$ and $y_2 = f(x_2)$ for some function $f(x)$.

3. There is unfortunately the possibility of a confusion in terminology. The reader may well have met a description of this type of contour as '*convex to the origin*' which of course it is, and yet the function is *quasi-concave*. The reason for this term can be seen by comparing [B.10] and [B.4].

The most fundamental question which can be asked of an optimization problem is whether a solution exists. We can specify conditions on the properties of the feasible set and the objective function in an optimization problem which ensure that there is a solution to the problem. The conditions are embodied in *Weierstrass' Theorem*:

An optimization problem always has a solution if (a) the objective function is continuous, and (b) the feasible set is (i) non-empty, (ii) closed and (iii) bounded.

The theorem is based on the fact that the set of values of the function $f(x)$, which results when we plug into it the x-values in the feasible set, is itself non-empty, closed and bounded, given that the conditions of the theorem are satisfied. That is, a continuous function maps a closed and bounded set of vectors onto a closed and bounded set of real numbers. Any such set contains its lowest upper bound, which is the maximum of the function over the set, and its greatest lower bound, which is therefore the minimum.

A simple illustration of the roles played by the conditions in the theorem is given in Fig. C.1. We take a one-variable problem, where the objective function is given by $f(x)$, x a scalar, and the feasible set by the set of values on the interval $0 \leqslant x \leqslant x'$. This feasible set is non-empty, closed and bounded. In (a) of the figure the function

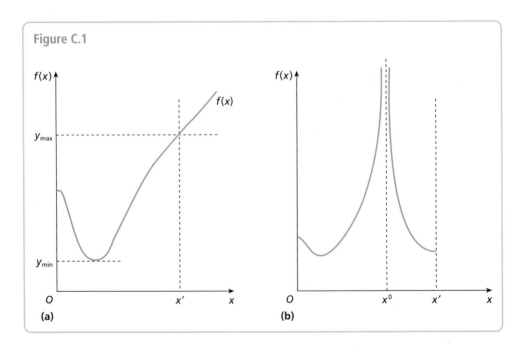

Figure C.1

$f(x)$ is continuous and a solution to the problem of maximizing f over the feasible set is found at x', the upper boundary of the feasible set. In (b) on the other hand, the function is discontinuous at x^0. In that case there is no solution to the maximization problem; by letting $x \to x^0$, we can go on increasing the value of the function, since $\lim_{x \to x_0} f = \infty$. The condition of continuity rules out such cases as (b).

To see the importance of closedness, suppose that the feasible set is defined by the interval $0 \leqslant x \leqslant x'$, so that the upper boundary x' is not in the set. Then, in (a), if we let $x \to x'$, we can go on increasing the value $f(x)$ without end, since we can let x get closer and closer to x' without ever attaining it. In other words y_{max} is not an element of the set of values of $f(x)$. Thus the maximization problem has no solution.

Boundedness is important because in its absence we again have the possibility that the value of the objective function can be made to increase without limit. Thus suppose that the feasible set in the problem is given simply by the constraint $x \geqslant 0$, and also that the objective function is monotonically increasing for $x > x'$ in Fig. C.1(a). Then clearly there will be no maximum. Boundedness of the feasible set rules out this kind of case.

The conditions of continuity of the objective function and closedness and boundedness of the feasible set are *sufficient but not necessary* conditions for existence of a solution. In other words, solutions *may* exist if they are not satisfied, but solutions may also not exist. Satisfaction of the conditions, however, rules out all possible cases of non-existence. Note, finally, that the condition of non-emptiness of the feasible set is a necessary condition for existence of a solution; any problem in which no point is feasible cannot have a solution.

EXERCISE C

1. Draw variants of Fig. C.1 which show that solutions may exist when the objective function is discontinuous, and the feasible set open and unbounded. From this, explain what is meant by the statement that the conditions of the existence theorem are sufficient but not necessary.

2. Explain why the only condition of the existence theorem which is necessary is that the feasible set be non-empty.

Local and global optima

Suppose that the conditions which guarantee existence of a solution are satisfied; we have a continuous objective function, and a non-empty, closed and bounded feasible set. We consider a two-variable problem, in which we wish to maximize the function $f(x_1, x_2)$, with $f_1, f_2 > 0$. Given that we can find a local maximum of this function, under what conditions can we be sure that it is also a global maximum?

In Fig. D.1 the shaded areas are the feasible sets. Recall that maximization of a function over a given feasible set is equivalent to finding a point within that set which is on the highest possible contour. Given the assumption $f_1, f_2 > 0$, contours increase in value as we move northeastwards in the figure. Then both (a) and (b) show examples of cases in which two local optima exist, only one of which is a global optimum. In (a) the objective function is strictly quasi-concave and the feasible set is non-convex. There is a local maximum at x^* and also at x', since relative to a small neighbourhood of points within the feasible set around them, they are on the highest possible contours. We can see that x^* only is a global maximum. In (b), the feasible set is convex, and the objective function is not quasi-concave: there are local optima at x^* and x', but only x^* is a global maximum.

Figure D.1 shows that sufficient conditions for any local optimum also to be global must depend on the shapes of the feasible set *and* of the contours of the function. As (a) shows, it is not sufficient that the function be quasi-concave; and (b) shows

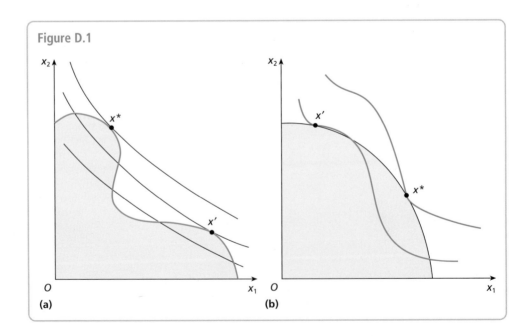

Figure D.1

that it is not sufficient that the feasible set be convex. However, taking both together, we can state the theorem:

A local maximum is always a global maximum if (a) the objective function is quasi-concave, and (b) the feasible set is convex.

Proof

The proof is by contradiction. Let x^* be a local maximum, i.e. $f(x^*) \geq f(x)$ for all x in a neighbourhood of x^*, and suppose there exists $x' \in S$, the feasible set, such that $f(x') > f(x^*)$. Then since S is a convex set

$$\bar{x} = kx^* + (1 - k)x' \in S \qquad \text{for } 0 \leq k \leq 1$$

In addition, since f is quasi-concave and $f(x') > f(x^*)$

$$f(\bar{x}) \geq kf(x^*) + (1 - k)f(x') > f(x^*)$$

But then, by choosing k arbitrarily close to 1, we can ensure that $\bar{x}$ is in a neighbourhood of x^*, contradicting the fact that x^* is a local maximum. Thus if x^* is a local maximum there cannot exist $x' \in S$ such that $f(x') > f(x^*)$ and so x^* is also a global maximum.

Figure D.2 provides some intuition. The feasible set S is convex, and the objective function, with contour c, is quasi-concave. This latter implies that the set B, consisting of those points *along and above* the contour c, is also convex. The solutions to the problem are the points on the segment ab, since these are the points in S on the highest possible contour. Since they lie on the same contour they yield the same value of the objective function; each is a global as well as a local maximum. Now consider the line T, part of which is coincident with the segment ab. Because S is a convex set, and the segment ab lies along its upper boundary, the set S must lie on or below T – no point in S can lie above T. Likewise, because B is a convex set (as a

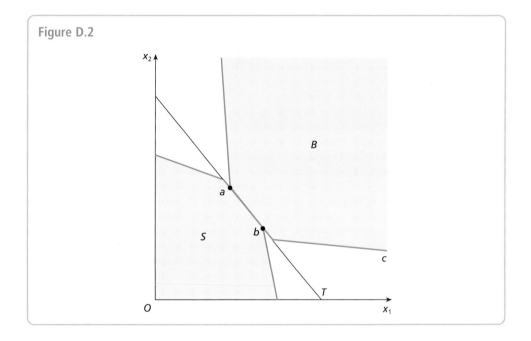

Figure D.2

result of the quasi-concavity of the objective function) and *ab* lies along its lower boundary, the entire set *B* must lie on or above *T* – no point in *B* can lie below *T*. But *B* is the set of points which yield at least as high a value of the objective function as the points along *ab*. Thus no points in *B* can possibly also be in *S* except those along the segment *ab*. But this in turn implies that the points along *ab* must be global as well as local optima.

The difference between the cases in Figs D.1 and D.2 is that in the former the absence of convexity or quasi-concavity implies that the set *B* may intersect with the set *S* at points other than a given local optimum, and so that optimum may not be global. Convexity of the sets *B* and *S* rules this out. In this case the line *T* is said to *separate* the sets *S* and *B*, and the importance of the convexity of *B* and *S* lies in the fact that such a separating line can always be found. Note that, again, the conditions of the theorem are sufficient but not necessary: even if they do not hold, the configuration of contours and feasible set may be such that local optima are also global.

Finally, since a concave function is always quasi-concave (see Question 4, Appendix B), we can conclude that the theorem also holds for concave functions.

EXERCISE D

1. (a) Draw examples of cases in which the conditions of the theorem are not met, but local optima are also global optima.

   (b) Explain why the set *B* in Fig. D.2 consists of points which yield at least as high values of the objective function as those along the segment *ab*.

2. Suggest what happens to the solution illustrated in Fig. D.2 if the feasible set *S* is not closed.

3. Consider the adaptation of the theorem of this section to the case in which it is desired to minimize the function $f(x_1, x_2)$.

4. Adapt the discussion of Fig. D.2 to the case in which the set *B* is strictly convex.

Uniqueness of solutions

From a normative or prescriptive point of view the question of the uniqueness of solutions is not very important: by definition one global optimum is as good as another. However, if we are using the optimization problems for positive or predictive purposes, the question of whether the decision-taker has a unique best decision or a number of equally good decisions is of more relevance. We are interested in the way in which decisions change in response to changes in the constraints defining the feasible set. Where the optimal solution is unique for each given feasible set we can specify functions which relate the optimal values of the choice variables to the parameters in the constraints. If the solution is not unique, then we have a more general relationship between optimal *sets* of values of the choice variables and the constraint parameters, known as a *correspondence*. Though this presents no insuperable obstacles to analysis, it does require us to change our procedures and approach. Since the models in this book usually deal with functions rather than with correspondences, it is worthwhile to be aware that this is valid when the solutions to the relevant optimization problems are unique.

In Fig. D.2 of the previous Appendix there were multiple global optima; there was an infinite number of optimal points on the line segment *ab*. The feasible set was convex, but not strictly convex; and the objective function was quasi-concave, but not strictly quasi-concave. Consider now Fig. E.1, where we show three unique global optima, respectively x^*, x' and x''. In the first the objective function is strictly quasi-concave but the feasible set not strictly convex; in the second we have the

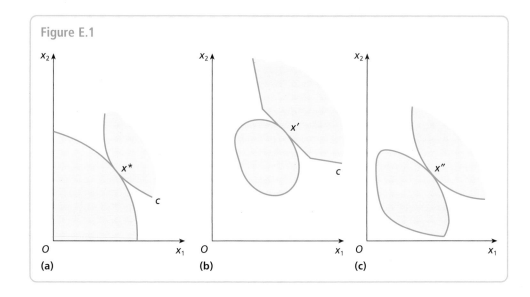

Figure E.1

(a) (b) (c)

reverse; and in the third the objective function is strictly quasi-concave and the feasible set strictly convex. These figures illustrate the *Uniqueness Theorem*:

Given an optimization problem in which the feasible set is convex and the objective function is non-constant and quasi-concave, a solution is unique if: (a) the feasible set is strictly convex, or (b) the objective function is strictly quasi-concave, or (c) both.

Proof

The proof is by contradiction. Let x^* be a solution and suppose there exists $x' \in S$, the feasible set, such that $x' \neq x^*$ and $f(x') = f(x^*)$. Since S is convex, it contains $\bar{x} = kx^* + (1 - k)x'$, $0 \leqslant k \leqslant 1$. Now if f is strictly quasi-concave we have

$$f(\bar{x}) > kf(x^*) + (1 - k)f(x') = f(x^*)$$

which contradicts the optimality of x^*. Therefore in this case the optimum must be unique. Now suppose the feasible set is strictly convex. Then $\bar{x}$ lies in the interior of S and, since $f(x)$ is non-constant in x, it is always possible to find another point in S which yields a higher value of the function. Again this contradicts the optimality of x^*.

The theorem gives only sufficient conditions: it is possible that a unique solution will exist even when the conditions are not satisfied, but we cannot be sure.

EXERCISE E

1. Draw examples in which the optimum is unique even though the conditions of the theorem are not met.

2. Apply the theorem of this section to the case of minimization problems (refer back to Question 3, Appendix D).

3. When $f_1, f_2 > 0$, show that it is sufficient for uniqueness that the feasible set be *upper convex*, i.e. a line joining any two points on its *upper boundary* lies in the interior of the set. [*Hint*: consider Fig. E1(a).]

Interior and boundary optima

The boundaries of a feasible set are always defined by the constraints which are part of the specification of the optimization problem. Given that the feasible set is closed, we can partition its points into two mutually exclusive subsets, interior points and boundary points. Loosely, the former points lie inside the boundaries of the set and the latter lie on them. More rigorously, the defining characteristic of an interior point of a point set is that we can find a (possibly very small) neighbourhood around it which contains *only* points in the set. A boundary point, on the other hand, has the property that *all* neighbourhoods around it, however small, contain points which are, and points which are not, in the set (draw diagrams to show that these definitions are consistent with your intuition).

In general, a solution to an optimization problem which is at an interior point of the feasible set is unaffected by small shifts in the boundaries of the set, while a solution at a boundary point will be sensitive to changes in at least one constraint. Since much of microeconomics is concerned with predicting the changes in solutions to optimization problems resulting from shifts in constraints, the question of whether such solutions are at interior or boundary points is fundamental.

In parts (a) and (b) of Fig. F.1 the feasible sets are initially the areas Oab. In (a) we have an interior optimum at x^*, and in (b) and (c) we have boundary optima also denoted x^*. The solution in (a) is unaffected by a *small* shift in the constraint, e.g. to $a'b'$; that in (b) is affected; that in (c) is changed by a shift in constraint cd but not by that in ab, as illustrated.

The absence of response of the solution in (a) is due to the assumed existence of a *bliss* point at x^* (the 'peak' of the 'hill' whose contours are drawn in the figure), i.e.

Figure F.1

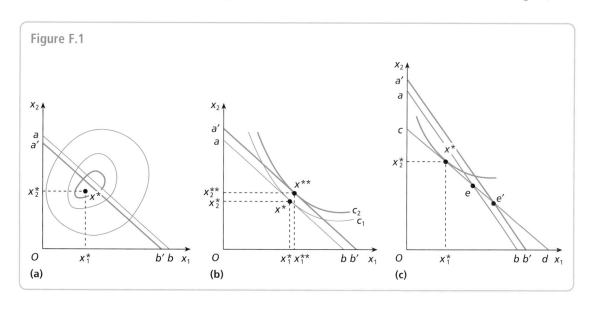

(a)

(b)

(c)

a point at which the objective function takes on a maximum. The occurrence of a bliss point in the interior of the feasible set is clearly necessary for there to be an interior maximum. We can characterize cases of boundary maxima as ones in which no bliss points exist (but see Question 1 below). One such class of cases is that in which the objective function is monotonically increasing, i.e. every $f_i > 0$, where f_i is the ith partial derivative of the function. In these cases we can go further and say that the solution must be on the *upper* boundary of the feasible set. In terms of the contours of the function, this would imply that higher contours are reached as we move rightwards in the diagram. Clearly, however, it is not necessary, if we want to rule out bliss points, that the partial derivatives are all positive or even that the objective function is differentiable. It is simply necessary to assume that at any point in the feasible set it is always possible to find a small change in the value of at least one variable which will increase the value of the objective function. This is the property of *local non-satiation*.

Parts (b) and (c) of the figure show two kinds of boundary optima. In (b) there is only one upper boundary and, given the assumption that $c_2 > c_1$, the boundary shift changes the optimum. In (c), the initial feasible set is taken to be the area $Oceb$ defined by two weak linear inequalities and non-negativity constraints on x_1 and x_2. The initial optimum is on the boundary at x^*. At such a point the constraint defined by the line ab is satisfied as a strict inequality. This constraint is inoperative *at the solution* and so is non-binding. Once we know where the solution lies, a non-binding constraint can be dropped from any analysis concerned with movements around a small neighbourhood of the optimum, and this can often greatly simplify such analysis. *Before* solving the problem, however, it is impossible to know which constraints will turn out to be non-binding (given that we have eliminated constraints which lie *wholly* outside other constraints and so could not possibly be binding) and so all must be retained. Moreover, in a general theoretical analysis we do not have enough information to conclude that some constraint will turn out to be non-binding and so all solution possibilities have generally to be considered. In Fig. F.1(a) there are three such solution possibilities – point out the two not shown. What can be said in the latter two cases about the responsiveness of the solution to shifts in the constraints?

EXERCISE F

1. Draw an example of a case in which a bliss point exists, but the solution is affected by *some* kinds of constraint shifts.

2. The theory of 'satisficing' says that, given a feasible set, an individual chooses not the best alternative but a 'satisfactory' one. Explain why, in terms of the discussion of this section, this theory may fail to yield predictions about economic behaviour.

3. Given a feasible set such as that in Fig. F.1(a), where would you expect the solution to be in the cases:
   (a) $f_1 > 0, f_2 < 0$
   (b) $f_1 < 0, f_2 > 0$
   (c) $f_1, f_2 < 0$
   (d) $f_1 = 0, f_2 > 0$
   where $f(x_1, x_2)$ is the objective function and f_i ($i = 1, 2$) its partial derivatives.

4. If all consumers in an economy possessed bliss points, what would be the relevance of microeconomics?

G Location of the optimum: the method of Lagrange

As suggested earlier, in general theoretical models we do not have numerical information with which to find solutions to optimization problems. Instead, we seek to describe the characteristics or properties the solution possesses in terms of general conditions which it satisfies.

It is assumed that the reader is familiar with the necessary condition for the point $x^* = (x_1^*, x_2^*, \ldots, x_n^*)$ to yield a maximum of the function $f(x)$ when *no* constraints are present, namely

$$f_i(x^*) = 0 \qquad i = 1, 2, \ldots, n \qquad \text{[G.1]}$$

that is, that each partial derivative of the function, evaluated at x^*, must be zero.

Suppose now, however, we also have a constraint on the problem: we seek the vector giving the largest possible value of $f(x)$ from only those vectors which satisfy the constraint $g(x) = b$, where g is a differentiable function and b is a real number, the *constraint constant*. We write the problem as

$$\max_x f(x) \quad \text{s.t.} \quad g(x) = b \qquad \text{[G.2]}$$

Referring back to parts (a) and (b) of Fig. F.1 allows us to see immediately that the conditions [G.1] are no longer necessary for a solution to [G.2]. In Fig. F.1(a), conditions [G.1] are satisfied at the bliss point x^*, the 'peak of the hill', but if we are constrained to choose a solution *upon* the line ab in the figure, in which case the constraint in [G.2] takes the linear form

$$a_1 x_1 + a_2 x_2 = b \qquad \text{[G.3]}$$

then this solution will clearly lie at a point on the 'side' of the hill where *some* $f_i \neq 0$. Similarly, at point x^* in Fig. F.1(b), which is a solution to the problem again with a linear constraint ab, the partial derivatives f_i cannot possibly be zero, because we have (recalling [B.8] and [B.9])

$$\frac{dx_2}{dx_1} = -\frac{f_1}{f_2} = -\frac{a_1}{a_2} \qquad \text{[G.4]}$$

where $-a_1/a_2$ is the slope of the linear constraint [G.3].

So, a point which solves the problem [G.2] need not (and generally will not) satisfy conditions [G.1], which are then no longer necessary conditions for a solution. We have to develop a new set of conditions. We do so by extending the idea just introduced in [G.4]. Suppose that the problem in [G.2] can be represented as in Fig. G.1. We now assume $g(x_1, x_2)$ is non-linear. $g(x_1, x_2) = b$ defines a contour. Similarly, $f(x_1, x_2) = c$ defines a contour of the objective function, and the optimum is at x^*. Note that we have built into the diagram the assumptions which ensure that x^* exists, and is a unique global optimum.

Figure G.1

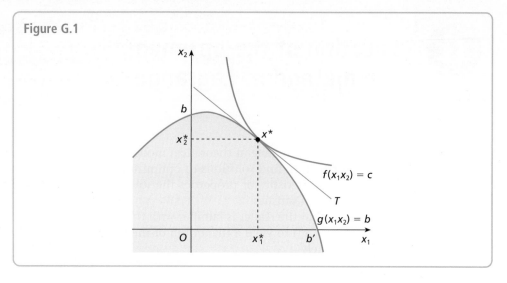

The essential fact about x^* in the figure is that it is a point of tangency. That is, at x^*, the contour of the objective function f and the contour of the constraint function g have a slope equal to that of the common tangent T. We have already shown (see equation [B.9]) that the slope of any contour of f is given by:

$$\frac{dx_2}{dx_1} = \frac{-f_1}{f_2} \qquad [G.5]$$

By a similar argument (supply the details) we can show that the slope of the constraint contour is:

$$\frac{dx_2}{dx_1} = \frac{-g_1}{g_2} \qquad [G.6]$$

It follows that the optimal solution x^* satisfies the conditions:

$$\text{(i)} \quad \frac{f_1}{f_2} = \frac{g_1}{g_2} \qquad [G.7]$$

$$\text{(ii)} \quad g(x_1^*, x_2^*) = b$$

Note that (ii) is an important part of these conditions. (i) simply states that we must be at *some* point of tangency, but does not precisely locate the optimum point – the single equation cannot determine values of both x_1 and x_2. The addition of (ii) closes the system, and ensures that what we have is actually the point of tangency on the constraint contour. (Note that the condition $f(x_1^*, x_2^*) = c$ would do just as well provided we know the value of c at the optimum.)

Condition (i) can be expressed as

$$\frac{f_1}{g_1} = \frac{f_2}{g_2} = \lambda^* > 0 \qquad [G.8]$$

where λ^* is a number representing the common value of the ratios f_i/g_i, $i = 1, 2$ at the optimum. But [G.8] then implies the two equations:

$$f_1 = \lambda^* g_1 \qquad f_2 = \lambda^* g_2 \qquad [G.9]$$

which are then logically equivalent to (i) of [G.7]. Given that $\lambda^* \neq 0$ and $g_i(x_1^*, x_2^*) \neq 0$, $i = 1, 2$, [G.9] implies that at the optimum $f_i \neq 0$, $i = 1, 2$. Thus, as we conjectured, the conditions in [G.1] are *not* necessary for a *constrained* maximum. The optimum x^* in Fig. G.1 has been shown, in [G.9] and [G.7], to satisfy conditions which can be written as:

$$f_1 - \lambda^* g_1 = 0$$
$$f_2 - \lambda^* g_2 = 0 \qquad \text{[G.10]}$$
$$g(x_1^*, x_2^*) - b = 0$$

As is always the case with geometrical reasoning, we have built into the analysis a number of restrictive assumptions by drawing a particular picture. In particular we have assumed only two choice variables, no non-negativity conditions, and only one functional constraint. However, the way of writing the necessary conditions in [G.10] suggests a major step in generalizing the results, by means of a procedure first formulated by Lagrange. Given the problem illustrated in Fig. G.1, we formulate the *Lagrange function*:

$$L(x_1, x_2, \lambda) = f(x_1, x_2) - \lambda[g(x_1, x_2) - b] \qquad \text{[G.11]}$$

If we now set equal to zero the derivatives of the Lagrange function L with respect to its three variables x_1, x_2 and λ, we obtain precisely the necessary conditions for an optimum shown in [G.10]. (Note that for this we have to multiply the third partial derivative by -1. To avoid this we could have formed the Lagrange function by taking $g(x_1, x_2)$ over to the *right*-hand side of the constraint, multiplying by λ, and *adding* to f. Confirm that nothing significant is affected thereby. You will encounter both methods.)

One way of regarding Lagrange's procedure is as a routine method for delivering conditions such as [G.10].

Note that we could have derived conditions [G.7] by algebraic rather than geometrical reasoning. *Assume it is possible* to solve the constraint $g(x_1, x_2) - b = 0$ for x_1 as a function of x_2, say $x_1 = h_1(x_2)$. Then substituting for x_1 in the objective function gives $f(h_1(x_2), x_2) \equiv \Phi(x_2)$. In effect, Φ gives the values of f along the contour in (x_1, x_2) – space defined by $g(x_1, x_2) = b$. Then for a maximum of Φ we must have

$$\Phi'(x_2^*) = f_1 h_1'(x_2^*) + f_2 = -f_1 \frac{g_2}{g_1} + f_2 = 0 \qquad \text{[G.12]}$$

where we have used [G.6] to obtain $h_1' = dx_1/dx_2 = -g_2/g_1$. Then [G.12] gives us the 'tangency condition' (i) of [G.7], and the rest of the derivation of the Lagrange procedure follows.

The key assumption here was that we could solve the constraint for one variable as a function of the other, i.e. the *implicit function* $g(x_1, x_2) - b = 0$ yields $h_1(x_2)$. This suggests that the key theorem underlying Lagrange's method is the *Implicit Function Theorem*. To state this in its general form, suppose we have a system of m continuously differentiable implicit functions in $n > m$ variables, of the form

$$g^1(x_1, \ldots, x_m; x_{m+1}, \ldots, x_n) = 0$$
$$g^2(x_1, \ldots, x_m; x_{m+1}, \ldots, x_n) = 0$$
$$\cdots\cdots\cdots\cdots\cdots\cdots\cdots\cdots\cdots\cdots$$
$$g^m(x_1, \ldots, x_m; x_{m+1}, \ldots, x_n) = 0$$

Define D as the $m \times m$ determinant formed by taking the first m partial derivatives of these m functions, i.e.

$$\begin{vmatrix} g_1^1 & g_2^1 & \cdots & g_m^1 \\ g_1^2 & g_2^2 & \cdots & g_m^2 \\ \cdots & \cdots & \cdots & \cdots \\ g_1^m & g_2^m & \cdots & g_m^m \end{vmatrix}$$

Then, the Implicit Function Theorem states:

If $D \neq 0$, then we can find m continuous functions $h_j(x_{m+1}, \ldots, x_n)$ such that $x_j = h_j(x_{m+1}, \ldots, x_n)$ and $g^j(h_1, \ldots, h_m; x_{m+1}, \ldots, x_n) = 0, j = 1, \ldots, m$.

Thus the theorem says that a sufficient condition to be able to 'solve' the m implicit functions for m of the variables as functions of the remaining $n-m$ variables is that the determinant D be non-zero.

We can now generalize [G.12]. Suppose the problem is

$$\max_x f(x) \quad \text{s.t.} \quad g^1(x) - b_1 = 0, g^2(x) - b_2 = 0, \ldots, g^m(x) - b_m = 0 \qquad \text{[G.13]}$$

where $x = (x_1, x_2, \ldots, x_n)$ and $m < n$. We now introduce a vector of m Lagrange multipliers, $\lambda = (\lambda_1, \ldots, \lambda_m)$, one for each constraint, and form the Lagrange function

$$L(x, \lambda) = f(x) - \sum_{j=1}^{m} \lambda_j [g^j(x) - b_j] \qquad \text{[G.14]}$$

Setting to zero all the partial derivatives of $L(x, \lambda)$ yields the conditions

$$\frac{\partial L}{\partial x_i} = f_i - \sum_{j=1}^{m} \lambda_j^* g_i^j = 0 \qquad i = 1, \ldots, n \qquad \text{[G.15]}$$

$$-\frac{\partial L}{\partial \lambda_j} = g^j(x^*) - b_j = 0 \qquad j = 1, \ldots, m \qquad \text{[G.16]}$$

Thus we have the generalization of the earlier procedure to n variables and m constraints (note that the restriction $n > m$ is to avoid cases in which the feasible set is either empty or contains only one point).

Interpretation of the Lagrange multipliers

We derived necessary conditions for an optimal vector x^* by introducing the Lagrange multipliers λ_j and forming the Lagrange function. The multipliers are, however, more than an ingenious mathematical device, and turn out to have an interpretation which is of great interest in specific economic contexts. To show this, we revert to the two-variable problem in Fig. G.1. Given the necessary conditions for an optimal solution in [G.10], we can regard these as three equations in the three 'unknowns' x_1^*, x_2^* and λ^*, with the constraint value b as an exogenous parameter which determines the solution. We can solve for the unknowns as functions of this parameter, i.e. we may write:

$$\begin{aligned} x_1^* &= h_1(b) \\ x_2^* &= h_2(b) \\ \lambda^* &= h_\lambda(b) \end{aligned} \qquad \text{[G.17]}$$

which express the idea that the solution values depend upon the parameter b. We define the *optimized value*, v^*, of the objective function as its value at the optimal point, i.e.

$$v^* = f(x_1^*, x_2^*) \qquad [\text{G.18}]$$

Clearly, therefore, v^* depends on b, and so we can write, using [G.17];

$$v^* = f(h_1(b), h_2(b)) = v^*(b) \qquad [\text{G.19}]$$

Consider the derivative dv^*/db. This gives the rate at which changes in the constraint parameter b cause changes in the optimized value of the objective function, via its effect on the solution values x_1^* and x_2^*. The significance of λ^* stems from the fact that:

$$\frac{dv^*}{db} = \lambda^* \qquad [\text{G.20}]$$

In other words, λ^* *measures the rate at which the optimized value of the objective function varies with changes in the constraint parameter*. The theorem which establishes this result is the Envelope Theorem, which we consider in some detail in Appendix J.

We can interpret this result with the help of Fig. G.2. Initially, the constraint is defined by $g(x_1, x_2) = b$, and the solution is at x^*. Now suppose the constraint becomes $g(x_1, x_2) = b'$, with $b' > b$, and the curve in the figure shifts outward. There will be a new solution at x^{**}, with optimal values x_1^{**}, x_2^{**}. The change in b has caused a change in the optimized value of the objective function, given by:

$$f(x_1^{**}, x_2^{**}) - f(x_1^*, x_2^*) = v^{**} - v^* \qquad [\text{G.21}]$$

Thus, we can take the ratio of these changes:

$$\frac{\Delta v^*}{\Delta b} = \frac{v^{**} - v^*}{b' - b} \qquad [\text{G.22}]$$

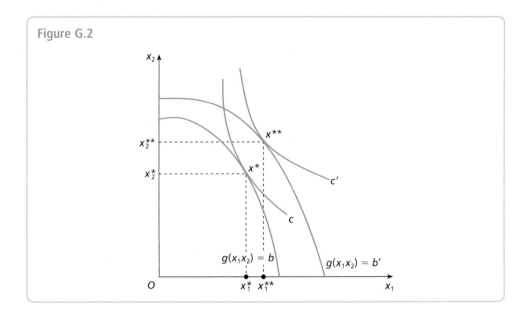

Figure G.2

which relates to a finite change in b. Then, in the usual way, we can take:

$$\lim_{\Delta b \to 0} \frac{\Delta v^*}{\Delta b} = \frac{dv^*}{db} \qquad \text{[G.22]}$$

Thus, we can think of the constraint shifting infinitesimally and the derivative dv^*/db then measures the rate at which v^* changes, given that an optimal point is always chosen.

In economics, derivatives are usually designated by the term '*marginal* this or that'. The equality in [G.20] implies that λ^* can be thought of as the marginal change in the optimized value of the objective function with respect to changes in the constraint. In specific contexts, this leads to useful interpretations of the Lagrangean multipliers. For example, in the case in which the consumer maximizes utility (the objective function) subject to a budget constraint (b = income), λ^* would measure the *marginal utility of income* at the optimal point. In a problem in which costs were to be minimized subject to a fixed output constraint (b = output), λ^* would measure *marginal cost* at the optimal point.

A further interpretation of the Lagrange multiplier is as a kind of price. Since its value at the optimum measures the change in value of the objective function caused by a slight shift in the constraint, it can be interpreted as measuring the maximum 'payment' which would be made *in exchange* for a shift in the constraint. For example, suppose that the problem is to maximize profit by choosing input and output levels, subject to a limitation on the amount of one input available (b = quantity of input). Then λ^* in this problem measures the marginal profitability of the input, or the rate at which maximum profit increases with a small increase in the fixed amount of the input. It follows that λ^* measures the maximum amount the firm would be prepared to pay for the increase in input, since anything less would result in a net increase in profit, and anything more a net decrease. For this reason, λ^* would be called the *shadow price* of the input which may differ from the input's actual market price.

EXERCISE G

1. Sketch in two and three dimensions the case in which a monotonically increasing objective function takes on a maximum over a closed, bounded feasible set. Explain from this why the condition in [G.1] is not necessary for a local maximum in a constrained maximization problem.

2. Explain why the conditions in [G.15] and [G.16] are also necessary for solution to the problem:

$$\min f(x) \quad \text{s.t.} \quad g^j(x) - b_j = 0 \qquad j = 1, \ldots, m$$

and why therefore these conditions are necessary but not sufficient for a maximum.

3. Interpret the Lagrange multipliers which would be associated with the constraints in the following optimization problems:

   (a) A central planner in a developing country wishes to maximize GNP, subject to the constraints that the balance of payments deficit may not exceed a given figure, and that a fixed amount of skilled labour is available.

   (b) A firm wishes to choose a set of investment projects which maximize its profitability, subject to the constraint that the total amount it spends on investment does not exceed a fixed amount of funds available.

4. Consider the problem:

$$\max_{x_1, x_2} f(x_1, x_2) \qquad \text{where } f_1, f_2 > 0$$

$$\text{s.t.} \quad a_{11}x_1 + a_{12}x_2 \leqslant b_1$$

$$a_{21}x_1 + a_{22}x_2 \leqslant b_2 \qquad x_1 \geqslant 0 \qquad x_2 \geqslant 0$$

The objective function f is strictly quasi-concave, and the a_{ij} ($i, j = 1, 2$) are all positive.

(a) Draw the feasible set, assuming

$$\frac{a_{11}}{a_{12}} > \frac{a_{21}}{a_{22}} \qquad \text{and} \qquad \frac{b_1}{a_{12}} > \frac{b_2}{a_{22}} \qquad \text{and that the lines intersect.}$$

Find the points at which a solution may be found, and suggest their main characteristics, in terms of whether they imply zero or non-zero variable values, and binding or non-binding constraints.

(b) Recalling the interpretation of Lagrangean multipliers, give an economic interpretation of the case $\lambda_1^* = 0$.

Concave programming and the Kuhn–Tucker conditions

In the previous section we considered the problem of maximizing some function subject to functional constraints in strict equality form. Such problems are often referred to as 'classical optimization problems'. Though this type of problem is standard in economics, it involves two important assumptions which are not in general satisfied in many economic problems. First, it assumes that there are no direct constraints on the values of the choice variables. Second, it assumes that constraints cannot be satisfied as inequalities.

In many economic problems, variables are constrained to be non-negative. For example, consumers cannot consume negative quantities of goods, firms cannot produce negative outputs. In other problems there may be natural non-zero upper or lower bounds to the value of some variable, for example a shareholder can only hold a fraction between 0 and 1 of a company's shares. For the moment we concentrate on the case of non-negativity constraints.

In Fig. G.1 of the previous Appendix, we *assumed* that the tangency occurred at a point in the interior of the positive quadrant, with $x_1^* > 0$, $x_2^* > 0$. However, we could easily have drawn a diagram with the tangency at a point, say, with $x_1^* < 0$, $x_2^* > 0$. None of the ensuing discussion would have been affected. But clearly, if negative values of x_1 are ruled out, this could not be a solution to the problem, and we would have to think again. We do this with the help of an example.

Suppose $R(x)$ and $C(x)$ are a firm's revenue and cost functions respectively, where x is a vector of outputs (we have a multi-product firm). The firm's objective function is profit: $f(x) = R(x) - C(x)$. The unconstrained profit-maximizing output vector is characterized by:

$$f_i(x^*) = R_i(x^*) - C_i(x^*) = 0 \qquad \text{[H.1]}$$

which yields the familiar description of the profit-maximizing output in terms of the equality of each output's marginal revenue ($R_i(x^*)$) with marginal cost ($C_i(x^*)$).

But is this problem really unconstrained? Given the inadmissibility of negative outputs we should impose the constraints:

$$x_i \geq 0 \qquad i = 1, 2, \ldots, n \qquad \text{[H.2]}$$

The result of this is that the conditions in [H.1] are *no longer necessary conditions for a maximum*. To see this consider Fig. H.1. In each part of the figure profit $f(x)$ is plotted holding all variables except the ith constant, at their optimal values. In (a) we have the case implicitly envisaged by the conditions in [H.1]. The ith output's optimal value $x_i^* > 0$ and the constraint in [H.2] is non-binding at the optimum. It follows that the usual argument applies – the derivative of profit must be zero at x_i^* since otherwise x_i could be varied so as to increase the value of f. However, in (b) of the figure the highest feasible value of profit occurs at $x_i^* = 0$, i.e. none of ith output should optimally be produced since positive outputs actually reduce profit

Figure H.1

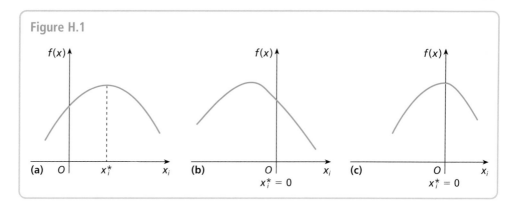

$(C_i(x) > R_i(x)$ when $x_i > 0$ and all other outputs are at their optimal values). But at $x_i^* = 0$, the slope of the profit function is negative, not zero, implying that [H.1] is not a necessary condition for an optimum, since an optimal point exists at which it is not satisfied. In the case shown the constraint [H.2] is binding, since without it the firm would seek to increase profit by producing negative x_i. In (c), on the other hand, we have a case in which it just so happens that at the optimal $x_i^* = 0$ the profit derivative is zero.

From this discussion we make the following generalization. In a problem in which non-negativity constraints are imposed, the 'necessary conditions' in [H.1] are no longer correct. The correct conditions can be deduced from Fig. H.1 (where $f(x)$ now represents any objective function and x_i^* the optimal value of x_i) as:

$$\begin{array}{ll} \text{(i) if } x_i^* > 0 & \text{then } f_i(x^*) = 0 \\ \text{(ii) if } x_i^* = 0 & \text{then } f_i(x^*) \leq 0 \end{array} \quad i = 1, 2, \ldots, n \qquad \text{[H.3]}$$

Condition (ii) ensures that $f(x)$ cannot be increased for *permissible* changes, i.e. increases, in x_i. A more concise way of writing [H.3] is:

$$f_i(x^*) \leq 0 \qquad x_i^* \geq 0 \qquad x_i^* \cdot f_i(x^*) = 0 \qquad i = 1, 2, \ldots, n \qquad \text{[H.4]}$$

Such conditions, involving a pair of inequalities both of which cannot be strict, are known as *complementary slackness conditions*. The third term, the condition that the product of x_i^* and its partial derivative be zero at the optimum, implies that condition [H.1] is obtained *as a special case*, one in which all variables turn out to be positive at the optimum and so all non-negative constraints are non-binding.

By an exactly similar type of argument, we can show that, if the problem is to *minimize* some function $f(x)$ subject to the non-negativity constraints $x_i \geq 0$, then the appropriate necessary condition is

$$f_i(x^*) \geq 0 \qquad x_i^* \geq 0 \qquad x_i^* \cdot f_i(x^*) = 0 \qquad i = 1, 2, \ldots, n \qquad \text{[H.5]}$$

Turning now to inequalities in functional constraints, note that it is natural in many economic problems to define the constraints in this way. For example, in the case of a consumer choosing quantities of two goods, it would seem reasonable to allow expenditure, $p_1 x_1 + p_2 x_2$, to be less than income, m, if the consumer wants it to be – we need not *constrain* all income to be spent. There are also important mathematical reasons for preferring to express constraints as weak inequalities when this is consistent with the economic sense of the problem. In a problem such as that in

Question 4, Appendix G, if the constraints were in equality form there would be just one point in the feasible set and the problem is trivial. If it makes sense, given the economics of the problem, to allow, as feasible, points that satisfy the constraints as inequalities, then far more solution possibilities exist and these have interesting economic interpretations, as we shall see below (see Question 5, for example). Moreover, recall from our earlier discussion of existence, local vs global optimality, and uniqueness of solutions, that the convexity of the feasible set is an important property. But in general, a constraint of the form $g(x) = b$ defines a convex feasible set *only if g* is a linear function, and so the earlier theorems would generally not be applicable (for example, is the set of points *on* the constraint contour in Fig. G.1 a convex set?). Thus, whenever possible it is preferable, at least initially, to define constraints as weak inequalities. Of course, in many problems, in the end, this 'may not matter'. For example, in the problem in Fig. G.1, since $f_1 > 0$, $f_2 > 0$, the solution ends up on the boundary of the feasible set, $g(x_1, x_2) = b$, and the fact that this often happens in economics explains why the classical formulation is so widespread. Nevertheless, this result is something that should be deduced, not assumed.

Concave programming

A problem in which functional constraints are expressed as weak inequalities, and non-negativity restrictions are imposed, is usually modelled as a *concave programming problem*. We are now concerned with the question of how to characterize a solution to such a problem, that is how to formulate a set of conditions which a solution must satisfy. The required conditions are known as the Kuhn–Tucker conditions.

We write the *concave programming problem* as

$$\max f(x) \quad \text{s.t.} \quad g^1(x) \geq 0, g^2(x) \geq 0, \ldots, g^m(x) \geq 0 \; x \geq 0 \qquad \text{[H.6]}$$

where $x = (x_1, \ldots, x_n)$. We assume throughout that a solution x^* exists and we want to characterize it. The functions $f, g^j (j = 1, \ldots, m)$ are *assumed to be concave*. Note that this formulation of the problem is otherwise quite general, for

(a) if a constraint is 'naturally' written in the form $h(x) \leq 0$, then this is equivalent to $g(x) = -h(x) \geq 0$;

(b) if a constraint is in equality form $h(x) = 0$, then this is equivalent to the two constraints $g^1(x) \equiv h(x \geq 0$ and $g^2(x) \equiv -h(x) \geq 0$.

The key restriction is that the functions must all be concave.

We proceed by defining the Lagrangean function

$$L(x, \lambda) = f(x) + \sum_{j=1}^{m} \lambda_j g^j(x) \qquad \text{[H.7]}$$

The essence of the approach is to show that the solution x^* to the concave programming problem must, in conjunction with a vector λ^* of Lagrange multipliers, satisfy the condition that it yield a *saddle-point of the Lagrangean function*, i.e. a point satisfying

$$L(x, \lambda^*) \leq L(x^*, \lambda^*) \leq L(x^*, \lambda) \qquad \text{for } x \geq 0, \lambda \geq 0 \qquad \text{[H.8]}$$

Thus x^* and λ^* can then be characterized as: x^* *maximizes* $L(x, \lambda^*)$ *for* $x \geqslant 0$; *and* λ^* *minimizes* $L(x^*, \lambda)$ *for* $\lambda \geqslant 0$. Assuming, as we always do, that the functions $f(x)$ and $g^j(x)$ are all differentiable, this implies that x^*, λ^* are characterized by the following *Kuhn–Tucker conditions*:

$$\frac{\partial L}{\partial x_i} = f_i(x^*) + \sum_{j=1}^{m} \lambda_j^* g_i^j(x^*) \leqslant 0 \quad x_i^* \geqslant 0 \quad x_i^* \frac{\partial L}{\partial x_i} = 0 \quad i = 1, \ldots, n \qquad \text{[H.9]}$$

$$\frac{\partial L}{\partial \lambda_j} = g^j(x^*) \geqslant 0 \quad \lambda_j^* \geqslant 0 \quad \lambda_j^* g^j(x^*) = 0 \qquad\qquad j = 1, \ldots, m \qquad \text{[H.10]}$$

The reason the partial derivatives $\partial L/\partial x_i$ must be non-positive at the optimum is because we are maximizing subject to the condition that $x_i \geqslant 0$, and so [H.9] reflects the same arguments that gave [H.4] earlier. Likewise, we require $\partial L/\partial \lambda_j \geqslant 0$ because we are minimizing subject to $\lambda_j \geqslant 0$ (recall [H.5]). The Kuhn–Tucker conditions are the required necessary conditions for the concave programming problem. We shall illustrate their use below, once we have examined in more depth the meaning and justification of the *saddle point characterization* of the optimum x^*.

The general idea of a saddle point is illustrated in Fig. H.2. The function $f(x, y)$ is strictly concave in x, for each y, and strictly convex in y, for each x. A saddle point occurs at (x^*, y^*): x^* maximizes $f(x, y^*)$, and y^* minimizes $f(x^*, y)$. The reason for the term 'saddle point' is obvious from the figure (a saddle point of a function need not look like that in Fig. H.2, however – see Question 10, Exercise H).

The Saddle Point Theorem given below establishes that, if f and the g^j are concave functions, then there exists a vector of Lagrange multipliers λ^* which, together with the vector x^* which solves the concave programming problem [H.6], represent *a saddle point of the Lagrange function*, over the domain $x \geqslant 0$, $\lambda \geqslant 0$. So, given differentiability, x^* can then be characterized by the Kuhn–Tucker conditions [H.9] and [H.10].

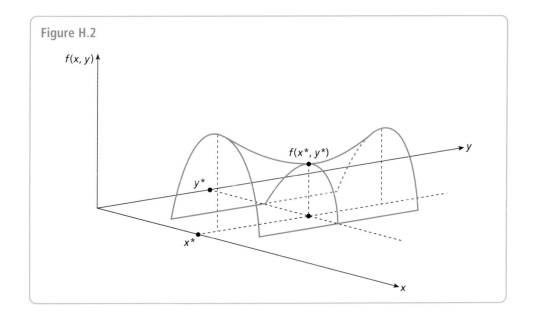

Figure H.2

The key result is given by the following

Fundamental Theorem of Concave Functions: Let $h^0(x)$, $h^1(x)$, . . . , $h^m(x)$ be concave functions defined on a convex set X. If there is no $\bar{x} \in X$ such that $h^j(\bar{x}) > 0$, all $j = 0, 1, . . . , m$, then there exist numbers $p_j \geqslant 0$, not all zero, such that

$$\sum_{j=0}^{m} p_j h^j(x) \leqslant 0 \qquad \text{for all } x \in X \qquad \text{[H.11]}$$

In words, if there is no point in the domain at which all the functions simultaneously take on a positive value, then we can always find a set of non-negative weights such that the weighted sum of the functions is never positive, whatever the value of x. It is easy to see why we have to rule out the existence of a point like $\bar{x}$, since then obviously no such p_j could exist. The interesting thing is that *fixed* weights can be found that keep the weighted sum non-positive for *all* values of $x \in X$.

Figure H.3 illustrates for three strictly concave functions. At x', $h^1(x') > 0$ and $h^2(x') > 0$, but $h^0(x') < 0$, and the functions satisfy the conditions of the theorem at all other points also. $X = \{x \mid 0 \leqslant x \leqslant \hat{x}\}$. Then clearly choosing $p_0 = 1$, $p_1 = 1$, and $p_2 = 0$ would do the trick – at no x is $1 \cdot h^0(x) + 1 \cdot h^1(x) + 0 \cdot h^2(x) > 0$. (Explain why in this example we could never set $p_0 = 0$ if we want to satisfy [H.11].)

This theorem yields the central result on the solution to the concave programming problem [H.6] directly.

Saddle Point Theorem: If x^* is a solution to the concave programming problem [H.6], and Slater's condition S: there exists $\bar{x}$ in X such that $g^j(\bar{x}) > 0$, $j = 1, . . . , m$, is satisfied, then there exist multipliers $\lambda_j^* \geqslant 0$, $j = 1, . . . , m$, not all zero, such that (x^*, λ^*) is a saddle point of the Lagrange function, i.e.

$$L(x, \lambda^*) \leqslant L(x^*, \lambda^*) \leqslant L(x^*, \lambda) \qquad \text{for } x \geqslant 0, \lambda \geqslant 0$$

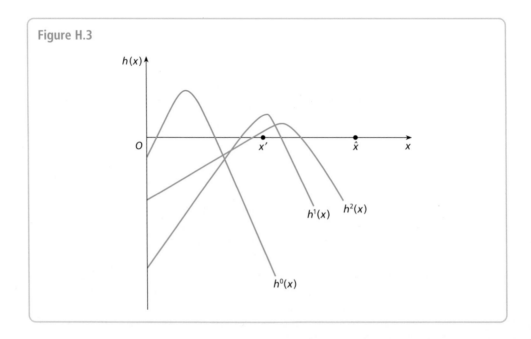

Figure H.3

Proof

Since $f(x^\star) \geqslant f(x)$ for all $x \geqslant 0$ such that $g^j(x) \geqslant 0$, then the system

$$
\begin{aligned}
g^j(x) > 0 \qquad j = 1, \ldots, m \\
f(x) - f(x^\star) > 0
\end{aligned}
\qquad \text{[H.12]}
$$

has no solution for $x \geqslant 0$. The g^j and f are all concave and so the conditions of the previous theorem are satisfied with $X = \mathbb{R}^n_+$, and so there exist numbers $p^\star_0, p^\star_1, \ldots, p^\star_m \geqslant 0$, not all zero, such that

$$
p^\star_0[f(x) - f(x^\star)] + \sum_{j=1}^{m} p^\star_j g^j(x) \leqslant 0 \qquad \text{for all } x \in X \qquad \text{[H.13]}
$$

Since this must also be true for $x = x^\star$, we have $\sum_{j=1}^{m} p^\star_j g^j(x^\star) \leqslant 0$. But since $x^\star$ is feasible, $p^\star_j \geqslant 0$ and $g^j(x^\star) \geqslant 0$ imply $\sum_{j=1}^{m} p^\star_j g^j(x^\star) \geqslant 0$, so these two weak inequalities together mean $\sum_{j=1}^{m} p^\star_j g^j(x^\star) = 0$. Thus we can rewrite [H.13] as

$$
p^\star_0 f(x) + \sum_{j=1}^{m} p^\star_j g^j(x) \leqslant p^\star_0 f(x^\star) + \sum_{j=1}^{m} p^\star_j g^j(x^\star) \qquad \text{all } x \in X \qquad \text{[H.14]}
$$

Note that $g^j(x^\star) \geqslant 0$ and $p_j \geqslant 0$ implies $\sum_{j=1}^{m} p_j g^j(x^\star) \geqslant 0$, so that we can re-write [H.14] as

$$
p^\star_0 f(x) + \sum_{j=1}^{m} p^\star_j g^j(x) \leqslant p^\star_0 f(x^\star) + \sum_{j=1}^{m} p^\star_j g^j(x^\star) \leqslant p^\star_0 f(x^\star) + \sum_{j=1}^{m} p_j g^j(x^\star)
$$

$$
\text{all } x \in X, p_j \geqslant 0 \qquad \text{[H.15]}
$$

Now suppose $p^\star_0 = 0$. Then [H.13] implies $\sum_{j=1}^{m} p^\star_j g^j(x) \leqslant 0$. In particular at $x = \bar{x}$ we have $\sum_{j=1}^{m} p^\star_j g^j(\bar{x}) \leqslant 0$. But since each $p^\star_j \geqslant 0$ and not all are zero, this must violate Slater's condition and we have a contradiction. Thus Slater's condition implies $p^\star_0 > 0$. So we can define $\lambda^\star_j = p^\star_j / p^\star_0$, $\lambda_j = p_j / p^\star_0$ $(j = 1, \ldots, m)$ and rewrite [H.15] as

$$
f(x) + \sum_{j=1}^{m} \lambda^\star_j g^j(x) \leqslant f(x^\star) + \sum_{j=1}^{m} \lambda^\star_j g^j(x^\star) \leqslant f(x^\star) + \sum_{j=1}^{m} \lambda_j g^j(x^\star)
$$

$$
\text{all } x \in X, \lambda_j \geqslant 0 \qquad \text{[H.16]}
$$

Then, recalling the definition of the Lagrange function $L(x, \lambda)$, we see that [H.16] is the saddle point result.

Note that Slater's condition was not required to derive [H.15], but only when we wanted to move to the Lagrange function form [H.16]. Slater's condition can be interpreted as requiring that the feasible set possesses an interior point, and is designed to rule out the following kind of case, in which the Lagrange procedure breaks down. Suppose the problem is max x s.t. $-x^2 \geqslant 0$ $(x \in \mathbb{R})$. The Lagrange function is $x - \lambda x^2$, and the 'necessary conditions' are $1 - 2\lambda x \leqslant 0$, $-x^2 \geqslant 0$, but since the only x which satisfies the constraint is $x = 0$, this leads to the nonsense result $1 \leqslant 0$. The solution is obviously $x^\star = 0$, but no $\lambda^\star \geqslant 0$ exists such that

$$
x - \lambda^\star x^2 \leqslant x^\star - \lambda^\star x^{\star 2} \leqslant x^\star - \lambda x^{\star 2}
$$

If $\lambda^\star = 0$, the first inequality is violated by choosing $x > 0$; if $\lambda^\star > 0$, then that inequality is violated by choosing $x < 1/\lambda^\star$. Thus the saddle-point condition does not characterize the solution of this concave programming problem. Slater's condition is clearly not satisfied (no x exists for which $-x^2 > 0$). Note, however, it *is* true that

$$p_0^* x - p_1^* x^2 \leqslant p_0^* x^* - p_1^* x^{*2} \leqslant p_0^* x^* - p_1 x^{*2}$$

for $p_0^* = 0$, $x^* = 0$, and *any* $p_1^* > 0$. In terms of our illustration in Fig. H.3, Slater's condition is ensuring that it is the objective function that corresponds to the function $h^0(x)$ and not one of the constraints. In other words, it is ensuring that p_0^* cannot be set to zero when taking the weighted sum of the concave functions. Hence it is permissible to divide through by p_0 in deriving the Lagrange multipliers.

It is also possible to prove the converse of this theorem, namely that if (x^*, λ^*) is a saddle point of the Lagrange function then x^* solves the problem in [H.6], and this does not require concavity of the functions f, g^j. Taking the two theorems together, *the Kuhn–Tucker conditions are both necessary and sufficient conditions for a solution x^* to problem [H.6] when the functions f, g^j are concave.* It is also possible to extend these theorems to the case in which any of the functions are quasi-concave. This is particularly important because ordinal utility functions in economics cannot be restricted to be concave, but only quasi-concave. It is then reassuring to know that the Kuhn–Tucker conditions are directly applicable (the interested reader is referred to Takayama, 1985, ch. 1).

To illustrate the use of the Kuhn–Tucker conditions we consider two problems, the first involving only non-negativity conditions, the second introducing also weak inequalities in the functional constraints. Consider the two-variable problem:

$$\max f(x_1, x_2) \quad \text{s.t.} \quad a_1 x_1 + a_2 x_2 = b \qquad x_1, x_2 \geqslant 0 \qquad \text{[H.17]}$$

where f is taken to be strictly increasing and strictly quasi-concave. However, we assume that the contours of the objective function are everywhere steeper than the constraint line. Fig. H.4 illustrates. The Lagrange function for the problem is:

$$L(x_1, x_2, \lambda) = f(x_1, x_2) - \lambda[a_1 x_1 + a_2 x_2 - b] \qquad \text{[H.18]}$$

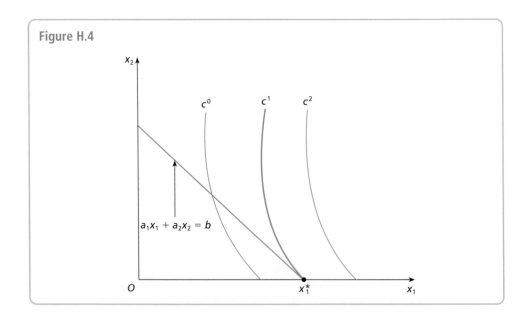

Figure H.4

and so the counterparts to condition [H.4] are:

$$L_1 = f_1 - \lambda^* a_1 \leq 0 \qquad x_1^* \geq 0 \qquad x_1^* \cdot [f_1 - \lambda^* a_1] = 0 \qquad \text{[H.19]}$$

$$L_2 = f_2 - \lambda^* a_2 \leq 0 \qquad x_2^* \geq 0 \qquad x_2^* \cdot [f_2 - \lambda^* a_2] = 0 \qquad \text{[H.20]}$$

$$L_\lambda = -(a_1 x_1^* + a_2 x_2^* - b) = 0 \qquad \text{[H.21]}$$

Now suppose, as in the figure, that at the optimum, $x_1^* > 0$ and $x_2^* = 0$. From [H.19] we must have (explain why):

$$f_1 = \lambda^* a_1 \qquad \text{[H.22]}$$

while from [H.20] we have:

$$f_2 \leq \lambda^* a_2 \qquad \text{[H.23]}$$

Dividing each side of [H.23] into the corresponding side of [H.22] gives

$$f_1/f_2 \geq a_1/a_2 \qquad \text{[H.24]}$$

which is simply the condition that, at the optimum, the contour of the objective function must be at least as steep as the constraint line. This is in fact all that *can* be said in characterizing an optimum when non-negativity constraints exist and one is binding at the optimum. Note that, if at the optimum $x_2^* > 0$, then we have of course the necessary conditions in the form given in Appendix G.

Turning now to the case of inequalities in the functional constraints, we can note first that in single-constraint problems the non-existence of bliss points makes this generalization unnecessary. Since in this case a solution will always lie on the boundary, we might as well express the constraint in equality form, as in the problem [H.17]. The generalization does, however, become important in problems of two or more constraints.

Consider the problem:

$$\max f(x_1, x_2) \quad \text{s.t.} \quad a_1 x_1 + a_2 x_2 \leq b_1$$
$$c_1 x_1 + c_2 x_2 \leq b_2 \qquad x_1, x_2 \geq 0 \qquad \text{[H.25]}$$

where f is concave and $f_1, f_2 > 0$. The problem is illustrated in Fig. H.5. It is assumed that the constraints are such as to intersect in the positive quadrant. The feasible set is then the shaded area. Points α, β and γ correspond to possible types of solution for different assumptions about the contours of the objective function, and assuming the non-negativity constraints are non-binding at the optimum.

The Lagrange function is:

$$L(x_1, x_2, \lambda_1, \lambda_2) = f(x_1, x_2) - \lambda_1[a_1 x_1 + a_2 x_2 - b_1] - \lambda_2[c_1 x_1 + c_2 x_2 - b_2] \qquad \text{[H.26]}$$

and the Kuhn–Tucker conditions are:

$$f_1 - \lambda_1^* a_1 - \lambda_2^* c_1 \leq 0 \qquad x_1^* \geq 0 \qquad x_1^*[f_1 - \lambda_1^* a_1 - \lambda_2^* c_1] = 0 \qquad \text{[H.27]}$$

$$f_2 - \lambda_1^* a_2 - \lambda_2^* c_2 \leq 0 \qquad x_2^* \geq 0 \qquad x_2^*[f_2 - \lambda_1^* a_2 - \lambda_2^* c_2] = 0 \qquad \text{[H.28]}$$

$$a_1 x_1^* + a_2 x_2^* - b_1 \leq 0 \qquad \lambda_1^* \geq 0 \qquad \lambda_1^*[a_1 x_1^* + a_2 x_2^* - b_1] = 0 \qquad \text{[H.29]}$$

$$c_1 x_1^* + c_2 x_2^* - b_2 \leq 0 \qquad \lambda_2^* \geq 0 \qquad \lambda_2^*[c_1 x_1^* + c_2 x_2^* - b_2] = 0 \qquad \text{[H.30]}$$

Let us now establish the connection between the solution possibilities in the figure and the conditions in [H.27]–[H.30]. In case of a solution at α, we have that

Figure H.5

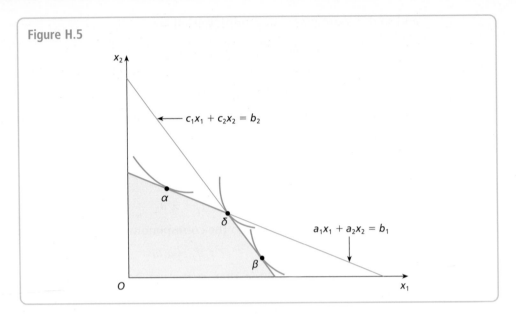

the b_2 constraint is non-binding. It follows therefore that $\lambda_2^* = 0$ (intuitively, the shadow price of a non-binding constraint is zero). Therefore the terms involving λ_2^* in [H.27] and [H.28] drop out and we have the conditions for

$$\textit{case } \alpha \quad f_1 - \lambda_1^* a_1 = 0 \qquad f_2 - \lambda_1^* a_2 = 0 \qquad a_1 x_1^* + a_2 x_2^* = b_1 \qquad [\text{H.31}]$$

These are the standard conditions resulting from applying the Lagrange procedure to the appropriate single-constraint problem, i.e. that with only the b_1 constraint expressed as an equality.

Consider now case β. Here, the b_1 constraint is non-binding. Therefore small shifts in it have no effect on the optimum and $\lambda_1^* = 0$. In that case we have the conditions for

$$\textit{case } \beta \quad f_1 - \lambda_2^* c_1 = 0 \qquad f_2 - \lambda_2^* c_2 = 0 \qquad c_1 x_1^* + c_2 x_2^* = b_2 \qquad [\text{H.32}]$$

Again, therefore, we obtain the appropriate conditions from applying the Lagrange procedure to the appropriate single-constraint problem.

In the third case δ, *both* constraints are binding at the optimum, and are satisfied as equalities (but see Question 7, Exercise H). Strictly speaking, conditions [H.29] and [H.30], the solution of which determines the point (x_1^*, x_2^*), are in the present case sufficient to solve the problem. From [H.27] and [H.28] we see that

$$f_1/f_2 = \frac{\lambda_1^* a_1 + \lambda_2^* c_1}{\lambda_1^* a_2 + \lambda_2^* c_2} \qquad [\text{H.33}]$$

i.e. at the optimum the slope of the contour of the objective function is *not equal* to the slope of either constraint, but rather lies between these slopes (see Question 9, Exercise H).

There are two remaining solution possibilities, namely those in which one of the variables is zero at the optimum, but considering these would add nothing to the discussion of the previous example (confirm).

We can draw the following conclusions from this discussion. The necessary conditions which follow from applying the Lagrange procedure *as if* the problem involved only equality constraints are valid only for the special case in which all constraints turn out to be binding at the optimum (a case which may not exist even as a logical possibility if the set of points satisfying the constraints as equalities is empty). The other solution possibilities are then systematically explored by considering all the possible combinations of non-binding constraints and by examining the conditions with the appropriate constraints and terms deleted.

EXERCISE H

1. Explain why condition [H.20] *does not* justify the statement: $x_2^* = 0 \Rightarrow f_2 < \lambda^* a_2$. How would you interpret the case in which $x_2^* = 0$ and $f_2 = \lambda^* a_2$?

2. Discuss the interpretation of the case analysed in Fig. H.4 as a problem in consumer demand. Is the type of solution, with one good's optimal consumption zero, plausible in reality? What if we were talking (realistically) about thousands of goods and not just two?

3. Suppose that instead of the direct constraints $x_i \geqslant 0$ we had $x_i \geqslant b_i (b_i \neq 0)$. Show how the Lagrange procedure can be modified to handle this case. [*Hint*: either redefine the variables x_i so as to put the direct constraints in non-negativity form, or treat the new constraints as a special form of functional constraints.]

4. Suppose that we added to the problem in [H.25] the further constraint $e_1 x_1 + e_2 x_2 \leqslant b_3$. Discuss the solution possibilities and necessary conditions for this problem along the lines of the analysis of cases α, β and γ in this section.

5. *Points rationing*. First read Chapter 2 and then return to this question. In the problem in [H.25], interpret a_1 and a_2 as money prices of the respective goods and b_1 as money income; while c_1 and c_2 are numbers of ration coupons which must also be paid per unit of each good and b_2 is the consumer's initial endowment of these ration coupons. f is a utility function. Give an economic interpretation of the problem and of the three solution possibilities shown in Fig. H.5. What would you expect to happen if some consumers are at α-type equilibria and others are at β-type equilibria?

6. Show that, if λ_1^*, $\lambda_2^* > 0$, the value of the ratio $(\lambda_1^* a_1 + \lambda_2^* c_1)/(\lambda_1^* a_2 + \lambda_2^* c_2)$ must lie between the values a_1/a_2 and c_1/c_2.

7. In Fig. H.5, two somewhat odd cases could occur. The solution could be at δ, but the contour of the objective function could be (a) tangent to the b_1 constraint, or (b) tangent to the b_2 constraint, at that point. What happens to the conditions [H.27]–[H.30] in such a case? [*Hint*: consider what happens in case (a) if the b_2 constraint shifts outward and inward, and in case (b) if the b_1 shifts. What can be said about the relevant Lagrange multiplier in each case?]

Second-order conditions and comparative statics

From the theory of unconstrained maximization of a function of a single variable we know that the condition $f'(x^\star) = 0$ is insufficient to fully characterize the point $x^\star$ at which f is maximized, since the condition may also be satisfied at points which yield a minimum, or a point of inflexion, of the function. Thus we supplement this first-order condition with a second-order condition $f''(x^\star) < 0$. Our preceding discussion of *constrained* maximization problems was concerned only with first-order conditions. For example, the Lagrange multiplier conditions in [G.12] would be satisfied both by a point which maximized and by a point which minimized $f(x)$ over the feasible set. Some discussion of second-order conditions is therefore required.

It is instructive to link this discussion with an account of the methods of 'comparative static equilibrium analysis', or comparative statics. Economic models typically yield a set of equations which determine the equilibrium values of a set of endogenous variables. The equilibrium values depend on the values of one or more exogenous parameters in the equations. It is of interest how the equilibrium values of the endogenous variables are affected by a change in value of an exogenous parameter. For example, a consumer's demand function traces out the relationship between the equilibrium quantity of a good (the endogenous variable), and the value of its price (the exogenous parameter); a firm's supply function shows the relationship between equilibrium output and market price; we may be interested in how a change in consumers' incomes (the exogenous parameter) affects the equilibrium price (endogenous variable) in the model of a market. The methods of comparative statics investigate the effects of changes in the exogenous variables on the endogenous variables.

The link between second-order conditions and comparative statics arises in the following way. There are two types of equilibrium equation systems in microeconomics. The first type is derived from an optimization problem and consists of the first-order conditions characterizing the solution to that problem. The second type consists of a set of 'supply = demand' conditions: although ultimately the supply and demand functions are derived from optimization problems, the equilibrium system is a set of 'balance equations' rather than a set of first-order conditions. In carrying out comparative static analysis of the first type of system, the second-order conditions for the optimization problem often have a useful part to play. Before exploring this point further, however, we consider the general method of comparative statics.

General method of comparative statics

Suppose we have a system of n equations involving n endogenous variables $x_1, \ldots, x_n$, and m parameters $\alpha_1, \ldots, \alpha_m$. We write this as

$$f^1(x_1, \ldots, x_n; \alpha_1, \ldots, \alpha_m) = 0$$

$$\ldots\ldots\ldots\ldots\ldots\ldots\ldots\ldots\ldots \quad\quad\quad \text{[I.1]}$$

$$f^n(x_1, \ldots, x_n; \alpha_1, \ldots, \alpha_m) = 0$$

From the Implicit Function Theorem, (Appendix G) we know that if the determinant of partial derivatives

$$D = \begin{vmatrix} f^1_1 & \cdots & f^1_n \\ \cdots & \cdots & \cdots \\ f^n_1 & \cdots & f^n_n \end{vmatrix}$$

is non-zero, then there exist n functions $h^i(\alpha_1, \ldots, \alpha_m)$, such that $x_i = h^i(\alpha_1, \ldots, \alpha_m)$, $i = 1, \ldots, n$. The equations in [I.1] determine the equilibrium values of the x_i, and the Implicit Function Theorem implies that the equilibrium values are functions of the parameters α_j ($j = 1, \ldots, m$) if $D \neq 0$. The problem of comparative statics is to say as much as we can about the derivatives $h^i_j = \partial x_i / \partial \alpha_j$, since these express the effects of a change in a parameter on the equilibrium value of a variable.

We proceed as follows. Totally differentiating through the system [I.1] gives

$$f^1_1 dx_1 + \ldots + f^1_n dx_n + f^1_{n+1} d\alpha_1 + \ldots + f^1_{n+m} d\alpha_m = 0$$

$$\ldots\ldots\ldots\ldots\ldots\ldots\ldots\ldots\ldots\ldots\ldots\ldots\ldots \quad\quad \text{[I.2]}$$

$$f^n_1 dx_1 + \ldots + f^n_n dx_n + f^n_{n+1} d\alpha_1 + \ldots + f^n_{n+m} d\alpha_m = 0$$

The total differentials of the f^i functions are set to zero because we constrain the equilibrium conditions to continue to hold when we make some specified change $d\alpha_j$ in a parameter, where these $d\alpha_j$ are given (small) numbers. That is, the differentials dx_i must be such as to keep the equilibrium conditions satisfied when the α_j change. Moreover, all the partial derivatives in [I.2] are evaluated at the initial equilibrium values of the x_i and given values α_j ($i = 1, \ldots, n$, $j = 1, \ldots, m$). This means that those partial derivatives are just numbers, and so [I.2] can be regarded as a *system of linear equations*, of the form

$$\begin{bmatrix} f^1_1 & \cdots & f^1_n \\ \cdots & \cdots & \cdots \\ f^n_1 & \cdots & f^n_n \end{bmatrix} \begin{bmatrix} dx_1 \\ \vdots \\ dx_n \end{bmatrix} = \begin{bmatrix} -(f^1_{n+1} d\alpha_1 + \ldots + f^1_{n+m} d\alpha_m) \\ \ldots\ldots\ldots\ldots\ldots\ldots\ldots\ldots \\ -(f^n_{n+1} d\alpha_1 + \ldots + f^n_{n+m} d\alpha_m) \end{bmatrix} \quad \text{[I.3]}$$

Then, we wish to solve for the unknowns, the dx_i, in terms of the given changes. Suppose that only one parameter has changed, i.e. $d\alpha_j \neq 0$, $d\alpha_k = 0$, $k \neq j$. Then, from Cramer's Rule, the solution for any dx_i is given by

$$dx_i = \frac{D_{ij}}{D} d\alpha_j \quad\quad \text{or} \quad\quad \frac{\partial x_i}{\partial \alpha_j} = \frac{D_{ij}}{D} \quad\quad \text{[I.4]}$$

where D_{ij} is the determinant formed by replacing the ith column of the determinant D (defined above and assumed non-zero) by the column vector $[-f^1_{n+j}, \ldots, -f^n_{n+j}]$.

At the level of generality of most economic models, all we have are general restrictions on the signs of the partial derivatives of the f^i functions. The most that can be expected then is that we can deduce from [I.4] the sign of the comparative statics effect $\partial x_i / \partial \alpha_j$. Even this much is often not possible: we may have to develop a taxonomy of cases in which the comparative statics effect is positive or negative.

To illustrate, suppose we have a problem of the form

$$\max_{x_1, x_2} u(x_1, x_2) \quad \text{s.t.} \quad \alpha_1 x_1 + \alpha_2 x_2 = \alpha_3$$

Then the first-order conditions are

$$u_1(x_1^*, x_2^*) - \lambda^* \alpha_1 = 0$$
$$u_2(x_1^*, x_2^*) - \lambda^* \alpha_2 = 0 \qquad \qquad [\text{I.5}]$$
$$-\alpha_1 x_1^* - \alpha_2 x_2^* + \alpha_3 = 0$$

where asterisks denote equilibrium values. Here, the counterparts of the f^i functions in [I.1] are the partial derivatives of the Lagrange function, $\partial L / \partial x_i$, $i = 1, 2$, and $\partial L / \partial \lambda$, and the endogenous variables are x_1, x_2, and λ. Then, carrying out the total differentiation gives the linear system

$$\begin{bmatrix} u_{11} & u_{12} & -\alpha_1 \\ u_{21} & u_{22} & -\alpha_2 \\ -\alpha_1 & -\alpha_2 & 0 \end{bmatrix} \begin{bmatrix} dx_1 \\ dx_2 \\ d\lambda \end{bmatrix} = \begin{bmatrix} \lambda^* d\alpha_1 \\ \lambda^* d\alpha_2 \\ x_1^* d\alpha_1 + x_2^* d\alpha_2 - d\alpha_3 \end{bmatrix} \qquad [\text{I.6}]$$

Solving for x_1, considering first only $d\alpha_1 \neq 0$, then $d\alpha_3 \neq 0$, gives

$$\frac{\partial x_1}{\partial \alpha_1} = \frac{-\lambda^* \alpha_2^2 + x_1^* (\alpha_1 u_{22} - \alpha_2 u_{12})}{D}; \qquad \frac{\partial x_1}{\partial \alpha_3} = \frac{-(\alpha_1 u_{22} - \alpha_2 u_{12})}{D} \qquad [\text{I.7}]$$

where D is the determinant of the matrix on the left-hand side of [I.6] and must of course be assumed non-zero.

In order to put signs to the terms in [I.7] we need to know the signs of D, α_1, α_2, u_{12}, u_{22} and λ^*. The economics underlying the formulation of the problem may help us in this, but note that the expressions in [I.7] involve sums and differences of terms and so we may well not be able to obtain unique signs for the partial derivatives (see Question 1, Exercise I). For our present purposes, however, it is enough to note that the sign of D *must follow from the second-order conditions* of the problem, and so, having motivated the study of second-order conditions, we now turn to this.

Second-order conditions for unconstrained maximization

In the problem of the *unconstrained* maximization of a function of a single variable, $f(x)$, the role of a second-order condition is to determine whether a point x^* which yields a stationary value of the function, $f'(x^*) = 0$, does in fact maximize the function. If the second-order condition $f''(x^*) < 0$ holds, then the first- and second-order conditions taken together are *sufficient* for x^* to be a locally maximizing point. They are not *necessary*, since we may have a function for which a point $\hat{x}$ yields a maximum but $f''(\hat{x}) = 0$, and we would have to examine higher-order derivatives to establish its optimality (we meet an example below). Such cases are excluded when we do comparative statics, for reasons which will soon become clear, and so we focus on the sufficient second-order condition where the strict inequality holds.

As an example, suppose a firm has a revenue function $\bar{p}x$, where $\bar{p} = 500$ is a constant price and x is output, and a total cost function $C = 750x - 30x^2 + 0.5x^3$. This cubic cost function gives the 'usual' U-shaped average and marginal curves. The firm chooses x to maximize profit $\pi = \bar{p}x - C = (500 - 750)x + 30x^2 - 0.5x^3$, giving the first-order condition

$$-250 + 60x - 1.5x^2 = 0$$

and yielding solution values $x^0 = 4.72$, $x^1 = 35.27$. The second derivative of the profit function is $60 - 3x$, and so, clearly, only $x^1 = 35.27$ satisfies the second-order condition and gives a local maximum (for further discussion and illustration of this problem see Chapter 7, section 7A).

Comparative statics: single-choice variable

To illustrate the use of the second-order conditions in comparative static analysis, suppose a decision-taker wishes to maximize a function $f(x, \alpha)$, where the single-choice variable is the scalar x and α is a parameter. Let x^* be a solution to this problem, so that x^* satisfies the first-order condition $f_x(x^*, \alpha) = 0$. When α alters, the decision-taker will change x^* so that the first-order condition continues to hold. Applying the Implicit Function Theorem as in [B.8] and [B.9] of Appendix B gives

$$\frac{dx^*}{d\alpha} = -\frac{f_{x\alpha}}{f_{xx}} \qquad \qquad [\text{I.8}]$$

Note that to obtain this result we *must assume* $f_{xx} \neq 0$. If we make this assumption then at the optimum $f_{xx} < 0$ and so the sign of $dx^*/d\alpha$ in [I.8] is the same as the sign of $f_{x\alpha}$.

Although this appears to be very simple we will frequently find that it is possible to formulate interesting economic problems as single-variable decision problems, and we make repeated use of [I.8] in this book. Figure I.1 provides some intuition for

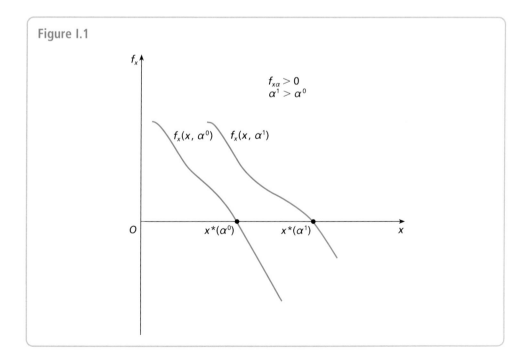

Figure I.1

the result. The decision-taker initially faces a decision problem in which $\alpha = \alpha^0$ and maximizes $f(x, \alpha^0)$ by setting $x = x^*(\alpha^0)$ where $f_x(x, \alpha^0)$, the marginal value of x, is zero. We assume that increases in the parameter α increase the marginal value of x and thus, when α increases from α^0 to α^1, the optimal x increases to $x^*(\alpha^1)$. We see that if the parameter change increases the marginal value of the decision variable the decision-taker will increase x, since $f_x(x^*(\alpha^0), \alpha^1)$, the marginal value of x at its initial optimal level, is now positive.

The cases we have to exclude to apply this procedure are not unduly strange. Take for example $f(x; \alpha) = -\alpha x^4$. This function is maximized at $x^* = 0$, but at this point its second derivative $-12\alpha x^2 = 0$, and so $-f_{x\alpha}/f_{xx}$ in [I.8] would be undefined. Thus in the general analysis we have to exclude this kind of case (but it is not at all difficult to give the effect of a change in α on x^* – what is it?).

Second-order conditions: *n* choice variables

We now extend the discussion to the case of the maximization of a function of an n-vector of variables, $f(x)$. Suppose the function has a maximum at x^*, so that $f_i(x^*) = 0$ $(i = 1, \ldots, n)$. Taking a Taylor series expansion of the function around this point gives, to the second order

$$f(x^* + h) = f(x^*) + h\nabla f + \tfrac{1}{2}hFh \qquad [\text{I.9}]$$

where ∇f is the vector of first-order partials and is therefore zero, h is an n-vector $(h_1, \ldots, h_n)$ of *small numbers*, and F is the *Hessian matrix* $[f_{ij}]$ $(i, j = 1, \ldots, n)$, i.e. the $n \times n$ symmetric matrix of second-order partials, evaluated at x^*. It is then sufficient for x^* to yield a local maximum that

$$hFh = (h_1, \ldots, h_n) \begin{bmatrix} f_{11} & \cdots & f_{1n} \\ \cdots & \cdots & \cdots \\ f_{n1} & \cdots & f_{nn} \end{bmatrix} \begin{bmatrix} h_1 \\ \vdots \\ h_n \end{bmatrix} = \sum_{i=1}^{n} \sum_{j=1}^{n} f_{ij} h_i h_j < 0 \qquad [\text{I.10}]$$

since then, from [I.9], $f(x^* + h) < f(x^*)$ for any small (non-zero) vector h. Again, the conditions $\nabla f = 0$, $hFh < 0$ are not necessary for an optimum because a maximum could occur at a point at which $hFh = 0$. However, for purposes of comparative statics we have to rule out cases in which this happens, and so we focus on the *sufficient* second-order condition $hFh < 0$.

The expression in [I.10] is a *quadratic form*, and condition [I.10] is the condition that this quadratic form be *negative definite*. From the theory of quadratic forms we have the following sufficient condition for this. A *principal minor of order $k = 1, \ldots, n$*, of a determinant is the sub-determinant formed by deleting the last $n - k$ rows and columns. Thus the principal minors of the $n \times n$ determinant $|F|$ are

$$|f_{11}|; \quad \begin{vmatrix} f_{11} & f_{12} \\ f_{21} & f_{22} \end{vmatrix}; \quad \ldots; \quad \begin{vmatrix} f_{11} & \cdots & f_{1k} \\ \cdots & \cdots & \cdots \\ f_{k1} & \cdots & f_{kk} \end{vmatrix}; \quad \ldots; \quad \begin{vmatrix} f_{11} & \cdots & f_{1n} \\ \cdots & \cdots & \cdots \\ f_{n1} & \cdots & f_{nn} \end{vmatrix} \qquad [\text{I.11}]$$

Then, *the quadratic form in [I.10] is negative definite if the kth principal minor of $|F|$ has the sign $(-1)^k$, $k = 1, \ldots, n$*.

This requires that the principal minors alternate in sign:

$$f_{11} < 0, \qquad f_{11}f_{22} - f_{21}f_{12} > 0; \ldots \qquad\qquad [I.12]$$

[I.12] then gives the second-order sufficient condition for a maximum in the *n*-variable case.

This suggests that, if we seek to maximize $f(x)$, we first solve the *n* equations $f_i(x^*) = 0$ for x^*, then evaluate the signs of the *n* principal minors in [I.12] by plugging x^* into the partial derivatives $f_{ij}(x)$, to check that we do in fact have a local maximum.

In economics, we often take a different approach. We appeal to some aspect of the economic nature of the problem (diminishing marginal productivity; diminishing returns to scale; diminishing marginal utility, and so on) to make a *global* sufficiency assumption (the conditions [I.12] are *local* since they were derived from an expansion in a neighbourhood of x^*). The assumption is that the objective function $f(x)$ is strictly concave over its domain. The stationary value of a strictly concave function must be a global maximum, and so the point x^* at which $f_i(x^*) = 0$ ($i = 1, \ldots, n$) must also be a local maximum. Diagrammatically, the graph of the function in three dimensions is like a hill or dome, the tangent plane to the peak of the hill is horizontal, and no other tangent plane to the hill has this property. Thus, if we make this global sufficiency assumption, which has the attraction that we then know that any optimum is a true global optimum, *local* second-order conditions are automatically satisfied.

Comparative statics analysis: *n* choice variables

The local conditions are useful primarily in comparative statics analysis which involves local changes in the parameter values. If a function $f(x)$ is concave it can be shown that at any point in its domain, including its maximum, we have

$$hFh = \sum_{i=1}^{n} \sum_{j=1}^{n} f_{ij}h_i h_j \leqslant 0 \qquad\qquad [I.13]$$

That is, the quadratic form involving the Hessian matrix F at any point of the domain of the function is *negative semidefinite*. Unfortunately, it is not true in general that, for a *strictly* concave function, [I.13] is satisfied as a strict inequality, i.e. that hFh is negative *definite*. However, apart from cases in which $hFh = 0$ at the optimal point x^* the global sufficiency assumption of strict concavity implies that the local sufficiency condition [I.12] is satisfied and F has the required properties. We now illustrate this with an example.

A decision-taker wants to maximize the function $f(x_1, x_2, \alpha)$, which is assumed strictly concave in x_1 and x_2. The first-order conditions are

$$f_1(x_1^*, x_2^*, \alpha) = 0$$
$$f_2(x_1^*, x_2^*, \alpha) = 0 \qquad\qquad [I.14]$$

Differentiating totally through these two conditions gives the system

$$\begin{bmatrix} f_{11} & f_{12} \\ f_{21} & f_{22} \end{bmatrix} \begin{bmatrix} dx_1^* \\ dx_2^* \end{bmatrix} = \begin{bmatrix} -f_{1\alpha}d\alpha \\ -f_{2\alpha}d\alpha \end{bmatrix} \qquad\qquad [I.15]$$

Applying the Implicit Function Theorem, say, for dx_1^* gives

$$\frac{dx_1^*}{d\alpha} = \frac{f_{12}f_{2\alpha} - f_{22}f_{1\alpha}}{|F|} \qquad [\text{I.16}]$$

where $|F|$ is the Hessian determinant and must be assumed non-zero at the optimal point. This assumption, together with the strict concavity of f, implies that hFh is negative definite at (x_1^*, x_2^*), and this allows us to sign the denominator in [I.16]. From the condition on principal minors we know that if hFh is negative definite

$$f_{11} < 0, \qquad f_{11}f_{22} - f_{21}f_{12} > 0$$

and so the denominator in [I.16] is positive. We can then proceed to discuss the sign of the numerator (which may not be uniquely defined).

For a case in which this procedure breaks down, take the case in which $f = -\alpha(x_1^4 + x_2^4)$ which is strictly concave and has a maximum at $x_1^* = x_2^* = 0$. The intuition is just as in the one-variable case.

We can briefly state the second-order conditions for the case in which we minimize a function $f(x)$, where x has $n \geq 2$ components. Proceeding from the derivation of [I.9] above, we have that sufficient conditions for x^* to yield a minimum of the function are that $\nabla f = 0$ and the quadratic form $hFh > 0$ at x^*. A sufficient condition for this quadratic form to be positive definite is that *all* the principal minors of $|F|$ be strictly positive. This is the local second-order sufficient condition for a minimum. A global sufficient condition is that f be strictly convex over its domain. Excluding the cases in which $hFh = 0$ at x^* (for example the case $f(x) = x_1^4 + x_2^4$) this will imply that $hFh > 0$ at the optimum and that fact can be used directly in the comparative statics analysis of the minimization problem.

Second-order conditions for constrained maximization

The formal statement of second-order conditions for the constrained maximization problem can be quite complex, but the essential ideas can be brought out simply if we first consider the two-variable one-constraint case. Thus suppose the problem is

$$\max_{x_1 x_2} f(x_1, x_2) \quad \text{s.t.} \quad g(x_1, x_2) = 0 \qquad [\text{I.17}]$$

and refer to Fig. I.2. In each case in the figure a local solution to the problem is shown as the point of tangency, x^*, between a contour of f and the constraint contour. Since x^* is a *constrained* local maximum, it must not be possible to reach a higher contour of f (we assume $f_i > 0$, $i = 1, 2$) by *moving along* the constraint contour – the only feasible variations in the x_i. This is the case in each part of the figure. In (a) f is strictly quasi-concave and g is either strictly quasi-convex ($\hat{g}$) or linear ($\bar{g}$). In (b) both functions are strictly quasi-concave, but around the optimum x^* the contour of f is 'more curved' than that of g. In (c) both functions are strictly quasi-convex but around x^* the f-contour is 'less curved' than that of g. In each case, small movements along the g-contour away from x^* must reduce the value of the objective function. This, geometrically, is the essence of the second-order condition. If x_1 increases (decreases) from x_1^*, then the slope of the g-contour must become greater (smaller) in absolute value, or smaller (greater) algebraically, than the slope of the f-contour. Since the slopes are equal at x^*, we can write this as the condition

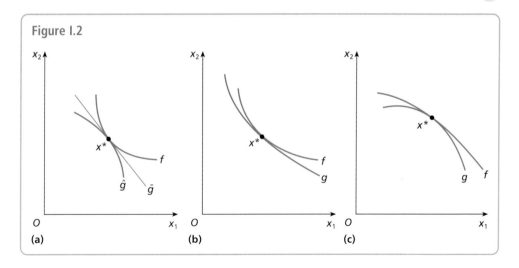

Figure I.2

$$\frac{d}{dx_1}\left[\frac{dx_2}{dx_1}\bigg|_f - \frac{dx_2}{dx_1}\bigg|_g\right] > 0 \qquad \text{at } x = x^* \qquad [\text{I}.18]$$

where $dx_2/dx_1|_f$ denotes the slope of the f-contour, and $dx_2/dx_1|_g$ that of the g-contour. Increasing x_1 from x_1^* increases $dx_2/dx_1|_f$ relative to $dx_2/dx_1|_g$ since the former becomes 'less negative' than the latter.

We can derive [I.18] more formally as follows. Assume $g_2 \neq 0$. Then we can solve $g(x_1, x_2) = 0$ for x_2 as a function of x_1, $x_2 = h(x_1)$, where $h' = dx_2/dx_1 = -g_1/g_2$. Substituting into f gives $f(x_1, h(x_1)) \equiv \phi(x_1)$. The value x_1^* which maximizes ϕ satisfies $\phi'(x_1^*) = 0$, $\phi''(x_1^*) < 0$ (again excluding cases where $\phi''(x_1^*) = 0$). But this second-order derivative is

$$\phi''(x_1^*) = \frac{d}{dx_1}[f_1 + f_2h'(x_1^*)] = f_{11} + f_{12}h' + h'(f_{21} + f_{22}h') + f_2h'' < 0 \qquad [\text{I}.19]$$

At the optimal point, $-g_1/g_2 = -f_1/f_2 = h'$, and substituting this into [I.19] and rearranging gives

$$\frac{1}{f_2^3}\{f_{11}f_2^2 - 2f_{12}f_1f_2 + f_1^2f_{22}\} + \frac{d^2x_2}{dx_1^2}\bigg|_g < 0 \qquad [\text{I}.20]$$

where we have also used $h'' = d^2x_2/dx_1^2$. But the first term in [I.20] is $-d^2x_2/dx_1^2|_f$ (recall Question 7, Appendix B). Thus we have established [I.18].

Note that, as Fig. I.2 shows, [I.18] may hold even though f is not quasi-concave or g is not quasi-convex. Therefore the *local* sufficiency condition [I.18] is less restrictive than the *global* condition that f be strictly quasi-concave and g be quasi-convex over their entire domains. However, we do usually assume this global condition, in order to ensure local maxima are also global maxima (in cases (b) and (c) this may well not be the case) and so we at the same time ensure satisfaction of the local second-order condition [I.18].

Though perfectly adequate for the two-variable case, condition [I.18] does not generalize readily to $n > 2$ variables, and it is usual to express the second-order conditions in terms of the signs of the principal minors of a particular determinant analogously to the unconstrained case. This is also the more useful form for comparative statics analysis. A full treatment of these determinantal conditions cannot be given here. We shall simply state the conditions for the general case, and then show that in the two-variable one-constraint case the condition is equivalent to [I.18].

Thus suppose we have the problem of maximizing a function of an n-vector of variables $f(x)$, subject to $m < n$ equality constraints $g^k(x) = 0$ $(k = 1, \ldots, m)$. We form the Lagrange function as before: $L = f(x) - \sum_{k=1}^{n} \lambda_k g^k(x)$. The first-order conditions are then

$$L_i = f_i(x^*) - \sum_{k=1}^{m} \lambda_k^* g_i^k(x^*) = 0 \qquad i = 1, \ldots, n$$

$$L_k = -g^k(x^*) = 0 \qquad\qquad k = 1, \ldots, m \qquad\qquad \text{[I.21]}$$

at the optimal point x^*. $L_{ij} = f_{ij} - \sum_k \lambda_k^* g_{ij}^k$ denotes the second-order partial of L. We now define the $(m + n) \times (m + n)$ *bordered Hessian matrix*

$$H = \begin{bmatrix} L_{11} \ldots L_{1n} & -g_1^1 \ldots -g_1^m \\ \cdots\cdots\cdots & \cdots\cdots\cdots \\ L_{n1} \ldots L_{nn} & -g_n^1 \ldots -g_n^m \\ -g_1^1 \ldots -g_n^1 & 0 \ldots 0 \\ \cdots\cdots\cdots & \cdots\cdots\cdots \\ -g_1^m \ldots -g_n^m & 0 \ldots 0 \end{bmatrix} = \begin{bmatrix} L & \vdots & G \\ \cdots & \vdots & \cdots \\ G' & \vdots & O \end{bmatrix} \qquad \text{[I.22]}$$

H can be thought of as consisting of four sub-matrices: the $n \times n$ symmetric matrix of second-order partials of the Lagrange function; the $n \times m$ matrix G of partials $L_{ki} = -g_i^k$; its transpose, G'; and an $m \times m$ matrix of zeroes. The kth column of G, and corresponding row of G', consists of the (negatives of the) n first derivatives of the constraint function g^k $(k = 1, \ldots, m)$, which are also the second-order cross partials L_{ki}. We think of G, G' and O as forming a 'border' of the Hessian of the Lagrange function, L, hence the term bordered Hessian.

We now define a bordered principal minor of the Hessian determinant $|H|$ as a principal minor which has at least $m + 1$ of the first rows and columns from L, and a border consisting of the appropriate rows and columns of partials $-g_i^k$, and of zeroes. Thus, let

$$|H_{m+1}| \equiv \begin{vmatrix} L_{11} \ldots L_{1,m+1} & -g_1^1 \ldots -g_1^m \\ \cdots\cdots\cdots & \cdots\cdots\cdots \\ L_{m+1,1} \ldots L_{m+1,m+1} & -g_{m+1}^1 \ldots -g_{m+1}^m \\ -g_1^1 \ldots -g_{m+1}^1 & 0 \ldots 0 \\ \cdots\cdots\cdots & \cdots\cdots\cdots \\ -g_1^m \ldots -g_{m+1}^m & 0 \ldots 0 \end{vmatrix}$$

$$\text{[I.23]}$$

$|H_{m+2}|$ is then constructed by adding the $m + 2$th row and column of L and adjusting the border appropriately, and so on. Thus we can define the sequence of bordered principal minors

$$|H_{m+1}|, |H_{m+2}|, \ldots, |H_{m+j}|, \ldots, |H_{m+(n-m)}| \equiv |H|$$

The sufficient second-order conditions can then be given as follows: x^* yields a maximum in the problem with n variables and $m(< n)$ constraints, if the bordered principal minor $|H_{m+j}|$ has the sign $(-1)^{m+j}$ for $j = 1, \ldots, n - m$.

The reason we ignore principal minors with less than m rows and columns from L is that they are necessarily zero. The principal minor with exactly m rows and columns from L always has a sign which is independent of the terms L_{ij}.

Comparative statics analysis: constrained maximization

As an illustration of the use of these conditions and their application in comparative statics, consider the problem with $n = 3$ and $m = 2$.

$$\max f(x_1, x_2, x_3) \quad \text{s.t.} \quad g^1(x_1, x_2, x_3, \alpha) = 0 \qquad g^2(x_1, x_2, x_3) = 0$$

where α is a parameter in the first constraint. The first-order conditions are

$$
\begin{aligned}
L_i &= f_i - \lambda_1^* g_i^1 - \lambda_2^* g_i^2 = 0 & i = 1, 2, 3 \\
L_k &= -g^k = 0 & k = 1, 2
\end{aligned}
\tag{I.24}
$$

The (sufficient) second-order condition is then

$$
\begin{vmatrix}
L_{11} & L_{12} & L_{13} & -g_1^1 & -g_1^2 \\
L_{21} & L_{22} & L_{23} & -g_2^1 & -g_2^2 \\
L_{31} & L_{32} & L_{33} & -g_3^1 & -g_3^2 \\
-g_1^1 & -g_2^1 & -g_3^1 & 0 & 0 \\
-g_1^2 & -g_2^2 & -g_3^2 & 0 & 0
\end{vmatrix} < 0
\tag{I.25}
$$

since $(-1)^{m+1} < 0$ for $m = 2$. Note that, as we asserted earlier, the principal minor with 1 row and column from L is zero and the principal minor with $2 = m$ rows and columns from L does not depend on the L_{ij} terms:

$$
\begin{vmatrix}
L_{11} & -g_1^1 & -g_1^2 \\
-g_1^1 & 0 & 0 \\
-g_1^2 & 0 & 0
\end{vmatrix} = 0 \quad \text{and} \quad
\begin{vmatrix}
L_{11} & L_{12} & -g_1^1 & -g_1^2 \\
L_{21} & L_{22} & -g_2^1 & -g_2^2 \\
-g_1^1 & -g_2^1 & 0 & 0 \\
-g_1^2 & -g_2^2 & 0 & 0
\end{vmatrix} = (g_1^1 g_2^2 - g_1^2 g_2^1)^2 > 0
\tag{I.26}
$$

In this three-variable case $|H_{m+1}| = |H|$. To carry out the comparative statics, differentiate through the first-order conditions to obtain the linear system

$$
\begin{bmatrix}
L_{11} & L_{12} & L_{13} & -g_1^1 & -g_1^2 \\
L_{21} & L_{22} & L_{23} & -g_2^1 & -g_2^2 \\
L_{31} & L_{32} & L_{33} & -g_3^1 & -g_3^2 \\
-g_1^1 & -g_2^1 & -g_3^1 & 0 & 0 \\
-g_1^2 & -g_2^2 & -g_3^2 & 0 & 0
\end{bmatrix}
\begin{bmatrix}
dx_1 \\ dx_2 \\ dx_3 \\ d\lambda_1 \\ d\lambda_2
\end{bmatrix}
=
\begin{bmatrix}
\lambda_1^* g_{1\alpha}^1 d\alpha \\
\lambda_1^* g_{2\alpha}^1 d\alpha \\
\lambda_1^* g_{3\alpha}^1 d\alpha \\
g_\alpha^1 d\alpha \\
0
\end{bmatrix}
\tag{I.27}
$$

which can be solved for $dx_i/d\alpha$ if the left-hand matrix has non-zero determinant. But note that this determinant is precisely the bordered Hessian $|H|$, and the second-order conditions tell us that $|H| < 0$. Thus, using Cramer's Rule gives

$$\frac{dx_i}{d\alpha} = \frac{|H_i|}{|H|} \qquad [\text{I}.28]$$

where $|H_i|$ is the determinant formed by replacing the ith column of $|H|$ by the column of coefficients of $d\alpha$ in the vector on the right-hand side of [I.27]. Then, in [I.28] the sign of $dx_i/d\alpha$ is the opposite of that of $|H_i|$ (which may well *not* be unambiguously determined, however).

We can see from this example that the relevance of the second-order conditions for comparative statics analysis arises from the fact that the bordered Hessian H is always the matrix of second-order partials in the linear system we need to solve to obtain the comparative statics results.

To see the relationship between the second-order condition in determinant form and the curvature conditions illustrated in Fig. I.2 and derived in [I.18], let us take the case in which $n = 2$, $m = 1$, as in [I.17]. The condition [I.25] then becomes

$$\begin{vmatrix} L_{11} & L_{12} & -g_1 \\ L_{21} & L_{22} & -g_2 \\ -g_1 & -g_2 & 0 \end{vmatrix} > 0 \qquad [\text{I}.29]$$

since $(-1)^{m+1} > 0$ for $m = 1$. Expanding the determinant gives

$$-(g_2^2 L_{11} - 2g_1 g_2 L_{12} + g_1^2 L_{22}) > 0 \qquad [\text{I}.30]$$

where we have used $L_{12} = L_{21}$. Since $L_{ij} = f_{ij} - \lambda g_{ij}$ $(i, j = 1, 2)$, by substituting these into [I.30] and rearranging we have

$$\frac{1}{\lambda}\{f_{11} g_2^2 - 2g_1 g_2 f_{12} + f_{22} g_1^2\} - \{g_{11} g_2^2 - 2g_1 g_2 g_{12} + g_{22} g_1^2\} < 0 \qquad [\text{I}.31]$$

Then, using $g_i = f_i/\lambda$ $(i = 1, 2)$ and $\lambda^3 = (g_2/f_2)^3$ gives

$$\frac{1}{f_2^3}\{f_{11} f_2^2 - 2f_1 f_2 f_{12} + f_{22} f_1^2\} - \frac{1}{g_2^3}\{g_{11} g_2^2 - 2g_1 g_2 g_{12} + g_{22} g_1^2\} < 0 \qquad [\text{I}.32]$$

implying

$$\left.\frac{d^2 x_2}{dx_1^2}\right|_g < \left.\frac{d^2 x_2}{dx_1^2}\right|_f \qquad [\text{I}.33]$$

as in [I.18]. Thus, the determinantal condition is equivalent to the condition on the relative curvature of the f- and g-contours.

The concave programming case

In the problem with non-negativity conditions and weak inequalities in the constraints, we cannot simply differentiate through the Kuhn–Tucker conditions to carry out comparative statics, because of the presence of inequalities in those conditions. Also, *global* sufficiency conditions are used. If the objective and constraint functions are all concave (the constraints are expressed as $g^j(x) \geq 0$) then the Kuhn–Tucker conditions are both necessary and sufficient for x^* to be a global maximum. If it is desired to carry out the conventional kind of comparative statics analysis, we exclude from the Kuhn–Tucker conditions those variables which are zero at the optimum, and those constraints that are non-binding there, so that in effect we end up with the conditions corresponding to a classical maximization problem. We can then apply the standard comparative statics procedure to these conditions. This involves the assumptions that, for small changes, zero variables and non-binding constraints do not change their status.

Minimization problems

The problem of minimizing a function $f(x)$ where x is an n-vector, subject to $m < n$ constraints $g^k(x) = 0$ $(k = 1, \ldots, m)$, has the same first-order conditions as the maximization problem. We could analyse the problem of second-order conditions for the case $n = 2$, $m = 1$, as we did for maximization in Fig. I.1, and derive an analogous condition to [I.18]. This is left as an exercise. Here we simply state the sufficient local second-order conditions in determinant form, and note that they play exactly the same role in the comparative statics analysis of minimization problems as was the case for maximization. These conditions are again framed in terms of the bordered Hessian matrix H in [I.22] and its principal minors $|H_{m+1}|, \ldots,$ $|H_{m+(n-m)}| \equiv |H|$. We can then state the condition: if $\hat{x}$ satisfies the first-order conditions and the bordered principal minors $|H_{m+j}| > 0$ $(j = 1, \ldots, n - m)$, then $\hat{x}$ yields a minimum of $f(x)$ subject to the constraints $g^k(x) = 0$ $(k = 1, \ldots, m)$.

Again, it can be shown that these local conditions are concerned with the relative curvatures of the contours of the f and g^k functions in the neighbourhood of the optimal point. A *global* sufficient condition is that $f(x)$ be strictly quasi-convex and the $g^k(x)$ quasi-concave on their domains (or quasi-convex and strictly quasi-concave respectively).

EXERCISE I

1. In the example analysed in conditions [I.5]–[I.7], show that

$$\partial x_1/\partial \alpha_1 = (-\lambda^* \alpha_2^2/D) - x_1^*(\partial x_1/\partial \alpha_3)$$

What is the sign of D? If we cannot put signs to u_{22} and u_{12}, explain why we cannot sign the derivatives in [I.7]. If u is interpreted as a utility function, α_1, α_2 as prices, and α_3 as income, relate the analysis here to the Slutsky equation in section 3B.

2. Develop second-order conditions for a minimum of a two-variable one-constraint problem along lines analogous to Fig. I.2 and equation [I.18] of the text.

The envelope theorem

What we have called the 'standard' method of comparative statics is useful because it is routine, even programmable: one just follows the steps. However, in a problem of any size it can be a very tedious method. Moreover, one may end up with a complicated expression in determinants which is not unambiguously signed. Considerable art and ingenuity may then be necessary to find and interpret economically interesting conditions under which a particular sign can be attached to a comparative statics effect. *Duality theory* applies the art and ingenuity at the outset to provide a more elegant and insightful mode of comparative statics analysis. Whenever possible, we adopt this approach in this book (see, for example, Chapters 3 and 8). A cornerstone of the approach is *the Envelope Theorem*: in fact, much of what we do will consist of repeated applications of the theorem in various contexts.

Suppose we have a classical maximization problem of the form

$$\max_x f(x, \alpha) \quad \text{s.t.} \quad g^j(x, \alpha) = 0 \qquad j = 1, \ldots, m$$

where x is an $n(> m)$-component vector and α is an l-vector of parameters. Let $v^* = f(x^*, \alpha)$ denote the value of the objective function at the optimal point. The Lagrange function is $L = f(x, \alpha) - \sum_{j=1}^{m} \lambda_j g^j(x, \alpha)$. Then the Envelope Theorem states:

$$\frac{\partial v^*}{\partial \alpha_k} = \frac{\partial L}{\partial \alpha_k} = f_{\alpha_k}(x^*, \alpha) - \sum_{j=1}^{m} \lambda_j^* g_{\alpha_k}^j(x^*, \alpha) \qquad k = 1, \ldots, l \qquad [\text{J.1}]$$

That is, *the effect of varying α_k on the optimised objective function is given by the partial derivative of the Lagrange function with respect to α_k, evaluated at the optimal solution point (x^*, λ^*).*

We have already seen one important application of this theorem, when we established the interpretation of the Lagrange multipliers in Appendix G. We now present the proof.

Differentiating v^* totally we have

$$dv^* = \sum_{i=1}^{n} f_i dx_i^* + f_{\alpha_k} d\alpha_k$$

Differentiating each constraint totally gives

$$dg^j = \sum_{i=1}^{n} g_i^j dx_i^* + g_{\alpha_k}^j d\alpha_k = 0 \qquad j = 1, \ldots, m$$

since $g^j = 0$ must continue to hold for any $d\alpha_k$. Multiplying through by λ_j^*, summing over j and noting that the result still equals zero allows us to write

$$dv^* = \sum_{i=1}^{n} f_i dx_i^* + f_{\alpha_k} d\alpha_k - \sum_{j} \lambda_j^* \left[\sum_{i=1}^{n} g_i^j dx_i^* + g_{\alpha_k}^j d\alpha_k \right]$$

$$= \sum_{i=1}^{n} \left[f_i - \sum_{j} \lambda_j^* g_i^j \right] dx_i^* + \left[f_{\alpha_k} - \sum_{j} \lambda_j^* g_{\alpha_k}^j \right] d\alpha_k$$

$$= \left[f_{\alpha_k} - \sum_{j} \lambda_j^* g_{\alpha_k}^j \right] d\alpha_k$$

which gives the result. The last step follows because, at the optimal point, $f_i - \sum_j \lambda_j^* g_i^j = 0$ $(i = 1, \ldots, n)$ from the first-order conditions.

As we just noted, the special case in which α_k enters only one constraint, as a constraint constant, so that $g_{\alpha_k}^k = -1$, and $f_{\alpha_k} = g_{\alpha_k}^j = 0$, $k \neq j$, establishes that $dv^*/d\alpha_k = \lambda_k^*$. If α_k enters only the objective function, then $dv^*/d\alpha_k = f_{\alpha_k}(x^*, \alpha)$. This is also the form of the envelope theorem for the *unconstrained* maximization problem, max $f(x, \alpha)$ (confirm). In this case the intuition behind the envelope theorem is straightforward. Changes in the parameter α_k alter the value of the objective function directly if f depends on α_k and indirectly because a change in α_k leads to changes in the optimal values of the choice variables x^*. However, the marginal value of changes in the choice variables is zero at the optimum and thus the indirect effects of α_k on v^* via x^* are also zero. Hence only the direct effect of α_k on the objective function matters.

Fixed points and Brouwer's Theorem

Consider a mapping of a set into itself, which we could write as $f: X \to X$. For example, if X is the set of non-negative real numbers, the mapping

$$y = a + bx \qquad x \in X \qquad a, b \geqslant 0 \qquad \text{[K.1]}$$

gives a non-negative real number y for every x, and so maps the set of non-negative real numbers into itself.

If there exists, for a given mapping of a set X into itself, a point x^* which is its own image, i.e. such that $x^* = f(x^*)$, such a point is called a *fixed point*, because it remains unchanged under the mapping. Consider, for example, the mapping in [K.1]. If $a = 0$, then there is either one fixed point, at $x = 0$, or an infinite number, at every value of x, according to whether b is or is not equal to 1. If $a > 0$, and $b < 1$ there will be a fixed point at $x = a/(1 - b)$. (Suggest values of a and b for which there is no fixed point.)

The existence of a fixed point depends both on the mapping and on the set X. *Brouwer's Fixed Point Theorem asserts that a continuous mapping of a closed, bounded, convex set into itself always has a fixed point.* A proof of this theorem is well outside the scope of this book. However, we illustrate for a simple case the roles of the various conditions of the theorem.

Let the set X be the closed interval of real numbers $0 \leqslant x \leqslant 1$, the *unit interval*. A mapping of this set into itself associates with *each* x in this interval one and only one value $f(x)$ which also lies in the interval. It is clear that X is closed, bounded and convex. Whatever the mapping $f: X \to X$, the theorem assures us that if it is continuous then at least one point, x^*, exists such that $x^* = f(x^*)$.

To illustrate, consider Fig. K.1. In (a) of the figure, the set X is shown as the unit interval on both axes. For emphasis, the unit square is drawn in. Consider the diagonal, which is a 45° line. Along this line, $x = f(x)$ and so to say that the mapping has a fixed point is to say that it contains at least one point on this line. Let the curve marked $f(x)$ in (a) be the graph of the mapping. Then, a point such as x^*, where the graph intersects the diagonal, is a fixed point. Now let us consider the roles played by the various conditions of the theorem:

1. *Convexity of X.* Suppose that X were not convex. In the present case, this can only imply that it consists of two or more disjoint intervals on the real line. Suppose these were: $0 \leqslant x \leqslant x_0$, and $x_1 \leqslant x \leqslant 1$, as shown in (a) of the figure. X is then the union of these two subsets. The mapping in the diagram still maps X into itself, since each x in the two intervals has an image in one of the two intervals. However, there is no fixed point.

2. *Boundedness of X.* Consider (b) of the figure, and suppose that X consisted of all $x \geqslant 0$, so that it is unbounded above. Then the 45° line extending to infinity will still contain any fixed point which exists. Suppose the mapping were shown by

Figure K.1

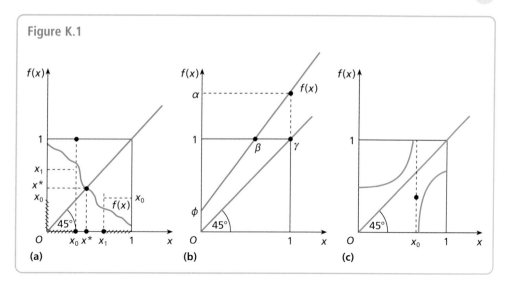

(a)   (b)   (c)

the straight line $\phi\beta$ in the diagram, continued to $+\infty$. Then clearly no fixed point will exist, since there is no intersection with the 45° line.

An objection might be made at this point. Suppose that X is the unit interval, as in (b). Then the mapping shown by $\phi\beta$ is continuous, the set is closed, bounded and convex, but there is still no fixed point. Hence, we seem to have a counter-example which disproves the theorem. This is, however, quickly resolved: in this case, the line $\phi\beta$ is not the graph of a mapping of a set into *itself*. The image set of the mapping is in fact $\phi\alpha$, as shown in (b). $\phi\alpha$ is not a subset of the unit interval. For the set to map into itself, we would have to have the mapping defined, say, by the kinked line $\phi\beta\gamma$, in which case a fixed point exists at γ.

3. *Closedness of X.* Suppose that the set X is defined as the half-open interval $0 \leqslant x < 1$, and consider the mapping given by $\phi\beta\gamma$ in (b). The only point at which this meets the 45° line is at γ, where $x = 1$. But this point is not in the set X, and so there is no fixed point.

4. *Continuity of f.* Consider (c) in Fig. K.1. There is a discontinuity in the mapping at $x = x_0$, and in this case no fixed point exists.

These various cases are meant to illustrate the possibility that, when one of the conditions of the theorem is violated, a fixed point *may* not exist. It is possible that a fixed point will exist, when a condition is not satisfied. Thus the reader should, in each case (1)–(4), draw a diagram on the lines of Fig. K.1 in which a fixed point does exist. In other words, the theorem gives *sufficient* conditions for existence of a fixed point: if they are satisfied, we can be certain that a fixed point exists, and we cannot construct a counter-example where one does not.

L Bayes' Theorem

Consider a random variable x which takes on the values $x_1, x_2, \ldots, x_n$. For example, x may be (a) the amount of rainfall in an area in a given year; (b) the value a buyer attaches to an asset; (c) a dichotomous variable taking on the value 0 when the individual is a good driver and 1 when he is a bad driver. Before any other information is received the *prior* probability that x has the value x_i is $P(x_i)$.

Suppose that a signal s about the value of the random variable x is received. The signal s received varies with the random variable of interest but also with other random and unobservable factors. The signal can take on the values $s_1, s_2, \ldots, s_m$. In the previous examples s may be (a) the hours of sunshine in the area in the year; (b) the event that a buyer accepts or refuses an offer of a given size. In the case (c), where the random variable is driving skill, the signal could be the number of accidents in a given period. We denote the conditional probability of receiving signal s_j when x has value x_i by $P(s_j|x_i)$. From the laws of probability

$$P(s_j|x_i) = \frac{P(s_j \text{ and } x_i)}{P(x_i)} \qquad \text{[L.1]}$$

The conditional probability that the random variable has the value x_i given that the signal s_j is received is

$$P(x_i|s_j) = \frac{P(x_i \text{ and } s_j)}{P(s_j)} \qquad \text{[L.2]}$$

But from [L.1] we can substitute $P(s_j|x_i)P(x_i)$ for $P(x_i \text{ and } s_j) = P(s_j \text{ and } x_i)$ to get

$$P(x_i|s_j) = \frac{P(s_j|x_i)P(x_i)}{P(s_j)} \qquad \text{[L.3]}$$

which is *Bayes' Theorem*.

Bayes' Theorem shows how new information (the value of the signal) can be used to produce a *posterior* probability distribution from the *prior* probabilities $P(x_i)$ and the *relative likelihood ratio* $P(s_j|x_i)/P(s_j)$. For example, suppose that: x_i is a high level of rainfall; s_j is a large number of hours of sunshine; high sunshine is less likely when there is high rainfall $[P(s_j|x_i) < P(s_j)]$. Then the signal s_j would lead us to place a lower probability on the occurrence of high rainfall. The posterior probability of high rainfall, given high sunshine, would be smaller than the prior probability: $P(x_i|s_j) < P(x_i)$.

The posterior probability is often written in a more complicated form by using the fact that $P(s_j) = \Sigma_k P(s_j \text{ and } x_k) = \Sigma_k P(s_j|x_k)P(x_k)$ to get

$$P(x_i|s_j) = \frac{P(s_j|x_i)P(x_i)}{\Sigma_k P(s_j|x_k)P(x_k)} \qquad \text{[L.4]}$$

References and further reading

Chapter 1 The nature and scope of microeconomics

There are critical discussions of rationality as a basis for the analysis of decisions in Cook and Levi (1990), Elster (1989), Hargreaves Heap *et al.* (1992), Simon (1972) and Thaler (1994). The extension of the equilibrium concept to dynamic economies under uncertainty is discussed in Hahn (1984). Alternative 'Austrian' views of rational behaviour and equilibrium are presented in Lachman (1986) and Loasby (1976). For a general survey of the methodology of economics see Blaug (1980).

Chapter 2 The theory of the consumer

A general introduction to the theory of consumer behaviour and its applications at about the level of this chapter is given by Green (1976). Consumer preferences are considered in some detail in Newman (1965), ch. 2, and at a more advanced level in Debreu (1959), ch. 4. An excellent account of the history of utility theory is given by Stigler (1950).

Chapter 3 Consumer theory: duality

Deaton and Muellbauer (1980) give an excellent treatment of the entire field of consumer theory, including empirical estimation of demand systems. For a more succinct survey, see Blundell (1988). On the theory of duality in general, see Diewert (1974). A thorough analysis of functional forms is given in Blackorby *et al.* (1978). For accounts of the integrability problem, see Samuelson (1950a) and Hurwicz and Uzawa (1971). The various measures of consumer surplus are analysed in Hicks (1940/1), Samuelson (1947), Chipman and Moore (1980), and McKenzie (1983).

Chapter 4 Further models of consumer behaviour

Revealed preference theory was developed in Samuelson (1938). Its usefulness for making aggregate welfare judgements was considered in Samuelson (1950b). Price indices are related to consumer theory in Deaton and Muellbauer (1980), ch. 7, which also has a good discussion of the model of labour supply (ch. 11). The seminal work on the economics of time is Becker (1965), and the time and household production models are integrated in Michael and Becker (1973). Both the preceding references are reprinted, along with other papers applying the microeconomic modelling approach to a wide variety of behaviour, in Becker (1976). More on the economics of two-person households with domestic production can be found in Apps and Rees (1988, 1997).

Chapter 5 Production

A good introduction to production theory is Chambers (1988) and there is very rigorous account in Shephard (1970).

Chapter 6 Cost

The relationship between cost and production functions is surveyed in Chambers (1988) and Shephard (1970). Cornes (1992) is a clear account of the application of duality theory to both producer and consumer theory. There are many illustrations of the use of the theory of multi-product cost function in the analysis of industrial structure and the regulation of firms in Baumol *et al.* (1982), Sharkey (1982) and Spulber (1989). The student should also be aware of the alternative concepts of cost set out in Alchian (1959) and Buchanan (1969).

Chapter 7 Supply and firm objectives

There is a comprehensive analysis of profit functions and their relationship with cost functions in Chambers (1988), ch. 4, and at a more advanced level in McFadden (1978). The classic paper on cost and supply curves is Viner (1953). Alternative concepts of income and profit are examined in Parker and Harcourt (1969). The basic reference on the theory of the entrepreneurial firm is Scitovsky (1943), whereas labour-managed firms are considered in Meade (1986), Vanek (1970) and Ward (1958).

Chapter 8 The theory of a competitive market

For a discussion of the relationship between the Walrasian tâtonnement adjustment process and the Marshallian adjustment hypothesis, see Davis (1963). The classic work on stability analysis and its relationship with comparative statics is Samuelson (1947) and there is a more recent analysis in Bhagwati *et al.* (1987). Rational expectations were introduced in Muth (1961). For a sceptical view, see Frydman (1982). A seminal article on disequilibrium price and quantity adjustment is Arrow (1959).

Chapter 9 Monopoly

Tirole (1988) has a comprehensive treatment of all the topics discussed in this chapter. Price discrimination is surveyed in Phlips (1983) and Varian (1989) and covered exhaustively in Wilson (1993). For the theory of rent seeking see Tullock (1967) and Tollison (1997) and Liebenstein (1966) for X-efficiency.

Chapter 10 Input markets

There is an extensive discussion of the demand for inputs by the competitive firm in Ferguson (1969) and Hicks (1964). Diewert (1971) uses the cost function to examine competitive market input demand. On the behaviour and objectives of unions, see Farber (1986) and Booth (1995).

Chapter 11 Capital markets

Bliss (1975) and Hirshleifer (1970) consider intertemporal resource allocation in some depth. See the references at the end of Chapter 21 for the extension of the models to the case of uncertainty. Strotz (1954) introduced the problem of time inconsistency in intertemporal decision-taking which can arise when there are more than two time periods, unless the preferences have a particular form. As an example, see Laibson (1997) for an analysis of hyperbolic discounting.

Chapter 12 General equilibrium

Leading references on general equilibrium theory are Arrow and Hahn (1971), Debreu (1959) and Hildenbrand and Kirman (1976), all of which require a good background in mathematics. An advanced, modern mathematical treatment is given in Mas-Colell (1985). For the mathematics required for these books, see Takayama (1985).

Chapter 13 Welfare economics

Boadway and Bruce (1984) is a good survey of the issues addressed in this chapter. The original account of Bergson social welfare functions is Bergson (1938), and they are further examined in Samuelson (1947) and Deaton and Muellbauer (1980), ch. 9. Indispensable works on social choice theory are Arrow (1963a) and Sen (1970, 1986).

Chapter 14 Market failure and government failure

Salanie (2000) has an extended analysis of market failure. For good discussions of property rights see Barzel (1989) and Eggertsson (1990). The approach to market failure in this chapter is based on Coase (1960), Demsetz (1964) and Arrow (1970). Cheung (1973) is very nice application to externalities. For the efficiency conditions for public goods, see Samuelson (1954). The positive modelling of public sector decisions is surveyed in Mueller (1989, 1997).

Chapter 15 Game theory

For a fuller treatment of game theory with a wealth of economic applications, at about the level of this book, see Gibbons (1992). Luce and Raiffa (1966) is a classic game theory text. For developments since then see Moulin (1986), Myerson (1991), Osborne and Rubinstein (1994). Friedman (1986) and Fudenberg and Tirole (1991) have plenty of economic applications as well as coverage of the theory. The discussion of the repeated Prisoner's Dilemma is based on Kreps *et al.* (1982), and that on herding was drawn from Gale (1996). On bargaining, see Nash (1950), Rubinstein (1982) and Fudenberg and Tirole (1983). The Nash paper is simple enough to serve as an introduction to the Nash bargaining solution, but the others are best approached after reading Binmore and Dasgupta (1987) and Osborne and Rubinstein (1990).

Chapter 16 Oligopoly

On oligopoly in general, very comprehensive treatments are given by Tirole (1988), Martin (2003), Friedman (1977) and Vives (1999), and all the chapters in Volume 1, Part 2, of Schmalensee and Willig (1989). The discussion of mixed strategy equilibrium in the Edgeworth model is based on Levitan and Shubik (1972). See also Kreps and Scheinkman (1983) and Davidson and Deneckere (1986). The discussion of trigger strategies was based on Abreu (1986), Farrell and Maskin (1989) and Fudenberg and Maskin (1986). On entry see Gilbert (1989). The original Chain Store Paradox is set out in Selten (1978). The capacity pre-commitment model is dealt with in more general terms than the example given here, by Dixit (1980).

Chapter 17 Choice under uncertainty

Hirshleifer and Riley (1992) have good coverage of wide range of topics in uncertainty. The original account of the Pratt–Arrow measures of risk aversion in Pratt (1964) is still a good introduction. Kimball (1990) introduced the concept of prudence. Mean-preserving spread measures of risk are examined in Rothschild and Stiglitz (1970, 1971) and in Diamond and Stiglitz (1974). A comprehensive account of stochastic dominance is in Hader and Russell (1969) and the usefulness of the concept is further demonstrated in Ormiston (1992). The mean-variance approach, without the need for quadratic preferences or normal distributions, is set out and applied in Sinn (1989) and Meyer (1987).

For criticism of the expected utility approach and some alternative approaches, see Kahneman *et al.* (1982) and Machina (1987). Chambers and Quiggin (2000) develop the state-contingent approach to modelling uncertainty and use it to give a different approach to some of the topics we consider in later chapters.

Chapter 18 Production under uncertainty

On the theory of the producer under uncertainty, see Newbery and Stiglitz (1981), and Applebaum and Katz (1986).

Chapter 19 Insurance, risk spreading and risk pooling

The basic model of insurance is extended to allow for state-dependent preferences by Cook and Graham (1977) and for a continuous loss distribution by Raviv (1979). Incomplete insurance markets are considered in Doherty and Schlesinger (1983). Risk spreading and its policy implications are examined by Arrow and Lind (1970). Akerlof (1970) is the pathbreaking analysis of adverse selection, whilst Rothschild and Stiglitz (1976) pointed out its implications for equilibria in insurance markets. Spence (1974) introduced the analysis of signalling. Equilibrium concepts in such markets are discussed by Riley (1979) and Hellwig (1987). On moral hazard, see the fundamental paper by Arrow (1963b).

Chapter 20 Agency and contract theory

Two fundamental papers on the question of why firms exist are Coase (1937) and Alchian and Demsetz (1972). There are good accounts of the more recent approaches to the theory of the firm based on incomplete contracts, relationship specific investments and principal–agent theory in Grossman and Hart (1986), Holmstrom and Tirole (1989), Williamson (1989) and Holmstrom and Roberts (1998). For the revelation principle, see Harris and Townsend (1981). The optimal debt contract discussion is based on Gale and Hellwig (1985), and the regulation problem on Laffont and Tirole (1993). For a survey of attempts to test contract theory, see Chiappori and Salanie (2003).

The seminal works on the moral hazard principal agent theory are Mirrlees (1971, 1999). Extensions and refinements are in Holmstrom (1979), Shavell (1979), Rogerson (1985), and Jewitt (1988). The paper by Holmstrom and Milgrom (1983) provides a rationale for linear incentive contracts, while the discrete action set model is analysed in Grossman and Hart (1983). For an up-to-date review of the now vast literature on agency theory, see Laffont and Martimort (2002).

Chapter 21 General equilibrium under uncertainty and incomplete markets

The valuation of price changes under uncertainty is closely related to the issue of option values: see Schmalensee (1972). Hanoch (1977) shows that assumptions about attitudes to price and income risk have implications for the form of the consumer's preferences. The analysis of the efficiency of rational expectations equilibria in this chapter is based on Newbery and Stiglitz (1982). For a simpler two-state model which reaches similar conclusions, see Diamond (1980). Hammond (1981) examines the distinction between *ex post* and *ex ante* welfare.

The extension of general equilibrium theory to the case of uncertainty was made by Arrow (1964), Debreu (1959) and Radner (1968). Huang and Litzenberger (1988), ch. 4, set out the capital asset pricing model of the determination of security prices, and the arbitrage pricing model is described in Varian (1987). On portfolio choice, see Cass and Stiglitz (1970) and Gollier (2001), chs 4, 13, 14.

The ability of stock markets to achieve an efficient allocation is discussed in Mossin (1977) and Hart (1975). Our approach to incomplete stock markets is based on Drèze (1987), chs 14, 15, 16, and Diamond (1967). A mathematically advanced survey of the theory of incomplete markets, which gives very comprehensive coverage of the literature, is provided by Magill and Quinzii (1996).

Appendices A–L

The material covered in the appendices will be found in any good text on 'mathematics for economists'. The one closest to this book in level and style is Hoy *et al.* (2001). For a more advanced treatment, particularly on the topics of general equilibrium and the welfare theorems, see Takayama (1985). Dixit (1990) is also excellent as a concise but comprehensive treatment of optimization for economists.

Bibliography

Abreu, D. (1986). 'Extremal equilibria of oligopolistic supergames', *Journal of Economic Theory*, 39, 191–235.

Akerlof, G. (1970). 'The market for lemons: qualitative uncertainty and the market mechanism', *Quarterly Journal of Economics*, 84, 488–500.

Alchian, A. A. (1959). 'Costs and outputs', in Abmramovitz, M. *et al.* (eds), *The Allocation of Economic Resources*, Stanford University Press, Stanford, CA.

Alchian, A. and Demsetz, H. (1972). 'Production, information costs, and economic organization', *American Economic Review*, 62, 777–795.

Applebaum, E. and Katz, E. (1986). 'Measures of risk aversion and comparative statics of industry equilibrium', *American Economic Review*, 524–529.

Apps, P. F. and Rees, R. (1988). 'Taxation and the household', *Journal of Public Economics*, 35, 355–369.

Apps, P. F. and Rees, R. (1997). 'Collective labor supply and household production', *Journal of Political Economy*, 105, 178–190.

Arrow, K. J. (1959). 'Towards a theory of price adjustment', in Abramovitz, M. *et al.* (eds), *The Allocation of Economic Resources*, Stanford University Press, Stanford, CA.

Arrow, K. J. (1963a) *Social Choice and Individual Values*, 2nd edn, John Wiley, New York.

Arrow, K. J. (1963b). 'Uncertainty and the welfare economics of medical care', *American Economic Review*, 53, 941–973.

Arrow, K. J. (1964). 'The role of securities in the optimal allocation of risk bearing', *Review of Economic Studies*, 31, 91–96.

Arrow, K. J. (1970). 'The organisation of economic activity: issues pertinent to the choice of market versus non-market allocation', in Haverman, R. H. and Margolis, J. (eds), *Public Expenditures and Policy Analysis*, Markham, Chicago.

Arrow, K. J. and Hahn, F. H. (1971). *General Competitive Analysis*, Oliver & Boyd, Edinburgh.

Arrow, K. J. and Lind, R. (1970). 'Uncertainty and the evaluation of public investment decisions', *American Economic Review*, 60, 364–368.

Barzel, Y. (1989). *Economic Analysis of Property Rights*, Cambridge University Press, Cambridge.

Baumol, W. J. (1959). *Business Behavior, Value and Growth*, Macmillan, New York.

Baumol, W. J., Panzar, J. C. and Willig, R. D. (1982). *Contestable Markets and the Theory of Industrial Structure*, Harcourt Brace Jovanovich, New York.

Becker, G. S. (1965). 'Theory of the allocation of time', *Economic Journal*, 75, 493–517.

Becker, G. S. (1976). *The Economic Approach to Human Behaviour*, University of Chicago Press, Chicago.

Bergson, A. (1938). 'A reformulation of certain aspects of welfare economics', *Quarterly Journal of Economics*, 52, 30–34.

Bhagwati, J. N., Brechner, R. A. and Hatta, T. (1987). 'The global correspondence principle', *American Economic Review*, 77, 124–132.

Binmore, K. and Dasgupta, P. (eds) (1987). *The Economics of Bargaining*, Basil Blackwell, Oxford.

Blackorby, C., Primont, D. and Russell, R. R. (1978). *Durability, Separability and Functional Structure*, American Elsevier, New York.

Blaug, M. (1980). *The Methodology of Economics*, Cambridge University Press, Cambridge.

Bliss, C. J. (1975). *Capital Theory and the Distribution of Income*, North-Holland, Amsterdam.

Blundell, R. (1988), 'Consumer behaviour: theory and empirical evidence – a survey', *Economic Journal*, 98, 16–65.

Boadway, R. and Bruce, N. (1984). *Welfare Economics*, Basil Blackwell, Oxford.

Booth, A. L. (1995). *The Economics of the Trade Union*. Cambridge University Press, Cambridge.

Buchanan, J. M. (1969). *Cost and Choice: An Enquiry into Economic Theory*, Markham, Chicago.

Cass, D. and Stiglitz, J. E. (1970). 'The structure of investor preferences and asset returns, and separability in portfolio allocation: a contribution to the pure theory of mutual funds', *Journal of Economic Theory*, 2(2), 122–160.

Chambers, R. G. (1988). *Applied Production Analysis: A Dual Approach*, Cambridge University Press, Cambridge.

Chambers, R. G. and Quiggin, J. (2000). *Uncertainty, Production, Choice, and Agency: The State Contingent Approach*, Cambridge University Press, Cambridge.

Cheung, S. N. (1973). 'The fable of the bees: an economic investigation', *Journal of Law and Economics*, 16, 11–33.

Chiappori, P. and Salanie, B. (2003). 'Testing contract theory: a survey of some recent work', in Dewatripont, M., Hansen, L. P. and Turnovsky, S. J. (eds), *Advances in Economics and Econometrics: Theory and Applications*, Vol. 1, Cambridge University Press, Cambridge.

Chipman, J. S. and Moore, J. C. (1980). 'Compensating variation, consumer surplus, and welfare', *American Economic Review*, 70, 933–949.

Coase, R. (1937). 'The nature of the firm', *Economica*, 4, 386–405.

Coase, R. (1960). 'The problem of social cost', *Journal of Law and Economics*, 3, 1–44.

Cook, K. S. and Levi, M. (eds) (1990). *The Limits of Rationality*, Chicago University Press, Chicago.

Cook, P. J. and Graham, D. (1977). 'The demand for insurance and protection: the case of irreplaceable commodities', *Quarterly Journal of Economics*, 91, 143–156.

Cornes, R. (1992). *Duality and Modern Economics*, Cambridge University Press, Cambridge.

Davidson, C. and Deneckere, R. (1986). 'Long-term competition in capacity, short-run competition in price, and the Cournot model', *Rand Journal of Economics*, 17, 404–415.

Davis, D. G. (1963). 'A note on Marshallian vs Walrasian stability conditions', *Canadian Journal of Economics and Political Science*, 29.

Deaton, A. and Muellbauer, J. (1980). *Economics and Consumer Behaviour*, Cambridge University Press, Cambridge.

Debreu, G. (1959). *Theory of Value*, John Wiley, New York.

Demsetz, H. (1964). 'The exchange and enforcement of property rights', *Journal of Law and Economics*, 7, 11–26.

Diamond, P. (1967). 'The role of a stock market in a general equilibrium model with technological uncertainty', *American Economic Review*, 57, 759–773.

Diamond, P. (1980). 'Efficiency with uncertain supply', *Review of Economic Studies*, 645–651.

Diamond, P. and Stiglitz, J. E. (1974). 'Increases in risk and risk aversion', *Journal of Economic Theory*, 8, 337–360.

Diewert, W. E. (1971). 'A note on the elasticity of derived demand in the *n*-factor case', *Economica*, 192–198.

Diewert, W. E. (1974). 'Applications of duality theory', in Intriligator, M. D. and Kendrick, J. W. (eds), *Frontiers of Quantitative Economics*, Vol. II, North-Holland, Amsterdam.

Dixit, A. (1980). 'The role of investment in entry deterrence', *Economic Journal*, 90, 95–106.

Dixit, A. (1990). *Optimization in Economic Theory*, 2nd edn, Oxford University Press, Oxford.

Doherty, N. A. and Schlesinger, H. (1983). 'Optimal insurance in incomplete markets', *Journal of Political Economy*, 91, 1045–1054.

Drèze, J. H. (1987). *Essays on Economic Decisions under Uncertainty*, Cambridge University Press, Cambridge.

Eggertsson, T. (1990). *Economic Behaviour and Institutions*, Cambridge University Press, Cambridge.

Elster, J. (1989). *Solomonic Judgements: Studies in the Limits of Rationality*, Cambridge University Press, Cambridge.

Farber, H. (1986). 'The analysis of union behaviour,' in Ashenfelter, A. and Layard, R. (eds), *Handbook of Labor Economics*, Vol. 1, Elsevier, Amsterdam.

Farrell, J. and Maskin, E. (1989). 'Renegotiation in repeated games', *Games and Economic Behaviour*, 1, 327–360.

Ferguson, C. E. (1969). *The Neo-classical Theory of Production and Distribution*, Cambridge University Press, Cambridge, chs 1–6.

Friedman, J. (1977). *Oligopoly and the Theory of Games*, North-Holland, Amsterdam.

Friedman, J. (1986). *Game Theory with Applications to Economics*, Oxford University Press, Oxford.

Frydman, R. (1982). 'Towards an understanding of market processes: individual expectations, learning, and convergence to rational expectations equilibrium', *American Economic Review*, 72, 652–668.

Fudenberg, D. and Maskin, E. (1986). 'The Folk Theorem in repeated games with discounting or with incomplete information', *Econometrica*, 54, 533–556.

Fudenberg, D. and Tirole, J. (1983). 'Sequential bargaining with incomplete information', *Review of Economic Studies*, 50, 221–247.

Fudenberg, D. and Tirole, J. (1991). *Game Theory*, MIT Press, Cambridge, MA.

Gale, D. (1996). 'What have we learned from social learning?', *European Economic Review*, 40, 617–628.

Gale, D. and Hellwig, M. (1985). 'Incentive-compatible debt contracts: the one-period problem', *Review of Economic Studies*, 52, 647–663.

Gibbons, R. S. (1992). *Game Theory for Applied Economists*, Princeton University Press, Princeton, NJ.

Gilbert, R. J. (1989). 'Mobility barriers and the value of incumbency', in Schmalensee, R. and Willig, R. D. (eds), *Handbook of Industrial Organization*, North-Holland, Amsterdam, ch. 8.

Gollier, C. (2001). *The Economics of Risk and Time*, MIT Press, Cambridge, MA.

Green, H. A. J. (1976). *Consumer Theory*, Macmillan, London.

Grossman, S. J. and Hart, O. D. (1979). 'A theory of competitive equilibrium in stock market economies' *Econometrica*, 47, 293–330.

Grossman, S. and Hart, O. (1983). 'An analysis of the principal–agent problem', *Econometrica*, 51, 7–45.

Grossman, S. and Hart, O. (1986). 'The costs and benefits of ownership: a theory of vertical and lateral integration', *Journal of Political Economy*, 94, 691–719.

Hader, J. and Russell, W. (1969). 'Rules for ordering uncertain prospects', *American Economic Review*, 59, 25–34.

Hahn, F. H. (1984). 'On the notion of equilibrium in economics', in F. H. (ed.), Hahn, *Equilibrium and Macroeconomics*, Basil Blackwell, Oxford.

Hammond, P. (1981). 'Ex ante and ex post welfare optimality under uncertainty', *Economica*, 48, 235–250.

Hanoch, G. (1977). 'Risk aversion and consumer preferences', *Econometrica*, 45, 413–426.

Hargreaves Heap, S., Hollis, M., Lyons, B., Sugden, R. and Weale, A. (1992). *The Theory of Choice: A Critical Guide*, Blackwell, Oxford.

Harris, M. and Townsend, R. M. (1981). 'Resource allocation under asymmetric information', *Econometrica*, 49, 33–64.

Hart, O. D. (1975). 'On the optimality of equilibrium when the market structure is incomplete', *Journal of Economic Theory*, 11, 418–443.

Hellwig, M. (1987). 'Some recent developments in the theory of competition in markets with adverse selection', *European Economic Review,* 31, 319–325.

Hicks, J. R. (1964). *Theory of Wages*, Macmillan, London.

Hicks, J. R. (1940/1). 'The rehabilitation of consumer's surplus', *Review of Economic Studies*, VIII, 108–116.

Hildenbrand, W. and Kirman, A. (1976). *Introduction to Equilibrium Analysis*, North-Holland, Amsterdam.

Hirshleifer, J. (1970). *Investment, Interest and Capital*, Prentice-Hall, Englewood Cliffs, NJ.

Hirshleifer, J. and Riley, J. G. (1992). *The Analytics of Uncertainty and Information*, Cambridge University Press, Cambridge.

Holmstrom, B. (1979). 'Moral hazard and observability', *Bell Journal of Economics*, 10, 74–91.

Holmstrom, B. and Milgrom, P. (1987). 'Aggregation and linearity in the provision of intertemporal incentives', *Econometrica*, 51, 7–45,

Holmstrom, B. and Roberts, J. (1998). 'The boundaries of the firm revisited', *Journal of Economic Perspectives*, 12, 73–94.

Holmstrom, B. R. and Tirole, J. (1989). 'The theory of the firm', in Schmalensee, R. and Willig, R. D. (eds), *The Handbook of Industrial Organisation*, Vol. 1, North-Holland, Amsterdam.

Hoy, M., Livernois, I. J., McKenna, C. J., Rees, R. and Stengos, T. (2001). *Mathematics for Economics*, 2nd edn, MIT Press, Cambridge, MA.

Huang, C. and Litzenberger, R. H. (1988). *Foundations for Financial Economics*, North-Holland, Amsterdam.

Hurwicz, L. and Uzawa, H. (1971). 'On the integrability of demand functions', in Chipman, J. S., Hurwicz, L., Richter, M. K. and Sonnenschein, H. F. (eds), *Preference, Utility and Demand*, Harcourt Brace, New York.

Jewitt, I. (1988). 'Justifying the first-order approach to principal–agent problems', *Econometrica*, 56, 1177–1190.

Kahneman, D., Slovic, P. and Tversky, A. (eds) (1982). *Judgement under Uncertainty: Heuristics and Biases*, Cambridge University Press, Cambridge.

Kimball, M. (1990). 'Precautionary saving in the small and in the large', Econometrica, 58, 53–73.

Kreps, D. and Scheinkman, J. (1983). 'Quantity precommitment and Bertrand competition yield Cournot outcomes', *Bell Journal of Economics*, 14, 326–337.

Kreps, D. M., Milgrom, P., Roberts, J. and Wilson, R. (1982). 'Rational cooperation in the finitely repeated prisoners' dilemma', *Journal of Economic Theory*, 27, 245–252.

Lachman, L. L. (1986). *The Market as an Economic Process*, Basil Blackwell, Oxford.

Laffont, J. J. and Martimort, D. (2002). *The Theory of Incentives: The Principal–Agent Model*, Princeton University Press, Princeton, NJ.

Laffont, J. J. and Tirole, J. (1988). 'The dynamics of incentive contracts', *Econometrica*, 56, 1153–1175.

Laffont, J. J. and Tirole, J. (1993). *Theory of Incentives in Procurement and Regulation*, MIT Press, Cambridge, MA.

Laibson, D. I. (1997). 'Golden eggs and hyperbolic discounting', *Quarterly Journal of Economics*, 112, 443–478.

Leibenstein, H. (1966). 'Allocative vs X-efficiency', *American Economic Review*, 56, 392–415.

Levitan, R. and Shubik, M. (1972), 'Price duopoly and capacity constraints', *International Economic Review,* 13, 111–122.

Loasby, B. J. (1976). Choice, *Complexity and Ignorance*, Cambridge University Press, Cambridge.

Luce, R. D. and Raiffa, D. (1966). *Games and Decisions*, John Wiley, New York.

Machina, M. (1987). 'Choice under uncertainty: problems solved and unsolved', *Journal of Economic Perspectives*, 1(1), 121–154.

Magill, M. and Quinzii, M. (1996). *Theory of Incomplete Markets*, Vol. 1, MIT Press, Cambridge, MA.

Martin, S. (2003). *Advanced Industrial Economics*, (3rd edn, Blackwell, Oxford.

Mas-Colell, A. (1985). *The Theory of General Economic Equilibrium: A Differentiable Approach*, Cambridge University Press, London.

McFadden, D. (1978). Cost, revenue and profit functions, in Fuss, M. and McFadden, D. (eds), *Production Economics: A Dual Approach to Theory and Applications*, Vol. 1, North-Holland, Amsterdam.

McKenzie, G. W. (1983). *Measuring Economic Welfare: New Methods*, Cambridge University Press, Cambridge.

Meade, J. E. (1986). *Alternative Systems of Business Organization and of Workers' Remuneration*, Allen & Unwin, London,

Meyer, J. (1987). 'Two-moment decision models and expected utility maximization', *American Economic Review*, 77(3), 421–430.

Michael, R. T. and Becker, G. S. (1973). 'On the new theory of consumer behaviour', *Swedish Journal of Economics*, 75, 378–396.

Mirrlees, J. (1971). 'An exploration in the theory of income taxation', *Review of Economic Studies*, 38, 175–208.

Mirrlees, J. (1999). 'The theory of unobservable behaviour: part 1', *Review of Economic Studies*, 66, 3–22.

Mossin, J. (1977). *The Economic Efficiency of Financial Markets*, D. C. Heath, Lexington.

Moulin, H. (1986). *Game Theory for the Social Sciences*, 2nd edn, New York University Press, New York.

Mueller, D. C. (1989). *Public Choice II*, Cambridge University Press, Cambridge.

Mueller, D. C. (ed.) (1997). *Perspectives on Public Choice: A Handbook*, Cambridge University Press, Cambridge.

Muth, J. F. (1961). 'Rational expectations and the theory of price movements', *Econometrica*, 29, 315–335.

Myerson, R. (1991). *Game Theory: Analysis of Conflict*, Harvard University Press, Cambridge, MA.

Nash, J. F. (1950). 'The bargaining problem', *Econometrica*, 18, 155–162.

Newbery, D. M. G. and Stiglitz, J. E. (1981). *The Theory of Commodity Price Stabilization: A Study in the Economics of Risk*, Oxford University Press, Oxford.

Newbery, D. M. G. and Stiglitz, J. E. (1982). 'The choice of techniques and the optimality of market equilibrium with rational expectations', *Journal of Political Economy*, 90, 223–246.

Newman, P. (1965). *The Theory of Exchange*, Prentice-Hall, Englewood Cliffs, NJ.

Ormiston, M. B. (1992). 'First and second degree transformations and comparative statics', *International Economic Review*, 28, 33–44.

Osborne, M. J. and Rubinstein, A. (1990). *Bargaining and Markets*, Academic Press, San Diego, CA.

Osborne, M. J. and Rubinstein, A. (1994). *A Course in Game Theory*, MIT Press, Cambridge, MA.

Parker, R. H. and Harcourt, G. C. (1969). *Readings in the Concept and Measurement of Income*, Cambridge University Press, London, ch. 7.

Philips, L. (1983). *The Economics of Price Discrimination*, Cambridge University Press, Cambridge.

Pratt, J. W. (1964). 'Risk aversion in the small and in the large', *Econometrica*, 32, 122–136.

Radner, R. (1968). 'Competitive equilibrium under uncertainty', Econometrica, 36, 31–58.

Radner, R. (1972). 'Existence of equilibrium of plans, prices and price expectations in a sequence of markets', *Econometrica*, 40, 289–303.

Raviv, A. (1979). 'The design of an optimal insurance policy', *American Economic Review*, 69(1), 84–96.

Riley, J. (1979). 'Informational equilibrium', *Econometrica*, 47, 331–359.

Rogerson, W. P. (1985). 'The first order approach to principal–agent problems', *Econometrica*, 53, 1357–1368.

Rothschild, M. and Stiglitz, J. E. (1970). 'Increasing risk: I. A definition', *Journal of Economic Theory*, 2, 225–243.

Rothschild, M. and Stiglitz, J. E. (1971). 'Increasing risk: II. Its consequences', *Journal of Economic Theory*, 3, 66–84.

Rothschild, M. and Stiglitz, J. E. (1976). 'Equilibrium in competitive insurance markets: an essay on the economics of imperfect information', *Quarterly Journal of Economics*, 90, 629–649.

Rubinstein, A. (1982). 'Perfect equilibrium in a bargaining model', *Econometrica*, 50, 97–109.

Salanie, B. (2000). *Microeconomics of Market Failure*, MIT Press, Cambridge, MA.

Samuelson, P. A. (1938). 'A note on the pure theory of consumer behaviour', *Economica*, 5, 61–71.

Samuelson, P. A. (1947). *Foundations of Economic Analysis*, Harvard University Press, Cambridge, MA.

Samuelson, P. A. (1950a). 'The problem of integrability in utility theory', *Economica*, 17, 355–385.

Samuelson, P. A. (1950b). 'Evaluation of real national income', *Oxford Economic Papers*, 1–29.

Samuelson, P. A. (1954). 'The pure theory of public expenditure', *Review of Economics and Statistics*, 36, 386–389.

Schmalensee, R. (1972). 'Option demand and consumer surplus: valuing price changes under uncertainty', *American Economic Review*, 65, 813–824.

Schmalensee, R. and Willig, R. D. (eds) (1989). *The Handbook of Industrial Organisation*, Vol. 1, North-Holland, Amsterdam.

Scitovsky, T. (1943). 'A note on profit maximization and its implications', *Review of Economic Studies*, 11, 57–60.

Selten, R. (1978). 'The Chain-Store Paradox', *Theory and Decision*, 9, 127–159.

Sen, A. K. (1970). *Collective Choice and Social Welfare*, Holden-Day, Oliver & Boyd, Edinburgh.

Sen, A. K. (1986). 'Social choice theory', in Arrow, K. J. and Intrilligator, M. (eds), *Handbook of Mathematical Economics*, Vol. 3, North-Holland, Amsterdam, ch. 22.

Sharkey, W. W. (1982). *The Theory of Natural Monopoly*, Cambridge University Press, Cambridge.

Shavell, S. (1979). 'Risk sharing and incentives in the principal–agent relationship', *Bell Journal of Economics*, 10, 55–73.

Shephard, R. W. (1970). *Theory of Cost and production Functions*, Princeton University Press, Princeton, NJ.

Simon, H. A. (1972). 'Theories of bounded rationality', in McGuire, C. B. and Radner, R. (eds), *Decision and Organisation*, North-Holland, London.

Sinn, H. W. (1989). *Economic Decisions under Uncertainty*, 2nd edn, Physica-Verlag, Heidelberg.

Spence, M. (1974). *Market Signalling: Information Transfer in Hiring and Related Economic Processes*, Harvard University Press, Cambridge, MA.

Spulber, D. F. (1989). Regulation and Markets, MIT Press, Cambridge, MA.

Stigler, G. (1950). 'The development of utility theory', *Journal of Political Economy*, 58, 307–327, 373–396.

Strotz, R. H. (1954). 'Myopia and inconsistency in dynamic utility maximization', *Review of Economic Studies*, 23, 165–180.

Takayama, A. (1985). *Mathematical Economics*, 2nd edn, Cambridge University Press, Cambridge.

Thaler, R. H. (1994). *Quasi-rational Economics*, Russell Sage Foundation, New York.

Tirole, J. (1988). *The Theory of Industrial Organization*, MIT Press, Cambridge, MA.

Tollison, R. D. (1997). 'Rentseeking', in Mueller, D. C. (ed.) (1997). *Perspectives on Public Choice: A Handbook*, Cambridge University Press.

Tullock, G. (1967). 'The welfare costs of tariffs, monopolies and theft', *Western Economic Journal*, 5, 224–232.

Vanek, J. (1970). *The General Theory of Labor-managed Market Economies*, Cornell University Press, Ithaca, NY.

Varian, H. A. R. (1987). 'The arbitrage principle in financial economics', *Journal of Economic Perspectives*, 1(2), 55–72.

Varian, H. (1989). 'Price discrimination', in Schmalensee, R. and Willig, R. D. (eds), *Handbook of Industrial Organization*, North-Holland, Amsterdam, ch. 10.

Varian, H. (1994). 'A solution to the problem of externalities when agents are well informed', *American Economic Review*, 84, 1278–1293.

Viner, J. (1953). 'Cost curves and supply curves', in Stigler, G. J. and Boulding, K. E. (eds), *Readings in Price Theory*, George Allen & Unwin, London.

Vives, X. (1999). *Oligopoly Pricing*, MIT Press, Cambridge, MA.

Ward, B. (1958). 'The Firm in Illyria: market syndicalism', *American Economic Review*, 48, 566–589.

Williamson, O. E. (1964). *The Economics of Discretionary Behavior: Managerial Objectives in a Theory of the Firm*, Prentice-Hall, Englewood Cliffs, NJ.

Williamson, O. E. (1989). 'Transactions costs economics', in Schmalensee, R. and Willig, R. D. (eds), *The Handbook of Industrial Organisation*, Vol. 1, North-Holland, Amsterdam.

Wilson, C. (1977). 'A model of insurance markets with incomplete information', Journal of Economic Theory, 16, 167–207.

Wilson, R. (1993). *Nonlinear Pricing*, Oxford University Press, Oxford.

Index